D

Guide
2009

Advertisement Sales: advertisingsales@theAA.com
Editorial: lifestyleguides@theAA.com

Front Cover Photos: (t) The Deep, Kingston Upon Hull; Front Cover
(bl) AA/V Greaves; Front Cover (br) AA/J Carnie; Back Cover (l) AA/N
Setchfield; Back Cover (c) AA/N Hicks; Back Cover (r) AA/J Smith

Typeset/Repro by Keenes, Andover, Hampshire UK
Printed in Italy by Printer Trento SRL, Trento

Published by AA Publishing, which is a trading name of Automobile
Association Developments Limited whose registered office is
Fanum House, Basingstoke, Hampshire, RG21 4EA
CIP catalogue record for this book is available from the British Library

Registered number 1878835.
ISBN-13: 978-0-7495-5876-5
A03686

Maps prepared by the
Mapping Services Department of
The Automobile Association.
Maps © Automobile Association
Developments Limited 2008.

  This
product
includes mapping data licensed
from Ordnance Survey ® with the
permission of the Controller of
Her Majesty's Stationery Office.
© Crown copyright 2008.
All rights reserved.
Licence number 100021153.

 This material is based
upon Crown Copyright
and is reproduced
with the permission of Land and
Property Services under delegated
authority from the Controller of
Her Majesty's Stationery Office,
© Crown copyright and database
rights LA59 Permit number 80033.

© Ordnance Survey Ireland/
Government of Ireland.
Copyright Permit No. MP000108

Contents

Museums National Parks Art Galleries Visitor c
National Parks Art Galleries Visitor centres The
Art Galleries Visitor centres Theme Parks State
Parks Art Galleries Visitor centres Theme Parks
National Parks Art Galleries Visitor centres The
Art Galleries Visitor centres Theme Parks State
Visitor centres Theme Parks Stately HomesMus

How to Use the Guide

The AA Days Out Guide provides useful information about a large number of museums, art galleries, theme parks, national parks, visitor centres, stately homes and other attractions across Britain and Ireland. Entries include contact details, along with a short description and details of opening times, prices and special facilities. We hope this guide will help you and your family get the most out of your visit.

The Directory

The directory is arranged in countries, counties, and in alphabetical location order within each county.

❶ Map References and Atlas
Map references for attractions are based on the National Grid, and can be used with the Atlas at the back of this book. First comes the map page number, followed by the National Grid reference. To find the location, read the first figure horizontally and the second figure vertically within the lettered square.

❷ Directions may be given after the address of each attraction and where shown have been provided by the attractions themselves.

❸ Telephone Numbers have the STD code shown before the telephone number. (If dialling Northern Ireland from England use the STD code, but for the Republic you need to prefix the number with 00353, and drop the first zero from the Irish area code).

❹ Opening Times quoted in the guide are inclusive - for instance, where you see Apr-Oct, that place will be open from the beginning of April to the end of October.

❺ Fees quoted for the majority of entries are current. If no price is quoted, you should check with the attraction concerned before you visit. Places which are open 'at all reasonable times' are usually free, and many places which do not charge admission at all may ask for a voluntary donation. Remember that prices can go up, and those provided to us by the attractions are provisional.

---

❶ SW7   MAP 05 TQ58

The Natural History Museum

Cromwell Rd SW7 SBD

❷ (Underground - South Kensington)

❸ ☎ 020 7942 5000

e-mail: feedback@nhm.ac.uk

web: www.nhm.ac.uk

This vast and elaborate Romanesque-style building, with its terracotta facing showing relief mouldings of animals, birds and fishes, covers an area of four acres. Holding over 70 million specimens from all over the globe, from dinosaurs to diamonds and earthquakes to ants, the museum provides a journey into Earth's past, present and future. Discover more about the work of the museum through a daily programme of talks from museum scientists or go behind the scenes of the Darwin Centre, the museum's scientific research centre.

❹ Times Open daily 10-5.30 (last admission 5.30). Closed 24-26 Dec.

❺ Fee Free. Charge made for some special exhibitions. **Facilities** ℗ (180yds) **❻** (limited parking, use public transport) 및 ❀❑ licensed ♿ (top floor/one gallery not accessible, wheelchair hire) Shop ✖ (ex assist dogs) ➡ **❼** **❽**

✱**Admission prices** followed by an asterisk relate to 2008. It should be noted that in some entries the opening dates and times may also have been supplied as 2008. Please check with the establishment before making your journey.

Free Entry FREE

These attractions do not charge a fee for entry, although they may charge for use of audio equipment, for example. We have not included attractions that expect a donation in this category.

2-FOR-1 Voucher Scheme 2 for 1

This symbol indicates which attractions have chosen to participate in our 2-for-1 voucher scheme. Visitors using one of the vouchers from the back of this guide will be able to buy 2 tickets for the price of

es Theme Parks Stately Homes Museums
Parks Stately HomesMuseums National Parks
omesMuseums National Parks
tely HomesMuseums
Parks Stately HomesMu
omesMuseums Nationa
s National Parks Art Ga

one, with certain restrictions that are detailed on the voucher itself. Some attractions also have individual restrictions, which are detailed in their entries.

❻ **Facilities** This section includes parking, dogs allowed, refreshments etc. See this page for a key to Symbols and Abbreviations used in this guide.

❼ **Visitors with Mobility Disabilities** should look for the wheelchair symbol showing where all or most of the establishment is accessible to the wheelchair-bound visitor. We strongly recommend that you telephone in advance of your visit to check the exact details, particularly regarding access to toilets and refreshment facilities. Assistance dogs are usually accepted where the attractions show the 'No Dogs' symbol ⊗ unless stated otherwise. For the hard of hearing induction loops are indicated by a symbol at the attraction itself.

❽ **Credit & Charge cards** are taken by a number of attractions for admission charges. To indicate which accept credit cards we have used this symbol at the end of the entry. ▬

Photography is restricted in some places and there are many where it is only allowed in specific areas. Visitors are advised to check with places of interest on the rules for taking photographs and the use of video cameras.

Special events are held at many of these attractions, and although we have listed a few in individual entries, we cannot hope to give details of them all, so please ring the attractions for details of exhibitions, themed days, talks, guided walks and more.

Attractions with *italic* headings. These are entries that were unable to provide the relevant information in time for publication.

...and finally Opening times and admission prices can be subject to change. Please check with the attraction before making your journey.

Key to Symbols

☎	Telephone number	♯	English Heritage
♿	Suitable for visitors in	⅏	National Trust
	wheelchairs	⅋	The National Trust
℗	Parking at		for Scotland
	Establishment	▯	Historic Scotland
℗	Parking nearby		

Abbreviations

🚽 Refreshment
🍴 Picnic Area
🍴 Restaurant
⊗ No Dogs
🚌 No Coaches
✳ Admission prices relate to 2008
✛ Cadw (Welsh Monuments)

BH Bank Hoildays
PH Public Holidays
Etr Easter
ex except
ch Children
Pen Senior Citizens
Concessions (Students, unemployed etc)

Public Holidays 2009

1 January	New Year's Day
2 January	New Year's Holiday
	(Scotland only)
17 March	St Patrick's Day
	(N.I & R.O.I)
10 April	Good Friday
13 April	Easter Monday
4 May	May Day Bank Holiday
25 May	Spring Bank Holiday
	(excluding R.O.I)
15 July	Battle of the Boyne
	(Orangemen's Day) (N.I)
3 August	Summer Bank Holiday
	(Scotland & R.O.I only)
31 August	Summer Bank Holiday
	(excluding R.O.I)
26 October	Bank Holiday (R.O.I)
25 December	Christmas Day
28 December	Boxing Day
	(BH in lieu of 26th December)
	(St Stephen's Day in R.O.I)

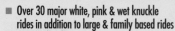

BEDFORDSHIRE

Bears at Whipsnade

AMPTHILL MAP 04 TL03

Houghton House `FREE`

➲ *(1m NE off A421)*

web: www.english-heritage.org.uk

Now a ruin, the mansion was built for Mary Countess of Pembroke, the sister of Sir Philip Sidney. Inigo Jones is thought to have been involved in work on the house, which may have been the original 'House Beautiful' in Bunyan's *Pilgrim's Progress*.

Times Open at all reasonable times. **Facilities** ❷ ▦

BEDFORD MAP 04 TL04

Cecil Higgins Art Gallery `FREE`

Castle Ln MK40 3RP

➲ *(in town centre close to Embankment)*

☎ 01234 211222

e-mail: chag@bedford.gov.uk

web: www.cecilhigginsartgallery.org

A recreated Victorian mansion, with the rooms arranged as though the house is still lived in. Includes a bedroom with furniture designed by Victorian architect William Burges, and the adjoining gallery has an outstanding collection of ceramics, glass and a changing exhibition of prints, drawings and watercolours. Also includes the Thomas Lester lace collection.

Times The museum is due to open in 2009 after refurbishment. Open all year Tue-Sat 11-5, Sun & BH Mon 2-5 (last entry 4.45). Closed Xmas, New Year & Good Fri. Please check the website for further details. **Facilities** ℗ (100yds) (pay & display) (free on Sun) ▱ ⊓ (outdoor) ♿ (wheelchair available) toilets for disabled shop ❽ (ex assist dogs) ▰

LEIGHTON BUZZARD MAP 04 SP92

Leighton Buzzard Railway `2 for 1`

Pages Park Station, Billington Rd LU7 4TN

➲ *(0.75m SE on A4146 signed in and around Leighton Buzzard, near rdbt junct with A505)*

☎ 01525 373888

e-mail: info@buzzrail.co.uk

web: www.buzzrail.co.uk

The Leighton Buzzard Railway offers a 70 minute journey into the vanished world of the English light railway, with its sharp curves, steep gradients, level crossings and unique roadside running. Built in 1919 to serve the local sand industry, the railway has carried a steam passenger service, operated by volunteers, since 1968. In 2009 the railway celebrates its 90th anniversary.

Times Open 16 Mar-26 Oct, Sun; 24 Mar, 5 & 26 May, 25 Aug, Mon; 29 Jul-19 Aug, Tue; 26 Mar, 26 Mar, 28 May-25 Aug, 22-29 Aug; 31 Jul-21 Aug, Thu; 21 Mar, Fri; 22 Mar, 3 & 24 May, 2-23 Aug, 6 Sep, 4 Oct, Sat. **Fee** ✳ Return ticket £7 (ch 2-15 £3, ch under 2 free, concessions £6). Party 10+ 20% discount. Family and Day Rover tickets available. **Facilities** ❷ ▱ ⊓ (outdoor) ♿ (some museum exhibits not suitable, platform & train access for wheelchairs) (designated parking) toilets for disabled shop ▰

LUTON MAP 04 TL02

John Dony Field Centre `FREE`

Hancock Dr, Bushmead LU2 7SF

➲ *(signed from rdbt on A6, at Barnfield College on New Bedford Rd)*

☎ 01582 486983 & 422818

e-mail: johndony@luton.gov.uk

web: www.luton.gov.uk/museums

This is a purpose-built study centre for exploring the landscapes, plants and animals of the Luton area. Featuring permanent displays on local archaeology, natural history and the management of the local nature reserve, it explains how ancient grasslands and hedgerows are conserved and follows 4000 years of history from Bronze Age to modern times. Please contact for details of special events.

Times Open all year, Mon-Fri 9.30-4.45 & for programmed events **Facilities** ❷ ❽ (ex assist dogs)

Stockwood Discovery Centre `FREE`

Stockwood Park, London Rd LU1 4LX

➲ *(signed from M1 junct 10 & from Hitchin, Dunstable, Bedford, Luton town centre)*

☎ 01582 548600

e-mail: museum.gallery@luton.gov.uk

web: www.luton.gov.uk/museums

Stockwood Discovery Centre is a new museum and visitor attraction that includes new gardens featuring world, medicinal and sensory gardens, a visitor centre with a new shop and a café selling locally produced free range products and an outdoor discovery play area. It also features fascinating interactive displays about the history of Luton and the surrounding areas as well as exciting events and special exhibitions.

Times Open all year; Apr-Oct, Mon-Fri 10-5, Sat-Sun 11-5, until 8 on 1st Thu of mth; Nov-Mar, Mon-Fri 10-4, Sat-Sun 11-4. **Facilities** ❷ ▱ ⊓ (outdoor) ♿ (stair lift, induction loop, mobility scooter, w/chairs) toilets for disabled shop ❽ (ex assist dogs)

Wardown Park Museum

Wardown Park, Old Bedford Rd LU2 7HA

➲ *(Follow brown signs from town centre north. Turn off A6 towards Bedford)*

☎ 01582 546722 & 546739

e-mail: museum.gallery@luton.gov.uk

web: www.luton.gov.uk/museums

A Victorian mansion, with displays illustrating the natural and cultural history, archaeology and industries of the area, including the development of Luton's hat industry, and the Bedfordshire and Hertfordshire Regimental Collections. New 'Luton Life' displays tell the story of the town and its residents over the past 200 years. Exhibitions and events throughout the year, please telephone for details.

Times Open all year, Tue-Sat 10-5, Sun 1-5 (Closed Xmas, 1 Jan & Mon ex BH Mons). **Facilities** ❷ ▱ ⊓ (outdoor) ♿ (parking adjacent to entrance, lift to 1st floor) toilets for disabled shop ❽ (ex assist dogs)

OLD WARDEN   MAP 04 TL14

The Shuttleworth Collection
Old Warden Park SG18 9EP

⮑ *(2m W from rdbt on A1, Biggleswade by-pass)*

☎ 01767 627927

web: www.shuttleworth.org

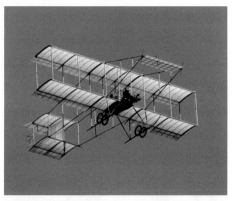

Housed in eight hangars on a classic grass aerodrome, 40 working historic aeroplanes span the progress of aviation with exhibits ranging from a 1909 Bleriot to a 1941 Spitfire. A garage of roadworthy motor vehicles explores the eras of the 1898 Panhard Levassor to the Railton sports car of 1937. The 19th-century coach house displays horse-drawn vehicles from 1880 to 1914.

Times Open Apr-Oct 10-5 (last admission 4), Nov-Feb 10-4 (last admission 3). Closed Xmas-New Year. **Fee** ✳ £10 (concessions £9). Flying displays £20. **Facilities** ♿ ☕ 🍽 licensed 🎪 (outdoor) ♿ (wheelchairs) toilets for disabled shop ⊗ (ex on leads/assist dogs) 🚻

SANDY   MAP 04 TL14

RSPB Nature Reserve The Lodge
SG19 2DL

⮑ *(1m E, on B1042 Potton road)*

☎ 01767 680541

e-mail: claire.wallace@rspb.org.uk

web: www.rspb.org.uk

The headquarters of the Royal Society for the Protection of Birds. The house and buildings are not open to the public, but there are waymarked paths and formal gardens, and two species of woodpecker, nuthatches and woodland birds may be seen, as may muntjac deer. Another feature is the specialist wildlife garden created in conjunction with the Henry Doubleday Association.

Times ✳ Open all year, Mon-Fri 9-5, Sat, Sun & BHs 10-5. Closed 25-26 Dec. **Facilities** ♿ 🎪 shop ⊗ (ex in restricted areas) 🚻

SILSOE   MAP 04 TL03

Wrest Park Gardens
MK45 4HS

⮑ *(0.75m E off A6)*

☎ 01525 860152

web: www.english-heritage.org.uk

Take an audio tour through a century and a half of gardening styles as you explore the 90 acres of formal gardens that make up Wrest Park.

Times Open: House & Gardens, 21 Mar-Jun, Sat-Sun & BH 10-6; Jul-Aug, Thu-Mon 10-6; Sep, Sat-Sun 10-6; Oct, Sat-Sun 10-5. (The House may close Fri, Jul-Aug & Sat all months. Please call to check.) **Fee** £4.90 (concessions £3.90, ch £2.50). Family £12.30. Prices and opening times are subject to change in March 2009. Please call 0870 333 1181 for the most up to date prices and opening times when planning your visit. **Facilities** ♿ ⊗ (ex on lead in certain areas) 🚻

WHIPSNADE   MAP 04 TL01

Whipsnade Wild Animal Park
LU6 2LF

⮑ *(signed from M1 junct 9 & 12)*

☎ 01582 872171

e-mail: marketing@zsl.org

web: www.whipsnade.co.uk

Located in beautiful Bedfordshire countryside, Whipsnade is home to more than 2,500 rare and exotic animals and is one of the largest conservation centres in Europe. Hop aboard the Jumbo Express, a fantastic steam train experience, and see elephants, rhino, yaks, camels and deer, along with wild horses, and learn about their lives in the wilds of Asia and Africa. Other highlights include the Lions of the Serengeti, the sealion pool, and Birds of the World. The Discover Centre is home to tamarins, turtles, big snakes and sea horses among others. Visitors can also enjoy the picnic areas, keeper talks and animal shows.

Times ✳ Open all year, daily. (Closed 25 Dec). Closing times vary. **Facilities** ♿ (charged) ☕ 🎪 (outdoor) shop ⊗ 🚻

WILDEN   MAP 04 TL05

Wild Britain

2 for 1

65A Renhold Rd MK44 2PX

➲ *(From A421 take Gt Barford slip road. Follow signs to Renhold & Wilden)*

☎ 01234 772770

e-mail: enquiries@bedford-butterflies.co.uk

web: www.wild-britain.co.uk

Join Urchin the hedgehog's Play Trail as he explores the countryside. Meet British animals in the presentation shows and learn about life cycles with a new puppet show. Visit the steamy tropical butterfly house to experience what the future could hold for Britain. Children's arts and craft activities every day. 2009 is the 10th anniversary of Wild Britain.

Times Open 8 Jan-1 Feb & 5 Nov-20 Dec, Thu-Sun 10-4. Daily 5 Feb-1 Nov, 10-5. **Fee** £8 (ch under 16 £5.50, under 2 free, concessions £7.50). **Facilities** ⊕ �)(& toilets for disabled shop ⊗ (ex assist dogs) ▬

WOBURN   MAP 04 SP93

Woburn Abbey

MK17 9WA

➲ *(Just off M1 junct 12/13)*

☎ 01525 290333

e-mail: admissions@woburnabbey.co.uk

web: www.discoverwoburn.co.uk

Set in a beautiful 3,000 acre deer park, Woburn Abbey has been the home of the Dukes of Bedford for over 300 years, and is currently occupied by the 15th Duke and his family. The Abbey houses one of the most important private art collections in the world including paintings by Canaletto, Gainsborough, Reynolds, Van Dyck and Cuyp and collections of silver, gold and porcelain. Woburn was the setting for the origin of "Afternoon Tea", introduced by Anna Maria, wife of the 7th Duke. An audio tour is available (charged) and guided tours on request. There are extensive informal gardens, pottery and a fine antiques centre representing over 70 dealers. Wheelchairs by arrangement.

Times Open 15 Mar-28 Sep, 11-5.30 (last entry 4) **Fee** ✶ £10,50 (ch 3-15 £6, pen £9.50). Passport ticket for Woburn Abbey and Woburn Safari Park allows one visit to each attraction on same or different days £18.50-£20 (ch £14-£15.50, pen £16-£17.50). Please phone or check website for further details. **Facilities** ⊕ ☐ ⊙(☐ (outdoor) & (limited access to house, only 3 rooms on ground floor. Other areas can only be accessed by means of stairs) (Advise in advance of special requirements) toilets for disabled shop ⊗ ▬

Woburn Safari Park

MK17 9QN

➲ *(Signed from M1 junct 13)*

☎ 01525 290407

e-mail: info@woburnsafari.co.uk

web: www.discoverwoburn.co.uk

Experience a Safari Adventure at Woburn Safari Park and enjoy the beauty of wild animals in real close-up. Tour the reserves from the safety of your own car and experience the thrill of being alongside white rhino, buffalo, giraffe or looking into the chilly eyes of a Siberian tiger. The Leisure Park has indoor and outdoor adventure playgrounds, walkthrough areas with wallabies, squirrel monkeys and lemurs, and a full programme of keeper talks and demonstrations. Don't miss the sea lions or the penguins. All attractions are included in the entry price including the new Mammoth Play Ark, Great Woburn Railway and the Swanboats.

Times Open 7 Mar-30 Oct 10-5, Winter wknds 11-3. **Fee** ✶ £9.50-£17.50 (ch 3-15 £8.50-£13.50, pen £8.50-£15). Passport ticket for Woburn Safari Park and Woburn Abbey allows one visit to each attraction on same or different days £18.50-£20 (ch £14-£15.50, pen £16-£17.50). Please phone or check website for further details. **Facilities** ⊕ ☐ ⊙(☐ (indoor & outdoor) & toilets for disabled shop ⊗ ▬

BERKSHIRE

River Thames, Cookham

BRACKNELL   MAP 04 SU86

The Look Out Discovery Centre   `2 for 1`

Nine Mile Ride RG12 7QW

➲ *(3m S of town centre. From M3 junct 3, take A322 to Bracknell and from M4 junct 10, take A329M to Bracknell. Follow brown tourist signs)*

☎ 01344 354400

e-mail: thelookout@bracknell-forest.gov.uk

web: www.bracknell-forest.gov.uk/be

A hands-on, interactive science and nature exhibition where budding scientists can spend many hours exploring and discovering over 70 fun filled exhibits within five themed zones, linked to the National Curriculum. Zones include Light and Colour, Forces and Movement and the Body and Perception. A new exciting zone, Woodland and Water; has a vortex, stream, ant colony and many more interactive exhibits. Climb the 88 steps to the Look Out tower and look towards Bracknell and beyond, or enjoy a nature walk in the surrounding 2,600 acres of Crown Estate woodland. Interactive shows for the public and schools running throughout the year. Please note the tower is closed when wet.

Times Open all year 10-5 (Closed 24-26 Dec, 12-16 Jan) **Fee** ✳ £5.70 (ch & concessions £3.80). Family (2ad+2ch or 1ad+3ch) £15.30 **Facilities** ⊕ ⊡ 🛱 (outdoor) ♿ (lift to 1st floor) toilets for disabled shop ⊗ (ex assist dogs) ➽

ETON   MAP 04 SU97

Dorney Court   `2 for 1`

Dorney SL4 6QP

➲ *(signed from M4 junct 7)*

☎ 01628 604638

e-mail: palmer@dorneycourt.co.uk

web: www.dorneycourt.co.uk

An enchanting brick and timber manor house (c1440) in a tranquil setting. With tall Tudor chimneys and a splendid great hall, it has been the home of the present family since 1510.

Times Open BH Sun & Mon in May 1.30-4.30. Aug every afternoon ex Sat 1.30-4.30. **Fee** £7.50 (ch £4.50, under 10's free). **Facilities** ⊕ ⊡ ♿ (Partly accessible) (ramps) toilets for disabled garden centre ⊗ (ex assist dogs)

HAMPSTEAD NORREYS   MAP 04 SU57

The Living Rainforest   `2 for 1`

RG18 0TN

➲ *(follow brown tourist signs from M4/A34)*

☎ 01635 202444

e-mail: enquiries@livingrainforest.org

web: www.livingrainforest.org

By providing education and supporting research into the relationship between humanity and the rainforests, this wonderful attraction hopes to promote a more sustainable future. Visitors to the Living Rainforest will see plants and wildlife that are under threat in their natural habitat,

and be encouraged to take part in a large variety of activities, workshops and exhibitions.

Times Open all year daily 10-5. (Closed 24-26 Dec) **Fee** ✳ £7.95 (ch 3-4 £4.95, ch 5-14 £5.95, concessions £6.95). Family ticket £24.95 **Facilities** ⊕ ⊡ 🛱 (outdoor) ♿ toilets for disabled shop ⊗ (ex assist dogs) ➽

LOWER BASILDON   MAP 04 SU67

Basildon Park

RG8 9NR

➲ *(7m NW of Reading on W side of A329 between Reading & Wallingford)*

☎ 0118 984 3040

e-mail: basildonpark@nationaltrust.org.uk

web: www.nationaltrust.org.uk/basildonpark

This 18th-century house, built of Bath stone, fell into decay in the 20th century, but has been beautifully restored by Lord and Lady Iliffe. The classical front has a splendid central portico and pavilions, and inside there are delicate plasterwork decorations on the walls and ceilings. The Octagon drawing room has fine pictures and furniture, and there is a small formal garden. The house more recently featured in the 2005 film adaptation of Jane Austen's *Pride & Prejudice*. Please contact for details of special events.

Times House open end Mar-end Oct, Wed-Sun & BH Mon 12-5. Park & garden end Mar-end Oct, Wed-Sun & BH Mon 11-5. **Facilities** ⊕ ⊡ ⋉⊙⋈ 🛱 (outdoor) ♿ (driven buggy) toilets for disabled ☙ ➽

Beale Park

Lower Basildon RG8 9NH

➲ *(M4 junct 12, follow brown tourist signs to Pangbourne, A329 towards Oxford)*

☎ 0870 777 7160

web: www.bealepark.co.uk

Beale Park is home to an extraordinary collection of birds and animals including peacocks, swans, owls and parrots. It also offers a steam railway, rare breeds of farm animals, a great pet corner, meerkats, wallabies, ring-tailed lemurs, a deer park, three splash pools, a huge adventure playground, acres of gardens, and sculptures in a traditional, family park beside the Thames. There are summer riverboat trips and excellent lake and river fishing.

Times ✳ Open Mar-Oct. **Facilities** ⊕ ⊡ ⋉⊙⋈ 🛱 (outdoor) ♿ (wheelchair available, parking) toilets for disabled shop ⊗ (ex assist dogs)

NEWBURY MAP 04 SU46
West Berkshire Museum `FREE`
The Wharf RG14 5AS

➲ *(from London take M4 junct 13, then southbound on A34, follow signs for town centre)*

☎ 01635 30511
e-mail: museum@westberks.gov.uk
web: westberkshiremuseum.org.uk

Occupying two adjoining buildings in the centre of Newbury; the Cloth Hall built in 1627 and the Granary built in 1720. The museum includes displays of fine and decorative art, costume, local history and archaeology.

Times Open all year Tue-Sat 10-5. Open BH Feb-Nov **Facilities** ℗ (15yds) ♿ (ground floor accessible) shop ⊗ (ex assist dogs)

OLD WINDSOR MAP 04 SU97
Runnymede
North Lodge, Windsor Rd SL4 2JL

➲ *(From M25 junct 13. 2m W of Runnymede Bridge on S side of A308. 6m E of Windsor)*

☎ 01784 432891
e-mail: runnymede@nationaltrust.org.uk
web: www.nationaltrust.org.uk/runnymede

Partly designated as a Site of Special Scientific Interest, Runnymede is an area of meadows, grassland, and woodland that sits alongside the Thames. Best known as the site where King John signed the Magna Carta in 1215, this momentous event was commemorated by the American Bar Association, who built a monument here in 1957. There is also a memorial to American President, John F Kennedy. Also there are the Fairhaven Lodges, designed by Edward Lutyens, one of which is now an art gallery.

Times Car parks: Oct-Mar 9-5, Apr-Sep 9-7 **Fee** ✳ Car parking £1-5, Coaches £4-6 **Facilities** ℗ (charged) ⊡ ⌇ ⊓ (outdoor) ♿ (steps to front of tea rooms & art gallery) (Braille guide) toilets for disabled

READING MAP 04 SU77
Museum of English Rural Life `FREE`
University of Reading, Redlands Rd RG1 5EX

➲ *(close to Royal Berkshire Hospital, museum 100mtrs on right)*

☎ 0118 378 8660
e-mail: merl@reading.ac.uk
web: www.merl.org.uk

This museum houses a national collection of agricultural, domestic and crafts exhibits, including wagons, tools and a wide range of other equipment used in the English countryside over the last 150 years. Special facilities are available for school parties. The museum also contains extensive documentary and photographic archives, which can be studied by appointment. There is a regular programme of events and activities, please see website for details.

Times Open all year, Tue-Fri, 9-5, Sat & Sun 2-4.30 (Closed BH's & Xmas-New Year). **Facilities** ℗ ⊓ (outdoor) ♿ (Chair lifts, hearing loop) toilets for disabled shop garden centre ⊗ (ex assist dogs)

RISELEY MAP 04 SU76
Wellington Country Park `2 for 1`
RG7 1SP

➲ *(signed off A33, between Reading & Basingstoke)*
☎ 0118 932 6444
e-mail: info@wellington-country-park.co.uk
web: www.wellington-country-park.co.uk

350 acres of woodland walks and parkland provided for a family outing. Attractions appealing to younger and older children include; miniature railway, variety of children's play areas, crazy golf and nature trails. There is also an 80 acre family campsite.

Times Open Mar-Nov, daily 10-5.30. **Fee** ✳ £6 (ch £5, under 3's free, concessions £5) **Facilities** ℗ ⊡ ⊓ (outdoor) ♿ (Partly accessible) (Nature trail) toilets for disabled shop ⊗ (ex on lead) ⬛

WINDSOR   MAP 04 SU97

Frogmore House

Home Park SL4 1NJ

➲ *(entrance via The Long Walk, from B3021 between Datchet & Old Windsor)*

☎ 020 7766 7305

e-mail: bookinginfo@royalcollection.org.uk

web: www.royalcollection.org.uk

Frogmore House has been a royal retreat since the 18th century, and is today used by the Royal Family for private entertaining. It is especially linked with Queen Charlotte, the wife of George III, and her daughters, whose love of botany and art is reflected throughout the house. Queen Victoria loved Frogmore so much that she broke with royal tradition and chose to build a mausoleum for herself and Prince Albert there.

Times Open 15-17 May & Aug BH wknd, 10-5.30 (last admission 4). Prebooked groups Aug-28 Sep Tue-Thu. **Fee** Contact Ticket Sales and Information Office (020 7766 7305) for details of admission prices. **Facilities** ❷ ⋈ (outdoor) ♿ (Partly accessible) (phone 020 7766 7324 for information) shop ❽ (ex assist dogs) ▬

Legoland Windsor

Winkfield Rd SL4 4AY

➲ *(on B3022 (Windsor to Ascot road) signed from M3 junct 3 & M4 junct 6)*

e-mail: customer.services@legoland.co.uk

web: www.legoland.co.uk

With over 50 interactive rides, live shows, building workshops, driving schools and attractions. Set in 150 acres of beautiful parkland, LEGOLAND Windsor is a different sort of family theme park. An atmospheric and unique experience for the whole family, a visit to LEGOLAND Windsor is more than a day out, it's a lifetime of memories.

Times ✳ Open daily 12 Mar-5 Nov **Facilities** ❷ (charged) ⌑▯◎⋈ (outdoor) ♿ (signing staff, wheelchair hire, parking) toilets for disabled shop ❽ (ex assist dogs) ▬

St George's Chapel

SL4 1NJ

➲ *(M4 junct 6 & M3 junct 3)*

☎ 01753 865538

St George's Chapel, within the precincts of Windsor Castle, is one of the most beautiful ecclesiastical buildings in England. Founded by Edward IV in 1475, it is the burial place of ten monarchs, including Henry VIII and his favourite wife Jane Seymour. The Chapel is the spiritual home of the Order of the Garter, the oldest and most senior order of British Chivalry.

Times Open Mar-Oct 9.45-5.15 (last admission 4) Nov-Feb 9.45-4.15 (last admission 3). May close at short notice - 24hr info line - 01753 831118. (Closed Sun, worshippers welcome) **Fee** Free entry to the Chapel is included in the price of entry to Windsor Castle. **Facilities** ℗ 400 yds shop ❽ (ex assist dogs)

The Royal Landscape

The Savill Garden, Wick Ln, Englefield Green TW20 0UU

➲ *(M25 junct 13, signed off A30 between Egham & Virginia Water)*

☎ 01784 439746 435544

e-mail: enquiries@theroyallandscape.co.uk

web: www.theroyallandscape.co.uk

The work of master landscape gardener, Sir Eric Savill, this is one of the greatest woodland gardens in England. It was created in the 1930s and offers year-round interest with colourful displays of interesting and rare plants. The Savill Building is a visitor centre built to a unique and innovative gridshell design, made with timber harvested from Windsor Great Park. The Royal Landscape is an area of a thousand acres of gardens and parkland accessible to the public, at the southern end of Windsor Great Park. It includes the Savill Garden, the Valley Gardens and Virginia Water, and was shaped and planted over a period of 400 years.

Times Open all year, daily 10-6 (10-4.30 Nov-Feb). Closed 25-26 Dec **Fee** ✳ Mar-Oct: £7 (ch 6-16 £3.50, concessions £5.50). Family £18 (2ad+2ch). Groups (10+) £6.50. For prices from Nov 2008, please call, email or visit website. **Facilities** ❷ (charged) ⌑▯◎ licensed ⋈ (outdoor) ♿ (wheelchairs available) toilets for disabled shop garden centre ❽ (ex assist dogs) ▬

Windsor Castle

SL4 1NJ

➲ *(M4 junct 6 & M3 junct 3)*

☎ 020 7766 7304

e-mail: bookinginfo@royalcollection.org.uk

web: www.royalcollection.org.uk

Covering 13 acres Windsor Castle is the official residence of HM The Queen, and the largest inhabited castle in the world. Begun as a wooden fort by William the Conqueror, it has been added to by almost every monarch since. A visit takes in the magnificent State Apartments, St George's Chapel, Queen Mary's dolls house, the Drawings Gallery, and between October and March, the semi-state rooms created by George IV. A special exhibition to celebrate the 60th birthday of The Prince of Wales is on display until February 2009.

Times Open daily except Good Fri & 25-26 Dec. Nov-Feb, 9.45-4.15 (last admission 3), Mar-Oct 9.45-5.15 (last admission 4). May be subject to change at short notice (24hr info line: 01753 831118) **Fee** £15.50 (ch under 17 £9, under 5's free, concessions £14) Family (2ad+3ch) £40 **Facilities** ℗ (400yds) ♿ (phone 020 7766 7324 for details) toilets for disabled shop ❽ (ex assist dogs) ▬

14

BRISTOL

Clifton Suspension Bridge, Avon Gorge

BRISTOL   MAP 03 ST57

Arnolfini   FREE

16 Narrow Quay BS1 4QA

➲ *(From M32 follow brown signs)*

☎ 0117 917 2300 & 0117 917 2301

e-mail: boxoffice@arnolfini.org.uk

web: www.arnolfini.org.uk

In a fantastic location at the heart of Bristol's harbourside, Arnolfini is one of Europe's leading centres for the contemporary arts. Arnolfini stages art exhibitions, cinema, live art and dance performances, talks and events, and has one of the country's best art bookshops. Entrance to the galleries is free, making Arnolfini a great place to spend a few minutes or a few hours.

Times Open all year, daily 10-8. (Thu, galleries close at 6). **Facilities** ⓟ (100mtrs) (Disabled parking on site) 🚻🍽🎪♿ toilets for disabled shop ⊗ (ex assist dogs) ⬛

Bristol's Blaise Castle House Museum   FREE

Henbury Rd, Henbury BS10 7QS

➲ *(4m NW of city, off B4057)*

☎ 0117 903 9818

e-mail: general_museum@bristol-city.gov.uk

web: www.bristol-city.gov.uk/museums

Built in the 18th century for a Quaker banker, this mansion is now Bristol's Museum of Social History. Set in 400 acres of parkland, nearby Blaise Hamlet is a picturesque estate village, designed by John Nash.

Times Open all year: 10-5 Sat-Wed. (Closed 25-26 Dec & 25-26 Jan). **Facilities** ⓟ 🎪 (outdoor) ♿ (Partly accessible) shop ⊗ (ex assist dogs)

Bristol's City Museum & Art Gallery   FREE

Queen's Rd, Clifton BS8 1RL

➲ *(follow signs to city centre, then follow tourist board signs to City Museum & Art Gallery)*

☎ 0117 922 3571

e-mail: general_museum@bristol-city.gov.uk

web: www.bristol-city.gov.uk/museums

Regional and international collections representing ancient history, natural sciences, and fine and applied arts. Displays include dinosaurs, Bristol ceramics, silver, and Chinese and Japanese ceramics. A full programme of special exhibitions take place throughout the year. Ring for details.

Times Open all year, daily 10-5. (Closed 25-26 Dec). **Facilities** ⓟ (400yds) 🚻♿ (lift) toilets for disabled shop ⊗ (ex assist dogs)

Bristol's Georgian House

7 Great George St, off Park St BS1 5RR

➲ *(5 mins walk from city centre)*

☎ 0117 921 1362

e-mail: general_museum@bristol-city.gov.uk

web: www.bristol-city.gov.uk/museums

A carefully preserved example of a six-storey late 18th-century merchant's town house, with many original features and furnished to illustrate life both above and below stairs. Displays allow visitors to examine and question the role that slavery played in 18th-century Bristol.

Times Open all year: Sat-Wed 10-5. (Closed 25-26 Dec & 26-30 Jan). **Facilities** ⓟ (pay & display street parking) ⊗ (ex assist dogs)

Bristol Zoo Gardens

Clifton BS8 3HA

➲ *(M5 junct 17, take A4018 then follow brown elephant signs. Also signed from city centre)*

☎ 0117 974 7399

e-mail: information@bristolzoo.org.uk

web: www.bristolzoo.org.uk

Within the safety of Bristol Zoo's 12 acre gardens, meet over 450 species of exotic endangered animals from around the globe. Enjoy daily animal shows and expert talks and experience the zoo's newest exhibit 'Butterfly Forest', a fantastic, walk-through butterfly house. Come face to face with penguins and seals in their natural environment when you vist Seal and Penguin Coast. Other attractions include Monkey Jungle and barrier-free lemur garden, Reptile house, Asiatic lion enclosure, pygmy hippos, Bug World, Twilight World, and the children's play area.

Times Open all year, daily (ex 25 Dec). 9-5.30 (British Summer Time), 9-5 (standard hrs) **Fee** ✳ £12 (ch 3-14yrs £7.50, under 3-free, concessions £10.50). Family ticket (2ad+2ch) £35. **Facilities** ⓟ (charged) 🚻🍽 licensed 🎪 (outdoor) ♿ (wheelchairs/electric scooters for use in zoo grounds) toilets for disabled shop ⊗ (kennels for assist dogs) ⬛

British Empire & Commonwealth Museum

Station Approach, Temple Meads BS1 6QH

➲ *(Exit M32 following signs for Commonwealth Museum & Bristol Temple Meads Station)*

☎ 0117 925 4980

e-mail: admin@empiremuseum.co.uk

web: www.empiremuseum.co.uk

Exploring the dramatic 500-year history of the rise and fall of the British Empire and the emergence of the modern Commonwealth, this internationally acclaimed museum uses video stations, interactive exhibits, and computer games, as well as more traditional techniques. Visitors have the opportunity to dress in period costume, learn Morse code or sample exotic spices. The museum is divided into three sections: Britain's first empire 1500-1790, the British Empire at its height 1790-1914, and Independence and Beyond, and is housed in a restored railway terminus built by Brunel. A visit to the museum includes entry to 'Breaking the Chains', an exhibition on the British slave trade, its abolition and legacies (until November 2008).

Times Open all year, daily 10-5. (Closed 25-26 Dec) **Facilities** ❷ (charged) ⬚ ♿ (all but one conference room accessible, lifts) toilets for disabled shop ⊗ (ex assist dogs) ▬

Brunel's ss Great Britain

Great Western Dock, Gas Ferry Rd BS1 6TY

➲ *(off Cumberland Rd)*

☎ 0117 926 0680

e-mail: admin@ssgreatbritain.org

web: www.ssgreatbritain.org

Built and launched in Bristol in 1843, Isambard Kingdom Brunel's maritime masterpiece was the first ocean-going, propeller-driven, iron ship. Launched in 1843 to provide luxury travel to New York, the world's first great ocean liner set new standards in engineering, reliability and speed. Take your choice of audio companion and find out about passengers and crew - from the rich and famous to those leaving 1850s England to begin a new life. Steer the ship on a westerly course, prepare her for sail and climb to the crow's nest. Descend beneath the glass 'sea' for a close up view of the ship's giant hull and propeller and the state-of-the-art equipment which will save her for the next hundred years. Another feature is the Dockyard Museum charting

the history of Brunel's Masterpiece. A replica of the square rigger *Matthew* is moored at the same site when in Bristol. Special events are held all year - please see the website for details.

Times Open all year daily 10-6, 4.30 in winter. (Closed 17, 24-25 Dec). **Facilities** ❷ (charged) ⬚ ♿ (audio guides, free entry for dedicated carers) toilets for disabled shop ⊗ (ex assist dogs) ▬

Explore-At-Bristol

Anchor Rd, Harbourside BS1 5DB

➲ *(from city centre, A4 to Anchor Rd. Located on left opposite Cathedral)*

☎ 0845 345 1235

e-mail: information@at-bristol.org.uk

web: www.at-bristol.org.uk

Explore-At-Bristol is one of the UK's most exciting hands-on science centres, and is located on Bristol's historic Harbourside. Discover interactive exhibits and special exhibitions, take in a Planetarium show, or join the Live Science team for fun experiments and activities. Explore involves people of all ages in an incredible journey through the workings of the world around us.

Times ✳ Open all year, term-time wkdays 10-5, wknds & school hols 10-6. (Closed 24-26 Dec). **Facilities** ❷ (charged) ⬚ 🍴 (outdoor) ♿ (Partly accessible) (induction loop & mini com 0117 914 3475) toilets for disabled shop ⊗ (ex assist dogs) ▬

HorseWorld · 2 for 1

Staunton Manor Farm, Staunton Ln, Whitchurch BS14 0QJ

➲ *(A37 Bristol to Wells road, follow brown signs from Maes Knoll traffic lights)*

☎ 01275 540173

e-mail: visitor.centre@horseworld.org.uk

web: www.horseworld.org.uk

Set in beautiful stone farm buildings on the southern edge of Bristol, HorseWorld's Visitor Centre is an award winning attraction that offers a great day for everyone. Meet the friendly horses, ponies and donkeys.

Times Open all year Apr-Oct daily 10-5; Nov-Mar daily (ex Mon) 10-4. **Fee** £6.75 (ch 3-15yrs £5, concessions £5.75). Family (2ad+2ch) £20. **Facilities** ❷ ⬚ 🍴 🍴 (indoor & outdoor) ♿ toilets for disabled shop ▬

The Red Lodge · FREE

Park Row BS1 5LJ

➲ *(5 mins walk from city centre)*

☎ 0117 921 1360

e-mail: general_museum@bristol-city.gov.uk

web: www.bristol-city.gov.uk/museums

The house was built in 1590 and then altered in 1730. It has fine oak panelling and carved stone chimney pieces, and is furnished in the style of both periods. The Great Oak Room is considered to be one of the finest Elizabethan rooms in the West Country. Outside is a recreation of a Tudor garden. Special events take place all year, please contact for details.

Times Open all year Sat-Wed 10-5 (Closed 25-26 Dec & 12-16 Jan). **Facilities** ℗ (adjacent) ⊗ (ex assist dogs)

BUCKINGHAMSHIRE

John Milton's cottage, Chalfont St Giles

AYLESBURY   MAP 04 SP81

Boarstall Duck Decoy

Boarstall HP18 9UX

➲ *(A41/B4011, towards Long Crendon. Turn right to Boarstall & follow brown sign. Establishment 200yds on right, through Manor Farm)*

☎ 01280 822850

e-mail: stowegarden@nationaltrust.org.uk
web: www.nationaltrust.org.uk

A rare survival of a 17th-century decoy in working order. Working decoy demonstration on Saturday and Sunday, please phone for more details.

Times Open 4 Apr-30 Aug Sat-Sun 10-4; 8 Apr-26 Aug Wed 3.30-6
Fee £2.60 (ch £1.25) Family £6.50 **Facilities** ❷ 🍴 (outdoor) ♿ ❊ (ex assist dogs) ♨

King's Head

King's Head Passage, Market Square HP20 2RW

➲ *(A41 follow signs for town centre, located at top of Market Sq)*

☎ 01296 381501

e-mail: kingshead@nationaltrust.org.uk
web: www.nationaltrust.org.uk

This historic coaching inn was established in 1455 and is still trading today. It has many notable architectural features, including a medieval stained glass window, extensive timber framing and an ancient cobbled courtyard. Once a base for Oliver Cromwell it now houses a history centre among other features.

Times ✳ Open all year NT office 9-6. (Inn Mon-Sat 11-11 & Sun 11-10.30)
Facilities ℗ (2-10min walk) ⌖ ♿ (Hearing loop) toilets for disabled ❊ (ex assist dogs) ♨

Tiggywinkles Visitor Centre & Hedgehog World Museum

Aston Rd HP17 8AF

➲ *(Turn off A418 towards Haddenham then follow signs to 'Wildlife Hospital')*

☎ 01844 292511

e-mail: mail@sttiggywinkles.org.uk
web: www.tiggywinkles.com

Look through the glass into our bird and mammal nursery wards in the hospital. Find out all about the hospital, our patients and their treatment on our education boards dotted around the gardens. See some of the other hospital wards on our CCTV monitor. Wander round the world's first Hedgehog Memorabilia Museum or watch the foxes in their permanent enclosure. Try to catch a glimpse of one of our permanent badgers or see the deer in the recovery paddocks. The animals live as natural a life as possible, so don't be surprised if they do not come out to visit.

Times ✳ Open Etr-Sep, daily 10-4 **Facilities** ❷ 🍴 shop ❊

BEACONSFIELD   MAP 04 SU99

Bekonscot Model Village and Railway   `2 for 1`

Warwick Rd HP9 2PL

➲ *(M40 junct 2, 4m M25 junct 16, take A355 and follow signs to Model Village)*

☎ 01494 672919

e-mail: info@bekonscot.co.uk
web: www.bekonscot.com

A miniature world, depicting rural England in the 1930s. A Gauge 1 model railway meanders through six little villages, each with their own tiny population. Rides on the sit-on miniature railway take place weekends and local school holidays. Remote control boats available. Bekonscot celebrates its 80th Anniversary in 2009.

Times Open mid Feb-Oct, 10-5. **Fee** ✳ £7 (ch £4.50, concessions £5)
Facilities ❷ ⌖ 🍴 (indoor & outdoor) ♿ (wheelchair loan by prior booking) toilets for disabled shop ❊ (ex assist dogs) ▄

BLETCHLEY   MAP 04 SP93

Bletchley Park

The Mansion, Bletchley Park MK3 6EB

➲ *(Approach Bletchley from V7 Saxon St. At rdbt, southern end of Saxon St under railway bridge towards Buckingham & follow signs to Bletchley Park)*

☎ 01908 640404

e-mail: info@bletchleypark.org.uk
web: www.bletchleypark.org.uk

Known as 'Station X' during World War II, this was the home of the secret scientific team that worked to decipher German military messages sent using the Enigma code machine. Visitors can find out more about the Enigma machine; the 'bombes', computers used to crack the code; Alan Turing, one of the leading mathematicians of his day, who worked on the project; as well as see a number of other displays including the use of pigeons during the war, wartime vehicles, and a Churchill collection.

Times ✳ Open daily 9.30-5.30 (Tours at 11 & 2). Wknds open 10.30-5. Closed 25 & 26 Dec. **Facilities** ❷ (charged) ⌖ 🍴 shop ▄

CHALFONT ST GILES
MAP 04 SU99

Chiltern Open Air Museum
Newland Park, Gorelands Ln HP8 4AB

➲ *(M25 junct 17, M40 junct 2. Follow brown signs)*

☎ 01494 871117

e-mail: coamuseum@netscape.net

web: www.coam.org.uk

Chiltern Open Air Museum is an independent charity, established thirty two years ago with the aim of preserving some of the historic building which are unique examples of the heritage of the Chilterns. The museum is now home to more than 30 historic buildings all rescued from demolition that have been re-erected on this 45 acre woodland and parkland site. Events take place weekends and school holidays throughout the season, please check website for details.

Times Open 21 Mar-Oct, daily 10-5 (last admission 3.30) **Fee** ✳ £7.50 (ch 5-16, under 5's free) £5 , concessions £6.50) Family ticket (2ad+2 ch) £22 **Facilities** ❷ ▱ ⼓ (indoor & outdoor) ♿ (Some paths/areas and buildings not accessible for all on this 45 acre site - full details on website or phone) (Braille & audio guides, w/chairs pre-booking advised) toilets for disabled shop ⊗ (ex on lead) ▄

Milton's Cottage
Dean Way HP8 4JH

➲ *(0.5m W of A413. 3m N of M40 junct 2)*

☎ 01494 872313

e-mail: info@miltonscottage.org

web: www.miltonscottage.org

A timber-framed, 16th-century cottage, with a charming garden, the only surviving home in which John Milton lived and worked. He completed *Paradise Lost* and started *Paradise Regained* here. First editions of these works are among the many rare books and artefacts on display.

Times Open Mar-Oct, Tue-Sun 10-1 & 2-6. Also open Spring & Summer BH. **Fee** £4 (ch 15 £2). Group rate 20+ £3 each. **Facilities** ❷ ⼌⼗ licensed ♿ (ground floor only accessible) (special parking area closer to cottage) shop ⊗ (ex assist dogs)

CLIVEDEN
MAP 04 SU98

Cliveden
SL6 0JA

➲ *(2m N of Taplow, follow brown signs on A4)*

☎ 01628 605069

e-mail: cliveden@nationaltrust.org.uk

web: www.nationaltrust.org.uk

The 375 acres of garden and woodland overlook the River Thames, and include a magnificent parterre, topiary, lawns with box hedges, and water gardens. The palatial house, former home of the Astors, is now a hotel - The Great Hall and French Dining Room can be visited on certain afternoons.

Times Open Grounds Mar-Oct daily 11-6, Nov-23 Dec daily 11-4 House Apr-Oct, Thu & Sun 3-5.30 by timed ticket. **Fee** Grounds: £8 (ch £4). House: £1 extra (ch 50p extra). Family ticket £20. Group £7 each. Woodlands £3 (ch £1.50) Family £7.50. **Facilities** ❷ ⼌⼗ licensed ⼓ (outdoor) ♿ (most garden paths accessible) (wheelchairs available, parking) toilets for disabled shop ⊗ (ex woodland & assist dogs) ▰ ▄

GREAT MISSENDEN
MAP 06 SP80

The Roald Dahl Museum & Story Centre
81-83 High St HP16 0AL

➲ *(From London/Amersham turn left off A413 into Great Missenden link road)*

☎ 01494 892192

e-mail: admin@roalddahlmuseum.org

web: www.roalddahlmuseum.org

This award-winning museum is aimed at 6 to 12 year olds and their families. Two interactive and biographical galleries tell the fascinating story of Roald Dahl's life, while the Story Centre puts imagination centre-stage, and encourages everyone (young and old) to dress up, make up stories, words and poems, or get arty in the craft room. Situated in Great Missenden where Dahl lived for over 36 years, it was created as a home for the author's archive (which visitors can see on regular tours) and as a place to inspire creativity and a love of reading in children, about which Dahl was passionate. 13th September every year - Roald Dahl Day national celebrations.

Times Open all year, Tue-Sun & BH Mon 10-5. **Fee** £5.50 (ch 5-18 & concessions £3.95, under 5's free). Family ticket (2ad+up to 3ch) £18 **Facilities** ℗ (5 mins walk) ▱ ⼗ (indoor & outdoor) ♿ (audio loops, tactile maps, wheelchair) toilets for disabled shop ⊗ (ex assist dogs) ▰ ▄

HIGH WYCOMBE
MAP 04 SU89

Hughenden Manor
HP14 4LA

➲ *(1.5m N of High Wycombe, on W side of A4128)*

☎ 01494 755573

e-mail: hughenden@nationaltrust.org.uk

web: www.nationaltrust.org.uk

Fascinating Victorian Manor, home of Prime Minister Benjamin Disraeli from 1847-1881. Many of his possessions are still on display, along with beautiful gardens designed by his wife Mary-Anne. Other facilities include circular woodland walks, family tracker packs, I-spy sheets in the Manor and an exhibition revealing Hughenden's role in WWII. See website for special event details.

Times House open Mar-Oct, Wed-Sun & BH Mon 1-5. (Last admission 4.30). Also open 12-20 Dec 11-3. Gardens same dates as house 11-5. Park open all year. **Fee** £7.40 (ch £3.70). Family ticket £18.40. Garden only £2.90 (ch £2.20). Park free. **Facilities** ❷ ⼌⼗ licensed ⼗ (outdoor) ♿ (Ground floor only fully accessible) (Braille leaflet, wheelchairs, ramp to house) toilets for disabled shop ⊗ (ex assist dogs) ▰ ▄

West Wycombe Park

West Wycombe HP14 3AJ

➲ *(S of A40, at W end of West Wycombe)*

☎ 01494 513569

e-mail: westwycombe@nationaltrust.org.uk
web: www.nationaltrust.org.uk

Set in 300 acres of beautiful parkland, the house was rebuilt in the Palladian style, between 1745 and 1771, for Sir Francis Dashwood. Of particular note are the painted ceilings by Borgnis. The park was laid out in the 18th century and given an artificial lake and classical temples.

Times Open, House & grounds Jun-Aug, Sun-Thu 2-6. Grounds only Apr-May, Sun-Thu 2-6 & BH Sun & Mon 2-6. (Last admission 5.15). Entry by timed tickets. Parties must book in advance. **Fee** House & grounds £6.60 (ch £3.30). Family £16.50. Group £6. Grounds only £3.30 (ch £1.70). **Facilities** ❷ ♿ (partial access to ground floor & gardens) ❸ (ex assist dogs) ❤

Wycombe Museum

Castle Hill House, Priory Av HP13 6PX

➲ *(A404 (Amersham Hill) N of High Wycombe just past railway station or from Marlow Hill A404, follow brown signs)*

☎ 01494 421895

e-mail: museum@wycombe.gov.uk
web: www.wycombe.gov.uk/museum

High Wycombe is famous for chair making and the museum has an extensive collection of chairs and artefacts from the furniture industry. There is also a gallery featuring local scenes and artists. Other aspects of Wycombe's history are also represented along with changing exhibitions. A new local history gallery will be opening October 2008. All exhibitions are interactive and fun for all ages. The beautiful Museum Gardens provide an ideal spot for a picnic.

Times Open all year, Mon-Sat 10-5, Sun 2-5. Closed on BHs except special events - ring for details. **Fee** Free admission (charges made for special events) **Facilities** ❷ ♍ ⛺ (outdoor) ♿ (ground floor and museum gardens only accessible) (portable induction loop, special parking & drop off point) toilets for disabled shop ❸ (ex assist dogs) ▬

LONG CRENDON   MAP 04 SP60

Courthouse

HP18 9AN

➲ *(2m N of Thame, via B4011, on entering village turn right into High St. Courthouse on left at end of High St next to parish church)*

☎ 01280 822850

e-mail: stowegardens@nationaltrust.org.uk
web: www.nationaltrust.org.uk

One of the finest examples of early timber-framed building in the area. Probably built as a wool store in the early 1400s, but also used as a manorial courthouse until the late 19th century, this building stands out, even in this picturesque village. Although the windows and doors have been altered and the chimney stack is Tudor, the magnificent timber roof is original.

Times Open, Upper storey 4 Apr-27 Sep, Sat-Sun 1-6; 8 Apr-Sep, Wed 2-6 **Fee** £1.60 (ch 55p) **Facilities** ❶ (street) ❸ ❤

MIDDLE CLAYDON   MAP 04 SP72

Claydon House

MK18 2EY

➲ *(M40 junct 9 off A413 in Padbury, follow National Trust signs. Entrance by north drive only)*

☎ 01296 730349

e-mail: claydon@nationaltrust.org.uk
web: www.nationaltrust.org.uk

The rather sober exterior of this 18th-century house gives no clue to the extravagances that lie inside, in the form of fantastic rococo carvings. Ceilings, cornices, walls and overmantels are adorned with delicately carved fruits, birds, beasts and flowers by Luke Lightfoot. The Chinese room is particularly splendid. There is also a spectacular parquetry staircase.

Times House open 7 Mar-1 Nov, Sat-Wed 1-5. (Last admission 4.30). **Fee** £6 (ch £2.90). Family ticket £14.75. Private Gardens £3.50. Half price for wheelchair guests. **Facilities** ❷ ♍ ❿ licensed ⛺ (outdoor) ♿ (ground floor accessible) (Braille guide, photograph albums) toilets for disabled ❸ (ex assist dogs & in park) ❤ ▬

QUAINTON   MAP 04 SP72

Buckinghamshire Railway Centre 2 for 1
Quainton Rd Station HP22 4BY
➲ *(Signed off A41 (Aylesbury-Bicester road) at Waddesdon, 7m NW of Aylesbury)*
☎ 01296 655450
e-mail: bucksrailcentre@btopenworld.com
web: www.bucksrailcentre.org

Housed in a former Grade II listed building, the Centre features an interesting and varied collection of about 20 locomotives with 40 carriages and wagons from places as far afield as South Africa, Egypt and America. Items date from the 1800s up to the 1960s. Visitors can take a ride on full-size and miniature steam trains, and stroll around the 20-acre site to see locomotives and rolling stock. The Centre runs locomotive driving courses for visitors. Regular 'Days out with Thomas' events take place throughout the year. 2009 is the 40th anniversary of the Railway Society.

Times Open with engines in steam Apr-Oct, Sun & BH; also Wed in school hols: 10.30-4.30. Restricted viewing most days. Santa's Magical Steaming Days in Dec - advance booking essential. **Fee** Steaming Days: £7 (ch £4.50, under 5's free, concessions £6). Family ticket (2ad+up to 4 ch) £18. Special events £9 (ch £6, under 5's free, concessions £8). Family ticket £24.
Facilities ❷ ♥ ⛺ (outdoor) ♿ (some trains not accessible) (ramped bridge with lift for wheelchairs) toilets for disabled shop ▄

STOWE   MAP 04 SP63

Stowe House
MK18 5EH
➲ *(3m NW Buckingham)*
☎ 01280 818229
e-mail: amcevoy@stowe.co.uk
web: www.shpt.org

Set in the famous landscaped gardens, now owned by the National Trust, Stowe House is a splendid 18th-century neo-classical palace. The leading architects of the day - Vanbrugh, Gibbs, Kent and Leoni - all had a hand in the design in both the house and the gardens. A public school since 1923, Stowe House Preservation Trust now owns the building and is raising money for a six-phase restoration plan.

Times Open various dates & times. Call information line 01280 818166.
Fee ✳ £4 (ch £2.50). NT members £3.40 (ch £2) **Facilities** ❷ ♥ ♿ (lift to 1st floor) toilets for disabled shop ❸ (ex assist dogs)

Stowe Landscape Gardens
MK18 5DQ
➲ *(3m NW of Buckingham via Stowe Ave, off A422)*
☎ 01280 822850
e-mail: stowegarden@nationaltrust.org.uk
web: www.nationaltrust.org.uk

Stowe is a breathtaking 18th-century creation, an idealised version of nature and is one of the first and foremost of the great English landscape gardens. Hidden amongst spectacular views and vast open spaces there are over 40 monuments, temples and secret corners to be discovered.

Times Open all year Jan-Mar, Sat-Sun, 10.30-4, Mar-Nov Wed-Sun 10.30-5.30 (last entry 4); Nov-Feb, Sat-Sun 10.30-4. Open BHs. **Fee** £7.15 (ch £3.50). Family ticket £17.10 **Facilities** ❷ ♥ licensed ⛺ (outdoor) ♿ Some hills Batricars toilets for disabled shop garden centre ♣ ▄

WADDESDON   MAP 04 SP71

Waddesdon Manor
HP18 0JH
➲ *(entrance off A41, 6m NW of Aylesbury)*
☎ 01296 653211, 653226 & 653203
e-mail: waddesdonmanor@nationaltrust.org.uk
web: www.waddesdon.org.uk

Built in the 19th century by Baron Ferdinand de Rothschild, this French-style chateau was created as a showcase for his fine collection of French decorative arts. Its Victorian gardens are known for its parterre, seasonal displays, walks, views, fountains and statues. The aviary is stocked with species that were once part of Baron Ferdinand's collection and the wine cellar contains Rothschild wines dating back to 1868. Special events throughout the year.

Times Gardens: 3 Jan-29 Mar wknds only; Apr-23 Dec Wed-Sun, BHs; 27-31 Dec Wed-Sun & 28-29 Dec, 10-5. House: Apr-1 Nov Wed-Sun & BHs Bachelors Wing Apr-1 Nov Wed-Fri; 11 Nov-23 Dec Wed-Fri 12-4 Sat-Sun; 21-22 Dec, 27-31 Dec Wed-Sun & 28-29 Dec Sat-Sun 11-4 & Wed-Fri 12-4. **Fee** Gardens, 6 Jan-18 Mar (wknds only) 21 Mar-23 Dec, 27-31 Dec (Wed-Fri) £5.50, (ch £2.75). Family £13.75. 19 Mar-23 Dec, 27-31 Dec (wknds & BH's) £7, (ch £3.50). Family £17.50. House & gardens, 21 Mar-28 Oct (Wed-Fri) £13.20, (ch £9.35), wknds & BHs £15, (ch £11). **Facilities** ℗ ⦿ licensed ♿ (wheelchairs, Braille guide, parking, scented plants) toilets for disabled shop garden centre ⊗ (ex assist dogs) ⛟ ➡

WEST WYCOMBE   MAP 04 SU89

The Hell-Fire Caves

HP14 3AJ

➲ *(on A40 in West Wycombe)*

☎ 01494 524411 (office) & 533739 (caves)

e-mail: mary@west-wycombe-estate.co.uk

web: www.hellfirecaves.co.uk

The entrance to West Wycombe caves is halfway up the hill that dominates the village. On the summit stands the parish church and the mausoleum of the Dashwood family. The caves are not natural but were dug on the orders of Sir Francis Dashwood between 1748 and 1752. Sir Francis, the Chancellor of the Exchequer, was also the founder of the Hell Fire Club, whose members were reputed to have held outrageous and blasphemous parties in the caves, which extend approximately half a mile underground. The entrance, from a large forecourt, is a brick tunnel that leads into the caves, where tableaux and curiosities are exhibited.

Times Open all year, Apr-Oct, daily, 11-5.30; Nov-Mar, wknds & school hols 11-5.30. **Fee** ✳ £5 (ch, concessions £4). Family ticket £15 (max 3 ch) **Facilities** ℗ ⛽ ⌲ (outdoor) ♿ toilets for disabled shop ⊗ (ex assist dogs) ➡

WING   MAP 04 SP82

Ascott

LU7 0PS

➲ *(0.5m E of Wing, 3m SW of Leighton Buzzard on S side of A418)*

☎ 01296 688242

e-mail: info@ascottestate.co.uk

web: www.ascottestate.com

A National Trust property since 1949, Ascott holds an exceptional collection of paintings, Chinese porcelain, and English and French furniture. The garden is a fine example of Victorian gardening and the grounds are stunning at any time of year.

Times House & Gardens: 24 Mar-26 Apr daily (ex Mon), 28 Apr-23 Jul Tue-Thu, 28 Jul-11 Sep daily (ex Mon). Open BH Mons. **Fee** ✳ House & Garden £8 (ch £4). Gardens only: £4 (ch £2). **Facilities** ℗ ♿ (w/chairs avail, assistance required, large print guide) toilets for disabled ⊗ ⛟

George I, Stowe House

CAMBRIDGESHIRE

Mathematical Bridge, River Cam, Cambridge

CAMBRIDGE   MAP 05 TL45

Cambridge & County Folk Museum   `2 for 1`

2/3 Castle St CB3 0AQ

➲ *(off A14 onto A3019, museum NW of town)*

☎ 01223 355159

e-mail: info@folkmuseum.org.uk

web: www.folkmuseum.org.uk

This timber-framed inn houses items covering the everyday life of the people of Cambridgeshire from the early times to the present day. There are also temporary exhibitions. Special exhibitions and children's activity days take place throughout the year. Please telephone for details.

Times Open all year, Apr-Sep, Mon-Sat 10.30-5, Sun 2-5. Oct-Mar, Tue-Sat 10.30-5, Sun 2-5. (Last admissions 30 mins before closing). Closed 24-31 Dec & 1 Jan **Fee** £3.50 (ch 5-12 £1, concessions £2) one free ch with every full paying adult. **Facilities** ℗ (300yds) (pay and display on street parking) ♿ (outdoor) ♿ (lift & disabled toilet) toilets for disabled shop ⊗ (ex assist dogs)

Cambridge University Botanic Garden

1 Brookside CB2 1JE

➲ *(1m S of city centre, 5min from train station)*

☎ 01223 336265

e-mail: enquiries@botanic.cam.ac.uk

web: www.botanic.cam.ac.uk

The Cambridge University Botanic Garden is a 40-acre oasis of beautifully landscaped gardens and glasshouses close to the heart of the historic city. Opened on its present site in 1846, the garden showcases a collection of some 8000 plant species. This Grade II heritage landscape features the Rock Garden, displaying alpine plants, the Winter and Autumn Gardens, tropical rainforest and seasonal displays in the Glasshouses, the historic Systematic Beds, the Scented Garden, Herbaceous Beds and the finest collection of trees in the east of England.

Times Open all year daily Apr-Sep 10-6; Feb-Mar, Oct 10-5, Nov-Jan 10-4. (Glasshouses close 30 mins before garden). Please call to check Xmas closure. Entry by Bateman St & Station Rd gates on wkdays & by Bateman St gate only at wknds & BH. **Fee** £4 (concessions £3.50) **Facilities** ℗ (on street parking or park & ride) ♿ (outdoor) ♿ (Some historic areas of the garden inaccessible for wheelchairs, such as the rock garden) (guiding service, manual & motorised wheelchairs-prebooked) toilets for disabled shop ⊗ (ex assist dogs)

Fitzwilliam Museum   `FREE`

Trumpington St CB2 1RB

➲ *(M11 junct 11, 12 or 13. Near city centre)*

☎ 01223 332900

e-mail: fitzmuseum-enquiries@lists.cam.ac.uk

web: www.fitzmuseum.cam.ac.uk

The Fitzwilliam is the art museum of the University of Cambridge and one of the oldest public museums in Britain. It contains magnificent collections spanning centuries and civilisations including antiquities from Ancient Egypt, Greece and Rome; sculpture, furniture, armour, ceramics, manuscripts, coins and medals, paintings, drawings and prints.

Times Open all year Tue-Sat 10-5, Sun 12-5. (Closed Mon ex BH, & 24-26, 31 Dec & 1 Jan). **Facilities** ℗ (400yds) (2hr max, metered) ♿ (outdoor) ♿ (induction loop) toilets for disabled shop ⊗ (ex assist dogs)

Scott Polar Research Institute Museum

Lensfield Rd CB2 1ER

➲ *(1km S of City Centre)*

☎ 01223 336540

e-mail: enquiries@spri.cam.ac.uk

web: www.spri.cam.ac.uk

An international centre for polar studies, including a museum featuring displays of Arctic and Antarctic expeditions, with special emphasis on those of Captain Scott and the exploration of the Northwest Passage. Other exhibits include Inuit work and other arts of the polar regions, as well as displays on current scientific exploration. Public lectures run from October to December and February to April.

Times Open all year, Tue-Fri 11-1 & 2-4. Sat 12-4. Closed some BH wknds, public hols & University hols. For possible closures in 2009 please call 01223 336540 or check the website www.spri.cam.ac.uk **Fee** Free admission, donations welcome. **Facilities** ℗ (400mtrs) ♿ (majority of museum accessible. One small area of display & part of museum shop up a step) shop ⊗ (ex assist dogs) ⊟

University Museum of Archaeology & Anthropology   `FREE`

Downing St CB2 3DZ

➲ *(opposite Crowne Plaza Hotel in city centre)*

☎ 01223 333516

e-mail: cumaa@hermes.cam.ac.uk

web: http://museum.archanth.cam.ac.uk

The museum is part of the Faculty of Archaeology and Anthropology of the University of Cambridge. It was established in 1884 and is still housed in its 1916 building on the Downing Site in the city centre. Some of the highlights are Pacific material collected on Captain Cook's voyages of exploration and a 46-foot high totem pole from Canada. Find out about local, national and world archaeology in the Archaeology Galleries, including painted pottery from Peru, gilded Anglo-Saxon brooches, and Roman altar stones.

Times ✳ Open all year Tue-Sat 2-4.30. (Closed 1wk Etr & 1wk Xmas). Telephone for extended summer hours. **Facilities** ℗ (100yds) ♿ (lift available) shop ⊗ (ex assist dogs)

DUXFORD   MAP 05 TL44

Imperial War Museum Duxford
CB2 4QR

➲ *(off M11 junct 10, on A505)*
☎ 01223 835000
e-mail: duxford@iwm.org.uk
web: www.iwm.org.uk

Duxford is one of the world's most spectacular aviation heritage complexes with a collection of nearly 200 aircraft, the American Air Museum and a fine collection of military vehicles plus special exhibitions including The Battle of Britain, Normandy Experience and Monty. The Museum holds four Air Shows throughout the summer plus other special events such as the Military Vehicle Show and Flying Proms.

Times Open all year, mid Mar-mid Oct daily 10-6; mid Oct-mid Mar daily 10-4. (Closed 24-26 Dec) **Facilities** ℗ ☐✆🍽🖼 (indoor) ♿ (w/chair available-phone in advance, ramps, lifts) toilets for disabled shop ⊗ (ex assist dogs) ▬

ELY   MAP 05 TL58

Ely Cathedral
CB7 4DL

➲ *(A10 or A142, 15m from Cambridge)*
☎ 01353 667735
e-mail: receptionist@cathedral.ely.anglican.org
web: www.cathedral.ely.anglican.org

The Octagon Tower of Ely Cathedral can be seen for miles as it rises above the surrounding flat fenland. A monastery was founded on the site by St Etheldreda in 673, but the present cathedral church dates from 1083 and is a magnificent example of Romanesque architecture. Choral music is a big attraction at the Cathedral, and visitors can hear Evensong at 5.30pm on weekdays and Saturdays, and 4pm on a Sunday.

Times ✴ Open daily, Summer 7-7, Winter 7.30-6 (5pm Sun). **Facilities** ℗ (walking distance) ☐✆🍽🖼 (outdoor) ♿ (touch tour for blind/partially sighted) toilets for disabled shop ⊗ (ex assist dogs) ▬

Ely Museum   `2 for 1`
The Old Gaol, Market St CB7 4LS

➲ *(On corner of Market St and Lynn Rd. In centre of Ely, 250mtrs from west door of Ely Cathedral)*
☎ 01353 666655
e-mail: admin@elymuseum.org.uk
web: www.elymuseum.org.uk

Centre of history for the Isle of Ely and the Fens, telling the story of the area from prehistoric times to the twentieth century. The museum is within a building dating from the 13th century that has been a private house, a tavern, a registry office and most famously the Bishop's Gaol. Sensitively renovated in 1997 much of the building's history can still be seen, including prisoner's graffiti, hidden doorways and original planking on the walls.

Times Open during summer, Mon-Sat 10.30-5 & Sun 1-5. Winter Mon-Sat 10.30-4 (closed Tue), Sun 1-4. **Fee** £3 (accompanied children free, concessions £2.50). **Facilities** ℗ 200 mtrs ♿ (Stair lift, auto doors) toilets for disabled shop ⊗ (ex assist dogs)

Oliver Cromwell's House   `2 for 1`
29 St Mary's St CB7 4HF

➲ *(follow brown tourist signs from main roads. Adjacent to Saint Mary's Church)*
☎ 01353 662062
e-mail: tic@eastcambs.gov.uk
web: www.eastcambs.gov.uk/tourism

Cromwell inherited the house and local estates from a maternal uncle and moved here in 1636, along with his mother, sisters, wife and eight children. There are displays and period rooms dealing with Cromwell's life, the Civil War and domestic life in the 17th century, as well as the history of The Fens and the house itself, from its medieval origins to its role as an inn in the 19th century. Various special events are held during the year including Living History days. 2009 is the 350th anniversary of Cromwell's death.

Times Open all year: Apr-Oct, daily 10-5; Nov-Mar, Mon-Fri 11-4, Sat 10-5. Sun, 11.15-4. **Fee** ✴ £4.30 (ch £3, concessions £3.85). Family ticket £12.50 **Facilities** ℗ (100yds) ♿ (wheelchair access to two rooms) (written script of audio features) shop ⊗ (ex assist dogs) ▬

The Stained Glass Museum   `2 for 1`
The South Triforium, Ely Cathedral CB7 4DL

➲ *(Museum inside Ely Cathedral on corner of Market St & Lymm Rd)*
☎ 01353 660347
e-mail: curator@stainedglassmuseum.com
web: www.stainedglassmuseum.com

Eight hundred years of stained glass history are illustrated in this unique museum inside Ely Cathedral. Over 100 panels of original stained glass windows rescued from the UK and abroad are on display. The medieval section includes important loans from the Victoria and Albert Museum in London. There are also exhibits from Buckingham Palace and Windsor Castle, work by William Morris and John Piper, and a changing summer exhibition of contemporary work.

Times Open all year (ex Good Fri & 25-26 Dec) Etr-Oct, Mon-Fri 10.30-5, Sat 10.30-5.30, Sun 12-6. Nov-Etr, Mon-Sat 10.30-5, Sun 12-4.30 **Fee** ✴ £3.50 (ch under 16 & concessions £2.50). Family ticket (up to 4 with 1 under 16) £7. **Facilities** ℗ (400yds) ☐✆🍽♿ (Partly accessible) (interactive virtual visit at ground floor) toilets for disabled shop ⊗ (ex assist dogs) ▬

HAMERTON — MAP 04 TL17

Hamerton Zoo Park

PE28 5RE

➲ *(off A1 junct 15, signed Sawtry)*

☎ 01832 293362

e-mail: office@hamertonzoopark.com

web: www.hamertonzoopark.com

A wildlife breeding centre, dedicated to the practical conservation of endangered species including gibbons, marmosets, lemurs, wildcats, meerkats, sloths and many more. There is also a large and varied bird collection, with several species unique to Hamerton. Over 120 species in all. Other attractions include a children's play area, and new "creature contact" sessions.

Times ✳ Open Summer daily 10.30-6; Winter daily 10.30-4. Closed 25 Dec **Facilities** ♿ ⏚ 🛒 shop ⊗ ▄

HOUGHTON — MAP 04 TL27

Houghton Mill

PE28 2AZ

➲ *(in Houghton signed off A1123 Huntingdon to St Ives)*

☎ 01480 301494

e-mail: houghtonmill@nationaltrust.org.uk

web: www.nationaltrust.org.uk

The last working watermill on the Great Ouse, Houghton Mill has hands-on exhibits for all the family and has most of its machinery intact.

Times Open Mill/Bookshop: 2 May-26 Sep Sat 11-5, 27 Apr-27 Sep Mon-Wed & Sun 11-5, Mar-Apr & Oct Sat 11-5. Also open BH hols & Good Fri. **Fee** £3.90 (ch £1.80). Family £8.90 **Facilities** ♿ ⏚ 🛒 ♿ (Partly accessible) ⊗ (ex assist dogs) ♨

LINTON — MAP 05 TL54

Chilford Hall Vineyard　[2 for 1]

Chilford Hall, Balsham Rd CB21 4LE

➲ *(signed from A1307 & A11)*

☎ 01223 895600

e-mail: annette@chilfordhall.co.uk

web: www.chilfordhall.co.uk

Taste and buy award-winning wines from the largest vineyard in Cambridgeshire. See the grapes growing in the 18-acre vineyard and take a winery tour to learn how English wine is made and appreciate the subtle difference between each of the Chilford quality wines. Telephone for details of special events.

Times Open Mar-Oct , Fri-Sun & BHs **Fee** Guided tours £6.65 (ch free). Party 15+ discount £5.85. **Facilities** ♿ ⏚ ♿ (ramps, lift, all areas are ground floor) toilets for disabled shop ▄

Linton Zoological Gardens

Hadstock Rd CB21 4NT

➲ *(M11 junct 9/10, on B1052 off A1307 between Cambridge & Haverhill, signed)*

☎ 01223 891308

web: www.lintonzoo.co.uk

Linton Zoo places emphasis on conservation and education where visitors can see a combination of beautiful gardens and a wealth of wildlife from all over the world. There are many rare and exotic creatures to see including tapirs, snow leopards, tigers, lions, zebra, tamarin monkeys, lemurs, owls, parrots, giant tortoises, snakes, tarantulas and many others. The zoo is set in 16-acres of gardens with plenty of picnic areas, children's play area and bouncy castle.

Times Open all year, daily 10.30-4, (last admission 3). Hours extended during summer. Closed 25-26 Dec. **Fee** ✳ £7.50 (ch 2-13 £5, concessions £7) **Facilities** ♿ ⏚ 🛒 (outdoor) ♿ toilets for disabled shop ⊗ ▄

LODE — MAP 05 TL56

Anglesey Abbey, Gardens & Lode Mill

CB2 9EJ

➲ *(6m NE of Cambridge on B1102, signed from A14)*

☎ 01223 810080

e-mail: angleseyabbey@ntrust.org.uk

web: www.nationaltrust.org.uk/angleseyabbey

A medieval undercroft has survived from the priory founded here in 1135, but the house dates mainly from 1600. Thomas Hobson of *Hobson's Choice* was one of the owners. A later owner was Lord Fairhaven, who amassed the huge collection of pictures, and laid out the beautiful gardens which also display over a hundred pieces of classical sculpture. Lode Mill was restored to full working order in 1982.

Times Open House: 8 Apr-1 Nov, Wed-Sun & BH Mon, 11-5. Gardens open 18 Mar-1 Nov 10.30-5.30. Lode Mill open Jan-Dec, Wed-Sun 11-3.30 **Fee** House, garden & mill £9.75 (ch £4.90). Family £24.40. Garden & mill £5.80 (ch £2.90). Family £14.50. **Facilities** ♿ 🍴 🛒 (outdoor) ♿ (Partly accessible) (electric buggy, wheelchairs, large print & braille guides) toilets for disabled shop garden centre ⊗ (ex assist dogs) ♨ ▄

PETERBOROUGH — MAP 04 TL19

Flag Fen Archaeology Park　[2 for 1]

The Droveway, Northey Rd PE6 7QJ

➲ *(From A1139 exit at Boongate junct. At rdbt 3rd exit, through lights, turn right. At T-junct turn right, Flag Fen signed)*

☎ 0844 414 0646

e-mail: info@flagfen.org

web: www.flagfen.org

Although visitors enter this site through a 21st-century roundhouse, the rest of their day will be spent in the Bronze Age, some 3,000 years ago. Flag Fen's Museum contains artefacts found over the last 20 years of excavating on site, and includes among them the oldest wheel in Britain. In the Park there is a reconstructed Bronze Age settlement and Iron Age roundhouse, while in the Preservation Hall visitors can see the

CONTINUED

27

excavated Bronze Age processional way that spanned over one mile. The Hall also contains a 60-ft mural depicting the fens in ancient times. The 2 for 1 voucher is only valid on non-event days.

Times Open daily Mar-Oct 10-5 (last admission 4). **Fee** £5.50 (ch £4.15, concessions £4.95). Family £15.15. **Facilities** ℗ ⊡ 🗮 (outdoor) ♿ (electric mobility scooter and wheelchairs available) toilets for disabled shop ⊗ (ex assist dogs) 🚍

Peterborough Cathedral

PE1 1XS

➲ *(access from A1 junct with A605 or A47, follow signs for city centre)*

☎ 01733 343342 & 355300

e-mail: a.watson@peterborough-cathedral.org.uk

web: www.peterborough-cathedral.org.uk

With one of the most dramatic West fronts in the country, its three arches an extraordinary creation of medieval architecture, it would be easy for the interior to be an anticlimax, but it is not. The dramatic Romanesque interior is little altered since its completion 800 years ago. Particular highlights of a visit include the unique painted nave ceiling, the elaborate fan vaulting of the 'new' building, Saxon carvings from an earlier church and the burial place of two Queens. An exhibition in the North aisle tells the story of the cathedral. A range of tours can be booked in advance: please contact the Chapter office for details.

Times Open all year, Mon-Fri 9-6.30 (ltd access from 5.30), Sat 9-5, Sun services from 7.30 visitors from 12. (Closed 25-26 Dec). **Fee** Donations appreciated. Group tours £4 (concessions £3) **Facilities** ℗ (300yds) (no parking within cathedral precincts) ⊡ 🍴 🗮 ♿ (touch & hearing centre, Braille guide, ramps) toilets for disabled shop ⊗ (ex assist dogs or in grounds)

Railworld   2 for 1

Oundle Rd PE2 9NR

➲ *(from A1(M) Peterborough onto A1139 then exit at junct 5 to city centre. At 1st rdbt, follow "Little Puffer" tourist signs. Entrance for Railworld off Oundle Rd at city end through car park)*

☎ 01733 344240 & 319362

e-mail: railworld@aol.com

web: www.railworld.net

Railworld is a sustainable transport centre and 21st-century rail showcase. Its main focus is on the future of rail transport and how it can meet the challenges of climate change and other environmental issues. It features a large model railway, displays on rail history, showcases of rail technology and innovation, an environmental maze, hovertrains, and much more.

Times Open Mar-Oct daily 11-4, Nov-Feb Mon-Fri 11-4. Closed Good Fri & 25-31 Dec unless by appointment. **Fee** ✳ £5 (ch £2.50, concessions £4). Family £13 (up to 4 ch). **Facilities** ℗ ⊡ 🗮 (outdoor) ♿ (reasonable access) toilets for disabled shop ⊗ (ex assist dogs & outside) 🚍

RAMSEY   MAP 04 TL28

Ramsey Abbey Gatehouse   FREE

Abbey School PE17 1DH

➲ *(SE edge of Ramsey, at Chatteris Road & B1096 junct)*

☎ 01480 301494

e-mail: ramseyabbey@nationaltrust.org.uk

web: www.nationaltrust.org.uk/regions/eastanglia

The ruins of this 15th-century gatehouse, together with the 13th-century Lady Chapel, are all that remain of the abbey. Half of the gatehouse was taken away after the Dissolution. Built in ornate late-Gothic style, it has panelled buttresses and friezes.

Times Open Apr-Sep, first Sun of the month 1-5 (Group visits by appt only other wknds) **Facilities** ⊗ 🌿

THORNHAUGH   MAP 04 TL00

Sacrewell Farm & Country Centre   2 for 1

PE8 6HJ

➲ *(E of A1/A47 junct. Follow brown tourist signs from both directions)*

☎ 01780 782254

e-mail: info@sacrewell.org.uk

web: www.sacrewell.org.uk

Treasures of farming and the country await discovery at this farm and 18th-century watermill. All aspects of agriculture and country life through the ages are here, listed buildings, working watermill, mill house and farm bygones. Farm animals, tractor rides, mini maze and pedal tractors are just a few of the activities to be experienced. Lamb feeding takes place in March and April, and there are egg hunts at Easter. Please check website for special events.

Times Open all year daily Mar-Sep, 9.30-5; Oct-Feb 10-4. Closed 24 Dec-2 Jan. **Fee** ✳ £6 (ch £4.50, pen £5). Family ticket £18.50. **Facilities** ℗ ⊡ 🍴 licensed 🗮 (indoor & outdoor) ♿ (upstairs in watermill not accessible) toilets for disabled shop 🚍

WANSFORD   MAP 04 TL09

Nene Valley Railway   2 for 1

Wansford Station, Stibbington PE8 6LR

➲ *(A1 at Stibbington, W of Peterborough, 1m S of A47 junct)*

☎ 01780 784444

e-mail: nvrorg@nvr.co.uk

web: www.nvr.org.uk

Originally opened as a working railway in 1845, closed in 1966, then re-opened in 1977 as a tourist railway, Nene Valley Railway has steam and diesel engines, carriages and wagons from Europe including the UK. All the sights and sounds of the golden age of steam come alive here. Travelling between Yarwell Junction, Wansford and Peterborough the 7.5 miles of track pass through the heart of the 500-acre Ferry Meadows Country Park. Nene Valley Railway is also the home of 'Thomas'- children's favourite engine.

Times Train services operate on Sun from Jan; wknds from Apr-Oct; Wed from May, plus other mid-week services in summer. **Fee** ✳ £10.50 (ch 3-15 £5.50, concessions £8). Family ticket £26. **Facilities** ❷ ⌺⅁ (outdoor) ♿ (disabled access to trains) toilets for disabled shop ▰

WATERBEACH   MAP 05 TL46

The Farmland Museum and Denny Abbey

`2 for 1`

Ely Rd CB25 9PQ

➲ *(on A10 between Cambridge & Ely)*

☎ 01223 860988

e-mail: info@farmlandmuseum.org.uk

web: www.dennyfarmlandmuseum.org.uk

Explore two areas of rural life at this fascinating museum. The Abbey tells the story of those who have lived there, including Benedictine monks, Franciscan nuns, and the mysterious Knights Templar. The farm museum features the craft workshops of a wheelwright, a basketmaker, and a blacksmith. There is also a 1940s farmworker's cottage and a village shop. Special events on Easter, May and August Bank Holidays.

Times Open daily, Apr-Oct, 12-5. **Fee** ✳ £4 (ch £2, concessions £3) **Facilities** ❷ ⌺⅁ (outdoor) ♿ (Partly accessible) (wheelchairs, guides upstairs) toilets for disabled shop ▰

WICKEN   MAP 05 TL57

Wicken Fen National Nature Reserve

Lode Ln CB7 5XP

➲ *(S of Wicken A1123)*

☎ 01353 720274

e-mail: wickenfen@nationaltrust.org.uk

web: www.nationaltrust.org.uk

An ancient fenland landscape and internationally renowned wetland site, Wicken Fen is home to the Wicken Vision Project, the Trust's most ambitious landscape-scale habitat restoration project.

Times Open Jan-15 Feb & 2 Nov-Dec Tue-Sun 10-4.30, 16-22 Feb & 6 Apr-1 Nov daily 10-5, 23 Feb-5 Apr Tue-Sun 10-5. **Fee** £5.50 (ch £2.80). Family £14. **Facilities** ❷ (charged) ⌺⅁ (outdoor) ♿ (Partly accessible) shop ♨

WIMPOLE   MAP 05 TL35

Wimpole Hall

SG8 0BW

➲ *(M11 junct 12, 8m SW of Cambridge off A603)*

☎ 01223 206000

e-mail: wimpolehall@nationaltrust.org.uk

web: www.wimpole.org

Wimpole Hall is one of the grandest mansions in East Anglia, and has 360 acres of parkland devised and planted by no less than four celebrated landscape designers, Charles Bridgeman, `Capability' Brown, Sanderson Miller and Humphrey Repton. The house dates back to 1640, but was altered into a large 18th-century mansion with a Georgian façade. The chapel has a trompe l'oeil ceiling.

Times Hall 28 Feb-15 Jul, 29 Aug-1 Nov, Mon-Wed, Sat & Sun 10.30-5; 18 Jul-27 Aug, Mon-Thu, Sat & Sun 10.30-5. Garden 1-25 Feb, 2 Nov-23 Dec, 2-31 Jan, Mon-Wed, Sat & Sun 11-4; 28 Feb-15 Jul, Mon-Wed, Sat & Sun; 18 Jul-27 Aug, 10.30-5. BH Mon & Good Fri 10.30-5 (Hall 11-5 & Good Fri 1-5) Park: all year dawn-dusk daily, **Fee** Hall & Garden: £8.80 (ch £4.95) Family £25.50. Hall, garden & farm £13.30 (ch £7.20). Family £35. Garden & farm £7.30 (ch £4.95) Family £22.50. Garden only £3.70 (ch £1.95) **Facilities** ❷ (charged) ⌺⍾⅁ (outdoor) ♿ (Partly accessible) (Braille & large print guide, buggies, stairlift, w/chair) toilets for disabled shop ✖ (ex in park) ♨ ▰

Wimpole Home Farm

SG8 0BW

➲ *(M11 junct 12, 8m SW of Cambridge off A603)*

☎ 01223 206000

e-mail: wimpolehall@nationaltrust.org.uk

web: www.wimpole.org

When built in 1794, the Home Farm was one of the most advanced agricultural enterprises in the country. The Great Barn, now restored, holds a display of farm machinery and implements of the kind used at Wimpole over the past two centuries. On the farm there are rare breeds of domestic animals, and visitors can see the new lambs in spring, and sheep shearing in June. Please ring for details of special events.

Times Open 1-25 Feb, Sat & Sun 11-4; 28 Feb-15 Jul, Mon-Wed, Sat & Sun 10.30-5; Jul-27 Aug, Mon-Thu, Sat & Sun 10.30-5, 29 Aug-1 Nov Mon-Wed, Sat & Sun 10.30-5; 7 Nov-20 Dec, Sat-Sun 11-4, 27-31 Dec, Tue-Thu, Sat & Sun 11-4, 2-31Jan Sat-Sun 11-4. BH Mon & Good Fri 10.30-5 **Fee** £7.30 (ch £4.95) Family £22.50. Hall & Farm: £13.30(ch £7.20) Family £35 **Facilities** ❷ ⌺⍾⅁ (outdoor) ♿ (Large print guide, wheelchairs, electric buggies) toilets for disabled shop ✖ (ex assist dogs) ♨ ▰

WISBECH MAP 09 TF40

Peckover House & Garden

North Brink PE13 1JR

➲ *(Exit A47, follow town centre signs, then brown tourist signs)*

☎ 01945 583463

e-mail: peckover@nationaltrust.org.uk
web: www.nationaltrust.org.uk

Dating from 1722, Peckover House is an elegant Georgian brick townhouse with an outstanding two-acre walled town garden. Over 70 types of rose grow here, along with a number of notable specimen trees such as Maidenhead Tree and Tulip Tree. The Victorian glasshouses include a fern house, and an orangery with 300-year-old trees that still bear fruit. Visitors can borrow a croquet set and play on the lawn. There is a children's handling collection in the basement. Lots of special events each year, ring for details.

Times House open 14 Mar-1 Nov, Mon-Wed, wknds, 12-4.30 Gardens 12-5
Fee £5.80 (ch £2.90). Family ticket £14.70. Garden only £3.70, (ch £1.85)
Facilities Ⓟ (400yds) ⬚🍴 ♿ (Batricar, induction loops, large print & Braille guides) toilets for disabled shop 🚫 (ex assist dogs) ⛄ ➡

WOODHURST MAP 05 TL37

The Raptor Foundation `2 for 1`

The Heath, St Ives Rd PE28 3BT

➲ *(B1040 to Somersham, follow brown signs)*

☎ 01487 741140

e-mail: heleowl@aol.com
web: www.raptorfoundation.org.uk

Permanent home to over 250 birds of which there are 40 different varieties. This is a unique opportunity to meet and learn about birds of prey. Depending on weather and time of year flying demonstrations are held, usually three times a day and audiences have the chance to participate in displays. There are nearly 60 birds in the flying team, so each display has a different set of birds. Educational trail linking to new education room. New indoor flying area. Ask about activity days, membership and adoption.

Times Open all year, daily 10-5. Closed 25-26 Dec & 1 Jan. **Fee** £4.50 (ch £2.75 ages 2-4 £1, concessions £3.50). Family ticket £12.50. **Facilities** Ⓟ ⬚ 🍴 ☂ (outdoor) ♿ (ramped areas, blocked paved paths) toilets for disabled shop 🚫 ➡

CHESHIRE

Wildboarclough, Peak District National Park

BEESTON   MAP 07 SJ55

Beeston Castle

Chapel Ln CW6 9TX

➲ *(on minor road off A49 or A41)*

☎ 01829 260464

web: www.english-heritage.org.uk

Legend tells of a vast treasure hidden here by Richard II, but the real treasure at Beeston lies in its 4,000 years of history waiting to be discovered. Breathtaking views extend from the Pennines to the mountains of Wales.

Times Open all year, 21 Mar-Sep, daily 10-6; Oct-Mar, Thu-Mon 10-4. Closed 24-26 Dec & 1 Jan. **Fee** £5 (concessions £4, ch £2.50). Prices and opening times are subject to change in March 2009. Please call 0870 333 1181 for the most up to date prices and opening times when planning your visit. **Facilities** ❷ ㆑ shop ❽ (in certain areas) ⚏

CAPESTHORNE   MAP 07 SJ87

Capesthorne Hall

SK11 9JY

➲ *(On A34 between Congleton and Wilmslow)*

☎ 01625 861221

e-mail: info@capesthorne.com

web: www.capesthorne.com

Capesthorne has been the home of the Bromley-Davenport family and their ancestors since Domesday times. The present house dates from 1719 and was designed by the Smiths of Warwick. It was subsequently altered by Edward Blore in 1837 and after a disastrous fire in 1861 the whole of the centre portion was rebuilt by Anthony Salvin.
Capesthorne contains a great variety of sculptures, paintings and other items including a collection of boxes, from a Victorian oak letterbox to hat and cigar boxes.

Times Open Apr-Oct, Sun & Mon (inc BH) Closed Xmas & New Year. Park & Garden 12-5.30, Hall 1.30-3.30 **Fee** ✳ Park, Garden & Chapel £4 (ch £2). Park, Gardens, Chapel & Hall £6.50 (ch £3 & concessions £5.50). Family ticket £15. Special deal on Mon £10 per car (up to 4 persons). Coach £50, Mini-bus £25 **Facilities** ❷ ⬚ ⬚ ⬚ (Partly accessible) (ramp access to ground floor of hall & gardens) toilets for disabled ❽ (ex assist dogs & in gardens)

CHESTER   MAP 07 SJ46

The Cheshire Military Museum

The Castle CH1 2DN

➲ *(follow signs to Military Museum from town centre)*

☎ 01244 327617

e-mail: museum@chester.ac.uk

web: www.chester.ac.uk/militarymuseum

This military museum boasts exhibits from the history of the Cheshire Regiment, Cheshire Yeomanry, 5th Royal Inniskilling Dragoon Guards, and 3rd Carabiniers. Display of the work of George Jones, Victorian battle artist, and an exhibition of life in barracks in the 1950s. Research available by written appointment and donation. There are special events throughtout the year, please phone for details.

Times Open all year, daily 10-5 (last entry 4). (Closed 22 Dec-3 Jan). **Fee** ✳ £3 (ch & concessions £2). **Facilities** ❷ (400yds) ♿ (wheelchair accessible) toilets for disabled shop ❽ (ex assist dogs)

Chester Cathedral

Saint Werburgh St CH1 2HU

➲ *(opposite town hall)*

☎ 01244 324756

e-mail: office@chestercathedral.com

web: www.chestercathedral.com

With 1000 years of history, a visit to Chester Cathedral opens a window onto a rich and varied story of monks, kings and craftsmen. The Cathedral is an extraordinary mixture of old and new, with something for everyone to enjoy. From Norman arches to gothic columns, spectacular 14th-century woodcarvings to afternoon teas in the Refectory Café. This is so much here to discover from modern works of art to the newly replanted Cloister Garden, a haven of peace and calm on a busy day.

Times Open Mon-Sat, 9-5, Sun 1-4.30, Please telephone to check. **Fee** ✳ £4 (concessions & groups 10+ £3, ch 5-16 £1.50). Family ticket £10 **Facilities** ❷ (200yds) (multi-storey) ⬚ ⭘ licensed ♿ (steps to some areas) (induction loop, wide doors) toilets for disabled shop ❽ (ex assist dogs) ▰

Chester Visitor Centre   FREE

Vicars Ln CH1 1QX

➲ *(opposite St Johns Church Roman Amphitheatre)*

☎ 01244 351609

e-mail: tis@chestercc.gov.uk

web: www.chestertourism.com

Among the attractions at this large visitor information centre are guided walks of Chester; World of Names, which explores the history of family and first names; displays on the history of Chester; a café and a gift shop. Chester is the most complete walled city in Britain, and was originally settled by the Romans in the first century AD. The city also played its part in battles with the Vikings, the Norman invasion, and the Civil War.

Times ✳ Open all year, Mon-Sat 10-5, Sun 10-4 **Facilities** ❷ (200mtrs) (short stay) ⬚ ㆑ (outdoor) ♿ (ramped access from Vicars Lane) toilets for disabled shop

Chester Zoo

Upton-by-Chester CH2 1LH

➲ *(2m N of city centre off A41& M53 junct 10 southbound, junct 12 all other directions)*

☎ 01244 380280

e-mail: marketing@chesterzoo.org

web: www.chesterzoo.org

Chester Zoo is the UK's number one charity zoo, with over 7,000 animals and 500 different species, some of them amongst the most endangered species on the planet. There's plenty to see and do, like the Realm of the Red Ape enclosure, a new home for the Bornean and Sumatran orang-utans. Experience the sights and sounds of Assam, with the herd of Asian Elephants, Hornbills, Tree Shrews and rare fish inside Elephants of the Asian Forest. The world's fastest land mammal, the cheetah, is returning to Chester Zoo in late spring 2008. A wide variety of beautifully coloured African birds will be housed in African Aviaries in the autumn. New for 2009 is Butterfly Journey.

Times Open all year, daily from 10. Last admission varies with season. (Closed 25-26 Dec). **Fee** £11.95 (ch £8.95). Family £38 **Facilities** Ⓟ ☕ 🍴 ⛩ (indoor & outdoor) ♿ (electric scooters, wheelchairs for hire) toilets for disabled shop ⊗ (ex assist dogs) 💳

Dewa Roman Experience

Pierpoint Ln,

➲ *(off Bridge St) CH1 1NL (city centre)*

☎ 01244 343407

e-mail: info@dewaromanexperience.co.uk

web: www.dewaromanexperience.co.uk

Stroll along reconstructed streets experiencing the sights, sounds and smells of Roman Chester. From the streets of Dewa (the Roman name for Chester) you return to the present day on an extensive archaeological 'dig', where you can discover the substantial Roman, Saxon and medieval remains beneath modern Chester. Try on Roman armour, solve puzzles and make brass rubbings and make mosaics in the hands-on/activity room. Roman soldier patrols available.

Times Open all year, daily Feb-Nov 9-5, Dec-Jan 10-4 . (Closed 25-26 & 31 Dec & 1 Jan). **Fee** ✻ £4.25 (ch £2.50, under 5's free, concessions £3.75). Family ticket £12. Party £3.25 (10 or more). Roman soldier patrols £35.95 (for 30 maximum) **Facilities** Ⓟ (200yds) ♿ shop ⊗ (ex assist dogs)

CHOLMONDELEY — MAP 07 SJ55

Cholmondeley Castle Gardens

SY14 8AH

➲ *(off A49 Tarporley to Whitchurch road)*

☎ 01829 720383

e-mail: penny@cholmondeleycastle.co.uk

Dominated by a romantic Gothic Castle built in 1801 of local sandstone, the gardens are laid out with fine trees and water gardens, and have been replanted with rhododendrons, azaleas, cornus, and acer. There is also a rose and lavender garden, lakeside and woodland walks, and rare breeds of farm animals. The Duckery, a derelict 19th-century lakeside pleasure ground has recently been developed and restored. The castle is not open to the public. Plenty of events throughout the year, including classic car rallies, open-air theatre and fireworks. Contact for details.

Times Open 21 Mar-28 Sep, Wed-Thu, Sun & BHs 11-5. **Fee** ✻ £5 (ch £2). **Facilities** Ⓟ ☕ ⛩ (outdoor) ♿ (Partly accessible) (disabled car park, part of garden accessible) toilets for disabled shop garden centre

CONGLETON — MAP 07 SJ86

Little Moreton Hall

CW12 4SD

➲ *(4m SW of Congleton, on E side of A34)*

☎ 01260 272018

e-mail: littlemoretonhall@nationaltrust.org.uk

web: www.nationaltrust.org.uk

One of the best-known examples of moated, half-timbered architecture in England. By 1580 the house was much as it is today, and the long gallery, chapel and the great hall are very impressive. The garden has a knot garden, orchard and herbaceous borders. Wall paintings are also of some significant interest, and the house recently featured in David Dimbleby's *How We Built Britain* documentary series (2007). Ring for details of special events.

Times Open 4-5 Apr, Sat-Sun 11-5; 8 Apr-1 Nov, Wed-Sun 11-5; 7 Nov-20 Dec, Sat-Sun 11-4. **Fee** ✻ £5.80 (ch £3). Family ticket £13.50, Groups £5, Special Openings £10.50. **Facilities** Ⓟ (charged) 🍴 licensed ⛩ (outdoor) ♿ (access restricted, no lift to other floors, some steps & cobbles in ground) (w/chairs, Braille/large print guides, induction loop,map) toilets for disabled shop ⊗ (ex assist dogs) ✿ 💳

DISLEY — MAP 07 SJ98

Lyme Park

SK12 2NX

➲ *(off A6, 6.5m SE of Stockport. 12m NW of Buxton. House & car park 1m from entrance)*

☎ 01663 762023 & 766492

e-mail: lymepark@nationaltrust.org.uk

web: www.nationaltrust.org.uk

Originally Tudor, Lyme Park now resembles a huge, Italianate palace following its transformation in the 18th century. Inside, a colourful family history is brought to life in beautifully furnished rooms. Outside, enjoy the opulent Victorian and Edwardian gardens with their sunken

CONTINUED

DISLEY CONTINUED

parterre, lake, and Wyatt-designed orangery. The surrounding deer park stretches up to the moors and is stocked with native species of deer.

Times House: open 28 Feb-8 Mar, Sat-Sun 11-5; 14 Mar-1 Nov, Fri-Tue 11-5: Park open Apr-Oct daily, 8am-8.30pm, Oct-Feb daily 8-6: Garden, 28 Feb-8 Mar, Sat-Sun 11-5; 14 Mar-1 Nov daily 11-5; 7 Nov-20 Dec, Sat-Sun 12-3. **Fee** ✱ Park £3.80 per car (refundable on purchase of House & Garden ticket). Garden £3 (ch £1.50). House £4.50 (ch £2.30). House & Garden £6.20 (ch £3.10). Family ticket £15, ch under 5 free. **Facilities** ❷ (charged) ♥ ⏀ licensed 🎋 (outdoor) ♿ (access restricted, no lift to other floors, grounds have some slopes and uneven gravel paths) (large print guide, induction loop, w/chairs, shuttle bus) toilets for disabled shop ✪ (ex assist dogs/on lead park) ♨ ▬

ELLESMERE PORT   MAP 07 SJ47

Blue Planet Aquarium   `2 for 1`

Cheshire Oaks CH65 9LF

⊃ *(M53 junct 10 at Cheshire Oaks, M56 junct 15 follow Aquarium signs)*

☎ 0151 357 8800

e-mail: info@blueplanetaquarium.co.uk
web: www.blueplanetaquarium.com

A voyage of discovery on one of the longest moving walkways in the world. Beneath the waters of the Caribbean Reef, see giant rays and menacing sharks pass inches from your face, stroke some favourite fish in the special rock pools, or pay a visit to the incredible world of poisonous frogs. Divers hand feed the fish and sharks throughout the day and can answer questions via state of the art communication systems. Home to Europe's largest collection of sharks, including the large sand tiger sharks. We offer at least two special events in each season please check website for details.

Times Open all year, daily from 10. (Closed 25 Dec). Seasonal variations in closing times, please call to confirm. **Fee** ✱ £13.50 (ch 15 £9.50, concessions £11.50) Family ticket (2ad+2ch) £45. Groovy grandparent ticket (2+2) £41. Please check website for further details. **Facilities** ❷ ⏀ 🍽 🎋 (outdoor) ♿ (wheelchair hire, lifts, hearing loop) toilets for disabled shop ✪ (ex assist dogs) ▬

The National Waterways Museum   `2 for 1`

South Pier Rd CH65 4FW

⊃ *(M53 junct 9)*

☎ 0151 355 5017

e-mail: bookings@thewaterwaystrust.org
web: www.nwm.org.uk

The National Waterways Museum aims to bring Britain's canal history to life. The fascinating museum is set within a 200-year-old seven acre dock complex and includes the world's largest floating collection of canal craft. With the dock workers cottages, blacksmiths forge, boat trips and events throughout the year there is something for everyone to enjoy. Check website or telephone for details of future events.

Times Open Summer daily 10-5. Winter Thu-Sun 10-4. Closed 1 Jan. **Fee** £5.50 (ch over 5 £3.50, concessions £4.50) Family £19. Boat trip not included. **Facilities** ❷ ⏀ 🎋 (indoor & outdoor) ♿ (85% of the site is accessible to wheelchairs) (tactile map for blind, induction loop, free wheelchair use) toilets for disabled shop ▬

GAWSWORTH   MAP 07 SJ86

Gawsworth Hall

SK11 9RN

⊃ *(2.5m S of Macclesfield on A536)*

☎ 01260 223456

e-mail: enquiries@gawsworthhall.com
web: www.gawsworthhall.com

This fine Tudor black-and-white manor house was the birthplace of Mary Fitton, thought by some to be the 'Dark Lady' of Shakespeare's sonnets. Pictures and armour can be seen in the house, which also has a tilting ground - now thought to be a rare example of an Elizabethan pleasure garden. Watch out for open air theatre in July and August, and craft fairs in spring and autumn.

Times Open 4 May-22 Jun & 31 Aug-21 Sep, Sun-Wed 2-5 (& special events); 22 Jun-27 Aug daily 2-5. **Fee** ✱ £6 (ch £3). Party 20+ £5 each. **Facilities** ❷ ⏀ 🎋 (outdoor) ♿ (Partly accessible) (disabled parking in front of house) toilets for disabled shop ✪ (assist dogs in garden only) ▬

JODRELL BANK VISITOR   MAP 07 SJ77
CENTRE & ARBORETUM

Jodrell Bank Visitor Centre & Arboretum

SK11 9DL

⊃ *(M6 junct 18, A535 Holmes Chapel to Chelford road)*

☎ 01477 571339

web: www.manchester.ac.uk/jodrellbank

At Jodrell Bank, a scientific and engineering wonder awaits you - the magnificent Lovell telescope, one of the largest radio telescopes in the world. A pathway leads you 180 degrees around the telescope as it towers above you surveying and exploring the universe. Then, the visitor can wander along pathways amongst the trees of the extensive arboretum. The Centre is currently under a redevelopment, which will take 2-3 years to complete.

Times Open daily Nov-mid Mar 10.30-3, wknds 11-4; mid Mar-end Oct 10.30-5.30 **Facilities** ❷ ⏀ 🎋 (outdoor) ♿ (wheelchair loan) toilets for disabled shop ✪ (ex assist dogs) ▬

KNUTSFORD MAP 07 SJ77

Tabley House
WA16 0HB

➲ *(Exit M6 junct 19 onto A556 S towards Chester. Entrance for cars off A5033, 2m W of Knutsford)*

☎ 01565 750151

e-mail: enquiries@tableyhouse.co.uk
web: www.tableyhouse.co.uk

This finest Palladian House in the North West, holds the first great collection of English pictures ever made, including works by Turner, Lawrence, Fuseli and Reynolds. This is also furniture by Chippendale, Gillow and Bullock, and fascinating Leicester family memorabilia. Friendly stewards are available to talk about the Leicester's 700 years at Tabley.

Times House: Open Apr-end Oct, Thu-Sun & BHs, 2-5 (last entry 4.30) **Facilities** ♿ ⌷ †◯ ⊞ ♿ (phone administrator in advance for help) toilets for disabled shop ⊗ (ex assist dogs)

Tatton Park
WA16 6QN

➲ *(Signed on A556, 4m S of Altrincham. Entrance to Tatton Park on Ashley Rd, 1.5m NE of junct A5034 with A50)*

☎ 01625 374400 & 374435

e-mail: tatton@cheshire.gov.uk
web: www.tattonpark.org.uk

Tatton is one of England's most complete historic estates, with gardens and a 1,000-acre country park. The centrepiece is the Georgian mansion, with gardens laid out by Humphry Repton and Sir Joseph Paxton. More recently, a Japanese garden with a Shinto temple was created. The Tudor Old Hall is the original manor house, where a guided tour is available. There is also a working 1930s farm and a children's adventure playground. Special events most weekends include the RHS flower show and open air concerts.

Times 28 Mar-4 Oct, 10-7; 5 Oct-26 Mar 11-5 **Fee** ✳ Car entry £4.50. Each attraction £4 (ch £2). Family ticket £10. Totally Tatton Ticket (up to 3 attractions) £6 (ch £3). Family £15. **Facilities** ♿ (charged) †◯ licensed ⊞ (outdoor) ♿ (old hall & areas of farm not accessible) (Braille guides) toilets for disabled shop ♨ ▬

MACCLESFIELD MAP 07 SJ97

Hare Hill
Over Alderley SK10 4QB

➲ *(Off B5087. Turn N into Prestbury Road, left at T-junct after 200yds, continue 0.75m. Entrance on left)*

☎ 01625 584412

web: www.nationaltrust.org.uk

The beautiful parkland at Hare Hill also features a pretty walled garden and pergola. There are woodland paths and ponds, and, in late spring, a brilliant display of rhododendrons and azaleas. The grounds were originally developed as the setting for a Georgian mansion.

Times Open 4 Apr-10 May & 2 Jun-30 Oct, Wed-Thu & Sat-Sun, 10-5; 11-31 May, daily, 10-5 (last admission 1hr before closing). **Fee** ✳ £3.20 (ch £1.50). £1.80 per car (refundable on entry to garden) **Facilities** ♿ (charged) ⊞ (outdoor) ♿ (access difficult in some areas, slopes, steps, grass & uneven paths) (Braille guides) toilets for disabled ⊗ (ex assist dogs) ♨

Macclesfield Silk Museum `2 for 1`
Heritage Centre, Roe St SK11 6UT

➲ *(Turn off A523 & follow brown signs. Museum in town centre)*

☎ 01625 613210

e-mail: info@macclesfield.silk.museum
web: www.macclesfield.silk.museum

The story of silk in Macclesfield, told through a colourful audio-visual programme, exhibitions, textiles, garments, models and room settings. The Silk Museum is part of the Heritage centre, a restored Georgian Sunday school, which runs a full programme of musical and artistic events throughout the year. New science and silk displays opened in 2008.

Times Open all year, Mon-Sat 11-5, Sun & BH Mon 1-5. Closed 25-26 Dec, 1 Jan & Good Fri. Please ring for winter opening times. **Fee** ✳ £4.50 (concessions £4). Accompanied ch free. **Facilities** ♿ (50mtrs) ⌷ †◯ ♿ (ramps, chairlift, audio guides, induction loop) toilets for disabled shop ⊗ (ex assist dogs) ▬

Paradise Mill & Silk Industry Museum `2 for 1`
Park Ln SK11 6TJ

➲ *(turn off A523 'The Silk Rd' & follow brown signs)*

☎ 01625 612045

e-mail: info@macclesfield.silk.museum
web: www.macclesfield.silk.museum

A working silk mill until 1981, with restored jacquard hand looms in their original location. Knowledgeable guides, many of them former silk mill workers, illustrate the silk production process with the help of demonstrations from weavers. Exhibitions and room settings give an impression of working conditions at the mill during the 1930s. The adjacent Silk Industry Museum opened in 2002 and focuses on design and manufacturing processes.

Times Open all year, BH Mon & Mon-Sat 11-5 (Closed Sun, 25-26 Dec & 1 Jan, Good Fri). Please ring for winter opening times. **Fee** ✳ £4.50 (concessions £4), joint ticket with all museums £7.90 (concessions £6.75) **Facilities** ♿ (100yds) ♿ (care needed on uneven floors in Paradise Mill) toilets for disabled shop ⊗ (ex assist dogs) ▬

NANTWICH   MAP 07 SJ65

Hack Green Secret Nuclear Bunker

French Ln, Hack Green CW5 8AP

➲ *(from Nantwich take A530 towards Whitchurch, follow brown signs)*

☎ 01270 629219

e-mail: coldwar@hackgreen.co.uk

web: www.hackgreen.co.uk

One of the nation's most secret defence sites. Declassified in 1993, this underground bunker would have been the centre of regional government had nuclear war broken out. Observe the preparations the government made for nuclear war and step into the lives of people who worked here. View the Minister of State's office, life support, communication centre, decontamination facilities, telephone exchange and much more.

Times Open 20 Apr-30 Oct, daily 10.30-5.30; Nov, Jan, Feb wknds, 11-4. Closed Dec. **Fee** ✷ £6.30 (ch £4.50, concessions £5.90). Family £19 **Facilities** ❷ ⬚ 🍽 🍴 (outdoor) ♿ (Partly accessible) (facilities for blind & hard of hearing) toilets for disabled shop ⊗ (ex assist dogs) ⊜

Stapeley Water Gardens

London Rd, Stapeley CW5 7LH

➲ *(off M6 junct 16, 1m S of Nantwich on A51)*

☎ 01270 623868 & 628628

e-mail: info@stapeleywg.com

web: www.stapeleywg.com

There is plenty to do at Stapeley Water Gardens. The Palms Tropical Oasis is home to sharks, piranhas, parrots, skunks and exotic flowers, as well as tamarin monkeys, poisonous frogs and a crocodile. The two-acre Water Garden Centre houses the national collection of water-lilies, as well as Koi carp and other water features. There is also a large garden centre, and various children's activities, including 'Meet the Keeper', take place during school holidays.

Times Open Summer: Mon-Sat 9-6, BHs 10-6, Sun 10-4, Wed 9-8; Winter: Mon-Sat 9-5, BHs 10-5, Sun 10-4. The Palms Tropical Oasis open from 10. **Fee** The Palms Tropical Oasis £4.95 (ch £2.95, concessions £4.45). Family ticket (2ad+2ch) £12.60 (2ad+3ch) £15. Discounts for groups 15+ **Facilities** ❷ ⬚ 🍽 🍴 (outdoor) ♿ (free wheelchair loan service) toilets for disabled shop garden centre ⊗ (ex assist dogs) ⊜

NESTON   MAP 07 SJ27

Liverpool University Botanic Gardens (Ness Gardens)

Ness Gardens CH64 4AY

➲ *(off A540 near Ness, follow signs)*

☎ 0151 353 0123

e-mail: nessgdns@liv.ac.uk

web: www.nessgardens.org.uk

A long association with plant collectors ensures a wide range of plants, providing interest for academics, horticulturists and amateurs alike. There are tree and shrub collections, water and rock gardens, herbaceous borders and glasshouses. A regular programme of lectures, courses and special events take place throughout the year for which tickets must be obtained in advance. A visitor centre offers meeting and conference facilities, and weekly exhibitions by local artists.

Times Open all year, Feb-Oct, daily 10-5; Nov-Jan, daily 10-4.30. Closed 25 Dec. **Fee** ✷ £5.75 (ch 5-16 £2.75 under 5's free, concessions £5.25). Family (2ad+3ch) £15. **Facilities** ❷ ⬚ 🍴 (outdoor) ♿ (visitor centre & 65% of gardens accessible) (wheelchair route, induction loop in lecture theatre) toilets for disabled shop garden centre ⊗ (ex assist dogs) ⊜

NORTHWICH   MAP 07 SJ67

Arley Hall & Gardens   `2 for 1`

CW9 6NA

➲ *(5m N of Northwich on B5075. 5m NW of Knutsford A556, signed from M56 juncts 9/10 and M6 juncts 19/20)*

☎ 01565 777353 & 777284

e-mail: enquiries@arleyhallandgardens.com

web: www.arleyhallandgardens.com

Owned by the same family since medieval times, the present Arley Hall is a good example of the early Victorian Jacobean style and contains fine furniture, plasterwork, panelling and family portraits. The gardens include a walled garden, unique clipped Ilex avenue, herb garden, scented garden and a woodland garden with rhododendrons, azaleas and exotic trees as well as the double herbaceous borders, one of the earliest to be established in England (1846).

Times Gardens, grounds & chapel: Open Apr-Sep, Tue-Sun & BH 11-5. For Hall dates please call 01565 777353 **Fee** ✷ Gardens, Grounds & Chapel £5.50 (ch 5-15 £2, under 5's free, concessions £5) Family ticket £12 Hall £2.50 (ch 5-16 £1, concessions £2). Party 15+. **Facilities** ❷ ⬚ 🍽 licensed 🍴 (outdoor) ♿ (lower levels of hall & garden accessible) (ramps, parking by entrance) toilets for disabled shop garden centre ⊗ (ex in gardens on lead) ⊜

Salt Museum `2 for 1`

162 London Rd CW9 8AB

➲ *(on A533, 0.5m S of town centre & 0.5m N of A556. Well signed from A556)*

☎ 01606 271640

e-mail: cheshiremuseums@cheshire.gov.uk

web: www.saltmuseum.org.uk

Britain's only Salt Museum tells the fascinating story of Cheshire's oldest industry. Models, reconstructions, original artefacts and audio-visual programmes throw new light on something we all take for granted. Various temporary exhibitions are held here, please contact for details.

Times Open Tue-Fri 10-5, wknds 2-5 (Sat & Sun, 12-5 in Aug). Open BH & Mons in Aug 10-5. **Fee** ✳ £2.50 (ch £1.30, concessions £2) Family ticket (2 ad + 2 ch) £6 **Facilities** ℗ ⊑ ㅈ (outdoor) ㊫ (introductory video with induction loop facilities) toilets for disabled shop ⊗ (ex assist dogs) ▄

RUNCORN   MAP 07 SJ58

Norton Priory Museum & Gardens

Tudor Rd, Manor Park WA7 1SX

➲ *(from M56 junct 11 towards Warrington, follow brown signs)*

☎ 01928 569895

e-mail: info@nortonpriory.org

web: www.nortonpriory.org

Thirty-eight acres of peaceful woodland gardens are the setting for the medieval priory remains, museum and Walled Garden. Displays tell the story of the transformation of the priory into a Tudor manor house and then into an elegant Georgian mansion.

Times Open all year, Apr-Oct, Mon-Fri 12-5; Sat, Sun & BHs 12-6; Nov-Mar daily 12-4. Closed 24-26 Dec & 1 Jan. Walled Garden open Apr-Oct, daily 1.30-4.30 **Facilities** ℗ ⊑ ㅈ (outdoor) ㊫ (wheelchairs, large print & audio guides, induction loop) toilets for disabled shop garden centre ⊗ (ex in wall garden) ▄

STYAL   MAP 07 SJ88

Quarry Bank Mill & Styal Estate

SK9 4LA

➲ *(1.5m N of Wilmslow off B5166, 2.5m from M56 junct 5. Follow heritage signs from A34 & M56)*

☎ 01625 527468 & 445896

e-mail: quarrybankmill@nationaltrust.org.uk

web: www.quarrybankmill.org.uk

Founded in 1784, Quarry Bank Mill is one of the finest surviving cotton mills of the period. Inside the water and steam-powered mill there are hands-on exhibits and demonstrations that show how traditional spinning and weaving was transformed through the ingenuity of early textile engineers. Using the most powerful working waterwheel in Europe, two mill engines bring the past to life. At the Apprentice House you can discover what home life was like for the pauper children who worked in the mill in the 1830s. Visit the Mill Owner's secret garden, a picturesque valley retreat. After all this history take a walk through surrounding wood and farmland along the River Bollin.

Times Open Mar-Oct daily 11-5; Nov-Feb Wed-Sun 11-4 (last admission 1hr before closing). Apprentice House timed tours. Garden open Mar-Oct. **Fee** ✳ Mill & Apprentice House £9 (ch £4.70). Family ticket £20. Mill only £6 (ch £3.70). Family ticket £16. **Facilities** ℗ (charged) ⊑ ⑩ㅈ ㊫ (Apprentice House level access to ground floor only) (wheelchairs, chairlift, ramps, Braille & induction loops) toilets for disabled shop ⊗ (ex assist dogs & in park) ▓ ▄

WIDNES   MAP 07 SJ58

Catalyst Science Discovery Centre

Mersey Rd WA8 0DF

➲ *(signed from M62 junct 7 & M56 junct 12)*

☎ 0151 420 1121

e-mail: info@catalyst.org.uk

web: www.catalyst.org.uk

Enter a colourful world of science and technology in interactive galleries, and experience an amazing journey of discovery in the interactive theatre. Take a trip in an all-glass external lift to the Observatory, 100 feet above the River Mersey. A range of special events is planned throughout the year. Please ring for details.

Times ✳ Open all year, Tue-Fri daily & BH Mon 10-5, wknds 11-5. (Closed Mon ex BHs, 24-26 & 31 Dec & 1 Jan). **Facilities** ℗ ⊑ shop ⊗ (ex assist dogs) ▄

CORNWALL &
THE ISLES OF SCILLY

Manacle Rocks, Lizard Point

BODMIN
MAP 02 SX06

Military Museum
The Keep PL31 1EG

➲ *(on B3268, Lostwithiel Rd, beside steam railway station)*

☎ 01208 269516

e-mail: dclimus@talk21.com

The history of the Duke of Cornwall's Light Infantry Regiment with fascinating displays of uniforms, weapons, medals, badges and much more. Please telephone for details of events planned throughout the year. There is also an extensive archive/reference library available and volunteer archivists to assist with research.

Times Open all year Mon-Fri 9-5 and BH. (Closed Xmas). **Facilities ❷ 서** (indoor & outdoor) ♿ (Partly accessible) (presentation of inaccessible areas, virtual tour) toilets for disabled shop

Pencarrow
2 for 1
Washaway PL30 3AG

➲ *(4m NW of Bodmin, signed off A389 & B3266)*

☎ 01208 841369

e-mail: info@pencarrow.co.uk

web: www.pencarrow.co.uk

Still a family home, this Georgian house has a superb collection of pictures, furniture and porcelain. The 50 acres of formal and woodland gardens include a Victorian rockery, a lake, 700 different rhododendrons and an acclaimed conifer collection. There is also a craft centre and a children's play area. Special events throughout the year. Ring for details. 2 for 1 voucher only applicable for garden entry.

Times House: 23 Mar-19 Oct, Sun-Thu, 11-3; Gardens: Mar-Oct daily 9.30-5.30.Cafe, craft shop & plants 11-5. **Fee** ✳ House & Garden £8. Gardens only £4 (ch £1). Family ticket £22. Party 20-30 £7 each, Party 31+ £6 each. **Facilities ❷ ⛁ 서** (outdoor) ♿ (ground floor rooms of house accessible) (1 w/chair, disabled parking, DVD tour) toilets for disabled shop garden centre ❽ (ex in grounds) ▄

CALSTOCK
MAP 02 SX46

Cotehele
St Dominick PL12 6TA

➲ *(between Tavistock & Callington. Turn off A390 at St. Ann's Chapel, signed 2.5m S of junct)*

☎ 01579 351346 & 352739 (info)

e-mail: cotehele@ntrust.org.uk

web: www.nationaltrust.org.uk

A 15th-century house that contains tapestries, embroideries, furniture and armour; and outside, a beautiful garden on different levels, including a formal Italian-style garden, medieval stewpond, dovecote, and an 18th-century tower with lovely views. There is a restored water mill in the valley below, and at the Victorian riverside quay a Maritime Museum.

Times Open 14 Mar-1 Nov. Garden open all year daily 10-dusk. Limited opening 9 Nov-24 Dec. **Fee** House, Garden & Mill £9.20. Garden & Mill £5.20 (ch 1/2 price, under 5's & NT members free). Family tickets available. Garden & mill only £5.50 (ch 1/2 price, under 5's & NT members free). **Facilities ❷ ⛁🍴서** (outdoor) ♿ (garden limited access) (Braille guide, audio loop, wheelchairs) toilets for disabled shop garden centre ❽ (ex assist dogs) 🐾 ▄

CAMELFORD
MAP 02 SX18

British Cycling Museum
2 for 1
The Old Station PL32 9TZ

➲ *(1m N of Camelford on B3266 at junct with B3314)*

☎ 01840 212811

web: www.chycor.co.uk/britishcyclingmuseum

This is the nation's foremost museum of cycling history from 1818 to the present day, with over 400 cycles; more than 1,000 cycling medals, fobs and badges; an extensive library; displays of gas, candle, battery and oil lighting; and many advertising posters and enamel signs.

Times Open all year, Sun-Thu 10-5. **Fee** £3.35 (ch 5-17 £1.90). **Facilities ❷ 서** (outdoor) ♿ shop ❽ (ex assist dogs)

CHYSAUSTER ANCIENT VILLAGE
MAP 02 SW43

Chysauster Ancient Village
TR20 8XA

➲ *(2.5m NW of Gulval, off B3311)*

☎ 07831 757934

web: www.english-heritage.org.uk

This unique Celtic settlement includes probably the oldest known 'Village Street' in the country. Explore the remains of 2,000-year-old stone houses.

Times Open 21 Mar-Jun & Sep, daily 10-5; Jul-Aug, daily 10-6; Oct, daily 10-4. Closed Nov- Mar. **Fee** £2.50 (concessions £2, ch £1.30). Prices and opening times are subject to change in March 2009. Please call 0870 333 1181 for the most up to date prices and opening times when planning your visit. **Facilities ❷ ❽ ♿**

ENGLAND

FALMOUTH   MAP 02 SW83

National Maritime Museum Cornwall   `2 for 1`

Discovery Quay TR11 3QY

➲ *(follow signs from A39 for park/float ride and museum)*

☎ 01326 313388

e-mail: enquiries@nmmc.co.uk

web: www.nmmc.co.uk

Recently voted Cornwall's Visitor Attraction of the Year, this award winning museum offers something for everyone from ever-changing exhibitions, hands-on family activities, talks, lectures, displays, events, crabbing and the opportunity to sail and see marine and bird life. Admire the views from the 29 metre tower, descend the depths in one of only three natural underwater viewing galleries in the world and discover Cornwall, journey through time, explore the seas and go mad about boats. The purchase of a full price individual ticket gives you free entry to the Museum for a year.

Times Open daily 10-5. Closed 25-26 Dec. **Fee** ✳ £7.95 (ch under 5 free, ch 6-15 & students £5.25, pen £6.25). Family ticket £21. **Facilities** ℗ (charged) ⌑ 🍴 licensed ᒫ (wheelchairs provided on arrival) toilets for disabled shop ✪ (ex assist dogs) ⚏

Pendennis Castle

Pendennis Headland TR11 4LP

➲ *(1m SE)*

☎ 01326 316594

web: www.english-heritage.org.uk

Together with St Mawes Castle, Pendennis forms the end of a chain of castles built by Henry VIII along the south coast as protection from attack from France. Journey through 450 years of history and discover the castle's wartime secrets.

Times Open all year, 21 Mar-Jun & Sep, daily 10-5 (Sat 10-4); Jul-Aug, daily 10-6 (Sat 10-4); Oct-Mar, daily 10-4 (certain buildings by guided tour only, phone for details. The Keep will close 1 hour for lunch on Sat if an event is booked). Closed 24-26 Dec & 1 Jan. **Fee** £5.40 (ch £2.70, concessions £4.10). Family £13.50. Prices and opening times are subject to change in March 2009. Please call 0870 333 1181 for the most up to date prices and opening times when planning your visit. **Facilities** ℗ ⌑ 🍴 shop ✪ (ex on lead in certain areas) ⚏

FOWEY   MAP 02 SX15

St Catherine's Castle   `FREE`

➲ *(0.75m SW of Fowey along footpath off A3082)*

web: www.english-heritage.org.uk

A small 16th-century fort built by Henry VIII to defend Fowey Harbour. It has two storeys with gun ports at ground level.

Times Open at any reasonable time. **Facilities** ℗ (0.5m) ✪ (ex on leads) ⚏

GODOLPHIN CROSS   MAP 02 SW53

Godolphin House

TR13 9RE

➲ *(on minor road from Godolphin Cross to Townsend)*

☎ 01736 763194

e-mail: godo@euphony.net

web: www.godolphinhouse.com

A romantic Tudor and Stuart mansion, begun in 1475 and considerably extended over the centuries. The Godolphin family's taste is evident throughout the mansion, and of particular note are examples of 16th and 17th-century English oak furniture and Wootton's 1731 painting, *Godolphin Arabian*, one of the three Arab stallion ancestors of all British bloodstock. The gardens are Tudor, with some areas even earlier. Major repair programme on the mansion funded by English Heritage.

Times Estate open all year. Garden 29 Mar-1 Nov 10-5 (not Fri & Sat). House Apr-28 Oct Wed; 27 Apr-8 May, 22 Jun-3 Jul, 24 Aug-4 Sep, 28 Sep-9 Oct daily **Fee** ✳ House & gardens £5 (ch 5-15yrs £1.50). Gardens only £2 (ch free) **Facilities** ℗ ⌑ 🍴 ᒫ (telephone prior to visit, lift to first floor) toilets for disabled shop garden centre ✪ (ex assist dogs) ⚏

GORRAN   MAP 02 SW94

Caerhays Castle Gardens   `2 for 1`

PL26 6LY

➲ *(off A390 onto B3287. Right at T-junct, left at next T-junct, next left to Porthluney Beach car park)*

☎ 01872 501144 & 501310

e-mail: estateoffice@caerhays.co.uk

web: www.caerhays.co.uk

For centuries this magnolia filled garden was a deer park, and it was not until the late 19th century that John Charles Williams ("JCW") inherited Caerhays and not until the early 20th that new and exotic plants were introduced here. Now the gardens are a blaze of plants from Chile, China, New Zealand, the Himalayas, and many other distant lands. Magnolias, Rhododendrons, Camellia, and Japonicas can all be seen on marked walks, and the house can be visited in small groups during the spring.

Times Gardens open mid Feb-Jun 10-5. House open mid Mar-Jun. **Fee** ✳ £5.50 house or garden; £9.50 combined ticket **Facilities** ℗ ⌑ ᒫ (House & lower area of garden accessible) toilets for disabled shop garden centre ✪ (ex on lead & assist dogs) ⚏

GWEEK MAP 02 SW72

National Seal Sanctuary

2 for 1

TR12 6UG

➲ *(pass RNAS Culdrose, take A3293, then B3291 to Gweek. Sanctuary signed from village)*

☎ 01326 221361 & 221874

e-mail: slcgweek@merlin-entertainments.com

web: www.sealsanctuary.co.uk

Britain's first rescue centre dedicated to the rehabilitation and release of grey seals. The Sanctuary offers a unique, educational experience and fun opportunity to learn more about the UK's largest mammal. The Sanctuary also provides a permanent home for the world's oldest grey seal. Visit the UK's only Arctic hooded seal and the most diverse collection of pinniped in the UK. As well as Asian short-clawed otters, goats, ponies and sheep.

Times Open all year, daily from 10. Closed 25 Dec. **Fee** ✻ £11.50 (ch 3-14 £8.50, concessions £10.50). Family ticket (2ad+2ch) £34.50. **Facilities** Ⓟ ☕ ⛩ (outdoor) ♿ toilets for disabled shop ▬

HELSTON MAP 02 SW62

The Flambards Experience

Culdrose Manor TR13 0QA

➲ *(0.5m SE of Helston on A3083, Lizard road)*

☎ 01326 573404

e-mail: info@flambards.co.uk

web: www.flambards.co.uk

Three award-winning, all-weather attractions can be visited on one site here. Flambards Victorian Village is a recreation of streets, shops and houses from 1830-1910. Britain in the Blitz is a life-size wartime street featuring shops, a pub and a living room with Morrison shelter. The Science Centre is a science playground that brings physics alive for the whole family. Along with the Thunderbolt and Extreme Force, we also offer the Hornet Rollercoaster, the Family Log Flume, Go-Kart circuit, and rides and play areas for the very young. The Wildlife Experience show features lizards, snakes, large spiders and birds of prey. See the website for special events.

Times Open Etr-Nov, summer opening. Nov-Mar, winter opening. **Fee** ✻ £12.95 (ch 3-10 £8.25, concessions £6.95). Family of 3 £31.50, of 4 £41, of 5 £50, of 6 £58.50. **Facilities** Ⓟ ☕ ⛩ (indoor & outdoor) ♿ (some rivers not accessible) (free loan of wheelchairs, route guides) toilets for disabled shop garden centre ⊗ (ex assist dogs) ▬

Goonhilly Satellite Earth Station Experience

Goonhilly Downs TR12 6LQ

➲ *(From Helston follow the brown direction signs)*

☎ 0800 679593

e-mail: goonhilly.visitorscentre@bt.com

web: www.goonhilly.bt.com

Future World is on the site of what was the largest satellite earth station in the world, with over 60 dishes, which makes a dramatic impression on the Lizard Peninsula landscape. Enter a world of historic predictions, past inventions and ideas and see artefacts from jet packs and space helmets to the Sinclair C5 and the first mobile phones complete with 'brick' size batteries. Journey into a zone of interactive displays where you can record your own visions of the future. Discover the history and heritage of Goonhilly itself in the main visitors' centre, and learn how international communications have developed over the past 200 years. You an also book a tour into the heart of 'Arthur', the Grade II listed iconic satellite dish.

Times Open 15 Mar-27 Jun & 6 Sep-31 Oct 10-5; 28 Jun-5 Sep 10-6; Nov-27 Mar 11-4.Closed 24-26 Dec & 1 Jan **Fee** ✻ £7.95(ch £5.50, under 4's free, pen £6.50) **Facilities** Ⓟ ☕ 🍽 licensed ⛩ (outdoor) ♿ (induction loop, wheelchair height terminals, lifts, ramps) toilets for disabled shop ⊗ (ex assist dogs) ▬

Trevarno Estate Garden & Museum of Gardening

Trevarno Manor, Crowntown TR13 0RU

➲ *(E of Crowntown. Leave Helston on Penzance road signed B3302)*

☎ 01326 574274

e-mail: enquiry@trevarno.co.uk

web: www.trevarno.co.uk

Victorian gardens with the splendid fountain garden conservatory, unique range of crafts and the National Museum of Gardening. In the tranquil gardens and grounds, follow the progress of restoration projects, visit craft areas including handmade soap workshop, explore Britain's largest and most comprehensive collection of antique tools, implements, memorabilia and ephemera, creatively displayed to illustrate how gardens and gardening influences most people's lives. Adventure play area for the youngsters, extended estate walk and viewing platform.

Times Open daily 10.30-5. Closed 25-26 Dec **Facilities** Ⓟ ☕ ⛩ (outdoor) ♿ (parking, extended disabled route) toilets for disabled shop garden centre ▬

LANHYDROCK MAP 02 SX06

Lanhydrock

PL30 5AD

➲ *(2.5m SE of Bodmin, signed from A30, A38 & B3268)*

☎ 01208 265950

e-mail: lanhydrock@nationaltrust.org.uk

web: www.nationaltrust.org.uk

Part-Jacobean, part-Victorian building that gives a vivid picture of life in Victorian times. The 'below stairs' sections have a huge kitchen, larders, dairy, bakehouse, cellars, and servants' quarters. The long gallery has a moulded ceiling showing Old Testament scenes, and overlooks the formal gardens with their clipped yews and bronze urns. The higher garden, famed for its magnolias and rhododendrons, climbs the hillside behind the house.

Times House open 28 Feb-1 Nov daily (ex Mon), open BH Mon & Mon in Aug. Gardens open daily all year 10-6. **Fee** House & Grounds £10.40 (ch £5.20). Family tickets available. Garden & Grounds £5.90 (ch £2.95). Reduced rate when arriving by cycle or public transport. **Facilities** Ⓟ ☕ 🍽 ⛩ (outdoor) ♿ (lift, self drive buggy (pre-book), wheelchairs) toilets for disabled shop garden centre ⊗ (ex assist dogs) ✤ ▬

ENGLAND

LAUNCESTON   MAP 02 SX38

Launceston Castle

Castle Lodge PL15 7DR

☎ 01566 772365

web: www.english-heritage.org.uk

Commanding the town and surrounding countryside, this castle controlled the route onto Cornwall.

Times Open 21 Mar-Jun & Sep, daily 10-5; Jul-Aug, daily 10-6; Oct, daily 10-4. Closed Nov-Mar. **Fee** £2.50 (concessions £2, ch £1.30). Prices and opening times are subject to change in March 2009. Please call 0870 333 1181 for the most up to date prices and opening times when planning your visit. **Facilities** ⊨ ﴾ (outer bailey only) shop ⊗ ✿

Tamar Otter & Wildlife Centre

North Petherwin PL15 8GW

➲ *(5m NW off B3254 Bude road)*

☎ 01566 785646

e-mail: info@tamarotters.co.uk

web: www.tamarotters.co.uk

Visitors to this wildlife centre will see British and Asian short-clawed otters in large natural enclosures. They will also be able to see fallow and Muntjac deer, and wallabies roaming around the grounds. There are also owls, peacocks, and a large selection of waterfowl on two lakes.

Times Open Good Fri-Oct, daily 10.30-6 (dates extended in accordance with school hols) **Fee** ✴ £7 (ch 3-15yrs £3.50, concessions £6) Family (2 ad+3 ch) £18 **Facilities** ℗ ⬜⧠ (outdoor) ﴾ (steep slope to otter pens/ woodland walk) toilets for disabled shop ⊗ (ex assist dogs) ➠

LOOE   MAP 02 SX25

The Monkey Sanctuary Trust

St Martins PL13 1NZ

➲ *(signed on B3253 at No Man's Land between East Looe & Hessenford)*

☎ 01503 262532

e-mail: info@monkeysanctuary.org

web: www.monkeysanctuary.org

Visitors can see a colony of Amazonian woolly monkeys in extensive indoor and outdoor territory. There are also conservation gardens, children's play area, activity room, a display room and vegetarian café. The Monkey Sanctuary Trust is also a rescue centre for ex-pet capuchin monkeys rescued from the UK pet trade. In addition a bat cave is on site where visitors can watch a colony of rare horseshoe bats.

Times Open Sun-Thu from the Sun before Etr-Sep. Also open Autumn Half Term. **Fee** ✴ £6 (ch £3.50, under 5's free & concession £4.50). Family (2ad+2ch) £16. **Facilities** ℗ ⬜⧠ (outdoor) ﴾ (Partly accessible) toilets for disabled shop ⊗ ➠

MARAZION   MAP 02 SW53

St Michael's Mount

TR17 0HT

➲ *(access is by Causeway on foot at low tide. 0.5m S of A394 at Marazion)*

☎ 01736 710507 & 710265

e-mail: mail@stmichaelsmount.co.uk

web: www.stmichaelsmount.co.uk

Explore the amazing island world of St Michael's Mount and discover legend, myth and history. Follow in the pilgrims' footsteps and walk the causeway at low tide or enjoy a short boat trip when the tide is always an adventure! Climb the ancient cobbled path to the medieval castle, gaze down at beautiful gardens and enjoy magnificent views across the bay to Penzance. Various events take place throughout the year, please contact for details.

Times Open 29 Mar-30 Jun & Sep-1 Nov 10.30-5; Jul-Aug 10.30-5.30. Castle winter opening Tue & Fri by guided tour only. **Fee** £6.60 (ch £3.30) Family ticket £16.50 (1ad family £9.90). Groups 15+ £5.60. Garden £3 (ch £1). Castle & gardens free to NT members. **Facilities** ℗ (on mainland) ⬜ ⑩ ⧠ (outdoor) ﴾ (Braille guide, sandchair available) shop garden centre ⊗ (ex assist dogs) ✄ ➠

MAWNAN SMITH   MAP 02 SW72

Glendurgan

TR11 5JZ

➲ *(4m SW of Falmouth. 0.5m SW of Mawnan Smith on road to Helford Passage)*

☎ 01872 862090

e-mail: glendurgan@nationaltrust.org.uk

web: www.nationaltrust.org.uk

This delightful garden, set in a valley above the River Helford, was started by Alfred Fox in 1820. The informal landscape contains trees and shrubs from all over the world, including the Japanese loquat and tree ferns from New Zealand. There is a laurel maze, and a Giant's Stride which is popular with children. The house is not open.

Times Open 14 Feb-Jul & Sep-Oct, Tue-Sat, 10.30-5.30; Aug, Mon-Sat, 10.30-5.30. Open BH Mons. (Closed Good Fri). **Fee** £6.40 (ch £3.20). Family ticket available. Reduced rate for arriving by cycle or public transport. **Facilities** ℗ ⬜ ﴾ (limited access to gardens/ground floor) (Braille guide) toilets for disabled shop garden centre ⊗ (ex assist dogs) ✄ ➠

Trebah Garden

TR11 5JZ

➔ *(signed at Treliever Cross rdbt at junct of A39/A394 & follow brown tourist signs)*

☎ 01326 252200

e-mail: mail@trebah-garden.co.uk

web: www.trebah-garden.co.uk

A 25-acre wooded valley garden, descending 200 feet from the 18th-century house down to a private cove on the Helford River. The cascading Water Garden has pools of giant koi and exotic water plants, winding through two acres of blue and white hydrangeas to the beach. There are glades of sub-tropical tree ferns and palms, as well as rhododendrons and many other trees and shrubs from all over the world. The beach is open to visitors and there are children's trails and activities all year.

Times Open daily 10.30-5 (last admission). In winter 10.30 til dusk. **Fee** ✴ Mar-Oct £7 (ch £2, ch under 5 free, disabled £3.50, concessions £6; Nov-Feb £3 (ch & disabled £1, ch under 5 free, concessions £2.50). **Facilities** ⓟ ⌴ ⓧ ⍥ (outdoor) ৬ (Partly accessible) (3 powered wheelchairs & wheelchair route) toilets for disabled shop garden centre ▭

NEWQUAY   **MAP 02 SW86**

Blue Reef Aquarium   `2 for 1`

Towan Promenade TR7 1DU

➔ *(from A30 follow signs to Newquay, follow Blue Reef Aquarium signs to car park in town centre)*

☎ 01637 878134

e-mail: newquay@bluereefaquarium.co.uk

web: www.bluereefaquarium.co.uk

Take the ultimate undersea safari at the Blue Reef Aquarium. Discover Cornish marine life from native sharks and rays to the incredibly intelligent and playful octopus. From here journey through warmer waters to watch the magical seahorses, unusual shape shifting, jet-propelled cuttlefish and the vibrant, swaying tentacles of living sponges and anemones. Continue your safari through the underwater tunnel below a tropical sea. Here you will encounter the activities of a coral reef alive with shoals of brightly coloured fish and the graceful, black tip reef sharks which glide silently overhead. Daily talks and regular feeding demonstrations bring the experience to life. Events all year, please see website for details.

Times Open all year, daily 10-5. (Closed 25 Dec). Open until 6 during summer holidays. **Fee** £8.50 (ch £6, concessions £7.50). **Facilities** ⓟ (5mins walk) (prior contact for disabled parking) ⌴ ⍥ (outdoor) ৬ (small area, only accessible via steps) (lifts, 2 wheelchairs & beach wheelchair, ramps) toilets for disabled shop ⓧ (ex assist dogs) ▭

Dairy Land Farm World

Summercourt TR8 5AA

➔ *(Signed from A30 at exit for Mitchell/Summercourt)*

☎ 01872 510246

e-mail: info@dairylandfarmworld.co.uk

web: www.dairylandfarmworld.com

Visitors can watch while the cows are milked to music on a spectacular merry-go-round milking machine. The life of a Victorian farmer and his neighbours is explored in the Heritage Centre, and a Farm Nature Trail features informative displays along pleasant walks. Children will have fun getting to know the farm animals in the Farm Park. They will also enjoy the playground, assault course and indoor play areas.

Times ✴ Open daily, late Mar-Oct 10-5. (Bull pen additional winter openings Thu-Sun & school hols, please telephone for more information) **Facilities** ⓟ ⌴ ⍥ (indoor & outdoor) ৬ (wheelchairs for loan; disabled viewing gallery - milking) toilets for disabled shop ⓧ ▭

Newquay Zoo

Trenance Gardens TR7 2LZ

➔ *(off A3075 and follow signs to Zoo)*

☎ 01637 873342

e-mail: info@newquayzoo.org.uk

web: www.newquayzoo.org.uk

Newquay Zoo is set among exotic lakeside gardens with animals from all around the world. Enjoy fascinating talks, animal encounters and feeding times throughout the day. See the otter family playing in the stream in the Oriental Garden, look out for meerkats on sentry duty, try to spot the secretive red panda, and glimpse the endangered lemurs and fossa. Kids will enjoy the Tarzan Trail, the village farm and the dragon maze. Other highlights include penguin, zebra, black-crested macaques, tapirs, marmosets, tamarin and much more. The zoo celebrates its 40th birthday in May 2009.

Times Open all year daily Apr-Sep 9.30-6; Oct-Mar 10-dusk. Under review please check website for details. **Fee** ✴ Under review please check website for details **Facilities** ⓟ (charged) ⌴ ⍥ licensed ⍥ (outdoor) ৬ (stairs in Tropical House & upto the Owls & Tarzan Trail) (80% access, wheelchairs, guided tours) toilets for disabled shop ⓧ (ex assist dogs) ▭

PADSTOW   **MAP 02 SW97**

Prideaux Place

PL28 8RP

➔ *(off B3276 Padstow to Newquay road. Follow brown heritage signs)*

☎ 01841 532411

e-mail: office@prideauxplace.co.uk

web: www.prideauxplace.co.uk

Situated above the picturesque port of Padstow is the Elizabethan Prideaux Place. Completed in 1592 by Nicholas Prideaux and still lived in by the family who can trace back their ancestry to William the Conqueror. Surrounded by 40 acres of landscaped gardens and overlooking a deer park, this splendid house contains a wealth of family and royal portraits, a fine porcelain collection, a growing teddy bear collection and a magnificent 16th-century plaster ceiling in the

PADSTOW CONTINUED

Great Chamber, which has some marvellous views across countryside to Bodmin Moor. There's plenty of opportunity for walking in both formal gardens and woodland, and there is also a peaceful tearoom. The house has been featured in many film and TV productions.

Times Open early May-early Oct, Sun-Thu 1.30-4 (house tours), Open 5 days over Etr. Grounds 12.30-5. Open all year to pre-booked groups (15+) **Facilities** ❷ ⬛ ⬛ ⤴ ᧒ (Partly accessible) (ramps to main entrance and tea room) toilets for disabled shop ⊗ (ex on leads in grounds) ▭

PENDEEN MAP 02 SW33

Geevor Tin Mine 2 for 1

TR19 7EW

⮕ *(From Penzance take A3071 towards St Just, then B3318 towards Pendeen. From St Ives follow B3306 to Pendeen)*

☎ 01736 788662

e-mail: bookings@geevor.com

web: www.geevor.com

A preserved tin mine and museum provide an insight into the methods and equipment used in the industry that was once so important in the area. The Geevor Tin Mine only actually stopped operation in 1990. Guided tours let visitors see the tin treatment plant, and a video illustrates the techniques employed. The underground tour is well worth the trip.

Times Open daily (ex Sat) 9-5 (9-4 Nov-Mar). Closed 21-26 Dec & 1 Jan **Fee** ✳ £7.50 (ch & students £4.50, concessions £7) Family £22 **Facilities** ❷ ⬛ ⭐ ▭ (outdoor) ᧒ (access to new museum, shop & cafe) (lift, ramps) toilets for disabled shop ⊗ (ex assist dogs) ▭

PENTEWAN MAP 02 SX04

The Lost Gardens of Heligan

PL26 6EN

⮕ *(signed from A390 & B3273)*

☎ 01726 845100

e-mail: info@heligan.com

web: www.heligan.com

Heligan, seat of the Tremayne family for more than 400 years, is one of the most mysterious estates in England. At the end of the 19th-century its thousand acres were at their zenith, but only a few years after the Great War, bramble and ivy were already drawing a green veil over this sleeping beauty. Today the garden offers 200 acres for exploration, which include productive gardens, pleasure grounds, sustainably-managed farmland, wetlands, and ancient woodlands. Please telephone for details of spring-time and harvest-time events and for summer evening theatre.

Times Open Mar-Oct daily 10-6 (last tickets 4.30); Nov-Feb daily 10-5 (last tickets 3.30) **Fee** ✳ £8.50 (ch £5, pen £7.50). Family £23.50 (2ad+3ch) **Facilities** ❷ ⬛ ▭ (indoor & outdoor) (free loan of wheelchairs & trained access advisors) shop garden centre ⊗ (ex assist dogs & Mar-Oct) ▭

PENZANCE MAP 02 SW43

Trengwainton Garden

TR20 8RZ

⮕ *(2m NW Penzance, 0.5m W of Heamoor off Penzance - Morvah road)*

☎ 01736 363148

e-mail: trengwainton@nationaltrust.org.uk

web: www.nationaltrust.org.uk

Trengwainton has one of the best collections of tender plants on the British mainland. Thanks to the Gulf Stream and its sheltered position, plants grow here all year round. The garden is long and thin, flanking a drive that winds uphill beside a tranquil stream. Unusual plants from four continents fill a range of walled gardens, and from the top there are breathtaking views over Mounts Bay and the Lizard Peninsula.

Times Open 8 Feb-1 Nov, daily (ex Fri & Sat) 10.30-5. Open Good Fri 10-5. **Fee** £5.80 (ch £2.90). Family & group tickets available. Reduced rate when arriving by cycle or public transport. **Facilities** ❷ ⬛ ▭ (outdoor) ᧒ (Partly accessible) (special route, 2 wheelchairs) toilets for disabled shop garden centre 🐾 ▭

POOL MAP 02 SW64

Cornish Mines & Engines

TR15 3NP

⮕ *(2m W of Redruth on A3047, signed from A30, Pool exit)*

☎ 01209 315027 & 210900

e-mail: jane.affleck@nationaltrust.org.uk

Impressive relics of the tin mining industry, these great beam engines were used for pumping water from 2000ft down and for lifting men and ore from the workings below ground. The mine at East Pool has been converted into the Cornwall Industrial Heritage Centre which includes audio-visual theatre giving background to all aspects of Cornwall's industrial heritage.

Times Open 29 Mar-Jun & Sep-1 Nov, Sun-Mon, Wed-Fri 11-5, Jul-Aug daily (ex Tue). **Fee** £5.80 (ch £2.90) Family & group tickets available **Facilities** ❷ ▭ (outdoor) ᧒ (lift to all levels) toilets for disabled shop ⊗ (ex assist dogs) 🐾 ▭

PROBUS MAP 02 SW84

Trewithen Gardens

Grampound Rd TR2 4DD

⮕ *(on A390 between Truro & St Austell)*

☎ 01726 883647

e-mail: gardens@trewithen-estate.demon.co.uk

web: www.trewithengardens.co.uk

The Hawkins family has lived in this charming, intimate country house since it was built in 1720. The internationally renowned landscaped garden covers some 30 acres and grows camellias, magnolias and rhododendrons as well as many rare trees and shrubs seldom seen elsewhere. The nurseries are open all year.

Times Open Mar-Sep, Mon-Sat 10-4.30; daily Mar-May. **Fee** £5 (group 20+ £4.50) **Facilities** ❷ ⬚ ⴳ (outdoor) ও (some steeper areas of garden not accessible) toilets for disabled shop garden centre ▬

RESTORMEL   MAP 02 SX16

Restormel Castle

PL22 0BD

➲ *(1.5m N of Lostwithiel off A390)*

☎ 01208 872687

web: www.english-heritage.org.uk

High on a moated mound, this splendid Norman stronghold offers spectacular views across the Cornish countryside.

Times Open 21 Mar-Jun & Sep, daily 10-5; Jul-Aug, daily 10-6; Oct, daily 10-4. Closed Nov- Mar. **Fee** £2.50 (concessions £2, ch £1.30). Prices and opening times are subject to change in March 2009. Please call 0870 333 1181 for the most up to date prices and opening times when planning your visit. **Facilities** ❷ ⴳ shop ⊗ (ex dogs on leads) ⧓

ST AUSTELL   MAP 02 SX05

Charlestown Shipwreck & Heritage Centre

Quay Rd, Charlestown PL25 3NJ

➲ *(signed off A390 from St. Austell close to Eden Project)*

☎ 01726 69897

e-mail: admin@shipwreckcharlestown.com

web: www.shipwreckcharlestown.com

Charlestown is a small and unspoilt village with a unique sea-lock, china-clay port, purpose built in the 18th century. The Shipwreck and Heritage Centre was originally a dry house for china clay built on underground tunnels. Now it houses the largest display of shipwreck artefacts in the UK, along with local heritage, diving exhibits, and a Titanic display. A recent addition is a Nelson display to commemorate the Battle of Trafalgar.

Times ✳ Open Mar-Oct, daily 10-5 (later in high season). (Last admission 1 hour before closing) **Facilities** ❷ (charged) ⬚⎚ shop ▬

The China Clay Country Park

Carthew PL26 8XG

➲ *(2m N on B3274, follow brown signs 'China Clay Museum')*

☎ 01726 850362

e-mail: info@chinaclaycountry.co.uk

web: www.chinaclaycountry.co.uk

This museum tells the story of Cornwall's most important present-day industry: china clay production. The open-air site includes a complete 19th-century clayworks, with huge granite-walled settling tanks, working water-wheels and a wooden slurry pump. There is a fully interactive gallery, nature trails and a children's adventure trail. Exhibition halls and interactive displays depict the life of claypit workers from 1800 to the present.

Times Open all year 10-6, last admission summer 4, winter 3 **Fee** £7.50 (ch 6-16 £4.50, under 6 free concessions £6.) Family ticket (2ad+2ch) £20. Group discount available **Facilities** ❷ ⬚⎚ licensed ⴳ (outdoor) ও (interactive museum gallery) toilets for disabled shop ▬

Eden Project

Bodelva PL24 2SG

➲ *(overlooking St Austell Bay signposted from A390/ A30/A391)*

☎ 01726 811911

e-mail: information@edenproject.com

web: www.edenproject.com

An unforgettable experience in a breathtaking location, the Eden Project is a gateway into the fascinating world of plants and human society. Space age technology meets the lost world in the biggest greenhouse ever built. Located in a 50 metre deep crater the size of 30 football pitches are two gigantic geodesic conservatories: the Humid Tropics Biome and the Warm Temperate Biome. This is a startling and unique day out. There's an ice-rink in the winter (Nov-Feb) and concerts in the summer - see the website for details.

Times Open daily Mar-Oct 10-6 (last admission 4.30). Nov-Mar 10-4.30 (last admission 3). 20 Jul-4 Sep open until 8 on Tue, Wed & Thu. **Fee** ✳ £15 (ch 5-15 £5, student £7 concessions £10). Family ticket £36. Annual membership available. **Facilities** ❷ ⬚⎚ licensed ⴳ ও (Partly accessible) (wheelchairs, car shuttle to visitor centre/biomes) toilets for disabled shop garden centre ⊗ (ex assist dogs) ▬

ST IVES   MAP 02 SW54

(Park your car at Lelant Station and take advantage of the park and ride service. The fee includes parking and journeys on the train between Lelant and St Ives during the day).

Barbara Hepworth Museum & Sculpture Garden

Barnoon Hill TR26 1AD

➲ *(M5 to Exeter, A30 onto Penzance & St Ives, in town centre)*

☎ 01736 796226

e-mail: tatestivesinfo@tate.org.uk

web: www.tate.org.uk/stives

Visiting the museum and garden is a unique experience, which offers a remarkable insight into the work and outlook of one of Britain's most important twentieth-century artists, Dame Barbara Hepworth.

Times ✳ Open Mar-Oct, daily 10-5.30 (last admission 5); Nov-Feb, Tue-Sun 10-4.30 (last admission 4). Closed 25 Dec **Facilities** ℗ (880yds) ⊗ (ex assist dogs)

ST IVES CONTINUED

Tate St Ives

Porthmeor Beach TR26 1TG

➲ *(M5 to Exeter, then A30 onto Penzance & St Ives. Located on Porthmeor Beach)*

☎ 01736 796226

e-mail: tatestivesinfo@tate.org.uk

web: www.tate.org.uk/stives

Home of post-war British Modernism, St Ives provides the artistic foundations for Tate St Ives. Built in 1993, the gallery celebrates the surroundings and atmosphere that inspired the Modernists, and its unique architecture recalls the 'White Relief' work of Ben Nicholson as well as the unexpected twists and turns of the town itself. The gallery presents a varied programme of both Cornish and international artists, from the past and present, including displays on loan from Tate Modern.

Times Open Mar-Oct, daily 10-5.30; Nov-Feb, Tue-Sun 10-4.30. Closed 24-26 Dec ✳ £5.50 (concessions £2.75). **Facilities** ℗ (800yds) 💻 🍽 ♿ (access ramp, lift, wheelchairs) toilets for disabled shop ⊗ (ex assist dogs) ⬛

ST MARY'S   MAP 02

Isles of Scilly Museum

Church St, Hugh Town TR21 0JT

➲ *(In centre of Hugh Town)*

☎ 01720 422337

e-mail: info@iosmuseum.org

web: www.iosmuseum.org

A small, independent museum, which seeks to safeguard and promote the islands' history and traditions, and reflect every aspect of island life.

Times Open Etr-Sep, Mon-Sat 10-4.30. Oct-Etr, Mon-Sat 10-12 **Fee** ✳ £3.50 (ch 50p concessions £2.50) **Facilities** ♿ (stairlift)

ST MAWES   MAP 02 SW83

St Mawes Castle

TR2 3AA

➲ *(on A3078)*

☎ 01326 270526

web: www.english-heritage.org.uk

Wonderful location alongside the pretty fishing village of St Mawes, this castle was Henry VIII's most picturesque fort.

Times Open all year 21 Mar-Jun & Sep, Sun-Fri 10-5; Jul-Aug, Sun-Fri 10-6; Oct, daily 10-4; Nov-Mar, Fri-Mon 10-4. Closed Sat. (May close at 4 on Sun & Fri for private events). Closed 24-26 Dec & 1 Jan. **Fee** £4 (concessions £3.20, ch £2). Prices and opening times are subject to change in March 2009. Please call 0870 333 1181 for the most up to date prices and opening times when planning your visit. **Facilities** 🅿 🍴 shop ⊗ (ex dogs on leads in grounds) ⬛

SANCREED   MAP 02 SW42

Carn Euny Ancient Village

➲ *(1.25m SW of Sancreed, off A30)*

web: www.english-heritage.org.uk

The remains of an Iron-Age settlement. Surviving features include the foundations of stone huts and an intriguing curved underground passage or 'fogou'.

Times Open at any reasonable time. **Facilities** ℗ (600mtrs) ⬛

TINTAGEL   MAP 02 SX08

Tintagel Castle

PL34 0HE

➲ *(on Tintagel Head, 0.5m along uneven track from Tintagel, no vehicles)*

☎ 01840 770328

web: www.english-heritage.org.uk

Overlooking the wild Cornish coast, Tintagel is one of the most spectacular spots in the country associated with King Arthur and Merlin. Recent excavations revealed Dark Age connections between Spain and Cornwall, alongside the discovery of the 'Arthnou' stone suggesting that this was a royal palace for the Dark Age rulers of Cornwall.

Times Open all year, 21 Mar-Sep, daily 10-6; Oct, daily 10-5; Nov-Mar, daily 10-4. Closed 24-26 Dec & 1 Jan. **Fee** £4.70 (concessions £3.80, ch £2.40). Family ticket £11.80. Prices and opening times are subject to change in March 2009. Please call 0870 333 1181 for the most up to date prices and opening times when planning your visit. **Facilities** ℗ (in village) shop ⊗ (ex dogs on leads) ⬛

Tintagel Old Post Office NEW

PL34 0DB

➲ *(In centre of Tintagel village)*

☎ 01840 770024

e-mail: tintageloldpo@nationaltrust.org.uk

web: www.nationaltrust.org.uk

A rare survival of Cornish domestic medieval architecture, this 14th-century yeoman farmhouse is well furnished with local oak pieces. One room was used during the Victorian era as the letter receiving office for the district.

Times Open 14 Feb-1 Mar daily 11-4, 7-8 Mar Sat-Sun 11-4, 14 Mar-Sep daily 11-5.30, Oct-1 Nov 11-4. **Fee** £3 (ch £1.50, under 5's & NT members free). Family tickets available. Group 10+ £2.50. **Facilities** ℗ (within village) ♿ (partly accessible with ramp) (Braille guide, induction loop, virtual tour) shop ⊗ 🧸 ⬛

TORPOINT   MAP 02 SX45

Antony House

PL11 2QA

➲ *(2m NW, off A374 from Trerulefoot rdbt, 2m from Torpoint Ferry)*

☎ 01752 812191

e-mail: philip.brunsdon@nationaltrust.org.uk

web: www.nationaltrust.org.uk/antony

A fine, largely unaltered mansion, built in brick and Pentewan stone for Sir William Carew between 1711 and 1721. The stable block and outhouses remain from an earlier 17th-century building. The house contains contemporary furniture and family portraits. The grounds include a dovecote and the Bath Pond House.

Times Open Apr-28 May & Sep-29 Oct, Tue-Thu; 2 Jun-Aug, Tue-Thu & Sun. Open BH Mon. **Fee** House £6.30 (ch £3.15) Family tickets available. Garden only £3.25 (ch £1.60) **Facilities** ❷ ⏣❖ (Partly accessible) (Braille guide, recommended route in garden) toilets for disabled shop ❽ (ex assist dogs) ⬛❤

Mount Edgcumbe House & Country Park

Cremyll PL10 1HZ

➲ *(from Plymouth via Cremyll Foot Ferry, Torpoint ferry or Saltash Bridge. Via Liskeard to A374, B3247 follow brown heritage signs)*

☎ 01752 822236

e-mail: mt.edgcumbe@plymouth.gov.uk

web: www.mountedgcumbe.gov.uk

Covering some 800 acres, the country park surrounding Mount Edgcumbe contains a deer park, an amphitheatre, formal gardens, sculpture, the 18th-century Earl's Garden, and woodlands containing California redwoods. The coastal footpath runs along the shores of the Park from Cremyll to Whitsand Bay. Sir Richard Edgcumbe of Cotehele built Mount Edgcumbe between 1547 and 1553. It survived a direct hit by bombs in 1941, and was restored in the 1950s. It now contains antique paintings and furniture, 16th-century tapestries, and 18th-century porcelain. Events and exhibitions held each year.

Times ✳ Open: House & Earl's Garden Apr-Sep, Sun-Thu & BH Mon, 11-4.30. (Closed Fri & Sat). Country Park open all year. **Facilities** ❷ (charged) ⏣⏣ (outdoor) shop ❽ (ex assist dogs & in park) ⬛

TRELISSICK GARDEN   MAP 02 SW83

Trelissick Garden

TR3 6QL

➲ *(4m S of Truro on both sides of B3289, King Harry Ferry Road)*

☎ 01872 862090

e-mail: trelissick@nationaltrust.org.uk

web: www.nationaltrust.org.uk

Set amidst more than 500 acres of park and farmland, with panoramic views down the Carrick Roads to Falmouth and the sea, the garden is well known for its large collection of hydrangeas, camellias, rhododendrons and exotic and tender plants. The Cornish Apple Orchard contains the definitive collection of Cornish apple varieties and is particularly lovely in the spring. Two galleries on the property display Cornish Arts and Crafts.

Times Open 14 Feb-1 Nov, 10.30-5.30; 2 Nov-23 Dec & 2 Jan-13 Feb, 11-4; 27-31 Dec 11-4 (Mon, Tue, Sun) **Fee** £7 (ch £3.50). Family & Group tickets available. Reduced rate when arriving by cycle or public transport. **Facilities** ❷ (charged) ⏣⏣⏣❖ (audio guide, wheelchairs, batricar, induction loops) toilets for disabled shop garden centre ❽ (ex assist dogs) ⬛❤

TRERICE   MAP 02 SW85

Trerice

TR8 4PG

➲ *(3m SE of Newquay off A3058 at Kestle Mill)*

☎ 01637 875404

e-mail: trerice@nationaltrust.org.uk

web: www.nationaltrust.org.uk

The Trerice you see today was built in 1571 by Sir John Arundell IV and, having suffered no major changes since then due to a succession of absentee landlords, it is still somehow caught in the spirit of its age. The plaster ceilings in the Great Hall and Great Chamber are of particular merit and the façade of the building is now thought to be the oldest such example of Dutch influenced architecture still extant in the country. The house contains many fine pieces of furniture and a large collection of clocks. A barn houses a fascinating display of lawnmowers. The garden is planted to provide colour and interest throughout the year and features an orchard containing many varieties of Cornish apple trees.

Times Open 28 Feb-1 Nov, daily (ex Fri) 11-4.30 **Fee** House £7 (ch £3.50) Family & group tickets available. Reduced rate when arriving by cycle or public transport. **Facilities** ❷ ⏣⏣ (outdoor) ❖ (Braille/large print guide, tape tour, 2 wheelchairs) toilets for disabled shop ❽ (ex assist dogs) ⬛❤

TRURO   MAP 02 SW84

Royal Cornwall Museum   `FREE`

River St TR1 2SJ

➲ *(follow A390 towards town centre)*

☎ 01872 272205

e-mail: enquiries@royalcornwallmuseum.org.uk

web: www.royalcornwallmuseum.org.uk

Cornwall's oldest and most prestigious museum is famed for its internationally important collections. Visitors can see large collections of minerals, a real Egyptian mummy and the Cornish Giant. The art gallery has a fine collection of Newlyn School paintings and regular temporary exhibitions of local, national and international artists. The museum runs a range of family activities throughout the year along with a regular programme of lectures. Contact the museum for details of events and activities.

Times Open all year, Mon-Sat 10-4.45. Library closes 1-2, 10-1 Sat. (Closed BHs & Sun). **Facilities** ⓟ (200yds) (disabled parking on street) ⏣⏣ licensed ❖ (lift, ramps to main entrances) toilets for disabled shop ❽ (ex assist dogs) ⬛

ENGLAND

WENDRON   MAP 02 SW63

Poldark Mine and Heritage Complex

TR13 0ER

➲ *(3m from Helston on B3297 Redruth road, follow brown signs)*

☎ 01326 573173

e-mail: info@poldark-mine.com

web: www.poldark-mine.com

The centre of this attraction is the 18th-century tin mine where visitors can join a guided tour of workings which retain much of their original character. The site's Museum explains the history of tin production in Cornwall from 1800BC through to the 19th century and the fascinating story of the Cornish overseas. In addition to the Museum, the audio-visual presentation gives more insight into Cornwall's mining heritage. Ghost tours through July and August, please phone for details.

Times Open Etr-end Oct, 10-5.30 (last tour 4). **Fee** ✳ Guided Underground Tour: £8 (ch 5-15 £5) Family (2ad+2ch) £20, 2+1 £19. Site free. **Facilities** ❷ ➘ ⑩ licensed ⋒ (indoor & outdoor) ♿ (surface area only) (w/chair hire) toilets for disabled shop ➡

ZENNOR   MAP 02 SW43

Wayside Folk Museum

TR26 3DA

➲ *(4m W of St Ives, on B3306)*

☎ 01736 796945

Founded in 1937, this museum covers every aspect of life in Zennor and surrounding district from 3000BC to the 1930s. Over 5,000 items are displayed in 12 workshops and rooms covering wheelwrights, blacksmiths, agriculture, fishing, wrecks, mining, schoolroom, dairy, domestic and archaeological artefacts. A photographic exhibition entitled 'People of the Past' tells the story of the village. The museum also contains a watermill to which visitors have access.

Times Open Etr-end Oct, daily 10.30-5.30. **Fee** ✳ £3.50 (ch £2). Family ticket (2ad+2ch) £10. Party rates 10+ **Facilities** ℗ (50yds) ⋒ (outdoor) ♿ (not suitable for wheelchair users) shop ➡

Cheesewring, Bodmin Moor

CUMBRIA

Catbells and Friar's Crag from Derwent Water, Lake District National Park

ALSTON   MAP 12 NY74

Nenthead Mines **2 for 1**

Nenthead CA9 3PD

➲ *(5m E of Alston, on A689)*

☎ 01434 382726

e-mail: mines@npht.com

web: www.npht.com/nentheadmines

Set in 200 acres in the North Pennines, this hands-on heritage centre contains exhibitions and displays on geology, local wildlife, and social history. Visitors can operate three enormous water wheels, gaze down a 328ft deep brewery shaft, and take an underground trip through the Nenthead mines, last worked for lead in 1915. Special events take place throughout the year.

Times Open Etr-Oct, daily 11-5 (last entry to mine 3.30). **Fee** £4-£7 (ch free- £3). Family ticket from £15. **Facilities** ♿ 🍴 (indoor & outdoor) ♿ (ltd disabled access underground) (ramps & motorised scooter) toilets for disabled shop ✉

South Tynedale Railway

The Railway Station, Hexham Rd CA9 3JB

➲ *(0.25m N, on A686)*

☎ 01434 381696

web: www.strps.org.uk

Running along the beautiful South Tyne valley, this narrow-gauge railway follows the route of the former Alston to Haltwhistle branch. At present the line runs between Alston and Kirkhaugh.

Times Open Etr-Oct, wknds & BHs; mid Jul-Aug daily. Please enquire for exact details **Fee** ✳ Return £5.50 (ch 3-15 £2.50). Single £3.30 (ch 3-15 £1.50). All day £9 (ch 3-15 £4). Family ticket £15. **Facilities** ♿ 🍴 (outdoor) ♿ (railway carriage for wheelchairs, pre-booking required) toilets for disabled shop ✉

AMBLESIDE   MAP 07 NY30

The Armitt Collection

Rydal Rd LA22 9BL

➲ *(On A591 opposite Rydal Rd car park in Ambleside. Next to St Martins College)*

☎ 015394 31212

e-mail: info@armitt.com

web: www.armitt.com

A fascinating and entertaining place that celebrates over 2,000 years of Lake District history, from the time of Ambleside's Roman occupation to the 20th century. Facts, artefacts, historic photographs and renowned works of art by not only the area's better known former inhabitants such as Beatrix Potter, Kurt Schwitters and John Ruskin, but also displays about the daily lives of its hard-working townspeople in past times. Over 11,000 books are contained within a reference library and there is a changing programme of exhibitions.

Times ✳ Open all year, daily 10-5 (last entrance 4.30). Closed 24-26 Dec. **Facilities** ♿ (50yds) ♿ (chairlift to upstairs library, parking at establishment) toilets for disabled shop ✳ (ex assist dogs) ✉

BARROW-IN-FURNESS   MAP 07 SD26

The Dock Museum **FREE**

North Rd LA14 2PW

➲ *(A590 to Barrow-in-Furness. Follow brown tourist signs)*

☎ 01229 876400

e-mail: dockmuseum@barrowbc.gov.uk

web: www.dockmuseum.org.uk

Explore this museum and relive the fascinating history of Barrow-in-Furness. Discover how the industrial revolution prompted the growth of the town from a small hamlet into a major industrial power through models, graphics and computer kiosks.

Times Open mid Apr-Nov (Tue-Fri 10-5, Sat-Sun 11-5); Nov-Mar (Wed-Fri 10.30-4, Sat-Sun 11-4.30) **Facilities** ♿ 🍴 (outdoor) ♿ (hearing & induction loops, 2 w/chairs for loan) toilets for disabled shop ✳ (ex assist dogs) ✉

Furness Abbey

LH13 0TJ

➲ *(1.5m NE on unclass road)*

☎ 01229 823420

web: www.english-heritage.org.uk

Located in a peaceful valley, the majestic red sandstone remains of this beautiful abbey once housed a wealthy monastic order. View the fine stone carvings and visit the exhibition to find out more about the powerful religious community that was once based here.

Times Open all year, 21 Mar-Sep, daily 10-5; Oct-Mar, Thu-Sun 10-4. Closed 24-26 Dec & 1 Jan. **Fee** £3.50 (concessions £2.80, ch £1.80). Prices and opening times are subject to change in March 2009. Please call 0870 333 1181 for the most up to date prices and opening times when planning your visit. **Facilities** ♿ 🍴 shop ✳ (ex on lead in certain areas) 🚻

BASSENTHWAITE MAP 11 NY23

Trotters World of Animals **2 for 1**

Coalbeck Farm CA12 4RD

➲ *(follow brown signs on A591/A66 from Bassenthwaite Lake)*

☎ 017687 76239

e-mail: info@trottersworld.com

web: www.trottersworld.com

Home to hundreds of friendly creatures including lemurs, wallabies, zebras, otters and other exotic animals along with reptiles and birds of prey and a family of gibbons which will keep families amused for hours. Informative, amusing demonstrations bring visitors closer to the animals. "Clown About" is an indoor play centre with soft play area and ballpools for toddlers upwards.

Times Open all year, except 25 Dec & 1 Jan, 10-5.30 or dusk if earlier. **Fee** £7.25 (ch £5.25, pen £6.25) **Facilities ❷** ⌴ ⫙ licensed ⋔ (outdoor) ♿ toilets for disabled shop ⊗ (ex assist dogs) ▭

BIRDOSWALD MAP 12 NY66

Birdoswald Roman Fort

CA8 7DD

➲ *(signed off A69 between Brampton & Hexham)*

☎ 016977 47602

e-mail: birdoswald@dial.pipex.com

web: www.birdoswaldromanfort.org

A visitor centre introduces you to Hadrian's Wall and the Roman Fort. This unique section of Hadrian's Wall overlooks the Irthing Gorge, and is the only point along the Wall where all the components of the Roman frontier system can be found together. Birdoswald isn't just about the Romans, though, it's also about border raids in the Middle Ages, and recent archaeological discoveries. Please telephone for details of re-enactments and family activities.

Times Open Apr-30 Sep, daily 10-5.30 (last admission 5). 1-30 Oct daily, 10-4 **Facilities ❷** ⌴ ⋔ ♿ (ramp outside, disabled parking, lift) toilets for disabled shop ▭

BORROWDALE MAP 11 NY21

Honister Slate Mine

Honister Pass CA12 5XN

➲ *(from Keswick take B5289 through Borrowdale & Rosthwaite, follow road to top of pass. From Cockermouth take B5292 towards Keswick for 4m, turn right onto B5289 to Low Larton & Buttermere. Follow road to top of pass)*

☎ 01768 777230

e-mail: info@honister.com

web: www.honister.com

The last working slate mine in England. Fully guided tours allow you to explore the caverns hacked out by Victorian miners. Learn the history

of the famous Honister green slate, see local skills in action, and learn how to rive slates.

Times Open Mon-Fri 9-5, wknds 10-5. Closed 19 Dec-12 Jan. **Facilities ❷** ⌴ ⫙ ⋔ ♿ (Partly accessible) toilets for disabled shop garden centre

---

BOWNESS-ON-WINDERMERE MAP 07 SD49

Blackwell The Arts & Crafts House

LA23 3JT

➲ *(M6 junct 36. 1.5m S of Bowness on B5360, off A5074)*

☎ 015394 46139

e-mail: info@blackwell.org.uk

web: www.blackwell.org.uk

Blackwell was designed by architect M H Baillie Scott (1865-1945) and completed in 1900. Part of the late 19th-century Arts and Crafts Movement, it houses changing exhibitions of high quality applied arts and crafts, as well as original design features including stained glass, stonework, carved oak panelling, and plasterwork.

Times Open 18 Jan-Dec daily, 10.30-5 (closes 4pm Jan-Mar & Nov-Dec) **Fee** ✳ £6 (ch & concessionS £3.50). Family ticket £16. **Facilities ❷** ⌴ ♿ (Partly accessible) (lift to upper floor, photos for inaccessible rooms) toilets for disabled shop ⊗ (ex assist dogs) ▭

BRAMPTON MAP 12 NY56

Lanercost Priory

CA8 2HQ

➲ *(2.5m NE)*

☎ 01697 73030

web: www.english-heritage.org.uk

Close to Hadrian's Wall are the atmospheric ruins of this Augustinian priory founded in the 12th-century.

Times Open 21 Mar-Sep, daily 10-5; Oct, Thu-Mon, 10-4; Nov-13 Dec, Sat-Sun 10-4. **Fee** £3 (concessions £2.40, ch £1.50) Family £7.50. Prices and opening times are subject to change in March 2009. Please call 0870 333 1181 for the most up to date prices and opening times when planning your visit. **Facilities ❷** shop ▦

BROUGH MAP 12 NY71

Brough Castle **FREE**

CA17 4EJ

➲ *(8m SE of Appleby, S of A66)*

☎ 0191 261 1585

web: www.english-heritage.org.uk

Dating from Roman times, the 12th-century keep at this site replaced an earlier stronghold destroyed by the Scots in 1174. It was restored by Lady Anne Clifford in the 17th century. You can still see the outline of her kitchen gardens.

Times Please call 0870 333 1181 for details of opening times & charges. **Facilities ❷** ⊗ (ex dogs on leads) ▦

BROUGHAM   MAP 12 NY52

Brougham Castle

CA10 2AA

⮩ *(1.5m SE of Penrith on minor road off A66)*

☎ 01768 862488

web: www.english-heritage.org.uk

Explore the maze of stairs and passages in the ruins of this once glorious 11th-century castle on the banks of the River Eamont. Enjoy the lively exhibition where you'll see relics from the nearby Roman Fort.

Times Open 21 Mar-Sep, daily 10-5. **Fee** £3 (concessions £2.40, ch £1.50). Family £7.50. Prices and opening times are subject to change in March 2009. Please call 0870 333 1181 for the most up to date prices and opening times when planning your visit. **Facilities** ℗ ⋒ ⅃ (ex keep) shop ▦

CARLISLE   MAP 11 NY35

Carlisle Castle

CA3 8UR

⮩ *(north side of city centre, close to station)*

☎ 01228 591992

web: www.english-heritage.org.uk

Discover a thrilling and bloody past and enjoy panoramic views over the city and hills of the Lake District and Southern Scotland. Uncover an exciting history through lively exhibitions, which tell of William Rufus, Mary Queen of Scots and Bonnie Prince Charlie.

Times Open all year, 21 Mar-Sep, daily 9.30-5; Oct-Mar, daily 10-4. Closed 24-26 Dec & 1 Jan. **Fee** £4.50 (concessions £3.60, ch £2.30). Prices and opening times are subject to change in March 2009. Please call 0870 333 1181 for the most up to date prices and opening times when planning your visit. **Facilities** ℗ (400yds) ⅃ (parking for disabled at Castle) shop ⊗ (ex on lead in certain areas) ▦

Carlisle Cathedral

Castle St CA3 8TZ

⮩ *(M6 junct 42,43 or 44, located in City Centre)*

☎ 01228 535169 & 548151

e-mail: office@carlislecathedral.org.uk

web: www.carlislecathedral.org.uk

The Cathedral, founded in 1122 as a Norman Priory for Augustinian canons has had services conducted for nearly 900 years. Items of special interest include the East Window, with its tracery containing some very fine 14th-century stained glass and the Brougham Triptych, a magnificent 16th-century carved Flemish altarpiece in St. Wilfrid's Chapel. There is an interesting 14th-century barrel-vaulted painted ceiling in the Choir, and in the north and south aisles medieval paintings depict the Life of St. Cuthbert and St. Anthony and the figures of the 12 Apostles.

Times Open daily throughout the year, Mon-Sat 7.30-6.15, Sun 7.30-5, summer BHs 9.45-6.15, winter BHs, Xmas & New Year 9.45-4. **Fee** Suggested donation of £4 per adult. Treasury £1 charge. **Facilities** ℗ (5 mins walk) (2 disabled spaces only) ⁏⊙⁏ licensed ⋒ (outdoor) ⅃ (cathedral mostly accessible) (parking, ramps, loop system, large print books, chairlifts) toilets for disabled shop ⊗ (ex assist dogs)

The Guildhall Museum   `FREE`

Green Market CA3 8JE

⮩ *(town centre, behind Tourist Information Centre)*

☎ 01228 625400

e-mail: enquiries@tulliehouse.co.uk

web: www.tulliehouse.co.uk

The Guildhall is an impressive building standing alongside the Castle and Cathedral at the heart of the city. It is part of a surviving legacy of medieval life, and was once the meeting and trading place of Carlisle's eight trade Guilds. Today it is home to the rare and beautiful Carlisle Bells, the oldest horseracing prizes in the country. The civic history of the city is told with the impressive medieval muniment chest, Victorian civic regalia, and Guild silver collections.

Times Open Apr-Oct, 12-4.30 **Facilities** ℗ (500yds) (disc parking on street, 1 hr limit) shop ⊗ (ex assist dogs)

Tullie House Museum & Art Gallery

Castle St CA3 8TP

⮩ *(M6 junct 42, 43 or 44 follow signs to city centre. Car park in Devonshire Walk)*

☎ 01228 618718

e-mail: enquiries@tulliehouse.co.uk

web: www.tulliehouse.co.uk

Set in newly re-designed Roman and Jacobean gardens, Old Tullie House is home to an impressive collection of Pre-Raphaelite art, with many of the classical features of the 17th century still remaining, including the stunning staircase. Along with painting and sculpture, there are plenty of interactive exhibits that explore Roman life as well as 'Freshwater Life'. Lots of events throughout the year, contact for details.

Times Open Nov-Mar, Mon-Sat 10-4, Sun 12-4; Apr-Jun & Sep-Oct, Mon-Sat 10-5, Sun 12-5; Jul-Aug, Mon-Sat 10-5, Sun 11-5. Closed 25-26 Dec & 1 Jan. **Fee** ✳ Ground floor (including Art Gallery & Old Tullie House) Free. Upper floors & New Millennium Gallery £5.20 (ch under 18 free, concessions £3.60) **Facilities** ℗ (5mins walk) (disabled parking on site by request) ⊡ ⁏⊙⁏ licensed ⅃ (Old Tullie House not accessible) (chair lift, ramped access, lifts to all floors) toilets for disabled shop ⊗ (ex assist dogs) ▭

COCKERMOUTH   MAP 11 NY13

Jennings Brewery Tour and Shop

The Castle Brewery CA13 9NE

➲ *(A66 to Cockermouth, follow tourist signs to brewery)*

☎ 0845 129 7190

e-mail: jenningsbreweryshop@marstons.co.uk

web: www.jenningsbrewery.co.uk

Jennings Brewery was originally established as a family business in 1828 and moved to its current location in 1874. It is a traditional brewer, using Lakeland water drawn from the Brewery's own well, malt made from Maris Otter barley, and hops from Kent and Herefordshire.

Times Tours: Jan-Feb & Nov- Dec, Mon-Sat at 2; Mar-Jun & Sep-Oct, Mon-Sat, at 11 & 2; Jul-Aug, daily, at 11 & 2. **Fee** ✳ £5.50 (ch over 12 £2.50). **Facilities** ℗ (250mtrs) ♿ (ground floor shop & amenities accessible) toilets for disabled shop ⊗ (ex assist dogs) ➡

Lakeland Sheep & Wool Centre

Egremont Rd CA13 0QX

➲ *(M6 junct 40, W on A66 to rdbt at Cockermouth on A66/A5086 junct)*

☎ 01900 822673

e-mail: sheepshow@btconnect.com

web: www.sheep-woolcentre.co.uk

Come face to face with 19 different breeds of live sheep. Stage show with *One Man and his Dog* demonstration and our Jersey cow. Shows four times daily, March-end Oct (Sun-Thu only). All indoors.

Times Open all year, daily 9.30-5.30 (Closed 25-26 Dec & 5-18 Jan). **Fee** £5 (ch £4.50) for farm show. **Facilities** ℗ ⬚ 🍽 licensed 🍴 (outdoor) ♿ (hearing loop system) toilets for disabled shop ⊗ (ex assist dogs) ➡

Wordsworth House

Main St CA13 9RX

➲ *(W end of Main Street)*

☎ 01900 820882

e-mail: wordsworthhouse@nationaltrust.org.uk

web: www.wordsworthhouse.org.uk

William Wordsworth was born here on 7th April 1770, and happy memories of the house had a great effect on his work. The house is imaginatively presented for the first time as the home of the Wordsworth family in the 1770s. It offers a lively and interactive visit with hands-on activities and costumed living history.

Times Open 27 Mar-28 Oct, 11-4.30. Jul, Aug & BHs Mon-Sat, other times Tue-Sat. **Fee** ✳ £4.70 (ch £2.60). Family ticket £13.50. Groups 15+ £3.70 (ch£1.60). **Facilities** ℗ (300yds) ♿ (Braille guide, touch list, computer) toilets for disabled shop ⊗ (ex assist dogs) ♨ ➡

CONISTON   MAP 07 SD39

Brantwood

LA21 8AD

➲ *(2.5m SE off B5285, unclass road. Regular ferry services from Coniston Pier)*

☎ 015394 41396

e-mail: enquiries@brantwood.org.uk

web: www.brantwood.org.uk

Brantwood, home of John Ruskin, is a beautifully situated house with fine views across Coniston Water. Inside, there is a large collection of Ruskin paintings and memorabilia, and visitors can enjoy delightful nature walks through the Brantwood Estate.

Times Open mid Mar-mid Nov, daily 11-5.30. Winter, Wed-Sun 11-4.30. (Closed 25-26 Dec). **Fee** ✳ House & Estate £5.95 (ch £1.20, student £4.50). Family ticket £11.95. Estate only £4. **Facilities** ℗ ⬚ 🍽 ♿ (Partly accessible) (wheelchairs, photos of inaccessible areas, Braille guides) toilets for disabled shop ⊗ (ex assist dogs & in grounds) ➡

The Ruskin Museum

Yewdale Rd LA21 8DU

➲ *(In village centre opposite fire station, accessed from Mines Rd between Black Bull and Co-op)*

☎ 015394 41164

web: www.ruskinmuseum.com

John Ruskin (1819-1900) was one of Britain's most versatile and important political thinkers and artists. The museum contains many of his watercolours, drawings, letters, sketchbooks and other relics. The geology, mines and quarries of the area, Arthur Ransome's *Swallows and Amazons* country, and Donald Campbell's *Bluebird* are also explored in the Museum.

Times Open 2 Jan-13 Mar & 25 Nov-23 Dec Wed-Sun 10.30-3.30; 14 Mar-22 Nov, daily 10-5.30. Closed 24-26 & 31 Dec & 1 Jan. **Fee** £4.25 (ch £2). Family ticket £11. Ticket gives 50p discount for cruise on S.Y. Gondola/ Coniston Launch and/or visit to Brantwood. **Facilities** ℗ ♿ (handling specimens, guided walks) toilets for disabled shop ⊗ (ex assist dogs) ➡

Steam Yacht Gondola

Coniston Pier LA21 8AJ

➲ *(A593 to Coniston, follow signs near garage 'to boats' & S Y Gondola. Coniston Pier at end of Lake Road)*

☎ 015394 41288

e-mail: gondola@nationaltrust.org.uk

web: www.nationaltrust.org.uk/gondola

Originally launched in 1859, the graceful Gondola plied the waters of Coniston Water until 1936. Beautifully rebuilt, she came back into service in 1980, and visitors can once again enjoy her silent progress and old-fashioned comfort.

Times Open Apr-Oct to scheduled daily timetable. **Fee** ✳ Round trip £6 (ch £3). Family ticket (2ad+3ch) £15 **Facilities** ℗ (charged) ♿ (Gondola not accessible to wheelchair bound visitors) shop ⊗ (ex outside salloons) ♨ ➡

ENGLAND

53

DALEMAIN · MAP 12 NY42

Dalemain Historic House & Gardens

CA11 0HB

➲ (M6 junct 40, between Penrith & Ullswater on A592)

☎ 017684 86450

e-mail: admin@dalemain.com

web: www.dalemain.com

Originally a mediaeval pele tower, Dalemain was added to in Tudor times, and the imposing Georgian façade was completed in 1745. It has oak panelling, Chinese wallpaper, Tudor plasterwork and fine period furniture. The tower contains the Westmorland and Cumberland Yeomanry Museum, and there is a countryside collection in the 16th-century Great Barn. The gardens include a collection of old fashioned roses, and in early summer a magnificent display of blue Himalayan poppies.

Times Open Gardens, Tea room & Giftshop: 5 Apr-29 Oct , Sun-Thu 10.30-5. House open 11.15-4 (3 in Oct). **Fee** House & Garden £8.50, Garden only £6. (ch under 16 free when accompanied). **Facilities** ℗ ♿ ⛿ licensed ☂ (outdoor) ♿ (downstairs of house accessible, pictures of upstairs available) (ramp access at entrance, electric scooter) toilets for disabled shop garden centre ⊗ (ex assist dogs) ➠

DALTON-IN-FURNESS · MAP 07 SD27

South Lakes Wild Animal Park [2 for 1]

Crossgates LA15 8JR

➲ (M6 junct 36, A590 to Dalton-in-Furness, follow tourist signs)

☎ 01229 466086

e-mail: office@wildanimalpark.co.uk

web: www.wildanimalpark.co.uk

A day you'll never forget at one of Cumbria's top attractions. Hand feed giraffes, penguins and kangaroos every day. Get up close to rhinos, tigers, bears, hippos, monkeys, vultures, and lemurs. There are new aerial walkways and viewpoints, the Wild Things gift shop and Maki restaurant, all overlooking a recreated African Savannah where rhinos, giraffes and baboons wander.

Times Open all year, daily 10-5; Nov-Feb 10-4.30 (last admission 3.45). (Closed 25 Dec). **Fee** ✳ £10.50 (ch & concessions £7). Reduced prices Nov-Mar. **Facilities** ℗ ⛿ ☂ (indoor & outdoor) ♿ (wheelchair users may need help) toilets for disabled shop ⊗ ➠

GRASMERE · MAP 11 NY30

Dove Cottage, The Wordsworth Museum and Art Gallery

LA22 9SH

➲ (A591S of rdbt for Grasmere village)

☎ 015394 35544

e-mail: enquiries@wordsworth.org.uk

web: www.wordsworth.org.uk

Dove Cottage was the inspirational home of William Wordsworth for over eight years (1799-1808), and it was here that he wrote some of his best-known poetry. The cottage has been open to the public since 1891, and is kept in its original condition. The museum displays manuscripts, works of art and items that belonged to the poet. There is a changing programme of special events, both historical and modern. Please visit website for details.

Times Open daily 9.30-5.30 (closed Jan-early Feb & 24-26 Dec). **Fee** £7.50 (ch £4.10). Family ticket £18.20. Discounts for pre-bkd groups. **Facilities** ℗ ⛿ ⛿ licensed ♿ (Museum, galleries & ground floor of cottage accessible) (ramps, induction loop, virtual tour) toilets for disabled shop ⊗ (ex assist dogs) ➠

HAWKSHEAD · MAP 07 SD39

Beatrix Potter Gallery

Main St LA22 0NS

➲ (on main street in village centre)

☎ 015394 36355

e-mail: beatrixpottergallery@nationaltrust.org.uk

web: www.nationaltrust.org.uk

An annually changing exhibition of Beatrix Potter's original illustrations from her children's storybooks, housed in the former office of her husband, solicitor William Heelis.

Times Open Apr-29 Oct & Good Fri, Sat-Wed 10.30-4.30 (last admission 4). Also open Thu in Jul/Aug. Admission by timed ticket including NT members. **Fee** ✳ £3.80 (ch £1.90). Family ticket (2ad+3ch) £9.50. **Facilities** ℗ (300mtrs) ♿ (Partly accessible) (Braille guide) shop ⊗ (ex assist dogs) ✖ ➠

HOLKER · MAP 07 SD37

Holker Hall & Gardens

Cark in Cartmel, Grange over Sands LA11 7PL

➲ (from M6 junct 36, follow A590, signed)

☎ 015395 58328

e-mail: publicopening@holker.co.uk

web: www.holker-hall.co.uk

Dating from the 16th century, the new wing of the Hall was rebuilt in 1871, after a fire. It has a notable woodcarving and many fine pieces of furniture which mix happily with family photographs from the present day. There are magnificent gardens, both formal and woodland, and the Lakeland Motor Museum, exhibitions, deer park and adventure playground are further attractions.

Times Open Apr-28 Oct, Garden open 10.30-5.30. Hall open 12-4. **Fee** ✻ Gardens & Grounds £5.95 (ch 6-15 £3) Family ticket £15.50. All 3 attractions £11.50 (ch £6.50) Family ticket £32. **Facilities ℗** ⌷ 🍴 🎪 (outdoor) ♿ (ramps, wheelchairs & scooters available for hire) toilets for disabled shop ⊗ (assist dogs only in hall) ═

KENDAL　　　　　　　　　　　　　MAP 07 SD59

Abbot Hall Art Gallery

LA9 5AL

➲ *(M6 junct 36, follow signs to Kendal. Located at south end of town centre beside parish church)*

☎ 01539 722464

e-mail: info@abbothall.org.uk

web: www.abbothall.org.uk

The ground floor rooms of this splendid house have been restored to their former glory, with original carvings and fine panelling. The walls are hung with paintings by Romney, Gardner, Turner and Ruskin. The gallery has notable temporary exhibitions and a fine permanent collection of 18th- and 19th-century watercolours of the Lake District, and 20th-century British art, including works by Hepworth, Frink, Nicholson, Sutherland, Riley and Freud.

Times Open 18 Jan-20 Dec, Mon-Sat 10.30-5 (closes 4 Jan-Mar & Nov-Dec) **Fee** ✻ £5.45 (ch 18 and students up to age 25 free) **Facilities ℗** (charged) ⌷ ♿ (chair lifts in split level galleries, large print labels) toilets for disabled shop ⊗ (ex assist dogs) ═

Kendal Museum

Station Rd LA9 6BT

➲ *(opposite railway station)*

☎ 01539 721374

e-mail: info@kendalmuseum.org.uk

web: www.kendalmuseum.org.uk

The archaeology and natural history of the Lakes is explored in this popular museum which also features a world wildlife exhibition and a display devoted to author Alfred Wainwright, who was honorary clerk to the museum.

Times ✻ Open 17 Feb-22 Dec 10.30-5 (4pm Feb-Mar & Nov-Dec) **Facilities ℗** shop ⊗ (ex assist dogs) ═

Museum of Lakeland Life

Abbot Hall LA9 5AL

➲ *(M6 junct 36, follow signs to Kendal. Located at south end of Kendal beside Abbot Hall Art Gallery)*

☎ 01539 722464

e-mail: info@lakelandmuseum.org.uk

web: www.lakelandmuseum.org.uk

The life and history of the Lake District is captured by the displays in this museum, housed in Abbot Hall's stable block. The working and social life of the area are well illustrated by a variety of exhibits including period rooms, a Victorian Cumbrian street scene and a farming display. Three of the museum's rooms have undergone a recent refurbishment, two now host a large collection of Arts and Crafts movement textiles and furniture, while the third one is a recreation of Arthur Ransome's study, furnished with many of his personal possessions.

Times Open 18 Jan-20 Dec, Mon-Sat 10.30-5. (Closing at 4 Jan-Mar & Nov-Dec) **Fee** ✻ £4.50 (ch £3.20). Family ticket £13. **Facilities ℗** (charged) ⌷ ♿ (Partly accessible) toilets for disabled shop ⊗ (ex assist dogs) ═

KESWICK　　　　　　　　　　　　MAP 11 NY22

Cars of the Stars Motor Museum

Standish St CA12 5LS

➲ *(M6 junct 40, A66 to Keswick, continue to town centre, close to Bell Close car park)*

☎ 017687 73757

e-mail: cotsmm@aol.com

web: www.carsofthestars.com

This unusual museum features celebrity TV and film vehicles. Some notable exhibits to look out for are Chitty Chitty Bang Bang, James Bond's DB5 Aston Martin, Harry Potter's Ford Anglia, Del Boy's Robin Reliant, A-Team van and Batmobiles. Each vehicle is displayed in its individual film set.

Times Open Feb half term. Daily Etr-Nov (wknds Dec) 10-5 **Fee** ✻ £5 (ch £3) **Facilities ℗** (100yds) ♿ shop

KESWICK CONTINUED

Cumberland Pencil Museum `2 for 1`

Southey Works, Greta Bridge CA12 5NG

➲ *(M6 N onto A66 at Penrith. Left at 2nd Keswick exit, left at T-Junct, left over Greta Bridge)*

☎ 017687 73626

e-mail: museum@acco-uk.co.uk

web: www.pencilmuseum.co.uk

Investigating the history and technology of an object most of us take utterly for granted, this interesting museum includes a replica of the Borrowdale mine where graphite was first discovered, the world's longest pencil, children's activity area, and various artistic techniques that use pencils.

Times Open daily 9.30-4 (hours may be extended during peak season). (Closed 25-26 Dec & 1 Jan) **Fee** £3.25 (ch & pen £1.75, student £2.25). Family ticket (2ad+3ch) £8.25. **Facilities** 🅿 ⏛ 🎋 (outdoor) ♿ toilets for disabled shop ▦

Keswick Museum & Art Gallery

Fitz Park, Station Rd CA12 4NF

➲ *(M6 junct 40, A66 to Keswick, then follow tourist signs for Museum & Art Gallery)*

☎ 017687 73263

e-mail: keswick.museum@allerdale.gov.uk

web: www.allerdale.gov.uk/keswick-museum

Keswick's surprising past, from industrial mining centre to peaceful tourist town, is revealed in this fine example of a late Victorian museum. Set in the beautiful Fitz Park, the collections cover local and natural history, famous inhabitants and visitors, including the Lake Poets, and houses the work of many artists who have been captivated by the local landscape and history. The art gallery hosts a variety of special exhibitions, which change monthly.

Times ✳ Open Good Fri-Oct, Tue-Sat 10-4 **Facilities** 🅿 (on road outside) (2 hour limit) 🎋 (outdoor) ♿ (ramp at front entrance, with handrails) shop ⊗ (ex assist dogs)

Mirehouse

CA12 4QE

➲ *(3m N of Keswick on A591)*

☎ 017687 72287

e-mail: info@mirehouse.com

web: www.mirehouse.com

Visitors return to Mirehouse for many reasons: close links to Tennyson and Wordsworth, the spectacular setting of mountain and lake, the varied gardens, changing displays on the Poetry Walk, free children's nature notes, four woodland playgrounds, live classical piano music in the house, generous Cumbrian cooking in the tearoom, and a relaxed, friendly welcome. Please contact for details of special events.

Times Open Apr-Oct. Grounds: daily 10.30-5.30 House: Wed, Sun, (also Fri in Aug) 2-last entry 4.30. **Fee** ✳ House & grounds £5.60 (ch £2.80). Grounds only £2.80 (ch £1.40). Family ticket £15.50 (2ad & up to 4ch) **Facilities** 🅿 ⏛ 🎋 (outdoor) ♿ toilets for disabled ⊗ (ex on leads & assist dogs)

LAKESIDE   MAP 07 SD38

Lakes Aquarium

LA12 8AS

➲ *(M6, junct 36, take A590 to Newby Bridge. Turn right over bridge, follow Hawkshead Rd to Lakeside)*

☎ 015395 30153

e-mail: info@lakesaquarium.co.uk

web: www.lakesaquarium.co.uk

Re-launched in 2008, the Lakes Aquarium is now home to creatures that live in and around freshwater lakes across the globe. See things that swim, fly and bite in beautifully-themed displays. Discover mischievous otters in the Asia area, piranhas in the Americas and cheeky marmosets in the rainforest displays, not forgetting all your favourite creatures that live a bit closer to home. This includes diving ducks in the spectacular underwater tunnel and fresh water rays and seahorses in the Seashore Discover Zone. Don't miss the worlds first virtual diving bell. Experience a spectacular interactive adventure and come face to face with awesome virtual creatures including a terrifying shark, charging hippo and fierce crocodile - without getting wet. Special themed events take place throughout the year, please see website for details.

Times Open all year, daily from 9-5 (winter) 9-6 (summer) last admission 1hr prior to closing. Closed 25 Dec. **Fee** ✳ £8.50 (ch 3-15 £5.50, concessions £7). Family ticket (2ad+2ch £25, 2ad+3ch £29.75) **Facilities** 🅿 (charged) ⏛ 🍴 🎋 (outdoor) ♿ (lift to first floor, wheelchair) toilets for disabled shop ⊗ (ex assist dogs) ▦

LE VENS
MAP 07 SD48

Levens Hall

LA8 0PD

⮥ *(M6 junct 36. 5m S of Kendal, on A6)*

☎ 015395 60321

e-mail: houseopening@levenshall.co.uk

web: www.levenshall.co.uk

An Elizabethan mansion, built onto a 13th-century pele tower, with fine plasterwork, panelling and leatherwork. The topiary garden, laid out in 1694, survives virtually unchanged.

Times Open: House & gardens mid Apr-mid Oct, Sun-Thu. Gardens 10-5. House 12-4.30. Last admission 4. **Fee** ✳ House & garden £10 (ch £4.50), garden only £7 (ch £3.50). **Facilities** ℗ � ⏃ (outdoor) ᴕ (house-no access for wheelchairs/buggies) toilets for disabled shop garden centre ⊗ (ex assist dogs) ▰

NEAR SAWREY
MAP 07 SD39

Hill Top

LA22 0LF

⮥ *(2m S of Hawkshead. or 2m from Bowness Car Ferry).*

☎ 015394 36269

e-mail: hilltop@nationaltrust.org.uk

web: www.nationaltrust.org.uk

This small 17th-century house is where Beatrix Potter wrote many of her famous children's stories. It remains as she left it, and in each room can be found something that appears in one of her books.

Times Open 31 Mar-28 Oct Sat-Wed & Good Fri, 10.30-4.30 (last admission 4). Also open Thu in Jun-Aug. **Fee** ✳ £5.40 (ch £2.70). Family ticket £13.50 (2ad+3ch). **Facilities** ℗ ᴕ (access by arrangement) (Braille guide, handling items) shop ⊗ (ex assist dogs) ▰▰

PENRITH
MAP 12 NY53

The Rheged Centre

Redhills CA11 0DQ

⮥ *(M6 junct 40, on A66 near Penrith)*

☎ 01768 868000

e-mail: enquiries@rheged.com

web: www.rheged.com

Rheged's ten shops reflect the unique nature of the region, while the indoor and outdoor activities provide challenges for children of all ages. Five films are shown daily on the big cinema screen, as well as the 3D Discovering Cumbria exhibition. From a relaxed family lunch to a quick coffee and cake, Rheged's three cafés offer fresh food, made on the premises using the finest local ingredients.

Times Open daily 10-5.30. (Closed 25-26 Dec) **Fee** ✳ Imax style films £4.95 (ch £3 & pen £3.95). Family ticket £17. **Facilities** ℗ ⌷◉ licensed ⏃ (outdoor) ᴕ (Wheelchairs and motorised scooters) toilets for disabled shop ⊗ (ex assist dogs) ▰

Wetheriggs Country Pottery and Craft Centre
FREE

Clifton Dykes CA10 2DH

⮥ *(approx 2m off A6, S from Penrith, signed)*

☎ 01768 895617

web: www.wetheriggs-pottery.co.uk

Watch designer-maker artists and craftspeople at work in their studios, from where you can buy their wares, including paintings, glass, pottery, ceramics, fabrics, pine furniture, stone and metal work. Throw or paint your own pot. Newt pond, play area and the only steam-powered pottery workings in Britain. There is also a petting farm and reptile house, café and gift shop, all set within 7.5 acres of the beautiful Eden Valley.

Times Open daily, Etr-Oct 10-5.30; Nov-Etr 10-4.30. Closed 25-26 Dec & 1 Jan. **Facilities** ℗ ⌷⏃ (outdoor) ᴕ (stairs to gift shop, no lift. All other areas accessible by wheelchair) toilets for disabled shop ▰

RAVENGLASS
MAP 06 SD09

Ravenglass & Eskdale Railway

CA18 1SW

⮥ *(close to A595, Barrow to Carlisle road)*

☎ 01229 717171

e-mail: steam@ravenglass-railway.co.uk

web: www.ravenglass-railway.co.uk

The Lake District's oldest, longest and most scenic steam railway, stretching from the coast at Ravenglass, through two of Lakeland's loveliest valleys for seven miles to Dalegarth Visitor Centre and the foot of England's highest mountains. At least seven trains daily from March to November, plus winter weekends and holiday periods. Packages for walkers and cyclists, children's activities with the Water-vole Stationmaster. Postman Pat and Paddington Bear Days.

Times Open: trains operate daily mid Mar-early Nov, most winter wknds, daily between Xmas & New Year & Feb half term. **Fee** ✳ Return fare £10.20 (ch £5.10, under 5's free). Family discounts available **Facilities** ℗ (charged) ⌷◉⏃ (outdoor) ᴕ (special coaches - prior notice advisable) toilets for disabled shop ▰

RYDAL
MAP 11 NY30

Rydal Mount and Gardens

LA22 9LU

⮥ *(1.5m from Ambleside on A591 to Grasmere)*

☎ 015394 33002

e-mail: info@rydalmount.com

web: www.rydalmount.co.uk

The family home of William Wordsworth from 1813 until his death in 1850. The house contains important family portraits, furniture, and many of the poet's personal possessions, together with first editions of his work. In a lovely setting overlooking Windermere and Rydal Water, the gardens were designed by Wordsworth himself. Evening visits for groups can be organised.

Times Open daily Mar-Oct 9.30-5; Nov, Dec & Feb daily (ex Tue) 10-4. Closed 24-25 Dec & Jan **Facilities** ℗ ⏃ (outdoor) ᴕ (Partly accessible) (assistance to front door & ramp) shop ⊗ (ex on lead, assist dogs) ▰▰

SHAP   MAP 12 NY51

Shap Abbey   `FREE`

CA10 3NB

➲ (1.5m W of Shap on bank of River Lowther)
web: www.english-heritage.org.uk

Dedicated to St Mary Magdalene, the abbey was founded by the
Premonstratensian order in 1199, but most of the ruins are of
13th-century vintage. The most impressive feature is the 16th-century
west tower of the church.

Times Open at any reasonable time. **Facilities** ♿ ⊗ (ex dogs on leads) ⚐

SIZERGH   MAP 07 SD48

Sizergh Castle & Garden

LA8 8AE

➲ (3.5m S of Kendal, signed from A590)

☎ 015395 60951
e-mail: sizergh@nationaltrust.org.uk
web: www.nationaltrust.org.uk

The castle has a 60-foot high tower, built in the 14th century, but most
of the castle dates from the 15th to the 18th centuries. There are
panelled rooms with fine carved overmantels and adze-hewn floors,
and the gardens, laid out in the 18th century, contain the National
Trust's largest limestone rock garden.

Times Open Apr-Oct, Sun-Thu 1.30-5.30; Garden open Apr-Oct, from 12.30.
(Last admission 5). **Fee** ✳ House & Garden £5.80 (ch £2.90). Family ticket
£14.50. Group rate £4.80 each. Garden only £3.50 (ch £1.70). **Facilities** ♿
⊑ ⊞ ♿ (ramps) (Braille guide, wheelchair, powered buggy) toilets for
disabled shop ⊗ (ex assist dogs) ⚐ ▬

SKELTON   MAP 12 NY43

Hutton-in-the-Forest

CA11 9TH

➲ (6m NW of Penrith on B5305 to Wigton, 2.5m from
M6 junct 41)

☎ 017684 84449
e-mail: info@hutton-in-the-forest.co.uk
web: www.hutton-in-the-forest.co.uk

A beautiful house, set in woods which were once part of the medieval
forest of Inglewood, belonging to the Inglewood family since 1605. The
house consists of a 14th-century pele tower with later additions, and
contains a fine collection of furniture, portraits, tapestries and china, a
17th-century gallery and cupid staircase. The walled garden has a large
collection of herbaceous plants, and there are 19th-century topiary
terraces, a 17th-century dovecote and a woodland walk with impressive
specimen trees. Special events include a plant and food fair in May,
open-air Shakespeare in June and vintage cars in July. See website for
details.

Times Open: Gardens Apr-Oct daily (ex Sat) 11-5; House 8 Apr-4 Oct,
Wed-Thu, Sun & BH Mon 12.30-4). **Fee** £7 (ch £3). Family ticket £17.
Gardens £4 (ch £1.50). **Facilities** ♿ ⊑ ⊞ (outdoor) ♿ (garden gravel
paths) (most rooms on view in house upstairs) toilets for disabled shop ⊗
(ex in grounds on leads) ▬

TEMPLE SOWERBY   MAP 12 NY62

Acorn Bank Garden and Watermill

CA10 1SP

➲ (6m E of Penrith on A66)

☎ 017683 61893
e-mail: acornbank@nationaltrust.org.uk
web: www.nationaltrust.org.uk

A delightful garden of some two and a half acres, where an extensive
collection of over 250 varieties of medicinal and culinary herbs is
grown. Scented plants are grown in the small greenhouse, and a
circular walk runs beside the Crowdundle Beck to the partially restored
watermill. Please ring for details of special events.

Times Open late Mar-Oct, daily (ex Mon & Tue) 10-5 (last admission 4.30).
Fee ✳ £3.40 (ch £1.70). Family ticket £8.50. Party 15+ £2.85. **Facilities** ♿
⊑ ⊞ (outdoor) ♿ (Partly accessible) (Braille/large print guide, wheelchairs
available) toilets for disabled shop ⊗ (ex on lead on woodland walk) ⚐ ▬

ENGLAND

TROUTBECK   MAP 07 NY40

Townend

LA23 1LB

➲ (3m SE of Ambleside at S end of village)

☎ 015394 32628

e-mail: townend@nationaltrust.org.uk

web: www.nationaltrust.org.uk

The house is one of the finest examples of a 'statesman' (wealthy yeoman) farmer's house in Cumbria, built in 1626 for George Browne, whose descendents lived here until 1943. Inside is the original home-made carved furniture, with domestic utensils, letters and papers of the farm.

Times Open Apr-Oct, Wed- Sun & BH Mon 1-5 or dusk if earlier (last admission 4.30). **Fee** ✳ £3.60 (ch £1.80). Family ticket £9. **Facilities** ❷ ⓓ (Braille and sensory guide) ❽ (ex assist dogs) ⅍

WHITEHAVEN   MAP 11 NX91

The Beacon   `2 for 1`

West Strand CA28 7LY

➲ (A595, after Parton right onto New Rd. Follow one way system & town museum tourist signs)

☎ 01946 592302

e-mail: thebeacon@copelandbc.gov.uk

web: www.thebeacon-whitehaven.co.uk

Home to Copeland's museum collection, The Beacon traces the area's history from prehistoric times up to modern day using interactive displays and activities. Enjoy panoramic views of the town and coast from the fourth floor gallery. Regular art exhibitions are held in the Harbour Gallery.

Times Open all year Tue-Sun 10-4.30. Closed Mon except school & BHs. Closed 25-26 Dec. **Fee** Art gallery free. Museum £5 (under 16's free, concessions £4) **Facilities** ❷ (charged) 💬 ⅋ licensed ⓓ (chair/stair lift, Braille signs) toilets for disabled shop ❽ (ex assist dogs) ▤

The Rum Story   `2 for 1`

27 Lowther St CA28 7DN

➲ (A595, follow town centre signs)

☎ 01946 592933

e-mail: dutymanagers@rumstory.co.uk

web: www.rumstory.co.uk

Set in the original shop, courtyards, cellars and bonded warehouses of the Jefferson family, - the oldest rum trading family in the UK - this fascinating story takes the visitor back in time to the days of the rum trade, its links with the slave trade, sugar plantations, the Royal Navy, barrel-making and more. Set pieces include a tropical rainforest, an African village, a slave ship, and a cooper's workshop.

Times Open daily, 10-4.30. Closed 25-26 Dec & 1 Jan. **Fee** £5.45 (ch £3.45, concessions £4.45) Family £16.45. (2ad+2ch). Group rate 15+ £3.50, Child group 15+ £2.50 **Facilities** ⓟ 50 to 200 metres 💬 ⅋ licensed ⓓ (wheelchairs, wide doors, lifts) toilets for disabled shop ❽ (ex in courtyard) ▤

WINDERMERE   MAP 07 SD49

Lake District Visitor Centre at Brockhole

LA23 1LJ

➲ (on A591, between Windermere and Ambleside, follow brown tourist signs)

☎ 015394 46601

e-mail: infodesk@lake-district.gov.uk

web: www.lake-district.gov.uk

Set in 32 acres of landscaped gardens and grounds, on the shore of Lake Windermere, this house became England's first National Park Visitor Centre in 1969. It offers permanent and temporary exhibitions, lake cruises, an adventure playground and an extensive events programme. Contact the Centre for a copy of their free events guide. Boats available for hire in summer, weekends and school holidays.

Times Open 14 Feb-1Nov daily, 10-5. Grounds & gardens open all year. **Fee** Free admission but pay & display parking. **Facilities** ❷ (charged) 💬 ⅋ licensed ⌐ (indoor & outdoor) ⓓ (manual & electric wheelchairs, lifts, induction loops) toilets for disabled shop ▤

DERBYSHIRE

Howden Reservoir Dam, Peak District National Park

BOLSOVER | MAP 08 SK47

Bolsover Castle

Castle St S44 6PR

➲ (on A632)

☎ 01246 822844

web: www.english-heritage.org.uk

This award winning property has the air of a romantic storybook castle, with its turrets and battlements rising from a wooded hilltop. See the stunning Venus garden with its beautiful statuary and fountain. State of the art audio tours are available.

Times Open all year, 21 Mar-Apr, Thu-Mon 10-5; May-Sep, daily 10-6 (Fri-Sat 10-4); Oct, daily 10-5; Nov-Mar, Thu-Mon 10-4. Closed 24-26 Dec & 1 Jan. (Part of the Castle may close for 1hr if event is booked, please phone to check.) **Fee** £7 (concessions £5.60, ch £3.50). Family £17.50. Prices and opening times are subject to change in March 2009. Please call 0870 333 1181 for the most up to date prices and opening times when planning your visit. **Facilities** ❷ ⌨ ☶ & (keep not accessible) shop ❽ ⌗

BUXTON | MAP 07 SK07

Poole's Cavern (Buxton Country Park)

Green Ln SK17 9DH

➲ (1m from Buxton town centre, off A6 and A515)

☎ 01298 26978

e-mail: info@poolescavern.co.uk

web: www.poolescavern.co.uk

Limestone rock, water, and millions of years created this natural cavern containing thousands of crystal formations. A 45-minute guided tour leads the visitor through chambers used as a shelter by Bronze-Age cave dwellers, Roman metal workers and as a hideout by the infamous robber Poole. Attractions include the underground source of the River Wye, the 'Poached Egg Chamber', Mary, Queen of Scots' Pillar, the Grand Cascade and underground sculpture formations. Set in 100 acres of woodland, Buxton Country Park has leafy trails to Grinlow viewpoint and panoramic peakland scenery.

Times Open Mar-Oct, daily 9.30-5; Nov-Feb wknds 10-4. **Fee** ✳ £6.75 (ch £4, concession £5.50). Family ticket £20. **Facilities** ❷ (charged) ⌨ ⁅⊚⁆ ☶ (outdoor) & (access to visitor centre & 1st 100mtrs of cave tour to main chamber, no access to woods) toilets for disabled shop ❽ (ex assist dogs or in park) ▰

CALKE | MAP 08 SK32

Calke Abbey

DE73 7LE

➲ (on A514 between Swadlincote and Melbourne)

☎ 01332 863822

e-mail: calkeabbey@nationaltrust.org.uk

web: www.nationaltrust.org.uk

This fine baroque mansion was completed in 1704, and built for Sir John Harpur. Among its treasures are an extensive natural history collection, a magnificent Chinese silk state bed, and a spectacular red and white drawing room. The house stands in 600 acres of wooded parkland and also has walled flower gardens. Lots of special events all year round. Contact for details.

Times Open 1-9 Mar, Sat-Sun, 15 Mar-2 Nov, Mon-Wed & Sat-Sun & Good Fri. House 12.30-5; Gardens & Church 11-5; Restaurant & Shop 10.30-5. **Fee** ✳ With Gift Aid donation: £8.50 (ch £4.20). Family ticket £21.50. Garden only £5.30 (ch £2.70). Family ticket £13.30. **Facilities** ❷ ⁅⊚⁆ ☶ (outdoor) & (Access to 3 rooms on ground floor only. Stairs to other floors. Groundspartly accessible, grass, uneven and hard gravel paths, slopes & some steps) (Braille guide, hearing system, wheelchair, map) toilets for disabled shop ❽ (ex assist dogs) ▰

CASTLETON | MAP 07 SK18

Blue-John Cavern & Mine

Buxton Rd S33 8WP

➲ (follow brown 'Blue-John Cavern' signs from Castleton)

☎ 01433 620638 & 620642

e-mail: lesley@bluejohn.gemsoft.co.uk

web: www.bluejohn.gemsoft.co.uk

A remarkable example of a water-worn cave, over a third of a mile long, with chambers 200ft high. It contains eight of the 14 veins of Blue John stone, and has been the major source of this unique form of fluorspar for nearly 300 years.

Times Open all year, daily, 9.30-5 (or dusk). Guided tours of approx 1hr every 10 mins tour. **Fee** ✳ £8 (ch £4, pen & students £6) Family ticket £22. Party rates on request. **Facilities** ❷ ⌨ (not suitable for disabled visitors) shop ▰

ENGLAND

CASTLETON CONTINUED

Peak Cavern

S33 8WS

➲ *(on A6187, in centre of Castleton)*

☎ 01433 620285

e-mail: info@peakcavern.co.uk

web: www.devilsarse.com

One of the most spectacular natural limestone caves in the Peak District, with an electrically-lit underground walk of about half a mile. Ropes have been made for over 500 years in the 'Grand Entrance Hall', and traces of a row of cottages can be seen. Rope-making demonstrations are included on every tour.

Times Open all year, daily 10-5. Nov-Mar limited tours, please call in advance for times. Closed 25 Dec. **Fee** ✻ £7.25 (ch £5.25, other concessions £6.25). Family ticket (2ad+2ch) £22. **Facilities** ♿ (charged) 🍴 (indoor & outdoor) shop ➦

Peveril Castle

Market Place S33 8WQ

➲ *(on S side of Castleton)*

☎ 01433 620613

web: www.english-heritage.org.uk

The romantic ruins of this Norman fortress are situated high on a rocky crag and the views from the great square tower of the surrounding Peak District are breathtaking. Sir Walter Scott glamourised the castle in his novel, *Peveril of the Peak*.

Times Open 21 Mar-Apr & Sep-Oct, daily 10-5; May-Aug, daily 10-6; Nov-Mar, Thu-Mon 10-4. Closed 24-26 Dec & 1 Jan. **Fee** £3.70 (concessions £3, ch £1.90). Family £9.30. Prices and opening times are subject to change in March 2009. Please call 0870 333 1181 for the most up to date prices and opening times when planning your visit. **Facilities** shop ⌗

Speedwell Cavern

Winnats Pass S33 8WA

➲ *(A625 becomes A6187 at Hathersage. 0.5m W of Castleton)*

☎ 01433 620512

e-mail: info@speedwellcavern.co.uk

web: www.speedwellcavern.co.uk

Descend 105 steps to a boat that takes you on a one-mile underground exploration of floodlit caverns part of which was once a lead mine. The hand-carved tunnels open out into a network of natural caverns and underground rivers. See the Bottomless Pit, a huge subterranean lake in a huge, cathedral-like cavern.

Times Open all year, daily 10-5.30 (Closed 25 Dec). Phone to check Winter opening times due to weather. Last boat 4 **Fee** ✻ £7.75 (ch £5.75). **Facilities** ♿ (charged) shop ⊗ (ex assist dogs) ➦

Treak Cliff Cavern

S33 8WP

➲ *(0.75m W of Castleton on A6187)*

☎ 01433 620571

e-mail: treakcliff@bluejohnstone.com

web: www.bluejohnstone.com

An underground world of stalactites, stalagmites, flowstone, rock and cave formations, minerals and fossils. There are rich deposits of the rare and beautiful Blue John Stone, including 'The Pillar', the largest piece ever found. Show caves include the Witch's Cave, Aladdin's Cave, Dream Cave and Fairyland Grotto. These caves contain some of the most impressive stalactites in the Peak District. Visitors can also polish their own Blue John Stone, and purchase Blue John Stone jewellery and ornaments in the Castleton Gift Shop.

Times Open all year, Mar-Oct, daily 10-last tour 4.20, Nov-Feb daily - call for special tour times. All tours are guided & last about 40 mins. Enquire for last tour of day & possible closures. Closed 24-26 & 31 Dec & 1 Jan. All dates & times are subject to change without notice. **Fee** ✳ £7 (ch 5-15 £3.60). Family ticket (2ad+2ch) £19. **Facilities** ❷ ⌑ ⌒ (indoor & outdoor) ♿ (no wheelchair access) (hearing loop & picture word guides) shop ▬

CHATSWORTH   MAP 08 SK27

Chatsworth

DE45 1PP

➲ *(8m N of Matlock off B6012. 16m from M1 junct 29, signposted via Chesterfield, follow brown signs)*

☎ 01246 565300

e-mail: visit@chatsworth.org

web: www.chatsworth.org

Home of the Duke and Duchess of Devonshire, Chatsworth contains a massive private collection of fine and decorative arts. There is a splendid painted hall, and a great staircase leads to the chapel, decorated with statues and paintings. There are pictures, furniture and porcelain, and a trompe l'oeil painting of a violin on the music room door. The park was laid out by 'Capability' Brown, but is most famous as the work of Joseph Paxton, head gardener in the 19th century. The park is also home to the Duke and Duchess' personal collection of contemporary sculpture.

Times Open mid Mar-23 Dec, House & Garden 11-5.30, Farmyard 10.30-5.30. **Fee** ✳ House & Garden: £11.25 (ch £6.50, concessions £9.25). Family ticket £28. Pre-booked group discounts available. Garden only: £7.50 (ch £4.50, concessions £6). Family ticket £21. Farmyard & Adventure Playground: £5.25 (ch under 3 free, pen £3.50). Groups 5+ £3. **Facilities** ❷ (charged) ⌑ ⍨ licensed ♿ (Partly accessible) (3 electric wheelchairs available for garden) toilets for disabled shop ⊗ (ex on lead & in garden) ▬

CRESWELL   MAP 08 SK57

Creswell Crags Museum and Education Centre

Crags Rd, Welbeck S80 3LH

➲ *(off B6042, Crags Road, between A616 & A60, 1m E of Creswell village)*

☎ 01909 720378

e-mail: info@creswell-crags.org.uk

web: www.creswell-crags.org.uk

Creswell Crags, a picturesque limestone gorge with lakes and caves, is one of Britain's most important archaeological sites. The many caves on the site have yielded Ice Age remains, including bones of woolly mammoth, reindeer, hyena and bison, stone tools of Ice Age hunters from over 10,000 years ago and new research has revealed the only Ice Age rock art in Britain (about 13,000 years old). Visit the Museum and

Education Centre to learn more about your Ice Age ancestors through an exhibition, touch-screen computers and video. Join a 'Virtually the Ice Age' cave tour, picnic in Crags Meadow, or try the new activity trail. Plenty of special events year round, contact for details.

Times Open all year, Feb-Oct, daily, 10.30-4.30; Nov-Jan, Sun only 10.30-4.30. **Fee** ✳ Museum & site free. Ice Age tour £4.75 (ch £3); Rock Art tour £6 (ch £3) no under 5's on tours. £2 parking donation requested. **Facilities** ❷ ⌒ ♿ (accessible round Gorge. Tour may be unsuitable for mobility scooters, due to steps) toilets for disabled shop ⊗ (only assist dogs in museum) ▬

CRICH   MAP 08 SK35

Crich Tramway Village

DE4 5DP

➲ *(off B5035, 8m from M1 junct 28)*

☎ 01773 854321

e-mail: enquiry@tramway.co.uk

web: www.tramway.co.uk

A mile-long scenic journey through a period street to open countryside with panoramic views. You can enjoy unlimited vintage tram rides, and the exhibition hall houses the largest collection of vintage electric trams in Britain. The village street contains a bar and restaurant, tearooms, a sweet shop, ice cream shop, and Police sentry box, among others. There is also a Workshop Viewing Gallery where you can see the trams being restored. Ring for details of special events.

Times Open Apr-Oct, daily 10-5.30 (6.30 wknds Jun-Aug & BH wknds). 10.30-4 until Nov. **Fee** ✳ £10 (ch 3-15 £5, pen £9). Family ticket (2ad+3ch) £28 **Facilities** ❷ ⌑ ⍨ licensed ⌒ (outdoor) ♿ (converted tram, ramps) (Braille guidebooks, talktype facility) toilets for disabled shop ▬

DENBY   MAP 08 SK34

Denby Pottery Visitor Centre   2 for 1

Derby Rd DE5 8NX

➲ *(8m N of Derby off A38, on B6179, 2m S of Ripley)*

☎ 01773 740799

e-mail: tours.reception@denby.co.uk

web: www.denbyvisitorcentre.co.uk

The Visitor Centre is situated around a cobbled courtyard with shops and a restaurant. Pottery tours are available daily including hands-on activities such as paint-a-plate and make-a-clay-souvenir. Extensive cookshop with free half hour demonstrations daily. There are lots of bargains on Denby seconds in the factory shop, hand-made blown glass from the Glass Studio, Dartington Crystal Shop, gift shop, garden shop and hand painted Denby. (2-for-1 Voucher applies to factory tour only.) Denby Pottery celebrates its bi-centenary in 2009. Various events will take place through the year.

Times Open all year. Factory tours, Mon-Thu 10.30 & 1. Craftroom tour, daily 11-3. Visitor Centre Mon-Sat 9.30-5, Sun 10-5. Closed 25-26 Dec. **Fee** ✴ Free. Factory tour £5.95 (ch £4.95). Craftroom tour £4.50 (ch £3.50) **Facilities** ℗ ⌷ ☀ licensed 🍴 (outdoor) ᕃ (factory tour not accessible) (lift) toilets for disabled shop garden centre ⊗ (outside only, ex assist dogs) ◼

DERBY   MAP 08 SK33

Derby Museum & Art Gallery   FREE

The Strand DE1 1BS

➲ *(follow directions to city centre)*

☎ 01332 716659

e-mail: museums@derby.gov.uk

web: www.derby.gov.uk/museums

The museum has a wide range of displays, notably of Derby porcelain, and paintings by the local artist Joseph Wright (1734-97). Also antiquities, natural history and militaria, as well as many temporary exhibitions. A new military gallery, 'Soldiers' Story' opens in late summer 2008.

Times Open all year, Mon 11-5, Tue-Sat 10-5, Sun & BHs 1-4. Closed Xmas & New Year, telephone for details. **Facilities** ℗ (50yds) ᕃ (Partly accessible) (lift to all floors, portable mini-loop, large print labels) toilets for disabled shop ⊗ (ex assist dogs)

Pickford's House Museum of   FREE
Georgian Life & Historic Costume

41 Friar Gate DE1 1DA

➲ *(from A38 into Derby, follow signs to city centre)*

☎ 01332 255363

e-mail: museums@derby.gov.uk

web: www.derby.gov.uk/museums

The house was built in 1770 by the architect Joseph Pickford as a combined workplace and family home. It now shows domestic life at different periods, with Georgian reception rooms and service areas and a 1930s bathroom. Other galleries display part of the museum's collections of historic costume and toy theatres. There is a lively programme of changing temporary exhibitions and events throughout the year.

Times Open all year, Mon 11-5, Tue-Sat 10-5, Sun & BHs 1-4. (Closed Xmas & New Year, telephone for details). **Facilities** ℗ ᕃ (Partly accessible) (tape guides, video with sign language subtitles) shop ⊗ (ex assist dogs)

Royal Crown Derby Visitor Centre

194 Osmaston Rd DE23 8JZ

➲ *(on A514, opposite Derby Royal Infirmary)*

☎ 01332 712800

e-mail: enquiries@royal-crown-derby.co.uk

web: www.royal-crown-derby.co.uk

This museum traces the history of the company from 1750 to the present day, while the factory tour demonstrates the making of Royal Crown Derby in detail from clay through to the finished product. A demonstration studio gives you the opportunity to watch craftspeople at close quarters and try out a variety of different skills.

Times ✴ Open all year, daily, Mon-Sat 9-5 & Sun 10-4 (shop, Sun 10.30-4.30). **Facilities** ℗ ⌷ 🍴 ᕃ (ramps) toilets for disabled shop ⊗ (ex assist dogs) ◼

The Silk Mill, Derby's Museum of   FREE
Industry and History

Silk Mill Ln, off Full St DE1 3AR

➲ *(From Derby inner ring road, head for Cathedral & Assembly Rooms car park. 5 mins walk)*

☎ 01332 255308

e-mail: roger.shelley@derby.gov.uk

web: www.derby.gov.uk/museums

The museum is set in a re-built 18th-century silk mill and adjacent flour mill on the site of the world's first modern factory. Displays cover local industries, and include a major collection of Rolls Royce aero-engines from 1915 to the present. There is also a section covering the history of railway engineering in Derby. The building is now part of the Derwent Valley Mills World Heritage Site.

Times Open all year, Mon 11-5, Tue-Sat 10-5, Sun & BHs 1-4. (Closed Xmas & New Year, telephone for details). **Facilities** ℗ 5 min walk (museum parking restricted to disabled) 🍴 (outdoor) ᕃ (lift to all floors) toilets for disabled shop ⊗ (ex assist dogs)

EYAM   MAP 08 SK27

Eyam Hall

S32 5QW

⮐ *(Turn off A623 just after Calver Crossroads &
village of Stoney Middleton. Turn left at top of hill.
Eyam Hall in village centre opposite stocks).*

☎ 01433 631976

e-mail: nicola@eyamhall.com

web: www.eyamhall.com

An intimate 17th-century manor house in the heart of the famous
"plague village". Home to the Wright family since 1671, the Hall offers a
glimpse of domestic history through the eyes of one family, in
portraits, furniture, tapestries, costumes and memorabilia. Converted
farm buildings house the Eyam Hall Craft Centre. Please telephone for
details of musical and theatrical events throughout the season.

Times Open House & Garden: Etr week Sun, Mon, Wed & Thu. May &
Spring BH Sun & Mon. Jul & Aug: Wed, Thu, Sun, BH Mon. Xmas wknds in
Dec. All 12-4. Craft Centre year round Tue-Sun 11-5 **Facilities** ❷ ⬛🍴️☐
(outdoor) ♿ (Partly accessible) (disabled entrance via special gate, ramps)
toilets for disabled shop ❽ (ex assist & dogs in grounds) ◼

HADDON HALL   MAP 08 SK26

Haddon Hall

DE45 1LA

⮐ *(1.5m S of Bakewell off A6)*

☎ 01629 812855

e-mail: info@haddonhall.co.uk

web: www.haddonhall.co.uk

Originally held by the illegitimate son of William the Conqueror,
Haddon has been owned by the Manners family since the 16th century.
Little has been added since the reign of Henry VIII, and, despite its
time-worn steps, few medieval houses have so successfully withstood
the ravages of time.

Times Open Apr-Sep, Sat-Mon; Etr Good Fri-Tue; May-Sep daily 12-5 (closed
5-6 Jul); 6-14 Dec 10.30-3.30. **Fee** ✴ £8.50 (ch £4.50 & pen £7.50). Family
ticket £22. Party 15+. **Facilities** ❷ (charged) 🍴 licensed ♿ (steps &
uneven floors, not accessible for w/chairs due to distance from carpark)
toilets for disabled shop ❽ (ex assist dogs) ◼

HARDWICK HALL   MAP 08 SK46

Hardwick Hall

Doe Lea S44 5QJ

⮐ *(2m S M1 junct 29 via A6175. Access by Stainsby
Mill entrance only)*

☎ 01246 850430

e-mail: hardwickhall@nationaltrust.org.uk

web: www.nationaltrust.org.uk

An outstanding example of Elizabethan architecture, described as
'more glass than wall', Hardwick Hall was built by Bess of Hardwick
between 1590 and 1597, and is surrounded by 300 acres of historic
parkland. Other attractions on the estate include Stainsby Mill, a fully
functioning water-powered mill with 17-foot waterwheel; the Stone
Centre where visitors can learn about the art of stonemasonry; and the
Park Centre which details local wildlife. Lots of talks and special events.
Contact for details.

Times Open Mar-2 Nov, Wed-Thu & Sat-Sun, BH Mon & Good Fri, 12-4.30;
6-21 Dec Sat-Sun, 11-3. Garden Mar-2 Nov, Wed-Sun 11-5.30 & 6-21 Dec,
Sat-Sun 11-3. Old Hall 21 Mar-Oct, Wed-Thu & Sat-Sun 11-5.30 (11-5 Oct) .
Parkland gates all year 8-6. Mill Mar-Jun, 5 Sep-2 Nov, Wed-Thu & Sat-Sun
10-4; Jul-4 Sep, Wed-Sun 10-4 & 6-21 Dec, Sat-Sun 10-3. **Fee** ✴ With Gift
Aid donation: House & Garden £9.50 (ch £4.75). Family ticket £23.75.
Garden only £4.75 (ch £2.30). Family £11.80. Joint ticket with Stainsby Mill
£12.15 (ch £6.10). Family £30.80. Mill only £3.15 (ch £1.60). **Facilities** ❷ 🍴
☐ (outdoor) ♿ (Ramped entrance. Ground floor accessible, stairs with
handrail to other floors, Grounds partly accessible with slopes, grass paths &
some cobbles.) (large print & Braille guide, wheelchair, touch screens) toilets
for disabled shop ❽ (ex in park on leads) ❧

KEDLESTON HALL   MAP 08 SK34

Kedleston Hall

DE22 5JH

⮐ *(5m NW of Derby, entrance off Kedleston Rd,
signed from rdbt where A38 crosses A52, close to
Markeaton Park)*

☎ 01332 842191

e-mail: kedlestonhall@nationaltrust.org.uk

web: www.nationaltrust.org.uk

Kedleston has been the Derbyshire home of the Curzon family for over
eight centuries. The original house was demolished at the end of the
17th century. In 1760 Robert Adam built the south front and designed
most of the interior including the marble hall. There are pictures,
furniture and china displayed in the house together with an Indian
Museum containing the collection accumulated by Lord Curzon when
he was Viceroy of India.

Times Open all year: House; Mar-2 Nov, Sat-Wed 12-5 (last admission 4.15).
Garden; same as house but open daily 10-6. Park open daily, Mar-2 Nov
10-6 & 3 Nov-27 Feb 10-4. (Closed 25-26 Dec & some restrictions may apply
in Dec & Jan). **Fee** ✴ With Gift Aid donation: House & Garden £8.50 (ch
£4.20). Family ticket £21.50. Park and Garden only: £3.80 (ch £1.90). Family
ticket £9.60. Park (winter) £4. **Facilities** ❷ 🍴 ♿ (steps to main entrance,
access via shop. Ground floor fully accessible but stairs to state floor.
Grounds have steps, grass paths & cobbles.) (Braille guide, w/chair, self-drive
vehicle) toilets for disabled shop ❽ (ex in park on leads) ❧

MATLOCK BATH   MAP 08 SK25

The Heights of Abraham Cable Cars, Caverns & Hilltop Park

DE4 3PD

➲ *(on A6, signed from M1 junct 28 & A6. Base station next to Matlock Bath railway station)*

☎ 01629 582365

e-mail: office@heightsofabraham.com

web: www.heightsofabraham.com

The Heights of Abraham, a unique Hilltop Park, reached using the country's most up-to-date cable cars. Once you are at the summit you can join exciting underground tours of two spectacular show caverns. Above ground there are play areas, picnic spots, exhibitions, shops, café and summit bar all with stunning views across the surrounding Peak District. New attractions are the Heath and Heaven and Fossil Factory exhibitions, plus brand new, state-of-the-art lighting in the Great Masson Cavern which reveals its magnitude as it has never seen before.

Times Open daily 14-22 Feb & Etr-Oct 10-5 (later in high season) 28 Feb-26 Mar wknds only. Please telephone or check website for details & other times. **Fee** Please telephone or check website for details. **Facilities** Ⓟ (300mtrs) 🖵🍴🎎 (outdoor) ♿ (please ring for details) toilets for disabled shop ⊗ (ex in grounds & cable car) ▬

Peak District Mining Museum

The Pavilion DE4 3NR

➲ *(On A6 alongside River Derwent)*

☎ 01629 583834

e-mail: mail@peakmines.co.uk

web: www.peakmines.co.uk

A large display explains the history of the Derbyshire lead industry from Roman times to the present day. The geology of the area, mining and smelting processes, the quarrying and the people who worked in the industry, are illustrated by a series of static and moving exhibits. The museum also features an early 19th-century water pressure pumping engine. There is a recycling display in the Pump Room.

Times Open all year, daily Apr-end Sep 10-5, Oct-end Mar 11-3. Closed 25 Dec. **Facilities** Ⓖ (charged) 🖵♿ (chair lift to mezzanine, larger print) shop ⊗ (ex assist dogs)

Temple Mine

Temple Rd DE4 3NR

➲ *(off A6. Telephone for directions)*

☎ 01629 583834

e-mail: mail@peakmines.co.uk

web: www.peakmines.co.uk

A typical Derbyshire mine which was worked from the early 1920s until the mid 1950s for fluorspar and associated minerals. See examples of mining methods which give an insight into working conditions underground.

Times ✳ Open Apr-end Sep timed visits noon & 2pm daily, Oct-end Mar timed visits noon & 2pm wknds only **Facilities** Ⓟ Pay & Display ⊗ (ex assist dogs)

MELBOURNE   MAP 08 SK32

Melbourne Hall & Gardens

DE73 8EN

➲ *(9m S of Derby on A514, in Melbourne take turn by bus shelter in Market Place, follow road to Church Square)*

☎ 01332 862502

e-mail: melbhall@globalnet.co.uk

web: www.melbournehall.com

Sir John Coke (Charles I's Secretary of State) leased Melbourne Hall in 1628 and the house has been home to two Prime Ministers: Lord Melbourne and Lord Palmerston. The glorious formal gardens are among the finest in Britain.

Times Open, house daily throughout Aug only (ex first three Mons) 2-5 (last admission 4.15). Prebooked parties by appointment in Aug. Gardens Apr-Sep, Wed, Sat, Sun & BH Mon 1.30-5.30. Upstairs rooms available by appointment. **Fee** House Tue-Sat (guided tour) £3.50 (ch £2, pen £3), Sun & BH Mon (no guided tour) £3 (ch £1.50, pen £2.50). House & Garden (Aug only) £5.50 (ch £3.50, pen £4.50). Garden only £3.50 (pen £2.50). Family £9.50. **Facilities** Ⓟ (200yds) (no parking in visitor centre courtyard) 🖵♿ (Partly accessible) (ramps at house & garden entrance) shop ⊗ (ex assist dogs)

MIDDLETON BY WIRKSWORTH   MAP 08 SK25

Middleton Top Engine House

Middleton Top Visitor Centre DE4 4LS

➲ *(Signed off A6 in Cromford then, 0.5m S from B5036 Cromford/Wirksworth road)*

☎ 01629 823204

e-mail: middletontop@derbyshire.gov.uk

web: www.derbyshire.gov.uk/countryside

A beam engine built in 1829 for the Cromford and High Peak Railway, and its octagonal engine house. The engine's job was to haul wagons up the Middleton Incline, and its last trip was in 1963 after 134 years' work. The visitor centre tells the story of this historic railway.

Times ✻ Open: Information Centre, daily, wknds only winter. Engine House Etr-Oct 1st wknd in month (engine in motion). **Facilities** Ⓟ (charged) ⛩ (outdoor) shop

OLD WHITTINGTON MAP 08 SK37

Revolution House

FREE

High St S41 9JZ

➲ *(3m N of Chesterfield town centre, on B6052 off A61, signed)*

☎ 01246 345727

e-mail: tourism@chesterfield.gov.uk

web: www.visitchesterfield.info

Originally the Cock and Pynot alehouse, this 17th-century cottage was the scene of a meeting between local noblemen to plan their part in the Revolution of 1688, a series of events that led to the overthrow of James II in favour of William and Mary of Orange. The house is now furnished in 17th-century style. A video relates the story of the Revolution and there is a small exhibition room.

Times Open daily (ex Tue) 11-4 from 21 Mar-28 Sep. Call for Xmas opening **Facilities** Ⓟ (100yds) ♿ (Partly accessible) (signing available by prior arrangement) shop ⊗ (ex assist dogs)

RIPLEY MAP 08 SK35

Midland Railway Butterley

Butterley Station DE5 3QZ

➲ *(M1 junct 28, A38 towards Derby, then signed)*

☎ 01773 747674 & 749788

e-mail: mr_b2004@btconnect.com

web: www.midlandrailwaycentre.co.uk

A regular steam-train passenger service runs here, to the centre where the aim is to depict every aspect of the golden days of the Midland Railway and its successors. Exhibits range from the steam locomotives of 1866 to an electric locomotive, with a large section of rolling stock spanning the last 100 years. Also a farm and country park, along with narrow gauge, miniature and model railways. Regular rail-related special events throughout the year. Contact for details. 2009 marks 40 years of the project.

Times Open all year, trains run wknds Feb-Dec & most school holidays **Fee** ✻ £10.90 (ch 5-16 £5.50, pen £9.95) children under 2 free. Party 15+. **Facilities** Ⓟ ☕ ⛩ (outdoor) ♿ (special accommodation on trains) toilets for disabled shop 💳

SUDBURY MAP 07 SK13

Sudbury Hall

DE6 5HT

➲ *(6m E of Uttoxeter at junct of A50 & A515)*

☎ 01283 585305

e-mail: sudburyhall@nationaltrust.org.uk

web: www.nationaltrust.org.uk

This country house was started in 1664 by Lord George Vernon. It has unusual diapered brickwork, a carved two-storey stone frontispiece, a cupola and tall chimneys. The interior features work by craftsmen including Edward Pierce and Grinling Gibbons. Parts of the interior featured as Mr Darcy's rooms in the BBC adaptation of *Pride and Prejudice*. The Museum of Childhood contains a Victorian schoolroom, collections of toys, and displays.

Times Open Hall: 21 Mar-2 Nov, Wed-Sun 1-5 (open BH Mons & Good Fri). (When dusk, Hall may close early). Museum: Spring-27 Jul, Wed-Sun; 28 Jul-7 Sep, daily; 10 Sep-2 Nov, Wed-Sun, 11-5 & 8 Nov-21Dec, Sat-Sun 10.30-3.30. Gardens open: 15 Mar-21Dec, daily 10.30-5. **Fee** ✻ With Gift Aid donation: House £6.80 (ch £3.40). Family ticket (2ad+2ch) £17. Museum £7.20 (ch £4.20). Family ticket £18.60. Joint ticket £12.50 (ch £6.50). Joint Family ticket £31. **Facilities** Ⓟ ☕ ♿ (Access via steps & 4 flights of steps to first floor. Lift to all Museum floors. Grounds partly accessible, grass & loose gravel paths, some steps) (w/chair available, large print/Braille guide & touch list) toilets for disabled shop ⊗ (ex in grounds) ✤

WIRKSWORTH MAP 08 SK25

Wirksworth Heritage Centre

Crown Yard DE4 4ET

➲ *(on B5023 off A6 in centre of Wirksworth)*

☎ 01629 825225

e-mail: enquiries@storyofwirksworth.co.uk

web: www.storyofwirksworth.co.uk

The Centre has been created in an old silk and velvet mill. The three floors of the mill have interpretative displays of the town's past history as a prosperous lead-mining centre. Each floor offers many features of interest including a computer game called *Rescue the Injured Lead-Miner*, a mock-up of a natural cavern, and a Quarryman's House. During the Spring Bank Holiday you can also see the famous Well Dressings. Newly renovated exhibits on the top floor include one on quarrying, information about local round-the-world yachtswoman Ellen MacArthur, and local memories from the Second World War. There's also a small art gallery carrying local works.

Times Open Etr-Sep, Wed-Sun & BHs 10.30-4.30 & Oct half term **Fee** £3 (ch £1, concessions £2). Party 20+ 10% discount **Facilities** Ⓟ (80yds) (pay & display) ☕ 🍽 ♿ (4 steps to ground floor) (portable ramp) shop ⊗ (ex assist dogs)

DEVON

Sidmouth

ARLINGTON MAP 02 SS64

Arlington Court
EX31 4LP

🕓 *(7m NE of Barnstaple, on A39)*

☎ 01271 850296

e-mail: arlingtoncourt@nationaltrust.org.uk

web: www.nationaltrust.org.uk

Arlington Court was built in 1823 and is situated in the thickly wooded Yeo Valley. The centrepiece is the Victorian mansion, surrounded by formal and informal gardens. Also open to visitors is the working stable yard, housing a collection of carriages and horse-drawn vehicles. The extensive parkland around the house is grazed by Jacob sheep and Red Devon cattle. Please telephone for details of events running throughout the year. 2009 - 60 years since the property was given to the National Trust by Miss Rosalie Chichester.

Times Open 14 Mar-1 Nov, daily 10.30-5. (Last admission 4.30). Grounds open Nov-Mar during daylight hours. **Fee** House, carriage museum & grounds £8.20 (ch £4.10). Family £20.50. Carriage museum & grounds £5.90 (ch £2.95). Parties 15+ pre-booked 15% discount. **Facilities** 🅿 ⬚ 🍴 (outdoor) ♿ (ground floor only of house) (wheelchairs, ramps at house, batricar, Braille guide) toilets for disabled shop garden centre ⊗ (ex in grounds on leads) 🐾 ➡

BARNSTAPLE MAP 02 SS53

Marwood Hill Gardens
Marwood EX31 4EB

➲ *(off A361, follow brown tourist signs)*

☎ 01271 342528

web: www.marwoodhillgarden.co.uk

The 18-acre gardens with their three small lakes contain many rare trees and shrubs. There is a large bog garden and a walled garden, collections of clematis, camellias and eucalyptus. Alpine plants are also a feature, and there are plants for sale.

Times Open Mar-Oct, daily 9.30-5.30. **Facilities** 🅿 ⬚ garden centre ➡

BEER MAP 03 SY28

Pecorama Pleasure Gardens
Underleys EX12 3NA

➲ *(from A3052 take B3174, Beer road, signed)*

☎ 01297 21542

e-mail: pecorama@btconnect.com

web: www.peco-uk.com

The gardens are high on a hillside, overlooking Beer. A miniature steam and diesel passenger line offers visitors a stunning view of Lyme Bay as it runs through the Pleasure Gardens. Attractions include an aviary, crazy golf, children's activity area and the Peco Millennium Garden. The main building houses an exhibition of railway modelling in various small gauges. There are souvenir and railway model shops, plus full catering facilities. Please telephone for details of events running throughout the year.

Times Open Etr-end Oct , Mon-Fri 10-5.30, Sat 10-1. Open Sun at Etr & 24 May-6 Sep. **Fee** ✳ £6.30 (ch 4-14 £4.30, concessions £5.80, over 80 & under 4 free) **Facilities** 🅿 ⬚ 🍴 licensed 🍴 (outdoor) ♿ (no wheelchairs on miniature railway) (access with helper, wheelchair. Garden steep in places) toilets for disabled shop ⊗ (ex assist dogs) ➡

BICTON MAP 03 SY08

Bicton Park Botanical Gardens
East Budleigh EX9 7BJ

➲ *(2m N of Budleigh Salterton on B3178, leave M5 at junct 30 & follow brown tourist signs)*

☎ 01395 568465

e-mail: info@bictongardens.co.uk

web: www.bictongardens.co.uk

Unique Grade I-listed, 18th-century historic gardens with palm house, orangery, plant collections, extensive countryside museum, indoor and outdoor activity play areas, pinetum, arboretum, nature trail, woodland railway garden centre and restaurant. All this set in 63 acres of beautiful parkland that has been cherished for 300 years. Open air concerts take place in July and August.

Times Open Winter 10-5, Summer 10-6. Closed 25 & 26 Dec. **Facilities** 🅿 ⬚ 🍴 🍴 (outdoor) ♿ (adapted carriage on woodland railway, wheelchairs) toilets for disabled shop garden centre ➡

BLACKMOOR GATE MAP 03 SS64

Exmoor Zoological Park
South Stowford, Bratton Fleming EX31 4SG

➲ *(off A361 link road onto A399, follow tourist signs)*

☎ 01598 763352

e-mail: exmoorzoo@btconnect.com

web: www.exmoorzoo.co.uk

Exmoor Zoo is both personal and friendly. Open since 1982 it is an ideal family venue, catering particularly for the younger generation. The zoo specialises in smaller animals, many endangered, such as the golden-headed lion tamarins. Over 14 species of this type of primate are exhibited. Contact pens are provided throughout and children are encouraged to participate. Twice daily guided tours at feeding times along with handling sessions.

CONTINUED

BLACKMOOR GATE CONTINUED

Times Open daily, Apr-4 May & 16 Sep-2 Nov 10-5; Nov-Mar 10-4; 5 May-15 Sep 10-6 **Fee** £8.50 (ch £6.50, concessions £7.50). Family ticket (2ad+2ch) £28. **Facilities** Ⓟ ☕ ⛩ (outdoor) ♿ (tarmac paths on hill) toilets for disabled shop ⊗ (ex assist dogs) ▬

BRANSCOMBE MAP 03 SY29

Branscombe - The Old Bakery, Manor Mill and Forge NEW

EX12 3DB

➲ *(In Branscombe village, off A3052)*

☎ 01392 881691

e-mail: branscombe@nationaltrust.org.uk

web: www.nationaltrust.org.uk

Charming vernacular buildings with mill and forge restored to working order. The forge is open daily and the blacksmith sells the ironwork he produces.

Times Open Old Bakery: Apr-1 Nov Wed-Sun 11-5; Manor Mill 29 Mar-28 Jun & 6 Sep-1 Nov Sun 2-5, Jul-30 Aug Wed & Sun 2-5; Forge - phone for opening times. **Fee** Manor Mill £2.80 (ch £1.40, under 5's & NT members free). **Facilities** Ⓟ ☕ ♿ (Manor Mill has narrow doorways, corridors & steep stairs) toilets for disabled

BUCKFASTLEIGH MAP 03 SX76

Buckfast Abbey FREE

TQ11 0EE

➲ *(0.5m from A38, midway between Exeter and Plymouth. Turn off at 'Dart Bridge' junct and follow brown tourist signs)*

☎ 01364 645500

e-mail: enquiries@buckfast.org.uk

web: www.buckfast.org.uk

The Abbey, founded in 1018, was dissolved by Henry VIII in the 16th century. Restoration began in 1907, when four monks with little building experience began the work. The church was built on the old foundations, using local blue limestone and Ham Hill stone. The precinct contains several medieval monastic buildings, including the 14th-century guest hall which contains an exhibition of the history of the Abbey.

Times Open all year daily. Closed Good Fri & 24-26 Dec. **Facilities** Ⓟ ☕ 🍽 licensed ⛩ (outdoor) ♿ (Braille & audio information) toilets for disabled shop ⊗ (ex assist dogs) ▬

Buckfast Butterfly Farm & Dartmoor Otter Sanctuary

TQ11 0DZ

➲ *(off A38, at Dart Bridge junct, follow tourist signs, adjacent to steam railway)*

☎ 01364 642916

e-mail: contact@ottersandbutterflies.co.uk

web: www.ottersandbutterflies.co.uk

Visitors can wander around a specially designed, undercover tropical garden, where free-flying butterflies and moths from around the world can be seen. The otter sanctuary has large enclosures with underwater viewing areas. Three types of otters can be seen - the native British otter along with Asian and North American otters.

Times Open Good Fri-end Oct, daily 10-5.30 or dusk (if earlier). **Fee** * £6.95 (ch £4.95, concession £5.95). Family ticket £19.95 **Facilities** Ⓟ ☕ ⛩ (outdoor) ♿ (Partly accessible) (wheelchair ramps) shop ⊗ (ex assist dogs) ▬

BUCKLAND ABBEY MAP 02 SX46

Buckland Abbey

PL20 6EY

➲ *(off A386 0.25m S of Yelverton, signed)*

☎ 01822 853607

e-mail: bucklandabbey@nationaltrust.org.uk

web: www.nationaltrust.org.uk

Originally a prosperous 13th-century Cistercian Abbey, and then home of the Grenville family, Buckland Abbey was sold to Sir Francis Drake in 1581, who lived there until his death in 1596. Several restored buildings house a fascinating exhibition about the abbey's history. Among the exhibits is Drake's drum, which is said to give warning of danger to England. An Elizabethan garden is also open.

Times Open 14 Mar-1 Nov, daily (ex Thu) 10.30-5.30, (daily Jul-Aug). 14 Feb-8 Mar, 6 Nov-13 Dec, 18 Dec-23 Dec, Fri-Sun, 11-4. **Fee** Abbey & grounds £8.20. Grounds only £4.10. (ch 1/2 price) Party rate £6.90 each. **Facilities** Ⓟ ☕ 🍽 licensed ⛩ (outdoor) ♿ (upper floors in house not accessible. Some steep slopes in grounds) (wheelchairs & motorised buggy available) toilets for disabled shop ⊗ (ex assist dogs) ▬

CHITTLEHAMPTON MAP 03 SS62

Cobbaton Combat Collection

Cobbaton EX37 9RZ

➲ *(signed from A361 & A377)*

☎ 01769 540740

e-mail: info@cobbatoncombat.co.uk

web: www.cobbatoncombat.co.uk

World War II British and Canadian military vehicles, war documents and military equipment can be seen in this private collection. There are over 50 vehicles including tanks, one a Gulf War Centurian, and a recently added Warsaw Pact section. There is also a section on 'Mum's War' and the Home Front.

Times Open Apr-Oct, daily (ex Sat) 10-5; Jul-Aug daily. Winter most wkdays, phone for details. **Fee** ✳ £6 (ch £4, concessions £5). **Facilities** ❷ ☐ ⼊ (outdoor) ♿ toilets for disabled shop ⊗ (ex assist dogs, & in grounds) ▬

CHUDLEIGH   MAP 03 SX87

Canonteign Falls   2 for 1

EX6 7NT

➲ *(off A38 at Chudleigh/Teign Valley junct onto B3193 and follow tourist signs for 3m)*

☎ 01647 252434

e-mail: info@canonteignfalls.co.uk

web: www.canonteignfalls.co.uk

A magical combination of waterfalls, woodlands and lakes. Three graded walks marked with colour ferns.

Times Open summer 10-6. Last admission 1 hour before closing. **Fee** ✳ £5.75 (ch £4.50, concessions £4.75). Family £19.50. **Facilities** ❷ ☐ ⼤ 🍴 licensed ⼊ (indoor & outdoor) ♿ (grounds partly accessible but not up to falls) toilets for disabled shop ▬

CHURSTON FERRERS   MAP 03 SX95

Greenway

TQ5 0ES

➲ *(off A3022 into Galmpton. Follow Manor Vale Rd into village then follow brown signs for gardens)*

☎ 01803 842382

e-mail: greenway@nationaltrust.org.uk

web: www.nationaltrust.org.uk/devoncornwall

Greenway House will re-open after a major restoration project: 'Another Chapter'. For the first few months of the season the house will gradually open for timed, limited-access visits while the collection continues to be reinstated. Pre-booking for car parking is essential; those arriving by 'green' means will have slots made available to see this unique and magical property with its many collections, including archaeology, Tunbridgeware, silver, botanical china and books, the atmospheric house set in the 1950s, and the glorious woodland garden with its wild edges and rare plantings, all allow a glimpse into the private holiday home of the famous and well-loved author, Agatha Christie, and her family. Enjoy the adventure of arriving here by ferry alighting at Greenway Quay, with the dramatic views of the house from the river. Greenway is not easily accessible having some steep and slippery paths. All visitors are asked to wear walking shoes and to follow routes and directions according to their suitability on the day.

Times Open 28 Feb-19 Jul & 2 Sep-25 Oct, Wed-Sun; 21 Jul-30 Aug, Tue-Sun 10.30-5 **Fee** £7.80 (ch £3.90) Car, £6.60(ch £3.30) Green and groups (not by car) **Facilities** ❷ ☐ ⼊ (outdoor) ♿ (Ground floor of house and part of garden only accessible) (Braille guide, large print, T Loop) toilets for disabled shop ⊗ (ex assist dogs & in parkland) ❧ ▬

CLOVELLY   MAP 02 SS32

The Milky Way Adventure Park

EX39 5RY

➲ *(on A39, 2m from Clovelly)*

☎ 01237 431255

e-mail: info@themilkyway.co.uk

web: www.themilkyway.co.uk

One of the West Country's leading attractions for the biggest rides and the best shows. Attractions include Clone Zone - Europe's first interactive adventure ride featuring a suspended roller coaster; Time Warp - indoor adventure play area; daily displays from the North Devon Bird of Prey Centre; archery centre; golf driving nets; railway; pets corner and more. 'Droid Destroyer Dodgems' invites pilots to save the Earth from the Vega Asteroid. New to the attraction is Devon's biggest, longest and fastest roller coaster.

Times Open Etr-end Oct, daily 10.30-6. Also open wknds & school hols in winter. **Fee** ✳ £10 per person. Under 1.2m £9 (under 3's free, concessions £6). **Facilities** ❷ ☐ ⼊ (indoor & outdoor) ♿ (ramps) toilets for disabled shop ▬

CLYST ST MARY   MAP 03 SX99

Crealy Adventure Park

Sidmouth Rd EX5 1DR

➲ *(M5 junct 30 onto A3052 Exeter to Sidmouth road)*

☎ 01395 233200

e-mail: fun@crealy.co.uk

web: www.crealy.co.uk

Crealy Adventure Park offers an unforgettable day for all the family with Tidal Wave log flume, El Pastil Loco Coaster, Queen Bess Pirate Ship, Techno Race Karts, Bumper Boats, Victorian Carousel, Funosaurus show and all weather play area. Visit the Animal Realm to ride, feed, milk, groom or cuddle the animals. Relax on the Prairie Train tour around the worlds first Sunflower Maze.

Times ✳ Open all year, Jan-mid July & 6 Sep-Dec, daily 10-5. Closed winter term time Mon-Tue; mid Jul-5 Sep, daily 10-6. **Facilities** ❷ ☐ 🍴 ⼊ (indoor & outdoor) ♿ (carers admitted free, rollercoaster has disabled facility) toilets for disabled shop ▬

COMBE MARTIN
MAP 02 SS54

Combe Martin Wildlife Park & Dinosaur Park

EX34 0NG

⮑ *(M5 junct 27 then A361 towards Barnstaple, turn right onto A399)*

☎ 01271 882486

e-mail: info@dinosaur-park.com

web: www.dinosaur-park.com

Come and see the UK's only full-size animatronic Tyrannosaurus Rex, along with a pair of vicious, interacting Meglosaurs, a Velociraptor and Dilophosaurus, the 'Spitting Dinosaur'. Explore 26 acres of stunning gardens with cascading waterfalls and hundreds of exotic birds and animals. There are daily sea lion shows, falconry displays, lemur encounters and handling sessions. Other attractions include the Earthquake Canyon Train Ride, Tomb of the Pharoahs, Tropical House, Wolf Research and Education Centre, and much more.

Times Open 15 Mar-2 Nov; daily 10-5.30 (last admission 3). **Fee** ✳ £12 (ch 3-15 £7.50, ch under 3 free, pen £8.50). Family (2ad+2ch) £34. **Facilities** ℗ ⌴ ⊓ (outdoor) ⚹ (bottom part of park has sharp decline, not suitable for wheelchairs or severe disabilities) toilets for disabled shop ⊗ ⊟

COMPTON
MAP 03 SX86

Compton Castle

TQ3 1TA

⮑ *(off A381 at Ipplepen. Or, off A380 Torquay, Paignton ring road at Marldon (no coaches on this road))*

☎ 01803 842382

e-mail: compton@nationaltrust.org.uk

web: www.nationaltrust.org.uk/devoncornwall

Home to the Gilbert family for an almost unbroken 600 years, this imposing castle set against a backdrop of rolling hills and orchards evokes a bewitching mixture of romance and history. This is the last truly fortified dwelling to be built in Devon, and its extremely high curtain walls, symmetrical towers and portcullis create an unforgettable approach. Inside there are machiolations, spiral staircases and squints, making Compton a place of discovery and adventure for imaginative children and adults alike.

Times Open 30 Mar-29 Oct Mon, Wed & Thu 11-5 **Fee** Castle & garden £4.20 (ch £2.10). Groups £3.50 (ch £1.80) **Facilities** ℗ ⊓ (outdoor) ⚹ (Please phone for guidance, accessiblity limited) (large print, Braille notes, portable ramp) ⊗ (ex assist dogs) 🦮

CULLOMPTON
MAP 03 ST00

Diggerland

Verbeer Manor EX15 2PE

⮑ *(M5 junct 27. E on A38 & at rdbt turn right onto A3181. Diggerland is 3m on left)*

☎ 08700 344437

e-mail: mail@diggerland.com

web: www.diggerland.com

An adventure park with a difference, where kids of all ages can experience the thrills of driving real earth-moving equipment. Choose from various types of diggers and dumpers ranging from one ton to eight and a half tons. Supervised by an instructor, complete the Dumper Truck Challenge or dig for buried treasure. New rides include JCB Robots, the Supertrack, Landrover Safari and Spin Dizzy. Even under fives can join in, with mum or dad's help. Please telephone for details of events during school and Bank Holidays.

Times ✳ Open mid Feb-Nov, BHs & school hols. **Facilities** ℗ ⌴ ⊓ shop ⊗ (ex assist dogs) ⊟

DARTMOUTH
MAP 03 SX85

Bayard's Cove Fort
FREE

TQ6 9AT

⮑ *(in Dartmouth on riverfront)*

web: www.english-heritage.org.uk

Built by the townspeople to protect the harbour, the remains of the circular stronghold still stand at the southern end of the harbour.

Times Open at any reasonable times. **Facilities** ⊗ ⊞

Dartmouth Castle

Castle Rd TQ6 0JN

⮑ *(1m SE off B3205, narrow approach road)*

☎ 01803 833588

web: www.english-heritage.org.uk

Built at the water's edge in a superb scenic setting, the castle's military history spans well over 500 years.

Times Open all year, 21 Mar-Jun & Sep, daily 10-5; Jul-Aug, daily 10-6; Oct, daily 10-4; Nov-Mar, Sat-Sun, 10-4. Closed 24-26 Dec & 1 Jan. **Fee** £4 (concessions £3.20, ch £2.00). Prices and opening times are subject to change in March 2009. Please call 0870 333 1181 for the most up to date prices and opening times when planning your visit **Facilities** ℗ (charged) shop ⊗ ⊞

Woodlands Leisure Park

Blackawton TQ9 7DQ

➲ *(5m from Dartmouth on A3122. From A38 follow brown tourist signs)*

☎ 01803 712598

e-mail: fun@woodlandspark.com
web: www.woodlandspark.com

Woodlands Leisure Park, Blackawton, Totnes, South Devon TQ9 7DQ
Tel: 01803 712598 • www.woodlandspark.com
Woodlands Leisure reserve the right to close the park or any attractions without prior notice.

A family day out of variety and fun, with 60 acres of unique indoor and outdoor attractions. Sixteen family rides including exhilarating water coasters, toboggan run, avalanche and bumper boats. Enjoy the dizzy dune buggies, polar pilots and soft play, there are playzones to entertain big and small kids for hours. Rainy days are great with a vast area of indoor fun. Experience The Empire with five floors of challenging tower climbs, rides and slides, hang on to the Trauma Tower as it shoots up and drops down fifty feet! Play the Master Blaster, the zippiest game on the planet, blasting foam balls at your friends. At Big Fun Farm discover amazing night and daytime creatures, insects and birds. Get close to animals, ride big U-Drive Tractors while toddlers have fun tractoring round Pedal Town. Firework Festival in November.

Times Open daily 28 Mar-1 Nov, Winter wknds & school holidays only.
Fee ✳ £9.95 (under 92cms free). Family ticket £37.80 (2ad+2ch).
Facilities ❷ ⌴ ⩊ (indoor & outdoor) ♿ (some rides not suitable) (ramps) toilets for disabled shop ⊗ (ex assist dogs) ➦

See advert on this page

DREWSTEIGNTON   MAP 03 SX79

Castle Drogo

EX6 6PB

➲ *(5m S of A30 Exeter-Okehampton. Coaches turn off A382 at Sandy Park)*

☎ 01647 433306

e-mail: castledrogo@nationaltrust.org.uk
web: www.nationaltrust.org.uk

India tea baron Julius Drewe's dream house, this granite castle, built between 1910 and 1930, is one of the most remarkable works of Sir Edward Lutyens, and combines the grandeur of a medieval castle with the comfort of the 20th century. A great country house with terraced formal garden, woodland spring garden, huge circular croquet lawn and colourful herbaceous borders. Standing at more than 900 feet overlooking the wooded gorge of the River Teign with stunning views of Dartmoor, and delightful walks. Lots of events in school holidays, ring for details.

Times Castle open 14 Mar-1 Nov daily 11-5; Garden, tearooms & shop open 14 Mar-1 Nov 10.30-5.30 **Fee** House & garden £8.20 (ch £4.10). Family £20.50. Garden only £5.25 (ch £2.88) **Facilities** ❷ ⌴ ⩊ (outdoor) ♿ (Gardens, Hall & Library fully accessible, other areas only accessible via stairs) (Braille & large print guide, touch list) toilets for disabled shop garden centre ⊗ (ex assist dogs) ➦ ➦

EXETER   MAP 03 SX99

Exeter Cathedral

1 The Cloisters EX1 1HS

➲ *(Follow signs for city centre).*

☎ 01392 285983

e-mail: visitors@exeter-cathedral.org.uk
web: www.exeter-cathedral.org.uk

A fine example of a medieval cathedral, famous for its two Norman towers, impressive West Front carvings and the longest unbroken stretch of Gothic vaulting in the world. It has been the seat of the bishops of Exeter for over one thousand years and remains a vibrant worshipping community. The Cathedral has an on-going programme of concerts and recitals throughout the year. 2009 is the 1100th anniversary of the Diocese.

Times Open all year, Mon-Fri 9.30-5.30, Sat 9-5, Sun 12.3-2.30 for general visiting. No group tours. Restrictions may apply when the cathedral is being used for special services & events. Check website before travelling. **Fee** ✳ £4 (ch under 16 within a family group free, students & pen £2). Group rates apply. **Facilities** ℗ 5 mins ⌴ ❢⬠ ⩊ (outdoor) ♿ (wheelchair access avoiding steps can be made available) toilets for disabled shop ⊗ (ex assist dogs) ➦

EXETER CONTINUED

Exeter's Underground Passages

2 Paris St EX1 1GA

➲ *(Follow signs for city centre)*

☎ 01392 665887

e-mail: underground.passages@exeter.gov.uk

web: www.exeter.gov.uk/passages

Exeter's underground passages reopened in Autumn 2007, with a brand new visitor centre and a high profile entrance. The centre is packed with interactive exhibits but the passages remain the same: narrow, dark and exciting.

Times Open Jun-Sep (incl school hols outside this period) Mon-Sat 9.30-5.30 (last tour 4.30). Sun 10.30-4 (last tour 3). Oct-May (closed Mon) Tues-Fri 11.30-5.30, Sat 9.30-5.30 (last tour 4.30), Sun 11.30-4 (last tour 3). **Fee** £5 (ch £3.50 5-18yrs, under 5's free access to exhibition only, concessions £4), Family ticket £15 (2ad+3ch). **Facilities** Ⓟ (50mtrs) &. (exhibition accessible to wheelchairs, tours of passages not suitable) toilets for disabled shop ⓧ (ex assist dogs in exhibition) ▬

Quay House Visitor Centre   FREE

46 The Quay EX2 4AN

➲ *(Turn off A30 onto A366. Follow signs to historic quayside)*

☎ 01392 271611

e-mail: quayhouse@exeter.gov.uk

web: www.exeter.gov.uk/quayhouse

Two thousand years of Exeter's history in an audio-visual presentation of the city from Roman times to the present day. Learn about the history of the Quayside through lively displays, illustrations and artefacts.

Times Open all year, Apr-Oct, daily 10-5; Nov-Mar, Sat-Sun 11-4. **Facilities** Ⓟ 100mtrs (no parking on quayside) &. (access to downstairs only) (induction loop, audio visual presentation) shop ⓧ (ex assist dogs)

RAMM in the Library NEW   FREE

Royal Albert Memorial Museum, Castle St EX4 3PQ

➲ *(Off High Street)*

☎ 01392 665858

e-mail: RAMM@exeter.gov.uk

web: www.exeter.gov.uk/RAMM

With a range of objects on display and hands on gallery activities, RAMM in the Library is an ideal place for family visits and to catch up on news of the Royal Albert Memorial Museum's redevelopment. Many of the Museum's favourite activities can be enjoyed here during the closure.

Times Open all year Mon-Sat 10-5. Closed BHs. **Facilities** Ⓟ (300mtrs) &. (portable loop, large print) toilets for disabled ⓧ (ex assist dogs)

St Nicholas Priory NEW

The Mint, off Fore St EX4 3BL

➲ *(follow signs for city centre)*

☎ 01392 665858

e-mail: priory@exeter.gov.uk

web: www.exeter.gov.uk/priory

Originally part of a Medieval Priory, this splendid building was later lived in by the wealthy Hurst family. It is now presented as their furnished Elizabethan town house with replica furniture, sumptious fabrics and rich colours. Come and feel at home in this historical family house.

Times Open Sat & Mon-Sat Devon school hols, 10-5; Term time Mon-Fri prebooked groups & school parties. Closed BHs. **Fee** ✻ £2 (ch free). Prebooked groups £3 (ch £2). **Facilities** Ⓟ (250mtrs) &. (Ground floor) (audio visuals of inaccessible rooms) toilets for disabled shop garden centre ⓧ (ex assist dogs) ▬

EXMOUTH   MAP 03 SY08

A la Ronde NEW

Summer Ln EX8 5BD

➲ *(2m N of Exmouth on A376)*

☎ 01395 265514

e-mail: alaronde@nationaltrust.org.uk

web: www.nationaltrust.org.uk

A unique 16-sided house built on the instructions of two spinster cousins on their return from a grand tour of Europe. It has fascinating interior decorations and collections.

Times Open 28 Feb-8 Mar, Sat-Sun 11-5; 14 Mar-1 Nov, Mon-Wed & Sat-Sun 11-5; Good Fri 11-5 **Fee** £6.40 (ch £3.20, under 5's free). Family tickets available. Groups 15 £5.40 each. **Facilities** ❶ ⌨ 🅿 (outdoor) &. (grounds partly accessible) (Braille guide, large print, photo album) toilets for disabled shop garden centre ⓧ 🐾 ▬

The World of Country Life

Sandy Bay EX8 5BU

➲ *(M5 junct 30, take A376 to Exmouth. Follow signs to Sandy Bay)*

☎ 01395 274533

e-mail: info@worldofcountrylife.myzen.co.uk

web: www.worldofcountrylife.co.uk

All-weather family attraction including falconry displays, and a safari train that rides through a forty acre deer park. Kids will enjoy the friendly farm animals, pets centre and animal nursery. There are also a Victorian street, working models and thousands of exhibits from a bygone age, including steam and vintage vehicles.

Times Open 18 Mar-2 Nov, daily 10-5. **Fee** ✻ £9 (ch 3-17 & pen £7.50). Family ticket (2ad+2ch) £30, (2ad+3ch) £35. **Facilities** ❶ ⌨ 🅿 ⍩ licensed ⍩ (indoor & outdoor) &. toilets for disabled shop ⓧ (ex assist dogs) ▬

GREAT TORRINGTON MAP 02 SS41

Dartington Crystal

EX38 7AN

(Turn off A386 in centre of Great Torrington, down School Lane (opposite church). Dartington Crystal 200mtrs on left)

☎ 01805 626242

e-mail: sfrench@dartington.co.uk

web: www.dartington.co.uk

Dartington Crystal has won many international design awards in recognition of its excellence. The factory tour allows visitors to watch the glassware being crafted, from the safety of elevated viewing galleries. All age groups are encouraged to have fun in the glass activity area and to discover the fascinating story of glass and the history of Dartington in the Visitor Centre.

Times Open all year. Visitor centre, Factory tour, Pavilion Cafe and Shops Mon-Fri 9-5 (last tour 3.15), Sat 10-5, Sun 10-4 (tours closed wknds). For Xmas, New Year and BH opening please telephone for details. **Facilities** (Partly accessible) (wheelchairs available) toilets for disabled shop (ex assist dogs)

RHS Garden Rosemoor

2 for 1

EX38 8PH

(1m SE of Great Torrington on A3124)

☎ 01805 624067

e-mail: rosemooradmin@rhs.org.uk

web: www.rhs.org.uk/rosemoor

RHS Garden Rosemoor is 65 acres of enchanting garden and woodland set in Torridge Valley. Rich in variety with year-round interest, Rosemoor includes inspiring displays of formal and informal planting. The garden has two beautiful rose gardens, a winter garden, cottage garden, fruit and vegetable garden, lake, arboretum and much more. Over 80 events are held each year, phone 01805 626800 for details.

Times Open: Gardens all year; Apr-Sep 10-6, Oct-Mar 10-5. Closed 25 Dec; Visitor Centre as for Gardens but closed 24-26 Dec. **Fee** * £6 (ch 6-16 £2, under 6 free). Party 10+ £5. RHS members 1 guest free. **Facilities** licensed (outdoor) (herb garden for disabled, wheelchair available) toilets for disabled shop garden centre (ex assist dogs)

HONITON MAP 03 ST10

Allhallows Museum

High St EX14 1PG

(next to parish church of St Paul in High Street)

☎ 01404 44966 & 42996

e-mail: info@honitonmuseum.co.uk

web: www.honitonmuseum.co.uk

The museum, housed in a chapel dating back to around 1200, has a wonderful display of Honiton lace, and there are lace demonstrations from June to August. The town's history is also illustrated.

Times Open Mon before Etr-Sep; Mon-Fri 9.30-4.30 & Sat 9.30-1; Oct, Mon-Fri 9.30-3.30, Sat 9.30-12.30. **Fee** £2 (accompanied ch free, pen £1.50). **Facilities** (400yds) (stair lift, wheelchair, hearing loop) shop (ex assist dogs)

ILFRACOMBE MAP 02 SS54

Watermouth Castle & Family Theme Park

EX34 9SL

(3m NE off A399, midway between Ilfracombe & Combe Martin)

☎ 01271 863879

web: www.watermouthcastle.com

A popular family attraction including mechanical music demonstrations, musical water show, dungeon labyrinths, Victorian displays, bygone pier machines, animated fairy tale scenes, tube slide, mini golf, children's carousel, swingboats, aeroplane ride, water fountains, river ride, gardens and a maze.

Times Open Apr-end Oct, closed Sat. (Also closed some Mon & Fri off season). Ring for further details. **Fee** * £12 (ch £10, under 92cm free & pen £8) **Facilities** (outdoor) (Partly accessible) (special wheelchair route) toilets for disabled shop (ex assist dogs)

KILLERTON HOUSE & GARDEN

MAP 03 SS90

Killerton House & Garden

EX5 3LE

➲ (off B3181 Exeter to Cullompton road)

☎ 01392 881345

e-mail: killerton@nationaltrust.org.uk

web: www.nationaltrust.org.uk

Elegant 18th-century house set in an 18-acre garden with sloping lawns and herbaceous borders. A majestic avenue of beech trees runs up the hillside, past an arboretum of rhododendrons and conifers. The garden has an ice house and rustic summer house where the family's pet bear was once kept, as well as a Victorian chapel. Inside the house are displays from the Killerton Dress Collection, and a Victorian laundry. Please telephone for details of annual events.

Times Open: House, daily (ex Tue), Mar-Oct (Oct closed Mon & Tue), Aug daily 11-5 (last entry 4.30). Gardens open all year, daily, 10.30-dusk/7. **Facilities** ⓟ ⌑ 🍴 🌂 (outdoor) ♿ (wheelchairs & motorised buggy, photo album) toilets for disabled shop garden centre ⊗ (ex in park & assist dogs) 🐾 ➡

KINGSBRIDGE

MAP 03 SX74

Cookworthy Museum of Rural Life

The Old Grammar School, 108 Fore St TQ7 1AW

➲ (A38 onto A384, then A381 to Kingsbridge, museum at top of town)

☎ 01548 853235

e-mail: wcookworthy@talk21.com

web: www.devonmuseums.net

The 17th-century schoolrooms of this former grammar school are now the setting for another kind of education. Reconstructed room-sets of a Victorian kitchen, a costume room and extensive collection of local historical items are gathered to illustrate South Devon life. A walled garden and farm gallery are also features of this museum, founded to commemorate William Cookworthy, 'father' of the English china clay industry. The Local Heritage Resource Centre with public access databases, microfilm of local newspapers since 1855 and Devon record

service point are available to visitors. Please ring for details of special events.

Times Open 30 Mar-Sep, Mon-Sat 10.30-5; Oct 10.30-4. Nov-Mar groups by arrangement. Local Heritage Resource Centre open all year, Mon-Thu 10-12 & Wed also 2-4, other times by appointment. **Fee** £2.50 (ch £1, concessions £2). Family £6 (2ad+ up to 4ch). **Facilities** ⓟ (100mtrs) (max 3hrs) 🌂 (outdoor) ♿ (Partly accessible) (Braille labels on selected exhibits, viewing gallery) toilets for disabled shop ⊗ (ex assist dogs)

KINGSWEAR

MAP 03 SX85

Coleton Fishacre House & Garden

Brownstone Rd TQ6 0EQ

➲ (3m from Kingswear. Take Ferry Rd and turn off at Toll House, follow brown tourist signs)

☎ 01803 752466

e-mail: coletonfishacre@nationaltrust.org.uk

web: www.nationaltrust.org.uk

In this enchanting corner of South Devon, house, garden and sea meet in perfect harmony. Lose yourself in the magical garden, where tender plants from the Mediterranean, South Africa and New Zealand thrive. Explore the secluded cove below and enjoy the far-reaching views out over the sea. In this most evocative of holiday homes, built for Rupert D'Oyly Carte, there is true 1920s elegance. A light, joyful atmosphere fills the rooms and music is usually playing, echoing the family's Gilbert and Sullivan connections.

Times ✳ Garden open 1-30 Mar, Sat & Sun only 11-5; 31 Mar-29 Oct, Wed-Sun & BH Mon 10.30-5. House open 29 Mar-29 Oct, Wed-Sun & BH Mon 11-4.30. **Facilities** ⓟ ⌑ 🌂 (outdoor) ♿ (Partly accessible) (wheelchairs available, Braille guides, mobile T loop) toilets for disabled shop garden centre ⊗ (ex assist dogs) 🐾 ➡

KNIGHTSHAYES COURT

MAP 03 SS91

Knightshayes Court

EX16 7RQ

➲ (M5 junct 27, 2m N of Tiverton off A396)

☎ 01884 254665 & 257381

e-mail: knightshayes@nationaltrust.org.uk

web: www.nationaltrust.org.uk

This fine Victorian mansion, a rare example of William Burges' work, offers much of interest to all ages. The garden is one of the most beautiful in Devon, with formal terraces, amusing topiary, a pool garden and woodland walks.

Times Open 14 Feb-8 Mar, 11-4, 14 Mar-1 Nov, 11-5. **Fee** House, gardens & parkland £7.45 (ch £3.70). Family (2ad+3ch) £18.60, (1ad+3ch) £11.15. Groups 15+ £6.90 (ch £3.45). Gardens & parkland only £5.90 (ch£2.95) Groups 15+ £5.50 (ch£2.75). **Facilities** ⓟ ⌑ 🍴 licensed 🌂 (outdoor) ♿ (woodland paths not accessible. Lift available in mansion but must be able to stand and ascend 3 steps) (wheelchairs available, lift & Braille) toilets for disabled shop garden centre ⊗ (ex assist dogs) 🐾 ➡

Lydford Castle and Saxon Town   FREE

EX20 4BH

➲ *(in Lydford off A386)*
web: *www.english-heritage.org.uk*
Standing above the gorge of the River Lyd, this tower, dating back to the 12th-century, was notorious as a prison. The earthworks of the original Norman fort lie to the south.
Times Open at any reasonable time. **Facilities ❷ ♨**

Lydford Gorge

EX20 4BH

➲ *(off A386, between Okehampton & Tavistock)*
☎ 01822 820320 & 820441
e-mail: lydfordgorge@nationaltrust.org.uk
web: www.nationaltrust.org.uk
This lush oak-wooded steep-sided river gorge, with its fascinating history and many legends, can be explored through a variety of short and long walks. See the spectacular White Lady Waterfall, pass over the tumbling water at Tunnel Falls and watch the river bubble in the Devil's Cauldron. There's an abundance of wildlife to spot.
Times Open 14 Mar-Nov, daily 10-5 (Oct & Nov 10-4). Winter opening - please ring for details. **Fee** £5.80 (ch £2.90). Family ticket (2ad+3ch) £14.50. **Facilities ❷ ▯ ⌷** (outdoor) ♿ (Partly accessible) (audio tapes, Braille guide) toilets for disabled shop garden centre ♨ ▰

Morwellham Quay

PL19 8JL

➲ *(4m W of Tavistock, off A390. Midway between Gunnislake & Tavistock. Signed)*
☎ 01822 832766 & 833808
e-mail: enquiries@morwellham-quay.co.uk
web: www.morwellham-quay.co.uk
A unique, open-air museum based around the ancient port and copper mine workings in the heart of the Tamar Valley. Journey back into another time as costumed interpreters help you re-live the daily life of a 19th-century mining village and shipping quay. A tramway takes you deep into the workings of the George and Charlotte mine. Special events include music festivals, classic car shows, and a Victorian food festival.
Times ✳ Open all year (ex Xmas wk) 10-6 (4.30 Nov-Etr). Last admission 3.30 (2.30 Nov-Etr). **Facilities ❷ ▯⌷◖ ⌷** (indoor & outdoor) ♿ (smooth paths, but difficult areas in Victorian village) toilets for disabled shop ▰

Bradley Manor

TQ12 6BN

➲ *(SW of Newton Abbot on A381 Totnes road. 1m from town centre)*
☎ 01803 843235
e-mail: bradley@nationaltrust.org
web: www.nationaltrust.org.uk/devoncornwall
Set in an area of 'wild space' on the outskirts of the market town of Newton Abbot, Bradley Manor is a charming, unspoilt historic house still lived in by the donor family. Predominantly 15th century, parts of the building date back to the 13th century, and some original decoration survives from that time. This little-changed, relaxed family home contains a superb collection of furniture and paintings. The meadows and woodland surrounding it are ideal for family walks.
Times Open 31 Mar-1 Oct, Tue-Thu 2-5; Oct weekdays by appointment only **Fee** £4.20 (ch £2.10) **Facilities ❷ ⌷** (outdoor) ♿ (Partly accessible) (T loop, large print guide, portable ramps) ⊗ ▰ ♨

Prickly Ball Farm and Hedgehog Hospital

Denbury Rd, East Ogwell TQ12 6BZ

➲ *(1.5m from Newton Abbot on A381 towards Totnes, follow brown heritage signs)*
☎ 01626 362319 & 330685
e-mail: enquiries@pricklyballfarm.co.uk
web: www.pricklyballfarm.co.uk
See, touch and learn about this wild animal. In mid-season see baby hogs bottle feeding. Find out how to encourage hedgehogs into your garden and how they are put back into the wild. Talks on hedgehogs throughout the day, with a big-screen presentation. There are also pony and cart rides, goat walking, pony grooming, lamb feeding (in season), and a petting zoo.
Times ✳ Open Etr-28 Oct, 10-5. Except Aug 10-5.30 (Recommended last admission 3.30) **Facilities ❷ ▯⌷ ⌷** (outdoor) ♿ (large print menu, use of wheelchair, Braille menu) toilets for disabled shop ⊗ (ex assist dogs) ▰

Tuckers Maltings

Teign Rd TQ12 4AA

➲ *(follow brown tourist signs from Newton Abbot railway station)*
☎ 01626 334734
e-mail: info@tuckersmaltings.com
web: www.tuckersmaltings.com
The only working Malthouse in England open to the public, producing malt from barley for over 30 West Country breweries. Learn all about the process of malting - and taste the end product at the in-house brewery. Guided tours last an hour.
Times ✳ Open Good Fri-end Oct, Mon-Sat (Closed Sun). Speciality bottled beer shop open throughout the year. Phone to check winter opening. **Facilities ℗** (100yds) (pay & display car park) ⌷♿ (Partly accessible) toilets for disabled shop ▰

OKEHAMPTON   MAP 02 SX59

Museum of Dartmoor Life

3 West St EX20 1HQ

⮑ *(follow brown signs off all major roads into Okehampton. Museum on main road next to White Hart Hotel)*

☎ 01837 52295

e-mail: dartmoormuseum@eclipse.co.uk

web: www.museumofdartmoorlife.eclipse.co.uk

Housed on three floors in an early 19th-century mill, the museum tells the story of how people have lived, worked and played on and around Dartmoor through the centuries. It shows how the moorland has shaped their lives just as their work has shaped the moorland. In the Cranmere Gallery, temporary exhibitions feature local history, art and crafts.

Times Open Etr-Oct, Mon-Sat 10.15-4.30. Phone for Winter opening times. **Fee** £3.50 (students £1). Family £7.50 (2ad+2ch) **Facilities** ℗ ⌨ ⅃ & (Braille, desk loop, lift) toilets for disabled shop ▄

Okehampton Castle

Castle Lodge EX20 1JB

⮑ *(1m SW of town centre)*

☎ 01837 52844

web: www.english-heritage.org.uk

Once the largest castle in Devon set amongst the stunning Dartmoor foothills. A free audio tour brings this romantic ruin to life.

Times Open 21 Mar-Jun & Sep, daily 10-5; Jul-Aug, daily 10-6. Closed Oct-Mar. **Fee** £3 (concessions £2.40, ch £1.50). Prices and opening times are subject to change in March 2009. Please call 0870 333 1181 for the most up to date prices and opening times when planning your visit. **Facilities** ℗ ⼕ shop ⊞

OTTERTON   MAP 03 SY08

Otterton Mill   FREE

EX9 7HG

⮑ *(on B3178 between Budleigh Salterton & Newton Poppleford)*

☎ 01392 568521

e-mail: escape@ottertonmill.com

web: www.ottertonmill.com

Set beside the River Otter in one of Devon's loveliest valleys, Otterton Mill is a centuries-old working watermill, a famous bakery and shop full of local produce, a restaurant, and a gallery of arts and crafts from local artists. Please see website for details of music nights and art events

Times ✳ Open daily, 10-5. **Facilities** ℗ ⌨ †◎† & (Partly accessible) (free entry to ground floor) toilets for disabled shop ▄

PAIGNTON   MAP 03 SX86

Paignton & Dartmouth Steam Railway

Queens Park Station, Torbay Rd TQ4 6AF

⮑ *(from Paignton follow brown tourist signs)*

☎ 01803 555872

e-mail: mail@pdsr.eclipse.co.uk

web: www.paignton-steamrailway.co.uk

Steam trains run for seven miles from Paignton to Kingswear on the former Great Western line, stopping at Goodrington Sands, Churston, and Kingswear, connecting with the ferry crossing to Dartmouth. Combined river excursions available. Ring for details of special events.

Times Open Jun-Sep, daily 9-5.30 & selected days Oct & Apr-May. Santa specials in Dec. **Fee** ✳ Paignton to Kingswear £8 (ch £5.50, pen £7.50). Family £25. Paignton to Dartmouth (including ferry) £10 (ch £6.50, pen £9.50). Family £30. **Facilities** ℗ (5mins walk) ⌨ & (wheelchair ramp for boarding train) toilets for disabled shop ▄

Paignton Zoo Environmental Park

Totnes Rd TQ4 7EU

⮑ *(1m from Paignton town centre on A3022 Totnes road. Follow brown signs)*

☎ 01803 697500

e-mail: info@paigntonzoo.org.uk

web: www.paigntonzoo.org.uk

Paignton is one of Britain's biggest zoos, set in a beautiful and secluded woodland valley, where new enclosures are spacious and naturalistic. Your visit will take you through some of the world's threatened habitats - Forest, Savannah, Wetland and Desert, with hundreds of species, many of them endangered and part of conservation breeding programmes. There is a new crocodile swamp. There are regular keeper talks, a children's play area, and special events throughout the year. Visitors can obtain special joint tickets which allow them to visit nearby Living Coasts.

Times Open all year, daily 10-6 (5 in winter). Last admission 5 (4 in winter). Closed 25 Dec. **Fee** ✳ £11.35 (ch 3-15 £7.60, concessions £9.35). Family ticket (2ad & 2ch) £34.10. Joint family saver ticket with Living Coasts £49.15. **Facilities** ℗ ⌨ †◎† ⼕ (indoor & outdoor) & (footpaths have slight gradient, some steep hills) (wheelchair loan-booking essential) toilets for disabled shop ⊗ (ex assist dogs) ▄

PLYMOUTH

MAP 02 SX45

The Elizabethan House

32 New St, The Barbican PL1 2NA

➲ *(A38/A374 follow signs to city centre then The Barbican, house just behind Southside Street)*

☎ 01752 304774

e-mail: museum@plymouth.gov.uk

web: www.plymouth.gov.uk/museums

On Plymouth's historic Barbican, find an ancient doorway and go back in time to Drake's Plymouth. Home of an Elizabethan merchant or sea captain, the house is an opportunity to see how an Elizabethan mariner might have lived. A rare Tudor time-capsule with furniture and fabrics dating back to the 1600s. A recently restored kitchen and gardens add to the authentic feel. 2009 marks the 80th anniversary of the house being saved from demolition.

Times Open Apr-Sep Tue-Sat & BH Mon, 10-5 (last entry 4.30) **Fee** ✳ £1.50 (ch £1). Family & other concessions available. **Facilities** ℗ (200yds) (short stay) ⅋ (ground floor & kitchen garden partly accessible) shop ⊗ ▬

National Marine Aquarium

Rope Walk, Coxside PL4 0LF

➲ *(A38 to Marsh Mills (Sainsbury's) then towards city centre & follow brown signs for Barbican & Coxside car park)*

☎ 01752 600301

e-mail: enquiries@national-aquarium.co.uk

web: www.national-aquarium.co.uk

Britain's biggest aquarium is now even bigger, thanks to a brand-new, three-floor, multi-million pound interactive centre. Explorocean is a new attraction within the aquarium, which showcases the very latest in ocean technology, and includes underwater obstacle courses and Remote Operated Vehicle games, along with virtual sonar tours, satellite images from space, and 3D deep-sea journeys. This is all on top of over 3,000 fish in more than 50 tanks, including one that is the height of a three-storey building.

Times ✳ Open all year daily, mid Mar-Oct 10-6; Nov-mid Mar 10-5
Facilities ℗ 200yds ▯ ⊓ (outdoor) ⅋ (Partly accessible) toilets for disabled shop ⊗ (ex assist dogs) ▬

Plymouth City Museum & Art Gallery

FREE

Drake Circus PL4 8AJ

➲ *(off A38 onto A374, museum on NW of city centre, opposite university)*

☎ 01752 304774

e-mail: museum@plymouth.gov.uk

web: www.plymouthmuseum.gov.uk

The City Museum and Art Gallery runs an exciting programme of exhibitions, talks, concerts, family workshops and other events alongside its gallery collections. There is an interactive natural history gallery and an impressive porcelain and silver collection, as well as the

internationally important Cottonian collection. For further details please visit the website.

Times Open all year Tue-Fri 10-5.30, Sat & BH Mons 10-5. Closed Good Fri & Xmas. **Facilities** ℗ (200yds) (time restricted on-street parking) ⊓ (outdoor) ⅋ (wheelchair available) toilets for disabled shop ⊗ (ex assist dogs)

PLYMPTON

MAP 02 SX55

Saltram

PL7 1UH

➲ *(3.5m E of Plymouth, between A38 & A379. Take Plympton turn at Marsh Mill rdbt, right at 4th lights to Cot Hill. At T-junct right into Merafield Rd. Saltram 0.25m on right)*

☎ 01752 333500 & 333503

e-mail: saltram@nationaltrust.org.uk

web: www.nationaltrust.org.uk

This magnificent George II house still has its original contents. The collection of paintings was begun at the suggestion of Reynolds and includes many of his portraits. The saloon and dining room were designed by Robert Adam and have superb decorative plasterwork and period furniture. The extensive gardens include a working Orangery and several follies, and part of their 500 acres is alongside the River Plym.

Times Open House: Apr-Oct, 12-4.30 (ex Fri). Garden open all year, 11-4.30. Park open all year, dawn to dusk. **Fee** House and garden £9.20 (ch £4.60). Garden only £4.60 (ch £2.40). NT members free. **Facilities** ℗ ⅋ ⅃ ⊓ (outdoor) ⅋ (wheelchairs available, Braille & audio guides) toilets for disabled shop ⊗ (ex on lead & assist dogs) ♨ ▬

POWDERHAM

MAP 03 SX98

Powderham Castle

EX6 8JQ

➲ *(signed off A379 Exeter/Dawlish road)*

☎ 01626 890243

e-mail: castle@powderham.co.uk

web: www.powderham.co.uk

Set in a tranquil deer park along the Exe estuary. Built in 1391 by Sir Philip Courtenay, it has long been the family home of the Earl of Devon. There is a beautiful rose garden and spring walks through the woodland garden. Guided tours showcase the castle's intriguing history, majestic interiors and fine collection of treasures. Special events throughout the year.

Times ✳ Open Etr-Oct, 10-5.30 (last admission 4.30). Closed Sat.
Facilities ℗ ▯ ⅃ ⊓ (outdoor) ⅋ (ramps) toilets for disabled shop garden centre ⊗ (ex assist dogs) ▬

ENGLAND

SALCOMBE   MAP 03 SX73

Overbeck's

Sharpitor TQ8 8LW

➲ *(1.5m SW of Salcombe, signed from Malborough & Salcombe, narrow approach road)*

☎ 01548 842893

e-mail: overbecks@nationaltrust.org.uk

web: www.nationaltrust.org.uk

This famous garden is home to an unusual collection of rare and tropical plants creating a dramatic display of hot colours and exotic scents. Perching on high cliffs overlooking Salcombe, the views are breathtaking. Once home to the eccentric Dr Overbeck, the house contains some quirky collections from around the world.

Times Gardens open Jan-13 Mar & 2 Nov-Dec Mon-Fri 11-5 (or sunset if earlier). Closed 25-26 Dec & 1 Jan. Garden, House & facilities 14 Mar-1 Nov, Sat-Thu 11-4.15 **Fee** ✴ Gardens & House £6 (ch £3). Family ticket £15. **Facilities** ℗ ⬚ ㅈ (outdoor) ♿ (steep paths to access garden & house) (ramp from garden, Braille guide, hearing loop, audio tour) shop ⊗ (ex assist dogs) ⅗

SOUTH MOLTON   MAP 03 SS72

Quince Honey Farm   2 for 1

EX36 3AZ

➲ *(3.5m W of A361, on N edge of South Molton)*

☎ 01769 572401

e-mail: info@quincehoney.co.uk

web: www.quincehoney.com

Follow the story of honey and beeswax from flower to table. The exhibition allows you to see the world of bees close up in complete safety; hives open at the press of a button revealing the honeybees' secret life. After viewing the bees at work, sample the fruits of their labour in the café or shop.

Times Open daily, Apr-Sep 9-6; Oct 9-5; Shop only Nov-Etr 9-5, closed Sun. Closed 25 Dec-4 Jan. **Fee** ✴ £4 (ch 5-16 £3, pen £3.50) **Facilities** ℗ ⬚ ㅈ (outdoor) ♿ (no lift to exhibition on first floor) toilets for disabled shop ⊗ (ex assist dogs) ▬

STICKLEPATH   MAP 03 SX69

Finch Foundry

EX20 2NW

➲ *(off A30 at Okehampton junct, follow brown signs to Finch Foundry. Located in main street of village)*

☎ 01837 840046

e-mail: finchfoundry@nationaltrust.org.uk

web: www.nationaltrust.org.uk

Finch Foundry was, in the 19th century, a water-powered factory for making sickles, scythes, shovels and other hand tools. Although no longer in production, three waterwheels can still be seen driving huge hammers, shears, grindstone and other machinery, with daily working demonstrations. These demonstrations explain the key role the foundry played in the local community. Special Event: St. Clements Day (St Clements is the patron saint of blacksmiths) 3rd Sat in Nov.

Times Open 15 Mar-2 Nov, daily (ex Tue), 11-5 (Last entry 4.30). **Fee** ✴ £4 (ch £2). **Facilities** ℗ ⬚ ㅈ (outdoor) ♿ (access to shop/tea room, view main foundry via shop) shop ⅗ ▬

TIVERTON   MAP 03 SS91

Tiverton Castle   2 for 1

EX16 6RP

➲ *(M5 junct 27, then 7m on A361 towards Tiverton to rdbt. Castle signed)*

☎ 01884 253200 & 255200

e-mail: tiverton.castle@ukf.net

web: www.tivertoncastle.com

The original castle, built in 1106 by order of Henry I, was rebuilt in the late 13th-14th centuries. It resisted General Fairfax during the Civil War but fell to him when a lucky shot hit the drawbridge chain. Now a private house, the gardens are lovely and there's a fine Civil War armoury.

Times Open Etr Sun-end Oct, Sun,Thu & BH Mon only 2.30-5.30. Last admission 5. **Fee** £5 (ch 7-16 £2, under 7 free). Disabled half price if accessing ground floor only. **Facilities** ℗ ♿ (garden & ground floor accessible) toilets for disabled shop ⊗ (ex assist dogs)

TIVERTON Museum of Mid Devon Life

Beck's Square EX16 6PJ

➲ *(in centre of town next to Beck's Square car park)*

☎ 01884 256295

e-mail: curator04@tivertonmuseum.org.uk

web: www.tivertonmuseum.org.uk

This large and comprehensive museum now with 15 galleries, re-opened after extensive rebuilding throughout. It is housed in a 19th-century school and the exhibits include a Heathcoat Lace Gallery featuring items from the local lace-making industry. There is also an agricultural section with a collection of farm wagons and implements. Other large exhibits include two waterwheels and a railway locomotive with many GWR items.

Times Open Feb-mid Dec, Mon-Fri 10.30-4.30, Sat 10-1. Open BHs. **Fee** ✴ £4.25 (ch £1, pen £3.25). Family (2+4) £9. **Facilities** ℗ (100yds) ♿ (lift, induction loop) toilets for disabled shop ⊗ (ex assist dogs)

TORQUAY   MAP 03 SX96

Babbacombe Model Village

Hampton Av, Babbacombe TQ1 3LA

➲ *(follow brown tourist signs from outskirts of town)*

☎ 01803 315315

e-mail: ss@babbacombemodelvillage.co.uk

web: www.model-village.co.uk

See the world recreated in miniature. Thousands of miniature buildings, people and vehicles capture the essence of England's past, present and future, set in four acres of award-winning gardens. Various events are planned, please contact for details.

Times Open all year, times vary. **Facilities** ℗ (charged) ⬚ ⑩ ㅈ ♿ (push button audio information) toilets for disabled shop garden centre ▬

'Bygones'

Fore St, St Marychurch TQ1 4PR

➲ *(follow tourist signs into Torquay and St Marychurch)*

☎ 01803 326108

web: www.bygones.co.uk

Step back in time in this life-size Victorian exhibition street of over 20 shops including a forge, pub and period display rooms, housed in a former cinema. Exhibits include a large model railway layout, illuminated fantasyland, railwayana and military exhibits including a walk-through World War I trench. At Christmas the street is turned into a winter wonderland. A new set piece features Babbacombe's John Lee ('the man they couldn't hang') in his cell. There is something here for all the family including a 40/50s shopping arcade.

Times Open all year, Summer 10-6; Spring & Autumn 10-6; Winter 10-4, wknds & school hols 10-5. (Last entry 1hr before closing). **Fee** ✳ £6.50 (ch 4-14 £4.50, pen £5.50). Family ticket (2ad & 2ch) £20. Prices may change, contact in advance. **Facilities** ℗ (50yds) 🍴 & (ground floor only accessible) (ramp) shop ⊗ (ex assist dogs)

Kents Cavern   `2 for 1`

Cavern House, 91 Ilsham Rd, Wellswood TQ1 2JF

➲ *(1.25m NE off B3199, follow brown tourist signs. 1m from Torquay harbour)*

☎ 01803 215136

e-mail: caves@kents-cavern.co.uk

web: www.kents-cavern.co.uk

Probably the most important Palaeolithic site in Britain and recognised as one of the most significant archaeological areas. This is not only a world of spectacular natural beauty, but also a priceless record of past times, where a multitude of secrets of mankind, animals and nature have become trapped and preserved over the last 500,000 years. 170 years after the first excavations and with over 80,000 remains already unearthed, modern research is still discovering new clues to our past. Please visit website for details of special events.

Times Open all year daily from 10, last tour 3.30 Nov-Feb, 4 Mar-Jun & Sep-Oct, 4.30 Jul-Aug. **Fee** ✳ Daytime: £7.90 (ch 4-15 £6.30) Family £26.90. **Facilities** ℗ 🍴 licensed ⊓ (outdoor) & (Partly accessible) toilets for disabled shop ⊗ (ex assist dogs) ▬

Living Coasts

Beacon Quay TQ1 2BG

➲ *(once in Torquay follow A379 and brown tourist signs to harbour)*

☎ 01803 202470

e-mail: info@livingcoasts.org.uk

web: www.livingcoasts.org.uk

Living Coasts is a coastal zoo that allows visitors to take a trip around the coastlines of the world without leaving Torquay. Specially designed environments are home to fur seals, puffins, penguins, ducks, rats, and waders among others. All the animals can be seen above and below the water, while the huge meshed aviary allows the birds to fly free over your head. Visitors can obtain special joint tickets which will allow them to visit nearby Paignton Zoo.

Times Open daily from 10. Closed 25 Dec. **Facilities** ℗ 🍴 & (pre-booked wheelchair hire) toilets for disabled shop ⊗ (ex assist dogs) ▬

TOTNES   MAP 03 SX86

Berry Pomoroy Castle

Berry Pomoroy TQ9 6NJ

➲ *(2.5m E off A385)*

☎ 01803 866618

web: www.english-heritage.org.uk

Building of this now ruined shell, inside the 15th-century defences of the Pomeroy family castle, began around the mid 16th-century and ambitiously enlarged at the beginning of the 17th-century. Intended to become the most spectacular house in Devon. The project was abandoned by 1700 and has become the focus of spooky ghost stories.

Times Open daily, 21 Mar-Jun & Sep, 10-5; Jul-Aug, 10-6; Oct 10-4. Closed Nov-Mar. **Fee** £4 (concessions £3.20, ch £2). Prices and opening times are subject to change in March 2009. Please call 0870 333 1181 for the most up to date prices and opening times when planning your visit. **Facilities** ℗ 🍴 & shop ⊗ ⊞

TOTNES CONTINUED

The Guildhall

Ramparts Walk, off High St TQ9 5QH

➲ *(behind St Mary's Church on the main street)*

☎ 01803 862147

e-mail: office@totnestowncouncil.gov.uk

web: www.totnestowncouncil.gov.uk

Originally the refectory, kitchens, brewery and bakery for the Benedictine Priory of Totnes (1088-1536), the building was established as the Guildhall in 1553 during the reign of Edward VI. A magistrates' court and a prison opened in 1624, and the council chamber is still used today.

Times Open Apr-Oct, Mon-Fri 10.30-4.30, other times by appointment. **Fee** ✴ £1 (ch 25p). **Facilities** ℗ (50yds) & (Partly accessible)

Totnes Castle

Castle St TQ9 5NU

➲ *(on hill overlooking town)*

☎ 01803 864406

web: www.english-heritage.org.uk

One of the best surviving examples of a Norman motte and bailey castle with spectacular views. The once great ditch that surrounded the keep is today filled with the cottages and gardens of the town.

Times Open 21 Mar-Jun & Sep, daily 10-5; Jul-Aug, daily 10-6; Oct, daily 10-4. Closed Nov- Mar. **Fee** £2.50 (concessions £2, ch £1.30). Prices and opening times are subject to change in March 2009. Please call 0870 333 1181 for the most up to date prices and opening times when planning your visit. **Facilities** ℗ (70yds) (payment required) ⩇ shop ⊞

Totnes Museum

[2 for 1]

70 Fore St TQ9 5RU

➲ *(from bottom of Totnes Town, turn into Fore St, museum on left of main street, just before East Gate Arch Clock Tower)*

☎ 01803 863821

e-mail: totnesmuseum@btconnect.com

web: www.devonmuseums.net/totnes

An Elizabethan merchant's house, dating from 1575, said to have been built for Walter Kelland, a wealthy merchant. The building houses archaeological and social history collections and a room dedicated to Charles Babbage, inventor of the first computer. Study centre archives located at the rear of the museum.

Times Open 16 Mar-30 Oct, Mon-Fri 10.30-5 (last entry 4.30) **Fee** £2 (ch 5-16 75p, concessions £1.50). **Facilities** ℗ (440yds) (restricted parking on main street) & (spiral staircase) (personal guided tours, virtual/audio tours available) shop

UFFCULME   MAP 03 ST01

Coldharbour Mill Working Wool Museum

Coldharbour Mill EX15 3EE

➲ *(2m from M5 junct 27, off B3181. Follow signs to Willand, then brown signs to museum)*

☎ 01884 840960

e-mail: info@coldharbourmill.org.uk

web: www.coldharbourmill.org.uk

The Picturesque Coldharbour Mill is set in idyllic Devon countryside. It has been producing textiles since 1799 and is now a working museum, still making knitting wools and fabrics on period machinery. With machine demonstrations, a water wheel and steam engines, Coldharbour Mill is a wonderful and very different family day out. The Power Trail Tour is available Tue, Wed and Thu at 11.30 and 2.30. There are engines in steam regularly throughout the year plus special events, please see the website for details. The new self-guided tour of the Woollen Mill is available every day.

Times Open all year daily 11-4. **Fee** General visit £3.50 (ch £1.75 concessions £3: Power Trail Tour £5.50 (ch £2.75 concessions £5): Steam Up Event £6.50 (ch £3.75, concessions £6) **Facilities** ℗ ⊑ ⅩOI licensed ⩇ (outdoor) & (indoor restaurant not accessible but assistance given) (helpful guides & lift) toilets for disabled shop ⊗ (ex assist dogs or in grounds) ▬

YELVERTON   MAP 02 SX56

Yelverton Paperweight Centre   [FREE]

4 Buckland Ter, Leg O'Mutton Corner PL20 6AD

➲ *(at Yelverton off A386, Plymouth to Tavistock road)*

☎ 01822 854250

e-mail: paperweightcentre@btinternet.com

web: www.paperweightcentre.co.uk

This unusual centre is the home of the Broughton Collection - a glittering permanent collection of glass paperweights of all sizes and designs. The centre also has an extensive range of modern glass paperweights for sale. Prices range from a few pounds to over £1000. There is also a series of oil and watercolour paintings by talented local artists.

Times Open Apr-Oct, daily 10.30-5; 10-24 Dec, daily; Nov & Jan-Mar by appointment. **Facilities** ℗ (100yds) & (ramp on request) shop ▬

DORSET

Knoll Beach, Studland, Isle of Purbeck

ABBOTSBURY   MAP 03 SY58

Abbotsbury Swannery

New Barn Rd DT3 4JG

➲ *(turn off A35 at Winterborne Abbas near Dorchester. Abbotsbury on B3157 (coastal road), between Weymouth & Bridport)*

☎ 01305 871858

e-mail: info@abbotsbury-tourism.co.uk

web: www.abbotsbury-tourism.co.uk

Abbotsbury is the breeding ground of the only managed colony of mute swans. The swans can be seen safely at close quarters, and the site is also home or stopping point for many wild birds. The highlight of the year is the cygnet season, end of May to the end of June, when there may be over 100 nests on site. Visitors can often take pictures of cygnets emerging from eggs at close quarters. There is an audio-visual show, as well as mass feeding at noon and 4pm daily, and an ugly duckling trail. Children's play area available and a new giant maze planted with willow in the shape of a swan. Find your way to the giant egg at the centre.

Times Open 15 Mar-26 Oct, daily 10-6 (last admission 5). **Fee** £9 (ch £6 & concessions £8.50). **Facilities** ❷ ⬜ ◎ licensed ⅀ (outdoor) ♿ (free wheelchair loan, herb garden for blind) toilets for disabled shop ⊗ ▭

ATHELHAMPTON   MAP 03 SY79

Athelhampton House & Gardens

DT2 7LG

➲ *(off A35 Northbrook junct, follow brown tourist signs towards Puddletown. Left at lights. House & Gardens approx 1m on left)*

☎ 01305 848363

e-mail: enquiry@athelhampton.co.uk

web: www.athelhampton.co.uk

Athelhampton, one of the finest 15th-century houses in England, contains magnificently furnished rooms including The Great Hall of 1485 and the library, which contains 3,000 books and an original 1915 Riley Imperial billiard table. The glorious Grade I gardens contain the world-famous topiary pyramids, fountains, and collections of tulips, magnolias, roses, clematis and lilies in season. The West Wing Gallery features paintings by Marevna (1892-1984), a Russian painter who lived and painted at Athelhampton.

Times Open Mar-Oct, daily 10.30-5. Also Sun in Winter (ex Xmas). (Closed Fri & Sat, open Good Fri). **Facilities** ❷ ⬜ ◎ ⅀ (outdoor) ♿ (wheelchairs available) toilets for disabled shop ⊗ (ex assist dogs) ▭

BEAMINSTER   MAP 03 ST40

Mapperton   `2 for 1`

DT8 3NR

➲ *(2m SE off A356 & B3163)*

☎ 01308 862645

e-mail: office@mapperton.com

web: www.mapperton.com

Several acres of terraced valley gardens with specimen trees and shrubs and formal borders surround a manor house that dates back to the 16th century. There are also fountains, grottoes, stone sculpture, fishponds and an orangery, and the garden offers good views and walks. A plant fair is held annually, usually in April.

Times Gardens open: Mar-Oct, daily (ex Sat) 11-5. House open 22 Jun-Jul, 25 May, 31 Aug, wkdays only, 2-4.30 (last admission 4). **Fee** Gardens £4.50 (ch 5-18 £2, under 5 free). House £4. Groups 20+ £8.00 (house & garden), £4 (house or garden). **Facilities** ❷ ⬜ ♿ (ramp from parking area to garden) toilets for disabled shop ⊗ (ex assist dogs) ▭

BLANDFORD FORUM   MAP 03 ST80

Royal Signals Museum

Blandford Camp DT11 8RH

➲ *(signed off B3082 (Blandford/Wimborne road) & A354 (Salisbury road). Follow brown signs for Royal Signals Museum)*

☎ 01258 482248

e-mail: info@royalsignalsmuseum.com

web: www.royalsignalsmuseum.com

The Royal Signals Museum depicts the history of military communications, science and technology from the Crimea to current day. As well as displays on all major conflicts involving British forces, there are the stories of the ATS, the Long Range Desert Group, Air Support, Airborne, Para and SAS Signals. D-Day and Dorset explores the Royal Signals involvement in Operation Overlord. For children there are trails and interactive exhibits.

Times Open Mar-Oct Mon-Fri 10-5, Sat-Sun 10-4. Closed 10 days over Xmas & New Year **Facilities** ❷ ⬜ ⅀ ♿ (ramps & lifts) toilets for disabled shop ⊗ (ex assist dogs) ▭

BOURNEMOUTH   MAP 04 SZ09

Oceanarium

Pier Approach, West Beach BH2 5AA

➲ *(from A338 Wessex Way, follow Oceanarium tourist signs)*

☎ 01202 311993

e-mail: info@oceanarium.co.uk

web: www.oceanarium.co.uk

Take an underwater adventure around the waters of the world and come face to face with hundreds of awesome creatures. Home to all your favourites from flamboyant clownfish and tiny terrapins, to stunning sharks and the infamous piranha, immerse yourself in a sea of colour, with ten spectacular recreated environments including the

Great Barrier Reef underwater tunnel. Experience the world's first Interactive Dive Cage - take a virtual adventure to discover more about magnificent sea creatures, without getting wet. And don't miss the all new Global Meltdown experience and find out what would happen if the ice caps melted and the world was flooded.

Times Open all year, daily from 10. Late night opening during school summer hols. Closed 25 Dec. **Fee** ✳ Telephone for admission charges. **Facilities** Ⓟ (100mtrs) ⭑ licensed ⭑ (lift) toilets for disabled shop ⊗ (ex assist dogs) ▄

BOVINGTON CAMP　　　　MAP 03 SY88

Clouds Hill

BH20 7NQ

⊃ (1m N of Bovington Camp & Tank Museum, 1.5m E of Waddock x-rds B3390, 4m S of A35)

☎ 01929 405616

e-mail: cloudshill@nationaltrust.org.uk

web: www.nationaltrust.org.uk

T E Lawrence (of Arabia) bought this cottage in 1925 when he was a private in the Tank Corps at Bovington. He would escape here to play records and entertain friends to feasts of baked beans and China tea. The furniture and contents were Lawrence's own and a new display tells the story of Lawrence's life.

Times Open 20 Mar-26 Oct, Thu-Sun. 12-5 **Fee** ✳ £4 (ch £2). **Facilities** Ⓟ ⭑ (Partly accessible) (Braille guide, ramped access available) shop ⊗ ▄ ⛭

The Tank Museum

BH20 6JG

⊃ (off A352 or A35, follow brown tank signs from Bere Regis & Wool)

☎ 01929 405096

e-mail: info@tankmuseum.org

web: www.tankmuseum.org

The Tank Museum houses the world's best collection of tanks. From the first tank ever built to the modern Challenger II, the Museum houses examples from all over the world. This definitive collection comprises of over 250 vehicles dating back to 1909. The Tank Museum is the only place where many of these rare and historic vehicles can be

seen. You will come face to face with tanks that have seen action in all the major wars of the 20th century. There are plenty of live action displays all year, please see website for details. 2009 is the 70th anniversary of the Royal Armoured Corps.

Times Open all year, daily 10-5 (limited opening over Xmas). **Fee** ✳ £11 (ch £7, pen £9). Family saver (2ad+2ch) £29, (1ad+3ch) £26. Group rates available. **Facilities** Ⓟ ▭ ⭑ licensed ⛱ (outdoor) ⭑ (wheelchairs available) toilets for disabled shop ⊗ (ex assist dogs & in grounds) ▄

BROWNSEA ISLAND　　　MAP 03 SZ08

Brownsea Island

BH13 7EE

⊃ (located in Poole Harbour)

☎ 01202 707744

e-mail: brownseaisland@nationaltrust.org.uk

web: www.nationaltrust.org.uk

This is a 250-acre nature reserve partly managed by the Dorset Trust for Nature Conservation. The island is most famous as the site of the first scout camp, held by Lord Baden-Powell in 1907. Scouts and Guides are still the only people allowed to stay here overnight. It is a haven for red squirrels and seabirds.

Times Open daily mid Mar-mid Jul, 10-5; mid Jul-Aug, 10-6; 1-27 Sep 10-5; 28 Sep-2 Nov, 10-4 **Fee** ✳ £4.90 (ch £2.40). Family ticket £12.20. Group £4.20 (ch £2.10) **Facilities** ▭ ⭑ ⛱ (outdoor) ⭑ (Braille/Audio guide, 2 selfdrive vehicles- booking advised) toilets for disabled shop ⊗ ⛭

CANFORD CLIFFS　　　　MAP 04 SZ08

Compton Acres Gardens　　**2 for 1**

164 Canford Cliffs Rd BH13 7ES

⊃ (on B3065, follow brown tourist signs)

☎ 01202 700778

e-mail: events@comptonacres.co.uk

web: www.comptonacres.co.uk

The ten acres of Compton Acres incorporate Japanese and Italian gardens, rock and water gardens, and heather gardens. There are fine views over Poole Harbour and the Purbeck Hills. The beautiful wooded valley is an amazing place to explore the wide range of plants. The Italian garden was used as a location in Stanley Kubrick's 1975 movie, *Barry Lyndon*. There is also a model railway, restaurants, a tea room, and a craft shop.

Times Open Apr-Oct 9-dusk, Nov-Mar 10-4 (last entry 1hr before close). Closed 25-26 Dec. **Fee** £6.95 (ch £3.95, concessions £6.45). Party 15+ £5.95 (concessions £5.45) **Facilities** Ⓟ ▭ ⭑ licensed ⭑ (level paths & ramps into shops & cafe) toilets for disabled shop garden centre ⊗ (ex assist dogs) ▄

CHRISTCHURCH — MAP 04 SZ19

Christchurch Castle & Norman House — FREE

➲ *(near Christchurch Priory)*

web: www.english-heritage.org.uk

Set on the river bank, the ruins of this Norman keep and constable's house date back to the 12th-century.

Times Open at any reasonable time. **Facilities** ♿

Red House Museum & Gardens — FREE

Quay Rd BH23 1BU

➲ *(follow brown tourist signs from Christchurch, Red House is on corner of Quay Rd)*

☎ 01202 482860

e-mail: paul.willis@hants.gov.uk

web: www.hants.gov.uk/museum/redhouse

A museum with plenty of variety, featuring local history and archaeology, displayed in a beautiful Georgian house. There's an excellent costume collection, some Arthur Romney-Green furniture and gardens with a woodland walk and herb garden. Regularly changing temporary exhibitions include contemporary art and crafts, plus historical displays.

Times Open Tue-Sat 10-5, Sun 2-5 (last admission 4.30). Open BHs (spring & summer) Closed 25 Dec-1 Jan & Good Fri. **Facilities** ℗ (200yds) ⬛ & (ground floor and gardens accessible) (hearing loop in reception only) toilets for disabled shop ⊗ (ex assist dogs)

CORFE CASTLE — MAP 03 SY98

Corfe Castle

BH20 5EZ

➲ *(follow A351 from Wareham to Swanage. Corfe Castle approx 5m)*

☎ 01929 481294

e-mail: corfecastle@nationaltrust.org.uk

web: www.nationaltrust.org.uk

Built in Norman times, the castle was added to by King John. It was defended during the Civil War by Lady Bankes, who surrendered after

a stout resistance. Parliament ordered the demolition of the castle, and today it is one of the most impressive ruins in England. Ring for details of special events.

Times Open all year, daily Feb-Mar 10-5; Apr-Sep 10-6; Oct 10-5; Nov-Jan 10-4. (Last admission 30 mins before closing). Closed 25-26 Dec. Shop and Tearoom close 5.30 Apr-Sep. **Fee** ✳ £5.60 (ch £2.80). Family ticket (2ad+3ch) £14 or (1ad) £8.40. Groups £4.80 (ch £2.40) **Facilities** ❷ (charged) ⬛ ⦿ & (Braille/large print guide & menu) toilets for disabled shop ⊗ ➡

Corfe Castle Museum — FREE

West St BH20 5HE

➲ *(to side of church on left of West St upon leaving village square)*

☎ 01929 480666

e-mail: steven.hitchins@gmail.com

The tiny, rectangular building was partly rebuilt in brick after a fire in 1780, and is the smallest town hall building in England. It has old village relics, and dinosaur footprints 130 million years old. A council chamber on the first floor is reached by a staircase at one end. The Ancient Order of Marblers meets here each Shrove Tuesday.

Times ✳ Open all year, Apr-Oct, daily 9.30-6; Nov-Mar, wknds and Xmas holidays 10-5. **Facilities** ℗ Park & Ride ⊗

DORCHESTER — MAP 03 SY69

Dinosaur Museum

Icen Way DT1 1EW

➲ *(off A35 into Dorchester, museum in town centre just off High East St)*

☎ 01305 269880

e-mail: info@thedinosaurmuseum.com

web: www.thedinosaurmuseum.com

Britain's award-winning museum devoted to dinosaurs has an fascinating mixture of fossils, skeletons, life-size reconstructions and interactive displays such as the 'feelies', colour box and parasaurlophus sound. There are multi-media presentations providing an all-round family attraction with something new each year. It is part of the Jurassic Coast experience. There is a Great Dinosaur Easter Egg Hunt every Easter weekend.

Times Open all year, daily 9.30-5.30 (10-4.30 Nov-Mar). Closed 24-26 Dec. **Fee** ✳ £6.95 (ch £5.50, concessions £5.95, under 4's free). Family ticket £22.50 **Facilities** ℗ (50yds) & (ground floor only accessible) (many low level displays) shop ➡

Dorset County Museum `2 for 1`

High West St DT1 1XA

⮞ *(off A354 signed Dorchester, attraction on right half way up main street)*

☎ 01305 262735

e-mail: enquiries@dorsetcountymuseum.org

web: www.dorsetcountymuseum.org

Displays cover prehistoric and Roman times, including sites such as Maiden Castle, and there's a gallery on Dorset writers with sections on the poet William Barnes, Thomas Hardy (with a reconstruction of his study), and 20th-century writers. Also geology, local wildlife and social history are explored in the museum. The Jurassic Coast geology gallery was opened by Sir David Attenborough in Summer 2006.

Times Open all year, Mon-Sat, 10-5. Also open Sun, Jul-Sep. Closed 24-26 Dec. **Fee** ✳ £6 (up to 2 accompanied ch free, additional ch £1, concessions £5) **Facilities** ℗ (600yds) (nearby parking charged) ⅃ (Partly accessible) (free entry for disabled visitors, ramp, audio commentary) toilets for disabled shop ⊗ (ex assist dogs) ▰

Dorset Teddy Bear Museum

High East St & Salisbury St DT1 1JU

⮞ *(off A35, museum in town centre near Dinosaur Museum)*

☎ 01305 266040

e-mail: info@teddybearmuseum.co.uk

web: www.teddybearmuseum.co.uk

Meet Edward Bear and his extended family of people-sized bears. See them relaxing and busying themselves in their Edwardian-style house. From the earliest teddies of 100 years ago to today's TV favourites, they are all on display in this family museum.

Times Open daily, 10-5 (4.30 in winter). Closed 24-26 Dec. **Fee** ✳ £5.75 (ch £4, under 4's free, concessions £5). Family £18 **Facilities** ℗ (150mtrs) shop ⊗ (ex assist dogs) ▰

Hardy's Cottage

Higher Bockhampton DT2 8QJ

⮞ *(3m NE of Dorchester, 0.5m S of A35. Turn off A35 at Kingston Maurward rdbt towards Stinsford and Bockhampton. Left onto Bockhampton Ln, signed to Hardy's Cottage)*

☎ 01305 262366

e-mail: hardyscottage@nationaltrust.org.uk

web: www.nationaltrust.org.uk

The small cob and thatch cottage where novelist and poet Thomas Hardy was born in 1840 and from where he would walk six miles to school in Dorchester every day. It was built by his great-grandfather and is little altered since. The interior has been furnished by the Trust. It was here that he wrote his early novels *Under the Greenwood Tree* and *Far from the Madding Crowd*. It has a charming cottage garden.

Times Open Apr-Oct, Sun-Thu, 11-5 **Fee** ✳ £3.50 **Facilities** ℗ (10 min walk) (no coach parking) ⅃ (parking by arrangement, large print/Braille guide) shop ⊗ 🐾

The Keep Military Museum `2 for 1`

The Keep, Bridport Rd DT1 1RN

⮞ *(near top of High West St leading out of town towards Bridport)*

☎ 01305 264066

e-mail: keep.museum@talk21.com

web: www.keepmilitarymuseum.org

Three hundred years of military history, with displays on the Devon Regiment, Dorset Regiment, Dorset Militia and Volunteers, the Queen's Own Dorset Yeomanry, and Devonshire and Dorset Regiment (from 1958). The Museum uses modern technology, interactive and creative displays to tell the stories of the Infantry, Cavalry and Artillerymen.

Times Open Apr-Sep Mon-Sat 9-5, Oct-Mar Tue-Sat 9-5 (last admission 4pm). Closed Xmas & New Year. **Fee** ✳ £5.50 (ch & concessions £3.50). Family £13. **Facilities** ℗ ⅃ (wheelchairs cannot access roof) (lift availble to 3 floors) toilets for disabled shop ⊗ (ex assist dogs) ▰

Maiden Castle `FREE`

DT1 9PR

⮞ *(2m S of Dorchester, access off A354, N of bypass)*

web: www.english-heritage.org.uk

The Iron Age fort ranks among the finest in Britain. It covers 47 acres, and has daunting earthworks, with a complicated defensive system around the entrances. One of its main purposes may well have been to protect grain from marauding bands. The first single-rampart fort dates from around 700BC, and by 100BC the earthworks covered the whole plateau. It was finally overrun by Roman troops in AD43.

Times Open at any reasonable time. **Facilities** ℗ ⛺

Tutankhamun Exhibition

High West St DT1 1UW

⮞ *(off A35 into Dorchester town centre)*

☎ 01305 269571

e-mail: info@tutankhamun-exhibition.có.uk

web: www.tutankhamun-exhibition.co.uk

The exhibition recreates the excitement of one of the world's greatest discoveries of ancient treasure. A reconstruction of the tomb and recreations of its treasures are displayed. The superbly preserved mummified body of the boy king can be seen, wonderfully recreated in every detail. Facsimiles of some of the most famous treasures, including the golden funerary mask and the harpooner can be seen in the final gallery.

Times Open all year daily, Apr-Oct, 9.30-5.30; Nov-Mar wkdays 9.30-5, wknds 10-4.30. Closed 24-26 Dec. **Fee** ✳ £6.95 (ch £5.50, concessions £5.95, under 5's free). Family ticket £22.50 **Facilities** ℗ (200yds) ⅃ shop ⊗ (ex assist dogs) ▰

ENGLAND

MINTERNE MAGNA   MAP 03 ST60

Minterne Gardens   2 for 1

DT2 7AU

➲ *(2m N of Cerne Abbas on A352)*

☎ 01300 341370

e-mail: enquiries@minterne.co.uk

web: www.minterne.co.uk

Wander through 20 acres of wild woodland, where magnolias, rhododendrons, eucryphias, hydrangeas, water plants and water lillies provide a new vista at each turn. This has been the home of the Churchill and Digby families for 350 years, and contains small lakes and cascades landscaped in the 18th century.

Times Open Mar-9 Nov, daily 10-6. **Fee** £4 (accompanied ch free). **Facilities** ☻ ⋔ (outdoor) ⊗ (ex on lead)

ORGANFORD   MAP 03 SY99

Farmer Palmer's Farm Park

BH16 6EU

➲ *(From Poole, just off A35 straight over rdbt past Bakers Arms, signed on left, take 2nd turn, 0.5m after rdbt)*

☎ 01202 622022

e-mail: info@farmerpalmers.co.uk

web: www.farmerpalmers.co.uk

Family owned and run, Farmer Palmers has been specially designed for families with children eight years and under. Many activities include meeting and learning about the animals, climbing the straw mountain, going for a tractor trailer ride and exercising in the soft play area. A fun and busy day for the family.

Times Open 29 Mar-24 Oct, daily 10-5.30; 7 Feb-28 Mar & 28 Oct-20 Dec, daily 10-4, Fri & wknds 10-4. **Fee** 7 Feb-28 Mar & 28 Oct-20 Dec: £5.95 (ch £5.95, under 2yrs free, concessions £5.75). Saver £22. 29 Mar-24 Oct: £6.75 (ch £6.75, under 2yrs free, concessions £5.75) Saver £25. **Facilities** ☻ ⊑ ⑩ licensed ⋔ (indoor & outdoor) ⅙ (Partly accessible) (ramps & woodland walk) toilets for disabled shop ⊗ (ex assist dogs) ▭

POOLE   MAP 03 SZ09

Poole Museum   FREE

4 High St BH15 1BW

➲ *(off Poole Quay)*

☎ 01202 262600

e-mail: museums@poole.gov.uk

web: www.boroughofpoole.com/museums

After major redevelopment the museum opens its doors again. The museum tells the story of Poole's history, including the Studland Bay wreck and trade with Newfoundland with displays and hands-on activities.

Times Open 6 Apr-1 Nov Mon-Sat 10-5, Sun 12-5. Closed 25-26 Dec. **Facilities** ℗ (250mtrs) ⊑ ⅙ (Scaplen's Court not accessible) toilets for disabled shop ⊗ (ex assist dogs) ▭

PORTLAND   MAP 03 SY67

Portland Castle

Castleton DT5 1AZ

➲ *(overlooking Portland harbour)*

☎ 01305 820539

web: www.english-heritage.org.uk

Visit one of Henry VIII's finest coastal forts in use right up to the Second World War. Home to the Wrens and scene of the US troops' embarkation for the D-Day invasion in 1944. Explore the Captain's House and Gardens.

Times Open daily: 21 Mar-Jun & Sep, 10-5; Jul-Aug, 10-6; Oct, 10-4. Closed Nov-Mar. **Fee** £4 (concessions £3.20, ch £2). Family ticket £10.00. Prices and opening times are subject to change in March 2009. Please call 0870 333 1181 for the most up to date prices and opening times when planning your visit. **Facilities** ☻ ⊑ shop ⊗ ✿

Portland Museum

217 Wakeham DT5 1HS

➲ *(A354, through Fortuneswell to Portland Heights Hotel, then English Heritage signs)*

☎ 01305 821804

e-mail: tourism@weymouth.gov.uk

web: www.weymouth.gov.uk

Avice's cottage in Thomas Hardy's book *The Well-Beloved*, this building is now a museum of local and historical interest, with varied displays. Regular temporary exhibitions are held. The adjoining Marie Stopes cottage houses the shop and a display of maritime history. Exhibitions and events throughout the year. Contact for details.

Times ✳ Open Good Fri-Oct, Fri-Tue (ex school hols open daily), 10.30-5 (Closed 1-1.30 daily) **Facilities** ☻ ⋔ (outdoor) shop ⊗ (ex assist dogs)

SHAFTESBURY MAP 03 ST82

Shaftesbury Abbey Museum & Garden

Park Walk SP7 8JR

⮑ *(follow signs to town centre. Shaftesbury Abbey is signed from opposite Wharf's Restaurant)*

☎ 01747 852910

e-mail: user@shaftesburyabbey.fsnet.co.uk

web: www.shaftesburyabbey.co.uk

The Abbey at Shaftesbury was part of a nunnery founded by King Alfred in 888. Patronage and pilgrims to the shrine of St Edward helped to make the abbey both rich and famous. It became one of the wealthiest in the country but was destroyed during the Dissolution in 1539. The excavated ruins show the foundations of the abbey church. The story is told through the use of carved stone and medieval floor tiles and illustrations from ancient manuscripts. Please visit the website for event listings.

Times Open Apr-Oct, daily, 10-5. **Fee** ✻ £2.50 (ch £1, concessions £2). Please ask for more information on our new joint ticket which also allows entry into 'Gold Hill Museum & Garden' **Facilities** ⓟ (250yds) (2hr restriction on nearest car park) ⅍ (large print guides, audio tour, interactive display) toilets for disabled shop ⊗ (on leads only) ➤

SHERBORNE MAP 03 ST61

Sherborne Castle

New Rd DT9 5NR

⮑ *(off A30/A352, 0.5m SE of Sherborne)*

☎ 01935 813182 (office) & 812072 (castle)

e-mail: enquiries@sherbornecastle.com

web: www.sherbornecastle.com

Built by Sir Walter Raleigh in 1594, Sherborne Castle has been the home of the Digby family since 1617. Prince William of Orange was entertained here in 1688, and George III visited in 1789. Splendid collections of art, furniture and porcelain are on show in the Castle. Lancelot 'Capability' Brown created the lake in 1753 and 30 acres of beautiful gardens and grounds surround it. Special events include a country fair, classic car shows, outdoor theatre, music and sports events and fireworks. Contact for details.

Times Open 22 Mar-30 Oct, Tue-Thu, Sat-Sun & BH Mon 11-4.30. (Last admission 4.30). Castle interior open from 2pm on Sat. **Facilities** ⓟ ⏜ ㋫ (outdoor) ⅍ (Braille guide book) toilets for disabled shop ➤

Sherborne Museum

Abbey Gate House, Church Ln DT9 3BP

⮑ *(From bottom of Cheap St, walk through Church Ln towards Abbey, museum on left)*

☎ 01935 812252

e-mail: info@sherbornemuseum.co.uk

web: www.sherbornemuseum.co.uk

The museum features a model of Sherborne's original Norman castle, as well as a fine Victorian doll's house and other domestic and agricultural bygones. There are also items of local geological, natural history and archaeological interest, including Roman material. The

Sherborne Missal, one of the greatest medieval manuscripts, can be seen using the latest digital technology which enables the visitor to 'turn the pages' of the manuscript with the sweep of a hand - with touch, zoom and audio facilities.

Times Open Apr-1 Nov, Tue-Sat 10.30-4.30 **Fee** ✻ £2 (ch & concessions free) **Facilities** ⓟ (200yds) ⅍ (Ground floor only accessible) (video of upper floor displays) toilets for disabled shop ⊗ (ex assist dogs)

Sherborne Old Castle

Castleton D19 3SA

⮑ *(0.5m E off B3145)*

☎ 01935 812730

web: www.english-heritage.org.uk

The ruins of this early 12th-century castle are a testament to the 16 days Oliver Cromwell's army took to capture it during the Civil War.

Times Open daily: 21 Mar-Jun & Sep, 10-5; Jul-Aug, 10-6; Oct, 10-4. Closed Nov-Mar. **Fee** £2.50 (concessions £2, ch £1.30). Joint ticket for Sherborne Castle Grounds £5.50. Member's discount. Prices and opening times are subject to change in March 2009. Please call 0870 333 1181 for the most up to date prices and opening times when planning your visit. **Facilities** ⓟ shop ⊗ ❖

SWANAGE MAP 03 SZ07

Swanage Railway

Station House BH19 1HB

⮑ *(signed from A351)*

☎ 01929 425800

e-mail: info@swanage-railway.co.uk

web: www.swanagerailway.co.uk

The railway from Swanage to Wareham was closed in 1972, and in 1976 the Swanage Railway took possession and have gradually restored the line, which now runs for six miles, passing the ruins of Corfe Castle. On-train meals are offered on the Wessex Belle and the Dorsetman. Ring for details of special events.

Times Open every wknd ex Jan, daily Etr-Oct. **Fee** ✻ Swanage-Corfe/Norden £9 return (ch & concessions £7 return). Family ticket £26. Day Rover £13.50 (ch & concessions £10.50) **Facilities** ⓟ (charged) ⏜ ㋙ ㋫ (outdoor) ⅍ (disabled persons coach) shop ➤

TOLPUDDLE MAP 03 SY79

Tolpuddle Martyrs Museum FREE

DT2 7EH

⮑ *(off A35 from Dorchester Tolpuddle signed at Troytown turn off. Continue on old A35.) If coming from the East, the museum has a Brown Heritage sign.*

☎ 01305 848237

e-mail: jpickering@tuc.org.uk

web: www.tolpuddlemartyrs.org.uk

One dawn, in the bitter February of 1834, six Tolpuddle farm labourers were arrested after forming a trade union. A frightened squire's trumped up charge triggered one of the most celebrated stories in the history of human rights. That dawn arrest created the Tolpuddle

CONTINUED

ENGLAND

TOLPUDDLE *CONTINUED*

Martyrs, who were punished with transportation as convicts to Australia. Packed with illustrative displays, this interactive exhibition tells the Tolpuddle Martyrs' story. Every summer on the weekend of the third Sunday in July, the museum holds the Tolpuddle Martyrs Festival. The weekend combines celebration with tradition offering traditional and contemporary music as well as many other attractions. 2009 sees the 175th anniversary of Martyrs transportation.

Times Open all year, Apr-Oct, Tue-Sat 10-5, Sun 11-5; Nov-Mar, Thu-Sat 10-4, Sun 11-4. Also open BHs. Closed 21 Dec-6 Jan. **Facilities** Ⓟ (outside museum) ⋔ (outdoor) ♿ (parking, interactive computers at wheelchair height) toilets for disabled shop ⊗ (ex assist dogs) ▬

WEST LULWORTH   MAP 03 SY88

Lulworth Castle & Park   `2 for 1`

BH20 5QS

➲ *(from Wareham, W on A352 for 1m, left onto B3070 to E Lulworth, follow tourist signs)*

☎ 0845 450 1054

e-mail: estate.office@lulworth.com

web: www.lulworth.com

Glimpse life below stairs in the restored kitchen, and enjoy glorious views from the top of the tower of this historic castle set in beautiful parkland. The 18th-century chapel is the first Catholic chapel built in England after the Reformation. Children will enjoy the animal farm, play area, indoor activity room and pitch and putt. Visit website for details of future events.

Times Open Jan-22 Mar, Sun-Fri 10.30-4; 23 Mar-26 Sep Sun-Fri, 10.30-6; 28 Sep-Dec Sun-Fri, 10.30-4. Closed Sat (ex Etr Sat), 24-25 Dec & 6-19 Jan. **Fee** ✳ £8 (ch £4, concessions £5) Family ticket (1ad+3ch) £16 non-jousting season. £9.50 (ch £4.50, concessions £8) Family ticket (1ad+3ch) £18.50 jousting season (24 Jul-25 Aug) **Facilities** Ⓟ ⌂ ⋔ (outdoor) ♿ (access limited in castle due to grade one listing) toilets for disabled shop ▬

WEYMOUTH   MAP 03 SY67

RSPB Nature Reserve Radipole Lake

The Swannery Car Park DT4 7TZ

➲ *(close to seafront & railway station)*

☎ 01305 778313

web: www.rspb.org.uk

Covering 222 acres, the Reserve offers firm paths, hide and a visitor centre. Several types of warblers, mute swans, gadwalls, teals and great crested grebes may be seen, and the visitor centre has viewing windows overlooking the lake. Phone for details of special events.

Times ✳ Open daily 9-5 **Facilities** Ⓟ (charged) ⋔ shop ▬

Sharkys of Weymouth   `2 for 1`

9 Custom House Quay, Old Harbour North DT4 8BG

➲ *(A35 to Weymouth, then Old Harbour North. Attraction between pavillion & town bridge. Follow brown tourist signs.)*

☎ 01305 750550

e-mail: sharkysweymouth@fsmail.net

web: www.sharkysweymouth.co.uk

Sharkys of Weymouth is one of the largest indoor soft play arenas on the south coast. A new Laserzone is due for completion in summer 2008. Birthday parties are a speciality.

Times Open all year, daily from 9. (8am-8pm during summer). Closed 25-26 Dec & 1 Jan. **Fee** ✳ Adults free (ch £4). **Facilities** Ⓟ (100yds) ⌂ ⓘ licensed ♿ (lift & sign language for deaf) toilets for disabled shop ⊗ (ex assist dogs) ▬

Weymouth Sea Life Adventure Park & Marine Sanctuary

Lodmoor Country Park DT4 7SX

➲ *(on A353)*

☎ 0871 423 2110 & 01305 761070

e-mail: slcweymouth@merlinentertainments.biz

web: www.sealifeeurope.com

A unique mix of indoor and outdoor attractions set in seven acres. The park offers a day of fun, bringing you face to face with penguins, otters, seals and much more. Spring 2008 saw the opening of Adventure Island.

Times Open all year, daily from 10. (Closed 25 Dec). **Fee** ✳ £14.95 (ch £10.50, concessions £13.95). Family (2ad+2ch) £45.95. **Facilities** Ⓟ (charged) ⌂ ⓘ ⋔ (indoor & outdoor) ♿ toilets for disabled shop ⊗ (ex assist dogs) ▬

WIMBORNE   MAP 03 SZ09

Kingston Lacy

BH21 4EA

➲ *(1.5m W of Wimborne, B3082)*

☎ 01202 883402 (Mon-Fri) & 880413 (infoline)

e-mail: kingstonlacy@nationaltrust.org.uk

web: www.nationaltrust.org.uk

Kingston Lacy House was the home of the Bankes family for over 300 years. The original house is 17th century, but in the 1830s was given a stone façade. The Italian marble staircase, Venetian ceiling, treasures from Spain and an Egyptian obelisk were also added. There are outstanding pictures by Titian, Rubens, Velasquez, Reynolds and Van Dyck. No photography is allowed in the house.

Times Open: House 24 Mar-2 Nov, Wed-Sun, 11-4. Garden & Park 15 Mar-2 Nov, daily, 10.30-6; 2 Feb-9 Mar, Sat-Sun 10.30-4 **Fee** ✳ House, Garden & Park £10 (ch £5) Family £25. Park & Gardens £5 (ch £2.50) Family £12.50. **Facilities** Ⓟ ⌂ ⓘ ⋔ (outdoor) ♿ (wheelchairs, large print & Braille guides, parking) toilets for disabled shop ⊗ (ex on leads in park & wood) ⊌

The Priest's House Museum and Garden

23-27 High St BH21 1HR

➲ (opposite The Minster)

☎ 01202 882533

e-mail: priestshouse@eastdorset.gov.uk

web: www.priest-house.co.uk

An award-winning local history museum, set in an historic house. The 17th-century hall, Georgian parlour and working Victorian kitchen reveal the history of the building and its inhabitants. The museum houses exhibitions on East Dorset from prehistoric to modern times. There are regular special exhibitions and a walled garden to explore.

Times Open Apr-Oct Mon-Sat 10-4.30. **Facilities** ℗ (200yds) ⊇ ⊼ (outdoor) ♿ (hands on archaeology & childhood galleries) shop ⊗ (ex assist dogs)

WOOL   MAP 03 SY88

Monkey World Ape Rescue Centre

Longthorns BH20 6HH

➲ (1m N of Wool on Bere Regis road)

☎ 01929 462537 & 0800 456600

e-mail: apes@monkeyworld.org

web: www.monkeyworld.org

Set up in order to rescue monkeys and apes from abuse and illegal smuggling, Monkey World houses over 160 primates in 65 acres of Dorset woodland. There are 58 chimps, the largest grouping outside Africa, as well as orang-utans, gibbons, woolly monkeys, lemurs, macaques and marmosets. Those wishing to help the centre continue in its quest to rescue primates from lives of misery may like to take part in the adoption scheme which includes free admission to the park for one year. There are keeper talks every half hour, and the south's largest Great Ape Play Area for kids.

Times Open daily 10-5 (Jul-Aug 10-6). (Last admission 1 hour before closing) Closed 25 Dec **Facilities** ❷ ⊇ ⊙ ⊼ (indoor & outdoor) ♿ (motorised buggy) toilets for disabled shop ⊗ (ex assist dogs) ▄

COUNTY DURHAM

Durham Cathedral and the River Tyne

BARNARD CASTLE   MAP 12 NZ01

Barnard Castle

DL12 9AT

☎ 01833 638212

web: www.english-heritage.org.uk

Imposing remains of one of England's largest medieval castles perched high on a rugged escarpment above the banks of the River Tees.

Times Open all year, 21 Mar-Sep, daily 10-6; Oct, daily 10-4; Nov-Mar, Thu-Mon 10-4. Closed 24-26 Dec & 1 Jan. **Fee** £4 (concessions £3.20, ch £2). Prices and opening times are subject to change in March 2009. Please call 0870 333 1181 for the most up to date prices and opening times when planning your visit. **Facilities** shop ⚏

The Bowes Museum   2 for 1

DL12 8NP

⮑ *(in Barnard Castle, just off A66)*

☎ 01833 690606

e-mail: info@thebowesmuseum.org.uk

web: www.thebowesmuseum.org.uk

John and Josephine Bowes founded The Bowes Museum over 100 years ago. The magnificent building houses a collection of treasures from fine and decorative art to major temporary exhibitions of international quality and interest. The icon of the collection is the Silver Swan, a unique life-size, musical automaton which plays every day. There are also works by El Greco, Goya and Canaletto. The Café Bowes and beautiful grounds add to a wonderful day out for all. Spring 2009 sees the opening of the Textiles and Dress gallery and the Silver gallery.

Times Open daily 10-5, Nov-Feb 10-4. Closed 25-26 Dec & 1 Jan. **Fee** £7 (ch under 16 free, concessions £6) **Facilities** ❷ ⏛ ⏢ (outdoor) ♿ (vaults on lower ground not accessible) (lift, ramped entrance, reserved parking, audio guide/loop) toilets for disabled shop ⊗ (ex assist dogs) ➥

Egglestone Abbey   FREE

DL12 8QN

⮑ *(1m S of Barnard Castle on minor road off B6277)*

web: www.english-heritage.org.uk

The scant, but charming remains of a small medieval monastery. The picturesque ruins of Egglestone are located above a bend in the River Tees. A large part of the church can be seen, as can remnants of monastic buildings.

Times Open daily, 10-6. **Facilities** ❷ ⚏

BEAMISH   MAP 12 NZ25

Beamish, The North of England Open-Air Museum

DH9 0RG

⮑ *(off A693 & A6076. Signed from A1M junct 63.)*

☎ 0191 370 4000

e-mail: museum@beamish.org.uk

web: www.beamish.org.uk

Set in 200 acres of countryside, award-winning Beamish recreates life in the early 1800s and 1900s. Costumed staff welcome visitors to a 1913 town street, colliery village, farm and railway station; a re-creation of how people lived and worked. Ride on early electric tramcars, take a ride on a replica of an 1825 steam railway and visit Pockerley Manor where a yeoman farmer and his family would have lived.

Times Open Apr-Oct daily, 10-5; Oct-Mar 10-4 (last admission 3). Closed Mon, Fri & part of Dec. **Fee** ✳ Summer £16 (ch £10, pen £12.50). Winter £6 (ch & pen £6). Winter visit is centered on town & tramway only, other areas are closed. **Facilities** ❷ ⏛ ⏢ (outdoor) ♿ (not ideal for wheelchairs, assistance recommended) toilets for disabled shop ⊗ (ex in grounds & assist dogs) ➥

BISHOP AUCKLAND

MAP 08 NZ22

Auckland Castle

DL14 7NR

➲ *(follow signs to Market Place then brown tourist sign for Castle)*

☎ 01388 601627

e-mail: auckland.castle@zetnet.co.uk

web: www.auckland-castle.co.uk

Serving as the principal county residence of the Prince Bishops since the 12th century, Auckland Castle is the home of the Bishop of Durham. Built on a promontory overlooking the River Wear and the Roman Fort of Binchester, the Castle has been added to and adapted over the centuries. St Peter's Chapel houses many of the treasures of past Bishops. Special events take place throughout the year, please contact for details.

Times Open Etr Mon-Jun, Sun & Mon 2-5; Jul-Aug Sun 2-5, Mon & Wed 11-5, Sep Sun & Mon 2-5. **Fee** £4 (ch under 12 free, concessions £3). **Facilities** ♿ ♿ (chair walker available by prior arrangement) toilets for disabled shop ⊗ (ex assist dogs) ▬

BOWES

MAP 12 NY91

Bowes Castle

FREE

DL12 9LD

➲ (in Bowes village, just off A66)

web: www.english-heritage.org.uk

Massive ruins of Henry II's tower keep, three storeys high, set within the earthworks of a Roman fort and overlooking the valley of the River Greta.

Times Open at any reasonable time. **Facilities** ⧓ ▥ ⚏

COWSHILL

MAP 12 NY84

Killhope The North of England Lead Mining Museum

2 for 1

DL13 1AR

➲ *(beside A689 midway between Stanhope & Alston)*

☎ 01388 537505

e-mail: killhope@durham.gov.uk

web: www.killhope.org.uk

Equipped with hard hats and lamps, you can explore the working conditions of Victorian lead miners. The lead mine and 19th-century crushing mill have been restored to look as they would have done in the 1870s, and the 34ft water wheel has been restored to working order. There is also a visitor centre and mineral exhibition, a woodland walk, children's play area and a red squirrel and bird hides. Please ring for information on workshops and events. 2009 is the 25th anniversary of Killhopes's opening.

Times Open daily Apr-Nov 10.30-5. **Fee** ✳ Mine & Site: £6.50 (ch £3.50, concessions £6). Family £17. Site: £4.50 (ch £1.50, concessions £4). Family £11.50 **Facilities** ♿ ⧑ ⧓ (indoor & outdoor) ♿ (accessible hide for wildlife viewing) (electric scooter, sympathetic hearing scheme) toilets for disabled shop ▬

DARLINGTON

MAP 08 NZ21

Head of Steam-Darlington Railway Museum

North Rd Station DL3 6ST

➲ *(0.75m N, off A167)*

☎ 01325 460532

e-mail: museum@darlington.gov.uk

web: www.head-of-steam.co.uk

Housed in the carefully restored North Road Station, this museum's prize exhibit is Locomotion No 1, which pulled the first passenger train on the Stockton to Darlington railway and was built by Robert Stephenson & Co in 1825. Several other steam locomotives are also shown, together with models and other exhibits relating to the Stockton and Darlington and the North Eastern Railway companies.

Times Open Oct-Mar, Tue-Sun 11-3.30; Apr-Sep, Tue-Sun 10-4. **Fee** £4.95 (ch 6-16 £3, concessions £3.75). Family ticket (2ad+4ch) £10 **Facilities** ♿ ⧑ ⧓ (outdoor) ♿ (hearing loop at reception) toilets for disabled shop ⊗ (ex assist dogs) ▬

DURHAM

MAP 12 NZ24

Crook Hall & Gardens

2 for 1

Sidegate DH1 5SZ

➲ *(In city centre)*

☎ 0191 384 8028

e-mail: info@crookhall.co.uk

web: www.crookhallgardens.co.uk

Grade I listed medieval manor house with attractive gardens. A few minutes' walk from the city centre and close to the River Wear. Special events include Fairytale Week in May/June, Hallowe'en, Teddy Bear Day and Easter and Christmas events.

Times Open May-Sep, Wed-Sun 11-5. **Fee** £5.50 (concessions £5, ch £4.50). Family ticket (2ad & 2ch) £16. **Facilities** ♿ (charged) ⧑ ⧓ (outdoor) ♿ (Partly accessible) ⊗ ▬

Durham Cathedral

DH1 3EH

➲ *(A690 into city, follow signs to car parks)*

☎ 0191 386 4266

e-mail: enquiries@durhamcathedral.co.uk

web: www.durhamcathedral.co.uk

Founded in 1093 as a shrine to St Cuthbert, the cathedral is a remarkable example of Norman architecture, set in an impressive position high above the River Wear. A full programme of concerts throughout the year. St Cuthbert's Day Procession (phone for details).

Times Open all year, Mon-Sat, 9.30-6.15; Sun, 12.30-5. During school summer holidays open until 8. Access restricted during services and events. **Fee** Donation requested **Facilities** ♿ (in city centre) (please phone for disabled parking) ⧑ ⧒ ♿ (Partly accessible) (large print guide, touch/hearing centre, stairclimber) toilets for disabled shop ⊗ (ex assist dogs)

Durham Light Infantry Museum & Durham Art Gallery

Aykley Heads DH1 5TU

➲ *(0.5m NW, turn right off A691)*

☎ 0191 384 2214

e-mail: dli@durham.gov.uk
web: www.durham.gov.uk/dli

The history of the Regiment is told in displays of artefacts, medals, uniforms and vehicles. The Art Gallery has a continuous programme of temporary exhibitions, and holds regular lectures and concerts.

Times Open all year, Apr-Oct, daily 10-5; Nov-Mar, daily 10-4. Closed 24-25 Dec. **Fee** £3.25 (ch £1.35, concessions £2.15). Family ticket £7.50 **Facilities** ♥ ⏜ ⊓ (outdoor) ♿ (wheelchair available, lift, ramps) toilets for disabled shop ⊗ (ex assist dogs) ▬

Finchale Priory

Brasside, Newton Hall DH1 5SH

➲ *(3m NE)*

☎ 0191 386 6528

web: www.english-heritage.org.uk

Dating from the 13th-century, these beautiful priory ruins are in a wooded setting beside the River Wear.

Times Open 21 Mar-30 Sep, Sat-Sun & BH 10-5. **Fee** £3 (concessions & ch £1.50). Prices and opening times are subject to change in March 2009. Please call 0870 333 1181 for the most up to date prices and opening times when planning your visit. **Facilities** ♥ (charged) ⏜ shop ♿

Old Fulling Mill Museum of Archaeology NEW

The Banks DH1 3EB

➲ *(On river bank directly below Cathedral)*

☎ 0191 334 1823

e-mail: archaeology.museum@durham.ac.uk
web: www.dur.ac.uk/fulling.mill

Once a key part of Durham's cloth making industry, the Old Fulling Mill is now home to Durham University's Museum of Archaeology. The collections on display provide a fascinating insight into the rich heritage of the north east of England, as well as showcasing items from across Europe. Highlights include outstanding Roman collections together with Anglo-Saxon, Medieval and Tudor finds from Durham City and the local area. Up to date details of exhibitions and the lively programme of family activities at weekends and during school holidays can be found on the museum's website.

Times Open Apr-Oct daily 10-4; Nov-Mar Fri-Mon 11.30-3.30 **Fee** ✻ £1 (ch & concessions 50p, students free). Family ticket £2.50. **Facilities** ℗ 300mtrs (parking ltd, use P&R) ♿ (Partly accessible) shop ⊗ (ex assist dogs) ▬

Oriental Museum

2 for 1

University of Durham, Elvet Hill DH1 3TH

➲ *(signed from A167 & A177)*

☎ 0191 334 5694

e-mail: oriental.museum@durham.ac.uk
web: www.dur.ac.uk/oriental.museum

The Oriental Museum is the only museum in Britain dedicated solely to the art and archaeology of the Orient. The remarkable collections reveal to the visitor the history and prehistory of the great cultures of Asia, the Near and Middle East and North Africa. Highlights include one of the largest and finest Chinese collections in Europe and an ancient Egyptian collection of international importance.

Times Open Mon-Fri 10-5, wknds & BHs 12-5. Closed Xmas & New Year. **Fee** ✻ £1.50 (concessions 75p). Family ticket £3.50. **Facilities** ♥ ⏜ ⊓ (outdoor) ♿ (lifts to all floors) toilets for disabled shop ⊗ (ex assist dogs) ▬

Hartlepool's Maritime Experience

Maritime Av TS24 0XZ

➲ *(from N A19 take A179 and follow signs for marina then historic quay. From S A19 take A689 and follow signs for marina then historic quay)*

☎ 01429 860077

e-mail: info@hartlepoolsmaritimeexperience.com
web: www.hartlepoolsmaritimeexperience.com

Britain's maritime heritage is brought to life, with the sights, sounds and smells of a 19th-century quayside. Learn about the birth of the Royal Navy, and visit the Quayside shops, the admiral's house, the oldest warship afloat *HMS Trincomalee* and the naval prison. Other features include children's maritime adventure centre, regular demonstrations of sword fighting, and cannon firing. The *HMS Trincomalee* exhibition is one of the new features at this museum.

Times Open all year daily Summer 10-5, Winter 11-3. Closed 25-26 Dec & 1 Jan. **Facilities** ♥ ⏜ ⎁ ⊓ (outdoor) ♿ (Partly accessible) (all areas ramped or lift access, auto doors) toilets for disabled shop ⊗ (ex assist dogs) ▬

Diggerland

DH7 9TT

➲ *(A1(M) junct 62. W & follow Consett signs. After 6m left at rdbt, signed Langley Park, then right into Riverside Industrial Estate)*

☎ 08700 344437

e-mail: mail@diggerland.com

web: www.diggerland.com

An adventure park with a difference, where kids of all ages can experience the thrills of driving real earth-moving equipment. Choose from various types of diggers and dumpers ranging from 1 ton to 8.5 tons. Supervised by an instructor, complete the Dumper Truck Challenge or dig for buried treasure. New rides include JCB Robots, the Supertrack, Landrover Safari and Spin Dizzy. Even under fives can join in, with mum or dad's help.

Times ✳ Open mid Feb-Nov, 10-5, wknds BHs & school hols only **Facilities** ❷ ⬭ 🏕 ♿ toilets for disabled shop ⊗ (ex assist dogs) ⊟

Locomotion: The National Railway Museum at Shildon

DL4 1PQ

➲ *(A1(M) junct 68, take A68 & A6072 to Shildon, attraction is 0.25m SE of town centre)*

☎ 01388 777999

e-mail: info@locomotion.uk.com

web: www.locomotion.uk.com

Timothy Hackwood (1786-1850) was an important figure in the development of steam travel. He constructed *Puffing Billy* for William Hedley, ran Stephenson's Newcastle Works, and also became the first superintendent of the Stockton & Darlington Railway. The museum and house detail Hackwood's life and the steam transport revolution, as well as displaying working models and locomotives from various periods. Steam train rides are available throughout the year, on event days. The Collections building contains 60 vehicles from the National Collection.

Times Open 17 Mar-5 Oct, daily 10-5; 6 Oct-1 Apr, Wed-Sun, 10-4. **Fee** Free, small charge for train rides. **Facilities** ❷ ⬭ 🏕 (indoor & outdoor) ♿ (bus available to transport guests, please contact) toilets for disabled shop ⊗ (ex assist dogs) ⊟

Raby Castle

DL2 3AH

➲ *(on A688, Barnard Castle to Bishop Auckland road, 1m N of Staindrop)*

☎ 01833 660202

e-mail: admin@rabycastle.com

web: www.rabycastle.com

This dramatic 14th-century castle, built by the Nevills has been home to Lord Barnard's family since 1626. It has an impressive gateway, nine towers, a vast hall and an octagonal Victorian drawing room displaying one of the most striking interiors from the 19th century. Rooms contain fine furniture, impressive artworks and elaborate architecture. In the grounds are a deer park, large walled gardens, coach and carriage collections, a woodland adventure playground, a picnic area and gift shop.

Times Open May, Jun & Sep, Sun-Wed. Jul-Aug, open daily (ex Sat) 11-5, open BH wknds & Etr. **Fee** Castle, Park & Gardens: £9.50 (ch £4 & concessions £8.50). Family (2ad+3ch) £25. Park & Gardens: £5 (ch £2.50 & concessions £4). Family (2ad+3ch) £12.50. Group discounts available. Prices vary for special events. **Facilities** ❷ ⬭ 🏕 (outdoor) ♿ (most of ground floor accessible, 40 steps in castle, walkways in garden) (DVD interpretation) toilets for disabled shop ⊗ (ex assist dogs & on lead) ⊟

Tanfield Railway

Old Marley Hill NE16 5ET

➲ *(on A6076 1m S of Sunniside)*

☎ 0191 388 7545

e-mail: tanfield@ingsoc.demon.co.uk

web: www.tanfield_railway.co.uk

A three mile working steam railway which is the oldest existing railway in the world. The Causey Arch, the first large railway bridge of its era, is the centrepiece of a deep wooded valley, with picturesque walks. You can ride in carriages that first saw use in Victorian times, and visit Marley Hill shed, the home of 35 engines; inside the shed you can see the stationary steam engine at work driving some of the vintage machine tools. The blacksmith is also often at work forging new parts for the restoration work. Special events are held throughout the year, please telephone for details.

Times ✳ Open all year, Summer daily 10-5; Winter daily 10-4. Trains: Sun & Summer BHs wknds; also Thu & Sat mid Jul-Aug. Santa's Specials Sat & Sun in Dec (booking essential). Mince pie specials Boxing Day. **Facilities** ❷ ⬭ 🏕 ♿ (all trains carry ramps for wheelchair access) toilets for disabled shop

ESSEX

The Beth Chatto Gardens, Elmstead Market

AUDLEY END

MAP 05 TL53

Audley End House & Gardens

CB11 4JF

➲ (1m W of Saffron Walden on B1383)

☎ 01799 522842

web: www.english-heritage.org.uk

One of the most significant Jacobean houses in England with 31 opulent rooms on view. Set in 'Capability' Brown landscaped park, with walled Victorian kitchen garden.

Times Open House: 21 Mar-Sep, Wed-Sun 11-5 (Sat 11-3.30); Oct, Wed-Sun 11-4. (Last entry 1 hr before closing). Closed Nov-Mar except for Festive Fun wknds (22-23 Nov, 29-30 Nov, 6-7 Dec, 13-14 Dec). **Fee** House & Gardens: £10.50 (concessions £8.40, ch £5.30). Family £26.30. Gardens only: £5.50 (concessions £4.40, ch £2.80). Family £13.80. Prices & opening times are subject to change in March 2009. Please call 0870 333 1181 for the most up to date prices and opening times. **Facilities** ❷ (charged) ♬ ⬛ shop ▦

BRENTWOOD

MAP 05 TQ69

Kelvedon Hatch Secret Nuclear Bunker

CM14 5TL

➲ (on A128 at Kelvedon Hatch)

☎ 01277 364883

e-mail: bunker@japer.demon.co.uk

web: www.secretnuclearbunker.co.uk

Witness the three phases of the bunker's life. From its role with the RAF where the overall tactical controller would react to a nuclear attack from Britain's enemies, through to its role as Regional Government HQ, when there could have been up to 600 personnel, possibly including the Prime Minister, organising the survival of the civilian population in the aftermath of nuclear war. See for yourself the equipment and rooms needed to support the plotting of nuclear fall-out patterns.

Times Open Mar-Oct, wkdays 10-4 wknds 10-5; Nov-Feb, Thu-Sun 10-4. **Fee** £6.50 (ch £4.50). Family ticket (2ad+2ch) £16. **Facilities** ❷ ⬛ 🏵 licensed ♬ (outdoor) ♿ (top two floors accessible) (stairlift, ramps) toilets for disabled shop ⊗ (ex assist dogs)

CASTLE HEDINGHAM

MAP 05 TL73

Colne Valley Railway & Museum

Castle Hedingham Station CO9 3DZ

➲ (4m NW of Halstead on A1017)

☎ 01787 461174

e-mail: info@colnevalleyrailway.co.uk

web: www.colnevalleyrailway.co.uk

Many former Colne Valley and Halstead railway buildings have been rebuilt here. Stock includes seven steam locomotives plus 80 other engines, carriages and wagons. Visitors can dine in style in restored Pullman carriages while travelling along the line. Please telephone for a free timetable and details of the many special events.

Times ✳ Open all year, daily 10-dusk. Steam days, rides from 12-4. Closed 23 Dec-1 Feb. Steam days every Sun and BH from Mothering Sun to end Oct, Wed of school summer hols & special events. Railway Farm Park open May-Sep. Phone 01787 461174 for timetable information or visit website for details. **Facilities** ❷ ⬛ 🏵 ♬ (outdoor) ♿ (ramps for wheelchairs to get onto carriages) toilets for disabled shop ⊗ (ex assist dogs) ⬛

Hedingham Castle

CO9 3DJ

➲ (on B1508, 1m off A1017 Colchester/Cambridge. Follow brown heritage signs to Hedingham Castle)

☎ 01787 460261

e-mail: mail@hedinghamcastle

web: www.hedinghamcastle.co.uk

This impressive Norman castle was built in 1140. It was besieged by King John, visited by Henry VII, Henry VIII and Elizabeth I, and was home to the de Veres, Earls of Oxford, for over 500 years. During the summer months Hedingham's colourful heritage comes to life with a full programme of special events. There are medieval jousts and sieges with authentic living history displays and encampments. Please telephone for details.

Times ✳ Open Apr-28 Oct, Sun-Thur 10-5, Closed Fri-Sat **Facilities** ❷ ⬛ ♬ (outdoor) ♿ (paved access) toilets for disabled shop ⊗ (ex in grounds) ⬛

CHELMSFORD

MAP 05 TL70

RHS Garden Hyde Hall

Buckhatch Ln, Rettendon CM3 8ET

➲ (from M25 junct 28 (signed A12) or A29 (signed A127). SE of Chelmsford signed from A130. Exit Rettendon Turnpike, N through Rettendon Village, follow brown tourist signs)

☎ 01245 402006

e-mail: suecarter@rhs.org.uk

web: www.rhs.org.uk

RHS Garden Hyde Hall is an oasis of calm and serenity and a visit to the 360-acre estate is unforgettable in any season. The developed area of the garden, in excess of 24 acres, demonstrates an eclectic range of inspirational horticultural styles, from the formality of clipped hedges to large swathes of naturalistic planting. Highlights include the Rose Garden, colour themed herbaceous borders, ponds, dry garden and developing woodland. A range of workshops and family fun events are run throughout the year, please see the website for details.

Times Open all year (ex 25 Dec) from 10, closing times vary with season - contact garden for details. **Fee** ✻ £5 (ch 6-16 £1.50, ch under 6 free). RHS member & guest free. **Facilities** ❷ ⑂ licensed ☈ (outdoor) & (ramps and easy access to visitor centre) (manual wheelchairs for loan) toilets for disabled shop garden centre ⊗ (ex assist dogs)

COGGESHALL   MAP 05 TL82

Paycocke's

West St CO6 1NS

➲ *(Signed from A120, on S side of West Street)*

☎ 01376 561305

This timber-framed house is a fine example of a medieval merchant's home. It was completed in about 1505 and has interesting carvings on the outside timbers, including the Paycocke trade sign. Inside there are further elaborate carvings and linenfold panelling. Behind the house is a pretty garden.

Times Open 5 Apr-11 Oct, Tue, Thu, Sun & BH Mon **Fee** £3.20 (ch £1.60), joint ticket with Coggeshall Grange Barn £4.20 (ch £2.10). **Facilities** ❷ (400yds) & (Large print & Braille guide, photo album) ⊗ (ex assist dogs) ✺

COLCHESTER   MAP 05 TL92

The Beth Chatto Gardens

Elmstead Market CO7 7DB

➲ *(5m E of Colchester on A133)*

☎ 01206 822007

e-mail: info@bethchatto.fsnet.co.uk

web: www.bethchatto.co.uk

Begun almost 40 years ago, when Beth Chatto and her late husband began working on acres of wasteland. Now an area of landscaped gardens with many unusual plants grown in a variety of conditions.

Times Open all year, Mar-Oct, Mon-Sat 9-5; Nov-Feb, Mon-Fri 9-4. **Fee** £5 (accompanied ch under 14 free) **Facilities** ❷ ♿ ☈ (outdoor) & (steep slope in garden) (large print guide) toilets for disabled garden centre ⊗ (ex assist dogs)

Colchester Castle Museum   2 for 1

Castle Park, High St CO1 1TJ

➲ *(at E end of High St)*

☎ 01206 282939

e-mail: museums@colchester.gov.uk

web: www.colchestermuseums.org.uk

The largest Norman castle keep in Europe - built over the remains of the magnificent Roman Temple of Claudius which was destroyed by Boudicca in AD60. Colchester was the first capital of Roman Britain, and the archaeological collections are among the finest in the country. Please telephone or visit website for details of a range of events held throughout the year.

Times Open all year, Mon-Sat 10-5, Sun 11-5. Closed Xmas/New Year **Fee** ✻ £5.20 (ch & concessions £3.40) **Facilities** ❷ (town centre) ☈ (indoor & outdoor) & toilets for disabled shop ⊗ (ex assist dogs)

Colchester Zoo

Stanway, Maldon Rd CO3 0SL

➲ *(turn off A12 onto A1124, follow elephant signs)*

☎ 01206 331292

e-mail: enquiries@colchester-zoo.co.uk

web: www.colchester-zoo.co.uk

One of England's finest zoos, Colchester Zoo has over 250 species of animal. Visitors can meet the elephants, handle a snake, and see parrots, seals, penguins and birds of prey all appearing in informative daily displays. Enclosures include Spirit of Africa with the breeding group of African elephants, Playa Patagonia where sea lions swim above your head in a 24 metre underwater tunnel, Penguin Shores, Chimp World, and the Kingdom of the Wild, with giraffes, zebras and rhinos. There is also an undercover soft play complex, two road trains, four adventure play areas, eating places and gift shops, all set in 60 acres of gardens.

Times Open all year, daily from 9.30. Last admission 5.30 (1hr before dusk out of season). Closed 25 Dec. **Fee** ✻ £14.99 (ch 3-14 £7.99) **Facilities** ❷ ♿ ⑂ licensed ☈ & (easy routes developed but zoo has hills) (wheelchairs for hire) toilets for disabled shop ⊗ (ex assist dogs)

HADLEIGH   MAP 05 TQ88

Hadleigh Castle   FREE

➲ *(0.75m S of A13)*

☎ 01760 755161

web: www.english-heritage.org.uk

The subject of several of Constable's paintings, the castle has fine views of the Thames estuary. It is defended by ditches on three sides, and the north-east and south-east towers are still impressive.

Times Open at any reasonable time. **Facilities** & (limited access due to hilly surroundings) ✣

HARWICH   MAP 05 TM23

Harwich Redoubt Fort   2 for 1

CO12 3TE

➲ *(behind 29 Main Rd)*

☎ 01255 503429

e-mail: theharwichsociety@quista.net

web: www.harwich-society.com

The 180ft-diameter circular fort was built in 1808 in case of invasion by Napoleon. It has a dry moat and 8ft-thick walls, with 18 rooms for stores, ammunition and quarters for 300 men. The Redoubt is being restored by the Harwich Society, and contains three small museums. Ten guns can be seen on the battlements.

Times Open May-Aug, daily 10-4; Sep-Apr, Sun only 10-4. **Fee** £2 (accompanied ch free). **Facilities** ❷ (200yds) & (ground floor only) shop

ENGLAND

LAYER MARNEY   MAP 05 TL91

Layer Marney Tower

CO5 9US

➲ *(off B1022 Colchester to Maldon road, signposted)*

☎ 01206 330784

e-mail: info@layermarneytower.co.uk

web: www.layermarneytower.co.uk

The tallest Tudor gatehouse in the country, intended to be the entrance to a courtyard which would have rivalled Hampton Court Palace. The death of Henry, 1st Lord Marney in 1523, and of his son in 1525, meant that the building work ceased before completion. The beautiful parish church lies within the grounds. Visit the medieval barn and playground. Special events throughout the year, please see website.

Times Open 5 Apr-27 Sep, Sun 12-5, Jul-Aug Sun-Thu 12-5, also open BH Mon. **Fee** £4.25 (ch £2.75). Family ticket (2ad+2ch) £13. **Facilities** ❷ ⚲ ⏚ (outdoor) ♿ (ramps in garden and farm) toilets for disabled shop ⊗ (ex assist dogs/dogs on lead) ⛟

NEWPORT   MAP 05 TL53

Mole Hall Wildlife Park

Widdington CB11 3SS

➲ *(M11 junct 8 between Stansted & Saffron Walden, off B1383)*

☎ 01799 540400 & 541359

e-mail: enquiries@molehall.co.uk

web: www.molehall.co.uk

The Park covers 20 acres and has been lovingly developed by the Johnstone family for over 40 years. The wide variety of animals range from South American Lama Guanaco to red squirrels, leopard-like Serval cat and the Formosan Sika deer, which is extinct in the wild. Mole Hall is also home to two species of otter, being the first regular breeders in the UK of the North American otter. Other residents include chimpanzees, capuchins, lemurs and much more. In the tropical butterfly pavilion, see butterflies on the wing and free flying small birds. Tarantulas, snakes, pools of aquatic life, small monkeys, tortoises and lovebirds. Small children will also be entertained by the straw castle, water maze, sand pit and play area.

Times Open all year, daily 10-5.30 (or dusk). Closed 25 Dec. Butterfly House and Water Maze open mid Mar-Oct. **Fee** ✳ £6.90 (ch £4.30 under 3's free, pen, student & disabled £3). **Facilities** ❷ ⚲ ⏚ (outdoor) ♿ (Difficult in wet weather for wheelchairs) toilets for disabled shop garden centre ⊗ (ex assist dogs) ⛟

SAFFRON WALDEN   MAP 05 TL53

Saffron Walden Museum   `2 for 1`

Museum St CB10 1JL

➲ *(Close to M11, take B184/B1052 & follow signs to Saffron Walden)*

☎ 01799 510333

e-mail: museum@uttlesford.gov.uk

web: www.saffronwaldenmuseum.org

Opened in 1835, this friendly, family-size museum lies near the castle ruins in the centre of town. Its collections include local history and archaeology, natural history, ceramics, glass, costume, furniture, toys, an ancient Egyptian room, a natural history gallery, Discovery Centre and important ethnography collections. This museum has won the Museum of the Year award for being the best museum of social history, and awards for disabled access. There is a regular programme of special exhibitions, events and family holiday activities.

Times Open all year, Mar-Oct, Mon-Sat 10-5, Sun & BHs 2-5; Nov-Feb, Mon-Sat, 10-4.30, Sun & BHs 2-4.30. Closed 24 & 25 Dec. **Fee** £1 (ch 18 & under free, concessions 50p) **Facilities** ❷ ⏚ (outdoor) ♿ (2 small raised platforms unaccessible to wheelchairs) (ramps, wheelchairs, stairlifts, hearing loop) toilets for disabled shop ⊗ (ex assist dogs)

SOUTHEND-ON-SEA   MAP 05 TQ88

Southend Museum, Planetarium & Discovery Centre Centre

Victoria Av SS2 6EW

➲ *(take A127 or A13 towards town centre. Museum is adjacent to Southend Victoria Railway Station)*

☎ 01702 434449

e-mail: southendmuseum@hotmail.com

web: www.southendmuseums.co.uk

A fine Edwardian building housing displays of archaeology, natural history and local history, telling the story of man in the south-east Essex area. Ring for details of special events, or see website.

Times Open Central Museum: Tue-Sat 10-5 (Closed Sun-Mon & BH); Planetarium: Wed-Sat, shows at 11, 2 & 4. **Fee** ✳ Central Museum free. Planetarium £3.20 (ch & pen £2.10). Family tickets £9.50. Party rates on request. **Facilities** ❷ (50mtrs) (disabled only behind museum) ♿ (planetarium & toilets not accessible) shop ⊗ (ex assist dogs)

Southend Pier Museum

Western Esplanade, Southend Pier SS1 2EL

➲ *(A127 follow signs to seafront and pier, attraction is at shore end of pier, access from shore train station)*

☎ 01702 611214 & 614553

web: www.southendpiermuseum.com

Southend Pier is one and a third miles long and was built in 1830. This living museum portrays the history of the pier, its railway, its disasters, and the people who have lived and worked there. Exhibits include ex-pier rolling stock, a reconstructed signal box with working levers, and antique slot machines. Children can have fun learning about their heritage.

Times Open May-Oct. Tue, Wed, Sat, Sun & BHs 11-5 (during school hols 5.30) **Fee** ✳ £1 (accompanied ch under 12 free, applies to families only). Subject to change. For school rate please pre-book **Facilities** ℗ (50yds) ♿ (Access to museum through fire door via Adventure Island) shop ⊗ (ex assist dogs)

STANSTED   MAP 05 TL52

Mountfitchet Castle Experience

CM24 8SP

➲ *(off B1383, in village. 2m from M11 junct 8)*

☎ 01279 813237

e-mail: office@mountfitchetcastle.com

web: www.mountfitchetcastle.com

Come and see a Norman motte and bailey castle and village reconstructed as it was in Norman England of 1066, on its original historic site. A vivid illustration of village life in Domesday England, complete with houses, church, seige tower, seige weapons, and many types of animals roaming freely. Animated wax figures in all the buildings give historical information to visitors. Adjacent to the castle is the House on the Hill Toy Museum, a nostalgic trip through memories of childhood days. The whole experience is a unique all-weather, all-in-one heritage entertainment complex.

Times Open daily, mid Mar-mid Nov, 10-5. **Fee** ✳ £8.50 (ch £6.50, concessions £8). **Facilities** ℗ (charged) ⊡☶ (outdoor) ♿ (partly accessible due to grassy slopes, cobbled areas & steps) (laser commentaries) toilets for disabled shop ⊗ (ex assist dogs) ⊟

TILBURY   MAP 05 TQ67

Tilbury Fort

No 2 Office Block, The Fort RM18 7NR

➲ *(0.5m E off A126)*

☎ 01375 858489

web: www.english-heritage.org.uk

View the finest example of 17th-century military engineering, a spectacular sight on the River Thames. View the World War I and II gun emplacements and even fire a real anti-aircraft gun.

Times Open all year, 21 Mar-Oct, daily 10-5; Nov-Mar, Thu-Mon 10-4. Closed 24-26 Dec & 1 Jan. **Fee** £3.70 (concessions £3, ch £1.90). Family £9.30. Prices and opening times are subject to change in March 2009. Please call 0870 333 1181 for the most up to date prices and opening times when planning your visit. **Facilities** shop ⊗ (ex on lead in certain areas) ⊞

WALTHAM ABBEY   MAP 05 TL30

Lee Valley Park Farms

Stubbins Hall Ln, Crooked Mile EN9 2EG

➲ *(M25 junct 26, follow to Waltham Abbey. 2m from Waltham Abbey on B914)*

☎ 01992 892781 & 702200

e-mail: hayeshill@leevalleypark.org.uk

web: www.leevalleypark.org.uk

Lee Valley Park offers a unique visitor experience, two farms for the price of one. Hayes Hill Farm, a traditional style farm with a variety of different animals including pigs, goats and rare breeds, as well as the Pet Centre which houses small mammals and reptiles. You can take a stroll or a tractor and trailer ride to Holyfield Hall Farm, a modern dairy and arable farm. New activities include Rabbit World, re-furbished tearooms and farm shop and visit The World Beneath Your Feet to see if you can spot any ants or worms wriggling around.

Times Open all year, daily 10-5. **Facilities** ℗ ⊡☶ (indoor & outdoor) ♿ (Partly accessible) (graded concrete paths, signed routes) toilets for disabled shop ⊟

Royal Gunpowder Mills   [2 for 1]

Beaulieu Dr EN9 1JY

➲ *(M25 junct 26. Follow signs for A121 to Waltham Abbey at rdbt, entrance in Beaulieu Drive)*

☎ 01992 707370

e-mail: info@royalgunpowdermills.com

web: www.royalgunpowdermills.com

Set in 175 acres of parkland, this amazing scientific complex has 21 buildings of historical importance. Before it ceased operating as a gunpowder mill in 1991 this was a site of major scientific research and development, including work on Congreve's *Rocket* in the early 19th century, up to more recent work on ejector seats and fuel for rocket motors. Explosives were made in many of the buildings on the site which are connected by five miles of navigational canals.

Times Open 26 Apr-28 Sep, 11-5, last entry at 3.30. (Wknds and BHs only) **Fee** ✳ £6.50 (ch 5-16 £4, concessions £5.50, under 5's free) Family ticket (2ad & 3ch) £21 **Facilities** ℗ ⊡☶ (outdoor) ♿ (stairs provide access to top of Wildlife Tower. Some paths on nature walk are uneven. Lift available in main exhibition, number of ramps on site) (tactile with audio tour) toilets for disabled shop ⊗ (ex assist dogs) ⊟

Waltham Abbey Gatehouse,   [FREE]
Bridge & Entrance to Cloisters

➲ *(in Waltham Abbey off A112)*

☎ 01992 702200

web: www.english-heritage.org.uk

Beside the great Norman church at Waltham are the slight remains of the abbey buildings - bridge, gatehouse and part of the north cloister. The bridge is named after King Harold, founder of the abbey.

Times Open at any reasonable time. **Facilities** ♿ (sensory trail guide)

GLOUCESTERSHIRE

Cotswold Water Park

ALDSWORTH MAP 04 SP11

Lodge Park & Sherborne Estate

GL54 3PP

➲ *(approach from A40 only, between Northleach & Burford rdbts)*

☎ 01451 844130 & 844257

e-mail: lodgepark@nationaltrust.org.uk

web: www.nationaltrust.org.uk

Situated on the picturesque Sherborne Estate in the Cotswolds, Lodge Park was created in 1634 by John 'Crump' Dutton. Inspired by his passion for gambling and banqueting it is a unique survival of what would have been called a grandstand, with its deer course and park.

Times Open Grandstand/Deer Park: 14 Mar-2 Nov, Fri, Sat & Sun 11-4. Estate: daily all year. **Fee** ✷ Grandstand: £5 (ch £2.80). Family £12.50. Estate: free. (£1 donation per car to support work on the estate) **Facilities** ♿ ⛱ (outdoor) ♿ (Braille guide, manual wheelchair, drop off point) toilets for disabled ♿

Je...
Church...

➲ *(follow to... into High St & le...*

☎ 01453 810631

e-mail: manager@jenner...

web: www.jennermuseum.com...

This beautiful Georgian house was the hom... discoverer of vaccination against smallpox. The... with its Temple of Vaccinia, are much as they were... displays record Jenner's life as an 18th-century country... on vaccination and his interest in natural history. 2009 is the... anniversary of Jenner's birth.

Times Open Apr-Sep, Tue-Sat 12.30-5.30, Sun 1-5.30. Oct, Sun 1-5.30; dai... in Jul & Aug (Closed Mon, ex BH Mon 12.30-5.30). **Fee** ✷ £4.25 (ch £2.50, concessions £3.50). Family ticket £10.75. Party 20+. **Facilities** ♿ ⛱ (indoor & outdoor) ♿ (ground floor accessible) toilets for disabled shop ♿ (ex assist dogs) ☕

BERKELEY MAP 03 ST69

Berkeley Castle

GL13 9BQ

➲ *(M5 junct 13 or 14, just off A38 midway between Bristol & Gloucester)*

☎ 01453 810332

e-mail: info@berkeley-castle.com

web: www.berkeley-castle.com

Berkeley Castle is the amazing fortress home of the Berkeley family, who have lived in the building since the Keep was completed in 1153. The castle is still intact, from dungeon to elegant drawing rooms, and reflects nearly a thousand years of English history: a king's murder, the American Colonies, London's Berkeley Square. Rose-clad terraces surround this most romantic castle.

Times Open 21 Mar-26 Oct, every Sun & BH wknds (daily Jul & Aug). **Fee** Castle & Gardens & Butterfly House: £7.50 (ch 5-15 £4.50, pen £6). Family ticket (2ad+2ch) £21. **Facilities** ♿ 🍴 ⛱ (outdoor) shop garden centre ♿ (ex assist dogs) ☕

BOURTON-ON-THE-WATER MAP 04 SP12

Birdland `2 for 1`

Rissington Rd GL54 2BN

➲ *(on A429)*

☎ 01451 820480

e-mail: simonb@birdland.co.uk

web: www.birdland.co.uk

Birdland is a natural setting of woodland, river and gardens, which is inhabited by over 500 birds; flamingos, pelicans, penguins, cranes, storks, cassowary and waterfowl can be seen on various aspects of the water habitat. Over 50 aviaries of parrots, falcons, pheasants, hornbills, touracos, pigeons, ibis and many more. Tropical, Toucan and Desert Houses are home to the more delicate species. Only group of king penguins in England.

Times Open all year, Apr-Oct, daily 10-6; Nov-Mar, daily 10-4. (Last admission 1hr before closing). Closed 25 Dec. **Fee** ✷ £5.50 (concessions £4.50). Family ticket (2ad+2ch) £16. **Facilities** Ⓟ (adjacent) 🍴 ⛱ ♿ toilets for disabled shop ♿ (ex on leads) ☕

CHEDWORTH MAP 04 SP01

Chedworth Roman Villa

Yanworth GL54 3LJ

➲ *(3m NW of Fossebridge on A429)*

☎ 01242 890256

e-mail: chedworth@nationaltrust.org.uk

web: www.nationaltrust.org.uk

The remains of a Romano-British villa, excavated 1864-66 and known as 'Britains oldest county house'. Set in a beautiful wooded combe, there are fine 4th-century mosaics, two bath houses, and a temple with spring. The museum houses the smaller finds and there is a nine-minute video programme. Telephone for further details of special events.

Times Open 1-16 Mar, daily 11-4; 18 Mar-2 Nov, daily 10-5; 4-16 Nov, daily 11-4. (Closed Mon ex BH Mon). **Fee** ✷ £6.30 (ch £5.70). Family ticket £16.30. **Facilities** ♿ ⛱ ♿ (audio tour, induction loop, Braille guide) toilets for disabled shop ♿ ♿ ☕

(partial, torn page — Jenner Museum, Berkeley)

ner Museum

GLOUCESTERSHIRE

, High St GL13 9BN

urist signs from A38 to town centre, left
again into Church Lane)

useum.com

of Edward Jenner, the
ouse and the garden,
Jenner's day. The
octor, his work
260th

2 for 1

ENGLAND

year.

Times Open all year daily Apr-Oct 10-5; Nov-Mar 10-4 (Vis
open from 11). Closed BHs. **Fee** Free, donations welcome. **Facilities** ℗
(500 mtrs) (disabled parking on site) 🚻 ♿ (handling tables; speech
reinforcement system) toilets for disabled shop ⊗ (ex assist dogs) ■

Holst Birthplace Museum

4 Clarence Rd GL52 2AY

➲ *(opposite gateway of Pittville Park. 10 min walk
from town centre)*

☎ 01242 524846

e-mail: holstmuseum@btconnect.com

web: www.holstmuseum.org.uk

Gustav Holst, composer of *The Planets* was born at this Regency house
in 1874. The museum contains unique displays on Holst's life, including
his original piano. The rooms of the house have been carefully
restored, each area evoking a different period in the history of the
house from Regency to Edwardian times.

Times Open Tue-Sat 10-4 (Closed Mon & Dec-Jan, ex pre-booked groups).
Fee ✳ £3.50 (ch & concessions £3). Family ticket (2ad+3ch) £8.
Facilities ℗ (250yds) ♿ (ground floor accessible but steps to front door)
(large print & Braille guide, special hands-on tours) shop ⊗ (ex assist dogs)

CIRENCESTER   MAP 04 SP00

Corinium Museum   2 for 1

Park St GL7 2BX

➲ *(in town centre)*

☎ 01285 655611

e-mail: museums@cotswold.gov.uk

web: www.cotswold.gov.uk/go/museum

Discover the treasures of the Cotswolds at the new Corinium Museum.
Two years and over five million pounds in the making, it has been
transformed into a must-see attraction. Featuring archaeological and
historical material from Cirencester and the Cotswolds, from prehistoric
times to the 19th century. The museum is known for its Roman mosaic

e and other material from one of Britain's largest Roman
New on display are Anglo-Saxon treasures from Lechlade
g to life this little-known period. The museum also houses
val, Tudor, Civil War and 18th-19th century displays.

Open Mon-Sat 10-5, Sun 2-5. Closed Xmas & New Year. **Fee** £3.95
, students £2.50, con £3.10). Family ticket £10 **Facilities** ℗ (2mins
🚻 ⍾ ♿ (large print & Braille guides) toilets for disabled shop ⊗ (ex
dogs) ■

LEARWELL   MAP 03 SO50

Clearwell Caves Ancient Iron Mines

GL16 8JR

➲ *(1.5m S of Coleford town centre, off B4228 follow
brown tourist signs)*

☎ 01594 832535

e-mail: jw@clearwellcaves.com

web: www.clearwellcaves.com

These impressive natural caves have also been mined since the earliest
times for paint pigment and iron ore. Today visitors explore nine large
caverns with displays of local mining and geology. There is a colour
room where ochre pigments are still produced and a blacksmith shop.
Deep level excursions available for more adventurous visitors, must be
pre-booked. Christmas fantasy event when the caverns are transformed
into a world of light and sound.

Times Open Mar-Oct daily 10-5; Jan-Feb Sat-Sun 10-5; Xmas Fantasy 1-24
Dec, daily 10-5. **Fee** £5.50 (ch £3.50, concessions £5) Family ticket £14.50.
Facilities ❷ 🚻 ⍾ (outdoor) ♿ (Partly accessible) (hands-on exhibits,
Braille guide book, contact in advance) toilets for disabled shop ⊗ (ex assist
dogs) ■

CRANHAM   MAP 03 SO81

Prinknash Abbey and Visitor Centre

GL4 8EX

➲ *(on A46 between Cheltenham & Stroud)*

☎ 01452 812066

e-mail: prinknashshop@waitrose.com

web: www.prinknashabbey.org.uk

Set in a large park, the old priory building is a 12th to 16th-century house, used by Benedictine monks and guests of Gloucester Abbey until 1539. It became an abbey for Benedictine monks from Caldey in 1928. Home to the reconstruction of the Great Orpheus Pavement, the largest mosaic in Britain, as mentioned in the Guinness Book of Records. Also visit the bird and deer park.

Times Open all year Wed-Sun. Closed Good Fri, 25-26 Dec. **Fee** ✳ Admission free to grounds. Orpheus Pavement £3.25 (ch 1.75). Family ticket £7. **Facilities** ❷ ⏝ ⼐ (outdoor) ⴕ (Radar approved) toilets for disabled ▭

Prinknash Bird & Deer Park

GL4 8EX

➲ *(M5 junct 11a, A417 towards Cirencester, take 1st exit signed A46 Stroud. Follow brown tourist signs)*

☎ 01452 812727

web: www.thebirdpark.com

Nine acres of parkland and lakes make a beautiful home for black swans, geese and other water birds. There are also exotic birds such as white and Indian blue peacocks and crown cranes, as well as tame fallow deer and pygmy goats. The Golden Wood is stocked with ornamental pheasants, and leads to the reputedly haunted monks' fishpond, which contains trout. An 80-year old, free-standing, 16 foot tall Wendy House in the style of a Tudor house has recently been erected near the picnic area. This year a pair of reindeer have been introduced in a new enclosure and are the only ones to be found in the Cotswolds.

Times Open all year, 10-5 Summer, 10-4 Winter, Closed 25 Dec & Good Fri **Fee** £5.70 (ch £4.20, pen £5) **Facilities** ❷ ⏝ ⼐ (outdoor) ⴕ (no charge for wheelchairs or pushers) toilets for disabled shop ⊗

DEERHURST   MAP 03 SO82

Odda's Chapel   `FREE`

➲ *(off B4213 near River Severn at Abbots Court SW of parish church)*

This rare Saxon chapel was built by Earl Odda and dedicated in 1056. When it was discovered, it had been incorporated into a farmhouse. It has now been carefully restored.

Times ✳ Open Apr-Oct, daily 10-6; Nov-Mar, daily 10-4. Closed 24-26 Dec & 1 Jan. **Facilities** ❷ (charged) ⊗ ⌗

DYRHAM   MAP 03 ST77

Dyrham Park

SN14 8ER

➲ *(8m N of Bath, 2m S from M4 junct 18 on A46)*

☎ 0117 937 2501

e-mail: dyrhampark@nationaltrust.org.uk

web: www.nationaltrust.org.uk

Dyrham Park is a splendid Baroque country house, with interiors that have hardly altered since the late 17th century. It has contemporary Dutch-style furnishings, Dutch pictures and blue-and-white Delft ware. Around the house is an ancient park with fallow deer, from where Dyrham derives its name. In the beautiful gardens, famous for the tulip festival in April, is a medieval church.

Times Open: House 14 Mar-2 Nov, 12-5, Fri-Tue. Garden, shop & tearoom, 14 Mar-29 Jun, 11-5, Fri-Tue; 30 Jun- Aug, daily, 11-5; Sep-2 Nov, Fri-Tue, 11-5; 8 Nov-14 Dec, Sat & Sun, 11-4. Park all year, 11-5, all week. **Fee** ✳ House £10 (ch £5). Family £25. Ground only £4 (ch £2). Family £8.90. Park only £2.60 (ch £1.30). Family £5.80 **Facilities** ❷ ⏝ ⽓ ⼐ ⴕ (Braille/audio guides, stairclimber, free bus from car park) toilets for disabled shop ⊗ (ex in dog walk area) ⬿

GLOUCESTER   MAP 03 SO81

Gloucester City Museum & Art Gallery   `FREE`

Brunswick Rd GL1 1HP

➲ *(A38 Bristol Rd to Southgate St, situated between Spa Rd & Brunswick Rd)*

☎ 01452 396131

e-mail: city.museum@gloucester.gov.uk

web: www.gloucester.gov.uk/citymuseum

An impressive range of Roman artefacts including the Rufus Sita tombstone; the amazing Iron Age Birdlip mirror; one of the earliest backgammon sets in the world; dinosaur fossils; and paintings by famous artists such as Turner and Gainsborough. There is something for everyone, full-sized dinosaurs; wildlife from the city and the Gloucestershire countryside; beautiful antique furniture, glass, ceramics and silver; hands-on displays, computer quizzes and activity workstations throughout the galleries. There is an exciting range of

CONTINUED

GLOUCESTER CONTINUED

temporary exhibitions from contemporary art and textiles to dinosaurs and local history; children's holiday activities and regular special events.

Times Open all year, Tue-Sat 10-5. **Facilities** Ⓟ (500yds) ♿ (lift to 1st floor galleries, induction loops) toilets for disabled shop ⊗ (ex assist dogs) ▬

Gloucester Folk Museum

FREE

99-103 Westgate St GL1 2PG

➲ *(from W - A40 & A48; from N - A38 & M5, from E - A40 & B4073; from S - A4173 & A38)*

☎ 01452 396868 & 396869

e-mail: folk.museum@gloucester.gov.uk

web: www.gloucester.gov.uk/folkmuseum

Three floors of splendid Tudor and Jacobean timber-framed buildings along with new buildings housing the dairy, ironmonger's shop and wheelwright and carpenter workshops. Local history, domestic life, crafts, trades and industries from 1500 to the present, including Toys and Childhood gallery with hands-on toys and a puppet theatre, the Siege of Gloucester, a Victorian class room, Victorian kitchen and laundry equipment. A wide range of exhibitions, hands-on activities, events, demonstrations and role play sessions are held throughout the year. There is an attractive cottage garden and courtyard for events, often with live animals, and outside games.

Times Open all year, Tue-Sat, 10-5 **Facilities** Ⓟ (500yds) ⛩ (outdoor) ♿ (Partly accessible) (virtual tour in Postal gallery, induction loops) shop ⊗ (ex assist dogs) ▬

The National Waterways Museum

Llanthony Warehouse, The Docks GL1 2EH

➲ *(From M5, A40. In city follow brown signs for historic docks)*

☎ 01452 318200

e-mail: gloucester@thewaterwaystrust.org.uk

web: www.nwm.org.uk

Based in Gloucester Docks, this museum takes up three floors of a seven-storey Victorian warehouse, and documents the 200-year history of Britain's water-based transport. The emphasis is on hands-on experience, including working models and engines, interactive displays, actual craft, computer interactions and the national collection of inland waterways. Boat trips are also available between Easter and October. The museum was refurbished in spring 2008.

Times Open all year, daily 10-5. (Last admission 4). Closed 25 Dec. **Fee** ✳ £3.95 (ch & concessions £2.75, under 5's free). Family £12. **Facilities** Ⓟ (charged) ☕ 🍽 licensed ⛩ (outdoor) ♿ (wheelchair, lifts, limited access to floating exhibits) toilets for disabled shop ⊗ (ex assist dogs) ▬

Nature in Art

2 for 1

Wallsworth Hall, Tewkesbury Rd, Twigworth GL2 9PA

➲ *(0.5m off main A38 between Gloucester and Tewkesbury, 2m N of Gloucester. Follow brown tourist signs)*

☎ 01452 731422 & 0845 450 0233

e-mail: enquiries@nature-in-art.org.uk

web: www.nature-in-art.org.uk

The world's only museum dedicated to all kinds of art inspired by nature, this museum and art gallery is set in a Georgian Mansion, where there are many outstanding exhibits including sculpture, tapestries and ceramics. There is an 'artist in residence' programme Feb-Nov which ranges from painting to wood carving. See website for full details. Work from over 60 countries spanning 1500 years is included in the collection. From Picasso to David Shepherd, Flemish masters to ethnic art, contemporary sculpture to Japanese prints - there is something for everyone. 2009 is the 21st anniversary of the museum.

Times Open all year, Tue-Sun & BHs 10-5. Closed 24-26 Dec. **Fee** £4.50 (ch, concessions £4, ch under 8 free). Family ticket £13. Party 15+ 50p discount per person. **Facilities** Ⓟ ☕ 🍽 licensed ⛩ (outdoor) ♿ (lift & ramps at entrance) toilets for disabled shop ⊗ (ex assist dogs) ▬

Cotswold Farm Park

2 for 1

GL54 5UG

➲ *(signed off B4077 from M5 junct 9)*

☎ 01451 850307

e-mail: info@cotswoldfarmpark.co.uk
web: www.cotswoldfarmpark.co.uk

Meet over 50 breeding flocks and herds of rare farm animals. There are lots of activities for the youngsters, with rabbits and guinea pigs to cuddle, lambs and goat kids to bottle feed, tractor and trailer-rides, battery powered tractors, Touch Barn, Maze Quest, a Jumping Pillow and safe rustic-themed play areas both indoors and outside. Lambing occurs in early May, followed by shearing and then milking demonstrations later in the season. The Cotswold Farm Park also has its own 40-pitch camping and caravanning site.

Times Open mid Mar-mid Sep, daily (then open wknds only until end Oct & Autumn half term 10.30-5). **Fee** ✳ £6.50 (ch £5.25, concessions £6). Family ticket £21.25 **Facilities** ♿ 🅿️ ☕ 🍴 (outdoor) ♿ (Partly accessible) (ramps) toilets for disabled shop ⊗ (ex assist dogs) 🚐

Hailes Abbey

GL54 5PB

➲ *(2m NE of Winchcombe off B4632)*

☎ 01242 602398

web: www.english-heritage.org.uk

Explore the atmospheric ruins of this great medieval pilgrimage abbey, in the midst of the Cotswolds. Built in the 13th-century Hailes became famous when presented with a phial that was said to contain the blood of Christ.

Times Open 21 Mar-Jun & Sep, daily 10-5; Jul-Aug, daily 10-6; Oct, daily 10-4. Closed Nov- Mar. **Fee** £3.50 (concessions £2.80, ch £1.80). Nat Trust members free, but charge of £1 for audio tour & special events. Prices and opening times are subject to change in March 2009. Please call 0870 333 1181 for the most up to date prices and opening times when planning your visit. **Facilities** ♿ shop ▒

Dean Forest Railway

Forest Rd GL15 4ET

➲ *(At Lydney, turn off A48. Follow [...] to Norchard Station, on B4234)*

☎ 01594 843423 (info) & 845840

e-mail: info@deanforestrailway.co.uk
web: www.deanforestrailway.co.uk

Travel on a heritage railway operated by steam trains (and the occasional diesel) through the beautiful and historic Forest of Dean. A relaxing round trip of over eight miles to the recently opened Parkend Station. There's free car parking at Norchard Station (near Lydney) with a well-stocked gift shop, museum and cafe. Regular family events include Thomas the Tank Engine and Santa Specials.

Times Open Apr-Oct, Sun; Jun-Sep, Wed, Sat, Sun; also Thu in Aug & BHs; Dec wknds (Santa Specials) & New Year. **Fee** ✳ £9 (under 5's free, ch £5, pen £8). Family ticket (2ad+2ch) £26. Different charges may apply to events. **Facilities** ♿ 🅿️ ☕ 🍴 (outdoor) ♿ (Partly accessible) (specially adapted coach for wheelchairs, phone for details) toilets for disabled shop 🚐

Hidcote Manor Garden

Chipping Campden GL55 6LR

➲ *(1m E of B4632, near village of Mickleton)*

☎ 01386 438333

e-mail: hidcote@nationaltrust.org.uk
web: www.nationaltrust.org.uk/hidcote

One of the most delightful arts and crafts gardens in England, created by the horticulturist Major Laurence Johnston and comprising a series of small gardens within the whole, separated by walls and hedges of different species. It is famous for its rare shrubs and trees, outstanding herbaceous borders and unusual worldwide plant species.

Times Garden mid Mar-Jun & Sep, Sat-Wed 10-6; Jul-Aug Fri-Wed, 10-6; 2 Oct-2 Nov, Sat-Wed,10-5. **Fee** ✳ £8.50 (ch £4.25). Family £21.20. Groups £7.70 (ch £3.85) **Facilities** ♿ 🅿️ ☕ 🍴 ♿ (partial access due to stone paths, w/chair, Braille) toilets for disabled shop garden centre ⊗ (ex assist dogs) 🐾

Kiftsgate Court Garden

GL55 6LN

➲ *(0.5m S off A46, adjacent Hidcote NT garden)*

☎ 01386 438777

e-mail: info@kiftsgate.co.uk
web: www.kiftsgate.co.uk

Kiftsgate Garden is spectacularly set on the edge of the Cotswold Escarpment, with views over the Vale of Evesham. It contains many rare plants collected by three generations of women gardeners, including the largest rose in England, the R. Filipes Kiftsgate.

Times Open Apr, Aug & Sep; Sun, Mon & Wed, 2-6. May-Jul, open daily (ex Thu & Fri), 12-6. **Fee** ✳ £6 (ch £2). **Facilities** ♿ 🅿️ ♿ (top garden only accessible, very steep banks) shop garden centre ⊗ (ex assist dogs) 🚐

The National Birds of Prey Centre

GL18 1JJ

➲ *(follow A40, right onto B4219 towards Newent. Follow brown tourist signs from Newent town)*

☎ 0870 9901992

e-mail: kb@nbpc.co.uk

web: www.nbpc.co.uk

Trained birds can be seen at close quarters in the Hawk Walk and the Owl Courtyard and there are also breeding aviaries, a gift shop, bookshop, picnic areas, coffee shop and children's play area. Birds are flown three times daily in summer and winter, giving an exciting and educational display. There are over 80 aviaries on view with 40 species.

Times Open all year daily 10.30-5.30 (closed 25-26 Dec). **Facilities** ℗ ⬚ ⊞ ⅋ (special tours available, pre-booking required) toilets for disabled shop ⊗ ▬

Keith Harding's World of Mechanical Music

2 for 1

The Oak House, High St GL54 3ET

➲ *(at crossroads of A40 & A429)*

☎ 01451 860181

e-mail: keith@mechanicalmusic.co.uk

web: www.mechanicalmusic.co.uk

A fascinating collection of antique clocks, musical boxes, automata and mechanical musical instruments, restored and maintained in the world-famous workshops, displayed in a period setting, presented as a live entertainment, and played during regular tours. There is an exhibition of coin operated instruments which visitors can play.

Times Open all year, daily 10-6. Last tour 5. (Closed 25-26 Dec). **Fee** £8 (ch £3.50, concessions £7). Family (2ad+2ch) £19. Discounts for groups. **Facilities** ℗ ⅋ (Safety rails, non-slip floor) toilets for disabled shop ⊗ (ex assist dogs) ▬

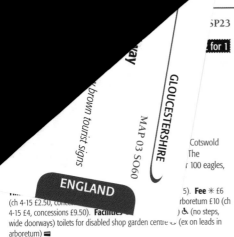

Cotswold
The
r 100 eagles,

5). **Fee** ✳ £6 (ch 4-15 £2.50, conce... rboretum £10 (ch 4-15 £4, concessions £9.50). **Facilities** ... ⅋ (no steps, wide doorways) toilets for disabled shop garden centre ↻ (ex on leads in arboretum) ▬

Sezincote

GL56 9AW

➲ *(1.5m out of Moreton-in-Marsh on A44, Evesham road)*

☎ 01386 700444

e-mail: edwardpeake64@hotmail.com

web: www.sezincote.co.uk

The Indian-style house at Sezincote was the inspiration for Brighton Pavilion; its charming water garden adds to its exotic aura and features trees of unusual size.

Times Open: House, May-Sep, Thu, Fri & BH Mon 2.30-6. Garden only, all year (ex Dec) Thu, Fri & BH Mon 2-6 or dusk if earlier. **Fee** ✳ House & garden £7, Garden only £5 (ch £1.50). Children not allowed in the House. Groups by appointment only. **Facilities** ℗ ⬚ ⊞ ⅋ (some hills & gravel paths) toilets for disabled ⊗ (ex assist dogs)

Owlpen Manor   **2 for 1**

GL11 5BZ

⮕ *(3m E of Dursley, signed at village green in Uley off B4066)*

☎ 01453 860261

e-mail: sales@owlpen.com

web: www.owlpen.com

A romantic Tudor manor house, with unique 17th-century painted cloth wallhangings, furniture, pictures and textiles. The house is set in formal terraced gardens, and is part of a picturesque Cotswold manorial group including a Jacobean Court House, a Victorian church and medieval tithe barn.

Times Open: House, May-Sep, Tue, Thur & Sun 2-5. Gardens & Restaurant May-Sep, Tue,Thu & Sun from 12. **Fee** £5.75 (ch £2.75) Family ticket £15.25 (2ad + up to 4ch). **Facilities** ❷ ⏲ licensed ♿ (downstairs accessible) shop ⊗ ⚌

Painswick Rococo Garden

GL6 6TH

⮕ *(on B4073 0.5m NW of Painswick)*

☎ 01452 813204

e-mail: info@rococogarden.org.uk

web: www.rococogarden.org.uk

This beautiful Rococo garden (a compromise between formality and informality) is the only one of its period to survive complete. There are ponds, woodland walks, a maze, kitchen garden and herbacious borders, all set in a Cotswold valley famous for snowdrops in the early spring. Ring for details of special events.

Times Open 10 Jan-Oct, daily 11-5. **Fee** £5.50 (ch £2.75, pen £4.50) **Facilities** ❷ ⏲ licensed ⎘ (outdoor) ♿ (steep slopes) toilets for disabled shop garden centre ⚌

WWT Slimbridge

GL2 7BT

⮕ *(off A38, signed from M5 junct 13 & 14)*

☎ 01453 891900

e-mail: info.slimbridge@wwt.org.uk

web: www.wwt.org.uk

Slimbridge is home to the world's largest collection of exotic wildfowl - and the only place in Europe where all six types of flamingo can be seen. Up to 8,000 wild birds winter on the 800-acre reserve of flat fields, marsh and mudflats on the River Severn. Facilities include a tropical house, discovery centre, shop and restaurant. In summer there is a Land Rover safari into the reserve. 2009 is the centenary of the birth of the WWT's founder Sir Peter Scott.

Times Open all year, daily from 9.30-5.30 (winter 5). Closed 25 Dec. **Fee** ✳ £7.95 (ch £4.35, under 4's free, concessions £6.15). Family £20.50. **Facilities** ❷ ⏲ ⎘ ⎘ (outdoor) ♿ (wheelchair & scooter loan, hearing loops) toilets for disabled shop garden centre ⊗ (ex assist dogs) ⚌

Snowshill Manor

WR12 7JU

⮕ *(3m SW of Broadway, off A44)*

☎ 01386 852410

e-mail: snowshillmanor@nationaltrust.org.uk

web: www.nationaltrust.org.uk

Arts and crafts garden designed by its owner Charles Paget Wade in collaboration with M.H. Baillie Scott, as a series of outdoor rooms to compliment his traditional Cotswold manor house filled with a unique collection of craftsmanship including musical instruments, clocks, toys, bicycles and Japanese armour. This was the first National Trust garden to be managed following organic principles. It is a lively mix of cottage flowers, bright colours and delightful scents with stunning views across Cotswold countryside.

Times Open 19 Mar-2 Nov, Wed-Sun; house 12-5, garden: 1-5.30. **Fee** ✳ House & Garden: £8.10, (ch £4.10). Family £20.60. Groups £7. Garden, Restaurant & Shop: £4.40, (ch £2.20). Family £11.10 **Facilities** ❷ ⏲ ♿ (Braille guides, audio tapes, 2 manual wheelchairs) toilets for disabled shop ⊗ (ex assist dogs) ⚌ ⚌

MAP 03 SO61

TODDINGTON
MAP 04 SP03

2 for 1

Gloucestershire Warwickshire Steam Railway

The Railway Station GL54 5DT

➲ *(10m E of M5 junct 9 near junct of B4077 & B4632 between Winchcombe & Broadway)*

☎ 01242 621405

e-mail: enquiries@gwsr.com

web: www.gwsr.com

The railway runs along a part of the former Great Western Railway's mainline from Birmingham to Cheltenham, via Stratford-upon-Avon. The line commands wonderful views of the sleepy hamlets and villages, as it runs though the beautiful Cotswold countryside. The line was primarily built (1900-1906) to improve through services from Birmingham to Bristol and the West Country.

Times Open Mar-Dec, selected days & times. Call 01242 621405 for details. **Fee** ✳ £10 (ch 5-15 £6, under 5 free, concessions £8.50). Family (2 ad+3 ch) £27. **Facilities** ❷ ☐ ⧕ (outdoor) ♿ (Partly accessible) (specially converted carriage) toilets for disabled shop garden centre ▭

.com

m

lg point for a visit to the Forest. With five modern museum galleries, and a range of features designed to create a living history experience, there is plenty for all ages to enjoy, including Forester's Cottage, Freemine Entrance, and Charcoal Burner's Camp. There is a regular events programme and there are plenty of activities involving history, crafts and the Forest's wildlife. The lovely mill pond and surrounding five acres of woodland are home to lots of wildlife.

Times Open Summer 10-5, Winter 10-4, open BHs (ex 24-26 Dec), 1 Jan 11-4. **Fee** ✳ £4.90 (ch £2.50, under 5's free, concessions £4.20). Family £14. Party 10+ **Facilities** ❷ ☐ ⧕ (outdoor) ♿ (access to woodland area restricted due to uneven ground) (lift, ramps, staff assistance) toilets for disabled shop ⊗ (ex assist dogs) ▭

TETBURY
MAP 03 ST89

Chavenage House
2 for 1

Chavenage GL8 8XP

➲ *(2m NW of Tetbury signed off B4014. 7m SE of Stroud, signed off A46)*

☎ 01666 502329

e-mail: info@chavenage.com

web: www.chavenage.com

Built in 1576, this unspoilt Elizabethan house contains stained glass from the 16th-century and earlier with some good furniture and tapestries. The owner during the Civil War was a Parliamentarian, and the house contains Cromwellian relics. In more recent years, the house has been the location for *Grace and Favour*, *Poirot*, *The House of Elliot*, *Berkeley Square*, *Casualty*, *Cider with Rosie*, and in 2006, the BBC adaptation of *Dracula*. Tours of the house are enlivened by ghost stories.

Times Open May-Sep, Thu, Sun & BHs 2-5. Also Etr Sun & Mon. Other days by appointment only. **Fee** ✳ £6 (ch £3). **Facilities** ❷ ♿ (no lift to 2 rooms upstairs) ⊗ (ex assist dogs)

ULEY
MAP 03 ST79

Uley Long Barrow (Hetty Pegler's Tump)
FREE

➲ *(3.5m NE of Dursley on B4066)*

web: www.english-heritage.org.uk

This 180 foot Neolithic long barrow is popularly known as Hetty Pegler's Tump. The mound, surrounded by a wall, is about 85 feet wide. It contains a stone central passage, and three burial chambers.

Times Open at any reasonable time. **Facilities** ⌗

WESTBURY ON SEVERN
MAP 03 SO71

Westbury Court Garden
GL14 1PD

➲ *(9m SW of Gloucester on A48)*

☎ 01452 760461

e-mail: westburycourt@nationaltrust.org.uk

web: www.nationaltrust.org.uk

This formal water garden with canals and yew hedges was laid out between 1696 and 1705. It is the earliest of its kind remaining in England and was restored in 1971 and planted with species dated pre-1700, including apple, pear and plum trees.

Times Open 12 Mar-Jun, Wed-Sun, 10-5; Jul-Aug, daily 10-5; Sep-26 Oct, Wed-Sun, 10-5. Nov-Feb by appointment. Open BHs. **Fee** ✳ £4.50 (ch £2.25). Family £11.60 **Facilities** ♿ ⟊ ♿ (Braille guide, w/chair available) toilets for disabled ⊗ (ex assist dogs) ♨

WESTONBIRT
MAP 03 ST88

Westonbirt, The National Arboretum
GL8 8QS

➲ *(3m S Tetbury on A433)*

☎ 01666 880220

web: www.westonbirtarboretum.com

Begun in 1829, this arboretum contains one of the finest and most important collections of trees and shrubs in the world. There are 18,000 specimens, planted from 1829 to the present day, covering 600 acres of landscaped Cotswold countryside. Magnificent displays of rhododendrons, azaleas, magnolias and wild flowers, and a blaze of colour in the autumn from the national collection of Japanese Maples. Special events include the Festival of the Tree (Aug BH) and the Enchanted Christmas Trail (every Fri, Sat, Sun in December until Xmas).

Times Open all year, daily 10-8 or sunset. Visitor centre & shop all year. Closed Xmas & New Year. **Fee** ✳ Mar-Nov £7; Dec-Feb £5 . **Facilities** ♿ ⟊ ⊙ licensed ⟊ (outdoor) ♿ (electric & manual wheelchair for loan-telephone to book) toilets for disabled shop garden centre ⊟

WINCHCOMBE
MAP 04 SP02

Sudeley Castle, Gardens & Exhibitions
2 for 1

GL54 5JD

➲ *(B4632 to Winchcombe. Castle signed from town)*

☎ 01242 602308

e-mail: enquiries@sudeley.org.uk

web: www.sudeleycastle.co.uk

Sudeley Castle was home to Katherine Parr, who is buried in the Chapel. Henry VIII, Anne Boleyn, Lady Jane Grey and Elizabeth I all stayed or visited here; and it was the headquarters of Prince Rupert during the Civil War. The Queen's Garden is famous for its rose collection. There are exhibitions, a full and varied special events programme and plant centre. 2009 is the 500th anniversary of the coronation King Henry VIII.

Times Open 15 Mar-Oct, daily 10.30-5. **Fee** ✳ Ad £7.20 (ch £4.20, concessions £6.20). Family £20.80. **Facilities** ♿ ⟊ ⟊ (outdoor) ♿ (part of exhibition up stairs) toilets for disabled shop garden centre ⊗ ⊟

GREATER MANCHESTER

Dunham Massey Hall, Altrincham

ALTRINCHAM
MAP 07 SJ78

Dunham Massey

WA14 4SJ

⮑ *(3m SW of Altrincham (off A56), M6 junct 19 or M56 junct 7, then follow brown signs)*

☎ 0161 941 1025

e-mail: dunhammassey@nationaltrust.org.uk

web: www.nationaltrust.org.uk

A fine 18th-century house, garden and park, home of the Earls of Stamford until 1976. The house contains fine furniture and silverware, and some thirty rooms, including the library, billiard room, fully-equipped kitchen, butler's pantry and laundry. The garden is on an ancient site with waterside plantings, mixed borders and fine lawns. The ancient deer park has beautiful avenues and several ponds as well as a working sawmill where the waterwheel is demonstrated on afternoons in high season.

Times Open House: 28 Feb-1 Nov, Sat-Wed 11-5; Garden: 28 Feb-1 Nov daily, 11-5.30; 2 Nov-26 Feb daily, 11-4. Park: 28 Feb-1 Nov daily, 9-7.30; 2 Nov-26 Feb daily, 9-5. **Fee** ✳ House & Garden £7.50 (ch £3.75). House only £5 (ch £2.50). Group rate (pre-booked only), House & garden £6. Family ticket £18.75. Reduced rate when arriving on public transport. **Facilities** ℗ (charged) ⑩ ⊓ ᵫ (access restricted, steps with handrail to Great Hall & other floors) (w/chairs, lift, Braille & large print guide, pmv, parking) toilets for disabled shop ⊗ (ex assist, on lead in park) ❧ ▬

ASHTON-UNDER-LYNE
MAP 07 SJ99

Central Art Gallery

FREE

Central Library Building, Old St OL6 7SG

⮑ *(Near centre of town, off A635 (large Victorian building)).*

☎ 0161 342 2650

e-mail: central.artgallery@tameside.gov.uk

web: www.tameside.gov.uk

Set in a fine Victorian Gothic building, Central Art Gallery has three gallery spaces, each of which offers a varied programme of contemporary exhibitions. A range of tastes and styles are covered, with group and solo shows of work by artists from the region including paintings, sculpture, installation and textiles. Extensive education programmes for schools, children, families, adults and teenagers.

Times Open all year, Tue, Wed & Fri 10-5, Thu 1-7.30 & Sat 9-4.
Facilities ℗ (100mtrs) (pay and display. supermarket) ᵫ (induction loop) toilets for disabled shop ⊗ (ex assist dogs)

Museum of The Manchester Regiment

FREE

The Town Hall, Market Place OL6 6DL

⮑ *(in town centre, on market square, follow signs for museum)*

☎ 0161 342 2812 & 3710

e-mail: portland.basin@tameside.gov.uk

web: www.tameside.gov.uk

The social and regimental history of the Manchesters is explored at this museum, tracing the story back to its origins in the 18th century. Children can try on military headwear, experience a First World War trench, and try out the interactive 'A Soldier's Life'.

Times Open all year, Mon-Sat, 10-4. (Closed Sun). **Facilities** ℗ (50yds) (pay & display) ᵫ (lift) toilets for disabled ⊗ (ex assist dogs)

Portland Basin Museum

FREE

Portland Place OL7 0QA

⮑ *(M60 junct 23 into town centre. Museum near Cross Hill Street & car park. Follow brown signs with canal boat image)*

☎ 0161 343 2878

e-mail: portland.basin@tameside.gov.uk

web: www.tameside.gov.uk

Exploring the social and industrial history of Tameside, this museum is part of the recently rebuilt Ashton Canal Warehouse, constructed in 1834. Visitors can walk around a 1920s street, dress up in old hats and gloves, steer a virtual canal boat, and see the original canal powered waterwheel that once drove the warehouse machinery. Portland Basin Museum also features changing exhibitions and event programme.

Times Open all year, Tue-Sun 10-5. (Closed Mon, ex BHs) **Facilities** ℗ ⑩ ⊓ (outdoor) ᵫ (wheelchair, lift, loop system) toilets for disabled shop ⊗ (ex assist dogs) ▬

BRAMHALL
MAP 07 SJ88

Bramall Hall & Park

2 for 1

SK7 3NX

⮑ *(from A6 right at Blossoms public house through Davenport village then right - signed)*

☎ 0845 833 0974

e-mail: bramall.hall@stockport.gov.uk

web: www.bramallhall.org.uk

This large timber-framed hall dates from the 14th century, and is one of the finest black-and-white houses in the North West. It has rare 16th-century wall paintings and period furniture, and was the home of the Davenport family for 500 years. Much of the house is open to the public and available for hire. Open air concerts and plays are a feature in summer. 2-for-1 voucher not available for special events.

Times Open all year, Apr-Sep Sun-Thu 1-5, Fri & Sat 1-4, BH 11-5; Oct-1 Jan Tue-Sun 1-4, BH 11-4; 2 Jan-Good Fri Sat & Sun 12-4. Closed 25-26 Dec.
Fee £3.95 (ch & concessions £2.95). **Facilities** ℗ (charged) ⌑ ⊓ (outdoor) ᵫ (Partly accessible) (access for wheelchair users, guide book) toilets for disabled shop ⊗ (ex assist dogs) ▬

MANCHESTER MAP 07 SJ89

Gallery of Costume

Platt Hall, Rusholme M14 5LL

➲ *(in Platt Fields Park, Rusholme, access from Wilmslow Rd. 2m S of city centre)*

☎ 0161 224 5217

e-mail: a.jarvis@notes.manchester.gov.uk

With one of the most comprehensive costume collections in Great Britain, this gallery makes captivating viewing. Housed in a fine Georgian mansion, the displays focus on the changing styles of everyday fashion and accessories over the last 400 years. Contemporary fashion is also illustrated. Because of the vast amount of material in the collection, no one period is permanently illustrated.

Times ✳ Open to public on last Sat of month. Mon-Fri by appointment, please ring 0161 224 5217 **Facilities** ℗ shop ⊗ (ex assist dogs)

Imperial War Museum North FREE

The Quays, Trafford Wharf Rd, Trafford Park M17 1TZ

➲ *(M60 junct 9, join Parkway (A5081) towards Trafford Park. At 1st island take 3rd exit onto Village Way. At next island take 2nd exit onto Warren Bruce Rd. Right at T-junct onto Trafford Wharf Rd. Alternatively, leave M602 junct 2 and follow signs)*

☎ 0161 836 4000

e-mail: iwmnorth@iwm.org.uk

web: www.iwm.org.uk

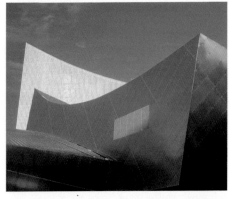

Imperial War Museum North features a wide range of permanent and temporary exhibitions exploring all the ways people's lives have been and still are affected by war and conflict. The award-winning building (designed by architect Daniel Libeskind) symbolises the world torn apart by conflict.

Times Open daily Mar-Oct 10-6, Nov-Feb 10-5. Closed 24-26 Dec. **Facilities** ℗ (charged) ⊑ ⋒ (indoor) ♿ (lifts, parking, wheelchairs, induction loop, audio tour) toilets for disabled shop ⊗ (ex assist dogs)

The John Rylands Library FREE

150 Deansgate M3 3EH

➲ *(off A56, at southern end of Deansgate)*

☎ 0161 306 0555

e-mail: jrl.visitors@manchester.ac.uk

web: www.manchester.ac.uk/library

Founded as a memorial to Manchester cotton-magnate and millionaire John Rylands, this is a public library, and also the Special Collections Division. It is widely regarded as one of the most beautiful libraries in the world. It extends to four million books, manuscripts and archival items representing some fifty cultures and ranging in date from the third millennium BC to the present day. Changing exhibitions throughout the year.

Times Open all year Mon, Fri & Sat 10-5, Tue & Sun 12-5. Closed 25-26 Dec & 1 Jan. **Facilities** ℗ (400yds) (pay and display) ⊑ ♿ toilets for disabled shop ⊗ (ex assist dogs)

Manchester Art Gallery FREE

Mosley St M2 3JL

➲ *(from M60 follow signs to city centre. Gallery close to Town Hall & Central Library)*

☎ 0161 235 8888

e-mail: mag@manchester.gov.uk

web: www.manchestergalleries.org

Manchester Art Gallery houses the city's magnificent art collection in stunning Victorian and contemporary surroundings. Highlights of the collection include outstanding Pre-Raphaelite works, crafts and design, and early 20th-century British art. The Clore Interactive Gallery has lively exhibits and multimedia facilities. There are also a wide range of events, from talks and tours to hands-on activities for children and adults. Contact for details of events and changing exhibitions.

Times Open Tue-Sun, 10-5 (closed Mon except BH). Closed Good Fri, 24-26 & 31 Dec & 1 Jan. **Facilities** ℗ (NCP-5 mins walk) ⊑ ⋒ licensed ♿ (w/chairs, induction loops, audio/Braille guides) toilets for disabled shop ⊗ (ex assist dogs)

Manchester Museum FREE

The University of Manchester, Oxford Rd M13 9PL

➲ *(S of city centre on B5117)*

☎ 0161 275 2634 & 2643

e-mail: museum@manchester.ac.uk

web: www.manchester.ac.uk/museum

Discover the natural wonders of the world and the many cultures it is home to. The objects in the Museum's 15 galleries tell the story of the past, present and future of our planet. Come face to face with live poison Dart frogs, fossils of pre-historic creatures and much more besides. Handle objects from the collection, take part in hands-on activities or enjoy a glass of wine or cup of coffee whilst exploring the latest ideas in science, culture and the arts. See website for details of family and adult events.

Times Open Tue-Sat 10-5, Sun-Mon & BHs 11-4. Closed Good Fri. **Facilities** ℗ (charged) ⊑ ⋒ licensed ⋒ (indoor) ♿ (lift access, accessible parking) (hearing loops, Braille & large print, object handling) toilets for disabled shop ⊗ (ex assist dogs) ▬

Manchester United Museum & Tour Centre

Sir Matt Busby Way, Old Trafford M16 0RA

➲ *(2m from city centre, off A56)*

☎ 0870 442 1994

e-mail: tours@manutd.co.uk

web: www.manutd.com

This museum was opened in 1986 and was the first purpose-built British football museum. It covers the history of Manchester United in words, pictures, sound and vision, from its inception in 1878 to the present day. Legends Tours are now available with ex-players, see website for full details.

Times Open daily 9.30-5 (open until 30mins before kick off on match days). Closed some days over Xmas & New Year. Some match day entry may vary due to matchday hospitality. **Fee** Stadium tour & Museum: £12 (ch & concessions £8) Family ticket (4) £35, (5) £40. Museum only £8.50 (ch & concessions £6.75) Family ticket (4) £25, (5) £30. **Facilities** ⊖ ⌾ & (w/chair, audio visual scripts) toilets for disabled shop ⊗ (ex assist dogs) ⊟

See advert on this page

Museum of Science and Industry

Liverpool Rd, Castlefield M3 4FP

➲ *(follow brown tourist signs from city centre)*

☎ 0161 832 2244

e-mail: marketing@mosi.org.uk

web: www.mosi.org.uk

Uncover Manchester's industrial past and learn the fascinating stories of the people who contributed to the history and science of a city which helped shape the modern world. Located on the site of the world's oldest passenger railway station, MoSI's action-packed galleries, working exhibits and costumed characters tell the amazing story of revolutionary discoveries and remarkable inventions both past and

CONTINUED

MANCHESTER CONTINUED

present. There is a programme of changing exhibitions, please see the website for details.

Times Open all year, daily 10-5. Last admission 4.30. Closed 24-26 Dec & 1 Jan. **Fee** All permanent galleries - Free. Charges apply for special exhibitions. **Facilities** ❷ (charged) ⬜❍ licensed ⊓ (indoor & outdoor) ♿ (lifts, wheelchair loan service) toilets for disabled shop ⊗ (ex assist dogs) ▬

Museum of Transport   `2 for 1`

Boyle St, Cheetham M8 8UW

➲ *(museum adjacent to Queens Rd bus depot. 1.25m N of city centre on Boyle St)*

☎ 0161 205 2122

e-mail: e-mail@gmts.co.uk

web: www.gmts.co.uk

This museum is a must-see for fans of public transport. Among the many interesting exhibits are more than 80 beautifully restored buses and coaches from the region - the biggest collection in the UK. Displays of old photographs, tickets and other memorabilia complement the vehicles, some of which date back to 1890. Please telephone for details of special events, most of which, unsurprisingly, relate to transport in some way.

Times Open all year Mar-Oct, 10-5; Nov-Feb, 10-4; Wed, Sat, Sun & BH ex Xmas **Fee** ✳ £4 (ch under 5 free, ch 5-15 & concessions £2, registered disabled, unemp free). Family ticket £10 (2ad+3ch). **Facilities** ❷ ⬜ ♿ toilets for disabled shop ⊗ (ex assist dogs) ▬

Urbis   `FREE`

Cathedral Gardens M4 3BG

➲ *(opposite Victoria railway station)*

☎ 0161 605 8200

e-mail: info@urbis.org.uk

web: www.urbis.org.uk

Urbis is an exhibition centre about city life. On your visit you can explore exhibitions of contemporary art and design, urban gardening, the city environment and the people who make our cities what they are. Family workshops take place every weekend, see the website for details.

Times Open daily, Sun-Wed, 10-6; Thu-Sat, 10-8. **Facilities** ⓟ (200yds) ⬜ ❍ licensed ⊓ (outdoor) ♿ toilets for disabled shop ⊗ (ex assist dogs) ▬

The Whitworth Art Gallery   `FREE`

The University of Manchester, Oxford Rd M15 6ER

➲ *(follow brown tourist signs, on Oxford Rd (B5117) to S of city centre. Gallery in Whitworth Park, opp Manchester Royal Infirmary)*

☎ 0161 275 7450

e-mail: whitworth@manchester.ac.uk

web: www.manchester.ac.uk/whitworth

The gallery houses an impressive range of modern and historic drawings, prints, paintings and sculpture, as well as the largest

collection of textiles and wallpapers outside London, and an internationally famous collection of British watercolours. The gallery hosts an innovative programme of touring exhibitions. A selection of tour lectures, workshops and concerts complement the exhibition programme.

Times Open Mon-Sat 10-5, Sun 2-5. Closed Good Fri & Xmas-New Year. **Facilities** ❷ ⬜ ⊓ ♿ (wheelchair available, induction loop, Braille lift buttons) toilets for disabled shop ⊗ (ex assist dogs)

PRESTWICH   MAP 07 SD80

Heaton Park   `FREE`

Heaton Park M25 2SW

➲ *(4m N of Manchester city centre. M60 junct 19, S on A576, then onto A6044 & A665, into St Margaret's Road. Park 100yds on right)*

☎ 0161 773 1085

e-mail: heatonpark@manchester.gov.uk

web: www.heatonpark.org.uk

600 acres of rolling parkland on the edge of Manchester; a traditional park for the whole family. Facilities include a Tram Museum, sports pitches, stables, farm and animals centres, and a horticultural centre. The hall was designed by James Wyatt for Sir Thomas Egerton in 1772, the house has magnificent period interiors decorated with fine plasterwork, paintings and furniture. Other attractions include a unique circular room with Pompeian-style paintings, and the original Samuel Green organ still in working order.

Times Park: Open all year daily, 8-dusk; Hall: Open Etr-early Sep, Thu-Sun & BH 11-5.30 **Facilities** ❷ (charged) ⬜ ⊓ (outdoor) ♿ (top floor not accessible) (disabled parking, land train from car park to facilities) toilets for disabled shop ⊗ (ex in grounds)

SALFORD   MAP 07 SJ89

The Lowry   `FREE`

Pier Eight, Salford Quays M50 3AZ

➲ *(M60 junct 12 for M602. Salford Quays is 0.25m from junct 3 of M602, follow brown Lowry signs)*

☎ 0870 787 5774

e-mail: info@thelowry.com

web: www.thelowry.com

The Lowry is an award-winning building housing galleries, shops, cafés and a restaurant, plus three theatres showing everything from West End plays and musicals, comedians, ballet and live bands. With regular family activity too, you can make a whole day of your visit.

Times ✳ Open daily from 10. Galleries, Sun-Fri from 11, Sat from 10. Closed 25 Dec. **Facilities** ❷ (charged) ⬜ ❍ ♿ (Sennheiser System, signed, audio & stage text) toilets for disabled shop ⊗ (ex assist dogs) ▬

Salford Museum & Art Gallery FREE

Peel Park, Crescent M5 4WU

➲ *(from N leave M60 junct 13, A666. From S follow signs from end of M602. Museum on A6)*

☎ 0161 736 2649

e-mail: salford.museum@salford.gov.uk

web: www.salfordmuseum.org

The museum features a reconstruction of a 19th-20th century northern street with original shop fronts. Upstairs in the galleries there are temporary exhibitions and a gallery displaying paintings, sculptures and ceramics. Recent additions include the lifetimes gallery, featuring audio, IT zones, temporary exhibitions, a spectacular Pilkington's display and lots of hands-on activities and dressing up areas.

Times ✳ Open all year Mon-Fri 10-4.45, Sat & Sun 1-5. Closed Good Fri, Etr Sat, 25 & 26 Dec, 1 Jan. **Facilities** ℗ ⬚ ♿ (Braille & large print labels & visitor packs, hearing loop) toilets for disabled shop ⊗ (ex assist dogs) ⬛

STALYBRIDGE   MAP 07 SJ99

Astley Cheetham Art Gallery FREE

Trinity St GK15 2BN

➲ *(N of town centre)*

☎ 0161 338 6767

e-mail: astley.cheetham@tameside.gov.uk

web: www.tameside.gov.uk

Built as a gift to the town in 1901 by mill owner John Frederick Cheetham, this one-time lecture hall has been an art gallery since 1932 when Cheetham left his collection to the town. Among the works are Italian paintings from the Renaissance, British masters such as Cox and Burne-Jones, and more recent gifts such as works by Turner and local artist Harry Rutherford. The gallery hosts a programme of temporary exhibitions of the collection and regional artists, and a variety of workshops are run for families throughout the year.

Times Open all year, Mon-Wed & Fri 10-12.30, 1-5; Sat 9-12.30, 1-4. **Facilities** ℗ (2hrs on street parking) ♿ (induction loop) ⊗ (ex assist dogs)

STOCKPORT   MAP 07 SJ89

Hat Works Museum

Wellington Mill, Wellington Rd South SK3 0EU

➲ *(M60 junct 1, on A6, Stockport town centre, follow signs for town centre. Museum opp bus station)*

☎ 0845 833 0975

e-mail: bookings.hatworks@stockport.gov.uk

web: www.hatworks.org.uk

Hat Works is the UK's only museum of the hatting industry, hats and headwear, offering an insight into a once flourishing industry. See how hats are made with a unique working collection of Victorian millinery machinery and take a tour with expert guides who will give visitors an insight into the Hatter's World. Browse an extensive collection of hats before relaxing in the Level 2 café. Exhibitions and events throughout the year, contact for details.

Times Open daily Mon-Fri 10-5, Sat, Sun & BHs 1-5. (Telephone for Xmas opening times) **Facilities** ℗ (5min walk) (limited pay & display parking) ⬚ ♿ (hearing loops) toilets for disabled shop ⊗ (ex assist dogs) ⬛

UPPERMILL   MAP 07 SD90

Saddleworth Museum & Art Gallery

High St OL3 6HS

➲ *(M62 E junct 22 or M62 W junct 21. On A670)*

☎ 01457 874093

e-mail: curator@saddleworthmuseum.co.uk

web: www.saddleworthmuseum.co.uk

Based in an old mill building next to the Huddersfield canal, the museum explores the history of the Saddleworth area. Wool weaving is the traditional industry, displayed in the 18th-century Weaver's Cottage and the Victoria Mill Gallery. The textile machinery is run regularly by arrangement. The Art Gallery has regular exhibitions.

Times Open all year: Apr-Oct, Mon-Sat 10-4.30; Sun 12-4; Nov-Mar, Mon-Sun 1-4. (Closed 24-25 & 31 Dec & 1 Jan) **Fee** Museum £2 (concessions £1) Family ticket £4. Art gallery free **Facilities** ℗ ♿ (chairlift to art gallery, ramp to ground floor galleries) (Braille & large print guides, wheelchair) toilets for disabled shop ⊗ (ex assist dogs)

HAMPSHIRE

New Forest National Park

ALDERSHOT MAP 04 SU85

Aldershot Military Museum `2 for 1`

Evelyn Woods Rd, Queens Av GU11 2LG

➲ *(A331 exit for 'Aldershot Military Town (North)',
attraction near to North Camp)*

☎ 01252 314598

e-mail: sally.1.day@hants.gov.uk

web: www.hants.gov.uk/museum/aldershot-museum

Follow the development of the 'Home of the British army' and the
'Birthplace of British aviation' through brand new displays. Also
discover the fascinating local history of Aldershot and Farnborough
including the first British powered flight, which took place in October
1908.

Times Open daily 10-5 (last admission 4.30) **Fee** ✳ £2 (ch under 5 free, ch
& concessions £1, pen £1.50) **Facilities** ♿ ⌷ (outdoor) ♿ toilets for
disabled shop ⊗ (ex assist dogs)

AMPFIELD MAP 04 SU42

The Sir Harold Hillier Gardens `2 for 1`

Jermyns Ln SO51 0QA

➲ *(2m NE of Romsey, signed off A3090 & A3057)*

☎ 01794 369318

e-mail: info@hilliergardens.org.uk

web: www.hilliergardens.org.uk

Open all year, Sir Harold Hillier Gardens offers 180 acres of beauty,
inspiration and discovery. Over 42,000 plants from temperate regions
around the world grow in a variety of landscapes. Visit the Children's
Education Garden and Europe's largest Winter Garden. Events,
exhibitions and workshops all year round. During May to October visit
the spectacular Art in the Garden annual outdoor exhibition, which has
its 10th anniversary in 2009, and features 150 sculptures set around
the gardens.

Times Open all year, daily, 10-6 (or dusk if earlier). Closed 25-26 Dec.
Fee £8.25 (ch under 16 free, concessions £7.15). Group bookings £6.60
Facilities ♿ ⌷ ⍝ licensed ⌷ (outdoor) ♿ (most pathways are fully
accessible) (wheelchairs & mobility scooters for hire pre-bookable) toilets for
disabled shop garden centre ⊗ (ex assist dogs)

ANDOVER MAP 04 SU34

Finkley Down Farm Park

SP11 6NF

➲ *(signed from A303 & A343, 1.5m N of A303 & 2m E
of Andover)*

☎ 01264 352195

e-mail: admin@finkleydownfarm.co.uk

web: www.finkleydownfarm.co.uk

This fun family farm park is jam packed with things to do. You can join
in with feeding time, groom a pony, or cuddle a rabbit. Lots of activities
are scheduled throughout the day, or kids can just let off steam in the
playground or on the trampolines. From chipmunks to chinchillas,
pygmy goats to peacocks, and lambs to llamas, Finkley Down Farm has
something for everyone.

Times Open mid Mar-Oct, daily 10-6 (last admission 5). **Fee** ✳ £6.50 (ch
£5.50, pen £6). Family ticket (2ad+2ch) £23 **Facilities** ♿ ⌷ ⌷ (outdoor)
♿ toilets for disabled shop ⊗ (ex assist dogs)

ASHURST MAP 04 SU31

Longdown Activity Farm `2 for 1`

Longdown SO40 7EH

➲ *(off A35 between Lyndhurst & Southampton)*

☎ 023 8029 2837

e-mail: enquiries@longdownfarm.co.uk

web: www.longdownfarm.co.uk

Fun for all the family with a variety of hands-on activities every day,
including small animal handling and bottle feeding calves and goat
kids. Indoor and outdoor play areas, with trampolines and ball pools.
Tearoom, picnic area and excellent gift shop. Farm shop selling locally
sourced produce.

Times Open Feb-Oct, daily 10-5. Wknds Nov-Dec, daily 13-21 Dec **Fee** ✳
£6.75 (ch 3-14 & concessions £5.75). Saver ticket £23 (2ad+2ch).
Facilities ♿ ⌷ ⌷ (indoor & outdoor) ♿ (concrete path for wheelchairs)
toilets for disabled shop ⊗ (kennels provided)

AVINGTON MAP 04 SU53

Avington Park

SO21 1DB

➲ *(off B3047 at Itchen Abbas between Winchester &
Alresford. 4m from both on River Itchen)*

☎ 01962 779260

e-mail: enquiries@avingtonpark.co.uk

web: www.avingtonpark.co.uk

Avington Park is a privately-owned house, which was once described
by William Cobbett as "one of the prettiest places in the county", and
has played host to Charles II and George IV. The state rooms consist of
the beautifully painted main hall, the library overlooking the south
lawns, adjoining and leading onto a unique pair of conservatories, the
old dining room and the ballroom upstairs with a magnificent gold
plasterwork ceiling and painted panels.

Times Open May-Sep, Sun & BHs 2.30-5.30 (10-11 Sep 2.30-5). Also open
Mon in Aug. **Fee** £4.50 **Facilities** ♿ ⌷ ♿ (2 staterooms only accessible
by stairs) toilets for disabled ⊗ (ex on leads)

BASINGSTOKE
MAP 04 SU65

Milestones - Hampshire's Living History Museum
`2 for 1`

Basingstoke Leisure Park, Churchill Way West RG22 6PG

➲ *(M3 junct 6, take ringway road (West). Follow brown Leisure Park signs)*

☎ 01256 477766

e-mail: jane.holmes@hants.gov.uk

web: www.milestones-museum.com

Milestones brings Hampshire's recent past to life through stunning period street scenes and exciting interactive areas, all under one roof. Nationally important collections of transport, technology and everyday life are presented in an entertaining way. Staff in period costumes, mannequins and sounds all bring the streets to life.

Times Open Tue-Fri & BHs 10-5, Sat-Sun 11-5. Closed Mon, 25-26 Dec & 1 Jan. **Fee** ✴ £7.50 (ch £4.50, under 5s free, concessions £6.75). Family ticket (2ad+2ch) £22. **Facilities** ❶ ⬛ ⊞ (indoor & outdoor) ♿ (Partly accessible) (induction loops, subtitles screens, scooters, wheelchairs) toilets for disabled shop ⊗ (ex assist dogs) ▬

BEAULIEU
MAP 04 SU30

Beaulieu : National Motor Museum
`2 for 1`

SO42 7ZN

➲ *(M27 junct 2, A326, B3054, then follow tourist signs)*

☎ 01590 612345

e-mail: info@beaulieu.co.uk

web: www.beaulieu.co.uk

Set in the heart of William the Conqueror's New Forest, on the banks of the Beaulieu River, stands this 16th-century house. It has become most famous as the home of the National Motor Museum. The site also contains the picturesque abbey building ruins, which have an exhibition on life in the middle ages, and various family treasures and memorabilia. The Secret Army Exhibition tells the story of the secret agents trained at the Beaulieu 'Finishing School' during WWII.

Times Open all year - Palace House & Gardens, National Motor Museum, Beaulieu Abbey & Exhibition of Monastic Life, May-Sep 10-6; Oct-Apr 10-5. Closed 25 Dec. **Fee** ✴ Please contact for current prices. **Facilities** ❶ ⬛ ⦿⬛ ⊞ (outdoor) ♿ (ramp access, lift to upper level, induction loop) toilets for disabled shop ▬

BISHOP'S WALTHAM
MAP 04 SU51

Bishop's Waltham Palace
`FREE`

SO32 1DH

➲ *(on A333)*

☎ 01489 892460

web: www.english-heritage.org.uk

Discover the medieval seat of the Bishops of Winchester. Enjoy the wonderful moated grounds and an exhibition about the powerful Winchester Bishops.

Times Grounds only: May-Sep, Sun-Fri 10-5. Farmhouse open by request. **Facilities** ❶ ⊞ shop ⊗ (ex on lead in certain areas) ⊞

BOLDRE
MAP 04 SZ39

Spinners Garden and Nursery

School Ln SO41 5QE

➲ *(off A337, between Brockenhurst & Lymington)*

☎ 01590 673347

The garden has been entirely created by the owners since 1960. It has azaleas, rhododendrons, camellias, magnolias and Japanese Maples interspersed with a huge range of woodland and bog plants. The nursery is well known for its rare trees, shrubs and plants. 2009 is the 50th anniversary of the garden.

Times Open Apr-14 Sep, daily 10-5. Other times on application. mid Sep-Mar Nursery & part of garden open. **Fee** £3 (ch under 6 free). Nursery & part of garden, free (mid Sep-Mar) **Facilities** ❶ ⊞ (outdoor) ♿ (part of garden unaccessible) (help provided where possible) garden centre ⊗ (ex assist dogs)

BREAMORE
MAP 04 SU11

Breamore House & Countryside Museum

SP6 2DF

➲ *(exit A338 between Salisbury & Fordingbridge. Follow signs for 1m)*

☎ 01725 512468

e-mail: breamore@btinternet.com

web: www.breamorehouse.com

The handsome manor house was completed in around 1583 and has a fine collection of paintings, china and tapestries. The museum has good examples of steam engines, and uses reconstructed workshops and other displays to show how people lived and worked a century or so ago. There is also a children's playground.

Times ✴ Open Apr, Tue, Sun & Etr, May-Sep, Tue-Thu & Sat, Sun & all BH; 2-5.30 (Countryside Museum 1pm). **Facilities** ❶ ⬛ ♿ (Partly accessible) (ramps, parking, recorded message & book about 1st floor) toilets for disabled shop ⊗ (ex assist dogs)

BUCKLERS HARD	MAP 04 SU40

Buckler's Hard Village & Maritime Museum

SO42 7XB

➲ *(M27 junct 2, A326, B3054 then follow tourist signs to Beaulieu & Buckler's Hard)*

☎ 01590 616203

e-mail: info@bucklershard.co.uk

web: www.bucklershard.co.uk

An enticing port of call, the historic and picturesque shipbuilding village of Buckler's Hard is where ships from Nelson's fleet were built. Enjoy the Buckler's Hard Story and the authentically reconstructed 18th-century historic cottages. Savour the sights and sounds of the countryside on a ramble along the riverside walk or enjoy a cruise on the Beaulieu river during the summer months.

Times Open all year daily from 10. Closed 25 Dec. **Fee** ✳ Please contact for current prices. **Facilities** ♿ ⬛ 🍴 ⏸ (outdoor) shop ⬛

BURGHCLERE	MAP 04 SU46

Sandham Memorial Chapel

Harts Ln RG20 9JT

➲ *(4m S Newbury, 0.5m E of A34. Follow signs to Highclere/Burghclere, then brown signs or white NT signs to Chapel)*

☎ 01635 278394

e-mail: sandham@nationaltrust.org.uk

web: www.nationaltrust.org.uk/sandham

This red brick chapel was built in the 1920s for the artist Stanley Spencer to fill with paintings inspired by his experiences in WWI. Influenced by Giotto's Arena Chapel in Padua, Spencer took five years to complete what is arguably his finest achievement. The chapel is set amongst lawns and orchards with views over Watership Down. The chapel has no internal lighting, so its best to visit on a bright day. 2008 is the 90th Anniversary of the end of the Great War, 2009 is the 50th anniversary of Stanley Spencer's death.

Times Open wknds in Mar & Nov-21 Dec 11-3; Apr-29 Sep , Wed-Sun incl BH 11-5; 30 Sep-1 Nov, Wed-Sun 11-3. **Fee** £4 (ch £2). **Facilities** ♿ (20yds) ⏸ (outdoor) ♿ (portable ramps available for manual wheelchairs to chapel) (Braille guide, large print guide, hearing loop, ramps) ✖ (ex assist dogs) 🐕

CHAWTON	MAP 04 SU73

Jane Austen's House

GU34 1SD

➲ *(1m SW of Alton, in centre of village)*

☎ 01420 83262

e-mail: enquiries@jane-austens-house-museum.org.uk

web: www.jane-austens-house-museum.org.uk

Jane Austen lived and wrote here from 1809 to 1817. Restored to look as it would have done in the early 1800s, with items such as the author's donkey cart and writing table to be seen.

Times ✳ Open daily Mar-Dec; Jan-Feb wknds only. Also open 27 Dec-1 Jan & Feb half term. **Facilities** ♿ (100yds) ⏸ (outdoor) ♿ (wheelchair ramp) toilets for disabled shop ✖ (ex assist dogs) ⬛

EXBURY	MAP 04 SU40

Exbury Gardens & Railway

Exbury Estate Office SO45 1AZ

➲ *(from M27 W junct 2, 3m from Beaulieu, off B3054)*

☎ 023 8089 1203

e-mail: nigel.philpott@exbury.co.uk

web: www.exbury.co.uk

A 200-acre landscaped woodland garden on the east bank of the Beaulieu River, with one of the finest collections of rhododendrons, azaleas, camellias and magnolias in the world - as well as many rare and beautiful shrubs and trees. A labyrinth of tracks and paths enable you to explore the beautiful gardens and walks. Year round interest is ensured in various parts of the gardens and a steam railway has several features. Exbury is National Collection holder for Nyssa and Oxydendrum, spectacular trees for autumn colour.

Times Open Mar-mid Nov, daily 10-5.30; Santa Steam Specials in Dec **Fee** ✳ £7.50 (ch under 3 free, ch 3-15 £1.50, concessions £7). Family £17.50 (2ad+3ch) Railway £3, please note the railway has 4 carriages accessible to wheelchairs. **Facilities** ♿ 🍴 licensed ⏸ (outdoor) ♿ (most pathways accessible) (free wheelchair loans, access maps, buggy tours £3.50) toilets for disabled shop garden centre ⬛

FAREHAM	MAP 04 SU50

Royal Armouries Fort Nelson

Portsdown Hill Rd PO17 6AN

➲ *(from M27 junct 11, follow brown tourist signs for Royal Armouries).*

☎ 01329 233734

e-mail: fnenquiries@armouries.org.uk

web: www.royalarmouries.org

Home to the Royal Armouries' collection of over 350 big guns and cannon, this superbly restored Victorian fort overlooks Portsmouth Harbour. Built in the 1860s to deter a threatened French invasion, there are secret tunnels, underground chambers and grass ramparts to explore with daily guided tours. Events throughout the year include

CONTINUED

FAREHAM CONTINUED

re-enactments of American Civil War, WWI and Napoleonic battles, and the Royal Armouries Military Tattoo. Contact Fort Nelson for details.

Times Open Apr-Oct, daily 10-5 (Wed 11-5); Nov-Mar, daily 10.30-4 (Wed 11.30-4) Closed 24-26 Dec. **Fee** ✳ Free. There may be a charge for special events/workshops. **Facilities** ❷ ☷ ⼤ (outdoor) ⅙ (access & audio guide, ramps, induction loop, wheelchair) toilets for disabled shop ⊗ (ex assist dogs) ▄

GOSPORT   MAP 04 SZ69

Explosion! Museum of Naval Firepower   `2 for 1`

Priddy's Hard PO12 4LE

⮌ (M27 junct 11, A32 and follow signs)

☎ 023 9250 5600

e-mail: info@explosion.org.uk

web: www.explosion.org.uk

Explosion! The Museum of Naval Firepower is set in the green Heritage Area of Priddy's Hard in Gosport on the shores of Portsmouth Harbour, telling the story of naval firepower from the days of gunpowder to modern missiles. Come face to face with the atom bomb, the Exocet missile and the Gatling Gun and take a trip into the fascinating story of the men and women who supplied the Royal Navy. Walk around the buildings that were a state secret for 200 years and discover the Grand Magazine, an amazing vault once packed full with gunpowder, now a stunning multimedia film show.

Times Open all year, Sat-Sun only, 10-4. **Fee** ✳ £4 (ch £2, concessions £3). Family ticket £10 **Facilities** ❷ ☷ ⼝⌽ licensed ⼤ (outdoor) shop ⊗ (ex assist dogs) ▄

Royal Navy Submarine Museum

Haslar Jetty Rd PO12 2AS

⮌ (M27 junct 11, follow brown tourist signs)

☎ 023 9252 9217 & 9251 0354

e-mail: rnsubs@rnsubmus.co.uk

web: www.rnsubmus.co.uk

The great attraction of this museum is the chance to see inside a submarine, and there are guided tours of HMS Alliance, as well as displays exploring the development of submarines. Two periscopes from HMS Conqueror can be seen in the reconstruction of a nuclear submarine control room, giving panoramic views of Portsmouth Harbour. One gallery shows the development of submarine weapons from the tiny torpedo to the huge polaris nuclear missile. The Navy's first submarine is also on display.

Times Open all year, Apr-Oct 10-5.30; Nov-Mar 10-4.30. (Allow 3 hrs for visit. Last tour 1 hour before closing). Closed 24 Dec-3 Jan **Fee** £8 (ch & concessions £6). Family (2ad+4ch) £20. Discounted entry scheme Defence of the Realm, in association with Southern Military Museums. **Facilities** ❷ ☷ ⼤ (outdoor) ⅙ (information in Braille, lift to upper gallery) toilets for disabled shop ⊗ (ex assist dogs) ▄

HARTLEY WINTNEY   MAP 04 SU75

West Green House Gardens

West Green RG27 8JB

⮌ (off A30, at Phoenix Green take sign to West Green, along Thackhams Lane. House last left)

☎ 01252 844611

e-mail: enquiries@westgreenhouse.co.uk

web: www.westgreenhouse.co.uk

The gardens are considered to be one of the top 50 gardens in England and were the subject of a whole edition of the BBC's Gardener's World. Today the Queen Anne house is surrounded by four walled gardens, lakes, follies, the green theatre, nymphaeum, mixed border and potager. The owner is noted garden writer and lecturer Marylyn Abbott. Music and opera performances are a regular feature.

Times ✳ Open 3 May-19 Aug Wed, Thu, Sat, Sun. 11-4.30. **Facilities** ❷ ⼝⌽ ⼤ ⅙ (Partly accessible) (most areas accessible) shop garden centre ⊗ (ex assist dogs) ▄

HAVANT   MAP 04 SU70

Staunton Country Park

Middle Park Way PO9 5HB

⮌ (off B2149, between Havant & Horndean)

☎ 023 9245 3405

e-mail: sam.brown@hants.gov.uk

web: www.hants.gov.uk/staunton

Set in the Regency pleasure grounds of Sir George Staunton, 19th-century traveller, Orientalist and patron of horticulture, Staunton boasts an ornamental farm, the largest ornamental glasshouses on the South Coast, 1,000 acres of parkland, with ancient woodland and intriguing follies and much, much more. Children can feed farm animals, or visit the play area while the grown-ups stroll through the walled gardens or get lost in the Golden Jubilee Maze.

Times Open 10-5 (4 winter). **Fee** £6 (ch £4.50, pen £4.50). Prices valid until Mar 2009. **Facilities** ❷ ☷ ⼝⌽ ⼤ (outdoor) ⅙ (most areas accessible) (wheelchair for visitors, lift) toilets for disabled shop ⊗ (ex in parkland & assist dogs) ▄

HIGHCLERE   MAP 04 SU45

Highclere Castle & Gardens   `2 for 1`

RG20 9RN

⮌ (4.5m S of Newbury, off A34)

☎ 01635 253210

e-mail: theoffice@highclerecastle.co.uk

web: www.highclerecastle.co.uk

This splendid early Victorian mansion stands in beautiful parkland on the site of a previous house, which in turn was built on the site of an even earlier house owned by the Bishops of Winchester. It has sumptuous interiors and numerous Old Master pictures. Also shown are early finds by the 5th Earl of Carnarvon, one of the discoverers of Tutankhamun's tomb. During WWI it was a hospital, and during WWII it was a home for evacuee children.

Times Open Jul-Aug, Sun-Thu (last entry 3.30). Telephone 01635 253210 before travelling as Highclere Castle reserves the right to close at other times. **Fee** ✳ £8 (ch £4, concessions £7). Family ticket (2ad+2ch or 1ad+3ch) £20. **Facilities** ❷ ⊡ ♬ (outdoor) ♿ (first floor landing/bedrooms not accessible) (wheelchair available) toilets for disabled shop ✪ (ex assist dogs) ☕

HINTON AMPNER   MAP 04 SU62

Hinton Ampner

SO24 0LA

➲ (off A272, 1m W of Bramdean)

☎ 01962 771305

e-mail: hintonampner@nationaltrust.org.uk

web: www.nationaltrust.org.uk

A masterpiece of design by Ralph Dutton, 8th and last Lord Sherborne, the 12 acre garden unites a formal layout with varied and informal plantings in pastel shades. There are magnificent vistas over 80 acres of parkland and rolling Hampshire countryside. The house, which is tenanted, contains Ralph Dutton's fine collection of Regency furniture, Italian paintings and hardstone items.

Times Garden open: 14 Mar-1 Nov, 11-5 & Good Fri. House open 14 Mar-1 Nov, 11.30-5 & BH Mon. **Fee** ✳ House and Garden £6.50 (ch £3.75). Group £5.75 each. Garden only £5.50 (ch £2.75) **Facilities** ❷ ⊡ ♬ (outdoor) ♿ (ground floor of house only accessible) (Braille guides, special parking, wheelchair loan) toilets for disabled shop ✪ (ex assist dogs) ⚘☕

HURST CASTLE   MAP 04 SZ38

Hurst Castle

SO4 0FF

➲ (on Pebble Spit S of Keyhaven)

☎ 01590 642344

web: www.english-heritage.org.uk

Built by Henry VIII, Hurst Castle was the pride of Tudor England's coastal defences. Crouched menacingly on a shingle spit, the castle has a fascinating history, including involvement in the smuggling trade in the 17th and 18th centuries.

Times Open 21 Mar-Oct, daily 10.30-5.30. **Fee** £3.20 (concessions £3, ch £2). Prices and opening times are subject to change in March 2009. Please call 0870 333 1181 for the most up to date prices and opening times when planning your visit. **Facilities** ⊡ ✪ (ex on lead in certain areas) ⚏

LIPHOOK   MAP 04 SU83

Hollycombe Steam In The Country

Iron Hill, Midhurst Rd GU30 7LP

➲ (1m SE Liphook on Midhurst road, follow brown tourist signs)

☎ 01428 724900

e-mail: info@hollycombe.co.uk

web: www.hollycombe.co.uk

A comprehensive collection of working steam-power, including a large Edwardian fairground, three railways, one with spectacular views of the South Downs, traction engine hauled rides, steam agricultural

machinery, pets corner, sawmill and even a paddle steamer engine. Festival of Steam 1st weekend in July.

Hollycombe Steam In The Country

Times Open Apr-mid Oct Sun & BHs, 26 Jul-25 Aug, daily 12-5 **Fee** ✳ £11 (ch 3-15 £9 & pen £10). **Facilities** ❷ ⊡ ♬ (outdoor) ♿ (Partly accessible) toilets for disabled shop ✪ (ex assist dogs) ☕

LYNDHURST   MAP 04 SU30

The New Forest Centre

Main Car Park, High St SO43 7NY

➲ (leave M27 at Cadnam & follow A337 to Lyndhurst. Visitor Centre signed)

☎ 023 8028 3444

e-mail: office@newforestmuseum.org.uk

web: www.newforestmuseum.org.uk

The story of the New Forest - history, traditions, character and wildlife, told through an audio-visual show and exhibition displays. With life-size models of Forest characters, and the famous New Forest embroidery. Events and exhibitions throughout the year, and children's activities on Tuesdays and Thursdays during every school holiday. Contact for details.

Times Open all year daily, from 10. Closed 25-26 Dec & 1 Feb) **Fee** ✳ £3 (ch under 16 free, concessions £2.50). **Facilities** ❷ (charged) ♿ (lift to 1st floor) toilets for disabled shop ☕

MARWELL   MAP 04 SU52

Marwell Zoological Park

Colden Common SO21 1JH

➲ (M3 junct 11 or M27 junct 5. On B2177, follow brown tourist signs)

☎ 01962 777407

e-mail: marwell@marwell.org.uk

web: www.marwell.org.uk

Marwell has over 200 species of rare and wonderful animals including tigers, snow leopards, rhino, meerkats, hippo and zebra. Highlights include The World of Lemurs, Encounter Village, Tropical World with its rainforest environment, Into Africa for giraffes and monkeys, Penguin

CONTINUED

MARWELL CONTINUED

World and Desert Carnivores. Recent additions include an exciting new snow leopard enclosure and a walkway that enables visitors to come face to face with the giraffes. Marwell is dedicated to saving endangered species and every visit helps conservation work. With road and rail trains, holiday activities, gift shop and adventure playgrounds Marwell provides fun and interest for all ages.

Times Open all year, daily 10-6 (summer), 10-4 (winter). (Last admission 90 mins before closing). Closed 25 Dec. **Fee** ✳ £14.50 (ch £10.50, concession £12.50). Family ticket (2ad+2ch) £46.50. **Facilities** 🅿 ⬛ 🍴 🎌 (outdoor) ♿ (Partly accessible) toilets for disabled shop ⊗ ➡

MIDDLE WALLOP   MAP 04 SU23

Museum of Army Flying
`2 for 1`

SO20 8DY

➲ *(on A343, between Andover & Salisbury)*

☎ 01264 784421

e-mail: administration@flying-museum.org.uk

web: www.flying-museum.org.uk

One of the country's finest historical collections of military kites, gliders, aeroplanes and helicopters. Imaginative dioramas and displays trace the development of Army flying from before the First World War to more recent conflicts in Ireland, the Falklands and the Gulf. Sit at the controls of a real Scout helicopter and test your skills on the flight simulator, plus children's education centre and 1940s house.

Times Open all year, daily 10-4.30. Closed week prior to Xmas. Evening visits by special arrangement. Private functions welcome. **Fee** ✳ £7 (ch £4.50, concessions £5) Family £21. **Facilities** 🅿 ⬛ 🍴 licensed 🎌 (outdoor) ♿ (lifts to upper levels) toilets for disabled shop ⊗ (ex assist dogs) ➡

MINSTEAD   MAP 04 SU21

Furzey Gardens

SO43 7GL

➲ *(1m S of junct A31/M3 Cadnam off A31 or A337 near Lyndhurst)*

☎ 023 8081 2464 & 2297

e-mail: info@furzey-gardens.org

web: www.furzey-gardens.org

A large thatched gallery is the venue for refreshments and displays of local arts and crafts, and the eight acres of peaceful glades which surround it include winter and summer heathers, rare flowering trees and shrubs and a mass of spring bulbs. There is a 16th-century cottage, lake, and the nursery, run by the Minstead Training Project for Young People with Learning Disabilities, sells a wide range of produce.

Times Gardens open daily, 10-5 (or dusk if earlier). Gallery open Mar-Oct, 10-5 **Fee** ✳ £5.50 (ch £2, pen £4.50) Family £13 **Facilities** 🅿 ⬛ 🎌 (outdoor) ♿ (garden access for wheelchair visitors with assistance) toilets for disabled shop garden centre ⊗ (ex assist dogs) ➡

MOTTISFONT   MAP 04 SU32

Mottisfont Abbey & Garden

SO51 0LP

➲ *(4.5m NW Romsey, 1m W of A3057)*

☎ 01794 340757

e-mail: mottisfontabbey@nationaltrust.org.uk

web: www.nationaltrust.org.uk/mottisfontabbey

In a picturesque setting by the River Test, Mottisfont Abbey is an 18th-century house adapted from a 12th-century priory. The north front shows its medieval church origins quite clearly, and the garden has splendid old trees and a walled garden planted with the national collection of old-fashioned roses. The estate includes Mottisfont village and surrounding farmland and woods.

Times House: Open daily Mar-29 Oct 11-5 (close Fri 21 Apr-25 May & 30 Jun-29 Oct). Garden: Open all year daily Mar-29 Oct 11-5 (close Fri 21 Apr-25 May & 30 Jun-29 Oct). Nov-Feb Sat & Sun only. **Facilities** 🅿 ⬛ 🍴 🎌 (outdoor) ♿ (Braille guide, wheelchair available, driven buggy) toilets for disabled shop garden centre ⊗ (ex assist dogs) 🌱 ➡

NETLEY   MAP 04 SU40

Netley Abbey
`FREE`

SO31 5FB

➲ *(4m SE of Southampton, facing Southampton Water)*

☎ 023 9258 1059

web: www.english-heritage.org.uk

A romantic ruin, set among green lawns and trees, this 13th-century Cistercian abbey was founded by Peter des Roches, tutor to Henry III. Nearby is the 19th-century Gothic Netley Castle.

Times Open all year, 21 Mar-Sep, daily 10-6 (guided tour 11am Sat during Aug only); Oct-Mar, Sat-Sun 10-3. Closed 24-26 Dec & 1 Jan. **Facilities** 🅿 ⊗

NEW ALRESFORD   MAP 04 SU53

Watercress Line   **2 for 1**

The Railway Station SO24 9JG

➲ *(stations at Alton & Alresford signed off A31, follow brown tourist signs)*

☎ 01962 733810

e-mail: info@watercressline.co.uk
web: www.watercressline.co.uk

The Watercress Line runs through ten miles of rolling scenic countryside between Alton and Alresford. All four stations are `dressed' in period style, and there's a locomotive yard and picnic area at Ropley. Special events throughout the year including Thomas the Tank Engine and Santa Specials.

Times Open Jan-Oct wknds, May-Sep midwk, Aug daily. **Fee** ✳ Unlimited travel for the day, £12 (ch £6). Family ticket £30 (2ad+2ch). Charge for dogs. Pre-booked groups 15+ discount available. **Facilities** ❷ (charged) ⬚ ⎰◎⎱ licensed ⊓ (outdoor) ⚐ (ramp access to trains) toilets for disabled shop ▰

NEW MILTON   MAP 04 SZ29

Sammy Miller Motorcycle Museum

Bashley Cross Rd BH25 5SZ

➲ *(signed off A35, 15m W of Southampton, 10m E of Bournemouth, N of New Milton town centre)*

☎ 01425 620777 & 616644

e-mail: info@sammymiller.co.uk
web: www.sammymiller.co.uk

The museum houses over 300 rare and classic bikes and with machines dating back to 1900, some are the only surviving examples of their type. The Racing collection features World Record breaking bikes and their history, including the first bike to lap a Grand Prix Course at over 100 miles per hour. The collection constantly evolves as new bikes are acquired, almost every bike is in full running order.

Times Open daily 10-4.30. Closed wkdys Dec-Feb. **Fee** £5.90 (ch £3). **Facilities** ❷ ⬚ ◎⎱ ⊓ (outdoor) ⚐ (upstairs inaccessible) (special rates for disabled people) toilets for disabled shop ⊗ (ex assist dogs) ▰

OLD BASING   MAP 04 SU65

Basing House

Redbridge Ln RG24 7HB

➲ *(signed from Basingstoke ring road)*

☎ 01256 467294

The largest private house of Tudor England, almost entirely destroyed by Parliamentary forces during a two-year siege ending in 1645. Built on the site of a Norman castle in 1530, the ruins include a 300ft long tunnel. There is a re-creation of a garden of 1600 and exhibitions showing the history of the house. A fine 16th-century barn stands nearby.

Times ✳ Open Apr-Sep, Wed-Sun & BH 2-6. **Facilities** ❷ ⊓ (outdoor) ⚐ (Partly accessible) (disabled parking by prior arangement) toilets for disabled shop

---

OWER   MAP 04 SU31

Paultons Park

SO51 6AL

➲ *(exit M27 junct 2, near junct A31 & A36)*

☎ 023 8081 4442

e-mail: info@paultons.co.uk
web: www.paultonspark.co.uk

Paultons Park offers a great day out for all the family with over 50 different attractions. Many fun activities include the Cobra ride, drop rides, roller coaster, 6-lane astroglide, teacup ride, log flume, pirate ship swingboat, dragon roundabout, and wave-runner coaster. Attractions for younger children include Kid's Kingdom, Tiny Tots Town, Rabbit Ride, the Magic Forest where nursery rhymes come to life, Wonderful World of Wind in the Willows and the Ladybird ride. In beautiful parkland setting with extensive `Capability' Brown gardens landscaped with ponds and aviaries for exotic birds; lake and hedge maze. There is also the Romany Experience Museum with unique collection of gypsy wagons and the Village Life Museum. Something for everyone.

Times Open mid Mar-Oct, daily 10-6; Nov & Dec, wknds only until Xmas. **Fee** ✳ £16. Children under 1m tall enter for free. Range of Family Supersavers. **Facilities** ❷ ⬚ ◎⎱ ⊓ ⚐ (pre-booked wheelchair hire, some rides unsuitable) toilets for disabled shop ⊗ (ex assist dogs) ▰

PORTCHESTER   MAP 04 SU60

Portchester Castle

Castle St PO16 9QW

➲ *(off A27)*

☎ 023 9237 8291

web: www.english-heritage.org.uk

Discover 2,000 years of history from its Roman beginnings to the years of medieval splendour. Stand where Henry V rallied his troops before setting out to the battle of Agincourt in 1415.

Times Open all year, 21 Mar-Sep, daily 10-6; Oct-Mar, daily 10-4. Closed 24-26 Dec & 1 Jan. **Fee** £4.20 (concessions £3.40, ch £2.10). Family £10.50. Prices and opening times are subject to change in March 2009. Please call 0870 333 1181 for the most up to date prices and opening times when planning your visit. **Facilities** ❷ shop ⊗ (ex on lead in certain areas) ⧈

ENGLAND

PORTSMOUTH

MAP 04 SU60

Blue Reef Aquarium

Clarence Esplanade PO5 3PB

⮕ *(on approach to city follow brown tourist signs to seafront or Aquarium. Located on Southsea seafront between D-Day Museum and The Hoverport)*

☎ 023 9287 5222

e-mail: portsmouth@bluereefaquarium.co.uk

web: www.bluereefaquarium.co.uk

Spectacular underwater walkthrough tunnels offer amazing sights of exotic coral reefs - home to sharks and shimmering shoals of brightly-coloured fish. Mediterranean and tropical waters are recreated in giant ocean tanks, home to a stunning array of undersea life including seahorses, puffer fish, coral, piranhas, and incredible crustaceans. Visit the website for current special events.

Times Open daily from 10. Closing times vary with season, please telephone for details. **Fee** ✳ £8.75 (ch £6.75, pen & students £7.95) **Facilities** ℗ (under 50mtrs) ⍁ 🗮 (outdoor) ⮫ (all on 1 level) toilets for disabled shop ⊗ (ex assist dogs) 🖭

Charles Dickens' Birthplace Museum

393 Old Commercial Rd PO1 4QL

⮕ *(M27/M275 into Portsmouth, from M275 turn left at 'The News' rdbt. Signed)*

☎ 023 9282 7261

e-mail: mvs@portsmouthcc.gov.uk

web: www.charlesdickensbirthplace.co.uk

A small terraced house built in 1805 which became the birthplace and early home of the famous novelist, born in 1812. On display are items pertaining to Dickens' work, portraits of the Dickens' family, and the couch on which he died. Dickens readings are given in the exhibition room on the first Sunday of each month at 3pm.

Times Open Apr-Sep, daily 10-5.30 (Last admission 5). **Fee** ✳ £3.50 (ch & student £2.50, accompanied ch under 13 free, concessions £3). Family £9.50. **Facilities** ℗ (150mtrs) shop ⊗ (ex assist dogs) 🖭

City Museum & Records Office   FREE

Museum Rd PO1 2LJ

⮕ *(M27/M275 into Portsmouth, follow museum symbol, City Museum on Brown signposts)*

☎ 023 9282 7261

e-mail: mvs@portsmouthcc.gov.uk

web: www.portsmouthcitymuseums.co.uk/

Dedicated to local history, fine and decorative art, 'The Story of Portsmouth' displays room settings showing life here from the 17th century to the 1950s. The 'Portsmouth at Play' exhibition features leisure pursuits from the Victorian period to the 1970s. The museum has a fine and decorative art gallery, plus a temporary exhibition gallery with regular changing exhibitions. The Record Office contains the official records of the City of Portsmouth from the 14th century.

Times Open all year, Apr-Sep daily 10-5.30; Oct-Mar daily 10-5. Closed 24-26 Dec & Record Office closed on public hols. **Facilities** ℗ ⍁ 🗮 (outdoor) ⮫ (induction loops, lift & wheelchairs, parking) toilets for disabled shop ⊗ (ex assist dogs) 🖭

D-Day Museum & Overlord Embroidery

Clarence Esplanade PO5 3NT

⮕ *(M27/M275 or M27/A2030 into Portsmouth, follow signs for seafront then D-Day museum name signs).*

☎ 023 9282 7261

e-mail: mvs@portsmouthcc.gov.uk

web: www.ddaymuseum.co.uk

Portsmouth's D-Day Museum tells the dramatic story of the Allied landings in Normandy in 1944. Centrepiece is the magnificent 'Overlord Embroidery', 34 individual panels and 83 metres in length. Experience the world's largest ever seaborne invasion, and step back in time to scenes of wartime Britain. Military equipment, vehicles, landing craft and personal memories complete this special story. 2009 is the 65th anniversary of the D-Day landings.

Times Open all year, Apr-Sep daily 10-5.30; Oct-Mar, 10-5. Closed 24-26 Dec **Fee** ✳ £6 (ch £4.20, concessions £5). Family £16.20. **Facilities** ℗ (charged) ⍁ 🗮 (outdoor) ⮫ (induction loops, sound aids, w/chairs available) toilets for disabled shop ⊗ (ex assist dogs) 🖭

Eastney Beam Engine House   FREE

Henderson Rd, Eastney PO4 9JF

⮕ *(accessible from A3(M), A27 & A2030 into Southsea, turn left at Bransbury Park traffic lights towards the seafront or follow signposts)*

☎ 023 9282 7261

e-mail: mvs@portsmouthcc.gov.uk

web: www.portsmouthmuseums.co.uk

The main attraction here is a magnificent pair of James Watt Beam Engines still housed in their original High-Victorian engine house opened in 1887. One of these engines is in steam when the museum is open. A variety of other pumping engines, many in running order are also on display.

Times Open last wknd of month, 1-5 (last admission 30 minutes before closing). Closed Dec. **Facilities** ℗ (300mtrs) ⮫ shop ⊗ (ex assist dogs)

Natural History Museum & Butterfly House

FREE

Cumberland House, Eastern Pde PO4 9RF

⮕ *(accessed via A3(M), A27 or A2030, follow signs to seafront)*

☎ 023 9282 7261

e-mail: mvs@portsmouthcc.gov.uk

web: www.portsmouthnaturalhistory.co.uk

Focusing on the natural history and geology of the area, with wildlife dioramas including a riverbank scene with fresh water aquarium. During the summer British and European butterflies fly free in the Butterfly House.

Times Open all year daily, Apr-Oct 10-5.30; Nov-Mar 10-5. **Facilities** Ⓟ (200mtrs) ♿ shop ⊗ (ex assist dogs) ▄

Portsmouth Historic Dockyard

HM Naval Base PO1 3LJ

⮕ *(M27/M275 & follow brown historic waterfront and dockyard signs)*

☎ 023 9283 9766

e-mail: enquiries@historicdockyard.co.uk

web: www.historicdockyard.co.uk

Portsmouth Historic Dockyard is home to the world's greatest historic ships: *Mary Rose* - King Henry VIII's favourite ship, *HMS Victory* - Lord Nelson's flagship at the Battle of Trafalgar and *HMS Warrior* - the first iron-hulled warship. In addition, the Royal Naval Museum has the most significant, permanent collections relating to Nelson and the Battle of Trafalgar, and Action Stations gives an interactive insight into the modern day Royal Navy.   April/June 2009 - 500th anniversary of Henry VIII's coronation and commission of *Mary Rose*.   July/August 2009, 250th anniversary of Laying of the Keel of *HMS Victory*.

Times Open Apr-Oct, daily 10-6 (last entry 4.30); Nov-Mar, daily 10-5.30 (last entry 4). **Fee** ✳ All inclusive ticket: £16.50 (ch £12 under 5 free, concessions £14). Family £48. **Facilities** Ⓟ (charged) ⫧ ⑩ licensed ⋒ (outdoor) ♿ (wheelchairs, facilities for visually & hearing impaired) toilets for disabled shop ⊗ (ex assist dogs) ▄

The Royal Marines Museum

Southsea PO4 9PX

⮕ *(signed from seafront)*

☎ 023 9281 9385

e-mail: info@royalmarinesmuseum.co.uk

web: www.royalmarinesmuseum.co.uk

The Royal Marines Museum celebrates the famous fighting spirit and long history of the Royal Marines. Based in the lavishly decorated former Officers' Mess of Eastney Barracks, built in the 1860s for the Royal Marine Artillery, the Museum is situated in the very heart of the Corps history. With displays and exhibits highlighting the history of the Royal Marines from their beginnings in 1664 through to the present day, and the new 'The Making of the Royal Marines Commando' exhibition, the Museum brings to life the history, character and humour of the Royal Marines.

Times Open all year, daily 10-5. Closed 24-26 Dec. **Fee** ✳ £5.25 (ch 5-16 £3.25, concessions £3.25-£4.25). Family ticket (2ad+4ch) £14.50. Registered disabled £3 (free admission for one assistant). **Facilities** Ⓟ ⫧ ⋒ (outdoor) ♿ (wheelchairs, hearing loops, special tours-prior notice) toilets for disabled shop ⊗ (ex assist dogs or in grounds) ▄

Southsea Castle

Clarence Esplanade PO5 3PA

⮕ *(Follow seafront symbol then Southsea Castle brown signs.)*

☎ 023 9282 7261

e-mail: mvs@portsmouthcc.gov.uk

web: www.southseacastle.co.uk

Part of Henry VIII's national coastal defences, this fort was built in 1544. In the 'Time Tunnel' experience, the ghost of the castle's first master gunner guides you through the dramatic scenes from the castle's eventful history. Audio-visual presentation, underground passages, Tudor military history displays, artillery, and panoramic views of the Solent and Isle of Wight.

Times Open Apr-Sep, daily 10-5.30. **Fee** ✳ £3.50(ch & students £2.50, ch accompanied under 13 free, concessions £3). Family £9.50. **Facilities** Ⓟ ⋒ (outdoor) ♿ (wheelchair available) shop ⊗ (ex assist dogs) ▄

Spinnaker Tower

Gunwharf Quays PO1 3TT

⮕ *(From M275 follow tourist signs for Tower)*

☎ 023 9285 7520

e-mail: info@spinnakertower.co.uk

web: www.spinnakertower.co.uk

Elegant, sculptural and inspired by Portsmouth's maritime heritage, the Spinnaker Tower is a new national icon - a 'must-see' landmark for visitors worldwide. Soaring 170 metres above Portsmouth Harbour, with three viewing decks, the Spinnaker Tower is now open to view. Glide to the top in style in the panoramic lift or take the high speed internal lift and step right out into the best view in the country. Dare you 'walk on air' on the glass floor, the largest in Europe? Watch history unfold through our unique 'Time Telescopes'. Back down to earth and shop for souvenirs or talk about your travels over a snack in the waterfront Tower Café bar.

CONTINUED

PORTSMOUTH CONTINUED

Spinnaker Tower

Times ✳ Open Apr-26 May, Sun-Thu 10-5, Fri-Sat 10-10; 27 May-3 Sep daily 10-10; 4 Sep-29 Oct Sun-Thu 10-5, Fri-Sat 10-10; 30 Oct-Mar, Sun-Fri 10-5, Sat 10-10 **Facilities** ♿ (charged) ⬚ 🚻 (hearing loop) toilets for disabled shop ⊗ (ex assist dogs) ▬

RINGWOOD   MAP 04 SU10

Moors Valley Country Park

Horton Rd, Ashley Heath BH24 2ET

➲ *(1.5m from Ashley Heath rdbt on A31 near Three Legged Cross)*

☎ 01425 470721

e-mail: moorsvalley@eastdorset.gov.uk

web: www.moors-valley.co.uk

Fifteen hundred acres of forest, woodland, heathland, lakes, river and meadows provide a home for a wide variety of plants and animals, and there's a Visitor Centre, Adventure Playground, picnic area, Moors Valley Railway, Tree Top Trail and the 'Go Ape'- high ropes course (book on 0870 444 5562). Cycle hire is also available.

Times Open all year, 8-dusk (8pm at latest). Visitor centre open 9.30-4.30 (later in summer). Closed 25 Dec. **Fee** ✳ No admission charge but parking up to £8 per day. **Facilities** ♿ (charged) ⬚ 🍴 licensed 🚻 (outdoor) ♿ (some footpaths in forest unaccessible) (scooter & wheelchairs to hire) toilets for disabled shop ▬

ROCKBOURNE   MAP 04 SU11

Rockbourne Roman Villa

SP6 3PG

➲ *(from Salisbury exit A338 at Fordingbridge, take B3078 west through Sandleheath & follow signs. Or turn off A354 (Salisbury to Blandford road), W of Coombe Bissett)*

☎ 01725 518541

web: www.hants.gov.uk/museum/rockbourne

Discovered in 1942, the site features the remains of a 40-room Roman villa and is the largest in the area. Displays include mosaics and a very

rare hypocaust system. The museum displays the many artefacts found on the site during excavations. Roman re-enactments are performed - please ring for details.

Times ✳ Open Apr-Sep, daily 10.30-6. (Last admission 5.30) **Facilities** ♿ 🚻 (outdoor) ♿ (ramps in & out of museum) toilets for disabled shop ⊗ (ex assist dogs)

ROMSEY   MAP 04 SU32

Broadlands

SO51 9ZD

➲ *(main entrance on A3090 Romsey by-pass)*

☎ 01794 505010

e-mail: admin@broadlands.net

web: www.broadlands.net

Famous as the home of the late Lord Mountbatten, Broadlands is now home to his grandson Lord Brabourne. An elegant Palladian mansion in a beautiful landscaped setting on the banks of the River Test, Broadlands was also the country residence of Lord Palmerston, the great Victorian statesman.

Times Open wkdays, 26 Jun-2 Sep, 1-5.30. Last admission 4. Open BHs. **Fee** ✳ £8 (ch 12-16 £4, concessions £7). Party 15+. **Facilities** ♿ 🚻 (outdoor) ♿ (Partly accessible) toilets for disabled ⊗ (ex assist dogs)

ROWLAND'S CASTLE   MAP 04 SU71

Stansted Park

PO9 6DX

➲ *(follow brown heritage 'Stansted House' signs from A3 Horndean exit, or A27 Havant exit)*

☎ 023 9241 2265

e-mail: enquiry@stanstedpark.co.uk

web: www.stanstedpark.co.uk

Stansted Park is set in 1750 acres of park and woodland. The mansion rooms house the Bessborough family collection of furniture and paintings, and below stairs the restored servants quarters can be found, with an extensive collection of household artefacts giving an insight into the running of the house. The ancient Chapel of St Paul was an inspiration to the poet John Keats and is open in conjunction with the house. Various events through the summer and Christmas.

Times Open Etr Sun-Sep, Sun & Mon 1-4; Jul & Aug, Sun-Wed (last admission 4) **Fee** £7 (ch £3.50, concessions £5). Family £17 (2ad+2ch) **Facilities** ♿ 🍴 🚻 (outdoor) ♿ (wheelchair lift to house) toilets for disabled garden centre ⊗ (ex assist dogs)

SELBORNE MAP 04 SU73

Gilbert White's House & The Oates Museum

2 for 1

High St GU34 3JH

➲ *(on village High St)*

☎ 01420 511275

e-mail: info@gilbertwhiteshouse.org.uk
web: www.gilbertwhiteshouse.org.uk

Charming 18th-century house, home of famous naturalist, the Rev. Gilbert White, author of *The Natural History and Antiquities of Selborne*. Over 20 acres of garden and parkland, shop and tea parlour serving some 18th-century fare. There is also an exhibition on Captain Lawrence Oates and his ill-fated expedition to the South Pole in 1911. Events, courses, exhibitions and lecture's throughout the year.

Times Open Jan-24 Dec, Tue-Sun & BH 11-5; Jun-Aug, Mon 11-5. Last admissions 4.30 **Fee** ✳ £6.50 (ch free, concessions £5.50). **Facilities** Ⓟ (100mtrs) 🖵 ⛄ (garden fully accessible, upstairs of house not accessible) (wheelchair users pay 1/2 price) toilets for disabled shop garden centre ⊗ (ex assist dogs) 🍴

SHERBORNE ST JOHN MAP 04 SU65

The Vyne

RG24 9HL

➲ *(4m N of Basingstoke, off A340, signed from A33, A339 & A340)*

☎ 01256 883858

e-mail: thevyne@nationaltrust.org.uk
web: www.nationaltrust.org.uk

Built in the early 16th-century for Lord Sandys, the Vyne was visited by Henry VIII at least three times. The house later became home to the Chute family for 350 years. The building is a fascinating microcosm of architectural and design fads and fashions through the centuries. Visitors can view the family's original collection of art and sculpture, and the garden and grounds are very popular for walking. A wetlands area with new bird hide attracts a wide diversity of wildlife. The recently restored Victorian glass house is now open, within the walled kitchen garden.

The Vyne

Times House, 14 Mar-1 Nov, Sat & Sun 11-5; 16 Mar-28 Oct, Mon, Tue & Wed. 1-5. Gardens, shop & restaurant Feb-8 Mar; Sat & Sun 11-5; 14 Mar-1 Nov, Sat-Wed, 11-5. **Fee** House & Grounds £9 (ch £4.50). Family £22.50. Group £7.77. Grounds & Gardens only £5.50 (ch £2.75) **Facilities** Ⓟ 🖵 🍴 🪑 (outdoor) ⛄ (Deep gravel in some parts of gardens, along with slopes make access difficult. Access to shop, restaurant & ground floor of house ok) (Braille guides, hearing loop & touch tours) toilets for disabled shop ⊗ (ex assist dogs) 🐾 🍴

SOUTHAMPTON MAP 04 SU41

Museum of Archaeology

FREE

God's House Tower, Winkle St SO14 2NY

➲ *(near waterfront, close to Queen's Park & Town Quay)*

☎ 023 8063 5904 & 8083 2768

e-mail: museums@southampton.gov.uk
web: www.southampton.gov.uk/leisure

The museum housed is in an early fortified building, dating from the 1400s and taking its name from the nearby medieval hospital. Exhibits on the Roman, Saxon and medieval towns of Southampton are displayed.

Times ✳ Open Tue-Fri 10-4, Sat 10-12, 1-4, Sun 1-4 **Facilities** Ⓟ (400 yds) (designated areas only, parking charges) shop ⊗ (ex assist dogs)

Southampton City Art Gallery

FREE

Civic Centre, Commercial Rd SO14 7LP

➲ *(situated on the Watts Park side of the Civic Centre, a short walk from the station, on Commercial Rd)*

☎ 023 8083 2277

e-mail: art.gallery@southampton.gov.uk
web: www.southampton.gov.uk/art

The largest gallery in the south of England, with the finest collection of British contemporary art in the country outside London. Varied displays of landscapes, portrait paintings or recent British art are always available, as well as a special display, selected by students.

Times Open all year, Tue-Sat 10-5, Sun 1-4. Closed 25-26 & 31 Dec. **Facilities** Ⓟ (50yds) (nearby street parking is 1hr only) 🖵 🍴 ⛄ (free BSL signed tours by arrangement, 'touch tour') toilets for disabled shop ⊗ (ex assist dogs)

ENGLAND

SOUTHAMPTON CONTINUED

Southampton Maritime Museum

FREE

The Wool House, Town Quay SO14 2AR

➲ *(on the waterfront, near to the Town Quay)*

☎ 023 8022 3941 & 8063 5904

e-mail: museums@southampton.gov.uk

web: www.southampton.gov.uk/leisure

The Wool House was built in the 14th century as a warehouse for wool, and now houses a maritime museum, with models and displays telling the history of the Victorian and modern port of Southampton. There are exhibitions on the *Titanic*, The *Queen Mary* and an interactive area for children.

Times * Open Tue-Fri 10-4; Sat 10-1 & 2-4; Sun 1-4 **Facilities** Ⓟ (400yds) (metered parking adjacent) ♿ (hearing loop on Titanic presentation) shop ⊗ (ex assist dogs)

TITCHFIELD MAP 04 SU50

Titchfield Abbey

FREE

Place House Studio, Mill Ln PO15 5RA

➲ *(0.5m N off Titchfield, off A27)*

☎ 01329 842133

Also known as 'Place House', in Tudor times this was the seat of the Earl of Southampton, built on the site of the abbey founded in 1232. He incorporated the gatehouse and the nave of the church into his house.

Times * Open Apr-Sep, daily 10-6; Oct-Mar, daily 10-4. Closed 25-26 Dec & 1 Jan. **Facilities** Ⓟ ⛩ #

WEYHILL MAP 04 SU34

The Hawk Conservancy and Country Park

SP11 8DY

➲ *(3m W of Andover, signed from A303)*

☎ 01264 773850

e-mail: info@hawkconservancy.org

web: www.hawkconservancy.org

This is the largest centre in the south for birds of prey from all over the world including eagles, hawks, falcons, owls, vultures and kites. Exciting birds of prey demonstrations are held daily at noon, 2pm, and 3.30pm, including the 'Valley of the Eagles' at 2pm. Another highlight of the afternoons is the Woodlands Owls and Hawks display. Different birds are flown at these times and visitors may have the opportunity to hold a bird and adults can fly a Harris hawk.

The Hawk Conservancy and Country Park

Times Open 14 Feb-8 Nov daily 10.30-5.30. Nov-Feb wknds only 10.30-4.30 (last admission 4pm). **Fee** * £9.75 (ch £6.25, pen £9, students £8.75). Family ticket (2ad+2ch) £31. **Facilities** Ⓟ ☕ 🍴 licensed ⛩ (indoor & outdoor) ♿ (wheelchairs avail, viewing areas in hides, ramps) toilets for disabled shop ⊗ (ex assist dogs) ▬

WHITCHURCH MAP 04 SU44

Whitchurch Silk Mill

28 Winchester St RG28 7AL

➲ *(halfway between Winchester & Newbury, clearly signed on A34. Located in town centre)*

☎ 01256 892065

e-mail: silkmill@btinternet.com

web: www.whitchurchsilkmill.org.uk

The mill is idyllically located on the River Test. Whitchurch Silk Mill is the oldest surviving textile mill in Southern England. Fine silks and ribbons are still woven for interiors and fashion. See the 19th-century waterwheel pounding and learn about winding, warping and weaving. There is a programme of exhibitions, workshops and children's activities.

Times * Open Tue-Sun & BH Mon 10.30-5 (last admission 4.15). Closed 24 Dec-1 Jan. **Facilities** Ⓟ ☕ ⛩ ♿ (disabled parking adjacent site) toilets for disabled shop ⊗ (ex assist dogs) ▬

WINCHESTER MAP 04 SU42

Gurkha Museum

Peninsula Barracks, Romsey Rd SO23 8TS

➲ *(M3 junct 9 to Winchester, follow one-way system into High St, 1st left after Westgate)*

☎ 01962 842832

e-mail: curator@thegurkhamuseum.co.uk

web: www.thegurkhamuseum.co.uk

This museum tells the fascinating story of the Gurkhas' involvement with the British Army. Travel from Nepal to the North-West Frontier and beyond, with the help of life-sized dioramas, interactive exhibits and sound displays.

Times Open all year, Mon-Sat 10-5, Sun 12-4. Closed 25-26 Dec & 1 Jan **Fee** £2 (pen £1, ch under 16 free). **Facilities** ❷ ♿ (lift & chair lift) toilets for disabled shop ⊗ (ex assist dogs)

Horse Power, The King's Royal Hussars Regimental Museum FREE

Peninsula Barracks, Romsey Rd SO23 8TS

➲ *(M3 junct 9/10 follow city centre signs, then hospital A&E red signs to Romsey Rd. Vehicle access from Romsey Rd)*

☎ 01962 828539 & 828541

e-mail: curator@horsepowermuseum.co.uk

web: www.krh.org.uk

Horse Power, the museum of the King's Royal Hussars, tells the exciting story of an English cavalry regiment, mounted on horses and in tanks or armoured cars.

Times Open 6 Jan-18 Dec, Tue-Fri 10-4, wknds & BHs, 12-4. (Closed daily between 12.45-1.15) **Facilities** ❷ ⬚♿ (lift to first floor) toilets for disabled shop ⊗ (ex assist dogs)

Hospital of St Cross 2 for 1

St Cross SO23 9SD

➲ *(on B3335, 0.5m from M3 junct 11)*

☎ 01962 851375

e-mail: administrator@stcrosshospital.co.uk

web: www.stcrosshospital.co.uk

A beautiful group of Grade I listed medieval and Tudor buildings, in a tranquil setting by the water meadows, St. Cross is home to 25 elderly brothers. In keeping with tradition, they wear gowns and trencher hats and act as visitor guides. The hospital is world-famous for its ancient and unique tradition of the Wayfarers Dole - a beaker of beer and a morsel of bread is given by the porter to all visitors who request it. Visitors can admire the medieval and Tudor architecture, explore the medieval hall, the Georgian kitchen and the Tudor cloister as well as the walled garden with many plants of American origin.

Times Open all year, Apr-Oct, 9.30-5; Nov-Mar 10.30-3.30. (Closed Good Fri, 25 Dec, Sun mornings (summer) and Sun (winter)) **Fee** ✳ £3 (ch £1, pen £2.50). **Facilities** ❷ ⬚♿ (outdoor) ♿ (ramp access to church & some buildings, gravel paths to gardens) toilets for disabled shop ⊗ (ex assist dogs) ➡

INTECH - Family Science Centre

Telegraph Way, Morn Hill SO21 1HZ

➲ *(M3 junct 10 (S) or junct 9 (N) onto A31 then B3404 (Alresford road))*

☎ 01962 863791

e-mail: htct@intech-uk.com

web: www.intech-uk.com

This purpose-built, all weather family attraction houses 100 interactive exhibits, which demonstrate the science and technology of the world around us in an engaging and exciting way. The philosophy is most definitely 'hands-on', and the motto of the centre is 'Doing is Believing'. Activities and science shows take place during school holidays. INTECH also has the UK's largest capacity planetarium. This digital cinema has a 17 meter dome making the audience feel it is floating through the universe. Dramatic, awesome and entertaining.

Times Open all year, daily 10-4. Closed Xmas. **Fee** £6.95 (ch £4.65, pen £5.50) Family ticket (2ad+2ch) £20.86 **Facilities** ❷ ⬚♿ (outdoor) ♿ toilets for disabled shop ⊗ (ex assist dogs) ➡

Royal Hampshire Regiment Museum & Memorial Garden FREE

Serle's House, Southgate St SO23 9EG

➲ *(near city centre. 150mtrs from lights in High St)*

☎ 01962 863658

e-mail: serleshouse@royalhampshireregimentmuseum.co.uk

web: www.royalhampshireregimentmuseum.co.uk

Regimental Museum of the Royal Hampshire Regiment 1702-1992, set in an 18th-century house by the regiment's Memorial Garden. The museum tells the history of the regiment, its regulars, militia, volunteers and Territorials.

Times Normally open all year (ex 2 wks Xmas & New Year), Mon-Fri 10-4; Apr-Oct wknds & BH 12-4. **Facilities** ℗ (1000mtrs) ♿ shop ⊗ (ex assist dogs)

The Great Hall FREE

Castle Av SO23 8PJ

➲ *(at top of High St. Park & Ride recommended)*

☎ 01962 846476

e-mail: the.great.hall@hants.gov.uk

web: www.hants.gov.uk/greathall

The only surviving part of Winchester Castle, once home to the Domesday Book, this 13th-century hall was the centre of court and government life. Built between 1222-1235 during the reign of Henry III, it is one of the largest and finest bay halls in England to have survived to the present day. The Round Table based on the Arthurian Legend and built between 1230-1280 hangs in the hall. Queen Eleanor's Garden is a re-creation of a late 13th century ornamental garden.

Times Open all year, Mar-Oct daily 10-5; Nov-Feb, daily 10-4. Closed 25-26 Dec. **Facilities** ℗ (200yds) ♿ toilets for disabled shop ⊗ (ex assist dogs) ➡

131

ENGLAND

WINCHESTER CONTINUED

Winchester Cathedral

1 The Close SO23 9LS

➲ (in city centre - follow city heritage signs)

☎ 01962 857200 & 866854

e-mail: cathedral.office@winchester-cathedral.org.uk
web: www.winchester-cathedral.org.uk

The longest medieval church in Europe, founded in 1079 on a site where Christian worship had already been offered for over 400 years. Among its treasures are the 12th-century illuminated Winchester Bible, the font, medieval wall paintings and Triforium Gallery Museum. Items of interest include Jane Austen's tomb and the statue of the Winchester diver, William Walker, who in 1905 saved the cathedral from collapse by underpinning its foundations, working up to six hours a day over a period of six years, often in 20 feet of water. Visitors can also descend into the crypt to see a sculpture by Anthony Gormley, best known as creator of The Angel of The North, or ascend to the tower and bell chamber. Christmas Market from Nov to Dec, and Ice Rink from Nov to Jan. Contact for details.

Times ✳ Open all year, Mon-Sat 8.30-6, Sun 8.30-5.30 (Subject to services and special events). **Facilities** Ⓟ (500mtrs) ⬚ 🍴 ♿ (chair lift to east end of Cathedral, touch & hearing model) toilets for disabled shop ⊗ (ex assist dogs) ▆

Winchester City Mill

Bridge St SO23 8EJ

➲ (by city bridge between King Alfred's statue & Chesil St)

☎ 01962 870057

e-mail: winchestercitymill@nationaltrust.org.uk
web: www.nationaltrust.org.uk

Built over the fastflowing River Itchen in 1744, the mill has a delightful small island garden and an impressive millrace. There are regular milling demonstrations and guided wildlife walks, as well as other special events and hands-on activities throughout the year.

Times ✳ Open: Mill & Shop, 5-27 Mar, Sat-Sun 11-5, 28 Mar-10 Apr & 4 Jul-23 Dec, daily 11-5, 13 Apr-3 Jul, Wed-Sun 11-5. Last admission to Mill 4.30 **Facilities** Ⓟ (200yds) ♿ (Partly accessible) (hearing loop, large print guide, Braille of video text) shop ⊗ (ex assist dogs) ▨ ▆

Winchester College

College St SO23 9NA

➲ (S of Cathedral Close, beyond Kingsgate arch. Limited vehicle access along College St)

☎ 01962 621209

e-mail: enterprises@wincoll.ac.uk
web: www.winchestercollege.org

Founded in 1382, Winchester College is believed to be the oldest continuously running school in England. The College has greatly expanded over the years but the original buildings remain intact. Visitors can follow in the footsteps of John Keats, and see the College's many historic buildings, including a schoolhouse thought to have been designed by Christopher Wren. Also the 14th-century gothic chapel with one of the earliest examples of a fan-vaulted roof constructed from wood rather than stone, the original scholars dining room and the cloister containing memorials to former members of the college including one to Mallory the Mountaineer.

Times Open all year. Guided tours available Mon, Wed, Fri & Sat; 10.45, 12, 2.15 & 3.30. Tue & Thu 10.45 & 12. Sun 2.15 & 3.30. Groups of 10+ at times to suit by arrangement only. Closed 24 Dec-1 Jan. **Fee** ✳ £4 (concessions £3.50). **Facilities** Ⓟ (250yds) (street parking max stay 1hr) ♿ (access ramps) toilets for disabled shop ⊗ (ex assist dogs) ▆

HEREFORDSHIRE

Hereford Cathedral

ASHTON   MAP 03 SO56

Berrington Hall

Berrington HR6 0DW

➲ *(3m N of Leominster, on A49)*

☎ 01568 615721

e-mail: berrington@nationaltrust.org.uk
web: www.nationaltrust.org.uk

An elegant neo-classical house of the late 18th century, designed by Henry Holland and set in a park landscape by 'Capability' Brown. There is a restored bedroom suite, a nursery, a Victorian laundry and a tiled Georgian dairy. Join one of the daily below stairs tours. There are also events throughout the year, please contact for details.

Times Open 1-16 Mar, Sat-Sun; 17 Mar-2 Nov, Mon-Wed, wknds & Good Fri 11-5. (Last admission 30mins before closing). Garden open 11-5 (4.30 6-21 Dec). Park walk open 16 Jun-2 Nov; wknds 12-4.30 1-16 Dec. Open Good Fri. **Fee** ✳ £6.50 (ch £2.40) Family ticket £16.25. Garden only £4.80 (ch £2.40). Joint ticket with Croft Castle £9.50 **Facilities** ⓟ ⓘⓞⓘ ⨅ (outdoor) ♿ (by arrangement, wheelchairs/batricar, steps to entrance) toilets for disabled shop ⊗ (ex assist dogs) ⨠ ➡

BROCKHAMPTON   MAP 03 SO65

Brockhampton Estate

WR6 5TB

➲ *(2m E of Bromyard on A44)*

☎ 01885 482077 & 488099

e-mail: brockhampton@nationaltrust.org.uk
web: www.nationaltrust.org.uk

This traditionally formed 1700 acre estate has extensive areas of wood and parkland, with a rich variety of wildlife and over five miles of walks. At the heart of the estate lies Lower Brockhampton House, a late 14th-century moated manor house with a beautiful timber-framed gatehouse and ruined chapel.

Times Open House and Tearoom: 1-16 Mar, Sat-Sun 12-4; 19-30 Mar & Oct-2 Nov, Wed-Sun 12-4; 2 Apr-28 Sep, Wed-Sun 12-5; 11-17 Feb, daily 11-4; Jul-Aug, Sat-Sun 11-5; 8 Nov-28 Dec, Sat-Sun 11-4. Open BH Mons & Good Fri 12-5. (Parkland walks open dawn to dusk all year). **Fee** ✳ Lower Brockhampton £5.25 (ch £2.60) Family £13. Parkland only £2.50 **Facilities** ⓟ ⬜ ⨅ (outdoor) ♿ (grounds, shop and ground floor of Lower Brockhampton all accessible) (special parking, ramps, Braille guide) toilets for disabled shop ⊗ (no dogs in house ex assist) ⨠ ➡

CROFT   MAP 03 SO46

Croft Castle & Parkland

Yarpole HR6 9PW

➲ *(off B4362 N of Leominster)*

☎ 01568 780246

e-mail: croftcastle@nationaltrust.org.uk
web: www.nationaltrust.org.uk

Home to the Croft family since Domesday, the walls and towers date from the 14th and 15th centuries, while the interior is mainly 18th century. Set in 1500 acres of Herefordshire countryside, there is a splendid avenue of 350-year-old Spanish chestnuts, and an Iron Age Fort (Croft Ambrey), which may be reached by footpath. Explore the walled garden, church and parkland or enjoy a family walk. There are also many annual events, including outdoor theatre; please telephone for details.

Times Park open all year, daily 8-9 (or dusk). Castle open 7 Mar-Jul & 2 Sep-1 Nov, Wed-Sun, 1-5; Aug daily 1-5; 7 Nov-20 Dec wknds only 1-4. Castle tours 7 Mar-1Nov; 7 Nov-20 Dec 11-1. Garden, shop & tea-room open 2hrs before Castle, closing times vary. **Fee** Castle & gardens £6 (ch £3) Family ticket £15.50 Garden & grounds: £4 (ch £2). Family ticket £10. Castle & Garden £6.80 (ch £3.50). Joint ticket with Berrington Hall £9. Group outside normal hrs £11.50. **Facilities** ⓟ ⬜ ⓘⓞⓘ licensed ⨅ (outdoor) ♿ (parking available, Braille guide, wheelchair buggy) toilets for disabled shop garden centre ⊗ (ex assist dogs & in park) ⨠ ➡

GOODRICH   MAP 03 SO51

Goodrich Castle

HR9 6HY

➲ *(5m S of Ross-on-Wye, off A40)*

☎ 01600 890538

web: www.english-heritage.org.uk

A magnificent red sandstone fortress rising out of a rocky outcrop above the Wye Valley. Climb the huge towers for exhilarating views and explore a maze of small rooms and passageways. Hear about the doomed Civil War lovers on our audio tour.

Times Open all year, 21 Mar-May & Sep-Oct, daily 10-5; Jun-Aug, daily 10-6; Nov-Feb, Wed-Sun 10-4. Closed 24-26 Dec & 1 Jan. **Fee** £5 (concessions £4, ch £2.50). Family £12.50. Prices and opening times are subject to change in March 2009. Please call 0870 333 1181 for the most up to date prices and opening times when planning your visit. **Facilities** ⓟ shop ⊗ ▦

HEREFORD   MAP 03 SO53

Cider Museum & King Offa Distillery   `2 for 1`

21 Ryelands St HR4 0LW

⮑ *(off A438 (Hereford to Brecon road))*

☎ 01432 354207

e-mail: enquiries@cidermuseum.co.uk

web: www.cidermuseum.co.uk

Explore the fascinating history of cider making - view cidermaking equipment, cooper's workshop and vat house. Walk through original champagne cider cellars, see 18th-century English lead crystal cider glasses and 19th-century watercolours of apples and pears.

Times Open all year, Apr-Oct 10-5; Nov-Mar 11-3, closed Sun-Mon. **Fee** ✳ £3.50 (ch & students £3, pen £2.50). Party 15+, 50p reduction per person. **Facilities** ❷ ⛛ ㅠ (outdoor) ⴲ (limited access to ground floor) (audiotapes, large print guide sheets) toilets for disabled shop ⊗ (ex assist dogs) ➠

Hereford Cathedral

HR1 2NG

⮑ *(A49 signed from city inner ring roads)*

☎ 01432 374200

e-mail: office@herefordcathedral.org

web: www.herefordcathedral.org

Built on the site of a place of worship that dated back to Saxon times, Hereford Cathedral contains some of the finest examples of architecture from the Norman era to the present day, including the 13th-century Shrine of St Thomas of Hereford, the recently restored 14th-century Lady Chapel, and the award-winning new library building. The Mappa Mundi and Chained Library exhibition tells the stories of these famous national treasures through models, artefacts and changing exhibitions.

Times ✳ Cathedral open daily 7.30-Evensong; Mappa Mundi & Chained Library Exhibition Summer: Mon-Sat 10-4.30, Sun 11-3.30. Winter: Mon-Sat 11-3.30 (closed Sun). **Facilities** ℗ (0.25m) ⛛ ㅠ ⴲ (touch facility for blind, Braille & large print info) toilets for disabled shop ⊗ (ex assist dogs) ➠

Old House   `FREE`

High Town HR1 2AA

⮑ *(in centre of High Town)*

☎ 01432 260694

e-mail: herefordmuseums@herefordshire.gov.uk

web: www.herefordshire.gov.uk

The Old House is a fine Jacobean building dating from around 1621, and was once in a row of similar houses. Its rooms are furnished in 17th-century style and give visitors the chance to learn what life was like in Cromwell's time.

Times Open all year, Tue-Sat 10-5; Apr-Sep Sun & BH Mon 10-4. **Facilities** ℗ (400mtrs) ⴲ (ground floor accessible) (virtual tour, Braille guide, tactile images) shop ⊗ (ex assist dogs)

KINGTON   MAP 03 SO25

Hergest Croft Gardens

The Hergest Estate Office, Ridgebourne HR5 3EG

⮑ *(off A44 W of Kington and follow signs)*

☎ 01544 230160

e-mail: gardens@hergest.co.uk

web: www.hergest.co.uk

From spring bulbs to autumn colour, this is a garden for all seasons. A fine collection of trees and shrubs surrounds the Edwardian house. There's an old fashioned kitchen garden with spring and summer borders, and Park Wood, a hidden valley with magnificent rhododendrons. Please contact for details of special events.

Times Open Mar wknds, 28 Mar-1 Nov daily 12.30-5.30. **Fee** ✳ £5.50 (ch under 16 free). Party 20+ £4.50 (£6.50 with guided tour). **Facilities** ❷ ⛛ ㅠ (outdoor) ⴲ (most of the garden accessible except park wood as it has steep gravel paths) (portable ramp & wheelchair available) toilets for disabled shop garden centre ⊗ (ex on leads) ➠

LEDBURY   MAP 03 SO73

Eastnor Castle

Eastnor HR8 1RL

⮑ *(2.5m E of Ledbury on A438 (Tewkesbury road))*

☎ 01531 633160

e-mail: enquiries@eastnorcastle.com

web: www.eastnorcastle.com

A magnificent Georgian castle in a lovely setting, with a deer park, arboretum and lake. Inside are tapestries, fine art and armour, and the Italianate and Gothic interiors have been beautifully restored. There are an adventure playground, nature trails and lakeside walks. Events take place throughout the year.

Times Open 20-24 Mar, every Sun & BH from 30 Mar-28 Sep, daily 14 Jul-29 Aug (ex Sat). 11-4.30 (last admission 4). **Facilities** ❷ ⛛ ㅠ (outdoor) ⴲ (wheelchair climber, lift) shop ➠

MAP 03 SO44

MUCH MARCLE

Weston's Cider

The Bounds HR8 2NQ

➲ *(Turn opp the A449 at Much Marcle crossroads (with the old garage and Walwyn Arms). Westons is about 0.5m up the road & is clearly signposted.)*

☎ 01531 660108

e-mail: enquiries@westons-cider.co.uk
web: www.westons-cider.co.uk

It's not just about a drop of cider (adults only) on this fun day out. Visitors can take in the Henry Weston courtyard garden; the Bottle Museum tea room; shire horse dray rides (ring first for availability); traditional and rare breeds farm park and orchard walk; a children's playground; visitor centre and Scrumpy House restaurant and bar.

Times Open wkdays 9-4.30, Sat, Sun & BHs 10-4. **Fee** ✳ Mill tours £5 (ch £3), Traditional & Rare Breeds Farm Park £3 (ch £2), Shire Horse Dray Rides £2.50 (ch £1.50). Picnic area, childrens play area & Henry Weston Courtyard Garden free. **Facilities** ❷ ⬚ ⊙ licensed ⏛ (outdoor) ♿ (restaurant, courtyard, garden and shop all accessible) toilets for disabled shop ⊗ (ex assist dogs) ▬

SWAINSHILL

The Weir Gardens

HR4 7QF

➲ *(5m W of Hereford, on A438)*

☎ 01981 590509
e-mail: theweir@nationaltrust.org.uk
web: www.nationaltrust.org.uk

A unique riverside garden created in the 1920s. This peaceful 10 acre garden offers dramatic views of the Wye Valley and Herefordshire countryside beyond. In spring, drifts of early flowering bulbs are followed by a succession of summer wildflowers, managed to create a varied habitat for a wide range of wildlife. Autumn gives a final flourish of colour and the River Wye provides a moving backdrop to this tranquil garden. Bring a picnic and spend a day by the river in this special place. 2009 is the 50 year anniversary of ownership by the National Trust.

Times Open Feb, Wed-Sun, 11-4; Mar-5 May, Mon- Sun, 11-5; 7 May -26 Oct, Wed-Sun, 11-5; 24 Jan, Sat-Sun, 11-4 **Fee** ✳ £4.50 (ch £2.25). Family £11.25. **Facilities** ❷ ⏛ (outdoor) ♿ (garden has steep banks with narrow paths and steps in some places). (disabled parking near toilets) toilets for disabled ⊗ (ex assist dogs) ⅜

Butterflies at Symond's Yat

HERTFORDSHIRE

Benington Lordship, Stevenage

AYOT ST LAWRENCE MAP 04 TL11

Shaw's Corner

AL6 9BX

(A1(M) junct 4 or M1 junct 10. Follow B653 signed Wheathampstead & follow National Trust signs to Shaw's Corner)

☎ 01438 820307

e-mail: shawscorner@nationaltrust.org.uk

web: www.nationaltrust.org.uk/shawscorner

An Edwardian arts and crafts influenced house, the home of George Bernard Shaw from 1906 until his death in 1950. The rooms remain much as he left them, with many literary and personal effects evoking the individuality and genius of this great dramatist. The kitchen and outbuildings are evocative of early 20th-century domestic life. Shaw's writing hut is hidden at the bottom of the garden, which has richly planted borders and views over the Hertfordshire countryside. A selection of plants in addition to a small collection of George Bernard Shaw plays are available to buy.

Times House:14 Mar-1 Nov, Wed-Sun 1-5. Garden: 14 Mar-1Nov, Wed-Sun 12-5.30 & all BHs **Fee** * £5.20 (ch £2.95). Family ticket £14.95. **Facilities** (Partly accessible) (Braille/large print guides, scented plants, items to touch) (ex on lead & assist dogs)

BERKHAMSTED MAP 04 SP90

Ashridge Estate Visitor Centre

Moneybury Hill, Ringshall HP4 1LX

(between Northchurch & Ringshall, just off B4506)

☎ 01442 851227 & 755557

e-mail: ashridge@nationaltrust.org.uk

web: www.nationaltrust.org.uk

Miles of paths through woodland and open country with spring bluebells, ancient trees, fungi and breath-taking views. Discover more about the wildlife in the visitor centre next to the Bridgewater monument, with an interactive exhibition room. A wide range of activities and events for all the family take place through out the year.

Times Open; Estate all year. Visitor Centre; 15 Mar-21 Dec, 12-5, Monument 15 Mar-26 Oct. **Facilities** (Disabled parking next to visitor centre) toilets for disabled shop

Berkhamsted Castle

FREE

HP4 1HF

(by Berkhamsted station)

web: www.english-heritage.org.uk

Roads and a railway have cut into the castle site, but its huge banks and ditches remain impressive. The original motte-and-bailey was built after the Norman Conquest, and there is a later stone keep, once owned by the Black Prince, eldest son of King Edward III, where King John of France was imprisoned.

Times Open all year, Summer, daily 10-6; Winter, daily 10-4. Closed 25 Dec & 1 Jan. **Facilities**

HATFIELD MAP 04 TL20

Hatfield House, Park and Gardens

AL9 5NQ

(2m from junct 4 A1(M) on A1000, 7m from M25 junct 23. House opposite Hatfield railway station)

☎ 01707 287010

e-mail: visitors@hatfield-house.co.uk

web: www.hatfield-house.co.uk

The house, built by Robert Cecil in 1611, is the home of the 7th Marquess of Salisbury and is full of exquisite tapestries, furniture and famous paintings. The 42 acres of gardens include formal, knot, scented and wilderness areas, and reflect their Jacobean history. Includes the national collection of model soldiers and children's play area. The Tudor Palace of Hatfield, close by the house, was the childhood home of Elizabeth I, and is where she held her first Council of State when she became Queen in 1558. Events take place throughout the year - see website for details.

Times Open Etr Sat-Sep. House: Wed-Sun & BHs 12-4; Park & West Garden: daily 11-5.30. East Garden, Thu. **Facilities** (outdoor) (lift to 1st floor, wheelchairs) toilets for disabled shop (ex in park)

KNEBWORTH MAP 04 TL22

Knebworth House, Gardens & Country Park

SG3 6PY

➲ *(direct access from A1(M) junct 7 Stevenage South)*

☎ 01438 812661

e-mail: info@knebworthhouse.com
web: www.knebworthhouse.com

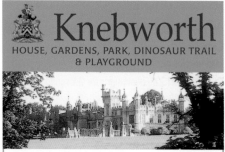
Home of the Lytton family since 1490, the original Tudor Manor was transformed in 1843 by the spectacular high Gothic decoration of Victorian novelist Sir Edward Bulwer-Lytton. The formal gardens, laid out by Edwin Lutyens in 1908, include a Gertrude Jekyll herb garden, a maze, an organically-run walled kitchen garden and a dinosaur trail, comprising 72 life-size models of dinosaurs set grazing and hunting amongst the rhododendrons and the redwoods. The 250-acres of rolling parkland include a giant adventure playground and miniature railway.

Times Open 4-19 Apr, 23-31 May, 27 Jun-2 Sep daily; 21-29 Mar, 25 Apr-17 May, 6-21 Jun, 5-27 Sep wknds & BHs; Park & gardens 11-5 (last admission 4.15); House 12-5 (last admission 4). **Fee** House, gardens & park £9.50 (ch & pen £9) Family ticket £33. Gardens & park £7.50. Family ticket £26. **Facilities** ℗ ⬜ ⊓ (outdoor) ♿ (house has no lift, history of building can be conveyed to visitors on ground floor) (transport to door, wheelchair available) toilets for disabled shop garden centre ⊗ (ex assist dogs & in park) ▰

See advert on this page

LETCHWORTH MAP 04 TL23

Museum & Art Gallery FREE

Broadway SG6 3PF

➲ *(next door to Public Library in town centre, near Broadway Cinema)*

☎ 01462 685647

e-mail: letchworth.museum@north-herts.gov.uk
web: www.north-herts.gov.uk

Opened in 1914 to house the collections of the Letchworth Naturalists' Society, this friendly town-centre museum has exhibits on local wildlife, geology, arts and crafts, and archaeology. There is also a museum shop and a regular programme of art exhibitions and workshops.

Times Open all year Mon-Tue, Thu-Sat (Closed BHs), 10-5. **Facilities** ℗ (100yds) ♿ (ground floor only accessible) (ramp, touch screen computer) shop ⊗ (ex assist dogs)

LONDON COLNEY
MAP 04 TL10

de Havilland Aircraft Heritage Centre
`2 for 1`

Salisbury Hall AL2 1BU

➲ (M25 junct 22. Follow signs for 'Mosquito Aircraft Museum' onto B556)

☎ 01727 826400 & 822051(info)

e-mail: w4050.dhamt@fsmail.net

web: www.dehavillandmuseum.co.uk

The oldest aircraft museum in Britain, opened in 1959 to preserve and display the de Havilland Mosquito prototype on the site of its conception. A working museum with displays of 20 de Havilland aircraft and sections together with a comprehensive collection of de Havilland engines and memorabilia. Selective cockpits are open to enter. Education storyboard 'maze style' now open.

Times Open first Sun Mar-last Sun Oct, Sun & BHs 10.30-5.30, Tue, Thu & Sat 2-5.30. **Fee** ✳ £5 (ch under 5 free, ch 5-16 £3, pen £4) Family ticket £13 (2ad+2ch) **Facilities** ❷ ⬚ ⋈ (indoor & outdoor) ⬥ (w/chairs available) toilets for disabled shop ❽ (ex assist dogs) ▬

ST ALBANS
MAP 04 TL10

Clock Tower
Market Place AL3 3DR

➲ (city centre, junct of High St (A1081) & Market Place)

☎ 01727 819340

e-mail: museum@stalbans.gov.uk

web: www.stalbansmuseums.org.uk

Built between 1403 and 1412, this is the only medieval town belfry in England. Inside you can hear the great bell Gabriel (also 600 years old), find out about the original clock, the Napoleonic War telegraph station (1808-14), and see the fine Victorian turret clock in action.

Times Open Etr-Sep, Sat, Sun & BH 10.30-5. **Facilities** ℗ (400yds) (wheelchair access not possible) shop ❽

The Gardens of The Rose (Royal National Rose Society)
`2 for 1`

Chiswell Green Ln AL2 3NR

➲ (2m S off B4630 Watford Rd in Chiswell Green Ln. Turn into lane by Three Hammers pub)

☎ 01727 850461 & 0845 833 4344

e-mail: mail@rnrs.org.uk

web: www.rnrs.org

The Royal National Rose Society's newly revamped Gardens of the Rose is now in its second year of opening. In addition to a comprehensive collection of roses of all types, the new garden boasts a good selection of complementary trees, shrubs, summer bulbs and herbaceous perennials in a garden setting together with a grass maze. A stunning new 72 arch pergola supports a wide selection of climbing roses with clematis and other flowering species. There are three new pools containing a variety of marginal plants and water lilies.

Times Open 4 Jun-28 Sep, Wed-Sun, 11-5 **Fee** ✳ £5. £4 for groups 20+ **Facilities** ❷ ⬚ ⬥ (ramps where necessary) toilets for disabled ▬

Gorhambury
AL3 6AH

➲ (entry via lodge gates on A4147)

☎ 01727 855000

This house was built by Sir Robert Taylor between 1774 and 1784 to house an extensive picture collection of 17th-century portraits of the Grimston and Bacon families and their contemporaries. Also of note is the 16th-century enamelled glass collection and an early English pile carpet.

Times Open May-Sep, Thu 2-5. **Fee** ✳ £7 (ch £4, concessions £5). **Facilities** ❷ ⬥ (Partly accessible) toilets for disabled ❽

Museum of St Albans
`FREE`

9A Hatfield Rd AL1 3RR

➲ (city centre on A1057 Hatfield road)

☎ 01727 819340

e-mail: history@stalbans.gov.uk

web: www.stalbansmuseums.org.uk

The story of St Albans is traced from the departure of the Romans up to the present day. Galleries representing different times can be seen along with a special gallery where a variety of exhibitions are held throughout the year. The Museum is also the home of the Salaman Collection of trade and craft tools. Outside is a wildlife garden suitable for picnics.

Times ✳ Open all year, daily 10-5, Sun 2-5. Closed 25-26 Dec & 1 Jan **Facilities** ❷ ⋈ (outdoor) ⬥ (Partly accessible) (ramp at entrance) toilets for disabled shop ❽ (ex assist dogs) ▬

Roman Theatre of Verulamium

St Michaels AL3 6AH

➲ *(Gorhambury Drive off Bluehouse Hill A4147)*

☎ 01727 835035

The theatre was first found in 1847, and was fully excavated by 1935. It is semicircular in shape with a stage area. The seating would have accommodated over 2,000 spectators.

Times Open all year, daily 10-5 (4 in winter). Closed 25-26 Dec. 1 Jan by appointment only. **Fee** ✷ £2 (ch £1, concessions £1.50, school parties 50p). **Facilities** ❷ ♿ (limited access to viewing path) shop

St Albans Cathedral

Sumpter Yard AL1 1BY

➲ *(M25 junct 22a, in the centre of St Albans)*

☎ 01727 860780

e-mail: mail@stalbanscathedral.org.uk

web: www.stalbanscathedral.org.uk

An imposing Norman abbey church built on the site of the execution of St Alban, Britain's first martyr (c250AD). The cathedral is constructed from recycled Roman brick taken from nearby Verulamium.

Times Open daily, 9-5.45. Closed 25 Dec from 1. **Fee** Admission free. Suggested donation £2.50 per adult. **Facilities** ❷ (200mtrs) ⌷❉ licensed ⌷ (outdoor) ♿ (vast majority of cathedral accessible but some restrictions) (touch & hearing centre, Braille guides) toilets for disabled shop

Verulamium Museum

St Michaels AL3 4SW

➲ *(follow signs for St Albans, museum signed)*

☎ 01727 751810

e-mail: museum@stalbans.gov.uk

web: www.stalbansmuseums.org.uk

Verulamium was one of the largest and most important Roman towns in Britain - by the lst century AD it was declared a 'municipium', giving its inhabitants the rights of Roman citizenship, the only British city granted this honour. A mosaic and underfloor heating system can be seen in a separate building, and the museum has wall paintings, jewellery, pottery and other domestic items. On the second weekend of every month legionaries occupy the galleries and describe the tactics and equipment of the Roman Imperial Army and the life of a legionary.

Times Open all year Mon-Fri 10-5.30, Sun 2-5.30. Closed 25-26 Dec. **Facilities** ❷ (charged) ⌷ (outdoor) ♿ (ramp access to main entrance) toilets for disabled shop ❁ (ex assist dogs) ⬛

The Natural History Museum at Tring   FREE

The Walter Rothschild Building, Akeman St HP23 6AP

➲ *(signed from A41)*

☎ 020 7942 6171

e-mail: tring-enquiries@nhm.ac.uk

web: www.nhm.ac.uk/tring

An unusual museum exhibiting a range of animals, collected by its founder Lionel Walter, 2nd Baron Rothschild, scientist, eccentric and natural history enthusiast. Home to the world-class research and collections of the Natural History Museum's Bird Group. A programme of temporary exhibitions, activities and events make any visit a unique day out.

Times Open Mon-Sat 10-5, Sun 2-5. Closed 24-26 Dec. **Facilities** ❷ ⌷❉ (outdoor) ♿ (ramps, virtual tour, disabled parking space) toilets for disabled shop ❁ (ex assist dogs) ⬛

Scott's Grotto

24 Scott's Rd SG12 9JQ

➲ *(off A119)*

☎ 01920 464131

e-mail: tourism@ware-herts.org.uk

web: www.scotts-grotto.org

Scott's Grotto, built in the 1760s by the Quaker poet John Scott, has been described by English Heritage as 'one of the finest in England'. Recently restored by the Ware Society, it consists of underground passages and chambers decorated with flints, shells, minerals and stones, and extends 67ft into the side of the hill. Please wear flat shoes and bring a torch, as the grotto is not lit this is essential.

Times Open Apr-Sep, Sat & BH Mon 2-4.30. Other times by appointment only. **Fee** ✷ Donations welcome **Facilities** ❷ on street (restricted at times) (many steps, not suitable for wheelchair users) (web link virtual tour) ❁ ⬛

KENT

Apple picking in Southborough

KENT

ENGLAND

AYLESFORD — MAP 05 TQ75

Aylesford Priory

The Friars ME20 7BX

⮱ *(M20 junct 6 or M2 junct 3 onto A229, signed)*

☎ 01622 717272

e-mail: gm@thefriars.org.uk
web: www.thefriars.org.uk

Built in the 13th and 14th centuries, the Priory has been restored and is now a house of prayer, guesthouse, conference centre and a place of pilgrimage and retreat. It has fine cloisters, and displays sculpture and ceramics by modern artists.

Times Open all year, daily 9-dusk. Gift, book shop & tea rooms May-Sep, 10-5; Oct-Apr, 10-4 (Sun 11am). Guided tours of the priory by arrangement. **Fee** ✳ Free, donations welcome. **Facilities** ❷ ♿ ☂ (outdoor) ♿ (Partly accessible) (wheelchairs available, ramps) toilets for disabled shop ❽ (ex assist dogs)

BEKESBOURNE — MAP 05 TR15

Howletts Wild Animal Park

Beekesbourne Rd CT4 5EL

⮱ *(off A2, 3m S of Canterbury, follow brown tourist signs)*

☎ 0870 750 4647

e-mail: info@totallywild.net
web: www.totallywild.net

Set in 90 acres of parkland, Howletts is home to some of the world's most rare and endangered animals. Howletts boasts the UK's largest group of African elephants, Indian and Siberian tigers, many small cats and rare monkeys and the world's largest group of Western Lowland gorillas. Glass-fronted tiger enclosures, children's adventure playground and the new Jurassic Mine with ice and gem cave are not to be missed. Visit the Natureworks Arts and Craft Studio for painting, pottery, arts and crafts and the open-topped Javan Langur enclosure where the endangered monkeys can be seen in a natural environment. There is also a farm shop.

Times Open all year, daily 10-6 during summer (last admission 4.30), 10-5 during winter (last admission 3.30). Closed 25 Dec. **Fee** ✳ £14.45 (ch 4-16 £11.45). Family (2ad+2ch) £44, (2ad+3ch) £51.50. **Facilities** ❷ ♿ ☂ �🍴 ☂ ♿ (wheelchairs for hire, book in advance) toilets for disabled shop ❽

BELTRING — MAP 05 TQ64

The Hop Farm

TN12 6PY

⮱ *(on A228 at Paddock Wood)*

☎ 01622 872068

e-mail: info@thehopfarm.co.uk
web: www.thehopfarm.co.uk

The Hop Farm is set among the largest collection of Victorian oast houses, and its attractions include museums and exhibitions, indoor and outdoor play areas, animal farm and shire horses, and restaurant and gift shop. The recently opened Driving School and Jumping Pillows

offer non-stop fun for children, and for the adults there are also Legends in Wax and the story of the Hop Farm.

Times Open from 10 daily. **Fee** ✳ £7.50 (ch 4-15 £6.50). Family ticket (2ad+2ch) £27. Event prices may vary. **Facilities** ❷ ♿ ☂ �🍴 licensed ☂ (outdoor) ♿ (Partly accessible) toilets for disabled shop ❽ (dogs not allowed inside)

BIDDENDEN — MAP 05 TQ83

Biddenden Vineyards & Cider Works

Gribble Bridge Ln TN27 8DF

⮱ *(0.5m S off A262, 0.5m from Biddenden Village. Bear right at Woolpack Corner)*

☎ 01580 291726

e-mail: info@biddendenvineyards.co.uk
web: www.biddendenvineyards.com

The present vineyard was established in 1969 and now covers 20 acres. Visitors are welcome to stroll around the vineyard and to taste wines, ciders and apple juice available at the shop. English wine week is held here at the end of May.

Times Open all year, Shop: Mon-Fri 10-5, Sat 10-5, Sun & BH 11-5. Closed noon 24 Dec-2 Jan & Sun in Jan & Feb. **Fee** ✳ Non-guided groups and individuals free. Pre-booked guided tours (min 15) £4.75 (ch 10-17 £2.25, ch under 10 £1). Evening guided tour max 35 people £6.75. **Facilities** ❷ ☂ (outdoor) ♿ (Partly accessible) shop ❽ (ex assist dogs)

BIRCHINGTON — MAP 05 TR36

Quex Museum, House & Gardens

Quex Park CT7 0BH

⮱ *(A28 to Birchington right into Park Lane before rdbt in town centre. Entrance 600yds on left)*

☎ 01843 842168

e-mail: enquiries@quexmuseum.org
web: www.quexmuseum.org

Major Powell-Cotton (1866-1940) devoted his life to the study of the animals and many different cultures of Africa. This museum, founded in 1895, is his legacy, consisting of animal dioramas, ethnography, weaponry, archaeology, ceramics and artefacts from around the world. Also on display in Quex House, the family home, are collections of paintings, Eastern and Asian furniture, and English period furniture. All set within 15 acres of mature gardens, including a Victorian walled garden, fountains, children's maze and resident doves, ducks and peacocks. A full programme of family events throughout the summer can be found on the website.

Times Open Apr-Oct, Sun-Thurs 11-5, Quex House 2-4.30. Nov-Mar museum & gardens, Sun 1-3.30 house closed. **Fee** ✳ £7 (ch & pen £5, under 5's free). Family ticket (2ad+3ch) £18. Garden only £2. **Facilities** ❷ ☂ �🍴 ☂ (outdoor) ♿ (Partly accessible) (two wheelchairs available) toilets for disabled shop ❽ (ex assist dogs)

BOROUGH GREEN MAP 05 TQ65

Great Comp Garden

TN15 8QS

➲ (2m E off B2016, follow brown signs)

☎ 01732 886154

e-mail: greatcompgarden@aol.com

web: www.greatcomp.co.uk

A beautiful seven-acre garden surrounds an early 17th-century Manor (not open). There is a plantsmans' collection of trees, shrubs, heathers and herbaceous plants in a setting of fine lawns and grass paths. Each area of the garden reveals a different character. From the large collection of magnolias, rhododendrons and azaleas in the spring to the rare and exotic shrubs and perennial plants through the remainder of the year. Great Comp is home to the Dyson Salvia Collection.

Times Open Apr-Oct, daily 11-5. **Facilities** ℗ ☐ ⛶ ⁺⊙⁺ & (free wheelchair for hire) toilets for disabled shop garden centre ⊗ (ex assist dogs)

BRASTED MAP 05 TQ45

Emmetts Garden

Ide Hill TN14 6AY

➲ (1m S of A25, Sundridge-Ide Hill road)

☎ 01732 750367

e-mail: emmetts@nationaltrust.org.uk

web: www.nationaltrust.org.uk/emmettsgarden

Emmetts is a charming hillside shrub garden, with bluebells, azaleas and rhododendrons in spring and rich autumn colours. It has magnificent views over Bough Beech Reservoir and the Weald. Events include family picnic days and guided walks.

Times Open 15 Mar-1 Jun, Tue-Sun; 4 Jun-1 Jul, Wed-Sun; 4 Jul-28 Oct, Sat-Sun & BHs 11-5 (last admission 4.15). **Fee** ✳ £5 (ch £1). Family ticket £9. Pre-booked group 15+ £4. Joint adult ticket with Quebec House **Facilities** ℗ ☐ ⛶ (outdoor) & (access steps & steep slopes) (wheelchairs, buggy service, Braille/large print guide) toilets for disabled shop ⊗ (ex on lead) ⅏ ⊜

BROADSTAIRS MAP 05 TR36

Dickens House Museum

2 Victoria Pde CT10 1QS

➲ (on seafront)

☎ 01843 863453

e-mail: l.ault@btinternet.com

web: www.dickenshouse.co.uk

The house was immortalised by Charles Dickens in David Copperfield as the home of the hero's aunt, Betsy Trotwood, whom Dickens based on owner Miss Mary Pearson Strong. Dickens' letters and possessions are shown, with local and Dickensian prints, costumes and general Victoriana.

Times Open Etr-Oct, daily 2-5, also Sat-Sun mid Jun-Aug 10.30-5. **Fee** ✳ £2.30 (ch £1.20). Family ticket (2ad+2ch) £5. **Facilities** ℗ (400yds) (pay & display) & (Partly accessible) shop ⊗ (ex assist dogs)

CANTERBURY MAP 05 TR15

Canterbury Roman Museum

Butchery Ln, Longmarket CT1 2JR

➲ (in centre close to cathedral & city centre car parks)

☎ 01227 785575

e-mail: museums@canterbury.gov.uk

web: www.canterbury-museums.co.uk

Step below today's Canterbury to discover an exciting part of the Roman town including the real remains of a house with fine mosaics. Experience everyday life in the reconstructed market place and see exquisite silver and glass. Try your skills on the touch screen computer, and in the hands-on area with actual finds. Use the computer animation of Roman Canterbury to join the search for the lost temple.

Times Open all year, Mon-Sat 10-5 & Sun (Jun-Oct) 1.30-5. (Last admission 4). Closed Good Fri & Xmas period. **Fee** £3 (ch 5-18, concession £2). Family ticket (2ad+up to 3 ch) £7.90. **Facilities** ℗ (walking distance) & (lift) toilets for disabled shop ⊗ (ex assist dogs) ⊜

The Canterbury Tales

St. Margaret's St CT1 2TG

➲ (In heart of city centre, located in St Margaret's St)

☎ 01227 479227

e-mail: info@canterburytales.org.uk

web: www.canterburytales.org.uk

Step back in time to experience the sights sounds and smells of the Middle Ages in this reconstruction of 14th-century England. Travel from the Tabard Inn in London, to St. Thomas Becket's Shrine in Canterbury with Chaucer's colourful pilgrims. Their tales of chivalry, romance and intrigue are brought vividly to life for you to enjoy along your journey.

Times Open all year, Mar-Jun 10-5, Jul-Aug 9.30-5, Sep-Oct 10-5 & Nov-Feb 10-4.30. Closed 25 & 26 Dec, 1 Jan **Fee** ✳ £7.75 (ch £5.75, concessions £6.75) Valid until 31/01/2009. **Facilities** ℗ (200mtrs) & (notice required for wheelchairs, hearing loop facility) toilets for disabled shop ⊗ (ex assist dogs) ⊜

Canterbury West Gate Towers

St. Peter's St CT1 2RA

➲ *(at end of main street beside river. Entrance under main arch)*

☎ 01227 789576

e-mail: museums@canterbury.gov.uk

web: www.canterbury-museum.co.uk

The last of the city's fortified gatehouses sits astride the London road with the river as a moat. Rebuilt in around 1380 by Archbishop Sudbury, it was used as a prison for many years. The battlements give a splendid panoramic view of the city and are a good vantage point for photographs. Arms and armour can be seen in the guardroom, and there are cells in the towers. Brass rubbings can be made and children can try on replica armour.

Times Open all year (ex Good Fri & Xmas period), Mon-Sat; 11-12.30 & 1.30-3.30. Last admission 15 mins before closure. **Fee** £1.25 (ch & concessions 75p). Family ticket (2ad+up to 3ch)£2.90. **Facilities** Ⓟ (100yds) shop ⊗ (ex assist dogs)

Druidstone Park

Honey Hill, Blean CT2 9JR

➲ *(3m NW on A290 from Canterbury)*

☎ 01227 765168

web: www.druidstone.net

Idyllic garden setting with enchanted woodland walks where dwells the sleeping dragon. See the Mystical Oak Circle with the Old Man of the Oaks. Children's farmyard, play areas, gift shop and cafeteria. There are usually twice-daily falconry displays.

Times Open Etr-Nov, Fri-Mon, 10-5.30. Daily during school hols. **Fee** £5.30 (ch £4 & pen £4.50). Family ticket £16. **Facilities** Ⓟ ☕ ⛩ (outdoor) ♿ toilets for disabled shop ⊗ (ex assist dogs) 💳

Museum of Canterbury

Stour St CT1 2NR

➲ *(in the Medieval Poor Priests' Hospital, just off St Margaret's St or High St)*

☎ 01227 475202

e-mail: museums@canterbury.gov.uk

web: www.canterbury-museums.co.uk

Discover the story of Canterbury in new interactive displays for all the family. See the city's treasures including the famous Canterbury Cross. Try the fun activities in the Medieval Discovery Gallery, find out about the mysteries surrounding Christopher Marlowe's life and death and spot friend or foe planes in the WW2 Blitz gallery. Meet favourite children's TV character Bagpuss and friend's and enjoy the Rupert Bear Museum - full of adventure and surprises.

Times Open all year, Mon-Sat 10.30-5 & Sun (Jun-Sep) 1.30-5 (last admission 4). (Closed Good Fri & Xmas period). **Fee** £3.50 (concessions £2.25). Family ticket £8.95 (2 ad & 3 ch) **Facilities** Ⓟ (5-10 min walk) ♿ toilets for disabled shop ⊗ (ex assist dogs)

St Augustine's Abbey

CT1 1TF

➲ *(off A28)*

☎ 01227 767345

web: www.english-heritage.org.uk

Part of the Canterbury World Heritage site, this is considered by many as the birthplace of Christianity in England. Visit the fascinating museum and take the free interactive audio tour.

Times Open all year, 21 Mar-Jun, Wed-Sun 10-5; Jul-Aug, daily 10-6; Sep-Mar, Sat-Sun 11-5. (Closed 24-26 Dec & 1 Jan). **Fee** £4.20 (concessions £3.40, ch £2.10). Family ticket £10.50. Prices and opening times are subject to change in March 2009. Please call 0870 333 1181 for the most up to date prices and opening times when planning your visit. **Facilities** Ⓟ shop ⌗

CHARTWELL — MAP 05 TQ45

Chartwell

TN16 1PS

➲ *(off A25 onto B2026 at Westerham, Chartwell 2m S of village)*

☎ 01732 866368 (info line) & 868381

e-mail: chartwell@nationaltrust.org.uk

web: www.nationaltrust.org.uk/chartwell

The former home of Sir Winston Churchill is filled with reminders of the great statesman, from his hats and uniforms to gifts presented by Stalin, Roosevelt, de Gaulle and many other State leaders. There are portraits of Churchill and other works by notable artists, and also many paintings by Churchill himself. The gardens command breathtaking views over the Weald of Kent.

Times Open House, 14 Mar-1 Nov, Wed-Sun 11-5. Open BH Mon & Tue in Jul & Aug. (Last admission 4.15). Garden & Studio Jan-13 Mar; 4 Nov-21 Dec, Wed-Sun 11-4. **Fee** * House, Garden & Studio £10 (ch £5). Garden & Studio £5 (Ch £2.50). Family ticket £25. **Facilities** Ⓟ (charged) 🍴 licensed ⛩ (outdoor) ♿ (access via 2 steps to lift & some steps in garden) (parking, guides, sensory facilities) toilets for disabled shop ⊗ (ex assist dogs & on lead) 🌿 💳

CHATHAM   MAP 05 TQ76

Dickens World

Leviathan Way ME4 4LL

➲ *(Signposted from junct's 1, 3, & 4 of the M2, follow brown anchor signs)*

☎ 01634 890421

e-mail: enquiries@dickensworld.co.uk

web: www.dickensworld.co.uk

Dickens World is an exciting indoor complex themed around the life, books and times of Charles Dickens. It takes visitors on a fascinating journey through the author's lifetime as you step back into Dickensian England and are immersed in the streets, sounds and smells of the 19th century. Dickens World includes The Great Expectations boat ride; The Haunted Man; Victorian School Room; a 4D Hi-def show in Peggotty's Boathouse; Fagin's Den, a soft play area for younger children; and The Britannia Theatre, an animatronic stage show.

Times Open daily 10-5.30 (last admission 4). Closed 25 Dec. Seasonal variations apply. **Fee** ✳ £12.50 (ch 5-15 £7.50, concessions £10.50) **Facilities** ❷ ⬚ ⬥ licensed ♿ (to board boat ride, wheelchair users must be able to get in/out of chair unaided) (lifts, hearing loops, essential carers, disabled parking) toilets for disabled shop ⊗ (ex assist dogs) ▭

The Historic Dockyard Chatham

ME4 4TZ

➲ *(M29 junct 6, M2 junct 3 onto A229 towards Chatham. Then A230 and A231, following brown tourist signs. Brown anchor signs lead to visitors entrance)*

☎ 01634 823807 & 823800

e-mail: info@chdt.org.uk

web: www.thedockyard.co.uk

Costumed guides bring this spectacular maritime heritage site alive. Discover over 400 years of maritime history as you explore the most complete dockyard of the Age of Sail, set in a stunning 80-acre estate, and 'meet' characters from the past. Various special events take place throughout the year, please see the website for details. In 2009 the Chatham Historic Dockyard Trust will celebrate its 25th anniversary.

Times Open daily mid Feb-end Oct, Nov wknds only. **Fee** £13.50 (ch £9, concessions £11). Family (2ad+2ch) £38, additional ch £6. **Facilities** ❷ ⬚ ⬥ licensed ⏛ (indoor & outdoor) ♿ (Partly accessible) (wheelchair available, virtual tours) toilets for disabled shop ▭

DEAL   MAP 05 TR35

Deal Castle

Victoria Rd CT14 7BA

➲ *(SW of Deal town centre)*

☎ 01304 372762

web: www.english-heritage.org.uk

Discover the history of this formidable fortress as you explore the long, dark passages that once linked a garrison of 119 guns.

Times Open 21 Mar-Sep, daily 10-6 (Sat 10-5). Closed Oct-Mar. **Fee** £4.20 (concessions £3.40, ch £2.10). Family Ticket £10.50. Prices and opening times are subject to change in March 2009. Please call 0870 333 1181 for the most up to date prices and opening times when planning your visit. **Facilities** ♿ (parking available) shop ⊗ ✤

Walmer Castle & Gardens

Kingsdown Rd CT14 7LJ

➲ *(1m S on coast, off A258)*

☎ 01304 364288

web: www.english-heritage.org.uk

Originally built by Henry VIII as a formidable and austere fortress, the castle has since been transformed into an elegant stately home, formerly used by HM The Queen Mother. Many of her rooms are open to view, but the special highlight is the magnificent gardens.

Times Open 21 Mar-Sep, daily 10-6 (Sat 10-4); Mar & Oct, Wed-Sun 10-4. Closed Nov-Feb. (Also closed 11-13 Jul when Lord Warden in residence). **Fee** £6.50 (concessions £5.20, ch £3.30). Family ticket £16.30. Prices and opening times are subject to change in March 2009. Please call 0870 333 1181 for the most up to date prices and opening times when planning your visit. **Facilities** ℗ ⬚ shop ⊗ ✤

DOVER   MAP 05 TR34

Dover Castle & Secret Wartime Tunnels

CT16 1HU

☎ 01304 211067

web: www.english-heritage.org.uk

Various exhibitions demonstrate how Dover Castle has served as a vital strategic centre for the Iron Age onwards. In May 1940 the tunnels under the castle became the nerve centre for 'Operation Dynamo' - the evacuation of Dunkirk. These wartime secrets are now revealed for all to see.

Times Open 21 Mar-Jul & Sep daily 10-6; Aug, daily 9.30-6; Oct, daily 10-5; Nov-Jan, Thu-Mon 10-4; Feb-Mar, daily 10-4. Closed 24-26 Dec & 1 Jan. (The Keep closes at 5pm on Sat if hospitality event booked. Last admission 30 mins before closing. Timed ticket sytem in operation for Secret Wartime Tunnel tour & last tour 1hr before closing). **Fee** £10.30 (concessions £8.20, ch £5.20). Family £25.80. Includes Tunnels tour. (Additional charges may apply on event days). All prices and opening times are subject to change in March 2009. Please call 0870 333 1181 for the most up to date prices and opening times when planning your visit. **Facilities** ❷ ⬥ shop ⊗ (ex on lead in certain areas) ✤

Roman Painted House `2 for 1`

New St CT17 9AJ

➲ *(follow A20 to York St bypass, located in town centre)*

☎ 01304 203279

Visit five rooms of a Roman hotel built 1800 years ago, famous for its unique, well-preserved Bacchic frescos. The Roman underfloor heating system and part of a late-Roman defensive wall are also on view. There are extensive displays on Roman Dover.

Times Open Apr-Sep, Tue-Sat 10-5, Sun 1-4.30, also BH Mon & Mon Jul & Aug. **Fee** £2 (ch, pen & students £1) **Facilities** ❷ ⚲ (outdoor) ♿ (Partly accessible) (touch table, glass panels on gallery for wheelchairs) toilets for disabled shop ✪ (ex assist dogs)

DYMCHURCH   MAP 05 TR12

Dymchurch Martello Tower `FREE`

High St CT16 1HU

➲ *(access from High St not seafront)*

☎ 01304 211067

web: www.english-heritage.org.uk

This artillery tower formed part of a chain of strongholds intended to resist invasion by Napoleon.

Times Open Aug BH and Heritage Open Days. **Facilities** ✪ ⚎

EDENBRIDGE

See **Hever**

EYNSFORD   MAP 05 TQ56

Eagle Heights

Lullingstone Ln DA4 0JB

➲ *(M25 junct 3/A20 towards West Kingsdown. Right after 2 rdbts onto A225. Follow brown signs)*

☎ 01322 866466

e-mail: office@eagleheights.co.uk

web: www.eagleheights.co.uk

Eagle Heights is an impressive display of birds of prey from all over the world. Many are flown out across the Darenth valley twice daily. Meet the owls, pygmy goat and rabbits in the paddock. New Africa show including cheetah.

Times Open Mar-Oct daily 10.30-5. Nov, Jan-Feb wknd only 11-4. **Fee** ☀ £7.95 (ch £5, concessions £6.95) **Facilities** ❷ ⚌ ⚲ (outdoor) ♿ (loop system) toilets for disabled shop ✪ ⚍

Eynsford Castle `FREE`

➲ *(in Eynsford, off A225)*

web: *www.english-heritage.org.uk*

One of the first stone castles to be built by the Normans. The moat and remains of the curtain wall and hall can still be seen.

Times Open 21 Mar-Sep, daily 10-6; Oct-Nov & Feb-Mar, daily 10-4; Dec-Jan, Wed-Sun, 10-4. Closed 24-26 Dec & 1 Jan. **Facilities** ❷ ⚎

Lullingstone Castle

DA4 0JA

➲ *(1m SW of Eynsford via A225 & Lullingstone Roman Villa)*

☎ 01322 862114

web: www.lullingstonecastle.co.uk

The house was altered extensively in Queen Anne's time, and has fine state rooms and beautiful grounds. The 15th-century gate tower was one of the first gatehouses in England to be made entirely of bricks, and there is a church with family monuments. The two-acre walled garden is currently being turned into a 'World Garden of Plants', which will contain 10,000 different plant species. Please telephone for details of special events.

Times Open Apr-Oct Fri & Sat, garden 12-5, house 2-5. Sun & BHs (ex Good Fri) garden & house 2-6. Guided groups by arrangement Wed & Thu. **Fee** ☀ House & Gardens £6 (ch £3 & concessions £5.50) Family £15. **Facilities** ❷ ⚌ ♿ (ground floor only accessible) shop garden centre ✪ (ex assist dogs)

FAVERSHAM   MAP 05 TR06

Fleur de Lis Heritage Centre `2 for 1`

10-13 Preston St ME13 8NS

➲ *(3 minutes drive from M2 junct 6)*

☎ 01795 534542

e-mail: ticfaversham@btconnect.com

web: www.faversham.org/society

Expanded and updated, and housed in 16th-century premises, the Centre features colourful displays and room settings that vividly evoke the 2,000 year history of Faversham. Special features include the 'Gunpowder Experience' and a working old-style village telephone exchange, one of only two remaining in Britain. In July, during the Faversham Open House Scheme, over 20 historic properties in the town are opened to the public.

Times Open all year, Mon-Sat, 10-4; Sun 10-1. **Fee** £2 (ch & pen £1) **Facilities** ℗ (200yds) ♿ (Partly accessible) (DVD show of parts that are inaccessible) toilets for disabled shop ⚍

ENGLAND

Royal Engineers Museum & Library

Prince Arthur Rd ME4 4UG

➲ *(follow brown signs from Gillingham & Chatham town centres)*

☎ 01634 822839

e-mail: mail@re-museum.co.uk

web: www.remuseum.org.uk

The museum covers the diverse and sometimes surprising work of the Royal Engineers. Learn about the first military divers, photographers, aviators and surveyors; see memorabilia relating to General Gordon and Field Marshal Lord Kitchener, Wellington's battle map from Waterloo and a Harrier jump-jet. The superb medal displays include 25 Victoria Crosses, among 6,000 medals. There are 25 galleries that cover numerous campaigns over the last 300 years. Among the exhibits are locomotives, tanks, the first wire-guided torpedo, bridges, and models. Special events sometimes take place in conjunction with Chatham Historic Dockyard.

Times Open all year, Tue-Fri 9-5, Sat-Sun & BH Mon 11.30-5. Closed Good Fri, Xmas week & 1 Jan. Library open by appointment (ex wknds). **Fee** £6.35 (ch under 5 free, concessions £3.30). Provision of postcode & name will entitle visitors to 1yr entry **Facilities** ☻ ⴱ (indoor & outdoor) ⴲ (Partly accessible) (help available if required, chair lift to upper level) toilets for disabled shop ⊗ (ex assist dogs) ⊟

Finchcocks Musical Museum

TN17 1HH

➲ *(off A21 on the A262, 2m W of Goudhurst village, entrance by Green Cross Inn)*

☎ 01580 211702

e-mail: info@finchcocks.co.uk

web: www.finchcocks.co.uk

This magnificent manor set in a beautiful garden surrounded by parkland provides the backdrop for a large and varied programme of open days, private visits, concerts, courses and much more. Now in its 27th year of operation, Finchcocks is a Georgian manor house with a very special collection of historical musical instruments: The Richard Burnett keyboard collection. There are entertaining musical demonstrations aimed at the general visitor rather than the specialist musician. 2009 is the 200th anniversary of Haydn's death.

Times Open Etr-Sep, Sun & BH Mon 2-6; Aug, Wed, Thu 2-6. Private groups on other days by appointment Apr-Dec. **Fee** ✳ £9 (ch £4, students £6). Family ticket (with school age children) £20. Garden only £2.50. Season ticket £24 **Facilities** ☻ ⴲ ⵏ⊙ⵏ licensed ⴱ (outdoor) ⴲ (accessible use of ramps & rails) (wheelchair available, Braille signs) toilets for disabled shop garden centre ⊗ (ex assist dogs)

Groombridge Place Gardens & Enchanted Forest

TN3 9QG

➲ *(M25 junct 5, follow A21 S, exit at A26 (signed Tunbridge Wells), then take A264 - follow signs to village and Groombridge Place Gardens)*

☎ 01892 861444

e-mail: office@groombridge.co.uk

web: www.groombridge.co.uk

This award-winning attraction, set in 200 acres, features a series of magnificent walled gardens set against the backdrop of a romantic 17th-century moated manor. Explore the herbaceous border, the white rose garden, the 'Drunken Topiary', the 'Secret Garden' and the peacock walk. By way of contrast in the ancient woodland of the 'Enchanted Forest', the imagination is stimulated by mysterious features such as the 'Dark Walk', 'Dinosaur and Dragon Valley' and 'Groms' Village'. Groombridge was used as a major location in the recent movie adaptation of Jane Austen's *Pride and Prejudice*. There are also bird of prey flying displays, canal boat cruises, and a full programme of special events.

Times Open Apr-Nov, daily 10-5.30 **Fee** ✳ £8.95 (ch 3-12 £7.45). Family ticket (2ad+2ch) £29.95. Groups (pre-booked) 12+ available on request. **Facilities** ☻ ⵏ⊙ⵏ ⴱ (outdoor) ⴲ (Partly accessible) toilets for disabled shop ⊗ (ex assist dogs) ⊟

See advert on opposite page

HAWKINGE   MAP 05 TR23

Kent Battle of Britain Museum

Aerodrome Rd CT18 7AG

➲ *(off A260, 1m along Aerodrome road)*

☎ 01303 893140

e-mail: kentbattleofbritainmuseum@btinternet.com
web: www.kbobm.org

Once a Battle of Britain Station, today it houses the largest collection of relics and related memorabilia of British and German aircraft involved in the fighting. Also shown, full-size replicas of the Hurricane, Spitfire and Me109 used in Battle of Britain films. The year 2000 was the 60th anniversary of the Battle of Britain and a new memorial was dedicated. Artefacts on show, recovered from over 600 battle of Britain aircraft, all form a lasting memorial to all those involved in the conflict.

Times ✳ Open Etr-Sep, daily 10-5; Oct, daily 11-4. (Last admission 1 hour before closing). **Facilities** ♥ ⌷ ⧖ shop ⊗ (ex assist dogs)

HEVER   MAP 05 TQ44

Hever Castle & Gardens

TN8 7NG

➲ *(M25 junct 5 or 6, 3m SE of Edenbridge, off B2026)*

☎ 01732 865224

e-mail: mail@hevercastle.co.uk
web: www.hevercastle.co.uk

This enchanting, double-moated, 13th-century castle was the childhood home of Anne Boleyn. Restored by the American millionaire William Waldorf Astor at the beginning of the 20th century, it shows superb Edwardian craftsmanship. Astor also transformed the grounds, creating topiary, a yew maze, 35 acre lake and Italian gardens filled with antique sculptures. There is also a 100 metre herbaceous border, and a 'splashing' water maze' on the Sixteen Acre Island, as well as a woodland walk known as Sunday Walk. Adventure play area with the Henry VIII Tower Maze.

Times ✳ Open Mar-Nov, daily. Castle 12-6, Gardens 11-6. (Last admission 5). (Closes 4pm Mar & Nov). **Facilities** ♥ ⌷ ⦿ ⧖ (outdoor) ♿ (wheelchairs available, book in advance) toilets for disabled shop garden centre ▰

HYTHE — MAP 05 TR13

Romney, Hythe & Dymchurch Railway

TN28 8PL

⮑ *(M20 junct 11, follow signs to Hythe Station)*

☎ 01797 362353 & 363256

e-mail: info@rhdr.org.uk

web: www.rhdr.org.uk

The world's smallest public railway has its headquarters here. The concept of two enthusiasts coincided with Southern Railway's plans for expansion, and so the thirteen-and-a-half mile stretch of 15 inch gauge railway came into being, running from Hythe through New Romney and Dymchurch to Dungeness Lighthouse.

Times Open daily Etr-Oct; Sun in Jan & wknds Feb- Mar **Fee** ✳ Charged according to journey. **Facilities** ♿ ☕ 🍽 licensed 🎭 (indoor & outdoor) ♿ (stairlift to Model Museum) toilets for disabled shop 🖶

IGHTHAM — MAP 05 TQ55

Ightham Mote

TN15 0NT

⮑ *(2.5m S off A227, 6m E of Sevenoaks)*

☎ 01732 810378 & 811145 (info line)

e-mail: ighammote@nationaltrust.org.uk

web: www.nationaltrust.org.uk

This moated manor house, nestling in a sunken valley, dates from 1320. The main features of the house span many centuries and include the Great Hall, old chapel and crypt, Tudor chapel with painted ceiling, drawing room with Jacobean fireplace, frieze and 18th-century handpainted Chinese wallpaper, and the billiards room. There is an extensive garden as well as interesting walks in the surrounding woodland. Following completion of all conservation work visitors can enjoy the most extensive visitor route to date, including the bedroom of Charles Henry Robinson who bequeathed Ightham Mote to the National Trust.

Times Open 15 Mar-2Nov, daily (ex Tue & Wed),11-5. Open Good Fri. (Last admission 4.30). **Fee** ✳ £8.50 (ch £4). Family ticket £21. **Facilities** ♿ ☕ 🍽 licensed 🎭 (outdoor) ♿ (only gardens & ground floor rooms in house accessible) (wheelchairs, special parking ask at office, virtual tour) toilets for disabled shop garden centre 🐕 (ex assist dogs) 🎎 🖶

LAMBERHURST — MAP 05 TQ63

Bayham Old Abbey

TN3 8DE

⮑ *(off B2169, 2m W in East Sussex)*

☎ 01892 890381

web: www.english-heritage.org.uk

Explore the romantic ruins of this 13th-century abbey built by French monks in an 18th-century landscaped setting.

Times Open 21 Mar-Sep, daily 11-5. Closed Oct-Mar. **Fee** £3.70 (concessions £3, ch £1.90). Prices and opening times are subject to change in March 2009. Please call 0870 333 1181 for the most up to date prices and opening times when planning your visit. **Facilities** ♿ ⚐

Scotney Castle

TN3 8JN

⮑ *(1m S, of Lamberhurst on A21)*

☎ 01892 893868

e-mail: scotneycastle@nationaltrust.org.uk

web: www.nationaltrust.org.uk/scotneycastle

Scotney Castle is a hidden gem, set in one of the most romantic gardens in England. Home of the Hussey family since the late 18th century, Scotney Castle was remodelled in the 1830s by Edward Hussey III. The beautiful gardens were planned around the remains of the old, moated castle. There is something to see all year round, with spring flowers followed by rhododendrons, azaleas and kalmia in May-June, Wisteria and roses in summer, and then superb autumn colours. There are fine estate walks all year, through 770 acres of woodlands, hop farm and meadows. The house has limited rooms open, reflecting the lives and times of family members.

Times Open House 12 Mar-2 Nov, Wed-Sun 11-5. Garden 1-9 Mar & 8 Nov-21 Dec, Sat-Sun; 12 Mar-2 Nov, Wed-Sun, 11-5.30 (or dusk if earlier). **Fee** ✳ With Gift Aid donation: House & Garden £8.80 (ch £4.40). Family ticket £22. Garden only: £6.60 (ch £3.30). Family ticket £16.50. **Facilities** ♿ ☕ 🎭 (outdoor) ♿ (wheelchair hire, Braille/large print guidebook, audio tape) toilets for disabled shop 🐕 (ex assist dogs) 🎎 🖶

LYDD — MAP 05 TR02

RSPB Nature Reserve

Boulderwall Farm, Dungeness Rd TN29 9PN

⮑ *(off Lydd to Dungeness road, 1m SE of Lydd, follow tourist signs)*

☎ 01797 320588

e-mail: dungeness@rspb.org.uk

web: www.rspb.org.uk

This coastal reserve comprises 2,016 acres of shingle beach and flooded pits. An excellent place to watch breeding gulls and other water birds. Marsh harriers, Wheatears, great crested and little grebes also nest here, and outside the breeding season there are large flocks of teals, shovelers, and goldeneyes, goosanders, smews and both Slavonian and red-necked grebes. The Dungeness Wildlife and Countryside fair takes place in August each year, with free entry to all.

Times Open: Visitor Centre all year, daily 10-5 (10-4 Nov-Feb). Reserve open all year, daily 9am-9pm (or sunset if earlier). Closed 25-26 Dec. **Fee** £3 (ch £1, concessions £2). RSPB members free. **Facilities** ❷ 🛏 (outdoor) & (visitor centre & most trails accessible for wheelchair users & access by car to all but one hide) toilets for disabled shop ⊗ (ex assist dogs) 🛏

LYMPNE   MAP 05 TR13

Port Lympne Wild Animal Park, Mansion & Garden

CT21 4PD

➲ *(M20 junct 11, follow brown tourist signs)*

☎ 0870 750 4647

e-mail: info@totallywild.net

web: www.totallywild.net

A 600-acre wild animal park that houses hundreds of rare animals: African elephants, rhinos, wolves, bison, snow leopards, Siberian and Indian tigers, gorillas and monkeys. New features include a glass-fronted lion enclosure and an open-topped woodland home for the Colobus monkeys. The mansion designed by Sir Herbert Baker is surrounded by 15 acres of spectacular gardens. Inside, notable features include the restored Rex Whistler Tent Room, a Moroccan patio, and the hexagonal library where the Treaty of Paris was signed after World War I. Visit the Spencer Roberts mural room and the Martin Jordan animal mural room.

Times Open all year, daily 10-6 (summer, last admission 4.30) 10-5 (winter, last admission 3.30). Closed 25 Dec. **Fee** ✳ £14.45 (ch 4-16 £11.45). Family £44 (2ad+2ch) £51.50 (2ad+3ch). **Facilities** ❷ 🖵 🍴 licensed 🛏 (outdoor) & (very limited access for disabled, special route available) toilets for disabled shop ⊗ 🛏

MAIDSTONE   MAP 05 TQ75

Leeds Castle

ME17 1PL

➲ *(7m E of Maidstone at junct 8 of M20/A20, clearly signed)*

☎ 01622 765400

e-mail: enquiries@leeds-castle.co.uk

web: www.leeds-castle.com

Set on two islands in the centre of a lake, Leeds Castle has been called the 'loveliest castle in the world', and was home to six medieval Queens of England, as well as being Henry VIII's Royal Palace. Among the treasures inside are many paintings, tapestries and furnishings. Attractions in the grounds include formal gardens, exotic aviary, dog collar museum, vineyard, woodland walks, toddlers play area, yew maze with secret underground grotto and daily falconry displays, an adventure playground and the Hiflyer balloon. Special events all year round, including the Big Dig 14-22 Feb 2009. Contact for details or visit the website.

Times Open daily, Apr-Sep 10-7 (Castle 10.30-7) Last admission 5. Oct-Mar 10-5 (Castle 10.30-5) Last admission 3. Last entry to the castle is 30min after the last admission time. **Fee** £15 (ch £9.50, concessions £12.50). **Facilities** ❷ 🍴 licensed 🛏 (outdoor) & (only ground floor of castle accessible) (Braille information, induction loops, wheelchair & lift) toilets for disabled shop ⊗ (ex assist dogs) 🛏

Maidstone Museum & Bentlif Art Gallery   FREE

St Faith's St ME14 1LH

➲ *(close to County Hall & Maidstone E train stn, opp Fremlin's Walk)*

☎ 01622 602838

e-mail: museum@maidstone.gov.uk

web: www.museum.maidstone.gov.uk

Set in an Elizabethan manor house which has been much extended over the years, this museum contains an outstanding collection of fine and applied arts, including watercolours, furniture, ceramics, and a collection of Japanese art and artefacts. The museum of the Queen's Own Royal West Kent Regiment is also housed here. Please apply for details of temporary exhibitions, workshops etc.

Times Open all year, Mon-Sat 10-5.15, Sun & BH Mon 11-4. Closed 25-26 Dec & 1 Jan **Facilities** ℗ (150 mtrs) 🖵 & (Partly accessible) (Lifts) shop ⊗ (ex assist dogs) 🛏

Museum of Kent Life   2 for 1

Lock Ln, Sandling ME14 3AU

➲ *(from M20 junct 6 onto A229 Maidstone road, follow signs for Aylesford)*

☎ 01622 763936

e-mail: enquiries@museum-kentlife.co.uk

web: www.museum-kentlife.co.uk

Kent's award-winning open air museum is home to an outstanding collection of historic buildings which house exhibitions on life in Kent over the last 100 years. An early 20th-century village hall and reconstruction of cottages from the 17th and 20th-centuries are included. The museum is also home to a variety of farmyard animals including pigs, goats, geese, ducks and lambs. Contact the museum for details of events throughout the year.

Times Open Feb-Nov, daily 10-5 (last admission 4) **Fee** ✳ £7.50 (ch £5.20, under 3's free, concessions £6). **Facilities** ❷ 🖵 🍴 licensed 🛏 (outdoor) & (access is limited to upstairs areas) (wheelchairs & transport available, ramps) toilets for disabled shop 🛏

Tyrwhitt Drake Museum of Carriages   FREE

The Archbishop's Stables, Mill St ME15 6YE

➲ *(close to River Medway & Archbishops Palace, just off A229 in town centre)*

☎ 01622 602838

e-mail: museuminfo@maidstone.gov.uk

web: www.museum.maidstone.gov.uk

The museum is home to a unique collection of horse-drawn vehicles and transport curiosities. More than 60 vehicles are on display, from grand carriages and ornate sleighs to antique sedan chairs and Victorian cabs, there is even an original ice-cream cart.

Times Open May-mid Sep, 10.30-4.30. **Facilities** ℗ (50yds) & (Partly accessible) shop ⊗ (ex assist dogs)

ENGLAND

PENSHURST   MAP 05 TQ54

Penshurst Place & Gardens

TN11 8DG

➲ (M25 junct 5 take A21 Hastings road then exit at Hildenborough & follow signs)

☎ 01892 870307

e-mail: enquiries@penshurstplace.com

web: www.penshurstplace.com

Built between 1340 and 1345, the original house is perfectly preserved. Enlarged by successive owners during the 15th, 16th and 17th centuries, the great variety of architectural styles creates a dramatic backdrop for the extensive collections of English, French and Italian furniture, tapestries and paintings. The chestnut-beamed Baron's Hall is one of the oldest and finest in the country, and the house is set in magnificent formal gardens. There is a toy museum, venture playground, woodland trail, 10 acres of walled formal gardens and events throughout the season. Penshurst was recently used as a location for *The Other Boleyn Girl*, and is a popular choice as a movie and television location.

Times Open: wknds from Feb 2009, daily from Sat 28 Mar-Sun 1 Nov. Gardens open 10.30-6. House open noon-4. **Fee** House, garden, grounds £8.50 (ch 5-16 £5.50). Family (2ad+2ch) £23. Grounds including garden £7 (ch 5-16 £5). Family (2ad+2ch) £20. Rates 15+ freeflow or with guided tours available. **Facilities** ⊖ ☷ ⏍ licensed ⋒ (outdoor) ⚘ (garden accessible from visitor entrance, Baron's Hall and Nether Gallery all on ground floor, DVD show of other state rooms) (ramp into Barons Hall, Braille & large print guides) toilets for disabled shop garden centre ⊗ (ex assist dogs) ▬

RAMSGATE   MAP 05 TR36

Ramsgate Maritime Museum

Clock House, Pier Yard, Royal Harbour CT11 8LS

➲ (Follow A299 to Ramsgate, then Harbour signs)

☎ 01843 570622

e-mail: curatorramsgate@btconnect.com

web: www.ekmt.fogonline.co.uk

Ramsgate Maritime Museum is housed in the early 19th-century Clock House, focal point of the town's historic Royal Harbour. Four galleries explore the maritime heritage of east Kent. Themes include the fishing industry, transport, shipwreck and salvage, the area during two World Wars and the archaeology of the Goodwin Sands. A fifth display and conservation room features a 17th-century naval gun.

Times Open Etr-Sep, Tue-Sun 10-5. Oct-Etr Thu-Sun 11-4.30. **Facilities** ⊖ (charged) ⚘ (Partly accessible) shop ⊗ (ex assist dogs) ▬

RECULVER   MAP 05 TR26

Reculver Towers & Roman Fort   FREE

CT6 6SU

➲ (3m E of Herne Bay)

☎ 01227 740676

web: www.english-heritage.org.uk

An imposing 12th-century landmark: twin towers and the walls of a Roman fort.

Times Open any reasonable time, external viewing only. **Facilities** ⊖ ⚘ (long slope from car park to fort) ♨

RICHBOROUGH   MAP 05 TR36

Richborough Roman Fort & Amphitheatre

CT13 9JW

➲ (1.5m N of Sandwich off A257)

☎ 01304 612013

web: www.english-heritage.org.uk

Explore the site of the first Roman landing in Britain and visit the museum with its collection of artefacts uncovered on site. See the remains of the huge triumphal arch, once 25 metres high.

Times Open Fort: 21 Mar-Sep, daily 10-6. Amphitheatre: Any reasonable time, access across grazed land from footpath (call 01304 612013 for details). **Fee** £4.20 (concessions £3.40, ch £2.10). Family ticket £10.50. Prices and opening times are subject to change in March 2009. Please call 0870 333 1181 for the most up to date prices and opening times when planning your visit. **Facilities** ⊖ shop ♨

ROCHESTER   MAP 05 TQ76

Guildhall Museum   FREE

High St ME1 1PY

➲ (follow signs from A2 to Rochester city centre, museum is at N end of High St)

☎ 01634 848717

e-mail: guildhall.museum@medway.gov.uk

web: www.medway.gov.uk

Housed in two adjacent buildings, one dating from 1687 and the other from 1909. The collections are arranged chronologically from Prehistory to the Victorian and Edwardian periods. They cover local history and archaeology, fine and decorative art. There is a gallery devoted to the prison hulks of the River Medway, and a new room detailing the links between Charles Dickens and the Medway Towns. The museum stages a regular programme of temporary exhibitions.

Times Open all year, daily (ex Mon) 10-4.30. (Last admission 4). Closed Xmas, New Year & some BHs. **Facilities** ℗ (250 yds) ⚘ (limited wheelchair access to Guildhall ground floor, by prior arrangement) shop ⊗ (ex assist dogs)

Rochester Castle

ME1 1SX

➲ *(M2 junct 1 & M25 junct 2, A2, by Rochester Bridge)*

☎ 01634 402276

web: www.english-heritage.org.uk

Built on the Roman City Wall, this Norman bishop's castle was a vital royal stronghold.

Times Open all year, 21 Mar-Sep, daily 10-6; Oct-Mar, daily 10-4. (Last admission 45mins before closing). Closed 24-26 Dec & 1 Jan. **Fee** £5 (concessions & ch £4). Family ticket £14. Prices and opening times are subject to change in March 2009. Please call 0870 333 1181 for the most up to date prices and opening times when planning your visit. **Facilities** shop ⊗

ROLVENDEN   MAP 05 TQ83

C M Booth Collection of Historic Vehicles

Falstaff Antiques, 63 High St TN17 4LP

➲ *(on A28, 3m from Tenterden)*

☎ 01580 241234

e-mail: info@morganmuseum.org.uk

web: www.morganmuseum.org.uk

Not just vehicles, but various other items of interest connected with transport. There is a unique collection of three-wheel Morgan cars, dating from 1913, and the only known Humber tri-car of 1904, as well as a 1929 Morris van, a 1936 Bampton caravan, motorcycles and bicycles. There is also a toy and model car display. 2009 celebrates 100 years of Morgan cars.

Times Open all year, Mon-Sat 10-5.30. Closed 25-26 Dec. **Fee** ✳ £2.50 (ch £1) **Facilities** ℗ (roadside) ♿ (Partly accessible) shop ▭

SEVENOAKS   MAP 05 TQ55

Knole

TN15 0RP

➲ *(From town centre, off A225 Tonbridge road, opposite St. Nicholas' church)*

☎ 01732 462100 & 450608 (info line)

e-mail: knole@nationaltrust.org.uk

web: www.nationaltrust.org.uk/knole

Knole's fascinating links with Kings, Queens and nobility, as well as its literary connections with Vita Sackville-West and Virginia Woolf, make this one of the most intriguing houses in England. Thirteen superb state-rooms are laid out much as they were in the 18th century, to impress visitors with the status of the Sackville family, who continue to live at Knole today. The house includes rare furniture, important paintings, as well as many 17th-century tapestries. Lord Sackville's private garden is open Wednesdays between April and September, 11-4.

Times House open Apr-1 Nov & Tue 21 Jul-Aug, Wed-Sun 12-4. **Fee** ✳ With Gift Aid donation: £9.00 (ch £4.50). Family ticket £22.50. **Facilities** ❷ (charged) ⊡ ♿ (access to the Great Hall, shop & tea room ground floor only) (audio loop, Braille guide, large print guide, virtual tour) toilets for disabled shop ⊗ (ex assist dogs & on leads) ✦ ▭

SISSINGHURST   MAP 05 TQ73

Sissinghurst Castle Garden

TN17 2AB

➲ *(1m E of Sissinghurst village on A262)*

☎ 01580 710700

e-mail: sissinghurst@nationaltrust.org.uk

web: www.nationaltrust.org.uk

Created in the ruins of a large Elizabethan house and set in unspoilt countryside, Sissinghurst Castle Garden is one of the most celebrated gardens made by Vita Sackville-West and her husband Sir Harold Nicolson. Phone for details of special events and info on the bus link.

Times ✳ Open: Gardens mid Mar-end Oct, Fri-Tue 11-5.30. (Peace & Tranquillity after 3.30) **Facilities** ❷ (charged) ⦿ ⍭ ♿ (admission restricted to 4 wheelchairs at any one time) toilets for disabled shop ⊗ (ex assist dogs) ✦ ▭

SMALLHYTHE · MAP 05 TQ83

Smallhythe Place

TN30 7NG

⮕ *(2m S of Tenterden, on E side of the Rye Road on B2082)*

☎ 01580 762334

e-mail: smallhytheplace@nationaltrust.org.uk
web: www.nationaltrust.org.uk

Once a Tudor harbour master's house, this half-timbered, 16th-century building was Dame Ellen Terry's last home, and is now a museum of Ellen Terry memorabilia. The Barn Theatre houses a display and the cottage garden contains roses, an orchard and spring garden.

Times Open 1-9 Mar, Sat & Sun only; 15 Mar-26 Oct, Sat-Wed 11-5 (last admission 4.30) **Fee** ✱ £4.50 (ch £2.25). Family ticket £11. **Facilities** ❷ ☐ ☐ (outdoor) ♿ (access restricted to ground floor of House & Garden partly accessible, slopes, uneven paths, undulating terrain.) (album of descriptions & photos of upstairs, Braille guide) ⊗ (ex assist dogs) ♨

STROOD · MAP 05 TQ76

Diggerland

Medway Valley Leisure Park, Roman Way ME2 2NU

⮕ *(M2 junct 2, follow A228 towards Rochester. At rdbt turn right. Diggerland on right)*

☎ 08700 344437

e-mail: mail@diggerland.com
web: www.diggerland.com

An adventure park with a difference. Experience the thrills of driving real earth-moving equipment. Choose from various types of diggers and dumpers ranging from 1 ton to 8.5 tons. Complete the Dumper Truck Challenge or dig for buried treasure supervised by an instructor. New rides include JCB Robots, the Supertrack, Landrover Safari, Spin Dizzy and the Diggerland Tractors.

Times Open all year, 10-5, wknds, BHs & school hols only **Facilities** ❷ ☐ ☐ ♿ toilets for disabled shop ⊗ (ex assist dogs) ▬

SWINGFIELD MINNIS · MAP 05 TR24

MacFarlane's World of Butterflies `2 for 1`

MacFarlanes Garden Centre CT15 7HX

⮕ *(on A260 by junction with Elham-Lydden road)*

☎ 01303 844244

e-mail: macfarlanes@gardensandtress.fsnet.co.uk
web: www.macfarlanesgardens.co.uk

A tropical greenhouse garden with scores of colourful free-flying butterflies from all over the world among exotic plants such as bougainvillea, oleander and banana.

Times Open Apr-end Sep, daily 10-5. Closed Etr Sun. **Fee** £3 (ch £2 & concessions £2.50). Family ticket (2ad+2ch) £8.50. **Facilities** ❷ ☐ ☐⚟ licensed ☐ (outdoor) ♿ toilets for disabled shop garden centre ⊗ (ex assist dogs) ▬

TENTERDEN · MAP 05 TQ83

Kent & East Sussex Railway

Tenterden Town Station, Station Rd TN30 6HE

⮕ *(A28 turn into Station Rd beside The Vine Public House, station 200yds on right)*

☎ 01580 765155

e-mail: enquiries@kesr.org.uk
web: www.kesr.org.uk

Ten and a half miles of pure nostalgia, this is England's finest rural light railway. Beautifully restored coaches and locomotives dating from Victorian times enable visitors to experience travel and service from a bygone age. The picturesque line weaves between Tenterden and Bodiam, terminating in the shadow of the castle.

Times ✱ Open Etr-Sep wkdays & wknds. Other times of the year wknds & school hols. Five trains per day **Facilities** ❷ ☐ ☐⚟ ☐ (outdoor) ♿ (Converted coach for w/chairs, induction loop) toilets for disabled shop ▬

TUNBRIDGE WELLS (ROYAL) · MAP 05 TQ53

Tunbridge Wells Museum and Art Gallery `FREE`

Civic Centre, Mount Pleasant TN1 1JN

⮕ *(adjacent to Town Hall, off A264)*

☎ 01892 554171 & 526121

e-mail: museum@tunbridgewells.gov.uk
web: www.tunbridgewellsmuseum.org

This combined museum and art gallery tells the story of the borough of Tunbridge Wells. There are collections of costume, art, dolls and toys along with natural and local history from dinosaur bones to the original Pantiles. There is also a large collection of Tunbridge ware, the intricate wooden souvenirs made for visitors to the Wells. The art gallery features a changing programme of contemporary and historic art, touring exhibitions, and local art and craft.

Times Open all year, daily 9.30-5. Sun 10-4. Closed BHs & Etr Sat. **Facilities** ℗ (200 yds) ♿ (Partly accessible) (parking adjacent to building) shop ⊗ (ex assist dogs)

UPNOR · MAP 05 TQ77

Upnor Castle

ME2 4XG

⮕ *(on unclass road off A228)*

☎ 01634 718742 & 338110

web: www.english-heritage.org.uk

16th-century gun fort built to protect Elizabeth I's warships. It saw action in 1667, when the Dutch navy sailed up the Medway to attack the dockyard at Chatham.

Times Open 21 Mar-Sep, daily 10-6; Oct, daily 10-4. (Last admission 45mins before closing). Closed 24-26 Dec & 1 Jan. (May close early on Fri-Sat for weddings, please call in advance to check). **Fee** £4.50 (concessions & ch £3.50). Family ticket £12.50. Prices and opening times are subject to change in March 2009. Please call 0870 333 1181 for the most up to date prices and opening times when planning your visit. **Facilities** ℗ ⚏

WESTERHAM   MAP 05 TQ45

Quebec House

TN16 1TD

➲ *(at E end of village on N side of A25 facing junct with B2026 Edenbridge Road)*

☎ 01732 868381

e-mail: chartwell@nationaltrust.org.uk

web: www.nationaltrust.org.uk

A house of architectural and historical interest situated near the village green in Westerham. For some years the childhood home of General James Wolfe, it contains family and military memorabilia and an exhibition on the Battle of Quebec. 2008 was the 400th anniversary of the founding of the city of Quebec.

Times Open 15 Mar-2 Nov, Wed-Sun & BH 1-5. Last entry 4.30. **Fee** ✳ £3.50 (ch £1.50). Family ticket £8.50. Booked groups £3. Adult joint ticket with Emmetts Garden £7. **Facilities** ℗ (150mtrs) (Pay & Display) ♿ (Ground floor accessible, stairs to other floors. Grounds partly accessible, loose gravel paths.) (Wheelchair, tactile items, Braille & large print guide) toilets for disabled shop ⊗ (ex assist dogs) ♨ ➡

Squerryes Court   2 for 1

TN16 1SJ

➲ *(0.5m W of town centre, signed off A25)*

☎ 01959 562345 & 563118

e-mail: enquiries@squerryes.co.uk

web: www.squerryes.co.uk

This beautiful manor house, built in 1681 by Sir Nicholas Crisp, has been the home of the Wardes since 1731. It contains a fine collection of pictures, furniture, porcelain and tapestries. The lovely garden was landscaped in the 18th century and has a lake, restored formal garden, and woodland walks. September 13th 2009: celebration of the 250th Anniversary of the Battle of Quebec.

Times Open Apr-Sep, Wed, Sun & BH Mon. Garden open 11.30-5, House 1-5 (last entry 4.30) **Fee** ✳ House & grounds £6.50 (ch 16 £3 & concessions £6). Family ticket £13.50. Grounds £4 (ch 16 £2 & concessions £3.50). Family ticket £7.50 **Facilities** ℗ ⬚ 🍴 (outdoor) ♿ (ground floor of house accessible and level area around formal garden pls phone for more detail) toilets for disabled shop ⊗ (ex on leads in grounds) ➡

WEST MALLING   MAP 05 TQ65

St Leonard's Tower   FREE

ME19 6PE

➲ *(on unclass road W of A228)*

☎ 01732 870872

web: www.english-heritage.org.uk

Early example of a Norman tower keep, built c.1080 by Gundulf, Bishop of Rochester. The tower stands almost to its original height and takes its name from a chapel dedicated to St Leonard that once stood nearby.

Times Open any reasonable time for exterior viewing. Internal viewing by appointment only, please call 01732 870872. **Facilities** ⊞

YALDING   MAP 05 TQ75

Yalding Organic Centre

Benover Rd ME18 6EX

➲ *(on B2162, 0.5m S of Yalding.)*

☎ 01622 814650

e-mail: enquiry@gardenorganic.org.uk

web: www.yaldingorganics.com

Eighteen gardens tell the history of gardening in an imaginatively landscaped setting. Travel through representations of ancient woodlands, medieval physic, knot and paradise gardens, a 19th-century artisan's plot, and borders inspired by Gertrude Jekyll's ideas, before reaching a 1950s 'Dig for Victory' allotment. The remainder of the garden is devoted to the vision of the 'organic' future of horticulture, growing flowers, fruit and vegetables without added chemicals. The garden was founded, and is still owned by, Garden Organic, the national charity for organic growing, almost fifty years ago.

Times Open all year daily 9-6 **Fee** ✳ £4.50 (ch under 16 free, concessions £3.50) **Facilities** ℗ ⬚♿ toilets for disabled shop garden centre ⊗ (ex assist dogs) ➡

LANCASHIRE

Forest of Bowland at Whitewell

BLACKPOOL   MAP 07 SD33

Blackpool Zoo & Dinosaur Safari

East Park Dr FY3 8PP

➲ *(M55 junct 4, follow brown tourist signs)*

☎ 01253 830830

e-mail: info@blackpoolzoo.org.uk

web: www.blackpoolzoo.org.uk

This multi-award-winning zoo, built in 1972, houses over 1500 animals within its 32 acres of landscaped gardens. There is a miniature railway, lots of close encounters and animals in action, a children's play area, animal feeding times and keeper talks throughout the day. The Dinosaur Safari takes you on a walking trail with 32 lifesize dinosaurs in Jurassic gardens. Many special events throughout the year.

Times Open all year daily, summer 10-6; winter 10-dusk. Jul-Aug, Wed 10-9. Closed 25 Dec. **Facilities** ♿ 💬 🍴 ⛱ (outdoor) ♿ (wheelchair loan, talking & signing tours) toilets for disabled shop 🚫 (ex assist dogs) 🚌

BURNLEY   MAP 07 SD83

Towneley Hall Art Gallery & Museums

Towneley Park BB11 3RQ

➲ *(M65 junct 9 signed Halifax (A646) and follow signs for Towneley Hall.)*

☎ 01282 424213

e-mail: towneleyhall@burnley.gov.uk

web: www.burnley.gov.uk/towneley

This 14th-century house contains the art gallery and museum. Today a variety of displays encompass natural history, Eygptology, textiles and art. Special exhibitions and events are held throughout the year, telephone for details. There are nature trails and Natural History Collections. Look out for the Wildabout Burnley. Educational facilities are available for schools.

Times Open all year Sat-Thu 12-5. Closed Fri **Fee** ✳ £4 (ch & students free) **Facilities** ♿ (charged) 💬 🍴 licensed ⛱ (outdoor) ♿ (no access due to stairs in Historic Long Gallery) (virtual tour on computer) toilets for disabled shop garden centre 🚫 (ex assist dogs) 🚌

CHARNOCK RICHARD   MAP 07 SD51

Camelot Theme Park

PR7 5LP

➲ *(from M6 junct 27/28, or M61 junct 8 follow brown tourist signs)*

☎ 01257 452100

e-mail: kingarthur@camelotthemepark.co.uk

web: www.camelotthemepark.co.uk

Join Merlin, King Arthur and the Knights of the Round Table at the magical kingdom of Camelot. Explore five magic lands filled with thrilling rides, spectacular shows, and many more attractions. From white-knuckle thrills on Knightmare, The Whirlwind spinning rollercoaster, to wet-knuckle thrills on Pendragon's Plunge, there's something for everyone.

Times ✳ Open 31 Mar-28 Oct. **Facilities** ♿ 💬 ⛱ (indoor & outdoor) ♿ (Partly accessible) (disabled car parking) toilets for disabled shop 🚫 (ex assist dogs) 🚌

CHORLEY   MAP 07 SD51

Astley Hall Museum & Art Gallery   FREE

Astley Park PR7 1NP

➲ *(M61 junct 8, signed Botany Bay. Follow brown signs)*

☎ 01257 515555

e-mail: astley.hall@chorley.gov.uk

web: www.astleyhall.co.uk

A charming Tudor/Stuart building set in beautiful parkland, this lovely Hall retains a comfortable 'lived-in' atmosphere. There are pictures and pottery to see, as well as fine furniture and rare plasterwork ceilings. Special events throughout the year.

Times ✳ Open Apr (or Etr)-Oct, Sat-Sun & BH Mon 12-5; By appointment only during the week **Facilities** ♿ ⛱ (outdoor) ♿ (video of upper floors, print/Braille guide, CD audio guide) shop 🚫 (ex assist dogs) 🚌

ENGLAND

CLITHEROE   MAP 07 SD74

Clitheroe Castle Museum

Castle House, Castle Gate, Castle St BB7 1BA

➲ *(follow Clitheroe signs from A59 Preston-Skipton by-pass. Museum located in castle grounds near town centre)*

☎ 01200 424635

e-mail: museum@ribblevalley.gov.uk

web: www.ribblevalley.gov.uk/castlemuseum

The museum has a good collection of carboniferous fossils, and items of local interest. Displays include local history and the industrial archaeology of the Ribble Valley, while special features include the restored Hacking ferry boat believed to be the inspiration for 'Buckleberry Ferry' featured in JRR Tolkien's *Fellowship of the Ring*, printer's and clogger's shops and Edwardian kitchen. The area is renowned for its early 17th-century witches, and the museum has a small display on witchcraft.

Times ✳ Open late Feb-Etr, Mon-Sat 11.15-4.30, Sun 1-4.30; Etr-Oct, daily inc BH; Nov, Dec & Feb, wknds & school half terms. Closed Jan **Facilities** ℗ (500yds) (disabled only parking at establishment) ⌂ ⴜ (outdoor) shop ⊗ (ex assist dogs)

LANCASTER   MAP 07 SD46

City Museum (also 15 Castle Hill)

Market Sq LA1 1HT

➲ *(in city centre just off A6)*

☎ 01524 64637

e-mail: paul.thompson@mus.lancscc.gov.uk

web: www.lancsmuseums.gov.uk

The fine Georgian town hall is the setting for the museum, which explores the history and archaeology of the city from prehistoric and Roman times onwards. Also housed here is the museum of the King's Own Royal Lancaster Regiment. The Cottage Museum, furnished in the style of an artisan's house of around 1820, faces Lancaster Castle.

Times Open all year, Mon-Sat, 10-5. Closed 25 Dec-1 Jan. 15 Castle Hill, Apr-Sep, daily 2-5. **Fee** ✳ City Museum free. 15 Castle Hill £1 (accompanied ch free, concessions 75p). **Facilities** ℗ (5 mins walk) ⴜ (ramp to entrance/ground floor, 2 stairlifts) shop ⊗ (ex assist dogs)

Lancaster Castle

The Shire Hall, Castle Pde LA1 1YJ

➲ *(follow brown tourist signs from M6 junct 33/34)*

☎ 01524 64998

e-mail: christine.goodier@mus.lancscc.gov.uk

web: www.lancastercastle.com

Founded on the site of three Roman forts, Lancaster Castle dominates Castle Hill, above the River Lune. The Norman keep was built in about 1170 and King John added a curtain wall and Hadrian's Tower. The Shire Hall, noted for its Gothic revival design, contains a splendid display of heraldry. The Crown Court was notorious as having handed out the greatest number of death sentences of any court in the land. Various events through the year.

Times Open daily 10.30 (1st tour)-4 (last tour). Court sittings permitting - it is advisable to telephone before visiting. Closed Xmas & New Year. **Fee** £5 (concessions £4). Family ticket £14. **Facilities** ℗ ⴜ (Shire Hall courtroom accessible to wheelchair users) shop ⊗ (ex assist dogs) ⬛

Lancaster Maritime Museum   `2 for 1`

St George's Quay LA1 1RB

➲ *(close to M6, junct 33 & 34. From A6 follow signs to town centre)*

☎ 01524 382264

e-mail: paul.thompson@mus.lancscc.gov.uk

web: www.lancsmuseums.gov.uk

Graceful Ionic columns adorn the front of the Custom House, built in 1764. Inside, the histories of the 18th-century transatlantic maritime trade of Lancaster, the Lancaster Canal and the fishing industry of Morecambe Bay are well illustrated. Changing programme of special exhibitions and holiday events, please ring or see website for details.

Times Open all year, daily, Etr-Oct 11-5; Nov-Etr 12.30-4. **Fee** ✳ £3 (concessions £2). Free to accompanied children and residents of Lancaster district **Facilities** ℗ ⌂ ⴜ (indoor) ⴜ (mezzanine floor inaccessible) toilets for disabled shop ⊗ (ex assist dogs)

LEIGHTON HALL   MAP 07 SD47

Leighton Hall

LA5 9ST

➲ *(M6 junct 35 onto A6 & follow signs)*

☎ 01524 734474

e-mail: info@leightonhall.co.uk

web: www.leightonhall.co.uk

This is the historic family home of the Gillow furniture makers, and early Gillow furniture is displayed among other treasures in the fine interior of the neo-Gothic mansion. There are also fine gardens, a maze and a woodland walk. A varied programme of special events throughout the year, for full details please see website.

Times Open May-Sep, Tue-Fri & BH Sun & Mon; Aug, Tue-Fri, Sun & BH Mon 2-5. Groups all year by arrangement **Fee** £6.95(ch 5-12 £4.75, pen £6). Family ticket £22. **Facilities** ℗ ⌂ ⴜ (outdoor) ⴜ (upstairs not accessible) (ramps, parking close to entrance) toilets for disabled shop garden centre ⊗ (ex assist dogs & in park)

LEYLAND   MAP 07 SD52

British Commercial Vehicle Museum

King St PR25 2LE

➲ *(0.75m from M6 junct 28 in town centre)*

☎ 01772 451011

e-mail: enquiries@bcvm.co.uk

web: www.bcvm.co.uk

A unique line-up of historic commercial vehicles and buses spanning a century of truck and bus building. There are more than 50 exhibits on permanent display, and plenty of special events including transport model shows, transport shows, and the Ford Cortina Mk 1 gathering.

Times Open Apr-Sep, Sun, Tue-Thu & BH Mon (Oct open Tue & Sun only); 10-5. **Fee** £4.50 (ch & pen £2.50). Family ticket (2ad+3ch) £12. **Facilities** ℗ ☒ ♿ (ramps to decked viewing area) toilets for disabled shop ⊗ (ex assist dogs)

MARTIN MERE   MAP 07 SD41

WWT Martin Mere

L40 0TA

⮑ (signed from M61, M58 & M6, 6m from Ormskirk, off A59)

☎ 01704 895181

e-mail: info@martinmere.co.uk

web: www.martinmere.co.uk

One of Britain's most important wetland sites, where you can get really close to a variety of ducks, geese and swans from all over the world as well as two flocks of flamingos and beavers. Thousands of wildfowl, including pink-footed geese, Bewick's and Whooper swans, winter here. Other features include a children's adventure playground, craft area, shop and an educational centre. 2009 would have been Sir Peter Scott's 100th birthday. He formed the WWT 62 years ago.

Times Open all year, daily 9.30-5.30 (5 in winter). Closed 25 Dec. **Fee** ✳ £7.95 (ch £3.95, concessions £5.95). Family ticket £18.95. **Facilities** ℗ ☒ ⊟ (indoor & outdoor) ♿ (wheelchair loan, heated hide) toilets for disabled shop ⊗ (ex assist dogs) ▭

PADIHAM   MAP 07 SD73

Gawthorpe Hall

BB12 8UA

⮑ (on E outskirts of Padiham, 0.75m on A671)

☎ 01282 771004

e-mail: gawthorpehall@nationaltrust.org.uk

web: www.nationaltrust.org.uk

An early 17th-century manor house, built around Britain's most southerly pele tower, restored in 1850. A collection of portraits from the National Portrait Gallery and the Kay Shuttleworth Collections of costume, embroidery and lace are on show in the exhibition areas. The wooded park and riverside location offer wonderful walks.

Times Open Apr-1 Nov, Garden: daily 10-6. Hall: Tue-Thu & Sat-Sun 1-5. Also open BH Mon & Good Fri. (Last admission 4.30). **Fee** ✳ House: £4 (ch & concessions £3). Children free if accompanied by adult. Garden: free. Please telephone or check website for further details. **Facilities** ℗ ☒ ⊟ (outdoor) ♿ (House accessed via 4 steps and stairs to all floors. Grounds route to lawn and entrance to tea room are level.) (Braille & large print guide, photo album & car drop off) toilets for disabled ⊗ (ex assist dogs or in grounds) ▨

PRESTON   MAP 07 SD52

Harris Museum & Art Gallery

Market Square PR1 2PP

⮑ (M6 junct 31, follow signs for city centre, park at bus stn car park)

☎ 01772 258248

e-mail: harris.museum@preston.gov.uk

web: www.harrismuseum.org.uk

An impressive Grade I listed Greek Revival building containing extensive collections of fine and decorative art including a gallery of clothes and fashion. The Story of Preston covers the city's history and the lively exhibition programmes of contemporary art and social history are accompanied by events and activities throughout the year.

Times Open all year, Mon & Wed-Sat 10-5, Tue 11-5. Closed Sun & BHs. **Facilities** ℗ (5 mins walk) (blue badge disabled parking only) ☒ ♿ (lift to all floors available, with the exception of Egyptian Balcony. Wheelchair available, chair lift to mezzanine galleries, ramp to entrance) (audio visual guide to Egyptian Balcony is on 2nd floor) toilets for disabled shop ⊗ (ex assist dogs) ▭

National Football Museum

Sir Tom Finney Way, Deepdale PR1 6PA

⮑ (2m from M6 juncts 31, 31A or 32. Follow brown tourist signs)

☎ 01772 908442

e-mail: enquiries@nationalfootballmuseum.com

web: www.nationalfootballmuseum.com

Take an amazing journey through football history. Discover the world's biggest football museum, packed full of great footballing moments, stories and objects -from the World Cup ball used in the first ever final in 1930, to the ball used in the 1966 World Cup final. There are fun interactive opportunities and the brilliant penalty shoot-out game Goalstriker. Plus events, activities and exhibitions all year round means there's always something new to see and do. The 2-for-1 voucher can be redeemed against the Goalstriker penalty shoot-out.

Times Open all year Tue-Sat 10-5, Sun 11-5. Closed Mon ex BHs and school hols. (Museum closed 15 mins before 'kick off' on match days) **Facilities** ℗ ☒ ♿ (lifts, multi-sensory exhibitions, audio guide) toilets for disabled shop ⊗ (ex assist dogs)

ROSSENDALE   MAP 07 SD72

Rossendale Museum   FREE

Whitaker Park, Haslingden Rd, Rawtenstall BB4 6RE

⮑ (off A681, 0.25m W of Rawtenstall centre)

☎ 01706 260785

e-mail: rossendalemuseum@btconnect.com

Former mill owner's house, built in 1840 and set in the delightful Whitaker Park. Displays include fine and decorative arts, a Victorian drawing room, natural history, costume, local and social history and regular temporary exhibitions.

Times Open Apr-Oct, Tue-Thu, Sat-Sun & BHs, 1-4.30; Nov-Mar, 1-4. **Facilities** ℗ ♿ (large print, audio guides, induction loop, lift) toilets for disabled shop ⊗ (ex assist dogs)

Rufford Old Hall

L40 1SG

➲ *(M6 junct 27 & follow signs to Rufford. Hall on E side of A59)*

☎ 01704 821254

e-mail: ruffordoldhall@nationaltrust.org.uk

web: www.nationaltrust.org.uk

Rufford is one of Lancashire's finest Tudor buildings, and is where a young William Shakespeare is believed to have performed for its owner, Sir Thomas Hesketh. Visitors can wander around the house and view the fine collections of furniture, arms, armour and tapestries. Outside there are the gardens, topiary and sculptures. Enjoy a walk in the woodlands alongside the canal, and then have some freshly-prepared local food in the tea room.

Times Open 28 Feb-8 Mar wknds only, 11-5.30; 14-Mar-1 Nov, Sun-Wed 11-5.30 & Sat 1-5.30. Garden, shop & tea room, 6 Nov-21 Dec Fri-Sun, 12-4. **Fee** ✳ House & Garden: £5.20 (ch £2.60). Family ticket £13. Groups £4.40 each (ch £1.50). Garden only: £3.50 (ch £1.70). No groups Sun & BH Mon. **Facilities** ❷ ᐁᗡ (outdoor) ♿ (ground floor accessible, but steps from Great Hall & some loose cobbles & gravel in grounds) (Braille & large print guide, wheelchairs, induction loop) toilets for disabled shop ⊗ (ex assist dogs) ⚐

Samlesbury Hall

Preston New Rd PR5 0UP

➲ *(M6 junct 31/A677 for 3m, as indicated by brown tourist signs)*

☎ 01254 812010 & 812229

e-mail: enquiries@samlesburyhall.co.uk

web: www.samlesburyhall.co.uk

A well restored half-timbered manor house, built during the 14th and 15th centuries, and set in 5 acres of beautiful grounds. Sales of antiques and collector's items, craft shows and temporary exhibitions are held all year round. Live theatre productions and seasonal events throughout the year.

Times Open all year, Sun-Fri 11-4.30. Closed 25-26 Dec & 1 Jan and Sat for weddings. **Fee** £3 (ch 4-16 £1). **Facilities** ❷ ᐁᗡ licensed ♿ (ground floor only accessible, free admission) toilets for disabled shop garden centre ⊗ (ex assist dogs)

RSPB Leighton Moss Nature Reserve

Myers Farm LA5 0SW

➲ *(M6 junct 35, west on A501(M) for 0.5m. Turn right and head N on A6. Follow brown tourist signs)*

☎ 01524 701601

e-mail: leighton.moss@rspb.org.uk

web: www.rspb.org.uk

Leighton Moss is the largest remaining reedbed in north-west England, with special birds, breeding bitterns, bearded tits, marsh harriers, avocets and other spectacular wildlife. You can visit nature trails, look around the RSPB shop and visitor centre and enjoy a meal in the tearoom.

Times Reserve: open daily 9-dusk . Visitor Centre daily 9.30-5. Feb-Oct 9.30-4.30 Nov-Jan. Closed 25 Dec. **Fee** ✳ £4.50 (ch £1, concessions £3) Family £9. RSPB members Free **Facilities** ❷ ᐁᗡ (outdoor) ♿ (some nature trails accessible) (stairlift available to tea room) toilets for disabled shop ⊗ (ex assist dogs) ⬛

Turton Tower

BL7 0HG

➲ *(on B6391, off A666 or A676)*

☎ 01204 852203

e-mail: turton.tower@mus.lanscc.gov.uk

A historic house incorporating a 15th-century tower house and Elizabethan half-timbered buildings, and displaying a major collection of carved wood furniture. During the 19th century, the house became associated with the Gothic revival and later typified the idealism of the Arts and Crafts movement. The gardens are being restored in late-Victorian style.

Times ✳ Open May-Sep, Mon-Thu 11-5, wknds 1-5; Mar-Oct, Mon-Wed 1-5, wknds 1-4; Apr Sat-Wed 1-5; Nov & Feb, Sun 1-4. Other times by prior arrangement. **Facilities** ❷ ᐁᗡ shop ⊗ (ex in grounds) ⬛

Whalley Abbey   `2 for 1`

BB7 9SS

➲ *(off A59 4m S of Clitheroe)*

☎ 01254 828400

e-mail: office@whalleyabbey.org

web: www.whalleyabbey.co.uk

Whalley Abbey was established in the 13th century and the ruins of this former Cistercian Monastery are now open to the public. It is set in beautiful grounds in the glorious countryside of the Ribble Valley.

Times Open daily, 10-5. Closed 25-26 Dec & New Year. **Fee** ✳ £2 (ch 50p, pen £1.25) **Facilities** ❷ ᐁᗡ (outdoor) ♿ (chair lifts, ramps, wheelchairs available) toilets for disabled shop ⊗ (ex assist dogs)

LEICESTERSHIRE

Town Hall Square, Leicester

ASHBY-DE-LA-ZOUCH   MAP 08 SK31

Ashby-de-la-Zouch Castle

South St LE65 1BR

☎ 01530 413343
web: www.english-heritage.org.uk

Impressive ruins of a late medieval castle. The magnificent 24 metre Hastings Tower offers panoramic views of the surrounding countryside. Ashby was the setting for the famous jousting scene in Sir Walter Scott's classic romance *Ivanhoe*.

Times Open 21 Mar-Jun & Sep-Oct, Thu-Mon 10-5; Jul-Aug, daily 10-6; Nov-Mar, Thu-Mon 12-4. Closed 24-26 Dec & 1 Jan. **Fee** £3.70 (concessions £3, ch £1.90). Family ticket £9.30. Prices and opening times are subject to change in March 2009. Please call 0870 333 1181 for the most up to date prices and opening times when planning your visit. **Facilities ❷** shop ♯♯

BELVOIR   MAP 08 SK83

Belvoir Castle

NG32 1PD

➲ *(between A52 & A607, follow the brown heritage signs from A1, A52, A607 & A46)*

☎ 01476 871002
e-mail: info@belvoircastle.com
web: www.belvoircastle.com

Although Belvoir Castle has been the home of the Dukes of Rutland for many centuries, the turrets, battlements, towers and pinnacles of the house are a 19th-century fantasy. Amongst the many treasures to be seen inside are paintings by Murillo, Holbein and other famous artists. For children, there's a delightful Regency nursery, schoolroom and an adventure playground. Lovingly restored gardens are also open to visitors. Special events planned every weekend throughout the season, phone for details or visit the website.

Times Open 3-12 Apr & wknds May-Jun, daily ex Mon & Fri, Jul-Aug daily ex Fri, Sep wknds only, 7-14 Dec. **Fee** ✳ £12 (ch £6 under 5 free, concessions £10). **Facilities ❷** (charged) ▱ ⁱ◎ⁱ licensed ⋻ (outdoor) ♿ (Partly accessible) (permitted to be driven/drive right up to castle entrance) toilets for disabled shop ⊗ (ex assist dogs) ▱

COALVILLE   MAP 08 SK41

Snibston

Ashby Rd LE67 3LN

➲ *(4.5m from M1 junct 22 or from A42/M42 junct 13 on A511 on W side of Coalville)*

☎ 01530 278444
e-mail: snibston@leics.gov.uk
web: www.snibston.com

Award winning attraction and up-to-date science centre. In the Extra Ordinary hands-on gallery visitors can see how technology has affected everyday life, by lifting up a Mini Cooper. The Fashion Gallery has a wide selection of historic and modern costumes, while the underground life of a miner can be explored in the colliery tour. There are also rides on a diesel locomotive, or fun in the adventure play area.

Times Open daily, Apr-Oct 10-5; Nov-Mar 10-3. School hols & wknds 10-5. Closed 2 weeks in Jan for maintainence. **Facilities ❷** ▱ ⋻ (indoor & outdoor) ♿ (Braille labels, touch tables, parking available) toilets for disabled shop ⊗ (ex assist dogs) ▱

DONINGTON-LE-HEATH   MAP 05 SK41

Donington-le-Heath Manor House   FREE

Manor Rd LE67 2FW

➲ *(S of Coalville)*

☎ 01530 831259
e-mail: museum@leics.gov.uk
web: www.leics.gov.uk/museums

This is a rare example of a medieval manor house, tracing its history back to about 1280. It has now been restored as a period house, with fine oak furnishings. The surrounding grounds include period gardens, and the adjoining stone barn houses a restaurant.

Times Open Mar-Nov daily 11-4, Dec-Feb Sat-Sun 11-4 **Facilities ❷** ▱ ⁱ◎ⁱ ⋻ ♿ (Partly accessible) toilets for disabled shop ⊗ (ex assist dogs)

LEICESTER   MAP 04 SK50

Abbey Pumping Station

Corporation Rd, Abbey Ln LE4 5PX

⮑ *(off A6, 1m N from city centre)*

☎ 0116 299 5111

e-mail: museums@leicester.gov.uk

web: www.leicester.gov.uk/museums

Explore Leicester's industrial, technological and scientific heritage at Abbey Pumping Station. Built in 1891, this fascinating museum features some of the largest steam beam engines in the country and a working model railway. Exhibitions include historic transport, light and optics and public health. There are plenty of interactive exhibits, popular with children.

Times Open Feb-Oct daily, 11-4.30. Open Nov-Jan for special events. **Fee** Admission free, a small charge made for some events. Donations welcome. **Facilities** ℗ ⊼ (outdoor) ♿ (limited wheelchair access) (loan of wheelchairs, wheelchair lift) toilets for disabled shop ⊗ (ex assist dogs) ▬

Belgrave Hall Museum & Gardens

Church Rd, off Thurcaston Rd, Belgrave LE4 5PE

⮑ *(off Belgrave/Loughborough road, 1m from city centre)*

☎ 0116 266 6590

e-mail: museums@leicester.gov.uk

web: www.leicester.gov.uk/museums

A delightful three-storey Queen Anne house which dates from 1709 with beautiful period and botanic gardens. Authentic room settings contrast Georgian elegance with Victorian cosiness and include the kitchen, drawing room, music room and nursery. Believed to be haunted, ghost hunters regularly investigate the site.

Times Open Feb-Oct, Sat-Wed 11-4.30, Sun 1-4.30. Open every day during school holidays, ex Xmas. **Fee** Donations welcome. Small charge for some events. **Facilities** ℗ ⊼ (outdoor) ♿ (No access upstairs in Hall) (loan of wheelchair) toilets for disabled shop ⊗ (ex assist dogs)

The Guildhall

Guildhall Ln LE1 5FQ

⮑ *(next to Leicester Cathedral)*

☎ 0116 253 2569

e-mail: museums@leicester.gov.uk

web: www.leicester.gov.uk/museums

A preserved medieval building dating back to the 14th century, the Guildhall is one of Leicester's oldest buildings still in use. Over the centuries it has served as the Hall of the Guild of Corpus Christi, the Civic Centre and Town Hall, a judicial centre for court sessions and home to Leicester's first police force. The Guildhall now houses one of the oldest libraries in the country, as well as hosting events, activities and performances.

Times Open all year: Feb-Nov, Sat-Wed 11-4.30, Sun 1-4.30. Open Dec-Jan for special events. **Fee** Admission free. Donations welcome. **Facilities** ℗ (100yds) ♿ (No disabled access upstairs) (wheelchair loan, induction loop, voice minicom) toilets for disabled shop ⊗ (ex assist dogs) ▬

Jewry Wall Museum

St Nicholas Circle LE1 4LB

⮑ *(opposite The Holiday Inn)*

☎ 0116 225 4971

e-mail: museums@leicester.gov.uk

web: www.leicester.gov.uk/museums

Behind the massive fragment of the Roman Jewry Wall and a Roman Baths site of the 2nd century AD is the Museum of Leicestershire Archaeology, which includes finds from the earliest times to the Middle Ages.

Times Open daily, Feb-Oct 11-4.30. Open Nov-Jan for special events. **Fee** Admission free, however a charge is made for some events. Donations welcome. **Facilities** ℗ (300yds) ♿ (Access for wheelchair users via the staff entrance on Holy Bones.) toilets for disabled shop ⊗ (ex assist dogs)

National Space Centre

Exploration Dr LE4 5NS

⮑ *(off A6, 2m N of city centre midway between Leicester's central & outer ring roads. Follow brown rocket signs from M1 (junct 21, 21a or 22) & all arterial routes around Leicester)*

☎ 0870 607 7223

e-mail: info@spacecentre.co.uk

web: www.spacecentre.co.uk

The award-winning National Space Centre offers a great family day out, with six interactive galleries, a full-domed Space Theatre, a 42-metre high Rocket Tower, and the new Human Spaceflight Experience with 3D SIM ride. Explore the universe, orbit Earth, join the crew on the lunar base, and take the astronaut fitness tests, all without leaving Leicester. Throughout the year there are numerous events relating to space reality and science fiction, so contact the Centre for more details. 2009 is the International year of Astronomy. Please see website for list of events.

Times Open during school term: Tue-Sun, 10-5 (last entry 3.30). During school hols: daily, 10-5 (last entry 3.30) **Fee** ✶ £12 (ch 4-16yrs & concessions £10). Family of 4 £38, of 5 £47 for a full year **Facilities** ℗ (charged) ⬛ ⦿ ⊼ (outdoor) ♿ (induction loop, large text, wheelchairs, lifts) toilets for disabled shop ⊗ (ex assist dogs) ▬

Newarke Houses Museum & Gardens

The Newarke LE2 7BY

⮑ *(opposite De Montfort University)*

☎ 0116 225 4980

e-mail: museums@leicester.gov.uk

web: www.leicester.gov.uk/museums

Recently renovated, this museum tells the story of the Royal Leicestershire Regiment and the city's social history in the 20th century. New displays include a reconstruction of a First World War trench, typical room settings from the 1950s and 1970s, a 1950s street and two community galleries, telling the stories of 'Moving Here' and settling in Leicester.

Times Open all year, daily; Mon-Sat 10-5, Sun 11-5. Closed 24-26 & 31 Dec & 1 Jan. **Fee** Admission free, however small charge is made for some events. Donations welcome. **Facilities** ℗ (200yds) ⊼ (outdoor) ♿ (some exhibitions and parts of the garden are not accessible) (car parking can be arranged) shop ⊗ (ex assist dogs)

LEICESTER CONTINUED

New Walk Museum & Art Gallery

53 New Walk LE1 7EA

➲ *(situated on New Walk. Access by car from A6 onto Waterloo Way at Railway Stn. Right into Regent Rd, right onto West St, right onto Princess Rd which leads to car park)*

☎ 0116 225 4900

e-mail: museums@leicester.gov.uk

web: www.leicester.gov.uk/museums

This major regional venue houses local and national collections. There's an internationally famous collection of German Expressionism and other displays include the Rutland Dinosaur and the Egyptian Gallery. An extensive Natural History collection augmented by art from the renaissance to contemporary.

Times Open daily all year, Mon-Sat 10-5, Sun 11-5. Closed 24-26 & 31 Dec & 1 Jan. (Some downstairs art galleries may close at 12 on Sat for weddings.) **Fee** Donations welcome. Small charge for some events. **Facilities** ℗ ⬜ & (wheelchairs for loan, minicom, induction loop) toilets for disabled shop ⊗ (ex assist dogs) ■

The Record Office for Leicestershire & Rutland

FREE

Long St, Wigston Magna LE18 2AH

➲ *(old A50, S of Leicester City)*

☎ 0116 257 1080

e-mail: recordoffice@leics.gov.uk

web: www.leics.gov.uk/museums

Housed in a converted 19th-century school in Wigston, the Record Office holds photographs, electoral registers and archive film, files of local newspapers, history tapes and sound recordings, all of which can be studied.

Times Open all year, Mon, Tue & Thu 9.15-5, Wed 9.15-7.30, Fri 9.15-4.45, Sat 9.15-12.15. Closed Sun & BH wknds Sat-Tue. **Facilities** ℗ & toilets for disabled ⊗ (ex assist dogs) ▱

University of Leicester Harold Martin Botanic Garden

Beaumont Hall, Stoughton Dr South, Oadby LE2 2NA

➲ *(3m SE A6, entrance at 'The Knoll', Glebe Rd, Oadby)*

☎ 0116 271 7725 & 2933 (tours)

e-mail: bldal@le.ac.uk

web: www.le.ac.uk/biology/botanicgarden/

The grounds of four houses, now used as student residences and not open to the public, make up this 16-acre garden. A great variety of plants in different settings provide a delightful place to walk, including rock, water and sunken gardens, trees, borders, glasshouses and national collections of hardy fuchsias, aubrieta, skimmia and Lawson cypress.

Times Open Mon-Fri 10-4, Sat & Sun 10-4 (from 3rd wknd in Mar to 2nd wknd in Nov inclusive). Closed 25-26 Dec & 1 Jan. **Fee** Free except charity 'Open Days'. **Facilities** ℗ (adjacent) & (some steps) toilets for disabled ⊗ (ex assist dogs)

LOUGHBOROUGH   MAP 08 SK51

Great Central Railway

Great Central Rd LE11 1RW

➲ *(signed from A6, follow brown tourist signs)*

☎ 01509 230726

e-mail: sales@gcrailway.co.uk

web: www.gcrailway.co.uk

This private steam railway runs over eight miles from Loughborough Central to Leicester North, with all trains calling at Quorn & Woodhouse and Rothley. The locomotive depot and museum are at Loughborough Central. A buffet car runs on most trains.

Times Open all year daily, trains run every wknd & BHs throughout the year, May-Sep Wed, Jun, Jul & Aug daily ex Fri. **Fee** ✳ Runabout (all day unlimited travel) £12 (ch & concessions £8). Family ticket (2ad+3ch) £30 (1ad+3ch) £20 **Facilities** ℗ ⬜ ⦿ licensed ⤒ (outdoor) & (disabled coach available on most trains, check beforehand) toilets for disabled shop ■

MARKET BOSWORTH   MAP 04 SK40

Bosworth Battlefield Visitor Centre & Country Park

Ambion Hill, Sutton Cheney CV13 0AD

➲ *(follow brown tourist signs from A447, A444 & A5)*

☎ 01455 290429

e-mail: bosworth@leics.gov.uk

web: www.leics.gov.uk

The Battle of Bosworth Field was fought in 1485 between the armies of Richard III and the future Henry VII. The visitor centre offers a comprehensive interpretation of the battle, with exhibitions, models and a film theatre. Special medieval attractions are held in the summer months.

Times ✳ Open: Country Park and Battle Trails all year. Visitor Centre open Apr-Oct, daily, 11-5; Nov-Dec, Sun 11-4; Mar, wknds 11-5. Parties all year by arrangement. **Facilities** ℗ (charged) ⬜ ⦿ ⤒ (outdoor) & (wheelchair & electric scooter hire, tactile exhibits) toilets for disabled shop ■

MOIRA   MAP 08 SK31

Conkers

Millennium Av, Rawdon Rd DE12 6GA

➲ *(on B5003 in Moira, signed from A444 and M42)*

☎ 01283 216633

e-mail: info@visitconkers.com

web: www.visitconkers.com

Explore over one hundred indoor interactive exhibits, together with 120 acres that contain lakeside walks and trails, habitats, an assault course, adventure play areas and a miniature train. There are also events in the covered amphitheatre, and many other opportunities for you and your family to be entertained and educated.

Times Open daily, summer 10-6, autumn 10-5, winter 10-4.30. Closed 25 Dec. **Fee** £6.95 (ch 3-15yrs £4.95, ch under 3 free, concessions £5.95). Family ticket (2ad+2ch) £19.95. Prices include a 10% donation to The Heart of the National Forest. **Facilities** ❷ ☐ ❍❍ licensed ♁ (indoor & outdoor) ♿ (multi access walks & trails accessible to wheelchairs) toilets for disabled shop ❽ (ex assist dogs) ⊜

SHACKERSTONE   MAP 04 SK30

Battlefield Line Railway

Shackerstone Station CV13 6NW

➲ *(between Ashby-de-la-Zouch & Hinckley follow brown signs from A444 & A447)*

☎ 01827 880754

web: www.battlefield-line-railway.co.uk

The Battlefield Line is the last remaining part of the former Ashby and Nuneaton Joint Railway which was opened in 1873. It runs from Shackerstone via Market Bosworth to Shenton in Leicestershire and is operated by the Shackerstone Railway Society. Regular train trips to Bosworth battlefield with a variety of locomotives, steam and diesel-hauled trains and heritage railcars. Special events take place all year - please contact for details.

Times ✳ Open all year Sat, 12-5, Sun & BH Mon 10.30-5.30. Closed Xmas. Trains runs Etr-Oct, Santa trains Dec **Fee** ✳ £7.50 (ch £4.50, concessions £5.50). Family ticket (2ad+2ch) £22. **Facilities** ❷ ☐ ♁ (outdoor) ♿ (partly accessible) toilets for disabled shop ⊜

SWINFORD   MAP 04 SP57

Stanford Hall

LE17 6DH

➲ *(7.5m NE of Rugby, 1.5m from Swinford. 2m from the M1, M6, A14 junct)*

☎ 01788 860250

e-mail: enquiries@stanfordhall.co.uk

web: www.stanfordhall.co.uk

A beautiful William and Mary house, built in 1697 by Sir Roger Cave, ancestor of the present owner. The house contains antique furniture, paintings (including the Stuart Collection) and family costumes. Special events include car and motorcycle owners' club rallies.

Times Open Etr Sun-end Sep, Sun & BH Mon 1.30-5. Grounds open noon on BH & earlier on event days. Open any day or evening (ex Sat) during season for pre-booked parties 20+. **Fee** ✳ House & Grounds: £5 (ch £2). Grounds only: £3 (ch £1). Party 20+ £4.75 each. **Facilities** ❷ ☐ ♿ (Partly accessible) (please contact for details) toilets for disabled shop ❽ (ex assist dogs & in park)

TWYCROSS   MAP 04 SK30

Twycross Zoo Park

CV9 3PX

➲ *(on A444 Burton to Nuneaton road, directly off M42 junct 11)*

☎ 01827 880250

web: www.twycrosszoo.com

Twycross Zoo appeals to all ages and spans some 50 acres that are home to around 1,000 animals, including the most comprehensive collection of primate species in the world. Twycross is the only zoo in Great Britain to house bonobos - humanity's 'closest living relative'. Whilst at the zoo, visitors can immerse themselves in a genuine Borneo Longhouse, brought to life in the Leicestershire countryside, where many exotic birds, animal species and traditional artefacts can be seen.

Times Open all year, daily 10-5.30 (4 in winter). Closed 25 Dec. **Fee** ✳ £9.50 (ch £6, pen £7). Family Ticket £29. **Facilities** ❷ ☐ ♁ (outdoor) ♿ toilets for disabled shop ❽ (ex assist dogs) ⊜

LINCOLNSHIRE

Burghley House, near Stamford

BELTON   MAP 08 SK93

Belton House Park & Gardens

NG32 2LS

➲ *(3m NE Grantham on A607)*

☎ 01476 566116

e-mail: belton@nationaltrust.org.uk

web: www.nationaltrust.org.uk

The ground floor of the house has a succession of state rooms, with the Marble Hall as its centrepiece. Splendid furnishings and decorations throughout the house include tapestries and hangings, family portraits, porcelain and fine furniture.

Times Open House: 1-14 Mar, Sat & Sun 12.30-4; 15 Mar-2 Nov, Wed-Sun. Open BH Mons, 12.30-5. Garden: 2 Feb-14 Mar, Sat & Sun 12-4; 15 Mar-Jun & 8 Sep-2 Nov, Wed-Sun 11-5.30; Jul-7 Sep, daily 10.30-5.30; 3 Nov-21 Dec, Fri-Sun 12-4; 26 Dec-4 Jan, daily 12-4. **Fee** ✳ With Gift Aid donation: House & garden £9.50 (ch £5.50). Family ticket £25. Grounds only £7.50 (ch £4.50) Family ticket £20. **Facilities** ❷ ⬛ ⚞ ⚞ (Braille guide, hearing scheme, audio guide) toilets for disabled shop ⊗ (ex in grounds) ⚘

CLEETHORPES   MAP 08 TA30

Pleasure Island Family Theme Park

Kings Rd DN35 0PL

➲ *(Follow signs from A180)*

☎ 01472 211511

e-mail: reception@pleasure-island.co.uk

web: www.pleasure-island.co.uk

Pleasure Island is packed with over seventy rides and attractions. Hold on tight as the colossal wheel of steel rockets you into the sky at a G-force of 2.5, then hurtles you around 360 degrees, sending riders into orbit and giving the sensation of complete weightlessness. It's not just grown ups and thrill seekers who are catered for at Pleasure Island. For youngsters there's hours of fun in Tinkaboo Town, an indoor themed area full of rides and attractions.

Times Open 31 Mar-2 Sep, daily from 10. Plus wknds during Sep-Oct. Park closed Mon-Tues during quiet times. Call for further info. **Facilities** ❷ ⬛ ⚞ ⊓ (outdoor) ⚞ (Partly accessible) toilets for disabled shop ⊟

CONINGSBY   MAP 08 TF25

Battle of Britain Memorial Flight Visitor Centre

LN4 4SY

➲ *(on A153 in Coningsby village - follow heritage signs)*

☎ 01526 344041

e-mail: bbmf@lincolnshire.gov.uk

web: www.lincolnshire.gov.uk/bbmf

View the aircraft of the Battle of Britain Memorial Flight, comprising the only flying Lancaster in Europe, five Spitfires, two Hurricanes, two Chipmunks and a Dakota. Because of operational commitments, specific aircraft may not be available. Ring for information before planning a visit.

Times Open Mon-Fri, conducted tours 10.30-3.30; (winter 10.30-3). Closed 2 wks Xmas. **Fee** £4 (children 5-16 £2.25, concessions £2.65). Family £10.65 **Facilities** ❷ ⊓ (outdoor) ⚞ (electric wheelchairs not allowed in hangar) toilets for disabled shop ⊗ (ex assist dogs) ⊟

EAST KIRKBY   MAP 08 TF36

Lincolnshire Aviation Heritage Centre

East Kirkby Airfield PE23 4DE

➲ *(off A16 onto A155, museum on east side of village)*

☎ 01790 763207

e-mail: enquiries@lincsaviation.co.uk

web: www.lincsaviation.co.uk

Relive a World War Two bomber airfield here at East Kirkby. Experience the sights and sounds, smells and atmosphere. The only place in the country to see and ride in a Lancaster bomber on its original airfield.

Times Open 2 Jan-Etr, 10-4; Etr-Nov, 10-5. Closed Sun. **Facilities** ❷ ⬛ ⚞ ⊓ (outdoor) ⚞ (hand rails) toilets for disabled shop ⊟

EPWORTH   MAP 08 SE70

Old Rectory

1 Rectory St DN9 1HX

➲ *(on A161, 3m S of M180 junct 2. Follow brown signs)*

☎ 01427 872268

e-mail: curator@epwortholdrectory.org.uk

web: www.epwortholdrectory.org.uk

John and Charles Wesley were brought up in this handsome rectory, built in 1709. Maintained by the World Methodist Council as 'The Home of the Wesleys', the house displays items which belonged to John and Charles Wesley and their parents Samuel and Susanna. The house is a registered museum.

Times ✳ Open daily Mar-Oct, Mon-Sat, 10-12 & 2-4, Sun 2-4 (Mar, Apr & Oct); May-Sep Mon-Sat 10-4.30, Sun 2-4.30. Other times by prior arrangement. **Facilities** ❷ ⊓ (outdoor) shop ⊗ (ex assist dogs) ⊟

ENGLAND

GAINSBOROUGH   MAP 08 SK88

Gainsborough Old Hall

Parnell St DN21 2NB

➲ *(turn off A1 onto A57 to Gainsborough. Follow brown heritage signs in city centre. Old Hall is adjacent to town centre.)*

☎ 01427 612669

e-mail: gainsboroughholdhall@lincolnshire.gov.uk

web: www.english-heritage.org.uk

A complete medieval manor house dating back to 1460-80 and containing a remarkable Great Hall and original kitchen with a variety of room settings. Richard III, Henry VIII, the Mayflower Pilgrims and John Wesley all visited the Old Hall.

Times Open early 21 Mar-Oct, Mon-Sat 10-4 (Sun 1-4); Nov-Mar, Mon-Sat 10-4. Closed 24-26, 31 Dec & 1 Jan. (Times & prices may vary please call to check). **Fee** £3.80 (concessions & ch £2.60). Family ticket £10. Groups 30+ discount. Small charge to special events for EH members. Prices and opening times are subject to change in March 2009. Please call 0870 333 1181 for the most up to date prices and opening times when planning your visit. **Facilities** ℗ (100yds) (unrestricted parking 100yds from Hall) 🎟 🍴 ♿ (audio tour, induction loop, wheelchair for visitors use) toilets for disabled shop ⊗ (ex assist dogs)

GRIMSBY   MAP 08 TA20

Fishing Heritage Centre   `2 for 1`

Alexandra Dock DN31 1UZ

➲ *(follow signs off M180)*

☎ 01472 323345

web: www.nelincs.gov.uk/leisure/museums

Sign on as a crew member for a journey of discovery, and experience the harsh reality of life on board a deep sea trawler built inside the Centre. Through interactive games and displays, your challenge is to navigate the icy waters of the Arctic in search of the catch.

Times Open Nov-Apr, Mon-Fri 10-4, Wknds & BHs 11-9 **Fee** ✳ £6 (ch £2, concessions £4). Family ticket (2ad+5ch) £12. Annual pass available. **Facilities** ❾ (charged) 🎟 ♿ (Ross Tiger Trawler not recommended to those with mobility problems) toilets for disabled shop ⊗ (ex assist dogs) ▬

GRIMSTHORPE   MAP 08 TF02

Grimsthorpe Castle

PE10 0LY

➲ *(on A151, 8m E of Colsterworth on A1)*

☎ 01778 591205

e-mail: ray@grimsthorpe.co.uk

web: www.grimsthorpe.co.uk

Seat of the Willoughby de Eresby family since 1516, the castle has a medieval tower and a Tudor quadrangular house with a Baroque north front by Vanbrugh. There are eight state rooms, two picture galleries, and an important collection of furniture, pictures and tapestries. There is also a family cycle trail, woodland adventure playground and ranger-guided tours of the park by minibus.

Times Open Apr-May Sun, Thu & BH Mon; Jun-Sep Sun-Thu. Park & Gardens 11-6. Castle 1-4.30. **Fee** Park & Gardens £4 (ch £2, concessions £3.50). Combined ticket with castle £9 (ch £3.50, concessions £8). **Facilities** ❾ 🎟 🍴 licensed 🍴 (outdoor) ♿ (no wheelchair access to 1st floor) (Virtual castle tour, Braille guide, w/chair loan) toilets for disabled shop ▬

LINCOLN   MAP 08 SK97

The Collection: Art & Archaeology in Lincolnshire

Danes Ter LN2 1LP

➲ *(follow signs for Lincoln City Centre, then parking for cultural quarter then pedestrian signs to The Collection)*

☎ 01522 550990

e-mail: thecollection@lincolnshire.gov.uk

web: www.thecollection.lincoln.museum

Housed in an impressive new building, the Collection consists of the combined collections of the City and County Museum and the Usher Gallery. The art collection includes contemporary art and craft, paintings, sculpture, porcelain, clocks and watches. There are paintings by Turner, Stubbs and Lowry, major porcelain collections and clocks by Robert Sutton. The archaeological collection covers 300,000 years of history up to the 18th-century.

Times Open all year daily, 10-4. (Last entry 3.30). Closed 25-26 Dec & 1 Jan. **Fee** ✳ Entry to Museum free, small charge to visit some temporary exhibitions **Facilities** ℗ 300mtrs (Broadgate multi storey car park) 🎟 🍴 🍴 (outdoor) ♿ (parking for disabled) toilets for disabled shop ⊗ (ex assist dogs) ▬

Lincoln Castle

Castle Hill LN1 3AA

➲ *(off A46 Lincoln Ring Road in heart of historic city)*

☎ 01522 511068

e-mail: lincoln_castle@lincolnshire.gov.uk

web: www.lincolnshire.gov.uk/lincolncastle

Situated in the centre of Lincoln, the Castle, built in 1068 by William the Conqueror, dominates the Bailgate area alongside the great Cathedral. In addition to its many medieval features, Lincoln Castle has strong 19th-century connections and the unique Victorian prison chapel is perhaps the most awe-inspiring. The beautiful surroundings are ideal for historical adventures, picnics and special events that include jousting, Roman re-enactments, and Vintage vehicle rallies. The Castle is the home of the Magna Carta and there is an exhibition interpreting and displaying this important document.

Times Open: May-Aug, Mon-Sun 10-6; Apr & Sep, Mon-Sun, 10-5; Oct-Mar, Mon-Sun, 10-4 **Fee** ✳ £4 (ch & concessions £2.65) Family ticket (2ad+3ch) £10.65. **Facilities** ℗ (100yds) 🎟 🍴 (outdoor) ♿ (hearing loop, audio visual tour, wheelchair, lift) toilets for disabled shop ⊗ (ex assist dogs) ▬

Museum of Lincolnshire Life

2 for 1

Burton Rd LN1 3LY

⮑ *(100mtr walk from Lincoln Castle)*

☎ 01522 528448

e-mail: lincolnshirelife.museum@lincolnshire.gov.uk
web: www.lincolnshire.gov.uk/museumoflincolnshirelife

A large and varied social history museum, where two centuries of Lincolnshire life are illustrated by enthralling displays of domestic implements, industrial machinery, agricultural tools and a collection of horse-drawn vehicles. The exciting and interactive Royal Lincolnshire Regiment Museum contains videos, an audio tour, and touch screen computers. Various events throughout the year.

Times Open all year, Apr-Sep, daily 10-4; Oct-Mar, Mon-Sat 10-4 (last admission 3.15). Closed 24-26 & 31 Dec, 1 Jan. **Fee** ✳ £2.25 (concessions £1.50). Family (2ad+3ch) £6.00. **Facilities** ❷ ⬜ & (wheelchair available, parking space) toilets for disabled shop ⊗ (ex assist dogs)

Usher Gallery

FREE

Lindum Rd LN2 1NN

⮑ *(follow signs for Lincoln City Centre, then parking for cultural quarter, then pedestrian signs to The Collection)*

☎ 01522 550990

e-mail: thecollection@lincolnshire.gov.uk
web: www.thecollection.lincoln.museum

Built as the result of a bequest by Lincoln jeweller James Ward Usher, the Gallery houses his magnificent collection of watches, porcelain and miniatures, as well as topographical works, watercolours by Peter de Wint, Tennyson memorabilia and coins. The gallery has a popular and changing display of contemporary visual arts and crafts. There is a lively lecture programme and children's activity diary.

Times Open all year, daily 10-4 ex 24-26 Dec & 1 Jan (last entry 3.30) **Facilities** ℗ (150yds) ⬜ ⊟ (outdoor) & (large print guides, induction loop, parking) toilets for disabled shop ⊗ (ex assist dogs)

SCUNTHORPE   MAP 08 SE81

Normanby Hall Country Park

2 for 1

Normanby DN15 9HU

⮑ *(4m N of Scunthorpe off B1430)*

☎ 01724 720588

e-mail: normanby.hall@northlincs.gov.uk
web: www.northlincs.gov.uk/normanby

A whole host of activities and attractions are offered in the 300 acres of grounds that surround Normanby Hall, including riding, nature trails and a farming museum. Inside the Regency mansion, the fine rooms are decorated and furnished in period style. Fully restored and working Victorian kitchen garden. There is also a Victorian walled garden selling a wide range of Victorian and other unusual plants from barrows located at the gift shop and Farming Museum.

Times Open: Park all year, daily, 9-dusk. Walled garden, daily 10.30-5 (4 in winter). Hall & Farming Museum, Apr-Sep, daily 1-5. **Fee** ✳ Mar-Sep £4.80 (ch £2.40, under 5s free, concessions £4.40). Family season ticket £18. **Facilities** ❷ (charged) ⬜ ⎮◉⎮ licensed ⊟ (outdoor) & (ground floor of Great Hall, walled garden, farming museum, cafe, giftshops & toilets accessible) (audio tour, wheelchair/scooter (must be pre-booked) toilets for disabled shop ⊗ (ex on leads)

SKEGNESS   MAP 09 TF56

Church Farm Museum

Church Rd South PE25 2HF

⮑ *(follow brown museum signs on entering Skegness)*

☎ 01754 766658

e-mail: churchfarmmuseum@lincolnshire.gov.uk
web: www.lincolnshire.gov.uk/churchfarmmuseum

A farmhouse and outbuildings, restored to show the way of life on a Lincolnshire farm at the end of the 19th century, with farm implements and machinery plus household equipment on display. Temporary exhibitions are held in the barn and a timber-framed mud and stud cottage is restored on site. Telephone for details of special events held throughout the season.

Times Open Apr-Oct, daily 10-4 (last entry 3.30) **Fee** ✳ Free admission apart from special events **Facilities** ❷ ⬜ ⊟ (outdoor) & (grounds accessible with care) (wheelchair available) toilets for disabled shop ⊗ (ex assist dogs)

Skegness Natureland Seal Sanctuary

North Pde PE25 1DB

⮑ *(N end of seafront)*

☎ 01754 764345

web: www.skegnessnatureland.co.uk

Natureland houses seals, penguins, tropical birds, aquarium, reptiles, pets' corner etc. Also free-flight tropical butterflies (Apr-Oct). Natureland is well known for its rescue of abandoned seal pups, and has successfully reared and returned to the wild a large number of them. The hospital unit incorporates a public viewing area, and a large seascape seal pool (with underwater viewing).

Times Open all year, daily at 10. Closing times vary according to season. Closed 25-26 Dec & 1 Jan. **Fee** £6.20 (ch £4, pen £5). Family ticket £18.40 (2ad+2ch) **Facilities** ℗ (100yds) ⬜ ⎮◉⎮ ⊟ (outdoor) & (low windows on seal pools) toilets for disabled shop

---

SPALDING   MAP 08 TF22

Butterfly & Wildlife Park

2 for 1

Long Sutton PE12 9LE

⮑ *(off A17 at Long Sutton)*

☎ 01406 363833 & 363209

e-mail: info@butterflyandwildlifepark@.co.uk
web: www.butterflyandwildlifepark.co.uk

The Park contains one of Britain's largest walk-through tropical gardens, in which hundreds of butterflies from all over the world fly freely. The tropical gardens are also home to crocodiles, snakes and lizards.

CONTINUED

ENGLAND

SPALDING CONTINUED

Outside are 15 acres of butterfly and bee gardens, wildflower meadows, nature trail, farm animals, a pets' corner and a large adventure playground. At The Lincolnshire Birds of Prey Centre, there are daily birds of prey displays. See an ant room where visitors can observe leaf-cutting ants in their natural working habitat.

Times Open 15 Mar-2 Nov, daily 10-5. Sep & Oct 10-4 **Fee** ✱ £6.50 (ch 3-16 £4.95, concessions £5.95). Family ticket (2ad+2ch) £20. **Facilities** ℗ ⌑ 🎢 (outdoor) ♿ (wheelchairs available) toilets for disabled shop ⊗ (ex assist dogs) ➡

STAMFORD   MAP 04 TF00

Burghley House

PE9 3JY

➲ *(1.5m off A1 at Stamford)*

☎ 01780 752451

e-mail: burghley@burghley.co.uk

web: www.burghley.co.uk

This great Elizabethan palace, built by William Cecil, has all the hallmarks of that ostentatious period. The vast house is three storeys high and the roof is a riot of pinnacles, cupolas and paired chimneys in classic Tudor style. However, the interior was restyled in the 17th century, and the state rooms are now Baroque, with silver fireplaces, elaborate plasterwork and painted ceilings. These were painted by Antonio Verrio, whose Heaven Room is quite awe-inspiring. The Sculpture Garden is dedicated to exhibiting the best in contemporary sculpture, in pleasant surroundings.

Times ✱ Open 31 Mar-28 Oct, daily (ex Fri). Please telephone for details. **Facilities** ℗ ⌑ 🎢🍴 🎢 (outdoor) ♿ (chairlift access, some mobility required) toilets for disabled shop garden centre ⊗ (ex in park & on lead) ➡

Stamford Museum   FREE

Broad St PE9 1PJ

➲ *(from A1 follow town centre signs from any Stamford exit)*

☎ 01780 766317

e-mail: stamford_museum@lincolnshire.gov.uk

web: www.lincolnshire.gov.uk/stamfordmuseum

Displays illustrate the history of this fine stone town and include Stamford Ware pottery, the visit of Daniel Lambert and the Town's more recent industrial past. The Stamford Tapestry depicts the history of the town in wool.

Times Open all year Mon-Sat 10-4. Closed 24-26 & 31 Dec & 1 Jan. **Facilities** ℗ (200yds) (on street parking is limited waiting) ♿ (audio loop, lift, semi auto doors,Braille leaflets) shop ⊗ (ex assist dogs)

TATTERSHALL   MAP 08 TF25

Tattershall Castle

LN4 4LR

➲ *(S of A153, 15m NE of Sleaford)*

☎ 01526 342543

e-mail: tattershallcastle@nationaltrust.org.uk

web: www.nationaltrust.org.uk

This large fortified house was built in 1440 by Ralph Cromwell, Treasurer of England, and has a keep 100ft high. Restored in 1911-14, it contains four great chambers with large Gothic fireplaces, tapestries and brick vaulting. Spectacular views from battlements and museum room in guardhouse.

Times Open 1-14 Mar & 3 Nov-16 Dec, Sat & Sun, 12-4; 15 Mar-1 Oct, Mon-Wed & Sat-Sun, 11-5.30; Open Good Fri 11-5.30. **Fee** ✱ With Gift Aid donation: £4.70 (ch £2.50). Family ticket £11.90 **Facilities** ℗ ♿ (ramped entrance, ground floor has ramp available. Many stairs to other floors. Some visitors may require assistance from their companion) (Braille guide, one wheelchair available, must prebook) toilets for disabled shop ⊗ (ex assist dogs) ♨

THORNTON   MAP 08 TA11

Thornton Abbey and Gatehouse

Thornton Abbey Rd, Ulceby DN39 6TU

➲ *(7m SE of Humber Bridge, on road E of A1077)*

web: www.english-heritage.org.uk

This abbey, founded in 1139 for a community of Augustinian canons, was reconstructed from the 1260s as its prestige and riches grew. The remains of a beautiful octagonal chapter-house are notably fine. Most impressive is the 14th-century gatehouse, recognised as one of the grandest in England.

Times Open Abbey Grounds: 21 Mar-Jun & Sep, Wed-Sun 10-5; Jul-Aug, daily 10-5; Oct-Mar, Fri-Sun 10-4. Closed 24-26 Dec & 1 Jan. **Fee** £4 (concessions £3.20, ch £2). Prices and opening times are subject to change in March 2009. Please call 0870 333 1181 for the most up to date prices and opening times when planning your visit. **Facilities** ℗ ♿ (mostly accessible apart from gatehouse) ✤

WOOLSTHORPE   MAP 08 SK92

Woolsthorpe Manor

23 Newton Way NG33 5PD

➲ *(7m S of Grantham, 1m W of A1)*

☎ 01476 862826

e-mail: woolsthorpemanor@nationaltrust.org.uk

web: www.nationaltrust.org.uk

A fine stone-built, 17th-century farmhouse which was the birthplace of the scientist and philosopher Sir Isaac Newton. He also lived at the house from 1665-67 during the Plague. An early edition of his *Principia Mathematica* (1687) is in the house. Science Discovery Centre and exhibition.

Times Open 1-23 Mar & 4-26 Oct, Sat & Sun 1-5; 26 Mar-29 Jun & 3-28 Sep, Wed-Sun (open BHs) 1-5, 2 Jul-Aug, Sat & Sun 11-5, Wed-Fri, 1-5. **Fee** ✱ With Gift Aid donation: £5.50 (ch £2.70). Family ticket £13 **Facilities** ℗ ♿ (narrow doorways and small rooms, ramps available. stairs to other floors. Grounds: partly accessible, uneven and loose gravel paths, some steps) (Braille & large print guide, wheelchair available) toilets for disabled ⊗ (ex assist dogs) ♨

LONDON

St Pancras and King's Cross Eurostar Station

ENGLAND

E2

Geffrye Museum

136 Kingsland Rd, Shoreditch E2 8EA

➲ *(S end of Kingsland Rd A10 in Shoreditch between Cremer St & Pearson St)*

☎ 020 7739 9893

e-mail: info@geffrye-museum.org.uk

web: www.geffrye-museum.org.uk

The only museum in the UK to specialise in the domestic interiors and furniture of the urban middle classes. Displays span the 400 years from 1600 to the present day, forming a sequence of period rooms which capture the nature of English interior style. The museum is set in elegant, 18th-century buildings, surrounded by delightful gardens including an award-winning walled herb garden and a series of historical gardens which highlight changes in town gardens from the 17th to 20th centuries. One of the museum's historic almshouses has been fully restored to its original condition and is open on selected days (ring for details). Each December, the museum's period rooms are decorated in authentic, festive style to reflect 400 years of Christmas traditions in English homes.

Times Open all year, Tue-Sat 10-5, Sun & BH Mon 12-5. Closed Mon, Good Fri, 24-26 Dec & New Year. **Fee** Free admission to museum & exhibitions. Prices for special lectures on request. **Facilities** ℗ (150yds) (meter parking, very restricted) ⏐⚈ ⻓ (outdoor) ⴷ (ramps, lift, wheelchair available, induction loop) toilets for disabled shop ⊗ (ex assist dogs)

V & A Museum of Childhood   `FREE`

Cambridge Heath Rd E2 9PA

➲ *(Underground - Bethnal Green)*

☎ 020 8983 5200

e-mail: moc@vam.ac.uk

web: www.museumofchildhood.org.uk

The V&A Museum of Childhood re-opened following a 4.7 million transformation in December 2006. There is a stunning new entrance, fully updated galleries and displays, a brand new gallery and expanded public spaces. Galleries include Creativity, Moving Toys and Childhood Galleries. There is also a full programme of activities. Exhibitions include Top to Toe and Fashion for Kids.

Times Open all year, daily 10-5.45. Closed 25-26 Dec & 1 Jan. **Facilities** ℗ (metered parking) ⏐⚈ ⻓ (outdoor) ⴷ (disabled parking by arrangement) toilets for disabled shop ⊗ (ex assist dogs)

E9

Sutton House

2 & 4 Homerton High St E9 6JQ

➲ *(10 min walk from Hackney Central train station)*

☎ 020 8986 2264

e-mail: suttonhouse@nationaltrust.org.uk

web: www.nationaltrust.org.uk

In London's East End, the building is a rare example of a Tudor red-brick house. Built in 1535 by Sir Ralph Sadleir, Principal Secretary of State for Henry VIII, the house has 18th-century alterations and later additions. There are regular exhibitions of contemporary art by local artists.

Times Open Feb-23 Dec, Thu-Sun & BH Mon, 12.30-4.30, closed Good Fri. **Fee** ✳ £2.80 (ch 60p) Family ticket £6.30. Group £2.40 each **Facilities** ℗ (on street parking) (meters) ⏐⚈ ⏐⚈ licensed ⴷ (wheelchair accessible on ground floor) (induction loop, Braille/large print/audio guide) toilets for disabled shop ⊗ (ex assist dogs) ⴵ ⎓

E14

Museum in Docklands

No 1 Warehouse, West India Quay E14 4AL

➲ *(Signposted from West India Quay DLR)*

☎ 0870 444 3855 & 3856

e-mail: info@museumindocklands.org.uk

web: www.museumindocklands.org.uk

Housed in a converted 18th-century warehouse the museum explores the 2,000 year history of London's river, port and people. Four floors of interactive displays and a unique collection that journeys through the history of the Thames, from the first Roman settlements to the massive regeneration that brought the Docklands into the 21st century. A changing programme of activities for all ages, includes character re-enactments, talks by history experts, films and guided walks through Docklands. A soft play gallery, Mudlarks is for children under eleven, and offers an opportunity to learn how to winch and weigh cargo or to take a diver's eye view of work under water. Discover archaeological finds on the foreshore, or even reconstruct a simple model of Canary Wharf.

Times ✳ Open all year, daily 10-6 (last admission 5.30) **Facilities** ℗ (opp rear museum) (Disabled parking on quayside) ⏐⚈ ⏐⚈ ⻓ (indoor) ⴷ (w/ chairs, power scooters & various aids) shop ⊗ (ex assist dogs)

E17

William Morris Gallery   `FREE`

Lloyd Park, Forest Rd, Walthamstow E17 4PP

⮑ *(Underground - Blackhorse Rd, take bus no. 123 along Forest Rd, get off at the Lloyd Park stop OR Walthamstow Central, N 15m along Hoe St, left into Gaywood Rd to Lloyd Park)*

☎ 020 8527 3782

e-mail: wmg.enquiries@walthamforest.gov.uk

web: www.walthamforest.gov.uk/william-morris

Victorian artist, craftsman, poet and free thinker William Morris lived here from 1848 to 1856, and the gallery houses displays illustrating his life and work. Exhibits include fabrics, stained glass, wallpaper and furniture, as well as Pre-Raphaelite paintings, ceramics and a collection of pictures by Frank Brangwyn, who worked briefly for Morris.

Times Telephone for opening times 020 8527 3782 **Facilities** Ⓟ & (Partly accessible) (ground floor only) shop ⊗ (ex assist dogs) ▬

EC1

Museum of The Order of St John

St John's Gate, St John's Ln, Clerkenwell EC1M 4DA

⮑ *(Underground - Farringdon, Barbican)*

☎ 020 7324 4070

e-mail: museum@nhq.sja.org.uk

web: www.sja.org.uk/museum

The Priory of Clerkenwell was built in the 1140s by the Crusading Hospitallers and it is their remarkable story which lies behind the modern work of St John Ambulance. The Knights' surprising tale is revealed in the ground floor galleries housed in the Tudor gatehouse and includes furniture, paintings, silver, armour, stained glass and an interactive, multimedia gallery 'Time to Care' which explores the work of St John Ambulance from 1877 to the present day.

Times ✳ Open all year, Mon-Sat 10-5, Sat 10-4. Closed Etr, Xmas wk & BH wknds. Guided tours 11 & 2.30 Tue, Fri & Sat. **Facilities** Ⓟ (meters/NCP 300yds) & (Partly accessible) toilets for disabled shop ⊗ (ex assist dogs) ▬

Wesley's Chapel, House & Museum Of Methodism

49 City Rd EC1Y 1AU

⮑ *(Underground - Old Street - exit number 4)*

☎ 020 7253 2262

e-mail: museum@wesleyschapel.org.uk

web: www.wesleyschapel.org.uk

Wesley's Chapel has been the Mother Church of World Methodism since its construction in 1778. The crypt houses a museum which traces the development of Methodism from the 18th century to the present day. Wesley's house - built by him in 1779 - was his home when not touring and preaching. Special events are held on May 24th (the anniversary of Wesley's conversion), and November 1st (the anniversary of the Chapel's opening).

Times Open all year, Mon-Sat , 10-4, Sun 12-2. Closed Thu 12.45-1.30, Xmas-New Year, BHs. (Last entry 30mins before closing). **Fee** ✳ Donations welcome **Facilities** Ⓟ (5min) (NCP at Finsbury Square) ⋈ & (chapel & museum fully accessible). Many stairs and no lift make the house inaccessible) (lift to the crypt of the chapel) toilets for disabled shop ⊗ (ex assist dogs) ▬

EC2

Bank of England Museum   `FREE`

Bartholomew Ln EC2R 8AH

⮑ *(Museum housed in Bank of London, entrance in Bartholomew Lane. Bank underground, exit 2)*

☎ 020 7601 5545

e-mail: museum@bankofengland.co.uk

web: www.bankofengland.co.uk/museum

The museum tells the story of the Bank of England from its foundation in 1694 to its role in today's economy. Interactive programmes with graphics and video help explain its many and varied roles. Popular exhibits include a unique collection of banknotes and a genuine gold bar, which may be handled.

Times Open all year, Mon-Fri 10-5. Closed wknds & BHs. Open on day of Lord Mayor's Show & Open House London **Facilities** Ⓟ (10 mins walk) & (Audio guides, induction loop. Advance notice helpful) toilets for disabled shop ⊗ (ex assist dogs)

The Guildhall   `FREE`

Gresham St EC2V 5AE

⮑ *(Underground - Bank, St Paul's)*

☎ 020 7606 3030

e-mail: pro@corpoflondon.gov.uk

web: www.cityoflondon.gov.uk

The Court of Common Council (presided over by the Lord Mayor) administers the City of London and meets in the Guildhall. Dating from 1411, the building was badly damaged in the Great Fire and again in the Blitz. The great hall, traditionally used for the Lord Mayor's Banquet and other important civic functions, is impressively decorated with the banners and shields of the livery companies, of which there are more than 90. The Clock Museum, which has a collection of 700 exhibits, charts the history of 500 years of time-keeping.

Times ✳ Open all year, May-Sep, daily 10-5; Oct-Apr, Mon-Sat 10-5. Closed Xmas, New Year, Good Fri, Etr Mon & infrequently for Civic occasions. Please contact 020 7606 3030 ext 1463 before visit to be certain of access. **Facilities** Ⓟ (NCP parking nearby) & (lift for east and west crypts) toilets for disabled shop ⊗

ENGLAND

EC2 CONTINUED

Museum of London

150 London Wall EC2Y 5HN

➲ *(Underground - St Paul's, Barbican. N of St Paul's Cathedral at the end of St Martins le Grand and S of the Barbican. S of Aldersgate St)*

☎ 0870 444 3851

e-mail: info@museumoflondon.org.uk

web: www.museumoflondon.org.uk

Dedicated to the story of London and its people, the Museum of London exists to inspire a passion for London in all who visit it. As well as the permanent collection, the Museum has a varied exhibition programme with major temporary exhibitions and topical displays each year. There are also smaller exhibitions in the foyer gallery. A wide programme of lectures and events explore London's history and its evolution to the city we know today.

Times ✳ Open all year, Mon-Sat 10-5.50, Sun 12-5.50. Last admission 5.30. **Facilities** ❷ ⌖ ⏵ ⚲ & (w/chairs & power scooters, lifts & induction loops) toilets for disabled shop ⊗ (ex assist dogs) ▭

EC3

The Monument

Monument St EC3R 8AH

➲ *(Underground - Monument)*

☎ 020 7626 2717

e-mail: enquiries@towerbridge.org.uk

web: www.towerbridge.org.uk

Designed by Wren and Hooke and erected in 1671-7, the Monument commemorates the Great Fire of 1666 which is reputed to have started in nearby Pudding Lane. The fire destroyed nearly 90 churches and about 13,000 houses. This fluted Doric column stands 202ft high (Pudding Lane is exactly 202ft from its base) and you can climb the 311 steps to a platform at the summit, and receive a certificate as proof of your athletic abilities.

Times ✳ Open all year, daily, 9.30-5. **Facilities** ⊗

Tower of London

Tower Hill EC3N 4AB

➲ *(Underground - Tower Hill)*

☎ 0870 756 6060

web: www.hrp.org.uk

Perhaps the most famous castle in the world, the Tower of London has played a central part in British history. The White Tower, built by William the Conqueror as a show of strength to the people of London, remains one of the most outstanding examples of Norman military architecture in Europe. For hundreds of years the Tower was used, among other things, as the State Prison. It was here that Henry VIII had two of his wives executed, here that Lady Jane Grey died and here that Sir Walter Raleigh was imprisoned. The Yeoman Warders, or 'Beefeaters' play an important role in the protection of the Tower - home of the Crown Jewels - and are informative and entertaining. Look out for the ravens, whose continued residence is said to ensure

that the Kingdom does not fall. The Crowns and Diamonds exhibition features a number of crowns never displayed to the public before and more than 12,000 rough and polished diamonds. Also open to the public are the Royal Armouries, which received their first recorded visitor as long ago as 1489. The displays include an extensive range of arms and armour dating from the Norman ages, a collection of Spanish arms and the Line of Kings.

Times ✳ Open all year, Mar-Oct, Mon-Sat 9-6, Sun 10-6 (last admission 5); Nov-Feb, Tue-Sat 9-5, Sun 10-5 (last admission 4). Closed 24-26 Dec & 1 Jan. **Facilities** ℗ (100yds) (NCP Lower Thames St) ⌖ ⍟ & (access guide can be obtained in advance call 020 7488 5694) toilets for disabled shop ⊗ (ex assist dogs) ▭

EC4

Dr Johnson's House

17 Gough Square EC4A 3DE

➲ *(Underground - Temple, Blackfriars, Chancery Lane)*

☎ 020 7353 3745

e-mail: curator@drjohnsonshouse.org

web: www.drjohnsonshouse.org

The celebrated literary figure, Dr Samuel Johnson, lived here between 1748 and 1759. He wrote his English Dictionary here, and a facsimile edition is on display at the house. The dictionary took nine and a half years to complete and contained over 40,000 words. The house is a handsome example of early 18th-century architecture, with many original features, and includes a collection of prints, letters and other Johnson memorabilia. 2009 is the tercentenary of Dr Johnson's birth and there is an international year of celebration planned.

Times Open all year, May-Sep, Mon-Sat 11-5.30; Oct-Apr 11-5. Closed Sun, BHs, Good Fri. Please check website for Xmas opening times. **Fee** £4.50 (ch £1.50, concessions £3.50). Family £10. **Facilities** ℗ (500yds) (few meters, disabled in Gough Sq) & (Partly accessible) (large print info sheets, handrails, seating) shop ⊗ (ex assist dogs)

Middle Temple Hall

The Temple EC4Y 9AT

➲ *(Underground - Temple, Blackfriars. Turn left at the embankment & left into Middle Temple Lane. Hall half way up on left)*

☎ 020 7427 4800 & 4820

e-mail: banqueting@middletemple.org.uk

web: www.middletemple.org.uk

Between Fleet Street and the Thames are the Middle and Inner Temples, separate Inns of Court, so named after the Knights Templar who occupied the site from about 1160. Middle Temple Hall is a fine example of Tudor architecture, completed in about 1570, and has a double hammerbeam roof and beautiful stained glass. The 29ft-long high table was made from a single oak tree from Windsor Forest. Sir Francis Drake was a visitor to and friend of the Middle Temple, and a table made from timbers from the *Golden Hind* - the ship in which he sailed around the world - survives to this day.

Times Open all year, Mon-Fri 10-12 & 3-4. Closed BH & legal vacations. **Facilities** ℗ (300 mtrs) (meters) ⍟ licensed & toilets for disabled shop ⊗ (ex assist dogs)

St Paul's Cathedral

St Pauls Courtyard EC4M 8AD

➲ (St Paul's Tube)

☎ 020 7246 8348

e-mail: chapterhouse@stpaulscathedral.org.uk

web: www.stpauls.co.uk

Completed in 1710, Sir Christopher Wren's architectural masterpiece is the cathedral church of the Bishop of London, and arose, like so much of this area of London, from the ashes of the Great Fire of London in 1666. Among the worthies buried here are Nelson and the Duke of Wellington, while Holman Hunt's masterpiece, *Light of the World* hangs in the nave. St Paul's also hosted the weddings of Charles and Diana, and the funeral of Sir Winston Churchill. Impressive views of London can be seen from the Golden Gallery.

Times Open Cathedral, Crypt, Ambulatory, Mon-Sat 8.30. Galleries 9.30. (Last admission 4). Cathedral may close for special services. **Fee** ✳ £10 (ch £3.50, concessions £9, students £8.50). Family (2ad+2ch) £23.50. **Facilities** ℗ (400mtrs) (meter parking in area) ⌨ ♚◎♿ (cathedral floor and crypt are accessible, but not the galleries) toilets for disabled shop ✪ (ex assist dogs) ▬

See advert on this page

N1

The London Canal Museum

12/13 New Wharf Rd N1 9RT

➲ (Underground - Kings Cross. Follow York Way along East side of King's Cross Stn, turn right at Wharfdale Rd, then left into New Wharf Rd).

☎ 020 7713 0836

e-mail: info@canalmuseum.org.uk

web: www.canalmuseum.org.uk

The museum covers the development of London's canals (particularly Regent's Canal), canal vessels and trade, and the way of life of the canal people. Housed in a former ice warehouse and stables, it also illustrates horse transport and the unusual trade of importing ice from Norway; there are two large ice wells under the floor. Facilities include temporary moorings, so you can arrive by boat if you want. There are regular special exhibitions, and special events include evening illustrated talks, towpath walks, and tunnel boat trips.

It's more than the Dome

www.stpauls.co.uk

Times Open all year, Tue-Sun & BH Mon 10-4.30 (last admission 3.45), 1st Thu each mth 10-7.30. Closed 24-26 & 31 Dec. **Facilities** ℗ (0.25m) (Street parking Mon-Fri after 6.30pm) ⌨ (indoor & outdoor) ♿ (large print guides, induction loop, Braille signs) toilets for disabled shop ✪ (ex assist dogs) ▬

N6

Highgate Cemetery

Swains Ln N6 6PJ

➲ (Underground - Archway, see directions posted at exit)

☎ 020 8340 1834

web: www.highgate-cemetery.org.uk

Highgate Cemetery is the most impressive of a series of large, formally arranged and landscaped cemeteries which were established around the perimeter of London in the mid-19th century. There's a wealth of fine sculpture and architecture amongst the tombstones, monuments and mausoleums, as well as the graves of such notables as the Rossetti family, George Eliot, Michael Faraday and Karl Marx. It is also a Grade II listed park.

Times ✳ Open all year. Eastern Cemetery: daily 10 (11 wknds)-5 (4 in winter). Western Cemetery by guided tour only: Sat & Sun 11-4 (3 in winter); midweek tours at 2, advisable to book. Closed 25-26 Dec & during funerals. **Facilities** ✪ (ex assist dogs)

N7

Freightliners City Farm

`FREE`

Sheringham Rd, Islington N7 8PF

➲ *(off Liverpool Rd)*

☎ 020 7609 0467

e-mail: robert@freightlinersfarm.org.uk

web: www.freightlinersfarm.org.uk

A city farm bringing rural life into an urban setting. A variety of animals can be seen at the farm, including cows, pigs, goats, sheep and poultry. Some interesting building projects are taking place at the farm, including a strawbale building, solar dome, an outside bread oven and a continental beehive. A Saturday market offers organic produce, arts and crafts and much more.

Times ✳ Open Winter: 10-4. Summer: 10-4.45 **Facilities** ♿ (charged) ⬚ 🍴 shop garden centre ⊗ (ex assist dogs)

NW1

The Jewish Museum

Raymond Burton House, 129-131 Albert St,
Camden Town NW1 7NB

➲ *(Underground - Camden Town, 3 mins walk from station)*

☎ 020 7284 1997

e-mail: admin@jewishmuseum.org.uk

web: www.jewishmuseum.org.uk

The new Jewish Museum will open in Camden Town in the Summer 2009. For more details visit the Museum's website.

Times Open Mon-Thu, 10-4, Sun 10-5. Closed Jewish Festivals. **Fee** ✳ £3.50 (ch, students, disabled & UB40 £1.50, pen £2.50) Family ticket £8. **Facilities** Ⓟ (outside museum) (pay & display parking) ⬚ ♿ (induction loop in lecture room linked to audio-visual unit) toilets for disabled shop ⊗ (ex assist dogs) ▄

Madame Tussauds and Stardome

Marylebone Rd NW1 5LR

➲ *(Underground - Baker Street)*

☎ 0870 400 3000

e-mail: csc@madame-tussauds.com

web: www.madame-tussauds.com

Madame Tussaud's world-famous waxwork collection was founded in Paris in 1770. It moved to England in 1802 and found a permanent home in London's Marylebone Road in 1884. The 21st century has brought new innovations and new levels of interactivity. Listen to Kylie Minogue whisper in your ear, become an A-list celeb in the 'Blush' nightclub, and take your chances in a high security prison populated by dangerous serial killers. Madame Tussaud's has recently been combined with the equally memorable London Planetarium, where visitors can interact with characters from Disney's *Treasure Planet*.

Times ✳ Open all year 9.30-5.30 (9-6 wknds/summer) **Facilities** Ⓟ (200mtrs) 🍴 shop ⊗ (ex assist dogs) ▄

ZSL London Zoo

Regents Park NW1 4RY

➲ *(Underground - Camden Town or Regents Park)*

☎ 020 7449 6231

e-mail: marketing@zsl.org

web: www.zsl.org

ZSL London Zoo is home to over 12,000 animals, insects, reptiles and fish. First opened in 1828, the Zoo can claim the world's first aquarium, insect and reptile house. There's lots to do, plenty to see and so much to learn. Get closer to your favourite animals, learn about them at the keeper talks and watch them show off their skills at special events. The newest exhibit is Gorilla Kingdom, a walk through the rainforest where you can get closer than ever before to a group of Western Lowland gorillas.

Times Open all year, daily from 10, (closing time dependant on time of year). Closed 25 Dec. **Facilities** ♿ (charged) ⬚ 🍴 🍴 ♿ (wheelchairs & booster scooter available) toilets for disabled shop ⊗ ▄

NW3

Fenton House

Windmill Hill NW3 6RT

➲ *(Underground - Hampstead, right out of station. Cross Heath St, up Holly Hill. Take right fork at top of hill into Hampstead Grove. Entrance on left)*

☎ 020 7435 3471

e-mail: fentonhouse@nationaltrust.org.uk

web: www.nationaltrust.org.uk

A William and Mary merchants house built about 1686 and set in a walled garden, Fenton House is now owned by the National Trust. It contains outstanding displays of Oriental and European porcelain, 17th-century needlework pictures and Georgian furniture as well as the Benton Fletcher collection of early keyboard instruments. In 2007 a collection of British pictures of the 19th and early 20th centuries was bequeathed to Fenton House by the actor Peter Barkworth.

Times Open Mar, Sat & Sun 2-5; Apr-Oct, Sat-Sun & BH Mon 11-5, Wed-Fri 2-5. (Last admission 4.30). **Fee** ✳ £5.40 (ch £2.70). Family ticket £12.50. Group 15+ £4.40. Garden only £1 (ch free). **Facilities** ♿ (Partly accessible) (photographs of areas which are not accessible) ⊗ (ex assist dogs) ❧

Freud Museum

20 Maresfield Gardens, Hampstead NW3 5SX

➲ *(Underground - Finchley Road, follow blue signs to museum)*

☎ 020 7435 2002 & 5167

e-mail: info@freud.org.uk

web: www.freud.org.uk

In 1938, Sigmund Freud left Vienna as a refugee from the Nazi occupation and chose exile in England, transferring his entire domestic and working environment to this house. He worked here until his death a year later. His extraordinary collection of Egyptian, Greek, Roman and Oriental antiquities, his working library and papers, and his fine furniture including the famous desk and couch are all here.

Times Open all year, Wed-Sun 12-5. Closed BHs, telephone for Xmas holiday times. **Fee** ✳ £5 (ch 12-18, students, UB40 & pen £3, ch under 12 free). **Facilities** ℗ (100yds) (metered parking) ☺ (Partly accessible) (personal tours can be arranged if booked in advance) shop ⊗ (ex assist dogs) ▬

Keats House

Keats Grove, Hampstead NW3 2RR

⮩ *(Underground - Hampstead, about 15 mins walk from station)*

☎ 020 7435 2062

e-mail: keatshouse@corpoflondon.gov.uk

web: www.cityoflondon.gov.uk

The poet John Keats lived in this house from 1818-1820 and wrote some of his most famous poems, including *Ode to a Nightingale* here. His fiancee, Fanny Brawne, lived next door, and they often walked together on nearby Hampstead Heath. The house contains many of his personal items including inkstand, engagement ring, paintings, jewellery and manuscripts.

Times Closed for refurbishment until Jan 2009. **Fee** Prices not confirmed for 2009. **Facilities** ℗ (500yds) (residents parking in operation) 🍴 (outdoor) ☺ (ground floor accessible) toilets for disabled shop ⊗ (ex assist dogs) ▬

Kenwood House   FREE

Hampstead Ln NW3 7JR

⮩ *(Underground - Hampstead)*

☎ 020 8348 1286

web: www.english-heritage.org.uk

In splendid grounds beside Hampstead Heath, this outstanding neo-classical house contains one of the most important collections of paintings ever given to the nation. Works by Rembrandt, Vermeer, Turner, Gainsborough and Reynolds are all set against a backdrop of sumptuous rooms. Scenes from *Notting Hill* and *Mansfield Park* were filmed here.

Times Open all year, daily 11.30-4. Closed 24-26 Dec & 1 Jan. (The park stays open later, please see site notices). **Facilities** ❷ ⬚🍴 🍴 shop ⌗

2 Willow Road

2 Willow Rd, Hampstead NW3 1TH

⮩ *(Hampstead tube (Northern Line), along High Street, left Flask Walk, right at end into Willow Rd)*

☎ 020 7435 6166

e-mail: 2willowroad@nationaltrust.org.uk

web: www.nationaltrust.org.uk

Discover the 1939 home built by the architect Ernő Goldfinger for himself and his family. On display is his modern art collection including works by Henry Moore, Bridget Riley, Max Ernst and Marcel Duchamp as well as an extensive collection of original furniture designed by the architect.

Times Open 7 Mar-28 Nov Sat only, plus Thu & Fri 2 Apr-30 Oct. Entry by timed tour only at 12, 1 & 2 (plus 11 on Sat). Non-guided viewing 3-5. (Last admission 4.30). **Fee** £5.30 (ch £2.80). Joint admission with Fenton House £7.70. **Facilities** ℗ (100mtrs) (very limited, car park closes often) ☺ (wheelchair accessible on ground floor only) (video tour of house in cinema) ⊗ (ex assist dogs) ♨

NW8

Ben Uri Gallery, London Jewish Museum of Art

108A Boundary Rd, St John's Wood NW8 0RH

⮩ *(straight on West End Lane (B510), left onto Abbey Rd (B507), pass Beatle landmark, left onto Boundary Rd)*

☎ 020 7604 3991

e-mail: info@benuri.org.uk

web: www.benuri.org.uk

Ben Uri Gallery, The London Jewish Museum of Art, is Britain's oldest Jewish cultural organisation. The Ben Uri Art Society was established in 1915 in London's East End to provide support for the many Jewish artists and craftspeople who were flourishing there in the face of poverty, anti-semitism and isolation from mainstream culture. It was founded by Lazar Berson, a Lithuanian-born designer-maker.

Times Open Summer: Mon-Fri, 10-5.30, Sun 12-4. Winter: Mon-Thu, 10-5.30, Fri 10-3, Sun 12-4. **Fee** ✳ £5 (£4 concessions) **Facilities** ℗ (£1.20/hr) ⊗

Lord's Tour & M.C.C. Museum   2 for 1

Lord's Ground NW8 8QN

⮩ *(Underground - St John's Wood)*

☎ 020 7616 8595 & 8596

e-mail: tours@mcc.org.uk

web: www.lords.org

Established in 1787, Lord's is the home of the MCC and cricket. Guided tours take you behind the scenes, and highlights include the Long Room and the MCC Museum, where the Ashes and a large collection of paintings and memorabilia are displayed. The Museum is open on match days for spectators. 2-for-1 Voucher applies to public guided tours only, not match day admission to museum.

Times Open all year, Nov-Mar tours at 12 & 2; Apr-Sep 10, 12 & 2 (restrictions on some match days). Telephone for details & bookings. **Fee** ✳ Guided tour £12(ch £6, concessions £7). Family ticket (2ad+2ch) £31. Party 25+. Museum only £3 (concessions £1) plus ground admission (match days only). **Facilities** ❷ 🍴 🍴 ☺ (everything is accessible apart from 1st floor of museum) (by arrangement) toilets for disabled shop ⊗ (ex assist dogs) ▬

ENGLAND

NW9

Royal Air Force Museum London

FREE

Grahame Park Way NW9 5LL

➲ *(within easy reach of the A5, A41, M1 and North Circular A406 roads. Tube on Northern Line to Colindale. Rail to Mill Hill Broadway station. Bus route 303 passes the door)*

☎ 020 8205 2266

e-mail: groups@rafmuseum.org

web: www.rafmuseum.org

Take off to the Royal Air Force Museum London and soar through the history of aviation from the earliest balloon flights to the latest Eurofighter. This is a world-class collection of over 100 aircraft, aviation/wartime memorabilia, and artefacts together with an impressive sound and light show that takes you back in time to the Battle of Britain. The Aeronauts Interactive Centre offers hands-on entertainment and education for all ages and includes cockpit controls, co-ordination tests, engine lifting, air speed, drop zone, pilot testing and more.

Times Open daily 10-6. (Last admission 5.30). Closed 24-26 Dec, 1 & 5-9 Jan. **Facilities** Ⓟ ☕ 🍽 licensed ⛩ (indoor & outdoor) ♿ (lifts, ramps & wheelchairs available) toilets for disabled shop ⊗ (ex assist dogs) 💳

SE1

Bankside Gallery

FREE

48 Hopton St SE1 9JH

➲ *(E of Blackfriars Bridge, South Bank of the Thames, adjacent to Tate Modern and the Millennium Bridge)*

☎ 020 7928 7521

e-mail: info@banksidegallery.com

web: www.banksidegallery.com

Bankside Gallery is the home of the Royal Watercolour Society (RWS) and the Royal Society of Painter-Printmakers (RE). A series of regularly changing exhibitions throughout the year displays the work of both societies, and other prestigious contemporary artists.

Times Open daily during exhibitions 11-6. **Facilities** Ⓟ ♿ shop ⊗ (ex assist dogs) 💳

Dali Universe

County Hall Gallery, Riverside Building, South Bank SE1 7PB

➲ *(Waterloo Station - follow signs to South Bank and County Hall, attraction next to London Eye. Westminster Underground - cross Westminster Bridge, County Hall on left).*

☎ 0870 744 7485

e-mail: info@countyhallgallery.com

web: www.countyhallgallery.com

Set in County Hall Gallery, the Dali Universe is host to the world's largest exhibit of surreal and anthropomorphic sculpture by Salvador Dali, including the *Profile of Time* and *Alice in Wonderland*. The exhibition also features a multiplicity of gold ornaments and works in crystal, an unrivalled collection of rare graphics and surreal furniture - including the Mae West Lips Sofa - and the monumental *Spellbound* canvas commissioned for the 1945 Hitchcock film of the same name.

Times ✳ Open daily 10-6.30 (last entry 5.30). Closed 25 Dec. **Facilities** Ⓟ (5 mins) ♿ (elevator, ramp access) toilets for disabled shop ⊗ (ex assist dogs) 💳

Design Museum

Shad Thames SE1 2YD

➲ *(Turn off Tooley St onto Shad Thames. Underground - London Bridge or Tower Hill)*

☎ 0870 909 9009

e-mail: info@designmuseum.org

web: www.designmuseum.org

The Design Museum is the first museum in the world to be dedicated to 20th and 21st-century design. Since opening in 1989, it has become one of London's most inspiring attractions and has won international acclaim for its ground-breaking exhibition and education programmes. As one of the leading museums of design, fashion and architecture, the Design Museum has a changing programme of exhibitions, combining compelling insights into design history with innovative contemporary design.

Times Open all year, daily 10-5.45 (last entry 5.15). Closed 25-26 Dec. **Facilities** Ⓟ (3 mins) (Gainsford St car park is chargeable) ☕ 🍽 ♿ (ramped entrance, wheelchair & lift) toilets for disabled shop ⊗ (ex assist dogs) 💳

Florence Nightingale Museum

St Thomas' Hospital, Gassiot House, 2 Lambeth Palace Rd SE1 7EW

➲ *(Underground - Westminster, Waterloo. On the site of St Thomas' Hospital)*

☎ 020 7620 0374

e-mail: info@florence-nightingale.co.uk

web: www.florence-nightingale.co.uk

Florence Nightingale needs no introduction, but this museum shows clearly that she was more than 'The Lady with the Lamp'. Beautifully designed, the museum creates a personal setting in which a large collection of Florence's personal items including childhood souvenirs, her dress, furniture from her houses and honours awarded to her in old age, are displayed. There is a small military history collection of souvenirs from the Crimean War, including military medals and a military nursing uniform.

Times Open Mon-Fri 10-5; wknds & BHs 10-4.30. (Last admission 1hr before closing). Closed Good Fri, Etr Sat & Sun & 22 Dec-2 Jan. **Facilities** ℗ (charged) ✦ toilets for disabled shop ⊗ (ex assist dogs) ▬

The Garden Museum

Lambeth Palace Rd SE1 7LB

➲ *(Underground - Waterloo, Westminster, Vauxhall. Next to Lambeth Palace, near Lambeth Bridge)*

☎ 020 7401 8865

e-mail: info@museumgardenhistory.org

web: www.museumgardenhistory.org

Situated in the restored church of St. Mary-At-Lambeth, adjacent to Lambeth Palace, the Museum of Garden History provides an insight into the history and development of gardens and gardening in the UK. It houses a fine public display of tools and artefacts. In addition, there is a replica 17th-century knot garden filled with flowers and shrubs of the period, created around the tombs of the famous plant hunters, the John Tradescants, father and son, and Captain William Bligh of the *Bounty.*

Times Tue-Sun, 10.30-5. Closed 23 Dec-2 Jan **Fee** ✶ Donations appreciated. Suggested donations: £3 (concessions £2.50) **Facilities** ℗ (100yds) (metered) ♀ ✦ toilets for disabled shop ⊗ (ex assist dogs)

Golden Hinde Educational Trust   `2 for 1`

182 Pickfords Wharf, Clink St SE1 9DG

➲ *(On the Thames path between Southwark Cathedral and the new Globe Theatre)*

☎ 020 7403 0123

e-mail: info@goldenhinde.org

web: www.goldenhinde.org

An authentic replica of the galleon in which Sir Francis Drake sailed around the world in 1577-1580. This ship has travelled over 140,000 miles. She is now permanently berthed on London's South Bank.

Times Open all year, 10-5.30. Visitors are advised to check opening times as they may vary due to closures for functions. **Fee** ✶ £6 (ch & concessions £4.50). Family (2ad+3ch) £18 **Facilities** ℗ (on street parking) ✦ (stairs on main deck so no access to wheelchairs) shop ⊗ (ex assist dogs) ▬

HMS Belfast

Morgans Ln, Tooley St SE1 2JH

➲ *(Underground - London Bridge/Tower Hill/ Monument. Rail - London Bridge)*

☎ 020 7940 6300

e-mail: hmsbelfast@iwm.org.uk

web: www.iwm.org.uk/hmsbelfast

Europe's last surviving big gun armoured warship from the Second World War, *HMS Belfast* was launched in 1938 and served in the North Atlantic and Arctic with the Home Fleet. She led the Allied naval

bombardment of German positions on D-Day, and was saved for the nation in 1971. A tour of the ship will take you from the Captain's Bridge through nine decks to the massive Boiler and Engine Rooms. You can visit the cramped Mess decks, Officers' Cabins, Galley, Sick Bay, Dentist and Laundry.

Times Open all year, daily. Mar-Oct 10-6 (last admission 5.15); Nov-Feb 10-5 (last admission 4.15). Closed 24-26 Dec. **Fee** £10.70 (ch under 15 free, concessions £8.60). **Facilities** ♀ ⊓ (indoor) ✦ (wheelchair access to main decks, but not all decks) (wheelchair lift for access on board) toilets for disabled shop ⊗ (ex assist dogs) ▬

Imperial War Museum

Lambeth Rd SE1 6HZ

➲ *(Underground - Lambeth North, Elephant & Castle or Waterloo)*

☎ 020 7416 5320 & 5321

e-mail: mail@iwm.org.uk

web: www.iwm.org.uk

Founded in 1917, this museum illustrates and records all aspects of the two World Wars and other military operations involving Britain and the Commonwealth since 1914. There are always special exhibitions and the programme of special and family events includes film shows and lectures. The museum also has a wealth of military reference material, although some reference departments are open to the public by appointment only.

Times Open all year, daily 10-6. Closed 24-26 Dec. **Facilities** ℗ (on street, 100mtrs) (metered Mon-Fri) ♀ ◉ ⊓ ✦ (parking & w/chair hire book in advance, study room, T-Loop) toilets for disabled shop ⊗ (ex assist dogs) ▬

London Aquarium

County Hall, Riverside Building, Westminster Bridge Rd SE1 7PB

➲ *(Underground-Waterloo & Westminster. On south bank next to Westminster Bridge, nr Big Ben & London Eye)*

☎ 020 7967 8000

e-mail: info@londonaquarium.co.uk

web: www.londonaquarium.co.uk

The London Aquarium is one of Europe's largest displays of global aquatic life with over 350 species in over 50 displays, ranging from the mystical seahorse to the deadly stonefish. The huge Pacific display is home to a variety of jacks, stingrays and seven sharks. Come and witness the spectacular Atlantic feed where a team of divers hand feed rays and native British sharks. The rainforest feed incorporates a frenzied piranha attack with the amazing marksmanship of the archerfish. There is also a range of education tours and literature to enhance any visit.

Times ✶ Open all year, daily 10-6. (Last admission 1hr before closing). Closed 25 Dec. Late opening over summer months. **Facilities** ℗ (300mtrs) ♀ ✦ (wheelchairs available) toilets for disabled shop ⊗ (ex assist dogs) ▬

ENGLAND

The London Dungeon

`2 for 1`

28-34 Tooley St SE1 2SZ

➜ *(Next to London Bridge Station)*

☎ 020 7403 7221

e-mail: london.dungeon@merlinentertainments.biz

web: www.thedungeons.com

Transport yourself back to the darkest moments in the capital's history in the depths of the London Dungeon. Live actors, shows, rides and interactive special effects ensure that you face your fears head on in this unique experience. Everything you see is based on real events, from Jack the Ripper to the Great Fire, torture and the Plague. Now with two scary rides including Extremis: Drop Ride to Doom, the Dungeon provides a thrilling experience.

Times Open all year, daily, Apr-Sep 10-5.30; Oct-Mar 10.30-5. Late night opening in the Summer. Telephone for exact times. **Fee** ✳ £19.95 (ch £14.95, concessions £15.95). **Facilities** ℗ (NCP 200yds) ♿ (cards for deaf visitors) toilets for disabled shop ⊗ (ex assist dogs) ☛

London Eye

Riverside Building, County Hall, Westminster Bridge Rd SE1 7PB

➜ *(Underground - Waterloo/Westminster)*

☎ 0870 500 0600

e-mail: customer.services@londoneye.com

web: www.londoneye.com

The London Eye is one of the most inspiring and visually dramatic additions to the London skyline. At 135m/443ft high, it is the world's tallest observation wheel, allowing you to see one of the world's most exciting cities from a completely new perspective. The London Eye takes you on a gradual, 30 minute, 360 degree rotation, revealing parts of the city, which are not visible from the ground. For Londoners and visitors alike, it is the best way to see London and its many celebrated landmarks. The London Eye provides the perfect location for private parties and entertaining and offers a wide variety of in-flight hospitality packages, like champagne and canapés, which are available to enjoy from the privacy of a private capsule.

Times Open daily, Oct-May, 10-8; Jun-Sep, 10-9. Closed 25 Dec & annual maintenance. **Fee** ✳ £15.50 (ch under 5 free, ch £6.50, disabled visitors £10). Fast track entry £25. **Facilities** ℗ (500yds) ⊑ ♿ (Braille guidebooks, w/chair hire, T-loop, carer ticket) toilets for disabled shop ⊗ (ex assist dogs) ☛

Shakespeare's Globe Theatre & Exhibition

21 New Globe Walk, Bankside SE1 9DT

➜ *(Underground - London Bridge, walk along Bankside. Mansion House, walk across Southwark Bridge. St Pauls, walk across Millennium Bridge)*

☎ 020 7902 1500

e-mail: info@shakespearesglobe.com

web: www.shakespeares-globe.org

Guides help to bring England's theatrical heritage to life at the recreation of this famous theatre. Discover what an Elizabethan audience would have been like, find out about the rivalry between the Bankside theatres, the bear baiting and the stews, hear about the penny stinkards and find out what a bodger is. Shakespeare's Globe Exhibition is the world's largest exhibition devoted to Shakespeare and the London in which he lived and worked. Housed beneath the reconstructed theatre, the exhibition explores the remarkable story of the Globe, and brings Shakespeare's world to life using a range of interactive display and live demonstrations.

Times Open all year, May-Sep, daily 9-12.30 (1-5 Rose Theatre tour); Oct-Apr 10-5. **Fee** £10.50 (ch 5-15 £6.50, pen & students £8.50). Family ticket (2ad+3ch) £28.Exhibition & Rose Tour £7.50 (ch £4.50, pen & students £6.50). Family Ticket (2ad+ 3ch) £20. **Facilities** ℗ (0.5m) (very limited on-street parking) ⊑ ⑩ licensed ♿ (parking spaces, 'touch tours' available by appointment) toilets for disabled shop ⊗ (ex assist dogs) ☛

See advert on opposite page

Southwark Cathedral

London Bridge SE1 9DA

➜ *(adjacent to London Bridge, off Borough High St)*

☎ 020 7367 6700

e-mail: cathedral@southwark.anglican.org

web: www.southwark.anglican.org/cathedral

Originally an Augustinian priory, this is London's oldest gothic church building, and has been a place of worship for more than 1,400 years. It became a cathedral for the Diocese of Southwark in 1905, and has links with Chaucer, Dickens and Shakespeare. John Gower and Shakespeare's brother Edmund are buried here. John Harvard of US university fame was baptised here in 1607, and there is a chapel to his memory. Visitors can view part of a Roman road, 14th-century cloister work, and kilns used for Southwark delftware in the 17th/18th centuries.

Times Open daily: Cathedral 9-6. No tourism permitted on Good Fri & 25 Dec. **Fee** ✳ Free, suggested donation £4 per person. Mandatory charge for groups, which should pre-book on 020 7367 6734 **Facilities** Ⓟ (10min walk) ⍟ licensed ⋈ (outdoor) ♿ (induction loop, wheelchair available, large print) toilets for disabled shop ⊗ (ex assist dogs)

Tate Modern

Bankside SE1 9TG

➲ (Underground - Southwark, Blackfriars)

☎ 020 7887 8008 (info) & 8888

e-mail: information@tate.org.uk

web: www.tate.org.uk

This is the UK's largest museum of modern art and is housed in the impressive Bankside power station. Entrance to the permanent collection, which includes works from artists like Picasso, Warhol and Dalí, is free. Tate Modern also holds world-acclaimed temporary exhibitions as well as education programmes, events and activities.

Times Open all year, Sun-Thu 10-6 (last admission 5.15), Fri & Sat 10am-10pm (last admission 9.15). Closed 24-26 Dec. **Fee** ✳ Free. A charge is made for special exhibitions. **Facilities** Ⓟ (reserved for mobility impaired) 💻⍟♿ (parking & wheelchairs available call 020 7887 8888) toilets for disabled shop ⊗ (ex assist dogs) ▬

The Tower Bridge Exhibition

Tower Bridge Rd SE1 2UP

➲ (Underground - Tower Hill or London Bridge)

☎ 020 7940 3985

e-mail: enquiries@towerbridge.org.uk

web: www.towerbridge.co.uk

One of the capital's most famous landmarks, its glass-covered walkways stand 142ft above the Thames, affording panoramic views of the river. Much of the original machinery for working the bridge can be seen in the engine rooms. The Tower Bridge Exhibition uses state-of-the-art effects to present the story of the bridge in a dramatic and exciting fashion.

Times Open all year, Apr-Sep 10-6.30 (last ticket 5.30); Oct-Mar 9.30-5.30 (last ticket 5) **Facilities** Ⓟ (100yds) ♿ (Loop systems) toilets for disabled shop ⊗ (ex assist dogs) ▬

Vinopolis, City of Wine

1 Bank End SE1 9BU

➲ (Underground-London Bridge. Borough High St West exit, right into Stoney St, then left into Park St & follow road round to Vinopolis main entrance)

☎ 0870 241 4040

e-mail: sales@vinopolis.co.uk

web: www.vinopolis.co.uk

Vinopolis is London's premiere wine attraction, situated on a 2.5 acre site on the vibrant Bankside. It offers an imaginative, interactive tour

CONTINUED

SE1 CONTINUED

around the world of wine as well as great tastings. The setting is delightful, with Victorian vaulted ceilings and intricate, almost rustic red brickwork.

Times ✳ Open all year, Mon, Fri & Sat 12-9, Tue-Thu & Sun 12-6, (last admission 2 hrs before closing). Please call for opening hours in Dec and BHs. **Facilities** Ⓟ (5-10 min walk) (NCP parking) ⌨️🍴Ⓞ🚻 ♿ (lifts & ramps) toilets for disabled shop ⊗ (ex assist dogs) ▰

Winston Churchill's Britain at War Experience

64/66 Tooley St SE1 2TF

➲ *(mid way down Tooley St, between London Bridge & Tower Bridge. 2min walk from London Bridge Stn)*

☎ 020 7403 3171

e-mail: info@britainatwar.org.uk
web: www.britainatwar.co.uk

Step back in time to the 1940s and experience a realistic adventure of life in war-torn London. Take the lift to the underground where many spent sleepless nights. Explore evacuation, food and clothes rationing, the blackout and much more. Voted top World War Two tourist attraction.

Times Open all year, Apr-Oct 10-5; Nov-Mar 10-4.30 **Fee** £10.45 (ch 5-16 £4.95, concessions £5.95). Family £26. **Facilities** Ⓟ (400mtrs) ♿ toilets for disabled shop ⊗ (ex assist dogs) ▰

SE5

South London Gallery

FREE

65 Peckham Rd SE5 8UH

➲ *(from Vauxhall take A202 to Camberwell Green. Gallery halfway between Camberwell Green and Peckham)*

☎ 020 7703 6120 & 9799 (info)
e-mail: mail@southlondongallery.org
web: www.southlondongallery.org

The gallery presents a programme of up to six exhibitions a year of cutting-edge contemporary art, and has established itself as South East London's premier venue for contemporary visual arts. The Gallery also programmes regular talks, screenings, live art projects and a range of activities for families and young people. An expansion programme in 2009 will include further exhibition spaces and artist designed gardens.

Times Open Tue-Sun, 12-6. Closed Mon **Facilities** Ⓟ (on-street parking) ♿ (not accessible for electric wheelchairs) (disabled access, induction loop) toilets for disabled shop ⊗ (ex assist dogs)

SE9

Eltham Palace

Court Yard SE9 5QE

☎ 020 8294 2548 ex209
web: www.english-heritage.org.uk

Stephen and Virginia Courtauld's stunning country house shows the glamour and allure of 1930s Art Deco style and is a feast of luxurious design ideas. The house incorporates the medieval Great Hall and stunning moated gardens.

Times Open 21 Mar-Oct, Sun-Wed 10-5; Nov-21 Dec & Feb, Sun-Wed 11-4. Closed 22 Dec-Jan. **Fee** House & Garden: £8.20 (concessions £6.60, ch £4.10). Family ticket £20.50. Garden only: £5.10 (concessions £4.10, ch £2.60). Prices and opening times are subject to change in March 2009. Please call 0870 333 1181 for the most up to date prices and opening times when planning your visit. **Facilities** Ⓟ shop ⊗ 🚍 🚻

SE10

The Fan Museum

2 for 1

12 Crooms Hill SE10 8ER

➲ *(approached via DLR)*

☎ 020 8305 1441

e-mail: admin@fan-museum.org

web: www.fan-museum.org

Two elegant Georgian houses have been beautifully restored as the setting for the first museum in the world devoted entirely to all aspects of the ancient art and craft of fan making. It exhibits the Helene Alexander collection of fans which has been gifted to the nation.

Times Open all year Tue-Sat, 11-5 & Sun noon-5. Closed 9 Oct, 25-26 Dec, 31 Dec-1Jan. **Fee** ✳ £4 (ch under 7 free, concessions £3). Free for OAPs & disabled on Tue after 2pm (ex groups). **Facilities** Ⓟ 500mtrs ☕ ♿ (lift, ramp) toilets for disabled shop garden centre ⊗ (ex assist dogs)

National Maritime Museum

Romney Rd SE10 9NF

➲ *(central Greenwich)*

☎ 020 8312 6565

e-mail: bookings@nmm.ac.uk

web: www.nmm.ac.uk

Britain's seafaring history is displayed in this impressive modern museum. Themes include exploration and discovery, Nelson, trade and empire, passenger shipping and luxury liners, maritime London, costume, art and the sea, and the future of the sea. There are interactive displays for children.

Times Open all year, daily 10-5 Closed 24-26 Dec. **Fee** Free, except special exhibtions. **Facilities** Ⓟ (50 yds) (parking in Greenwich limited) ☕ 🍽 licensed ⛩ (outdoor) ♿ (wheelchairs, advisory service for hearing/sight impaired) toilets for disabled shop ⊗ (assist dogs) 💳

See advert on this page

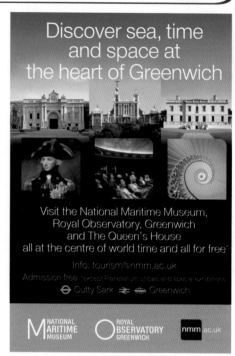

Old Royal Naval College

Greenwich SE10 9LW

➲ *(In centre of Greenwich, off one way system, (College Approach), on the Thames next to Greenwich Pier)*

☎ 020 8269 4747

e-mail: info@greenwichfoundation.org.uk

web: www.oldroyalnavalcollege.org

The Old Royal Naval College is one of London's most famous riverside landmarks and a masterpiece of Baroque architecture. The Grade I listed group of buildings, designed by Sir Christopher Wren as the Greenwich Hospital, occupy the site of the Tudor palace where Henry VIII and Elizabeth I were born. The buildings incorporate the magnificent Painted Hall by James Thornhill and the Chapel by James Stuart. The public can also visit the beautiful grounds of the estate, and from winter 2009 Discover Greenwich, a major new education and interpretation centre, will open to the public, telling the continuing history of the Old Royal Naval College and Maritime Greenwich.

Times Open all year ex 24-26 Dec. (Painted Hall, Chapel and Visitor Centre), daily 10-5 . Chapel open to visitors from 12.30 on Sun, public worship from 11. **Fee** ✳ Admission free, guided tours £4 (ch under 16 free). Group tours £4 booking necessary. **Facilities** Ⓟ (200mtrs) (all local streets, yellow line roads) ☕ 🍽 licensed ⛩ (outdoor) ♿ (lots of stairs makes access difficult, stairmate carrys wheelchair users up and into painted Hall & Chapel.) (parking, wheelchair, stairmate all with notice) toilets for disabled shop ⊗ (ex assist dogs) 💳

SE10 CONTINUED

The Queens House

Romney Rd, Greenwich SE10 9NF

➲ (central Greenwich)

☎ 020 8312 6565

e-mail: bookings@nmm.ac.uk

web: www.nmm.ac.uk

The first Palladian-style villa in England, designed by Inigo Jones for Anne of Denmark and completed for Queen Henrietta Maria, wife of Charles I. The Great Hall, the State Rooms and a Loggia overlooking Greenwich Park are notable features. Also displays the extensive art collection of the National Maritime Museum including Tudor and Stuart royalty.

Times Open daily 10-5. Closed 24-26 Dec. **Fee** Free, except special exhibitions **Facilities** ℗ (50 yds) ⦿ licensed ⊓ (outdoor) ⎏ (lift/wheelchairs) toilets for disabled shop ⊗ (ex assist dogs) ⊑

Royal Observatory Greenwich

Greenwich Park, Greenwich SE10 8XJ

➲ (off A2, Greenwich Park, enter from Blackheath Gate only)

☎ 020 8312 6565

e-mail: bookings@nmm.ac.uk

web: www.nmm.ac.uk

Charles II founded the Royal Observatory in 1675 'for perfecting navigation and astronomy'. It stands at zero meridian longitude and is the original home of Greenwich Mean Time. It houses an extensive collection of historic timekeeping, astronomical and navigational instruments. Recent additions include astronomy galleries and the Peter Harrison Planetarium.

Times Open all year, daily 10-5. Partial closures 31 Dec, 1 Jan and Marathon day. **Fee** Free, except for Planetarium shows £6(ch £4) **Facilities** ℗ (charged) ⊑ ⊓ (outdoor) ⎏ (assistance on request) toilets for disabled shop ⊗ ⊑

The Wernher Collection at Ranger's House

Chesterfield Walk, Blackheath SE10 8QY

☎ 020 8853 0035

web: www.english-heritage.org.uk

Handsome 18th-century house with lovely views over London, Greenwich Park, Blackheath and the Thames. View the 'Wernher Collection' of self-made millionaire Julius Wernher, who made his fortune in the diamond mines of South Africa.

Times Open 21 Mar-Sep, Sun-Wed 10-5; Oct-21; Dec & Mar, exclusive group access. (Please call for details). Pre-booked groups only Thu & Closed 22 Dec-Feb **Fee** £5.50 (concessions £4.40, ch £2.80). Prices and opening times are subject to change in March 2009. Please call 0870 333 1181 for the most up to date prices and opening times when planning your visit. **Facilities** ℗ shop ⊞

SE18

Firepower Royal Artillery Museum

Royal Arsenal, Woolwich SE18 6ST

➲ (A205, right at Woolwich ferry onto A206, attraction signed)

☎ 020 8855 7755

e-mail: info@firepower.org.uk

web: www.firepower.org.uk

Firepower is the Royal Artillery Museum in the historic Royal Arsenal. It spans 2,000 years of artillery and shows the development from Roman catapult to guided missile to self-propelled gun. Put science into action with touchscreen displays and be awed by the big guns.

Times ✳ Open Wed-Sun & BHs 11-5.30. Phone for winter opening times. **Facilities** ℗ (charged) ⊓ ⎏ (wheelchairs available) toilets for disabled shop ⊗ (ex assist dogs) ⊑

Thames Barrier Information & Learning Centre

1 Unity Way SE18 5NJ

➲ (Turn off A102(M) onto A206, turn onto Eastmoor St and follow signs)

☎ 020 8305 4188

e-mail: learningcentre@environment-agency.gov.uk

web: www.environment-agency.gov.uk

Spanning a third of a mile, the Thames Barrier is the world's largest movable flood barrier. The visitors' centre and exhibition on the South Bank explains the flood threat and the construction of this £535 million project, now valued at £1 billion. Each month a test closure of all ten gates, lasting over two hours, is carried out and the annual full day closure of all ten gates takes place in the autumn.

Times ✳ Open Apr-Sep, 10.30-4.30; Oct-Mar 11-3.30. Closed 25 Dec-3 Jan **Facilities** ℗ (charged) ⊑ ⊓ (outdoor) ⎏ (lift from river pier approach) toilets for disabled shop ⊗ (ex assist dogs) ⊑

SE21

Dulwich Picture Gallery

`2 for 1`

Gallery Rd, Dulwich SE21 7AD

➲ *(off South Circular A205, follow signs to Dulwich village)*

☎ 020 8693 5254

e-mail: info@dulwichpicturegallery.org.uk

web: www.dulwichpicturegallery.org.uk

This is the oldest public picture gallery in England, housing a magnificent collection of Old Masters, including works by Poussin, Claude, Rubens, Murillo, Van Dyck, Rembrandt, Watteau and Gainsborough. The gallery was designed by Sir John Soane in 1811. The collection, the building and the critically acclaimed loan exhibitions make the gallery a must see for art lovers. Various exhibitions throughout the year.

Times Open all year Tue-Fri 10-5, wknds & BH Mon 11-5. Closed 24-26 Dec, 1 Jan & Good Fri. **Fee** £5 (concessions £4, ch, students, unemployed & disabled free). + £4 for special exhibitions **Facilities** ❷ ⓘ◎ⓘ licensed ⌂ (outdoor) ♿ (wheelchairs available, hearing loop) toilets for disabled shop ⊗ (ex assist dogs) ▭

SE23

The Horniman Museum & Gardens `FREE`

London Rd, Forest Hill SE23 3PQ

➲ *(situated on A205)*

☎ 020 8699 1872

e-mail: enquiry@horniman.ac.uk

web: www.horniman.ac.uk

Founder Frederick Horniman, a tea merchant, gave the museum to the people of London in 1901. The collection covers the natural and cultural world including Natural History with displays on Vanishing Birds and African Worlds, The Music Gallery, which displays Britain's largest collection of musical instruments and the Centenary Gallery which showcases world cultures. There are 16 acres of gardens, and the museum hosts a variety of workshops and activities for all ages.

Times Open all year, daily 10.30-5.30. Closed 24-26 Dec. Gardens close at sunset. **Facilities** ℗ (opposite museum) ⌷⌂ (outdoor) ♿ (large print leaflets, induction loop) toilets for disabled shop ⊗ (ex assist dogs or in gardens)

SW1

The Banqueting House, Whitehall

Whitehall SW1A 2ER

➲ *(Underground - Westminster, Charing Cross or Embankment)*

☎ 0870 751 5178

e-mail: banquetinghouse@hrp.org.uk

web: www.hrp.org.uk

Designed by Inigo Jones, this is the only surviving building of the vast Whitehall Palace, destroyed by fire 300 years ago. The Palace has seen many significant royal events, including the execution of Charles I in 1649. The Banqueting House's Rubens ceiling paintings are stunning examples of the larger works of the Flemish Master and its classical Palladian style set the fashion for much of London's later architecture.

Times ✴ Open all year, Mon-Sat 10-5. Closed Sun, BHs, 24 Dec-1 Jan. Subject to closure at short notice. **Facilities** ℗ (5 mins) (no parking in Whitehall) ♿ (Braille guide, Induction loops) toilets for disabled shop ⊗ (ex assist dogs) ▭

Buckingham Palace

Buckingham Palace Rd SW1 1AA

➲ *(Underground - Victoria, Green Park, St James' Park)*

☎ 020 7766 7300

e-mail: bookinginfo@royalcollection.org.uk

web: www.royalcollection.org.uk

Buckingham Palace has been the official London residence of Britain's sovereigns since 1837. Today it serves as both the home and office of Her Majesty The Queen. Its nineteen State Rooms, which open for eight weeks a year, form the heart of the working palace and more than 50,000 people visit each year as guests at State, ceremonial and official occasions and garden parties. After visiting the State Rooms, visitors can enjoy a walk along the south side of the garden, which offers superb views of the west front of the Palace and the 19th-century lake.

Times Open Aug-Sep 9.45-6 (last admission 3.45). Entry by timed-ticket. **Fee** £16.50 (ch under 17 £10, ch under 5 free, students £14.50, pen £15) Family (2ad+3ch) £43. **Facilities** ℗ (200yds) (very limited, driving not recommended) ♿ (ex gardens, pre-booking essential - 020 7766 7324) toilets for disabled shop ⊗ (ex assist dogs) ▭

ENGLAND

SW1 CONTINUED

Churchill Museum & Cabinet War Rooms

Clive Steps, King Charles St SW1A 2AQ

➲ (Underground - Westminster (exit 6) or St James Park)

☎ 020 7930 6961

e-mail: cwr@iwm.org.uk

web: www.iwm.org.uk/cabinet

Learn more about the man who inspired Britain's finest hour at the interactive and innovative Churchill Museum, the world's first major museum dedicated to the life of the 'Greatest Briton'. Step back in time and discover the secret underground headquarters that were the nerve centre of Britain's war effort. Located in the heart of Westminster, visitors can view this complex of historic rooms left as they were in 1945, while at the same time taking in the Churchill Museum.

Times Open all year, daily 9.30-6. (last admission 5). Closed 24-26 Dec. **Fee** £12.50 (ch under 16 free, concessions £9.95, UB40 £6.25). Group rates available. **Facilities** ℗ (2 mins walk) (meter parking) 🍽 & (2 wheelchairs available) (education service, object handling session, induction loop) toilets for disabled shop ⊗ (ex assist dogs) ➡

The Household Cavalry NEW Museum   `2 for 1`

Horse Guards, Whitehall SW1A 2AX

➲ (Underground - Charing Cross, Embankment & Westminster)

☎ 020 7930 3070

e-mail: museum@householdcavalry.co.uk

web: www.householdcavalrymuseum.org.uk

The Household Cavalry Museum is unlike any other military museum as it offers a unique 'behind-the-scenes' look at the work that goes into the ceremonial duties and operational role of the Household Cavalry. Watch troopers working with their horses in the original 18th-century stables (via a glazed screen) and hear accounts of their demanding training. Plus children's trails, activity packs and dressing up areas.

Times Open all year daily, Mar-Sep 10-6, Oct-Feb 10-5. **Fee** £6 (ch 5-16 & concessions £4). Family ticket (2ad+3ch) £15. Group rate 10% discount. **Facilities** ℗ (few mins walk) & toilets for disabled shop ⊗ (ex assist dogs) ➡

Houses of Parliament

Westminster SW1A 0AA

➲ (Underground - Westminster)

☎ 020 7219 4272

web: www.parliament.uk

The Houses of Parliament occupy the Palace of Westminster, a royal palace for nearly 1,000 years. Visitors will see the Queen's Robing Room, the Royal Gallery, the Chambers of both the House of Lords and House of Commons, the voting lobbies, historic Westminster Hall (c.1097) where Charles I and Guy Fawkes were put on trial, plus other areas normally hidden from public view.

Times Summer opening: Aug-Sep, open to all. At other times by application to MP (UK constituents only) **Fee** ✳ £12 (concessions £5). Tours via MP free. **Facilities** ℗ (limited 50yds) 🍽 & (visitor route 95% accessible, one short detour required for wheelchair users) toilets for disabled shop ⊗ (ex assist dogs) ➡

Mall Galleries

The Mall SW1Y 5BD

➲ (Underground - Charing Cross, situated on the Mall, near Trafalgar Square and Admiralty Arch)

☎ 020 7930 6844

e-mail: info@mallgalleries.com

web: www.mallgalleries.org.uk

The venue for the annual open exhibitions of nine national art societies. There is also a wide range of individual and group shows. The galleries display work which is both traditional and contemporary by a large number of prominent international artists. A variety of subjects are displayed in a number of mediums, including oil, watercolour, drawings and sculpture. Phone for details of special events.

Times Open all year, daily 10-5. Closed between exhibitions and at Xmas. Some late night opening, please phone for details **Fee** ✳ £2.50 (ch & concessions £1.50). Groups 10+ £1.50 each (Special exhibitions may have different prices - phone for details) **Facilities** ℗ (50 yds) (no parking on the Mall) 🍽 & (platform lift to galleries) toilets for disabled shop ⊗ (ex assist dogs) ➡

The Queen's Gallery

Buckingham Palace, Buckingham Palace Rd SW1A 1AA

➲ (Underground - Victoria, Green Park & St. James' Park)

☎ 020 7766 7301

e-mail: bookinginfo@royalcollection.org.uk

web: www.royalcollection.org.uk

Some of the greatest works of art acquired by kings and queens over 500 years are brought together at The Queen's Gallery from royal residences across the UK. The exhibitions include world-famous paintings, some of the finest furniture ever made, spectacular jewels, dazzling works by Fabergé, and historic pieces of silver and gold that are still used for ceremonial occasions today. Exhibitions for 2008/9 include Amazing Rare Things, which has an audio tour narrated by Sir David Attenborough and Bruegel to Rubens: Masters of Flemish Painting.

Times Open all year, daily, 10-5.15 (last admission 4.30), Closed 25-26 Dec. **Fee** £8.50 (ch under 5 free, ch under 17 £4.50 concession £7.50). Family Ticket (2ad+3ch) £21.50. **Facilities** Ⓟ (200yds) (driving not advisable, limited parking) ♿ (contact 020 7766 7324 for details) toilets for disabled shop ⊗ (ex assist dogs) ▬

The Royal Mews

Buckingham Palace, Buckingham Palace Rd SW1W 0QH

➲ *(Underground - Victoria, Green Park, St. James Park)*

☎ 020 7766 7302

e-mail: bookinginfo@royalcollection.org.uk

web: www.royalcollection.org.uk

Designed by John Nash and completed in 1825, the Royal Mews houses the State Coaches, horse drawn carriages and motor cars used for coronations, State Visits, Royal Weddings and the State Opening of Parliament. These include the Gold State Coach made in 1762, with panels painted by the Florentine artist Cipriani. As one of the finest working stables in existence, the Royal Mews provides a unique opportunity for you to see a working department of the Royal Household.

Times Open daily ex Fri. Mar-Oct 11-4; Aug-Sep 10-5. (Last admission 3.15, Aug-Sep 4.15). **Fee** £7.50 (ch under 17 £4.80, ch under 5 free, concessions £6.75) Family (2ad+3ch) £19.80 **Facilities** Ⓟ (200yds) (driving not advisable, parking limited) ♿ (phone 020 7766 7324 for access information) toilets for disabled shop ⊗ (ex assist dogs) ▬

Tate Britain

Millbank SW1P 4RG

➲ *(Underground - Pimlico)*

☎ 020 7887 8888 & rec info 8008

e-mail: information@tate.org.uk

web: www.tate.org.uk

Tate Britain is the national gallery of British art from 1500 to the present day, from Tudors to the Turner Prize. Tate holds the greatest collection of British art in the world, including works by Blake, Constable, Epstein, Gainsborough, Gilbert and George, Hatoum, Hirst, Hockney, Hodgkin, Hogarth, Moore, Rossetti, Sickert, Spencer, Stubbs and Turner. The gallery is the world centre for the understanding and enjoyment of British art.

Times Open daily 10-5.50. Closed 24-26 Dec. **Fee** * Free. Donations welcomed. Prices vary for special exhibitions. **Facilities** Ⓟ (100mtrs) (metered parking) ☕ 🍴 ⊼ (indoor & outdoor) ♿ (wheelchairs on request, parking by prior arrangement) toilets for disabled shop ⊗ (ex assist dogs) ▬

Westminster Abbey

Broad Sanctuary SW1P 3PA

➲ *(Underground - Westminster, St James's Park. Next to Parliament Square and opposite the Houses of Parliament)*

☎ 020 7222 5152 & 7654 4900

e-mail: info@westminster-abbey.org

web: www.westminster-abbey.org

Westminster Abbey was originally a Benedictine monastery. In the 11th century, it was re-founded by St. Edward the Confessor. The great Romanesque abbey Edward built next to his royal palace became his burial place shortly after it was completed. Over the centuries that followed, many more kings and queens have been buried, and many great figures commemorated, in the abbey. The abbey has been the setting for nearly every coronation since that of William the Conqueror in 1066, and for numerous other royal occasions. The present building, begun by Henry III in 1245, is one of the most visited churches in the world.

Times * Open Abbey: Mon-Fri 9.30-3.45, Sat 9-1.45. Wed late night til 7. (Last admission 1hr before closing). No tourist visiting on Sun, however visitors are welcome at services. The Abbey may at short notice be closed for special services & other events. **Facilities** Ⓟ (500mtrs) ☕ ♿ (Partly accessible) (induction loop) toilets for disabled shop ⊗ (ex assist dogs) ▬

Westminster Cathedral

FREE

Victoria St SW1P 1QW

➲ *(300 yds from Victoria Station)*

☎ 020 7798 9055

e-mail: barrypalmer@rcdow.org.uk

web: www.westminstercathedral.org.uk

Westminster Cathedral is a fascinating example of Victorian architecture. Designed in the Early Christian Byzantine style by John Francis Bentley, its strongly oriental appearance makes it very distinctive. The foundation stone was laid in 1895 but the interior decorations are not fully completed. The Campanile Bell Tower is 273ft high and has a four-sided viewing gallery with magnificent views over London. The lift is open daily 9am-5pm Mar-Nov but shut Mon-Wed from Dec-Feb.

Times * Open all year, daily 7am-7pm. **Facilities** Ⓟ (0.25m) (2hr metered parking) ☕ ♿ (all parts accessible except side chapels, loop system) shop ⊗ (ex assist dogs)

SW1 CONTINUED

Westminster Hall

Houses of Parliament, Westminster SW1A 0AA

➲ *(Underground - Westminster Tube)*

☎ 020 7219 4272

web: www.parliament.uk

Visitors to the home of the British Parliament are guided by a qualified Blue Badge Guide. They follow the route taken by the Queen when she performs the State Opening of Parliament, which includes the Queen's Robing Room, the Royal Gallery, and the Prince's Chamber. The route goes from the House of Lords, through the various lobbies and into the chamber of the House of Commons.

Times Summer opening: Aug-Sep, open to all. At other times by application to MP. (UK constituents only) **Fee** ✳ £12 (concessions £5). Tours via MP free. **Facilities** ℗ (limited 50yds) ⛫ ♿ (Westminster Hall is fully accessible, other parts of the Palace are limited) toilets for disabled shop ⊗ (ex assist dogs) ⚍

SW3

Carlyle's House

24 Cheyne Row SW3 5HL

➲ *(Underground - Sloane Square. Off Cheyne Walk between Battersea & Albert Bridges)*

☎ 020 7352 7087

e-mail: carlyleshouse@nationaltrust.org.uk

web: www.nationaltrust.org.uk/carlyleshouse

'The Sage of Chelsea' - distinguished essayist and writer of historical works, Thomas Carlyle - lived here, with his wife Jane, from 1834 until his death in 1881. Such literary notables as Tennyson, Thackeray, Browning, Ruskin and Dickens were frequent visitors.

Times Open late Mar-Oct, Wed-Fri 2-5, Sat-Sun & BH Mon, 11-5. (Last admission 4.30). **Fee** ✳ £4.75 (ch 5-16, £2.40). Family £11.90 **Facilities** ℗ 100 yds (residents parking Mon-Sat) (not suitable for wheelchair users) ⊗ (ex assist dogs) 🍽 🎎

Chelsea Physic Garden

66 Royal Hospital Rd, (entrance in Swan Walk) SW3 4HS

➲ *(Underground - Sloane Square)*

☎ 020 7352 5646

e-mail: enquiries@chelseaphysicgarden.co.uk

web: www.chelseaphysicgarden.co.uk

Begun in 1673 for the study of plants used by the Society of Apothecaries, this garden is one of Europe's oldest botanic gardens and is the only one to retain the title 'Physic' after the old name for the healing arts. The garden is still used for botanical and medicinal research, and offers displays of many fascinating plants in lovely surroundings.

Times ✳ Open Apr-Oct, Wed 12-5, Sun 12-6. Additional opening during Chelsea Flower Show week, late May & Chelsea Festival week late Jun. Groups at other times by appointment. **Facilities** ℗ (0.5m) (west end of Battersea Park) ⛫ ♿ (disabled parking, wheelchair access) toilets for disabled shop ⊗ (ex assist dogs)

National Army Museum

Royal Hospital Rd, Chelsea SW3 4HT

➲ *(Underground - Sloane Square)*

☎ 020 7730 0717

e-mail: info@national-army-museum.ac.uk

web: www.national-army-museum.ac.uk

The museum offers a unique insight into the lives of Britain's soldiers, and the impact of the British Army on Britain, Europe and the world. Complementing four gallery displays, the events programme offers a range of changing exhibitions, events and children's activities.

Times Open all year, daily 10-5.30. Closed Good Fri, May Day, 24-26 Dec & 1 Jan. **Facilities** ❷ ⛫ ♿ (wheelchair lift to access lower ground floor) toilets for disabled shop ⊗ (ex assist dogs)

Royal Hospital Chelsea

FREE

Royal Hospital Rd SW3 4SR

➲ *(near Sloane Square, off A3216 & A3031)*

☎ 020 7881 5200

e-mail: info@chelsea-pensioners.org.uk

web: www.chelsea-pensioners.org.uk

Founded in 1682 by Charles II as a retreat for army veterans who had become unfit for duty, through injury or long service, the Royal Hospital Chelsea was built on the site of a theological college founded by James I in 1610. The buildings were designed and built by Sir Christopher Wren, and then added to by Robert Adam and Sir John Soane. The hospital houses some 300 'In-Pensioners', some of whom do voluntary work as tour guides, clerical assistants and ground staff. Visitors can stroll around the grounds, gain admission to the Chapel, Great Hall and visit the Museum.

Times Open daily Mon-Sat, 10-12 & 2-4, Sun 2-4. (Museum closed on Sun Oct-Mar). Closed 25-26 Dec & Good Friday. **Facilities** ℗ (limited) ⊓ (outdoor) ♿ (Partly accessible) (induction loop in post office) toilets for disabled shop ⊗ (ex staff & assist dogs) ⚍

SW7

The Natural History Museum

FREE

Cromwell Rd SW7 5BD

➲ *(Underground - South Kensington)*

☎ 020 7942 5000

e-mail: feedback@nhm.ac.uk

web: www.nhm.ac.uk

This vast and elaborate Romanesque-style building, with its terracotta facing showing relief mouldings of animals, birds and fishes, covers an area of four acres. Holding over 70 million specimens from all over the globe, from dinosaurs to diamonds and earthquakes to ants, the museum provides a journey into Earth's past, present and future. Discover more about the work of the museum through a daily programme of talks from museum scientists or go behind the scenes of the Darwin Centre, the museum's scientific research centre.

Times ✳ Open daily 10-5.50 (last admission 5.30). Closed 24-26 Dec. **Facilities** ℗ (180yds) (limited parking, use public transport) ⛫ 🍽 ⊓ (indoor) ♿ (top floor/one gallery not accessible, wheelchair hire) toilets for disabled shop ⊗ (ex assist dogs) ⚍

Science Museum

Exhibition Rd, South Kensington SW7 2DD

➲ *(Underground - South Kensington, signed from tube stn)*

☎ 0870 870 4868

e-mail: sciencemuseum@sciencemuseum.org.uk

web: www.sciencemuseum.org.uk

See iconic objects from the history of science, from Stephenson's *Rocket* to the *Apollo 10* command module; be amazed by a 3D IMAX movie; take a ride in a simulator; visit an exhibition; and encounter the past, present and future of technology in seven floors of free galleries, including the famous hands-on section where children can have fun investigating science with the Museum's dedicated Explainers. The Museum is free, but charges apply to the IMAX cinema, special exhibitions and simulators.

Times Open all year, daily 10-6. Closed 24-26 Dec. **Facilities** ℗ (metered 0.5m away) ⬚🖵🍽🛒 (indoor) ♿ (personal 2hr tour of museum, hearing loop) toilets for disabled shop ⊗ (ex assist dogs) ▄

Victoria and Albert Museum

Cromwell Rd, South Kensington SW7 2RL

➲ *(Underground - South Kensington, Museum situated on A4, Buses C1, 14, 74, 414 stop outside the Cromwell Road entrance)*

☎ 020 7942 2000

e-mail: vanda@vam.ac.uk

web: www.vam.ac.uk

The V&A is the world's greatest museum of art and design. It was established in 1852 to make important works of art available to all, and also to inspire British designers and manufacturers. The Museum's rich and diverse collections span over three thousand years of human creativity from many parts of the world, and include ceramics, furniture, fashion, glass, jewellery, metalwork, sculpture, textiles and paintings. Highlights include the British Galleries 1500-1900, the Jameel Gallery of Islamic Art, and the magnificent John Madejski Garden.

Times Open all year, daily 10-5.45. Fri 10am-10pm **Fee** ✳ Free admission but some exhibitions may carry an extra charge. **Facilities** ℗ (500yds) (limited, charged parking) ⬚🍽🛒 (outdoor) ♿ (Facilities available. Call 020 7942 2211 for details) toilets for disabled shop ⊗ (ex assist dogs) ▄

SW13

London Wetland Centre

Queen Elizabeth Walk SW13 9WT A306

➲ *(underground - Hammersmith).*

☎ 020 8409 4400

e-mail: info.london@wwt.org.uk

web: www.wwt.org.uk

An inspiring wetland landscape that stretches over 105 acres, almost in the heart of London, in Barnes SW13. Thirty wild wetland habitats have been created from reservoir lagoon to ponds, lakes and reedbeds and all are home to a wealth of wildlife. The visitor centre includes a café, gift shop, cinema, large glass viewing observatory and optics shop. There is a new explore adventure centre for 3-11s.

Times ✳ Open: winter 9.30-5 (last admission 4); summer 9.30-6 (last admission 5) **Facilities** ℗ ⬚🍽🛒 (outdoor) ♿ (Partly accessible) (ramps, lifts) toilets for disabled shop ⊗ (ex assist dogs) ▄

SW19

Wimbledon Lawn Tennis Museum

Museum Building, The All England Club, Church Rd SW19 5AE

➲ *(Underground - Southfields, 15mins walk)*

☎ 020 8946 6131

e-mail: museum@aeltc.com

web: www.wimbledon.org/museum

Visitors to the Wimbledon Lawn Tennis Museum are invited to explore the game's evolution from a garden party pastime to a multi-million dollar professional sport played worldwide. Highlights include the Championship Trophies, a cinema that captures the Science of Tennis using Matrix-style special effects, film and video footage of some of the most memorable matches, an extensive collection of memorabilia dating back to 1555, and a holographic John McEnroe who walks through a recreated 1980s changing room.

Times ✳ Open daily all year, 10.30-5. Closed middle Sun of Championships, Mon immediately following the Championships, 24-26 Dec & 1 Jan. **Facilities** ℗ ⬚♿ (lift, stairlift to cafe, audio guides in 8 languages) toilets for disabled shop ⊗ (ex assist dogs) ▄

W1

Apsley House, The Wellington Museum

148 Piccadilly, Hyde Park Corner W1J 7NT

➲ *(Underground - Hyde Park Corner, exit 1 overlooking rdbt)*

☎ 020 7499 5676

web: www.english-heritage.org.uk

Number One, London, is the popular name for one of the Capital's finest private residences, 19th-century home of the first Duke of Wellington. Built in the 1770s, its rich interiors have been returned to their former glory, and house the Duke's magnificent collection of paintings, silver, porcelain, sculpture and furniture.

Times Open all year 21 Mar-Oct, Wed-Sun & BHs 11-5; Nov-Feb, Wed-Sun 11-4. Closed 24-26 Dec & 1 Jan. **Fee** £5.30 (ch £2.70, concessions £4). Joint ticket to House & Wellington Arch: £6.90 (ch £3.50, concessions £5.20. Family £17.30). Prices & opening times are subject to change in March 2009. Please call 0870 333 1181 for the most up to date prices and opening times. **Facilities** ℗ (NCP 10mins walk) ♿ (lift) shop ⊗ (ex assist dogs) ⌘ ▄

W1 CONTINUED

Handel House Museum

`2 for 1`

25 Brook St W1K 4HB

⮑ *(off Park Lane into Brook Gate, then Upper Brook Street. Pass Claridge's Hotel on right. The entrance is in Lancashire Court)*

☎ 020 7495 1685

e-mail: mail@handelhouse.org

web: www.handelhouse.org

Home to George Frideric Handel from 1723 until his death in 1759, the Handel House Museum celebrates Handel's music and life. It was here that Handel composed *Messiah, Zadok the Priest* and *Music for the Royal Fireworks*. Over 200 years later, live music, educational projects and public events continue to bring Handel's former home to life. 14th April 2009 is the 250th anniversary of Handel's death.

Times Open all year Tue, Wed, Fri & Sat 10-6, Thu 10-8, Sun 12-6. Closed Mon & BHs, 25-26 Dec & 1-2 Jan. **Fee** ✳ £5 (ch £2, concessions £4.50). Free for children on Sat. **Facilities** ℗ (10-20mtrs) (congestion charge during week) ♿ (lift) toilets for disabled shop ⊗ (ex assist dogs) ⚌

Pollock's Toy Museum

1 Scala St W1T 2HL

⮑ *(Underground - Goodge St)*

☎ 020 7636 3452

e-mail: pollocks@btconnect.com

web: www.pollockstoytheatre.com

Teddy bears, wax and china dolls, dolls' houses, board games, toy theatres, tin toys, mechanical and optical toys, folk toys and nursery furniture, are among the attractions to be seen in this appealing museum. Items from all over the world and from all periods are displayed in two small, interconnecting houses with winding staircases and charming little rooms.

Times ✳ Open all year, Mon-Sat 10-5. Closed BH, Sun & Xmas. **Facilities** ℗ (100yds) (Central London restrictions) ♿ (Partly accessible) (Wheelchair access to shop only) shop ⚌

Royal Academy Of Arts

Burlington House, Piccadilly W1J 0BD

⮑ *(Underground - Piccadilly Circus, head towards Green Park)*

☎ 020 7300 5729

e-mail: maria.salvatierra@royalacademy.org.uk

web: www.royalacademy.org.uk

Known principally for international loan exhibitions, the Royal Academy of Arts was founded in 1768 and is Britain's oldest Fine Arts institution. Two of its founding principles were to provide a free school and to mount an annual exhibition open to all artists of distinguished merit, now known as the Summer Exhibition. The Royal Academy's most prized possession, Michelangelo's Tondo, *The Virgin and Child with the Infant St John*, one of only four marble sculptures by the artist outside Italy, is on permanent display in the Sackler Wing. The John Madejski Fine Rooms are a suite of six rooms displaying the highlights from the RA collection.

Times Open daily 10-6. Late night opening Fri 10am-10pm. Closed 24-25 Dec **Fee** £7-£11 (ch, concessions & group visitors reduced price). Prices vary for each exhibition. Free entry to permanent collection. **Facilities** ℗ (400yds) (disabled parking call in advance) ⏏🍴♿ (large-print guides/labels, sign language) toilets for disabled shop ⊗ (ex assist dogs) ⚌

The Wallace Collection

`FREE`

Hertford House, Manchester Square W1U 3BN

⮑ *(Underground - Bond St, Baker St, Oxford Circus, located minutes from Oxford St, in garden square behind Selfridges)*

☎ 020 7563 9500

e-mail: visiting@wallacecollection.org

web: www.wallacecollection.org

Founded by the 1st Marquis of Hertford, the Wallace Collection was bequeathed to the nation in 1897 and came on public display three years later. This is one of the world's finest collections of art ever assembled by one family. The collection is shown in the family home, a tranquil oasis just a few minutes from Oxford Street. There are paintings by Titian, Canaletto, Rembrandt, Rubens, Hals, Fragonard, Velazquez, Gainsborough and many more. There is a very important collection of French porcelain and furniture, much of it of Royal providence, as well as amazing arms and armour, sculpture and Renaissance treasures. Many rooms have been recently restored creating intimate and opulent settings for the works of art.

Times Open all year, daily 10-5, closed 24-26 Dec & 1 Jan. **Facilities** ℗ (NCP & meters) (Free on Sun, pre-book for disabled) ⏏🍴 licensed ♿ (lift, ramp, wheelchair available, induction loop) toilets for disabled shop ⊗ (ex assist dogs) ⚌

W2

Serpentine Gallery

`FREE`

Kensington Gardens W2 3XA

⮑ *(Underground - Knightsbridge, Lancaster Gate, South Kensington. Bus 9, 10, 12, 52, 94)*

☎ 020 7402 6075

e-mail: press@serpentinegallery.org

web: www.serpentinegallery.org

The Serpentine Gallery, named after the lake in Hyde Park, is situated in the heart of Kensington Gardens in a 1934 tea pavilion, and was founded in 1970 by the Arts Council of Great Britain. Today the Gallery attracts over 400,000 visitors a year and is one the best places in London for modern and contemporary art and architecture.

Times Open daily 10-6. **Facilities** 🚾♿ toilets for disabled shop ⊗ (ex assist dogs) ⚌

W4
Chiswick House
Burlington Ln, Chiswick W4 2RP

⮑ *(Underground - Gunnersbury)*

☎ 020 8995 0508

web: www.english-heritage.org.uk

Discover the story of this celebrated Palladian villa, a fine example of 18th-century English architecture with lavish interiors and classical landscaping.

Times Open 21 Mar-Oct, Wed-Sun & BHs 10-5; Nov-21 Dec exclusive group access. (Please call for details). Closed 22 Dec-Mar. **Fee** £4.20 (concessions £3.40, ch £2.10). Family ticket £10.50. Prices and opening times are subject to change in March 2009. Please call 0870 333 1181 for the most up to date prices and opening times when planning your visit. **Facilities** ℗ ⬚ ⧟ ⬚ (telephone in advance for wheelchair facilities) shop ⌗

Hogarth's House FREE
Hogarth Ln, Great West Rd W4 2QN

⮑ *(50yds W of Hogarth rdbt on Great West Road A4)*

☎ 020 8994 6757

e-mail: info@cip.org.uk

web: www.hounslow.info

This 18th-century house was the country home of artist William Hogarth (1697-1764) during the last 15 years of his life. The house contains displays on the artist's life, and many of his satirical engravings. The gardens contain Hogarth's famous mulberry tree.

Times ✳ Open Apr-Oct, Tue-Fri 1-5, Sat-Sun 1-6; Nov-Mar, Tue-Fri 1-4, Sat-Sun 1-5. Closed Mon (ex BHs), Jan, Good Fri & 25-26 Dec. **Facilities** ℗ (25 & 50yds) (spaces marked in Axis Centre car park) ⬚ (telephone in advance to confirm) toilets for disabled shop ⊗ (ex assist dogs)

W8
Kensington Palace State Apartments & Royal Ceremonial Dress Collection
Kensington Gardens W8 4PX

⮑ *(Underground - High Street Kensington or Notting Hill Gate)*

☎ 0870 751 5170

e-mail: kensingtonpalace@hrp.org.uk

web: www.hrp.org.uk

Highlights of a visit to Kensington include the King's and Queen's Apartments with a fine collection of Old Masters; Tintoretto and Van Dyke amongst them. The rooms used by Princess Victoria are also shown, including her bedroom, where she was woken to be told she was Queen. The Royal Ceremonial Dress Collection includes representations of tailor's and dressmaker's workshops, and a display of dresses that belonged to Diana, Princess of Wales.

Times ✳ Open Mar-Oct 10-6, Nov-Feb 10-5 (last admission 1hr before close). Closed 24-26 Dec. **Facilities** ℗ (500yds) ⬚ ⬚ (audio guide, cafe has wheelchair access ramp) toilets for disabled shop ⊗ (ex assist dogs) ⬚

Linley Sambourne House
18 Stafford Ter W8 7BH

⮑ *(Underground - High Street Kensington)*

☎ 020 7602 3316

e-mail: museums@rbkc.gov.uk

web: www.rbkc.gov.uk/linleysambournehouse

The home of Linley Sambourne (1844-1910), chief political cartoonist at *Punch* magazine, has had its magnificent artistic interior preserved, almost unchanged, since the late 19th century. Also displayed are many of Sambourne's own drawings and photographs. Tours are lead by costumed actors with scripts developed from the Sambourne family archive.

Times All access by guided tour, mid Mar-mid Dec. Sat & Sun tours 11.15, 1, 2.15, 3.30. **Fee** £6 (ch £1, concessions £4) **Facilities** ℗ (2 min walk) (metered parking) shop ⊗ ⬚

W12
BBC Television Centre Tours
BBC Television Centre, Wood Ln W12 7RJ

⮑ *(Underground - Central Line/White City)*

☎ 0370 603 0304

e-mail: bbctours@bbc.co.uk

web: www.bbc.co.uk/tours

On a tour of BBC Television Centre you will see behind the scenes of the most famous TV Centre in the world. You may see studios, the News Centre, Weather Centre, the interactive studio, and dressing rooms, but due to the operational nature of the building guarantees cannot be made. The CBBC Experience is aimed at 7-12 year olds - visit the Blue Peter Garden, have fun making a programme in the interactive studio, take part in the Raven challenge, become "Diddy Dick & Dom". Both tours last up to two hours. Broadcasting House - new for 2008 are monthly tours of the UK's first purpose-built broadcast centre, which has been undergoing a major restoration and modernisation as part of a ten year development project. Tours are fitted round the working building's activities and you will see a range of areas such as the newly restored radio theatre, the council chamber and an interactive radio drama experience. These tours will be held initially one Sunday a month, please telephone for details.

Times Open Mon-Sat. Tours at 10, 10.20, 10.40, 1.15, 1.30, 1.45, 3.30, 3.45 & 4. Closed Xmas & BH's. All tours must be pre-booked. Also tours at 11, 2, 4.15 Mon-Fri. **Fee** ✳ £9.50 (ch & students £7, concessions £8.50). Family £27. **Facilities** ℗ (10min walk) (no site disabled parking only) ⬚ (wheelchair & sign language available) toilets for disabled shop ⊗ (ex assist dogs) ⬚

W14

Leighton House Museum

12 Holland Park Rd W14 8LZ

➲ (Underground - High St Kensington. Museum is N of Kensington High St, off Melbury Rd)

☎ 020 7602 3316

e-mail: museums@rbkc.gov.uk

web: www.leightonhouse.co.uk

An opulent and exotic example of high Victorian taste, Leighton House was built for the President of the Royal Academy, Frederic Lord Leighton. The main body of the house was built in 1866 but the fabulous Arab Hall, an arresting 'Arabian Nights' creation, was not completed until 13 years later.

Times Open daily 11-5.30. Closed Tue & 25-26 Dec & 1 Jan. **Fee** £3 (concessions £1). Joint tours of Leighton House Museum & Linley Sambourne House £10. **Facilities** ℗ (100mtrs) (metered) shop ⊗ ⬛

WC1

British Museum

Great Russell St WC1B 3DG

➲ (Underground - Russell Sq, Tottenham Court Rd, Holborn)

☎ 020 7323 8000

e-mail: information@britishmuseum.org

web: www.thebritishmuseum.ac.uk

Of the world and for the world, the British Museum brings together astounding examples of universal heritage. Enter through the largest covered square in Europe. Pick up your audio guide, children's pack or What's On programme. Then discover the world through objects like the Aztec mosaics, the Rosetta Stone, El Anatsui's African textiles or the colossal Ramesses II. For a more intimate look, a fantastic evening meal or some world cinema, come late - every Thursday and Friday.

Times Open all year, Gallery: 10-5.30 selected galleries open late Thur-Fri until 8.30. Great Court: Sun-Wed 9-6, Thu-Sat 9am-11pm. Closed Good Fri, 24-26 Dec & 1 Jan. **Fee** ✳ Free admission except for special exhibitions **Facilities** ℗ (5 mins walk) ⊑ ⊚ licensed ⊞ (indoor) ♿ (parking by arrangement) toilets for disabled shop ⊗ (ex assist/companion dogs) ⬛

The Cartoon Museum   `2 for 1`

35 Little Russell St WC1A 2HH

➲ (left off New Oxford St into Museum St, then left into Little Russell St)

☎ 020 7580 8155

e-mail: info@cartoonmuseum.org

web: www.cartoonmuseum.org

The main galleries display over 200 original cartoons, comics, cartoon strips and caricatures by many of the greatest and funniest of British cartoonists past and present. There is also a programme of temporary exhibitions which change regularly.

Times Open all year Tue-Sat 10.30-5.30, Sun 12-5.30. **Fee** ✳ £4 (ch under 18, students & Friends of the Cartoon Museum free, concessions £3) Free admission for Art Fund members **Facilities** ℗ (metered parking) ♿ (only ground floor acessible to wheelchairs) (hearing loop, large print labels) toilets for disabled shop ⊗ (ex assist dogs) ⬛

The Charles Dickens Museum

48 Doughty St WC1N 2LX

➲ (Underground - Russell Square or Chancery Lane)

☎ 020 7405 2127

e-mail: info@dickensmuseum.com

web: www.dickensmuseum.com

Charles Dickens lived in Doughty Street in his twenties and it was here he worked on his first full-length novel, The Pickwick Papers, and later Oliver Twist and Nicholas Nickleby. Pages of the original manuscripts are on display, together with valuable first editions, his marriage licence and many other personal mementoes.

Times ✳ Open all year, Mon-Sat 10-5, Sun 11-5. **Facilities** ℗ (in street) (metered, 2 hrs max) shop ⊗ ⬛

Petrie Museum of Egyptian Archaeology   `FREE`

Malet Place, Univerity College London WC1E 6BT

➲ (on 1st floor of the D M S Watson building, in Malet Place, off Torrington Place, UCL Main Campus)

☎ 020 7679 2884

e-mail: petrie.museum@ucl.ac.uk

web: www.petrie.ucl.ac.uk

One of the largest and most inspiring collections of Egyptian archaeology anywhere in the world. The displays illustrate life in the Nile Valley from prehistory, through the era of the Pharoahs to Roman and Islamic times. Especially noted for its collection of the personal items that illustrate life and death in Ancient Egypt, including the world's earliest surviving dress (c 2800BC).

Times Open all year, Tue-Fri 1-5, Sat 10-1. Closed for 1 wk at Xmas & Etr. **Facilities** ♿ (objects on rear staircase which make it inaccessible to wheelchairs) (wheelchair lift) toilets for disabled shop ⊗ (ex assist dogs)

WC2

Benjamin Franklin House NEW

36 Craven St WC2N 5NF

➲ (Between Charing Cross & Embankment)

☎ 020 7839 2006

e-mail: info@benjaminfranklinhouse.org

web: www.benjaminfranklinhouse.org

The house is not only a museum, but an educational facility as well. Between 1757 and 1775 Dr Benjamin Franklin - scientist, diplomat, philosopher and inventor lived here. The Historical Experience Show presents the excitement and uncertainty of Franklin's London years.

Times Open Wed-Sun, shows at 12, 1, 2 & 3.15 & 6.15. Closed Xmas & BHs. **Fee** ✳ £7 (ch 16 free) **Facilities** shop ⊗ (ex assist dogs)

The Courtauld Gallery

Somerset House, Strand WC2R 0RN

➲ (Underground - Temple, Embankment, Covent Garden & Charing Cross)

☎ 020 7848 2526

e-mail: galleryinfo@courtauld.ac.uk

web: www.courtauld.ac.uk

Famous for its Impressionist and Post-impressionist masterpieces as well as outstanding earlier paintings and drawings, The Courtauld Gallery is one of the finest small museums in the world. Ranging from Botticelli, Cranach and Rubens to Monet, Gauguin and Van Gogh, this magnificent collection is displayed in the elegant 18th-century setting of Somerset House. World-famous paintings include Monet's *Bar at the Folies-Bergere*, Van Gogh's *Self Portrait with Bandaged Ear* and Renoir's *La Loge*. In addition, The Courtauld Gallery offers a highly acclaimed programme of temporary exhibitions.

Times Open daily 10-6. (Last admission 5.30). 24 & 31 Dec 10-4, closed 25-26 Dec, 1 Jan 12-6. **Fee** £5 (concessions £4). Free for under 18s, full time UK students, registered unwaged, staff of UK universities & Friends of The Courtauld. Helper for disabled visitors also free. **Facilities** ℗ (NCP Drury Lane) ⌨ ⍣ licensed ⅚ (lift, parking by arrangement only call 020 7845 4600) toilets for disabled shop ⊗ (ex assist dogs) ▬

Hunterian Museum [FREE]

The Royal College of Surgeons, 35-43 Lincoln's Inn Fields WC2A 3PE

➲ (Underground - Holborn)

☎ 020 7869 6560

e-mail: museums@rcseng.ac.uk

web: www.rcseng.ac.uk

The Hunterian Museum at the Royal College of Surgeons houses over 3,000 anatomical and pathological preparations collected by the surgeon John Hunter (1728-1793). New interpretive displays explore Hunter's life and work, the history of the Hunterian Museum and the College, and the development of surgery from the 18th century to the present. The MacRae Gallery provides a dedicated space for learning based on the museum's reserve collections. The museum also stages a changing programme of temporary exhibitions, lectures and other public events on themes related to the history and current practice of surgery.

Times Open all year Tue-Sat 10-5. Closed 22 Dec-5 Jan, Good Fri. **Facilities** ℗ (15mtrs) (pay & display 8.30-6.30pm) ⅚ (Descriptive tours by arrangement) toilets for disabled shop ⊗ (ex assist dogs)

London's Transport Museum

The Piazza, Covent Garden WC2E 7BB

➲ (Underground - Covent Garden, Leicester Sq or Holburn)

☎ 020 7379 6344 & 7565 7299

e-mail: resourcedesk@ltmuseum.co.uk

web: www.ltmuseum.co.uk

Covent Garden's original Victorian flower market is home to this excellent museum which explores the colourful story of London and its famous transport system from 1800 to the present day. There are buses, trams, tube trains, and posters, as well as touch-screen displays, videos, working models and tube simulators to bring the story to life. Details not confirmed for 2009.

Times ✳ Closed for refurbishment until autumn 2007. **Facilities** ℗ (5 mins walk) (parking meters) ⌨ ⅚ (lift & ramps, touch & sign tours) toilets for disabled shop ⊗ (ex assist dogs)

WC2 CONTINUED

National Gallery

Trafalgar Square WC2N 5DN

➲ *(Underground - Charing Cross, Leicester Square, Embankment & Piccadilly Circus. Rail - Charing Cross. Located on N side of Trafalgar Sq)*

☎ 020 7747 2885

e-mail: information@ng-london.org.uk
web: www.nationalgallery.org.uk

All the great periods of Western European painting from 1260-1900 are represented here. Artists on display include Leonardo da Vinci, Rembrandt, Titian, Caravaggio, Turner, Monet and Van Gogh.

Times Open all year, daily 10-6, (Fri until 9). Special major changing exhibitions open normal gallery times. Closed 24-26 Dec & 1 Jan. **Fee** Free. Admission charged for some major exhibitions. **Facilities** ℗ (100yds) ⚏ ⏝ licensed ♿ (wheelchair, induction loop, lift, deaf/blind visitor tours) toilets for disabled shop ⊗ (ex assist dogs) ⊨

National Portrait Gallery

St Martin's Place WC2H 0HE

➲ *(Underground - Charing Cross, Leicester Square. Buses to Trafalgar Square)*

☎ 020 7306 0055

web: www.npg.org.uk

The National Portrait Gallery is home to the largest collection of portraiture in the world featuring famous British men and woman who have created history from the Middle Ages until the present day. Over 1,000 portraits are on display across three floors from Henry VIII and Florence Nightingale to The Beatles and HM The Queen. And, if you want to rest those weary feet, visit the fabulous Portrait Restaurant on the top floor with roof-top views across London. Special events take place throughout the year, see website for details.

Times Open all year, Mon-Wed & Sat-Sun 10-6, Thu-Fri 10-9. Closed Good Fri, 24-26 Dec & 1 Jan. (Gallery closure commences 10mins prior to stated time). **Facilities** ℗ (200yds) ⚏ ⏝ ♿ (Partly accessible) (stair climber, touch tours, audio guide, print captions) toilets for disabled shop ⊗ (ex assist dogs) ⊨

Sir John Soane's Museum

13 Lincoln's Inn Fields WC2A 3BP

➲ *(Underground - Holborn)*

☎ 020 7405 2107

e-mail: jbrock@soane.org.uk
web: www.soane.org

Sir John Soane was responsible for some of the most splendid architecture in London, and his house, built in 1812, contains his collections of antiquities, sculpture, paintings, drawings and books. Amongst his treasures are the *Rake's Progess* and *Election* series of paintings by Hogarth.

Times Open all year, Tue-Sat 10-5. Also first Tue of month 6-9pm. (Closed BH, Good Fri & 24 Dec). Lecture tour Sat 11am (limited no of tickets sold from 10.30). **Fee** ✳ Donations welcome. **Facilities** ℗ (200yds) (metered parking very limited) ♿ (Partly accessible) (wheelchair available, phone for details of accessibility) shop ⊗ (ex assist dogs) ⊨

Theatre Museum

Victoria and Albert Museum, Cromwell Rd SW7 2RL

➲ *(Underground - Covent Garden, Leicester Sq)*

☎ 020 7943 4700

e-mail: tmenquiries@vam.ac.uk
web: www.vam.ac.uk/theatre

The Theatre Museum has moved and is now housed in the Victoria and Albert Museum. New Performance galleries celebrate the performing arts in Britain, from Shakespeare to the present day. 2009 will see a major retrospective, Diaghilev and the Ballet Russes, which will examine the origins, development and long term influence of the Ballet Russes and celebrate its centenary.

Times Open all year, daily 10-6. Closed 24-26 Dec & 1 Jan. **Facilities** ℗ (charged) ⚏ ⏝ ♿ (Braille guides, audio tours, workshops) toilets for disabled shop garden centre ⊗ (ex assist dogs) ⊨

BARNET   MAP 04 TQ29

Museum of Domestic Design & Architecture

Middlesex University, Cat Hill EN4 8HT

➲ *(from M25, junct 24 signed A111 Cockfosters to Cat Hill rdbt, straight over onto Chase side. Entrance 1st right opposite Chicken Shed Theatre on Cat Hill Campus)*

☎ 020 8411 5244

e-mail: moda@mdx.ac.uk

web: www.moda.mdx.ac.uk

MoDA is a museum of the history of the home. It holds one of the world's most comprehensive collections of decorative design for the period 1870 to 1960, and is a rich source of information on how people decorated and lived in their homes. MoDA has two galleries, a lecture theatre for study days, a seminar room with practical workshops for both adults and children, and a study room which gives visitors access to the collections.

Times Open Tue-Sat 10-5, Sun 2-5. Closed Mon, Etr, Xmas & New Year. **Fee** Free entrance. Charges for study days, workshop & group tours **Facilities** ℗ ♿ (induction loop fitted in lecture theatre & at reception) toilets for disabled shop ⊗ (ex assist dogs)

BEXLEY   MAP 05 TQ47

Hall Place and Gardens

Bourne Rd DA5 1PQ

➲ *(A2 Black Prince interchange 5m from M25 junct 2 towards London)*

☎ 01322 526574

e-mail: info@hallplace.org.uk

web: www.hallplace.com

Hall Place is an attractive Grade I listed mansion of chequered flint and brick, with wonderful gardens. It was built during the reign of Henry VIII and extended during the 17th century. It sits in 65 hectares of gardens which boast a stunning topiary lawn including the Queen's Beasts, planted to mark the Coronation of Queen Elizabeth II. The house is being comprehensively restored and refurbished. See the new galleries about the house's history and Tudor life. The gardens remain open.

Times Garden: Mon-Fri 7.30-dusk, Sat & Sun 9-dusk. House closed for restoration please phone 01322 526574 for details. **Fee** Free. Special events may be charged. **Facilities** ℗ ⊇ ⫯⨀ ♿ (Partly accessible) toilets for disabled shop garden centre ⊗ (ex assist dogs)

BEXLEYHEATH   MAP 05 TQ47

Danson House

Danson Park, Danson Rd DA6 8HL

➲ *(From Danson interchange of the A2 via Danson Rd (A221) located in Danson Park.)*

☎ 020 8303 6699

web: www.dansonhouse.org.uk

Danson House is a Palladian villa that was completed in 1766 to designs by Sir Robert Taylor for his client, Sir John Boyd, whose family fortune was founded on the West Indian sugar trade. The house was built for Boyd's young bride, Catherine Chapone, and so the interiors and layout reflect themes of love and enjoyment. The principal floor has a cycle of 17 original wall paintings, and there is a restored George England organ in the library.

Times Open 16 Mar-Oct, Wed Thu Sun & BH Mon 11-5 (last admission 4.15) **Fee** ✳ £5 (ch & Historic House Association members free, concessions £4.50), English Heritage members £3.75. **Facilities** ℗ (charged) ⊇⫯⨀ licensed ⋒ (outdoor) ♿ (Lifts) toilets for disabled shop ⊗ (ex assist dogs) ⊟

Red House

Red House Ln DA6 8JF

➲ *(off A221 Bexleyheath. At 1st rdbt take 2nd exit then 3rd exit at next rdbt, then 1st left into Danson Rd)*

☎ 020 8304 9878

web: www.nationaltrust.org.uk/redhouse

Commissioned by William Morris in 1859 and designed by Philip Webb, Red House is of enormous international significance in the history of domestic architecture and garden design. The building is constructed of warm red brick, under a steep red-tiled roof, with an emphasis on natural materials and a strong gothic influence. The garden was designed to 'clothe' the house with a series of subdivided areas which still exist. Inside, the house retains many of the original features and fixed items of furniture designed by Morris and Webb.

Times Open Mar-20 Dec, 30 Dec-1 Oct **Fee** £6.90 (ch 5-15 £3.45). Family ticket (2ad & 3ch) £17.50. Group price £5.90 **Facilities** ℗ (20 min walk) (narrow lane, limited parking space) ⊇⋒ (outdoor) ♿ (upper floor not accessible, ramp to allow access over small step on ground floor) shop ⊗ (ex assist dogs) ⫿⊟

BRENTFORD   MAP 04 TQ17

Kew Bridge Steam Museum

Green Dragon Ln TW8 0EN

➲ *(Underground - Kew Gardens, District line then 391 bus. Museum 100yds from N side of Kew Bridge, on A315)*

☎ 020 8568 4757

e-mail: info@kbsm.org

web: www.kbsm.org

This Victorian pumping station has steam engines and six beam engines, five of which are working and one of which is the largest in the world. The Grand Junction 90 inch engine is over 40 feet high, and

CONTINUED

BRENTFORD CONTINUED

weighs around 250 tons. A diesel house and waterwheel can also be seen along with London's only steam narrow-gauge railway, which operates every Sunday (Mar-Nov). The Water for Life Gallery tells the story of London's water supply from Pre-Roman times.

Times Open all year (ex Mon) daily 11-5. Engines in steam, wknds & BHs. **Facilities** ❷ ⬚ ⊟ (indoor & outdoor) ♿ (wheelchairs, large print guide) toilets for disabled shop ▬

Musical Museum

399 High St TW8 0DU

➲ (Underground - Gunnersbury, nr Kew Bridge)

☎ 020 8560 8108

web: www.musicalmuseum.co.uk

This museum (relocated in a new building) will take you back to a bygone age to hear and see a marvellous working collection of automatic musical instruments from small music boxes to a mighty Wurlitzer theatre organ. Working demonstrations.

Times Open Tue-Sun, 11-5.30 (last admission 4.30) **Fee** ✳ £7 (ch free, concession £5.50) **Facilities** ❷ ⬚♿ toilets for disabled shop ⊗ (ex assist dogs) ▬

CHESSINGTON　　　　　MAP 04 TQ16

Chessington World of Adventures

Leatherhead Rd KT9 2NE

➲ (M25 junct 9/10, on A243)

☎ 0870 444 7777

web: www.chessington.com

With many of its rides suitable for under-12s, this is the ideal place for an action-packed family day out. Very small children are entertained in Animal Land, Land of the Dragons, and on the Toytown fun-rides. Among the multitude of fun-packed areas are Beanoland, the Mystic East, the Forbidden Kingdom, Mexicana, Transylvania, and the Market Square. Riders float in 'bubble tubs' over chutes, fountains and foam on the bubbletastic Bubbleworks water ride. Enjoy the animals in the Monkey and Bird Garden and Creature Features which includes skunks, porcupines and meerkats. Plenty of special events and shows all year, including Halloween fun and TV characters.

Times Open 24 Mar-Oct (main season) Zoo only days in May, Sep, Oct, Nov & Dec. Main season 10-5, 10-6, Zoo 10-3. **Fee** ✳ £32 (ch £21). Family of 3 £66, of 4 £86, of 5 £104. **Facilities** ❷ ⬚⎚⊟ (outdoor) ♿ (some rides not accessible, guide available) toilets for disabled shop ⊗ (ex assist dogs) ▬

CHISLEHURST　　　　　MAP 05 TQ47

Chislehurst Caves　　　2 for 1

Old Hill BR7 5NL

➲ (off A222 near Chislehurst railway stn. Turn into station approach, then right & right again into Caveside Close)

☎ 020 8467 3264

e-mail: enquiries@chislehurstcaves.co.uk

web: www.chislehurstcaves.co.uk

Miles of mystery and history beneath your feet. Grab a lantern and get ready for an amazing adventure. Visit the caves and the whole family can travel back in time as they explore the maze of passageways dug through the chalk deep beneath Chislehurst. Accompanied by an experienced guide on a 45 minute tour, see the tunnels made famous as a shelter during the Second World War, visit the cave's church, druid altar, the haunted pool and much more.

Times Open all year, Wed-Sun, 10-4. Daily during local school hols (incl half terms). Closed Xmas. **Fee** £5 (ch & pen £3). **Facilities** ❷ ⬚⎚ licensed ⊟ (outdoor) ♿ (Uneven floors in the caves may cause some difficulties) toilets for disabled shop ⊗ (ex assist dogs) ▬

ESHER　　　　　MAP 04 TQ16

Claremont Landscape Garden

Portsmouth Rd KT10 9JG

➲ (1m S of Esher on A307)

☎ 01372 467806

e-mail: claremont@nationaltrust.org.uk

web: www.nationaltrust.org.uk/claremont

Laid out by Vanbrugh and Bridgeman before 1720, extended and naturalised by Kent, this is one of the earliest surviving examples of an English landscaped garden. Its 50 acres include a lake with an island pavilion, a grotto, a turf amphitheatre and a new children's play area. Full programme of events throughout the year, please see website for details.

Times Open all year Apr-Oct daily incl BH Mon 10-6; Nov-Mar daily (ex Mon) 10-5 or sunset if earlier. Closed 25 Dec. House not National Trust. **Fee** ✳ £5.80 (ch £2.80). Family ticket £14.50 **Facilities** ❷ ⬚♿ (Partly accessible) (wheelchairs available, Braille guide) toilets for disabled shop ⊗ (ex on leads, Nov-Mar only) 🐾 ▬

HAM   MAP 04 TQ17

Ham House & Garden

Ham St TW10 7RS

➲ *(W of A307, between Kingston & Richmond)*

☎ 020 8940 1951

e-mail: hamhouse@nationaltrust.org.uk

web: www.nationaltrust.org.uk/hamhouse

Ham House is a fine example of 17th-century fashion and power. Built in 1610, the house was enlarged in the 1670s by the Duchess of Lauderdale, when it was at the heart of Restoration court life and intrigue. It was then occupied by the same family until 1948. The formal garden is significant for its survival in an area known as the cradle of the English Landscape Movement. The outbuildings include an orangery, an ice house, a still house (a 17th-century equivalent of an in-house pharmacy), and a dairy with unusual cast-iron "cow's legs". Open-air theatre and ghost tours, contact for details.

Times House: 14-25 Feb, Sat-Wed 12-4; 28 Feb-8 Mar, Sat & Sun 12-4; 14 Mar-1Nov, Sat-Wed 12-4 (last admission 3.30). Garden: 1-11 Feb, Sat-Wed 11-4; 14 Feb-20 Dec, Sat-Wed 12-4; 21 Dec-31 Jan, Sat-Wed 11-4 (last admission 30 minutes before closing). Closed 25-26 Dec & 1 Jan. Open Good Fri. **Fee** House & Garden £9.90 (ch £5.50). Family ticket £25.30. Garden only £3.30 (ch £2.20). Family ticket £8.80. **Facilities** ❷ ▱ 🗛 (outdoor) ♿ (onsite lift suitable for most manual wheelchairs) (Braille guide, induction loop, lift, mobility vehicle) toilets for disabled shop ⊗ (ex assist dogs) ♨ ➡

HAMPTON COURT   MAP 04 TQ16

Hampton Court Palace

KT8 9AU

➲ *(A3 to Hook underpass then A309. Train from Waterloo - Hampton Court, 2mins walk from station)*

☎ 0870 752 7777

e-mail: hamptoncourt@hrp.org.uk

web: www.hrp.org.uk

With over 500 years of royal history Hampton Court Palace has something to offer everyone, from the magnificent State Apartments to the domestic reality of the Tudor Kitchens. Costumed guides and audio tours bring the palace to life and provide an insight into how life in the palace would have been in the time of Henry VIII and William III. There is also an exhibition that explores community life after the departure of the monarchy from the Palace, along with an audio installation in the world famous maze. A recent addition is a multi-sensory experience involving the Tudor kitchens. 2009 will see a series of events celebrating the 500th anniversary of Henry VIII's accession to the throne.

Times ✳ Open all year from 10, closes 6 mid Mar-mid Oct, 4.30 mid Oct-mid Mar. Closed 24-26 Dec. **Facilities** ❷ (charged) ▱ ⑩ 🗛 ♿ (lifts, buggies for gardens, wheelchairs, wardens, Braille toilets for disabled shop ⊗ (ex assist dogs) ➡

ISLEWORTH   MAP 04 TQ17

Syon House

TW8 8JF

➲ *(A310 Twickenham road into Park Rd)*

☎ 020 8560 0882 & 0883

e-mail: info@syonpark.co.uk

web: www.syonpark.co.uk

Set in 200 acres of parkland, Syon House is the London home of the Duke of Northumberland, whose family have lived here since the late 16th century. During the second half of the 18th century the first Duke of Northumberland engaged Robert Adam to remodel the interior and 'Capability' Brown to landscape the grounds. Adam was also responsible for the furniture and decorations, and the result is particularly spectacular in the superbly coloured Ante-Room and Long Gallery.

Times Open 19 Apr-Oct, Wed-Thu, Sun & BH 11-5 (last ticket 4.15). **Facilities** ❷ ▱ ♿ (stairclimber available) toilets for disabled shop garden centre ⊗ ➡

ENGLAND

ISLEWORTH CONTINUED

Syon Park

TW8 8JF

⮩ *(A310 Twickenham road into Park Rd)*

☎ 020 8560 0882

e-mail: info@syonpark.co.uk

web: www.syonpark.co.uk

Contained within the 40 acres that make up Syon Park Gardens is one of the inspirations for the Crystal Palace at the Great Exhibition of 1851: a vast crescent of metal and glass, the first construction of its kind in the world and known as the Great Conservatory. Although the horticultural reputation of Syon Park goes back to the 16th century, its beauty today is thanks to the master of landscape design, 'Capability' Brown.

Times Open all year, Mar-Oct daily, 10.30-5.30; (4pm Nov-Feb, wkends & 1 Jan) **Facilities** ❷ ♿ ♿ toilets for disabled shop garden centre ❽ (ex assist dogs) ➿

KEW   **MAP 04 TQ17**

Kew Gardens (Royal Botanic Gardens)

TW9 3AB

⮩ *(1m from M4 on South Circular) (A205)*

☎ 020 8332 5655

e-mail: info@kew.org

web: www.kew.org

Kew Gardens is a paradise throughout the seasons. Lose yourself in the magnificent glasshouses and discover plants from the world's deserts, mountains and oceans. Wide-open spaces, stunning vistas, listed buildings and wildlife contribute to the Gardens' unique atmosphere. As well as being famous for its beautiful gardens, Kew is world renowned for its contribution to botanical and horticultural science. 2009 is the 250th anniversary of Kew Gardens.

Times Open all year, Gardens daily 9.30. Closing times vary (seasonal, phone to verify). Closed 24-25 Dec. **Fee** ✳ £13 (ch under 17 free, concessions £12). **Facilities** ❷ (charged) ♿ ⓘ♿ (Partly accessible) (16 seat bus tour: enquiries ring 020 8332 5643) toilets for disabled shop garden centre ❽ (ex assist dogs) ➿

Kew Palace

Royal Botanic Gardens TW9 3AB

⮩ *(Underground - Kew Bridge)*

☎ 0870 751 5179

e-mail: kewpalace@hrp.org.uk

web: www.hrp.org.uk

A fairly modest red-brick building, built in the Dutch style with gables, Kew Palace was built in 1631 and used until 1818 when Queen Charlotte died. A major renovation project was completed in April 2006, and the palace was reopened to the public after ten years of closure. Visitors can see artefacts that belonged to George III and his family, and visit rooms on the second floor, faithfully recreated with décor and furnishings as George III and his family would have known them in the early 1800s.

Times ✳ Open 24 Mar-28 Oct, Tue-Sun 11-5 (last admission 4.15). **Facilities** ❷ (charged) ♿ toilets for disabled shop ❽ (ex assist dogs) ➿

The National Archives   `FREE`

Ruskin Av TW9 4DU

⮩ *(Underground - Kew Gardens)*

☎ 020 8392 5202 & 020 8487 9202

e-mail: events@pro.gov.uk

web: www.pro.gov.uk/

The National Archives houses one of the finest, most complete archives in Europe, comprising the records of the central government and law courts from the Norman Conquest to the present century. It is a mine of information and some of the most interesting material including Domesday Book.

Times ✳ Open Mon, Wed & Fri, 9-4.45; Tue, 10-7; Thu, 9-7. Closed 1st wk in Dec, Sun & public holiday wknds. **Facilities** ❷ ♿ ♿ (hearing loops & large print text in museum) toilets for disabled shop ❽ (ex assist dogs)

Queen Charlotte's Cottage

Royal Botanic Gardens TW9 3AB

⮩ *(Underground - Kew Gardens)*

☎ 0870 751 5175

web: www.hrp.org.uk

Typical of the fashionable rustic style popular with the gentry in the 18th century, the cottage was built for George III and Queen Charlotte as a home for their menagerie of exotic pets, as well as a picnic spot and summer house.

Times ✳ Open wknds Jul & Aug. **Facilities** ⓟ ❽ ➿

MORDEN   **MAP 05 TQ26**

Morden Hall Park   `FREE`

Morden Hall Rd SM4 5JD

⮩ *(A298 (Bushey Rd), right at 2nd lights into Martin Way. Morden Hall signed)*

☎ 020 8417 8091

e-mail: mordenhallpark@nationaltrust.org.uk

web: www.nationaltrust.org.uk

A green oasis in the heart of South West London. A former deer park, with a network of waterways including meadow, wetland and woodland habitats. Also discover the picturesque rose garden with over 2000 roses, fragrant from May to September.

Times ✳ Open daily, 8-6. **Facilities** ❷ ♿ ⓘ♿ ⌂ (outdoor) ♿ (wheelchair, Braille guides, large handled cutlery) toilets for disabled shop garden centre ❧ ➿

OSTERLEY MAP 04 TQ17

Osterley Park and House

Jersey Rd TW7 4RB

➲ (signed from A4. Underground - Osterley)

☎ 020 8232 5050

e-mail: osterley@nationaltrust.org.uk

web: www.nationaltrust.org.uk/osterley

This spectacular mansion and its surrounding gardens, park and farmland is one of the last surviving country estates in London. Transformed in the late 18th century for the wealthy Child family by the architect Robert Adam, the house and garden were designed for entertaining and impressing this banking family's friends and clients. With a series of stunning show rooms affording views over extensive parkland, Osterley continues to impress visitors today. The gardens are currently being restored to their former 18th-century splendour and there are pleasant walks around the park as well as wide open green spaces for families to enjoy.

Times Open all year: House 12 Mar-2 Nov, Wed-Sun + BH's 1-4.30. Garden 12 Mar-2 Nov, Wed-Sun + BH's 11-5. Park, daily until 29 Mar 8-6; 30 Mar-25 Oct 8-7.30; 26 Oct onwards 8-6, **Fee** House & Garden £8.40 (ch £4.20). Family ticket £21. Group 15+(booked in advance) £7.15. Garden only £3.70 (ch £1.85). **Facilities** ❷ (charged) 💺 🍴 (outdoor) ♿ (house-steps to principle floor, please call for full details) (Braille guide, wheelchairs, electric carts, stair climber) toilets for disabled shop ⊗ (ex assist dogs in house) 🚼 ⬛

TWICKENHAM MAP 04 TQ17

Marble Hill House

Richmond Rd TW1 2NL

☎ 020 8892 5115

web: www.english-heritage.org.uk

A magnificent Thames-side Palladian villa built for Henrietta Howard, mistress of King George II, set in 66 acres of riverside parklands.

Times Open 21 Mar-Oct, Sat 10-2, Sun & BHs 10-5. Nov-21 Dec & Mar exclusive group access, please call for details. Closed 22 Dec-Feb. **Fee** £4.20 (concessions £3.40, ch £2.10). Family £10.50. Prices and opening times are subject to change in March 2009. Please call 0870 333 1181 for the most up to date prices and opening times when planning your visit. **Facilities** ❷ 💺 🍴 🛒 shop ⊗ (ex on lead in certain areas) 🎏

Orleans House Gallery `FREE`

Riverside TW1 3DJ

➲ (Richmond road (A305), Orleans Rd is on right just past Orleans Park School)

☎ 020 8831 6000

e-mail: m.denovellis@richmond.gov.uk

web: www.richmond.gov.uk

Stroll beside the Thames and through the woodland gardens of Orleans House, where you will find stunning 18th-century interior design and an excellent public art gallery. Visitors of all ages can try out their own artistic talents in pre-booked workshops, and wide-ranging temporary exhibitions are held throughout the year - please telephone for details.

Times ✳ Open Oct-Mar, Tue-Sat 1-4.30, Sun & BH 2-4.30; Apr-Sep Tue-Sat 1-5.30, Sun & BH 2-5.30. **Facilities** ❷ 🍴 ♿ (handling objects & large print labels for some exhibitions) toilets for disabled shop ⊗ (ex assist dogs)

World Rugby Museum & Twickenham Stadium Tours

Twickenham Stadium, Rugby Rd TW1 1DZ

➲ (A316, follow signs to Twickenham Stadium)

☎ 020 8891 8877

e-mail: museum@rfu.com

web: www.rfu.com/museum/

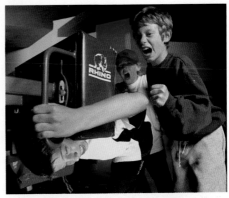

Combine a behind-the-scenes guided tour of the world's most famous rugby stadium with a visit to the World Rugby Museum. The tour includes breathtaking views from the top of the North Stand, a visit to the England dressing room and ends by walking through the players tunnel to pitch side. The multi-media museum appeals to enthusiasts of all ages and charts the history and world-wide growth of rugby. You can also test your skills on the scrum machine. 100 years of Twickenham Stadium 2009/2010 season.

Times Open, Tue-Sat 10-5 (last museum admission 4.30), Sun 11-5 (last admission 4.30). Closed post Twickenham match days, Etr Sun, 24-26 Dec & 1 Jan. On match days museum only available to match ticket holders. Please pre book all tours. **Fee** ✳ Museum & Tour £10 (concessions £7). Family £34. **Facilities** ❷ 💺 🍴 licensed ♿ toilets for disabled shop ⊗ (ex assist dogs) ⬛

MERSEYSIDE

Liverpool Anglican Cathedral

LIVERPOOL   MAP 07 SJ39

The Beatles Story   `2 for 1`

Britannia Pavilion, Albert Dock L3 4AD

⮑ *(follow signs to Albert Dock. Located outside Britannia Pavilion, next to Premier Travel Inn)*

☎ 0151 709 1963

e-mail: info@beatlesstory.com

web: www.beatlesstory.com

Located within Liverpool's historic Albert Dock, the Beatles Story is a unique visitor attraction that transports you on an enlightening and atmospheric journey into the life, times, culture and music of The Beatles.

Times Open all year 9-7 (last admission 5). Closed 25-26 Dec. **Fee** £12.50 (ch 5-16 yrs £6.50 & concessions £8.50). Family ticket (2ad+2ch) £32 (2ad+3ch) £37 **Facilities** ❷ (charged) 🖵 & (hearing loop, large print guide) toilets for disabled shop ⊗ (ex assist dogs) ➡

Central Library   `FREE`

William Brown St L3 8EW

⮑ *(located between museum and art gallery-in the Cultural Quarter and part of the World Heritage Site)*

☎ 0151 233 3000

e-mail: refhum.central.library@liverpool.gov.uk

web: www.liverpool.gov.uk/libraries

The Picton, Hornby and Brown buildings, situated in the Victorian grandeur of William Brown Street, house Liverpool's collection of over one million books, forming one of Britain's largest and oldest public libraries. The Liverpool Record Office is one of the country's largest and most significant County Record offices. Regular exhibitions of treasures from the collections are held, please telephone or see website for details.

Times Open all year, Mon-Fri 9-6, Sat 10-4 & Sun 12-4. Closed BHs. **Facilities** ⓟ (50 yds) (pay & display parking only) & (Ground floor access - lift to floors 1-4 only) (lift, text magnification, reading machine) toilets for disabled ⊗ (ex assist dogs)

The Grand National Experience & Visitor Centre Visitor Centre

Aintree Racecourse, Ormskirk Rd L9 5AS

⮑ *(Aintree Racecourse on A59 (Liverpool to Preston road), clearly signed)*

☎ 0151 523 2600

e-mail: aintree@jockeyclubracecourses.com

web: www.aintree.co.uk

A fascinating look at Britain's most famous horserace, the Grand National. Visitors can sit in the jockeys' weighing-in chair, walk around the dressing rooms, watch video presentations, and view a gallery of paintings and photography depicting the race.

Times Open late May-mid Oct, Tue-Fri, 10-5. **Fee** Please telephone for details. **Facilities** ❷ ⑩ 🍴 (indoor & outdoor) & toilets for disabled ⊗ (ex assist dogs) ➡

International Slavery Museum   `FREE`

Albert Dock L3 4AQ

⮑ *(enter Albert Dock from the Strand)*

☎ 0151 478 4499

web: www.liverpoolmuseums.org.uk

2007 was the bicentenary of the abolition of the slave trade in Britain, and this museum was opened at Albert Dock. It looks at the impact of the transatlantic slave trade and includes thought-provoking displays on issues such as freedom, identity, human rights, racial discrimination and cultural change.

Times Open daily 10-5 & 24 Dec 10-2. Closed 25-26 Dec & 1 Jan. **Facilities** ❷ 🖵 ⑩ & (restricted wheelchair access, no access to basement) toilets for disabled shop ⊗ (ex assist dogs) ➡

Liverpool Cathedral   `2 for 1`

St James' Mount L1 7AZ

⮑ *(follow city centre signs 'Cathedrals'. St James' Mount is off Upper Duke St in S side of city centre, adjacent to 'Chinatown')*

☎ 0151 709 6271

e-mail: eryl.parry@liverpoolcathedral.org.uk

web: www.liverpoolcathedral.org.uk

Although it appears at first sight to be as old as any other monumental cathedral in Britain, Liverpool Cathedral is in fact a 20th-century structure that was only completed in 1978. Its foundation stone was laid in 1904, and through two World Wars the building continued. It is the largest Anglican Cathedral in Europe, and has the largest pipe organ and the heaviest ringing peal of bells in the world. In addition to great views from the tower, the Cathedral now has an award-winning new visitor centre, the Great Space, with a film, audio tours and interactive stations. The Cathedral hosts a full calendar of family activities and cultural events. Please note the 2-for-1 voucher applies to the Great Space Film Audio and Interactive tour only.

Times Open daily 8-6, 25 Dec 8-3. **Fee** ✳ Free. £3 donation per person welcomed. Tower £4.25 (concessions £3) Family ticket (2ad+3ch) £10. Great Space £4.75(concessions £3.50). Family £10. Combined ticket £6.75 (concessions £5). family £15. **Facilities** ❷ (charged) 🖵 ⑩ licensed & (Tower & Nave Bridge have steps) (Braille leaflets, handrails, lift, induction loop) toilets for disabled shop ⊗ (ex assist dogs)

ENGLAND

Liverpool Football Club Museum and Stadium Tour Tour

Anfield Rd L4 0TH

☎ 0151 260 6677

e-mail: stephen.done@liverpoolfc.tv

web: www.liverpoolfc.tv

Touch the famous "This is Anfield" sign as you walk down the tunnel to the sound of the crowd at the LFC museum and tour centre. Celebrate all things Liverpool, past and present. Bright displays and videos chart the history of one of England's most successful football clubs and more recent glories are recalled.

Times ✳ Open all year: Museum daily 10-5 last admission 4. Closed 25-26 Dec. Match days 9 until last admission - 1hr before kick off. Museum & Tour - tours are run subject to daily demand. Advance booking is essential to avoid disappointment. **Facilities** ❷ ⏺ ♿ (lifts, ramps to all areas for wheelchairs) toilets for disabled shop ⊗ (ex assist dogs) ▭

Mendips NEW

251 Menlove Av, Woolton L25 7SA

➲ (No direct access by car or on foot. Visits are by combines minibus tour only with 20 Forthlin Road, childhood home of Sir Paul McCartney)

☎ 0151 427 7231   0844 800 4791

e-mail: mendips@nationaltrust.org.uk

web: www.nationaltrust.org.uk/beatles

Visit Mendips and 20 Forthlin Road as part of a combined minibus tour. The childhood home of John Lennon, Mendips is a 1930s semi where his passion for music began and where some of his early songs were written. The house evokes the time he spent here during his formative years.

Times Open 28 Feb-15 Mar & 7-29 Nov, Wed-Sun 10, 12.30 & 3; 18 Mar-1 Nov, 10, 10.50, 2.30 & 3.20. **Fee** Joint ticket Mendips & Forthlin Road £16 (ch £3, NT members £8) **Facilities** ♿ (Partly accessible) toilets for disabled ⊗ (ex assist dogs) ▭

Merseyside Maritime Museum   FREE

Albert Dock L3 4AQ

➲ (enter Albert Dock from the Strand)

☎ 0151 478 4499

web: www.liverpoolmuseums.org.uk

Discover the story behind one of the world's greatest ports and the people who used it. For many, Liverpool was a gateway to a new life in other countries. For others its importance to the slave trade had less happy consequences. From slavers to luxury liners, submarine hunters to passenger ferries, explore Liverpool's central role. The Magical History Tour continues until September 2009.

Times Open daily 10-5 & 24 Dec 10-2. Closed 25-26 Dec & 1 Jan. **Facilities** ❷ ⏺ ⏺ (outdoor) ♿ (lifts, wheelchairs, ramps, ex pilot boat & basement) toilets for disabled shop ⊗ (ex assist dogs) ▭

Metropolitan Cathedral of Christ the King

Mount Pleasant L3 5TQ

➲ (10 mins walk from either Liverpool Lime St or Liverpool Central Railway Station. Cathedral well signed from city centre)

☎ 0151 709 9222

e-mail: info@metcathedral.org.uk

web: www.liverpoolmetrocathedral.org.uk

A modern Roman Catholic cathedral which provides a focal point on the Liverpool skyline. The imposing structure of concrete ribs and stained glass was designed by Sir Frederick Gibberd and consecrated in 1967. Monumental crypt of brick and granite by Sir Edwin Lutyens 1933. Numerous modern works of art.

Times Open daily 8-6 (Sun 5 in winter). **Fee** Free admission, although donation of £3 requested **Facilities** ❷ (charged) ⏺ ⏺ licensed ♿ (lift, loop system) toilets for disabled shop ⊗ (ex assist dogs) ▭

National Conservation Centre   FREE

White Chapel L1 6HZ

➲ (follow brown tourist signs to Whitechapel)

☎ 0151 478 4999

web: www.liverpoolmuseums.org.uk

Award winning centre, the only one of its kind, gives the public an insight into the world of museum and gallery conservation.

Times Open daily 10-5 & 24 Dec 10-2. Closed 25-26 Dec & 1 Jan. **Facilities** ❷ (charged) ⏺ ♿ toilets for disabled shop ⊗ (ex assist dogs) ▭

National Wildflower Centre   2 for 1

Court Hey Park, Roby Rd L16 3NA

➲ (M62 junct 5, take A5080 to rdbt. Exit into Roby Rd, entrance 0.5m on left)

☎ 0151 738 1913

e-mail: info@nwc.org.uk

web: www.nwc.org.uk

Set in a public park on the outskirts of Liverpool, the award-winning National Wildflower Centre promotes the creation of wildflower habitats around the country and provides educational materials, wildflower seeds and interactive facilities. The Centre has demonstration areas, children's activities, a working nursery, compost display and rooftop walk. The centre has a comprehensive programme of events through the summer. Special Events: Green Fayre in June, Knowsley Flower Show in August, Winter celebration in December. The National Wildflower Centre celebrates its 10th anniversary in 2009.

Times Open Apr-Sep daily 10-5. Last entry 4. **Fee** £3.50 (ch & concessions £1.75). Family ticket (2ad+2ch) £9. Group discount tickets available & supporter packages. **Facilities** ℗ ☷ ⊟ (outdoor) ♿ (electric buggy & wheelchair available) toilets for disabled shop garden centre ⊗ (ex assist dogs & in park) ⊟

Sudley House
FREE

Mossley Hill Rd L18 8BX

⮑ *(near Aigburth Station and Mossley Hill Station)*

☎ 0151 724 3245

web: www.liverpoolmuseums.org.uk

Sudley, Liverpool's hidden gem, is unique, a Victorian merchant's house with an art collection displayed in its original setting. Works on show include paintings by Landseer and Turner, major pre-Raphaelite pictures and a group of 18th-century portraits by Gainsborough, Reynolds, Romney and Lawrence. Sudley houses an introductory display telling the history of the house, a Toy Zone - a display of dolls, toys and doll's house with a children's activities area, a display of items from the historic costume and fashion collection, and a new temporary exhibition gallery.

Times Open daily 10-5 & 24 Dec 10-2. Closed 25-26 Dec & 1 Jan. **Facilities** ℗ ☷ ♿ shop ⊗ (ex assist dogs)

Tate Liverpool

Albert Dock L3 4BB

⮑ *(within walking distance of Liverpool Lime Street train station, on the Albert Dock)*

☎ 0151 702 7400 & 7402

e-mail: visiting.liverpool@tate.org.uk

web: www.tate.org.uk/liverpool/

Tate Liverpool is one of the largest galleries of modern and contemporary art outside London and is housed in a converted warehouse in the historic Albert Dock. The gallery is home to the National Collection of Modern Art in the North, and has four floors displaying work selected from the Tate Collection, as well as special exhibitions which bring together artwork loaned from around the world.

Times Open Tue-Sun, BH Mon & all Mons in Jun-Aug, 10-5.50. Closed 24-26 Dec, 1 Jan & Good Fri **Fee** ✴ Admission free. £5 (concessions £4) for special exhibitions, phone for details. **Facilities** ℗ (5 min walk) (Pay & Display) ☷ ♿ (wheelchairs available, leaflets in Braille, hearing loop) toilets for disabled shop ⊗ (ex assist dogs) ⊟

20 Forthlin Road NEW

L24 1YP

⮑ *(No direct access by car or on foot. Visits are by combines minibus tour only with Mendips, childhood home of John Lennon)*

☎ 0844 8004791

e-mail: 20forthlinroad@nationaltrust.org.uk

web: www.nationaltrust.org.uk/beatles

Visit 20 Forthlin Road and Mendips as part of a combined minibus tour. 20 Forthlin Road is the former home of the McCartney family, a 1950s terraced house where the Beatles met, rehearsed and wrote many of their earliest songs. Displays include contemporary photographs by Michael McCartney and early Beatles memorabilia.

Times Open 28 Feb-15 Mar & 7-29 Nov, Wed-Sun 10, 12.30 & 3; 18 Mar-1 Nov, 10, 10.50, 2.30 & 3.20. **Fee** Joint ticket Forthlin Road & Mendips £16 (ch £3, NT members £8) **Facilities** ♿ (Partly accessible) toilets for disabled ⊗ (ex assist dogs)

Walker Art Gallery

William Brown St L3 8EL

⮑ *(city centre adjacent to St George's Hall & Lime St)*

☎ 0151 478 4199

web: www.liverpoolmuseums.org.uk

The National Gallery of the North, this is one of the finest art galleries in Europe, housing an outstanding collection of British and European art from the 14th to the 20th century. Many visitors will already be familiar with some of the much-loved paintings in the gallery's permanent collection, including the tense Civil War scene *And when did you last see your father?* and the famous Tudor portraits. There are also temporary exhibitions and a programme of special events, please see the website for details.

Times Open daily 10-5 & 24 Dec 10-2. Closed 25-26 Dec & 1 Jan. **Facilities** ℗ (charged) ☷ ⊹❋ ♿ (prior notice appreciated, wheelchair on request) toilets for disabled shop ⊗ (ex assist dogs)

World Museum Liverpool
FREE

William Brown St L3 8EN

⮑ *(in city centre next to St George's Hall and Lime St, follow brown signs)*

☎ 0151 478 4393

web: www.liverpoolmuseums.org.uk

The World Museum Liverpool offers a journey of discovery from the oceans to the stars. Collections cover natural and physical sciences, ancient history and archaeology, and there are also frequently changing exhibitions, special events and other permanent attractions, such as the Bug House. Upcoming exhibition: The Beat Goes On, from July 2008 to November 2009.

Times Open daily 10-5 & 24 Dec 10-2. Closed 25-26 Dec & 1 Jan. **Facilities** ℗ ☷ ⊹❋ ⊟ (indoor) ♿ toilets for disabled shop ⊗ (ex assist dogs)

PORT SUNLIGHT — MAP 07 SJ38

Lady Lever Art Gallery `FREE`

CH62 5EQ

➲ *(Follow brown heritage signs)*

☎ 0151 478 4136

web: www.liverpoolmuseums.org.uk

The Lady Lever Art Gallery is one of the most opulent and beautiful galleries in the country and the perfect place to introduce younger members of the family to art. Home to the extensive personal collection of founder William Hesketh Lever, first Lord Leverhulme, this wonderful gallery is best known for its outstanding Victorian and pre-Raphaelite paintings by artists such as Leighton and Rossetti as well as other treasures.

Times Open daily 10-5 & 24 Dec 10-2. Closed 25-26 Dec & 1 Jan.
Facilities ℗ (charged) ⬚ & (prior notice appreciated, wheelchair on request) toilets for disabled shop ⊗ (ex assist dogs)

PRESCOT — MAP 07 SJ49

Knowsley Safari Park

L34 4AN

➲ *(M57 junct 2. Follow 'safari park' signs)*

☎ 0151 430 9009

e-mail: safari.park@knowsley.com

web: www.knowsley.com

A five-mile drive through the reserves enables visitors to see lions, tigers, elephants, rhinos, monkeys and many other animals in spacious, natural surroundings. Also a children's amusement park, reptile house, pets' corner plus sealion shows. Other attractions include an amusement park and a miniature railway.

Times Open all year, Mar-Oct, daily 10-4. Nov-Feb, 11-3. Closed 25 Dec.
Fee ✳ £12 (ch & concession £9). **Facilities** ℗ ⬚ ⊓ (outdoor) & toilets for disabled shop ⊗ (kennels provided) ▭

Prescot Museum `FREE`

34 Church St L34 3LA

➲ *(situated on corner of High St (A57) & Church St. Follow brown heritage signs)*

☎ 0151 430 7787

e-mail: prescot.museum.dlcs@knowsley.gov.uk

web: www.knowsley.gov.uk/leisure

Permanent exhibitions reflecting the local history of the area, including its important clock and watch-making heritage. There is a programme of special exhibitions, events and holiday activities, telephone for details.

Times Open all year, Tue-Sat 10-5 (closed 1-2), Sun 2-5. Closed BHs. Mon by appointment **Facilities** ℗ (100 yds) & (wheelchair access to ground floor) (ramp) shop ⊗ (ex assist dogs)

ST HELENS — MAP 07 SJ59

World of Glass

Chalon Way East WA10 1BX

➲ *(5mins from M62 junct 7)*

☎ 01744 22766

e-mail: info@worldofglass.com

web: www.worldofglass.com

Ideal for all the family, this fascinating attraction is in the heart of St Helens, a town shaped by glass-making. Features include the world's first continuous glass-making furnace, and two museum galleries that show glass from antiquity and Victorian life in St Helens. Live glass-blowing demonstrations and a special effects film show are the highlight of any visit.

Times Summer Opening (Etr-Oct) Open Tue-Sun & BH, 10-5. Winter Opening (Nov-1 Apr) Open Tue-Sun, 10-4. Closed 25-26 Dec & 1 Jan.
Fee ✳ £5.30 (ch £3.80, pen £3.80) Family & group discounts. **Facilities** ℗ ⬚ & (induction loop) toilets for disabled shop ⊗ (ex assist dogs) ▭

See advert on opposite page

SOUTHPORT — MAP 07 SD31

Atkinson Art Gallery `FREE`

Lord St PR8 1DH

➲ *(located in centre of Lord St, next to Town Hall)*

☎ 0151 934 2110

e-mail: atkinson.gallery@leisure.sefton.gov.uk

web: www.seftonarts.co.uk

The gallery specialises in 19th-and 20th-century oil paintings, watercolours, drawings and prints, as well as 20th-century sculpture. Temporary exhibitions are shown regularly at the art gallery.

Times Open all year, Tue-Thu 10-5, Fri 12-5, Sat 10-5, Sun 2-5. Closed Mon
Facilities ℗ (next street) (pay & display) & shop ⊗ (ex assist dogs) ▭

The British Lawnmower Museum `2 for 1`

106-114 Shakespeare St PR8 5AJ

➲ *(From M6, M58 or M57 follow signs towards town centre, then brown heritage signs to museum)*

☎ 01704 501336

e-mail: info@lawnmowerworld.com

web: www.lawnmowerworld.com

This award-winning museum houses a private collection of over 250 rare exhibits of garden machinery of special interest dating from 1799. There is also the largest collection of vintage toy lawnmowers and games in the world. See the fastest and most expensive mowers, a genuine 2 inch lawnmower, the first electric and robot lawnmowers, and the Lawnmowers of the Rich and Famous, including machines that belonged to Princess Diana, Nicholas Parsons, Prince Charles, Brian May, Hilda Ogden and many more.

Times Open daily, 9-5.30, ex Sun & BH Mon. **Fee** £2 (ch 50p) includes Audio tour. Guided tours by appointment. **Facilities** ❷ shop ⊗ (ex assist dogs) ▬

SPEKE   **MAP 07 SJ48**

Speke Hall

The Walk L24 1XD

➲ *(on N bank of Mersey, 1m off A561 on W side of Liverpool Airport, follow brown signs)*

☎ 0151 427 7231 0844 8004799

e-mail: spekehall@nationaltrust.org.uk

web: www.nationaltrust.org.uk

A remarkable timber-framed manor house set in tranquil gardens and grounds. The house has a Tudor Great Hall, Stuart plasterwork, and William Morris wallpapers. Outside are varied grounds, including a rose garden, bluebell woods and woodland walks. Also, live interpretation by costumed guides, children's quiz-trail and adventure playground. Lots of events throughout the year, contact for details.

Times House open: 28 Feb-15 Mar, 7 Nov-13 Dec, Sat & Sun 11-4.30; 18 Mar-1 Nov, Wed-Sun, 11-5 Garden open daily 11-5.30 or dusk. Closed Mon (ex BH). **Fee** ✳ Hall & Garden: £6.70 (ch £3.70). Family ticket £20.50. Gardens only: £4 (ch £1.90). Family ticket for garden £11. Reduced rate when arriving by public transport, cycle or on foot. Please check website for further details. **Facilities** ❷ ⛫ ⦿ ⟊ (outdoor) ♿ (wheelchairs, electric car, Braille guide, induction loop) toilets for disabled shop ⊗ (ex assit dogs) ☙ ▬

NORFOLK

Hickling Broad, Norfolk Broads National Park

BACONSTHORPE

MAP 09 TG13

Baconsthorpe Castle

FREE

NR25 6LN

➲ *(0.75m N of Baconsthorpe off unclass road, 3m E of Holt)*

☎ 01799 322399

web: www.english-heritage.org.uk

The remains of a 15th-century castle, built by Sir John Heydon during the Wars of the Roses. The exact date when the building was started is not known, since Sir John did not apply for the statutory royal licence necessary to construct a fortified house. In the 1560s, Sir John's grandson added the outer gatehouse, which was inhabited until the 1920s, when one of the turrets fell down. The remains of red brick and knapped flint are reflected in the lake, which partly embraces the castle as a moat.

Times Open at any reasonable time. **Facilities** 🅿 ♿

BANHAM

MAP 05 TM08

Banham Zoo

The Grove NR16 2HE

➲ *(on B1113, signed off A11 and A140. Follow brown tourist signs)*

☎ 01953 887771 & 887773

e-mail: info@banhamzoo.co.uk

web: www.banhamzoo.co.uk

Set in 35 acres of magnificent parkland, see hundreds of animals ranging from big cats to birds of prey and siamangs to shire horses. Tiger Territory is a purpose-built enclosure for Siberian tigers, including a rock pool and woodland setting. See also Lemur Island and Tamarin and Marmoset Islands. The Heritage Farm Stables and Falconry displays Norfolk's rural heritage with majestic shire horses and birds of prey. Other attractions include Children's Farmyard Barn and Adventure Play Area.

Times ✳ Open all year, daily from 10. (Last admission 1 hour before closing). Closed 25 & 26 Dec. **Facilities** 🅿 ⬛ 🍽 🎋 ♿ (3 wheelchairs for hire, parking) toilets for disabled shop ⊗ ➡

BLICKLING

MAP 09 TG12

Blickling Hall

NR11 6NF

➲ *(on B1354, 1.5m NW of Aylsham, signposted off A140 Norwich to Cromer road)*

☎ 01263 738030

e-mail: blickling@nationaltrust.org.uk

web: www.nationaltrust.org.uk/blickling

Flanked by dark yew hedges and topped by pinnacles, the warm red brick front of Blickling is a memorable sight. Fifty five acres of grounds include woodland and a lake, a formal parterre, topiary yew hedges, a Secret Garden, an orangery, and a dry moat filled with roses, camellias and other plants. Inside there are fine collections of furniture, paintings

and tapestries, along with a spectacular Jacobean plaster ceiling, and a library of some 12,000 books.

Times Hall: 28 Feb-12 Jul, 15 Jul-6 Sep, 9 Sep-1 Nov, Wed-Sun 11-5, Garden: 2 Jan-27 Feb, 2 Nov-31 Jan, Thu-Sun11-4; 28 Feb-1 Nov Wed-Sun10.15-5.15. Park: all year dawn to dusk. Open all BHs **Fee** £9.75 (ch £4.85) Family £25.50. Gardens only: £6.50 (ch£3.25) Family £17.10 **Facilities** 🅿 ⬛ 🍽 🎋 (outdoor) ♿ (Partly accessible) (wheelchairs & batricars, Braille guide, lift, parking) toilets for disabled shop garden centre ⊗ (ex assist dogs) 🎋 ➡

BRESSINGHAM

MAP 05 TM08

Bressingham Steam Museum & Gardens

2 for 1

IP22 2AB

➲ *(on A1066 2.5m W of Diss, between Thetford & Diss)*

☎ 01379 686900 & 687386

e-mail: info@bressingham.co.uk

web: www.bressingham.co.uk

Alan Bloom is an internationally recognised nurseryman and a steam enthusiast, and has combined his interests to great effect at Bressingham. There are three miniature steam-hauled trains, including a 15in gauge running through two and a half miles of the wooded Waveney Valley. The Dell Garden has 5,000 species of perennials and alpines; Foggy Bottom has wide vistas, pathways, trees, shrubs, conifers and winter colour (restricted opening). A steam roundabout is another attraction, and the Norfolk fire museum is housed here. Various events are held, including Dad's Army Day, Friends of Thomas the Tank Engine, and the home of the Royal Scot locomotive, please telephone for details.

Times Open: Steam Museum, Dad's Army collection, Foggy Bottom & Dell Garden Mar, Apr, May, Sep & Oct, daily 10.30-4.30. Jun, Jul & Aug, 10.30-5.30. Check before travelling. **Fee** ✳ £7-£12 (ch £5-£8, concessions £7-£10). Family £22-£35. Season tickets available. **Facilities** 🅿 ⬛ 🍽 licensed 🎋 (outdoor) ♿ (Nursery and Waveney lines accessible to wheelchairs) toilets for disabled shop garden centre ⊗ (ex assist dogs) ➡

BURGH CASTLE · MAP 05 TG40

Burgh Castle · FREE

NR31 9PZ

⮕ *(at far W end of Breydon Water on unclass road, 3m W of Great Yarmouth)*

web: www.english-heritage.org.uk

Burgh Castle was built in the third century AD by the Romans, as one of a chain of forts along the Saxon Shore - the coast where Saxon invaders landed. Sections of the massive walls still stand.

Times Open at any reasonable time. **Facilities** ⊗ ✛

CAISTER-ON-SEA · MAP 09 TG51

Caister Roman Site · FREE

⮕ *(3m N of Great Yarmouth)*

web: www.english-heritage.org.uk

The name Caister has Roman origins, and this was in fact a Roman naval base. The remains include the south gateway, a town wall built of flint with brick courses and part of what may have been a seamen's hostel.

Times Open at any reasonable time. **Facilities** ⊗ ✛

CASTLE ACRE · MAP 09 TF81

Castle Acre Priory and Castle

Stocks Green PE32 2XD

☎ 01760 755394

web: www.english-heritage.org.uk

Britain's best-preserved Cluniac priory with walled herb garden where visitors can find out about the medieval uses of herbs. Nearby Castle Acre Castle is also well worth a visit.

Times Priory: Open all year 21 Mar-Sep, daily 10-6; Oct-Mar, Thu-Mon 10-4. Closed 24-26 Dec & 1 Jan. **Fee** Castle: Free entry; Priory: £4.90 (concessions £3.90, ch £2.50) Family ticket £12.30. Prices and opening times are subject to change in March 2009. Please call 0870 333 1181 for the most up to date prices and opening times when planning your visit. **Facilities** ℗ ⛽ shop ✛

CASTLE RISING · MAP 09 TF62

Castle Rising Castle

PE31 6AH

⮕ *(off A149)*

☎ 01553 631330

web: www.english-heritage.org.uk

A fine 12th-century domestic keep, set amid huge defensive earthworks, once the palace and home to Isabella, the 'She Wolf' of France, dowager Queen of England. The keep walls stand to their original height.

Times Open all year, 21 Mar-Nov, daily 10-6 (closes at dusk if earlier in Oct); 2 Nov-Mar, Wed-Sun 10-4. Closed 24-26 Dec. **Fee** £4 (concessions £3.30, ch £2.50, additional children £2). Family ticket £12. Prices and opening times are subject to change in March 2009. Please call 0870 333 1181 for the most up to date prices and opening times when planning your visit. **Facilities** ℗ ♿ (exterior only) toilets for disabled shop ✛

CROMER · MAP 09 TG24

Cromer Museum

East Cottages, Tucker St NR27 9HB

⮕ *(On Church St next to Cromer Church)*

☎ 01263 513543

e-mail: cromer.museum@norfolk.gov.uk

web: www.norfolk.gov.uk/tourism/museums

The museum is housed in five 19th-century fishermen's cottages, one of which has period furnishings. There are pictures and exhibits from Victorian Cromer, with collections illustrating local natural history, archaeology, social history and geology. Items to discover include the scandal of mixed bathing, the daring rescues of Henry Blogg and the Cromer Lifeboatmen, and the incredible story of the West Runton elephant, Britain's oldest and most complete elephant fossil. Contact for details of special events.

Times Open daily Mar-Oct, Mon-Sat 10-5, Sun 2-5; Nov-Feb, Mon-Sat 10-4. Closed Sun **Fee** £2.75 (ch £1.75, concessions £2.65) **Facilities** ℗ (100mtrs) ♿ (Partly accessible) (lift and ramps) toilets for disabled shop ⊗ (ex assist dogs) ⊜

RNLI Henry Blogg Museum ·

Rocket House Building, Promenade NR27 9HE

⮕ *(located at the bottom of East Gangway)*

☎ 01263 511294

e-mail: rnlicromermuseum@rnli.org.uk

A lifeboat has been stationed at Cromer since 1804, and the museum at the bottom of The Gangway covers local lifeboat history and the RNLI in general. The main exhibit is the WWII Watson Class lifeboat *H F Bailey*, the boat Henry Blogg coxed. In ten years he helped to save over 500 lives, and is still the RNLI's most decorated crew member. The new exhibition hosts a number of new features including; interactive displays and radio/navigation instruction.

Times Open Etr-Nov Tues-Sun 10-5, Feb-Etr & Nov 10-4. **Facilities** ℗ (under 1m) ♿ (full disabled access) toilets for disabled shop ⊗

ERPINGHAM · MAP 09 TG13

Wolterton Park

NR11 7LY

⮕ *(signed from A140 Norwich to Cromer)*

☎ 01263 584175

web: www.manningtongardens.co.uk

Covering some 800 hectares this estate contains managed conservation areas, 18th-century landscaped gardens, and Wolterton Hall, built in the 1720s for Horatio Walpole, younger brother of Britain's first Prime Minister, Sir Robert Walpole. Special events include gardening demonstrations, concerts, plays, opera, craft fairs, guided walks and history lectures.

Times Open: Park daily; Hall, late Apr-end Oct, Fri 2-5 (last entry 4). **Fee** Hall £5. Car park £2 (free for hall visitors) **Facilities** ❷ (charged) ⊭ ᕃ (Partly accessible) (chair lift) toilets for disabled shop ⊗ (ex assist dogs) ▬

FAKENHAM   MAP 09 TF93

See also **Thursford Green**

Pensthorpe Nature Reserve & Gardens

Pensthorpe NR21 0LN

➲ *(1m from Fakenham on the A1067 to Norwich)*

☎ 01328 851465

e-mail: info@pensthorpe.com

web: www.pensthorpe.co.uk

Also known as the Natural Centre of Norfolk, this is a great family day out for lovers of nature, conservation, wildlife and the outdoors. Explore the beautiful lakes, nature trails and gardens designed by Chelsea Flower Show gold medallists, and look out for the large collection of cranes in the recently opened Conservation Centre.

Times Open Jan-Mar, daily 10-4. Apr-Dec, 10-5. Closed 25-26 Dec **Fee** ✳ £7.50 (ch 4-16 £4, concessions £6) **Facilities** ❷ ⊡ ⊭ (outdoor) ᕃ (suitable paths around some of the reserve) (network of hard surfaced pathways ensures access) toilets for disabled shop ⊗ (ex assist dogs) ▬

FELBRIGG   MAP 09 TG23

Felbrigg Hall

NR11 8PR

➲ *(off B1436 between A148 Cromer to Kings Lynn & A140 Cromer to Norwich)*

☎ 01263 837444

e-mail: felbrigg@nationaltrust.org.uk

web: www.nationaltrust.org.uk

Felbrigg is a 17th-century house built on the site of an existing medieval hall. It contains a superb collection of 18th-century furniture and pictures and an outstanding library. A 550-acre wood shelters the house from the North Sea and contains waymarked walks and a working dovecot. Please telephone for details of special events.

Times House Open 4 Apr-1 Nov, Mon-Sun, 11-5. Garden, 28 Feb-3 Apr, 18 Apr-22 May, 30 May-17 Jul, 5 Sep-23 Oct, Mon-Sun, 11-5; 4-17 Apr, 23-29 May, 18 Jul-4 Sep, 24 Oct-1 Nov, 28 Dec-3 Jan, daily, 11-5 **Fee** £8.30 (ch £3.90). Family ticket £20.50*. Garden only £3.90 (ch £1.70) * includes a voluntary donation but visitors can choose to pay the standard prices displayed at the property and on the website **Facilities** ❷ (charged) ⊡ ⊺◯ ⊭ (outdoor) ᕃ (Partly accessible) (electric wheelchair for garden, Braille guide) toilets for disabled shop ⊗ (ex assist dogs) ⅍ ▬

FILBY   MAP 09 TG41

Thrigby Hall Wildlife Gardens

NR29 3DR

➲ *(on unclass road off A1064, between Acle & Caister-on-Sea)*

☎ 01493 369477

web: www.thrigbyhall.co.uk

The 250-year-old park of Thrigby Hall is now the home of animals and birds from Asia, and the lake has ornamental wildfowl. There are tropical bird houses, a unique blue willow pattern garden and tree walk and a summer house as old as the park. The enormous jungled swamp hall has special features such as underwater viewing of large crocodiles.

Times Open all year, daily from 10. **Fee** £9.50 (ch 4-14 £7.50, concessions £8.50). **Facilities** ❷ ⊡ ⊭ (indoor & outdoor) ᕃ (wheelchairs available, ramps, parking) toilets for disabled shop ⊗ (ex assist dogs) ▬

GREAT BIRCHAM   MAP 09 TF73

Bircham Windmill   2 for 1

PE31 6SJ

➲ *(0.5m W off unclassified Snettisham road).*

☎ 01485 578393

e-mail: info@birchamwindmill.co.uk

web: www.birchamwindmill.co.uk

This windmill is one of the last remaining in Norfolk. Sails turn on windy days, and the adjacent tea room serves home-made cakes, light lunches and cream teas. There is also a bakery shop and cycle hire. In addition, crafts people feature on a number of weekends throughout the year.

Times Open Etr-Sep, 10-5. **Fee** ✳ £3.75 (ch £2, pen £3) **Facilities** ❷ ⊡ ᕃ (no access to upper floors) toilets for disabled shop ▬

GREAT YARMOUTH   MAP 05 TG50

Elizabethan House Museum

4 South Quay NR30 2QH

➲ *(from A12 & A47 follow town centre signs, then Historic South Quay signs, leading onto South Quay)*

☎ 01493 855746

e-mail: yarmouth.museums@norfolk.gov.uk

web: www.museums.norfolk.gov.uk

Experience the lives of families who lived in this splendid quayside house from Tudor to Victorian times. Decide for yourself if the death of Charles I was plotted in the Conspiracy Room. Dress the family in Tudor costumes. Discover Victorian life, upstairs and downstairs, and what it was like to work in the kitchen and scullery. Children can play in the toy room, while parents relax in the small but delightful walled garden.

Times Open Mar-Oct, Mon-Fri 10-5, Sat & Sun 1.15-5. **Fee** £3.20 (ch £1.75, concessions £2.65) **Facilities** ⒫ (250yds) ᕃ (Partly accessible) (Braille guide) shop ⊗ (ex assist dogs)

ENGLAND

Great Yarmouth Row 111 Houses & Greyfriars' Cloister

South Quay NR30 2RQ

➲ *(follow signs to dock and south quay)*

☎ 01493 857900

web: www.english-heritage.org.uk

Visit these 17th-century houses unique to Great Yarmouth, and the remains of a Franciscan friary with rare early wall paintings. Guided tours explain how the rich and poor lived in these properties over various time periods.

Times Open 21 Mar-Sep, Sun-Thu 12-5. **Fee** £3.70 (concessions £3, ch £1.90). Prices and opening times are subject to change in March 2009. Please call 0870 333 1181 for the most up to date prices and opening times when planning your visit. **Facilities** shop ⊗ ✷

Merrivale Model Village   2 for 1

Marine Pde NR30 3JG

➲ *(Marine parade seafront, next to Wellington Pier)*

☎ 01493 842097

web: www.merrivalemodelvillage.co.uk

Set in more than an acre of attractive landscaped gardens, this comprehensive miniature village is built on a scale of 1:12, and features streams, a lake and waterfalls. Among the models are a working fairground, a stone quarry, houses, shops, and a garden railway. At some times of the year there are illuminations at dusk. The Penny Arcade gives you the chance to play old amusements.

Times Open daily Etr-Oct **Fee** Please telephone for details **Facilities** ℗ (opposite) ⬚ ♿ toilets for disabled shop ▬

Time and Tide Museum of Great Yarmouth Life

Tower Curing Works, Blackfriar's Rd NR30 3BX

➲ *(from A12 & A47 follow brown signs)*

☎ 01493 743930

e-mail: yarmouth.museums@norfolk.gov.uk

web: www.museums.norfolk.gov.uk

An award-winning museum set in a Grade II listed Victorian herring-curing factory. Time and Tide tells Great Yarmouth's fascinating story, from prehistoric times to the present day; displays include fishing, wreck and rescue, seaside holidays, port and trade, the World Wars and brings to life the herring curing industry and the lives of the people who worked here. The Museum's unique collections are interpreted using both traditional and interactive technology.

Times Open Nov-Mar, Mon-Fri 10-4, Sat & Sun12-4; Apr-Oct daily, 10-4 **Fee** £5 (ch £4.15, concessions £4.25) **Facilities** ℗ 50mtrs ⬚ ♿ (lift) toilets for disabled shop ⊗ (ex assist dogs) ▬

Tolhouse Museum

Tolhouse St NR30 2SH

➲ *(from A12 & A47 follow AA signs to town centre, then signs to South Quay. Museum attached to Central Library.)*

☎ 01493 858900

e-mail: yarmouth.museums@norfolk.gov.uk

web: www.museums.norfolk.gov.uk

Visit one of the oldest prisons in the country and explore Great Yarmouth's story of crime and punishment. With the free audio guide you can hear the gaoler and his prisoners describe their experiences. Discover the fate of the thieves, smugglers, witches, pirates and murderers at a time when punishments included transportation or execution. Other exhibits detail the history of this 12th-century former merchant's house that went on to become one of the town's most important civic buildings.

Times Open Mar-Oct, Mon-Fri 10-5, Sat & Sun 1.15-5 **Fee** £3.20 (ch £1.75, concessions £2.65) **Facilities** ℗ (500yds) ♿ (Partly accessible) (lift to ground & 2nd floor, notice preferable) shop ⊗ (ex assist dogs)

GRESSENHALL   MAP 09 TF91

Gressenhall Farm and Workhouse

NR20 4DR

➲ *(on B1146 3m NW of Dereham, follow brown signs)*

☎ 01362 860563

e-mail: gressenhall.museum@norfolk.gov.uk

web: www.museums.norfolk.gov.uk

This fascinating journey through the history of rural Norfolk includes an historic workhouse, a traditional farm, extensive collections, and a brand new adventure playground. The farm has lambs and piglets as well as horses working the fields. Visitors can explore the grounds, gardens and country trails, then take a break in the Café.

Times ✳ Open 12-19 Feb, 11-4. 26 Mar-29 Oct, 10-5. **Facilities** ℗ ⬚ ⏁ (indoor & outdoor) ♿ (sound guide, wheelchair loan) toilets for disabled shop ⊗ (ex assist dogs) ▬

GRIMES GRAVES   MAP 05 TL88

Grimes Graves

IP26 5DE

➲ *(7m NW of Thetford off A134)*

☎ 01842 810656

web: www.english-heritage.org.uk

These unique and remarkable Neolithic flint mines are the earliest major industrial site in Europe.

Times Open Mar & Oct, Thu-Mon 10-5; Apr-Sep, daily 10-6. **Fee** £3 (concessions £2.40, ch £1.50). Family ticket £7.50.(No entry to mines for children under 5). Prices and opening times are subject to change in March 2009. Please call 0870 333 1181 for the most up to date prices and opening times when planning your visit. **Facilities** ℗ ♿ (exhibition area, grounds only, access track rough) shop ✷

HEACHAM MAP 09 TF63

Norfolk Lavender

Caley Mill PE31 7JE

➲ *(follow signs on A149 & A148. Car park entrance on B1454, 100yds E of junct with A149)*

☎ 01485 570384

e-mail: admin@norfolk-lavender.co.uk

web: www.norfolk-lavender.co.uk

Norfolk lavender is England's premier lavender farm, and home to the National Collection of Lavender. There are plants for sale and tours are available (including the distillery) between May-August. There's a Lavender Festival in June.

Times ✳ Open all year, daily, Apr-Oct 9-5; Nov-Mar 9-4. (Closed 25-26 Dec & 1 Jan). **Facilities** ❷ ▭ ❂ ఉ (wheelchair for loan) toilets for disabled shop garden centre ▬

HOLKHAM MAP 09 TF84

Holkham Hall & Bygones Museum

NR23 1AB

➲ *(off A149, 2m W of Wells-next-the-Sea, coaches should use B1105 at New Holkham, signed "Holkham Coaches")*

☎ 01328 710227

e-mail: enquiries@holkham.co.uk

web: www.holkham.co.uk

This classic Palladian mansion was built between 1734 and 1764 by Thomas Coke, 1st Earl of Leicester, and is home to his descendants. It has a magnificent alabaster entrance hall and the sumptuous state rooms house Roman statuary, fine furniture and paintings by Rubens, Van Dyck, Gainsborough and others. The Bygones Museum, housed in the stable block, has over 5,000 items of domestic and agricultural display - from gramophones to fire engines. The adjacent free History of Farming exhibition illustrates how a great agricultural estate such as Holkham works and has evolved.

Times Open 25 May-30 Sep, Sun-Thu 12-5; also Sat-Mon & all BHs, 12-5 **Fee** ✳ Hall £7 (ch £3.50). Bygones £5 (ch £2.50). Combined ticket Hall & Bygones: £10 (ch £5). Family ticket £25. **Facilities** ❷ ▭ ⊼ (outdoor) ఉ (wheelchair ramps, stairclimbing equipment) toilets for disabled shop ❽ (park only ex assist dogs) ▬

HORSEY MAP 09 TG42

Horsey Windpump

NR29 4EF

➲ *(15m N of Great Yarmouth, on the B1159 4m NE of Martham)*

☎ 01263 740241

e-mail: horseywindpump@nationaltrust.org.uk

web: www.nationaltrust.co.uk

Set in a remote part of the Norfolk Broads, the windpump mill was built 200 years ago to drain the area, and then rebuilt in 1912 by Dan England, a noted Norfolk millwright. It has been restored since being struck by lightning in 1943, and overlooks Horsey Mere and marshes, noted for their wild birds and insects, as a site of International Importance for Nature Conservation.

Times Open 28 Feb-29 Mar, Sat & Sun, 10-5; 1-5 Apr, 9 Sep-18 Oct, 28 Oct-1 Nov, Wed-Sun, 10-5; 6 Apr-6 Sep, 19 Oct-25 Oct, daily, 10-5, Open Good Friday & BH Mons **Fee** £2.25 (ch £1). **Facilities** ❷ (charged) ▭ ఉ (nature garden is wheelchair accessible) (parking, ramps to ground floor) toilets for disabled shop ⚒ ▬

HORSHAM ST FAITH MAP 09 TG21

City of Norwich Aviation Museum

Old Norwich Rd NR10 3JF

➲ *(follow brown tourist signs from A140 Norwich to Cromer road)*

☎ 01603 893080

e-mail: norwichairmuseum@hotmail.com

web: www.cnam.co.uk

A massive Avro Vulcan bomber, veteran of the Falklands War, dominates the collection of military and civilian aircraft at this museum. There are several displays relating to the aeronautical history of Norfolk, including some on the role played by Norfolk-based RAF and USAAF planes during World War II, and a section dedicated to the operations of RAF Bomber Command's 100 group.

Times Open all year, Apr-Oct Tue-Sat, 10-5. Sun & BH Mons 12-5. Nov-Mar, Wed & Sat 10-4. Sun 12-4. **Fee** £4 (ch £2, concessions £3.50). Family £11. **Facilities** ❷ ▭ ⊼ (outdoor) ఉ (Partly accessible) (assistance available) shop ❽ (ex assist dogs) ▬

HOUGHTON MAP 09 TF72

Houghton Hall `2 for 1`

PE31 6UE

➲ *(1.25m off A148. 13m E of King's Lynn & 10m W of Fakenham on A148)*

☎ 01485 528569

e-mail: administrator@houghtonhall.com

web: www.houghtonhall.com

Houghton Hall built in the 1720s by Sir Robert Walpole, Britain's first Prime Minister, is one of the grandest surviving Palladian Houses in England. Now owned by the 7th Marquess of Cholmondeley. The spectacular 5-acre walled garden, restored by Lord Cholmondeley, has been divided into areas for fruit and vegetables, spacious herbaceous borders, and formal rose gardens with over 150 varieties. A collection of Model Soldiers contains over 20,000 models laid out in various battle formations. Look out for the herd of fallow deer that live in the grounds, and also a collection of contemporary sculpture. There are musical events in the summer, and the Houghton International Horse Trials in May.

Times Open Grounds, Walled Garden, Soldier Museum 12 Apr-Sep 11.30-5.30. House open 1.30-5 (last entry 4.30). **Fee** £8.80 (ch £3.50). Family ticket £22. Grounds only (not house) £6 (ch £2.50) Family ticket £15. **Facilities** ❷ ❂ licensed ⊼ (outdoor) ఉ (lift, motorised buggies) toilets for disabled shop ❽ (ex assist dogs, on leads) ▬

HUNSTANTON MAP 09 TF64

Hunstanton Sea Life Sanctuary

Southern Promenade PE36 5BH

➲ *(A149 King's Lynn to Hunstanton, then follow brown sealife signs.)*

☎ 01485 533576

web: www.sealsanctuary.co.uk

With over 30 fascinating displays of marine life, this fascinating aquarium offers close encounters with starfish, sharks, octopus, eels and many other underwater wonders. Feeding demonstrations, talks and special presentations. Latest addition: Claws. Six displays featuring strange clawed creatures from around the world.

Times ✳ Open all year, daily from 10. (Closed 25 Dec) **Facilities** ☉ (charged) ᛃ ⋒ shop ⊗ (ex assist dogs) ▰

KING'S LYNN MAP 09 TF62

African Violet Centre FREE

Terrington St Clement PE34 4PL

➲ *(situated beside A17 5m from Kings Lynn and 3m from A47/A17 junct)*

☎ 01553 828374

e-mail: manager@africanvioletandgardencentre.com

web: www.africanvioletandgardencentre.com

A warm and friendly welcome awaits you at the African Violet Centre. As a major plant specialist the centre offers a wide variety of plants for any enthusiast. Best known for their vast selection and display of African violets. The African Violet Centre is a winner of many Chelsea Gold Medals.

Times Open all year Mon-Sat 9-5, Sun 10-5. Closed Xmas & New Year. **Facilities** ☉ ᛃ ⅊ (ramps & wide doors) toilets for disabled shop garden centre ⊗ (ex assist dogs) ▰

King's Lynn Arts Centre FREE

St George's Guildhall, 29 King St PE30 1HA

➲ *(located just off Tuesday Market Place in King Street, next to Globe Hotel)*

☎ 01553 765565

e-mail: entertainment_admin@west-norfolk.gov.uk

web: www.kingslynnarts.co.uk

Although it has been used for many purposes, the theatrical associations of this 15th-century Guildhall are strongest: Shakespeare himself is said to have performed here. A year round programme of film, performing and visual arts takes place. Contact box office on 01553 764864 for details.

Times Open Mon-Sat, 10-2. Closed show days, Sun, BHs, Good Fri & 24 Dec-1st Mon in Jan. **Facilities** ℗ (50yds) (pay & display) ᛃ ⅋⅊ ⅊ (hearing loop, ramp) ⊗ 🐌

Lynn Museum

Market St PE30 1NL

➲ *(Town centre)*

☎ 01553 775001

e-mail: lynn.museum@norfolk.gov.uk

web: www.museums.norfolk.gov.uk

Following a £1.2 million redevelopment, this charming museum tells the story of West Norfolk, and is home to Seahenge, the astonishing Bronze Age timber circle. A whole gallery is devoted to these unique 4,000 year old timbers, and includes a life size replica of the circle. Original timbers are also displayed. The main gallery narrates the history of the area from the Iron Age to the 20th century. The museum also features the Iron Age gold coin hoard from Sedgeford, a display of pilgrims' badges and the beautiful 19th-century fairground gallopers made by Savages of Lynn.

Times Open all year, Tue-Sat, 10-5. **Fee** ✳ £3 (ch 4-16 £1.65, concessions £2.50). Free admission from Oct-Mar. **Facilities** ℗ (100yds) ᛃ shop ⊗ (ex assist dogs)

Town House Museum

46 Queen St PE30 5DQ

➲ *(in town centre close to historic South Quay)*

☎ 01553 773450

e-mail: lynn.museum@norfolk.gov.uk

web: www.museums.norfolk.gov.uk

A charming museum set in a 19th-century town house. Explore everyday life in King's Lynn through the ages in a series of carefully re-constructed rooms, from medieval times to the 1950s. Enjoy collections of historic toys and costumes, and take the air in the delightful garden. Dotted around the displays are colourful games and activities that will keep the children amused.

Times ✳ Open May-Sep, Mon-Sat 10-5. Oct-Apr, Mon-Sat 10-4. **Facilities** ℗ (100yds) shop ⊗ ▰

LENWADE MAP 09 TG01

Dinosaur Adventure Park

Weston Park NR9 5JW

➲ *(From A47 or A1067 follow brown signs to Park)*

☎ 01603 876310

e-mail: info@dinosaurpark.co.uk

web: www.dinosaurpark.co.uk

Visitors can help the Ranger 'Track' T-Rex' on the Dinosaur Trail and meet giants from the past including the spinosaurus. They can also make friends with animals from hedgehogs to wallabies, or bugs and snakes in the secret animal garden. There is also an adventure play area including a Climb-o-saurus, Raptor Racers, Jurassic Putt Crazy Golf, and the Lost World Amazing Adventure.

Times ✳ Open daily from 10 Sep & Oct half term; 11 Sep-22 Oct, Fri-Sun. **Facilities** ☉ ᛃ ⋒ (indoor & outdoor) shop ⊗ (ex assist dogs) ▰

LITTLE WALSINGHAM   MAP 09 TF93

Walsingham Abbey Grounds & Shirehall Museum

NR22 6BP

➲ *(follow B1105 from Fakenham. Entrance to museum through tourist info centre in village)*

☎ 01328 820510 & 820259

e-mail: jackie@walsingham-estate.co.uk

In the grounds of the Abbey are the ruins of the original Augustinian priory built in the 1100s. The priory was built over the shrine of Our Lady of Walsingham which had been established in 1061. Shirehall Museum consists of an original Georgian Courthouse, displays on the history of Walsingham and local artefacts. The museum is situated in 20 acres of tranquil and picturesque gardens with access to woodland and river walks across the historic parkland.

Times Open Feb daily 10-4. Mar-26 Oct, daily 10-4.30; Nov-Dec, wknds only 10-4; (possible closure 19-20 Jul & 26-27 Jul - phone for details) **Fee** ✳ £3 (concessions £2) **Facilities** ℗ (100yds) ⋒ (outdoor) ♿ (gravel/hard paths accessible but not woodland & river) toilets for disabled shop garden centre ➡

NORTH CREAKE   MAP 09 TF83

Creake Abbey   `FREE`

NR21 9LF

➲ *(off B1355)*

web: www.english-heritage.org.uk

The ruins of the church of an Augustinian abbey, later converted to an almshouse.

Times Open at any reasonable time. **Facilities** ⊗ (ex dogs on leads) ⚏

NORWICH   MAP 05 TG20

Air Defence Radar Museum   `2 for 1`

RAF Neatishead NR12 8YB

➲ *(follow brown signs from A1062 at Horning)*

☎ 01692 631485

e-mail: curator@radarmuseum.co.uk

web: www.radarmuseum.co.uk

This multi-award winning museum, housed in the original 1942 Radar Operations building, features the Battle of Britain Room, 1942 Ground Controlled Interception Room, Radar Engineering, Military Communications Systems, Cold War Operations Room, Royal Observer Corps, Space Defence, Bloodhound Missiles and Original Mobile Radar Vehicles. The newest addition is the RAF Coltishall Memorial Room.

Times Open year round 2nd Sat each month; Apr-Oct, Tue & Thu & BH Mons 10-5 **Fee** £4.50 (ch £3.50, under 13 free, concessions £4) **Facilities** ❶ ⊡ ⋒ (outdoor) ♿ (two rooms not accessible to wheelchairs) (video tour for inaccessible areas) toilets for disabled shop ⊗ (ex assist dogs)

The Bridewell

Bridewell Alley NR2 1AQ

➲ *(in city centre, Lanes area, 5 min from Norwich Market Place)*

☎ 01603 629127

e-mail: museums@norfolk.gov.uk

web: www.museums.norfolk.gov.uk

Built in the late 14th century, this flint-faced merchant's house was used as a prison from 1583 to 1828. It now houses displays illustrating the trades and industries of Norwich during the past 200 years, including a large collection of locally-made boots and shoes. There are also a reconstructed 1930s pharmacy, pawnbrokers shop and a blacksmith's smithy. Fans of Norwich City FC will enjoy the exhibition on the team's history.

Times Est-Oct ,Tue-Sat 10-5 **Fee** £3.20 (ch £1.75, concessions £2.65) **Facilities** ℗ (5 min walk) shop ⊗ (ex assist dogs) ➡

Norwich Castle Museum & Art Gallery

Castle Meadow NR1 3JU

➲ *(in city centre)*

☎ 01603 493625

e-mail: museums@norfolk.gov.uk

web: www.museums.norfolk.gov.uk

The Castle keep was built in the 12th century, and the museum houses displays of art, archaeology, natural history, Lowestoft porcelain, Norwich silver, a large collection of paintings (with special emphasis on the Norwich School of Painters) and British ceramic teapots. There are also guided tours of the dungeons and battlements. A programme of exhibitions, children's events, gallery and evening talks takes place throughout the year. Please ring for details.

Times Mon-Sat from 10, Sun from 1 **Fee** Castle Ticket £5.80 (ch £4.25, concessions £4.95), Special exhibitions £3 (ch £1.50, concessions £2.60) **Facilities** ℗ (200mtrs) ⊡ ⋒ ♿ (lift, disabled parking, virtual tour, audio loops) toilets for disabled shop ⊗ (ex assist dogs) ➡

Norwich Cathedral

The Close NR1 4DH

➲ *(A47, A11 to city centre, inner ring road to Barrack St rdbt, take road towards city centre to Tombland)*

☎ 01603 218300

e-mail: vis-profficer@cathedral.org.uk

web: www.cathedral.org.uk

The splendour and tranquility of Norwich Cathedral have attracted visitors and pilgrims for nearly 1,000 years. Norwich has the second highest spire, and the largest monastic cloister in England, and the 1,000 carved medieval roof bosses are amazing. The building remains a place of quiet reflection and prayer as well as for participation in daily worship or the rich pageantry of the Church's festivals.

Times ✳ Open daily, 7.30-7 (6 mid Sep-mid May). **Facilities** ℗ (440yds) ⊡ ⭕ ⋒ (outdoor) ♿ (lift, touch & hearing centre, audio-induction loop) toilets for disabled shop ➡

ENGLAND

Royal Norfolk Regimental Museum

Shirehall, Market Av NR1 3JQ

➲ *(adjacent to Norwich Castle Museum)*

☎ 01603 493649

e-mail: regimental.museum@norfolk.gov.uk

web: www.norfolk.gov.uk

Museum displays deal with the social as well as military history of the county regiment from 1685, including the daily life of a soldier. Audio-visual displays and graphics complement the collection and there's a programme of temporary exhibitions.

Times ✸ Open School term-time & Xmas hols: Tue-Fri 10-4.30, Sat 10-5; School half-terms, Easter & Summer hols: Mon-Sat 10-5 **Facilities** ⓟ (400yds) & (stair lift available, ring for details) shop ⊗ (ex assist dogs) ⊜

Sainsbury Centre for Visual Arts `FREE`

University of East Anglia NR4 7TJ

➲ *(A47 bypass W towards Swaffham. 1st exit onto B1108, follow brown signs)*

☎ 01603 593199

e-mail: scva@uea.ac.uk

web: www.scva.ac.uk

The collection of Sir Robert and Lady Sainsbury was given to the University in 1973. This outstanding collection is housed in two buildings designed by Norman Foster and combines modern Western art with fine and applied arts from Africa, the Pacific, the Americas, Asia, Egypt, Medieval Europe and the ancient Mediterranean.

Times ✸ Open Tue-Sun 10-5, Wed 10-8 **Facilities** ⓟ (charged) ⊑ ⅰ◎ℱ (indoor & outdoor) & (parking at main entrance, wheelchair available on loan) toilets for disabled shop ⊗ (assist dogs by arrangement) ⊜

Oxburgh Hall

PE33 9PS

➲ *(Signed from A134 at Stoke ferry & Swaffham)*

☎ 01366 328258

e-mail: oxburghhall@nationaltrust.org.uk

web: www.nationaltrust.org.uk

The outstanding feature of this 15th-century moated building is the 80ft high Tudor gatehouse which has remained unaltered throughout the centuries. Henry VII lodged in the King's Room in 1487. A parterre garden of French design stands outside the moat. Rare needlework by Mary Queen of Scots and Bess of Hardwick is on display. A particular attraction is a genuine 16th-century priests hole, which is accessible to members of the public.

Times Open House: 28 Feb-8 Mar, Sat & Sun, 11-5; 14 Mar-Jul, 1 Sep-1 Nov, Mon-Sun, 11-5. 1-31 Aug, daily 11-5. **Fee** £7.45, (ch £3.90). Family Ticket £19.95* Garden only £3.90 (ch £2.25) * includes a voluntary donation but visitors can choose to pay the standard prices displayed at the property and on the website. **Facilities** ⓟ ⊑ ⅰ◎ℱ (outdoor) & (DVD tour of first floor, wheelchairs available, touch tour) toilets for disabled shop ⊗ (ex assist dogs) ⅶ ⊜

Pettitts Animal Adventure Park

NR13 3UA

➲ *(off A47 at Acle then follow brown signs)*

☎ 01493 700094 & 701403

e-mail: pettittsreedham@aol.com

web: www.pettittsadventurepark.co.uk

Three parks in one, aimed at the younger child. Rides include a railway and roller coaster; the adventure play area has a golf course, ball pond and tearoom; and entertainment is provided by clowns, puppets and live musicians. Among the animals that can be seen are small horses, wallabies, birds of prey, goats, alpacas and reindeer.

Times Open daily 15 Mar-2 Nov, 10-5/5.30; wknds in Nov & Dec. Daily during Xmas hols. Closed 25 Dec. **Fee** ✸ £8.95 (ch £8.95, under 3's free, concessions £6.85) **Facilities** ⓟ ⊑ ℱ (outdoor) & (ramps to all areas) toilets for disabled shop ⊗ (ex assist dogs) ⊜

St Olave's Priory `FREE`

➲ *(5.5m SW of Great Yarmouth on A143)*

web: www.english-heritage.org.uk

Remains of an Augustinian priory founded nearly 2,000 years after the death in 1030 of the patron saint of Norway, after whom it was named.

Times Open at any reasonable time. **Facilities** ⌗

Sandringham House, Gardens & Museum

PE35 6EN

➲ *(off A148)*

☎ 01553 612908

e-mail: visits@sandringhamestate.co.uk

web: www.sandringhamestate.co.uk

The private country retreat of Her Majesty The Queen, this neo-Jacobean house was built in 1870 for King Edward VII. The main rooms used by the Royal Family when in residence are all open to the public. Sixty acres of glorious grounds surround the House and offer beauty and colour throughout the season. Sandringham Museum contains fascinating displays of Royal memorabilia. The ballroom exhibition changes each year.

Times Open Etr Sat-mid Jul & early Aug-Oct. House open 11-4.45, Museum 11-5 & Grounds 10.30-5. **Fee** ✳ House, Museum & Grounds: £9 (ch £5, pen £7). Family ticket £23. **Facilities ❷** ⊑ ⏍ licensed ⋒ (outdoor) ⏃ (wheelchair loan, free transport in grounds, Braille guide) toilets for disabled shop garden centre ⦸ (ex assist dogs) ▰

SAXTHORPE
MAP 09 TG13

Mannington Gardens & Countryside

Mannington Hall NR11 7BB

➲ *(signed from Corpusty/Saxthorpe on B1149 Norwich-Holt road. Follow signs)*

☎ 01263 584175

e-mail: laurelwalpole@manningtongardens.co.uk

web: www.manningtongardens.co.uk

The moated manor house, built in 1460 and still a family home, forms a centre-piece for the pretty gardens which surround it. Visitors can take in the Heritage rose garden, lakes, a scented garden, a ruined church, and horse graves. Music and theatre events are a regular feature. Contact for more details.

Times Open: Gardens Jun-Aug, Wed-Fri 11-5; also Sun noon-5; 30 Apr-1 Oct. Walks open every day from 9. Hall open by prior appointment only. **Fee** Garden £5 (accompanied ch 16 & under free, concessions £4). Walks free. **Facilities ❷** ⊑ ⋒ (outdoor) ⏃ (Partly accessible) (boardwalk across meadow, wheelchair entrance) toilets for disabled shop ⦸ (ex assist dogs) ▰

SHERINGHAM
MAP 09 TG14

North Norfolk Railway (The Poppy Line)

Sheringham Station NR26 8RA

➲ *(from A148 take A1082. Next to large car park by rdbt in town centre. Just off A149 coast road)*

☎ 01263 820800

e-mail: enquiries@nnrailway.co.uk

web: www.nnr.co.uk

A full size heritage railway running between Sheringham and Holt, with an intermediate station at Weybourne. The route runs for 5.5m along the coast, and up through the heathland, and features genuine Victorian stations. The William Marriott Railway Museum at Holt Station is housed in a replica goods shed. There are special events throughout the year, please contact for details. Early spring 2009 is the 50th anniversary of the closure by British Railways of most of the Midlands & Great Northern Railway in Norfolk.

Times Open Apr-Oct, daily. Santa Specials in Dec **Fee** ✳ £9.50 (ch 5-15yrs £6, concession £8.50). Family ticket £29, cycles & dogs £1. **Facilities ❷** (charged) ⊑ ⋒ (outdoor) ⏃ (ramps to trains, carriage converted for wheelchair access) toilets for disabled shop ▰

SOUTH WALSHAM
MAP 09 TG31

Fairhaven Woodland & Water Garden

[2 for 1]

School Rd NR13 6DZ

➲ *(follow brown heritage signs from A47 onto B1140 to South Walsham. Through village towards Gt Yarmouth. Left into School Rd, 100yds on left, opposite South Walsham Village Hall)*

☎ 01603 270449 & 270683

e-mail: fairhavengarden@btconnect.com

web: www.fairhavengarden.co.uk

131 acres of ancient woodland and water garden with private broad. Excellent bird-watching from the boat. In spring there are masses of primroses and bluebells, with azaleas and rhododendrons in several areas. Candelabra primulas and some unusual plants grow near the waterways, and in summer the wild flowers provide food for butterflies, bees and dragonflies. Summer flowers include Day Lilies, Ligularia, Hostas, Hydrangeas and flowering shrubs, including Viburnum Mariesii (Wedding Cake Viburnum), Cornus Kousa Chinensis and Cornus Florida Rubra. Special events take place throughout the summer.

Times Open daily 10-5, (10-4 winter). Closed 25 Dec. **Fee** £5 (ch £2.50, concessions £4.55). Single membership tickets £19. Family membership ticket £45 **Facilities ❷** ⊑ ⋒ (outdoor) ⏃ (2 paths inaccessible) (ramp, grab rail, sensory gardens) toilets for disabled shop garden centre ▰

THETFORD
MAP 05 TL88

Ancient House Museum

White Hart St IP24 1AA

➲ *(in town centre)*

☎ 01842 752599

e-mail: ancient.house.museum@norfolk.gov.uk

web: www.norfolk.gov.uk/tourism/museums

An early Tudor timber-framed house with beautifully carved beamed ceilings, it now houses an exhibition on Thetford and Breckland life. This has been traced back to very early times, and there are examples from local Neolithic settlements. Brass rubbing facilities are available and there is a small period garden recreated in the rear courtyard.

Times Open all year from 10am. Closed Sun **Fee** £3.20 (ch £1.75, concession £2.65). Free admission Nov-Mar **Facilities ℗** (20yds) ⏃ (Partly accessible) toilets for disabled shop garden centre ⦸ (ex assist dogs) ▰

Thetford Priory

[FREE]

➲ *(on W side of Thetford near station)*

web: www.english-heritage.org.uk

A glimpse of medieval religious life before the dissolution of the monasteries. The Priory of Our Lady of Thetford belonged to the Order of Cluny, and was founded in 1103 by Roger Bigod, an old soldier and friend of William the Conqueror.

Times Open all year at any reasonable time. **Facilities** ⌗

ENGLAND

THETFORD CONTINUED

Thetford Warren Lodge
FREE

➲ *(2m W of Thetford, off B1107)*

web: www.english-heritage.org.uk

The remains of a two-storey hunting lodge, built in the 15th century of flint with stone dressings.

Times Open at any reasonable time. **Facilities**

THURSFORD GREEN   MAP 09 TF93

Thursford Collection
2 for 1

NR21 0AS

➲ *(1m off A148. Halfway between Fakenham and Holt)*

☎ 01328 878477

e-mail: admin@thursfordcollection.co.uk

web: www.thursford.com

This exciting collection specialises in organs, with a Wurlitzer cinema organ, fairground organs, barrel organs and street organs among its treasures. There are live musical shows every day. The collection also includes showmen's engines, ploughing engines and farm machinery. There is a children's play area and a breathtaking 'Venetian gondola' switchback ride. Christmas sees a series of spectacular events, check venue for details.

Times Open Good Fri-last Sun in Sep, daily, 12-5. Closed Sat. **Fee** ✳ £7.50 (ch under 4 free, ch 4-14 £3.50, students & pen £7). Party 20+ £6.50 each. **Facilities** ➋ ⬚ ⦿ licensed ⩍ (outdoor) ♿ toilets for disabled shop ⊗ (ex assist dogs) ▬

TITCHWELL   MAP 09 TF74

RSPB Nature Reserve

PE31 8BB

➲ *(6m E of Hunstanton on A149, signed entrance)*

☎ 01485 210779

e-mail: titchwell@rspb.org.uk

web: www.rspb@org.uk

On the Norfolk coast, Titchwell Marsh is the RSPB's most visited reserve. Hundreds and thousands of migrating birds pass through in spring and autumn and many stay during winter, providing an opportunity to see many species of ducks, waders, seabirds and geese and also the RSPB emblem bird, the Avocet.

Times ✳ Open at all times. Visitor Centre daily 9.30-5 (4 Nov-Mar). **Fee** (car parking charge for non RSPB members). **Facilities** ➋ (charged) ⬚ ⩍ (outdoor) ♿ (ramps to hides, wheelchair bays in hides) toilets for disabled shop ▬

UPPER SHERINGHAM   MAP 09 TG14

Sheringham Park

Visitor Centre, Wood Farm NR26 8TL

➲ *(2m SW of Sheringham, main entrance at junct of A148 Cromer-Holt road & B1157)*

☎ 01263 820550

e-mail: sheringhampark@nationaltrust.org.uk

web: www.nationaltrust.org.uk

Fabulous displays of rhododendrons and azaleas from mid May to June, as well as a gazebo and viewing towers with stunning coastal vistas, make Sheringham one of the finest examples of landscape design in the country.

Times Open Park: all year, dawn-dusk; Visitor Centre: Feb-14 Mar & Nov-Jan 11-4 Sat-Sun; 15 Mar-Sep daily 10-5; Oct Wed-Sun 10-5 **Fee** ✳ £4 **Facilities** ➋ (charged) ⬚ ♿ (designated parking) toilets for disabled shop

---

WEETING   MAP 05 TL78

Weeting Castle
FREE

IP27 0RQ

➲ *(2m N of Brandon off B1106)*

web: www.english-heritage.org.uk

This ruined 11th-century fortified manor house stands in a moated enclosure. There are interesting but slight remains of a three-storey cross-wing.

Times Open at any reasonable time. **Facilities**

WELLS-NEXT-THE-SEA   MAP 09 TF94

Wells & Walsingham Light Railway

NR23 1QB

➲ *(A149 Cromer road)*

☎ 01328 711630

The railway covers the four miles between Wells and Walsingham, and is the longest ten and a quarter inch gauge track in the world. The line passes through some very attractive countryside, particularly noted for its wild flowers and butterflies. This is the home of the unique Garratt Steam Locomotive specially built for the line.

Times Open daily Good Fri-end Oct. **Fee** £7.50 return (ch £6 return). **Facilities** ➋ ⬚ shop

WELNEY — MAP 05 TL59

WWT Welney Wetland Centre

Hundred Foot Bank PE14 9TN

➲ *(off A1101, N of Ely)*

☎ 01353 860711

e-mail: info.welney@wwt.org.uk

web: www.wwt.org.uk

This important wetland site on the beautiful Ouse Washes is famed for the breathtaking winter spectacle of wild ducks, geese and swans. Impressive observation facilities, including hides and a heated main observatory, offer outstanding views of the huge numbers of wildfowl which include Bewick's and Whooper swans, wigeon, teal and shoveler. Floodlit evening swan feeds take place between November and February. In summer the reserve is alive with over 40% of all British wetland plant flowers. Butterflies, dragonflies and damselflies are in abundance, and the summer walk gives a unique access to the marshes. 2009 would have been Sir Peter Scott's 100th Birthday, celebrations of his life and his legacy throughout the year with special events, please visit website for details.

Times Open all year, Mar-Oct, daily 9.30-5; Nov-Feb, Mon-Wed 10-5, Thu-Sun 10-8. Closed 25 Dec. **Fee** £5.95 (ch £2.95, concessions £4.50). Family ticket £16. **Facilities** ℗ ☷ ⌂ (outdoor) ♿ (w/chair loan (1 electric, book in advance), hearing loops) toilets for disabled shop ⊗ (ex assist dogs) ⬛

WEST RUNTON — MAP 09 TG14

Hillside Animal & Shire Horse Sanctuary

Sandy Ln NR27 9QH

➲ *(off A149 in village of West Ranton half-way between Cromer & Sheringham, follow brown signs)*

☎ 01263 837339

e-mail: contact@hillside.org.uk

web: www.hillside.org.uk

Come and see the heavy horses, ponies and donkeys as well as sheep, pigs, rabbits, ducks, hens, goats and many more rescued animals in their home in the beautiful north Norfolk countryside. Visit the museum and relive the farming days of the past surrounded by an extensive collection of carts, wagons and farm machinery. There is lots of space for children to play in the activity areas. Try 'animal friendly' refreshments in the café and take home a souvenir from the gift shop. You may even 'adopt' a rescued animal.

Times Open 5 Apr-Nov daily; Apr & May after Etr & closed Fri & Sat; Jun-Aug closed Sat; Sep-Oct closed Fri & Sat **Fee** £5.95 (ch £3.95, pen £4.95). Family ticket (2ad+2ch) £18. **Facilities** ℗ ☷ ⌂ (outdoor) ♿ (video room, concrete yards all ramped) toilets for disabled shop ⊗ (ex on lead) ⬛

WEYBOURNE — MAP 09 TG14

The Muckleburgh Collection

Weybourne Military Camp NR25 7EG

➲ *(on A149, coast road, 3m W of Sheringham)*

☎ 01263 588210 & 588608

e-mail: info@muckleburgh.co.uk

web: www.muckleburgh.co.uk

The largest privately-owned military collection of its kind in Norfolk, which incorporates the Museum of the Suffolk and Norfolk Yeomanry. Exhibits include restored and working tanks, armoured cars, trucks and artillery of WWII, and equipment and weapons from the Falklands and the Gulf War. Live tank demonstrations are run daily (except Sat) during school holidays.

Times Open daily 21 Mar-2 Nov. **Fee** ✳ £6 (ch £3.50 & pen £5). Family ticket £17. **Facilities** ℗ ☷ ⌾ ⌂ (outdoor) ♿ (ramped access, wheelchairs available) toilets for disabled shop ⊗ (ex assist dogs) ⬛

NORTHAMPTONSHIRE

Sulgrave Manor, Ancestral Home of George Washington

ALTHORP   MAP 04 SP66

Althorp

NN7 4HQ

⮑ *(from S, exit M1 junct 16, & N junct 18, follow signs towards Northampton until directed by brown signs)*

☎ 01604 770107 & 0870 167 9000

e-mail: mail@althorp.com

web: www.althorp.com

Althorp House has been the home of the Spencer family since 1508. The house was built in the 16th century, but has been changed since, most notably by Henry Holland in the 18th century. Recently restored by the present Earl, the house is carefully maintained and in immaculate condition. The award-winning exhibition 'Diana, A Celebration' is located in six rooms and depicts the life and work of Diana, Princess of Wales. There is in addition, a room which depicts the work of the Diana, Princess of Wales Memorial Fund.

Times ✳ Open Jul-Sep, daily 11-5. Closed 31 Aug. **Facilities** ℗ ⊑ ⼓ ⼕ (disabled parking, wheelchairs, audio tour, shuttle) toilets for disabled shop ⊗ (ex assist dogs) ▬

CANONS ASHBY   MAP 04 SP55

Canons Ashby House

NN11 3SD

⮑ *(easy access from either M40 junct 11 or M1 junct 16)*

☎ 01327 861900

e-mail: canonsashby@nationaltrust.org.uk

web: www.nationaltrust.org.uk

Home of the Dryden family since the 16th century, this is an exceptional small manor house, with Elizabethan wall paintings and Jacobean plasterwork. It has restored gardens, a small park and a church - part of the original 13th-century Augustinian priory.

Times Open: House & Gardens 1 Mar-14 Mar, Sat-Sun 1-5; 15 Mar-Sep daily (ex Thu & Fri) 1-5, (Gardens Mar-Sep 11-5.30), Oct-2 Nov, daily (ex Thu & Fri) 12-4, (Gardens 11-4.30). House 6-21 Dec, Sat-Sun 12-4. Gardens: 8 Nov-21 Dec, Sat-Sun 11-4. Park & Church, Sat-Sun until 15 Mar daily (ex Thu & Fri) 11-5.30, (Oct-2 Nov 11-4.30 & 8 Nov-21 Dec 11-4). Open Good Fri. **Fee** ✳ With Gift Aid donation: £7.50 (ch £3.75) Family (2ad+2ch) £18.75. Garden only £2.75 (ch £1.50). Winter grounds only £1.50 (ch 75p). **Facilities** ℗ ⊑ ⼓ (access limited, ground floor has steps, uneven floors, little turning space. Stairs to other floors. Grounds have gravel paths & some steps.) (Braille/large print guide, taped guide, w/chair available) toilets for disabled shop ⊗ (ex on leads, car park only) ⼓

DEENE   MAP 04 SP99

Deene Park

NN17 3EW

⮑ *(0.5m off A43, between Kettering & Stamford)*

☎ 01780 450278 & 450223

e-mail: admin@deenepark.com

web: www.deenepark.com

A mainly 16th-century house of great architectural importance, and home of the Brudenell family since 1514 (including the 7th Earl of Cardigan who led the Charge of the Light Brigade). There's a large lake and park, and extensive gardens with old-fashioned roses, rare trees and shrubs. Phone for details of garden openings and any other special events.

Times Open Etr, May, Spring & Aug 2-5 BHs (Sun & Mon); Jun-Aug, Sun. Party 20+ by prior arrangement with House Keeper. **Fee** ✳ House & Gardens: £7.50 (ch 10-14 £2.50, concessions £6.50). Gardens only: £5 (ch £1.50). Children under 10 free admission with accompanying adult. **Facilities** ℗ ⊑ ⼓ (ground floor & gardens) (ramps to cafeteria and gardens) toilets for disabled shop ⊗ (ex assist dogs garden only)

Kirby Hall

NN17 5EN

⮑ *(on unclass road off A43, 4m NE of Corby)*

☎ 01536 203230

web: www.english-heritage.org.uk

An outstanding Elizabethan mansion with unusually strict symmetry and amazing Renaissance detail. The beautiful formal gardens gained a reputation in the 17th-century as being the finest in England.

Times Open all year, 21 Mar-Jun & Sep-Oct, Thu-Mon 10-5; Jul-Aug, daily 10-6; Nov-Mar, Thu-Mon 12-4. (May close early for private events, please call to check). Closed 24-26 Dec & 1 Jan. **Fee** £4.70 (ch £2.40, concessions £3.50) Family £11.80. Prices and opening times are subject to change in March 2009. Please call 0870 333 1181 for the most up to date prices and opening times when planning your visit. **Facilities** ℗ shop

---

KETTERING   MAP 04 SP87

Alfred East Art Gallery   FREE

Sheep St NN16 0AN

⮑ *(A43/A14, located in town centre, next to library, 5 min walk from railway station)*

☎ 01536 534274

e-mail: museumandgallery@kettering.gov.uk

web: www.kettering.gov.uk/art

The Gallery has a permanent exhibition space showing work by Sir Alfred East, Thomas Cooper Gotch and other local artists, as well as selections from the Gallery's contemporary collection. Two further display spaces are dedicated to temporary changing exhibitions of art, craft and photography by regional and national artists. There is also a monthly lunchtime talks programme and regular family events.

Times Open all year, Tue-Sat 9.30-5 (closed BHs) **Facilities** ℗ (300yds) (pay & display) ⼏ (outdoor) ⼓ (wheelchair access via Kettering Library, during gallery opening hrs, except Sat when library closes at 4) shop ⊗ (ex assist dogs)

LYVEDEN NEW BIELD MAP 04 SP98

Lyveden New Bield

PE8 5AT

➲ *(4m SW Oundle via A427)*

☎ 01832 205358

e-mail: lyvedennewbield@nationaltrust.org.uk

web: www.nationaltrust.org.uk

An incomplete Elizabethan garden house and moated garden. Building began in 1595 by Sir Thomas Tresham, and Lyveden remains virtually unaltered since work stopped when he died in 1605. The house has fascinating Elizabethan detail and in the grounds is one of the oldest garden layouts in Britain.

Times Open 15 Mar-2 Nov, daily (ex Mon & Tue), 10.30-5 (Aug daily, 10.30-5); Feb-1 Dec, Sat & Sun, 11-4. (Open BH Mon & Good Fri 10.30-5) **Fee** ✱ With Gift Aid donation: £4 (ch free). **Facilities** ℗ (0.5 m along track) ♿ (9 steps to low entrance & Grounds are partly accessible, grass and uneven paths) ⊗ (ex on leads) ⊌

NORTHAMPTON MAP 04 SP76

Northampton Museum & Art Gallery `FREE`

Guildhall Rd NN1 1DP

➲ *(situated in town centre, in Guildhall Rd)*

☎ 01604 838111

e-mail: museums@northampton.gov.uk

web: www.northampton.gov.uk/museums

Home to the world's largest collection of shoes, Northampton Museum and Art Gallery displays shoes that have been in fashion through the ages, from Ferragamo to Vivienne Westwood. 'Life and Sole' tells the history of footwear, and other displays detail the history of Northampton, and British and Oriental ceramics and glass. There is also a gallery of Italian paintings depicting scenes from the Bible and ancient mythology. There is a dynamic programme of changing exhibitions.

Times Open all year, Mon-Sat 10-5, Sun 2-5. (closed 25-26 Dec & 1 Jan) **Facilities** ℗ (200 yds) (Carparks at bottom of Guildhall Rd) ♿ (wheelchair available) toilets for disabled shop ⊗ (ex assist dogs) ▭

ROCKINGHAM MAP 04 SP89

Rockingham Castle `2 for 1`

LE16 8TH

➲ *(2m N of Corby, off A6003)*

☎ 01536 770240

e-mail: a.norman@rockinghamcastle.com

web: www.rockinghamcastle.com

Set on a hill overlooking five counties, the castle was built by William the Conqueror. The site of the original keep is now a rose garden, but the outline of the curtain wall remains as do the foundations of the Norman hall, and the twin towers of the gatehouse. A royal residence for 450 years, the castle was granted to Edward Watson in the 16th century, and the Watson family have lived there ever since.

Times Open Etr-Jun: Sun & BH Mon; Jul-Sep, Sun & BH 12-5. Grounds open from 12. Castle open from 1. **Fee** ✱ £8.50 (ch 5-16 £5 & pen £7.50). Family ticket (2ad+2ch) £22. **Facilities** ❷ ⎁ ⊓ (outdoor) ♿ (Ramps are available. Ground floor is accessible, 1st floor and tower not accessible due to spiral staircase.) (audio tour, large print guide, parking next to Castle) toilets for disabled shop ▭

RUSHTON MAP 04 SP88

Rushton Triangular Lodge

NN14 1RP

☎ 01536 710761

web: www.english-heritage.org.uk

A delightful Elizabethan folly designed to symbolise the Holy Trinity, with its three sides, three floors, trefoil windows and three triangular gables on each side. Designed and built by Sir Thomas Gresham.

Times Open 21 Mar-Oct, Thu-Mon 11-4. **Fee** £2.60 (concessions £2.10, ch £1.30). Prices and opening times are subject to change in March 2009. Please call 0870 333 1181 for the most up to date prices and opening times when planning your visit. **Facilities** ℗ shop ⊞

SULGRAVE MAP 04 SP54

Sulgrave Manor

Manor Rd OX17 2SD

➲ *(off B4525 Banbury to Northampton road).*

☎ 01295 760205

e-mail: enquiries@sulgravemanor.org.uk

web: www.sulgravemanor.org.uk

A splendid example of a Tudor manor house with a Georgian wing, housing excellent collections of authentic period furniture and fabrics. Set in pleasant gardens in the English formal style.

Times Open Apr-Oct (wknds only in April). From May Tue, Wed and Thu from 2 (Last entry 4). Open for pre-booked groups all year. **Fee** ✱ £6.25 (ch £3). Family £17.50. Special event days £7.50 (ch £3.50). Family ticket £20. **Facilities** ❷ ⎁ ⊓ (outdoor) ♿ (fully accessible visitor centre and grounds. House partially accessible on ground floor) toilets for disabled shop ▭

NORTHUMBERLAND

Hadrian's Wall, Northumberland National Park

ALNWICK

MAP 12 NU11

Alnwick Castle

2 for 1

NE66 1NQ

➲ *(off A1 on outskirts of town, signed)*

☎ 01665 510777

e-mail: enquiries@alnwickcastle.com

web: www.alnwickcastle.com

Set in a stunning landscape, Alnwick Castle overlooks the historic market town of Alnwick. Although it was originally built for the Percy family, who have lived here since 1309, -the current Duke and Duchess of Northumberland being the current tenants- the castle is best known as one of the locations that served as Hogwarts School in the Harry Potter movies. The castle is full of art and treasures and there are plenty of activities for all the family.

Times Open 20 Mar-26 Oct, daily 10-6 (last admission 4.30). **Fee** ✳ £10.50 (ch 5-15yrs £4.50, concessions £9). Family ticket (2ad+4ch) £27.50. Party 14+. **Facilities** ❷ ⬜ 🍴 ☔ (outdoor) ♿ (Castle lift for those able to walk a little) toilets for disabled shop ⊗ (ex assist dogs) ▬

The Alnwick Garden

Denwick Ln NE66 1YU

➲ *(1m from A1. Follow signs & access garden from Denwick Lane)*

☎ 01665 511350

e-mail: info@alnwickgarden.com

web: www.alnwickgarden.com

Alnwick Garden is a vision of the Duchess of Northumberland and a leading garden visitor attraction in North East England. The 40-acre landscape is the creation of Belgian designers Wirtz International, and the Pavilion and Visitor Centre was designed by British architect Sir Michael Hopkins. This unique project in a deprived rural area has transformed a derelict and forgotten plot into a stimulating landscape. Having completed its second phase of development, the garden includes one of the largest wooden tree houses in the world, a Poison Garden, Bamboo Labyrinth and Serpent Garden. An all weather attraction for all ages, accessible to all.

Times Open all year Apr-Sep 10-6; Oct-Mar 10-4. Closed 25 Dec **Fee** ✳ Gift Aid donation £10 (concessions £7.50). Without Gift Aid donation £9 (concessions £6.50). Groups 14+ £6.25. **Facilities** ❷ (charged) ⬜ 🍴 licensed ☔ (outdoor) ♿ (ramps, w/chairs & scooters for hire) toilets for disabled shop garden centre ⊗ (ex assist dogs) ▬

ASHINGTON

MAP 12 NZ29

Woodhorn

Northumberland Museum, Archives & Country Park, QEII Country Park NE63 9YF

➲ *(Just off A189 E of Ashington)*

☎ 01670 528080

e-mail: dtate@woodhorn.org.uk

web: www.experiencewoodhorn.com

Inspired by monster coal cutting machines, the Cutter building houses emotive displays about life in the mining community, colourful banners and galleries for exhibitions. It is also home to the archives for Northumberland with records dating back 800 years. Unique listed colliery buildings have also been brought back to life for the Colliery Experience.

Times Open Apr-Oct, Wed-Sun 10-5; Nov-Mar 10-4 **Fee** ✳ Entrance free but £2.50 parking **Facilities** ❷ (charged) ⬜ ♿ (Accessibility limited to 95%, due to Grade II building status) (Tactile map, large print text) toilets for disabled shop ⊗ (ex assist dogs)

BAMBURGH

MAP 12 NU13

Bamburgh Castle

NE69 7DF

➲ *(A1 Belford by-pass, E on B1342 to Bamburgh)*

☎ 01668 214515 & 214208

web: www.bamburghcastle.com

Rising dramatically from a rocky outcrop, Bamburgh Castle is a huge, square Norman castle. Last restored in the 19th century, it has an impressive hall and an armoury with a large collection of armour from the Tower of London. Guide services are available.

Times Open Mar-Oct, daily 10-5 (last admission 4). **Fee** £7.50 (ch under 5 free, ch 5-15yrs £3.50 & pen £6.50). **Facilities** ❷ (charged) ⬜ ♿ (5 castle rooms accessible to wheelchairs) toilets for disabled shop ⊗ (ex assist dogs)

Grace Darling Museum

Radcliffe Rd NE69 7AE

➲ *(follow A1, turn off at Bamburgh & follow signposts to Northumbria Coastal route, museum on left)*

☎ 01668 214910

Pictures, documents and other reminders of the heroine are on display, including the boat in which Grace Darling and her father, keeper of Longstone Lighthouse, Farne Islands, rescued nine survivors from the wrecked *SS Forfarshire* in 1838. New exhibitions include audio visual displays and a replica of the Longstone Lighthouse.

Times Open Etr-Sep, daily 10-5; Oct-Etr 10-4, closed Mon. **Fee** Free. Voluntary contribution of £1 (ch 50p) is requested. **Facilities** ℗ (400yds) ♿ (disabled lift) (ramps) toilets for disabled shop ⊗ (ex assist dogs)

BARDON MILL MAP 12 NY76

Vindolanda (Chesterholm)

Vindolanda Trust NE47 7JN

➲ *(signed from A69 or B6318)*

☎ 01434 344277

e-mail: info@vindolanda.com

web: www.vindolanda.com

Vindolanda was a Roman fort and frontier town. It was started well before Hadrian's Wall, and became a base for 500 soldiers. The civilian settlement lay just west of the fort and has been excavated. The excellent museum in the country house of Chesterholm nearby has displays and reconstructions. There are also formal gardens and an open-air museum with Roman Temple, shop, house and Northumbrian croft.

Times Open Feb-Mar, daily 10-5; Apr-Sep, 10-6; Oct & Nov 10-5. Limited winter opening, please contact site for further details. **Fee** ✳ £5.20 (ch £3, concessions £4.30). Family (2ad&2ch) £14.50. Saver ticket for joint admission to the Roman Army Museum £8 (ch £4.70, concessions £6.80) Family £23.50. **Facilities** Ⓟ ☕ ⛩ (outdoor) ♿ (please contact for further info) toilets for disabled shop ⊗ (ex assist dogs) ▬

BELSAY MAP 12 NZ07

Belsay Hall, Castle and Gardens

NE20 0DX

➲ *(on A696)*

☎ 01661 881636

web: www.english-heritage.org.uk

Beautiful neo-classical hall, built from its own quarries with a spectacular garden deservedly listed Grade I in the Register of Gardens. It is slightly unclear who built the 'Grecian-style hall', however it was designed by Sir Charles in 1807, in Greek Revival style. The magnificent 30 acres of grounds contain the ruins of a 14th-century castle.

Times Open all year, 21 Mar-Sep, daily 10-5; Oct, daily 10-4; Nov-Mar, Thu-Mon 10-4. Closed 24-26 Dec & 1 Jan. **Fee** £6.50 (concessions £5.20, ch £3.30). Family ticket £16.30. Prices and opening times are subject to change in March 2009. Please call 0870 333 1181 for the most up to date prices and opening times when planning your visit. **Facilities** Ⓟ ☕ ⛩ shop ⌗

BERWICK-UPON-TWEED MAP 12 NT95

Berwick-Upon-Tweed Barracks

The Parade TD15 1DF

➲ *(on the Parade, off Church St, in town centre)*

☎ 01289 304493

web: www.english-heritage.org.uk

Take an informative journey into our military past at the famous border town's barracks.

Times Open Barracks: 21 Mar-Sep, Wed-Sun 10-5. Please call site for details of Main Guard. **Fee** £3.50 (concessions £2.80, ch £1.80). Prices and opening times are subject to change in March 2009. Please call 0870 333 1181 for the most up to date prices and opening times when planning your visit. **Facilities** Ⓟ (town centre) shop ⌗

Paxton House, Gallery & Country Park

TD15 1SZ

➲ *(3m from A1 Berwick-upon-Tweed bypass on B6461 Kelso road)*

☎ 01289 386291

e-mail: info@paxtonhouse.com

web: www.paxtonhouse.com

Built in 1758 for the Laird of Wedderburn, the house is a fine example of neo-Palladian architecture. Much of the house is furnished by Chippendale and there is a large picture gallery. The house is set in 80 acres beside the River Tweed, and the grounds include an adventure playground. Visit website for details of special events.

Times Open daily from Apr-Oct, House & gallery 11-5 (last tour of house 4). Grounds 10-sunset. **Fee** ✳ House & Grounds: £6.50 (ch £3.30) Family £17.50. Grounds only: £4 (ch £2) Family £10. **Facilities** Ⓟ ☕ 🍽 ⛩ (outdoor) ♿ (Partly accessible) (lifts to main areas of house, parking close to reception) toilets for disabled shop ⊗ (ex in grounds & assist dogs) ▬

CAMBO MAP 12 NZ08

Wallington House Walled Garden & Grounds

NE61 4AR

➲ *(6m NW of Belsay)*

☎ 01670 773600

e-mail: wallington@nationaltrust.org.uk

web: www.nationaltrust.org.uk

Wallington is the largest country estate protected by the National Trust. With 13,000 acres that include the entire village of Cambo, the main attraction is the country house set among woods and gardens. There is a Pre-Raphaelite central hall, a small museum of curio sites and a display of dolls' houses. There are plenty of walks exploring the historic landscape, and a walled garden created by the Trevelyan family in the 1920s. Contact the estate for details of open-air theatre and rock and classical music concerts.

Times Open: House daily (ex Tue) 17 Mar-2 Sep 1-5.30; 3 Sep-4 Nov 1-4.30. Walled garden open daily Apr-Sep 10-7; Oct 10-6; Nov-Mar 10-4. Grounds open all year (except Christmas day) dawn-dusk. **Fee** ✳ House, walled garden & grounds: £9.25 (ch £4.65). Family £23.10; Garden & grounds only £6.40 (ch £3.20). Family £16. **Facilities** Ⓟ ☕ 🍽 ⛩ (outdoor) ♿ (Wheelchairs available) toilets for disabled shop garden centre ✤ ▬

ENGLAND

CARRAWBROUGH   MAP 12 NY87

Temple of Mithras   FREE
(Hadrian's Wall)

⮑ (3.75m W of Chollerford on B6318)

web: www.english-heritage.org.uk

This fascinating Mithraic temple was uncovered by a farmer in 1949. Its three altars to the war god Mithras, date from the third century AD, and are now in the Museum of Antiquities in Newcastle, but there are copies on site.

Facilities ⊘ ✿

CHILLINGHAM   MAP 12 NU02

Chillingham Castle

NE66 5NJ

⮑ (signed from A1 & A697)

☎ 01668 215359

e-mail: enquiries@chillingham-castle.com

web: www.chillingham-castle.com

Magnificent Medieval fortress with Tudor additions. Romantic grounds laid out by Sir Jeffry Wyatville command views over the Cheviots and include topiary gardens and woodland walks. Weddings, private functions and meals can be arranged, and fishing is available. Please ring for details of special events.

Times Open Etr-end Oct, Sun-Fri (last admission 4.30). Other times by prior arrangement. Castle 1-5, grounds & tearoom 12-5. **Fee** £6.75 (ch £3, pen £5.50). **Facilities** ⊘ ▱ & (limited access to gardens) shop ⊗ (ex assist dogs) ⇌

Chillingham Wild Cattle Park

NE66 5NP

⮑ (off B6348, follow brown tourist signs off A1 and A697)

☎ 01668 215250

web: www.chillingham-wildcattle.org.uk

The Park at Chillingham has been home to a unique herd of wild white cattle for around 700 years. Visitors are welcome to experience the Park and approach the cattle in the company of the Warden, who can provide information on the cattle and their history.

Times Open Apr-Oct, daily 10-12 & 2-5, Sun 2-5. (Closed Tue). Guided tours 10,11 & 12 then 2,3 & 4 **Fee** ✳ £5 (ch £2, pen £3). Family ticket £12 (2ad + 2ch), forest walk-free. **Facilities** ⊘ ☵ (outdoor) & (Partly accessible) (Guided tour with warden by prior arrangement) ⊗

CORBRIDGE   MAP 12 NY96

Corbridge Roman Site and Museum

NE45 5NT

⮑ (0.5m NW of Corbridge on minor road - signed)

☎ 01434 632349

web: www.english-heritage.org.uk

Originally a fort, which evolved into a prosperous town during the Roman era. An excellent starting point to explore Hadrian's Wall. The museum houses a fascinating collection of finds.

Times Open all year, 21 Mar-Sep, daily 10-5.30 (last admission 5); Oct, daily 10-4; Nov-Mar, Sat-Sun 10-4. Closed 24-26 Dec & 1 Jan. **Fee** £4.50 (concessions £3.60, ch £2.30). Prices and opening times are subject to change in March 2009. Please call 0870 333 1181 for the most up to date prices and opening times when planning your visit. **Facilities** ⊘ ✿

EMBLETON   MAP 12 NU22

Dunstanburgh Castle

Craster NE66 2RD

⮑ (1.5m E on footpaths from Craster or Embleton)

☎ 01665 576231

web: www.english-heritage.org.uk

An easy two mile coastal walk leads to the eerie skeleton of this wonderful 14th-century castle situated on a basalt crag more than 30 metres high with breathtaking views. The castle was built by Thomas Earl of Lancaster, nephew to King Edward II.

Times Open all year, 21 Mar-Sep, daily 10-5; Oct, daily 10-4; Nov-Mar, Thu-Mon 10-4. **Fee** £3.50 (concessions £2.80, ch £1.80). Prices and opening times are subject to change in March 2009. Please call 0870 333 1181 for the most up to date prices and opening times when planning your visit. **Facilities** ⊘ (charged) ⧖ ✿

GREENHEAD   MAP 12 NY66

Roman Army Museum

Carvoran CA8 7JB

⮑ (follow brown tourist signs from A69 or B6318)

☎ 016977 47485

e-mail: info@vindolanda.com

web: www.vindolanda.com

Situated alongside the Walltown Crags Section of Hadrian's Wall, the museum is a great introduction to the Roman Army. Find out about Roman weapons, training, pay, off-duty activities and much more. See if you can be persuaded to join up by watching the recruitment film, or view the Eagle's Eye film and soar with the eagle over Hadrian's Wall.

Times Open Feb-Mar & Oct-Nov, 10-5; Apr-Sep 10-6 (closed mid Nov-mid Feb) **Fee** £4.20 (ch £2.50, concessions £3.70) Family £11.50 (2ad+2ch). Joint site Saver ticket with Vindolanda £8 (ch £4.70, concessions £6.80). Family ticket £23.50. **Facilities** ⊘ ▱ ⧖ (outdoor) & (ramps, subtitles on main film) toilets for disabled shop ⊗ (ex assist dogs) ⇌

HOLY ISLAND (LINDISFARNE)
MAP 12 NU14

Lindisfarne Castle

TD15 2SH

⮑ *(8m S Berwick from A1 on Holy Island via 3m tidal causeway)*

☎ 01289 389244

e-mail: lindisfarne@nationaltrust.org.uk

web: www.nationaltrust.org.uk

This 16th-century fort was restored by Sir Edwin Lutyens in 1903. The austere outside walls belie the Edwardian comfort within, which includes antique Flemish and English furniture, porcelain and polished brass. A small walled garden designed by Gertrude Jekyll is set on the southward facing slope, some 500 metres to the north of the castle. Spectacular views from the ramparts to the Farne Islands, Bamburgh Castle and beyond.

Times Open 17 Mar-28 Oct, daily (closed Mon ex BHs). As Lindisfarne is a tidal island, the Castle opening times will vary. Garden open all year (10-dusk). **Fee** ✳ Castle & garden £6 (ch £3) Family ticket £15. **Facilities** ℗ (1m in village) ♿ (Braille guide) shop ⊗ ♨ ➾

Lindisfarne Priory

TD15 2RX

⮑ *(can only be reached at low tide across a causeway. Tide tables posted at each end of the causeway)*

☎ 01289 389200

web: www.english-heritage.org.uk

One of the holiest Anglo-Saxon sites in England, renowned for the original burial place of St Cuthbert whose corpse was discovered 11 years after his burial and found to be mysteriously undecayed. An award-winning museum.

Times Open all year, 21 Mar-Sep, daily 10-5; Oct, daily 9.30-4; Nov-Jan, Sat-Mon 10-2; Feb-Mar, daily 10-4. Closed 24-26 Dec & 1 Jan. **Fee** £4 (concessions £3.20, ch £2). Prices and opening times are subject to change in March 2009. Please call 0870 333 1181 for the most up to date prices and opening times when planning your visit. **Facilities** shop ⚏

HOUSESTEADS
MAP 12 NY76

Housesteads Roman Fort

Haydon Bridge NE47 6NN

⮑ *(2.5m NE of Bardon Mill on B6318)*

☎ 01434 344363

web: www.english-heritage.org.uk

The jewel in the crown of Hadrian's Wall and the most complete Roman fort in Britain. These superb remains offer a fascinating glimpse into the past glories of one of the world's greatest empires.

Times Open all year, 21 Mar-Sep, daily 10-6; Oct-Mar, daily 10-4. Closed 24-26 Dec & 1 Jan. **Fee** £4.50 (concessions £3.60, ch £2.30). Free entry to NT members. Prices and opening times are subject to change in March 2009. Please check web site or call 0870 333 1181 for the most up to date prices and opening times when planning your visit. **Facilities** ℗ (0.25m from fort) (charge payable) ⌂ ♿ (disabled parking) shop

LONGFRAMLINGTON
MAP 12 NU10

Brinkburn Priory

NE65 8AF

⮑ *(off B6344)*

☎ 01665 570628

web: www.english-heritage.org.uk

This late 12th-century church is a fine example of early gothic architecture set in beautiful riverside surroundings. Look out for some unusual modern sculptures.

Times Open 21 Mar-Sep, Thu-Mon, 10-4. **Fee** £3 (concessions £2.40, ch £1.50). Prices and opening times are subject to change in March 2009. Please check web site or call 0870 333 1181 for the most up to date prices and opening times when planning your visit. **Facilities** ℗ ⌂ shop ⚏

MORPETH
MAP 12 NZ28

Morpeth Chantry Bagpipe Museum
FREE

Bridge St NE61 1PD

⮑ *(off A1, in Morpeth town centre)*

☎ 01670 500717

e-mail: anne.moore@castlemorpeth.gov.uk

This unusual museum specialises in the history and development of Northumbrian small pipes and their music. They are set in the context of bagpipes from around the world, from India to Inverness. It is also host to the Morpeth Northumbrian Gathering, with music and crafts the weekend after Easter and a traditional music festival through the month of October.

Times Open all year, Mon-Sat 9.30-5, open Sun in Aug & Dec. Closed 25-26 Dec, 1 Jan & Etr Mon. **Facilities** ℗ (100mtrs) ♿ (lift to 1st floor) (induction loop, large print text, DVD guide to museum) toilets for disabled shop ➾

NORHAM
MAP 12 NT94

Norham Castle
FREE

TD15 2JY

☎ 01289 382329

web: www.english-heritage.org.uk

A mighty border fortress built in 1160, was one of the strongest of the border castles. Take an audio tour conjuring up four centuries of sieges and war with the Scots.

Times Open 21 Mar-Sep, Sat-Sun & BH. Admission limited. Please call 01289 304493 for details. **Facilities** ℗ ⊗ ⚏

PRUDHOE   MAP 12 NZ06

Prudhoe Castle

NE42 6NA

➲ *(on minor road off A695)*

☎ 01661 833459

web: www.english-heritage.org.uk

Explore the romantic remains of this 13th-century fortress perched on a steep wooded spur rising above the Tyne and set in lovely grounds.

Times Open 21 Mar-Sep, Thu-Mon 10-5. **Fee** £3.50 (concessions £2.80, ch £1.80). Prices and opening times are subject to change in March 2009. Please check web site or call 0870 333 1181 for the most up to date prices and opening times when planning your visit. **Facilities** ❷ shop ♨

ROTHBURY   MAP 12 NU00

Cragside

NE65 7PX

➲ *(15m NW of Morpeth on A697, left onto B6341, entrance 1m N of Rothbury)*

☎ 01669 620333 & 620150

e-mail: cragside@nationaltrust.org.uk

web: www.nationaltrust.org.

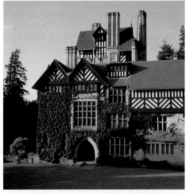

The aptly named Cragside was the home of Victorian inventor and landscape genius, Lord Armstrong, and sits on a rocky crag high above the Debden Burn. Crammed with ingenious gadgets it was the first house in the world to be lit by water-powered electricity. In the 1880s it also had hot and cold running water, central heating, fire alarms, telephones, and a passenger lift. In the estate there are forty miles of footpaths to explore, including a stroll through some of the best Victorian gardens in the country.

Times Open, Estate & Gardens: Mar-Oct, Tue-Sun & BH Mons 10.30-5.30; Nov-mid Dec Wed-Sun 11-4 (or dusk if earlier); (Last admission 1hr before closing). House 1-5.30 3 April-30 Sep, 1-4.30 2 Oct-4 Nov. **Fee** ✳ House, Gardens & Estate £12.10 (ch £6.10) Family £29.20. Garden & Estate £7.70 (ch £3.30) Family ticket £18.70. **Facilities** ❷ ⛶ ⤒ ◓ (very steep paths on estate) (virtual tour, Braille guide, wheelchair path, lift) toilets for disabled shop ♨

WALWICK   MAP 12 NY97

Chesters Roman Fort

Chollerford NE46 4EP

➲ *(0.5m W of Chollerford on B6318)*

☎ 01434 681379

web: www.english-heritage.org.uk

The best-preserved Roman cavalry fort in Britain. The museum holds displays of carved stones, altars and sculptures from all along Hadrian's Wall.

Times Open all year, 21 Mar-Sep, daily 10-6; Oct-Mar, daily 10-4. Closed 24-26 Dec & 1 Jan. **Fee** £4.50 (concessions £3.60, ch £2.30). Prices and opening times are subject to change in March 2009. Please check web site or call 0870 333 1181 for the most up to date prices and opening times when planning your visit. **Facilities** ❷ ⛶ ◓ (wheelchair access limited) shop ♨

WARKWORTH   MAP 12 NU20

Warkworth Castle & Hermitage

NE66 0UJ

☎ 01665 711423

web: www.english-heritage.org.uk

The magnificent eight-towered keep of Warkworth Castle stands on a hill high above the River Coquet, dominating all around it. A complex stronghold, it was home to the Percy family, which at times wielded more power in the North than the King himself.

Times Open all year. Castle: 21 Mar-Sep, daily 10-5; Oct, daily 10-4; Nov-Mar, Sat-Mon 10-4. Hermitage: 21 Mar-Sep, Wed, Sun & BH 11-5. Closed 24-26 Dec & 1 Jan. **Fee** Castle: £4 (concessions £3.20, ch £2). Family ticket 10. Hermitage: 3 (concessions £2.40, ch £1.50). Prices and opening times are subject to change in March 2009. Please check web site or call 0870 333 1181 for the most up to date prices and opening times when planning your visit. **Facilities** ❷ ◓ (limited access) shop ♨

WYLAM   MAP 12 NZ16

George Stephenson's Birthplace NEW

NE41 8BP

➲ *1.5m S of A69 at Wylam*

☎ 01661 853457

e-mail: georgestephensons@nationaltrust.org.uk

web: www.nationaltrust.org.uk

Birthplace of the world famous railway engineer. This small stone tenement was built c1760 to accommodate mining families. The furnishings reflect the year of Stephenson's birth here in 1781, his whole family living in one room.

Times Open 15 Mar-2 Nov, Thu-Sun, 12-5 & BH Mons. **Fee** ✳ £2 (ch £1) **Facilities** ❷ ⛶ ◓ (induction loop, Braille guide, wheelchair) toilets for disabled ⊗ (ex assist dogs) ♨

NOTTINGHAMSHIRE

West Leake, nr Loughborough

EASTWOOD — MAP 08 SK44

D. H. Lawrence Heritage

Durban House Heritage Centre, Mansfield Rd NG16 3DZ

➲ (A610 or A608, follow brown tourist signs)

☎ 01773 717353

e-mail: culture@broxtowe.gov.uk

web: www.broxtowe.gov.uk/dh/heritage

D H Lawrence Heritage, in the writer's home town of Eastwood, brings together the D H Lawrence Birthplace Museum and the Durban House Heritage Centre, along with two quality gift shops, a contemporary art gallery and a bistro. Discover more about the son of a miner who went on to become one of the 20th century's most influential writers. The D H Lawrence festival is held August and September each year.

Times Open all year: Apr-Oct daily 10-5, Nov-Mar daily 10-4. Closed over Xmas, telephone for details. **Fee** Free Mon-Fri. Single site: £2 (concessions £1.20) Family (2ad+2ch) £5.80. Both sites £3.50 (concessions £1.80) Family ticket (2ad+2ch) joint site £8, single site £5.80 **Facilities** ℗ ⬚ ❍ ☶ (outdoor) ♿ (Durban house is fully accessible, but the Birthplace Museum has steep stairs and no lift) (lift to exhibition, wheelchair available Braille signage) toilets for disabled shop ⊗ (ex assist dogs) ⬛

EDWINSTOWE — MAP 08 SK66

Sherwood Forest Country Park & Visitor Centre `FREE`

NG21 9HN

➲ (on B6034 N of Edwinstowe between A6075 and A616)

☎ 01623 823202 & 824490

e-mail: sherwood.forest@nottscc.gov.uk

web: www.nottinghamshire.gov.uk/sherwoodforestcp

At the heart of the Robin Hood legend is Sherwood Forest. Today it is a country park and visitor centre with 450 acres of ancient oaks and shimmering silver birches. Waymarked pathways guide you through the forest. A year round programme of events includes the spectacular annual Robin Hood Festival.

Times Open all year. Country Park: open daily dawn to dusk. Visitor Centre: open daily 10-5 (4.30 Nov-Mar). Closed 25 Dec. **Facilities** ℗ (charged) ⬚ ☶ (outdoor) ♿ (wheelchair and electric buggy loan) toilets for disabled shop ⬛

FARNSFIELD — MAP 08 SK65

White Post Farm Centre

NG22 8HL

➲ (12m N of Nottingham on A614)

☎ 01623 882977 & 882026

e-mail: admin@whitepostfarmcentre.co.uk

web: www.whitepostfarmcentre.co.uk

With over 25 acres there's lots to see and do at the White Post Farm Centre. There are more than 3000 animals including pigs, goats and sheep, along with more exotic animals like bats, reptiles and meerkats.

The indoor play area is ideal for small children, and there's also a sledge run, trampolines and pedal go-karts.

Times ✳ Open daily from 10 **Facilities** ℗ ⬚ ☶ (indoor & outdoor) ♿ (free hire wheelchairs, book if more than 6) toilets for disabled shop ⊗ (ex assist dogs) ⬛

NEWARK-ON-TRENT — MAP 08 SK75

Newark Air Museum `2 for 1`

The Airfield, Winthorpe NG24 2NY

➲ (easy access from A1, A46, A17 & Newark relief road, follow tourist signs, next to county showground)

☎ 01636 707170

e-mail: newarkair@onetel.com

web: www.newarkairmuseum.org

A diverse collection of transport, training and reconnaissance aircraft, jet fighters, bombers and helicopters, now numbering more than seventy. Two Undercover Aircraft Display Halls and an Engine Hall make the museum an all-weather attraction. Everything is displayed around a WWII airfield. The Annual Cockpit Fest and Aeroboot takes place on the 14th and 15th of June 2009.

Times Open all year, Mar-Sep daily 10-5; Oct-Feb, daily 10-4. Closed 24-26 Dec & 1 Jan. Other times by appointment. **Fee** £6.50 (ch £4.25, concessions £6). Family ticket (2ad+3ch) £19.50. Party 15+. **Facilities** ℗ ⬚ ☶ (outdoor) ♿ toilets for disabled shop ⬛

Newark Millgate Museum `FREE`

48 Millgate NG24 4TS

➲ (easy access from A1 & A46)

☎ 01636 655730

e-mail: museums@nsdc.info

web: www.newark-sherwooddc.gov.uk

The museum is home to diverse social history collections and features fascinating exhibitions - recreated streets, shops and houses in period settings. There are also children's activities. The mezzanine gallery, home to a number of temporary exhibitions shows the work of local artists, designers and photographers. A special exhibition to mark the bi-centenary of the birth of Sir William Gladstone will be held in December 2009.

Times Open Apr-Sep, Tue-Sun, 10.30-4.30; Oct-Mar, Tue-Fri, 10.30-4, Sat-Sun 1-4. Open spring and summer BH Mon. **Facilities** ℗ (250yds) ⬚ ♿ (access to ground floor only for wheelchair users) toilets for disabled shop ⊗ (ex assist dogs)

Vina Cooke Museum of Dolls & Bygone Childhood

The Old Rectory, Cromwell NG23 6JE

➲ (5m N of Newark off A1)

☎ 01636 821364

e-mail: info@vinasdolls.co.uk

web: www.vinasdolls.co.uk

All kinds of childhood memorabilia are displayed in this 17th-century house: prams, toys, dolls' houses, costumes and a large collection of

Victorian and Edwardian dolls including Vina Cooke hand-made character dolls.

Times Open Apr-Sep, Tue, Thu, Sat-Sun & BH 10.30-4.30. Mon, Wed, Fri and Oct-Mar by appointment, please telephone. **Fee** £3 (ch £1.50, pen £2.50). **Facilities** ℗ ⋒ (outdoor) ᕹ (Partly accessible) shop ⊗ (ex assist dogs)

NEWSTEAD   MAP 09 SK55

Newstead Abbey, Historic House & Gardens

Newstead Abbey Park NG15 8NA

➲ (off A60, between Nottingham & Mansfield, at Ravenshead)

☎ 01623 455900

e-mail: sally.winfield@nottinghamcity.gov.uk

web: www.newsteadabbey.org.uk

This beautiful house is best known as the home of poet Lord Byron. Visitors can see Byron's own rooms, mementoes of the poet and other splendidly decorated rooms. The grounds of over 300 acres include waterfalls, ponds, water gardens and Japanese gardens. Special events include outdoor theatre and opera, Christmas events and Ghost Tours. Please telephone for details of events running throughout the year.

Times Open: Grounds all year, daily 9-dusk or 6 whichever is earliest (ex last Fri in Nov & 25 Dec); House Apr-Sep, daily 12-5. (Last admission 4). **Fee** ✳ House & Grounds £7 (ch £2, concessions £3) Family ticket £17.50. Grounds only £3.50 (concessions £3) Family ticket £9.50. Subject to change. **Facilities** ℗ ⋤ ⋒ (outdoor) ᕹ (grounds & ground floor of house accessible) (audio tour & wheelchair for loan Apr-Sep) toilets for disabled shop ⊗ (ex assist dogs & on a lead) ⬛

NOTTINGHAM   MAP 08 SK53

Galleries of Justice

The Shire Hall, High Pavement, Lace Market NG1 1HN

➲ (follow signs to city centre, brown heritage signs to Lace Market & Galleries of Justice)

☎ 0115 952 0555

e-mail: info@nccl.org.uk

web: www.nccl.org.uk

The Galleries of Justice are located on the site of an original Court and County Gaol. Recent developments include the arrival of the HM Prison Service Collection, which will now be permanently housed in the 1833 wing. Never before seen artefacts from prisons across the country offer visitors the chance to experience some of Britain's most gruesome, yet often touching, reminders of what prison life would have been for inmates and prison staff over the last three centuries.

Times ✳ Open all year, Tue-Sun & BH Mon 10-5 (also open Mon in school hols). (Last admission one hour before closing). Contact for Xmas opening times. **Facilities** ℗ (5 mins walk) ⋤ ⋒ (indoor) ᕹ (Braille control lifts, induction loop, large print lables) toilets for disabled shop ⊗ (ex assist dogs) ⬛

Green's Windmill

Windmill Ln, Sneinton NG2 4QB

➲ (off B686, 500yds from Ice Centre)

☎ 0115 915 6878

e-mail: greensmill@nottinghamcity.gov.uk

web: www.greensmill.org.uk

Restored to working order, take a look around the mill and see how grain is turned into flour by harnessing the power of the wind. Find out about the "mathematician miller" George Green and his theories, and test your mind with hands-on puzzles and experiments. There's also a guinea pig piggery in the summer. (Please call before visiting if you are making a special trip to see the guinea pig piggery).

Times Open all year Wed-Sun, 10-4, also BHs. Phone for Xmas & New Year closing. **Fee** Admission free, but small charge for some events and activities. **Facilities** ℗ ⋒ (outdoor) ᕹ (The centre and ground floor of the Mill are accessible to wheelchair users, but there is a short flight of steps from the car park.) (parking in Millyard, induction loops) toilets for disabled shop ⊗ (ex assist dogs)

The Lace Centre   [FREE]

Severns Building, Castle Rd NG1 6AA

➲ (follow signs for Castle, situated opposite Robin Hood statue)

☎ 0115 941 3539

Exquisite Nottingham lace fills this small 14th-century building to capacity, with panels also hanging from the beamed ceiling. There are weekly demonstrations of lace-making on Thursday afternoons from Easter to October. Telephone for details.

Times Open Jan-Mar, daily 10-4; Apr-Oct, 10-5; Nov-Dec, 10-4. Every Sun 11-4. Phone for Xmas & New Year. **Facilities** ℗ (100yds) (metered street parking) shop ⬛

The Museum of Nottingham Life

Brewhouse Yard, Castle Boulevard NG7 1FB

➲ (follow signs to city centre, the museum is a 5 min walk from city centre with easy access from train, tram and bus)

☎ 0115 915 3640

e-mail: anni@ncmg.org.uk

web: www.nottinghammuseum.org.uk

Nestled in the rock below Nottingham Castle and housed in a row of 17th-century cottages, the museum presents a realistic glimpse of life in Nottingham over the last 300 years. Discover the caves behind the museum and peer through 1920s shop windows.

Times Open daily, 10-4.30. Last admission 4. Closed 24-26 Dec, 1-2 Jan. **Fee** ✳ Joint ticket with castle £3 (concessions £1.50) Family ticket £7. **Facilities** ℗ (100yds) ⋒ (outdoor) ᕹ (ground floor fully accessible to all, but no lifts in main museum or Rock Cottage) (video of upper floors and room displays) toilets for disabled shop ⊗ (ex assist dogs)

NOTTINGHAM CONTINUED

Nottingham Castle Museum & Art Gallery

Off Friar Ln NG1 6EL

➲ (Follow signs to city centre, then signs to castle.)

☎ 0115 915 3700

e-mail: castle@ncmg.org.uk

web: www.nottinghamcastle.org.uk

This 17th-century building is both museum and art gallery, with major temporary exhibitions, by historical and contemporary artists, as well as the permanent collections. There is a 'Story of Nottingham' exhibition and a gallery designed especially to entertain young children. Guided tours of the underground passages take place on most days.

Times Open all year, daily; Mar-Sep 10-5; Oct-Feb 10-4 (last entry 30 mins before closing) **Fee** ✳ Joint ticket with Brewhouse Yard £3 (ch and concessions £1.50, under 5's free) Family £7 (2ad+up to 3 ch). Group ticket: 1 free ticket for every 10. **Facilities** ℗ (400yds) (ltd disabled spaces, book in advance) ⊑ ㅈ (outdoor) ♿ toilets for disabled shop ⊗ (ex assist dogs) ▰

Nottingham Industrial Museum

Courtyard Buildings, Wollaton Park NG8 2AE

➲ (4m from city centre off A6514)

☎ 0115 915 3900

e-mail: wollaton@ncmg.org.uk

web: www.wollatonhall.org.uk

Nottingham's industrial history is on display in this 18th-century stable block. Lace, hosiery, pharmaceuticals (Nottingham was the home of the founder of Boots the Chemists), tobacco and much else are among the exhibits. There is a beam engine and other steam engines, regularly in steam.

Times Open Apr-Oct, daily 11-5; Nov-Mar 11-4. **Fee** Free admission to museum but guided tours and car parking charged. **Facilities** ℗ (charged) ⊑ ㅈ (outdoor) ♿ (hand & powered wheelchairs available) toilets for disabled shop ⊗ (ex assist dogs)

The Tales of Robin Hood

2 for 1

30-38 Maid Marian Way NG1 6GF

➲ (in city centre, follow brown & white signs. 2min walk from Castle)

☎ 0115 948 3284

e-mail: robinhoodcentre@mail.com

web: www.robinhood.uk.com

Explore the intriguing and mysterious story of the legendary tales of Robin Hood in medieval England. Enjoy film shows, live performances, an adventure ride, falconry and even try your hand at archery. Banquets and live entertainment in the evening.

Times Open all year, daily Spring/Summer 10-5.30, Autumn/Winter 10-5. Last admission 1 hr before closing. (Closed 24-26 Dec & 1 Jan). **Fee** ✳ £8.95 (ch £6.95, concessions £7.95) Family (2ad+2ch) £26.95 (2ad+3ch) £32.95. **Facilities** ℗ (NCP 200 yds) ⊑ ㅈ (indoor) ♿ (specially adapted 'car', lift) toilets for disabled shop ⊗ (ex assist dogs) ▰

Wollaton Hall, Gardens & Park

Wollaton NG8 2AE

➲ (M1 junct 25 signed from A52, A609, A6514, A60 and city centre)

☎ 0115 915 3900

e-mail: info@wollatonhall.org.uk

web: www.wollatonhall.org.uk

Built in the late 16th century, and extended in the 19th, Wollaton Hall and Park holds Nottingham's Natural History Museum, Nottingham's Industrial Museum, the Wollaton Park Visitor Centre, and the Yard Gallery, which has changing exhibitions exploring art and the environment. The Hall itself is set in 500 acres of historic deer park, with herds of red and fallow deer roaming wild. There are also formal gardens, a lake, nature trails and adventure playgrounds. A celebration of Britain's veterans is planned for summer 2009.

Times Open daily, Apr-Oct 11-5; Nov-Mar 11-4. (Please phone for Xmas & New Year closing times.) **Fee** Free entry. Charge for guided tours and car parking. **Facilities** ❷ (charged) ⊑ ㅈ (outdoor) ♿ toilets for disabled shop ⊗ (ex assist dogs) ▰

OLLERTON   MAP 08 SK66

Rufford Abbey Country Park

FREE

NG22 9DF

➲ (3m S of Ollerton, directly off A614)

☎ 01623 821338

e-mail: info.rufford@nottscc.gov.uk

web: www.nottinghamshire.gov.uk/ruffordcp

At the heart of the wooded country park stand the remains of a 12th-century Cistercian Abbey, housing an exhibition on the life of a Cistercian Monk at Rufford. Many species of wildlife can be seen on the lake, and there are lovely formal gardens with sculptures, plus exhibitions of contemporary crafts in the gallery.

Times Open all year, daily 10.30-5 (4.30 in winter). Closed 25 Dec. **Facilities** ❷ (charged) ⊑ ⦿ ㅈ (outdoor) ♿ (visitor facilities accessible) (lift to craft centre, w/chair and electric buggy loan) toilets for disabled shop garden centre ▰

SOUTHWELL   MAP 08 SK65

The Workhouse

Upton Rd NG25 0PT

➲ (13m from Nottingham on A612)

☎ 01636 817250

e-mail: theworkhouse@nationaltrust.org.uk

web: www.nationaltrust.org.uk

Enter this 19th-century brick institution and discover the thought-provoking story of the 'welfare' system of the New Poor Law. The least altered workhouse in existence today, it survives from hundreds that once covered the country. Explore the segregated stairs and rooms, use the audio guide, based on archive records, to bring the 19th-century inhabitants to life in the empty rooms, then try the interactive displays exploring poverty through the years and across the country.

Times Open 1-16 Mar, 1 Oct-2 Nov, Sat -Sun 11-4; 17-31 Mar, Apr-Sep, open daily (ex Mon-Tue) 12-5, (Apr-Sep 11-4). Tours 2-31 Aug, daily (ex Mon-Tue) 11-12. Open BH Mons & Good Fri. (Last admission 1hr before closing.) **Fee** ✳ With Gift Aid donation: £5.80 (ch £3). Family ticket (2ad+3ch) £14.50. Family ticket (1ad) £8.80. **Facilities** ♿ & (Ground floor accessible, stairs to other floors. Not suitable for motorised wheelchairs. Grounds partly accessible, loose gravel paths.) (virtual tour, photo album, wheelchairs available) toilets for disabled ⊗ (ex assist dogs) ♨

SUTTON-CUM-LOUND   MAP 08 SK68

Wetlands Waterfowl Reserve & Exotic Bird Park

Off Loundlow Rd DN22 8SB

➲ *(signed on A638)*

☎ 01777 818099

The Reserve is a 32-acre site for both wild and exotic waterfowl. Visitors can see a collection of birds of prey, parrots, geese, ducks, and wigeon among others. There are also many small mammals and farm and wild animals, including llamas, wallabies, emus, monkeys, red squirrels, deer and goats.

Times ✳ Open all year, daily 10-5.30 (or dusk - whichever is earlier). Closed 25 Dec. **Facilities** ♿ ⊑ ⊓ & (wheelchair available) shop ⊗ (ex assist dogs)

WORKSOP   MAP 08 SK57

Clumber Park

The Estate Office, Clumber Park S80 3AZ

➲ *(4.5m SE of Worksop, 6.5m SW of Retford, 1m from A1/A57)*

☎ 01909 476592

e-mail: clumberpark@nationaltrust.org.uk

web: www.nationaltrust.org.uk

An impressive, landscaped park, laid out by 'Capability' Brown. An outstanding feature is the lake running through the park, a haven for wildfowl, covering an area of 80 acres. The park is a mixture of woodland, open grass and heathland.

Times Open: Park daily. Kitchen Garden: 29 Mar-28 Sep, Mon-Fri 10-5, Sat-Sun 10-6; 4-26 Oct, Sat-Sun 11-4 & BH Mon. **Fee** ✳ Pedestrians, cyclists & coaches free; cars & motorbikes £4.80. Kitchen Garden £2.75 (ch under 16 free). **Facilities** ♿ (charged) ⊑ ⊓ ⊚ & (ramped access to chapel and walled kitchen garden & from conservatory to garden.) (powered self-drive vehicle available if booked) toilets for disabled shop garden centre ♨

Robin Hood, Nottingham

OXFORDSHIRE

Radcliffe Camera, Oxford

BANBURY   MAP 04 SP44

Banbury Museum

Spiceball Park Rd OX16 2PQ

⊃ *(M40 junct 11 straight across at first rdbt into Hennef Way, left at next rdbt into Concord Ave, right at next rdbt & left at next rdbt, Castle Quay Shopping Centre & Museum on right)*

☎ 01295 259855

e-mail: banburymuseum@cherwell-dc.gov.uk

web: www.cherwell-dc.gov.uk/banburymuseum

The museum is situated in an attractive canal-side location in the centre of Banbury. Exciting modern displays tell of Banbury's origins and historic past. The Civil War; the plush manufacturing industry; the Victorian market town; costume from the 17th century to the present day; Tooley's Boatyard and the Oxford Canal, are just some of the subjects illustrated.

Times Open all year, Mon-Sat, 10-5, Sun 10.30-4.30. **Facilities** ℗ (500yds) ⭐ & toilets for disabled shop ⊗ (ex assist dogs) ▬

BROUGHTON   MAP 04 SP43

Broughton Castle

OX15 5EB

⊃ *(2m W of Banbury Cross on B4035 Shipston-on-Stour in Broughton village, turn off B4035 by Saye & Sele Arms)*

☎ 01295 276070

e-mail: info@broughtoncastle.com

web: www.broughtoncastle.com

Built by Sir John de Broughton, then owned by William of Wykeham, and later by the first Lord Saye and Sele, the castle is an early 14th-and mid 16th-century house with a moat and gatehouse. Period furniture, paintings and Civil War relics are displayed. There are fine borders in the walled garden, and against the castle walls.

Times Open Etr Sun & Mon; May-15 Sep, Wed, Sun & BH Mon 2-5 (also open Thu in Jul & Aug). **Fee** ✳ £6.50 (ch 5-15 £2.50, concessions & group rate £5.50). Family ticket (2ad+up to 3ch) £15. **Facilities** ℗ ⫯ ₥ (outdoor) & (Ground floor & garden only for wheelchair users). toilets for disabled shop ⊗ (ex assist dogs)

BURFORD   MAP 04 SP21

Cotswold Wildlife Park

OX18 4JP

⊃ *(on A361 2m S of A40 at Burford)*

☎ 01993 823006

web: www.cotswoldwildlifepark.co.uk

This 160-acre landscaped zoological park, surrounds a listed Gothic-style manor house. There is a varied collection of animals from all over the world, many of which are endangered species such as Asiatic lions, leopards, white rhinos and red pandas. There's an adventure playground, a children's farmyard, and train rides during the summer. The park has also become one of the Cotswolds' leading attractions for garden enthusiasts, with its exotic summer displays and varied plantings offering interest all year.

Times Open all year, daily from 10, (last admission 4.30 Mar-Sep, 3.30 Oct-Feb). Closed 25 Dec. **Fee** £10.50 (ch 3-16 & over 65's £8). **Facilities** ℗ ⫯ ⭐ licensed ₥ (indoor) & (parking, free hire of wheelchairs, access to train) toilets for disabled shop ▬

BUSCOT   MAP 04 SU29

Buscot Park

SN7 8BU

⊃ *(on A417 between Faringdon & Lechlade)*

☎ 01367 240786

e-mail: estbuscot@aol.com

web: www.buscotpark.com

An 18th-century Palladian house with park and water garden. Home of the Faringdon collection of paintings and furniture. The park is landscaped with extensive water gardens designed by Harold Peto with parkland walks and a walled garden boasting seasonal herbaceous borders.

Times Open Grounds Only 6 Apr-29 Sep, Mon-Tue 2-6. House and Grounds Apr-Sep, Wed-Fri 2-6 (last entry 5). Also open Sat-Sun & BHs: 11/12, 25/26 Apr; 2/3; 9/10, 23/24 May; 13/14, 27/28 Jun; 11/12, 25/26 Jul; 8/9, 22/23, 29/30 Aug; 12/13, 26/27 Sep. **Fee** House & Grounds £7.50 (ch £3.75); Grounds only £5 (ch £2.50). **Facilities** ℗ ⫯ ₥ (outdoor) & (Partly accessible) (2 motorised mobility vehicles-must pre-book) toilets for disabled ⊗ (ex assist dogs) ⛟ ▬

CHASTLETON   MAP 04 SP22

Chastleton House

GL56 0SU

⮑ *(6m from Stow-on-the-Wold. Approach from A436 between A44)*

☎ 01608 674355

e-mail: chastleton@nationaltrust.org.uk

web: www.nationaltrust.org.uk

One of England's finest and most complete Jacobean houses, Chastleton House is filled with a mixture of rare and everyday objects, furniture and textiles maintaining the atmosphere of this 400-year-old home. The gardens have a typical Elizabethan and Jacobean layout with a ring of topiary. The National Trust has focussed on conserving rather than restoring the house.

Times Open 28 Mar-29 Sep 1-5, 3-27 Oct, 1-4. **Fee** ✳ £7 (ch £3.50) Family £17.50. **Facilities** ❷ & (visual material on ground floor) toilets for disabled ⊗ ⅍

DEDDINGTON   MAP 04 SP43

Deddington Castle   FREE

OX5 4TE

⮑ *(S of B4031 on E side of Deddington)*

web: www.english-heritage.org.uk

The large earthworks of the outer and inner baileys can be seen; the remains of 12th-century castle buildings have been excavated, but they are not now visible.

Times Open any reasonable time. **Facilities** ⊞

DIDCOT   MAP 04 SU58

Didcot Railway Centre   2 for 1

OX11 7NJ

⮑ *(on A4130 at Didcot Parkway Station)*

☎ 01235 817200

e-mail: info@didcotrailwaycentre.org.uk

web: www.didcotrailwaycentre.org.uk

Based around the original GWR engine shed, the Centre is home to the biggest collection anywhere of Great Western Railway steam locomotives, carriages and wagons. A typical GWR station has been re-created and a section of Brunel's original broad gauge track relaid, with a replica of the *Fire Fly* locomotive of 1840. There is a full programme of steamdays, including the now-traditional Thomas the Tank and Santa specials. Contact for a timetable.

Times Open all year, Sat & Sun. Daily 14-22 Feb; 4-19 Apr ;23-31 May; 20 Jun-6 Sep; 24 Oct-1 Nov; 27 Dec-3 Jan. Day out with Thomas 6-8 Mar, 2-4 Oct. Thomas Santa Special 5-23 Dec, Fri-Sun. **Fee** £5-£10 depending on event (ch £4-£9, concessions £4.50-£9.50). **Facilities** ℗ (100yds) ⬛ ⁑️ ☂ (outdoor) & (Partly accessible) (advance notice recommended, awkward steps at entrance) toilets for disabled shop ⚌

GREAT COXWELL   MAP 04 SU29

Great Coxwell Barn

⮑ *(2m SW of Faringdon between A420 & B4019)*

☎ 01793 762209

e-mail: greatcoxwellbarn@nationaltrust.org.uk

web: www.nationaltrust.org.uk

William Morris said that the barn was 'as noble as a cathedral'. It is a 13th-century stone-built tithe barn, 152ft long and 44ft wide, with a beautifully crafted framework of timbers supporting the lofty stone roof. The barn was built for the Cistercians.

Times Open all reasonable times. For details please contact Estate Office. **Fee** £1 **Facilities** ❷ & ⅍

HENLEY-ON-THAMES   MAP 04 SU78

Greys Court

Rotherfield Greys RG9 4PG

⮑ *(A4130 take B481. Property signed 3m on left. From town centre follow signs to Peppard/Greys for 3m)*

☎ 01491 628529

e-mail: greyscourt@nationaltrust.org.uk

web: www.nationaltrust.org.uk

A picturesque house originating from the 14th century but with later additions. The house re-opens after major conservation work, providing the opportunity to see the first floor for the first time. There is a beautiful courtyard and the surviving tower which dates from 1347. The outbuildings include a Tudor wheelhouse - one supplying water to the house, walled gardens and an ornamental vegetable garden. Check online for details of special events.

Times House open: Apr-27 Sep & BH Mon, Wed-Sun 2-5. (Last entry 4.30) Garden open: 12-5, **Fee** With Gift Aid donation: House & Garden £7 (ch £4.85). Family ticket £18.85. Garden only £5.20 (ch £2.90). Family ticket £13.30. Without Gift Aid donation: House & garden £6.75 (ch £4.40). Family ticket £17.90. Garden only £4.95 (ch £2.60). Family ticket £12.50. **Facilities** ❷ ⬛ & (accessibility to ground floor limited & no access to top floor of house. Full access to gardens.) toilets for disabled shop ⊗ (ex assist dogs) ⅍

River & Rowing Museum

Mill Meadows RG9 1BF

➲ (off A4130, signed to Mill Meadows)

☎ 01491 415600

e-mail: museum@rrm.co.uk

web: www.rrm.co.uk

Discover the River Thames, the sport of rowing and the town of Henley-on-Thames at this award-winning museum, a contemporary building overlooking the river and bordered by meadows. You can also meet Mr Toad, Ratty, Badger and Mole at the Wind in the Willows exhibition. E.H. Shepard's famous illustrations are brought to life by 3-D models of their adventures. See Ratty and Mole's picnic on the riverbank, get lost in the Wild Wood or watch the weasels at Toad Hall.

Times Open: May-Aug 10-5.30; Sep-Apr 10-5. Closed 24-25 & 31 Dec & 1 Jan. **Fee** £7 (ch 4 & over £5, concessions £6). Family from £20. Party 10+. (Tickets give unlimited entry for 12 months) **Facilities** ⊕ ⬚ ⏹ ⧉ (Partly accessible) (lift access to upstairs galleries, ramps at entrance) toilets for disabled shop ⊗ (ex assist dogs) ⬛

LONG WITTENHAM   MAP 04 SU59

Pendon Museum

OX14 4QD

➲ (follow brown signs from A4130 Didcot-Wallingford or A415 Abingdon-Wallingford road)

☎ 01865 407365

e-mail: sandra@pendon.plus.com

web: www.pendonmuseum.com

This charming exhibition shows highly detailed and historically accurate model railway and village scenes transporting the visitor back into 1930s country landscapes. Skilled modellers can often be seen at work on the exhibits.

Pendon Museum

Times Open Sat & Sun 2-5 (last admission 4.45), BH wknds from 11 also Wed in school hols. Closed Dec. **Fee** ✻ £5 (ch £3, under 6's free, pen £4). Family ticket (2ad+3ch) £16. **Facilities** ⊕ ⬚ ⧉ (phone in advance, special seating with handrails, lift) toilets for disabled shop ⊗ (ex assist dogs) ⬛

MAPLEDURHAM   MAP 04 SU67

Mapledurham House

RG4 7TR

➲ (off A4074, follow brown heritage signs from Reading)

☎ 0118 972 3350

e-mail: enquiries@mapledurham.co.uk

web: www.mapledurham.co.uk

The small community at Mapledurham includes the house, a watermill and a church. The fine Elizabethan mansion, surrounded by quiet parkland that runs down to the River Thames, was built by the Blount family in the 16th century. The estate has literary connections with the poet Alexander Pope, with Galsworthy's *Forsyte Saga* and Kenneth Graham's *Wind in the Willows*, and was a location for the film *The Eagle has Landed*. Open air theatre is a summer feature.

Times Open Etr-Sep, Sat, Sun & BHs 2-5.30. Picnic area 2-5.30. (Last admission 5). Group visits midweek by arrangement. **Fee** ✻ Combined house, watermill & grounds £6.75 (ch £3). House & grounds £4.25 (ch £2). Watermill & grounds £3.25 (ch £1.50). **Facilities** ⊕ ⬚ ⧉ (outdoor) ⧉ (Partly accessible) shop ⊗ (ex in grounds) ⬛

...igns from

...working corn and grist mill on the ma... ...den machinery and producing flour for local bakers and s..., ...e watermill's products can be purchased in the shop. When Mapledurham House is open the mill can be reached by boat from nearby Caversham.

Times Open Etr-Sep, Sat, Sun & BHs 2-5.30. Picnic area 2-5.30. (Last admission 5). Groups midweek by arrangement. **Fee** ✳ Watermill & grounds £3.25 (ch £1.50) **Facilities** ℗ ⌨ 🍴 (outdoor) 🚻 shop ⊗ (ex in country park) ▬

MINSTER LOVELL   MAP 04 SP31

Minster Lovell Hall & Dovecote   FREE

OX8 5RN

➲ *(adjacent to Minster Lovell Church, 3m W of Witney off A40)*

web: www.english-heritage.org.uk

Home of the ill-fated Lovell family, the ruins of the 15th-century house are steeped in history and legend. One of the main features of the estate is the medieval dovecote.

Times Open any reasonable time. Dovecote-exterior only **Facilities** ♿

NORTH LEIGH   MAP 04 SP31

North Leigh Roman Villa   FREE

OX8 6QB

➲ (2m N of North Leigh)

web: www.english-heritage.org.uk

This is the remains of a large and well-build Roman courtyard villa. The most important feature is an almost complete mosaic tile floor, which is intricately patterned in reds and browns.

Times Grounds open any reasonable time. Viewing window for mosaic tile floor. (Pedestrian access only from main road). **Facilities** ℗ ♿

Ashmolean Museum of Art & Archaeology   FREE

Beaumont St OX1 2PH

➲ *(city centre, opposite The Randolph Hotel)*

☎ 01865 278000

web: www.ashmolean.org

The oldest museum in the country, opened in 1683, the Ashmolean contains Oxford University's priceless collections. Many important historical art pieces and artefacts are on display, including work from Ancient Greece through to the twentieth century. The museum is currently undergoing a massive redevelopment, which includes the building of 39 new galleries, an education centre, conservation studios and a walkway, all due to open in 2009. The museum remains open for business with some restrictions, but not enough to spoil your visit.

Times Open all year, Tue-Sat 10-5, Sun 12-5 BH Mons 10-5. Closed during St.Giles Fair (7-9 Sept) Xmas & 1 Jan. **Facilities** ℗ (100-200mtrs) (pay & display) ⌨ 🍴 🚻 (entry ramp from Beaumont St. Tel. before visit) toilets for disabled shop ⊗ ▬

Harcourt Arboretum

Nuneham Courtenay OX44 9PX

➲ *(400yds S of Nuneham Courtenay on A4074)*

☎ 01865 343501

e-mail: piers.newth@obg.ox.ac.uk

web: www.botanic-garden.ox.ac.uk

The gardens consist of 75 acres of mixed woodland, meadow, pond, rhododendron walks and fine specimen trees.

Times Open Apr-Nov, daily 10-5; Dec-Mar, Mon-Fri 10-4.30. Closed 22 Dec-4 Jan. **Fee** £3 (ch free, concessions £2.50). Annual pass £10 (concessions £8.50) **Facilities** ℗ 🚻 (access for wheelchairs via path around Arboretum) toilets for disabled ⊗ (ex assist dogs) ▬

Museum of Oxford   FREE

St Aldate's OX1 1DZ

☎ 01865 252761

e-mail: museum@oxford.gov.uk

web: www.museumofoxford.org.uk

Permanent displays depict the archaeology and history of the city through the ages. There are temporary exhibitions, facilities for school parties and groups, and an audio tour. A programme of family, community events and activities also operates throughout the year.

Times Open all year, Tue-Fri 10-5, Sat & Sun 12-5. Closed 25-26 Dec. **Facilities** ⌨ 🚻 (main entrance steps, alternative access to ground floor via Town Hall next door) (virtual tour online, audio tour for adults) toilets for disabled shop ⊗ (ex assist dogs) ▬

Museum of the History of Science   FREE

Broad St OX1 3AZ

⮕ *(next to Sheldonian Theatre in city centre, on Broad St)*

☎ 01865 277280

e-mail: museum@mhs.ox.ac.uk

web: www.mhs.ox.ac.uk

The first purpose built museum in Britain, containing the world's finest collection of early scientific instruments used in astronomy, navigation, surveying, physics and chemistry. History of the telescope exhibition November 2008 to March 2009.

Times Open Tue-Fri 12-5, Sat 10-5, Sun 2-5. Closed Xmas and Etr Sun. **Facilities** Ⓟ (300mtrs) (limited street parking, meters) & (lift to basement) toilets for disabled shop ⊗ (ex assist dogs)

Oxford Castle - Unlocked

44-46 Oxford Castle OX1 1AY

⮕ *(in city centre off New Rd)*

☎ 01865 260666

e-mail: info@oxfordcastleunlocked.co.uk

web: www.oxfordcastleunlocked.co.uk

For the first time in 1,000 years, the secrets of Oxford Castle will be unlocked revealing episodes of violence, executions, great escapes, betrayal and even romance. Walk through these ancient buildings and experience the stories that connect the real people of the past to these extraordinary events.

Times Open daily 10-5.30 (last tour 4.20). Closed 25 Dec. **Fee** ✳ £7.50 (ch £5.35, concessions £6.20) **Facilities** Ⓟ 200mtrs ⬚ & (St Georges Tower & Castle Mound not accessible) (lift & ramp) toilets for disabled shop ⊗ (ex assist dogs) ▄

Oxford University Museum of   FREE
Natural History

Parks Rd OX1 3PW

⮕ *(opposite Keble College)*

☎ 01865 272950

e-mail: info@oum.ox.ac.uk

web: www.oum.ox.ac.uk

Built between 1855 and 1860, this museum of "the natural sciences" was intended to satisfy a growing interest in biology, botany, archaeology, zoology, entomology and so on. The museum reflects Oxford University's position as a 19th-century centre of learning, with displays of early dinosaur discoveries, Darwinian evolution and Elias Ashmole's collection of preserved animals. Although visitors to the Pitt-Rivers Museum must pass through the University Museum, the two should not be confused.

Times Open daily 10-5. Times vary at Xmas & Etr. **Facilities** Ⓟ (200mtrs) (meter parking) ⍾ (outdoor) & (lift access to gallery) toilets for disabled shop ⊗

Pitt Rivers Museum   FREE

South Parks Rd OX1 3PP

⮕ *(10 min walk from city centre, visitors entrance on Parks Rd through the Oxford Univiersity Museum of Natural History)*

☎ 01865 270927

e-mail: prm@prm.ox.ac.uk

web: www.prm.ox.ac.uk

The museum is one of the city's most popular attractions. It is part of the University of Oxford and was founded in 1884. The collections held at the museum are internationally acclaimed, and contain many objects from different cultures of the world and from various periods, all grouped by type, or purpose.

Times Open Tue-Sun & BH Mon 10-4.30, Mon 12-4.30. Contact museum at Xmas & Etr to check times. All public galleries will be closed due to building works from until Spring 2009. Please contact museum for details of re-opening. **Facilities** Ⓟ (city centre) (parking for disabled if booked) & (audio guide, wheelchair trail) toilets for disabled shop ⊗ (ex assist dogs)

St Edmund Hall   FREE

College of Oxford University OX1 4AR

⮕ *(Queen's Lane Oxford at end of High St)*

☎ 01865 279000

e-mail: bursary@seh.ox.ac.uk

web: www.seh.ox.ac.uk

This is the only surviving medieval academic hall and has a Norman crypt, 17th-century dining hall, chapel and quadrangle. Other buildings are of the 18th and 20th centuries.

Times Open all year. Closed 20-30 Mar, 23-26 Aug, 21 Dec-5 Jan. **Facilities** ⬚ & toilets for disabled ⊗ (ex assist dogs)

University of Oxford Botanic Garden

Rose Ln OX1 4AZ

⮕ *(E end of High St on banks of River Cherwell)*

☎ 01865 286690

e-mail: postmaster@obg.ox.ac.uk

web: www.botanic-garden.ox.ac.uk

Founded in 1621, this botanic garden is the oldest in the United Kingdom. There is a collection of over 6,000 species of plants from all over the world. Consisting of three sections, the Glasshouses contain plants that need protection from the British weather. The area outside the Walled Garden contains a water garden and rock garden as well as the spring border and autumn border. Within the Walled Garden plants are grouped by country of origin, botanic family or economic use.

Times Open all year daily: 9-4.30 Jan-Feb & Nov-Dec (last admission 4.15). Mar-Apr, Sep-Oct 9-5 (last admission 4.15) May-Aug 9-6 (last admission 5.15) Closed Good Fri & 25 Dec **Fee** ✳ £3 (ch free, disabled with 1 carer free, concessions £2.50). Annual pass £10, (concessions annual pass £8.50) **Facilities** Ⓟ (0.5m) (park and ride system) & toilets for disabled shop ⊗ (ex assist dogs) ▄

ENGLAND

ROUSHAM — MAP 04 SP42

Rousham House — 2 for 1

OX25 4QX

➲ (1m E of A4260. 0.5m S of B4030)

☎ 01869 347110

e-mail: ccd@rousham.org

web: www.rousham.org

This attractive mansion was built by Sir Robert Dormer in 1635. During the Civil War it was a Royalist garrison. The house contains over 150 portraits and other pictures, and also much fine contemporary furniture. The gardens are a masterpiece by William Kent, and are his only work to survive unspoiled.

Times Open all year, garden only, daily 10-4.30 (last entry). House, May-Sep. Groups by arrangement **Fee** Garden £5. (No children under 15). **Facilities** ❷ ♿ (restricted access as some areas of garden quite steep) ⊗ (ex assist dogs)

RYCOTE — MAP 04 SP60

Rycote Chapel

OX9 2PE

➲ (off B4013)

web: www.english-heritage.org.uk

This small private chapel was founded in 1449 by Richard Quatremayne. It has its original font, and a particularly fine 17th-century interior. The chapel was visited by both Elizabeth I and Charles I.

Times Open Apr-Sep, Fri-Sun, 2-6. May close at short notice for services or functions, please phone for details. **Fee** £3.50 (ch £1.50, concessions £2.50) Prices and opening times are subject to change in March 2009. Please check web site or call 0870 333 1181 for the most up to date prices and opening times when planning your visit. **Facilities** ❷ ♿ (if assisted) shop ⊗ ⚑

STONOR — MAP 04 SU78

Stonor House & Park

RG9 6HF

➲ On B480, approx 5m N of Henley-on-Thames

☎ 01491 638587

e-mail: administrator@stonor.com

web: www.stonor.com

The house dates back to 1190 but features a Tudor façade. It has a medieval Catholic chapel which is still in use today, and shows some of the earliest domestic architecture in Oxfordshire. Its treasures include rare furniture, paintings, sculptures and tapestries from Britain, Europe and America. The house is set in beautiful gardens with commanding views of the surrounding deer park. Special events June and August.

Times Open 5 Apr-13 Sep, Sun 2-5.30; Jul-Aug, also Wed 2-5.30; BH Mon. Parties by appointment Tue Thu, Apr-Sep **Fee** ✳ House £7 (ch 5-16 £3; under 5 free). Gardens only £3.50 (ch 5-16 £1.50; Under 5 free). Private guided tours £7 each. **Facilities** ❷ 🖾 🍴 (outdoor) ♿ (Partly accessible) shop ⊗ (on leads in park)

UFFINGTON — MAP 04 SU38

Uffington Castle, White Horse & Dragon Hill — FREE

➲ (S of B4507)

☎ 01793 762209

The 'castle' is an Iron Age fort on the ancient Ridgeway Path. It covers about eight acres and has only one gateway. On the hill below the fort is the White Horse, a 375ft prehistoric figure carved in the chalk hillside and thought to be about 3,000 years old.

Times Open at any reasonable time. **Facilities** ❷ (charged) 🍴 (outdoor) ♿ (disabled car parking and access to view points) 🐾

WATERPERRY — MAP 04 SP60

Waterperry Gardens

OX33 1JZ

➲ (7.5m from city centre. From E M40 junct 8, from N M40 junct 8a. Waterperry 2.5m from A40, exit a Wheatley and follow brown tourist signs)

☎ 01844 339226 & 339254

e-mail: office@waterperrygardens.co.uk

web: www.waterperrygardens.co.uk

Waterperry has eight acres of ornamental gardens, including formal and rose gardens, a river walk, lily canal and classical herbaceous border. The Gallery and Long Barn feature works of art, and the shop carries a large range of locally grown apples and juices. Look out for outdoor theatre in the gardens in the summer. Ring for details of this and a full programme of events or visit website.

Times Open daily all year, Jan-Feb & Nov-Dec 10-5; Mar-Oct 10-5.30. Closed Xmas, New Year & during "Art in Action" 16-19 Jul. **Fee** £3.50 (ch 16 & under free, concessions £3.50). Party 20+ £3.50, Jan-Feb. £5.45 (ch under 10 free, ch 10-16 £3.65, concessions £4.35). Party 20+ £4.25, Mar-Oct. £3.85 (ch 16 & under free, concessions £3.85). Party 20+ £3.85, Nov-Dec. (Party rates available for coaches) **Facilities** ❷ 🖾 🍴 🍽 licensed 🍴 (outdoor) ♿ (grounds mostly accessible) toilets for disabled shop garden centre ⊗ (ex assist dogs, ex garden) 🍴

WITNEY — MAP 04 SP31

Cogges Manor Farm Museum

Church Ln, Cogges OX28 3LA

➲ (0.5m SE off A4022)

☎ 01993 772602

web: www.cogges.org

The museum includes the Manor, dairy and walled garden, and has breeds of animals typical of the Victorian period. The first floor of the manor contains period rooms. Special events take place through the season.

Times ✳ Open Apr-Oct, Tue-Fri 10.30-5.30, Sat, Sun & BH Mon, 12-5.30. Early closing Oct. Closed Good Fri. **Facilities** ❷ 🖾 🍴 (outdoor) ♿ (wheelchair available, audio tour) toilets for disabled shop 🍴

WOODSTOCK   MAP 04 SP41

Blenheim Palace   `2 for 1`

OX20 1PP

➲ *(M40 junct 9, follow signs to Blenheim Palace, on A44 8m N of Oxford)*

☎ 08700 602080

e-mail: operations@blenheimpalace.com

web: www.blenheimpalace.com

Home of the 11th Duke of Marlborough and birthplace of Sir Winston Churchill, Blenheim Palace is an English Baroque masterpiece. Fine furniture, sculpture, paintings and tapestries are set in magnificent gilded staterooms that overlook sweeping lawns and formal gardens. 'Capability' Brown landscaped the 2,100-acre park, which is open to visitors for pleasant walks and beautiful views. A new exhibit 'Blenheim Palace: The Untold Story' explores the lives of those who have lived here, through the eyes of the servants. Please telephone for details of the full event programme which runs throughout the year and includes a Jousting Tournament and the Battle Proms.

Times Open Palace & Gardens mid Feb-mid Dec (ex Mon & Tue in Nov & Dec) daily 10.30-5.30 (last admission 4.45). Park daily all year 9-4.45. Closed 25 Dec. **Fee** ✳ Palace, Park & Gardens £13.90-£16.50 (ch £7.70-£10, concessions £11.30-£13.80). Park & Gardens £7.50-£9.50 (ch £2.50-£4.80, concessions £5.30-£7.50) **Facilities** ℗ ⊑ ⑩ licensed ⋒ (outdoor) ⑤ (Wheelchair access via lift in Palace) (ramps, disabled parking, buggies, wheelchairs) toilets for disabled shop ⊗ (ex assist dogs) ▰

Oxfordshire Museum   `FREE`

Fletcher's House, Park St OX20 1SN

➲ *(A44 Evesham-Oxford, follow signs for Blenheim Palace. Museum opposite church)*

☎ 01993 811456

e-mail: oxon.museum@oxfordshire.go.uk

web: www.oxfordshire.gov.uk/the_oxfordshire_museum

Situated in the heart of the historic town of Woodstock, the award-winning redevelopment of Fletcher's House provides a home for the new county museum. Set in attractive gardens, the new museum celebrates Oxfordshire in all its diversity and features collections of local history, art, archaeology, landscape and wildlife as well as a gallery exploring the county's innovative industries from nuclear power to nanotechnology. Interactive exhibits offer new learning experiences for visitors of all ages. The museum's purpose built Garden Gallery houses a variety of touring exhibitions of regional and national interest.

Times Open all year, Tue-Sat 10-5, Sun 2-5. Closed Good Fri, 25-26 Dec & 1 Jan. Galleries closed on Mon, but open BH Mons, 2-5. **Facilities** ℗ (outside entrance) (free parking) ⊑ ⑩ licensed ⋒ (outdoor) ⑤ (chair lifts to all galleries) toilets for disabled shop ⊗ (ex assist dogs) ▰

RUTLAND

Rutland Water

LYDDINGTON   MAP 04 SP89

Lyddington Bede House

Blue Coat Ln LE15 9LZ

☎ 01572 822438

web: www.english-heritage.org.uk

Once a prominent medieval palace later converted into an almshouse for the poor. Its history is bought to life in an evocative audio tour.

Times Open 21 Mar-Oct, Thu-Mon 10-5. **Fee** £3.70 (concessions £3, ch £1.90). Family ticket £9.30. Prices and opening times are subject to change in March 2009. Please check web site or call 0870 333 1181 for the most up to date prices and opening times when planning your visit. **Facilities** ⊗ ♯

OAKHAM   MAP 04 SK80

Oakham Castle

Catmos St LE15 6HW

⤷ *(off Market Place)*

☎ 01572 758440

e-mail: museum@rutland.gov.uk

web: www.rutland.gov.uk/castle

An exceptionally fine Norman Great Hall built in the 12th-century. Earthworks, walls and remains of an earlier motte can be seen along with medieval sculptures and unique presentation horseshoes forfeited by peers of the realm and royalty to the Lord of the Manor. The castle is now a popular place for civil marriages, meetings and special events.

Times Open all year, Mon-Sat 10.30-5 (closed 1-1.30), Sun 2-4. Closed Xmas, New Year & Good Fri **Facilities** ℗ (400yds) (disabled parking only by notification) ৬ (Partly accessible) shop ⊗ (ex assist dogs)

Rutland County Museum & Visitor Centre   FREE

Catmos St LE15 6HW

⤷ *(on A6003, S of town centre)*

☎ 01572 758440

e-mail: museum@rutland.gov.uk

web: www.rutland.gov.uk/museum

Rutland County Museum is the perfect introduction to England's smallest county. The 'Welcome to Rutland' gallery is a guide to its history. The museum includes a shop and study area. On show in the 18th-century Riding School are displays of archaeology, history and an extensive rural life collection.

Times Open all year, Mon-Sat 10.30-5, Sun 2-4. Closed Xmas, New Year & Good Fri. **Facilities** ℗ (charged) ৬ (Partly accessible) (induction loop in meeting room) toilets for disabled shop ⊗ (ex assist dogs)

By Rutland Water

SHROPSHIRE

Iron Bridge over the River Servern, Ironbridge

ACTON BURNELL — MAP 07 SJ50

Acton Burnell Castle — FREE

SY5 7PE

➲ *(in Acton Burnell on unclass road 8m S of Shrewsbury)*

web: www.english-heritage.org.uk

The warm red sandstone shell of a fortified 13th-century manor house. The site of the first parliament at which the commons were fully represented.

Times Open at all reasonable times. **Facilities** ▦

ATCHAM — MAP 07 SJ50

Attingham Park

SY4 4TP

➲ *(4m SE of Shrewsbury on B4380)*

☎ 01743 708123

e-mail: attingham@nationaltrust.org.uk

web: www.nationaltrust.org.uk/attinghampark

Attingham Park is centred on one of Britain's finest regency mansions, set in a landscaped deer park designed by Humphry Repton. The house is undergoing a major project to revive and re-discover the original lavish decorative schemes, with new upstairs rooms open for the first time. The park is an ideal place for a country walk, and there is a programme of events throughout the year.

Times Park & grounds open daily, Jan-13 Feb & 2 Nov-Dec 9-5; 14 Feb-1 Nov 9-6. House: 7-8 Mar, 14 Mar-1 Nov daily (ex Wed). Tours 11-1. Free flow 1-5.30 (last admission 4.30). Winter opening - tours at wknds. **Fee** House: £8.40 (ch £4.70) Family £19.50. Grounds £4.20 (ch £2.20) Family £10.40 **Facilities** ❷ ⊑ ⋒ (outdoor) ⚹ (level access, lift to first floor, top floor only accessible via stairs) (2 electric self drive buggies, 1 staff driven 8-seater) toilets for disabled shop ❧ ▭

BENTHALL — MAP 07 SJ60

Benthall Hall

TF12 5RX

➲ *(on B4375)*

☎ 01952 882159

e-mail: benthall@nationaltrust.org.uk

The main part of the house was built around 1585. A wing at the back, which has been altered at various times, dates originally from about 1520. It is an attractive sandstone building with mullioned windows, fine oak panelling and a splendid carved staircase.

Times Open 9 Feb-2 Nov, Wed-Sun, 11-5. **Fee** ✳ House and garden £5.10 (ch £2.50) Family £12.50. Garden only £3.15 (ch £1.60) **Facilities** ❷ ⚹ (Partly accessible) (Braille, large print guides) toilets for disabled ⊗ (ex assist dogs) ❧

BOSCOBEL — MAP 07 SJ80

Boscobel House and The Royal Oak

Brewood ST19 9AR

➲ *(on unclass road between A41 and A5)*

☎ 01902 850244

web: www.english-heritage.org.uk

This fully restored and refurbished lodge and famous Royal Oak tree is where King Charles II sought refuge from Cromwell's troops in 1651. The house was built around 1632.

Times Open 21 Mar-Oct, Wed-Sun & BH 10-5. (Last entry 1hr before closing). **Fee** £5 (concessions £4, ch £2.50). Family ticket £12.50. Grounds only: £2.50 (concessions £2, ch £1.30). Prices and opening times are subject to change in March 2009. Please check web site or call 0870 333 1181 for the most up to date prices and opening times when planning your visit. **Facilities** ❷ ⊑ ⋒ shop ⊗ ▦

Whiteladies Priory — FREE

➲ *(1m SW of Boscobel House, off an unclass road between A41 and A5)*

web: www.english-heritage.org.uk

Only the ruins are left of this Augustinian nunnery, which dates from 1158 and was destroyed in the Civil War. After the Battle of Worcester Charles II hid here and in the nearby woods before going on to Boscobel House.

Times Open 21 Mar-Oct, daily 10-5. Closed Nov-Mar. **Facilities** ▦

BUILDWAS — MAP 07 SJ60

Buildwas Abbey

Iron Bridge TF8 7BW

➲ *(on S bank of River Severn on B4378)*

☎ 01952 433274

web: www.english-heritage.org.uk

Set beside the River Severn, against a backdrop of wooded grounds, are the extensive remains of this Cistercian abbey founded in 1135.

Times Open 21 Mar-Sep, Wed-Sun & BH Mon 10-5. **Fee** £3 (concessions £2.40, ch £1.50). Prices and opening times are subject to change in March 2009. Please check web site or call 0870 333 1181 for the most up to date prices and opening times when planning your visit. **Facilities** ❷ shop ⊗ ▦

BURFORD
MAP 03 SO56

Burford House Gardens
WR15 8HQ

➲ *(off A456, 1m W of Tenbury Wells, 8m from Ludlow)*

☎ 01584 810777

e-mail: info@burford.co.uk

web: www.burford.co.uk

Burford House and Garden Centre set within 15 acres, incorporates a Georgian mansion, which houses a shop and riverside gardens housing the National Clematis Collection.

Times Open all year 9-6 or dusk if earlier. Closed 25-26 Dec. **Facilities** ❷ ⬚ ⁍⌁ ⋔ (outdoor) ⅁ (Partly accessible) (ramp into gardens, sloping paths, wheelchairs available) toilets for disabled shop garden centre ⊗ (ex assist dogs) ▬

COSFORD
MAP 07 SJ70

The Royal Air Force Museum
TF11 8UP

➲ *(on A41, 1m S of M54 junct 3)*

☎ 01902 376200

e-mail: cosford@rafmuseum.org

web: www.rafmuseum.org

The Royal Air Force Museum Cosford has one of the largest aviation collections in the UK, with 70 historic aircraft on display. Visitors will be able to see Britain's V bombers - Vulcan, Victor and Valiant and other aircraft suspended in flying attitudes in the national Cold War exhibition, housed in a landmark building covering 8,000sqm.

Times Open all year daily, 10-6 (last admission 4). Closed 24-26 Dec & 1 Jan, 7-11 Jan. **Facilities** ❷ ⬚ ⁍⌁ ⋔ (outdoor) ⅁ (free loan of 3 manual w/chairs and 3 motor scooters) toilets for disabled shop ⊗ (ex assist dogs)

CRAVEN ARMS
MAP 07 SO48

The Shropshire Hills Discovery Centre
School Rd SY7 9RS

➲ *(on A49, on S edge of Craven Arms)*

☎ 01588 676000

e-mail: zoe.griffin@shropshire-cc.gov.uk

web: www.shropshirehillsdiscoverycentre.co.uk

This attraction explores the history, nature and geography of the Shropshire Hills, through a series of interactive displays and simulations. The award-winning Centre has been revamped over the winter and now has a brand new Secret Hills exhibition. Become a landscape detective as you follow the new family Timeline Trail, which takes you from the Ice Age to the present day. On the way meet the Shropshire Mammoth, look inside an Iron Age Round House, dress up in Celtic clothing, make a mediaeval seal and float over Shropshire by watching the panoramic hot air balloon film. Other features include the Ice Age Orienteering trail around Onny Meadows, a Craft Room and a Riverside Ramble. Also try Geocaching, a kind of treasure-hunt that uses hand-held GPS.

Times ✳ Open all year, daily from 10. (Last admission 3.30 Nov-Mar, 4.30 Apr-Oct). **Facilities** ❷ ⬚ ⁍⌁ ⋔ (outdoor) ⅁ (wheelchair available) toilets for disabled shop ⊗ (ex assist dogs) ▬

HAUGHMOND ABBEY
MAP 07 SJ51

Haughmond Abbey
Upton Magna SY4 4RW

➲ *(off B5062)*

☎ 01743 709661

web: www.english-heritage.org.uk

Absorb these extensive 12th-century Augustinian abbey ruins, and visit the small museum.

Times Open 21 Mar-Sep, Wed-Sun & BH Mon 10-5. **Fee** £3 (concessions £2.40, ch £1.50). Prices and opening times are subject to change in March 2009. Please check web site or call 0870 333 1181 for the most up to date prices and opening times when planning your visit. **Facilities** ❷ ⅁ (limited access for wheelchair users) shop ⌗

IRONBRIDGE
MAP 07 SJ60

Ironbridge Gorge Museums

Coach Rd TF8 7DQ

⮥ *(M54 junct 4, signed)*

☎ 01952 884391 & 0800 590258

e-mail: tic@ironbridge.org.uk

web: www.ironbridge.org.uk

Ironbridge is the site of the world's first iron bridge. It was cast and built here in 1779, to span a narrow gorge over the River Severn. Now Ironbridge is the site of a remarkable series of museums relating the story of the bridge, recreating life in Victorian times and featuring ceramics and social history displays.

Times ✲ Open all year, 10-5. Some small sites closed Nov-Mar. Telephone for exact winter details. **Facilities** ❷ ⏢ ⑩ 🛒 (outdoor) ♿ (wheelchairs, potters wheel, Braille guide, hearing loop) toilets for disabled shop ❽ (ex Blists Hill & assist dogs) 🚐

LILLESHALL
MAP 07 SJ71

Lilleshall Abbey
FREE

TF10 9HW

⮥ *(off A518 on unclass road)*

☎ 0121 625 6820

web: www.english-heritage.org.uk

In the beautiful grounds of Lilleshall Hall, ruined Lilleshall Abbey was founded shortly before the middle of the 12th century and from the high west front visitors can look down the entire 228ft length of the abbey church.

Times Open 21 Mar-Sep, daily 10-5. Closed Oct-Mar. **Facilities** ▦

LUDLOW
MAP 07 SO57

Ludlow Castle

Castle Square SY8 1AY

⮥ *(A49 to town centre)*

☎ 01584 873355 & 874465

e-mail: hduce@ludlowcastle.com

web: www.ludlowcastle.com

Ludlow Castle dates from 1086. In 1473, Edward IV sent the Prince of Wales and his brother - later to become the Princes in the Tower - to live here, and Ludlow Castle became a seat of government. John Milton's *Comus* was first performed at Ludlow Castle in 1634; now contemporary performances of Shakespeare's plays, together with concerts, are put on in the castle grounds during the Ludlow Festival (end June-early July). Please telephone for details of events running throughout the year.

Times Open Dec-Jan, Sat-Sun 10-4; Feb-Mar & Oct-Nov, daily 10-4; Apr-Jul & Sep, daily 10-5; Aug, daily 10-7; (last admission 30 minutes before closing). Closed 25 Dec. Open 26 Dec-1 Jan, daily 10-4 **Fee** £4.50 (ch under 6 free, ch £2.50, pen £4). Family ticket £12.50 **Facilities** ℗ (100yds) ⏢ 🛒 (outdoor) ♿ (Partly accessible) toilets for disabled shop 🚐

MORETON CORBET
MAP 07 SJ52

Moreton Corbet Castle
FREE

⮥ *(off B5063, in Moreton Corbet)*

web: www.english-heritage.org.uk

Inherited by the Corbets in 1235, who are thought to have remodelled the great keep, this castle may already have been standing for over 100 years. It was remodelled in the 16th century and then partially demolished to make way for a great Elizabethan mansion. Although damaged in the civil war, the castle and mansion stand today as one of the most picturesque ruins of the Shropshire Marches.

Times Open at any reasonable time. **Facilities** ❷ ▦

MUCH WENLOCK
MAP 07 SO69

Wenlock Priory

TA3 6HS

☎ 01952 727466

web: www.english-heritage.org.uk

Experience the ruins of this large Cluniac priory and the atmospheric remains of the 13th-century church and Norman chapter house. The audio tour offers a fascinating insight into its history. Impressive topiary figures guard the priory ruins.

Times Open all year, 21 Mar-Apr, Wed-Sun & BH 10-5; May-Aug, daily 10-5; Sep-Oct, Wed-Sun 10-5; Nov-Feb, Thu-Sun 10-4. Closed 24-26 Dec & 1 Jan. **Fee** £3.50 (concessions £2.80, ch £1.80). Prices and opening times are subject to change in March 2009. Please check web site or call 0870 333 1181 for the most up to date prices and opening times when planning your visit. **Facilities** ❷ ▦

OSWESTRY
MAP 07 SJ22

Old Oswestry Hill Fort
FREE

⮥ *(1m N of Oswestry, off an unclass road off A483)*

web: www.english-heritage.org.uk

An impressive Iron Age hill-fort of 68 acres, defended by a series of five ramparts, with an elaborate western entrance and unusual earthwork cisterns.

Times Open at any reasonable time. **Facilities** ▦

QUATT — MAP 07 SO78

Dudmaston

WV15 6QN

➲ *(4m SE of Bridgnorth on A442)*

☎ 01746 780866

e-mail: dudmaston@nationaltrust.org.uk

The 17th-century flower paintings which belonged to Francis Darby of Coalbrookdale are exhibited in this house of the same period, with modern works, botanical art and fine furniture. The house stands in an extensive park and garden and there are woodland and lakeside walks.

Times Open Apr-Sep, Tue, Wed & Sun & BH Mons, 2-5.30. Garden Sun-Wed, noon-6. Closed Good Fri. **Fee** ✳ House & Garden £6.10. Garden only £4.90. Family ticket £15.25. **Facilities** ❷ ⊆ ♠ (outdoor) ⅙ (all ground floors are accessible, first floor galleries are currently unaccessible) (Braille & large print guides, taped tours) toilets for disabled shop ⊗ (ex in grounds & assist dogs) ⅍ ➟

SHREWSBURY — MAP 07 SJ41

Shrewsbury Castle and Shropshire Regimental Museum

2 for 1

The Castle, Castle St SY1 2AT

➲ *(located in town centre, adjacent to railway station)*

☎ 01743 358516

e-mail: shropsrm@zoom.co.uk

web: www.shrewsburymuseums.com

Shrewsbury Castle commands fantastic views over the town and surrounding area. Dating originally from the 1070s it was 'restored' in the 18th century by Thomas Telford, who built the romantic Laura's Tower. In the main building is the Shropshire Regimental Museum, where, as well as fascinating displays, you will find staff ready to help with enquiries about your family's role in Shropshire's military life. The Circular Room at Shrewsbury Castle is licensed for civil ceremonies. The grounds are a magnificent setting for photographs and a varied programme of summer events.

Times Open 27 May-10 Sep, Mon-Sat, 10-5; Sun 10-4; 11 Sep-22 Dec, Tue-Sat, 10-4 **Fee** ✳ £2.50 (£1.30 concessions). All local residents & members of the regiment, ch under 18 or in full time education free. Admission to castle grounds free. **Facilities** ℗ (3 mins NCP) (metered on street parking) ♠ (outdoor) ⅙ (please ask staff for assistance) toilets for disabled shop ⊗ (ex assist dogs)

STOKESAY — MAP 07 SO48

Stokesay Castle

SY7 9AH

➲ *(1m S of Craven Arms off A49)*

☎ 01588 672544

web: www.english-heritage.org.uk

Stokesay Castle is a perfectly preserved 13th-century fortified manor house. See its superb timber-framed Jacobean gatehouse and stroll through the impressive great hall. Delightful cottage gardens.

Times Open 21 Mar-Sep, daily 10-5; Oct, Wed-Sun 10-5; Nov-Feb, Thu-Sun 10-4. Closed 24-26 Dec & 1 Jan. (Castle may close early for functions, please call to check). **Fee** £4.90 (ch £2.50, concessions £3.70) Family £12.30. Prices and opening times are subject to change in March 2009. Please check web site or call 0870 333 1181 for the most up to date prices and opening times when planning your visit. **Facilities** ❷ ♠ ⅙ (tape tour for visually handicapped, ramp for wheelchairs) toilets for disabled ⊗ ✿

TELFORD — MAP 07 SJ60

Hoo Farm Animal Kingdom

Preston-on-the-Weald Moors TF6 6DJ

➲ *(M54 junct 6, follow brown tourist signs)*

☎ 01952 677917

e-mail: info@hoofarm.com

web: www.hoofarm.com

Hoo Farm is a real children's paradise where there is always something happening. A clean, friendly farm that appeals to all ages and offers close contact with a wide variety of animals from fluffy yellow chicks and baby lambs to foxes, llamas, deer and ostriches. A daily programme of events encourages audience participation in the form of bottle feeding lambs, pig feeding, ferret racing and collecting the freshly laid eggs. The Craft Area offers the chance to try your hand at candle dipping, glass or pottery painting or even throwing a pot on the potters wheel. There are Junior Quad Bikes and a Rifle Range, Pony Rides, powered mini tractors as well as indoor and outdoor play areas and a new games room. Please telephone for details of special events running throughout the year.

Times Open: 25 Mar-9 Sep, Tue-Sun 10-6. 10 Sep-24 Nov, Tue-Sun, 10-5. 25 Nov-24 Dec, daily 10-5 closes at 1 on 24 Dec. Closed 25 Dec to mid March. **Facilities** ❷ ⊆ ♠ (indoor & outdoor) ⅙ (Partly accessible) toilets for disabled shop ⊗ (ex assist dogs) ➟

WELLINGTON — MAP 07 SJ61

Sunnycroft

200 Holyhead Rd TF1 2DR

➲ *(M54 junct 7, 2m E of Wellington off B5061)*

☎ 01952 242884

e-mail: sunnycroft@nationaltrust.org.uk

web: www.nationaltrust.org.uk/sunnycroft

A late Victorian gentleman's villa, typical of houses built for prosperous business and professional people on the fringe of towns and cities. The house is a time capsule of early 20th century life both above and below stairs, when it was home to the Lander family. Displays of embroidery by Joan Lander can be seen within the house. The gardens and grounds are very attractive, and taking tea in the old smoking room overlooking the croquet lawn is a quintessential English experience.

Times House & Gardens open 20 Mar-2 Nov & 18-21 Dec Fri-Mon 1-5. **Fee** ✳ House & Garden £5.70 (ch £2.80). Family £14.20. Garden £3.50 (ch £1.75). Family £8.75 **Facilities** ❷ ⊆ ♠ (outdoor) ⊗ (ex on leads in grounds) ⅍

VESTON-UNDER-REDCASTLE MAP 07 SJ52

Hawkstone Historic Park & Follies 2for1

Y4 5UY

⊃ *(3m from Hodnet off A53, follow brown heritage signs)*

☎ 01948 841700

e-mail: info@hawkstone.co.uk

web: www.hawkstone.co.uk

Created in the 18th century by the Hill family, Hawkstone is one of the greatest historic parklands in Britain. After almost one hundred years of neglect it has now been restored and designated a Grade 1 historic landscape. Visitors can once again experience the magical world of intricate pathways, arches and bridges, towering cliffs and follies, and an awesome grotto. The Grand Valley and woodlands have centuries-old oaks, wild rhododendrons and lofty monkey puzzles. The park covers nearly 100 acres of hilly terrain and visitors are advised to wear sensible shoes and clothing and to bring a torch. Allow 3-4 hours for the tour, which is well signposted and a route map is provided in the admission price. Attractions include 'Hear King Arthur' and meeting the Duke of Wellington in the White Tower to discuss the Battle of Waterloo.

Times Open from 10 Mar, Sat & Sun; Apr-May, & Sep-Oct, Wed-Sun; Jun-Aug, daily. Closed Nov-Mar. **Fee** ✳ Wkdays £6 (ch £4 pen & students £5). Family ticket £17. **Facilities** ♿ 🚻 🍽 ⛱ (outdoor) ♿ (access to tearooms, gift shop and grand valley) (no access to follies due to terrain access Valley only) toilets for disabled shop 🛒

WROXETER   MAP 07 SJ50

Wroxeter Roman City

SY5 6PH

⊃ *(5m E of Shrewsbury, 1m S of A5)*

☎ 01743 761330

web: www.english-heritage.org.uk

Discover what urban life was like 2,000 years ago in the fourth largest city in Roman Britain. See the remains of the impressive 2nd-century municipal baths and view the excavated treasures in the museum.

Times Open all year, 21 Mar-Oct, daily 10-5; Nov-Feb, Wed-Sun 10-4. Closed 24-26 Dec & 1 Jan. **Fee** £4.20 (concessions £3.40, ch £2.10). Family ticket £10.50. Prices and opening times are subject to change in March 2009. Please check web site or call 0870 333 1181 for the most up to date prices and opening times when planning your visit. **Facilities** ♿ shop 🚻

Stokesay Castle, Ludlow

SOMERSET

Pultney Bridge, Bath

AXBRIDGE   MAP 03 ST45

King John's Hunting Lodge

The Square BS26 2AP

➲ *(on corner of Axbridge High St, in the Square)*

☎ 01934 732012

e-mail: kingjohns@nationaltrust.org.uk

web: www.nationaltrust.org.uk

Nothing to do with King John or with hunting, this jettied and timber-framed house was built around 1500. It gives a good indication of the wealth of the merchants of that time and is now a museum of local history, with old photographs, paintings and items such as the town stocks and constables' staves.

Times Open 21 Mar-Sep, daily 1-4 **Fee** Donations welcome **Facilities** ℗ (100yds) shop ⊗ ♨

BARRINGTON   MAP 03 ST31

Barrington Court

TA19 0NQ

➲ *(5m NE of Ilminster on B3168)*

☎ 01460 241938 & 242614

e-mail: barringtoncourt@nationaltrust.org.uk

web: www.nationaltrust.org.uk

The house is a Tudor manor, the interior of which is now let out to Stuart Interiors as showrooms with antique furniture for sale. The gardens were created in the 1920s, with the help (through the post) of Gertrude Jekyll. They are laid out in 'rooms' and there is a large walled kitchen garden supplying fresh fruit and vegetables to the restaurant.

Times Open Mar, Thu-Tue 11-4.30; Apr-Sep daily (ex Wed) 11-5; 2 Oct-2 Nov, Thu-Tue 11-4.30. 6-14 Dec, Sat & Sun 11-4. **Fee** ✳ £8.10 (ch £3.50). Family £19.70. Groups £7 **Facilities** ℗ ⊑ ⊚ ☶ ♿ (Batricars, Braille and large print guides, w/chairs) toilets for disabled shop garden centre ⊗ (except assist dogs) ♨

BATH   MAP 03 ST76

American Museum in Britain   2 for 1

Claverton Manor BA2 7BD

➲ *(Signed from city centre & A36 Warminster road)*

☎ 01225 460503

e-mail: info@americanmuseum.org

web: www.americanmuseum.org

Claverton Manor is just two miles south east of Bath, in a beautiful setting above the River Avon. The house was built in 1820 by Sir Jeffrey Wyatville, and is now a museum of American decorative arts. The gardens are well worth seeing, and include an American arboretum and a replica of George Washington's garden at Mount Vernon. The Folk Art Gallery and the New Gallery are among the many exhibits in the grounds along with seasonal exhibitions.

Times Open mid Mar-Oct, Tue-Sun 12-5. Open Mon in Aug & BHs. (Xmas opening last week in Nov and first two weeks Dec). **Fee** ✳ £7.50 (ch £4, concession £6.50). **Facilities** ℗ ⊑ ⊚ ☶ (outdoor) ♿ (lift to all floors & adapted toilets) toilets for disabled shop ➡

Bath Abbey

Abbey Churchyard BA1 1LY

➲ *(M4 junct 18, centre of Bath, next to Pump Rooms & The Roman Baths. Orange Grove drop off and collection point for coaches-east end)*

☎ 01225 422462 & 446300

e-mail: office@bathabbey.org

web: www.bathabbey.org

The 15th-century abbey church was built on the site of the Saxon abbey where King Edgar was crowned in 973. The church is Perpendicular style with Norman arches and superb fan-vaulting. The famous West Front carvings represent the founder-bishop's dream of angels ascending and descending from heaven.

Times The Abbey: Apr-Oct, Mon-Sat 9-6; Nov-Mar, Mon-Sat 9-4.30; Closed 25 Dec & Good Fri. The Heritage Vaults Museum: Open all year, Mon-Sat 10-4, closed 25 Dec & Good Fri. Closed at other times for services & events, please check **Fee** Visitors invited to donate £2.50 per adult & £1 per student. **Facilities** ℗ (3-4 mins) (limited street parking) ♿ (level access, induction loop, large print leaflet, lift) toilets for disabled shop ⊗ (ex assist dogs)

Bath Aqua Theatre of Glass

105-107 Walcot St BA1 5BW

☎ 01225 428146

e-mail: sales@bathaquaglass.com

web: www.bathaquaglass.com

View old stained glass windows renovated from Bath Abbey Chambers. In the heart of the city's artisan quarter, this is an ideal centre to learn about the history of glass and watch the ancient craft of free glass blowing.

Times Open Etr-Sep daily (ex Sun) 9.30-5 **Fee** ✳ £3.50 (ch & concessions £2). Family of 4 £8. **Facilities** shop ⊗ ➡

ENGLAND

BATH CONTINUED

Bath Postal Museum

2 for 1

27 Northgate St BA1 1AJ

➲ *(On entering city fork left at mini rdbt. After all lights into Walcot St. Podium car park facing)*

☎ 01225 460333

e-mail: info@bathpostalmuseum.org
web: www.bathpostalmuseum.org

Discover how 18th-century Bath influenced and developed the Postal System, including the story of the Penny Post. The first letter sent with a stamp was sent from Bath. Visitors can explore the history of written communication from Egyptian clay tablets, thousands of years old, to the first Airmail flight from Bath to London in 1912. See the Victorian Post Office and watch continuous video films including the in-house production entitled 'History of Writing'. The museum is full of hands-on and interactive features to engage the whole family.

Times Open all year, Mon-Sat 11-5. (Last admission Mar-Oct 4.30, Nov-Feb 4). **Fee** £3.50 (ch under 5 free, ch £1.50, concessions £3, students £1.50). Family and Party 10+ tickets available. **Facilities** ℗ (50yds) (no on street parking) ⅁ (films and computer games for hearing impaired) shop ⊗ (ex assist dogs) ▬

Fashion Museum

Bennett St BA1 2QH

➲ *(Museum near city centre. Parking in Charlotte Street Car park.)*

☎ 01225 477173

e-mail: fashion_bookings@bathnes.gov.uk
web: www.fashionmuseum.co.uk

The Fashion Museum showcases a world-class collection of historical and contemporary dress and includes opportunities to try on replica corsets and crinolines. It is housed in Bath's famous 18th-century Assembly Rooms designed by John Wood the Younger in 1771. Entrance to the Assembly Rooms is free.

Fashion Museum

Times Open all year, daily Jan-Feb 10.30-4; Mar-Oct, 10.30-5; Nov-Dec, 10.30-4. Closed 25-26 Dec. **Fee** ✳ £7 (ch £5). Family ticket £19.75. Combined ticket with Roman Baths, £14 (ch £8.50). **Facilities** ℗ (5 mins walk) (park & ride recommended) ⅁ ⅍ (audio guides available) toilets for disabled shop ⊗ (ex assist dogs) ▬

The Herschel Museum of Astronomy

19 New King St BA1 2BL

➲ *(in Bath city centre)*

☎ 01225 446865

e-mail: herschelbpt@btinternet.com
web: www.bath-preservation-trust.org.uk

This 18th-century town house celebrates the achievements of William Herschel and his sister Caroline, who were both distinguished astronomers. William discovered Uranus in 1781. The house is decorated and furnished in the style of the period of Georgian Bath, while the gardens are semi-formal in design and include different plants and herbs popular at the time. There is also a star vault astronomy auditorium. 2009 is the international year of astronomy.

Times Open daily Feb-16 Dec, Mon-Tue & Thu-Fri, 1-5, Sat, Sun & BHs 11-5. **Fee** £4, (ch £2.50, students £3, concessions £3.50) Family £10. **Facilities** ℗ (some 2 hour free spaces) ⅍ (Partly accessible) (audio & virtual tours, handling collections, sub titles) shop ⊗ (ex assist dogs)

The Jane Austen Centre

2 for 1

40 Gay St, Queen Square BA1 2NT

➲ *(in heart of Bath by Queen Square)*

☎ 01225 443000

e-mail: jackie@janeausten.co.uk
web: www.janeausten.co.uk

Celebrating Bath's most famous resident, the centre offers a snapshot of life during Regency times and explores how living in this city affected Jane Austen's life and writing. Every September, Bath holds a Jane Austen festival.

Times Open all year, daily 9.45-5.30 (Sun-Fri 11-4.30, Sat 9.45-5.30, Nov-Mar) **Fee** ✳ £6.50 (ch £3.50, concessions £4.95) Family ticket (2 ad+up to 4 ch) £18. **Facilities** ℗ (50mtrs) ⅁⅋⅍ (access to exhibition on ground floor only) (Ground floor access) shop ⊗ (ex assit dogs) ▬

Museum of Bath at Work

2 for 1

Julian Rd BA1 2RH

➲ *(from city centre, off Lansdown Rd into Julian Rd. Museum next to church on right)*

☎ 01225 318348

e-mail: mobaw@hotmail.com

web: www.bath-at-work.org.uk

Two thousand years of Bath's commercial and industrial development are explored with exhibits on 'The Story of Bath Stone', a Bath cabinet makers' workshop, a 1914 Horstmann car and a reconstruction of J B Bowlers' engineering and mineral water business. A computer info point is available. A local history gallery and display on local invention is also part of the museum.

Times Open all year, Etr-1 Nov, daily 10.30-5; Nov-Etr, wknds 10.30-5. Closed 25-26 Dec. **Fee** £4.50 (concessions £3.50). Family ticket £10. **Facilities** Ⓟ (0.25m) ☕ ⛩ (indoor) ♿ (Partly accessible) (audio guides, ramps) shop ⊗ (ex assist dogs)

No 1 Royal Crescent

No 1 Royal Cresent BA1 2LR

➲ *(1st house in Royal Crescent situated above Victoria Ave & Victoria Park, Charlotte St car park)*

☎ 01225 428126

e-mail: no1musuem@bptrust.org.uk

web: www.bath-preservation-trust.org.uk

Bath is very much a Georgian city, but most of its houses have naturally altered over the years to suit changing tastes and lifestyles. Built in 1768 by John Wood the Elder, No 1 Royal Crescent has been restored to look as it would have done some 200 years ago. Visitors can see a grand townhouse of the late 18th century with authentic furniture, paintings and carpets. On the ground floor are the study and dining room and on the first floor a lady's bedroom and drawing room. In the basement a period kitchen and museum shop.

Times Open 16 Feb-25 Oct, 10.30-5, 26 Oct-30 Nov, 10.30-4. Open BH Mon. Open wknds 6-7 & 13-14 Dec. Closed Good Fri. (Last admission 30 mins before closing). **Facilities** Ⓟ (5 mins walk) (street parking with card £1 per hour) ♿ (Partly accessible) (virtual tour, induction loop, Braille guide) shop ⊗ (ex assist dogs) ▬

Prior Park Landscape Garden

Ralph Allen Dr BA2 5AH

➲ *(in city centre)*

☎ 01225 833422 & 0900 133 5242

e-mail: priorpark@nationaltrust.org.uk

web: www.nationaltrust.org.uk

Created by local entrepreneur Ralph Allen with advice from Alexander Pope and 'Capability' Brown, this garden in set in a sweeping valley with magnificent views of the city of Bath. Many interesting features include a Palladian Bridge (250 years old in 2005), three lakes, and lovely wooded glades.

Times Open Mar-Oct, Wed-Mon 11-5.30; Nov-Feb, Sat-Sun 11-dusk. (BHs 11-5.30). Closed 25-26 Dec & 1 Jan. **Fee** ✻ £5 (ch £2.80). Family (2ad+2ch) £12.80. **Facilities** Ⓟ (park & ride) ⛩ (outdoor) ♿ (Braille, large print guides, designated parking) toilets for disabled ⊗ (Nov-Feb only - on leads)

Roman Baths & Pump Room

Abbey Church Yard BA1 1LZ

➲ *(M4 junct 18, A46 into city centre)*

☎ 01225 477785

e-mail: romanbaths_bookings@bathnes.gov.uk

web: www.romanbaths.co.uk

The remains of the Roman baths and temple give a vivid impression of life nearly 2,000 years ago. Built next to Britain's only hot spring, the baths served the sick, and the pilgrims visiting the adjacent Temple of Sulis Minerva. Above the Temple Courtyard, the Pump Room became a popular meeting place in the 18th century. The site still flows with natural hot water and no visit is complete without a taste of the famous hot spa water. Costumed characters every afternoon.

Times Open all year, Mar-Jun & Sep-Oct, daily 9-5; Jul & Aug, daily 9am-9pm; Jan-Feb & Nov-Dec, daily 9.30-4-30. Closed 25-26 Dec. (Last exit 1hr after these times). **Fee** ✻ £10.50 (£11.50 Jul-Aug) (ch £6.90). Family ticket £30. Combined ticket with Fashion Museum £14 (ch £8.50). **Facilities** Ⓟ (5 mins walk) (park & ride recommended) 🍽 ♿ (sign language & audio tours) toilets for disabled shop ⊗ (ex assist dogs) ▬

Sally Lunn's Refreshment House & Museum

4 North Pde Passage BA1 1NX

➲ *(centre of Bath, follow signs, next to Bath Abbey)*

☎ 01225 461634

e-mail: enquiries@sallylunns.co.uk

web: www.sallylunns.co.uk

This Tudor building is Bath's oldest house and was a popular 17th-century meeting place. The traditional 'Sally Lunn' is similar to a brioche, and it is popularly believed to carry the name of its first maker who came to Bath in 1680. The bun is still served in the restaurant, and the original oven, Georgian cooking range and a collection of baking utensils are displayed in the museum.

Times Open all year, Museum - Mon-Fri 10-6, Sat 10-5, Sun 11-5. Closed 25-26 Dec. House open Mon-Fri 10-9, Sat 10-10, Sun 11-9. **Fee** ✻ 30p (concessions free). **Facilities** Ⓟ (2-3 min walk) ☕ 🍽 licensed ♿ (toilets and museum only accessible via stairs) (Braille menu available) shop ⊗ (ex assist dogs) ▬

CHARD
MAP 03 ST30

Forde Abbey
2 for 1

TA20 4LU

➲ *(4m SE of Chard, signed from A30 and A358)*

☎ 01460 221290

e-mail: info@fordeabbey.co.uk

web: www.fordeabbey.co.uk

As one of the top gardens in England, Forde Abbey has much to offer keen gardeners. The 30 acres include a colourful bog garden, a walled kitchen garden, cascades, ponds, Ionic temple, rockery, herbaceous borders and the Centenary Fountain, the highest powered fountain in England. The privately owned magnificent 12th-century house contains outstanding Mortlake tapestries, spectacularly decorated plaster ceilings and fine furniture and paintings.

Times Gardens, open all year, daily 10-4.30. House open Apr-Oct, Tue-Fri, Sun & BH 12-4. **Fee** ✳ Gardens £7 (under 15's free, concessions £6.50). House & Gardens £8.80 (ch free, concessions £8.20). **Facilities** ❷ ♿ �🍴 licensed �🅿 (outdoor) ♿ (parts of bog garden not wheelchair accessible. Only great hall accessible in house) (large print guide, computer presentation, w/chair,) toilets for disabled shop garden centre ➡

CLEVEDON
MAP 03 ST47

Clevedon Court

Tickenham Rd BS21 6QU

➲ *(off B3130 1.5m E of Clevedon)*

☎ 01275 872257

e-mail: clevedoncourt@nationaltrust.org.uk

web: www.nationaltrust.org.uk

Clevedon Court is a remarkably complete manor house of around 1320. Additions have been made in each century, so it has a pleasing variety of styles, with an 18th-century, terraced garden.

Times Open 23 Mar-28 Sep, Wed-Thu, Sun & BH Mon 2-5. Car park & Gardens will open at 1.15. **Fee** ✳ £6 (ch £3). Party 20+ by arrangement. **Facilities** ❷ ♿ (access via steps, Braille/large print guide) ❌ 🐾

CRANMORE
MAP 03 ST64

East Somerset Railway
2 for 1

Cranmore Railway Station BA4 4QP

➲ *(on A361 between Frome & Shepton Mallet)*

☎ 01749 880417

e-mail: info@eastsomersetrailway.com

web: www.eastsomersetrailway.com

Steam through the rolling Mendip countryside on a day out at the East Somerset Railway. Take a ride on one of the steam trains and travel back in time to the halcyon days of steam. There are plenty of events throughout the year, from Thomas the Tank Engine and Santa Specials to Enthusiast Gala Weekends. Telephone for details.

Times Open Mar-Dec, wknds; Jun-Aug, Wed & BHs (& Thu in Aug) **Fee** £6.50 (ch £4.50 & pen £5.50) **Facilities** ❷ ♿ �🍴 🅿 ♿ (Partly accessible) (ramp from road to platform & to train) toilets for disabled shop ➡

CRICKET ST THOMAS
MAP 03 ST30

The Wildlife Park at Cricket St Thomas
2 for 1

TA20 4DB

➲ *(3m E of Chard on A30, follow brown heritage signs).*

☎ 01460 30111

e-mail: wildlifepark.cst@bourne-leisure.co.uk

web: www.wild.org.uk

The Wildlife Park offers you the chance to see more than 500 animals at close quarters. Visitors can learn about what is being done to save endangered species, take a walk through the Lemur Wood, or ride on the Safari Train. During peak season, park mascot Larry the Lemur stars in his own show.

Times Open all year, daily 10-6 last admission 4, (10-4.30, last admission 3 in winter). Closed 25 Dec. **Fee** ✳ £8.75 (ch 3-14 £6.50, under 3's free, concessions £7.50). Family ticket £27.50 (2ad+3ch). **Facilities** ❷ ♿ �🍴 🅿 (outdoor) ♿ (some steep slopes) toilets for disabled shop ❌ (ex assist dogs) ➡

DUNSTER
MAP 03 SS94

Dunster Castle

TA24 6SL

➲ *(3m SE of Minehead, approach from A39. Approx 2m from Dunster Stn)*

☎ 01643 821314 & 823004 (info only)

e-mail: dunstercastle@nationaltrust.org.uk

web: www.nationaltrust.org.uk

The castle's picturesque appearance is largely due to 19th-century work, but older features can also be seen, the superb 17th-century oak staircase for example. Sub-tropical plants flourish in the 28-acre park and the terraced gardens are noted for exotica such as a giant lemon tree, yuccas, mimosa and palms as well as the National Collection of Strawberry Trees.

Times Castle: 15 Mar-23 Jul, Fri-Wed 11-4.30; 25 Jul-3 Sep, Fri-Wed 11-5; 5 Sep-2 Nov 11-4.30, Fri-Wed. Garden & Park: 1 Feb-14 Mar & 3 Nov-Jan, all week, 11-4; 15 Mar-2 Nov, all week, 10-5. **Fee** ✳ Castle, Garden & Park £8.60 (ch under 16 £4.20). Family ticket £20.50. Garden & Park only £4.80 (ch under 16 £2.20). Family ticket £11.80 (1 ad £7) **Facilities** ❷ 🅿 ♿ (Braille, large print guides, Batricar & 2 w/chairs) toilets for disabled shop ❌ (ex in park) 🐾

EAST LAMBROOK
MAP 03 ST41

East Lambrook Manor Garden
2 for 1

TA13 5HH

➲ *(signed off A303, at South Petherton rdbt)*

☎ 01460 240328

e-mail: enquiries@eastlambrook.com

web: www.eastlambrook.com

It was the late Margery Fish who created the concept of 'cottage gardening' in the 1940s. Her wonderful Grade I listed gardens are known to garden lovers throughout the world. The gardens now house a collection of Geraniums, a specialist plant nursery, and art gallery. Various events take place throughout the year, please contact or see website for details.

Times Open daily 10-5. Closed 2 wks at Xmas. **Fee** ✳ £3(ch £1 & pen £3.50). Group rate available. **Facilities** ❷ ⊞ (outdoor) ♿ (Partly accessible) (gardens partly accessible) garden centre ⊗ (ex assist dogs) ⚇

FARLEIGH HUNGERFORD   MAP 03 ST85

Farleigh Hungerford Castle

BA2 7RS

⮫ *(3.5m W of Trowbridge on A366)*

☎ 01225 754026

web: www.english-heritage.org.uk

Set in a picturesque valley, this castle hides many secrets and a sinister past. An audio tour reveals all.

Times Open all year, 21 Mar-Jun & Sep, daily 10-5; Jul-Aug, daily 10-6; Oct, daily 10-4; Nov-Mar, Sat-Sun 10-4. Closed 24-26 Dec & 1 Jan. **Fee** £3.50 (concessions £2.80, ch £1.80). Prices and opening times are subject to change in March 2009. Please check web site or call 0870 333 1181 for the most up to date prices and opening times when planning your visit. **Facilities** ❷ shop ⊗ ⚏

GLASTONBURY   MAP 03 ST43

Glastonbury Abbey   `2 for 1`

Abbey Gatehouse, Magdalene St BA6 9EL

⮫ *(on A361 between Frome & Taunton)*

☎ 01458 832267

e-mail: info@glastonburyabbey.com

web: www.glastonburyabbey.com

Few places in Britain are as rich in myth and legend as Glastonbury. Tradition maintains that the impressive ruins mark the birthplace of Christianity in Britain. Joseph of Arimathea is said to have founded a chapel here in AD61, planting his staff in the ground where it flowered both at Christmas and Easter. Later, it is said, King Arthur and Guinevere were buried here, and the abbey has been a place of pilgrimage since the Middle Ages. The present abbey ruins date mostly from the 12th and 13th centuries. The display area contains artefacts

and a model of the Abbey as it might have been in 1539. During the summer months meet a character from the past, who will tell you something of this wonderful place. Thirty-six acres of grounds including two ponds, an orchard and wildlife areas. 4th July 2009: Diocesan Pilgrimage to celebrate the Royal opening of the Abbey in 1909 by the Prince and Princess of Wales.

Times Open all year, daily, Jun-Aug 9-6; Sep-May 9.30-6 or dusk, whichever is the earliest. Dec-Feb open at 10. Closed 25 Dec. **Fee** £5 (ch 5-15 £3, concessions £4.50). Family ticket £14.50 **Facilities** ❷ (charged) ♿ ⊞ (outdoor) ♿ (Partly accessible) (audio tape, deaf loop, wheelchairs, lge print leaflet) toilets for disabled shop ⊗ (ex on leads) ⚇

KINGSDON   MAP 03 ST52

Lytes Cary Manor

TA11 7HU

⮫ *(off A303, signed from Padimore rdbt at junct of A303 & A37, take A372)*

☎ 01458 224471

e-mail: lytescarymanor@nationaltrust.org.uk

web: www.nationaltrust.org.uk

Fine medieval manor house and delightful 14th-century chapel, surrounded by gardens with an enchanting mixture of formality and simplicity. Much of the present house was built in the 16th century although the oldest part, the chapel, dates from 1343. The Great Hall was a 15th-century addition. Unfortunately the gardens did not survive, but the present formal gardens are being restocked with plants that were commonly grown at the time of building, according to the 'Lytes Cary Herbal'-a manuscript still on display within the property. High yew topiary hedges enclose large borders and hidden paths.

Times Open 15 Mar-2 Nov, Sat-Wed 11-5. Open BH. Closes at dusk if earlier than 5. **Fee** ✳ £7 (ch £3.15). Family £17.50. Garden only £5 Ch £2.50 **Facilities** ❷ ♿ ⊞ (outdoor) ♿ (Partly accessible) (Braille guide, scented plants) toilets for disabled ⊗ (ex assist dogs & on lead) ⚇

MINEHEAD   MAP 03 SS94

West Somerset Railway NEW

The Railway Station TA24 5BG

⮫ *(M5 junct 25/26, follow brown WSR sign through Taunton & onto A358. Left after 3m for Bishops Lydeard Station car park)*

☎ 01643 704996

e-mail: info@west-somerset-railway.co.uk

web: www.west-somerset-railway.co.uk

Take a journey of discovery, relive your childhood, or simply sit back and relax as you travel along one of Britain's Best and longest Heritage Railways.

Times Open May-Sep daily, Mar, Apr & Oct Tue-Thu & Sat-Sun, 10.30-5.15. **Fee** ✳ £13.40 (ch £6.70, pen £11.40). Cheaper for shorter journeys. **Facilities** ❷ ♿ ⊞ (outdoor) ♿ toilets for disabled shop ⚇

MONTACUTE
MAP 03 ST41

Montacute House

TA15 6XP

➲ *(4m W of Yeovil, on S side of A3088, 3m E of A303)*

☎ 01935 823289

e-mail: montacute@nationaltrust.org.uk

web: www.nationaltrust.org.uk

Set amidst formal gardens, Montacute House was built by Sir Edward Phelips. He was a successful lawyer, and became Speaker of the House of Commons in 1604. Inside there are decorated ceilings, ornate fireplaces, heraldic glass and fine wood panelling. The Long Gallery displays a permanent collection of Tudor and Jacobean portraits from the National Portrait Gallery in London. Montacute has been used as the setting for successful films such as *Sense and Sensibility* (1995).

Times House: 15 Mar-2 Nov, Wed-Mon, 11-5. Garden & Shop: 1-14 Mar, Wed-Sun 11-4. 15 Mar-2 Nov, Wed-Mon, 11-6. 28 Nov-21 Dec, Wed-Sun, 11-4. **Fee** ✱ House, Garden & Park £9.50 (ch £4.50). Family ticket £23.50. Garden & Park only £5.70 (ch £2.80), Nov-Feb, £2 (ch £1). **Facilities** ℗ ⌒ ⑩ ⊼ (outdoor) ⑤ (Braille guide, 3 manual wheelchairs) toilets for disabled shop garden centre ⊗ (ex in park) ⅏

MUCHELNEY
MAP 03 ST42

Muchelney Abbey

TA10 0DQ

☎ 01458 250664

web: www.english-heritage.org.uk

The monastery was first established at Muchelney by Ine, a 7th-century king of Wessex. It did not survive the Viking invasions, but the abbey was re-founded about AD950 and lasted for nearly six centuries. The present remains date largely from the 12th century. The best preserved feature of the site today is the Abbot's lodging, which had only just been completed in 1539 when the abbey was surrendered to Henry VIII.

Times Open 21 Mar-Jun & Sep, daily 10-5; Jul-Aug, daily 10-6; Oct, daily 10-4. Closed Nov-Mar. **Fee** £3.50 (concessions £2.80, ch £1.80). Prices and opening times are subject to change in March 2009. Please check web site or call 0870 333 1181 for the most up to date prices and opening times when planning your visit. **Facilities** ℗ shop ⊗ ♯♯

NETHER STOWEY
MAP 03 ST13

Coleridge Cottage

35 Lime St TA5 1NQ

➲ *(at W end of Nether Stowey, on S side of A39, 8m W of Bridgwater)*

☎ 01278 732662

e-mail: coleridgecottage@nationaltrust.org.uk

web: www.nationaltrust.org.uk

Discover the former home of Coleridge, who lived in the cottage for three years from 1797. It was here that he wrote *The Rime of the Ancient Mariner*, part of *Christabel*, *Frost at Midnight* and "Kubla Khan". The Coleridge family moved to Nether Stowey in 1797 and became friendly with the Wordsworths who lived nearby.

Times Open 3 Apr-28 Sep, Thu-Sun & BHs 2-5. **Fee** ✱ £3.90 (ch £1.90). **Facilities** ℗ (500yds) ⑤ (steps to entrance, Braille & large print guides) ⊗ ⅏

NUNNEY
MAP 03 ST74

Nunney Castle
FREE

➲ *(3.5m SW of Frome, off A361)*

web: www.english-heritage.org.uk

Built in 1373, and supposedly modelled on France's Bastille, this crenellated manor house has one of the deepest moats in England. It was ruined by Parliamentarian forces in the Civil War.

Times Open at any reasonable time. **Facilities** ♯♯

SPARKFORD
MAP 03 ST62

Haynes International Motor Museum

BA22 7LH

➲ *(from A303 follow A359 towards Castle Cary, museum clearly signed)*

☎ 01963 440804

e-mail: info@haynesmotormuseum.co.uk

web: www.haynesmotormuseum.co.uk

An excellent day out for everyone - with more than 350 cars and bikes stunningly displayed, dating from 1886 to the present day, this is the largest international motor museum in Britain. If you want a nostalgic trip down memory lane the museum offers a host of familiar names such as Austin, MG and Morris, while for those seeking something more exotic, there is a vast array of performance cars, from modern classics such as the Dodge Viper, Jaguar XJ220 and the Ferrari 260, plus the classic Jaguar E Type and AC Cobra. Also on show is a large collection of American cars, including the jewels in the Haynes crown, the V16 Cadillac, and the million-dollar Duesenberg. There's a Kids' Race Track, themed play area, soft play-bus, Super Diggers and plenty of other activities.

Times Open all year, Mar-Oct, daily 9.30-5.30; Nov-Feb, 10-4.30. Closed 24-26 Dec & 1 Jan. **Facilities** ℗ ⑩ ⊼ (outdoor) ⑤ (ramps & loan wheelchairs available) toilets for disabled shop ⊗ (ex assist dogs & in grounds) ⊜

STOKE ST GREGORY
MAP 03 ST32

Willow & Wetlands Visitor Centre
FREE

Meare Green Court TA3 6HY

➲ *(between North Curry & Stoke St Gregory, signed from A361 & A378)*

☎ 01823 490249

e-mail: info@englishwillowbaskets.co.uk

web: www.englishwillowbaskets.co.uk

The centre is owned and run by Somerset Basketmakers and willow growers P H Coate & Son. The environmental exhibition gives a fascinating insight into the Somerset Levels and Moors.

Times Open all year, daily (ex Sun) 9-5. **Facilities** ℗ ⌒ ⊼ (outdoor) ⑤ (some areas of the garden inaccessible) toilets for disabled shop ⊜

STOKE-SUB-HAMDON   MAP 03 ST41

Stoke-Sub-Hamdon Priory   `FREE`

North St TA4 6QP

➲ *(between A303 & A3088)*

☎ 01935 823289

web: www.nationaltrust.org.uk

A complex of buildings, begun in the 14th century for the priests of the Chantry Chapel of St Nicholas (now destroyed).

Times Open 15 Mar-2 Nov, daily 10-6 or dusk if earlier. **Facilities** Ⓟ ⊗ 🅿(on road parking only) ⚇

STREET   MAP 03 ST43

The Shoe Museum   `FREE`

C & J Clark Ltd, High St BA16 0EQ

➲ *(A39 to Street, follow signs for Clarks Village)*

☎ 01458 842169

e-mail: janet.targett@clarks.com

The museum is in the oldest part of the shoe factory set up by Cyrus and James Clark in 1825. It contains shoes from Roman times to the present, buckles, engravings, fashion plates, machinery, hand tools and advertising material.

Times Open all year, Mon-Fri 10-4.45. Closed 10 days over Christmas and BH. **Facilities** Ⓟ At Clarks Village ♿ shop ⊗ (ex assist dogs)

–See advert on this page

TAUNTON   MAP 03 ST22

Hestercombe Gardens

Cheddon Fitzpaine TA2 8LG

➲ *(3m N of Taunton near Cheddon Fitzpaine. Signed from all main roads)*

☎ 01823 413923

e-mail: info@hestercombegardens.com

web: www.hestercombegardens.com

There are three period gardens to enjoy at Hestercombe: the 40-acre Georgian pleasure grounds with woodland walks, temples, Witch House and Great Cascade; the Victorian terrace and recently established Victorian shrubbery; and the Edwardian gardens, where the work of Gertrude Jekyll and architect Edwin Lutyens are shown off to full effect.

Times ✳ Open daily, 10-6 (last admission 5). Closed 25 Dec. **Facilities** Ⓟ ⫴⊙⊦ 🍴 (outdoor) ♿ (Partly accessible) toilets for disabled shop garden centre ⊗ (ex on lead) ⚍

TINTINHULL   MAP 03 ST41

Tintinhull Garden

Farm St BA22 8PZ

➲ *(0.5m S off A303. Follow signs to Tintinhull village, garden is well signed)*

☎ 01935 823289

e-mail: tintinhull@nationaltrust.org.uk

web: www.nationaltrust.org.uk

An attractive, mainly 17th-century manor house with a Queen Anne façade, it stands in two acres of beautiful formal gardens. The gardens were largely created by Mrs Reiss, who gave the property to the National Trust in 1953.

Times Open 15 Mar-2 Nov, Wed-Sun & BH Mons 11-5. Tea room: as garden. **Fee** ✳ £5.40 (ch £2.80). Family £13.50. **Facilities** ℗ ⬜ & (1 Wheelchair, Braille and large print guide) ⊗ (ex assist dogs) ⛟

WASHFORD   MAP 03 ST04

Cleeve Abbey

TA23 0PS

➲ *(0.25m S of A39)*

☎ 01984 640377

web: www.english-heritage.org.uk

This 13th-century monastic site features some of the finest cloister buildings in England; medieval wall paintings, a mosaic tiled floor and an interesting exhibition.

Times Open 21 Mar-Jun & Sep, daily 10-5; Jul-Aug, daily 10-6; Oct, daily 10-4. Closed Nov- Mar. **Fee** £3.50 (concessions £2.80, ch £1.80). Prices and opening times are subject to change in March 2009. Please check web site or call 0870 333 1181 for the most up to date prices and opening times when planning your visit. **Facilities** ℗ ⌂ & shop ⌗

Tropiquaria Animal and Adventure Park

`2 for 1`

TA23 0QB

➲ *(on A39, between Williton and Minehead)*

☎ 01984 640688

e-mail: info@tropiquaria.co.uk

web: www.tropiquaria.co.uk

Housed in a 1930s BBC transmitting station, the main hall has been converted into an indoor jungle with a 15-foot waterfall, tropical plants and free-flying birds. (Snakes, lizards, iguanas, spiders, toads and terrapins are caged!) Downstairs is the submarine crypt with local and tropical marine life. Other features include landscaped gardens, the Shadowstring Puppet Theatre, and 'Wireless in the West' museum. Also two new full size pirate adventure ships are moored on the front lawn accessible to pirates of all ages. The park has an indoor playcastle for adventure and fun whatever the weather.

Times Open Apr-Sep, daily 10.30-6 (last entry 4.30); Oct daily 11-5 (last entry 4); Nov-Mar Wed & wknds 11-4 (last entry 3). **Fee** £7.50 (ch & concessions £6.50). **Facilities** ℗ ⬜ ⌂ (indoor & outdoor) & (aquarium not accessible) (ramp to pirate galleon & indoor castle) toilets for disabled shop ⊗ (ex assist dogs) ⛟

WELLS   MAP 03 ST54

The Bishop's Palace

Henderson Rooms BA5 2PD

➲ *(Follow city centre signs, turn left into Market Pl and enter archway between National Trust shop and post office)*

☎ 01749 678691

e-mail: info@bishopspalacewells.co.uk

web: www.bishopspalacewells.co.uk

Close to the cathedral is the moated bishop's palace. The early part of the palace, the bishop's chapel and the ruins of the banqueting hall date from the 13th century and the undercroft remains virtually unchanged from this time. There are several state rooms and a long gallery which houses portraits of former Bishops. Events include a Living History re-enactment.

Times ✳ Open Apr-Oct, Mon-Fri 10.30-5, Sun noon-5 **Facilities** ℗ (100yds) ⬜ ⍢ ⌂ (outdoor) & (free use of electric wheelchair) shop

WESTON-SUPER-MARE   MAP 03 ST36

The Helicopter Museum

The Heliport, Locking Moor Rd BS24 8PP

➲ *(outskirts of town on A371, nr M5 junct 21, follow propellor signs)*

☎ 01934 635227

e-mail: office@helimuseum.fsnet.co.uk

web: www.helicoptermuseum.co.uk

The world's largest rotary-wing collection and the only helicopter museum in Britain. More than 70 helicopters and autogyros are on display - including examples from France, Germany, Poland, Russia and the United States, from 1935 to the present day - with displays of models, engines and other components explaining the history and development of the rotorcraft. Special events include 'Open Cockpit Days', when visitors can learn more about how the helicopter works. Helicopter flights available on set dates throughout the year.

Times Open all year, Nov-Mar, Wed-Sun 10-4.30; Apr-Oct 10-5.30. Open daily during Etr & summer school hols 10-5.30. Closed 24-26 Dec & 1 Jan. **Fee** ✳ £5.50 (ch under 5 free, ch 5-16 £3.50, concessions £4.50). Family ticket (2ad+2ch) £15.50, (2ad+3ch) £17.50. Party 12+. **Facilities** ℗ ⬜ ⌂ (outdoor) & (large print and Braille information sheet) toilets for disabled shop ⛟

North Somerset Museum

Burlington St BS23 1PR

➲ *(in centre of Weston-super-Mare)*

☎ 01934 621028

e-mail: museum.service@n-somerset.gov.uk

web: www.n-somerset.gov.uk/museum

This museum, housed in the former workshops of the Edwardian Gaslight Company, has displays on the seaside holiday, an old chemist's shop, a dairy and Victorian pavement mosaics. Adjoining the museum is Clara's Cottage, a Westonian home of the 1900s with period kitchen, parlour, bedroom and back yard. One of the rooms has an additional display of Peggy Nisbet dolls. Other displays include wildlife gallery, mining and local archaeology, costume and ceramics.

There is even a display on secret weapons developed on Birnbeck Island during WWII.

Times Open all year Mon-Sat 10-4.30. Closed 24-26 Dec & 1 Jan. **Fee** ✳ £4.10 (ch free when accompanied by an adult, concessions £3.10) **Facilities** ℗ (800yds) (1 disabled parking outside museum) 🖵 & (main museum accessible) (hearing loop at reception) toilets for disabled shop ⊗ (ex assist dogs) ▬

WOOKEY HOLE   MAP 03 ST54

Wookey Hole Caves & Papermill   2 for 1

BA5 1BB

➲ *(M5 junct 22 follow signs via A38 & A371, from Bristol & Bath A39 to Wells then 2m to Wookey Hole)*

☎ 01749 672243

e-mail: witch@wookey.co.uk

web: www.wookey.co.uk

Britain's most spectacular caves and legendary home of the infamous Witch of Wookey. The 19th-century paper mill houses a variety of fascinating attractions including a Cave Museum, Victorian Penny Arcade, Magical Mirror Maze, Haunted Corridor of Crazy Mirrors, and the Wizard's Castle play area. Visitors can also see paper being made in Britain's only surviving handmade paper mill. Puppet theatre shows, magic lessons, an enchanted fairy garden and Dinosaur Valley round off this family day out in Wookey Gorge.

Times Open all year daily Nov-Mar 10-4, Apr-Oct 10-5 (closed 25 Dec) **Fee** ✳ £15 (ch 4-14 & concessions £10, under 3's free) **Facilities** ℗ 🖵 †⊚ licensed ⋈ (outdoor) & (papermill only accessible) toilets for disabled shop ⊗ (ex assist dogs) ▬

YEOVILTON   MAP 03 ST52

Fleet Air Arm Museum

Royal Naval Air Station BA22 8HT

➲ *(on B3151, just off junct of A303 and A37)*

☎ 01935 840565

e-mail: info@fleetairarm.com

web: www.fleetairarm.com

At Fleet Air Arm Museum you will be 'transported' by helicopter to the replica flight deck of aircraft carrier *HMS Ark Royal*. You'll see fighter

FLY NAVY

100 years of WOW!

A MAJOR NEW EXHIBITION CELEBRATING A CENTURY OF NAVAL AVIATION

FLEET AIR ARM experience!

EUROPE'S LARGEST NAVAL AVIATION MUSEUM

PLUS! EXPERIENCE LIFE ON AN AIRCRAFT CARRIER GO ON BOARD CONCORDE & MUCH MORE

Fleet Air Arm Museum, RNAS Yeovilton, Somerset BA22 8HT www.fleetairarm.com tel: 01935 840565

aircraft and two enormous projection screens showing jet fighters taking off and landing, and even a nuclear bomb. The Museum has Europe's largest collection of naval aircraft and the first British-built Concorde. Go on board and visit the cockpit. There's an adventure playground, and the museum is located alongside Europe's busiest military air station at RNAS Yeovilton.

Times Open all year: Apr-Oct 10-5.30, Nov-Mar Wed-Sun 10-4.30 (Closed 24-26 Dec) **Fee** £10.50 (ch under 17 £7.50, under 5 free, concessions £8.50). Family (2ad+3ch) £32. **Facilities** ℗ 🖵 †⊚ licensed ⋈ (outdoor) & (wheelchairs available) toilets for disabled shop ⊗ (ex assist dogs) ▬

See advert on this page

STAFFORDSHIRE

Thor's Cave, Peak District National Park

ALTON
MAP 07 SK04

Alton Towers
ST10 4DB

➲ *(from S - M1 junct 23a or M6 junct 15. From N - M1 junct 24a or M6 junct 16)*

☎ 08705 204060

e-mail: info@alton-towers.com

web: www.altontowers.com

Alton Towers is one of the UK's most popular attractions. With world first rides as well as some beautiful gardens, this is more than just a theme park. The Alton Towers Resort is a popular UK short break destination for families including Alton Towers Theme Park, waterpark, spa, two fully themed hotels and two nine-hole golf courses.

Times Open daily 14-22 Feb & 28 Mar-1 Nov. Hotels, waterpark, spa and golf open all year. **Fee** ✳ Advance booked - Adults from £28 (ch from £21) **Facilities** ❷ (charged) ⬛ 🍴 licensed ⯅ (outdoor) ♿ (disabled guest guide books) toilets for disabled shop ⊗ (ex assist dogs) ▭

BIDDULPH
MAP 07 SJ85

Biddulph Grange Garden
Grange Rd ST8 7SD

➲ *(access from A527, Tunstall-Congleton road. Entrance on Grange Rd 0.5m N of Biddulph)*

☎ 01782 517999

e-mail: biddulphgrange@nationaltrust.org.uk

web: www.nationaltrust.org.uk

This exciting and rare survival of a high Victorian garden has undergone extensive restoration. Conceived by James Bateman, the fifteen acres are divided into a number of smaller gardens which were designed to house specimens from his extensive plant collection.

Times Open 1-9 Mar, Sat-Sun, 11-4; 15 Mar-2 Nov, Wed-Sun, 11-5; 8 Nov-21 Dec, Sat-Sun, 11-3 **Fee** ✳ Mar-Oct £6.40 (ch £3.20). Family ticket £14.90; Nov-Dec £2.40 (ch £1.20). Family ticket £5.60. **Facilities** ❷ ⬛ ⯅ (outdoor) ♿ (not suitable for people with mobility problems) toilets for disabled shop ⊗ (ex assist dogs) ▱ ▭

CHEDDLETON
MAP 07 SJ95

Cheddleton Flint Mill
Beside Caldon Canal, Leek Rd ST13 7HL

➲ *(3m S of Leek on A520)*

☎ 01782 502907

web: www.people.ex.ac.uk/akoutram/cheddleton-mill

Twin water-wheels on the River Churnet drive flint-grinding pans in the two mills. Museum collection of machinery used in the preparation of materials for the ceramic industry. This includes a 100 HP Robey horizontal steam engine, model Newcomen beam engine, edge-runner mill. Display panels explain the processes of winning and treating clays, stone and flint for the pottery industry.

Times Open all year, Sat & Sun 2-5, Mon-Fri 10-5 (by arrangement). Phone to check **Fee** ✳ Entrance free (all donations gratefully accepted). **Facilities** ❷ ♿ (Partly accessible) (not accessible upstairs for wheelchairs) toilets for disabled

Churnet Valley Railway
The Station ST13 7EE

➲ *(3m S from Leek, 3m N from Cellarhead along A520. Kingsley & Froghall Station is situated on the Stoke to Ashbourne road, A52)*

☎ 01538 360522

e-mail: enquiries@churnetvalleyrailway.co.uk

web: www.churnetvalleyrailway.co.uk

The Churnet Valley Railway runs through the hidden countryside between Cheddleton, with its Grade II Victorian station, Kingsley and Froghall, and Canal Wharf. The journey incorporates Consall, which has a sleepy rural station and nature reserve, and Leekbrook with one of the longest tunnels on a preserved railway. Special Events: 1940s wknd Apr, Ghost Train Oct, Santa and Steam Dec.

Times Open every Mar-Oct, Sun; Jun-Sep, Sat; Jul-Aug, Wed; Aug, Mon & all BH Mon. **Facilities** ❷ ⬛ ⯅ (outdoor) ♿ (ramps) toilets for disabled shop ▭

HALFPENNY GREEN   MAP 07 SO89

Halfpenny Green Vineyards   FREE

DY7 5EP

⮑ *(0.5m off B4176 Dudley to Telford road)*

☎ 01384 221122

e-mail: enquiries@halfpenny-green-vineyards.co.uk

web: www.halfpenny-green-vineyards.co.uk

Using German, French and hybrid varieties that can prosper even in the poorest British summer, this vineyard offers "The complete English wine experience." This includes a self-guided vineyard trail as well as guided tours, wine-tasting, a craft centre and a visitor centre. Visitors can purchase wines with personalised labels for special occasions. Coarse fishing is also available.

Times Open all year, daily 10-5. **Facilities** ℗ ⌑ ⁍⬦ licensed ⅋ toilets for disabled shop garden centre ⊗ (ex assist dogs) ▭

HIMLEY   MAP 07 SO89

Himley Hall & Park

DY3 4DF

⮑ *(off A449, on B4176)*

☎ 01384 817817

e-mail: himley.hall@dudley.gov.uk

The extensive parkland offers a range of attractions, including a nine-hole golf course and coarse fishing. The hall is open to the public when exhibitions are taking place. Permanent orienteering course, a charge is made for the maps. Guided tours at the hall available by prior arrangement. The Hall is available for private hire. There are also a large variety of outdoor events and concerts.

Times Open Hall: 4 Apr-13 Sep, Tue-Sun 2-5, BH Mon 2-5 **Fee** Free admission except for special events **Facilities** ℗ (charged) ⌑ ⅋ toilets for disabled ⊗ (ex assist dogs & in park)

LEEK   MAP 07 SJ95

Blackbrook Zoological Park

Winkhill ST13 7QR

⮑ *(off A523 Leek to Ashbourne road)*

☎ 01538 308293

e-mail: enquiries@blackbrookzoologicalpark.co.uk

web: www.blackbrookzoologicalpark.co.uk

Blackbrook Zoological Park is a fun and educational day for all. A continually growing attraction, always with something new to see. The zoo features: mammals, rare birds, reptiles, insects and aquatics; owl flights, pelican, penguin and lemur feeds. Blackbrook Zoological Park is fully accessible for pushchairs and wheelchairs.

Times Open daily 10-5.30; Winter 10.30-dusk (last admission 4) **Fee** ✳ £8.50 (ch £5, under 3 free, concessions £6.50) **Facilities** ℗ ⌑ ⌂ (outdoor) ⅋ (fully accessible) toilets for disabled shop ⊗ (ex assist dogs) ▭

LICHFIELD   MAP 07 SK10

Erasmus Darwin House   2 for 1

Beacon St WS13 7AD

⮑ *(signed to Lichfield Cathedral. Access by foot through cathedral close at West End)*

☎ 01543 306260

e-mail: enquiries@erasmusdarwin.org

web: www.erasmusdarwin.org

The House is dedicated to Erasmus Darwin, the grandfather of Charles Darwin, and a talented doctor, inventor, philosopher, poet and founder member of the Lunar Society. A resident of Lichfield for more than 20 years, the displays are contained within his beautiful 18th-century home, and recreate the story of Erasmus' life, ideas and inventions, through period rooms, audio visual and interactive displays. 2009 will see events to mark the 200th anniversary of Charles Darwin's birth.

Times Open Apr-Sep, Tue-Sun noon-5; Oct-Mar, Thu-Sun noon-5. (Last admission 4.15). **Fee** £3 (ch £1, concessions £2.50). Family ticket (2ad+2ch) £6. **Facilities** ℗ (across road) (Pay and Display) ⅋ (audio tour) toilets for disabled shop ⊗ (ex assist dogs)

Lichfield Cathedral

WS13 7LD

⮑ *(Signed from all major roads and within city).*

☎ 01543 306100

e-mail: enquiries@lichfield-cathedral.org

web: www.lichfield-cathedral.org

The Cathedral's three spires, known as the Ladies of the Vale, dominate the landscape. The first cathedral here was founded in AD700 to house the shrine of St Chad. The present building, with its elaborate carvings, has been much restored since it was attacked during the Civil War. Among its treasures are an 8th-century illuminated manuscript, the St Chad Gospels, a collection of modern silver and the 16th-century Flemish glass in the Lady Chapel. Many musical events take place here. Please check website for details of latest events.

Times Open daily 7.30-6.15. **Fee** ✳ Suggested donation of £5 for each adult visitor. **Facilities** ℗ (200mtrs) (no parking ex disabled in close) ⌑ ⁍⬦ ⅋ (touch & hearing centre for blind) toilets for disabled shop ⊗ (ex assist dogs)

Samuel Johnson Birthplace Museum   FREE

Breadmarket St WS13 6LG

⮑ *(located in city centre market place)*

☎ 01543 264972

e-mail: sjmuseum@lichfield.gov.uk

web: www.samueljohnsonbirthplace.org.uk

Dr Samuel Johnson, author of the famous English dictionary of 1755, lexicographer, poet, critic, biographer and personality. One of England's greatest writers, Dr Johnson was born in this house in 1709. The birthplace now houses a museum dedicated to his extraordinary life, work and personality. Five floors of exhibits featuring period room settings, introductory video and personal items owned by Johnson, his family and his famous friends. Please see the website for special events. Johnson's 300th birthday in 2009 will be celebrated by a variety of events.

Times Open daily Apr-Sep 10.30-4.30; Oct-Mar 11-3.30. **Facilities** ℗ (500yds) ♿ (Partly accessible) (large print text literature, induction loop system) shop ⊗ (ex assist dogs)

SHUGBOROUGH   MAP 07 SJ92

Shugborough Estate

ST17 0XB

⮕ *(6m E of Stafford off A513, signed from M6 junct 13)*

☎ 01889 881388

e-mail: shugborough.promotions@staffordshire.gov.uk
web: www.shugborough.org.uk

Journey through the historic estate of Shugborough and discover a bygone era as the costumed living history characters bring the past to life. The story begins in the walled garden - meet the gardeners of 1805 and find out how fruit and vegetables are grown on the estate. At the farm the servants are busy making butter and cheese and the farm hands tend to the animals. Then take a short ride on Lucy the Train or walk across the stunning parkland. The story continues in the Servants' Quarters where cooks and kitchen maids scurry about, preparing food on the range, starching the whites in the laundry and brewing ale in the wood-fired brewery. The Mansion House completes the story, where the 1805 Viscount and Lady Anson are often present.

Times ✳ Open 18 Mar-28 Oct, daily 11-5. Site open all year to pre-booked parties. **Facilities** ℗ (charged) 🍴🍽🅿 (outdoor) ♿ (6 wheelchairs, 2 Batricars avail) toilets for disabled shop ⊗ (ex assist dogs & in parkland) 🐾═

STAFFORD   MAP 07 SJ92

Shire Hall Gallery   `FREE`

Market Square ST16 2LD

⮕ *(Stafford is 3m from the M6 junct 13 or 14, the gallery is located in the pedestrianised area of the town centre, 5 min walk from the railway)*

☎ 01785 278345

e-mail: shirehallgallery@staffordshire.gov.uk
web: www.staffordshire.gov.uk/sams

With free entry and an exciting activities programme, there's something for everyone at the Shire Hall Gallery, Staffordshire's largest venue for contemporary arts and crafts. Visit our historic courtroom, or book a play session in our multi-sensory room. Shire Hall Gallery will be celebrating its 15th year in September 2009. Please contact the Gallery for the latest exhibition and activities leaflet.

Times Open all year Mon & Wed-Sat, 9.30-5; Tue 10-5; Sun 1-4. Gallery closes for exhibition changes and at BHs, please call for further details.
Facilities ℗ (5 mins walk) 🍴♿ (Partly accessible) (Wheelchair lifts to some areas, hearing loop) toilets for disabled shop ⊗ (ex assist dogs) ═

STOKE-ON-TRENT   MAP 07 SJ84

Ceramica

Market Place, Burslem ST6 3DS

⮕ *(A4527 (signposted Tunstall). After 0.5m right onto B5051 for Burslem. Ceramica is in Old Town Hall in centre of town.)*

☎ 01782 832001

e-mail: info@ceramicauk.com
web: www.ceramicauk.com

A unique experience for all the family, Ceramica is housed in the Old Town Hall in the centre of Burslem, Mother Town of the Potteries. Explore the hands-on activities in Bizarreland, and learn how clay is transformed into china. Dig into history with the time team and take a magic carpet ride over the town. Discover the past, present and future of ceramics with the interactive displays in the Pavillions. Explore the Memory Bank and read the local news on Ceramica TV.

Times ✳ Open all year Mon-Sat 9.30-5, Sun 10.30-4.30. For Xmas opening please telephone. **Facilities** ℗ (charged) 🅿 (indoor) ♿ (ramps, lift to all floors, tactile displays) toilets for disabled shop ⊗ (ex assist dogs) ═

Gladstone Working Pottery Museum

Uttoxeter Rd, Longton ST3 1PQ

⮕ *(A50 then follow brown heritage signs)*

☎ 01782 237777

e-mail: gladstone@stoke.gov.uk
web: www.stoke.gov.uk/gladstone

Located at the heart of the Potteries, Gladstone Pottery Museum is the last remaining Victorian Pottery industry. Whilst touring the original factory building discover what it was like for the men, women and children to live and work in a potbank during the era of the coal firing bottle ovens. In original workshops working potters can be found demonstrating traditional pottery skills. There are also lots of opportunities for you to have a go at pottery making, throw your own pot on the potters wheel, make china flowers and decorate pottery items to take home. Also explore Flushed with Pride, dedicated to the story of the development of the toilet, and The Tile Gallery, a fine collection which traces the development of decorative tiles.

Times ✳ Open all year, daily 10-5 (last admission 4). Limited opening Xmas & New Year. **Facilities** ℗ 🍴🍽♿ (electric buggy available to loan) toilets for disabled shop ⊗ (ex assist dogs) ═

The Potteries Museum &   `FREE`
Art Gallery

Bethesda St, Hanley ST1 3DW

⮕ *(M6 junct 15/16 take A500 to Stoke-on-Trent. Follow signs for city centre (Hanley), Cultural Quarter & The Potteries Museum)*

☎ 01782 232323

e-mail: museums@stoke.gov.uk
web: www.stoke.gov.uk/museums

The history of the Potteries under one roof, including a dazzling display of the world's finest collection of Staffordshire ceramics. Other displays

CONTINUED

STOKE-ON-TRENT CONTINUED

introduce natural, local and archaeological history from in and around The Potteries, and a Mark 16 Spitfire commemorating its locally born designer - Reginald Mitchell.

Times ✳ Open Mar-Oct, Mon-Sat 10-5, Sun 2-5; Nov-Feb, Mon-Sat 10-4, Sun 1-4. Closed 25 Dec-1 Jan. **Facilities** 🅿 (charged) 🖵 & (lift, induction loop, 2 wheelchairs available) toilets for disabled shop ⊗ (ex assist dogs) ⬛

Wedgwood Visitor Centre   `2 for 1`

Barlaston ST12 9ES

↪ *(From M1, via A50 follow tourist signs to Stoke. From M6 junct 15 follow brown tourist signs)*

☎ 01782 282986

e-mail: bookings@wedgwood.com

web: www.thewedgwoodvisitorcentre.com

At the Wedgwood Visitor Centre the whole family can share in almost 250 years of history and heritage that is still being lived today. Nothing is stage-managed or recreated just for visitors. What you see is the continuing life of this successful English manufacturer and exporter of fine quality ceramics. The tour features a film theatre, two exhibition areas, and a hands-on area. 2009 is the 250th anniversary of Wedgwood.

Times Open all year, Mon-Fri 9-5, Sat & Sun 10-5. Shop open Sun 10-4 (ex Etr Sun). Closed 25 Dec **Fee** Wkdays £8.25 (concessions £6.25). Family £28. Wknds & Fri pm £6.25 (concessions £4.25). Family £20. **Facilities** 🅿 🖵 🍽 licensed & toilets for disabled shop ⊗ (ex assist dogs) ⬛

TAMWORTH   MAP 07 SK20

Drayton Manor Theme Park

B78 3TW

↪ *(M42 junct 9/10, on A4091. Exit at T2 of M6 toll)*

☎ 0844 4721950   0844 4721960

e-mail: info@draytonmanor.co.uk

web: www.draytonmanor.co.uk

A popular family theme park with over 100 rides and attractions suitable for all the family, set in 280 acres of parkland and lakes. Drayton Manor has been run by the same family for 60 years, and

features world-class rides like rollercoaster sensation 'G-Force', 'Apocalypse'- the world's first stand-up tower drop, 'Stormforce 10' - the best water ride in the country and 'Shockwave' - Europe's only stand-up rollercoaster. 'ThomasLand', which opened in 2008, features Thomas and Percy trains and themed rides for adults and children. There's an award-winning zoo and a penny slot machine museum plus plenty of special events throughout the year.

Times Park & Rides open mid Mar-Oct. Rides from 10.30-5, 6 or 7. Zoo open all year. 'ThomasLand' also open winter wknds. **Fee** Please telephone 0844 4721950 for prices or 0844 4721960 for ticket offers, or visit website for details. **Facilities** 🅿 🖵 🍽 licensed 🍴 (indoor & outdoor) & (some rides limited access due to steps, ramps or lifts to most rides) toilets for disabled shop garden centre ⊗ (ex in park & assist dogs) ⬛

See advert on page 6

Tamworth Castle   `2 for 1`

Holbway Lodge B79 7NA

↪ *(M42 junct 10 & M6 junct 12, access via A5)*

☎ 01827 709629   & 709626

e-mail: heritage@tamworth.gov.uk

web: www.tamworthcastle.co.uk

Tamworth Castle is located in the centre of the town. Owned by six wealthy and influential families over the centuries, the medieval motte and bailey castle has welcomed a number of royal visitors including King Henry II, King James I and his son Prince Charles. The ancient sand stone tower and shell wall still dominate views of the Castle today. While visiting this scheduled ancient monument witness the magnificent late medieval Great hall, grand Tudor Chambers and Victorian suite of reception rooms. The castle hosts a varied and exciting events programme and is also an ideal wedding location.

Times Open Apr-Sep, Tue-Sun 12-5.15; Oct-Mar, Sat & Sun 12-5.15 (last admission 4.30). **Fee** ✳ £4.95 (ch £2.95 & pen £3.95). Family £13.65. Prices subject to change. **Facilities** 🅿 (100yds & 400yds) 🖵 🍴 (outdoor) & (ground floor access only) (one wheelchair for use inside the castle) shop ⊗ (ex assist dogs) ⬛

See advert on opposite page

TRENTHAM · MAP 07 SJ94

Trentham Monkey Forest

Trentham Estate, Southern Entrance, Stone Rd ST4 8AY

➲ *(M6 junct 15, 5 mins drive to A34 direction Stone)*

☎ 01782 659845

e-mail: info@monkey-forest.com
web: www.monkey-forest.com

A unique experience for everyone - come to the only place in Britain where you can walk amongst 140 Barbary macaques roaming free in 60 acres of forest. Walking in the park, you are transported into a different world through close contact with the monkeys. Guides are situated all along the path to give information and there are feeding talks every hour.

Times Open Feb-Mar & Nov, wknds & school hols, 10-4; daily Apr-Oct 10-5 (Jul & Aug 10-6) **Fee** £6 (ch under 3 free, ch 3-14 £4.50). Groups 20+ £5 (ch £3.50) **Facilities** ℗ ☐ 묘 (outdoor) ❤ (Partly accessible) toilets for disabled shop ⊗ ➡

WALL · MAP 07 SK10

Wall Roman Site   FREE

Watling St WS14 0AW

➲ *(off A5)*

☎ 01543 480768

web: www.english-heritage.org.uk

Explore the haunting remains of a 2,000 year old wayside staging post situated along Watling Street, the famous Kent to North Wales Roman road.

Times Site open: Mar-Oct, daily 10-5; Museum 21 Mar-Oct, last Sun & Mon of each month 10-5. Closed Nov-Feb. **Facilities** ℗ shop 🎌 🐾

WESTON PARK · MAP 07 SJ81

Weston Park

TF11 8LE

➲ *(on A5 at Weston-under-Lizard, 30min from central Birmingham 3m off M54 junct 3 and 8m off M6 junct 12).*

☎ 01952 852100

e-mail: enquiries@weston-park.com
web: www.weston-park.com

Built in 1671, this fine mansion stands in elegant gardens and a vast park designed by 'Capability' Brown. Three lakes, a miniature railway, and a woodland adventure playground are to be found in the grounds, and in the house itself there is a magnificent collection of pictures, furniture and tapestries. There is also an animal centre and Deer Park.

Times ✳ Open wknds from 15 Apr-Jul, then daily until 3 Sep. **Facilities** ℗ ☐ ℃ 묘 ❤ (disabled route, access to restaurant & shop) toilets for disabled shop ➡

ENGLAND

Staffordshire Regiment Museum

Whittington Barracks WS14 9PY

➲ *(on A51 between Lichfield/Tamworth)*

☎ 01543 434394 & 434395

e-mail: curator@staffordshireregimentmuseum.com

Located next to Whittington Barracks, the museum tells the story of the soldiers of the Staffordshire Regiment and its predecessors. Exhibits include vehicles, uniforms, weapons, medals and memorabilia relating to three hundred years of regimental history, including distinguished service in the First and Second World Wars and the Gulf War. Visitors can experience a World War I trench system with sound effects and a World War II Anderson shelter.

Times Open all year, Mon-Fri 10-4.30 (last admission 4); also Apr-Oct wknds and BH 12.30-4.30. Closed Xmas-New Year. Parties at other times by arrangement. **Fee** £3 (ch £2, concessions £2). Family ticket £6. Regimental Association Members & serving Mercian soldiers free. **Facilities** ℗ 🏕 (outdoor) ♿ (ramps, lowered kerbs, graded access to attraction) toilets for disabled shop ⊗ (ex assist dogs)

The Dorothy Clive Garden

TF9 4EU

➲ *(on A51 between Nantwich & Stone)*

☎ 01630 647237

e-mail: info@dorothyclivegarden.co.uk

web: www.dorothyclivegarden.co.uk

This 12-acre, 200-year-old gravel quarry was converted by Colonel Harry Clive, who began landscaping in 1939 to create a garden for his wife, Dorothy. Today the garden boasts superb woodland with cascading waterfall, an alpine scree and spectacular summer borders which drift along the hillside down to a tranquil lily pond. A host of spring bulbs, magnificent displays of rhododendrons and azaleas, and stunning autumn colours are among the seasonal highlights.

Times Open daily 28 Mar-27 Sep, 10-5.30. **Fee** £5 (ch up to 16 free, concessions £4.50). **Facilities** ℗ ⊡ ♿ (Partly accessible) (wheelchairs for use, special route) toilets for disabled ▬

Mow Cop folly

SUFFOLK

Beach Huts at Southwold

ENGLAND

BURY ST EDMUNDS   MAP 05 TL86

Moyse's Hall Museum

Cornhill IP33 1DX

➾ *(take Bury central exit from A14, follow signs for town centre, museum situated in town centre)*

☎ 01284 706183

e-mail: moyses.hall@stedsbc/gov.uk

web: www.stedmundsbury.gov.uk/moyses.htm

Moyse's Hall is a 12th-century Norman house built of flint and stone which now serves as a local history museum, and among the fascinating exhibits are memorabilia of the notorious William Corder "Murder in the Red Barn". Other collections include the history of the town, archaeology and the Suffolk Regiment.

Times ✳ Open all year, Mon-Fri 10.30-4.30, Sat & Sun 11-4. Closed 25-27 Dec & all BH. **Facilities** ℗ (200yds 1hr max) Long term parking, short walk ㅤ (stairlift, lift, hearing loop, w/chair) toilets for disabled shop ⊗ (ex assist dogs)

EAST BERGHOLT   MAP 05 TM03

Flatford: Bridge Cottage

Flatford CO7 6UL

➾ *(On N bank of Stour, 1m S of East Bergholt B1070)*

☎ 01206 298260

e-mail: flatfordbridgecottage@nationaltrust.org.uk

web: www.nationaltrust.org.uk/flatford

Bridge Cottage, Flatford Mill and Willy Lott's House were the subject of several of John Constable's paintings. Today you can take a tour of the sites of his paintings and enjoy some of the best walks you could wish for in the beautiful unspoilt countryside of the Dedham vale.

Times Open Jan-Feb Sat-Sun 11-3.30, Mar-Apr Wed-Sun 11-5, May-Sep daily 10.30-5.30, Oct daily 11-4, Nov-20 Dec Wed-Sun 11-3.30 **Fee** ✳ Bridge Cottage free. Guided walks (when available) £2.50 (ch free). **Facilities** ℗ (charged) ㅤㅤ (wheelchair/electric runaround available) shop ⊗ (ex assist dogs) ㅤ

EASTON   MAP 05 TM25

Easton Farm Park

IP13 0EQ

➾ *(signed from A12 at Wickam Market, and from A1120)*

☎ 01728 746475

e-mail: info@eastonfarmpark.co.uk

web: www.eastonfarmpark.co.uk

Award winning Farm Park on the banks of the River Deben. There are lots of breeds of farm animals, including Suffolk Punch horses, ponies, pigs, lambs, calves, goats, rabbits, guinea pigs and poultry. Chicks hatching and egg collecting daily. Free hug-a-bunny and pony rides every day.

Times ✳ Open Mar-end Sep, daily 10.30-6. Also open Feb & Oct half term hols and wknds in Dec. **Facilities** ℗ ㅤㅤ (indoor & outdoor) ㅤ (Partly accessible) (special parking and wheelchairs) toilets for disabled shop ▬

EUSTON   MAP 05 TL87

Euston Hall

IP24 2QP

➾ *(on A1088, 3m S of Thetford)*

☎ 01842 766366

e-mail: lcampbell@euston-estate.co.uk

web: www.eustonhall.co.uk

Home of the Duke and Duchess of Grafton, this 18th-century house is notable for its fine collection of pictures, by Stubbs, Lely, Van Dyck and other Masters. The grounds were laid out by John Evelyn, William Kent and `Capability' Brown, and include a 17th-century church in the style of Wren and a river walk to the restored watermill.

Times Open 18 Jun-17 Sep, Thu only. Also open Sun 28 Jun, 12 Jul & 6 Sep. **Fee** ✳ £6 (ch 5-16 £3, concessions £5). Parties 12+ £5 each. Ground only £3. **Facilities** ℗ ㅤㅤ (outdoor) ㅤ (first floor of hall not accessible) toilets for disabled shop ⊗ (ex assist dogs)

FLIXTON   MAP 05 TM38

Norfolk & Suffolk Aviation Museum   FREE

Buckeroo Way, The Street NR35 1NZ

➾ *(off A143, take B1062, 2m W of Bungay)*

☎ 01986 896644

e-mail: aviationmuseumfl@aol.com

web: www.aviationmuseum.net

Situated in the Waveney Valley, the museum has over 50 historic aircraft. There is also a Bloodhound surface-to-air missile, the 446th Bomb Group Museum, RAF Bomber Command Museum, the Royal Observer Corps Museum, RAF Air-Sea Rescue and Coastal Command and a souvenir shop. Among the displays are Decoy Sites and Wartime Deception, Fallen Eagles - Wartime Luftwaffe Crashes and an ex-Ipswich airport hangar made by Norwich company Boulton and Paul Ltd.

Times Open Apr-Oct, Sun-Thu 10-5 (last admission 4); Nov-Mar, Tue, Wed & Sun 10-4 (last admission 3). Closed late Dec-early Jan. **Facilities** ℗ ㅤ ㅤ (outdoor) ㅤ (helper advised, ramps/paths to all buildings) toilets for disabled shop ⊗ (ex on lead)

FRAMLINGHAM   MAP 05 TM26

Framlingham Castle

IP8 9BT

➲ *(on B1116)*

☎ 01728 724189

web: www.english-heritage.org.uk

Walk the 12th-century battlements that encircle the castle site with their impressive thirteen towers. Exceptional views over the countryside and a very popular audio tour.

Times Open all year, 21 Mar-Sep, daily 10-6; Oct, daily 10-5; Nov-Mar, Thur-Mon 10-4. (May close early for events. Please call to check). Closed 24-26 Dec & 1 Jan. **Fee** £5.50 (concessions £4.40, ch £2.80). Family ticket £13.80. Prices and opening times are subject to change in March 2009. Please check web site or call 0870 333 1181 for the most up to date prices and opening times when planning your visit. **Facilities** ❽ shop ⏣

HORRINGER   MAP 05 TL86

Ickworth House, Park & Gardens

The Rotunda IP29 5QE

➲ *(2.5m SW of Bury St Edmunds in village of Horringer on A143)*

☎ 01284 735270

e-mail: ickworth@ntrust.org.uk

web: www.nationaltrust.org.uk/ickworth

The eccentric Earl of Bristol created this equally eccentric house, begun in 1795, to display his collection of European art. The Georgian Silver Collection is considered the finest in private hands. 'Capability' Brown designed the parkland, and also featured are a vineyard, waymarked walks and an adventure playground.

Times Open: House 14 Mar-1 Nov, Mon-Tue, Fri-Sun & BHs, 11-5, Oct-2 Nov, Mon-Tue, Fri-Sun & BHs. Garden Feb-13 Mar & 2 Nov-Jan daily, 11-4; 14 Mar-1 Nov daily 10-5. Park: daily 8-8. **Fee** House, Garden & Park £8.95 (ch £3.30). Family £21. Garden & Park £4.50 (ch £1.30). Family £10.10 **Facilities** ❽ ❍❙ ⋒ (outdoor) ♿ (Braille guide, batricars, hearing loop, large print guides) toilets for disabled shop ❽ (ex assist dogs and on lead) ⚑ ➡

IPSWICH   MAP 05 TM14

Christchurch Mansion   FREE

Soane St IP4 2BE

➲ *(S side of Christchurch Park, close to town centre)*

☎ 01473 433554 & 213761

e-mail: museums.service@ipswich.gov.uk

web: www.ipswich.gov.uk

The house was built in 1548 on the site of an Augustinian priory. Set in a beautiful park, it displays period rooms and an art gallery which has changing exhibitions. The Suffolk Artists' Gallery has a collection of paintings by Constable and Gainsborough.

Times Open all year, Mon-Sun 10-5. Closed Good Fri, 24-26 Dec & 1 Jan. **Facilities** ❽ (10 min walk) ⟐ ♿ (Partly accessible) toilets for disabled shop ❽

Ipswich Museum   FREE

High St IP1 3QH

➲ *(follow tourist signs to Crown St car park. Museum 3 mins walk)*

☎ 01473 433550

e-mail: museum.service@ipswich.gov.uk

web: www.ipswich.gov.uk

The Museum has sections on Victorian Natural History, Suffolk wildlife, Suffolk geology, Roman Suffolk, Anglo-Saxon Ipswich and Peoples of the World. There is also one of the best bird collections in the country.

Times Open all year, Tue-Sat 10-5. Closed Sun, Mon, Good Friday, 24-26 Dec & 1 Jan. **Facilities** ❽ (3 min walk) ♿ (lift) toilets for disabled shop ❽ (ex assist dogs)

LAVENHAM   MAP 05 TL94

Lavenham The Guildhall of Corpus Christi

Market Place CO10 9QZ

➲ *(Lavenham Market Place. A1141 & B1071)*

☎ 01787 247646

e-mail: lavenhamguildhall@nationaltrust.org.uk

web: www.nationaltrust.org.uk/regions/eastofengland

The Guildhall of Corpus Christi is one of the finest timber framed buildings in Britain. It was built around 1530 by the prosperous Corpus Christi Guild, for religious rather than commercial reasons. The hall now houses a local history museum telling the story of Lavenham's 15th- and 16th-century cloth-trade riches. Visitors can also see the walled garden with its 19th-century lock-up and mortuary.

Times Open 7 Mar-29 Mar, Wed-Sun, 11-4. Apr-1 Nov, Mon-Sun 11-5, 7 Nov-29 Nov, Sat-Sun 11-4. **Fee** Gift Aid admission prices £4.20 (ch £1.55). Family ticket £10.15 Gift aid admission includes a voluntary donation but visitors can choose to pay the standard prices displayed at the property and on the website. **Facilities** ❽ (adjacent) ⟐ ♿ (Partly accessible) (photo album of museum, Braille guide) shop ❽ (ex assist dogs) ⚑

ENGLAND

Leiston Abbey

IP16 4TB

⮑ *(N of Leiston, off B1069)*

☎ 01728 831354 & 832500

e-mail: admin@leistonabbey.co.uk

web: www.leistonabbey.co.uk

For hundreds of years this 14th-century abbey was used as a farm and its church became a barn. A Georgian house, now used as a school for young musicians, was built into its fabric and remains of the choir, the church transepts and parts of the cloisters still stand.

Times ✳ Open at any reasonable time. **Facilities** ℗ ⊗ (ex on lead)

Long Shop Museum

Main St IP16 4ES

⮑ *(Turn off A12, follow B1119 from Saxmundham to Leiston. Museum is in the middle of town)*

☎ 01728 832189

e-mail: longshop@care4free.net

web: www.longshop.care4free.net

Discover the Magic of Steam through a visit to the world famous traction engine manufacturers. Trace the history of the factory and Richard Garrett engineering. See the traction engines and road rollers in the very place that they were built. Soak up the atmosphere of the Long Shop, built in 1852 as one of the first production line engineering halls in the world. An award-winning museum with five exhibition halls full of items from the glorious age of steam and covering 200 years of local, social and industrial history.

Times Open Apr-Oct, Mon-Sat 10-5, Sun 11-5. **Facilities** ℗ ᴙ (outdoor) ♿ (wheelchair available) toilets for disabled shop ⊗ (ex assist dogs)

St James' Chapel (Lindsey)   FREE

Rose Green

⮑ *(on unclass road 0.5m E of Rose Green)*

web: www.english-heritage.org.uk

Built mainly in the 13th century, this small thatched, flint-and-stone chapel incorporates some earlier work.

Times Open all year, daily 10-4. **Facilities** ⊗ ⌗

Kentwell Hall

CO10 9BA

⮑ *(signed off A134, between Bury St Edmunds & Sudbury)*

☎ 01787 310207

e-mail: info@kentwell.co.uk

web: www.kentwell.co.uk

Kentwell Hall is a moated red brick Tudor manor with gardens, woodland walks and a rare breeds farm. Restoration started in 1971 and still continues today. The house and grounds are open to the public at certain times of the year, and recreations of Tudor and 1940s life take place at weekends. Ring for details.

Times Open: Sun, daily in school hols Mar-Oct. **Facilities** ℗ ⌹ ᴙ (outdoor) ♿ (Partly accessible) (wheelchair ramps & 3 wheelchairs for loan) toilets for disabled shop ⊗ (ex assist dogs) ▬

Melford Hall

CO10 9AA

⮑ *(off A134, 3m N of Sudbury, next to village green)*

☎ 01787 379228 & 376395

e-mail: melford@nationaltrust.org.uk

web: www.nationaltrust.org.uk

Set in the unspoilt village of Long Melford, the house has changed little externally since 1578 when Queen Elizabeth I was entertained here, and retains its original panelled banqueting hall. It has been the home of the Hyde Parker Family since 1786. There is a Regency library, Victorian bedrooms, good collections of furniture and porcelain and a small display of items connected with Beatrix Potter, who was related to the family. The garden contains some spectacular specimen trees and a banqueting house, and there is an attractive walk through the park.

Times Open Apr, Wed-Mon, 1.30-5; May-Sep, Wed-Sun, 1.30-5; Oct-Nov, Sat & Sun, 1.30-5; BH Mon. Last entry to the house 4.30 **Fee** £6 (ch £3) Family £15. **Facilities** ℗ ⌹ ᴙ (outdoor) ♿ (stairlift, ramp, Braille & large print guides) toilets for disabled garden centre ⊗ (ex assist dogs) 🦮

LOWESTOFT   MAP 05 TM59

East Anglia Transport Museum

Chapel Rd, Carlton Colville NR33 8BL

➲ *(3m SW of Lowestoft, follow brown signs from A12, A146 & A1117)*

☎ 01502 518459

e-mail: enquiries@eatm.org.uk

web: www.eatm.org.uk

A particular attraction of this museum is the reconstructed 1930s street scene which is used as a setting for working vehicles: visitors can ride by tram, trolley bus and narrow gauge railway. Other motor, steam and electrical vehicles are exhibited. There is also a woodland picnic area served by trams.

Times Open: Apr-Sep, Sun and BH 11-5. From Jun, Thu and Sat, 2-5. **Fee** ✳ £6 (ch 5-15 £4.50) concessions £5. Price includes rides. Party rates available. **Facilities** ❷ ⬚ ⊓ (outdoor) ♿ (Partly accessible) toilets for disabled shop ▬

Maritime Museum   `2 for 1`

Sparrow Nest Gardens, Whapload Rd NR32 1XG

➲ *(on A12, 100mtrs N of Lowestoft Lighthouse, turn right down Ravine)*

☎ 01502 561963

Models of ancient and modern fishing and commercial boats, fishing gear and shipwrights' tools are among the exhibits. There is also an exhibition of the evolution of lifeboats, and a replica of the aft cabin of a steam drifter, as well as an art gallery.

Times Open 10-19 Apr; 2 May-Oct, daily 10-5. **Fee** £1 (ch & students 25p, pen 75p). **Facilities** ❷ ⊓ (outdoor) ♿ (hear for all) toilets for disabled shop ⊗ (ex assist dogs)

Pleasurewood Hills   `2 for 1`

Leisure Way, Corton NR32 5DZ

➲ *(off A12 at Lowestoft)*

☎ 01502 586000 (admin)

e-mail: info@pleasurewoodhills.com

web: www.pleasurewoodhills.com

Set in 50 acres of coastal parkland, Pleasurewood Hills, which celebrated its 25th anniversary in 2008, has all the ingredients for a great day out for all the family. Adrenalin-fuelled thrills and spills for the bravest adventurers, such as the newest attraction 'Wipeout', the most extreme rollercoaster in the East of England. Fun rides for all the family including some for younger children. Wonderful shows with sealions, parrots, acrobats and the breathtaking Magic Circus spectacular. When the action gets too much, take a leisurely ride on the alpine chairlift or jump aboard one of two railways that weave their way through the park.

Times Open Apr-Oct. Telephone for details or visit website. **Fee** ✳ (£15.75 over 1.4mtr, £13.50 1-4mtrs, under 1mtr free, concessions £9.75). Family ticket (2ad+2 ch) £52.00. **Facilities** ❷ ⬚ ⦿ licensed ⊓ (outdoor) ♿ (all shows accessible, most ride operators able to assist) toilets for disabled shop ⊗ (ex assist dogs) ▬

NEWMARKET   MAP 05 TL66

National Horseracing Museum and Tours   `2 for 1`

99 High St CB8 8JH

➲ *(located in centre of High St)*

☎ 01638 667333

web: www.nhrm.co.uk

This friendly award-winning museum tells the story of the people and horses involved in racing in Britain. Have a go on the horse simulator in the hands-on gallery and chat to retired jockeys and trainers about their experiences. Special mini bus tours visit the gallops, a stable and horses' swimming pool.

Times Open Etr-Oct, daily 11-5 (also BH Mons). 10am on race days. **Fee** ✳ £5.50 (ch £3, concessions £4.50). Family £12 (2ad+2ch). **Facilities** ℗ (300yds) (coach drop off in front of museum) ⬚ ⦿ ⊓ (outdoor) ♿ (ramps & lift) toilets for disabled shop ⊗ (ex assist dogs) ▬

ORFORD   MAP 05 TM45

Orford Castle

IP12 2ND

➲ *(on B1084)*

☎ 01394 450472

web: www.english-heritage.org.uk

A great keep of Henry II with three huge towers and commanding views over Orford Ness. Climb the spiral staircase leading to a maze of rooms and passageways.

Times Open all year, 21 Mar-Sep, daily 10-6; Oct-Mar, Thu-Mon 10-4. Closed 24-26 Dec & 1 Jan. **Fee** £4.90 (concessions £3.90, ch £2.50). Family ticket £12.30. Prices and opening times are subject to change in March 2009. Please check web site or call 0870 333 1181 for the most up to date prices and opening times when planning your visit. **Facilities** ❷ shop ⊗ ⧉

SAXTEAD GREEN   MAP 05 TM26

Saxtead Green Post Mill

The Mill House IP13 9QQ

➲ *(2.5m NW of Framlingham on A1120)*

☎ 01728 685789

web: www.english-heritage.org.uk

A post mill since 1287, Saxtead Green Post Mill is still in working order. Climb the wooden stairs to the various floors full of fascinating mill machinery. An audio tour explains the workings of the mill.

Times Open 21 Mar-Sep, Fri-Sat & BHs 12-5. **Fee** £3.20 (concessions £2.60, ch £1.60). Prices and opening times are subject to change in March 2009. Please check web site or call 0870 333 1181 for the most up to date prices and opening times when planning your visit. **Facilities** shop ⊗ ⧉

ENGLAND

STOWMARKET | MAP 05 TM05

Museum of East Anglian Life

IP14 1DL

➲ *(in centre of Stowmarket, signed from A14 & B1115)*

☎ 01449 612229

e-mail: enquiries@eastanglianlife.org.uk

web: www.eastanglianlife.org.uk

This 70-acre, all-weather museum is set in an attractive river-valley site with 3km of woodland and riverside nature trails. There are reconstructed buildings, including a working water mill, a smithy and also a wind pump, and the Boby Building houses craft workshops. There are displays on Victorian domestic life, gypsies, farming and industry. These include working steam traction engines, the only surviving pair of Burrell ploughing engines of 1879, and a Suffolk Punchhorse. The William Bone Building illustrates the history of Ransomes of Ipswich.

Times Open late March-end Oct. **Fee** ✳ £6.50 (ch 4-16 £3.50, concessions £5.50). Family ticket (2ad+2/3ch) £17.50. 1ad family £11. Party 10+.
Facilities ℗ (adjacent) ⊑ ⊓ (outdoor) ⅋ (w/chairs & 2 buggies available, special vehicle facilities) toilets for disabled shop ▄

SUDBURY | MAP 05 TL84

Gainsborough's House

46 Gainsborough St CO10 2EU

➲ *(situated in centre of Sudbury. Follow pedestrian signs from town centre car parks or from train stn)*

☎ 01787 372958

e-mail: mail@gainsborough.org

web: www.gainsborough.org

The birthplace of Thomas Gainsborough RA (1727-88). The Georgian-fronted town house, with an attractive walled garden, displays more of the artist's work at any one time than any other gallery, together with 18th-century furniture and memorabilia. A varied programme of temporary exhibitions on British art is shown throughout the year, with sculpture in the garden during the summer.

Times Open all year. Mon-Sat 10-5. closed Sun, Good Fri & Xmas-New Year. **Fee** ✳ £4 (concessions £3.20, ch and students £1.50). Family £8.
Facilities ℗ (300yds) (no parking in Gainsborough Street) ⊑⅋ (2nd floor not accessible) (lift to 1st floor) toilets for disabled shop ⊗ (ex assist dogs) ▄

SUFFOLK WILDLIFE PARK | MAP 05 TM58

Africa Alive!

Kessingland NR33 7TF

➲ *(25min S of Gt. Yarmouth just S of Lowestoft off A12)*

☎ 01502 740291

e-mail: info@africa-alive.co.uk

web: www.africa-alive.co.uk

Set in 80 acres of dramatic coastal parkland, visitors can explore the sights and sounds of Africa at Africa Alive! There are giraffes, rhinos, cheetah, hyenas and many more, including a bird's eye view of the new lion enclosure. There are lots of daily feeding talks and animal encounter sessions, a magnificent bird of prey display, and free journey round the park with live commentary.

Times ✳ Open all year, daily from 10. Closed 25-26 Dec. **Facilities** ℗ ⊑ ⏃⊓⅋ (wheelchairs available for hire) toilets for disabled shop ⊗ ▄

WESTLETON | MAP 05 TM46

RSPB Nature Reserve Minsmere

IP17 3BY

➲ *(signed from A12 at Yoxford & Blythburgh and from Westleton Village)*

☎ 01728 648281

e-mail: minsmere@rspb.org.uk

web: www.rspb.org.uk/reserves/minsmere

Set on the beautiful Suffolk coast, Minsmere offers an enjoyable day out for all. Nature trails take you through a variety of habitats to the excellent birdwatching hides. Spring is a time for birdsong, including nightingales and booming bitterns. In summer, you can watch breeding avocets and marsh harriers. Autumn is excellent for migrants, and in winter, hundreds of ducks visit the reserve. Look out for otters and red deer. The visitor centre has a well-stocked shop and licensed tearoom, and you can find out more about the reserve. There is a programme of events throughout the year, including several for children and families. Self-guided activity booklets for families.

Times Open daily (ex 25-26 Dec) 9-9 (or dusk if earlier). Visitor centre: 9-5 (9-4 Nov-Jan). **Fee** £5 (ch £1.50, concessions £3). Family ticket £10. RSPB members free **Facilities** ℗ ⊑⊓ (outdoor) ⅋ (Visitor Centre, parts of nature trail and some hides are accessible) (batricar available for loan, booking advised) toilets for disabled shop ⊗ (ex assist dogs) ▄

WEST STOW | MAP 05 TL87

West Stow Anglo Saxon Village

West Stow Country Park, Icklingham Rd IP28 6HG

➲ *(off A1101, 7m NW of Bury St Edmunds. Follow brown heritage signs)*

☎ 01284 728718

e-mail: weststow@stedsbc.gov.uk

web: www.weststow.org

The village is a reconstruction of a pagan Anglo-Saxon settlement dated 420-650 AD. Seven buildings have been reconstructed on the site of the excavated settlement. There is a Visitors' Centre which includes a new archaeology exhibition, DVD area and a children's play area. A new Anglo-Saxon Centre houses the original objects found on the site. Located in the 125 acre West Stow Country Park with river, lake, woodland and heath, plus many trails and paths.

Times Open all year, daily 10-5. Last entry 4 (3.30 in Winter) except Xmas period. **Fee** £5 (ch £4). Family £15. (Prices subject to change for special events) **Facilities** ℗ ⊑ ⼝ (outdoor) ♿ (Partly accessible) (ramps) toilets for disabled shop ⊗ (ex assist dogs) ⊜

WOODBRIDGE   MAP 05 TM24

Sutton Hoo

IP12 3DJ

➲ *(off B1083 Woodbridge to Bawdsey road. Follow signs from A12 avoiding Woodbridge itself)*

☎ 01394 389700

e-mail: suttonhoo@nationaltrust.org.uk

web: www.nationaltrust.org.uk

Discovered in 1939 and described as 'page one of English history', this is the site of one of the most important archaeological finds in Britain's history: the complete 7th-century ship burial of an Anglo-Saxon king, which had been missed by grave-robbers, and lay undisturbed for 1,300 years. Sutton Hoo displays reveal how Anglo-Saxon nobles lived, went to war and found a new kingdom in East Anglia. The centre-piece is a full-sized replica of an Anglo-Saxon warrior king's burial chamber. The discoveries at Sutton Hoo changed forever our perceptions of the 'dark ages', by revealing a culture rich in craftsmanship, trade and legend.

Times Open: Jun, Wed-Sun, 10.30-5; Jul-Aug, daily 10.30-5; Sep-Oct, Wed-Sun, 10.30-5; Nov-Feb, Sat-Sun, 11-4. Open: BHs. **Fee** Gift Aid Admission prices £6.50, (ch £3.40). Family tickets £16.45. Gift aid admission includes a voluntary donation but visitors can choose to pay the standard prices displayed at the property and on the website. **Facilities** ℗ ⼝ 🍴 ⼝ ♿ (ramps, electric buggy hire) toilets for disabled shop ⽕ ⊜

Woodbridge Tide Mill

Tide Mill Way IP12

➲ *(follow signs for Woodbridge off A12, 7m E of Ipswich-Tide Mill is on riverside)*

☎ 01728 746959

e-mail: wtm@redpoll.co.uk

web: www.tidemill.org.uk

The machinery of this 18th-century mill has been completely restored. There are photographs and working models on display. Situated on a busy quayside, the unique building looks over towards the historic site of the Sutton Hoo Ship Burial. Every effort is made to run the machinery for a while whenever the mill is open and the tides are favourable.

Times Open Etr, then daily May-Sep; Apr, Oct wknds only, 11-5. **Fee** £2.50 (accompanied ch free (ex school groups) concessions £2). **Facilities** ℗ (400yds) (no parking or turning in Tide Mill Way) ♿ (ground floor & viewing area only accessible) shop ⊗ (ex assist dogs)

Beach at Dunwich

SURREY

East Warren woods, nr Compton

ASH VALE
MAP 04 SU85

Army Medical Services Museum `FREE`

Keogh Barracks GU12 5RQ

➲ *(M3 junct 4 on A331 to Mytchett then follow tourist signs)*

☎ 01252 868612

e-mail: armymedicalmuseum@btinternet.com

web: www.ams-museum.org.uk

The museum traces the history of Army medicine, nursing, dentistry and veterinary science from 1660 until the present day. Medical equipment and ambulances complement displays including uniforms and medals.

Times ✴ Open all year, Mon-Fri 10-3.30. Closed Xmas, New Year & BH. Wknds by appointment only. **Facilities** ♿ ♿ (hand rails, wide doors, audio guide, Braille guides) toilets for disabled shop ⊗ (ex assist dogs)

CHERTSEY
MAP 04 TQ06

Thorpe Park

Staines Rd KT16 8PN

➲ *(M25 junct 11 or 13 and follow signs via A320 to Thorpe Park)*

☎ 0870 444 4466

web: www.thorpepark.com

For hard core adrenalin junkies, Thorpe Park is the must-do destination for adrenaline fuelled fun. Unleash the dare devil within and take on the loops, spins, vertical drops and incredible speeds of the nation's thrill capital.

Times Open 15 Mar-9 Nov. Opening times vary throughout, check in advance. **Fee** ✴ From £25.60 (ch £16.80, ch under 1mtr free) with advanced booking **Facilities** ♿ ⊡ ⛽ licensed ⊟ ♿ (some rides not accessible) (wheelchair hire available) toilets for disabled shop ⊗ (ex assist dogs) ⬛

EAST CLANDON
MAP 04 TQ05

Hatchlands Park

GU4 7RT

➲ *(E of Guildford, off A246)*

☎ 01483 222482

e-mail: hatchlands@nationaltrust.org.uk

web: www.nationaltrust.org.uk/hatchlands

Built in the 1750s for Admiral Boscawen, hero of the battle of Louisburg, and set in a beautiful 430-acre Repton Park offering a variety of park and woodlands walks, Hatchlands boasts the earliest known decorative works by Robert Adam. Hatchlands is home to the Cobbe collection, the world's largest group of keyboard instruments associated with famous composers. There is also a small garden by Gertrude Jekyll and a beautiful bluebell wood in May. For details of children's events and family activities during school holidays, please visit website.

Times House & Gardens: Apr-29 Oct, Tue-Thu & Sun, 2-5.30 (also open BH & Fri in Aug). Park Walks open 1 Apr, daily, 11-6. **Fee** £7 (ch £3.50) Family ticket £18. Park walks £3.70 (ch £1.80). Joint ticket with Clandon Park £11.60 (ch £5.80). Family £33.40 **Facilities** ♿ ⛽ ⊟ (outdoor) ♿ (park walks unsuitable and not accessible) (wheelchair available, parking and assistance to house) toilets for disabled shop ⊗ (ex park only & assist dogs) ♨ ⬛

FARNHAM
MAP 04 SU84

Birdworld & Underwaterworld `2 for 1`

Holt Pound GU10 4LD

➲ *(3m S of Farnham on A325)*

☎ 01420 22140

e-mail: bookings@birdworld.co.uk

web: www.birdworld.co.uk

Birdworld is the largest bird collection in the country and includes toucans, pelicans, flamingos, ostriches and many others. Underwater World is a tropical aquarium with brilliant lighting that shows off collections of marine and freshwater fish, as well as the swampy depths of the alligator exhibit. Visitors can also visit some beautiful gardens, the Jenny Wren farm and the Heron Theatre.

Times Open daily, 10-6 (summer), 10-4.30 (winter). Closed 25-26 Dec. **Fee** ✴ £11.95 (ch 3-14 £9.95, concessions £9.95). Family ticket (2ad+2ch) £39.95. **Facilities** ♿ ⛽ licensed ⊟ (outdoor) ♿ (wheelchairs available) toilets for disabled shop garden centre ⊗ (ex assist dogs) ⬛

Farnham Castle Keep

Castle St GU6 0AG

➲ *(0.5m N on A287)*

☎ 01252 713393

web: www.english-heritage.org.uk

A motte and bailey castle, once one of the seats of the bishop of Winchester, has been in continuous occupation since the 12th-century.

Times Open 21 Mar-Sep, Fri-Sun 1-5. Guided tour Aug only, Sun 2.30. **Fee** £3 (concessions £2.40, ch £1.50). Prices and opening times are subject to change in March 2009. Please check web site or call 0870 333 1181 for the most up to date prices and opening times when planning your visit. **Facilities** ♿ shop ⊞

GODSTONE
MAP 05 TQ35

Godstone Farm

RH9 8LX

➲ *(M25 junct 6, S of village, signed)*

☎ 01883 742546

e-mail: havefun@godstonefarm.co.uk

web: www.godstonefarm.co.uk

An ideal day out for children, Godstone Farm has lots of friendly animals, big sand pits and play areas, including an indoor play barn for rainy days.

Times Open Mar-Oct, 10-6 (last admission 5); Nov-Feb 10-5 (last admission 4). Closed 25 & 26 Dec. **Fee** Contact for admission prices. **Facilities** ♿ ⊡ ⊟ (indoor & outdoor) ♿ toilets for disabled shop ⊗ (ex assist dogs) ⬛

GREAT BOOKHAM   MAP 04 TQ15

Polesden Lacey

RH5 6BD

➲ *(2m S off A246 from village of Bookham)*

☎ 01372 452048

e-mail: polesdenlacey@nationaltrust.org.uk

web: www.nationaltrust.org.uk/polesdenlacey

King George VI and Queen Elizabeth (the Queen Mother) spent part of their honeymoon here, and photographs of other notable guests can be seen. The house is handsomely furnished and full of charm, and it is set in spacious grounds. There is also a summer festival, where concerts and plays are performed. Please phone 01372 452048 for details of special events.

Times Open all year; Grounds & Garden, daily 11-5. House, 15 Mar-25 Oct,11-5 (last admission 30 mins before closing). **Fee** ✳ Garden £6.50 (ch £3.20). Family ticket £16.20. House & Garden £10.50 (ch £5.20). Family £26.50. Group rates 15+. Please check website for further details. **Facilities** ❷ (charged) ♿ ❙◎❙ licensed ⊞ (outdoor) ♿ (no access for wheelchairs to upper floors in house. Some steps and uneven paths in garden.) (Braille guide, parking & mobility vehicles/wheelchairs) toilets for disabled shop garden centre ❦ ◱

GUILDFORD   MAP 04 SU94

Dapdune Wharf

Wharf Rd GU1 4RR

➲ *(off Woodbridge Rd to rear of Surrey County Cricket Ground)*

☎ 01483 561389

e-mail: riverwey@nationaltrust.org.uk

web: www.nationaltrust.org.uk/riverwey

The visitor centre at Dapdune Wharf is the centrepiece of one of the National Trust's most unusual properties, the River Wey Navigations. A series of interactive exhibits and displays allow you to discover the fascinating story of Surrey's secret waterway, one of the first British rivers to be made navigable. See where huge Wey barges were built and climb aboard *Reliance*, one of the last surviving barges. Children's trails and special events run throughout the season.

Times Open 28 Mar-1 Nov, Thu-Mon 11-5. River trips Thu-Mon, 11-5 (conditions permitting) **Fee** £4.20 (ch £2.20). Family £11.50. NT Members free. **Facilities** ❷ ♿ ⊞ (outdoor) ♿ (Partly accessible) (Braille guide) toilets for disabled shop ◱ (ex on leads) ❦ ◱

Guildford House Gallery   `FREE`

155 High St GU1 3AJ

➲ *(N side of High St, opposite Sainsbury's)*

☎ 01483 444742

e-mail: guildfordhouse@guildford.gov.uk

web: www.guildfordhouse.co.uk

An impressive building in its own right, Guildford House dates from 1660 and has been Guildford's art gallery since 1959. A changing selection from the Borough's Art Collection is on display, including pastel portraits by John Russell, topographical paintings and contemporary craftwork, as well as temporary exhibitions. 2009 is the 50th anniversary of the art gallery.

Times Open all year Tue-Sat 10-4.45. (Closed Good Fri & 25-26 Dec) **Facilities** ℗ (100yds) ♿❙◎❙ ♿ (Partly accessible) (ramps available for w/chair access to ground floor) shop ◱ (ex assist dogs) ◱

Loseley Park   `2 for 1`

GU3 1HS

➲ *(2m SW of Guildford, off A3 onto B3000)*

☎ 01483 304440 & 505501

e-mail: enquiries@loseley-park.com

web: www.loseley-park.com

Magnificent Elizabethan mansion, home of the More-Molyneux family for 500 years. Set in magnificent parkland scenery. Based on a Gertrude Jekyll design, the walled garden contains five gardens each with its own theme and character. These include the award-wining Rose Garden, Vine Walk, fruit, vegetable and flower gardens and the Serene White Fountain Garden. Events throughout the year including RHS talks, medieval festival, Shakespeare performances and music.

Times Open Grounds and Walled Garden: May-Sep, Tue-Sun & BH 11-5. House May-Aug, Tue-Thu, Sun & BH 1-5. **Fee** ✳ House & Gardens £7 (ch £3.50, ch under 5 free, concessions £6.50). Gardens only £4 (ch £2, concessions £3.50). Discount for pre-booked groups. Garden season ticket £12 (admits ticket holder & guest from May-Sep) **Facilities** ❷ ♿ ⊞ (outdoor) ♿ (Only ground floor of house accessible) (wheelchair available, parking outside shop) toilets for disabled shop ◱ (ex assist dogs) ◱

HASCOMBE   MAP 04 SU94

Winkworth Arboretum

Hascombe Rd GU8 4AD

➲ *(2m SE of Godalming, E side of B2130, follow brown tourist signs from Godalming)*

☎ 01483 208477

e-mail: winkwortharboretum@nationaltrust.org.uk

web: www.nationaltrust.org.uk/winkwortharboretum

This lovely woodland covers a hillside of nearly 100 acres, with fine views over the North Downs. The best times to visit are April and May, for the azaleas, bluebells and other flowers, and October for the autumn colours. A delightful Victorian boathouse is open Apr-Oct with fine views over Rowes Flashe lake. Many rare trees and shrubs in group plantings for spring and autumn colour effect.

Winkworth Arboretum

Times Open all year, daily during daylight hours. (Could close when weather is bad). **Fee** ✱ £5 (ch £2.50). Family £12.50. Reduction if arriving by public transport/cycle. **Facilities** ℗ ⬚& (suggested route, free entry for helpers) toilets for disabled ⊗ (ex on lead) ⛄⬛

PAINSHILL PARK
MAP 04 TQ06

Painshill Park

Portsmouth Rd KT11 1JE

➲ *(W of Cobham on A245)*

☎ 01932 868113

e-mail: info@painshill.co.uk

web: www.painshill.co.uk

Covering 158 acres, this magnificent 18th-century parkland was created by Charles Hamilton as a series of subtle and surprising vistas. Its landscapes include authentic 18th-century plantings, a working vineyard, unusual follies, and a magical grotto. The Park is also home to the John Bartram Heritage Collection of North American Trees and Shrubs. There are a number of events for the whole family, throughout the year, and Father Christmas visits the grotto in December.

Times Open: Apr-Oct, 10.30-6 (last entry 4.30). Nov-Mar, 10.30-4 (last entry 3). Closed 25-26 Dec. Ltd opening times to grotto. **Fee** £6.60 (ch 5-16 £3.85, under 5 free, concessions £5.80). Family £22 (2ad& 4ch). Free admission for carer. Pre-booked adult groups 10+ £5.80 **Facilities** ℗ ⬚⊓ (outdoor) & (accessible route covering 2/3rds of the landscape) (pre-booked w/chairs & guided buggy tour available) toilets for disabled shop ⊗ (ex on short lead) ⬛

REIGATE
MAP 04 TQ24

Reigate Priory Museum

Bell St RH2 7RL

➲ *(in Priory Park close to town centre, use Bell St car park on A217)*

☎ 01737 222550

web: www.reigatepriorymuseum.org.uk

The Priory Museum is housed in Reigate Priory which was originally founded before 1200, this Grade I listed building was converted to a mansion in Tudor times. Notable features include the magnificent

---

Holbein fireplace, 17th-early 18th-century oak staircase and murals. The small museum has changing exhibitions on a wide range of subjects, designed to appeal to both adults and children. The collection includes domestic bygones, local history and costume.

Times Open Etr-early Dec, Wed & Sat, 2-4.30 in term time. **Fee** Donations welcome. **Facilities** ℗ (50yds) & (hands on facilities) shop ⊗ (ex assist dogs)

TILFORD
MAP 04 SU84

Rural Life Centre
2 for 1

Reeds Rd GU10 2DL

➲ *(off A287, 3m S of Farnham, signed)*

☎ 01252 795571

e-mail: info@rural-life.org.uk

web: www.rural-life.org.uk

The museum covers village life from 1750 to 1960. It is set in over ten acres of garden and woodland and incorporates purpose-built and reconstructed buildings, including a chapel, pavilion, village hall, schoolroom and 'prefab'. Displays show village crafts and trades, such as wheelwrighting, thatching, ploughing and gardening. The historic village playground provides entertainment for children and there is an arboretum featuring over 100 trees from around the world. An extensive programme of events takes place throughout the year, please contact for details.

Times Open mid Mar-end Oct, Wed-Sun & BH 10-5; Winter Wed & Sun only 11-4 **Fee** £7.50 (ch £5.50 & concessions £6.50). Family ticket £22 (2ad+2ch) **Facilities** ℗ ⬚⊓⦿ licensed ⊓ (indoor & outdoor) & (2 buildings are not wheelchair accessible but can be viewed from outside.) (3 wheelchairs for use) toilets for disabled shop ⬛

WEST CLANDON
MAP 04 TQ05

Clandon Park

GU4 7RQ

➲ *(E of Guildford on A247)*

☎ 01483 222482

e-mail: clandonpark@nationaltrust.org.uk

web: www.nationaltrust.org.uk/clandonpark

A grand Palladian mansion built c.1730 by the Venetian architect Giacomo Leoni, and notable for its magnificent marble hall. The house is filled with the superb Gubbay collection of 18th-century furniture, porcelain, textiles and carpets. The attractive gardens contain a parterre, grotto, sunken Dutch garden and a Maori meeting house. Please see website for details of special events.

Times House & Garden open 15 Mar-1 Nov, Tue-Thu & Sun; House 11-4, Garden 11-5, Museum 12-5 **Fee** House & Garden £8.10 (ch £4). Family ticket £22.00. Joint ticket with Hatchlands Park £11.60 (ch £5.80). Family £33.40. **Facilities** ℗ ⦿⊓ (outdoor) & (7 steps to house entrance with handrail, grounds partly accessible, grass & loose gravel paths, slopes, some steps & ramped access) (wheelchairs, Braille guide, lifts, disabled parking) toilets for disabled shop ⊗ (ex assist dogs) ⛄⬛

WEYBRIDGE MAP 04 TQ06

Brooklands Museum

Brooklands Rd KT13 0QN

➲ *(M25 junct 10/11, museum off B374, follow brown signs)*

☎ 01932 857381

e-mail: info@brooklandsmuseum.com

web: www.brooklandsmuseum.com

Brooklands racing circuit was the birthplace of British motorsport and aviation. From 1907 to 1987 it was a world-renowned centre of engineering excellence. The Museum features old banked track and the 1-in-4 Test Hill. Many of the original buildings have been restored including the Clubhouse, the Shell and BP Petrol Pagodas, and the Malcolm Campbell Sheds in the Motoring Village. Many motorcycles, cars and aircraft are on display. Ring for details of special events.

Times Open all year, daily & BHs 10-5 (4 in winter). **Fee** ✳ £8 (ch under 5 free, ch 6-16 £5, concessions £5). Family ticket (2ad+3ch) £20. **Facilities** ❷ ⬚ ☕ (outdoor) ♿ (no wheelchair access to aircraft) toilets for disabled shop ⊗ (ex assist dogs) ⬛

WISLEY MAP 04 TQ05

RHS Garden Wisley

GU23 6QB

➲ *(on A3, close to M25 junct 10)*

☎ 01483 224234

web: www.rhs.org.uk

With over 100 years of gardening, Wisley is the flagship garden of the Royal Horticultural Society. The garden stretches over 200 acres and there are countless opportunities for visitors to draw inspiration and gather new ideas. A 'must see' is the new glasshouse with exotics from around the world in two climate zones. The mixed borders and vegetable garden are glories of summer, while the country garden, Battleston Hill and wild garden are magnificent in spring. Whatever the season the garden is full of interest.

Times Open all year, Mon-Fri 10-6 (4.30 Nov-Feb), Sat-Sun, 9-6 (4.30 Nov-Feb). Closed 25 Dec. **Fee** ✳ £7.50 (ch 6-16 £2) Group bookings 10+ £5.50 (ch £1.60) **Facilities** ❷ ⬚ ☕ licensed ☕ (outdoor) ♿ (garden partly accessible, some difficult paths) (free wheelchairs, mobility buggy/scooter, wheelchair route) toilets for disabled shop garden centre ⊗ (ex assist dogs) ⬛

Deer in Richmond Park

EAST SUSSEX

Wheat fields, nr Ditchling

ALFRISTON — MAP 05 TQ50

Alfriston Clergy House

The Tye BN26 5TL

➲ *(4m NE of Seaford, E of B2108, next to church)*

☎ 01323 870001

e-mail: alfriston@nationaltrust.org.uk
web: www.nationaltrust.org.uk

This 14th-century thatched Wealden 'hall house' was the first building to be acquired by the National Trust in 1896. It has an unusual chalk and sour milk floor, and its pretty cottage garden is in an idyllic setting beside Alfriston's parish church, with views across the meandering Cuckmere River. Please telephone or check website for details of events running throughout the year.

Times Open 1-9 Mar, Sat-Sun 11-4; 15 Mar-26 Oct, daily, except Tue & Fri 10-5; 27 Oct-21 Dec 11-4. **Fee** ✴ £3.70 (ch £1.85). Family ticket £9.20 **Facilities** ℗ (0.25m) ♿ (slopes in garden to some limited areas. Steps in house and garden make it inaccessible in wheelchair) (Braille/large print guides, sensory guide) shop ⊗ (ex assist dogs) 🐾

Drusillas Park

Alfriston Rd BN26 5QS

➲ *(off A27 near Alfriston 12m from Brighton & 7m from Eastbourne)*

☎ 01323 874100

e-mail: info@drusillas.co.uk
web: www.drusillas.co.uk

This excellent small zoo offers an opportunity to get nose to nose with nature with hundreds of exotic animals from monkeys and crocodiles to penguins and meerkats. But animals are only half the fun - Go Bananas! Monkey Kingdom and Amazon Adventure are paradise for anyone who needs to let off steam and Thomas the Tank Engine offers a train service 362 days a year. Don't miss the Zoolympics Trial, Animal Spotter books, Jungle Adventure golf, Panning for Gold, the Wacky Workshop, Dino-Dig or Explorers Lagoon.

Times Open all year, daily 10-5 (winter 10-4). Closed 24-26 Dec. **Fee** ✴ Family of 4: peak £49.80, standard £46.80, off peak £40.80 **Facilities** ℗ ⊑ 🍴 licensed 🎍 (indoor & outdoor) ♿ toilets for disabled shop ⊗ (ex assist dogs) 🚰

BATTLE — MAP 05 TQ71

1066 Battle of Hastings Abbey & Battlefield

TN33 0AD

➲ *(A21 onto A2100)*

☎ 01424 773792

web: www.english-heritage.org.uk

Explore the site of the Battle of Hastings, where on 14th October 1066, one of the most famous events in English history took place. Free interactive wand tour of the battlefield and atmospheric abbey ruins.

Times Open daily all year, 21 Mar-Sep, 10-6; Oct-Mar, 10-4. Closed 26 Dec & 1 Jan. **Fee** £6.50 (concessions £5.20, ch £3.30). Family £16.30. Opening times and prices are subject to change from March 2009, for further details please phone 0870 333 118. **Facilities** ♿ (charged) shop 🎕

Yesterday's World

89-90 High St TN33 0AQ

➲ *(M25 junct 5, A21 onto A2100 towards Battle, opposite Battle Abbey Gatehouse)*

☎ 01424 893938 & 774269

e-mail: info@yesterdaysworld.co.uk
web: www.yesterdaysworld.co.uk

Go on a magical time-travel adventure from the reign of Queen Victoria to the psychedelic 70s. Explore five floors of displays with over 100,000 artefacts, virtual and interactive exhibits, sounds and smells. See an English country garden, a children's play village, the 1930s Nippy's Tea Room, nostalgic gift shop and traditional English sweet shop.

Times Open all year, Winter, daily 9.30-5.30; Summer, daily 9.30-6. Closed 25-26 Dec & 1 Jan. **Facilities** ℗ (100yds) (£3 per day) ⊑ 🎍 (outdoor) ♿ (Partly accessible) (Medieval building accessible) toilets for disabled shop ⊗ (ex assist dogs) 🚰

BODIAM — MAP 05 TQ72

Bodiam Castle

TN32 5UA

➲ *(2m E of A21 Hurst Green)*

☎ 01580 830196

e-mail: bodiamcastle@nationaltrust.org.uk
web: www.nationaltrust.org.uk/bodiamcastle

With its tall round drum towers at each corner, Bodiam is something of a fairytale castle. It was built in 1386 by Sir Edward Dalyngrigge, for comfort and defence. The ramparts rise dramatically above a broad moat and the great gatehouse contains the original portcullis - a very rare example of its kind.

Times Open Jan-13 Feb, Sat & Sun 10.30-4; 14 Feb-Oct daily 10.30-6; Nov-20 Dec, Wed-Sun 10.30-4 (last entry to castle, 1 hr before closing) **Fee** ✴ £5 (ch £2.50). Family ticket £12.50. Group 15+ £4.30 (ch £2.15) **Facilities** ♿ (charged) ⊑ ♿ (ground floor level is fully accessibile, spiral staircase to upper levels) (Braille/large print guides, sensory objects, audio loops) toilets for disabled shop ⊗ (ex assist dogs) 🐾 🚰

BRIGHTON   MAP 04 TQ30

Booth Museum of Natural History `FREE`

194 Dyke Rd BN1 5AA

➲ *(from A27 Brighton by pass, 1.5m NW of town centre, opposite Dyke Rd Park)*

☎ 01273 292777

e-mail: boothmuseum@brighton-hove.gov.uk
web: www.virtualmuseum.info

The museum was built in 1874 to house the bird collection of Edward Thomas Booth (1840-1890). His collection is still on display, but the museum has expanded considerably since Booth's day and now includes thousands of butterfly and insect specimens, geology galleries with fossils, rocks and local dinosaur bones, a magnificent collection of animal skeletons, largely collected by the Brighton solicitor F W Lucas (1842-1932), and an interactive discovery gallery.

Times Open all year, Mon-Sat (ex Thu) 10-5, Sun 2-5. Closed Good Fri, Xmas & 1 Jan. **Facilities** ℗ (road opposite) (2 hr limit, metered) & (rear access, otherwise accessible) toilets for disabled shop ⊗ (ex assist dogs) ⇌

Brighton Museum & Art Gallery

Royal Pavilion Gardens BN1 1EE

➲ *(M23/A23 from London. In city centre near seafront. New entrance in Royal Pavilion Gardens)*

☎ 01273 290900

e-mail: museums@brighton-hove.gov.uk
web: www.brighton.virtualmuseum.info

A £10 million redevelopment transformed Brighton Museum into a state-of-the-art visitor attraction. Dynamic and innovative galleries, including fashion, 20th-century design and world art, feature exciting interactive displays appealing to all ages. The museum also benefits from a spacious entrance located in the Royal Pavilion gardens and full disabled access.

Times Open Tue 10-7, Wed-Sat 10-5, Sun 2-5. (Closed Mon ex BHs 10-5). **Facilities** ℗ (5 mins walk) (Church St NCP & on street) ⬚ & (lift, tactile exhibits, induction loops, ramps) toilets for disabled shop ⊗ (ex assist dogs)

Brighton Toy and Model Museum

52-55 Trafalgar St BN1 4EB

➲ *(underneath Brighton Railway Station)*

☎ 01273 749494

e-mail: info@brightontoymuseum.co.uk
web: www.brightontoymuseum.co.uk

A fascinating collection of over 10,000 exhibits, includes collections of toys from the last one hundred years. Toys from the top toy makers and a priceless model train collection are some examples to be viewed.

Times ✳ Open all year, Tue-Fri 10-5, Sat 11-5. Closed Sun & Mon. **Facilities** ℗ (10 mins walk) (no on street parking) & (ramp, wide door, rails & bars) toilets for disabled shop ⊗ (ex assist dogs)

Preston Manor

Preston Drove BN1 6SD

➲ *(off A23, 2m N of Brighton)*

☎ 01273 292770

e-mail: museums@brighton-hove.gov.uk
web: www.prestonmanor.virtualmuseum.info

This charming Edwardian manor house is beautifully furnished with notable collections of silver, furniture and paintings and presents a unique opportunity to see an Edwardian home both 'upstairs' and 'downstairs'. The servants' quarters can also be seen, featuring kitchen, butler's pantry and boot hall. The house is set in beautiful gardens, which include a pet cemetery and the 13th-century parish church of St Peter. The restored walled garden enables disabled people to explore the garden for the first time.

Times Open Apr-Sep, Tue-Sat 10-5, Sun 2-5. Closed Mon **Fee** ✳ £4.50 (ch £2.50, concessions £3.50). Family ticket (1ad+2ch) £7, (2ad+2ch) £11.50 (Brighton & Hove residents £2.25 plus 4 accompanying children free) **Facilities** ℗ & (lower floor only) (call prior to visit to discuss access requirements) shop ⊗ (ex assist dogs) ⇌

Royal Pavilion

BN1 1EE

➲ *(M23/A23 from London. In city centre near seafront. 15 min walk from rail station)*

☎ 01273 290900

e-mail: visitor.services@brighton-hove.gov.uk
web: www.royalpavilion.org.uk

Acclaimed as one of the most exotically beautiful buildings in the British Isles, the Royal Pavilion was the magnificent seaside residence of George IV. This breathtaking Regency palace is decorated in Chinese style, with a romanticised Indian exterior, and surrounded by restored Regency gardens.

Times Open all year, Apr-Sep, daily 9.30-5.45 (last admission 5); Oct-Mar, daily 10-5.15 (last admission 4.30). Closed 25-26 Dec. **Fee** ✳ £8.50 (ch £5.10, concessions £6.50) Family ticket (1ad+up to 2ch) £13.60 (2ad+up to 2ch) £22.10. Groups 20+ £7.50 each, concessions £6 each. **Facilities** ℗ (5 mins walk) (NCP & on Church St) ⬚ ⫟◯ licensed & (ground floor only accessible) (wheelchairs, audio guides) toilets for disabled shop ⊗ (ex assist dogs) ⇌

BRIGHTON CONTINUED

Sea Life Centre

Marine Pde BN2 1TB

➲ *(next to Brighton Pier between Marine Parade & Madeira Drive)*

☎ 01273 604234

e-mail: slcbrighton@merlinentertainments.biz

web: www.sealife.co.uk

Experience spectacular marine displays, set in the world's oldest functioning aquarium. Take a look at over 100 species in their natural habitat, including seahorses, sharks and rays. Over forty exhibits include Adventures at 20,000 Leagues complete with NASA-designed walkthrough observation tunnel. Features also include a Captain Pugwash quiz trail, a soft play area, a café and a giftshop.

Times ✳ Open all year, daily 10-5. (Last admission 4). Open later on wknds in summer & school hols. Closed 25 Dec. **Facilities** ⓟ (200yds) (pay & display) ⌨ & (Partly accessible) toilets for disabled shop ⊗ (ex assist dogs) ▭

BURWASH   MAP 05 TQ62

Bateman's

TN19 7DS

➲ *(0.5m SW off A265)*

☎ 01435 882302

e-mail: batemans@nationaltrust.org.uk

web: www.nationaltrust.org.uk

Rudyard Kipling lived for over 34 years in this 17th-century manor house and it remains much the same as it was during his lifetime. His 1928 Rolls Royce Phantom is on display, and the watermill at the bottom of the garden grinds wheat into flour on Saturday afternoons and Wednesdays.

Times Open 15 Mar-2 Nov, Sat-Wed 11-5, also open Good Fri, (last admission 4.30). House closes at 5. **Fee** ✳ £6.50 (ch £3.25). Family ticket £16.25 Party £5.20 (ch £2.60) **Facilities** ⓟ ⌨ 🍴 licensed ⋔ (outdoor) & (Partly accessible) (Braille guide, touch test, computerised tour) toilets for disabled shop ⊗ (ex assist dogs) 🐾 ▭

EASTBOURNE   MAP 05 TV69

"How We Lived Then" Museum of Shops & Social History

20 Cornfield Ter BN21 4NS

➲ *(just off seafront, between town centre & theatres, signed)*

☎ 01323 737143

e-mail: howwelivedthen@btconnect.com

web: www.how-we-lived-then.co.uk

Over the last 50 years, Jan and Graham Upton have collected over 100,000 items which are now displayed on four floors of authentic old shops and room-settings, transporting visitors back to their grandparents' era. Other displays, such as seaside souvenirs, wartime rationing and Royal mementoes, help to capture 100 years of social history.

Times Open all year, daily, 10-5 (last entry 4.30). Winter times subject to change, telephone establishment. **Fee** £4.50 (ch 5-15 £3.50, under 5's free, concession £4). Party 10+. **Facilities** ⓟ (outside) & (ground floor access only) (no charge) shop

---

EAST DEAN   MAP 05 TV59

Seven Sisters Sheep Centre

Gilberts Dr BN20 0AA

➲ *3m W of Eastbourne on A259. Turn left in village of East Dean to Birling Gap (and sea), 0.5m on left*

☎ 01323 423302

e-mail: sevensisters.sheepcentre@talk21.com

web: www.sheepcentre.co.uk

Possibly the largest collection of sheep in the world, where over 40 different breeds can be visited at this family run farm. See lambs being born, sheep sheared and milked, cheese making and spinning. Take in the agricultural heritage and history of sheep on the South Downs.

Times ✳ Open 3 Mar-7 May & 30 Jun-2 Sep, 2-5 (11-5 wknds/E Sussex school hols) **Facilities** ❾ (charged) ⌨ ⋔ (indoor & outdoor) shop ⊗ (ex assist dogs)

FIRLE   MAP 05 TQ40

Firle Place   `2 for 1`

BN8 6LP

➲ *(off A27, Eastbourne to Brighton road near Lewes)*

☎ 01273 858307

e-mail: gage@firleplace.co.uk

web: www.firleplace.co.uk

Home of the Gage family for over 500 years, the house has a Tudor core but was remodelled in the 18th century. Its treasures include important European and English Old Master paintings, fine English and French furniture, and porcelain, including notable examples from Sèvres and English factories. There are family monuments and brasses in the church at West Firle.

Times Open Jun-Sep, Sun, Wed, Thu & BHs 2-4.30. **Fee** £6.50 (ch £3, concessions £5.50). Family £16.50, Special group rates available
Facilities ℗ ❍ licensed ⚭ (access to ground floor only) toilets for disabled shop ⊗ (ex in garden) ▭

FOREST ROW   MAP 05 TQ43

Ashdown Forest Llama Park

Wych Cross RH18 5JN

➲ *(on A22 between Uckfield & East Grinstead, 250mtrs S of junct with A275)*

☎ 01825 712040

e-mail: info@llamapark.co.uk

web: www.llamapark.co.uk

Ashdown Forest Llama Park is home to more than 100 llamas and alpacas and these beautiful and gentle woolly animals, native to the high Andes of South America, are very much at home in Sussex. There are also now three reindeer who, in December, are an important part of the Christmas celebrations and Santa's Groto. The park has wonderful views over Ashdown Forest and there is a marked trail around the Park, a picnic area and adventure play area. In the information centre you learn about the fascinating world of llamas and alpacas and other fibre producing animals and plants. The coffee shop is open daily and local produce is used as much as possible. You can visit the coffee shop at any time without paying to visit the park. The park is holder of a Green Tourist Award.

Times Open daily 10-5. Closed 25-26 Dec & 1 Jan **Fee** £5.95 (ch 3-16 £4.95, pen & concessions £4.95). Group £4.50 **Facilities** ℗ 🖵 ❍ licensed ⌂ (outdoor) ⚭ (Shop and coffee shop accessible, some gravel areas in park but limited access to wheelchair users) (ramps, wheelchairs provided foc) toilets for disabled shop ⊗ ▭

HAILSHAM   MAP 05 TQ50

Michelham Priory

Upper Dicker BN27 3QS

➲ *(off A22 & A27 signed, 2m W of Hailsham, 8m NW of Eastbourne)*

☎ 01323 844224

e-mail: adminmich@sussexpast.co.uk

web: www.sussexpast.co.uk

Set on a moated island surrounded by glorious gardens, Michelham Priory is one of the most beautiful historic houses in Sussex. Founded in 1229 for Augustinian canons, the Priory is approached through a 14th-century gatehouse spanning the longest water-filled medieval moat in the country. Most of the original priory was demolished during the Dissolution, but the remains were incorporated into a Tudor farm that became a country house. Outside, the gardens are enhanced by a fully restored medieval watermill, physic garden, smithy, rope museum and the dramatic Elizabethan Great Barn. A variety of special events take place throughout the year.

Times ✳ Open Mar-Oct, Tue-Sun (daily in Aug & BH Mons). Mar & Oct 10.30-4.30, Apr-Jul & Sep 10.30-5, Aug 10.30-5.30. **Facilities** ℗ 🖵 ❍ ⌂ (outdoor) ⚭ (wheelchairs, Braille guide & tactile tours) toilets for disabled shop ⊗ (ex assist dogs) ▭

HALLAND   MAP 05 TQ51

Bentley Wildfowl & Motor Museum

BN8 5AF

➲ *(7m NE of Lewes, signposted off A22, A26 & B2192)*

☎ 01825 840573

e-mail: barrysutherland@pavilion.co.uk

web: www.bentley.org.uk

Hundreds of swans, geese and ducks from all over the world can be seen on lakes and ponds along with flamingoes and peacocks. There is a fine array of Veteran, Edwardian and Vintage vehicles, and the house has splendid antiques and wildfowl paintings. The gardens specialise in old fashioned roses. Other attractions include woodland walks, a nature trail, education centre, adventure playground and a miniature train.

Times ✳ Open 17 Mar-Oct, daily 10.30-4.30. House open from noon, Apr-Nov, Feb & part of Mar, wknds only. Estate closed Dec & Jan. House closed all winter. **Facilities** ℗ 🖵 ⌂ ⚭ (wheelchairs available) toilets for disabled shop ⊗ (ex assist dogs) ▭

HASTINGS   MAP 05 TQ80

Blue Reef Aquarium NEW

Rock-a-nore Rd TN34 3DW

➲ *(Follow signs to end of Rock-a-nore Rd on seafront)*

☎ 01424 721483

e-mail: hastings@bluereefaquarium.co.uk

web: www.bluereefaquarium.co.uk

Undersea safari in Hastings. Come face to face with seahorses, sharks, giant crabs, stingrays and many of other aquatic creatures. At the aquarium's heart is a giant ocean tank where an underwater walkthrough tunnel offers close encounters with giant wrasse, tropical sharks and hundreds of colourful fish. Talks and feeding displays take place throughout the day.

Times Open all year daily 10-5. Closed 25 Dec. **Fee** ✳ £7.50 (ch £5.50, concessions £6.50) **Facilities** ℗ (charged) ⬚ ⅊ (Partly accessible) toilets for disabled shop ⊗ (ex assist dogs)

Old Town Hall Museum of Local History

Old Town Hall, High St TN34 1EW

➲ *(off A259 coast road into High St in Hastings old town. Signed)*

☎ 0845 2741053

e-mail: oldtownmuseum@hastings.gov.uk

web: www.hmag.org.uk

Situated in the heart of Hastings Old Town, the museum was originally a Georgian Town Hall built in 1823. Refurbished displays tell the story of Hastings Old Town as a walk back in time, with features including a Cinque Ports ship, and interactive displays.

Times Open Oct-Mar, Mon-Fri 10-4, Sat & Sun 11-4; Apr-Sep, Mon-Sat 10-5, Sun 11-5. ⁰ **Facilities** ℗ (150yds) (parking meters in operation) ⅊ (lift, evac chair, low-level displays, audio tour) toilets for disabled shop ⊗ (ex assist dogs)

Shipwreck & Coastal Heritage Centre

Rock-a-Nore TN34 3DW

➲ *(old town E end of A259, turn into Rock-A-Nore rd. On right between Fishermans Museum & Underwater World)*

☎ 01424 437452

web: www.shipwreck-heritage.org.uk

Sited in the historic town of Hastings, in the middle of the 'Maritime Park' shoreline, the Centre opened in 1986 and tells the story of shipwrecks around the area. It also explores the geological and environmental circumstances that have preserved these wrecks, two of which can be visited, where they sank, at certain very low tides. The audio-visual presentation is narrated by Christopher Lee. There are also fossils of dinosaurs and plants on display.

Times Open Jan-Mar, Sat & Sun 11-4; Apr-Dec, daily 10-5. **Facilities** ℗ (50yds) ⅊ shop ⊗ (ex assist dogs) ▬

Smugglers Adventure

St Clements Caves, West Hill TN34 3HY

➲ *(follow brown signs on A259, coast road, through Hastings. Use seafront car park, then take West Cliff railway or follow signed footpath)*

☎ 01424 422964

e-mail: smugglers@discoverhastings.co.uk

web: www.discoverhastings.co.uk

Journey deep into the heart of Hastings historic West Hill to discover the fascinating world of the Smugglers Adventure in St Clements Caves. Join notorious smuggler 'Hairy Jack' as he leads you through acres of underground caverns, passages and tunnels on a voyage back through time to the heyday of smuggling.

Times Open all year daily, Apr-Sep 10-5; Oct-Mar 11-4. **Fee** ✳ £6.75 (ch £4.75, concessions £5.75). Family ticket £19.99 **Facilities** ℗ (500yds) ⅊ (40 steps to entrance & exit the attraction) shop ⊗ ▬

1066 Story in Hastings Castle

Castle Hill Rd, West Hill TN34 3RG

➲ *(close to A259 seafront, 2m from B2093)*

☎ 01424 781111 & 781112 (info line)

e-mail: bookings@discoverhastings.co.uk

web: www.hastings.gov.uk

The ruins of the Norman castle stand on the cliffs, close to the site of William the Conqueror's first motte-and-bailey castle in England. It was excavated in 1825 and 1968, and old dungeons were discovered in 1894. An unusual approach to the castle can be made via the West Hill Cliff Railway.

Times ✳ Open daily, Oct-26 Mar 11-3.30, 27 Mar-Sep 10-5. Closed 24-26 Dec. **Facilities** ℗ (seafront) (time restrictions, pay & display) ⌂ ⅊ (concrete slope, some uneven ground) shop ⊗ (ex assist dogs)

HERSTMONCEUX   MAP 05 TQ61

The Observatory Science Centre

BN27 1RN

⮑ *(0.75m N of Wartling village)*

☎ 01323 832731

e-mail: info@the-observatory.org

web: www.the-observatory.org

From the 1950s to the 1980s this was part of the Royal Greenwich Observatory, and was used by astronomers to observe and chart movements in the night sky. Visitors can learn about not only astronomy, but also other areas of science in a series of interactive and engaging displays. There are also exhibitions, a discovery park, and a collection of unusual giant exhibits. 2009 is also the International Year of Astronomy.

Times Open daily from 26 Jan-Nov. Open wknd of Dec 6-7. **Fee** ✳ £7 (ch 4-15 £5.18). Family ticket (2ad+3ch or 1ad+4ch) £21.50, Family of 5 £24.50. **Facilities** Ⓟ ⲇ ⊓ (indoor & outdoor) ⟨ (Partly accessible) (ramps & disabled entrance, lift to 1st floor) toilets for disabled shop ⊗ (ex assist dogs) ⬛

The Truggery   `FREE`

Coopers Croft BN27 1QL

⮑ *(from A22 at Hailsham, Boship rdbt, take A271 towards Bexhill for 4m)*

☎ 01323 832314

e-mail: info@truggery.co.uk

web: www.truggery.co.uk

The art of Sussex trug making can be seen through all the work processes including preparing timber, use of the draw knife and assembly of trug. There is a wide selection of Sussex Trugs and locally made garden related items. 2009 is the Truggery's 110th anniversary.

Times Open all year Thu-Sat 10-1, or by appointment. **Facilities** Ⓟ ⟨ (path to workshop is over rough ground) shop ⬛

LEWES   MAP 05 TQ41

Anne of Cleves House

52 Southover High St BN7 1JA

⮑ *(S of town centre off A27/A26/A275)*

☎ 01273 474610

e-mail: anne@sussexpast.co.uk

web: www.sussexpast.co.uk

Henry VIII gave this beautiful timber-framed house to Anne of Cleves, his fourth wife, as part of her divorce settlement. Today there are collections of early English furniture, Sussex pottery and stone from Lewes Priory, plus a local social history exhibition. The Wealden Iron Gallery tells the story of the industrial past of Sussex and contains a large collection of iron artefacts.

Times ✳ Open Jan-Feb & Nov-Dec, Tue-Sat 10-5; Mar-Oct, Tue-Sat 10-5, Sun, Mon & BHs 11-5. Closed 24-26 Dec. **Facilities** Ⓟ (25yds) (on street-2hr restriction) ⟨ (Partly accessible) shop ⊗ (ex assist dogs) ⬛

Charleston

Firle BN8 6LL

⮑ *(Signed off A27, 7m E of Lewes between the villages of Firle and Selmeston)*

☎ 01323 811265 & 811626

e-mail: info@charleston.org.uk

web: www.charleston.org.uk

From 1916 Charleston was the home of the artists Vanessa Bell and Duncan Grant, and a rural retreat for the Bloomsbury Group. Over the years the house was transformed and filled with furniture, textiles and art by them and their contemporaries including Picasso, Renoir, Sickert, Derain and Lamb. The Downland setting captures their pioneering, creative and Bohemian way of life. The walled garden was redesigned in a style reminiscent of southern Europe, with mosaics, box hedges, gravel pathways and ponds, but with a touch of Bloomsbury humour in the placing of the statuary. Special events: The Charleston Literary Festival every May, plus other events throughout the year.

Times Open Wed & Sat 11.30-6, Thu-Fri, Sun & BH 2-6 (Thu & Fri 11.30-6 Jul-Aug) **Fee** House and grounds £7.50 (ch 6-16 £5) **Facilities** Ⓟ ⲇ ⊓ (outdoor) ⟨ (ground floor of house only) toilets for disabled shop ⊗ (ex assist dogs) ⬛

Lewes Castle & Barbican House Museum

169 High St BN7 1YE

⮑ *(N of High St off A27/A26/A275)*

☎ 01273 486290

e-mail: castle@sussexpast.co.uk

web: www.sussexpast.co.uk

One of the oldest castles in England, built soon after the Norman Conquest, and one of only two in England to be built on two mounds. The views over Lewes, the River Ouse and surrounding Downs are worth the climb up the Keep. Barbican House Museum, opposite the Castle tells the story of Sussex from the Stone Age to the end of the medieval period, and displays include flint tools, pottery, weapons, jewellery and other archaeological discoveries, as well as a model of

CONTINUED

LEWES CONTINUED

Lewes in about 1870. Special family sessions on archaeological and historical themes are run throughout the year. Other events include a Medieval Day in May and open-air theatre.

Times ✳ Open daily, Tue-Sat 10-5.30, Sun, Mon & BHs 11-5.30. (Last admission 30 mins before closing). Closed Xmas & Mon in Jan. **Facilities** ℗ (on street parking) ♿ shop ⊗ (ex assist dogs) ▬

NEWHAVEN   MAP 05 TQ40

Paradise Park, Heritage Trail & Gardens
Avis Rd BN9 0DH

➲ *(signed off A26 & A259)*

☎ 01273 512123

e-mail: promotions@paradisepark.co.uk

web: www.paradisepark.co.uk

A perfect day out for plant lovers whatever the season. Discover the unusual garden designs with waterfalls, fountains and lakes, including the Caribbean garden and the tranquil Oriental garden. The Conservatory Gardens complex contains a large variety of the world's flora divided into several zones. There's also a Sussex history trail and Planet Earth with moving dinosaurs and interactive displays, plus rides and amusements for children. 2009 is the 20th anniversary of Paradise Park.

Times Open all year, daily 9-6. Closed 25-26 Dec. **Fee** ✳ £7.99 (ch £5.99). Family ticket £23.99 (2ad+2ch). **Facilities** ℗ ⊑🍴🗏 (outdoor) ♿ (all areas level or ramped) toilets for disabled shop garden centre ⊗ (ex assist dogs) ▬

NORTHIAM   MAP 05 TQ82

Great Dixter House & Gardens
TN31 6PH

➲ *(off A28, signed)*

☎ 01797 252878

e-mail: office@greatdixter.co.uk

web: www.greatdixter.co.uk

Birthplace and home of Christopher Lloyd, gardening writer, Great Dixter was built in 1460 and boasts one of the largest timber-framed buildings in the country. Lutyens was employed to restore both the house and gardens in 1910. The gardens are now a combination of meadows, ponds, topiary and notably the Long Border and Exotic Garden.

Times Open Apr-Oct, Garden 11-5.30; House 2-5, Tue-Sun & BH Mon. **Facilities** ℗ 🗏 (outdoor) ♿ (Partly accessible) (2 wheelchairs available free of charge) toilets for disabled shop garden centre ⊗ (ex assist dogs) ▬

PEVENSEY   MAP 05 TQ60

Pevensey Castle
BN24 5LE

➲ *(off A259)*

☎ 01323 762604

web: www.english-heritage.org.uk

William the Conqueror landed here in 1066 and established his first stronghold. Discover the history of the Norman castle and the remains of an unusual keep through the free audio tour.

Times Open 21 Mar-Sep, daily 10-6; Oct, daily 10-4; Nov-Mar, Sat-Sun 10-4. Closed 24-26 Dec & 1 Jan. **Fee** £4.20 (concessions £3.40, ch £2.10). Family £10.50. Prices and opening times are subject to change in March 2009. Please check web site or call 0870 333 1181 for the most up to date prices and opening times when planning your visit. **Facilities** ℗ (charged) ⊑ shop ⌗

RYE   MAP 05 TQ92

Lamb House
West St TN31 7ES

➲ *(facing W end of Church)*

☎ 01580 762334

e-mail: lambhouse@nationaltrust.org.uk

web: www.nationaltrust.org.uk

This 18th-century house was the home of novelist Henry James from 1898 until his death in 1916, and was later occupied by the writer, E F Benson. Some of James' personal posessions can be seen. There is also a charming walled garden.

Times Open 24 Mar-29 Oct, Thu & Sat 2-6 (last admission 5.30) **Fee** ✳ £2.90 (ch£1.40). Family ticket £7.25. Groups £2.50 per person. **Facilities** ℗ (500mtrs) ♿ (Partly accessible) (scented plants & herbs, some steps to house) ⊗ (ex assist dogs) 🐾

Rye Castle Museum
3 East St TN31 7JY

➲ *(in town centre, on A259. Museum is on 2 sites, East St & Ypres Tower)*

☎ 01797 226728

e-mail: info@ryemuseum.co.uk

web: www.ryemuseum.co.uk

Part of the museum is housed in a stone tower built as a fortification in 1249. The museum's collection of ironwork, medieval pots and smuggling items are on display here, while the East Street site contains the rest of the collection, including pottery made in Rye, fashions, an 18th-century fire engine, toys, cinque port regalia, a special exhibition on Rye between the wars, descriptions of the changes to the harbour and shipbuilding in Rye and businesses and leisure in Rye during the 19th and 20th centuries.

Times ✳ Open all year Apr-Oct, Thu-Mon 10.30-1 & 2-5. East St site only open 2-5 wkdys, full hrs Sat & Sun. Nov-Mar Ypres Tower open wknds 10.30-3.30 (last admission 30 mins before closing). **Facilities** ℗ (30yds) (street 1hr) (long stay 10mins away) ♿ (only East Street accessible, part of garden) toilets for disabled shop ⊗ (ex assist dogs)

SHEFFIELD PARK   MAP 05 TQ42

Sheffield Park Garden

TN22 3QX

➲ *(midway between East Grinstead & Lewes, 5m NW of Uckfield, on E side of A275, between A272 & A22)*

☎ 01825 790231

e-mail: sheffieldpark@nationaltrust.org.uk

web: www.nationaltrust.org.uk/sheffieldpark

Sheffield Park was originally landscaped by 'Capability' Brown, in about 1775 to create a beautiful park with four lakes and cascades. Further extensive planting was done at the beginning of the 20th century, to give emphasis to autumn colour among the trees. In May and June masses of azaleas and rhododendrons bloom and later there are magnificent waterlilies on the lakes. Autumn brings stunning colours from the many rare trees and shrubs. 2009 is the centenary of 3rd Earl of Sheffield's death. Special events run throughout the year please check website for details.

Times Open all year. Please phone for details or check website **Fee** Please call for details or check website **Facilities** ♿ ☐ ☂ (outdoor) ♿ (most of the garden is accessible, please phone for further details) (powered self drive cars pre-book, wheelchairs) toilets for disabled shop garden centre ⊗ (ex assist dogs) ♨ ⬛

SHEFFIELD PARK STATION   MAP 05 TQ42

Bluebell Railway

Sheffield Park Station TN22 3QL

➲ *(4.5m E of Haywards Heath, off A275, 10m S of East Grinstead A22-A275)*

☎ 01825 720800 & 722370

e-mail: info@bluebell-railway.co.uk

web: www.bluebell-railway.co.uk

A volunteer-run heritage steam railway with nine miles of track running through pretty Sussex countryside. Please note that there is no parking at Kingscote Station. If you wish to board the train here, catch the bus (service 473) which connects Kingscote and East Grinstead.

Times Open all year, Sat & Sun, daily Apr-Oct & during school hols. Santa Specials run Dec. For timetable and information regarding trains contact above. **Facilities** ♿ ☐ ☂ (indoor) ♿ (Partly accessible) (special carriage for wheelchairs & carers with lift) toilets for disabled shop ⬛

TICEHURST   MAP 05 TQ63

Pashley Manor Gardens

TN5 7HE

➲ *(on B2099 between A21 and Ticehurst village, follow brown tourist signs)*

☎ 01580 200888

e-mail: info@pashleymanorgardens.com

web: www.pashleymanorgardens.com

Once belonging to the family of Anne Boleyn, Pashley Manor has a beautiful traditional English garden. Visitors can wander among fine old trees, fountains, springs and large ponds, all surrounded by romantic landscaping and imaginative plantings, and interspersed with statues and sculptures by leading European sculptors. Special events take place throughout the year. Please telephone for details.

Times Open early Apr-Sep, Tue-Thu, Sat & BH Mon 11-5; Garden only Oct, Mon-Fri 10-4. **Fee** ✳ £7 (ch £5) Group rate 20+ £6.50. Tulip festival £7.50. Special Rose wknd £7. Craft show £5.50 **Facilities** ♿ ⁍◉⁌ licensed ⎷ (outdoor) ♿ (formal gardens, gift shop & cafe can be accessed. No access to woodland, and some areas of garden have sloping and gravel paths) (ramps, 2 w/chairs for loan) toilets for disabled shop ⊗ (ex assist dogs) ⬛

WEST SUSSEX

Fulking Escarpment

AMBERLEY

MAP 04 TQ01

Amberley Working Museum

BN18 9LT

⮑ *(on B2139, between Arundel and Storrington, adjacent to Amberley railway station)*

☎ 01798 831370

e-mail: office@amberleymuseum.co.uk

web: www.amberleymuseum.co.uk

This 36 acre open-air museum is dedicated to the industrial heritage of the south east of England. Traditional craftspeople on site (including a blacksmith and potter), working narrow-gauge railway and vintage bus collection, Connected Earth telecommunications display, Seeboard Electricity Hall, stationary engines, print workshop, woodturners, wheelwrights, nature trails, restaurant, shop and much more.

Times ✳ Open 12 Mar-2 Nov, Wed-Sun & BH Mon 10-5.30 (last admission 4.30). Also open daily during school hols. **Facilities** ❷ ⏛ 🚻 ♿ (wheelchairs available for loan & large print guides) toilets for disabled shop ▬

ARDINGLY

MAP 05 TQ32

Wakehurst Place & Millennium Seed Bank

Royal Botanic Gardens RH17 6TN

⮑ *(M23 junct 10, 1.5m NW of Ardingly, on B2028, follow brown tourist signs)*

☎ 01444 894066

e-mail: wakehurst@kew.org

web: www.kew.org

Woodland and lakes linked by a pretty watercourse make this large garden a beautiful place to walk, with an amazing variety of interesting trees and shrubs, a winter garden, and a rock walk. Also on site is the Millennium Seed Bank, dedicated to the conservation of seeds from wild plants. The garden is administered and maintained by the Royal Botanic Gardens, Kew.

Times Open all year, Mar-Oct 10-6, Nov-Feb 10-430. Closed 24-25 Dec. **Fee** £9 (under 17's free) **Facilities** ❷ ⏛ 🍴 🚻 (indoor & outdoor) ♿ (Partly accessible) (manual & electric wheelchairs available) toilets for disabled shop garden centre ⊗ (ex assist dogs) ▬

ARUNDEL

MAP 04 TQ00

Arundel Castle

BN18 9AB

⮑ *(on A27 between Chichester & Worthing)*

☎ 01903 882173

e-mail: info@arundelcastle.org

web: www.arundelcastle.org

Set high on a hill in West Sussex, this magnificent castle and stately home, seat of the Dukes of Norfolk for nearly 1,000 years, commands stunning views across the river Arun and out to sea. Climb to the keep and battlements; marvel at a fine collection of 16th-century furniture; portraits by Van Dyke, Gainsborough, Canaletto and others; tapestries

and the personal possessions of Mary, Queen of Scots; wander in the grounds and renovated Victorian flower and vegetable gardens.

Arundel Castle

Times ✳ Open Apr-Oct, Sun-Fri 11-5, Castle open 12-5. (Last admission 4). Closed Sat. **Facilities** ❷ (charged) ⏛ ♿ (chair lift) toilets for disabled shop ⊗ (ex assist dogs) ▬

See advert on this page

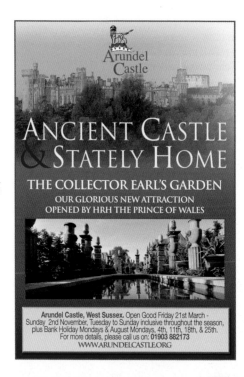

ARUNDEL CONTINUED

WWT Arundel

Mill Rd BN18 9PB

➲ *(signed from A27 & A29)*

☎ 01903 881524

e-mail: arundel@wwt.org.uk

web: www.wwt.org.uk

Many hundreds of ducks, geese and swans from all over the world can be found here, many of which are so friendly that they will eat from your hand. The wild reserve attracts a variety of birds and includes a reedbed habitat considered so vital to the wetland wildlife it shelters that it has been designated a Site of Special Scientific Interest. Visitors can walk right through this reedbed on a specially designed boardwalk. Every day there are Boat Safaris through the Wetland Discovery area (between 11am and 4pm). There is a packed programme of events and activities throughout the year.

Times Open all year, daily; summer 9.30-5.30; winter 9.30-4.30. (Last admission summer 5; winter 4). Closed 25 Dec. **Fee** ✳ With Gift Aid donation: £8.50 (ch £4.25 concessions £7.15). Family ticket £22.95. Without Gift Aid donation: £7.72 (ch £3.86 concessions £6.47) Family ticket £20.84 **Facilities** ℗ ⊈ ⑩ licensed ☖ (outdoor) ♿ (level paths, free wheelchair loan) toilets for disabled shop ⊗ (ex assist dogs) ➰

BIGNOR   MAP 04 SU91

Bignor Roman Villa & Museum

RH20 1PH

➲ *(6m S of Pulborough & 6m N of Arundel on A29, signed. 8m S of Petworth on A285, signed)*

☎ 01798 869259

e-mail: bignorromanvilla@care4free.net

web: www.pyrrha.demon.co.uk

Rediscovered in 1811, this Roman house was built on a grand scale. It is one of the largest known, and has spectacular mosaics. The heating system can also be seen, and various finds from excavations are on show. The longest mosaic in Britain (82ft) is on display here in its original position.

Times ✳ Open Mar-Apr, Tue-Sun & BH 10-5; May daily 10-5; Jun-Sep daily 10-6, Oct daily 10-5 **Facilities** ℗ ⊈ ☖ (outdoor) ♿ (most areas accessible) shop ⊗ (ex assist dogs) ➰

BRAMBER   MAP 04 TQ11

Bramber Castle   FREE

BN4 3FB

➲ *(on W side of village off A283)*

web: www.english-heritage.org.uk

The remains of a Norman motte and bailey castle. The gatehouse, still standing almost to its original height, and walls are still visible.

Times Open any reasonable time. **Facilities** ℗ ⚘

CHICHESTER   MAP 04 SU80

Chichester Cathedral

West St PO19 1PX

➲ *(in city centre)*

☎ 01243 782595

e-mail: visitors@chichestercathedral.org.uk

web: www.chichestercathedral.org.uk

The beauty of the 900-year-old cathedral, site of the shrine of St Richard, is enhanced by many art treasures, ancient and modern.

Times Open end Mar-end Sep daily 7.15-7; end Sep-end Mar 7.15-6. **Fee** Donations invited. **Facilities** ℗ (within city walls) ⊈ ⑩ licensed ♿ (touch & hearing centre, loop system) toilets for disabled shop ⊗ (ex assist dogs)

Mechanical Music & Doll Collection

Church Rd, Portfield PO19 7HN

➲ *(1m E of Chichester, signed off A27)*

☎ 01243 372646

A unique opportunity to see and hear barrel organs, polyphons, musical boxes, fair organs etc - all fully restored and playing. A magical musical tour to fascinate and entertain all ages. The doll collection contains fine examples of Victorian china and wax dolls, and felt and velvet dolls of the 1920s.

Times Group bookings only: anytime in the year by prior arrangement. **Fee** ✳ £2, min group £40 (ch £1, min group £30). **Facilities** ℗ ♿ (one step within main hall) shop ⊗ (ex assist dogs)

Pallant House Gallery

9 North Pallant PO19 1TJ

➲ *(from city centre (the Cross) take East St turning right at Superdrug. Gallery at end of North Pallant on left)*

☎ 01243 774557

e-mail: info@pallant.org.uk

web: www.pallant.org.uk

A Queen Anne townhouse and a modern building have been combined to house a fine collection of 20th-century British art. The permanent collection includes pieces by: Auerbach, Blake, Bomberg, Caulfield, Freud, Hamilton, Hitchens, Leger, Moore, Nicholson, Piper, Richards, Severini, Sickert and Sutherland. Telephone or visit website for details of temporary exhibitions.

Times Open Tue-Sat, 10-5 (Thu 10-8), Sun & BHs, 12.30-5. **Fee** ✳ £7.50 (ch £2.30, students £4). Family ticket £17. Cheap Tue - half price. **Facilities** ℗ (100 yds) ⊈ ⑩ ♿ toilets for disabled shop ⊗ (ex assist dogs) ➰

EAST GRINSTEAD
MAP 05 TQ33

Standen
West Hoathly Rd RH19 4NE

➲ *(2m S of East Grinstead, signed from B2110)*

☎ 01342 323029

e-mail: standen@nationaltrust.org.uk

web: www.nationaltrust.org.uk/standen

Life in a Victorian family home is brought vividly to life in this gem of the Arts & Crafts Movement. Standen is hidden at the end of a quiet Sussex lane with fine views over the High Weald and Weir Wood Reservoir. The design of the house, which incorporates the original medieval farmhouse, is a monument to the combined genius of architect Philip Webb and his friend William Morris. All the big names of the Arts & Crafts period are represented including ceramics by William de Morgan, furniture by George Jack and metal work by W. A. S. Benson. The beautiful hillside gardens provide year-round interest and the woodlands now offer a number of easily accessible, and picturesque, walks.

Times House open 11-4.30, 1-9 Mar, Sat & Sun; 15 Mar-20 Jul & 3 Sep-2 Nov, Wed-Sun & BH; 21 Jul-Aug, Wed-Mon; 11-3, 8 Nov-21 Dec, Sat & Sun. Garden open same dates as house, but closes 5.30 Mar-early Nov. **Fee** ✻ House & garden £7.80. Garden only £4.60 (ch half price). Family ticket £19.50. **Facilities** ❷ ❀ ㅠ (outdoor) ఈ (ground floor of house accessible. Some parts of garden steep with steps) (Braille guide & touch list & large print guide) toilets for disabled shop ✪ (ex assist dogs) ✺ ➡

FISHBOURNE
MAP 04 SU80

Fishbourne Roman Palace
Salthill Rd PO19 3QR

➲ *(off A27 onto A259 into Fishbourne. Turn right into Salthill Rd & right into Roman Way)*

☎ 01243 785859

e-mail: adminfish@sussexpast.co.uk

web: www.sussexpast.co.uk

The remains of the Roman Palace at Fishbourne were discovered in 1960. Here you can see Britain's largest collection of in-situ Roman floor mosaics. More everyday Roman objects found during the excavations are displayed in the museum gallery. An audio-visual presentation uses computer-generated images to interpret the site. Outside the garden has been replanted to its original plan, using plants that may have grown there when the palace was inhabited. The new Collections Discovery Centre displays more artefacts from both Fishbourne and Chichester district. Join a 'behind the scenes' tour for an opportunity to handle some of these. Special events include a Celtic Spring Festival in April, Roman Gladiator re-enactment weekend in September and a week of Roman army activities for all the family in October.

Times ✻ Open all year, daily Feb-15 Dec. Feb, Nov-mid Dec 10-4; Mar-Jul & Sep-Oct 10-5; Aug 10-6. Winter wknds 10-4. **Facilities** ❷ ❀ ㅠ (outdoor) ఈ (self guiding tapes & tactile objects, audio/visual room) toilets for disabled shop ✪ (ex assist dogs) ➡

FONTWELL
MAP 04 SU90

Denmans Garden
Denmans Ln BN18 0SU

➲ *(5m E of Chichester off A27 W between Chichester and Arundel, adjacent to Fontwell racecourse)*

☎ 01243 542808

e-mail: denmans@denmans-garden.co.uk

web: www.denmans-garden.co.uk

The garden, jointly owned by John Brookes MBE and Michael Neve, is planted for all-year interest with emphasis on shape, colour and texture, and although four acres in size, is full of planting and design ideas that can be adapted to suit any size of garden. Gravel is used extensively in the garden, both to walk on and as a growing medium, so that you can walk through plantings rather than past them. Individual plants are allowed to self-seed and ramble.

Times Open all year daily 9-5. Closed 25-26 Dec & 1 Jan. **Fee** ✻ £4.25 (ch £2.50, ch under 4 free, pen £3.80). Family ticket £12.50 Party 15+ £3.60 each. **Facilities** ❷ ❀ ఈ toilets for disabled shop garden centre ✪ (ex assist dogs) ➡

GOODWOOD
MAP 04 SU81

Goodwood House
PO18 0PX

➲ *(3m NE of Chichester)*

☎ 01243 755048

e-mail: curator@goodwood.co.uk

web: www.goodwood.co.uk

The Sussex Downs and 12,000 acre working country estate provide a glorious backdrop to the magnificent Regency house, which has been the home of the Dukes of Richmond for over 300 years. The gilded, richly-decorated State Apartments include the luxurious Yellow Drawing Room and the unique Egyptian Dining Room. The art collection includes paintings by George Stubbs and Canaletto.

Times Open end Mar-early Oct, Sun & Mon, 1-5; Aug, Sun-Thu. Closed for occasional events. **Fee** ✻ £8.50 (ch under 12 free, ch & student £4, pen £7.50). Groups am £9 each, pm £7.50 each. Family ticket £15 **Facilities** ❷ ❀ ఈ (ramp at front of house, disabled parking area) toilets for disabled shop ✪ (ex assist dogs) ➡

HANDCROSS   MAP 04 TQ22

Nymans

RH17 6EB

➲ *(on B2114 at Handcross, 4.5m S of Crawley)*

☎ 01444 405250

e-mail: nymans@nationaltrust.org.uk

web: www.nationaltrust.org.uk/nymans

One of the great 20th-century gardens, with an important collection of rare plants, set around a romantic house and ruins in a beautiful woodland estate. Theatrically designed with plants from around the world, Nymans is internationally renowned for its garden design, rare plant collection and intimacy. Visit the Messel family rooms in the house, and see the dramatic ruins, which form a backdrop to the main lawn. Enjoy fine views across the Sussex countryside and explore the wide estate with walks through ancient woodland, lakes and wild flowers. Nymans is one of the leading 'green' gardens in the National Trust, actively engaging visitors with its methods of sustainable gardening. There is an extensive and varied events programme, including family activities, horticultural workshops and summer theatre.

Times Garden: Open all year Wed-Sun & BH 10-5; Nov-Jan 10-4. Last admission 30mins before closing. House: open 11 Mar-1 Nov, 11-4. Closed 25-26 Dec & 1 Jan. Last admission to house 3.45pm **Fee** £7.70 (ch £3.90), Family ticket (2ad + 3ch) £19. **Facilities ℗** ☕ 🍴 licensed 🌲 (outdoor) ⚒ (accessible WCs, Wheelchairs, mobility buggy tours) toilets for disabled shop garden centre ⊗ (ex assist dogs) ♨ ✉

HAYWARDS HEATH   MAP 05 TQ32

Borde Hill Garden

Balcombe Rd RH16 1XP

➲ *(0.5m N of Haywards Heath on Balcombe Rd, 3m from A23)*

☎ 01444 450326

e-mail: info@bordehill.co.uk

web: www.bordehill.co.uk

This glorious garden flows into linked garden rooms, boasting their own distinctive character and style. Year-round colour and interest with spring flowering rhododendrons, azaleas, camellias, magnolias and many champion trees. The Rose and Italian Gardens with the herbaceous borders provide colour for summer and into autumn. Set in 200 acres of parkland with panoramic views, woodland and lakeside walks.

Times Open Apr-Oct, 10-6. **Facilities ℗** ☕ 🍴 🌲 (outdoor) ⚒ (wheelchairs available, audio/Braille guides) toilets for disabled shop ✉

HIGHDOWN   MAP 04 SU91

Highdown FREE

Highdown Gardens BN12 6PE

➲ *(N off A259 between Worthing & Littlehampton. Access off dual carriageway, when coming from E proceed to rdbt)*

☎ 01903 501054

e-mail: chris.beardsley@worthing.gov.uk

web: www.worthing.gov.uk/wbc

Set on downland countryside this unique garden overlooks the sea, and has been deemed a National collection due to the unique assortment of rare plants and trees. The garden was the achievement of Sir Frederick and Lady Stern, who worked for fifty years to prove that plants could grow on chalk. Many of the original plants were collected in China and the Himalayas.

Times Open all year: Apr-Sep, Mon-Fri 10-6. Winter: Oct-Nov & Feb-Mar, Mon-Fri, 10-4.30; Dec-Jan, 10-4. **Facilities ℗** 🌲 (outdoor) ⚒ (gardens on a sloping site, may prove difficult for wheelchair users) toilets for disabled ⊗ (ex assist dogs)

LITTLEHAMPTON   MAP 04 TQ00

Look & Sea! Visitor Centre 2 for 1

63-65 Surrey St BN17 5AW

➲ *(on harbour front 10 mins walk from Littlehampton Station)*

☎ 01903 718984

e-mail: info@lookandsea.co.uk

web: www.lookandsea.co.uk

An interactive museum exploring the history and geography of Littlehampton and the surrounding area. Inside the modern waterfront building you can meet the 500,000 year old Boxgrove Man, become a ship's captain in an interactive computer game, and enjoy spectacular panoramic views of the Sussex coast from the circular glass tower.

Times Open all year, daily 9-5 **Fee** £2.95 (ch & concessions £2.50). **Facilities ℗** (charged) ☕ 🍴 licensed ⚒ toilets for disabled shop ⊗ (ex assist dogs) ✉

LOWER BEEDING MAP 04 TQ22

Leonardslee Lakes & Gardens

RH13 6PP

➲ *(4m SW from Handcross, at junct of B2110 & A281)*

☎ 01403 891212

e-mail: gardens@leonardslee.com

web: www.leonardslee.com

This Grade I listed garden is set in a peaceful valley with walks around seven beautiful lakes. It is a paradise in spring, with banks of rhododendrons and azaleas along paths lined with bluebells. Wallabies live in parts of the valley, deer in the parks and wildfowl on the lakes. Enjoy the Rock Garden, the fascinating Bonsai, the 'Behind the Doll's House' exhibition and the collection of Victorian Motorcars (1889-1900).

Times ✳ Open Apr-Oct, daily 9.30-6 **Facilities** shop garden centre

PETWORTH MAP 04 SU92

Petworth House & Park

GU28 0AE

➲ *(in town centre, A272/283)*

☎ 01798 342207 & 343929

e-mail: petworth@nationaltrust.org.uk

web: www.nationaltrust.org.uk/petworth

Petworth house is an impressive 17th-century mansion set in a 700 acre deer park, landscaped by 'Capability' Brown, and immortalised in Turner's paintings. At Petworth you will find the National Trust's finest art collection including work by Van Dyck, Titian, and Turner, as well as sculpture, ceramics and fine furniture. Fascinating Servants' Quarters show the domestic side of life of this great estate.

Times Open Mar-Oct, Sat-Wed 11-5 (last entry 4.30) **Fee** £10.40 (ch £5.20). Family ticket £26. NT members free. Pleasure Ground £4 (ch £2.10). **Facilities** licensed (staircase to first floor bedrooms and steps down into chapel) (wheelchairs, Braille guide, induction loop, virtual tour) toilets for disabled shop (ex assist dogs)

PULBOROUGH MAP 04 TQ01

Parham House & Gardens

Parham Park, Storrington RH20 4HS

➲ *(midway between A29 & A24, off A283 between Pulborough & Storrington)*

☎ 01903 744888 & 742021

e-mail: enquiries@parhaminsussex.co.uk

web: www.parhaminsussex.co.uk

Surrounded by a deer park, fine gardens and 18th-century pleasure grounds in a beautiful downland setting, this Elizabethan family home contains an important collection of paintings, furniture, carpets and rare needlework. There are four acres of walled garden with huge herbaceous borders, greenhouse, orchard and herb garden. A brick and turf maze has been created in the grounds - designed with children in mind, it is called 'Veronica's Maze'.

Times ✳ Open Etr Sun-Sep, Wed, Thu, Sun & BH Mons (also open Tue & Fri in Aug). Gardens open 12-5; House 2-5. **Facilities** (outdoor) (Partly accessible) (wheelchairs, ramps, recorded tour tape, parking) toilets for disabled shop (ex assist dogs & in grounds)

RSPB Pulborough Brooks Nature Reserve

Uppertons Barn Visitor Centre, Wiggonholt RH20 2EL

➲ *(signed on A283, 2m SE of Pulborough & 2m NW of Storrington)*

☎ 01798 875851

e-mail: pulborough.brooks@rspb.org.uk

web: www.rspb.org.uk

Set in the scenic Arun Valley and easily reached via the visitor centre at Wiggonholt, this is an excellent reserve for year-round family visits. A nature trail winds through hedgerow-lined lanes to viewing hides overlooking water-meadows. Breeding summer birds include nightingales and warblers, ducks and wading birds, and nightjars and hobbies on nearby heathland. Unusual wading birds and hedgerow birds regularly pass through on spring and autumn migration.

Times Open daily, Reserve: 9-9, (or sunset if earlier). Visitor centre: 9.30-5. Reserve closed 25 Dec, Visitor Centre closed 25-26 Dec. **Facilities** (outdoor) (free hire electric buggy and wheelchair) toilets for disabled shop (ex assist dogs)

SINGLETON   MAP 04 SU81

Weald & Downland Open Air Museum

PO18 0EU

➲ *(6m N of Chichester on A286)*

☎ 01243 811348

e-mail: office@wealddown.co.uk

web: www.wealddown.co.uk

A showcase of English architectural heritage, where historic buildings have been rescued from destruction and rebuilt in a parkland setting. Vividly demonstrating the evolution of building techniques and use of local materials, these fascinating buildings bring to life the homes, farms and rural industries of the south east of the past 500 years.

Times Open all year, Mar-Oct, daily 10.30-6. Rest of year, 10.30-4. Winter opening days vary, see website for details. **Fee** ✳ £8.50 (ch £4.50, pen £7.50). Family ticket (2ad+3ch) £23.30. **Facilities** ☻ ☗ ⴲ (indoor & outdoor) ዿ (some areas of museum not suitable for disabled visitiors, but most key areas and exhibits are accessible) (separate entrance and ramps available for some buildings) toilets for disabled shop ➡

SOUTH HARTING   MAP 04 SU71

Uppark

GU31 5QR

➲ *(A3 take A272, B2146 to South Harting, follow signs to Uppark)*

☎ 01730 825415 & 825857

e-mail: uppark@nationaltrust.org.uk

web: www.nationaltrust.org.uk/uppark

A late 17th-century house set high on the South Downs with magnificent sweeping views to the sea. The elegant Georgian interior houses a famous Grand Tour collection that includes paintings, furniture and ceramics. An 18th-century dolls' house with original features is one of the more impressive items. The servants' quarters appear as they did in Victorian days, when H G Wells' mother was housekeeper, while the garden is restored in the early 19th-century 'Picturesque' style.

Times Open 29 Mar-29 Oct, Sun-Thu. Garden 11.30-5. House: 12.30-4.30 **Fee** ✳ £7.50 (ch £3.75). Family £18. Garden only £3.50 (ch £1.75) **Facilities** ☻ ☗ ⵏⵎ ⴲ (outdoor) ዿ (ramps, lift to basement, chair lift in exhibition) toilets for disabled shop ⊗ (ex assist & woodland walk) ⴲ ➡

TANGMERE   MAP 04 SU90

Tangmere Military Aviation Museum

PO20 2ES

➲ *(off A27, 3m E of Chichester towards Arundel)*

☎ 01243 790090

e-mail: info@tangmere-museum.org.uk

web: www.tangmere-museum.org.uk

Based at an airfield that played an important role during the World Wars, this museum spans 80 years of military aviation. There are photographs, documents, aircraft and aircraft parts on display along with a Hurricane replica, prototype Spitfire replica and cockpit simulator. Hangars house a Supermarine Swift, English Electric Lightning and the record-breaking aircraft Meteor and Hunter. Aircraft outside include; Lockheed T33, De Havilland Sea Vixen, McDonnell Douglas Phantom F4, Gloster Meteor and a Westland Wessex helicopter.

Times Open Mar-Oct, daily 10-5.30; Feb & Nov, daily 10-4.30. **Fee** ✳ £6 (ch £1.50 & over 60s £5) Family £13.50 (2ad+2ch). **Facilities** ☻ ☗ ⴲ (outdoor) ዿ (wheelchairs available) toilets for disabled shop ⊗ (ex assist dogs)

WEST DEAN   MAP 04 SU81

West Dean Gardens

PO18 0QZ

➲ *(6m N of Chichester and 7m S of Midhurst on A286)*

☎ 01243 818210 & 811301

e-mail: gardens@westdean.org.uk

web: www.westdean.org.uk

Award winning historic garden of 35 acres in a tranquil downland setting. Noted for its 300ft long Harold Peto pergola, mixed and herbaceous borders, rustic summerhouses and specimen trees. Walled kitchen garden with magnificent collection of 16 Victorian glasshouses and frames. St Roche Arboretum offers a wonderful walk, including a new treehouse installation. The visitors' centre provides a high level of facilities with a beautiful prospect of the River Lavant and West Dean Park.

Times Open Mar-Oct, daily 10.30-5, Nov-Feb, 10.30-4, Wed-Sun only. Closed 24 Dec-2 Jan. **Fee** ✳ Mar-Oct, £6 (concessions £2.50). Family ticket £14.25. Nov-Feb, £3 (ch £1.25). Family ticket £7.25. Adult season ticket £22.50, family season ticket £50. **Facilities** ℗ 🚻 ⛽ 🍴 ⋔ (outdoor) ♿ shop, restaurant & majority of gardens accessible. Parkland walk not accessible) (reserved parking, 2 wheelchairs available) toilets for disabled shop garden centre ⊗ (ex assist dogs) 🚍

WISBOROUGH GREEN   MAP 04 TQ02

Fishers Farm Park

Newpound Ln RH14 0EG

➲ *(follow brown & white tourist boards on all roads approaching Wisborough Green)*

☎ 01403 700063

e-mail: info@fishersfarmpark.co.uk

web: www.fishersfarmpark.co.uk

All weather, all year farm and adventure park, providing a mixture of farmyard and dynamic adventure play. Please contact for details of special events.

Times Open all year, daily, 10-5. Closed 26-26 Dec. **Fee** Please phone for details. **Facilities** ℗ 🚻 🍴 ⋔ (outdoor) ♿ toilets for disabled shop ⊗ 🚍

Sheep graze in a field along the South Downs Way

TYNE & WEAR

St Mary's Lighthouse, Whitley Bay

GATESHEAD   MAP 12 NZ26

Baltic Centre for Contemporary Art   FREE

South Shore Rd, Gateshead Quays NE8 3BA

➲ *(follow signs for Quayside, Millennium Bridge. 15 mins' walk from Gateshead Metro & Newcastle Central Station)*

☎ 0191 478 1810 & 440 4944
e-mail: info@balticmill.com
web: www.balticmill.com

Once a 1950s grain warehouse, part of the old Baltic Flour Mills, the Baltic Centre for Contemporary Art is an international centre presenting a dynamic and ambitious programme of complementary exhibitions and events. It consists of five art spaces, cinema, auditorium, library and archive, eating and drinking areas and a shop. Check website for current events information.

Facilities ℗ (charged) ☐ ⅋⁄ ⌐ (outdoor) & (wheelchairs/scooters, braille/large-print guides) toilets for disabled shop ⊗ (ex assist dogs)

JARROW   MAP 12 NZ36

Bede's World

Church Bank NE32 3DY

➲ *(off A185 near S end of Tyne tunnel)*

☎ 0191 489 2106
e-mail: visitor.info@bedesworld.co.uk
web: www.bedesworld.co.uk

Bede's World is an ambitious museum based around the extra-ordinary life and work of the Venerable Bede (AD673-735) early Medieval Europe's greatest scholar and England's first historian. Attractions include an 'Age of Bede' exhibition in the museum, which displays finds excavated from the site of St Paul's monastery. Alongside the museum, Bede's World has developed Gyrwe, an Anglo-Saxon demonstration farm, which brings together the animals, timber buildings, crops and vegetables that would have featured in the Northumbrian Landscape of Bede's Day.

Times Open all year, Apr-Oct, Mon-Sat 10-5.30, Sun noon-5.30; Nov-Mar, Mon-Sat 10-4.30 & Sun 12-4.30. Please contact for Xmas/New Year opening times. **Fee** £5.50 (ch & concessions £3.50). Family ticket £12.50.
Facilities ℗ ☐ ⅋⁄ licensed ⌐ (outdoor) & (w/chair & elec. w/chair on request, disabled parking) toilets for disabled shop ⊗ (ex assist dogs)

NEWCASTLE UPON TYNE   MAP 12 NZ26

Centre for Life

Times Square NE1 4EP

➲ *(A1M, A69, A184, A1058 & A167, follow signs to Centre for Life or Central Station)*

☎ 0191 243 8210
e-mail: info@life.org.uk
web: www.life.org.uk

The Centre for Life is a family science centre full of hands-on activities and exhibitions that bring science to life for all ages.

Times Open all year Mon-Sat 10-6, Sun 11-6 . Closed 25 Dec & 1 Jan. (Last entry subject to seasonal demand). **Fee** ✳ £8 (ch 5-16 £5.85, concessions £6.95). Family ticket (1ad&3 ch) £24.20 (2ad&2ch) £24.20. **Facilities** ℗ (charged) ☐ ⅋⁄ licensed ⌐ (indoor) & (ramps, wheelchairs, induction loops) toilets for disabled shop ⊗ (ex assist dogs)

ROWLANDS GILL   MAP 12 NZ15

Gibside

NE16 6BG

➲ *(3m W of Metro Centre & 6m SW of Gateshead, on B6314, clearly signposted from the A1)*

☎ 01207 541820
e-mail: gibside@nationaltrust.org.uk
web: www.nationaltrust.org.uk

This 18th-century landscaped garden is the former home of the Bowes-Lyon family, with miles of walks through the wooded slopes and riverside of the Derwent valley. Discover hidden vistas, wildlife or wild flowers, or just enjoy a Georgian style lunch in the tea room. Lots of events and activities for children and families, and those interested can hold an Anglican wedding in the unique Palladian Chapel.

Times Grounds open: all year daily 5 Mar-8 Oct 10-6 (last entry 4.30); 23 Oct-4 Mar 10-4 (last entry 3.30) closed 23-26 Dec, 30 Dec-2 Jan; Chapel open 6 Mar-22 Oct 11-4.30 **Fee** ✳ £6 (ch £3.50). Family (2ad+4ch), £17.50, family (1ad+3ch), £12. **Facilities** ℗ ☐ ⅋⁄ & (Braille guide, w/chairs and carriers, induction loop) toilets for disabled shop ♨

SOUTH SHIELDS   MAP 12 NZ36

Arbeia Roman Fort & Museum

Baring St NE33 2BB

➲ *(5 mins' walk from town centre)*

☎ 0191 456 1369
web: www.twmuseums.org.uk

In South Shields are the extensive remains of Arbeia, a Roman fort in use from the 2nd to 4th century. It was the supply base for the Roman army's campaign against Scotland. On site there are full size reconstructions of a fort gateway, a barrack block and part of the commanding officer's house. Archaeological evacuations are in progress throughout the summer.

Times Open all year, Apr-Oct, Mon-Sat 10-5.30, Sun 1-5; Nov-Mar, Mon-Sat 10-3.30. Closed 25-26 Dec & 1 Jan **Fee** ✳ Fort & Museum free of charge ex for 'Timequest' Archaeological Interpretation Gallery £1.50 (ch & concessions 80p). **Facilities** ℗ (on road outside) ⌐ (outdoor) & (Partly accessible) (pre-visit info pack and portable induction loop) toilets for disabled shop ♨

SUNDERLAND   MAP 12 NZ35

National Glass Centre   `FREE`

Liberty Way SR6 0GL

➲ *(A19 onto A1231, signposted from all major roads)*

☎ 0191 515 5555

e-mail: info@nationalglasscentre.com

web: www.nationalglasscentre.com

Housed in a striking modern building, the National Glass Centre celebrates the unique material and explains its history. Visitors can see the changing exhibitions of glass art, featuring pieces by leading artists. There is also the opportunity to witness the glass-making process and learn how it impacts on our lives. The brave can even walk on the glass roof 30 feet above the riverside. In 2009 the National Glass Centre will celebrate its 10th anniversary.

Times Open daily 10-5 (last admission 4.30). Closed 25 Dec & 1 Jan. **Facilities** ❷ ⅋⓾ & (lifts, ramps, parking facilites) toilets for disabled shop ⊗ (ex assist dogs)

Sunderland Museum & Winter Gardens   `FREE`

Burdon Rd SR1 1PP

➲ *(in city centre on Burdon Rd, short walk from Sunderland metro and mainline stations)*

☎ 0191 553 2323

e-mail: sunderland@twmuseums.org.uk

web: www.twmuseums.org.uk/sunderland

An award-winning attraction with wide-ranging displays and many hands-on exhibits that cover the archaeology and geology of Sunderland, the coal mines and shipyards of the area and the spectacular glass and pottery made on Wearside. Other galleries show the changes in the lifestyles of Sunderland women over the past century, works by LS Lowry and wildlife from all corners of the globe. The Winter Gardens are a horticultural wonderland where the exotic plants from around the world can be seen growing to their full natural height in a spectacular glass and steel rotunda.

Times Open all year, Mon-Sat 10-5, Sun 2-5. **Facilities** ℗ (150 yds) ⅋⓾ licensed & (lifts to all floors, induction loops) toilets for disabled shop ⊗ (ex assist dogs)

TYNEMOUTH   MAP 12 NZ36

Blue Reef Aquarium   `2 for 1`

Grand Pde NE30 4JF

➲ *(follow A19, taking A1058 (coast road), signed Tynemouth. Situated on seafront)*

☎ 0191 258 1031

e-mail: tynemouth@bluereefaquarium.co.uk

web: www.bluereefaquarium.co.uk

From its position overlooking one of the North East's prettiest beaches, Blue Reef is home to a dazzling variety of creatures. Enjoy close encounters with seals, seahorses, sharks, stingrays, giant octopi, frogs, otters and hundreds of other aquatic lifeforms. Explore a dazzling coral reef and journey through the spectacular tropical ocean display in a transparent underwater tunnel. Informative, entertaining talks and feeding displays throughout the day.

Times Open all year, daily from 10. Closed 25 Dec **Fee** ✳ £7.50 (ch £5.50, concessions £6.50). Family (2ad&2ch) £21.99 (2ad+3ch) £23.99. **Facilities** ❷ (charged) ⅋ 禸 (outdoor) & (wheelchair available) toilets for disabled shop ⊗ (ex assist dogs)

Tynemouth Priory and Castle

NE30 4BZ

➲ *(near North Pier)*

☎ 0191 257 1090

web: www.english-heritage.org.uk

Discover a rich and varied history as you explore the priory, castle and underground chambers beneath a World War I gun battery.

Times Open all year, 21 Mar-Sep, daily 10-5; Oct-Mar, Thu-Mon 10-4. (Access to Gun battery limited, please ask site staff for details). Closed 24-2 Dec & 1 Jan. **Fee** £3.50 (concessions £2.80, ch £1.80). Family ticket £8.80. Prices and opening times are subject to change in March 2009. Please check web site or call 0870 333 1181 for the most up to date prices and opening times when planning your visit. **Facilities** 禸 & (wheelchair access to priory) shop ⌗

WALLSEND   MAP 12 NZ2

Segedunum Roman Fort, Baths & Museum   `2 for`

Buddle St NE28 6HR

➲ *(A187 from Tyne Tunnel, signposted)*

☎ 0191 236 9347

e-mail: segedunum@twmuseums.org.uk

web: www.twmuseums.org.uk

Hadrian's Wall was built by the Roman Emperor, Hadrian in 122AD, Segedunum was built as part of the Wall, serving as a garrison for 600 soldiers until the collapse of Roman rule around 410AD. This major historical venture shows what life would have been like then, using artefacts, audio-visuals, reconstructed buildings and a 34m high viewing tower. Plenty of special events including puppet shows, workshops, and Saturnalia. Contact for details.

Times Open all year, Apr-Oct 10-5.30; Nov-Mar, 10-3. **Fee** ✳ £3.95 (ch, pen & concessions £2.25). (ch 16 and under free) **Facilities** ❷ ⅋ 禸 (outdoor) & (lifts) toilets for disabled shop ⊗ (ex assist dogs)

WASHINGTON   MAP 12 NZ35

Washington Old Hall

The Avenue, Washington Village NE38 7LE

➲ *(7m S of Newcastle-upon-Tyne. From A1 and A19 follow signs to A1231 to Washington, then District 4. The Avenue, next to Holy Trinity Church)*

☎ 0191 416 6879

e-mail: washingtonoldhall@nationaltrust.org.uk

web: www.nationaltrust.org.uk

Sitting next to Washington's Holy Trinity church, the Old Hall was the home of George Washington's ancestors from 1183 to 1613, and was originally a medieval manor, but was rebuilt in the 17th century. The house has been restored and filled with period furniture, and contains displays on George Washington and the history of American Independence. Enjoy a peaceful walk in the formal Jacobean garden.

Times Open Apr-Oct, Sun-Wed & Good Fri 11-5. House: 11-5. Garden: 10-5. Tea-room: 11-4. **Fee** ✳ £4.65 (ch £3). Family ticket £12.10. Group 10+ £3.80 (ch £2.50). **Facilities** ♿ ⬚ 🍴 (outdoor) ♿ (Braille guide,sensory scented gdns,induction loop,w/chair) toilets for disabled shop ⊗ (ex assist dogs) ♨

WWT Washington Wetland Centre

Pattinson NE38 8LE

➲ *(signposted off A195, A1231 & A182)*

☎ 0191 416 5454

e-mail: info.washington@wwt.org.uk

web: www.wwt.org.uk/visit/washington

Explore 45 hectares of wetland, woodland and wildlife reserve at Washington Wetland Centre - one of the North East's biggest conservation success stories. Home to exotic birds, amazing insects and beautiful wild scenery. Get nose to beak with rare waterbirds at Close Encounters and meet the pink Chilean Flamingos. See Grey Herons at Wade Lake, Great-spotted Woodpeckers in Hawthorn Wood and tiny ducklings at Waterfowl Nursery (May-July). Plus wildflower meadows, dragonflies, frogs, bats, goats and ancient woodland. Excellent year-round events calendar, and award-winning educational programmes. The 100th birthday of founder Sir Peter Scott takes place in 2009.

Times Open all year. Summer: 9.30-5.30. (Last admission 5pm). Winter: 9.30-4.30. (Last admission 4pm). Closed 25 Dec. **Fee** ✳ £6.31 (ch £3.18, concessions £4.85). Family £17.08 **Facilities** ♿ ⬚ 🍴 licensed 🍴 (outdoor) ♿ (majority of pathways are terraced and most hides are accessible) (lowered windows in certain hides, wheelchairs to hire free) toilets for disabled shop ⊗ (ex assist dogs) ▬

WHITBURN   MAP 12 NZ46

Souter Lighthouse

Coast Rd SR6 7NH

➲ *(on A183 coast road, 2m S of South Shields, 3m N of Sunderland)*

☎ 0191 529 3161 & 01670 773966

e-mail: souter@nationaltrust.org.uk

web: www.nationaltrust.org.uk

When it opened in 1871, Souter was the most advanced lighthouse in the world, and warned shipping off the notorious rocks in the river approaches of the Tyne and Wear. Painted red and white and standing at 150ft high, it is a dramatic building and hands-on displays and volunteers help bring it to life. Visitors can explore the whole building with its engine room and lighthouse keeper's cottage. The hands-on activities concern shipwrecks and the workings of the lighthouse. Climb to the top of the lighthouse, or walk along the Leas, a 2.5 mile stretch of spectacular coastline.

Times Open 22 Mar-8 Nov daily ex Fri (open Good Fri) 11-5 (last entry 30mins before closing). **Fee** ✳ £4.65 (ch £3) Family ticket £12.10. Group 10+ £3.80. **Facilities** ♿ 🍴 🍴 ♿ (Braille guide, induction loops, tactile exhibits) toilets for disabled shop ⊗ (ex assist dogs) ♨ ▬

WARWICKSHIRE

Warwick Castle

ALCESTER   MAP 04 SP05

Ragley Hall

B49 5NJ

➲ *(8m SW of Stratford-upon-Avon, off A46/A435, follow brown tourist signs)*

☎ 01789 762090

e-mail: info@ragleyhall.com

web: www.ragleyhall.com

Built in 1680, Ragley is the family home of the Marquess and Marchioness of Hertford, and has been for nine generations. Set in 400 acres of parkland, woodland and landscaped gardens, Ragley has something for all the family. Younger visitors will enjoy Adventure Wood with its swings, trampoline, 3-D maze, rope bridges and wooden fortress, while the Lakeside Café is ideal for parents to rest and enjoy a cuppa while the kids play safely. There are also 27 acres of formal gardens, the Woodland Walk featuring the Jerwood Sculpture Park, and the 18th-century stable block that houses a collection of historic carriages and equestrian memorabilia.

Times Open Mar-Oct, please phone or see website to confirm opening times. **Fee** £8.50 (ch £5, concessions £7). Family £27. **Facilities** ❷ ⌷ ⼞ (outdoor) ⚬ (some areas of garden accessible) (lift) toilets for disabled shop ⊗ (ex on leads) ▄

BADDESLEY CLINTON   MAP 04 SP27

Baddesley Clinton Hall

B93 0DQ

➲ *(0.75m W off A4141, 7.5m NW of Warwick)*

☎ 01564 783294

e-mail: baddesleyclinton@nationaltrust.org.uk

web: www.nationaltrust.org.uk

A romantically-sited medieval moated house, dating from the 14th century, that has changed very little since 1634. With family portraits, priest's holes, chapel, garden, ponds, nature trail and lake walk.

Times Open Garden: 9 Feb-2 Nov, Wed-Sun 11-5; 5 Nov-21 Dec Wed-Sun 11-4. House 9 Feb-2 Nov, Wed-Sun 11-5. **Fee** ✳ Garden only £2.60 (ch £2.10). House & Garden £8 (ch £4). Family ticket £20. Joint ticket with Packwood House £12 (ch £6). Family ticket £30. Joint ticket for gardens only £6.30 (ch £3.15). National Trust members and children under 5 free. **Facilities** ❷ ⼎ licensed ⼞ (outdoor) ⚬ (grounds partly accessible,some steps and gravel paths) (Braille guides, tactile route and 4 wheelchairs) toilets for disabled shop ⊗ (ex assist dogs) ▄ ▄

CHARLECOTE   MAP 04 SP25

Charlecote Park

CV35 9ER

➲ *(5m E of Stratford Upon Avon, 1m W of Wellesbourne, off B4086)*

☎ 01789 470277

e-mail: charlecote.park@nationaltrust.org.uk

web: www.nationaltrust.org.uk

Queen Elizabeth I and William Shakespeare knew Charlecote Park well. Follow in their footsteps at this impressive Warwickshire house and

ancient deer park. Special events held every month, from outdoor theatre and picnic concerts to family events, and specialist tours. Call for event details.

Times Open Mar-28 Oct, Fri-Tue; Grounds 10.30-5.30, (Park until 6). House noon-5. Open wknds Nov & Dec **Fee** ✳ House & Grounds; £8.20 (ch £4.10). Family £20. Groups £7. Grounds only £4.20 (ch £2.10). **Facilities** ❷ ⌷ ⼎ licensed ⚬ (access restricted to ground floor of mansion & outbuildings) (ramp to kitchens and shop) toilets for disabled shop ⊗ (ex assist dogs) ▄

COMPTON VERNEY   MAP 04 SP35

Compton Verney

CV35 9HZ

➲ *(9m from Stratford-upon-Avon/Warwick/ Leamington Spa on B4086 between Wellesbourne & Kineton)*

☎ 01926 645500

e-mail: info@comptonverney.org.uk

web: www.comptonverney.org.uk

This large, award-winning gallery is housed in an 18th-century Grade I Robert Adam mansion house, set in 120 acres of 'Capability' Brown parkland. Six permanent collections include; Naples 1600-1800, German 1450-1650, British portraits, China, British Folk Art and the Marx-Lambert collection. There is also a programme of changing exhibitions, special events, tours and workshops.

Times Open 24 Mar-9 Dec, Tue-Sun, 10-5. Closed Mon except BH. **Facilities** ❷ ⌷ ⼎ ⼞ (outdoor) ⚬ (w/chairs, large print guides, hearing loop) toilets for disabled shop ⊗ (ex assist dogs) ▄

COUGHTON   MAP 04 SP06

Coughton Court

B49 5JA

➲ *(2m N of Alcester on E side of A435)*

☎ 01789 400777 & 400702

e-mail: coughtoncourt@nationaltrust.ork.uk

web: www.nationaltrust.org.uk

This imposing Tudor house is set in beautiful gardens, and has been home to the Throckmortons for hundreds of years. The house contains

CONTINUED

COUGHTON CONTINUED

many family portraits, and much in the way of fascinating furniture, fabrics and ornaments. The estate has two churches, a 19th-century Catholic church, and the parish church of St Peter's. The Throckmorton family created and maintains the grounds, including the walled garden and the award-winning displays of roses. 2009 marks the 600th anniversary of the Throckmorton family at Coughton Court and events to celebrate will be held throughout the year.

Times House & Gardens open 15 Mar-29 Jun, Wed-Sun 11-5; Jul-Aug, Tue-Sun 11-5, 3-28 Sep, Wed-Sun 11-5; 4 Oct-2 Nov, wknds only 11-5. **Fee** ✶ House and Garden: £9.20 (ch £4.60). Family £23. Garden only: £6.40 (ch £3.20). Family £16. Walled garden: £2.50 for NT members. (inc. in admission price for non-members) **Facilities** ❷ ⏣ licensed ☕ (outdoor) ⚅ (access only to to ground floor of mansion house, loose gravel and hoggin paths in garden) (Braille guide, DDA Album, parking, 3 w/chairs available) toilets for disabled shop ⦻ (ex assist dogs) ⚐ ➡

FARNBOROUGH   MAP 04 SP44

Farnborough Hall

OX17 1DU

➲ *(6m N of Banbury, 0.5m W of A423)*

☎ 01295 690002

web: www.nationaltrust.org.uk

A classical mid 18th-century stone house with notable plasterwork; the entrance hall, staircase and two principal rooms are shown. The grounds contain charming 18th-century temples, a 0.75m terrace walk and an obelisk.

Times House, grounds & terrace walk open 2 Apr-27 Sep, Wed & Sat 2-5.30; 4-5 May, Sun & Mon only 2-5.30. (Last admission 5). **Fee** ✶ House, Garden & Terrace walk £4.75 (ch £2.40), Family £12. **Facilities** ❷ ⚅ (access only to ground floor, 2 steps to entrance and grounds partly accessible) ⦻ (ex assist dogs) ⚐

GAYDON   MAP 04 SP35

Heritage Motor Centre   `2 for 1`

Banbury Rd CV35 0BJ

➲ *(M40 junct 12 and take B4100. Attraction signed)*

☎ 01926 641188

e-mail: enquiries@heritage-motor-centre.co.uk

web: www.heritage-motor-centre.co.uk

The Heritage Motor Centre is home to the world's largest collection of British cars. Following a £1.7 million makeover in 2007, the museum is now host to exciting and interactive exhibitions, which uncover the story of the British motor industry from the 1890s to the present day. Fun for all the family with free guided tours twice a day, and a host of outdoor activities, such as a children's play area, go-karts, 4x4 experiences, and a miniature railway. Details of special events including those which run during the school holidays are available, check website for details.

Times Open daily 10-5. (Closed over Xmas, check website for details) **Fee** £9 (ch 5-16 £7, under 5 free, & concessions £8). Family ticket £28. (Additional charges apply to outdoor activities). **Facilities** ❷ ⏣ ☕ (outdoor) ⚅ (lift to all floors, limited number of manual wheelchairs) toilets for disabled shop ⦻ (ex assist dogs) ➡

KENILWORTH   MAP 04 SP27

Kenilworth Castle

CV8 1NE

☎ 01926 852078

web: www.english-heritage.org.uk

Explore the largest and most extensive castle ruin in England, with a past rich in famous names and events in history. Its massive red sandstone towers, keep and wall glow brightly in the sunlight. Discover the history of Kenilworth through the interactive model in Leicester's Barn.

Times Open all year, 21 Mar-Oct, daily 10-5; Nov-Feb, daily 10-4. Closed 24-26 Dec & 1 Jan. (Gatehouse may close early for private events). **Fee** £6.20 (concessions £5, ch £3.10). Family ticket £15.50. Prices and opening times are subject to change in March 2009. Please check web site or call 0870 333 1181 for the most up to date prices and opening times when planning your visit. **Facilities** ❷ ⏣ ☕ shop ⚏

Stoneleigh Abbey   `2 for 1`

CV8 2LF

➲ *(entrance off B4115 close to junct of A46 and A452)*

☎ 01926 858535 & 858585

e-mail: enquire@stoneleighabbey.org

web: www.stoneleighabbey.org

Stoneleigh Abbey is one of the finest country house estates in the Midlands and has been the subject of considerable restoration work. The abbey, founded in the reign of Henry II, is now managed by a charitable trust. Visitors will experience a wealth of architectural styles spanning more than 800 years. The magnificent state rooms and chapel, the medieval Gatehouse and the Regency stables are some of the major areas to be admired. Set in 690 acres of parkland, 'Through the Keyhole' tours enable visitors to see parts of the Abbey that are not generally open to the public and on Sundays to explore the Abbey's close links with Jane Austen.

Times Open Good Fri-Oct, Tue-Thu, Sun & BHs for guided tours at 11, 1 & 3. Grounds open 10-5. **Fee** Grounds only, £3. Guided tour of house, £6.50 (1ch 5-12 free, additional ch £3) pen £5. **Facilities** ❷ ⏣ ☕ (outdoor) ⚅ (access over exterior paths will require assistance & lift access to state rooms) toilets for disabled shop ⦻ (ex assist dogs)

MIDDLETON   MAP 07 SP19

Ash End House Children's Farm

Middleton Ln B78 2BL

➲ *(signed from A4091)*

☎ 0121 329 3240

e-mail: contact@childrensfarm.co.uk

web: www.childrensfarm.co.uk

Ideal for young children, this is a small family-owned farm with many friendly animals to feed and stroke, including some rare breeds. Café, new farm shop stocking local produce, play areas, picnic barns and lots of undercover activities. New for 2008/2009 is the New Farm

Education Classroom to complement Food and Farming Year and an improved Toddlers Barn.

Times Open daily 10-5 or dusk in winter. Closed 25 Dec until 2nd weekend in Jan **Fee** ✳ £4.50 (ch £4.90 includes animal feed, farm badge & all activities). **Facilities** ❷ ⊑ ⛫ (indoor & outdoor) ♿ toilets for disabled shop ⊗ (ex assist dogs) ➡

NUNEATON　　　　　　　　　　MAP 04 SP39

Arbury Hall

CV10 7PT

➲ *(2m SW of Nuneaton, off B4102 Meriden road)*

☎ 024 7638 2804

e-mail: brenda.newell@arburyhall.net

The 16th-century Elizabethan house, Gothicised in the 18th century, has been the home of the Newdegate family for over 450 years. It is the finest complete example of Gothic revival architecture in existence, and contains pictures, furniture, and beautiful plasterwork ceilings. The 17th-century stable block, with a central doorway by Wren, houses the tearooms and there are lovely gardens with lakes and wooded walks.

Times Open Apr-Sep. Hall & Gardens: Sun & Mon of BH wknds only. For other opening days & times, contact Administrator. **Fee** ✳ £6.50 (ch £4.50) Gardens only £5 (ch £3.50) **Facilities** ❷ ⊑ ♿ (Partly accessible) toilets for disabled shop ⊗ (ex assist dogs & in grounds)

PACKWOOD HOUSE　　　　　　MAP 07 SP17

Packwood House

B94 6AT

➲ *(on unclass road off A3400)*

☎ 01564 782024

e-mail: packwood@nationaltrust.org.uk

web: www.nationaltrust.org.uk

Dating from the 16th century, Packwood House has been extended and much changed over the years. An important collection of tapestries and textiles is displayed. Equally important are the stunning gardens with renowned herbaceous borders, attracting many visitors, and the almost surreal topiary garden based on the Sermon on the Mount. During summer months there is open air theatre in the garden.

Times House & Gardens open: 9 Feb-2 Nov 11-5, Wed-Sun, BH Mon & Good Fri. Park open all year. **Fee** ✳ House & Garden £7 (ch £3.50, ch under 5 free.). Family ticket £17.50. Garden only £4.20 (ch £2.10). Joint ticket with Baddesley Clinton £12 (ch £6). Family ticket £30, joint ticket for gardens only £6.30 (ch £3.15). **Facilities** ❷ ⛫ (outdoor) ♿ (ground floor of house, apart from great hall, accessible and loose gravel and some steps in garden) (2 w/chairs available, tactile tour, Braille guide) toilets for disabled shop ⊗ (ex assist dogs) 🐾 ➡

RUGBY　　　　　　　　　　　　MAP 04 SP57

The Webb Ellis Rugby Football Museum　　　FREE

5 Saint Matthew's St CV21 3BY

➲ *(on A428 opposite Rugby School)*

☎ 01788 567777

e-mail: sales@webb-ellis.co.uk

web: www.webb-ellis.co.uk

An intriguing collection of Rugby football memorabilia is housed in the shop in which rugby balls have been made since 1842. Visitors can watch a craftsman at work, hand-stitching the footballs. Situated near to Rugby School and its famous playing field.

Times Open all year, Mon-Sat 9-5. Phone for holiday opening times. **Facilities** ℗ (500yds) ♿ (Partly accessible) shop ⊗ (ex assist dogs)

RYTON-ON-DUNSMORE　　　　MAP 04 SP37

Garden Organic Ryton　　　2 for 1

Wolston Ln CV8 3LG

➲ *(5m SE of Coventry signed off A45, on road to village of Wolston)*

☎ 024 7630 3517

e-mail: enquiry@gardenorganic.org.uk

web: www.gardenorganic.org.uk

Garden Organic Ryton is home to the UK's leading authority on organic growing and is celebrating 50 years of growing. The site has over 30 glorious organic gardens in ten acres of grounds to explore and discover. Designed around getting more people to grow organically, the gardens demonstrate the effectiveness of gardening in harmony and how easy it is to grow your own fruit and vegetables. Also on site is the charity's world renowned Heritage Seed Library, which protects hundreds of endangered vegetable varieties, the Vegetable Kingdom interactive experience, and an award winning organic restaurant and shop. The site also hosts special event days and garden tours.

Times Open daily May-Sep 9-6; Oct-Apr 9-5. Restricted opening hours over Xmas. **Fee** £6 (ch £3 (one ch incl in adult ticket), concessions £5.50). **Facilities** ❷ ⊑ 🍴 licensed ⛫ (outdoor) ♿ (wheelchairs available & scooter) toilets for disabled shop garden centre ⊗ (ex assist dogs) ➡

Anne Hathaway's Cottage

Cottage Ln CV37 9HH

➲ *(House in Shottery Village, 1m from Stratford)*

☎ 01789 292100

e-mail: info@shakespeare.org.uk

web: www.shakespeare.org.uk

This world-famous thatched cottage was the childhood home of Anne Hathaway, William Shakespeare's wife. The cottage still contains many family items including the beautiful 'Hathaway Bed'. In the stunning grounds there is a quintessential English cottage garden, orchard, sculpture garden, a romantic willow cabin and a maze.

Times ✳ Open Nov-Mar, daily 10-4; Apr-May & Oct-Nov, Mon-Sat 9.30-5, Sun 10-5; Jun-Aug, Mon-Sat 9-5, Sun 9.30-5. **Facilities** ℗ ⌨ ᕱ (access room with virtual reality tours of cottage) toilets for disabled shop ⊗ (ex assist dogs) ▬

Hall's Croft

Old Town CV37 6EP

➲ *(located in the centre of Stratford upon Avon)*

☎ 01789 292107

e-mail: info@shakespeare.org.uk

web: www.shakespeare.org.uk

This elegant 17th-century house belonged to Shakespeare's eldest daughter Susanna, and her husband, the physician John Hall. It is an impressive building with many exquisite furnishing and paintings of the period, and an exhibition on early medicine.

Times ✳ Open Nov-Mar, daily 11-4; Apr-May and Sep-Oct, daily 11-5; Jun-Aug, Mon-Sat 9.30-5, Sun 10-5. **Facilities** ℗ ⌨ ᕱ (Partly accessible) toilets for disabled shop ⊗ (ex assist dogs) ▬

Nash's House & New Place

Chapel St CV37 6EP

➲ *(located in centre of Stratford upon Avon)*

☎ 01789 292325

e-mail: info@shakespeare.org.uk

web: www.shakespeare.org.uk

The elegant home of Shakespeare's granddaughter, Elizabeth Hall's first husband Thomas Nash. The adjacent site of New Place, where Shakespeare retired and subsequently died in 1616, is now preserved as a picturesque garden space with an attractive Elizabethan knot garden.

Times ✳ Open Nov-Mar, daily 11-4; Apr-May & Sep-Oct, daily 11-5; Jun-Aug, Mon-Sat 9.30-5, Sun 10-5.30. **Facilities** ℗ (250yds) ᕱ (Partly accessible) toilets for disabled shop ⊗ (ex assist dogs) ▬

Shakespeare's Birthplace   `2 for 1`

Henley St CV37 6QW

➲ *(in town centre)*

☎ 01789 204016

e-mail: info@shakespeare.org.uk

web: www.shakespeare.org.uk

Visit the house where the world's most famous playwright was born and grew up. Discover the fascinating story of William Shakespeare's life and see it brought to life by the costumed guides.

Times Open Nov-Mar, Mon-Sat 10-4, Sun 10.30-4; Apr-May & Sep-Oct, Mon-Sat 10-5, Sun 10-5; Jun-Aug, Mon-Sat 9-5, Sun 9.30-5. **Fee** ✳ £7 (ch £2.75, concessions £6) Family ticket £17. All five Shakespeare Houses £14 (ch £6.50, concessions £12) Family ticket £29. All three Town Shakespeare Houses £11 (ch £5.50, concessions £9) Family ticket £23. **Facilities** ℗ (coach park 100m) (drop off only, max 30 mins) ᕱ (Partly accessible) (computer based virtual reality tour of upper floor) toilets for disabled shop ⊗ (ex assist dogs) ▬

Stratford Butterfly Farm   `2 for 1`

Tramway Walk, Swan's Nest Ln CV37 7LS

➲ *(south bank of River Avon opposite RSC)*

☎ 01789 299288

e-mail: sales@butterflyfarm.co.uk

web: www.butterflyfarm.co.uk

The UK's largest live butterfly and insect exhibit. Hundreds of the world's most spectacular and colourful butterflies, in the unique setting of a lush tropical landscape, with splashing waterfalls and fish-filled pools. See also the strange and fascinating Insect City, a bustling metropolis of ants, stick insects, beetles and other remarkable insects. See the dangerous and deadly in Arachnoland.

Stratford Butterfly Farm

Times Open all year, daily 10-6 (winter 10-dusk). Closed 25 Dec. **Fee** ✳
£5.50 (ch £4.50, concessions £5). Family £16. **Facilities** ℗ (opposite
entrance) (site parking blue badge holders only) ⊟ (outdoor) ♿ shop ⊗ ▬

UPTON HOUSE

MAP 04 SP34

Upton House & Gardens

OX15 6HT

➲ *(M40 junct 12, on A422, 7m NW of Banbury, 12m
SE of Stratford)*

☎ 01295 670266

e-mail: uptonhouse@nationaltrust.org.uk

web: www.nationaltrust.org.uk

Upton House, together with its outstanding collections and fine
gardens, reflects its 1930s heyday, when it was home to millionaire oil
magnate the 2nd Viscount Bearsted. Lord Bearsted was Chairman of
Shell and son of the Company's founder. He was a passionate art
collector, and visitors can get close to internationally important works
by artists such as Canaletto, Brueghel and El Greco. An extensive
porcelain collection includes 18th-century Sèvres porcelain, Chelsea
and Derby figures. There are also lovely gardens, much of the planting
designed by Kitty Lloyd-Jones with Lady Beartsted in the 1930s. The
sweeping lawn gives way to a dramatic series of terraces and
herbaceous borders, descending to a kitchen garden and tranquil water
garden. Upton is also home to the National Collection of Asters.

Times House & Garden open: Mar-2 Nov, Mon-Wed & Sat-Sun, 17 Mar-30
Mar & 21 July-Aug, all week 1-5; 8 Nov-21 Dec, Sat-Sun, 12-4. **Fee** ✳ £8.50
(ch £4.20). Family ticket £21. Garden only £5 (ch £2.50) Family ticket £12.50.
Facilities ℗ ⛄ ⍾ licensed ⊟ (outdoor) ♿ (access restricted to ground
floor of house) (close parking, buggy, w/chair, virtual tour) toilets for
disabled shop garden centre ⊗ (ex assist dogs) ♨ ▬

WARWICK

MAP 04 SP26

Warwick Castle

CV34 4QU

➲ *(2m from M40 junct 15)*

☎ 0870 442 2000

e-mail: customer.information@warwick-castle.com

web: www.warwick-castle.com

From the days of William the Conqueror to the reign of Queen Victoria,
Warwick Castle has provided a backdrop for many turbulent times.
Today it offers family entertainment with a medieval theme. Attractions
include the world's largest siege engine, thrilling jousting tournaments,
birds of prey, daredevil knights, and entire castleful of colourful
characters. The newest addition is the immersive and interactive
"Dream of Battle".

Times ✳ Open all year, daily 10-6 (5pm Nov-Mar). Closed 25 Dec.
Facilities ℗ (charged) ⛄ ⍾ ⊟ ♿ (hearing loop, large print guides, DVD,
audio guides) toilets for disabled shop ⊗ (ex assist dogs) ▬

Warwickshire Yeomanry Museum

The Court House Vaults, Jury St CV34 4EW

➲ *(situated on corner of Jury St & Castle St, 2m E of
M40 junct 15)*

☎ 01926 492212

e-mail: wtc.admin@bt.click.com

The vaults of the courthouse display militaria from the county
Yeomanry, dating from 1794 to 1945. It includes regimental silver,
paintings, uniforms and weapons. A small room in the cellars now
houses the HUJ Gun project, a field gun captured by the Yeomanry in
1917.

Times Open Good Fri-Remembrance Sun, Sat, Sun & BH only
Facilities ℗ (150yds) (2hr max) ⊟ (outdoor) shop ⊗

WILMCOTE

MAP 04 SP15

Mary Arden's

Station Rd CV37 9UN

➲ *(3m NW of Stratford-upon-Avon off A3400)*

☎ 01789 293455

e-mail: info@shakespeare.org.uk

web: www.shakespeare.org.uk

The site includes two Tudor buildings, one of which was the childhood
home of Shakespeare's mother, Mary Arden. Experience the sights and
sounds of a Tudor farm as the farmer, maids and labourers bring the
farm to life. Take a walk on the nature trail and track down the
Longhorn cattle, Cotswold sheep and other rare breeds.

Times ✳ Open Nov-Mar, Mon-Sun 10-4; Apr-May & Sep-Oct, Mon-Sun
10-5; Jun-Aug, Mon-Sun 9.30-5. **Facilities** ℗ ⛄ ⊟ (outdoor) ♿ (Partly
accessible) toilets for disabled shop ⊗ (ex assist dogs) ▬

WEST MIDLANDS

Canon Hill Park, Edgbaston

BIRMINGHAM   MAP 07 SP08

Aston Hall   FREE

Trinity Rd, Aston B6 6JD

➲ *(E of Birmingham, just off the A4040 in Yardley.)*

☎ 0121 464 2193

e-mail: bmag-enquiries@birmingham.gov.uk

web: www.bmag.org.uk

Built by Sir Thomas Holte, Aston Hall is a fine Jacobean mansion complete with a panelled Long Gallery, balustraded staircase and magnificent plaster friezes and ceilings. King Charles I spent a night here during the Civil War and the house was damaged by Parliamentary troops. It was also leased to James Watt Junior, the son of the great industrial pioneer.

Times Open Etr-Oct, Tue-Sun 11.30-4. Closed Mon ex BHs. Re-opening spring 2009 after refurbishment. **Facilities** ❷ ⬚ ⴲ (Partly accessible) shop ⊗ (ex assist dogs)

Birmingham Botanical Gardens & Glasshouses

Westbourne Rd, Edgbaston B15 3TR

➲ *(2m W of city centre, follow signs for Edgbaston, then brown heritage signs)*

☎ 0121 454 1860

e-mail: admin@birminghambotanicalgardens.org.uk

web: www.birminghambotanicalgardens.org.uk

Originally opened in 1832, the gardens include the Tropical House, which has a 24ft-wide lily pool and lush vegetation. The Mediterranean house features a wide variety of citrus fruits and the Arid House has a desert scene with its giant agaves and opuntias. Outside, a tour of the gardens includes rhododendrons and azalea borders and a collection of over 200 trees. There's a young children's discovery garden and a sculpture trail as well as a large amount of events to choose from, contact the gardens for a brochure.

Times Open all year, wkdays 9-7 or dusk, Sun 10-7 or dusk whichever is earlier. Closed 25 Dec. **Fee** ✳ £7 (concessions £4.50). Family £21. Groups 10+ £6 (concessions £4) **Facilities** ❷ ⬚ ⴑ ⴲ (3 wheelchairs, 2 electric scooters & Braille guides) toilets for disabled shop garden centre ⊗ (ex assist dogs) ▬

Birmingham Museum & Art Gallery   FREE

Chamberlain Sq B3 3DH

☎ 0121 303 2834

e-mail: bmag-enquiries@birmingham.gov.uk

web: www.bmag.org.uk

One of the world's best collections of Pre-Raphaelite paintings can be seen here, including important works by Burne-Jones, a native of Birmingham. Also on display are fine silver, ceramics and glass. The archaeology section has prehistoric Egyptian, Greek and Roman antiquities, and also objects from the Near East, Mexico and Peru. New galleries explore the creation of art, while the Touch gallery includes talking sculptures, and Samurai armour. The Bull Ring explores the 800 year history of this well-known area.

Times Open all year, Mon-Thu & Sat 10-5, Fri 10.30-5 and Sun 12.30-5. **Facilities** ℗ (carparks nearby) ⬚ ⴑ ⴲ (lift) toilets for disabled shop ⊗ ▬

Blakesley Hall   FREE

Blakesley Rd, Yardley B25 8RN

➲ *(A4040 onto Blakesley Rd, Hall 100yds on right)*

☎ 0121 464 2193

e-mail: laura_r_cox@birmingham.gov.uk

web: www.bmag.org.uk

Blakesley Hall is a fine Yeoman farmer's residence, built by Richard Smalbroke in 1590. It has a half-timbered exterior and a Stuart interior, with a wonderful herb garden. The visitor centre has a varied exhibition programme, tea room and gift shop. Regular weekend events take place throughout the open season.

Times ✳ Open Apr-Oct, Tue-Sun & BHs, 11.30-4 **Facilities** ❷ ⬚ ⴲ (outdoor) shop ⊗

Museum of the Jewellery Quarter   FREE

75-79 Vyse St, Hockley B18 6HA

➲ *(off A41 into Vyse St, museum on left after 1st side street)*

☎ 0121 554 3598

e-mail: bmag-enquiries@birmingham.gov.uk

web: www.bmag.org.uk

The Museum tells the story of jewellery making in Birmingham from its origins in the Middle Ages right through to the present day. Discover the skill of the jeweller's craft and enjoy a unique tour of an original jewellery factory frozen in time. For over eighty years the family firm of Smith and Pepper produced jewellery from the factory. This perfectly preserved 'time capsule' workshop has changed little since the beginning of the century. The Jewellery Quarter is still very much at the forefront of jewellery manufacture in Britain and the Museum showcases the work of the city's most exciting new designers.

Times Open all year **Facilities** ℗ (limited 2hr stay/pay & display) ⴲ (tours for hearing/visually impaired booked in advance) toilets for disabled shop ⊗ (ex assist dogs) ▬

ENGLAND

ENGLAND

BIRMINGHAM CONTINUED

RSPB Sandwell Valley Nature Reserve

FREE

20 Tanhouse Av, Great Barr B43 5AG

(off B4167 Hamstead Rd into Tanhouse Ave)

0121 357 7395

e-mail: sandwellvalley@rspb.org.uk

web: www.rspb.org.uk

Opened in 1983 on the site of an old colliery, Sandwell Valley is home to hundreds of bird, animal and insect species in five different habitats. Summer is the best time to see the yellow wagtail or reed warblers, while wintertime attracts goosanders, snipe, and redshanks. There are guided walks and bug hunts for the kids in summer, and a shop and visitor centre all year round.

Times Open Tue-Fri 9-5, Sat & Sun 10-5 (closes at dusk in winter). Closed Mon, 24 Dec-2 Jan **Facilities** (outdoor) (Partly accessible) toilets for disabled shop

Sarehole Mill

FREE

Cole Bank Rd, Hall Green B13 0BD

(A34 towards Birmingham. After 5m turn left on B4146, attraction on left)

0121 777 6612

e-mail: bmag-enquiries@birmingham.gov.uk

web: www.bmag.org.uk

Home to Birmingham's only working watermill; Sarehole Mill was built in the 1760s. Used for both flour production and metal rolling up to the last century, the Mill can still be seen in action during the summer months. Restored with financial backing from JRR Tolkien, who grew up in the area and cites Sarehole as an influence for writing *The Hobbit* and *Lord of the Rings*. Tolkein Weekend takes place during May each year.

Times Open Etr-Oct, Tue-Sun 11.30-4. (Closed Mon, ex BH Mon) **Facilities** (Partly accessible) (ex assist dogs)

Soho House

FREE

Soho Av, Handsworth B18 5LB

(from city centre follow A41 to Soho Rd, follow brown heritage signs to Soho Ave)

0121 554 9122

e-mail: bmag-enquiries@birmingham.gov.uk

web: www.bmag.org.uk

Soho House was the elegant home of industrial pioneer Matthew Boulton between 1766 and 1809. Here, he met with some of the most important thinkers and scientists of his day. The house has been carefully restored and contains many of Boulton's possessions including furniture, clocks, silverware and the original dining table where the Lunar Society met.

Times Open Etr-Oct, Tue-Sun 11.30-4. (Closed Mon ex BH Mons) **Facilities** (induction loop) toilets for disabled shop (ex assist dogs)

Thinktank at Millennium Point

Millennium Point, Curzon St B4 7XG

0121 202 2222

e-mail: findout@thinktank.ac

web: www.thinktank.ac

Thinktank offers a fun-packed day out for all the family. From steam engines to intestines this exciting museum has over 200 amazing artefacts and interactive exhibits on science and discovery. There's a state-of-the-art planetarium where you can tour the night sky and fly through the galaxy. There's an ever-changing programme of demonstrations, workshops and events, so there's always something new to discover.

Times Open daily 10-5 (last entry 4). Closed 24-26 Dec. **Facilities** (charged) (indoor) (induction loop, wheelchair loan, BSL events, parking) toilets for disabled shop (ex assist dogs)

BOURNVILLE MAP 07 SP08

Cadbury World

Linden Rd B30 2LU

(1m S of A38 Bristol Rd, on A4040 Ring Rd. Follow brown signs from M5 junct 2 and junct 4)

0845 450 3599

e-mail: cadbury.world@csplc.com

web: www.cadburyworld.co.uk

Get involved in the chocolate making process, and to find out how the chocolate is used to make famous confectionery. Visitors can learn about the early struggles and triumphs of the Cadbury business, and follow the history of Cadbury television advertising. Essence, where visitors can create their own unique product by combining liquid chocolate with different tastes, and Purple Planet, where you can chase a creme egg, grow cocoa beans, and see yourself moulded in chocolate. A visitor centre explores the innovative values of the Cadbury Brothers that make Bournville the place it is.

Times Opening times vary throughout the year please contact the information line 0845 450 3599. **Facilities** (outdoor) (adapted ride & lift to 2nd floor, subtitles) toilets for disabled shop (ex assist dogs)

Selly Manor

Maple Rd, Bournville B30 2AE

➲ *(off A4040 at Bournville Village Green)*

☎ 0121 472 0199

e-mail: sellymanor@bvt.org.uk

web: www.bvt.org.uk/sellymanor

These two timber-framed manor houses date from the 13th and early 14th centuries, and have been re-erected in the 'garden suburb' of Bournville. There is a herb garden and events are held all year.

Times Open all year, Tue-Fri 10-5; Etr-Sep, Sat-Sun & BH Mon 2-5.
Fee £3.50 (ch £1.50, concessions £2). Family ticket (2ad+3ch) £9.
Facilities ℗ (10mtrs) 🍴 (outdoor) ♿ (ground floors, gardens & toilets) toilets for disabled shop

---

CASTLE BROMWICH   MAP 07 SP18

Castle Bromwich Hall Gardens

Chester Rd B36 9BT

➲ *(M6 junct 5, follow brown tourist signs)*

☎ 0121 749 4100

e-mail: admin@cbhgt.org.uk

web: www.cbhgt.org.uk

This recently-restored 17th-century formal garden illustrates a period of history in an unusual and fascinating way. Although the garden is an accurate reconstruction of the garden as it was around 1680-1740, there is an addition: the holly maze, which was created in the 19th century, based on 17th-century plans.

Times ✳ Open: Apr-Sep, Sat-Sun & BH Mon 1.30-5.30, Tue-Thu 11-4, Fri 11-3.30 **Facilities** ℗ 🚻 🍴 (outdoor) ♿ (wheelchairs available for free) toilets for disabled shop garden centre ⊗ (ex on a lead)

COVENTRY   MAP 04 SP37

Coventry Cathedral

Priory St CV1 5ES

➲ *(signposted on all approaches to the city)*

☎ 024 7652 1200

e-mail: information@coventrycathedral.org.uk

web: www.coventrycathedral.org.uk

Coventry's old cathedral was bombed during an air raid on 14th November 1940 which devastated the city. The remains have been carefully preserved. The new cathedral was designed by Sir Basil Spence and consecrated in May 1962. It contains outstanding modern works of art, including a huge tapestry designed by Graham Sutherland, the west screen (a wall of glass engraved by John Hutton with saints and angels), bronzes by Epstein, and the great baptistry window by John Piper.

Times Open all year, daily 9-5. **Fee** Cathedral £3 suggested donation. Tours from £5.50pp **Facilities** ℗ (250mtrs) (disabled parking adjacent) 🚻 🍴 (indoor & outdoor) ♿ (main floor areas, shops and cafe accessible. All side chapels have steps) toilets for disabled shop ⊗ (ex assist dogs)

Coventry Transport Museum   FREE

Millennium Place, Hales St CV1 1JD

➲ *(just off junct 1, Coventry ring road, Tower St in city centre)*

☎ 024 7623 4270

e-mail: enquiries@transport-museum.co.uk

web: www.transport-museum.com

Coventry is the traditional home of the motor industry, and the museum's world-renowned collection displays over 150 years of its history. You can design your own car, feel what its like to break the sound barrier at 763mph and even travel into the future. The Festival of Motoring takes place over the fist weekend in September and features vintage, veteran and classic vehicles with family activities and stunt show riders culminating in a car and motorcycle rally around the region.

Times Open all year, daily 10-5. Closed 24-26 Dec & 1 Jan **Facilities** ℗ (adjacent) (pay & display) 🚻 ♿ toilets for disabled shop ⊗ (ex assist dogs) ⊟

Herbert Art Gallery & Museum   FREE

Jordan Well CV1 5QP

➲ *(in city centre near Cathedral)*

☎ 024 7683 2381 & 2565

e-mail: artsandheritage@coventry.gov.uk

web: www.coventrymuseum.org.uk

The Herbert is currently undergoing a major redevelopment, which is due for completion during the autumn of 2008. During the time of the redevelopment there will be an active programme of temporary exhibitions, and plenty of events and activities for children.

Times ✳ Open all year, Mon-Sat 10-5.30, Sun 12-5. Closed 24-26, 31 Dec & 1 Jan **Facilities** ℗ (500yds) 🚻 ♿ (disabled parking, automatic doors) toilets for disabled shop ⊗ (ex assist dogs)

Jaguar Daimler Heritage Centre   FREE

Browns Ln, Allesley CV5 9DR

➲ *(on A45, follow signs for Browns Lane Plant)*

☎ 024 7620 3322

e-mail: jagtrust@jaguar.com

web: www.jdht.com

Established in 1983, the Jaguar-Daimler Heritage Trust maintains a unique collection of motor vehicles and artefacts manufactured by Jaguar Cars Ltd, and the many other renowned marques associated with the company.

Times ✳ Open wkdays by appointment, no appointment required on last Sun of mth. **Facilities** ℗ 🚻 shop ⊗ (ex assist dogs)

Lunt Roman Fort

Coventry Rd, Baginton CV8 3AJ

➲ *(S side of city, off Stonebridge highway, A45)*

☎ 024 7678 5173 & 7683 2565

e-mail: info@theherbert.org

web: www.theherbert.org

The turf and timber Roman fort from around the end of the 1st century has been faithfully reconstructed. An Interpretation Centre is housed in the granary.

Times ✳ Open 27 Mar-Oct, Sat-Sun & BH Mon 10-5; mid Jul-end Aug, Thu-Tue 10-5; Spring BH wk, Thu-Tue 10-5. **Facilities** ⓟ ⚲ (outdoor) ♿ (ramp to Granary Interpretation Centre) toilets for disabled shop ⊗ (ex assist dogs)

Priory Visitor Centre FREE

Priory Row CV1 5EX

➲ *(in city centre near Cathedral)*

☎ 024 7655 2242

e-mail: prioryvisitorscentre@coventry.gov.uk

web: www.theherbert.org

Earl Leofric and his wife Lady Godiva founded a monastery in Coventry in the 11th century. This priory disappeared somewhere beneath the cathedral that was built on the site, until this cathedral was in turn demolished by Henry VIII in the 16th century. Soon after that most of the buildings on the site had been reduced to ground level, leaving modern archaeologists to discover the outlines of history. This visitor centre displays finds from the site as well as telling the story of Coventry's first cathedral.

Times ✳ Open Mon-Sat 10-5.30, Sun noon-4 **Facilities** ⓟ (500yds) shop ⊗ (ex assist dogs)

St Mary's Guildhall FREE

Bayley Ln CV1 5QP

➲ *(in city centre near ruined Cathedral)*

☎ 024 7683 2386

e-mail: info@theherbert.org

web: www.theherbert.org

This impressive medieval Guildhall has stood in the heart of Coventry for over 650 years, and has played its part in the history of the area. It served as Henry VI's court during the War of the Roses, was a prison to Mary Queen of Scots, and was used as a setting by George Eliot in her novel *Adam Bede*. The Great Hall contains a Tournai tapestry commissioned for the visit of Henry VII and Queen Elizabeth in 1500.

Times ✳ Open Etr Sun-Sep, Sun-Thu 10-4 **Facilities** ⓟ (600yds) ⓘⓞⓘ shop ⊗ (ex assist dogs)

DUDLEY MAP 07 SO99

Black Country Living Museum

Tipton Rd DY1 4SQ

➲ *(on A4037, near Showcase cinema)*

☎ 0121 557 9643 & 520 8054

e-mail: info@bclm.co.uk

web: www.bclm.co.uk

On the 26-acre site is a recreated canal-side village, with shops, houses and workshops. Meet the costumed characters and find out what life was like around 1900. Ride on a tramcar, explore the underground mine, venture into the limestone caverns or visit the olde tyme fairground (additional charge). There are also demonstrations of chainmaking, glass engraving and sweet-making. Watch a silent movie in the Limelight cinema, taste fish and chips cooked on a 1930s range, and finish your visit with a glass of real ale or dandelion and burdock in the Bottle and Glass Inn. Lots of varied events throughout the year. Contact for details.

Times Open all year: Mar-Oct Mon-Sun 10-5, Nov-Feb Wed-Sun 10-4. (Telephone for Xmas closing) **Fee** £12.50 (ch & student with NUS card £6.75, pen £10). Family (1ad+1ch) £17 & (2ad+3ch) £33.50 **Facilities** ⓟ (charged) ⛴ ⓘⓞⓘ ⚲ (indoor & outdoor) ♿ (access to most buildings requires use temporary ramp. Staff will assist visitors with restricted mobility.) (wheelchairs & ramps available, carers free entry) toilets for disabled shop ⊗ (ex assist dogs) ▬

Dudley Zoological Gardens

2 The Broadway DY1 4QB

➲ *(M5 junct 2 towards Wolverhampton/Dudley, signed)*

☎ 01384 215313

e-mail: marketing@dudleyzoo.org.uk

web: www.dudleyzoo.org.uk

From lions and tigers to snakes and spiders, enjoy animal encounters and feeds. Get closer to some furry, and some not so furry creatures, and have fun on the fair rides, land train, and the adventure playground. Step back in time and see history come to life in the castle.

Times Open all year, Etr-mid Sep, daily 10-4; mid Sep-Etr, daily 10-3. Closed 25 Dec. **Fee** ✳ £10.95 (ch 3-15 £6.95 under 3 free, concessions £7.95). **Facilities** ⓟ (charged) ⛴ ⓘⓞⓘ licensed ⚲ (outdoor) ♿ (not all accessible for wheelchairs due to hilly site) (land train from gates-castle, w/chair pre book) toilets for disabled shop ⊗ (ex assist dogs) ▬

Museum & Art Gallery ` FREE `

St James's Rd DY1 1HU

➲ *(M5 N junct 2. Take A4123 signed to Dudley)*

☎ 01384 815575

e-mail: museum.pls@mbc.dudley.gov.uk

web: www.dudley.gov.uk

The museum houses the Brooke Robinson collection of 17th-, 18th-
and 19th-century European painting, furniture, ceramics and enamels.
A fine geological gallery, 'The Time Trail' has spectacular displays of
fossils from the local Wenlock limestone and coal measures.

Times ✳ Open all year, Mon-Sat 10-4. Closed BHs. **Facilities** Ⓟ (25mtrs)
♿ (Braille & large print text. Tactile objects) shop ⊗ (ex assist dogs)

KINGSWINFORD ` MAP 07 SO88 `

Broadfield House Glass Museum ` FREE `

Compton Dr DY6 9NS

➲ *(Off A491 Stourbridge to Wolverhampton road, just
S of Kingswinford Village Centre)*

☎ 01384 812745

e-mail: glass.museum@dudley.gov.uk

web: www.glassmuseum.org.uk

Situated in the historic Stourbridge Glass Quarter, Broadfield House
Glass Museum is one of the best glass museums in the world. Home
to a magnificent collection of British glass from the 17th century to the
present day, the museum hosts an exciting programme of exhibitions
and events, and is a main venue for the International Festival of Glass,
which is held in August. The museum also has a gift shop, and a hot
glass studio.

Times Open all year, Tue-Sun 12-4. Please phone for Xmas & Etr openings
Facilities Ⓟ ♿ (access restricted to ground floor, studio & temporary
exhibitions) (photo album) toilets for disabled shop ⊗ (ex assist dogs) ▬

SOLIHULL ` MAP 07 SP17 `

National Motorcycle ` 2 for 1 `

Coventry Rd, Bickenhill B92 0EJ

➲ *(M42 junct 6, off A45 near NEC)*

☎ 01675 443311

web: www.nationalmotorcyclemuseum.co.uk

The National Motorcycle Museum is recognised as the finest and
largest motorcycle museum in the world, with machines always being
added to the collection. It is a tribute to this once great British industry
that dominated world markets for some sixty years. The museum
records for posterity the engineering achievements of the last century.

Times Open all year, daily 10-6. Closed 24-26 Dec. **Fee** £6.95 (ch 12 & pen
£4.95). Party 20+ £5.95 **Facilities** Ⓟ ⑩ licensed ♿ toilets for disabled
shop ⊗ (ex assist dogs) ▬

STOURBRIDGE ` MAP 07 SO88 `

The Falconry Centre

Hurrans Garden Centre, Kidderminster Rd South, Hagley
DY9 0JB

➲ *(off A456)*

☎ 01562 700014

e-mail: info@thefalconrycentre.co.uk

web: www.thefalconrycentre.co.uk

The centre houses some 70 birds of prey including owls, hawks and
falcons and is also a rehabilitation centre for sick and injured birds of
prey. Spectacular flying displays are put on daily from midday. There
are picnic areas, special fun days and training courses available.

Times ✳ Open all year, daily 10-5 & Sun 11-5. Closed 25, 26 Dec & Etr Sun.
Facilities ❶ ⊡ ♿ (ramps in most places) toilets for disabled shop
garden centre ⊗ (ex assist dogs) ▬

WALSALL ` MAP 07 SP09 `

The New Art Gallery Walsall ` FREE `

Gallery Square WS2 8LG

➲ *(signed from all major routes into town centre)*

☎ 01922 654400

e-mail: info@artatwalsall.org.uk

web: www.artatwalsall.org.uk

Opened in 2000, this exciting art gallery has at its core the Garman
Ryan Collection, and a Children's Discovery Gallery that offers access to
the very best in contemporary art in the only interactive art gallery
designed especially for young people.

Times ✳ Open all year, Tue-Sat 10-5, Sun noon-5. Closed Mon ex BH Mon,
25-28 Dec & 1 Jan. Please telephone to confirm. **Facilities** Ⓟ (5 minutes
on foot) (free on site for disabled) ⊡ ♿ (lift, access guide-facilities,
induction loop, large print) toilets for disabled shop ⊗ (ex assist dogs)

Walsall Leather Museum ` FREE `

Littleton St West WS2 8EQ

➲ *(On Walsall ring-road A4148 on N side of town)*

☎ 01922 721153

e-mail: leathermuseum@walsall.gov.uk

web: www.walsall.gov.uk/leathermuseum

Award winning working museum in the saddlery and leathergoods
'capital' of Britain. Watch skilled craftsmen and women at work in this
restored Victorian leather factory. Displays tell the story of Walsall's
leatherworkers past and present. Large shop stocks range of Walsall
made leathergoods, many at bargain prices. Saddle Room Café serves
delicious home-cooked cakes and light lunches. Groups very welcome,
guided tours available.

Times Open all year, Tue-Sat 10-5 (Nov-Mar 4). Closed Sun-Mon. Open BH
Mon. Closed 24-26 Dec, 1 Jan, Good Fri, Etr Sun & May Day. **Facilities** Ⓟ
(10mtrs) ⊡ ⩗ (outdoor) ♿ (staff with sign language skills, tactile activities)
toilets for disabled shop ⊗ (ex assist dogs) ▬

WOLVERHAMPTON

MAP 07 SO99

Bantock House and Park

FREE

Finchfield Rd WV3 9LQ

➲ *(follow signs for Wolverhampton. Bantock House 1m out of city & well signed from ring road)*

☎ 01902 552195

e-mail: bantockhouse@wolverhampton.gov.uk
web: www.wolverhamptonart.org.uk

A restored Georgian farmhouse set within 43 acres and surrounded by beautiful formal gardens. Visitors can explore the period settings of the Bantock's former home and discover stories about the family and other Victorians that helped to shape Wolverhampton. The house has permanent displays of exquisite locally made japanned-ware, enamels and steel jewellery, as well as a programme of changing exhibitions. There is also a delightful courtyard, café, picnic areas, children's playground and pitch and putt. Please telephone or email for a quarterly events leaflet.

Times Open Apr-end Oct, 11-5; Nov-end Mar, 12-4. Closed Mon except BH **Facilities** 🅿 ♿ 🍴 (outdoor) ♿ (wheelchair, induction loop, Braille guide) toilets for disabled shop ⊗ (ex assist dogs)

Moseley Old Hall

Moseley Old Hall Ln, Fordhouses WV10 7HY

➲ *(4m N of Wolverhampton, off A460 and A449, M54 between junct 1 & 2)*

☎ 01902 782808

e-mail: moseleyoldhall@nationaltrust.org.uk
web: www.nationaltrust.org.uk

Originally built at the start of the 17th century, Moseley Old Hall is steeped in history. In 1651, the Prince of Wales, (later King Charles II) hid at Moseley Old Hall following his defeat at the Battle of Worcester. This romantic and daring story of the uncrowned king's escape is brought to life for visitors who enjoy stories from one of England's most turbulent times. Visitors can see the bed Charles slept on and the priest hole that concealed him. The impressive knot garden is based on a design of 1640. Details of special events can be found on the website.

Times Open Mar-2 Nov, Sat-Sun & Wed & additional Tue 22 Jul-9 Sep, 12-5; 9 Nov-21 Dec, Sun 12-4; BH Mon 11-5 & BH Tue 12-5. **Fee** ✳ £6 (ch £3, ch under 5 free). Family ticket £15. Group tickets £5 & on Wed £4.70.
Facilities 🅿 ♿ 🍴 (outdoor) ♿ (access restricted to the ground floor of the house) (Braille & large print, 1 wheelchair, thick handled cutlery) toilets for disabled shop 🐾 ▬

Wightwick Manor

WV6 8EE

➲ *(3m W, beside Mermaid Inn off A454 Bridgnorth)*

☎ 01902 761400

e-mail: wightwickmanor@nationaltrust.org.uk
web: www.nationaltrust.org.uk

This house was begun in 1887 and is one of the finest examples of 19th-century decorative style. All aspects of William Morris's talents are shown in the house - wallpapers, textiles, carpets, tiles, embroidery and even books. The garden reflects late Victorian and Edwardian design.

Times Open Mar-2 Aug, Wed-Sat 12.30-5; 3-31 Aug & Sep-20 Dec, Wed-Sat 11-5 (Last admission 4.30). **Fee** ✳ House & gardens £7.90 (accompanied ch & concession £3.90). Family ticket £19.70. Garden only £3.90 (ch free in garden) **Facilities** 🅿 ♿ ♿ (access to lower hall via 2 steps) (car parking call 01902 760100 for details) toilets for disabled shop ⊗ (ex assist dogs & in gardens) 🐾

WORDSLEY

MAP 07 SO88

The Red House Glass Cone

FREE

High St DY8 4AZ

➲ *(A491 just N of Stourbridge)*

☎ 01384 812750

e-mail: redhouse.cone@dudley.gov.uk
web: www.redhousecone.co.uk

One of only four cones left in the UK and one of the most complete glass cone sites in Europe, over one hundred feet tall. This is a busy heritage site hosting exhibitions, events, children's activities, tours, a schools' programme, live glass-making and craft studios.

Times ✳ Open Nov-Mar, Mon-Sun, 10-4, Apr-Oct, Mon-Sat, 10-5, Sun 10-4 Open BH. Please check for Xmas opening times. **Facilities** 🅿 ♿ 🍴 (outdoor) ♿ (Partly accessible) (lift from first floor to gallery) toilets for disabled shop ⊗ (ex assist dogs & in grounds) ▬

ISLE OF WIGHT

Bembridge Lifeboat Pier

ALUM BAY

MAP 04 SZ38

The Needles Old Battery & New Battery

West High Down PO30 0JH

⮩ *(at Needles Headland, W of Freshwater Bay and Alum Bay, B3322)*

☎ 01983 754772

e-mail: isleofwight@nationaltrust.org.uk

web: www.nationaltrust.org.uk/isleofwight

The threat of a French invasion prompted the construction in 1862 of this spectacularly sited fort, which now contains exhibitions on the Battery's involvement in both World Wars. Two of the original gun barrels are displayed in the parade ground and a 60-yard tunnel leads to a searchlight emplacement perched above the Needles Rocks giving magnificent views of the Dorset coastline beyond. An exhibition about the secret rocket testing programme is housed further up the headland at the Needles New Battery. Opening times vary, phone for details.

Times Old battery Open: end Mar-1 Nov, daily 10.30-5. New battery end Mar-1 Nov, Sat-Sun 11-4. (Last admission 4.30, both properties close in high winds). **Fee** Old battery with Gift Aid: £4.85 (ch £2.45). Family ticket £12.10. New battery free. **Facilities** ⓟ (0.5m) (phone to discuss disabled parking) ⌑ & (Access to Old battery via spiral staircase, uneven surfaces & steep paths. Access to New battery via steps down to exhibition room). (ramp, audio tours, hearing loops, photo album, w/chair). toilets for disabled shop 💥 ➥

The Needles Park

PO39 0JD

⮩ *(signed on B3322)*

☎ 0871 720 0022

e-mail: info@theneedles.co.uk

web: www.theneedles.co.uk

Overlooking the Needles on the western edge of the island, the park has attractions for all the family: included in the wide range of facilities is the spectacular chair lift to the beach to view the famous coloured sand cliffs, Needles Rocks and lighthouse. Other popular attractions are Alum Bay Glass and the Isle of Wight Sweet Manufactory. Kids will enjoy the Junior Driver roadway, the Jurassic golf course and the Spins and Needles tea cup ride. Please contact for special events.

Times Open Etr-Oct, daily 10-5. (Some attractions do run in winter) **Fee** No admission charged for entrance to Park. All day car park charge £3. Pay as you go attractions or Supersaver Attraction discount ticket. **Facilities** ⓟ (charged) ⌑ 🍴 licensed 🍽 (outdoor) & (Some slopes) (10 designated parking bays) toilets for disabled shop ➥

ARRETON

MAP 04 SZ58

Arreton Manor

`2 for 1`

PO30 3AA

⮩ *(on main Sandown to Newport road)*

☎ 01983 522604

e-mail: arretonmanor@mac.com

web: www.arretonmanor.co.uk

Set in five acres on the Arreton Downs, the manor was first mentioned in Alfred the Great's will in 885. Historical records in 1050 say it was owned by Edward the Confessor and the manor was also mentioned the Domesday Book. Although parts of the property are Jacobean, it still possesses many Tudor designs and features. Now a lived in famil home.

Times Open Etr hols & Jun-Sep, daily 10-5 (last tour 4) **Fee** £5.75 (ch £2.50, pen £5.25). Garden only £3. **Facilities** ⓟ ⌑ & (Access to garden only as stone steps inside house) shop ⊗ (ex assist dogs) ➥

Robin Hill Country Park

Downend PO30 2NU

⮩ *(0.5m from Arreton next to Hare & Hounds pub)*

☎ 01983 527352

e-mail: dj@robin-hill.com

web: www.robin-hill.com

Set in 88 acres of beautiful woodland gardens and countryside, Robin Hill provides fun for all the family, with a wide variety of activities and attractions. There are twice-daily falconry displays at 11.30 and 2.45, and plenty of rides, like the Toboggan Run, Colossus Galleon and Time Machine. New attractions are planned for 2009-2010, including a Roman villa interpretation barn and Rio Grande train ride. Robin Hill is also well-known as a great place to spot red squirrels.

Times Open 23 Mar-1 Nov, daily 10-5 (last admission 4). **Fee** £8.50 (pen disabled £5.50). Saver ticket (4) £31. **Facilities** ⓟ ⌑ 🍴 🍽 (outdoor) & (most areas accessible, but some steep paths and some rides may not be suitable). (ramps access) toilets for disabled shop ⊗ (ex on lead) ➥

BEMBRIDGE

MAP 04 SZ68

Bembridge Windmill

PO35 5SQ

⮩ *(0.5m S of Bembridge on B3395)*

☎ 01983 873945

e-mail: isleofwight@nationaltrust.org.uk

web: www.nationaltrust.org.uk/Isleofwight

Built around 1700, this is the only surviving windmill on the island and has much of its original machinery intact. It was last used in 1913, and the stone-built tower with its wooden cap and machinery has been restored so that visitors can explore its four floors. The mill also provides breathtaking views across glorious, unspoilt countryside.

Times Open end Mar-1 Nov, daily 11-5 (last admission 4.30 or dusk if earlier). **Fee** With Gift aid: £2.90 (ch £1.45) Family £7.15 **Facilities** ⓟ (200yds) & (restricted access to ground floor, steps & narrow doorways. Stairs to other floors) (hearing loop, pictorial guide, audio guide, Braille guide) shop ⊗ (ex assist dogs) 💥 ➥

BLACKGANG MAP 04 SZ47

Blackgang Chine Fantasy Park

PO38 2HN

➲ *(follow signs from Ventnor for Whitnell & Niton. From Niton follow signs for Blackgang)*

☎ 01983 730330

e-mail: info@blackgangchine.com

web: www.blackgangchine.com

Opened as scenic gardens in 1843 covering some 40 acres, the park has imaginative play areas, water gardens, maze and coastal gardens. Set on the steep wooded slopes of the chine are the themed areas Smugglerland, Nurseryland, Dinosaurland, Fantasyland and Frontierland. St Catherine's Quay has a maritime exhibition showing the history of local and maritime affairs. Newer attractions include Cliffhanger: the roller coaster, and Pirate's Lair, an adventure play area. Also, 'Chocolate Heaven', and a helicopter film cinema 'Wight Experience'.

Times Open mid Mar-end Oct daily, 10-5; school summer hols open until 7. **Fee** ✳ Combined ticket (as from 15 May) to chine, sawmill & quay £9.50. Saver ticket (4 people) £35. **Facilities** ℗ ♿ (outdoor) & (park on cliff edge, sloping paths) toilets for disabled shop ✉

BRADING MAP 04 SZ68

Brading The Experience

46 High St PO36 0DQ

➲ *(on A3055, in Brading High St)*

☎ 01983 407286

e-mail: info@bradingtheexperience.co.uk

web: www.bradingtheexperience.co.uk

Brading The Experience is more than just a waxworks. Comprising Great British Legends Gallery, 16th-century Rectory Mansion filled with famous and infamous characters from the past, Chamber of Horrors, award-winning Courtyards, Animal World, World of Wheels and The Pier.

Times Open all year, Etr-Oct 10-5, (Nov-Etr please contact establishment for details). (Last admission 1.5 hrs before closing). **Fee** £7.25 (ch 5-15 £5.25, under 5 free, concessions £6.25). Family £23 (2ad+2ch), Family £28 (2ad+3ch). Party 20+. **Facilities** ℗ ♿ & (disabled route planner, virtual tour) toilets for disabled shop ✉

Lilliput Antique Doll & Toy Museum

High St PO36 0DJ

➲ *(A3055 Ryde/Sandown road, in Brading High Street)*

☎ 01983 407231

e-mail: lilliput.museum@btconnect.com

web: www.lilliputmuseum.org.uk

This private museum contains one of the finest collections of antique dolls and toys in Britain. There are over 2,000 exhibits, ranging in age from 2000BC to 1945 with examples of almost every seriously collectable doll, many with royal connections. Also dolls' houses, teddy bears and rare and unusual toys.

Times Open all year, daily, 10-5. **Fee** £2.50 (ch £1.25, ch under 5 free, concessions £1.50). Party on request. **Facilities** ℗ (200 yds) & (ramps provided on request) shop ✉

Morton Manor

PO36 0EP

➲ *(off A3055 in Brading, well signed)*

☎ 01983 406168

e-mail: mortonmanor-iow@amserve.com

The manor dates back to 1249, but was rebuilt in 1680 with further changes during the Georgian period. The house contains furniture of both the 18th and 19th centuries, but its main attraction lies in the gardens. The garden is landscaped into terraces, with ornamental ponds, a sunken garden and a traditional Elizabethan turf maze.

Times ✳ Open Apr-Oct, daily 10-5.30. Closed Sat. (Last admissions 4.30). **Facilities** ℗ ♿ 🍴 shop garden centre ⊗ (ex assist dogs)

Nunwell House & Gardens `2 for 1`

Coach Ln PO36 0JQ

➲ *(Off Ryde-Sandown Rd, A3055, follow brown tourist signs)*

☎ 01983 407240

Set in beautiful gardens, Nunwell is an impressive, lived-in and much loved house where King Charles I spent his last night of freedom. It has fine furniture and interesting collections of family militaria. In summer, concerts are occasionally held in the music room. There are also five acres of gardens with some lovely views.

Times Open 24-25 May, 6 Jul-9 Sep, Mon-Wed 1-5. Tours of House 2 & 3. **Fee** £5 (ch under 10 £1, concessions £4) **Facilities** ℗ ♿ & toilets for disabled shop ⊗ (ex assist dogs)

BRIGHSTONE MAP 04 SZ48

Brighstone Shop and Museum `FREE`

North St PO30 4AX

➲ *(off B3399 in Brighstone onto North Street, next to Post Office)*

☎ 01983 740689

e-mail: isleofwight@nationaltrust.org.uk

web: www.nationaltrust.org.uk/isleofwight

Situated within a row of attractive, thatched cottages you will find this museum which contains an evocative tableau and an interesting exhibition on village life in the 19th century.

Times Open Mon-Sat all year. 2 Jan-9 Apr 10-1; 10 Apr-24 May & 28 Sep-24 Dec10-4; 23 May-26 Sep 10-5. Open Sun 24 May-27 Sep 12-5. **Facilities** ℗ (100mtrs) & (hearing loop) shop ⊗ (ex assist dogs) ♨ ✉

CARISBROOKE — MAP 04 SZ48

Carisbrooke Castle

Castle Hill PO30 1XY

➲ (1.25m SW of Newport, off B3401)

☎ 01983 522107

web: www.english-heritage.org.uk

A royal fortress and prison to King Charles I, Carisbrooke is set on a sweeping ridge at the heart of the Isle of Wight. Don't miss the donkeys that can be seen working a 16th-century wheel to draw water from the well.

Times Open all year, 21 Mar-Sep, daily 10-5; Oct-Mar, daily 10-4. Closed 24-26 Dec & 1 Jan. **Fee** £6.50 (concessions £5.20, ch £3.30). Family £16.30. Prices and opening times are subject to change in March 2009. Please check web site or call 0870 333 1181 for the most up to date prices and opening times when planning your visit. **Facilities** ❷ ☑ shop ⚫

FRESHWATER — MAP 04 SZ38

Dimbola Lodge Museum

Terrace Ln, Freshwater Bay PO40 9QE

➲ (off A3054, visible from Freshwater Bay)

☎ 01983 756814

e-mail: administrator@dimbola.co.uk

web: www.dimbola.co.uk

Home of Julia Margaret Cameron, the pioneer Victorian portrait photographer. The house has the largest permanent collection of Cameron prints on display in the UK, as well as galleries exhibiting work by young, up and coming, and acclaimed modern photographers; and a large display of cameras and accessories.

Times ✳ Open all year Tue-Sun. Closed 5 days at Xmas. Open BH Mons & daily during school summer hols. **Facilities** ❷ ⑩ & (chairlifts) toilets for disabled shop ⊗ (ex assist dogs) ⊟

MOTTISTONE — MAP 04 SZ48

Mottistone Manor Garden

PO30 4ED

➲ (Situated between Brighstone & Brook on B3399.)

☎ 01983 741302

e-mail: isleofwight@nationaltrust.org.uk

web: www.nationaltrust.org.uk/isleofwight

This magical garden is set in a sheltered valley with views to the sea, and surrounds an Elizabethan manor house, which is tenanted. With its colourful borders, shrub-filled banks and grassy terraces, it provides a tranquil and interesting place to visit. There is also a small organic kitchen garden, children's activity packs, a flowerpot trail, and some delightful walks onto the downs across the adjoining Mottistone Estate.

Times Open end Mar-1 Nov, Sun-Thu 11-5. (Last admission 4.30 or dusk if earlier). **Fee** With Gift Aid: £3.85 (ch £1.95). Family £9.65. **Facilities** ❷ ☑ & (Access to entrance has steps, with loose gravel paths & some slopes & steps in garden). (hearing loop, large print menu, photo album, 1 w/chair) toilets for disabled shop garden centre ⚫ ⊟

NEWTOWN — MAP 04 SZ49

Newtown Old Town Hall

Town Ln PO30 4PA

➲ (1m N of A3054 between Yarmouth & Newport)

☎ 01983 531785

e-mail: isleofwight@nationaltrust.org.uk

web: www.nationaltrust.org.uk/isleofwight

The small, now tranquil, village of Newtown once sent two members to parliament and the Town Hall was the setting for often turbulent elections. This historic building contains exhibits on local history including the exploits of 'Ferguson's Gang', a mysterious group of anonymous benefactors. There are splendid views across unspoilt countryside to the town and footpaths leading to the nearby estuary.

Times Open end Mar-21Oct Sun, Mon & Wed 2-5; Jul & Aug, Sun-Thu 2-5. Also open Good Fri & Etr Sat. (Last admission 4.45). **Fee** £2.10 (ch 1.05). Family £5.25. **Facilities** ❷ & (access restricted to ground floor, 10 steps with handrail to entrance, stairs to upper floors) (Photo album, hearing loops) toilets for disabled ⊗ (ex assist dogs) ⊟

OSBORNE HOUSE — MAP 04 SZ59

Osborne House

PO32 6JY

➲ (1m SE of East Cowes)

☎ 01983 200022

web: www.english-heritage.org.uk

The beloved seaside retreat of Queen Victoria offers a glimpse into the private life of Britain's longest reigning monarch. The royal apartments are full of treasured mementos; and Queen Victoria's role as Empress of India is celebrated in the decoration of the Durbar Room. Visit the gardens and the charming Swiss Cottage.

Times Open 21 Mar-Sep, daily 10-5 (grounds 10-6); Oct, daily 10-4; Nov-Mar, Wed-Sun 10-4 (pre-booked guided tours, last tour 2.30. Xmas tour season 8 Nov-4 Jan). Closed 24-26 Dec & 1 Jan. On 18-19 Jul & 4 Aug, house closes at 3 (grounds close 4) for special events. **Fee** House & Grounds: £10 (concessions £8, ch £5). Family £25. Grounds only: £6 (concessions £4.80, ch £3). Family £15. Prices and opening times are subject to change in March 2009. Please check web or call 0870 333 1181 for the most up to date prices and opening times. **Facilities** ❷ ☑ ⏚ shop ⊗ ⚫

PORCHFIELD — MAP 04 SZ49

Colemans Animal Farm

Colemans Ln PO30 4LX

➲ (A3054 Newport to Yarmouth road, follow brown tourist signs)

☎ 01983 522831

e-mail: info@colemansfarm.net

web: www.colemansfarm.com

Ideal for young children, this extensive petting farm has donkeys, goats, rabbits, guinea pigs, pigs, Highland cattle, Shetland ponies, chickens, ducks and geese. There is also a fun barn with slides and swings, an adventure playground, a Tractor Fun Park, and an Old Barn Café for adults who need to relax. Visitors can cuddle, stroke and feed the animals at special times throughout the day. Other special events run all day.

Times ✳ Open mid Mar-end Oct, Tue-Sun, 10-4.30 (last admission recommended 3.30). (Closed Mon, ex during school and BHs). Open for pre-booked events out of season. **Facilities** ♿ ⌷ ⫟ (indoor & outdoor) shop ▬

SANDOWN   MAP 04 SZ58

Dinosaur Isle   `2 for 1`

Culver Pde PO36 8QA

➲ *(In Sandown follow brown tourist signs to Dinosaur Isle, situated on B3395 on seafront)*

☎ 01983 404344

e-mail: dinosaur@iow.gov.uk

web: www.dinosaurisle.com

Britain's first purpose-built dinosaur attraction where, in a building reminiscent of a Pterosaur flying across the Cretaceous skies, you can walk back through fossilised time. In recreated landscape meet life sized models of the island's famous five - Neovenator, Eotyrannus, Iguanodon, Hypsilophodon and Polacanthus. Look out for the flying Pterodactyls and skeletons as they are found, watch volunteers preparing the latest finds or try the many hands-on activities. A guided fossil hunt (which must be pre-booked) has proven a popular addition.

Times Open all year daily, Apr-Sep 10-6; Oct 10-5; Nov-Mar 10-4. (Closed 24-26 Dec & 1 Jan). Please phone to confirm opening 5 Jan-6 Feb. (Last admission 1hr before closing.) **Fee** £5 (ch 3-15 £3, concessions £4). Family (2ad+2ch) £14.50 **Facilities** ♿ (charged) ⫟ (outdoor) ♿ (Lift for access to 2nd floor) toilets for disabled shop ⊗ (ex assist dogs) ▬

SHANKLIN   MAP 04 SZ58

Shanklin Chine

12 Pomona Rd PO37 6PF

➲ *(turn off A3055 at lights, left into Hope Rd & continue onto Esplanade for entrance)*

☎ 01983 866432

e-mail: jillshanklinchine1@msn.com

web: www.shanklinchine.co.uk

Part of Britain's national heritage, this scenic gorge at Shanklin is a magical world of unique beauty and a haven for rare plants and wildlife. A path winds through the ravine with overhanging trees, ferns and other flora covering the steep sides. 'The Island-Then and Now' is an exhibition detailing the history of the Isle of Wight, including its military importance in WWII.

Times ✳ Open 31 Mar-25 May, 10-5. 26 May-10 Sep, 10-10. 11 Sep-29 Oct, 10-5. **Facilities** ♿ (450yds) ⌷ ♿ (access via lower entry only) toilets for disabled shop

---

WROXALL   MAP 04 SZ57

Appuldurcombe House

PO38 3EW

➲ *(off B3327, 0.5m W)*

☎ 01983 852484

web: www.english-heritage.org.uk

The shell of Appuldurcombe, once the grandest house on the Isle of Wight, stands in its own grounds, designed by 'Capability' Brown. An exhibition of prints and photographs depicts the house and its history.

Times Open 16 Mar-Sep, daily 10-4. (Last entry 1hr before closing). Closed Oct-Mar. **Fee** £3.50 (concessions £3.25, ch £2.50). Family ticket £12. Prices and opening times are subject to change in March 2009. Please check web site or call 0870 333 1181 for the most up to date prices and opening times when planning your visit. **Facilities** ♿ shop ⊗ (ex on leads) ⛭

YARMOUTH   MAP 04 SZ38

Yarmouth Castle

Quay St PO4 1OP

➲ *(adjacent to car ferry terminal)*

☎ 01983 760678

web: www.english-heritage.org.uk

The last addition to Henry VIII's coastal defences completed in 1547, the Tudor castle is set in a beautiful old seaside town. See the Isle of Wight paintings and memorable photographs of Old Yarmouth.

Times Open 21 Mar-Sep, Sun-Thu 11-4. **Fee** £3.50 (concessions £2.80, ch £1.80). Prices and opening times are subject to change in March 2009. Please check web site or call 0870 333 1181 for the most up to date prices and opening times when planning your visit. **Facilities** ♿ (200yds) shop ⛭

WILTSHIRE

Waterfall at Bowood House, Derry Hill

AVEBURY MAP 04 SU06

Alexander Keiller Museum

High St SN8 1RF

⮑ *(6m W of Marlborough. 1m N of Bath Rd (A4) on A4361 and B4003)*

☎ 01672 539250

e-mail: avebury@nationaltrust.org.uk

web: www.nationaltrust.org.uk

Avebury is one of the most important megalithic monuments in Europe, and was built before Stonehenge. The museum, including an exhibition in the 17th-century threshing barn, presents the full archaeological story of the stones using finds from the site, along with inter-active and audio-visual displays.

Times Open Feb-Oct, daily 10-5; Nov-Feb, 10-4. Closed 24-26 Dec. **Fee** ✳ £4.70 (ch £2.35) Family £11.60 (2ad+3ch). £8.30 (1ad+3ch). Groups £3.60 (ch £1.80). **Facilities** ♿ (charged) ▯ ⑭ ⚲ ⛊ (Braille guide, large print guide, drop off point) toilets for disabled shop ⊗ (ex assist dogs) ⛞ ⊟

Avebury Manor & Garden

SN8 1RF

⮑ *(from A4 take A4361/B4003)*

☎ 01672 539250

e-mail: avebury@nationaltrust.org.uk

web: www.nationaltrust.org.uk

Avebury Manor has a monastic origin, and has been much altered since then. The present buildings date from the early 16th century, with notable Queen Anne alterations and Edwardian renovation. The flower gardens contain medieval walls, and there are examples of topiary.

Times House: Apr-28 Oct, Sun-Tue, 2-4.40. Garden: 31 Mar-28 Oct daily (ex Wed & Thu) 11-5. **Fee** ✳ Manor & Garden £4 (ch £2). Garden £3 (ch £1.50). Groups £2.55 (ch £1.30). **Facilities** ♿ (charged) ▯ ⑭ ⚲ ⛊ (audio visual, Braille/large print guide, induction loop) toilets for disabled shop ⊗ ⛞ ⊟

BRADFORD-ON-AVON MAP 03 ST86

Bradford-on-Avon Tithe Barn `FREE`

⮑ *(0.25m S of town centre, off B3109)*

web: www.english-heritage.org.uk

This impressive tithe barn, over 160ft long by 30ft wide, once belonged to Shaftesbury Abbey. The roof is of stone slates, supported outside by buttresses and inside by massive beams and a network of rafters.

Times Open all year, daily 10.30-4. Closed 25 Dec. **Facilities** ♿ (charged) ⊗ ⚏

Great Chalfield Manor and Garden

SN12 8NH

⮑ *(3m SW of Melksham off B3107 via Broughton Gifford Common)*

☎ 01225 782239

e-mail: greatchalfieldmanor@nationaltrust.org.uk

web: www.nationaltrust.org.uk

Built during the Wars of the Roses, the manor is a beautiful, mellow, moated house restored in the 1920s. There is a small 13th-century church next to the house.

Times House open Apr-2 Nov, Tue-Thu & Sun, guided tours only at 11.30, 12.15, 2.15, 3, 3.45, 4.30. Garden open 30 Mar-2 Nov Tue-Thu 11-5, Sun 2-5. **Fee** ✳ £6.40(ch £3.20). Family ticket £16.30. Groups £5.40 (ch £2.70). Garden only £4.2 (ch £2.10). **Facilities** ♿ ♿ (drop off point, wheelchair, Braille guide) toilets for disabled ⊗ ⛞

The Peto Garden at Iford Manor `2 for 1`

Iford Manor BA15 2BA

⮑ *(Brown tourist signs 0.5m S of Bradford-on-Avon on B3109)*

☎ 01225 863146

e-mail: ifordmanor@countryside.uk.net

web: www.ifordmanor.co.uk

An award-winning garden in the romantic setting of the Frome Valley. Designed by Harold Peto between 1899 and 1933, this Italian style garden features terraces, statues and ponds. Recitals and operas take place in the garden throughout the summer season as part of the Iford Arts programme. Homemade Housekeeper's teas at weekends (non-garden visitors welcome).

Times Open May-Sep, Tue-Thu, Sat & Sun. Apr & Oct open Sun only 2-5. Closed Mon & Fri except BH Mons. **Fee** £4.50 (ch under 10 free, concessions £4) **Facilities** ♿ ▯ ♿ (Partly accessible) toilets for disabled ⊗ (ex on leads

CALNE   MAP 03 ST97

Bowood House & Gardens

2 for 1

SN11 0LZ

➲ *(off A4 Chippenham to Calne road, in Derry Hill village)*

☎ 01249 812102

e-mail: houseandgardens@bowood.org

web: www.bowood.org

Built in 1624, the house was finished by the first Earl of Shelburne, who employed celebrated architects, notably Robert Adam, to complete the work. Adam's library is particularly admired, and also in the house is the laboratory where Dr Joseph Priestley discovered the existence of oxygen in 1774. The house overlooks terraced gardens towards the 40-acre lake and some beautiful parkland. The gardens were laid out by 'Capability' Brown in the 1760s, and are carpeted with daffodils, narcissi and bluebells in spring. For children between 2 and 12 years there is the superb adventure playground, which boasts a life size pirate and famous space dive. There is also an indoor soft play palace for younger children.

Times Open daily Apr-Oct 11-6, incl BH. Rhododendron Gardens (separate entrance off A342) open 6 weeks during mid Apr-early Jun, 11-6. **Fee** ✱ House & Gardens £8 (ch 2-4 £4.5; 5-15 £6.5; pen £7). Family ticket (2ad+2ch) £25. Rhododendrons only £5.25 (pen £4.75). £1 discount if house visited on same day. **Facilities** ℗ ⬚🍴 licensed 📮 (outdoor) ♿ (restricted access to upper exhibition rooms) (parking by arrangement, DVD tour of upstairs) toilets for disabled shop ⊗ (ex assist dogs) ▄

CORSHAM   MAP 03 ST87

Corsham Court

SN13 0BZ

➲ *(4m W of Chippenham off the A4)*

☎ 01249 701610

e-mail: staterooms@corsham-court.co.uk

web: www.corsham-court.co.uk

The Elizabethan manor was built in 1582, and then bought by the Methuen family in the 18th century to house their collections of paintings and statues. 'Capability' Brown made additions to the house and laid out the park, and later John Nash made further changes. There is furniture by Chippendale, Adam, Cobb and Johnson inside, as well as the Methuen collection of Old Master paintings. The garden has flowering shrubs, herbaceous borders, a Georgian bath house and peacocks.

Times Open: 20 Mar-Sep, daily (ex Mon & Fri), but incl BHs 2-5.30. Oct-19 Mar open wknds only 2-4.30. (Last admission 30 minutes before closing). Closed Dec. Open throughout year by appointment for groups 15+. **Fee** £7 (ch 5-15 £3, pen £6) Group rate £6 **Facilities** ℗ ♿ (platform lift) toilets for disabled shop ⊗ (ex assist dogs)

HOLT   MAP 03 ST86

The Courts Garden

BA14 6RR

➲ *(3m SW of Melksham, 2.5m E of Bradford on Avon, on south side of B3107 follow signs to Holt)*

☎ 01225 782875

e-mail: courtsgarden@nationaltrust.org.uk

web: www.nationaltrust.org.uk

The house is not open, but it makes an attractive backdrop to the gardens - a network of stone paths, yew hedges, pools and borders with a strange, almost magical atmosphere. The peaceful water gardens are planted with irises and lilies.

Times Open 15 Mar-2 Nov, daily (ex Wed) 11-5.30; out of season by appointment only. **Fee** ✱ £5.80 (ch £2.90). Family ticket £14.80. Groups £5 (ch £2.50). **Facilities** ℗ ⬚♿ (wheelchair, ramp access, Braille & large print guide) toilets for disabled ⊗ (ex assist dogs) ▄

LACOCK   MAP 03 ST96

Lacock Abbey, Fox Talbot Museum & Village

SN15 2LG

➲ *(3m S of Chippenham, E of A350, car park signed)*

☎ 01249 730227 (abbey) & 730459

e-mail: lacockabbey@nationaltrust.org.uk

web: www.nationaltrust.org.uk

Magnificent late Victorian country house with extensive servants quarters, gardens and wooded estate.

Times Cloisters & Grounds, Mar-2 Nov, daily 11-5.30. Closed Good Fri. Abbey, 15 Mar-2 Nov, daily, ex Tue, 1-5.30. Closed Good Fri. Museum 23 Feb-2 Nov, daily 11-5.30; 8 Nov-21 Dec, Sat & Sun 11-4; 3 Jan-31 Jan, Sat & Sun 11-4 **Fee** ✱ Museum, Abbey, Grounds & Cloisters £10 (ch £5). Family ticket £25.50 (2ad+2ch). Grounds, Cloisters & Museum £6 (ch £3). Family ticket £15.3 (2ad+2ch). Abbey, Cloisters & Grounds £8 (ch £4). Family ticket £20.40 (2ad+2ch). Museum (winter) £3.60 (ch £1.80). Family ticket £9.20 (2ad+2ch). **Facilities** ℗ (charged) 📮 (outdoor) ♿ (manual wheelchairs, Braille/large print & audio guides) toilets for disabled shop ⊗ ▄

LONGLEAT   MAP 03 ST84

Longleat

The Estate Office BA12 7NW

➲ *(turn off A36 Bath-Salisbury road onto A362 Warminster-Frome road)*

☎ 01985 844400

e-mail: enquiries@longleat.co.uk

web: www.longleat.co.uk

Nestling within magnificent 'Capability' Brown landscaped grounds in the heart of Wiltshire, Longleat House is widely regarded as one of the most beautiful stately homes open to the public. Longleat House was built by Sir John Thynne and completed in 1580. It has remained the home of the same family ever since. Many treasures are contained within the house: paintings by Tintoretto and Wootton, exquisite

Longleat

many of the original furnishings returned, together with a family portrait collection dating from Elizabethan to Victorian times. Exceptional plaster work, early wallpaper, a rare painted glass window, and a room devoted to the talented 18th-century artist, Lady Diana Spencer (Beauclerk), can also be seen. There is also a restored 18th-century ornamental fruit and flower walled garden.

Times Open all year, House & walled garden, Tue-Sun & BH Mons 11-5, Winter closing 4 (Nov-Feb). Park: all year, daily closing at dusk. Times may be subject to change, please call 01793 770401 or check website. **Fee** ✴ House £3.50 (ch £1.75 , concessions £3). House & Walled Garden £4.50 (ch £2.25, pen £4). Walled Garden only £1.85 (ch £1, pen £1.50) Entry to grounds is free. **Facilities** ℗ ⊏⋤ ⊓ (outdoor) ♿ (audio box in state room) toilets for disabled shop ⊗ (ex assist dogs in house) ➟

Flemish tapestries, fine French furniture and elaborate ceilings by John Dibblee Crace. The murals in the family apartments in the West Wing were painted by Alexander Thynne, the present Marquess, and are fascinating and remarkable additions to the collection. Apart from the ancestral home, Longleat is also renowned for its safari park, the first of its kind in the UK. Here, visitors have the rare opportunity to see hundreds of animals in natural woodland and parkland settings. Among the most magnificent sights are the famous pride of lions, wolves, rhesus monkeys and zebra. Other attractions which ensure a fun family day out include the 'Longleat Hedge Maze', the 'Adventure Castle', 'Longleat Railway', 'Pets' Corner' and the 'Safari Boats'.

Times Open daily 14-22 Feb, wknds only 28 Feb-29 Mar. Daily 4 Apr-1 Nov. **Fee** ✴ Longleat passport: £22 (ch 3-14 yrs & concessions £16). **Facilities** ℗ ⊏⋤ ⊚⊓ (outdoor) ♿ (Partly accessible) (informative leaflet available or see website) toilets for disabled shop ➟

LUDGERSHALL   MAP 04 SU25

Ludgershall Castle and Cross   FREE

SP11 9QR

➲ *(7m NW of Andover on A342)*

web: www.english-heritage.org.uk

Ruins of an early 12th-century royal hunting palace and medieval cross. The visitor can see large earthworks of the Norman motte-and-bailey castle and the flint walls of the later hunting palace. The stump of a medieval cross stands in the village street.

Times Open at any reasonable time. **Facilities** ℗ ⌗

LYDIARD PARK   MAP 04 SU18

Lydiard Park

Lydiard Tregoze SN5 3PA

➲ *(M4 junct 16, follow brown tourist signs)*

☎ 01793 770401

e-mail: lydiardpark@swindon.gov.uk

web: www.lydiardpark.org.uk

Set in country parkland, Lydiard Park belonged to the St John family (the Bolingbrokes) for 500 years up until 1943 when the Swindon Corporation purchased it. Since then the house has been restored and

MARLBOROUGH   MAP 04 SU16

Crofton Beam Engines

Crofton Pumping Station, Crofton SN8 3DW

➲ *(signed from A4/A338/A346 & B3087 at Burbage)*

☎ 01672 870300

e-mail: enquiries@croftonbeamengines.org

web: www.croftonbeamengines.org

The oldest working beam engine in the world still in its original building and still doing its original job, the Boulton and Watt 1812, can be found in this rural spot. Its companion is a Harvey's of Hayle of 1845. Both are steam driven, from a hand-stoked, coal-fired boiler, and pump water into the summit level of the Kennet and Avon Canal with a lift of 40ft.

Times Open daily Etr-Sep, 10.30-5 (last entry 4.30). 'In Steam' Etr, BH wknds & last wknd of Jun, Jul & Sep. **Facilities** ℗ (charged) ⊏⋤ ⊓ (outdoor) ♿ (phone warden in advance, sighted guides provided) shop ⊗ (ex assist dogs) ➟

MIDDLE WOODFORD   MAP 04 SU13

Heale Gardens

SP4 6NT

➲ *(4m N of Salisbury, between A360 & A345)*

☎ 01722 782504

Heale House and its eight acres of beautiful garden lie beside the River Avon at Middle Woodford. Much of the house is unchanged since King Charles II sheltered here after the Battle of Worcester in 1651. The garden provides a wonderfully varied collection of plants, shrubs, and musk and other roses, growing in the formal setting of clipped hedges and mellow stonework. Special Event: Snowdrop Sundays in Feb.

Times ✴ Open: Plant centre daily, 10-5. Gardens daily (closed Mon ex BHs) **Facilities** ℗ ⊏⋤ ⊓ (outdoor) ♿ (most parts accessible) shop garden centre ⊗ (ex assist dogs) ➟

SALISBURY   MAP 04 SU12

The Medieval Hall

Cathedral Close SP1 2EY

➲ *(look for signs within Salisbury Cathedral Close)*

☎ 01722 412472 & 324731

e-mail: medieval.hall@ntworld.com

web: www.medieval-hall.co.uk

Visit the historic 13th-century Medieval Hall and watch the fascinating 40 minute sound and picture guide to the city and region. A witty and informative soundtrack, (available in six different languages) specially composed music and some startling effects accompany hundreds of images to provide an insight into Salisbury's extraordinary past, the colourful city of today, and many of the attractions in the area. Enjoy refreshments 'while you watch'. Contact the Hall for full details of special events.

Times ✳ Open Apr-Sep, 11-5. Also open throughout year for pre-booked groups. Occasionally closed for special events. **Facilities** ⓟ (charged) ⌨ ♿ (ramp access) shop

Mompesson House

The Close SP1 2EL

➲ *(on N side of Choristers Green in Cathedral Close, near High St Gate)*

☎ 01722 335659 & 420980 (info only)

e-mail: mompessonhouse@nationaltrust.org.uk

web: www.nationaltrust.org.uk

With its high wrought-iron railings and perfect proportions, this Queen Anne house makes an impressive addition to the elegant Cathedral Close in Salisbury. Inside are stucco ceilings, a carved oak staircase and period furniture plus an important collection of 18th-century glasses, china and some outstanding paintings.

Times Open 15 Mar-2 Nov, daily (ex Thu & Fri) 11-5. Open Good Friday. **Fee** ✳ £4.95 (ch £2.45). Group rate £4. Garden only £1. Family £12.40. **Facilities** ⓟ (260 yds) (limited disabled parking available) ⌨ ♿ (Partly accessible) (ramps, Braille & large print guide) toilets for disabled shop ⊗ ♨

Old Sarum

Castle Rd SP1 3SD

➲ *(2m N on A345)*

☎ 01722 335398

web: www.english-heritage.org.uk

The site of the original city of Salisbury. The 56-acre ruins of this once bustling town are rich in history and woodland. Founded in the Iron Age and occupied until the 16th-century. Romans, Saxons and Normans have all left their mark.

Times Open 21 Mar-Jun & Sep, daily 10-5; Jul-Aug, daily 9-6; Oct, daily 10-4; Nov-Feb, daily 11-3. Closed 24-26 Dec & 1 Jan. **Fee** £3 (concessions £2.40, ch £1.50). Prices and opening times are subject to change in March 2009. Please check web site or call 0870 333 1181 for the most up to date prices and opening times when planning your visit. **Facilities** ⓟ ⤒ ♿ (assess to outer bailey and grounds only) shop ⌗

Salisbury Cathedral

33 The Close SP1 2EJ

➲ *(S of city centre & Market Sq)*

☎ 01722 555120

e-mail: visitors@salcath.co.uk

web: www.salisburycathedral.org.uk

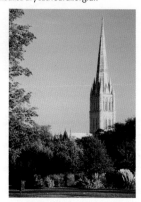

Discover nearly 800 years of history on a visit to this magnificent 13th-century Gothic Cathedral. Situated in the largest and best preserved Close in Britain, amid historic buildings and ancient stone walls, Salisbury Cathedral is surrounded by eight acres of lawns. Explore the Cathedral with a volunteer guide and discover Britain's tallest spire (123m), finest preserved original Magna Carta (AD 1215) and Europe's oldest working clock (AD 1386). Experience and enjoy the choral traditions which have existed here for almost eight centuries or relax in the glass-roofed Refectory Restaurant with its stunning views of the spire above.

Times Open all year, daily 7.15am-6.15pm **Fee** Suggested voluntary donations on entry: £5 (ch 5-17 £3, concessions £4.25). Family £12. **Facilities** ⓟ (100yds) ⌨ ⓘⓞⓘ licensed ⤒ (indoor & outdoor) ♿ (loop system, interpretative model for blind, wheelchairs) toilets for disabled shop ➡

Salisbury & South Wiltshire Museum   `2 for 1`

The King's House, 65 The Close SP1 2EN

➲ *(in Cathedral Close)*

☎ 01722 332151

e-mail: museum@salisburymuseum.org.uk

web: www.salisburymuseum.org.com

One of the most outstanding of the beautiful buildings in Cathedral Close houses this local museum. Galleries feature Stonehenge, History of Salisbury, the Pitt Rivers collection, ceramics and pictures and the Wedgwood room, a reconstruction of a pre-NHS surgery, and a costume, lace and embroidery gallery. .

Times Open all year Mon-Sat 10-5; also Suns Jul & Aug, 2-5. Closed Xmas. **Fee** ✳ £5 (ch £2, concessions £3.50). Family ticket £11. Gift Aid annual tickets available. **Facilities** ⓟ (100mtrs) (nearby parking charge) ⌨ ♿ (Partly accessible) (parking, induction loop, wheelchair, interactive computers) toilets for disabled shop ⊗ (ex assist dogs) ➡

STONEHENGE MAP 04 SU14

Stonehenge

SP4 7DE

➲ *(2m W of Amesbury on junct A303 and A344/ A360)*

☎ 0870 333 1181 & 01722 343834

web: www.english-heritage.org.uk

Britain's greatest prehistoric monument and a World Heritage Site. What visitors see today are the substantial remains of the last in a series of monuments erected between around 3000 and 1600BC.

Times Open all year, 16 Mar-May & Sep-15 Oct, daily 9.30-6; Jun-Aug, daily 9-7; 16 Oct-15 Mar, daily 9.30-4; 26 Dec & 1 Jan, 10-4. (Last admission no later than 30mins before closing). Closed 24-25 Dec. (Usual facilities may not apply around Summer Solstice 20-22 Jun & access may be restricted during bad weather, please check). **Fee** £6.50 (concessions £5.20, ch £3.30). Family ticket £16.30. NT members free. Prices and opening times are subject to change in March 2009. Please check web site or call 0870 333 1181 for the most up to date prices and opening times when planning your visit. **Facilities** Ⓟ ☕ shop ⊗ (ex assist dogs) ⌗

STOURHEAD MAP 03 ST73

Stourhead

Stourhead Estate Office BA12 6QD

➲ *(At Stourton off B3092, 3m NW Mere A303, follow brown tourist signs)*

☎ 01747 841152

e-mail: stourhead@nationaltrust.org.uk

web: www.nationaltrust.org.uk

An outstanding example of the English landscape style, this splendid garden was designed by Henry Hoare II and laid out between 1741 and 1780. Classical temples, including the Pantheon and Temple of Apollo, are set around the central lake at the end of a series of vistas, which change as the visitor moves around the paths and through the mature woodland with its extensive collection of exotic trees.

Times Garden open all year 9-7 (or dusk if earlier). House open 15 Mar-2 Nov , 11.30-4.30 (closed Wed & Thu); King Alfred tower open 15 Mar-2 Nov, daily 11.30-4.30. **Fee** ✳ Garden & House £11.60 (ch £5.80) Family ticket £27.60, groups £9.90. Garden or House £7 (ch £3.80), King Alfred Tower £2.60 (ch £1.40). **Facilities** Ⓟ ☕ 🍽 ⛩ (outdoor) ♿ (wheelchairs, electric buggy, Braille, sensory trail) toilets for disabled shop garden centre ⊗ (ex in gardens Nov-Feb only) ✿ ▬

STOURTON MAP 03 ST73

Stourton House Flower Garden

Stourton House BA12 6QF

➲ *(3m NW of Mere, on A303)*

☎ 01747 840417

Set in the attractive village of Stourton, the house has more than four acres of beautifully maintained flower gardens. Many grass paths lead through varied and colourful shrubs and trees. Stourton House also specialises in unusual plants and dried flowers, many of which are for sale. It also has collections of daffodils, delphiniums and hydrangeas, along with a nature garden where visitors can sit and watch the birds, butterflies and other wildlife.

Times ✳ Open last 2 Sun Feb & Apr-end Nov, Wed, Thu, Sun & BH Mon 11-6 (or dusk if earlier). Also open Dec-Mar, wkdays for plant/dried flower sales. **Facilities** Ⓟ ☕ ♿ (wheelchairs available) toilets for disabled shop garden centre ⊗ (ex by arrangement)

SWINDON MAP 04 SU18

STEAM - Museum of the Great Western Railway

Kemble Dr SN2 2TA

➲ *(from M4 junct 16 & A420 follow brown signs to 'Outlet Centre' & Museum)*

☎ 01793 466646

e-mail: steampostbox@swindon.gov.uk

web: www.steam-museum.org.uk

This fascinating day out tells the story of the men and women who built, operated and travelled on the Great Western Railway. Hands-on displays, world-famous locomotives, archive film footage and the testimonies of ex-railway workers bring the story to life. A reconstructed station platform, posters and holiday memorabilia recreate the glamour and excitement of the golden age of steam. Located next door to the McArthurGlen Designer Outlet Great Western, STEAM offers a great day out for all. Good value group packages, special events and exhibitions and shop.

Times ✳ Open daily 10-5. Closed 25-26 Dec & 1 Jan **Facilities** Ⓟ (100 yds) (disabled parking 20yds) ♿ (wheelchair or scooter can be pre-booked) toilets for disabled shop ⊗ (ex assist dogs) ▬

SWINDON CONTINUED

Swindon & Cricklade Railway   2 for 1

Blunsdon Station, Tadpole Ln, Blunsdon SN25 2DA

➲ *(M4 junct 15, take A419 to lights at Blunsdon Stadium. Railway in 1m along minor road to stadium)*

☎ 01793 771615

e-mail: randallchri@yahoo.co.uk

web: www.swindon-cricklade-railway.org

Heritage railway in the process of being restored. Steam and diesel locomotives, historic carriages, wagons and a large variety of railway structures from a past era. A new extension to the line opened in May 2008.

Times Open Etr-end Oct, Sat-Sun, 11-4; Nov-Etr, Sun only. Also open BHs, Xmas & Wed in local school hols. **Fee** £5 (ch £3.50). Family £15. Different prices apply for some special events. **Facilities** 🅿 ☕ 🍴 (outdoor) ♿ toilets for disabled shop

---

TEFFONT MAGNA   MAP 03 ST93

Farmer Giles Farmstead

SP3 5QY

➲ *(11m W of Stonehenge, off A303 to Teffont. Follow brown signs)*

☎ 01722 716338

e-mail: tdeane6995@aol.com

web: www.farmergiles.co.uk

Forty acres of Wiltshire downland with farm animals to feed, ponds, inside and outside play areas, exhibitions, tractor rides, and gift shop.

Times ✴ Open 18 Mar-5 Nov, daily 10-6, wknds in winters, 10-dusk. Party bookings all year. **Facilities** 🅿 🍴 🌳 ♿ (complete access for disabled/ wheelchairs available for use) toilets for disabled shop ➡

TISBURY   MAP 03 ST92

Old Wardour Castle

SP3 6RR

➲ *(2m SW)*

☎ 01747 870487

web: www.english-heritage.org.uk

This 14th-century castle stands in a romantic lakeside setting. Landscaped grounds and elaborate rockwork grotto surround the unusual hexagonal ruins. Scenes from *Robin Hood, Price of Thieves,* starring Kevin Costner were filmed here.

Times Open all year, 21Mar-Jun & Sep, daily 10-5; Jul-Aug, daily 10-6; Oct, daily 10-4; Nov-Mar, Sat-Sun 10-4. Closed 24-26 Dec & 1 Jan. **Fee** £3.50 (concessions £2.80, ch £1.80). Prices and opening times are subject to change in March 2009. Please check web site or call 0870 333 1181 for the most up to date prices and opening times when planning your visit. **Facilities** 🅿 ♿

TOLLARD ROYAL   MAP 03 ST91

Larmer Tree Gardens

SP5 5PT

➲ *(off A354 Blandford to Salisbury road, follow brown signs with flower)*

☎ 01725 516228

e-mail: larmertree@rushmoreuk.com

web: www.larmertreegardens.co.uk

Created by General Pitt Rivers in 1880 as a pleasure ground for 'public enlightenment and entertainment' the gardens are an extraordinary example of Victorian extravagance and vision. The garden contains a wonderful collection of ornate buildings, majestic trees and intimate arbours, retained in an enchanted and tranquil atmosphere.

Times ✴ Garden open: Feb-Nov, Mon-Thu 11-5 (Sun from Etr-Oct). Tea Pavilion Sun & BHs Etr-Sep 11-5 **Facilities** 🅿 ☕ 🍴 shop 🚫 (ex assist dogs) ➡

WESTBURY   MAP 03 ST85

Brokerswood Country Park   2 for 1

Brokerswood BA13 4EH

➲ *(off A36 at Bell Inn, Standerwick. Follow brown signs from A350)*

☎ 01373 822238 & 823880

e-mail: woodland.park@virgin.net

web: www.brokerswood.co.uk

Brokerswood Country Park's nature walk leads through 80 acres of woodlands, with a lake and wildfowl. Facilities include a woodland visitor centre (covering wildlife and forestry), two children's adventure playgrounds (Etr-Oct school holidays & wknds only), guided walks and the woodland railway, over a third of a mile long.

Times Open all year; Park open daily 10-5. Closed 24-26 Dec & 1 Jan. Ring for museum opening hours. **Fee** ✴ £3.50 (ch 3-16 £2.50, concessions £2.50) **Facilities** 🅿 ☕ 🍴 (outdoor) ♿ (ramp access to cafe) toilets for disabled shop ➡

Westwood Manor

BA15 2AF

⮣ *(1.5m SW of Bradford on Avon, off B3109)*

☎ 01225 863374

e-mail: westwoodmanor@nationaltrust.org.uk

web: www.nationaltrust.org.uk

This late 15th-century stone manor house was altered in the early 17th century and has late Gothic and Jacobean windows and fine plasterwork. There is a modern topiary garden.

Times Open 23 Mar-Sep, Tue, Wed & Sun, 2-5. **Fee** ✳ £5.40 (ch £2.70). Family ticket (2ad+2ch) £13.80. **Facilities** ❷ ♿ (Partly accessible) (drop off point, Braille & large print guide) ⊗ 🚾 ⚲

Wilton House   `2 for 1`

SP2 0BJ

⮣ *(3m W of Salisbury, on A30, 10m from Stonehenge & A303)*

☎ 01722 746720 & 746729(24 hr line)

e-mail: tourism@wiltonhouse.com

web: www.wiltonhouse.com

This fabulous Palladian mansion amazes visitors with its treasures, including magnificent art, fine furniture and interiors by Inigo Jones. The traditional and modern gardens, some designed by the 17th Earl, are fabulous throughout the season and continue to delight visitors, whilst the adventure playground is a firm favourite with children. Classical concert with fireworks July 2009.

Times Open Grounds: 21-24 Mar & 5 Apr-28 Sep, daily 10.30-5.30. (Last admission 4.30). House: 21-24 Mar & 5 May-Aug, daily 10.30-5.30. **Fee** ✳ £12 (ch £6.50, concessions £9.75). Family ticket £29.50. **Facilities** ❷ 🖥 🍴 licensed 🎪 (outdoor) ♿ (induction loop) toilets for disabled shop garden centre ⊗ (ex assist dogs) ⊟

Woodhenge   `FREE`

⮣ *(1.5m N of Amesbury, off A345 just S of Durrington)*

web: www.english-heritage.org.uk

A Neolithic ceremonial monument dating from about 2300 BC, consisting of six concentric rings of timber posts, now marked by concrete piles. The long axis of the rings, which are oval, points to the rising sun on Midsummer Day.

Times Open any reasonable time. (Usual facilities may not apply around Summer Solstice 20-22 Jun. Please check). **Facilities** ❷ ⌗

Lavender in Malmesbury

WORCESTERSHIRE

Worcester Cathedral on the River Severn

BEWDLEY   MAP 07 SO77

Severn Valley Railway
Comberton Hill DY10 1QN

☎ 01299 403816

web: www.svr.co.uk
(For full entry see Kidderminster)

West Midland Safari & Leisure Park
Spring Grove DY12 1LF

➲ *(on A456 between Kidderminster & Bewdley)*

☎ 01299 402114

e-mail: info@wmsp.co.uk

web: www.wmsp.co.uk

Located in the heart of rural Worcestershire, this 200-acre site is the home to a drive-through safari and an amazing range of exotic animals. Animal attractions include the new Leopard Valley, Twilight Cave, Creepy Crawlies, the Reptile House, Sealion Theatre, and the new buffalo, Boma. There are also a variety of rides, amusements and live shows suitable for all members of the family.

Times Open mid Feb-early Nov. Times may change. **Fee** ✱ £10.50 pp entry to Safari Park, £9.75 multi ride wristband (ch under 3 free) **Facilities** ⓟ ⌷ ⅋ licensed ⅃ (outdoor) ⅚ shop ⊗ (ex assist dogs) ▭

BROADWAY   MAP 04 SP03

Broadway Tower
WR12 7LB

➲ *(off A44, 1m SE of village)*

☎ 01386 852390

e-mail: info@broadwaytower.co.uk

web: www.broadwaytower.co.uk

The 65ft tower was designed by James Wyatt for the 6th Earl of Coventry, and built in 1799. The unique building now houses exhibitions depicting its colourful past and various uses such as holiday retreat to artist and designer William Morris. The viewing platform is equipped with a telescope, giving wonderful views over 13 counties.

Times Open Apr-Oct, daily 10.30-5; Nov-Mar (tower only) wknds weather permitting 11-3 or by prior booking. **Fee** ✱ £4 (ch 4-4 £2.50, concessions £3.50) Family £11 (2ad+2ch) **Facilities** ⓟ ⌷⅋⅃ shop ▭

BROMSGROVE   MAP 07 SO97

Avoncroft Museum of Historic Buildings `2 for 1`
Stoke Heath B60 4JR

➲ *(2m S, off A38)*

☎ 01527 831886 831 363

e-mail: admin@avoncroft.org.uk

web: www.avoncroft.org.uk

A visit to Avoncroft takes you through nearly 700 years of history. Here you can see 25 buildings rescued from destruction and authentically restored on a 15 acre rural site. There are 15th and 16th-century timber framed buildings, 18th-century agricultural buildings and a cockpit. There are industrial buildings and a working windmill from the 19th century, and from the 20th a fully furnished pre-fab.

Times Open Sep-Oct, daily 10.30-5. Closed Mon. Nov-Dec, Fri-Sun 10.30-4.30; Mar, Fri-Sun 10.30-4. **Fee** ✱ £6.60 (ch £3, concessions £5.50). Family (2ad+3ch) £16.50 **Facilities** ⓟ ⌷⅋ (outdoor) ⅚ (ramps, wheelchairs available) toilets for disabled shop ▭

EVESHAM   MAP 04 SP04

The Almonry Heritage Centre
Abbey Gate WR11 4BG

➲ *(on A4184, opposite Merstow Green, main N/S route through Evesham)*

☎ 01386 446944

e-mail: tic@almonry.ndo.co.uk

web: www.evesham.uk.com

The 14th-century stone and timber building was the home of the Almoner of the Benedictine Abbey in Evesham. It now houses exhibitions relating to the history of Evesham Abbey, the Battle of Evesham, and the culture and trade of Evesham. Evesham Tourist Information Centre is also located here.

Times ✱ Open all year, Mon-Sat & BHs, 10-5, Sun 2-5. Closed Xmas & Sun in Nov-Feb. **Facilities** ⓟ (110yds) shop ⊗

GREAT WITLEY   MAP 03 SO76

Witley Court
WR6 6JT

➲ *(on A433)*

☎ 01299 896636

web: www.english-heritage.org.uk

Discover the spectacular ruins of this once-great house destroyed by fire in 1937. Explore the magnificent landscaped gardens which feature the stunning Perseus and Andromeda fountains and contemporary sculpture. Step back in time with the audio tour.

Times Open all year, 21 Mar-May & Sep-Oct, daily 10-5; Jun-Aug, daily 10-6; Nov-Feb, Wed-Sun 10-4. Closed 24-26 Dec & 1 Jan. **Fee** £5.50 (concessions £4.40, ch £2.80). Family ticket £13.80. Prices and opening times are subject to change in March 2009. Please check web site or call 0870 333 1181 for the most up to date prices and opening times when planning your visit. **Facilities** ⓟ ⌷ shop ⊗ ♯

ENGLAND

HANBURY MAP 03 SO96

Hanbury Hall

School Rd WR9 7EA

➲ *(4.5m E of Droitwich, 1m N of B4090 and 1.5m W of B4091)*

☎ 01527 821214

e-mail: hanburyhall@nationaltrust.org.uk
web: www.nationaltrust.org.uk

This William and Mary style red-brick house, completed in 1701, was built by a prosperous local family. The house contains outstanding painted ceilings and staircase by Thornhill, and the Watney collection of porcelain. The 18th-century garden has recently been restored with many features including parterre, bowling green and working orangery.

Times House & Grounds, Open 28 Feb-1 Nov, Sat-Wed 11-5.30 (last entry 4.30) Grounds open, wknds only 3 Jan-22 Feb, 2 Nov-20 Dec. Open daily during school hols, & 27 Dec-3 Jan. **Fee** ✳ House & Garden £6.80. Family £17. Garden only £4.50 **Facilities** ❷ ♥ ⊼ (outdoor) ♿ (gardens and ground floor of house are accessible) (Braille guide, 2 wheelchairs) toilets for disabled shop ⊗ (ex assist dogs & in the park) ❤ ▄

Severn Valley Railway

Times Trains operate wknds throughout year, daily, early May end of Sep, school hols & half terms, Santa Specials, phone for details. **Facilities** ❷ (charged) ♥ ❀ ⊼ (outdoor) ♿ (Partly accessible) (some specially adapted trains, call for details) toilets for disabled shop ▄

See advert on opposite page

KIDDERMINSTER MAP 07 SO87

Bodenham Arboretum

Wolverley DY11 5SY

➲ *(follow brown signs W from Wolverley Church island along the B4189)*

☎ 01562 852444 & 850456
e-mail: james_binn@fsmail.net
web: www.bodenham-arboretum.co.uk

An award winning arboretum, over 2,700 species of trees and shrubs, attractively landscaped in 156 acres. The arboretum is incorporated into a working farm. Five miles of paths lead through dells, glades around lakes and pools.

Times Open 13 Feb-23 Dec, Wed-Sun, 11-5. Oct, daily. Also open Jan-Feb half-term & wknds only. **Fee** ✳ £5.50 (ch 5-16 & w/chair users £2.50) **Facilities** ❷ ♥ ❀ licensed ⊼ (outdoor) ♿ (Partly accessible) toilets for disabled shop ▄

Severn Valley Railway

Comberton Hill DY10 1QN

➲ *(on A448, clearly signed)*

☎ 01299 403816
web: www.svr.co.uk

The leading standard gauge steam railway, with one of the largest collections of locomotives and rolling stock in the country. Services operate from Kidderminster and Bewdley to Bridgnorth through 16 miles of picturesque scenery along the River Severn. Special steam galas and "Day out with Thomas" Weekends take place during the year along with Santa Specials.

Worcestershire County Museum `2 for 1`

Hartlebury Castle, Hartlebury DY11 7XZ

➲ *(4m S of Kidderminster clearly signed from A449)*

☎ 01299 250416

e-mail: museum@worcestershire.gov.uk
web: www.worcestershire.gov.uk/museum

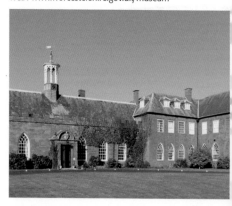

Housed in the north wing of Hartlebury Castle, the County Museum contains a delightful display of crafts and industries. There are unique collections of toys and costume, displays on domestic life, period room settings and horse-drawn vehicles. Visitors can also see a reconstructed forge, a schoolroom, scullery and nursery. Family events at least one weekend each month. Childrens craft activities Tue-Fri in school holidays. Phone for details of special events.

Times Open 1 Feb-23 Dec, Tue-Fri 10-5; Sat, Sun & BHs 11-5. Closed Good Fri. **Fee** £4 (ch & concession £2). Family ticket (2ad+2ch) £10. **Facilities** ❷ ♥ ⊼ (outdoor) ♿ (car parking spaces, close to main building, lift) toilets for disabled shop ⊗ (ex assist dogs & in grounds) ▄

REDDITCH   MAP 04 SP06

Forge Mill Needle Museum & Bordesley Abbey Visitor Centre

2 for 1

Forge Mill, Needle Mill Ln, Riverside B98 8HY

➲ *(N side of Redditch, off A441)*

☎ 01527 62509

e-mail: museum@redditchbc.gov.uk

web: www.forgemill.org.uk

The Needle Museum tells the fascinating and sometimes gruesome story of how needles are made. Working, water-powered machinery can be seen in an original needle-scouring mill. The Visitor Centre is an archaeological museum showing finds from excavations at the nearby Bordesley Abbey. Children can become an archaeologist for the day and explore the ruins of this fascinating ancient monument. Regularly changing temporary exhibits.

Times Open Etr-Sep, Mon-Fri 11-4.30, Sat-Sun 2-5; Feb-Etr & Oct-Nov, Mon-Thu 11-4 & Sun 2-5. Parties by arrangement. **Fee** ✳ £3.90 (ch £1, pen £2.95). Family ticket £7.50. **Facilities** ❷ ⬚⊓ (outdoor) ♿ (Partly accessible) (wheelchair, museum audio tour, Braille guide, hearing loop) toilets for disabled shop ⊗ (ex assist dogs) ▭

SEVERN STOKE   MAP 03 SO84

Croome Park

Builders Yard, High Green WR8 9JS

➲ *(8m S of Worcester signposted off A38 and B4084).*

☎ 01905 371006

e-mail: croomepark@nationaltrust.org.uk

web: www.nationaltrust.org.uk

'Capability' Brown's first complete landscape design. A decade of restoration has transformed the park to its 18th-century splendour. Restored WWII buildings house an exhibition about RAF Defford and a 1940's style canteen. Contact the Park for a full programme of events.

Times Open Mar-Apr, Wed-Sun 10-5.30; 31 Mar-Aug, daily 10-5.30; 3 Sep-26 Oct, Wed-Sun 10-5.30; Nov-21 Dec, Sat & Sun 10-4; 26 Dec-1 Jan, Mon-Sun, 10-4. 3 Jan, Sat & Sun, 10-4 **Fee** ✳ £4.80 (ch £2.40) Family £12 **Facilities** ❷ ⬚⊓ (outdoor) ♿ (w/chair, Braille & large print guides, induction loop) toilets for disabled shop garden centre ✿ ▭

SPETCHLEY   MAP 03 SO85

Spetchley Park Gardens

2 for 1

Spetchley Park WR5 1RS

➲ *(2m E of Worcester on A44)*

☎ 01453 810303

e-mail: hb@spetchleygardens.co.uk

web: www.spetchleygardens.co.uk

The 110-acre deer park and the 30-acre gardens surround an early 19th-century mansion (not open), with sweeping lawns and herbaceous borders, a rose lawn and enclosed gardens with low box and yew hedges. There is a large collection of trees (including 17th-century Cedars of Lebanon), shrubs and plants, many of which are rare or unusual. There's an illuminated trail each December (for ten days just before Christmas) when the gardens are open at night

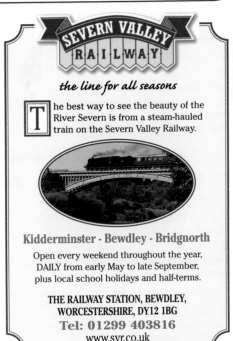

and beautifully lit. Various events through the year, check website for details.

Times Open all year: Wed-Sun, 11-6. BH Mon, 11-6. Other days by appointment **Fee** ✳ £6 (ch free, concession £5.50). Party 25+ £5. **Facilities** ❷ ⬚⊓ ♿ (Gravel paths and grass are prevalent throughout the gardens. Wet weather would make the grass difficult for disabled access) (most of garden accessible) toilets for disabled shop ⊗ (ex assist dogs)

STONE   MAP 07 SO87

Stone House Cottage Gardens

DY10 4BG

➲ *(2m SE of Kidderminster, on A448)*

☎ 01562 69902

e-mail: louisa@shcn.co.uk

web: www.shcn.co.uk

A beautiful walled garden with towers provides a sheltered area of about one acre for rare shrubs, climbers and interesting herbaceous plants. Adjacent to the garden is a nursery with a large selection of unusual plants.

Times Open mid Mar-mid Sept, Wed-Sat, 10-5. **Fee** £3 (ch free). **Facilities** ❷ ♿ (Partly accessible) garden centre ⊗

WICHENFORD MAP 03 SO76

Wichenford Dovecote

➲ *(N of B4204)*

☎ 01527 821214

web: www.nationaltrust.org.uk

17th-century half-timbered black-and-white dovecote, in a picturesque riverside location.

Times Open 28 Feb-1 Nov, 9-6. **Fee** £1 **Facilities** ⊗ 🚌 ✿

WORCESTER MAP 03 SO85

City Museum & Art Gallery

FREE

Foregate St WR1 1DT

➲ *(in city centre, 150m from Foregate St Train Station)*

☎ 01905 25371

e-mail: artgalleryandmuseum@cityofworcester.gov.uk

web: www.worcestercitymuseums.org.uk

The gallery has temporary art exhibitions from both local and national sources. Museum exhibits cover geology, local and natural history. Of particular interest is a complete 19th-century chemist's shop. There are collections relating to the Worcestershire Regiment and the Worcestershire Yeomanry Cavalry.

Times Open all year, Mon-Fri 9.30-5.30, Sat 9.30-5. Closed Sun, 25-26 Dec, 1 Jan & Good Fri, Easter Mon and Whitsun BH Mon. **Facilities** Ⓟ (city centre) ☕ ♿ (lift, induction loop) toilets for disabled shop ⊗ (ex assist dogs) ▬

The Elgar Birthplace Museum

2 for 1

Crown East Ln, Lower Broadheath WR2 6RH

➲ *(3m W of Worcester, signed off A44 to Leominster)*

☎ 01905 333224

e-mail: birthplace@elgarmuseum.org

web: www.elgarmuseum.org

In 2000, the Elgar Centre was opened, to complement the historic Birthplace Cottage and to provide additional exhibition space for more treasures from this unique collection, telling the story of Elgar's musical development and inspirations. Listen to his music as the audio tour guides you round the easily accessible displays. 2009 is the 75th anniversary of Sir Edward Elgar's death.

Times Open Feb-22 Dec, daily, 11-5 (last admission 4.15). Closed Xmas-end Jan. **Fee** ✳ £6 (ch £2, pen £5, concessions £3.50). **Facilities** Ⓟ ⛩ ♿ (Partly accessible) (large print guides, audio facilities, wheelchair) toilets for disabled shop ⊗ (ex assist dogs) ▬

The Greyfriars

Friar St WR1 2LZ

➲ *(in city centre, use public car park on Friar St)*

☎ 01905 23571

e-mail: greyfriars@nationaltrust.org.uk

web: www.nationaltrust.org.uk

Built in 1480, this is a beautiful timber framed merchant's house in the city centre, rescued from demolition and carefully restored. The panelled interior contains interesting textiles and furnishings. An archway leads through to a pleasant walled garden.

Times Open 4 Mar-12 Jun, Wed-Sat 1-5pm. Open Jul-Aug, Wed-Sun 1-5pm **Fee** £4.40 (ch £2.20). Family £11. **Facilities** Ⓟ (200yds) ☕ ♿ (ground floor is accessible) ⊗ (ex assist dogs) ✿ ▬

Hawford Dovecote

WR3 7SG

➲ *(3m N of Worcester, 0.5m E of A449).*

☎ 01527 821214

e-mail: hanburyhall@nationaltrust.org

web: www.nationaltrust.org.uk

An unusual square, half-timbered 16th-century dovecote. Access on foot only via the entrance drive to the adjoining house.

Times Open 28 Feb-1 Nov daily 9-6 or sunset. (Closed Good Fri). Other times by prior appointment only. **Fee** £1 **Facilities** ℗ 50yds (on street parking) ⊗ 🚻 ♨

Worcester Cathedral

WR1 2LH

➲ *(city centre, signed from M5 junct 7)*

☎ 01905 28854 & 21004

e-mail: info@worcestercathedral.org.uk

web: www.worcestercathedral.co.uk

Worcester Cathedral is one of England's loveliest cathedrals, with Royal Tombs, medieval cloisters, an ancient crypt and Chapter House and magnificent Victorian stained glass. The tower is open in the summer. There are a number of different celebrations each year, including the Heart of England Food Fair and many concerts.

Times Open all year, daily 7.30-6. **Facilities** ℗ (500yds) ⊑ & (access from College Green) toilets for disabled shop ⊗ (ex assist dogs) ➡

Worcester Porcelain Museum

Severn St WR1 2NE

➲ *(M5 junct 7, follow signs to city centre, at 7th set of lights take 1st left into Edger St & bear left with road into Severn St. At T junct bear right & after 700yds take 1st left. Museum on left)*

☎ 01905 746000

e-mail: info.admin@worcesterporcelainmuseum.org

web: www.worcesterporcelainmuseum.org

Worcester Porcelain Museum is situated amidst the city's Historic Quarter within two minutes walk of Royal Worcester, the Cathedral, Commandery, Birmingham Canal and River Severn. An informative and entertaining audio tour featuring Henry Sandon and skilled craftsmen is free with entry and tells the story of the factory's history, its famous customers, the talented workforce and everyday life. Gallery displays from 1751 to the 20th century include Oriental simplicity and Victorian extravaganza and offer a glimpse of times past, taking the visitor on a memorable journey from 1751 to the present day.

Times Open: Mar-Nov, Mon-Sat 10-5.30, Sun 11-5. Dec-Feb, Mon-Sat, 10-4, Sun, 11-5. Closed 25-26 Dec & Etr Sun. **Fee** ✳ Museum £5 **Facilities** ℗ (charged) ⊑ 🍴 & toilets for disabled shop ⊗ (ex assist dogs) ➡

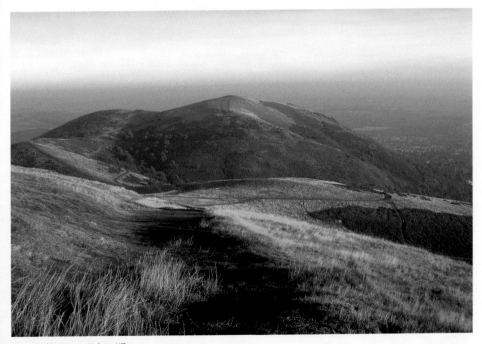

Worcestershire Beacon, Malvern Hills

EAST RIDING OF YORKSHIRE

Bempton Cliffs, nr Bridlington

BEMPTON
MAP 08 TA17

RSPB Nature Reserve
YO15 1JD

➲ *(take cliff road from B1229, Bempton Village and follow brown tourist signs)*

☎ 01262 851179

web: www.rspb.org.uk

Part of the spectacular chalk cliffs that stretch from Flamborough Head to Speeton. This is one of the best sites in England to see thousands of nesting seabirds including gannets and puffins at close quarters. Viewpoints overlook the cliffs, which are best visited from April to July. Over two miles of chalk cliffs rising to 400ft with numerous cracks and ledges. Enormous numbers of seabirds nest on these cliffs including guillemots, razorbills, kittiwakes, fulmars, herring gulls and several pairs of shag. This is the only gannetry in England and is growing annually. Many migrants pass off-shore including terns, skuas and shearwaters. Wheatears, ring ouzels and merlins frequent the clifftop on migration. Grey seal and porpoise are sometimes seen offshore.

Times ✱ Visitor centre open daily, Mar-Oct 10-5. Nov -Dec 9.30-4.
Facilities ℗ (charged) ⌑ ⊞ (outdoor) ♿ (large print guide) toilets for disabled shop ▰

BEVERLEY
MAP 08 TA03

The Guildhall
Register Sq HU17 9AU

➲ *(in Register Sq, next to post office)*

☎ 01482 392776

e-mail: stefan.ramsden@eastriding.gov.uk

A Guildhall has been on this site since 1500, although parts of the building date back to a private dwelling of 1320. Largely remodelled in the Palladian style in the 1760s, the Courtroom features a magnificent stucco work ceiling, and the Magistrate's Room houses rare 17th-century Civic furniture.

Times Open every Fri, 10-4. Please phone for guided tours at other times.
Fee ✱ Free on Fri. Charge for guided tours at other times. **Facilities** ♿ (ground floor only accessible) (disabled parking 100yds) ⊗ (ex assist dogs)

BURTON AGNES
MAP 08 TA16

Burton Agnes Hall
Estate Office YO25 0ND

➲ *(on A614)*

☎ 01262 490324

e-mail: burton.agnes@farmline.com

web: www.burton-agnes.co.uk

Built in 1598, this exquisite Elizabethan house is filled with furniture, pictures and china amassed by one family over five centuries. Lawns with topiary bushes surround the Hall and an award winning walled garden contains a maze, potager, giant games, jungle garden and more than four thousand plant species, including campanula and geranium collections. There is a woodland walk and a children's playground with guinea pigs. The Red Bus Gallery presents works by local artists in a London RouteMaster bus.

Burton Agnes Hall

Times Gardens 7 Feb-20 Mar, daily 11-4. Hall & gardens 21 Mar-21 Dec, daily 11-5 (Hall & Cafe closed 1-14 Nov) **Fee** Hall & gardens: £7 (ch £3.50 5-15, pens £6.50). Gardens only: £4 (ch 5-15 £2.50, pens £3.50).
Facilities ℗ ⌑ ⊞ (outdoor) ♿ (ground floor of hall, garden and woodland areas, courtyard cafe and shop all accessible) (scented garden for the blind, wheelchair available) toilets for disabled shop garden centre ▰

Burton Agnes Manor House   FREE
➲ *(in Burton Agnes, 5m SW of Bridlington on A166)*

web: www.english-heritage.org.uk

A rare and well-preserved example of a Norman house. Some interesting Norman architectural features can still be seen, but the building was encased in brick during the 17th and 18th centuries. The house is near Burton Agnes Hall and the gardens are privately owned and not managed by English Heritage.

Times Open 21 Mar-Oct, daily 11-5. **Facilities** ⊞

GOOLE
MAP 08 SE72

The Yorkshire Waterways Museum
Dutch River Side DN14 5TB

➲ *(M62 junct 36, enter Goole, turn right at next 3 sets of lights onto Dutch River Side. 0.75m and follow brown signs)*

☎ 01405 768730

e-mail: info@waterwaysmuseum.org.uk

web: www.waterwaysmuseum.org.uk

Discover the story of the Aire & Calder Navigation and the growth of the 'company town' of Goole and its busy port. Find out how to sail and, in the interactive gallery, see how wooden boats were built. Enjoy the unique 'Tom Pudding' story, brought to life through the vessels on the canal and the boat hoist in South Dock. Rediscover the Humber keels and sloops, and Goole's shipbuilding history through the objects, photos and memories of Goole people. 2009 is the 50th anniversary of Wheldale , the Tom Pudding tug.

Times Open all year Mon-Fri 9-4, Sat-Sun 10-4. (Closed Xmas & New Year).
Fee Free entry to museum. Boat trip £4 (ch under 12 £3). **Facilities** ℗ ⌑ ⊞ (outdoor) ♿ (disabled access on boats, nature trail, wheelchair) toilets for disabled shop ⊗ (ex assist dogs) ▰

ENGLAND

Hornsea Museum

2 for 1

11 Newbegin HU18 1AB

⮑ *(turn off A165 onto B1244)*

☎ 01964 533443

web: www.hornseamuseum.com

A former farmhouse whose outbuildings now illustrate local life and history. There are 19th-century period rooms and a dairy, plus craft tools and farming implements. Photographs, local personalities and industries are also featured along with a large display of Hornsea pottery.

Times Open Etr-Sep & Oct half-term hols, Tue-Sat 11-5, Sun 2-5 (last admission 4). Also open BH Mon. **Fee** ✳ £2.50 (concessions £2). Family £7.50 **Facilities** ⓟ (50yds) ⊼ (outdoor) ♿ (two thirds of museum accessible0 (audio interpretation for blind/partially sighted) toilets for disabled shop

Maister House

FREE

160 High St HU1 1NL

⮑ *(Hull city centre)*

☎ 01482 324114

web: www.nationaltrust.org.uk

The house is a mid-18th-century rebuilding, notable for its splendid stone and wrought-iron staircase, ornate stucco work and finely carved doors. Only the staircase and entrance hall are open as the house is now let as offices.

Times Open all year, Mon-Fri 10-4 (Closed BH). **Facilities** ⓟ ♿ (Partly accessible) ⊗ ⏩ ♨

Maritime Museum

FREE

Queen Victoria Square HU1 3DX

⮑ *(A63 to town centre, museum is within pedestrian area)*

☎ 01482 613902

e-mail: museums@hullcc.gov.uk

web: www.hullcc.gov.uk

Hull's maritime history is illustrated here, with displays on whales and whaling, ships and shipping, and other aspects of this Humber port. There is also a Victorian court room which is used for temporary exhibitions. The restored dock area, with its fine Victorian and Georgian buildings, is well worth exploring too.

Times Open all year, Mon-Sat 10-5 & Sun 1.30-4.30. Closed 25 Dec-2 Jan & Good Fri **Facilities** ⓟ (100yds) ♿ (Partly accessible) shop ⊗ (ex assist dogs)

`Streetlife' - Hull Museum of Transport

FREE

High St HU1 1PS

⮑ *(A63 from M62, follow signs for Old Town)*

☎ 01482 613902

e-mail: museums@hullcc.gov.uk

web: www.hullcc.gov.uk

This purpose built museum uses a 'hands-on' approach to trace 200 years of transport history. With a vehicle collection of national importance, state-of-the-art animatronic displays and authentic scenarios, you can see Hull's Old Town brought vividly to life. The mail coach ride uses the very latest in computer technology to recreate a Victorian journey by four-in-hand.

Times Open all year, Mon-Sat 10-5, Sun 1.30-4.30. Closed 24-25 Dec & Good Fri **Facilities** ⓟ (500mtrs) ⊼ ♿ toilets for disabled shop ⊗ (ex assist dogs)

The Deep

HU1 4DP

⮑ *(follow signs from city centre)*

☎ 01482 381000

e-mail: info@thedeep.co.uk

web: www.thedeep.co.uk

The Deep is a conservation and educational charity which runs one of the deepest and most spectacular aquariums in the world. It is a unique blend of stunning marine life, the latest interactives and audio-visual presentations which together tell the dramatic story of the world's oceans. Highlights include 40 sharks and 3,500 fish, Europe's deepest viewing tunnel and a glass lift ride through a 10m deep tank. The Deep has an annual programme of events all available online.

Times Open all year, daily 10-6. Closed 24-25 Dec (last entry 5). **Fee** ✳ £8.75 (ch under 16 £6.75). Family ticket (2ad+2ch) £28, (2ad+3ch) £33.25. **Facilities** ⓟ (charged) ⊑ ⍟ licensed ⊼ (indoor & outdoor) ♿ (signing for the deaf if booked in advance, tactile guides) toilets for disabled shop ⊗ (ex assist dogs) ▬

Wilberforce House `FREE`

23-25 High St HU1 1NE

➲ *(A63 from M62 or A1079 from York, follow signs for Old Town)*

☎ 01482 613902

e-mail: museums@hullcc.gov.uk

web: www.hullcc.gov.uk

The early 17th-century Merchant's house was the birthplace of William Wilberforce, who became a leading campaigner against slavery. Re-opened in 2007 after full refurbishment the House tells the story of slavery, abolition, the triangular trade and explores modern issues surrounding slavery.

Times Open all year, Mon-Sat 10-5 & Sun 1.30-4.30. Closed 25-26 Dec, 1 Jan & Good Fri. **Facilities** Ⓟ (500mtrs) (meters on street) 🍴 (outdoor) ♿ (large print, video area & audio guides) shop ⊗ (ex assist dogs)

POCKLINGTON　　　　　　　　MAP 08 SE84

Burnby Hall Garden & Stewart Collection `2 for 1`

33 The Balk YO42 2QF

➲ *(off A1079 at turning for Pocklington off B1247, follow brown tourist signs)*

☎ 01759 307125 & 307541

e-mail: brian@brianpetrie.plus.com

web: www.burnbyhallgardens.com

The two lakes in this garden have an outstanding collection of 80 varieties of hardy water lilies, designated a National Collection. The lakes stand within nine acres of beautiful gardens including heather beds, a rock garden, a spring and summer bedding area, woodland walk and Victorian garden. The museum contains sporting trophies and ethnic material gathered on Major Stewart's world-wide travels. The Stewart Museum has been completely refurbished and re-opened in June 2007. There are band concerts every other Sunday and various events through the season.

Times Open 28 Mar-11 Oct, daily 10-6 (last admission 5) **Fee** ✳ £4 (ch 5-15 £2, pen £3.25). Party 20+.£3 each **Facilities** Ⓟ ⊑🍴 (outdoor) ♿ (free wheelchair hire, viewing platform for wheelchairs) toilets for disabled shop ⊗ (ex assist dogs) ▬

SEWERBY　　　　　　　　　MAP 08 TA16

Sewerby Hall & Gardens

Church Ln YO15 1EA

➲ *(2m NE of Bridlington on B1255 towards Flamborough)*

☎ 01262 673769

e-mail: sewerby.hall@eastriding.gov.uk

web: www.sewerby-hall.co.uk

Sewerby Hall and Gardens, set in 50 acres of parkland overlooking Bridlington Bay, dates back to 1715. The Georgian house, with its 19th-century Orangery, contains art galleries, archaeological displays and an Amy Johnson Room with a collection of her trophies and mementoes. The grounds include magnificent walled Old English and Rose gardens and host many events throughout the year. Activities for all the family include a Children's Zoo and play areas, golf, putting, bowls, plus woodland and clifftop walks. Phone for details of special events.

Times Estate open all year, dawn-dusk. Hall open Etr-end Oct. Please contact for further details. **Facilities** Ⓟ ⊑🍴 (outdoor) ♿ (ramp, lift to 1st floor) toilets for disabled shop ⊗ (ex on leads) ▬

SPROATLEY　　　　　　　　MAP 08 TA13

Burton Constable Hall

HU11 4LN

➲ *(Follow signs for A165 Bridlington Road towards Sirlaugh, then right towards Hornsea and follow brown historic house signs to Burton Constable)*

☎ 01964 562400

e-mail: helendewson@btconnect.com

web: www.burtonconstable.com

This superb Elizabethan house was built in 1570, but much of the interior was remodelled in the 18th century. There are magnificent reception rooms and a Tudor long gallery with a pendant roof: the contents range from pictures and furniture to a unique collection of 18th-century scientific instruments. Outside are 200 acres of parkland landscaped by 'Capability' Brown, with oaks and chestnuts, and a lake with an island.

Times Open, Hall & Grounds Etr Sat-end Oct. Grounds 12.30-5, Hall 1-5. (Last admission 4). Closed Fri. **Fee** House £6 (ch £3, pen £5.50). Family ticket £14. Grounds only £2.50 (ch £1.25). Family ticket £6.50. **Facilities** Ⓟ ⊑🍴 (outdoor) ♿ (3 bedrooms not accessible) (stair lift to first foor, wheelchairs) toilets for disabled shop ⊗ (ex assist dogs) ▬

NORTH YORKSHIRE

How Stean Gorge in Nidderdale, nr Lofthouse

ALDBOROUGH MAP 08 SE46

Aldborough Roman Site

YO5 9ES

➲ *(0.75m SE of Boroughbridge, on minor road off B6265 within 1m of junct of A1 & A6055)*

☎ 01423 322768

web: www.english-heritage.org.uk

View two spectacular mosaic pavements and discover the remains of the Roman town, the 'capital' of the Romanized Brigantes, the largest tribe in Britain.

Times Open 21 Mar-Sep, Sat-Sun & BH 11-5. **Fee** £3 (concessions £2.40, ch £1.50). Prices and opening times are subject to change in March 2009. Please check web site or call 0870 333 1181 for the most up to date prices and opening times when planning your visit. **Facilities** ⼞ shop ⊞

AYSGARTH MAP 07 SE08

National Park Centre

DL8 3TH

➲ *(off A684, Leyburn to Hawes road at Falls junct, Palmer Flatt Hotel & continue down hill over river, centre 500yds on left)*

☎ 01969 662910

e-mail: aysgarth@ytbtic.co.uk

web: www.yorkshiredales.org.uk

A visitor centre for the Yorkshire Dales National Park, with maps, guides, walks and local information. Interactive displays explain the history and natural history of the area. Plan the day ahead with a light lunch in the coffee shop. Various guided walks begin here throughout the year.

Times Open Apr-Oct, daily 10-5; Winter open Fri-Sun, 10-4. **Fee** ✳ Parking: £2.20 2hrs, £3.20 all day **Facilities** ❷ (charged) ⼞⼞ (outdoor) ⼴ (viewing platform at Falls) toilets for disabled shop ⊗ (ex assist dogs) ▭

BEDALE MAP 08 SE28

Bedale Museum

DL8 1AA

➲ *(on A684, 1.5m W of A1 at Leeming Bar. Opposite church, at N end of town)*

☎ 01677 423797

Situated in a building dating back to the 17th century, the Bedale is a fascinating museum. The central attraction is the Bedale fire engine, which dates back to 1742. Other artefacts include documents, toys, craft tools and household utensils, which all help to give an absorbing picture of the lifestyle of the times.

Times ✳ Open all year Tue & Fri 10-12.30 & 2-4, Wed 2-4, Thu-Sat 10-12 **Facilities** ❷ shop ⊗ (ex assist dogs)

BENINGBROUGH MAP 08 SE55

Beningbrough Hall & Gardens

YO30 1DD

➲ *(off A19, 8m NW of York)*

☎ 01904 472027

e-mail: beningbrough@nationaltrust.org.uk

web: www.nationaltrust.org.uk

Beningbrough was built around 1716. It houses 100 portraits from the National Portrait Gallery in London. Ornately carved wood panelling is a feature of several of the rooms. There is also a fully equipped Victorian laundry and walled garden.

Times Open early Mar-Jun & Sep-end Oct daily (ex Thu & Fri) open Good Fri, Jul-Aug daily (ex Thu) 12-5. Grounds 11-5.30. Galleries & Grounds winter wknds Nov-Feb, Sat & Sun 11-3. **Facilities** ❷ ⼀⼞ (outdoor) ⼴ (Partly accessible) (access to Victorian laundry, shop & restaurant) toilets for disabled shop ⊗ (ex assist dogs) ♨ ▭

BRIMHAM MAP 08 SE26

Brimham Rocks

Summerbridge HG3 4DW

➲ *(10m NW of Harrogate, off B6265)*

☎ 01423 780688

e-mail: brimhamrocks@nationaltrust.org.uk

web: www.nationaltrust.org.uk

The rocks stand on National Trust open moorland at a height of 987ft, enjoying spectacular views over the surrounding countryside. The area is filled with strange and fascinating rock formations and is rich in wildlife. Brimham House is now an information point and shop.

Times Open daily 8-dusk, (facilities may close in bad weather): shop with exhibition room, Mar-18 May & 11 Oct-2 Nov, Sat & Sun 11-5, 24 May-5 Oct daily 11-5, 9 Nov-21 Dec, Sat & Sun 11-dusk. Also open daily; local school hols, BHs, 26 Dec & 1 Jan (weather permitting). **Fee** ✳ Cars (up to 4hrs £3.50, over 4hrs £4.50). Minibuses £7. Coaches £12. Motorcycles free. Nat Trust members free. Cars up to 4 hours £3.50. Cars over 4 hours £4.50. **Facilities** ❷ (charged) ⼞⼀ (outdoor) ⼴ (adapted path steep in places, Braille/large print guide) toilets for disabled shop ♨ ▭

CASTLE BOLTON MAP 07 SE09

Bolton Castle

DL8 4ET

➲ *(off A684, 6m W of Leyburn)*

☎ 01969 623981

e-mail: harry@boltoncastle.co.uk

web: www.boltoncastle.co.uk

Medieval castle completed in 1399, overlooking Wensleydale. Stronghold of the Scrope family. Mary, Queen of Scots was imprisoned here for six months during 1568 and 1569. The castle was besieged and taken by Parliamentary forces in 1645. Tapestries, tableaux, arms and armour can be seen. Medieval gardens including maze. Events throughout the year, please telephone for details.

Times ✳ Open Apr-Oct, 10-5; Nov-Mar, 10-4 or dusk. Phone for winter opening times. **Facilities** ❷ ⼞⼀ shop ⊗ (ex assist dogs) ▭

ENGLAND

CASTLE HOWARD

See **Malton**

COXWOLD   MAP 08 SE57

Byland Abbey

YO6 4BD

⮑ *(2m S of A170 between Thirsk & Helmsley, near Coxwold village)*

☎ 01347 868614

web: *www.english-heritage.org.uk*

A hauntingly beautiful monastic ruin set in peaceful meadows in the shadow of the Hambleton Hills. Contains a collection of medieval floor tiles still in their original setting.

Times Open 21 Mar-Jul & Sep, Wed-Sun, 11-6; Aug, daily, 11-6. **Fee** £3.50 (concessions £2.80, ch £1.80). Prices and opening times are subject to change in March 2009. Please check web site or call 0870 333 1181 for the most up to date prices and opening times when planning your visit. **Facilities** ♿ 🚻 ♿ (garden/grounds partly accessible) toilets for disabled 🚻 ➡

DANBY   MAP 08 NZ70

The Moors National Park Centre

Lodge Ln YO21 2NB

⮑ *(turn S off A171, follow Moors Centre Danby signs . Left at crossroads in Danby and then 2m, Centre at bend on right)*

☎ 01439 772737

e-mail: moorscentre@ytbtic.co.uk

web: www.moors.uk.net

The ideal place to start exploring the North York Moors National Park. There is an exhibition about the area as well continuous exhibition of arts. Also events, video and local walks. The Moorsbus service also operates from this site - phone for details.

Times Open all year, Apr-Oct, daily 10-5. Nov, Dec & Mar daily 10.30-3.30, Jan-Feb wknds only 10.30-3.30, Closed 24-26 Dec. Please phone to check to confirm before visit. **Fee** Free admission £2 car parking fee (parking charge under review) **Facilities** ♿ (charged) 🚻 🚻 (outdoor) ♿ (garden trails, wheelchairs, Braille maps, hearing Loops) toilets for disabled shop ⊗ (ex assist dogs & in grounds) ➡

EASBY   MAP 08 NZ10

Easby Abbey   FREE

⮑ *(1m SE of Richmond off B6271)*

web: *www.english-heritage.org.uk*

Set beside the River Swale, this Premonstratensian Abbey was founded in 1155 and dedicated to St Agatha. Extensive remains of the monks' domestic buildings can be seen.

Times Open 21 Mar-Sep, daily 10-6; Oct, daily 10-5; Nov-Mar, daily 10-4. Closed 24-26 Dec & 1 Jan **Facilities** ♿ 🚻

ELVINGTON   MAP 08 SE74

Yorkshire Air Museum & Allied Air Forces Memorial   2 for 1

Halifax Way YO41 4AU

⮑ *(from York take A1079 then immediate right onto B1228, museum is signposted on right)*

☎ 01904 608595

e-mail: museum@yorkshireairmuseum.co.uk

web: www.yorkshireairmuseum.co.uk

This award-winning museum and memorial is based around the largest authentic former WWII Bomber Command Station open to the public. There is a restored tower, an air gunners museum, archives, an Airborne Forces display, Squadron memorial rooms, and much more. Among the exhibits are replicas of the pioneering Cayley Glider and Wright Flyer, along with the Halifax Bomber and modern jets like the Harrier GR3, Tornado GR1 and GR4. A new exhibition 'Against The Odds' tells the story of the RAF Bomber Command.

Times Open daily, 10-5 (summer); 10-3.30 (winter). Closed 25-26 Dec. **Fee** ✳ £5 (ch £3 & pen £4). **Facilities** ♿ 🚻 🍽 licensed 🚻 (outdoor) ♿ toilets for disabled shop ➡

See advert on opposite page

FAIRBURN   MAP 08 SE42

RSPB Nature Reserve Fairburn Ings   FREE

The Visitor Centre, Newton Ln WF10 2BH

⮑ *(W of A1, N of Ferrybridge. Signed from Allerton Bywater off A656. Signed Fairburn Village off A1)*

☎ 01977 603796

e-mail: james.dean@rspb.org.uk

web: www.rspb.org.uk

One-third of the 700-acre RSPB reserve is open water, and over 270 species of birds have been recorded. A visitor centre provides information, and there is an elevated boardwalk, suitable for disabled visitors.

Times Access to the reserve via car park, open 9-dusk. Centre open 9.30-5 everyday. Car park open: 9-5. Closed 25-26 Dec. **Facilities** ❷ ⊟ (outdoor) ☕ (Partly accessible) (Lindyke area accessible) toilets for disabled shop ⊗ (ex assist dogs & in reserve) ➡

GRASSINGTON   MAP 07 SE06

National Park Centre   FREE

Hebden Rd BD23 5LB

➲ *(situated on B6265 in the main Grassington car park)*

☎ 01969 751690

e-mail: grassington@yorkshiredales.org.uk

web: www.yorkshiredales.org.uk

The centre is a useful introduction to the Yorkshire Dales National Park. Maps, guides and local information are available. There is also a 24-hr public access information service through computer screens and a full tourist information service. The centre has recently been refurbished with the emphasis on agriculture and climate change. A video display explains this.

Times Open Apr-Oct daily, 10-5; Nov-Mar, Fri, & Sat-Sun, 10-4 (also daily in school hols). **Facilities** ❷ (charged) ⊟ ☕ toilets for disabled shop ➡

GUISBOROUGH   MAP 08 NZ61

Gisborough Priory   2 for 1

TS14 6HG

➲ *(next to parish church)*

☎ 01287 633801

web: www.english-heritage.org.uk

The remains of the east end of the 14th-century church make a dramatic sight here. The priory was founded in the 12th century for Augustinian canons.

Times Open Jun-Sep, Tue-Sun, 9-5. Oct-May, Wed-Sun, 9-5. **Fee** £1.10 (ch 55p, concessions 75p). Opening times and prices are subject to change, for further details please phone 0870 333 1181 **Facilities** ❷ ⊟ (outdoor) ☕ ⚅➡

HARROGATE   MAP 08 SE35

RHS Garden Harlow Carr

Crag Ln, Otley Rd HG3 1QB

➲ *(off B6162 Otley Rd, 1.5m from Harrogate centre)*

☎ 01423 565418

e-mail: harlowcarr@rhs.org.uk

web: www.rhs.org.uk/harlowcarr

One of Yorkshire's most relaxing and surprising gardens at the gateway to the Yorkshire Dales. Wander through tranquil surroundings and find inspiration in the innovative and dramatic Rose Revolution and Main Borders. Stroll along the streamside garden and explore 'Gardens through Time'; savour the scented garden, and take practical ideas from the extensive kitchen garden. Year round events for all the family - sculpture, outdoor theatre, guided walks, quiz trails, workshops and free demonstrations.

YORKSHIRE AIR MUSEUM

YORKSHIRE TOURIST BOARD
White Rose Awards for Tourism

Tremendous atmosphere, Fascinating exhibits, Historic aircraft

Great for Coach Parties!!
(Group Rates Available)

Licensed Restaurant
• Open daily •

Halifax Way, Elvington, York • 01904 608595
www.yorkshireairmuseum.co.uk

Times Open all year, daily 9.30-6, Nov-Mar 9.30-4 (last admission 1hr before closing). Closed 25 Dec. **Fee** ✳ £6.50 (ch under 6 £2.20) **Facilities** ❷ ⛁ ⏴⏵ licensed ⊟ (outdoor) ☕ (electric and push wheelchairs available, scented garden) toilets for disabled shop garden centre ⊗ (ex assist dogs) ➡

The Royal Pump Room Museum

Crown Place HG1 2RY

➲ *(A61 into town centre and follow brown heritage signs)*

☎ 01423 556188

e-mail: museums@harrogate.gov.uk

web: www.harrogate.gov.uk/museums

Housed in an early Victorian pump room over the town's sulphur wells, the museum tells the story of Harrogate's heyday as England's European spa. Visitors discover some of the amazing spa treatments; taste the sulphur water; and explore stories of Russian royalty, communal ox-roasts and early bicycles, among many others.

Times Open all year, Mon-Sat 10-5, Sun 2-5, (Nov-Mar close at 4). Closed 24-26 Dec, 1 Jan, 7-25 Jan inclusive. **Facilities** ❷ (100yds) (restricted to 3hrs, need parking disc) ☕ toilets for disabled shop ⊗ (ex assist dogs) ➡

HAWES

MAP 07 SD88

Dales Countryside Museum, National Park Centre

2 for 1

Station Yard DL8 3NT

➲ *(off A684 in Old Station Yard)*

☎ 01969 666210

e-mail: hawes@yorkshiredales.org.uk

web: www.yorkshiredales.org.uk

Fascinating museum telling the story of the people and landscape of the Yorkshire Dales. Static steam locomotive and carriages with video and displays. Added features include hands-on interactive displays for children, temporary exhibitions and events.

Times Open all year daily 10-5. Closed Xmas. **Fee** ✳ Museum: £3 (ch free, concessions £2) . National park centre, temporary exhibitions free. **Facilities** ❷ (charged) ⊟ (outdoor) ♿ (lifts, ramps and parking) toilets for disabled shop ⊗ (ex assist dogs) ⊨

HELMSLEY

MAP 08 SE68

Duncombe Park

2 for 1

YO62 5EB

➲ *(located within North York Moors National Park, off A170 Thirsk-Scarborough road, 1m from Helmsley market place)*

☎ 01439 778625

e-mail: liz@duncombepark.com

web: www.duncombepark.com

Duncombe Park stands at the heart of a spectacular 30-acre early 18th-century landscape garden which is set in 300 acres of dramatic parkland around the River Rye. The house, originally built in 1713, was gutted by fire in 1879 and rebuilt in 1895. Its principal rooms are a fine example of the type of grand interior popular at the turn of the 20th century. Home of the Duncombes for 300 years, for much of this century the house was a girls' school. In 1985 the present Lord and Lady Feversham decided to make it a family home again, and after major restoration, opened the house to the public in 1990. Part of the garden and parkland were designated a 250-acre National Nature Reserve in 1994. Special events include a Country Fair (May), an Antiques Fair (June), Steam Fair (July), Antiques Fair (November). Please telephone for details. The 2-for-1 voucher is not valid on special event days.

Times Open 12 Apr-25 Oct, Sun-Thu; Gardens, Parkland Centre tea room & shop & Parkland walks 11-5.30. House by guided tour only every hour from 12.30-3.30. (Closed 10, 11 & 15 Jun). **Fee** House & Gardens £8.25 (ch 5-16, £3.75, concessions £6.25) Gardens & Parkland £5 Parkland only £3. **Facilities** ❷ ⓧ⏐ ⊟ (outdoor) ♿ (garden limited due to steps) (portable ramp, lift, wheelchair for loan) toilets for disabled shop ⊗ (ex assist dogs) ⊨

Helmsley Castle

Castlegate YO6 5AB

☎ 01439 770442

web: www.english-heritage.org.uk

An atmospheric ruin with formidable double earthworks. Also, an exhibition of the history of the castle.

Times Open all year, 21 Mar-Sep, daily 10-6; Oct, daily 10-5; Nov-Feb, Thu-Mon 10-4. Closed 24-26 Dec & 1 Jan. **Fee** £4 (concessions £3.20, ch £2). Family ticket £10. Prices and opening times are subject to change in March 2009. Please check web site or call 0870 333 1181 for the most up to date prices and opening times when planning your visit. **Facilities** ❷ (charged) shop ⏛

KIRBY MISPERTON

MAP 08 SE77

Flamingo Land Theme Park & Zoo

The Rectory YO17 6UX

➲ *(turn off A64 onto A169, Pickering to Whitby road)*

☎ 01653 668287

e-mail: info@flamingoland.co.uk

web: www.flamingoland.co.uk

Set in 375 acres of North Yorkshire countryside with over 100 rides and attractions there's something for everyone at Flamingo Land. Enjoy the thrills and spills of 12 white knuckle rides or enjoy a stroll through the extensive zoo where you'll find tigers, giraffes, hippos and rhinos. The theme park also boasts six great family shows.

Times Open daily, 30 Mar-28 Oct. **Fee** ✳ £22 (ch under 3 free, concessions £11). Family ticket (4 people) £82. **Facilities** ❷ ⏐ ⓧⓘ licensed ⊟ (outdoor) ♿ (parking, wheelchair hire) toilets for disabled shop ⊨

KIRKHAM

MAP 08 SE76

Kirkham Priory

Whitwell-on-the-Hill YO6 7JS

➲ *(5m SW of Malton on minor road off A64)*

☎ 01653 618768

web: www.english-heritage.org.uk

Discover the ruins of this Augustinian priory, which includes a magnificent carved gatehouse, set in a peaceful and secluded valley by the River Derwent.

Times Open 21 Mar-Jul & Sep, Thu-Mon 10-5; Aug, daily 10-5. **Fee** £3 (cconcessions £2.40, ch £1.50). Prices and opening times are subject to change in March 2009. Please check web site or call 0870 333 1181 for the most up to date prices and opening times when planning your visit. **Facilities** ❷ ⏛

KNARESBOROUGH

MAP 08 SE35

Knaresborough Castle & Museum

Castle Yard HG5 8AS

➲ *(off High St towards Market Square, right at police station into Castle Yard)*

☎ 01423 556188

e-mail: museums@harrogate.gov.uk

web: www.harrogate.gov.uk/museums

Towering high above the town of Knaresborough, the remains of this 14th-century castle look down over the gorge of the River Nidd. This imposing fortress was once the hiding place of Thomas Becket's murderers and served as a prison for Richard II. Visit the King's Tower, the secret underground tunnel and the dungeon. Discover Knaresborough's history in the museum and find out about 'Life in a Castle' in the hands-on gallery.

Times Open Good Fri-end Sep, daily 10.30-5. Guided tours regularly available **Facilities** ❷ (charged) ♿ (Limited access to Kings Tower. Museum is accessible) toilets for disabled shop ⊗ (ex assist dogs)

LAWKLAND   MAP 07 SD76

Yorkshire Dales Falconry & Wildlife Conservation Centre

Crows Nest LA2 8AS

⮕ *(on A65 follow brown signs)*

☎ 01729 822832 & 825164 (info line)

e-mail: mail@falconryandwildlife.com

web: www.falconryandwildlife.com

The first privately-owned falconry centre in the north of England. The main aim of the centre is to educate and promote awareness that many of the world's birds of prey are threatened with extinction. Successful captive breeding and educational programmes helps to safeguard these creatures. Regular free flying demonstrations throughout the day and falconry courses throughout the week.

Times Open all year summer 10-6; winter 10-4. Closed 25-26 Dec & 1 Jan. **Fee** £5.90 (ch £3.90, pen £4.80) Family ticket £18.50 (2ad+2ch). Group 20+ £4.90 (ch £3.50). 1 Ad free with 10 ch. **Facilities** ❷ ⛲ 🍴 (indoor & outdoor) ♿ (Ramp for w/chair into tea room, and giftshop access) toilets for disabled shop ⊗ (ex assist dogs) ⬛

MALHAM   MAP 07 SD96

Malham National Park Centre   `FREE`

BD23 4DA

⮕ *(off A65 at Gargrave opposite petrol station. Malham 7m)*

☎ 01969 652380

e-mail: malham@yorkshiredales.org.uk

web: www.yorkshiredales.org.uk

The Yorkshire Dales National Park centre has maps, guides and local information together with displays on the remarkable natural history of the area, local community and work of conservation bodies. A 24-hour teletext information service is available.

Times Open Apr-Oct, daily 10-5; Winter, Sat-Sun, 10-4. Daily in school hols. **Facilities** ❷ (charged) 🍴 (outdoor) ♿ (Radar key scheme for toilet) toilets for disabled shop ⬛

MALTON   MAP 08 SE77

Castle Howard

YO60 7DA

⮕ *(off A64, follow brown heritage signs)*

☎ 01653 648333

e-mail: house@castlehoward.co.uk

web: www.castlehoward.co.uk

A magnificent 18th-century house situated in breathtaking parkland. House guides share the history of the house, family and collections, while outdoor guided tours reveal the secrets of the gardens and architecture. Visitors can also enjoy a changing programme of exhibitions and events; boat trips, adventure playground and various cafés and shops including a farm shop and a chocolate shop. New exhibition "Brideshead Restored" - telling the story of restoration of Castle Howard and the filming of *Brideshead Revisited*.

Times House: Mar-Oct open Mar-1 Nov & 28 Nov-20 Dec, daily from 11. Gardens, shops & cafes open all year from 10. **Fee** ✳ £9.50 (ch £6.50, concessions £8.50). Grounds only £6.50 (ch £4.50, concessions £6). **Facilities** ❷ ⛲ 🍴 ♿ (Partly accessible) (wheelchair lift, free adapted transport to house) toilets for disabled shop garden centre ⊗ (ex assist dogs & in gardens) ⬛

Eden Camp Modern History Theme Museum   `2 for 1`

Eden Camp YO17 6RT

⮕ *(junct of A64 & A169, between York & Scarborough)*

☎ 01653 697777

e-mail: admin@edencamp.co.uk

web: www.edencamp.co.uk

Housed in an original prisoner of war camp built in 1942 to house Italian and German POW's, this regional and national award winning museum presents the most comprehensive display of British civilian life during World War Two. The period is brought to life through life-size tableaux and diorama which incorporate sound, light and even smell effects to create the atmosphere of the 1940s. Other sections of the museum cover military and political events of WWII and British military history of the 20th century, from World War One to the wars in Iraq and Afghanistan. The museum also houses an extensive collection

CONTINUED

MALTON CONTINUED

of military vehicles, artillery and associated equipment. Special Events: WWII re-enactment weekend; Reunion of Escapers and Evaders April; All Services Commemorative Day and Parade September; Palestine Veterans Reunion Day in Oct.

Times Open 2nd Mon in Jan-23 Dec, daily 10-5. (Last admission 4) **Fee** ✳ £5 (ch & concessions £4) Party 10+.£5 - £1 discount on individual admission prices. **Facilities** ♿ ⛳☕ (indoor & outdoor) ♿ (taped tours, Braille guides) toilets for disabled shop

Malton Museum

Old Town Hall, Market Place YO17 7LP

➲ *(leave A64, follow signs for Malton town centre)*

☎ 01653 695136

web: www.maltonmuseum.co.uk

The extensive Roman settlements in the area are represented and illustrated in this museum, including collections from the Roman fort of Derventio. There are also displays of local prehistoric and medieval finds, plus changing exhibitions of local interest.

Times Open Etr-Nov, Mon-Sat 10.30-3. **Fee** ✳ £1.50 (ch, concessions £1) Family ticket £4 (2ad+2ch) **Facilities** ♿ (adjacent) (pay & display-2hrs) ♿ (stair lift) shop ⊗ (ex assist dogs)

MASHAM   MAP 08 SE28

Theakston Brewery & Visitor Centre

The Brewery HG4 4YD

➲ *(On A6108, in town centre. Parking for Brewery visitors is in market place. Follow pedestrian signs. Approx 2 min walk)*

☎ 01765 680000
e-mail: info@theakstons.co.uk
web: www.theakstons.co.uk

First established in 1827, T&R Theakston Ltd is home of the legendary Old Peculier Ale. Experience the wonderful aromas of hops and malt, used every day to brew their famous beers, as has been done for generations, and sample their legendary ales in the Brewery Tap - The Black Bull in Paradise. There is plenty to do and see including the

Cooper's shop where the cooper crafts the wooden barrels - one of the last remaining working cooperages in the country.

Times Open all year from 10.30, closing times vary according to time of year. Closed 24-26 Dec & 31 Dec-2 Jan. **Fee** ✳ £4.75 (ch £2.50, students £4.50 & concessions £4). Family £12.50 (2ad+2ch). **Facilities** ♿ (400yds) ⛳♿ (Partly accessible) (ex brewery tours, stair lift to visitor centre) toilets for disabled shop ⊗ (ex assist dogs)

MIDDLEHAM   MAP 07 SE18

Middleham Castle

Castle Hill DL8 4RJ

➲ *(2m S of Leyburn on A6108)*

☎ 01969 623899

web: www.english-heritage.org.uk

Explore the maze of rooms and passageways at this impressive castle, once the boyhood home of the ill-fated Richard III. Oak viewing gallery of the magnificent views of the 12th-century keep and exhibition.

Times Open all year, 21 Mar-Sep, daily 10-6; Oct-Mar, Sat-Wed 10-4. Closed 24-26 Dec & 1 Jan. **Fee** £4 (concessions £3.20, ch £2). Prices and opening times are subject to change in March 2009. Please check web site or call 0870 333 1181 for the most up to date prices and opening times when planning your visit. **Facilities** ♿ ☕♿ (ex tower) shop ⌗

MIDDLESBROUGH   MAP 08 NZ42

Captain Cook Birthplace Museum   FREE

Stewart Park, Marton TS7 8AT

➲ *(3m S on A172)*

☎ 01642 311211

e-mail: captcookmuseum@middlesbrough.gov.uk

web: www.captcook-ne.co.uk

Opened in 1978 to mark the 250th anniversary of the birth of the voyager in 1728, this museum illustrates the early life of James Cook and his discoveries with permanent and temporary exhibitions. Located in spacious and rolling parkland, the site also offers outside attractions for the visitor. The museum has a special resource centre which has fresh approaches to presentation with computers, films, special effects, interactives and educational aids.

Times Open all year: Mar-Oct, Tue-Sun, 10-5.30. Nov-Feb 9-4.00. (Last entry 45 mins before closure). Closed Mon & some BH, 24-26 Dec,1 Jan & 1st full week Jan. **Facilities** ♿ ⛳☕●☕☕ (outdoor) ♿ (lift to all floors, car parking, wheelchair) toilets for disabled shop ⊗ (ex assist dogs)

NEWBY HALL & GARDENS   MAP 08 SE36

Newby Hall & Gardens

HG4 5AE

➲ *(4m SE of Ripon & 2m W of A1M, off B6265, between Boroughbridge and Ripon)*

☎ 01423 322583

e-mail: info@newbyhall.com

web: www.newbyhall.com

A late 17th-century house with beautifully restored Robert Adam interiors containing an important collection of classical sculpture, Chippendale furniture and Gobelin tapestries. 25 acres of award-winning gardens include a miniature railway, an adventure garden for children and a woodland discovery walk with contemporary sculpture park (Jun-Sep).

Times ✲ Open Apr-Sep, Tue-Sun & BHs, also Mon in Jul & Aug; Gardens 11-5.30; House 12-5. (Last admission 5 Gardens, 4.30 House) **Facilities** ❷ ♿🅿🍴🚻♿ (wheelchairs available, maps of wheelchair routes) toilets for disabled shop garden centre ❌ (ex assist dogs) ➡

NORTH STAINLEY   MAP 08 SE27

Lightwater Valley Theme Park

HG4 3HT

➲ *(3m N of Ripon on A6108)*

☎ 0871 720 0011

e-mail: leisure@lightwatervalley.co.uk

web: www.lightwatervalley.co.uk

Set in 175 acres of beautiful North Yorkshire parkland, Lightwater Valley Theme park, Shopping Village and Birds of Prey Centre offers an exciting choice of activities. The thrilling theme park line-up comprises some amazing rides, including Europe's longest rollercoaster - The Ultimate, as well as the stomach-churning mighty Eagle's Claw and The Hornet's Nest - the ride with a sting in its tail! However, if you prefer to take things at a more leisurely pace, take a gentle stroll around the picturesque lake, play crazy golf or just climb aboard the Lightwater Express for a round-the-park train ride. Also on site, the Birds of Prey Centre was established to raise awareness of a wide selection of breathtaking birds. The purpose built raptor complex offers the opportunity to see possibly the largest Golden Eagle in England, as well as learning how these amazing birds are trained and handled, as well as being treated to dramatic flying shows every day.

Times Open 31 Mar-15 Apr, wknds only; 21 Apr-27 May inc BH Mon; daily from 26 May-2 Sep, wknds only, 8 Sep-21 Oct, daily 22 Oct-28 Oct. Gates open at 10, closes 4.30, depending on time of year. **Fee** ✲ £16.95 over 1.3mtrs, £14.95 under 1.3mtrs, free under 1m (concessions £8.50). Family (2ad+2ch or 1ad+3ch under 16) £60. **Facilities** ❷ ♿🍴 licensed 🅿 (outdoor) ♿ (Partly accessible) (even pathways) toilets for disabled shop garden centre ❌ (ex assist dogs) ➡

NUNNINGTON   MAP 08 SE67

Nunnington Hall

YO62 5UY

➲ *(4.5m SE of Helmsley)*

☎ 01439 748283

e-mail: nunningtonhall@nationaltrust.org.uk

web: www.nationaltrust.org.uk

This large 16th to 17th-century house has panelled rooms and a magnificent staircase. The Carlisle collection of miniature rooms is on display. Changing programme of temporary exhibitions.

Times ✲ Open 15 Mar-2 Nov, Tue-Sun 12-5; Jun-Aug, Tue-Sun 12-5.30 **Facilities** ❷ 🅿🅿 (outdoor) ♿ (Partly accessible) (wheelchairs, Braille guide, scented garden) toilets for disabled shop ❌ (ex assist dogs) ♨ ➡

ORMESBY   MAP 08 NZ51

Ormesby Hall

TS7 9AS

➲ *(3m SE of Middlesborough, W of A19 take the A174 to the A172. Follow signs for Ormesby Hall. Car entrance on Ladgate Lane B1380)*

☎ 01642 324188

e-mail: ormesbyhall@nationaltrust.org.uk

web: www.nationaltrust.org.uk

An 18th-century mansion, Ormesby Hall has stables attributed to John Carr of York. Plasterwork, furniture and 18th-century pictures are on view. Exhibiting a large model railway.

Times ✲ Open 17 Mar-4 Nov Sat, Sun & BHs 1.30-5 **Facilities** ❷ 🅿🅿 (outdoor) ♿ (Partly accessible) (parking, Braille guide, special tours, sensory list) toilets for disabled ♨ ➡

OSMOTHERLEY   MAP 08 SE49

Mount Grace Priory

DL6 3JG

➲ *(1m NW)*

☎ 01609 883494

web: www.english-heritage.org.uk

The best preserved Carthusian monastery in the country, set in breathtakingly beautiful woodland surroundings and gardens, including fully reconstructed monks' cells and herb garden, illustrating the solitary life of the monk.

Times Open 21 Mar-Sep, Thu-Mon, 10-6; Oct-Mar, Thu-Sun, 10-4. Closed 24-26 Dec & 1 Jan. **Fee** £4 (concessions £3.20, ch £2). Family ticket £10. NT members free on non-event days. Prices and opening times are subject to change in March 2009. Please check web site or call 0870 333 1181 for the most up to date prices and opening times when planning your visit. **Facilities** ❷ 🅿 shop ❌ ♨ ♨

PARCEVALL HALL GARDENS **MAP 07 SE06**

Parcevall Hall Gardens

BD23 6DE

➲ *(Off B6265 between Grassington and Pateley Bridge)*

☎ 01756 720311

e-mail: parcevallhall@btconnect.com

web: www.parcevallhallgardens.co.uk

Enjoying a hillside setting east of the main Wharfedale Valley, these beautiful gardens surround a Grade II listed house which is used as the Bradford Diocesan Retreat House (not open to the public).

Times Open Apr-Oct, daily 10-6. Winter visitors by appointment. (Last entry 5) **Fee** ✳ £5.50 (ch £2.50, concession £4.50). **Facilities** ❿ ♨ ⽊ (outdoor) garden centre ⊗ (ex on lead)

PATELEY BRIDGE **MAP 07 SE16**

Stump Cross Caverns

Greenhow HG3 5JL

➲ *(on B6265 between Pateley Bridge & Grassington)*

☎ 01756 752780

web: www.stumpcrosscaverns.co.uk

Discovered by the brothers Mark and William Newbould in 1860, Stump Cross Caverns have been an attraction for visitors since 1863 when one shilling was charged for entrance. Among the few limestone show caves in Britain, these require no special clothing, experience or equipment, as walkways are gravel and concrete and floodlighting is provided. Stalagmites, stalagtites and calcite precipitation make this an eerie day out.

Times Open daily, Mar-end of Nov, then wknds and school hols Dec, Jan, Feb 10-5. **Fee** ✳ £6 (ch £3.95, ch under 4 free) free gift for ch in school hols **Facilities** ❿ ♨ ⿻ ♿ & (accessiblity to ground floor and gardens) shop ⊗ (ex assist dogs) ⊟

PICKERING **MAP 08 SE78**

North Yorkshire Moors Railway

Pickering Station YO18 7AJ

➲ *(from A169 take road towards Kirkbymoorside, right at traffic lights, station 400yds on left)*

☎ 01751 472508

e-mail: admin@nymr.pickering.fsnet.co.uk

web: www.northyorkshiremoorsrailway.com

Operating through the heart of the North York Moors National Park between Pickering and Grosmont, steam trains cover a distance of 18 miles. The locomotive sheds at Grosmont are open to the public. Events throughout the year include Day Out with Thomas, Steam Gala, and Santa Specials.

Times ✳ Open 29 Mar-Oct, daily; Dec, Santa specials and Xmas to New Year running. Further information available from Pickering Station. **Facilities** ❿ (charged) ♨ ⿻ ⽊ (outdoor) & (ramp for trains) toilets for disabled shop ⊟

Pickering Castle

Castlegate YO6 5AB

☎ 01751 474989

web: www.english-heritage.org.uk

Splendid 12th-century castle, on the edge of the Yorkshire Moors, originally built by William the Conqueror. Visit the exhibition on the castle's history and take in the views from the keep.

Times Open 21 Mar-Sep, daily 10-6; Oct, Thu-Mon 10-4. **Fee** £3.50 (concessions £2.80, ch £1.80). Family ticket £8.80. Prices and opening times are subject to change in March 2009. Please check web site or call 0870 333 1181 for the most up to date prices and opening times when planning your visit. **Facilities** ❿ ⽊ & (ex motte) shop ⽚

REDCAR **MAP 08 NZ62**

RNLI Zetland Museum `FREE`

5 King St TS10 3DT

➲ *(on corner of King St and The Promenade)*

☎ 01642 494311 & 471813

e-mail: zetland.museum@yahoo.co.uk

The museum portrays the lifeboat, maritime, fishing and local history of the area, including its main exhibit *The Zetland* - the oldest lifeboat in the world, dating from 1802. There is also a replica of a fisherman's cottage c1900 and almost 2,000 other exhibits. The museum is housed in an early lifeboat station, now a listed building.

Times Open May, Wed 11-4, Sat-Sun 12-4; Jun-Sep Tue-Fri 11-4, Sat-Sun 12-4. Closed Mon. **Facilities** ℗ (20m) (60p per hour) & (Partly accessible) (ground floor only accessible) shop

RICHMOND   MAP 07 NZ10

Green Howards Museum

Trinity Church Square, Market Place DL10 4QN

⮩ *(take any turning on A1, between Catterick & South Corner, signed to Richmond. Located in centre cobbled market square, in Holy Trinity Church)*

☎ 01748 826561

e-mail: greenhowardsmus@aol.com

web: www.greenhowards.org.uk

This award-winning museum traces the military history of the Green Howards from the late 17th century onwards. The exhibits include uniforms, weapons, medals and a special Victoria Cross exhibition. There is a children's interactive area, family history research centre, interactive computers and a temporary exhibition area.

Times Open Mon-Sat 10-4.30, Sun closed (closed Xmas to end of Jan) **Fee** £3.50 (accompanied ch free, concessions £3). Richmond residents £3. **Facilities** ⓟ (in market place) (disk parking, 2hr max) ♿ (stairlift, lightweight wheelchair) shop ⊗ (ex assist dogs)

Richmond Castle

Tower Castle DL10 4QW

☎ 01748 822493

web: www.english-heritage.org.uk

Overlooking the River Swale and market town of Richmond, the views from the keep are stunning. Built by William the Conqueror to subdue the rebellious North, the castle now houses an exciting interactive exhibition.

Times Open all year, 21 Mar-Sep, daily 10-6; Oct-Mar, Thu-Mon 10-4. Closed 24-26 Dec & 1 Jan. **Fee** £4 (concessions £3.20, ch £2). Prices and opening times are subject to change in March 2009. Please check web site or call 0870 333 1181 for the most up to date prices and opening times when planning your visit. **Facilities** ⓟ (800 yds) ⍨ shop ⚌

RIEVAULX   MAP 08 SE58

Rievaulx Abbey

⮩ *(2.25m W of Helmsley on minor road off B1257)*

☎ 01439 798228

web: www.english-heritage.org.uk

Explore the magnificent romantic ruin set in a tranquil wooded valley of the River Rye. Find out about monastic life with the help of the audio tour and exhibition.

Times Open 21 Mar-Sep, daily, 10-6; Oct, Thu-Mon, 10-5; Nov-Mar, Thu-Mon, 10-4. Closed 24-26 Dec & 1 Jan **Fee** £5 (concessions £4, ch £2.50). Prices and opening times are subject to change in March 2009. Please check web site or call 0870 333 1181 for the most up to date prices and opening times when planning your visit. **Facilities** ⓟ ⍨ shop ⚌ ⚌

Rievaulx Terrace & Temples

YO62 5LJ

⮩ *(2m NW of Helmsley on B1257)*

☎ 01439 798340

e-mail: nunningtonhall@nationaltrust.org.uk

web: www.nationaltrust.org.uk

This curved terrace, half a mile long, overlooks the abbey, with views of Ryedale and the Hambleton Hills. It has two mock-Greek temples, one built for hunting parties, the other for quiet contemplation. There are also remarkable frescoes by Borgnis, and an exhibition on English landscape design.

Times ✳ Open mid 17 Mar-Sep, daily 11-6. Oct, daily, 11-5 (last admission 1hr before close) **Facilities** ⓟ ⍨ (outdoor) ♿ (Partly accessible) (w/chair/runaround vehicle/Braille guide/ramp) shop ⚌ ⚌

RIPLEY   MAP 08 SE26

Ripley Castle

HG3 3AY

⮩ *(off A61, Harrogate to Ripon road)*

☎ 01423 770152

e-mail: enquiries@ripleycastle.co.uk

web: www.ripleycastle.co.uk

Ripley Castle has been home to the Ingilby family for 26 generations and stands at the heart of an estate with deer park, lakes and Victorian walled gardens. The Castle has a rich history and a fine collection of Royalist armour housed in the 1555 tower. There are also tropical hot houses, a children's play trail, tearooms, woodland walks, pleasure grounds and the National Hyacinth collection in spring. 2009 is the 700 year anniversary of Ripley Castle.

Times Open Nov-8 Mar, Tue, Thu, Sat & Sun 10.30-3; Apr-Oct, daily 10.30-3; Dec-Feb wknds only, also BH and school hols. Groups all year by prior arrangement. Gardens open daily 9-5. **Fee** ✳ Castle & Gardens £7.50 (ch £4.50, pen £6.50). Gardens only £5 (ch £3, concession £4.50). Party £4.50. **Facilities** ⓟ ⍨ ⍩ ♿ (two of the rooms in the castle on view are upstairs) (mobility buggy for hire, audio loop) toilets for disabled shop garden centre ⊗ (ex assist dogs) ⚌

RIPON   MAP 08 SE37

Fountains Abbey & Studley Royal

HG4 3DY

⮑ *(4m W of Ripon off B6265)*

☎ 01765 608888

e-mail: fountainsenquiries@nationaltrust.org.uk

web: www.fountainsabbey.org.uk

A World Heritage Site comprising the ruin of a 12th-century Cistercian abbey and monastic watermill, an Elizabethan mansion and one of the best surviving examples of a Georgian water garden. Elegant ornamental lakes, canals, temples and cascades provide eye-catching vistas. The site also contains the Victorian St. Mary's Church and medieval deer park.

Times ✳ Open daily all year: Nov-Feb 10-4, Mar-Oct 10-5. Closed Fri Nov-Jan & 24-25 Dec. **Fee** £7.90 (ch £4.20) Family £20.90 **Facilities** ℗ ⊑ ⌷◖ ⋒ (outdoor) � (Partly accessible) (pre-bk wheelchairs & batricars. Braille/large print guides) toilets for disabled shop ⊗ (ex on lead at all times) ✻ ▬

Norton Conyers

Wath HG4 5EQ

⮑ *(from Ripon take A61 to Thirsk. At top of hill just outside Ripon, turn sharp left onto Wath Road)*

☎ 01765 640333

e-mail: norton.conyers@bronco.co.uk

This charming late medieval house has belonged to the Grahams since 1624, and is now the home of Sir James and Lady Graham. Of medieval origins, it was altered in Tudor and Stuart times, and again in the 18th and 19th centuries. The interior, with its furniture and extensive collection of family portraits, reflects nearly four hundred years of occupation by the same family. Famous visitors include Charles I in 1633, James II and his wife in 1679, and Charlotte Brontë in 1839. The last of these is said to have been inspired by a local legend of a mad woman in the attic to create mad Mrs Rochester in her novel *Jane Eyre*. The house is set in a fine park with an 18th-century walled garden.

Times House due to re-open June after major repairs. Gardens due to open May. Please ring for details **Fee** Please ring for details **Facilities** ℗ ㄓ (ramp at entrance) toilets for disabled shop ⊗ (ex assist dogs)

SALTBURN-BY-THE-SEA   MAP 08 NZ62

Saltburn Smugglers Heritage Centre

2 for 1

Old Saltburn TS12 1HF

⮑ *(adjoining Ship Inn, on A174)*

☎ 01287 625252

web: www.redcar-cleveland.gov.uk

Set in old fisherman's cottages, this centre skillfully blends costumed characters with authentic sounds and smells. Follow the story of John Andrew "King of Smugglers", who was at the heart of illicit local trade 200 years ago.

Times Open daily Apr-May, Wed-Sun 10-6; Jun, Tue-Sun 10-6; Jul-Aug daily 10-6; Sep, Wed-Sun 10-6. **Fee** ✳ £1.95 (ch £1.45). Family ticket £5.80. Party. **Facilities** ℗ (200 mtrs) (charged) ⋒ (outdoor) ㄓ (gift shop area is inaccessible) (no access for wheelchairs in giftshop) shop ⊗ (ex assist dogs)

SCARBOROUGH   MAP 08 TA08

Scarborough Castle

Castle Rd YO11 1HY

⮑ *(E of town centre)*

☎ 01723 372451

web: www.english-heritage.org.uk

This 12th-century fortress housed many important figures in history. Enjoy the spectacular coastal view and see the remains of the great keep still standing over three storeys high. Discover the castle's exciting history through the free audio tour.

Times Open all year, 21 Mar-Sep, daily 10-6; Oct, Thu-Mon 10-5; Nov-Mar, Thu-Mon 10-4. Closed 24-26 Dec & 1 Jan. **Fee** £4 (concessions £3.20, ch £2). Family ticket £10. Prices and opening times are subject to change in March 2009. Please check web site or call 0870 333 1181 for the most up to date prices and opening times when planning your visit. **Facilities** ℗ (100yds) ⋒ ㄓ (ex in keep) ⚏

Sea Life & Marine Sanctuary

Scalby Mills Rd, North Bay YO12 6RP

⮑ *(follow brown tourist signs after entering Scarborough. Centre in North Bay Leisure Parks area of town)*

☎ 01723 376125

web: www.sealife.co.uk

Made up of three large white pyramids, this impressive marine sanctuary overlooks the white sandy beaches of the North Bay, Scarborough's Castle, and Peasholm Park. The sanctuary features Jurassic seas, jellyfish, Otter River, penguins, and sea turtles.

Times ✳ Open all year daily. Closed 25 Dec. **Facilities** ℗ (charged) ⊑ ⋒ ㄓ (lift to cafe) toilets for disabled shop ⊗ (except assist dogs) ▬

SKINNINGROVE   MAP 08 NZ71

Cleveland Ironstone Mining Museum

Deepdale TS13 4AP

⮑ *(in Skinningrove Valley, just off A174 near coast between Saltburn and Whitby)*

☎ 01287 642877

e-mail: visits@ironstonemuseum.co.uk

web: www.ironstonemuseum.co.uk

On the site of the old Loftus Mine, this museum offers visitors a glimpse into the underground world of Cleveland's ironstone mining past. Discover the special skills and customs of the miners who helped make Cleveland the most important ironstone mining district in Victorian and Edwardian England. This is not a glass case museum but an experience.

Times Open Apr/Etr-Oct, Mon-Fri 10.30-3.30, Sat 1-3.30, Sun 1-3.30 during Aug. **Fee** £5 (ch 5-16 £2.50, concessions £4.50). Family ticket £12. **Facilities** ℗ ⋒ (outdoor) ㄓ (Partly accessible) (2 wheelchairs on site, induction loop) toilets for disabled shop ⊗ (ex assist dogs)

SKIPTON   MAP 07 SD95

Skipton Castle

BD23 1AW

➪ *(in town centre at head of High Street)*

☎ 01756 792442

e-mail: info@skiptoncastle.co.uk

web: www.skiptoncastle.co.uk

Skipton is one of the most complete and well-preserved medieval castles in England. Some of the castle dates from the 1650s when it was rebuilt after being partially damaged following the Civil War. However, the original castle was erected in Norman times and became the home of the Clifford family in 1310 and remained so until 1676. Illustrated tour sheets are available in a number of languages. Please see website for special events.

Times Open daily from 10, (Sun from noon). Last admission 6 (4pm Oct-Feb). Closed 25 Dec. **Fee** ✳ £5.80 (inc illustrated tour sheet) (ch under 18 £3.20, under 5 free, concessions £5.20). Family ticket £17.90. Party 15+. **Facilities** ℗ (200m) ⬛ 🍴 (indoor & outdoor) ♿ (Partly accessible) shop garden centre ⊗ (ex on a lead) ⬛

SUTTON-ON-THE-FOREST   MAP 08 SE56

Sutton Park   2 for 1

YO61 1DP

➪ *(off A1237 onto B1363 York to Helmsley road. 8m N of York city centre)*

☎ 01347 810249 & 811239

e-mail: suttonpark@fsbdial.co.uk

web: www.statelyhome.co.uk

The early Georgian house contains fine furniture, paintings and porcelain. The grounds have superb, award-winning terraced gardens, a lily pond and a Georgian ice house. There are also delightful woodland walks as well as spaces for caravans.

Times Open Gardens Apr-end Sep, daily 11-5. House open Apr-end Sep, Wed, Sun & BH. **Fee** Gardens only £3.50 (ch £1.50, concessions £3). House & Gardens £6.50 (ch £4, concessions £5.50) **Facilities** ℗ ⬛ 🍴 (outdoor) ♿ (Partly accessible) (wheelchair & lift in house, ramps in garden) toilets for disabled shop ⊗ (ex assist dogs in garden)

THIRSK   MAP 08 SE48

Falconry UK - Birds of Prey Centre   2 for 1

Sion Hill Hall, Kirby Wiske YO7 4EU

➪ *(follow brown tourist signs, situated on A167 between Northallerton and Topcliffe)*

☎ 01845 587522

e-mail: mail@falconrycentre.co.uk

web: www.falconrycentre.co.uk

Set up as a conservation centre, and also to provide the public with a rare opportunity to see and enjoy these beautiful birds. Enjoy the excitement of falconry with over 70 birds and 30 species. Three different flying displays with public participation where possible. After each display, handling birds are brought out for the public to hold.

Times Open Mar-Oct daily, 10.30-5. **Fee** £6 (ch £4, under 3 free, pen £5). Family ticket £18 (2ad+2ch) **Facilities** ℗ ⬛ 🍴 (outdoor) ♿ toilets for disabled shop ⊗ ⬛

Monk Park Farm Visitor Centre

Bagby YO7 2AG

➪ *(just off A170 Scarborough road or A19 from York)*

☎ 01845 597730

web: www.monkpark.co.uk

Monk Park, once a haven for the monks who made their living from the land, is now a favourite for children. There is something for all ages to see and do, with indoor and outdoor viewing and feeding areas. The park has also been the venue for filming *Blue Peter* and *Vets in Practice*.

Times Open Feb half term-Oct, daily, 11-5.30. **Facilities** ℗ ⬛ 🍴 (indoor & outdoor) ♿ (ramps) toilets for disabled shop ⊗ (ex assist dogs)

WHITBY   MAP 08 NZ81

Whitby Abbey

YO22 4JT

➪ *(on clifftop E of Whitby town centre)*

☎ 01947 603568

web: www.english-heritage.org.uk

Uncover the full story of these atmospheric ruins in their impressive clifftop location above the picturesque fishing town, with associations ranging from Victorian jewellery and whaling, to Count Dracula.

Times Open all year, 21 Mar-Sep, daily 10-6; Oct-Mar, Thu-Mon 10-4. Closed 24-26 Dec & 1 Jan. **Fee** £5 (concessions £4, ch £2.50). Family ticket £12.50. Prices and opening times are subject to change in March 2009. Please check web site or call 0870 333 1181 for the most up to date prices and opening times when planning your visit. **Facilities** ℗ (charged) ⬛ 🍴 shop 🏠

WINTRINGHAM   MAP 08 SE87

Wolds Way Lavender   FREE

Deer Farm Park, Sandy Ln, Wintringham YO17 8HW

⮕ *(off A64 between Malton & Scarborough, follow brown signs)*

☎ 01944 758641

e-mail: admin@woldswaylavender.co.uk

web: www.woldswaylavender.co.uk

The medicinal and therapeutic benefits of lavender are extolled at this 12-acre site close to the Yorkshire Wolds. Four acres are currently planted with lavender, and a wood-burning still for the extraction of lavender oil. Visitors can be calmed by the Sensory Areas, enjoy a cuppa in the tearoom, and purchase all manner of lavender items at the farm shop.

Times Open daily from 1st Sun in Feb to 2nd Sun in Dec 10-4. (May-Aug 10-5) **Facilities** ⓟ ⬚ ⧖ (outdoor) ♿ (sensory garden, raised flower beds) toilets for disabled shop garden centre ⊗ (ex assist dogs) ▬

YORK   MAP 08 SE65

Clifford's Tower

Tower St YO1 1SA

☎ 01904 646940

web: www.english-heritage.org.uk

Visit this proud symbol of the might of England's medieval kings - and enjoy magnificent views over York. The original wooden tower was built to help William the Conqueror subdue the North. It was burned down during the persecution of the Jewish community in 1190 and rebuilt in a rare design of interlocking circles by Henry III in the 13th-century.

Times Open 21 Mar-Sep, daily 10-6; Oct, daily 10-5; Nov-Mar, daily 10-4. Closed 24-26 Dec & 1 Jan. **Fee** £3 (concessions £2.40, ch £1.50). Family £7.50. Prices and opening times are subject to change in March 2009. Please check web site or call 0870 333 1181 for the most up to date prices and opening times when planning your visit. **Facilities** ⓟ shop ⊗ 🍴 ⚹

DIG   2 for 1

St Saviourgate YO1 8NN

⮕ *(follow A19 or A64 to city centre then pedestrian signs for attraction)*

☎ 01904 543402

e-mail: jorvik@yorkat.co.uk

web: www.digyork.co.uk

Grab a trowel and dig to see what you can find in DIG's specially designed excavation pits. Rediscover some of the amazing finds that the archaeologists have uncovered under the streets of York. Understand what these finds tell us about how people lived in Roman, Viking, Medieval and Victorian times. Touch real artefacts and work out what they would be used for. Special events scheduled throughout the year.

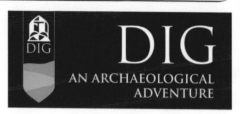

DIG AN ARCHAEOLOGICAL ADVENTURE

Times Open daily 10-5. Closed 24-27 Dec **Fee** ✳ £5.50. (ch, concessions £5). Family of 4 £18.50. Family of 5 £19.60. Group rates available on request. **Facilities** ⓟ (50yds NCP) ⧖ (indoor & outdoor) ♿ (induction loop, sensory garden, hearing posts) toilets for disabled shop ⊗ (ex assist dogs) ▬

Fairfax House

Castlegate YO1 9RN

⮕ *(city centre, close to Jorvik Centre and Cliffords Tower)*

☎ 01904 655543

e-mail: peterbrown@fairfaxhouse.co.uk

web: www.fairfaxhouse.co.uk

An outstanding mid 18th-century house with a richly decorated interior, Fairfax House was acquired by the York Civic Trust in 1983 and restored. The house contains fine examples of Georgian furniture, porcelain, paintings and clocks which were donated by Mr Noel Terry, the great grandson of the founder of the York-based confectionery business. There is a special display of a recreated meal dating from 1763 in the dining room and kitchen.

Times ✳ Open 7 Feb-5 Jan, Mon-Sat 11-5, (Fri guided tours only at 11 & 2). Sun 1.30-5. (Last admission 4.30) **Facilities** ⓟ (50yds) (3hr short stay) ⧖ ♿ (with assistance, phone before visit) shop ⊗ (ex assist dogs) ▬

Guildhall   FREE

Coney St YO1 9QN

⮕ *(5-10mins walk from rail station)*

☎ 01904 613161

web: www.york.gov.uk

The present Hall dates from 1446, but in 1942 an air raid virtually destroyed the building. The present Guildhall was carefully restored as an exact replica and was re-opened in 1960. There is an interesting arch-braced roof decorated with colourful bosses and supported by 12 solid oak pillars. There are also some beautiful stained-glass windows.

Times ✳ Open all year, May-Oct, Mon-Fri 9-5, Sat 10-5, Sun 2-5; Nov-Apr, Mon-Fri 9-5. **Facilities** ⓟ (15-20 mins walk) ♿ (electric chair lift & ramps) toilets for disabled ⊗ (ex assist dogs) 🍴

Jorvik Viking Centre

2 for 1

Coppergate YO1 9WT

➲ *(follow A19 or A64 to York. Jorvik in Coppergate shopping area (city centre) signed)*

☎ 01904 543402

e-mail: jorvik@yorkat.co.uk

web: www.jorvik-viking-centre.com

Explore York's Viking history on the very site where archaeologists discovered remains of the city of Jorvik. See over 800 of the items discovered on site and meet the famous Jorvik Vikings in our three exciting exhibitions, learn what life was like here more than 1,000 years ago, and journey through a reconstruction of actual Viking streets. A new feature is 'Are You A Viking?', uses scientific evidence to discover if you have Viking ancestors. 'Unearthed' tells how the people of ancient York lived and died, as revealed by real bone material. Special events throughout the year.

Times Open all year, summer, daily 10-5; winter, daily 10-4. Closed 25 Dec. Opening times subject to change, please telephone for up to date details. **Fee** ✳ £8.50 (ch 5-15 £6.00, under 5 free, concessions £7) Family of 4 £26 & family of 5 £29. Telephone bookings on 01904 615505 (£1 booking fee per person at peak times). **Facilities** ℗ (400 yds) ⊑ ♿ (wheelchair users are advised to pre-book) (lift & time car designed to take wheelchair, hearing loop) toilets for disabled shop ⊗ (ex assist dogs) ▭

Merchant Adventurers' Hall

2 for 1

Fossgate YO1 9XD

➲ *(located in town centre, between Piccadilly and Fossgate)*

☎ 01904 654818

e-mail: enquiries@theyorkcompany.co.uk

web: www.theyorkcompany.co.uk

Construction of the Merchant Adventurers' Hall began in 1357 and it is one of the best preserved medieval guild halls in the world. Explore the Great Hall, Undercroft, and Chapel, along with unique collections of art, silver and furniture. Fully accessible to all from Fossgate.

Times Open Etr-Sep, Mon-Thu, 9-5, Fri & Sat, 9-3.30. Sun 12-4. Oct-Etr, Mon-Sat, 9-3.30, Sun & Xmas period closed. Closed Jan-Feb for works. **Fee** £2.50 (ch under 7 free, ch 7-17yrs £1, concessions £2). **Facilities** ℗ (500yds) ⧓ (outdoor) ♿ (access from Fossgate, lift) toilets for disabled ⊗ (ex assist dogs)

National Railway Museum

Leeman Rd YO26 4XJ

➲ *(behind rail station. Signed from all major roads and city centre)*

☎ 01904 621261

e-mail: nrm@nrm.org.uk

web: www.nrm.org.uk

The National Railway Museum is the world's largest railway museum. Among its attractions are *The Flying Scotsman*, three enormous galleries, interactive exhibits and daily events. The National Railway

CONTINUED

ENGLAND

YORK CONTINUED

Museum mixes education with fun. This attraction is free although there is a charge for certain special events.

Times Open all year 10-6. Closed 24-26 Dec. **Fee** Admission may be charged for special events and rides **Facilities** ❷ (charged) ⌑ ⦿ ⋈ (indoor & outdoor) ♿ ("Please Touch" evenings usually in June) toilets for disabled shop garden centre ⊗ (ex assist dogs) ▬

See advert on page 347

Treasurer's House

Minster Yard YO1 7JL

⮑ *(in Minster Yard, on N side of Minster, in the centre of York)*

☎ 01904 624247

e-mail: treasurershouse@nationaltrust.org.uk

web: www.nationaltrust.org.uk

Named after the Treasurer of York Minster and built over a Roman Road, the house is not all it seems. Nestled behind the Minster, the size, splendour and contents of the house are a constant surprise to visitors - as are the famous ghost stories. Children's trails and access to the tea room free.

Times ✳ Open 15 Mar-7 Nov, daily 11-5 except Fri. **Fee** ✳ £5.80 (ch £2.90). Family ticket £14.50 (2 ad+3 ch). House and Ghost Cellar £8 (ch £4.60) **Facilities** ℗ (800 mtrs) ⌑ ⦿ ♿ (Partly accessible) (Braille guide/tactile pictures/induction loop/scented path) ⊗ (ex assist dogs) ⛎ ▬

The York Brewery Co Ltd   2 for 1

12 Toft Green YO1 6JT

⮑ *(5 min walk from York train station. Turn right out of station, right at lights. Walk under Mickelgate Bar, then left into Toft Green. Brewery is 300yds on right.)*

☎ 01904 621162

e-mail: tony@yorkbrew.co.uk

web: www.yorkbrew.co.uk

One of the North's finest independent breweries now offers a tour of its premises inside the city walls. Visitors can observe all the processes that go into producing beers like *Centurion's Ghost, Yorkshire Terrier, Guzzler,* and *Stonewall*. Those made intolerably thirsty by the sight of all this brewing expertise will be glad to know that the adult ticket price includes one pint of beer.

Times Open daily, tours at 12.30, 2, 3.30 & 5 Mon-Sat (Sun, May-Sep) **Fee** ✳ £6 (ch 14-17 yrs £3, concessions £5). **Facilities** ℗ (50yds) (£1.40 per hr) ♿ (12 steps) shop ⊗ (ex assist dogs) ▬

York Castle Museum

The Eye of York YO1 1RY

⮑ *(city centre, next to Clifford's Tower)*

☎ 01904 687687

e-mail: castle.museum@ymt.org.uk

web: www.yorkcastlemuseum.org.uk

Fascinating exhibits that bring memories to life, imaginatively displayed through reconstructions of period rooms and two indoor streets, complete with cobbles, a Hansom cab and a park. The museum is housed in the city's former prison and is based on an extensive collection of 'bygones' acquired at the beginning of the twentieth century. It was one of the first folk museums to display a huge range of everyday objects in an authentic scene. The Victorian street includes a pawnbroker, a tallow candle factory and a haberdasher's. There is even a reconstruction of the original sweet shop of the York chocolate manufacturer, Joseph Terry. An extensive collection of many other items ranging from musical instruments to costumes and a gallery of domestic gadgets from Victorian times to the 1960s (entitled 'Every home should have one') are further attractions to this remarkable museum. The museum also has one of Britain's finest collections of Militaria; this includes a superb example of an Anglo-Saxon helmet - one of only three known. A special exhibition called 'Seeing it Through' explores the life of York citizens during the Second World War. The museum includes the cell where highwayman Dick Turpin was held. Please contact the museum for details of exhibitions and events.

Times Open daily 9.30-5 **Fee** ✳ £7.50 (ch £4 under 5's free, concessions £6.50). Family tickets available **Facilities** ℗ (30mtrs) ⌑ ♿ (main galleries accessible, no access up stairs) toilets for disabled shop ⊗ (assist dogs only) ▬

York City Art Gallery   FREE

Exhibition Square YO1 7EW

(3 min walk from The Minster in city centre)

☎ 01904 687687

e-mail: www.york.trust.museum

web: www.york.trust.museum

The gallery is remarkable for the range and quality of its collections that provide a survey of most developments in Western European painting over the past six centuries. Works by Parmigianino, Bellotto, Lely, Reynolds, Frith, Boudin, Lowry and Nash and nudes by Etty are on permanent display. There are also fine collections of watercolours and pottery.

Times ✳ Open all year, daily 10-5. (Closed 25 & 26 Dec & 1 Jan). **Facilities** ℗ (500mtrs) ⌑ ⋈ (outdoor) ♿ (chair lift) toilets for disabled shop ⊗ (ex assist dogs) ▬

The York Dungeon   `2 for 1`

12 Clifford St YO1 9RD

➲ (A64/A19/A59 to city centre)

☎ 01904 632599

e-mail: yorkdungeons@merlinentertainments.biz

web: www.thedungeons.com

Deep in the heart of historic York lies the York Dungeon bringing more than 2,000 years of gruesomely authentic history vividly back to life. Be warned, in the dungeon's dark catacombs it always pays to keep your wits about you. The 'exhibits' have an unnerving habit of coming back to life. The journey includes Dick Turpin, Guy Fawkes, Witch Trials, Clifford's Tower, Pit of Despair and Jorvik - the real Viking experience. The most recent addition is the 'Labyrinth of the Lost', which explores the Roman presence in York.

Times Open Apr-Sep 10.30-5 (last admission); Nov-Jan 11-4; Oct, Feb & Mar 10.30-4.30; Etr & Summer hols 10-5.30 **Fee** ✳ £12.95 (ch £8.95, concessions £11.95) Family ticket (2ad+2ch) £40.95 **Facilities** Ⓟ (500yds) ♿ (accessible for wheelchairs, however unable to accommodate motorised wheelchairs) (wheelchair ramps, stairlifts, award winning access) toilets for disabled shop ⊗ (ex assist dogs) ▄

York Minster

Deangate YO1 7HH

➲ (easy access via A19, A1 or A64)

☎ 01904 557216

e-mail: visitors@yorkminster.org

web: www.yorkminster.org

Enjoy the peaceful atmosphere of the largest Gothic cathedral in Northern Europe, a place of worship for over 1,000 years, and a treasure house of stained glass. Take an audio tour of the Undercroft to find out more about the Minster's fascinating history and climb the Tower for amazing views.

Times Open from 7 for services. Visitors Mon-Sat 9-5 (9.30 in winter), Sun noon-3.45. Phone for details. **Fee** ✳ £5.50 (ch16 free, concessions £4.50). **Facilities** Ⓟ (440yds) ♿ (no disabled access to Undercroft or Central Tower) (tactile model, Braille & large print guide) toilets for disabled shop ⊗ (ex assist dogs) ▄

Yorkshire Museum

Museum Gardens YO1 7FR

➲ (park & ride service from 4 sites near A64/A19/ A1079 & A166, also 3 car parks within short walk)

☎ 01904 551800

e-mail: yorkshire.museum@york.gov.uk

web: www.york.gov.uk

The Yorkshire Museum is set in ten acres of botanical gardens in the heart of the historic City of York, and displays some of the finest Roman, Anglo-Saxon, Viking and Medieval treasures ever discovered in Britain. The Middleham jewel, a fine example of English Gothic jewellery, is on display, and in the Roman Gallery, visitors can see a marble head of Constantine the Great. The Anglo-Saxon Gallery houses the delicate silver-gilt Ormside bowl and the Gilling sword.

Times ✳ Open all year, daily 10-5. **Facilities** Ⓟ (5 mins walk) ♿ (ramps & lift) toilets for disabled shop ⊗ ▄

SOUTH YORKSHIRE

'Needle's Eye' folly, Wentworth Woodhouse

BARNSLEY　　　　　　　　MAP 08 SE30

Monk Bretton Priory

S71 5QD

➲ (1m E of town centre, off A633)

web: www.english-heritage.org.uk

The priory was an important Cluniac house, founded in 1153. The considerable remains of the gatehouse, church and other buildings can be seen.

Times Open all year, 21 Mar-Sep, daily 10-6; Oct, daily 10-5; Nov-Mar, daily 10-4. (Managed by a keykeeper). Closed 24-26 Dec & 1 Jan. **Fee** Charge may apply on event days **Facilities** ♿ ♿

CONISBROUGH　　　　　　MAP 08 SK59

Conisbrough Castle

DN12 3HH

➲ (NE of town centre off A630)

☎ 01709 863329

web: www.english-heritage.org.uk

The white, circular keep of this 12th-century castle is a spectacular structure. Made of magnesian limestone, it is the oldest of its kind in England. Recently restored, with two new floors and a roof, it is a fine example of medieval architecture and was the inspiration for Sir Walter Scott's classic novel *Ivanhoe*.

Times Open all year, 21 Mar-Sep, daily 10-5 (last admission 4.20); Oct-Mar, Thu-Mon 10-4 (last admission 3.20). Closed 24-26 Dec & 1 Jan. **Fee** £4 (concessions £3, ch £2). Family ticket £10. Prices and opening times are subject to change in March 2009. Please check web site or call 0870 333 1181 for the most up to date prices and opening times when planning your visit. **Facilities** ♿ ♿ ♿ (wheelchair access limited) shop ⊗

CUSWORTH　　　　　　　MAP 08 SE50

Cusworth Hall, Museum and Park Hall　FREE

Cusworth Ln DN5 7TU

➲ (3m NW of Doncaster off A638. Signed)

☎ 01302 782342

e-mail: museum@doncaster.gov.uk

web: www.doncaster.gov.uk

Cusworth Hall is an 18th-century country house set in a landscaped park. It has displays which illustrate the way local people here lived, worked and entertained themselves over the last 200 years. The Hall and Park have recently reopened following extensive refurbishment, giving visitors access to the magnificent Chapel and Great Kitchen. The Park features a pleasure grounds, 18th-century lake system, lawns and woodland. The Tea Room is noted for its homemade food.

Times Open Mon-Fri 10.30-5, Sat-Sun 1-5. Park open 24hrs. **Facilities** ♿ (charged) ♿ ♿ (wheelchair available) toilets for disabled shop ⊗ (ex assist dogs)

DONCASTER　　　　　　　MAP 08 SE50

Brodsworth Hall & Gardens

Brodsworth DN5 7XJ

➲ (between A635 & A638)

☎ 01302 722598

web: www.english-heritage.org.uk

This Victorian country house has survived largely intact. See how the serving classes fared below stairs, then experience, in contrast, the opulent 'upstairs' apartments. Outside, visitors can enjoy a leisurely stroll around the extensive newly restored gardens.

Times House: open 21 Mar-Sep, Tue-Sun & BHs, 1-5; Oct, Sat-Sun 12-4. Gardens: open 21 Mar-Oct, daily 10-5.30; Nov-Mar, Sat-Sun 10-4. (including Servant's Wing). (Last admission half an hour before closing). Closed 24-26 & 1 Jan. **Fee** ✱ House & Gardens £8.50 (concessions £6.80, ch £4.30). Gardens only £5 (concessions £4, ch £2.50). Prices and opening times are subject to change in March 2009. Please check web site or call 0870 333 1181 for the most up to date prices and opening times when planning your visit. **Facilities** ♿ ♿ shop ⊗ ♿ ═

Doncaster Museum & Art Gallery　FREE

Chequer Rd DN1 2AE

➲ (off inner ring road)

☎ 01302 734293

e-mail: museum@doncaster.gov.uk

web: www.doncaster.gov.uk/museums

The wide-ranging collections include fine and decorative art and sculpture. Also ceramics, glass, silver, and displays on history, archaeology and natural history. The historical collection of the Kings Own Yorkshire Light Infantry is housed here. A recent addition is the 'By River and Road' gallery, which details the history of the Doncaster area. Temporary exhibitions are held.

Times Open all year, Mon-Sat 10-5, Sun 2-5. (Closed Good Fri, 25-26 Dec & 1 Jan). **Facilities** ♿ ♿ (lift, hearing loop in lecture room) toilets for disabled shop ⊗ (ex assist dogs)

MALTBY　　　　　　　　　MAP 08 SK59

Roche Abbey

S66 8NW

➲ (1.5m S off A634)

☎ 01709 812739

web: www.english-heritage.org.uk

Visit the enchanting valley designed by 'Capability' Brown and discover the fascinating ruins of Roche Abbey, founded in 1147 by the Cistercians.

Times Open 21 Mar-Jul & Sep, Thu-Sun 11-4; Aug, daily 11-4. **Fee** £3 (concessions £2.40, ch £1.50). Prices and opening times are subject to change in March 2009. Please check web site or call 0870 333 1181 for the most up to date prices and opening times when planning your visit. **Facilities** ♿ shop ♿

ENGLAND

Magna Science Adventure Centre 2 for 1

Sheffield Rd, Templeborough S60 1DX

➲ *(M1 junct 33/34, follow Templeborough sign off rdbt, then brown heritage signs)*

☎ 01709 720002

e-mail: ebodley@magnatrust.co.uk

web: www.visitmagna.co.uk

Magna is the UK's first Science Adventure Centre, an exciting exploration of Earth, Air, Fire and Water. A chance for visitors to create their own adventure through hands-on interactive challenges. Visit the four Adventure Pavilions, live show and outdoor playgrounds Sci-Tek and Aqua-Tek.

Times Open all year, daily (ex some Mons), 10-5 **Fee** ✳ £9.95 (ch & concessions £7.95). Family ticket (2ad+1ch) £25 **Facilities** ❷ ⌷ ⯑ ☕ 🗙 (outdoor) ♿ (lifts, portable seating, wheelchair hire) toilets for disabled shop ⊗ (ex assist dogs) ⬛

Kelham Island Museum

Alma St S3 8RY

➲ *(0.5m NW of city centre, take A61 N to West Bar, follow signs)*

☎ 0114 272 2106

e-mail: postmaster@simt.co.uk

web: www.simt.co.uk

The story of Sheffield, its industry and life, with the most powerful working steam engine in Europe, reconstructed workshops, and craftspeople demonstrating traditional 'made in Sheffield' skills - this is a 'living' museum. During the year Kelham Island stages events, displays and temporary exhibitions culminating in the annual Christmas Victorian Market.

Times ✳ Open Mon-Thu 10-4, Sun 11-4.45. Closed Fri & Sat. Check opening days & times at Xmas & New Year before travelling. **Facilities** ❷ ⌷ ♿ (wheelchair on request) toilets for disabled shop ⊗

Millennium Gallery

Arundel Gate S1 2PP

➲ *(Follow signs to city centre, then follow the brown signs marked M).*

☎ 0114 278 2600

e-mail: info@museums-sheffield.org.uk

web: www.museums-sheffield.org.uk

With four different galleries under one roof, the Millennium Galleries has something for everyone. Enjoy new blockbuster exhibitions drawn from the collections of Britain's national galleries and museums, including the Victoria & Albert Museum and Tate Gallery. See the best of contemporary craft and design in a range of exhibitions by established and up-and-coming makers. There is also a magnificent and internationally important collection of decorative and domestic metalwork and silverware. Discover the Ruskin Gallery with its wonderful array of treasures by Victorian artist and writer John Ruskin.

Times Open daily Mon-Sat 10-5, Sun 11-5. **Fee** Special Exhibitions: £6 (ch 5-16 £2, concessions £1) **Facilities** ❷ (250m) ⌷ ☕ ♿ (hearing loop) toilets for disabled shop ⊗ (ex assist dogs) ⬛

WEST YORKSHIRE

Chevin ridge on the south side of Wharfedale, with a view of Otley

BRADFORD   MAP 07 SE13

Bolling Hall   `FREE`

Bowling Hall Rd BD4 7LP

⮑ *(1m from city centre off A650)*

☎ 01274 431826

web: www.bradfordmuseums.org

A classic West Yorkshire manor house, complete with galleried `housebody' (hall), Bolling Hall dates mainly from the 17th century but has medieval and 18th-century sections. It has panelled rooms, plasterwork in original colours, heraldic glass and a rare Chippendale bed.

Times Open all year, Wed-Fri 11-4, Sat 10-5, Sun 12-5. Closed Mon ex BH, Good Fri, 25-26 Dec. **Facilities** ℗ shop ⊗ (ex assist dogs)

Bradford Industrial Museum   `FREE`
and Horses at Work

Moorside Mills, Moorside Rd, Eccleshill BD2 3HP

⮑ *(off A658)*

☎ 01274 435900

web: www.bradfordmuseums.org

Moorside Mills is an original spinning mill, now part of a museum that brings vividly to life the story of Bradford's woollen industry. There is the machinery that once converted raw wool into cloth, and the mill yard rings with the sound of iron on stone as shire horses pull trams, haul buses and give rides. Daily demonstrations and changing exhibitions.

Times Open all year, Tue-Sat 10-5, Sun 12-5. Closed Mon ex BH, Good Fri & 25-26 Dec **Facilities** ℗ ⌗ ⬥ (induction loop in lecture theatre, lift) toilets for disabled shop ⊗ (ex assist dogs)

Cartwright Hall Art Gallery   `FREE`

Lister Park BD9 4NS

⮑ *(1m from city centre on A650)*

☎ 01274 431212

e-mail: cartwright.hall@bradford.gov.uk

web: www.bradfordmuseums.org

Built in dramatic Baroque style in 1904, the gallery has permanent collections of 19th and 20th-century British art, contemporary prints, and older works by British and European masters.

Times Open all year, Tue-Sat 10-5, Sun 1-5. Closed Mon ex BH, Good Fri & 25-26 Dec. **Facilities** ℗ ⬥ (wheelchair available, lift) toilets for disabled shop ⊗ (ex assist dogs)

The Colour Museum

Perkin House, 1 Providence St BD1 2PW

⮑ *(from city centre follow signs B6144 (Haworth), then brown heritage signs)*

☎ 01274 390955

e-mail: museum@sdc.org.uk

web: www.colour-experience.org

Europe's only Museum of Colour comprises two galleries packed with visitor-operated exhibits demonstrating the effects of light and colour,

including optical illusions, and the story of dyeing and textile printing. There is a programme of special exhibitions and events. Please telephone for details.

Times ✳ Open 2 Jan-18 Dec, Tue-Sat, 10-4. **Facilities** ℗ (200 yds) ⬥ (lifts, ramps at door) toilets for disabled shop ⊗ (ex assist dogs) ⬛

National Media Museum

Pictureville BD1 1NQ

⮑ *(2m from end of M606, follow signs for city centre)*

☎ 01274 202030

e-mail: talk@nationalmediamuseum.org.uk

web: www.nationalmediamuseum.org.uk

Journey through popular photography and visit IMAX - the world's powerful giant screen experience, discover the past, present and future of television in Experience TV, watch your favourite TV moments in TV Heaven, play with light, lenses and colour in the Magic Factory and explore the world of animation - watch a real animator at work in the Animation Gallery. There are also temporary exhibitions and various special events are planned, please see the website for details.

Times Open all year, Tue-Sun 10-6, BH Mon & school hols. Closed 24-26 Dec. **Fee** ✳ Admission to permanent galleries free, IMAX Cinema £6.95 (concessions £4.95). DMR (Feature length films) £8 (£6 concesssions). Groups 20% discount. **Facilities** ℗ (charged) ⌗⍥⎚ (Indoor) ⬥ (tailored tours,Braille signs,induction loop,cinema seating) toilets for disabled shop ⊗ (ex assist dogs) ⬛

BRAMHAM   MAP 08 SE44

Bramham Park

LS23 6ND

⮑ *(on A1, 4m S of Wetherby, take Bramham/Thorner slip road and follow signs)*

☎ 01937 846000

e-mail: enquiries@bramhampark.co.uk

web: www.bramhampark.co.uk

This fine Queen Anne house was built by Robert Benson and is the home of his descendants. The garden has ornamental ponds, cascades, temples and avenues. The landscape is a unique example of early 18th century design, remaining virtually unchanged. The Bramham International Horse Trials take place here on the second weekend in June, and the Leeds Rock Festival on August bank holiday weekend.

Times ✳ Open Apr-Sep, daily 11.30-4.30. Closed 7-14 Jun & 16 Aug-4 Sep **Facilities** ℗ ⬥ (Partly accessible) toilets for disabled

GOMERSAL   MAP 08 SE22

Red House   `FREE`

Oxford Rd BD19 4JP

⮑ *(M62 junct 26, take A58 towards Leeds then right onto A651 towards Gomersal. Red House on right)*

☎ 01274 335100

web: www.kirkleesmc.gov.uk/community/museums/museums.asp

Delightful redbrick house displayed as the 1830s home of a Yorkshire wool clothier and merchant. The house and family was frequently visited by Charlotte Brontë in the 1830s and featured in her novel *Shirley*. The gardens have been reconstructed in the style of the period and there are exhibitions on the Brontë connection and local history in restored barn and cartsheds.

Times ✳ Open all year, Mon-Fri 11-5, Sat-Sun 12-5. Telephone for Xmas opening. Closed Good Fri & 1 Jan. **Facilities** 🅿 & (Braille & T-setting hearing aid available) toilets for disabled shop ⊗ (ex assist dogs) ▬

HALIFAX   MAP 07 SE02

Bankfield Museum   `FREE`

Boothtown Rd, Akroyd Park HX3 6HG

➲ *(on A647 Bradford via Queensbury road, 0.5m from Halifax town centre)*

☎ 01422 354823 & 352334

e-mail: bankfield-museum@calderdale.gov.uk

web: www.calderdale.gov.uk

Built by Edward Akroyd in the 1860s, this Renaissance-style building is set in parkland on a hill overlooking the town. It has an outstanding collection of costumes and textiles from many periods and parts of the world, including a new gallery featuring East European textiles. There is also a section on toys, and the museum of the Duke of Wellington's Regiment is housed here. Temporary exhibitions are held and there is a lively programme of events, workshops and activities. Please ring for details.

Times Open all year, Tue-Sat 10-5, Sun 1-4, BH Mon 10-5. **Facilities** 🅿 & (Partly accessible) (audio guide & tactile objects) toilets for disabled shop ⊗ (ex assist dogs) ▬

Eureka! The Museum for Children   `2 for 1`

Discovery Rd HX1 2NE

➲ *(M62 junct 24 follow brown heritage signs to Halifax centre - A629)*

☎ 01422 330069

e-mail: info@eureka.org.uk

web: www.eureka.org.uk

With over 400 'must touch' exhibits, interactive activities and challenges, visitors are invited to embark upon a journey of discovery through six main gallery spaces. They can find out how their bodies and senses work, discover the realities of daily life, travel from the familiar 'backyard' to amazing and faraway places and experiment with creating their own sounds and music.

Times Open all year, daily 10-5. Closed 24-26 Dec **Fee** ✳ £7.25 (ch 1-2 £2.25, ch under 1 free) Family Saver ticket £31. Special group rates available. **Facilities** 🅿 (charged) ⬚ 🅰 (indoor & outdoor) & (lift, staff trained in basic sign language, large print) toilets for disabled shop ⊗ (ex assist dogs) ▬

Halifax Visitor Centre and Art Gallery   `FREE`

HX1 1RE

➲ *(follow brown tourist signs, close to railway station)*

☎ 01422 368725

e-mail: halifax@ytbtic.co.uk

web: www.calderdale.gov.uk

The merchants of Halifax built the elegant and unique hall in 1770, and it has over 300 merchant's rooms around a courtyard, now housing an art gallery and visitor centre. There are around eight temporary exhibitions each year.

Times Open all year, daily 10-5. (Closed 1 Jan & 25-26 Dec). **Facilities** 🅿 (50 yds) 🅰 (outdoor) & (lifts, shopmobility on site & audio guide available) toilets for disabled shop ⊗ (ex assist dogs) ▬

Shibden Hall

Lister's Rd HX3 6XG

➲ *(2km E of Halifax on A58)*

☎ 01422 352246 & 321455

e-mail: shibden.hall@calderdale.gov.uk

web: www.calderdale.gov.uk

The house dates back to the early 15th century, and its rooms have been laid out to illustrate life in different periods of its history. Craft weekends, featuring over 30 craftworkers demonstrating historic skills, are held, and there's a lively programme of craft events, workshops and family activities. Please apply for details.

Times Open Mar-Nov, Mon-Sat 10-5, Sun 12-5. Dec-Feb, Mon-Sat 10-4, Sun 12-4. **Fee** £3.50 (ch & concessions £2.50) Family ticket £10. **Facilities** 🅿 ⬚ 🅰 (outdoor) & (garden only partially accessible) toilets for disabled shop ⊗ (ex assist dogs) ▬

HAREWOOD   MAP 08 SE34

Harewood House & Bird Garden   `2 for 1`

LS17 9LG

➲ *(junct A61/A659 Leeds to Harrogate road)*

☎ 0113 218 1010

e-mail: info@harewood.org

web: www.harewood.org

Designed in 1759 by John Carr, Harewood House is home to the Queen's cousin, the Earl of Harewood. His mother, HRH Princess Mary, Princess Royal lived at Harewood for 35 years and much of her memorabilia is still displayed. The House, renowned for its stunning architecture and exquisite Adam interiors, contains a rich collection of Chippendale furniture, fine porcelain and outstanding art collections from Italian Renaissance masterpieces and Turner watercolours to contemporary works. The old kitchen contains the best collection of noble household copperware in the country giving visitors a glimpse

CONTINUED

HAREWOOD CONTINUED

into below stairs life. The grounds include a restored parterre terrace, oriental rock garden, Himalayan Garden with Buddist Stupa, walled garden, lakeside and woodland walks, a bird garden and for youngsters, an adventure playground. The new Himalayan Garden will be officially opened in May 2009.

Times Open wknds from 13 Feb (grounds only). Full opening 3 Apr 11-4.30. **Fee** ✳ With Gift Aid donation: 28 Jun-7 Sep plus all BH wknds, £13.50 (ch/student £8.50, pen £12.20) Family (2ad+3ch) £46.50. Without Gift Aid donation: £12 (ch/student £7.70, pen £11) Family (2ad+3ch) £42. Prices will change in the lower season. **Facilities** Ⓟ ☕ ⛩ (outdoor) ♿ (the house is fully accessible. The grounds are on a natural slope with some gravel paths) (electric ramp, wheelchair lift) toilets for disabled shop ⊗ (ex assist dogs or in gardens) ▬

HAWORTH MAP 07 SE03

Brontë Parsonage Museum

BD22 8DR

➲ *(A629 & A6033 follow signs for Haworth, take Rawdon Rd, pass 2 car parks, next left, then right)*

☎ 01535 642323

e-mail: bronte@bronte.org.uk

web: www.bronte.info

Haworth Parsonage was the lifelong family home of the Brontës. An intensely close-knit family, the Brontës saw the parsonage as the heart of their world and the moorland setting provided them with inspiration for their writing. The house contains much personal memorabilia, including the furniture Charlotte bought with the proceeds of her literary success, Branwell's portraits of local worthies, Emily's writing desk and Anne's books and drawings.

Times Open Apr-Sep, daily 10-5.30; Oct-Mar daily 11-5 (final admission 30 min before closing). Closed 24-27 Dec & 2-31 Jan. **Facilities** Ⓟ (charged) ♿ (Partly accessible) (Info in large type & Braille, loop induction system) shop ⊗ (ex assist dogs) ▬

Keighley & Worth Valley Railway & Museum

Keighley BD22 8NJ

➲ *(1m from Keighley on A629 Halifax road, follow brown signs)*

☎ 01535 645214 & 677777

e-mail: admin@kwvr.co.uk

web: www.kwvr.co.uk

The line was built mainly to serve the valley's mills, and passes through the heart of Brontë country. Beginning at Keighley (shared with Network Rail), it climbs up to Haworth, and terminates at Oxenhope, which has a storage and restoration building. At Haworth there are locomotive workshops and at Ingrow West, an award-winning museum. Events take place throughout the year, please telephone for details.

Times Open every wknd, please phone for other times. **Fee** ✳ All day fares: Family Day Rover £27, Adult Day Rover £12 (ch 5-15 £6 under 5's free, pen concessionary). Single and day returns, group rates available, phone for details. **Facilities** Ⓟ (charged) ☕ ⛩ (outdoor) ♿ (Partly accessible) (level access to all sites, ramps on trains and stations) toilets for disabled shop ▬

HUDDERSFIELD MAP 07 SE11

Tolson Memorial Museum FREE

Ravensknowle Park, Wakefield Rd HD5 8DJ

➲ *(on A629, 1m from town centre)*

☎ 01484 223830

e-mail: tolson.museum@kirkdees.gov.uk

web: tolson.museum.co.uk

Displays on the development of the cloth industry and a collection of horse-drawn vehicles, together with natural history, archaeology, toys and folk exhibits. There is a full programme of events and temporary exhibitions.

Times ✳ Open all year. Mon-Fri 11-5, Sat & Sun noon-5. Closed Xmas. **Facilities** Ⓟ ♿ (mini-com, partial stairlift, induction loop, parking) toilets for disabled shop ⊗ (ex assist dogs) ▬

ILKLEY MAP 07 SE14

Manor House Gallery & Museum FREE

Castle Yard, Church St LS29 9DT

➲ *(behind Ilkley Parish Church, on A65)*

☎ 01943 600066

web: www.bradfordmuseums.org

This Elizabethan manor house, one of Ilkley's few buildings to pre-date the 19th century, was built on the site of a Roman fort. Part of the Roman wall can be seen, together with Roman objects and displays on archaeology. There is a collection of 17th and 18th-century farmhouse parlour and kitchen furniture, and the art gallery exhibits works by contemporary artists and craftspeople.

Times Open all year, Tue-Sat 1-5, Sun 1-4. Open BH Mon. Closed Good Fri, 25-28 Dec. **Facilities** ℗ (5mins) ♿ shop ⊗ (ex assist dogs)

KEIGHLEY MAP 07 SE04

Cliffe Castle Museum & Gallery FREE

Spring Gardens Ln BD20 6LH

➲ *(NW of town off A629)*

☎ 01535 618230

web: www.bradfordmuseums.org

Built as a millionaire's mansion, the house displays Victorian interiors, together with collections of local and natural history, ceramics, dolls, geological items and minerals. There is a play area and aviary in the grounds. Temporary exhibitions throughout the year.

Times Open all year, Tue-Sat 10-5, Sun 12-5. Open BH Mon. Closed Good Fri & 25-28 Dec. **Facilities** Ⓟ ☕ ⛩ (outdoor) ♿ (upstairs galleries hard to access by disabled users) (access trail, brining the exhibition to life downstairs) toilets for disabled shop garden centre ⊗ (ex assist dogs)

East Riddlesden Hall

Bradford Rd BD20 5EL

➲ *(1m NE of Keighley on S side of Bradford Rd)*

☎ 01535 607075

e-mail: eastriddlesden@nationaltrust.org.uk

web: www.nationaltrust.org.uk

The interior of this 17th-century manor house is furnished with textiles, Yorkshire oak and pewter, together with fine examples of 17th-century embroidery. The honeysuckle and rose covered façade ruin of the Starke Wing, provides the backdrop to the garden. Wild flowers, perennials, and a fragrant herb border provide a transition of colour throughout the year.

Times Open 15 Mar-2 Nov daily (ex Mon, Thu & Fri). Open Good Fri, BH Mons and Mons in Jul & Aug 12-5 **Fee** ✻ £5 (ch £2.50) Family ticket £11 **Facilities** Ⓟ ☕ ⛩ (outdoor) ♿ (Partly accessible) (Braille and large print guides, sensory photo album) shop ⊗ ✿ ▬

LEEDS MAP 08 SE33

Abbey House Museum

Abbey Walk, Abbey Rd, Kirkstall LS5 3EH

➲ *(3m W of city centre on A65)*

☎ 0113 230 5492

e-mail: abbey.house@leeds.gov.uk

web: www.leeds.gov.uk

Displays at this museum include an interactive childhood gallery, a look at Kirkstall Abbey, and an exploration of life in Victorian Leeds. Three reconstructed streets allow the visitor to immerse themselves in the sights and sounds of the late 19th century, from the glamourous art furnishers shop to the impoverished widow washerwoman.

Times ✻ Open all year Tue-Fri 10-5, Sat noon-5, Sun 10-5. Closed Mon ex BH Mon (open 10-5) **Facilities** Ⓟ ☕ 🍽 ⛩ (outdoor) ♿ (Braille plaques on wall, tactile tours by request) toilets for disabled shop ⊗ (ex assist dogs) ▬

Kirkstall Abbey

FREE

Abbey Rd, Kirkstall LS5 3EH

➲ *(off A65, W of city centre)*

☎ 0113 274 8041

e-mail: kirkstall.abbey@leeds.gov.uk

web: www.leeds.gov.uk

The most complete 12th-century Cistercian Abbey in the country stands on the banks of the River Aire. Many of the original buildings can still be seen, including the cloister, church and refectory. Regular tours take visitors to areas not normally accessible to the public. During the summer the Abbey hosts plays, fairs and musical events. A new visitor centre gives an insight into the history of the Abbey and a true sense of how the monks lived in the 15th century.

Times Abbey site open dawn to dusk. Visitor centre open: Tue-Thu 10-4, Sat-Sun 10-4. Open BH's. **Facilities** Ⓟ ⛩ (outdoor) ♿ toilets for disabled shop

Leeds Art Gallery

FREE

The Headrow LS1 3AA

➲ *(in city centre, next to town hall and library)*

☎ 0113 247 8256

e-mail: city.art.gallery@leeds.gov.uk

web: www.leeds.gov.uk/artgallery

Leeds Art Gallery has something to offer everyone. Home to one of the best collections of 20th-century British art outside London, as well as Victorian and late 19th-century pictures, an outstanding collection of English watercolours, a display of modern sculpture and temporary exhibitions focusing on contemporary art. The gallery holds an active events programme with talks, demonstrations and workshops regularly planned. Wander through the newly-opened Victorian Tiled Hall to access Leeds Central Library.

Times Open all year, Mon-Tue 10-8, Wed 12-8, Thu-Sat 10-5, Sun 1-5. Closed BHs. **Facilities** Ⓟ (walking distance) Meter parking, car parks. ☕ 🍽 licensed ♿ (restricted access to upper floor) (access ramp) toilets for disabled shop ⊗ (ex assist dogs) ▬

Leeds Industrial Museum at Armley Mills

Canal Rd, Armley LS12 2QF

➲ *(2m W of city centre, off A65)*

☎ 0113 263 7861

web: www.leeds.gov.uk/armleymills

Once the world's largest woollen mill, Armley Mills evokes memories of the 18th-century woollen industry, showing the progress of wool from the sheep to knitted clothing. The museum has its own 1930s cinema illustrating the history of cinema projection, including the first moving pictures taken in Leeds. The Museum is set in some lovely scenery, between the Leeds & Liverpool Canal and the River Aire. There are demonstrations of static engines and steam locomotives, a printing gallery and a journey through the working world of textiles and fashion.

Times Open all year, Tue-Sat 10-5, Sun 1-5. Last entry 4pm. Closed Mon ex BHs. **Fee** £3 (ch £1, concessions £1.50). Family ticket (2ad+2ch) £5. **Facilities** Ⓟ ⛩ (indoor & outdoor) ♿ (Partly accessible) (chair-lifts between floors) toilets for disabled shop ⊗ (ex assist dogs) ▬

Middleton Railway

Moor Rd, Hunslet LS10 2JQ

➲ *(M621 junct 5 or follow signs from A61)*

☎ 0113 271 0320 (ansaphone)

e-mail: info@middletonrailway.org.uk

web: www.middletonrailway.org.uk

This was the first railway authorised by an Act of Parliament (in 1758) and the first to succeed with steam locomotives (in 1812). Steam trains run each weekend in season from Tunstall Road roundabout to Middleton Park. There is a programme of special events.

Times Open Etr-end Nov, Diesel Sat 1-4.20. Heritage & Steam Sun & BH Mon 11-4.20. Both at 40min intervals. Santa specials Sat & Sun in Dec. **Fee** ✻ £4.50 (ch £2.50) unlimited travel on day. Family ticket (2ad+3ch) £12. **Facilities** Ⓟ ☕ ♿ (ramped access to all areas, disabled parking) toilets for disabled shop ▬

LEEDS CONTINUED

Royal Armouries Museum

`FREE`

Armouries Dr LS10 1LT

➲ (off A61 close to Leeds centre, follow brown heritage signs.)

☎ 0113 220 1999 & 0990 106 666

e-mail: enquiries@armouries.org.uk

web: www.royalarmouries.org

The museum is an impressive contemporary home for the renowned national collection of arms and armour. The collection is divided between five galleries: War, Tournament, Self-Defence, Hunting and Oriental. The Hall of Steel features a 100ft-high mass of 3,000 pieces of arms and armour. Visitors are encouraged to take part in and handle some of the collections. Live demonstrations and interpretations take place throughout the year.

Times ✴ Open daily, from 10-5. Closed 24-25 Dec **Facilities** 🅿 (charged) ⏛ ⦿ ⼌ (indoor) ⟐ (induction loops, wheelchairs, signers, low level counter) toilets for disabled shop ⊗ (ex assist dogs) ▬

Thackray Museum

Temple Newsam Estate

Temple Newsam Rd, Off Selby Rd, Halton LS15 0AE

➲ (4m from city centre on A63 or 2m from M1 junct)

☎ 0113 264 7321 (House) & 5535 (Estate)

e-mail: temple.newsam.house@leeds.gov.uk

web: www.leeds.gov.uk/templenewsam

Temple Newsam is celebrated as one of the country's great historic houses and estates. Set in 1,500 acres of stunning parkland, Temple Newsam House is home to outstanding collections of fine and decorative art, many desigriated as being of national importance. The Estate includes a working rare breeds farm and national plant collections.

Times Open all year. House: Tue-Sun 10.30-5, Nov-28 Dec & Mar, Tue-Sat 10.30-4. Open BHs. Home Farm: Tue-Sun, 10-5 (4 in winter); Gardens: 10-dusk. Estate: daily, dawn-dusk. **Fee** ✴ House: £3.50 (ch £2.50) Family £9. Farm: £3 (ch £2) Family £8. Joint ticket: £5.50 (ch £3.50) Family £14. **Facilities** 🅿 (charged) ⏛ ⼌ (indoor & outdoor) ⟐ (ramps for full access to parkland, electric wheelchairs) toilets for disabled shop ⊗ (ex assist dogs) ▬

Thackray Museum

Beckett St LS9 7LN

➲ (M1 junct 43, onto M621 junct 4. Follow signs for York & St James Hospital, then brown tourist signs)

☎ 0113 244 4343

e-mail: info@thackraymuseum.org

web: www.thackraymuseum.org

Your visit transports you into the world of health and medicine - past, present and future. Experience life in the Victorian slums of 1840 and be flabbergasted at the incredible lotions and potions once offered as cures for your ills. See how surgery was performed without the aid of anaesthetics, experience pregnancy by trying on an empathy belly, and step inside the human body in the interactive Life Zone.

Times Open all year, daily 10-5. Closed 24-26 & 31 Dec & 1 Jan **Fee** ✴ £5.50 (ch 4-16 £4, concessions £4.50). Family ticket (2ad+3ch) £18. Group rates available. **Facilities** 🅿 (charged) ⏛ ⼌ (indoor) ⟐ (wheelchairs, induction loop, large texts) toilets for disabled shop ⊗ (ex assist dogs) ▬

Tropical World

Roundhay Park LS8 2ER

➲ (3m N of city centre off A58 at Oakwood, also accessible from A610)

☎ 0113 214 5715

e-mail: parks@leeds.gov.uk

web: www.leeds.gov.uk

The atmosphere of the tropics is recreated here as visitors arrive on the beach and walk through the depths of the swamp into the rainforest. A waterfall cascades into a rock-pool and other pools contain terrapins and carp. There are reptiles, insects, meerkats and more than 30 species of butterfly. Feel the dry heat of the desert and the darkness of the nocturnal zone, and watch out for the piranhas and other exotic fish in the depths of the aquarium.

Times Open Winter daily 10-4 (last admission 3.30); Summer 10-6 (last admission 5.30). Closed 25-26 Dec. **Fee** ✴ £3 (ch 8-15 £2, under 8's, Leedscard & Breezecard holders free) **Facilities** 🅿 ⏛ ⼌ toilets for disabled shop ⊗ (ex assist dogs) ▬

LOTHERTON HALL   MAP 08 SE43

Lotherton Hall

Aberford LS25 3EB

➲ (off the A1, 0.75m E of junct with B1217)

☎ 0113 281 3259 (house) & 264 5535 (estate)

e-mail: lotherton@leeds.gov.uk

web: www.leeds.gov.uk/lothertonhall

Lotherton Hall is a beautiful, Edwardian country house. It is home to a treasure trove of arts and crafts, housing collections of painting, silver, ceramics and costume. The hall is set within an estate with formal gardens and a red deer park. It includes an adventure playground and large bird garden. 2009 is the 45th Anniversary of the hall bequest to Leeds City Council and will involve a year long celebration of special events. Please see the website for details.

ENGLAND

Times Hall: Mar-Dec Tue-Sat 10-5, Sun 1-5 (last admission 45 mins before closing).Estate: 8-8, Bird gardens: 10-5, open BH's **Fee** ✳ £3 (ch £1, concessions £1.50). Grounds & Bird Garden free. Leeds card 20% discount. **Facilities** ❷ (charged) ⬚ ⑩ ☐ (outdoor) ♿ (access limited to ground floor of hall only) (Scooters available) toilets for disabled shop ⦸ (ex in park) ▰

MIDDLESTOWN — MAP 08 SE21

National Coal Mining Museum for England   FREE

Caphouse Colliery, New Rd WF4 4RH

➲ *(on A642 between Huddersfield & Wakefield)*

☎ 01924 848806

e-mail: info@ncm.org.uk

web: www.ncm.org.uk

A unique opportunity to go 140 metres underground down one of Britain's oldest working mines. Take a step back in time with one of the museum's experienced local miners who will guide parties around the underground workings, where models and machinery depict methods and conditions of mining from the early 1800s to present day. Other attractions include the Hope Pit, pithead baths, Victorian steam winder, nature trail and adventure playground and meet the last ever working pit ponies. You are strongly advised to wear sensible footwear and warm clothing. 2009 is the 21st anniversary of the museum.

Times Open all year, daily 10-5. Closed 24-26 Dec & 1 Jan. **Facilities** ❷ ⬚ ⑩ licensed ☐ (outdoor) ♿ (induction loop, audio tours, 2 w'chairs for underground) toilets for disabled shop ⦸ (ex assist dogs) ▰

NOSTELL PRIORY — MAP 08 SE41

Nostell Priory & Parkland

Doncaster Rd WF4 1QE

➲ *(5m SE of Wakefield towards Doncaster, on A638)*

☎ 01924 863892

e-mail: nostellpriory@nationaltrust.org.uk

web: www.nationaltrust.org.uk/nostellpriory/

Built by James Paine in the middle of the 18th century, the priory has an additional wing built by Robert Adam in 1766. It contains a notable saloon and tapestry room, and displays pictures and Chippendale furniture. There are lakeside walks within the grounds with rhododendrons and azaleas in bloom in late spring.

Times ✳ 15 Mar-2 Nov, Wed-Sun 1-5; 6-14 Dec daily 12-4. Grounds 15 Mar-2 Nov, Wed-Sun 11-5.30; 6-14 Dec daily 11-4.30. Parkland, daily 9-5 **Fee** ✳ £7.70 (ch £3.85). Family £18.50. Gardens only £5 (ch £2.50) **Facilities** ❷ ⬚ ☐ (outdoor) ♿ (Partly accessible) (Braille guide/tactile books, wheelchair) toilets for disabled shop ⦸ (ex on lead) ▰▰ ▰

OAKWELL HALL — MAP 08 SE22

Oakwell Hall

Nutter Ln, Birstall WF17 9LG

➲ *(6m SE of Bradford, off M62 junct 26/27, follow brown heritage signs, turn off A652 onto Nutter Lane)*

☎ 01924 326240

e-mail: oakwell.hall@kirklees.gov.uk

web: www.oakwellhallcountrypark.co.uk

A moated Elizabethan manor house, furnished as it might have looked in the 1690s. Extensive 110-acre country park with visitor information centre, period gardens, nature trails, arboretum and children's playground.

Times Open all year, daily Mon-Fri 11-5; Sat & Sun 12-5. Closed Good Fri & 24 Dec-1 Jan. **Fee** ✳ Hall £1.60 (ch & wheelchair users 70p). Family ticket £4. Charges Mar-Oct. Free admission Nov-Feb. Visitor centre & park free all year. **Facilities** ❷ ⬚ ☐ (outdoor) ♿ (gardens, ground floor of hall, visitor centre) (large print & Braille guide, induction loops) toilets for disabled shop ⦸ (ex assist dogs & in park) ▰

WEST BRETTON — MAP 08 SE21

Yorkshire Sculpture Park

WF4 4LG

➲ *(M1 junct 38, follow brown heritage signs to A637. Left at rdbt, attraction signed)*

☎ 01924 832631

e-mail: info@ysp.co.uk

web: www.ysp.co.uk

Set in the beautiful grounds and gardens of a 500 acre, 18th-century country estate, Yorkshire Sculpture Park is one of the world's leading open-air galleries and presents a changing programme of international sculpture exhibitions. The landscape provides a variety of magnificent scenic vistas of the valley, lakes, estate buildings and bridges. By organising a number of temporary exhibitions each year, the park ensures that there is always something new to see. The Visitor Centre provides all-weather facilities including a large restaurant, shop, coffee bar, audio-visual auditorium and meeting rooms.

Times ✳ Open all year 10-6 (summer) 10-5 (winter). Please phone for details of Xmas closures **Facilities** ❷ (charged) ⬚ ⑩ ☐ (outdoor) ♿ (free scooters, parking, trail accessible for wheelchairs) toilets for disabled shop ⦸ (ex assist dogs & outdoors)

GUERNSEY

St Peter Port

FOREST MAP 16

German Occupation Museum

GY8 0BG

➲ *(Behind Forest Church near the airport)*

☎ 01481 238205

The museum has the Channel Islands' largest collection of Occupation items, with tableaux of a kitchen, bunker rooms and a street during the Occupation. Liberation Day 9th May will be celebrated with special events and exhibitions.

Times Open Apr-Oct 10-4.30; Nov-Mar 10-12.30 (Closed Mon Nov-Mar) **Fee** £4 (ch £2). Free admission for disabled. **Facilities** Ⓟ ☕ ⛩ (outdoor) ♿ (Steps to street level alternative route available) (ramps & handrails) ⊗ (ex assist dogs)

ROCQUAINE BAY MAP 16

Fort Grey and Shipwreck Museum

GY7 9BY

➲ *(on coast road at Rocquaine Bay)*

☎ 01481 265036

e-mail: admin@museums.gov.gg

web: www.museum.gov.gg

The fort is a Martello tower, built in 1804, as part of the Channel Islands' extensive defences. It is nicknamed the 'cup and saucer' because of its appearance, and houses a museum devoted to ships wrecked on the treacherous Hanois reefs nearby.

Times Open 3 Apr-25 Oct 10-5 **Fee** ✻ £3 (ch free, concessions £2). 4 venue pass £10 (concessions £6). Season ticket available **Facilities** Ⓟ (opposite fort) ⛩ (outdoor) shop ⊗ (ex assist dogs) ▬

ST MARTIN MAP 16

Sausmarez Manor

2 for 1

Sausmarez Rd GY4 6SG

➲ *(halfway between airport & St Peter Port)*

☎ 01481 235571

e-mail: sausmarezmanor@cwgsy.net

web: www.sausmarezmanor.co.uk

The Manor has been owned and lived in by the same family for centuries. The style of each room is different, with collections of Oriental, French and English furniture and paintings. Outside the Formal Garden has herbaceous borders, and the subtropical Woodland Garden, set around two small lakes and a stream, is planted with colourful shrubs, bulbs and wild flowers. Also on view, a sculpture park which is now the most comprehensive in Britain.

Times Open Etr-Oct 10-5 **Fee** House £7.50 (ch £5.50, concessions £6.50). Woodland Garden £5.50 (accompanied ch & concessions £5, disabled free). Sculpture Park £4.50 (accompanied ch & concessions £3, disabled free). **Facilities** Ⓟ ☕ ♿ (partial access to garden) (free admission) shop ⊗ (ex assist dogs) ▬

ST PETER PORT MAP 16

Castle Cornet

GY1 1AU

➲ *(5 mins walk from St Peter Port bus terminus)*

☎ 01481 721657

e-mail: admin@museums.gov.gg

web: www.museums.gov.gg

The history of this magnificent castle spans eight centuries and its buildings now house several museums, the Refectory Café and a shop. Soldiers fire the noonday gun in a daily ceremony. Look for the Maritime Museum that charts Guernsey's nautical history, the 'Story of Castle Cornet' with its mystery skeleton, and the 201 squadron RAF Museum. A refurbished Regimental Museum of the Royal Guernsey Militia and Royal Guernsey Light Infantry is planned for Summer 2009.

Times Open 3 Apr-25 Oct, daily 10-5. **Fee** ✻ £6.50 (concessions £4.50). 4 venue ticket £10 (concessions £6). 4 site pass available, season ticket available. **Facilities** Ⓟ (100 yds) time limit ☕ shop ⊗ (ex assist dogs) ▬

Guernsey Museum & Art Gallery

Candie Gardens GY1 1UG

➲ *(On the outskirts of St Peter Port set in the Victorian 'Candie gardens')*

☎ 01481 726518

e-mail: admin@museums.gov.gg

web: www.museums.gov.gg

The museum, designed around a Victorian bandstand, tells the story of Guernsey and its people. There is an audio-visual theatre and an art gallery, and special exhibitions are arranged throughout the year. It is surrounded by beautiful gardens with superb views over St Peter Port harbour.

Times Open Feb-Dec, daily 10-5 (winter 10-4) **Fee** ✻ £4 (ch free, concessions £3). 4 venue ticket £10 (concessions £6). Season ticket available. **Facilities** Ⓟ (street parking) (2hr & 5hr) ☕ ♿ (audio guides) toilets for disabled shop ⊗ (ex assist dogs) ▬

VALE MAP 16

Rousse Tower

FREE

Rousse Tower Headland

➲ *(on Island's W coast, signed)*

☎ 01489 726518 & 726965

e-mail: admin@museums.gov.gg

web: www.museums.gov.gg

One of the original fifteen towers built in 1778-9 in prime defensive positions around the coast of Guernsey. They were designed primarily to prevent the landing of troops on nearby beaches. Musket fire could be directed on invading forces through the loopholes. An interpretation centre displays replica guns.

Times Open Apr-Oct 9-dusk, Nov-Mar Wed, Sat & Sun 9-4. **Facilities** Ⓟ ♿ (tower can only be viewed from the outside) ⊗ (ex assist dogs)

JERSEY

Somewhere, on a beach in Jersey

GOREY MAP 16

Mont Orgueil Castle

JE3 6ET

➲ *(A3 or coast road to Gorey)*

☎ 01534 853292

e-mail: marketing@jerseyheritagetrust.org

web: www.jerseyheritagetrust.org

Standing on a rocky headland, on a site which has been fortified since the Iron Age, this is one of the best-preserved examples in Europe of a medieval concentric castle, and dates from the 12th and 13th centuries.

Times Open daily, Mar-Nov 10-6 (last admission 5). Winter open Fri-Mon 10-4 (last admission 3). **Fee** ✳ £9.30 (ch & students £5.50 , ch under 6 free, pen £8.50). Family ticket £26. **Facilities** ℗ (200yds) ☐ ⊟ (outdoor) ♿ (castle keep accessible) toilets for disabled shop ⊗ (ex assist dogs) ▭

LA GREVE DE LECQ MAP 16

Greve de Lecq Barracks FREE

➲ *(on side of valley, overlooking beach)*

☎ 01534 483193 & 482238

e-mail: enquiries@nationaltrustjersey.org.je

web: www.nationaltrustjersey.org.je

Originally serving as an outpost of the British Empire, these barracks, built in 1810, were used for civilian housing from the end of WWI to 1972, when they were bought by the National Trust and made into a museum that depicts the life of soldiers who were stationed here in the 19th century. Also includes a collection of old horse-drawn carriages.

Times Open May-Sep, Wed-Sat, 10-5, Sun 1-5. **Facilities** ℗ ♿ (wheelchair ramps) toilets for disabled shop ⊗ (ex assist dogs) ▭

GROUVILLE MAP 16

La Hougue Bie

JE2 7UA

➲ *(A6 or A7 to Five Oaks, at mini-rdbt take B28 to site)*

☎ 01534 853823

e-mail: marketing@jerseyheritagetrust.org

web: www.jerseyheritagetrust.org

This Neolithic burial mound stands 40ft high, and covers a stone-built passage grave that is still intact and may be entered. The passage is 50ft long, and built of huge stones, the mound is made from earth, rubble and limpet shells. On top of the mound are two medieval chapels, one of which has a replica of the Holy Sepulchre in Jerusalem below. Also on the site is an underground bunker built by the Germans as a communications centre, now a memorial to the slave workers of the Occupation.

Times Open Mar-Nov, daily 10-5. **Fee** ✳ £6.50 (ch under 6 free, ch & students £4, pen £6). Family ticket £20. **Facilities** ℗ ⊟ (outdoor) ♿ shop ⊗ (ex assist dogs) ▭

ST BRELADE MAP 16

Jersey Lavender Farm

Rue du Pont Marquet JE3 8DS

➲ *(on B25 from St Aubin's Bay to Redhouses)*

☎ 01534 742933

e-mail: admin@jerseylavender.co.uk

web: www.jerseylavender.co.uk

Jersey Lavender grows nine acres of lavender, distils out the essential oil and creates a range of fine toiletry products. Visitors are able to see the whole process from cultivating, through to harvesting, distillation and the production of the final product. There is a national collection of lavenders, extensive gardens, herb beds and walks among the lavender fields. There are also other herbs that are grown and distilled, namely eucalyptus, rosemary and tea tree.

Times ✳ Open 10 May-18 Sep, Tue-Sun 10-5. **Facilities** ℗ ☐ ♿ (free wheelchair loan) toilets for disabled shop garden centre ▭

ST CLEMENT MAP 16

Samarès Manor 2 for 1

JE2 6QW

➲ *(2m E of St Helier on St Clements Inner Rd)*

☎ 01534 870551

e-mail: enquiries@samaresmanor.com

web: www.samaresmanor.com

Samares Manor is a beautiful house, surrounded by exceptional gardens. These include the internationally renowned herb garden, Japanese garden, water gardens and exotic borders. There are tours of the manor house and of the Rural Life and Carriage Museum. Talks on herbs and their uses take place each week day and there is a plant trail and activities for children.

Times Open 4 Apr-10 Oct. **Fee** £6.50 (ch under 5 free, 5-16 & students £2.35, concessions £5.95). **Facilities** ℗ ☐ ❍ ♿ (ground floor only of the house and part of the water garden as small paths) toilets for disabled shop garden centre ⊗ (ex assist dogs) ▭

ST HELIER MAP 16

Elizabeth Castle

JE2 3WU

➲ *(access by causeway or amphibious vehicle)*

☎ 01534 723971

e-mail: marketing@jerseyheritagetrust.org

web: www.jerseyheritagetrust.org

The original Elizabethan fortress was extended in the 17th and 18th centuries, and then refortified by the Germans during the Occupation. Please telephone for details of events.

Times Open Mar-Nov, daily 10-6 (last admission 5) **Fee** ✳ £8 (ch under 6 free, ch & students £5, pen £7.30). Family ticket £25. **Facilities** ℗ (paycards required) ☐ ⊟ (outdoor) ♿ (castle keep & parade ground accessible) toilets for disabled shop ⊗ (ex assist dogs) ▭

ST HELIER CONTINUED

Jersey Museum and Art Gallery

The Weighbridge JE2 3NF

➲ *(near bus station on weighbridge)*

☎ 01534 633300

e-mail: marketing@jerseyheritagetrust.org

web: www.jerseyheritagetrust.org

Home to 'The Story of Jersey', Jersey's art gallery, an exhibition gallery which features a changing programme, a lecture theatre, and an audio-visual theatre. Special exhibitions take place throughout the year.

Times Open all year, daily Summer 9.30-5. Winter daily 10-4. **Fee** ✳ £7 (ch under 6 free, ch & students £4, pen £6.40). Family ticket £20. **Facilities** Ⓟ (200yds) (paycard at most public parking) 🍽 licensed ᴇ (audio loop, magnilink viewer, lift, car park) toilets for disabled shop ⊗ (ex assist dogs) ☰

Maritime Museum & Occupation Tapestry Gallery

New North Quay JE2 3ND

➲ *(alongside Marina, opposite Liberation Square)*

☎ 01534 811043

e-mail: marketing@jerseyheritagetrust.org

web: www.jerseyheritagetrust.org

This converted 19th-century warehouse houses the tapestry consisting of 12 two-metre panels that tells the story of the occupation of Jersey during World War II. Each of the 12 parishes took responsibility for stitching a panel, making it the largest community arts project ever undertaken on the island. The Maritime Museum celebrates the relationship of islanders and the sea, including an award winning hands-on experience, especially enjoyed by children.

Times Open all year, daily Summer 9.30-5. Winter 10-4. **Fee** ✳ £7.50 (ch under 6 free, ch & students £4.50, pen £7). Family ticket £20. **Facilities** Ⓟ (paycards in public car parks) ᴇ (Braille books) toilets for disabled shop ⊗ (ex assist dogs) ☰

ST LAWRENCE   MAP 16

Hamptonne Country Life Museum

La Rue de la Patente JE3 1HS

➲ *(5m from St Helier on A1, A10 & follow signs)*

☎ 01534 863955

e-mail: marketing@jerseyheritagetrust.org

web: www.jerseyheritagetrust.org

Here visitors will find a medieval 17th-century home, furnished in authentic style and surrounded by 19th-century farm buildings. Guided tours every weekday. Living history interpretation and daily demonstrations.

Times Open Mar-Nov, daily 10-5. **Fee** ✳ £6.50 (ch under 6 free, ch & students £4, pen £6). Family ticket £20. **Facilities** Ⓟ ⌺ ☕ (outdoor) ᴇ (courtyard & garden accessible) (Sensory Garden, designated parking) toilets for disabled shop ⊗ (ex assist dogs) ☰

Jersey War Tunnels

Les Charrieres Malorey JE3 1FU

➲ *(bus route 8A from St Helier)*

☎ 01534 860808

e-mail: info@jerseywartunnels.com

web: www.jerseywartunnels.com

On 1 July 1940 the Channel Islands were occupied by German forces, and this vast complex dug deep into a hillside is the most evocative reminder of that Occupation. A video presentation, along with a large collection of memorabilia, illustrates the lives of the islanders at war and a further exhibition records their impressions during 1945, the year of liberation.

Times ✳ Open 14 Feb-19 Dec, daily 9.30-5.30 (last admission 4). **Facilities** Ⓟ ⌺ 🍽 ᴇ (ramp to restaurant & lift in Visitor Centre to restaurant) toilets for disabled shop ⊗ (ex assist dogs) ☰

ST OUEN   MAP 16

The Channel Islands Military Museum

Five Mile Rd

➲ *(N end of Five Mile Rd, at rear of Jersey Woollen Mill & across road from Jersey Pearl)*

☎ 07797 732072

e-mail: damienhorn@jerseymail.co.uk

The museum is housed in a German coastal defence bunker, which formed part of Hitler's Atlantic Wall. It has been restored, as far as possible, to give the visitor an idea of how it looked. The visitor can also see German uniforms, motorcycles, weapons, documents, photographs and other items from the 1940-45 occupation.

Times Open wk before Etr-Oct **Fee** ✳ £4 (ch £2) Groups by arrangement. **Facilities** Ⓟ ⌺ ☕ (outdoor) ᴇ (all parts accessible ex 1 small room) toilets for disabled shop ⊗ (ex assist dogs)

Kempt Tower Visitor Centre

Five Mile Rd

☎ 01534 483651 & 483140

web: www.eco-active.je

Kempt Tower is buzzing with hands-on activities for all ages. The centre has displays on history and the wildlife of St Ouen's Bay, including Les Mielles, which is Jersey's miniature national park. There are breath-taking views from the roof of a genuine Martello Tower.

Times Open May-Sep, daily 2-5. **Facilities** Ⓟ ☕ (outdoor) shop ⊗

ST PETER   MAP 16

The Living Legend   **2 for 1**

Rue de Petit Aleval JE3 7ET

⮕ *(from St Helier, along main esplanade & right to Bel Royal. Left and follow road to attraction, signed from German Underground Hospital)*

☎ 01534 485496

e-mail: info@jerseyslivinglegend.co.je

web: www.jerseyslivinglegend.co.je

Pass through the granite archways into the landscaped gardens and the world of the Jersey Experience where Jersey's exciting past is recreated in a three dimensional spectacle featuring Stephen Tompkinson, Tony Robinson and other well-known names. Learn of the heroes and villains, the folklore and the story of the island's links with the UK and its struggles with Europe. Other attractions include an adventure playground, street entertainment, the Jersey Craft and Shopping Village, a range of shops and the Jersey Kitchen Restaurant. Two 18-hole adventure golf courses are suitable for all ages. Jersey Karting is a formula one style experience. A unique track featuring adult and cadet karts.

Times Open Apr-Oct, daily; Mar & Nov, Sat-Wed; 9-5. **Fee** The Jersey Story £8.20 (ch £5.70), Jersey Adventure Golf £6.10 (ch £5.05) **Facilities** ❷ ⬛ ⦿ licensed ♿ (Adventure Golf has lots of steps and uneven surfaces) (wheelchair available) toilets for disabled shop ⊗ (ex assist dogs) ▭

Le Moulin de Quetivel

St Peters Valley, Le Mont Fallu

⮕ *(A11 through St Peter's Valley. Attraction located on left, with junct of Le Mont Fallu B58)*

☎ 01534 483193 & 745408

e-mail: enquiries@nationaltrustjersey.org.je

web: www.nationaltrustjersey.org.je

There has been a water mill on this site since 1309. The present granite-built mill was worked until the end of the 19th century, when it fell into disrepair; during the German Occupation it was reactivated for grinding locally grown corn, but after 1945 a fire destroyed the remaining machinery, roof and internal woodwork. In 1971 the National Trust for Jersey began restoration, and the mill is now producing stoneground flour again.

Times Open May-Sep, Sat only. **Fee** ✳ £2 (ch under 16 free, concessions £1.50). Free entry UK National Trust card. **Facilities** ❷ ♿ shop ⊗ (ex assist dogs) ⅍

TRINITY   MAP 16

Durrell Wildlife Conservation Trust

Les Augres Manor, La Profunde Rue JE3 5BP

⮕ *(From St Hellier follow A8 to Trinity until B31. Turn right & follow B31, signed)*

☎ 01534 860000

e-mail: info@durrell.org

web: www.durrell.org

Gerald Durrell's unique sanctuary and breeding centre for many of the world's rarest animals. Visitors can see these remarkable creatures, some so rare that they can only be found here, in modern, spacious enclosures in the gardens of the 16th-century manor house. Major attractions are the magical Aye-Ayes from Madagascar and the world-famous family of Lowland gorillas. There is a comprehensive programme of keeper talks, animal displays and activities. 2009 is the 50th Anniversary of Gerald Durrell's opening of the Durrell Wildlife Conservation Trust. There are various events throughout the year to celebrate this anniversary.

Times Open all year, daily 9.30-6 (summer); 9.30-5 (winter). Closed 25 Dec. **Fee** ✳ £11.90 (ch 4-16 £8.40 concessions £9.50). **Facilities** ❷ ⬛ ⦿ licensed ⧨ (outdoor) ♿ (some indoor areas cannot accommodate wheelchairs/scooters) (scooters, wheelchairs, quad walker for hire) toilets for disabled shop garden centre ⊗ ▭

ISLE OF MAN

'Lady Isabella' pump at Laxy

BALLASALLA MAP 06 SC27

Rushen Abbey

IM9 3DB

⮌ *(right at Whitestone Inn, left at next rdbt, then 1st right over bridge, car park on left)*

☎ 01624 648000

e-mail: enquiries@mnh.gov.im

web: www.storyofmann.com

The most substantial and important medieval religious site on the Isle of Man. Remains of medieval buildings, exhibitions and displays, set in beautifully landscaped gardens.

Times ✳ Open Etr-late Oct, daily 10-5. **Facilities** ❷ shop ✪ (ex assist dogs) ▬

BALLAUGH MAP 06 SC39

Curraghs Wild Life Park

IM7 5EA

⮌ *(on main road halfway between Kirk Michael & Ramsey)*

☎ 01624 897323

e-mail: curraghswlp@gov.im

web: www.gov.im/wildlife

This park has been developed adjacent to the reserve area of the Ballaugh Curraghs and a large variety of animals and birds can be seen. A walk-through enclosure lets visitors explore the world of wildlife, including local habitats along the Curraghs nature trail. The miniature railway runs on Sundays.

Times Open all year Etr-Oct, daily 10-6. (Last admission 5). Oct-Etr, Sat & Sun 10-4. **Fee** ✳ £6.60 (ch £3.30, under 3's free, pen £4.40). Family (2ad+2ch) £16.50 **Facilities** ❷ ⛲ ⊓ (outdoor) ♿ (Partly accessible) (loan of wheelchair & electric wheelchair) toilets for disabled shop ✪ (ex assist dogs) ▬

CASTLETOWN MAP 06 SC26

Castle Rushen

The Quay IM9 1LD

⮌ *(centre of Castletown)*

☎ 01624 648000

e-mail: enquiries@mnh.gov.im

web: www.storyofmann.com

One of Europe's best preserved medieval castles, Castle Rushen is a limestone fortress rising out of the heart of the old capital of the island, Castletown. Once the fortress of the Kings and Lords of Mann, Castle Rushen is brought alive with rich decorations, and the sounds and smells of a bygone era.

Times Open daily, Etr-Oct, 10-5. **Fee** ✳ £4.80 (ch £2.40) Family £12. Group from £3.80 each. **Facilities** ℗ (100 yds) (disc zone parking) shop ✪ (ex assist dogs) ▬

Nautical Museum

⮌ *(From Castletown centre, cross footbridge over harbour. Museum on right)*

☎ 01624 648000

e-mail: enquiries@mnh.gov.im

web: www.storyofmann.com

Set at the mouth of Castletown harbour the Nautical Museum is home to an 18th-century armed yacht, *The Peggy*, built by a Manxman in 1791. A replica sailmaker's loft, ship model and photographs bring alive Manx maritime life and trade in the days of sail.

Times Open daily, Etr-Oct, 10-5. **Fee** ✳ £3.30 (ch £1.70). Family £8.30. Groups from £2.60 **Facilities** ℗ (50 yds) shop ✪ (ex assist dogs) ▬

Old Grammar School `FREE`

IM9 1LE

⮌ *(centre of Castletown, opposite the castle)*

☎ 01624 648000

e-mail: enquiries@mnh.gov.im

web: www.storyofmann.com

Built around 1200AD, the former capital's first church, St Mary's, has had a significant role in Manx education. It was a school from 1570 to 1930 and evokes memories of Victorian school life.

Times Open daily, Etr-late Oct, 10-5. **Facilities** ❷ ⊓ (outdoor) ♿ (restricted access narrow door, 3 steps) shop ✪ (ex assist dogs)

The Old House of Keys

IM9 1LA

⮌ *(opposite Castletown Rushen in centre of Castletown)*

☎ 01624 648000

e-mail: enquiries@mnh.gov.im

web: www.storyofmann.com

The Old House of Keys is a portrayal of the long and often turbulent history of Manx politics. It has been restored to the way it looked in 1866 and visitors are invited to participate in a lively debate with interactive Members of Tynwald, the Manx parliament.

Times ✳ Open daily, Apr-late Oct, 10-5. **Facilities** ℗ (30yds) ✪ (ex assist dogs)

CREGNEASH
MAP 06 SC16

The National Folk Museum at Cregneash
➲ *(2m from Port Erin/Port St Mary, signed)*
☎ 01624 648000
e-mail: enquiries@mnh.gov.im
web: www.storyofmann.com

The Cregneash story begins in Cummal Beg - the village information centre where you can experience what life was really like in a Manx crofting village during the early 19th century. As you stroll around this attractive village, set in beautiful countryside, call into Harry Kelly's cottage, a Turner's shed, a Weaver's house, and the Smithy. The Manx Four-horned Loghtan Sheep can be seen grazing along with other animals from the village farm.

Times Open Etr-Oct, daily, 10-5. **Fee** ✳ £3.30 (ch £1.70) Family £8.30. Group rates from £2.60 **Facilities** ℗ ⊡ ㅠ (outdoor) shop ⊗ (ex assist dogs) ➡

DOUGLAS
MAP 06 SC37

Manx Museum   FREE
IM1 3LY
➲ *(signed in Douglas)*
☎ 01624 648000
e-mail: enquiries@mnh.gov.im
web: www.storyofmann.com

The Island's treasure house provides an exciting introduction to the "Story of Mann" where a specially produced film portrayal of Manx history complements the award winning displays. Galleries depict natural history, archaeology and the social development of the Island. There are also examples of famous Manx artists in the National Art Gallery together with the island's national archive and reference library. Events and exhibitions throughout the year please visit website.

Times Open daily all year, Mon-Sat, 10-5. Closed 25-26 Dec & 1 Jan. **Facilities** ℗ ⊡ ⊠ licensed ㅠ (outdoor) ♿ (lift) toilets for disabled shop ⊗ (ex assist dogs) ➡

Snaefell Mountain Railway
Banks Circus IM1 5PT
➲ *(Manx Electric Railway from Douglas and change at Laxey)*
☎ 01624 663366
e-mail: info@busandrail.dtl.gov.im
web: www.iombusandrail.info

Snaefell is the Isle of Man's highest mountain. Running up it is Britain's oldest working mountain railway, which was laid in 1895. From the top of Snaefell, on a clear day, England, Ireland, Scotland and Wales are all visible.

Times Open 30 Apr-Sep. **Facilities** ℗ ⊡ shop ➡

LAXEY
MAP 06 SC48

Great Laxey Wheel & Mines Trail
➲ *(signed in Laxey village)*
☎ 01624 648000
e-mail: enquiries@mnh.gov.im
web: www.storyofmann.com

Built in 1854, the Great Laxey Wheel, 22 metres in diameter, is the largest working water wheel in the world. It was designed to pump water from the lead and zinc mines and is an acknowledged masterpiece of Victorian engineering. The wheel was christened by Lady Isabella, the wife of the Lieutenant Governor of the Isle of Man.

Times Open Etr-Oct 10-5 **Fee** ✳ £3.30 (ch £1.70) Family £8.30. Group rates from £2.60 **Facilities** ℗ ㅠ (outdoor) shop ⊗ (ex assist dogs) ➡

PEEL
MAP 06 SC28

House of Manannan
Mill Rd IM5 1TA
➲ *(signed in Peel)*
☎ 01624 648000
e-mail: enquiries@mnh.gov.im
web: www.storyofmann.com

The mythological sea-god Manannan guides visitors through the Island's rich Celtic, Viking and maritime past. Step inside reconstructions of a Manx Celtic roundhouse and a Viking longhouse, discover the stories on magnificent Manx stone crosses, and see *Odin's Raven*, a splendid Viking longship. Displays and exhibitions throughout the year please see website.

Times Open daily 10-5. Closed 25-26 Dec & 1 Jan **Fee** ✳ £5.50 (ch £2.80) Family £13.80. Group rates from £4.40. **Facilities** ℗ ♿ toilets for disabled shop ⊗ (ex assist dogs) ➡

Peel Castle
IM5 1TB
➲ *(on St Patrick's Isle, facing Peel Bay, signed)*
☎ 01624 648000
e-mail: enquiries@mnh.gov.im
web: www.storyofmann.com

One of the Island's principle historic centres, this great natural fortress with its imposing curtain wall set majestically at the mouth of Peel Harbour is steeped in Viking heritage. The sandstone walls of Peel Castle enclose an 11th-century church and Round Tower, the 13th-century St German's Cathedral and the later apartments of the Lords of Mann.

Times Open Etr-Oct, daily 10-5 **Fee** ✳ £3.30 (ch £1.70). Family £8.30. Group rates from £2.60. **Facilities** ℗ (100yds) ⊗ (ex assist dogs) ➡

PORT ST MARY — MAP 06 SC26

Sound Visitor Centre

The Sound IM1 3LY

➲ *(follow coastal road towards Port Erin/Port St Mary. Past Cregneash village towards most S point of Island)*

☎ 01624 648000 & 838123

e-mail: enquiries@mnh.gov.im

web: www.storyofmann.com

The Sound Visitor Centre is set in one of the Island's most scenic areas overlooking the natural wonders of the Sound and the Calf of Man. Along with information and audio presentations about the area, other facilities add to the enjoyment and convenience of visitors.

Times Open daily, Etr-Oct 10-5. For winter opening times telephone 01624 838123. **Facilities** 🅿 🖵 🍴 🎋 (outdoor) & toilets for disabled ❸ (ex assist dogs)

RAMSEY — MAP 06 SC49

The Grove

IM8 3UA

➲ *(on W side of Andreas Rd. Signed in Ramsey)*

☎ 01624 648000

e-mail: enquiries@mnh.gov.im

web: www.storyofmann.com

This Victorian time capsule was a country house built as a summer retreat for a Liverpool shipping merchant. Rooms are filled with period furnishings together with a costume exhibition. In the adjacent farmyard are buildings containing displays on farming and 19th century vehicles. Around the grounds you may see Loghtan sheep, ducks and perhaps a Manx cat.

Times Open Etr-Oct, daily 10-5 **Fee** ✳ £3.30 (ch £1.70). Family £8.30. Group rates from £2.60. **Facilities** 🅿 🖵 🍴 & (ground floor fully accessible, 3 steps to gardens) shop ❸ (ex assist dogs) 🚍

Cashtal-Yn-Ard Long burial chamber, Maughold

369

SCOTLAND

Ben Macdui viewed from Glen Lui, nr Braemar, Cairngorms National Park

CITY OF ABERDEEN

ABERDEEN   MAP 15 NJ90

Aberdeen Art Gallery   `FREE`

Schoolhill AB10 1FQ

➲ *(located in city centre)*

☎ 01224 523700

e-mail: info@aagm.co.uk

web: www.aberdeencity.gov.uk

Aberdeen's splendid art gallery houses an important fine art collection, a rich and diverse applied art collection and an exciting programme of special exhibitions.

Times Open all year Tue-Sat 10-5, Sun 2-5. Closed Xmas & New Year
Facilities Ⓟ (500yds) ⬛ & (ramp, lift) toilets for disabled shop ⊗ (ex assist dogs)

Aberdeen Maritime Museum   `FREE`

Shiprow AB11 5BY

➲ *(located in city centre)*

☎ 01224 337700

e-mail: info@aagm.co.uk

web: www.aberdeencity.gov.uk

The award-winning Maritime Museum brings the history of the North Sea to life. Featuring displays and exhibitions on the offshore oil industry, shipbuilding, fishing and clipper ships.

Times Open Tue-Sat, 10-5, Sun 2-5. **Facilities** Ⓟ (250yds) ⬛ ⦿ licensed & (ramps, lifts, induction loop) toilets for disabled shop ⊗ (ex assist dogs) ⬛

Cruickshank Botanic Garden   `FREE`

University of Aberdeen, St Machar Dr AB24 3UU

➲ *(enter by gate in Chanonry, in Old Aberdeen)*

☎ 01224 272704

e-mail: pss@abdn.ac.uk

web: www.abdn.ac.uk/pss/cruickshank

Developed at the end of the 19th century, the 11 acres include rock and water gardens, a rose garden, a fine herbaceous border, an arboretum and a patio garden. There are collections of spring bulbs, gentians and alpine plants, and a fine array of trees and shrubs.

Times Open all year, Mon-Fri 9-4.30; also Sat & Sun, May-Sep 2-5.
Facilities Ⓟ (200mtrs) ⊗

The Gordon Highlanders Museum

St Luke's, Viewfield Rd AB15 7XH

☎ 01224 311200

e-mail: museum@gordonhighlanders.com

web: www.gordonhighlanders.com

Presenting a large collection of artefacts, paintings, films and reconstructions, the Gordon Highlanders Museum is the perfect day out for anyone interested in Scottish military history, and is also the former home of 19th-century artist, Sir George Reid. The exhibition includes interactive maps, original film footage, scaled reproductions, life-size models, touch screens, uniforms, medals and an armoury. The grounds also contain a tea-room, shop and gardens. See the website for details of changing exhibitions and events.

Times ✳ Open Apr-Oct, Tue-Sat 10-4.30, Sun 12.30-4.30. (Closed Mon). Nov, Feb & Mar Thurs-Sat 10-4. Open by appointment only at other times. **Facilities** ❶ ▱ ♿ (low level cases, hearing loop, lift) toilets for disabled shop ⊗ (ex assist dogs) ▤

Provost Skene's House
FREE

Guestrow, off Broad St AB10 1AS

➲ *(located in town centre)*

☎ 01224 641086

e-mail: info@aagm.co.uk

web: www.aberdeencity.gov.uk

16th-century town house with a stunning series of period room settings. Painted Gallery and changing displays of local history.

Times Open all year Mon-Sat 10-5. **Facilities** ℗ (200yds) ▱ ⊗ (ex assist dogs)

Satrosphere Science Centre
2 for 1

179 Constitution St AB24 5TU

➲ *(located very close to Beach Esplanade. Follow signs to fun beach, then attraction)*

☎ 01224 640340

e-mail: info@satrosphere.net

web: www.satrosphere.net

Satrosphere is Scotland's first science and discovery centre and with over 50 hands-on exhibits and live science shows, a visit to Satrosphere will not only inspire the scientist within, but will entertain the whole family. Satrosphere's exhibits offer interactive ways for visitors to discover more about the world around them and the science of how things work.

Times Open Mar-Oct, daily 10-5; Nov-Feb, Tue-Sun 10-5. Closed 25-26 Dec & 1 Jan. **Fee** ✳ £5.75 (under 3's free, ch & concessions £4.50). **Facilities** ❶ ▱ ♿ (lift & disabled toilets) toilets for disabled shop ⊗ (ex assist dogs) ▤

PETERCULTER　　　　　　　　MAP 15 NJ80

Drum Castle

AB31 5EY

➲ *(Off A93, 3m W of Peterculter)*

☎ 0844 493 2161

e-mail: information@nts.org.uk

web: www.nts.org.uk

The great 13th-century Square Tower is one of the three oldest tower houses in Scotland and has associations with Robert the Bruce. The handsome mansion, added in 1619, houses a collection of family memorabilia. The grounds contain the 100-acre Old Wood of Drum, a natural oak wood and an old rose garden.

Times ✳ Castle open 31 Mar-Jun daily (closed Tues & Fri) 12-5, Jul-Aug daily 11-5, Sep-Oct daily (closed Tue & Fri) 12.30-5. Last admission 45 mins before closing. Garden of Historic Roses 31 Mar-Oct daily 10-6, Grounds all year daily. Property open BH wknds from Fri-Mon inclusive. **Facilities** ❶ ▱ ⋒ ♿ (Partly accessible) (wheelchair available, Braille, touch tours, Scented gdn) shop ⊗ (ex assist dogs) ❦

ABERDEENSHIRE

ALFORD　　　　　　　　MAP 15 NJ51

Alford Valley Railway

AB33 8AD

➲ *(A944 Alford Village)*

☎ 019755 62326

e-mail: info@alfordvalleyrailway.org.uk

web: www.alfordvalleyrailway.org.uk

Alford Valley Railway is a narrow-gauge passenger railway between Alford and Haughton Park, about one mile long. Santa specials at Christmas.

Times Open Apr, May & Sep, wknds 1-5; Jun-Aug, daily from 1 (30 min service). Party bookings also available at other times. **Fee** ✳ £2.50 (ch £1) return fare. **Facilities** ❶ ⋒ (outdoor) ♿ (ramps at station platforms) toilets for disabled shop

Craigievar Castle

AB33 8JF

➲ *(on A980, 6m S of Alford)*

☎ 0844 493 2174

e-mail: information@nts.org.uk

web: www.nts.org.uk

A fairytale like castle, the Great Tower completed in 1626. The collection includes family portraits and 17th and 18th-century furniture. There are extensive wooded grounds with a waymarked trail.

Times ✳ Castle: Mar-Jun Fri-Tues 12-5.30. Jul-Aug daily 12-5.30. This property is currently closed for renovation, but should reopen at some point in 2009. Vist NTS website for details. **Facilities** ❶ (charged) ⋒ ♿ (Partly accessible) (Touch tours, radio microphone) shop ⊗ (ex assist dogs) ❦

SCOTLAND

SCOTLAND

BALMORAL   MAP 15 NO29
Balmoral Castle Grounds & Exhibition
AB35 5TB

⮕ *(on A93 between Ballater & Braemar)*

☎ 013397 42534

e-mail: info@balmoralcastle.com

web: www.balmoralcastle.com

Queen Victoria and Prince Albert first rented Balmoral Castle in 1848, and Prince Albert bought the property four years later. He commissioned William Smith to build a new castle, which was completed by 1856 and is still the Royal Family's Highland residence. Explore the exhibitions, grounds, gardens and trails as well as the magnificent Castle Ballroom.

Times Open Apr-Jul, daily 10-5 (last admission 4.30) **Fee** £7 (ch £3, concessions £6). Family (2ad+4ch) £15. **Facilities** ✿ (charged) ⛯ ⍏ (outdoor) ᴕ (wheelchairs & battricars available, reserved parking) toilets for disabled shop ▄

BANCHORY   MAP 15 NO69
Banchory Museum   FREE
Bridge St AB31 5SX

⮕ *(in Bridge St beside tourist information centre)*

☎ 01771 622807

e-mail: heritage@aberdeenshire.gov.uk

web: www.aberdeenshire.gov.uk/museums

The museum has displays on Scott Skinner (The 'Strathspey King'), natural history, royal commemorative china, local silver artefacts and a variety of local history displays.

Times Open Jan-May & Sep-Dec, Mon, Fri & Sat 11-1 & 2-4; Jul-Aug, Mon-Wed & Fri-Sat, 11-1, 2-4. **Facilities** ✿ (100yds) (limited) ᴕ toilets for disabled ✖ (ex assist dogs)

BANFF   MAP 15 NJ66
Banff Museum   FREE
High St AB45 1AE

☎ 01771 622807

e-mail: museums@aberdeenshire.gov.uk

web: www.aberdeenshire.gov.uk/museums

Displays of geology, natural history, local history, Banff silver, arms and armour, and displays relating to James Ferguson (18th-century astronomer) and Thomas Edward (19th-century Banff naturalist).

Times Open Jun-Sep, Mon-Sat 2-4.30. **Facilities** ✿ (200yds) ᴕ (ground floor only accessible) ✖ (ex assist dogs)

Duff House
AB45 3SX

⮕ *(0.5m S, access S of town)*

☎ 01261 818181

web: www.historic-scotland.gov.uk

The house was designed by William Adam for William Duff, later Earl of Fife. The main block was roofed in 1739, but the planned wings were never built. Although it is incomplete, the house is still considered one of Britain's finest Georgian baroque buildings. Duff House is a Country House Gallery of the National Galleries of Scotland.

Times ✳ Telephone for details of opening dates and times. **Facilities** ✿ ⍩⍏ shop ✖ ⋔

CORGARFF   MAP 15 NJ20
Corgarff Castle
AB36 8YL

⮕ *(8m W of Strathdon village)*

☎ 01975 651460

web: www.historic-scotland.gov.uk

The 16th-century tower was besieged in 1571 and is associated with the Jacobite risings of 1715 and 1745. It later became a military barracks. Its last military use was to control the smuggling of whisky between 1827 and 1831.

Times ✳ Open all year, Apr-Sep, daily 9.30-6.30; Oct-Mar, wknds only 9.30-4.30. Closed 25-26 Dec & 1-2 Jan. **Facilities** ✿ shop ⋔

CRATHES   MAP 15 NO79
Crathes Castle Garden & Estate
AB31 5QJ

⮕ *(On A93, 3m E of Banchory, 15m W of Aberdeen)*

☎ 0844 4932166

e-mail: information@nts.org.uk

web: www.nts.org.uk

This impressive 16th-century castle with magnificent interiors has royal associations dating from 1323. There is a large walled garden and a notable collection of unusual plants, including yew hedges dating from 1702. The grounds contain six nature trails, one suitable for disabled visitors, and an adventure playground.

Times ✳ Open daily 31 Mar-30 Sep, 10.30-5.30; Oct daily, 10.30-4.30; Nov-Mar, Wed-Sun 10.30-3.45. (Last admission 45min beofre close). Gardens open all year, daily 9-sunset. **Facilities** ✿ (charged) ⍩⍏ ᴕ (Partly accessible) (tape for visually impaired) toilets for disabled shop ✖ (ex assist dogs) ⚑

HUNTLY   MAP 15 NJ53

Brander Museum   FREE

The Square AB54 8AE

➲ *(in centre of Huntly, sharing building with library, museum on ground floor)*

☎ 01771 622807

e-mail: heritage@aberdeenshire.gov.uk

web: www.@aberdeenshire.gov.uk/museums

The museum has displays of local and church history, plus the 19th-century Anderson Bey and the Sudanese campaigns. Exhibits connected with George MacDonald, author and playwright, can also be seen.

Times Open all year, Tue-Sat 2-4.30. **Facilities** ℗ (25yds) ♿ (access difficult due to 3 large steps at entrance) ⊗ (ex assist dogs)

Huntly Castle

AB54 4SH

☎ 01466 793191

web: www.historic-scotland.gov.uk

The original medieval castle was rebuilt a number of times and destroyed, once by Mary, Queen of Scots. It was rebuilt for the last time in 1602, in palatial style, and is now an impressive ruin, noted for its ornate heraldic decorations. It stands in wooded parkland.

Times ✳ Open all year, Apr-Sep, daily 9.30-6.30; Oct-Mar, Mon-Wed & Sat-Sun 9.30-4.30. Closed 25-26 Dec & 1-2 Jan. **Facilities** ℗ ⋒ shop ∥

INVERURIE   MAP 15 NJ72

Carnegie Museum   FREE

Town House, The Square AB51 3SN

➲ *(in centre of Inverurie, on left side of townhouse building, above library)*

☎ 01771 622807

e-mail: museums@aberdeenshire.gov.uk

web: www.aberdeenshire.gov.uk/museums

This fine museum contains displays on local history and archaeology, including Pictish stones, Bronze Age material and the Great North of Scotland Railway.

Times Open all year, Mon & Wed-Fri 1.30-4, Sat 10-1 & 2-4. Closed Tue & public hols. **Facilities** ℗ (50yds) ♿ (chairlift to 1st floor) ⊗ (ex assist dogs)

KEMNAY   MAP 15 NJ71

Castle Fraser

AB51 7LD

➲ *(off A944, 4m N of Dunecht)*

☎ 0844 493 2164

e-mail: information@nts.org.uk

web: www.nts.org.uk

The massive Z-plan castle was built between 1575 and 1636 and is one of the grandest of the Castles of Mar. The interior was remodelled in 1838 and decoration and furnishings of that period survive in some of the rooms. A formal garden inside the old walled garden, estate trails, a children's play area and a programme of concerts are among the attractions.

Times ✳ Castle: 31 Mar-Jun, Wed-Sun 11-5; Jul-Aug, daily 11-5; Sep-Oct, Wed-Sun 12-5. (last admission 45min before closing). Garden & Grounds: all year daily. Property open BH wkends from Fri-Mon. **Facilities** ℗ (charged) ⌺ ⋒ ♿ (Partly accessible) (Printed room guides, scented garden) toilets for disabled shop garden centre ⊗ (ex assist dogs, some areas) ☕

KILDRUMMY   MAP 15 NJ41

Kildrummy Castle

AB54 7XT

➲ *(10m SW of Alford)*

☎ 01975 571331

web: www.historic-scotland.gov.uk

An important part of Scottish history, at least until it was dismantled in 1717, this fortress was the seat of the Earls of Mar. Now it is a ruined, but splendid, example of a 13th-century castle, with four round towers, hall and chapel all discernible. Some parts of the building, including the Great Gatehouse, are from the 15th and 16th centuries.

Times ✳ Open Apr-Sep, daily 9.30-6.30. **Facilities** ℗ shop ∥

Kildrummy Castle Gardens

AB33 8RA

➲ *(on A97 off A944. 10m W of Alford)*

☎ 019755 71277 & 71203

e-mail: information@kildrummy-castle-gardens.co.uk

web: www.kildrummy-castle-gardens.co.uk

With the picturesque ruin as a backdrop, these beautiful gardens include an alpine garden in an ancient quarry and a water garden. There's a small museum and a children's play area.

Times Open Apr-Oct, daily 10-5. **Fee** ✳ £4 (ch free, pen £3) **Facilities** ℗ ⌺ ⋒ ♿ (Partly accessible) toilets for disabled shop garden centre

MACDUFF — MAP 15 NJ76

Macduff Marine Aquarium

11 High Shore AB44 1SL

➲ *(off A947 and A98 to Macduff, aquarium signed)*

☎ 01261 833369

e-mail: macduff.aquarium@aberdeenshire.gov.uk

web: www.macduff-aquarium.org.uk

Exciting displays feature local sealife. The central exhibit, unique in Britain, holds a living kelp reef. Divers feed the fish in this tank. Other displays include an estuary exhibit, splash tank, rock pools, deep reef tank and ray pool. Young visitors especially enjoy the touch pools. There are talks, video presentations and feeding shows throughout the week.

Times Open 10-5 daily (last admission 4.15). Closed 25-26 Dec & 31 Dec-2 Jan **Fee** ✳ £5.40 (ch £2.70, concessions £3.35). Family ticket (2ad+2ch) £14.85 Groups 10+ **Facilities** ♿ 🅿 (outdoor) ♿ (audio tour for visually impaired) toilets for disabled shop ⊗ (ex assist dogs) 🖃

MARYCULTER — MAP 15 NO89

Storybook Glen

AB12 5FT

➲ *(5m W of Aberdeen on B9077)*

☎ 01224 732941

web: www.storybookglenaberdeen.co.uk

This is a child's fantasy land, where favourite nursery rhyme and fairytale characters are brought to life. Grown-ups can enjoy the nostalgia and also the 20 acres of Deeside country, full of flowers, plants, trees and waterfalls.

Times Open Mar-Oct, daily 10-6; Nov-Feb, daily 10-4. **Fee** ✳ £5.40 (ch £3.85, concessions £4.05). **Facilities** ♿ 🖵 🍽 licensed 🅿 (outdoor) ♿ toilets for disabled shop garden centre ⊗ (ex assist dogs) 🖃

METHLICK — MAP 15 NJ83

Haddo House

AB41 7EQ

➲ *(off B999, 4m N of Pitmedden)*

☎ 0844 493 2179

e-mail: information@nts.org.uk

web: www.nts.org.uk

Haddo House is a splendid Palladian-style mansion built in the 1730s to designs by William Adam. Home to the Earls of Aberdeen, the house was refurbished in the 1880s in the 'Adam Revival' style. The adjoining country park offers beautiful woodland walks.

Times ✳ House 31 Mar-Jun Fri-Mon 11-5, Jul-Aug daily 11-5, Sep to 1st wknd in Nov Fri-Mon 11-5. Last admission 4.15, Garden all year 9-sunset, Grounds open all year daily. **Facilities** ♿ 🍽 🅿 ♿ (Partly accessible) (lift to first floor of house & wheelchair) toilets for disabled shop ⊗ (ex in grounds & assist dogs) 🏵

MINTLAW — MAP 15 NJ94

Aberdeenshire Farming Museum   FREE

Aden Country Park AB42 5FQ

➲ *(1m W of Mintlaw on A950)*

☎ 01771 624590

e-mail: museums@aberdeenshire.gov.uk

web: www.aberdeenshire.gov.uk/museums

Housed in 19th-century farm buildings, once part of the estate which now makes up the Aden Country Park. Two centuries of farming history and innovation are illustrated, and the story of the estate is also told. The reconstructed farm of Hareshowe shows how a family in the north-east farmed during the 1950s - access by guided tour only.

Times Open May-Sep, daily 11-4.30; Apr & Oct, wknds only noon-4.30. (Last admission 30 mins before closing). Park open all year, Apr-Sep 7-10; winter 7-7. **Facilities** ♿ (charged) 🖵 🅿 (outdoor) ♿ (1st floor not accessible) (sensory garden) toilets for disabled shop ⊗ (ex assist dogs)

OLD DEER — MAP 15 NJ94

Deer Abbey   FREE

➲ *(2m W of Mintlaw on A950)*

☎ 01466 793191

web: www.historic-scotland.gov.uk

The remains of the Cistercian Abbey, founded in 1218, include the infirmary, Abbot's House and the southern claustral range. The University Library at Cambridge now houses the famous Book of Deer.

Times ✳ Open at all reasonable times. **Facilities** ♿ ⊗ 🎏

OYNE   MAP 15 NJ62

Archaeolink Prehistory Park

Berryhill AB52 6QP

➲ *(1m off A96 on B9002)*

☎ 01464 851500

e-mail: info@archaeolink.co.uk

web: www.archaeolink.co.uk

A stunning audio-visual show, a Myths and Legends Gallery and a whole range of interpretation techniques help visitors to explore what it was like to live 6,000 years ago. In addition there are landscaped walkways, and outdoor activity areas including an Iron Age farm, Roman marching camp and Stone Age settlement in the 40-acre park. Enjoy daily hands-on activities for all ages, guided tours with costumed guides or relax in the coffee shop. Special weekend events held regularly. 2009 is the 250th anniversary of the birth of Robert Burns.

Times Open daily, Apr-Oct 10-5 **Fee** ✳ £5.75 (ch £3.70, concessions £4.90) Family from £12.15 **Facilities** ♿ 💬 🍴 �🏞 (outdoor) ♿ (induction loop in theatre, wheelchair) toilets for disabled shop ⊗ (ex assist dogs) ➡

PETERHEAD   MAP 15 NK14

Arbuthnot Museum   `FREE`

St Peter St AB42 1QD

➲ *(at St.Peter St & Queen St x-roads, above library)*

☎ 01771 622807

e-mail: museums@aberdeenshire.gov.uk

web: www.aberdeenshire.gov.uk/museums

Specialising in local exhibits, particularly those relating to the fishing industry, this museum also displays Arctic and whaling specimens and a British coin collection. The regular programme of exhibitions changes approximately every six weeks.

Times Open all year, Mon-Tue & Thu-Sat 11-1 & 2-4.30, Wed 11-1. Closed Sun and BHs. **Facilities** ℗ (150 yds) ⊗ (ex assist dogs)

PITMEDDEN   MAP 15 NJ82

Pitmedden Garden

AB41 7PD

➲ *(1m W of Pitmedden on A920)*

☎ 0844 493 2177

e-mail: information@nts.org.uk

web: www.nts.org.uk

The fine 17th-century walled garden, with sundials, pavilions and fountains dotted among the parterres, has been authentically restored, and there is a Museum of Farming Life and a woodland walk.

Times ✳ Garden, Museum: May-Sep daily 10-5.30. Last admission at 5. Grounds: all year, daily. **Facilities** ♿ 💬 🏞 ♿ (Partly accessible) (2 wheelchairs available, scented plants) toilets for disabled shop ❦

Tolquhon Castle

AB41 7LP

➲ *(2m NE off B999)*

☎ 01651 851286

web: www.historic-scotland.gov.uk

Now roofless, this late 16th-century quadrangular mansion encloses an early 15th-century tower. There is a fine gatehouse and a splendid courtyard.

Times ✳ Open all year, Apr-Sep, daily 9.30-6.30; Oct-Mar, wknds only 9.30-6.30. Closed 25-26 Dec & 1-2 Jan. **Facilities** ♿ 🏞 shop ⊗ 🎫

RHYNIE   MAP 15 NJ42

Leith Hall, Garden & Estate

Kennethmont AB54 4NQ

➲ *(on B9002, 1m W of Kennethmont)*

☎ 0844 493 2175

e-mail: information@nts.org.uk

web: www.nts.org.uk

Home of the Leith family for over 300 years, the house dates back to 1650, and has a number of Jacobite relics and fine examples of needlework. It is surrounded by charming gardens and extensive grounds.

Times ✳ House: 31 Mar-Jun wknds only 12-5. Jul-Aug daily 12-5. Sep-Oct wknds only 12-5. Last admission 4.15. Garden: All year daily 9-sunset. Grounds: All year daily. Open BH wknds from Fr-Mon incl. **Facilities** ♿ (charged) 💬 🏞 ♿ (parking next to hall, scented garden, wheelchair avail.) toilets for disabled ⊗ (ex assist dogs) ❦

STONEHAVEN   MAP 15 NO88

Dunnottar Castle

AB39 2TL

➲ *(2m S of Stonehaven on A92)*

☎ 01569 762173

e-mail: info@dunechtestates.co.uk

web: www.dunnottarcastle.co.uk

This once-impregnable fortress, now a spectacular ruin, was the site of the successful protection of the Scottish Crown Jewels from the might of Cromwell. A must for anyone who takes Scottish history seriously.

Times Open all year, Spring & Autumn, Mon-Sat 9-6, Sun 2-5; Summer daily 9-6; Winter open Fri-Mon only. (Last entry 30mins before closing). **Fee** ✳ £5 (ch 5-15 £1) **Facilities** ♿ 🏞 (indoor & outdoor) ♿ (many steps) ⊗ (ex on a lead)

STONEHAVEN CONTINUED

Tolbooth Museum FREE

Old Pier AB39 2JU

➲ *(on harbour front)*

☎ 01771 622807

e-mail: museums@aberdeenshire.gov.uk
web: www.aberdeenshire.gov.uk/museums

Built in the late 16th century as a storehouse for the Earls Marischal at Dunnottar Castle, the building was the Kincardineshire County Tollbooth from 1600-1767. Displays feature local history and fishing.

Times Open 22 Mar-22 Sep, Wed-Mon, 1.30-4.30. **Facilities** Ⓟ (20yds) ♿ (lower ground floor not accessible) ⊗ (ex assist dogs)

TURRIFF   MAP 15 NJ75

Fyvie Castle

Fyvie AB53 8JS

➲ *(8m SE of Turriff off A947)*

☎ 0844 493 2182

e-mail: information@nts.org.uk

web: www.nts.org.uk

This superb castle, founded in the 13th century, has five towers, each built in a different century, and is one of the grandest examples of Scottish Baronial. It contains the finest wheel stair in Scotland, and a 17th-century morning room, lavishly furnished in Edwardian style. The collection of portraits is exceptional, and there are also displays of arms and armour and tapestries.

Times ✳ Castle: 31 Mar-Jun, Sat-Wed 12-5. Jul-Aug daily 11-5. Sep-Oct, Sat-Wed 12-5. Last admission 4.15. Garden: all year, daily 9-sunset. Open BH wknds from Fri-Mon incl. Grounds: open all year, daily. **Facilities** Ⓟ ⬱ 🍴 ♿ (Partly accessible) (small lift, Braille sheets, scented gardens) toilets for disabled shop ⊗ (ex assist dogs) 🐾

ANGUS

ARBROATH   MAP 12 NO64

Arbroath Abbey

DD11 1EG

☎ 01241 878756

web: www.historic-scotland.gov.uk

The 'Declaration of Arbroath' - declaring Robert the Bruce as king - was signed at the 12th-century abbey on 6 April 1320. The abbot's house is well preserved, and the church remains are also interesting.

Times ✳ Open all year, Apr-Sep, daily 9.30-6.30; Oct-Mar, daily 9.30-4.30. Closed 25-26 Dec & 1-2 Jan. **Facilities** Ⓟ ⊗ ⚑

Arbroath Museum FREE

Signal Tower, Ladyloan DD11 1PU

➲ *(on A92 adjacent to harbour. 16m NE of Dundee)*

☎ 01241 875598

e-mail: signal.tower@angus.gov.uk
web: www.angus.gov.uk/history/museums

Arbroath Smokies, textiles and engineering feature at this local history museum housed in the 1813 shore station of Stevenson's Bell Rock lighthouse.

Times Open all year, Mon-Sat 10-5; Jul-Aug, Sun 2-5. Closed 25-26 Dec & 1-2 Jan. **Facilities** Ⓟ 🍴 (outdoor) ♿ (induction loop) shop ⊗ (ex assist dogs)

BRECHIN   MAP 15 NO66

Brechin Town House Museum FREE

28 High St DD9 7AA

➲ *(off A90 at sign for Brechin, 2m into town centre)*

☎ 01356 625536

e-mail: brechin.museum@angus.gov.uk
web: www.angus.gov.uk/history/museum

Within a former courtroom, debtor's prison and seat of local government, this museum covers the history of the little City of Brechin from the earliest settlement, through the market town to industrialisation in the form of flax, jute mills, distilling, weaving and engineering. Brechin's fascinating history of development is portrayed in vivid displays. The Museum will be closed for refurbishment from October 2008 until spring 2009 please phone for details.

Times Closed for refurbishment Oct 2008-Spring 2009 please call for details **Facilities** Ⓟ (150yds) (2hrs max in free car park) ♿ (Induction loop) toilets for disabled shop ⊗ (ex assist dogs)

Pictavia Visitor Centre 2 for 1

Brechin Castle Centre, Haughmuir DD9 6RL

➲ *(off A90 at Brechin)*

☎ 01356 626241

e-mail: ecdev@angus.gov.uk
web: www.pictavia.org.uk

Find about more about the ancient pagan nation of the Picts, who lived in Scotland nearly 2,000 years ago. Visitors can learn about Pictish culture, art and religion through film, interactive displays and music. There are also nature and farm trails, a pets' corner, and an adventure playground in the adjacent country park (operated by Brechin Castle Centre). For events please check website.

Times Open daily, Etr-mid Oct, Mon-Sat 9.30-5.30, Sun 10.30-5.30; mid Oct-Etr, Sat 9-5, Sun 10-5. Closed 25-26 Dec & 1-2 Jan **Fee** £3.25 (ch & concessions £2.25). Group rates available parties 11+, educational rates for schools/students. **Facilities** ℗ ⌨ ⏣ ⴹ (outdoor) & toilets for disabled shop garden centre ⊗ (ex assist dogs) ▄

CARNOUSTIE   MAP 12 NO53

Barry Water Mill

Barry DD7 7RJ

⊃ *(N of Barry village between A92 & A930, 2m W of Carnoustie)*

☎ 0844 493 2140

e-mail: information@nts.org.uk

web: www.nts.org.uk

This restored 18th-century mill works on a demonstration basis. Records show that the site has been used for milling since the 16th century. Displays highlight the important place the mill held in the community. There is a waymarked walk and picnic area.

Times ✳ Open 31 Mar-Oct, Thu-Mon (closed Tue-Wed) 12-5, Sun 1-5. **Facilities** ℗ ⏣ & (Partly accessible) (ramp from car park to mill) toilets for disabled ⊗ (ex dogs on lead on grounds) ⴘ

EDZELL   MAP 15 NO56

Edzell Castle

DD9 7UE

⊃ *(on B966)*

☎ 01356 648631

web: www.historic-scotland.gov.uk

The 16th-century castle has a remarkable walled garden that was built in 1604 by Sir David Lindsay. Flower-filled recesses in the walls are alternated with heraldic and symbolic sculptures of a sort not seen elsewhere in Scotland. There are ornamental and border gardens and a garden house.

Times ✳ Open all year, Apr-Sep, daily 9.30-6.30; Oct-Mar, Mon-Wed & Sat-Sun 9.30-4.30. Closed 25-26 Dec & 1-2 Jan. **Facilities** ℗ ⏣ shop ▮

FORFAR   MAP 15 NO45

The Meffan Museum & Art Gallery

20 West High St DD8 1BB

⊃ *(off A90. Attraction in town centre)*

☎ 01307 464123   467017

e-mail: the.meffan@angus.gov.uk

web: www.angus.gov/history/museum

This lively, ever-changing contemporary art gallery and museum is full of surprises. Walk down a cobbled street full of shops, ending up at a witch-burning scene. Carved Pictish stones and a diorama of an archaeological dig complete the vibrant displays.

Times Open all year Mon-Sat. Closed 25-26 Dec & 1-2 Jan. **Facilities** ℗ (150yds) (30 mins limit on street) & (handrails, wide door, portable ramp) toilets for disabled shop ⊗ (ex assist dogs) ▄

GLAMIS   MAP 15 NO34

Angus Folk Museum

Kirkwynd Cottages DD8 1RT

⊃ *(off A94, in Glamis, 5m SW of Forfar)*

☎ 0844 493 2141

e-mail: information@nts.org.uk

web: www.nts.org.uk

A row of stone-roofed, late 18th-century cottages now houses the splendid Angus Folk Collection of domestic equipment and cottage furniture. Across the wynd, an Angus stone steading houses 'The Life on the Land' exhibition.

Times ✳ Open 31 Mar-Jun, wknds only 12-5, Jul-Aug Mon-Sat 11-5, Sun 1-5, Sep-Oct wknds only 12-5, BH wknds from Fri-Mon inclusive. **Facilities** ℗ (charged) & toilets for disabled ⊗ (ex assist dogs) ⴘ

Glamis Castle   2 for 1

DD8 1RJ

⊃ *(5m W of Forfar on A94)*

☎ 01307 840393

e-mail: enquires@glamis-castle.co.uk

web: www.glamis-castle.co.uk

Glamis Castle is the family home of the Earls of Strathmore and Kinghorne and has been a royal residence since 1372. It is the childhood home of the late Queen Mother, the birthplace of her daughter the late Princess Margaret, and the setting for Shakespeare's play *Macbeth*. Though the Castle is open to visitors it remains the home of the Strathmore family. Each year there are Highland games, a transport extravaganza, the Scottish Prom Weekend, and a countryside festival. Contact venue for exact dates.

Times Open Mar-Oct, 10-6. (Last admission 4.30) Nov-Dec, 10.30-5. (Last admission 3.30). **Fee** ✳ Castle & grounds £7.30 (ch £1.40, pen & students £6.10). Family ticket £21. Grounds only £3.50 (ch,pens & students £2.50) group 20+. **Facilities** ℗ ⏣ (outdoor) & (Partly accessible) (castle tour not suitable, audio visual film of tour) toilets for disabled shop ⊗ (ex in grounds & assist dogs) ▄

SCOTLAND

KIRRIEMUIR MAP 15 NO35

J M Barrie's Birthplace

9 Brechin Rd DD8 4BX

➲ *(on A90/A926 in Kirriemuir, 6m NW of Forfar)*

☎ 0844 493 2142

e-mail: information@nts.org.uk

web: www.nts.org.uk

The creator of Peter Pan, Sir James Barrie, was born in Kirriemuir in 1860. The upper floors of No 9 Brechin Road are furnished as they may have been when Barrie lived there, and the adjacent house, No 11, houses an exhibition about him. The wash-house outside was his first 'theatre' and gave him the idea for Wendy's house in *Peter Pan*.

Times ✷ 31 Mar-Jun Sat-Wed 12-5, Sun1-5. Jul-Aug daily 11-5. Sep-Oct Sat-Wed 12-5, Sun 1-5. Bh wknds Fri-Mon incl. **Facilities** Ⓟ (100yds) ⌺ ⊓ ⌖ (Partly accessible) (stairlift, induction loop, Braille info sheets) shop ⊗ (ex assist dogs) ♨

Kirriemuir Gateway to the Glens Museum FREE

The Town House, 32 High St DD8 4BB

➲ *(in town centre square, 30mins from Dundee, N on A90)*

☎ 01575 575479

e-mail: kirrie.gateway@angus.gov.uk

web: www.angus.gov.uk/history/museum

Housed in the town house dating from 1604, this museum covers the history of Kirriemuir and the Angus Glens from prehistoric times. A realistic model of Kirriemuir on market day in 1604 can be seen and local voices can be heard telling their part in the area's history from sweet making to linen weaving. Animals and birds can be seen at close range in the Wildlife diorama. The museum also houses Kirriemuir tourist information centre.

Times Open Jan-Mar & Oct-Dec, Mon-Wed, Fri-Sat 10-5, Thu 2-5; Apr-Sep, Mon-Sat 10-5Closed 25-26 Dec & 1-2 Jan **Facilities** Ⓟ (200yds) (free car park) ⌖ (ground floor accessible, steps to first floor) (induction loop) toilets for disabled shop ⊗ (ex assist dogs)

MONTROSE MAP 15 NO75

House of Dun

DD10 9LQ

➲ *(on A935, 3m W of Montrose)*

☎ 0844 493 2144

e-mail: information@nts.org.uk

web: www.nts.org.uk

This Georgian house, overlooking the Montrose Basin, was built for Lord Dun in 1730 and is noted for the exuberant plasterwork of the interior. Family portraits, fine furniture and porcelain are on display, and royal mementos connected with a daughter of King William IV and the actress Mrs Jordan, who lived here in the 19th century. There is a walled garden and woodland walks.

Times ✷ Open House:31 Mar-Jun, Wed-Sun 12.30-5.30. Jul-Aug daily 11.30-5.30. Sep-Oct Wed-Sun 12.30-5.30. (Last admission 45 mins before closing). Garden: All year daily 9-sunset. Grounds: All year daily. Open BH wknds from Fri-Mon incl. **Facilities** Ⓟ ⍟⊓⌖ (Partly accessible) (Braille sheets, wheelchair & stair lift, subtitled video) toilets for disabled shop ⊗ (ex assist dogs) ♨

Montrose Museum & Art Gallery FREE

Panmure Place DD10 8HE

➲ *(opposite Montrose Academy in town centre, approach via A92 from Aberdeen or Dundee)*

☎ 01674 673232

e-mail: montrose.museum@angus.gov.uk

web: www.angus.gov.uk/history/museum

Extensive local collections cover the history of Montrose from prehistoric times, the maritime history of the port, the natural history of Angus, and local art. The museum also houses Montrose tourist information centre.

Times Open all year, Mon-Sat 10-5. Closed 25-26 Dec & 1-2 Jan. **Facilities** Ⓟ 20yds (induction loop) shop ⊗ (ex assist dogs)

ARGYLL & BUTE

ARDUAINE MAP 10 NM71

Arduaine Garden

PA34 4XQ

➲ *(20m S of Oban, on A816, 19m N of Lochgilphead)*

☎ 0844 493 2216

e-mail: information@nts.org.uk

web: www.nts.org.uk

An outstanding 18-acre garden on a promontory bounded by Loch Melfort and the Sound of Jura, climatically favoured by the North Atlantic Drift. It is famous for its rhododendrons and azalea species and other rare trees and shrubs.

Times ✷ Open all year, Reception Centre 30 Mar-Sep daily 9.30-4.30, Garden all year daily 9.30-sunset. **Facilities** Ⓟ⊓⌖ (Partly accessible) (Scented flowers) toilets for disabled ⊗ (ex assist dogs) ♨

ARROCHAR MAP 10 NN20

Argyll Forest Park FREE

Forestry Commission, Ardgartan Visitor Centre G83 7AR

➲ *(on A83 at foot of "The Rest and Be Thankful")*

☎ 01301 702597

e-mail: katy.freeman@forestry.gsl.gov.uk

This park extends over a large area of hill ground and forest, noted for its rugged beauty. Numerous forest walks and picnic sites allow exploration; the Arboretum walks and the route between Younger Botanic Gardens and Puck's Glen are particularly lovely. Wildlife viewing facilities include live footage of nesting birds in season.

Times Open daily Etr-Oct **Facilities** Ⓟ ⊓ (outdoor) shop ▬

AUCHINDRAIN MAP 10 NN00

Auchindrain Museum

PA32 8XN

(6m SW of Inverarary on A83)

01499 500235

e-mail: manager@auchindrain-museum.org.uk

web: www.auchindrain-museum.org.uk

Auchindrain is an extraordinary attraction that brings an original Township or farming village back to life. On entering the Museum visitors step back in time to witness how the local community lived, worked and played. The original Township buildings are furnished and give a fascinating glimpse into the lives of the people who once lived and worked at Auchindrain. See the website for special events. The museum will be 45 years old in 2009.

Times Open Apr-Oct, daily 10-5. (last admission 4) **Fee** * £4.50 (ch £2.20, concession £3.50). Family ticket £12. **Facilities** (indoor & outdoor) (some areas are accessible but steep paths) shop

BARCALDINE MAP 10 NM94

Scottish Sea Life Sanctuary

2 for 1

PA37 1SE

(10m N of Oban on A828 towards Fort William)

01631 720386

e-mail: obansealife@merlinentertainments.biz

web: www.sealsanctuary.co.uk

Set in one of Scotland's most picturesque locations, the Scottish Sea Life Sanctuary provides dramatic views of native undersea life including stingrays, seals, octopus and catfish. There are daily talks and feeding demonstrations and during the summer young seals can be viewed prior to their release back into the wild. Recent additions include Otter Creek - a large naturally landscaped enclosure with deep diving pool with underwater viewing and cascading streams through other pools, and 'Into the Deep', a themed interactive area displaying living creatures from the deep. There is a restaurant, gift shop, children's play park and a nature trail. The Sanctury celebrates its 30th birthday in 2009.

Times Open daily at 10am. Please call for last admissions. **Fee** Prices not confirmed for 2009 **Facilities** (outdoor) (assistance available for wheelchairs) toilets for disabled shop (ex assist dogs)

BENMORE MAP 10 NS18

Benmore Botanic Garden

PA23 8QU

(7m N of Dunoon on A815)

01369 706261

e-mail: benmore@rbge.org.uk

web: www.rbge.org.uk

From the formal gardens, through the hillside woodlands, follow the paths to a stunning viewpoint with a spectacular outlook across the garden and the Holy Loch to the Firth of Clyde and beyond. Amongst many highlights are the stately conifers, the magnificent avenue of giant redwoods, and an extensive magnolia and rhododendron collection.

Times * Open Mar & Oct daily 10-5, Apr-Sep daily 10-6 **Facilities** shop garden centre (ex assist dogs)

CARNASSARIE CASTLE MAP 10 NM80

Carnassarie Castle

FREE

PA31 8RQ

(2m N of Kilmartin off A816)

web: www.historic-scotland.gov.uk

A handsome combined tower house and hall, home of John Carswell, first Protestant Bishop of the Isles and translator of the first book printed in Gaelic. Very fine architectural details of the late 16th century.

Times * Open at all reasonable times. **Facilities**

HELENSBURGH MAP 10 NS28

The Hill House

Upper Colquhoun St G84 9AJ

(off B832, between A82 & A814 23m NW of Glasgow)

0844 493 2208

e-mail: information@nts.org.uk

web: www.nts.org.uk

The Hill House is a handsome example of Charles Rennie Mackintosh's work, modern but part-inspired by Scottish tower houses. It was commissioned by the publisher Walter Blackie. The gardens are being restored to Blackie's design, with features reflecting the suggestions of Mackintosh. There is also a special display about Mackintosh.

Times * Open 30 Mar-31 Oct daily 1.30-5.30. Morning visits available for pre-booked groups. **Facilities** (Partly accessible) (Braille Guidebook) shop

SCOTLAND

INVERARAY   MAP 10 NN00

Bell Tower of All Saints' Church
The Avenue PA32 8YX

➲ (through the arches on Front St, into Avenue car park)

☎ 01838 200293

The tower stands next to All-Saints Church but is separate from it. Built by the 10th Duke of Argyll as a war memorial to the dead of Clan Campbell, it was completed in 1931. It has the second heaviest peal of bells in the world, and these are rung once a month. The tower is 126 feet high and has a narrow circular staircase of 176 steps, which are not suitable for the infirm. From the top is a spectacular view of Inverary, Loch Fyne and the surrounding hills.

Times Tower open May-Sep, daily, 10-1 & 2-5. Church open Mar-Oct. **Fee** ✻ £2 (ch & concessions 75p). Family £4 **Facilities** ℗ (adjacent to church) (pay and display) ⋒ (outdoor) ﬔ ⊗ (ex assist dogs)

Inveraray Castle
PA32 8XE

➲ (on A83 Glasgow to Campbeltown road)

☎ 01499 302203

e-mail: enquiries@inveraray-castle.com

web: www.inveraray-castle.com

The Castle is currently home to the Duke of Argyll, Head of the Clan Campbell, whose family have lived in Inveraray since the 15th century. Designed by Roger Morris and decorated by Robert Mylne, the fairytale exterior belies the grandeur of the gracious interior. The Armoury Hall contains some 1,300 pieces including Brown Bess muskets, Lochaber axes, 18th-century Scottish broadswords, and swords from the Battle of Culloden. Other rooms contain fine French tapestries, Scottish, English and French furniture, and a wealth of other works of art. There is also a unique collection of china, silver and family artefacts.

Times Open Apr-Oct., Mon-Sat 10-5.45, Sun 12-5.45 (last admission 5) **Fee** £6.30 (ch under 16 £4.10, concessions £5.20) Family ticket £17. School parties. Groups 20+. 20% discount. School parties £2.10 per child. **Facilities** ℗ ⊑ ⋒ (outdoor) shop ⊗ (ex assist dogs & in grounds) ⇔

Inveraray Jail
Church Square PA32 8TX

➲ (on A82/A83 Campbeltown road)

☎ 01499 302381

e-mail: info@inverarayjail.co.uk

web: www.inverarayjail.co.uk

Enter Inveraray Jail and step back in time. See furnished cells and experience prison sounds and smells. Ask the 'prisoner' how to pick oakum. Turn the heavy handle of an original crank machine, take 40 winks in a hammock or listen to Matron's tales of day-to-day prison life. Visit the magnificent 1820 courtroom and hear trials in progress. Imaginative exhibitions including 'Torture, Death and Damnation' and 'In Prison Today'. Also a fully preserved "Black Maria", built in 1891.

Times Open all year, Nov-Mar, daily 10-5 (last admisssion 4); Apr-Oct, daily 9.30-6 (last admission 5). Closed 25-26 Dec & 1-2 Jan. **Fee** £7.25 (ch £4.25, concession £5.50). **Facilities** ℗ (100 yds) ﬔ (wheelchair ramp at rear, induction loop in courtroom) toilets for disabled shop ⇔

KILMARTIN   MAP 10 NR89

Dunadd Fort   FREE
➲ (2m S of Kilmartin on A816)

web: www.historic-scotland.gov.uk

Dunadd was one of the ancient capitals of Dalriada from which the Celtic kingdom of Scotland was formed. Near to this prehistoric hill fort (now little more than an isolated hillock) are carvings of a boar and a footprint; these probably marked the spot where early kings were invested with their royal power.

Times ✻ Open at all reasonable times. **Facilities** ⊗ ⋒

Kilmartin House Museum
PA31 8RQ

➲ (in centre of village, adjacent to church)

☎ 01546 510278

e-mail: museum@kilmartin.org

web: www.kilmartin.org

People have lived in the Kilmartin area for thousands of years, gradually shaping the extraordinary landscape you see today. More than 350 prehistoric and historic sites lie within six miles of this quiet village; burial cairns, rock-carvings, standing stones, stone circles and the fortress of the earliest Scottish Kings, medieval castles, ancient gravestones depicting warriors, early Christian crosses and deserted croft houses. This remarkable concentration and diversity of ancient sites is celebrated at Kilmartin House Museum. Explore enigmatic monuments, see ancient objects and learn more about the people who made them.

Times Open Mar-Oct, daily, 10-5.30. Nov-Xmas 11-4. **Fee** £4.60 (ch £1.70, concessions £3.90). Family ticket £6 or £10. **Facilities** ℗ ⊑ ⊠ licensed ⋒ (outdoor) ﬔ (Partly accessible) toilets for disabled shop ⊗ (ex assist dogs) ⇔(ex small coaches, pre-booked) ⇔

LOCHAWE   MAP 10 NN12

Cruachan Power Station
Visitor Centre, Dalmally PA33 1AN

➲ (A85 18m E of Oban)

☎ 01866 822618

e-mail: visit.cruachan@scottishpower.com

web: www.visitcruachan.co.uk

A vast cavern hidden deep inside Ben Cruachan, which contains a 400,000-kilowatt hydro-electric power station, driven by water drawn from a high-level reservoir up the mountain. A guided tour takes you inside the mountain and reveals the generators in their underground cavern.

Times ✻ Open Etr-Nov, daily 9.30-5 (last tour 4.15). (Winter hours available on request). **Facilities** ℗ ⊑ ⋒ shop ⊗ (ex assist dogs) ⇔

MINARD   MAP 10 NR99

Crarae Gardens

PA32 8YA

➲ *(10m S of Inveraray on A83)*

☎ 0844 493 2210

e-mail: information@nts.org.uk

web: www.nts.org.uk

Set beside Loch Fyne, these gardens are among Scotland's loveliest, noted for their rhododendrons, azaleas, conifers and ornamental shrubs, which include a number of rare species.

Times ✷ Visitor centre 30 Mar-Sep daily 10-5, Garden all year daily 9.30-sunset. **Facilities** ❷ ▱ 🍴 & (Partly accessible) toilets for disabled shop garden centre ⊗ (ex dogs on short lead) ➡

OBAN   MAP 10 NM83

Dunstaffnage Castle

PA37 1PZ

➲ *(3m N on peninsula)*

☎ 01631 562465

web: www.historic-scotland.gov.uk

Now ruined, this four-sided stronghold has a gatehouse, two round towers and walls 10 feet thick. It was once the prison of Flora MacDonald who aided the escape of Bonnie Prince Charlie.

Times ✷ Open all year, Apr-Sep, daily 9.30-6.30; Oct-Mar, Mon-Wed & Sat-Sun daily 9.30-4.30. Closed 25-26 Dec & 1-2 Jan. **Facilities** ❷ shop ▯

TAYNUILT   MAP 10 NN03

Bonawe Iron Furnace

PA35 1JQ

➲ *(0.75m NE off B845)*

☎ 01866 822432

web: www.historic-scotland.gov.uk

The furnace is a restored charcoal blast-furnace for iron-smelting and making cast-iron. It was established in 1753 and worked until 1876. The works exploited the Forest of Lorne to provide charcoal for fuel.

Times ✷ Open Apr-Sep, daily 9.30-6.30. **Facilities** ❷ shop ▯

CLACKMANNANSHIRE

ALLOA   MAP 11 NS89

Alloa Tower

Alloa Park FK10 1PP

➲ *(Off A907, close to town centre)*

☎ 0844 493 2129

e-mail: information@nts.org.uk

web: www.nts.org.uk

Beautifully restored, the tower, completed in 1467, is the only remaining part of the ancestral home of the Earls of Mar. The structure

retains rare medieval features, notably the complete timber roof structure and groin vaulting. A superb loan collection of portraits and chattels of the Erskine family includes paintings by Raeburn.

Times ✷ Open 30 Mar-Oct daily 1-5. Morning visits available for pre-booked groups. **Facilities** ❷ & (Partly accessible) (large print interpretation, induction loop) toilets for disabled ⊗ 🛡

DOLLAR   MAP 11 NS99

Castle Campbell

FK14 7PP

➲ *(10m E of Stirling on A91)*

☎ 01259 742408

web: www.historic-scotland.gov.uk

Traditionally known as the 'Castle of Gloom', the 15th to 17th-century tower stands in the picturesque Ochil Hills, gives wonderful views, and can be reached by a walk through the magnificent Dollar Glen. Care must be taken in or after rain when the path may be dangerous.

Times ✷ Open all year, Apr-Sep, daily 9.30-6.30; Oct-Mar, Mon-Wed & Sat-Sun 9.30-4.30. Closed 25-26 Dec & 1-2 Jan. **Facilities** ❷ 🍴 ⴲ shop ▯ 🛡

DUMFRIES & GALLOWAY

ARDWELL   MAP 10 NX14

Ardwell House Gardens

DG9 9LY

➲ *(10m S of Stranraer, on A716)*

☎ 01776 860227

Country house gardens and grounds with flowering shrubs and woodland walks. Plants for sale. House not open to the public.

Times Open Apr-Oct, 10-5. Walled garden & greenhouses close at 5. **Fee** ✷ £3 (ch & concessions £2) **Facilities** ❷ ⴲ (outdoor) & toilets for disabled garden centre

SCOTLAND

SCOTLAND

CAERLAVEROCK   MAP 11 NY06

Caerlaverock Castle

Glencaple DG1 4RU

➲ *(8m SE of Dumfries, on B725)*

☎ 01387 770244

web: www.historic-scotland.gov.uk

This ancient seat of the Maxwell family is a splendid medieval stronghold dating back to the 13th century. It has high walls and round towers, with machicolations added in the 15th century.

Times ✷ Open all year, Apr-Sep, daily 9.30-6.30; Oct-Mar, daily 9.30-4.30. Closed 25-26 Dec & 1-2 Jan. **Facilities** ℗ ⑩ ⼌ shop ▮

WWT Caerlaverock   `2 for 1`

Eastpark Farm DG1 4RS

➲ *(9m SE of Dumfries, signed from A75)*

☎ 01387 770200

e-mail: info@caerlaverock@wwt.org.uk

web: www.wwt.org.uk

This internationally important wetland is the winter home of the Barnacle goose, whose entire Svalbard population spend the winter on the Solway Firth. Observation facilities include 20 hides, three towers and a heated observatory. A wide variety of other wildlife can be seen, notably the rare Natterjack Toad and a family of Barn Owls and ospreys which can be observed via a CCTV system. Swan feeds daily at 11-2. For special events please see website for details.

Times Open daily 10-5. Closed 25 Dec. **Fee** £5.95 (ch £2.95 & concessions £4.50). Family ticket £16 **Facilities** ℗ ⼐ ⼌ (outdoor) ♿ (all hides and observatories accessible except farmhouse tower and small avenue hides) toilets for disabled shop ⊗ (ex assist dogs) ▰

CARDONESS CASTLE   MAP 11 NX55

Cardoness Castle

DG7 2EH

➲ *(1m SW of Gatehouse of Fleet, off A75)*

☎ 01557 814427

web: www.historic-scotland.gov.uk

A 15th-century stronghold overlooking the Water of Fleet. It was once the home of the McCullochs of Galloway. The architectural details inside the tower are of very high quality.

Times ✷ Open Apr-Sep, daily 9.30-6.30; Oct closed Thu & Fri. Nov-Mar open wknds only. Closed 25-26 Dec & 1-2 Jan. **Facilities** ℗ shop ▮

CASTLE DOUGLAS   MAP 11 NX76

Threave Castle

DG7 1RX

➲ *(3m W on A75)*

☎ 0411 223101

web: www.historic-scotland.gov.uk

Archibald the Grim built this lonely castle in the late 14th century. It stands on an islet in the River Dee, and is four storeys high with round towers guarding the outer wall. The island is reached by boat.

Times ✷ Open Apr-Sep, daily 9.30-6.30. **Facilities** ℗ ⼌ ⊗ ▮

Threave Garden & Estate

DG7 1RX

➲ *(1m W of Castle Douglas, off A75)*

☎ 08449 4932245

e-mail: information@nts.org.uk

web: www.nts.org.uk

The best time to visit is in spring when there is a dazzling display of daffodils. The garden is a delight in all seasons, however, and is home to the National Trust for Scotland's School of Practical Gardening.

Times ✷ Visitor, countryside centre & exhibition room Feb-Mar daily 10-4, Apr-Oct daily 9.30-5.30, Nov-23 Dec daily 10-4, House Apr-Oct, Wed-Fri & Sun 11-3.30, Walled garden & glasshouses all year daily (9.30-4.30 Fri), Garden & Estate all year daily. **Facilities** ℗ ⑩ ⼌ ♿ (wheelchairs available incl. electric wheelchair) toilets for disabled shop garden centre ⊗ (ex assist dogs) ☙

CREETOWN   MAP 11 NX45

Creetown Gem Rock Museum

Chain Rd DG8 7HJ

➲ *(follow signs from A75 at Creetown bypass)*

☎ 01671 820357 & 820554

e-mail: enquiries@gemrock.net

web: www.gemrock.net

The Gem Rock is the leading independent museum of its kind in the UK, and is renowned worldwide. Crystals, gemstones, minerals, jewellery and fossils, the Gem Rock displays some of the most breathtaking examples of nature's wonders. See the audio-visual 'Fire in the Stones', explore the Crystal Cave, relax in the Prospector's Study, and sample the home-baked Scottish cakes in the café.

Times Open Etr-Sep, daily 9.30-5.30; Oct-Nov & Feb, Feb-Etr, daily 10-4; Dec, wknds 10-4 or by appointment wkdays. Closed 23 Dec-Jan. **Facilities** ℗ ⼐ ⼌ (outdoor) ♿ (ideal attraction for wheelchair users) toilets for disabled shop ⊗ (ex assist dogs) ▰

DRUMCOLTRAN TOWER MAP 11 NX86

Drumcoltran Tower `FREE`

➲ *(7m NE of Dalbeattie, in farm buildings off A711)*

web: www.historic-scotland.gov.uk

A well-preserved tower from the mid-16th century, simply planned and built, set in a busy modern farmyard.

Times ✳ Open at any reasonable time. **Facilities** ℗ ⊗ 🏳

DUMFRIES MAP 11 NX97

Burns Mausoleum `FREE`

St Michael's Churchyard

➲ *(at junct of Brooms Rd (ATS) and St Michael's St (B725))*

☎ 01387 255297

e-mail: dumfriesmuseum@dumgal.gov.uk

web: www.dumgal.gov.uk/museums

The mausoleum is in the form of a Greek temple, and contains the tombs of Robert Burns, his wife Jean Armour, and their five sons. A sculptured group shows the Muse of Poetry flinging her cloak over Burns at the plough.

Times House: Phone for details. Grounds: Unrestricted access. **Facilities** ℗ (50yds) ⅋ (visitors with mobility difficulties tel 01387 255297)

Dumfries Museum & Camera Obscura `2 for 1`

The Observatory, Rotchell Rd DG2 7SW

➲ *(A75 from S Carlisle or SW from Castle Douglas, museum in Maxwellton area of Dumfries)*

☎ 01387 253374

e-mail: dumfriesmuseum@dumgal.gov.uk

web: www.dumgal.gov.uk/museums

Situated in and around the 18th-century windmill tower, the museum's collections were started over 150 years ago and exhibitions trace the history of the people and landscape of Dumfries & Galloway. The Camera Obscura is to be found on the top floor of the windmill tower. 2-for-1 voucher valid at Camera Obscura.

Times Open all year Apr-Sep, Mon-Sat, 10-5, Sun, 2-5; Oct-Mar, Tue-Sat 10-1 & 2-5. **Fee** ✳ Free except Camera Obscura £2.10 (concessions £1.05) **Facilities** ℗ ⋔ (outdoor) ⅋ (spiral staircase) (parking available) toilets for disabled shop

Old Bridge House Museum `2 for 1`

Mill Rd DG2 7BE

➲ *(at W end of Devorgilla's Bridge)*

☎ 01387 256904

e-mail: dumfriesmuseum@dumgal.gov.uk

web: www.dumgal.gov.uk/museums

The Old Bridge House was built in 1660, and is the oldest house in Dumfries. A museum of everyday life in the town, it has an early

20th-century dentist's surgery, a Victorian nursery and kitchens of the 1850s and 1900s.

Times Open Apr-Sep 10-5 Mon-Sat & 2-5 Sun. **Fee** Donations welcome **Facilities** ℗ shop

Robert Burns Centre `2 for 1`

Mill Rd DG2 7BE

➲ *(on Westbank of River Nith)*

☎ 01387 264808

e-mail: dumfriesmuseum@dumgal.gov.uk

web: www.dumgal.gov.uk/museums

This award-winning centre explores the connections between Robert Burns and the town of Dumfries. Situated in the town's 18th-century watermill, the centre tells the story of Burns' last years spent in the busy streets and lively atmosphere of Dumfries in the 1790s. In the evening the centre shows feature films in the Film Theatre. 2-for-1 voucher valid on audio-visual presentations.

Times Open all year. Apr-Sep 10-8 Mon-Sat, 2-5 Sun. Oct-Mar, 10-1 & 2-5 Tue-Sat. **Fee** ✳ Free admission to museum, audio-visual theatre £1.80 (concessions 90p). **Facilities** ℗ ⊒ ⏵ licensed ⋔ (outdoor) ⅋ (induction loop hearing system in auditorium, chairlift) toilets for disabled shop ▬

Robert Burns House `FREE`

Burns St DG1 2PS

➲ *(signed from Brooms Rd [ATS] car park)*

☎ 01387 255297

e-mail: dumfriesmuseum@dumgal.gov.uk

web: www.dumgal.gov.uk/museums

It was in this house that Robert Burns spent the last three years of his short life; he died here in 1796. It retains much of its 18th-century character and contains many fascinating items connected with the poet. There is the chair in which he wrote his last poems, many original letters and manuscripts, and the famous Kilmarnock and Edinburgh editions of his work.

Times Open all year Apr-Sep 10-5 Mon-Sat & 2-5 Sun. Oct-Mar 10-1 & 2-5 Tue-Sat. **Facilities** ℗ (opposite) shop

---

DUNDRENNAN MAP 11 NX74

Dundrennan Abbey

DG6 4QH

➲ *(6.5m SE of Kirkcudbright, on A711)*

☎ 01557 500262

web: www.historic-scotland.gov.uk

The now ruined abbey was founded for the Cistercians. The east end of the church and the chapter house are of exceptional architectural quality. Mary, Queen of Scots is thought to have spent her last night in Scotland here on 15 May 1568, before seeking shelter in England, where she was imprisoned and eventually executed.

Times ✳ Open, Apr-Sep, daily 9.30-6.30; Oct open daily 9.30-4.30 closed Thu & Fri. Nov-Mar wknds only 9.30-4.30. Closed 25-26 Dec & 1-2 Jan. **Facilities** ℗ ⊗ 🏳

SCOTLAND

GLENLUCE MAP 10 NX15

Glenluce Abbey

DG8 0AF

➲ *(2m NW, off A75)*

☎ 01581 300541

web: www.historic-scotland.gov.uk

The abbey was founded for the Cistercians in 1192 by Roland, Earl of Galloway. The ruins include a vaulted chapter house, and stand in a beautiful setting.

Times ✳ Open all year, Apr-Sep daily 9.30-6.30; Oct closed Thu & Fri. Nov-Mar wknds only. Closed 25-26 Dec & 1-2 Jan. **Facilities** ♿ ⌷ ⊗ 🅿

KIRKCUDBRIGHT MAP 11 NX65

Broughton House & Garden

12 High St DG6 4JX

➲ *(off A711/A755)*

☎ 0844 493 2246

e-mail: information@nts.org.uk

web: www.nts.org.uk

An 18th-century house where Edward A Hornel, one of the 'Glasgow Boys' group of artists, lived and worked from 1901-1933. It features a collection of his work, an extensive library of local history, including rare editions of Burns' works, and a Japanese-style garden that he created.

Times ✳ Garden only : Feb-30 Mar Mon-Fri 11-4. House & garden: Mar-Jun Thu-Mon 12-5. Jul-Aug, daily 12-5. Sep-Oct Thu-Mon 12-5. **Facilities** ♿ (on street) (limited space) ♿ (Partly accessible) (large print info, garden viewing area) ⊗ (ex assist dogs) 👗

Galloway Wildlife Conservation Park

Lochfergus Plantation DG6 4XX
➲ *(follow brown signs from A75, 1m from Kirkcudbright on B727)*

☎ 01557 331645

e-mail: info@gallowaywildlife.co.uk

web: www.gallowaywildlife.co.uk

Galloway is the wild animal conservation centre for southern Scotland, set in 27 acres of mixed woodland. A varied zoological collection of over 150 animals from all over the world. Close animal encounters and bird of prey displays are some of the features giving an insight into wildlife conservation.

Times Open Feb-Nov, daily 10-6 (last admission 5). **Fee** £6 (ch 4-15 £4, under 4 free, concessions £5). **Facilities** ♿ ⌷ 🅿 (outdoor) ♿ (due to the rising terrain, the nature trail is not accessible) (British sign language) toilets for disabled shop ⊗ (ex assist dogs) ▬

MacLellan's Castle

➲ *(in Kirkcudbright on A711)*

☎ 01557 331856

web: www.historic-scotland.gov.uk

This handsome structure has been a ruin since the mid 18th-century. It was once an imposing castellated mansion, elaborately planned with fine architectural detail. Something of its 16th-century grandeur still remains.

Times ✳ Open Apr-Sep, daily 9.30-6.30. **Facilities** 🅿 shop ⊗ 🚭 🅿

Stewartry Museum FREE

St Mary St DG6 4AQ

➲ *(from A711 through town, pass parish church, museum approx 200mtrs on right)*

☎ 01557 331643

e-mail: davidd@dumgal.gov.uk

web: www.dumgal.gov.uk/museums

A large and varied collection of archaeological, social history and natural history exhibits relating to the Stewartry district.

Times Open May, Jun & Sep, Mon-Sat 11-5 Sun 2-5; Jul-Aug, Mon-Sat 10-5 Sun 2-5; Oct Mon-Sat 11-4 Sun 2-5; Nov-Apr, Mon-Sat 11-4 **Facilities** 🅿 (outside) 🅿 (outdoor) ♿ (access to ground floor only) shop ⊗ (ex assist dogs)

Tolbooth Art Centre FREE

High St DG6 4JL

➲ *(from A711, through town pass parish church & Stewartry Museum, 1st right into High St)*

☎ 01557 331556

e-mail: david.devereux@dumgal.gov.uk

web: www.dumgal.gov.uk/museums

Dating from 1629, the Tolbooth was converted into an art centre and provides an interpretive introduction to the Kirkcudbright artists's colony, which flourished in the town from the 1880s. It also provides studio and exhibition space for contemporary local and visiting artists. There is a programme of exhibitions from March to October.

Times Open May, Jun & Sep, Mon-Sat 11-5 Sun 2-5; Jul & Aug, Mon-Sat 10-5, Sun 2-5; Oct, Mon-Sat 11-4 Sun 2-5; Nov-Apr, Mon-Sat 11-4 **Facilities** 🅿 (on street parking) ⌷ ♿ (lift for access to upper floors) toilets for disabled shop ⊗ (ex assist dogs)

NEW ABBEY   MAP 11 NX96

National Museum of Costume Scotland   `2 for 1`

Shambellie House DG2 8HQ

➲ *(7m S of Dumfries, on A710)*

☎ 01387 850375

e-mail: info@nms.ac.uk

web: www.nms.ac.uk

Shambellie House, a 19th-century country home in wooded grounds, is the perfect setting for discovering 100 years of costume, from the 1850s through to the 1950s. Put yourself in the shoes of those who wore the trends of the time. In 2009, the Museum will host the Jean Muir: A Fashion Icon exhibition. Jean Muir was at the forefront of the London fashion scene in the 1960s and 1970s. Her signature style was found in the cut and fit of an outfit. Find out why she was considered technically brilliant, who wore her designs and why were they life-long fans of her fashion label. 2-for-1 Voucher not valid for special events.

Times Open Apr-Oct, daily, 10-5. **Fee** ✳ £3 (ch under 12 & members free, concessions £2) **Facilities** ❷ ⬛ 🛆 (outdoor) ⅃ (ramp & wheelchair lift provide access to ground floor of museum, tearoom & toilets) (ramp and w/ chair lift at main entrance) shop ⊗ (ex assist dogs) ▬

New Abbey Corn Mill

DG2 8BX

➲ *(7m S of Dumfries on A710)*

☎ 01387 850260

web: www.historic-scotland.gov.uk

Built in the late 18th century, this water-driven corn mill is still in working order, and regular demonstrations are held.

Times ✳ Open all year, Apr-Sep, daily 9.30-6.30; Oct-Mar, Mon-Wed & Sat-Sun 9.30-4.30. Closed 25-26 Dec & 1-2 Jan. **Facilities** ℗ (100yds) shop ⊗ 🗐

Sweetheart Abbey

DG2 8BU

➲ *(on A710)*

☎ 01387 850397

web: www.historic-scotland.gov.uk

Lady Devorgilla of Galloway founded Balliol College, Oxford in memory of her husband John Balliol; she also founded this abbey in his memory in 1273. When she died in 1289 she was buried in front of the high altar with the heart of her husband resting on her bosom; hence the name 'Sweetheart Abbey'. The abbey features an unusual precinct wall of enormous boulders.

Times ✳ Open all year, Apr-Sep, daily 9.30-6.30; Oct-Mar, Mon-Wed & Sat-Sun 9.30-4.30. Closed 25-26 Dec & 1-2 Jan. **Facilities** ❷ 🛆 (with assistance) ⊗ 🗐

PALNACKIE   MAP 11 NX85

Orchardton Tower   `FREE`

➲ *(6m SE of Castle Douglas on A711)*

web: www.historic-scotland.gov.uk

A charming little tower house from the mid-15th-century. It is, uniquely, circular in plan.

Times ✳ Open all reasonable times. Closed 25-26 Dec. **Facilities** ❷ ⊗ 🗐

PORT LOGAN   MAP 10 NX04

Logan Botanic Garden

DG9 9ND

➲ *(on B7065, 14m S of Stranraer)*

☎ 01776 860231

e-mail: logan@rbge.org.uk

web: www.rbge.org.uk

Logan's exceptionally mild climate allows a colourful array of tender plants to thrive out-of-doors. Amongst the many highlights are tree ferns, cabbage palms, unusual shrubs, climbers and tender perennials found within the setting of the walled, water, terrace and woodland gardens.

Times ✳ Open Mar & Oct daily 10-5. Apr-Sep 10-6 **Facilities** ❷ 🍴 🛆 (wheelchairs available for loan) toilets for disabled shop garden centre ⊗ (ex assist dogs) 🗐

RUTHWELL   MAP 11 NY16

Ruthwell Cross   `FREE`

➲ *(sited within the parish church on B724)*

web: www.historic-scotland.gov.uk

Now in a specially built apse in the parish church, the carved cross dates from the 7th or 8th centuries. Two faces show scenes from the Life of Christ; the others show scroll work, and parts of an ancient poem in Runic characters. It was broken up in the 18th century, but pieced together by Dr Henry Duncan, 19th-century minister.

Times ✳ Open all reasonable times. Contact Key Keeper for access on 01387 870249. **Facilities** ❷ ⊗ 🗐

Savings Banks Museum   `FREE`

DG1 4NN

➲ *(off B724, 10m E of Dumfries & 7m W of Annan)*

☎ 01387 870640

e-mail: tsbmuseum@btinternet.com

web: www.lloydstsb.com/savingsbankmuseum

Housed in the building where Savings Banks first began, the museum traces their growth and development from 1810 up to the present day. The museum also traces the life of Dr Henry Duncan, father of savings banks, and restorer of the Ruthwell Cross. Multi-lingual leaflets available.

Times Open, Tue-Sat, Apr-Sep, Thu-Sat, Oct-Mar, 10-4; Open on BHs except Xmas Day & New Year **Facilities** ❷ 🛆 (touch facilities for blind, guide available) ⊗ (ex assist dogs)

SCOTLAND

Sanquhar Tolbooth Museum

 FREE

High St DG4 6BN

➲ (on A76 Dumfries-Kilmarnock road)

☎ 01659 250186

e-mail: dumfriesmuseum@dumgal.gov.uk

web: www.dumgal.gov.uk/museums

Housed in the town's fine 18th-century tolbooth, the museum tells the story of the mines and miners of the area, its earliest inhabitants, native and Roman, the history and customs of the Royal Burgh of Sanquhar and local traditions.

Times Open Apr-Sep 10-1 & 2-5 Tue-Sat & 2-5 Sun . **Facilities** ❷ ঐ (museum up steps, phone for info) shop

Castle Kennedy & Gardens

Stair Estates, Rephad DG9 8BX

➲ (5m E of Stranraer on A75, signed at Castle Kennedy Village)

☎ 01776 702024 & 01581 400225

e-mail: info@castlekennedygardens.co.uk

web: www.castlekennedygardens.co.uk

Perfect for exploring, these stunning 18th-century gardens are uniquely situated between two lochs. As well as rhododendrons, rare plants, a walled garden, Lochinch Castle and the romantic ruined Castle Kennedy, there is a charming tearoom, gift shop, plant centre and seasonal children's activities. New for visitors is the Snowdrop Trail, open at weekends in February and March.

Times Open Etr-Sep, daily 10-5; Feb-Mar wknds only, 10-5, rest of year by appointment. **Facilities** ❷ ☐ ⼓ (outdoor) ঐ (Partly accessible) (free wheelchair) toilets for disabled shop garden centre ❽ (ex on a lead) ▤

Glenwhan Gardens

Dunragit DG9 8PH

➲ (7m E of Stranraer, signed)

☎ 01581 400222

e-mail: tess@glenwhan.freeserve.co.uk

web: www.glenwhangardens.co.uk

Enjoying spectacular views over the Mull of Galloway and Luce Bay, Glenwhan is a beautiful 12-acre garden set on a hillside. There are two lakes filled with rare species, alpines, scree plants, heathers, conifers, roses, woodland walks and fascinating garden sculpture.

Times Open Apr-Sep, daily 10-5 **Fee** £4.50 (ch £2, concessions £3.50). Family ticket up to 3 ch £10. Season ticket £10 **Facilities** ❷ ☐ ⼓ ⼓ ঐ (some hilly areas) (wheelchair provided) toilets for disabled shop garden centre ❽ (ex on lead)

Drumlanrig Castle, Gardens & Country Park

DG3 4AQ

➲ (4m N of Thornhill off A76)

☎ 01848 331555

e-mail: enquiries@drumlanrig.com

web: www.drumlanrig.com

This unusual pink sandstone castle was built in the late 17th century in Renaissance style. It contains a outstanding collection of fine art. There is also French furniture, as well as silver and relics of Bonnie Prince Charlie. The old stable block has a craft centre with resident craft workers, and the grounds offer an extensive garden plant centre, working forge, mountain bike hire and woodland walks. For details of special events phone 01848 331555.

Drumlanrig Castle, Gardens & Country Park

Times Castle open 10 Apr-Aug daily, 11-4 (last tour). **Fee** ✻ £7 (ch £4 & pen £6). Grounds only £4. Party 20+ £5 each. **Facilities** ℗ ⦿ licensed ⊓ (outdoor) ⚹ (some areas of garden not easily accessible to wheelchair users) (lift) toilets for disabled shop garden centre ⊗ (ex in park on lead) ▬

WANLOCKHEAD   MAP 11 NS81

Museum of Scottish Lead Mining

ML12 6UT

➲ *(signed from M74 and A76)*

☎ 01659 74387

e-mail: miningmuseum@hotmail.com
web: www.leadminingmuseum.co.uk

Wanlockhead is Scotland's highest village, set in the beautiful Lowther Hills. Visitors can see miners' cottages, and the miners' library as well as the 18th-century lead mine. Visitors can also pan for gold.

Times Open Apr-Nov, daily 11-4.30; Jul-Aug & BHs 10-5. **Facilities** ℗ ⦿ ⦿⊓ (outdoor) ⚹ (induction loops) toilets for disabled shop ⊗ (ex assist dogs) ▬

WHITHORN   MAP 10 NX44

Whithorn-Cradle of Christianity

45-47 George St DG8 8NS

➲ *(follow directions S from junct at Newton Stewart & Glenluce A75. Centre on main street in centre of Whithorn)*

☎ 01988 500508

e-mail: enquiries@whithorn.com
web: www.whithorn.com

The Whithorn Story tells the story of the first Christian settlement in Scotland - the Candida Casa (or White House) built by St Ninian circa 397. There is an audio-visual element, an exhibition, Priory ruins and a Historic Scotland Museum. The Festival of St Ninian takes place from the end of July to mid-September.

Times Open daily, Apr or Etr-Oct 10.30-5. **Facilities** ℗ ⦿ ⊓ (outdoor) ⚹ (one short staircase with 'stairmatic') toilets for disabled shop ▬

Whithorn Priory

DG8 8PY

➲ *(on A746)*

☎ 01988 500508

web: www.historic-scotland.gov.uk

The first Christian church in Scotland was founded here by St Ninian in 397AD, but the present ruins date from the 12th century. These ruins are sparse but there is a notable Norman door, the Latinus stone of the 5th century and other early Christian monuments.

Times ✻ Open Apr-Oct, daily 10.30-5. **Facilities** ℗ ⊗ ⋈

CITY OF DUNDEE

DUNDEE   MAP 11 NO43

Broughty Castle Museum   FREE

Castle Approach, Broughty Ferry DD5 2TF

➲ *(turn S off A930 at traffic lights by Eastern Primary School in Broughty Ferry)*

☎ 01382 436916

e-mail: broughty@dundeecity.gov.uk
web: www.dundeecity.gov.uk/broughtycastle

This 15th-century coastal fort has faced many battles and sieges, and was rebuilt in the 19th century as part of the River Tay's coastal defence system. It now houses a museum featuring the life and times of Broughty Ferry, its people, environment and wildlife. A new gallery features a selection of paintings from the Orchar Collection, one of the most important collections of Scottish Victorian art. Enjoy spectacular views over the River Tay.

Times ✻ Open all year Apr-Sep, Mon-Sat 10-4, Sun 12.30-4; Oct-Mar, Tue-Sat 10-4, Sun 12.30-4. Closed Mons, 25-26 Dec & 1-3 Jan. **Facilities** ℗ ⦿ ⚹ (unsuitable for wheelchairs) shop ⊗ (ex assist dogs)

DUNDEE CONTINUED

Camperdown Country Park

Coupar Angus Rd DD2 4TF

➲ *(A90 to Dundee then onto A923 (Coupar-Angus road), left at 1st rdbt to attraction)*

☎ 01382 431818

e-mail: camperdown@dundeecity.gov.uk
web: www.camperdownpark.com

Camperdown is Dundee's largest park, covers an area of over 400 acres and is home to some 190 species of tree. There is a good range of facilities, including an 18-hole golf course, a putting green, boating pond, children's play area, footpaths and woodland trails, and Camperdown Wildlife Centre. There is also a year-round calendar of special events, contact for details.

Times Open Park: all year. Wildlife Centre: Mar-Sep, daily 10-4.30 (last admission 3.45), Oct-Feb 10-3.30 (last admission 2.45). **Fee** Park - free admission. Wildlife Centre charged, £3.30 (ch £2.75 under 3 £1.05, concessions £2.75), family (2ad+3ch) £9.25, accompanied group £3.60pp, unaccompanied group £2.60pp. **Facilities** ❷ ⟱ ⌷ (outdoor) ⟱ (ramps) toilets for disabled shop ⊗ (ex in park on leads)

Discovery Point & RRS Discovery

Discovery Quay DD1 4XA

➲ *(follow brown heritage signs for Historic Ships)*

☎ 01382 309060

e-mail: info@dundeeheritage.co.uk
web: www.rrsdiscovery.com

Discovery Point is the home of *RRS Discovery*, Captain Scott's famous Antarctic ship. Spectacular lighting, graphics and special effects re-create key moments in the Discovery story. The restored bridge gives a captain's view over the ship and the River Tay. Learn what happened to the ship after the expedition, during the First World War and the Russian Revolution, and find out about her involvement in the first survey of whales' migratory patterns.

Times Open Apr-Oct, Mon-Sat 10-6. Sun 11-6; Nov-Mar, Mon-Sat 10-5, Sun 11-5. **Fee** £7.25 (ch £4.50, concessions £5.50). Family ticket £20 **Facilities** ❷ (charged) ⟱ ⭑⊙⭑ licensed ⌷ (outdoor) ⟱ (access to exhibition on top deck, no access to lower deck, but virtual tour available) (in-house wheelchairs & lifts, parking, ramps onto ship) toilets for disabled shop ⊗ (ex assist dogs) ⊟

HM Frigate Unicorn

Victory Dock DD1 3BP

➲ *(from W follow A85 from A90 at Invergowrie. From E follow A92. Near N end of Tay Road Bridge. Follow signs for City Quay).*

☎ 01382 200900 & 200893

e-mail: mail@frigateunicorn.org
web: www.frigateunicorn.org

The *Unicorn* is the oldest British-built warship afloat, and Scotland's only example of a wooden warship. Today she houses a museum of life in the Royal Navy during the days of sail, with guns, models and displays.

Times Open all year Apr-Oct, daily 10-5; Nov-Mar, Wed-Fri 12-4, Sat & Sun 10-4. Closed Mon-Tue & 2 weeks at Xmas & New Year. **Fee** £4 (concessions £3). Family ticket £9-£11. Groups 10+ £2.50 each. **Facilities** ⓟ (3min walk) (1hr free, 2hr £1, £2 per hr thereafter) ⟱ ⟱ (wheelchair access to main gun deck only) (AV presentations, introductory video, virtual tour) shop ⊗ (ex assist dogs on deck area)

Mills Observatory   ▣ FREE

Balgay Park, Glamis Rd DD2 2UB

➲ *(1m W of city centre, in Balgay Park, on Balgay Hill. Vehicle entrance at Glamis Rd gate to Balgay Park)*

☎ 01382 435967

e-mail: mills.observatory@dundeecity.gov.uk
web: www.dundeecity.gov.uk/mills

Mills Observatory is Britain's only full-time public observatory. See breathtaking views of the stars and planets through the impressive Victorian refracting telescope. The reflecting telescope with state-of-the-art 'go to' technology, allows you to 'hop' from one object to another more quickly than ever before! During October to March, the Planetarium Shows, provide the chance to learn about constellations, planets and other jewels of the night sky. There are also displays on the solar system and space exploration.

Times ✷ Open all year, Apr-Sep, Tue-Fri 11-5, Sat & Sun 12.30-4; Oct-Mar, Mon-Fri 4pm-10pm, Sat & Sun 12.30-4. Closed 25-26 Dec & 1-3 Jan. Small charge for Planetarium. **Facilities** ❷ ⌷ (outdoor) ⟱ (Partly accessible) (portable telescopes available, images on screen) toilets for disabled shop ⊗ (ex assist dogs) ⊟

Verdant Works

West Henderson's Wynd DD2 5BT

➲ *(follow brown tourist signs)*

☎ 01382 309060

e-mail: info@dundeeheritage.co.uk
web: www.verdantworks.com

Dating from 1830, this old Jute Mill covers 50,000 square feet and has been restored as a living museum of Dundee and Tayside's textile history and is an award-winning European Industrial Museum. Phase I explains what jute is, where it comes from and why Dundee became the centre of its production. Working machinery illustrates the production process from raw jute to woven cloth. Phase II deals with the uses of jute and its effects on Dundee's social history.

Times Open Apr-Oct; Mon-Sat 10-5, Sun 11-5; Nov-Mar, Mon-Sat 10-4, Sun 11-4. Venue closes 1hr after last entry. Please check for winter opening times. Closed 25-26 Dec & 1-2 Jan. **Fee** £6 (ch £3.85, pen & concessions £4.75). Family ticket (2ad+2ch) £17. **Facilities** ❷ ⟱ ⭑⊙⭑ ⟱ (wheelchairs, induction loops) toilets for disabled shop ⊗ (ex assist dogs) ⊟

SCOTLAND

EAST AYRSHIRE

GALSTON
MAP 11 NS53

Loudoun Castle Theme Park
KA4 8PE

➲ (signed from A74(M), from A77 and from A71)

☎ 01563 822296

e-mail: loudouncastle@btinternet.com

web: www.loudouncastle.co.uk

Loudoun Castle Theme Park is a great day out for the whole family. Theme park rides, live entertainment and McDougals Farm are just a taster of what's on offer.

Times ✳ Open Etr-end of Sep. Please phone for further details.
Facilities ❷ ⬛ 🍴 🎪 (indoor & outdoor) shop ✖ (ex assist dogs) ▬

KILMARNOCK
MAP 10 NS43

Dick Institute Museum & Art Galleries
Elmbank Ave KA1 3BU

➲ (follow brown tourist signs from A77 S of Glasgow, into town centre)

☎ 01563 554343

web: www.east-ayrshire.gov.uk

Temporary and permanent exhibitions spread over two floors of this grand Victorian building. Fine art, social and natural history feature upstairs, whilst the downstairs galleries house temporary exhibitions of art and craft.

Times ✳ Open all year, Tue-Sat 11-5. Closed Sun, Mon and Public Hols.
Facilities ❷ ♿ (wheelchair available) toilets for disabled shop ✖ (ex assist dogs)

EAST DUNBARTONSHIRE

BEARSDEN
MAP 11 NS57

Antonine Wall: Bearsden Bath-house
`FREE`

Roman Rd G61 2SG

➲ (signed from Bearsden Cross on A810)

web: www.historic-scotland.gov.uk

Considered to be the best surviving visible Roman building in Scotland, the bath-house was discovered in 1973 during excavations for a construction site. It was originally built for use by the Roman garrison at Bearsden Fort, which is part of the Antonine Wall defences. This building dates from the 2nd century AD. Visitors should wear sensible footwear.

Times ✳ Open all reasonable times. **Facilities** ✖ ▮

MILNGAVIE
MAP 11 NS57

Mugdock Country Park
`FREE`

Craigallian Rd G62 8EL

➲ (N of Glasgow on A81, signed)

☎ 0141 956 6100 & 6586

e-mail: rangers@mcp.ndo.co.uk

web: www.mugdock-country-park.org.uk

This country park incorporates the remains of Mugdock and Craigend castles, set in beautiful landscapes as well as an exhibition centre, craft shops, orienteering course and many walks.

Times ✳ Open all year, daily. **Facilities** ❷ ⬛ 🍴 🎪 (outdoor) ♿ (mobility equip, audio leaflet, large print media) toilets for disabled shop garden centre ▬

EAST LOTHIAN

ABERLADY
MAP 12 NT47

Myreton Motor Museum
EH32 0PZ

➲ (1.5m from A198, 2m from A1)

☎ 01875 870288 & 07947 066666

e-mail: myreton.motor.museum@aberlady.org

The museum has on show a large collection, beginning from 1899, of cars, bicycles, motor cycles and commercials. There is also a large collection of period advertising, posters and enamel signs.

Times Open, Mar-Nov daily 11-4, Dec-Feb, wknds only 11-3 **Facilities** ❷ 🎪 (outdoor) ♿ ✖ (ex assist dogs)

DIRLETON
MAP 12 NT58

Dirleton Castle
EH39 5ER

➲ (on A198)

☎ 01620 850330

web: www.historic-scotland.gov.uk

The oldest part of this romantic castle dates from the 13th century. It was besieged by Edward I in 1298, rebuilt and expanded, and then destroyed in 1650. Now the sandstone ruins have a beautiful mellow quality. Within the castle grounds is a garden established in the 16th century, with ancient yews and hedges around a bowling green.

Times ✳ Open all year, Apr-Sep daily 9.30-6.30; Oct-Mar daily 9.30-4.30. Closed 25-26 Dec & 1-2 Jan. **Facilities** ❷ 🎪 shop ▮

SCOTLAND

EAST FORTUNE MAP 12 NT57

National Museum of Flight Scotland `2 for 1`

East Fortune Airfield EH39 5LF

➲ *(signed from A1 near Haddington. Onto B1347, past Athelstaneford, 20m E of Edinburgh)*

☎ 01620 897240

e-mail: info@nms.ac.uk

web: www.nms.ac.uk

The National Museum of Flight is situated on 63 acres of one of Britain's best preserved wartime airfields. The museum has four hangars, with more than 50 aeroplanes, plus engines, rockets and memorabilia. Items on display include two Spitfires, a Vulcan bomber and Britain's oldest surviving aeroplane, built in 1896; recent exhibits also include a Phantom jet fighter, and a Harrier jump-jet. The Concorde Experience is free with admission to the Museum, but pre-booking is essential for your boarding pass. The Concorde Experience explores the story of this historic plane through the lives of those who worked or travelled on it. See the website www.nms.ac.uk/ flight. The 2-for-1 Voucher is not valid for special events.

Times ✳ Open Apr-Oct, daily, 10-5. Nov-Mar, wknds only, 10-4. Also open 27-31 Dec & 9-17 Feb. **Fee** ✳ £5.50, (ch under 12 & NMS members free, concessions £4.50). Plus Concorde Boarding Pass; +£3 ad, +£2 ch & concessions. **Facilities** ❶ 〓 〓 (outdoor) & (no wheelchair access to Concorde's passenger cabin, most display areas are on ground floor) (wheelchair loan) toilets for disabled shop ⊗ (ex assist dogs) ▄

EAST LINTON MAP 12 NT57

Hailes Castle `FREE`

➲ *(1.5m SW of East Linton on A1)*

web: www.historic-scotland.gov.uk

A beautiful sited ruin incorporating a fortified manor of 13th-century date, extended in the 14th and 15th centuries. There are two vaulted pit-prisons.

Times ✳ Open at all reasonable times. **Facilities** ❶ 〓 ⊗ █

Preston Mill & Phantassie Doocot

EH40 3DS

➲ *(Off A1, in East Linton, 23m east of Edinburgh).*

☎ 0844 493 2128

e-mail: information@nts.org.uk

web: www.nts.org.uk

This attractive mill, with conical, pantiled roof, is the oldest working water-driven meal mill to survive in Scotland, and was last used commercially in 1957. Nearby is the charming Phantassie Doocot (dovecote), built for 500 birds.

Times ✳ Open Jun-Sep, Thu-Mon 1-5. **Facilities** ❶ (charged) 〓 & (Partly accessible) toilets for disabled shop ⊗ (ex assist dogs) ▼

INVERESK MAP 11 NT37

Inveresk Lodge Garden

24 Inveresk Village EH21 7TE

➲ *(A6124, S of Musselburgh, 6m E of Edinburgh)*

☎ 0844 493 2126

e-mail: information@nts.org.uk

web: www.nts.org.uk

This charming terraced garden, set in the historic village of Inveresk, specialises in plants, shrubs and roses suitable for growing on small plots. The 17th-century house makes an elegant backdrop.

Times ✳ Open all year, daily 10-6 or dusk if earlier. **Facilities** ❶ 〓 (outdoor) & (Partly accessible) (Scented plants, interpretation guides) ⊗ (ex assist dogs) ▼

NORTH BERWICK MAP 12 NT58

Scottish Seabird Centre

The Harbour EH39 4SS

➲ *(A1 from Edinburgh, then A198 to North Berwick. Brown heritage signs clearly marked from A1)*

☎ 01620 890202

e-mail: info@seabird.org

web: www.seabird.org

This award-winning wildlife visitor attraction offers panoramic views over the sea and sandy beaches. See wildlife close up with amazing live cameras - puffins spring-cleaning their burrows, gannets with fluffy white chicks, seals sunning themselves and occasional sightings of dolphins and whales. The Discovery Centre has a Wildlife cinema, Environment Zone, Kid Playzone and Migration Flyway. There's a packed programme of festivals and events, see the website for details.

Times Open Feb, Mar & Oct Mon-Fri 10-5, Sat-Sun 10-5.30. Apr-Sep 10-6 every day. Nov-Jan Mon-Fri 10-4, Sat-Sun 10-5.30. **Fee** £7.95 (ch £4.50, concessions £5.95) **Facilities** ❶ 〓 ▢ 〓 (outdoor) & (1 w/chair, parking on site, walking frame avail, lift) toilets for disabled shop ⊗ (ex assist dogs) ▄

Tantallon Castle

EH39 5PN

➲ *(3m E, off A198)*

☎ 01620 892727

web: www.historic-scotland.gov.uk

A famous 14th-century stronghold of the Douglases facing towards the lonely Bass Rock from the rocky Firth of Forth shore. Nearby 16th and 17th-century earthworks.

Times ✳ Open all year, Apr-Sep, daily 9.30-6.30; Oct-Mar, Mon-Wed & Sat-Sun 9.30-4.30. Closed 25-26 Dec & 1-2 Jan. **Facilities** ❶ 〓 shop ⊗ █

PRESTONPANS — MAP 11 NT37

Prestongrange Museum FREE
Prestongrange

➲ *(on B1348)*

☎ 0131 653 2904

e-mail: elms@eastlothian.gov.uk

web: www.eastlothian.gov.uk/museums

The oldest documented coal mining site in Scotland, with 800 years of history, this museum shows a Cornish Beam Engine and on-site evidence of associated industries such as brickmaking and pottery. It is located next to a 16th-century customs port. Special Events - weekend events for families and children in July/August.

Times Open Apr-Oct, daily, 11-4.30 **Facilities** ℗ ⌐ ⊼ (outdoor) & (grounds partly accessible) toilets for disabled shop ⊗ (ex assist dogs)

CITY OF EDINBURGH

BALERNO — MAP 11 NT16

Malleny Garden
EH14 7AF

➲ *(off A70 Lanark road)*

☎ 0844 493 2123

e-mail: information@nts.org.uk

web: www.nts.org.uk

The delightful gardens are set round a 17th-century house (not open to the public). Shrub roses, a woodland garden, and a group of four clipped yews, survivors of a group planted in 1603, are among its notable features. The National Bonsai Collection for Scotland is also at Malleny.

Times ✳ Open daily 10-6 or dusk if earlier. **Facilities** ℗ & ⊗ (ex assist dogs) ⛟

EDINBURGH — MAP 11 NT27

Brass Rubbing Centre
Trinity Apse, Chalmers Close, High St EH1 1SS

➲ *(located on the Royal Mile)*

☎ 0131 556 4364

e-mail: moc@edinburgh.gov.uk

web: www.cac.org.uk

Housed in the 15th-century remnant of Trinity Apse, the Centre offers the chance to make your own rubbing from a wide range of replica monumental brasses and Pictish stones. Tuition is available.

Times Open Apr-Sep, Mon-Sat 10-5 (Sun during Aug 12-5). **Fee** Free entry. Charge for making a brass rubbing. **Facilities** ℗ (250mtrs) & (Partly accessible) toilets for disabled shop ⊗ (ex assist dogs) ▭

Camera Obscura & World of Illusions
Castlehill, Royal Mile EH1 2ND

➲ *(next to Edinburgh Castle)*

☎ 0131 226 3709

e-mail: info@camera-obscura.co.uk

web: www.camera-obscura.co.uk

A unique view of Edinburgh - as the lights go down, a brilliant moving image of the surrounding city appears. See three other floors of optical illusions and hands on inter-active fun.

Times Open all year, daily, Apr-Oct 9.30-6; Nov-Mar 10-5. Closed 25 Dec. Open Jul-Aug, 9.30-7.30. **Fee** £8.50 (ch £5.75, concessions £6.75) **Facilities** shop ▭

City Art Centre
2 Market St EH1 1DE

➲ *(opposite rear of Waverley Stn)*

☎ 0131 529 3993

e-mail: cityartcentre@edinburgh.gov.uk

web: www.cac.org.uk

The City Art Centre houses the city's permanent fine art collection and stages a constantly changing programme of temporary exhibitions from all parts of the world. It has six floors of display galleries (linked by an escalator).

Times Open Mon-Sat 10-5 & Sun 12-5 **Fee** Free. Admission charged for some exhibitions. **Facilities** ℗ (500yds) (single yellow lines) ⌐🍽 licensed & (induction loop, lifts, Braille signage, escalator) toilets for disabled shop ⊗ (ex assist dogs) ▭

Craigmillar Castle
EH16 4SY

➲ *(2.5m SE, off A68)*

☎ 0131 661 4445

web: www.historic-scotland.gov.uk

Mary, Queen of Scots retreated to this 14th-century stronghold after the murder of Rizzio. The plot to murder Darnley, her second husband, was also hatched here. There are 16th and 17th-century apartments.

Times ✳ Open all year, Apr-Sep, daily 9.30-6.30; Oct-Mar, Mon-Wed & Sat-Sun 9.30-4.30. Closed 25-26 Dec & 1-2 Jan. **Facilities** ℗ shop ▮

Dean Gallery
73 Belford Rd EH4 3DS

➲ *(20 min walk from Edinburgh Haymarket stn & Princes St)*

☎ 0131 624 6200

e-mail: enquiries@nationalgalleries.org

web: www.nationalgalleries.org

Opened in March 1999, the Dean Gallery provides a home for the Eduardo Paolozzi gift of sculpture and graphic art, the Gallery of Modern Art's renowned Dada and Surrealist collections, a major library

CONTINUED

EDINBURGH CONTINUED

and archive centre, and temporary exhibition space for modern and contemporary art.

Times Open all year, daily 10-5. Extended opening during Edinburgh Festival. Closed 25-26 Dec. **Facilities** ☉ ☷ & (ramps & lift) toilets for disabled shop ⊗ (ex assist dogs) ═

Dynamic Earth

Holyrood Rd EH8 8AS

⮩ *(on edge of Holyrood Park, opposite Palace of Holyrood House)*

☎ 0131 550 7800

e-mail: enquiries@dynamicearth.co.uk

web: www.dynamicearth.co.uk

How the Earth works. Take a walk through Scotland's geological history. Travel back in time to follow the creation of Planet Earth. Be shaken by a volcano, feel the chill of polar ice and get caught in a tropical rainstorm. Please visit website for details of events running throughout the year.

Times ✳ Open Apr-Oct daily & Nov-Mar Wed-Sun 10-5, (last entry 3.50); Jul-Aug daily, 10-6, (last entry 4.50). **Facilities** ☉ (charged) ☷ ⊓ (indoor & outdoor) & (audio guides, large print gallery guides) toilets for disabled shop ⊗ (ex assist dogs) ═

Edinburgh Castle

EH1 2NG

☎ 0131 225 9846

web: www.historic-scotland.gov.uk

This historic stronghold stands on the precipitous crag of Castle Rock. One of the oldest parts is the 11th-century chapel of the saintly Queen Margaret, but most of the present castle evolved later, during its stormy history of sieges and wars, and was altered again in Victorian times. The Scottish crown and other royal regalia are displayed in the Crown Room. Also notable is the Scottish National War Memorial.

Times ✳ Open all year, Apr-Sep daily 9.30-6; Oct-Mar 9.30-5. Closed 25-26 Dec. **Facilities** ☉ (charged) ☷ ⑩ & (free transport to top of Castle Hill lift) toilets for disabled shop ⊗ ▮

The Edinburgh Dungeon

31 Market St EH1 1QB

⮩ *(close to Waverley Train Station)*

☎ 0131 240 1000 & 240 1002

e-mail: edinburghdungeon@merlinentertainments.biz

web: www.thedungeons.com

From the same team as The London Dungeon, there comes a Scottish "feast of fun with history's horrible bits". A mixture of live actors, rides, shows and special effects take the brave visitor back into a dark past that includes such delights as the Judgement of Sinners, the Plague, Burke & Hare: Bodysnatchers, and Clan Wars, which attempts to recreate the horror of the Glencoe Massacre of 1692. Visit the Inferno, and explore the Great Fire of Edinburgh in 1828.

Times ✳ Open all year ex Xmas. Please telephone for times. **Facilities** ℗ (100mtrs) (metered bays limited to 1-2hrs) shop ⊗ (ex assist dogs) ═

Edinburgh Zoo

Murrayfield EH12 6TS

⮩ *(3m W of city centre on A8 towards Glasgow)*

☎ 0131 334 9171

e-mail: marketing@rzss.org.uk

web: www.edinburghzoo.org.uk

Scotland's largest wildlife attraction, set in 80 acres of leafy hillside parkland, just ten minutes from the city centre. With over 1,000 animals ranging from the UK's only koalas to massive Indian rhinos, including many other threatened species. See the worlds largest penguin pool or visit our chimpanzees in the world-class, budongo trail. Edinburgh Zoo is celebrating its centenary in 2009.

Times Open all year, Apr-Sep, daily 9-6; Oct & Mar, daily 9-5; Nov-Feb, daily 9-4.30. **Fee** ✳ £11.50 (ch £8, concessions £10). Family ticket (2ad+2ch) £35; (2ad+3ch) £40. Prices valid until March 2009. **Facilities** ☉ (charged) ☷ ⑩ licensed ⊓ (indoor & outdoor) & (Zoo is on a hillside, but there is a free hilltop safari to the top of the hill) (wheelchair loan free, 1 helper free - phone in advance) toilets for disabled shop ⊗ (ex assist dogs) ═

The Georgian House

7 Charlotte Square EH2 4DR

⮩ *(2 mins walk W end of Princes St)*

☎ 0844 493 2118

e-mail: information@nts.org.uk

web: www.nts.org.uk

The house is part of Robert Adam's splendid north side of Charlotte Square, the epitome of Edinburgh New Town architecture. The lower floors of No 7 have been restored in the style of the early 1800s, when the house was new. There are also videos of life in the New Town, and this house in particular.

Times ✳ Open Mar daily 11-3, Apr-Jun daily 10-5, Jul-Aug daily 10-7, Sep-Oct daily 10-5, Nov daily 11-3. Last admission 30 mins before closing. **Facilities** ℗ (100 yds) (meters, disabled directly outside) & (Partly accessible) (induction loop, Braille guide, subtitled video) shop ⊗ (ex assist dogs) ⛲

Gladstone's Land

477b Lawnmarket EH1 2NT

⮩ *(5 mins walk from Princes St via Mound)*

☎ 0844 493 2120

e-mail: information@nts.org.uk

web: www.nts.org.uk

Built in 1620, this six-storey tenement, once a merchant's house, still has its arcaded front - a rare feature now. Visitors can also see unusual tempera paintings on the walls and ceilings. It is furnished as a typical 17th-century merchant's home, complete with ground-floor shop front and goods of the period.

Times ✳ Open 31 Mar-Jun daily 10-5, Jul-Aug daily 10-7, Sep-Oct daily 10-5, last admission 30 mins before closing. **Facilities** ℗ (440yds) (outside for disabled) & (Partly accessible) (tours for the blind can be arranged, Braille guidebook) shop ⊗ (ex assist dogs) ⛲

SCOTLAND

John Knox House

Scottish Story Telling Centre, 43-45 High St EH1 1SR

⊃ *(Between The Castle and Holyrood House, halfway along Edinburgh's Royal Mile)*

☎ 0131 556 9579

e-mail: reception@scottishstorytellingcentre.com

web: www.scottishstorytellingcentre.co.uk

John Knox the Reformer is said to have died in the house, which was built by the goldsmith to Mary, Queen of Scots. Renovation work has revealed the original floor in the Oak Room, and a magnificent painted ceiling. New audio tour available.

Times Open all year, Mon-Sat 10-6. July-Aug, Sun 12-6. Closed 25-26 Dec and 1-2 Jan. **Fee** ✳ £3.50 (ch £1, under 7's free, concessions £2.75). **Facilities** ℗ (5 min walk) (paying car park) ⌨ ♿ (access to ground floor only. Virtual computer tour for rest of house) (Braille, hearing loops, tours for blind) toilets for disabled shop ⊗ (ex assist dogs) ▬

Lauriston Castle

Cramond Rd South, Davidson's Mains EH4 5QD

⊃ *(NW outskirts of Edinburgh, 1m E of Cramond overlooking the Forth at Silverknowles)*

☎ 0131 336 2060

e-mail: lauriston.castle@tiscali.co.uk

web: www.cac.org.uk

The castle is a late 16th-century tower house with 19th-century additions but is most notable as a classic example of the Edwardian age. It has a beautifully preserved Edwardian interior and the feel of a country house, and the spacious grounds are very pleasant.

Times Guided tours: Apr-Oct, daily (ex Fri), 11, 12, 2, 3 & 4; Nov-Mar 12, 2 & 3. **Fee** £5 (concessions £3). Family £12.50 **Facilities** ❷ ⌱ (outdoor) ♿ (chair lift to upper floor) toilets for disabled shop ⊗ (ex assist dogs)

Museum of Childhood   FREE

42 High St, Royal Mile EH1 1TG

⊃ *(On the Royal Mile)*

☎ 0131 529 4142

e-mail: moc@edinburgh.gov.uk

web: www.cac.org.uk

One of the first museums of its kind, this was the brainchild of a local councillor and first opened in 1955. It has a wonderful collection of toys, games and other belongings of children through the ages, to delight visitors both old and young. Ring for details of special events.

Times Open all year, Mon-Sat 10-5, Sun 12-5. **Facilities** ℗ (200mtrs) (parking metres) ♿ (Partly accessible) (3 floors only) toilets for disabled shop ⊗ (ex assist dogs) ▬

Museum of Edinburgh   FREE

142 Canongate, Royal Mile EH8 8DD

⊃ *(on the Royal Mile)*

☎ 0131 529 4143

e-mail: moe@edinburgh.gov.uk

web: www.cac.org.uk

Housed in one of the best-preserved 16th-century buildings in the Old Town, built in 1570 and later the headquarters of the Incorporation of Hammermen. Now a museum of local history, it has collections of silver, glassware, pottery, and other items such as street signs.

Times Open all year, Mon-Sat 10-5. Sun in Aug noon-5. **Facilities** ℗ (200yds) (parking meters, limited spaces) ♿ toilets for disabled shop ⊗ (ex assist dogs) ▬

National Gallery Complex

The Mound, Princess St EH2 2EL

⊃ *(off Princes St)*

☎ 0131 624 6200

e-mail: enquiries@nationalgalleries.org

web: www.nationalgalleries.org

The National Gallery complex consists of three magnificent buildings, right in the heart of Edinburgh: The National Gallery of Scotland, home to Scotland's prestigious national collection; The Royal Scottish Academy, one of Europe's premier exhibition centres; and The Weston Link which houses the café, restaurant and lecture rooms.

Times Open all year, daily 10-5, Thu until 7. 1 Jan noon-5. Closed 25-26 Dec. **Facilities** ℗ (150yds) (pay and display) ⌨ ▯◑ ♿ (ramps & lift, room A1 not accessible) toilets for disabled shop ⊗ (ex assist dogs) ▬

National Museum of Scotland   2 for 1

Chambers St EH1 1JF

⊃ *(situated in Chambers St in Old Town. A few mins walk from Princes St and The Royal Mile)*

☎ 0131 225 7534

e-mail: info@nms.ac.uk

web: www.nms.ac.uk

Scotland - past, present and future. The Museum's collections tell you the story of Scotland - land, people and culture. What influence has the world had on Scotland, and Scotland on the world? Your journey of discovery starts here. For generations the museum has collected key exhibits from all over Scotland and beyond. Viking brooches, Pictish stones, ancient chessmen and Queen Mary's clarsach. There's more! Connect with Dolly the sheep, design a robot, test drive a Formula One car or blast off into outer space. See website for special exhibitions and events. 2-for-1 Voucher Scheme not valid for special events.

Times Open all year, Mon-Sun 10-5. Closed 25 Dec. Please telephone for times on 26 Dec & 1 Jan. **Fee** Admission free but there is a charge for special exhibitions **Facilities** ℗ (off street) (metered parking) ⌨ ▯◑ licensed ♿ (level access, lifts to all floors and adapted toilets available). (wheelchair loan, audio guides, induction loops) toilets for disabled shop ⊗ (ex assist dogs) ▬

SCOTLAND

EDINBURGH CONTINUED

National War Museum Scotland   `2 for 1`

Edinburgh Castle EH1 2NG

➲ *(at Edinburgh Castle, a few minutes walk up the Royal Mile to Castlehill)*

☎ 0131 225 7534

e-mail: info@nms.ac.uk

web: www.nms.ac.uk

Explore the Scottish experience of war and military service over the last 400 years. A chance to experience the poignant stories of the Scots who went to war, through their letters and personal treasures. See website for special exhibitions and events. 2-for-1 Voucher not valid for special events.

Times Open all year, daily, Apr-Sep, 9.45-5.45; Oct-Mar, 9.45-4.45. Closed 25-26 Dec. **Fee** ✳ Standard Fares £11 (ch £5.50, ch under 5 free, concessions £9) NMS members £9. Free entry to museum with admission to Edinburgh Castle. Peak Fares £12 (ch £6.00, conc £9.50). NMS Members £9.50 **Facilities** ℗ & (courtesy vehicle runs from Castle ticket kiosk) toilets for disabled shop ⊗ (ex assist dogs) ⊟

Nelson Monument

Calton Hill EH7 5AA Calton Hill

➲ *(Overlooking east end of city)*

☎ 0131 556 2716

e-mail: museums&galleries@edinburgh.gov.uk

web: www.cac.org.uk

Designed in 1807 the monument dominates the east end of Princes Street. The views are superb, and every day except Sunday the time ball drops at 1pm as the gun at the castle goes off.

Times Open all year, Apr-Sep, Mon 1-6 & Tue-Sat 10-6; Oct-Mar Mon-Sat 10-3. **Fee** £3 **Facilities** ℗ ⊗ (ex assist dogs)

Palace of Holyroodhouse

EH8 8DX

➲ *(at east end of Royal Mile)*

☎ 0131 556 5100

e-mail: bookinginfo@royalcollection.org.uk

web: www.royalcollection.org.uk

The Palace grew from the guest house of the Abbey of Holyrood, said to have been founded by David I after a miraculous apparition. Mary, Queen of Scots had her court here from 1561 to 1567, and 'Bonnie' Prince Charlie held levees at the Palace during his occupation of Edinburgh. Today the Royal Apartments are used by HM The Queen for state ceremonies and official entertaining, and are finely decorated with works of art from the Royal Collection.

Times Open daily, Apr-Oct 9.30-6 (last admission 5); Nov-Mar 9.30-4.30 (last admission 3.30). Closed Good Fri, 25-26 Dec and when The Queen is in residence. **Fee** ✳ £9.50 (ch £5.50, concessions £8.50). Family (2ad+3ch) £24.50. Provides unlimited admission for 12 months. **Facilities** ℗ (charged) ⊑ & (historic apartments accessible by spiral staircase) (first floor by lift, wheelchair available) toilets for disabled shop ⊗ (ex assist dogs) ⊟

Parliament House   `FREE`

Supreme Courts, 2-11 Parliament Square EH1 1RQ

➲ *(behind St Giles Cathedral on the high street)*

☎ 0131 225 2595

e-mail: emackenzie@scotcourts.gov.uk

web: www.scotcourts.gov.uk

Scotland's independent parliament last sat in 1707, in this 17th-century building hidden behind an 1829 façade, now the seat of the Supreme Law Courts of Scotland. A large stained glass window depicts the inauguration of the Court of Session in 1540.

Times ✳ Open all year, Mon-Fri 10-4. **Facilities** ℗ (400mtrs) (metered parking in high street) ⊑ ⦿ & (stair lift to restaurant) toilets for disabled ⊗ (ex assist dogs)

The People's Story Museum   `FREE`

Canongate Tolbooth, 163 Canongate, Royal Mile EH8 8BN

➲ *(on the Royal Mile)*

☎ 0131 529 4057

e-mail: socialhistory@edinburgh.gov.uk

web: www.cac.org.uk

The museum, housed in the 16th-century tolbooth, tells the story of the ordinary people of Edinburgh from the late 18th century to the present day. Reconstructions include a prison cell, 1930s pub and 1940s kitchen supported by photographs, displays, sounds and smells.

Times Open all year, Mon-Sat 10-5. Also open Sun in Aug 12-5. **Facilities** ℗ (100yds) (parking meters) & (Partly accessible) (lift, induction loop in video room, touch facilities) toilets for disabled shop ⊗ (ex assist dogs) ⊟

The Real Mary King's Close

2 Warriston's Close, High St EH1 1PG

➲ *(off High St, opposite St. Giles Cathedral)*

☎ 08702 430160

e-mail: info@realmarykingsclose.com

web: www.realmarykingsclose.com

Hidden deep beneath the Royal Mile lies Edinburgh's deepest secret; a warren of hidden 'closes' or streets where people lived, worked and died. For centuries they have lain forgotten and abandoned... until now. This award-winning underground attraction is a curious network of streets, town houses and rooms. Step back in time as you meet the characters from days gone by and enjoy stories of life on the Close from the perspective of a one-time resident.

Times Open Apr-Oct, 10-9 (last tour), Aug 9-9 (last tour) Sun-Sat. Nov-Mar, 10-4 (last tour), Sun-Fri, 10-9 (last tour) Sat. Closed 25 Dec. **Fee** ✳ £9.50 (ch £6, concessions £8.50). **Facilities** ℗ 2 mins walk & (ramped access provided to information and retail outlet) (hearing loop) toilets for disabled shop ⊗ (ex assist dogs) ⊟

Royal Botanic Garden Edinburgh

Inverleith Row EH3 5LR

⮑ (1m N of city centre, off A902)

☎ 0131 552 7171

e-mail: info@rbge.org.uk

web: www.rbge.org.uk

Established in 1670, on an area the size of a tennis court, the Garden is now over 70 acres of beautifully landscaped grounds. Spectacular features include the Rock Garden and the Chinese Hillside. The amazing glasshouses feature Britain's tallest palm house and the magnificent woodland gardens and arboretum.

Times ✳ Open all year, daily; Apr-Sep, 10-7; Mar & Oct, 10-6; Nov-Feb, 10-4. Closed 25 Dec & 1 Jan. (Facilities close 30 mins before Garden) **Facilities** ℗ (free on street) (restricted at certain times) ⬛ 🍽 ᕕ (wheelchairs available at east/west gates) toilets for disabled shop garden centre ⊗ (ex assist dogs) ▬

The Royal Yacht Britannia

Ocean Terminal, Leith EH6 6JJ

⮑ (follow signs to North Edinburgh & Leith. Situated within Ocean Terminal)

☎ 0131 555 5566

e-mail: enquiries@tryb.co.uk

web: www.royalyachtbritannia.co.uk

Visit the Royal Yacht Britannia, now in Edinburgh's historic port of Leith. The experience starts in the Visitor Centre where you can discover Britannia's fascinating story. Then step aboard for a self-led audio tour which takes you around five decks giving you a unique insight into what life on board was like for the Royal Family, officers and yachtsmen. Highlights include the State Apartments, Admiral's Cabin, Engine Room, Laundry, Sick Bay and Royal Marines' Barracks.

Times Open all year daily from 10 (Jul & Aug from 9.30). Last admission 4 (Apr-Jul), 4.30 (Aug) or 3.30 (Nov-Mar). Closed 25 Dec & 1 Jan. **Fee** ✳ £9.75 (ch 5-17 £5.75, concessions £7.75) Family ticket £27.75 (2ad+3ch). **Facilities** ℗ ᕕ (lift to ship, areas ramped, written scripts, audio tour) toilets for disabled shop ⊗ (ex assist dogs) ▬

Scotch Whisky Experience

354 Castlehill, The Royal Mile EH1 2NE

⮑ (next to Edinburgh Castle)

☎ 0131 220 0441

e-mail: info@scotchwhiskyexperience.co.uk

web: www.scotchwhiskyexperience.co.uk

This fascinating whisky experience reveals the history of the Scottish Whisky industry. The tour has four main areas: The Making of Scotch Whisky, The Distillery, The Blender's Ghost, and Whisky Barrel Ride. The Whisky Bond Bar has over 340 different whiskies available. The Whisky Experience celebrates its 21st birthday on the 5th May 2009.

Times Open daily, 10-5.30 (extended in summer). Closed 25 Dec. **Fee** £9.95 (ch 5-17 £5.25, concessions £7.70). **Facilities** ℗ (100m) (metered parking & NCP) ⬛ 🍽 licensed ᕕ (Braille script, tour script, lift) toilets for disabled shop ⊗ (ex assist dogs) ▬

Scottish National Gallery of Modern Art

Belford Rd EH4 3DR

⮑ (in West End, 20min walk from Haymarket station)

☎ 0131 624 6200

e-mail: enquiries@nationalgalleries.org

web: www.nationalgalleries.org

An outstanding collection of 20th-century painting, sculpture and graphic art. Includes major works by Matisse, Picasso, Bacon, Moore and Lichtenstein and an exceptional group of Scottish paintings. Set in leafy grounds with a sculpture garden.

Times Open all year, daily 10-5. New Year's Day noon-5. Closed 25-26 Dec. **Facilities** ℗ ⬛ ᕕ (ramps & lift) toilets for disabled shop ⊗ (ex assist dogs) ▬

Scottish National Portrait Gallery

1 Queen St EH2 1JD

⮑ (parallel to Princes St, just behind St Andrew Square)

☎ 0131 624 6200

e-mail: enquiries@nationalgalleries.org

web: www.nationalgalleries.org

The collection provides a visual history of Scotland from the 16th century to the present day, told through the portraits of the people who shaped it. Among the most famous are Mary, Queen of Scots, Ramsay's portrait of David Hume and Raeburn's portrait of Sir Walter Scott. The building also houses the National Collection of Photography.

Times Open all year, daily, 10-5, Thu until 7. New Year's Day noon-5. Closed 25-26 Dec. **Facilities** ℗ (200yds) (pay and display) ⬛ ᕕ (ramps & lift) toilets for disabled shop ⊗ (ex assist dogs) ▬

EDINBURGH CONTINUED

Scott Monument NEW

East Princes St Gardens, Princes St EH2 2EJ

➲ *(Overlooking city centre)*

☎ 0131 529 4068

Since the Scott Monument opened in 1846, millions of people have climbed the 200 foot structure to admire its commanding views of the city, the exhibition on Scott's life and the statuettes of characters from his novels.

Times Open all year, Mon-Sat 10-6, Sun 9-6. **Fee** ✱ £3 **Facilities** ⊟ (outdoor) ⊗ (ex assist dogs) ➡

The Writers' Museum   FREE

Lady Stair's House, Lady Stair's Close, Lawnmarket EH1 2PA

➲ *(off the Royal Mile)*

☎ 0131 529 4901

e-mail: writersmuseum@edinburgh.gov.uk

web: www.cac.org.uk

Situated in the historic Lady Stair's House which dates from 1622, the museum houses various objects associated with Robert Burns, Sir Walter Scott and Robert Louis Stevenson. Temporary exhibitions are planned throughout the year.

Times Open all year, Mon-Sat 10-5. (Aug only, Sun 12-5). **Facilities** ℗ (500mtrs) (parking meters) shop ⊗ (ex assist dogs) ➡

GOGAR   MAP 11 NT17

Suntrap Garden

43 Gogarbank EH12 9BY

➲ *(between A8 & A71 W of city bypass)*

☎ 0131 339 7283

e-mail: suntrap@btopenworld.com

web: www.suntrap-garden.org.uk

The three-acre garden consists of many gardens within a single garden, including Italian, Rock, Peat and Woodland.

Times Open all year 10-5. **Fee** £1 (accompanied ch & NTS members free). **Facilities** ❷ ⊟ (outdoor) ♿ (Partly accessible) (limited access to toilet facilities at wknds) toilets for disabled garden centre ⊗ (ex on lead)

SOUTH QUEENSFERRY   MAP 11 NT17

Dalmeny House

EH30 9TQ

☎ 0131 331 1888

e-mail: events@dalmeny.co.uk

web: www.dalmeny.co.uk

This is the home of the Earl and the Countess of Rosebery, whose family have lived here for over 300 years. The house, however, dates from 1815 when it was built in Tudor Gothic style. There is fine French furniture, tapestries and porcelain from the Rothschild Mentmore collection. Early Scottish furniture is also shown, with 18th-century

portraits, Rosebery racing mementoes, a display of pictures and one of the world's most important Napoleonic collections.

Times Open Jul-Aug, Sun-Tue 2-5.30. (Last admission 4.30). Open other times by arrangement for groups. **Fee** ✱ £5 (ch 10-16 £3, concessions £4). Party 20+. **Facilities** ❷ ⊟ ⊗ (ex assist dogs or in grounds)

Hopetoun House

EH30 9SL

➲ *(2m W of Forth Road Bridge, off A904)*

☎ 0131 331 2451

e-mail: marketing@hopetounhouse.com

web: www.hopetounhouse.com

Hopetoun House at South Queensferry is just a short drive from Edinburgh and has all the ingredients for a great family day out. Whether it is a leisurely stroll, afternoon tea or a touch of nostalgia, Hopetoun fits the bill. Built around 300 years ago, it is a delight to wander the corridors and historical rooms of one of the most splendid examples of the work of Scottish architects, Sir William Bruce and William Adam. It shows some of the finest examples in Scotland of carving, wainscoting and ceiling painting. With 100 acres of parkland including a deer park, the gardens are a colourful carpet of seasonal flowers. Summer fair in July, Christmas shopping fair in November.

Times Open daily Etr-end Sep. **Fee** ✱ £8 (ch £4.25). Grounds £3.70 (ch £2.20). **Facilities** ❷ ⊟ ⊟ (outdoor) ♿ (ramps to tearoom, lift to first floor of house) (touch screens showing photos of upstairs room) toilets for disabled shop ⊗ (ex on leads) ➡

Inchcolm Abbey

Inchcolm Island

➲ *(1.5m S of Aberdour. Access by ferry Apr-Sep)*

☎ 01383 823332

web: www.historic-scotland.gov.uk

Situated on a green island on the Firth of Forth, the Augustinian abbey was founded in about 1192 by Alexander I. The well-preserved remains include a fine 13th-century octagonal chapter house and a 13th-century wall painting.

Times ✱ Open Apr-Sep, daily 9.30-6.30. **Facilities** ⊟ shop ⊗ ▮

Queensferry Museum   FREE

53 High St EH30 9HP

➲ *(A90 from Edinburgh)*

☎ 0131 331 5545

web: www.cac.org.uk

The museum commands magnificent views of the two great bridges spanning the Forth and traces the history of the people of Queensferry and Dalmeny, the historic passage to Fife, the construction of the rail and road bridges and the wildlife of the Forth estuary. An ancient annual custom, in August, is Burry Man, who is clad from head to toe in burrs, and parades through the town. See the full size model of the Burry Man in the museum.

Times Open all year, Mon & Thu-Sat 10-1, 2.15-5, Sun noon-5. (Last admission 1/2 hour before closing). Closed 25-26 Dec & 1-2 Jan **Facilities** ℗ (0.25m) ♿ (induction loop at reception) shop ⊗ (ex assist dogs)

FALKIRK

BIRKHILL
MAP 11 NS97

Birkhill Fireclay Mine

EH51 9AQ

➲ (A706 from Linlithgow, A904 from Grangemouth, follow brown signs to Steam Railway & Fireclay Mine. Main access is by train from Bo'ness)

☎ 01506 825855 822298

e-mail: mine@srps.org.uk

web: www.srps.org.uk

Tour guides will meet you at Birkhill Station and lead you down into the ancient woodland of the beautiful Avon Gorge, and then into the caverns of the Birkhill Fireclay mine. See how the clay was worked, what it was used for and find the 300-million-year-old fossils in the roof of the mine.

Times Open weekends Apr-Oct, daily in Jul-Aug **Fee** ✳ Mine & Train £8 (ch £4.50, concessions £6.50) Family ticket (2ad+2ch) £21. Mine only £3 (ch £2, concessions £2.50) Family ticket £8. **Facilities** ℗ 🎪 (outdoor) ♿ (Partly accessible) (Not suitable for wheelchair users due to steps) toilets for disabled 🚻

BO'NESS
MAP 11 NT08

Bo'ness & Kinneil Railway
2 for 1

Bo'ness Station, Union St EH51 9AQ

➲ (A904 from all directions, signed)

☎ 01506 825855 822298

e-mail: enquiries.railway@srps.org.uk

web: www.srps.org.uk

Historic railway buildings, including the station and train shed, have been relocated from sites all over Scotland. The Scottish Railway Exhibition tells the story of the development of railways and their impact on the people of Scotland. Take a seven mile return trip by steam train to the tranquil country station at Birkhill. Thomas the Tank Engine weekends in May, August and September, and Santa Specials in December. (Booking is essential for these and 2-for-1 Voucher cannot be used.)

Times Open weekends Apr-Oct, Daily Jul-Aug **Fee** Return fare £6 (ch 5-15 £3, concessions £5). Family ticket £15. Ticket for return train fare & tour of Birkhill Fireclay Mine TBA **Facilities** ℗ 🎪 🎪 (outdoor) ♿ (ramps to station & adapted carriage) toilets for disabled shop 🚻

Kinneil Museum & Roman Fortlet
FREE

Duchess Anne Cottages, Kinniel Estate EH51 0PR

➲ (follow tourist signs from Heritage Railway, off M9. Establishment at E end of town accessed via Dean Rd)

☎ 01506 778530

web: www.falkirk.gov.uk/cultural

The museum is in a converted stable block of Kinneil House. The ground floor has displays on the industrial history of Bo'ness, while the upper floor looks at the history and environment of the Kinneil Estate. The remains of the Roman fortlet can be seen nearby. An audio-visual presentation shows 2000 years of history.

Times Open all year, Mon-Sat 12.30-4. **Facilities** ℗ ♿ shop ⊗ (ex assist dogs)

FALKIRK
MAP 11 NS88

Callendar House
FREE

Callendar Park FK1 1YR

➲ (On southside of town centre, Callendar House is signposted. Easily accessible from M9)

☎ 01324 503770

e-mail: callendar.house@falkirk.gov.uk

web: www.falkirk.gov.uk/cultural

Mary, Queen of Scots, Oliver Cromwell, Bonnie Prince Charlie, noble earls and wealthy merchants all feature in the history of Callendar House. Costumed interpreters describe early 19th-century life in the kitchens and the 900-year history of the house is illustrated in the 'Story of Callendar House' exhibition. The house is set in parkland, offering boating and woodland walks. Regular temporary heritage, natural history and visual arts exhibitions in Callendar House's Large and Small Galleries.

Times Open all year, Mon-Sat, 10-5 (Sun Apr-Sep only 2-5) **Facilities** ℗ 🎪 🎪 (outdoor) ♿ (ramped access, lift to all floors, no wheelchair access to shop/reception) (induction loop) toilets for disabled shop ⊗ (ex assist dogs) 🚻

Rough Castle
FREE

➲ (1m E of Bonnybridge, signed from B816)

web: www.historic-scotland.gov.uk

The impressive earthworks of a large Roman fort on the Antonine Wall can be seen here. The buildings have disappeared, but the mounds and terraces are the sites of barracks, and granary and bath buildings. Running between them is the military road, which once linked all the forts on the wall and is still well defined.

Times ✳ Open any reasonable time. **Facilities** ℗ ⊗ 🎌

FIFE

ABERDOUR
MAP 11 NT18

Aberdour Castle
KY3 0SL

➾ *(in Aberdour, 5m E of Forth Bridge on A921)*

☎ 01383 860519

web: www.historic-scotland.gov.uk

The earliest surviving part of the castle is the 14th-century keep. There are also later buildings, and the remains of a terraced garden, a bowling green and a fine 16th-century doocot (dovecote).

Times ✱ Open all year, Apr-Sep, daily 9.30-6.30; Oct-Mar, daily 9.30-4.30. Closed Thu-Fri & 25-26 Dec & 1-2 Jan. **Facilities** ℗ ⊙ ☶ ᚷ (wheelchairs) toilets for disabled shop ▮

ANSTRUTHER
MAP 12 NO50

Scottish Fisheries Museum
St Ayles, Harbour Head KY10 3AB

➾ *(A917 through St Monans & Pittenweem to Anstruther)*

☎ 01333 310628

e-mail: info@scotfishmuseum.org

web: www.scotfishmuseum.org

This award-winning national museum tells the story of Scottish fishing and its people from the earliest times to the present. With 10 galleries, 2 large boatyards, and a restored fisherman's cottage, containing many fine paintings and photographs, boat models and 17 actual boats, clothing and items of daily life to see, a visit to the museum makes for an exceptional day out. Contact the museum for details of events. 2009 is the 40th anniversary of the opening of the museum, and there are events and celebrations on throughout the year.

Times Open all year, Apr-Sep, Mon-Sat 10-5.30, Sun 11-5; Oct-Mar, Mon-Sat 10-4.30, Sun 12-4.30. Closed 25-26 Dec & 1-2 Jan. (Last admission 1 hr before closing). **Fee** ✱ £5 (ch in school groups £1.50, accompanied ch free, concessions £4). **Facilities** ℗ (20yds) (charge Apr-Sep) ⊑ ᚷ (ramps throughout to provide full access) toilets for disabled shop ⊗ (ex assist dogs or on leads) ▬

BURNTISLAND
MAP 11 NT28

Burntisland Edwardian Fair Museum   `FREE`
102 High St KY3 9AS

➾ *(in the centre of Burntisland)*

☎ 01592 583213

e-mail: kirkcaldy.museum@fife.gov.uk

Burntisland Museum has recreated a walk through the sights and sounds of the town's fair in 1910, based on a painting of the scene by local artist Andrew Young. See reconstructed rides, stalls and side shows of the time.

Times Open all year, Mon, Wed, Fri & Sat 10-1 & 2-5; Tue & Thu 10-1 & 2-7. Closed public hols **Facilities** ℗ (20m) (on street parking) ⊗ (ex assist dogs)

CULROSS
MAP 11 NS98

Culross Palace, Town House & The Study
West Green House KY12 8JH

➾ *(off A985, 4m E of Kincardine Bridge)*

☎ 0844 4932189

e-mail: information@nts.org.uk

web: www.nts.org.uk

A Royal Burgh, Culross dates from the 16th and 17th centuries and has remained virtually unchanged since. It prospered from the coal and salt trades, and when these declined in the 1700s, Culross stayed as it was. It owes its present appearance to the National Trust for Scotland, which has been gradually restoring it. In the Town House is a visitor centre and exhibition; in the building called The Study can be seen a drawing room with a Norwegian painted ceiling, and The Palace has painted rooms and terraced gardens.

Times ✱ Palace, Study, Town House 31 Mar-May Thu-Mon 12-5, Jun-Aug daily 12-5, Sep Thu-Mon 12-5,Oct Thu-Mon 12-4. Access to Study & Town House is by guided tour only, Tours depart every 30 mins from Palace reception (starting 12.30, last tour departs 4, in Oct last tour departs at 3). Garden all year, daily 10-6 or sunset if earlier. **Facilities** ℗ (charged) ⊑ ☶ ᚷ (Braille guide, large print) toilets for disabled shop ⊗ (ex assist dogs) ☒

CUPAR
MAP 11 NO31

Hill of Tarvit Mansionhouse & Garden
KY15 5PB

➾ *(2.5m S of Cupar, off A916)*

☎ 0844 493 2185

e-mail: information@nts.org.uk

web: www.nts.org.uk

Built in the first decade of the 20th century, the Mansionhouse is home to a notable collection of paintings, tapestries, furniture and Chinese porcelain. The grounds include formal gardens, and there is a regular programme of concerts and art exhibitions.

Times ✱ Open 31 Mar-May, Thu-Mon 1-5; Jun-Aug daily 1-5; Sep Thu-Mon 1-5; Oct Thu-Mon 1-4 **Facilities** ℗ ⊑ ☶ ᚷ (Partly accessible) (ramps, visual information, room sheets) toilets for disabled shop ⊗ (ex assist dogs) ☒

The Scottish Deer Centre
Bow-of-Fife KY15 4NQ

➾ *(3m W of Cupar on A91)*

☎ 01337 810391

Guided tours take about 30 minutes and allow you to meet and stroke deer. There are indoor and outdoor adventure play areas. Other features include regular falconry displays, viewing platform and a tree top walkway. European Grey Wolves are fed every day (except Friday) at 3pm.

Times ✱ Open daily, Etr-Oct 10-6, Nov-Etr 10-5. **Facilities** ℗ ⊑ ☶ (indoor & outdoor) ᚷ (special parking bay, loan of wheelchairs) toilets for disabled shop ⊗ (ex assist dogs) ▬

DUNFERMLINE MAP 11 NT08

Abbot House Heritage Centre `2 for 1`

Abbot House, Maygate KY12 7NE

➲ *(in city centre)*

☎ 01383 733266

e-mail: dht@abbothouse.co.uk

web: www.abbothouse.co.uk

For the better part of a millennium, pilgrims have beaten a path to Dunfermline's door. Today visitors can still share the rich royal heritage of the capital of Fife's Magic Kingdom. The volunteer-run Abbot House Heritage Centre - dubbed 'The People's Tardis' - propels the traveller through time from the days of the Picts - a time warp peopled by a veritable Who's Who of characters from Dunfermline's past: Scotland's royal saint, Braveheart's Wallace and Bruce, Scotland's Chaucer, steel magnate Andrew Carnegie and a whole panoply of kings, ending with the birth of ill-starred Charles I.

Times Open Mar-Oct, daily, 10-5. Nov-Feb, Sun-Fri, 10-4, Sat, 10-5. Closed 25-26 Dec & 1 Jan **Fee** £4 (accompanied ch under 16 free, concessions £3). Party 20+ **Facilities** Ⓟ (150yds) ⚐ ♿ (ground floor fully accessible) (parking on site, virtual tour of inaccessible areas) toilets for disabled shop ⊗ (ex assist dogs) ▬

Andrew Carnegie Birthplace Museum `FREE`

Moodie St KY12 7PL

➲ *(400yds S from Abbey)*

☎ 01383 724302

e-mail: info@carnegiebirthplace.com

web: www.carnegiebirthplace.com

The museum tells the story of the handloom weaver's son, born here in 1835, who created the biggest steel works in the USA and then became a philanthropist on a huge scale. The present-day work of the philanthropic Carnegie Trust is also explained.

Times Open Apr-Oct, Mon-Sat 11-5, Sun 2-5. **Facilities** Ⓟ ♿ (cottage inaccessible, main hall and shop accessible) (photo album) toilets for disabled shop ⊗ (ex assist dogs) ▬

Dunfermline Abbey

Pittencrieff Park

☎ 01383 739026

web: www.historic-scotland.gov.uk

The monastery was a powerful Benedictine house, founded by Queen Margaret in the 11th century. A modern brass in the choir marks the grave of King Robert the Bruce. The monastery guest house became a royal palace, and was the birthplace of Charles I.

Times ✳ Open all year, Apr-Sep, daily 9.30-6.30; Oct-Mar, daily 9.30-4.30, closed Thu (pm), Fri & Sun (am). Closed 25-26 Dec & 1-2 Jan. **Facilities** Ⓟ shop ⊗ ♪

Pittencrieff House Museum `FREE`

Pittencrieff Park KY12 8QH

➲ *(off A994 into Pittencriefff Park Car Park. Attraction on W edge of town)*

☎ 01383 722935 & 313838

e-mail: dunfermline.museum@fife.gov.uk

A fine 17th-century house standing in the beautiful park gifted to the town by Andrew Carnegie. Accessible displays tell the story of the park's animals and plants, with plenty of photographs of people enjoying the park over the last 100 years.

Times Open all year daily Jan-Mar 11-4; Apr-Sep 11-5; Oct-Dec 11-4 **Facilities** Ⓟ (800yds) ♿ (ramp) toilets for disabled shop ⊗ (ex assist dogs)

FALKLAND MAP 11 NO20

Falkland Palace & Garden

KY15 7BU

➲ *(off A912, 10m from M90, junct 8)*

☎ 0844 493 2186

e-mail: information@nts.org.uk

web: www.nts.org.uk

The hunting palace of the Stuart monarchs, this fine building, with a French-Renaissance style south wing, stands in the shelter of the Lomond Hills. The beautiful Chapel Royal and King's Bedchamber are its most notable features, and it is also home to the oldest royal tennis court in Britain (1539). The garden has a spectacular delphinium border. Recorded sacred music is played hourly in the Chapel. Please telephone for details of concerts, recitals etc.

Times ✳ Palace & Garden: Mar-Oct, Mon-Sat 10-5., Sun 1-5. **Facilities** Ⓟ ♿ (Audio wand, scented garden, wheelchair available) shop ⊗ (ex assist dogs) ♥

KELLIE CASTLE & GARDENS   MAP 12 NO50

Kellie Castle & Gardens

KY10 2RF

➲ *(On B9171, 3m NNW of Pittenweem)*

☎ 0844 493 2184

e-mail: information@nts.org.uk

web: www.nts.org.uk

The oldest part dates from about 1360, but it is for its 16th and 17th-century domestic architecture (designed by Sir Robert Lorimer) that Kellie is renowned. It has notable plasterwork and painted panelling, and there are also interesting Victorian gardens.

Times ✳ Castle: 31 Mar-Oct, daily 1-5. Garden: Daily all year, 9.30-5.30. Estate: Daily all year. **Facilities** ♿ (charged) ⊑ ⊓ (outdoor) & (induction loop, video, tour facility, photo albums) toilets for disabled shop ⊗ (ex assist dogs) 🍴

KIRKCALDY   MAP 11 NT29

Kirkcaldy Museum & Art Gallery   FREE

War Memorial Gardens KY1 1YG

➲ *(next to train station)*

☎ 01592 583213

e-mail: kirkcaldy.museum@fife.gov.uk

web: www.fifedirect.org.uk/museums

Set in the town's lovely memorial gardens, the museum houses a collection of fine and decorative art, including 18th to 21st-century Scottish paintings, among them the works of William McTaggart and S J Peploe. An award-winning display 'Changing Places' tells the story of the social, industrial and natural heritage of the area.

Times Open all year, Mon-Sat 10.30-5, Sun 2-5. Closed local hols **Facilities** ♿ ⊑ & (ramp to main entrance & lift to 1st floor galleries) toilets for disabled shop ⊗ (ex assist dogs)

NORTH QUEENSFERRY   MAP 11 NT17

Deep Sea World   2 for 1

Forthside Ter KY11 1JR

➲ *(from N, M90 take exit for Inverkeithing. From S follow signs to Forth Rd Bridge, 1st exit left)*

☎ 01383 411880

e-mail: info@deepseaworld.co.uk

web: www.deepseaworld.com/

The UK's longest underwater tunnel gives you a diver's eye view of an underwater world. Come face to face with Sand Tiger sharks, and watch divers hand-feed a wide array of sea life. Visit the Amazon Experience with ferocious piranhas and the amazing amphibian display featuring the world's most poisonous frog. Also featuring the Seal Sanctuary, dedicated to the rehabilitation and release of injured and orphaned seal pups. Please telephone or visit website for details of events running throughout the year.

Times Open all year daily from 10. See website for seasonal closing times. **Fee** ✳ £11.25 (ch 3-15 £7.75, under 3 free, concessions £9.50). Family ticket discount available. **Facilities** ♿ ⊑ ⊓ (outdoor) & (ramps & disabled parking, hearing loop) toilets for disabled shop ⊗ (ex assist dogs) 🍴

ST ANDREWS   MAP 12 NO51

British Golf Museum

Bruce Embankment KY16 9AB

➲ *(opposite Royal & Ancient Golf Club)*

☎ 01334 460046 & 460053

e-mail: judychance@randa.org

web: www.britishgolfmuseum.co.uk

Where better to find out about golf than in St Andrews, the home of the sport? Using diverse and exciting interactive displays, this museum explores the history of British golf from its origins to the personalities of today. The 18th Hole is fun for all the family, with dressing up, a mini-putting green and loads to do!

Times Open Mar-Oct, Mon-Sat 9.30-5.30, Sun 10-5. Nov-Mar, Mon-Sun 10-4. **Fee** ✳ £5.50 (ch £2.90, concessions £4.50). Family ticket £14. **Facilities** ♿ (charged) & toilets for disabled shop ⊗ (ex assist dogs) 🍴

Castle & Visitor Centre

KY16 9AR

☎ 01334 477196

web: www.historic-scotland.gov.uk

This 13th-century stronghold castle was the scene of the murder of Cardinal Beaton in 1546. The new visitor centre incorporates an exciting multi-media exhibition describing the history of the castle and nearby cathedral.

Times ✳ Open all year, Apr-Sep, daily 9.30-6.30; Oct-Mar, daily 9.30-4.30. Closed 25-26 Dec & 1-2 Jan. **Facilities** Ⓟ shop ⊗ 🏴

St Andrews Cathedral

KY16 9QU

☎ 01334 472563

web: www.historic-scotland.gov.uk

The cathedral was the largest in Scotland, and is now an extensive ruin. The remains date mainly from the 12th and 13th centuries, and large parts of the precinct walls have survived intact. Close by is St Rule's church, which the cathedral was built to replace. St Rule's probably dates from before the Norman Conquest, and is considered the most interesting Romanesque church in Scotland.

Times ✳ Open all year, Apr-Sep, daily 9.30-6.30; Oct-Mar, daily 9.30-4.30. Closed 25-26 Dec & 1-2 Jan. **Facilities** Ⓟ shop ⊗ 🏴

St Andrews Aquarium

The Scores KY16 9AS

➲ *(signed in town centre)*

☎ 01334 474786

web: www.standrewsaquarium.co.uk

This continually expanding aquarium is home to shrimps, sharks, eels, octopi, seals and much much more. Special features include the Seahorse Parade, and the Sea Mammal Research Unit, which is committed to the care of sea mammals and their environment.

Times ✳ Open daily from 10. Please phone for winter opening **Facilities** ♿ (charged) 🅿 🍴 🍃 shop ⊗ (ex assist dogs) 🍴

CITY OF GLASGOW

GLASGOW   MAP 11 NS56

Burrell Collection   FREE

Pollok Country Park, 2060 Pollokshaws Rd G43 1AT

➲ *(3.5m S of city centre, signposted from M77 Junct 2)*

☎ 0141 287 2550

e-mail: museums@csglasgow.org

web: www.glasgowmuseums.com

Set in Pollok Country Park, this award-winning building makes the priceless works of art on display seem almost part of the woodland setting. Shipping magnate Sir William Burrell's main interests were medieval Europe, Oriental art and European paintings. Colourful paintings and stained glass show the details of medieval life. Furniture, paintings, sculpture, armour and weapons help to complete the picture. Rugs, ceramics and metalwork represent the art of Islam. There is also a strong collection of Chinese and other Oriental ceramics. Paintings on display include works by Bellini, Rembrandt and the French Impressionists.

Times Open all year, Mon-Thu & Sat 10-5, Fri & Sun 11-5. Closed 25-26 & 31 (pm) Dec & 1-2 Jan **Facilities** ♿ (charged) 🅿 🍴 licensed ♿ (wheelchairs available, tape guides, lifts) toilets for disabled shop ⊗ (ex assist dogs)

Clydebuilt - Scottish Maritime Museum at Braehead

Braehead Shopping Centre, King Inch Rd G51 4BN

➲ *(M8 junct 25A, 26, follow signs for Braehead Shopping Centre, then Green car park)*

☎ 0141 886 1013

e-mail: clydebuilt@scotmaritime.org.uk

web: www.scottishmaritimemuseum.org

On the banks of the River Clyde, home of the Scottish shipbuilding industry, visitors can discover how Glasgow's famous ships were built, from the design stages through to the launch. There are also displays on the textile and cotton industries, iron and steel, and tobacco. Hands-on activities allow you to operate a real ship's engine, become a ship's riveter, and steer a virtual ship up the Clyde. A new QE2 exhibition will be launched in October 2008 to celebrate her last visit to the place of her birth. September 2009 is the 10th Anniversary of the museum.

Times Open daily 10-5.30, **Fee** £4.25 (ch £2.50, concessions £3). Family ticket £10 **Facilities** ♿ 🍃 (outdoor) ♿ (lift/ramps/wheelchairs from shopping centre) toilets for disabled shop ⊗ (ex assist dogs)

Gallery of Modern Art

Royal Exchange Square G1 3AH

➲ *(just off Buchanan St & close to Central Station & Queen St Stn)*

☎ 0141 229 1996

e-mail: museums@csglasgow.org

web: www.glasgowmuseums.com

GoMA offers a thought-provoking programme of temporary exhibitions and workshops. It displays work by local and international artists, as well as addressing contemporary social issues through its major biennial projects.

Times Open all year, Mon-Tue & Sat 10-5, Thu 10-8, Fri & Sun 11-5. Closed 25-26 Dec, 31 Dec pm, 1-2 Jan. **Fee** Free entry donations welcome **Facilities** ♿ (200yds) 🅿 ♿ toilets for disabled shop ⊗ (ex assist dogs)

Glasgow Botanic Gardens   FREE

730 Great Western Rd G12 0UE

➲ *(From M8 junct 17 onto A82 Dumbarton. Approx 2-3m the Botanic Gardens are on the right)*

☎ 0141 276 1614

e-mail: gbg@land.glasgow.gov.uk

Home of the national collections of Dendrobium Orchids, Begonias and tree ferns, the Gardens consist of an arboretum, herbaceous borders, a herb garden, rose garden, and unusual vegetables. The Kibble Palace contains carnivorous plants, island flora and temperate plant collections.

Times Open all year. Gardens open daily 7-dusk. Glasshouses 10-6 (4.15 in winter). **Facilities** ♿ (street parking) ♿ toilets for disabled ⊗

Glasgow Cathedral   FREE

Castle St G4 0QZ

➲ *(M8 junct 15, in centre of Glasgow)*

☎ 0141 552 6891

web: www.historic-scotland.gov.uk

The only Scottish mainland medieval cathedral to have survived the Reformation complete (apart from its western towers). Built during the 13th to 15th centuries over the supposed site of the tomb of St Kentigern. Notable features in this splendid building are the elaborately vaulted crypt, which includes an introductory display and collection of carved stones, the stone screen of the early 15th century and the unfinished Blackadder Aisle.

Times ✳ Open all year, Apr-Sep daily 9.30-6, Sun 1-5; Oct-Mar daily 9.30-4, Sun 1-4. Closed 25-26 Dec & 1-2 Jan. **Facilities** ♿ (telephone for disabled access details) shop ⊗ 🍴

SCOTLAND

GLASGOW CONTINUED

Glasgow Museums Resource Centre

FREE

200 Woodhead Rd, South Nitshill Ind Estate G53 7NN

➲ *(on S side, close to Rail Stn)*

☎ 0141 276 9300

web: www.glasgowmuseums.com

GMRC is the first publicly-accessible store for the city's museum service, offering a behind-the-scenes look at 200,000 treasures held in storage. Please note that access to the stores is by guided tour only. Viewings of a specific object can be arranged, with two weeks prior notice. Activities, tours and talks are held throughout the year - see website or phone for details.

Times ✳ Open all year Mon-Thu & Sat 10-5, Fri-Sun 11-5. Guided tours for public at 2.30 Access is only by guided tours. **Facilities** ❷ ❽ (ex assist dogs)

Glasgow Science Centre

50 Pacific Quay G51 1EA

➲ *(M8 junct 24 or M77 junct 21, follow brown signs, across Clyde from SECC)*

☎ 0871 540 1000

e-mail: admin@glasgowsciencecentre.org

web: www.glasgowsciencecentre.org

The centre is home to many entertaining and exciting attractions and contains hundreds of interactive exhibits. Highlights include the Scottish Power Planetarium, Scotland's only IMAX cinema and the 127 metre Glasgow Tower, a remarkable free-standing structure that gives breathtaking views of the city (check availability before visiting). GSC presents the world of science and technology in new and exciting ways.

Times Open 29 Oct-30 Mar, 10-5 Tue-Sun; 30 Mar-29 Oct daily 10-5. **Fee** Science Mall* or Imax: £6.95 (ch & concessions £5.95). Science Mall & Imax (45mins film only) £9.95 (ch & concessions £7.95). 20% off for groups 10+. Scottish Power Planetarium extra £2. **Facilities** ❷ (charged) ⏛ ⌇ (indoor & outdoor) ⌖ (induction loops) toilets for disabled shop ❽ (ex assist dogs) ⬛

Greenbank Garden

Flenders Rd, Clarkston G76 8RB

➲ *(off A726 on southern outskirts of city, 6m S of Glasgow)*

☎ 0844 493 2201

e-mail: information@nts.org.uk

web: www.nts.org.uk

The spacious, walled woodland gardens are attractively laid out in the grounds of an elegant Georgian house, and best seen between April and October. A wide range of flowers and shrubs are grown, with the idea of helping private gardeners to look at possibilities for their own gardens. A greenhouse and garden designed for the disabled gardener also displays specialised tools.

Times ✳ Garden open daily all year, 9.30-sunset. House 30 Mar-Oct Sun 2-4. **Facilities** ❷ ⏛ ⌖ (Partly accessible) (wheelchairs available, scented/textured plants) toilets for disabled shop garden centre ❽ (ex assist dogs)

Holmwood House

61-63 Netherlee House, Cathcart G44 3YG

➲ *(off Clarkston Rd)*

☎ 0844 493 2204

e-mail: information@nts.org.uk

web: www.nts.org.uk

Completed in 1858, Holmwood is considered to be the finest domestic design by the architect Alexander 'Greek' Thomson. Many rooms are richly ornamented in wood, plaster and marble.

Times ✳ Open 30 Mar-Oct daily, 12-5. Morning visits available for pre-booked groups. **Facilities** ❷ (charged) ⏛ ⌇ ⌖ (Partly accessible) (lift, audio tour, room guides) shop garden centre ❽ ❽

House for an Art Lover

10 Dumbreck Rd, Bellahouston Park G41 5BW

➲ *(M8 W junct 23 signed B768, left at top of slip road onto Dumbreck Rd. Bellahouston Park on right)*

☎ 0141 353 4770

e-mail: info@houseforanartlover.co.uk

web: www.houseforanartlover.co.uk

Inspired by a portfolio of drawings by Charles Rennie Mackintosh in 1901, this fascinating artistic attraction and private dining venue opened in 1996. Visitors can view the Mackintosh suite of rooms and learn from a DVD presentation about the development of the building and its contents. There is a full programme of changing art exhibitions, dinner concerts and afternoon musical recitals. Contact for more details.

Times Open Apr-Sep, Mon-Wed 10-4 & Thu-Sun 10-1; Oct-Mar, Sat-Sun 10-1, telephone for wkday opening details. **Fee** £4.50 (ch under 10 free, concessions £3). **Facilities** ❷ ❿ licensed ⌖ (lift to 1st floor) toilets for disabled shop ❽ (ex assist dogs) ⬛

Hunterian Art Gallery

FREE

82 Hillhead St, The University of Glasgow G12 8QQ

➲ *(on University of Glasgow Campus in Hillhead District, 2m W of city centre)*

☎ 0141 330 5431

e-mail: hunter@museum.gla.ac.uk

web: www.hunterian.gla.ac.uk

The founding collection is made up of paintings bequeathed in the 18th century by Dr William Hunter, including works by Rembrandt and Stubbs. The Gallery now has works by James McNeill Whistler, major displays of paintings by the Scottish Colourists, and a graphics collection holding some 300,000 prints. A popular feature of the Charles Rennie Mackintosh collection is the re-construction of the interiors of The Mackintosh House.

Times Open Mon-Sat 9.30-5. Telephone for BH closures. **Facilities** ℗ (500 yds) (pay & display) ⏛ ⌖ (lift, wheelchair available) toilets for disabled shop ❽ (ex assist dogs) ⬛

Hunterian Museum `FREE`

Gilbert Scott Building, The University of Glasgow G12 8QQ

➲ *(on University of Glasgow campus in Hillhead District, 2m W of city centre)*

☎ 0141 330 4221

e-mail: hunter@museum.gla.ac.uk

web: www.hunterian.gla.ac.uk

Named after the 18th-century physician, Dr William Hunter, who bequeathed his large and important collections of coins, medals, fossils, geological specimens and archaeological and ethnographic items to the university. The exhibits are shown in the main building of the university, and temporary exhibitions are held.

Times Open all year, Mon-Sat 9.30-5. Closed certain BHs phone for details.
Facilities Ⓟ (100yds) (pay & display) ⑂ (lift) toilets for disabled shop ⊗ (ex assist dogs) ▬

Hutchesons' Hall `FREE`

158 Ingram St G1 1EJ

➲ *(near SE corner of George Square)*

☎ 0844 493 2199

e-mail: information@nts.org.uk

web: www.nts.org.uk

This handsome early 19th-century building was designed by David Hamilton and houses a visitor centre and shop. There is a video about Glasgow's merchant city, and the Hall can be booked for functions. Telephone for details of concerts, recitals, etc. The Trust is considering some new initiatives at Hutchesons' Hall and as a result opening times may change. Please call in advance before making a visit.

Times ✷ Open 5 Jan-24 Dec Mon, Tue, Thu, Fri 10.5.Closed on BHs.
Facilities Ⓟ (on street) (meters)(outside for disabled) ⑂ (Partly accessible) toilets for disabled shop ⊗ ⑂

Kelvingrove Art Gallery & Museum

Argyle St G3 8AG

➲ *(1m W of city centre)*

☎ 0141 276 9599

e-mail: museums@csglasgow.org

web: www.glasgowmuseums.com

Glasgow's favourite building re-opened in July 2006 after a three-year, £35 million restoration project. On display are 8000 objects, including a Spitfire, a 4-metre ceratosaur and Salvador Dali's Christ of St John of the Cross. A new 'Mackintosh and the Glasgow Style Gallery' explores the genius of Charles Rennie Mackintosh. Exciting temporary exhibitions take place throughout the year. Organ recitals take place each day and there are a range of tours and activities available for all ages. Forthcoming exhibitions include 'Impressionism in Scotland' October 2008-January 2009 and 'Dr Who' March-October 2009.

Times Open all year, Mon-Thu & Sat 10-5; Fri & Sun 11-5. Closed 25-26 Dec & 31 Dec (pm) & 1-2 Jan. **Fee** Free admission, some exhibitions have an entrance fee. Please check the website for details. **Facilities** ❷ (charged) ⑂ᵀⓄⵏ licensed ⟞ (outdoor) ⑂ toilets for disabled shop ⊗ (ex assist dogs)

The Lighthouse `2 for 1`

11 Mitchell Ln G1 3NU

➲ *(in city centre)*

☎ 0141 221 6362

e-mail: enquiries@thelighthouse.co.uk

web: www.thelighthouse.co.uk

Scotland's National Centre for Architecture, Design and the City. Extending over six floors and one of the biggest centres of its kind in Europe. Home to the award-winning Mackintosh Centre, devoted to the art, architecture and design of Charles Rennie Mackintosh. There are also temporary exhibition spaces with a thought provoking programme. A place of discovery and learning, another feature of The Lighthouse is the uninterrupted view over Glasgow's cityscape. Climb the helical staircase in the Mackintosh Tower or use the lift to the Level 6 Viewing Platform and spot some significant buildings that make up Glasgow's architectural tapestry. In 2009 the Lighthouse celebrates its 10th anniversary.

Times Open all year, Mon & Wed-Sat, 10.30-5, Tue 11-5, Sun noon-5.
Fee £3 (ch £1, concessions £1.50) free entrance on Sat **Facilities** Ⓟ (20mtrs) (NCP on Mitchell St) Ⓞⵏ licensed ⑂ (Mackintosh tower inaccessible) (induction loop, large print brochures) toilets for disabled shop ⊗ (ex assist dogs) ▬

Museum of Transport `FREE`

1 Bunhouse Rd G3 8DP

➲ *(1.5m W of city centre)*

☎ 0141 287 2720

e-mail: museums@csglasgow.org

web: www.glasgowmuseums.com

Visit the Museum of Transport and the first impression is of gleaming metalwork and bright paint. All around you there are cars, caravans, carriages and carts, fire engines, buses, steam locomotives, prams and trams. The museum uses its collections of vehicles and models to tell the story of transport by land and sea, with a unique Glasgow flavour. Visitors can even go window shopping along the recreated Kelvin Street of 1938. Upstairs 250 ship models tell the story of the great days of Clyde shipbuilding. The Museum of Transport has something for everyone.

Times Open all year, Mon-Thu & Sat 10-5, Fri & Sun 11-5. Closed 25-26 Dec, 31 Dec pm, 1-2 Jan. **Facilities** ❷ (charged) ⑂ᵀ ⑂ (assistance available) toilets for disabled shop ⊗ (ex assist dogs)

People's Palace `FREE`

Glasgow Green G40 1AT

➲ *(1m SE of city centre)*

☎ 0141 271 2951

e-mail: museums@csglasgow.org

web: www.glasgowmuseums.com

Glasgow grew from a medieval town located by the Cathedral to the Second City of the British Empire. Trade with the Americas, and later industry, made the city rich. But not everyone shared in Glasgow's wealth. The People's Palace on historic Glasgow Green shows how ordinary Glaswegians worked, lived and played. Visitors can discover how a family lived in a typical one-room Glasgow 'single end'

CONTINUED

GLASGOW CONTINUED

tenement flat, see Billy Connolly's amazing banana boots, learn to speak Glesga, take a trip 'doon the watter' and visit the Winter Gardens.

Times Open all year, Mon-Thu & Sat 10-5, Fri & Sun 11-5. Closed 25-26 & 31 Dec (pm) & 1-2 Jan **Facilities** Ⓟ (50yds) ♿ (lifts) toilets for disabled shop ⊗ (ex assist dogs)

Pollok House

Pollok Country Park, 2060 Pollokshaws Rd G43 1AT

➲ *(3.5m S of city centre, off M77 junct 2, follow signs for Burrell Collection)*

☎ 0141 616 6410

e-mail: pollokhouse@nts.org.uk

web: www.nts.org.uk

The house is one of Glasgow's most elegant, and was built by the Maxwell family in the 18th century and expanded between 1890 and 1901, including extensive servants' quarters. The rooms are decorated with 18th-century plasterwork, fine furniture and the Stirling Maxwell art collection, including works by El Greco, Goya and William Blake.

Times House: open daily 10-5. Closed 25 & 26 Dec & 1 & 2 Jan. **Facilities** Ⓟ ⅋♿ (lifts) toilets for disabled shop ⊗

Provand's Lordship   FREE

3 Castle St G4 0RB

➲ *(1m E of city centre)*

☎ 0141 552 8819

e-mail: museums@csglasgow.org

web: www.glasgowmuseums.com

Provand's Lordship is the only house to survive from Medieval Glasgow. For over 500 years it has watched the changing fortunes of the city and the nearby Cathedral. Bishop Andrew Muirhead built the house as part of St Nicholas' Hospital in 1571. The prebendary of Barlanark later bought it for use as a manse. Inside, the displays recreate home life in the middle ages. Behind the house is the St Nicholas Garden, built in 1997. It is a medical herb garden, in keeping with the original purpose of the house.

Times Open all year, Mon-Thu & Sat 10-5, Fri & Sun 11-5. Closed 25-26 Dec, 31 Dec pm, 1-2 Jan. **Facilities** Ⓟ (50 yds) ♿ (ground floor only) (please contact for details) ⊗ (ex assist dogs)

St Mungo Museum of Religious Life & Art   FREE

2 Castle St G4 0RH

➲ *(1m NE of city centre)*

☎ 0141 553 2557

e-mail: museums@csglasgow.org

web: www.glasgowmuseums.com

The award-winning St Mungo Museum explores the importance of religion in peoples' everyday lives and art. It aims to promote understanding and respect between people of different faiths and of none. The museum features stained glass, objects, statues and video footage. In the grounds is Britain's first Japanese Zen garden.

Times Open all year, Mon-Thu & Sat 10-5, Fri & Sun 11-5. Closed 25-26 Dec, 31 Dec (pm) & 1-2 Jan. **Facilities** Ⓟ (50yds) ♿ (taped information & lift) toilets for disabled shop ⊗ (ex assist dogs)

Scotland Street School Museum   FREE

225 Scotland St G5 8QB

☎ 0141 287 0500

e-mail: museums@csglasgow.org

web: www.glasgowmuseums.com

Designed by Charles Rennie Mackintosh between 1903 and 1906 for the School Board of Glasgow, and now a museum telling the story of education in Scotland from 1872 to the late 20th century. Also hosts temporary exhibitions.

Times Open all year daily 10-5, Fri & Sun 11-5. (closed 25,26,31 Dec & pm 1 & 2 Jan) **Facilities** Ⓟ (across road) (Shields Rd pay & display ♿ toilets for disabled shop ⊗ (ex assist dogs)

The Scottish Football Museum   2 for 1

Hampden Park G42 9BA

➲ *(3m S of city centre, follow brown tourist signs)*

☎ 0141 616 6139

e-mail: info@scottishfootballmuseum.org.uk

web: www.scottishfootballmuseum.org.uk

Using 2500 pieces of footballing memorabilia, the Scottish Football Museum covers such themes as football's origins, women's football, fan culture, other games influenced by football, and even some social history. The exhibits include the world's oldest football, trophy and ticket, a reconstructed 1903 changing room and press box, and items of specific import, such as Kenny Dalglish's silver cap, Jimmy McGrory's boots, and the ball from Scotland's 5-1 win over England in 1928. Visit the Scottish Football Hall of Fame, and take the guided Hampden Stadium tour.

Times Open Mon-Sat 10-5, Sun 11-5. Closed match days, special events and Xmas/New Year, please telephone in advance for confirmation **Fee** Museum £6 (ch 16 & concessions £3) Stadium £6 (ch 16 & concessions £3). Combined Ticket £9 (ch 16 & concessions £4.50) under 5's free. **Facilities** Ⓟ ⅋♿ (ramps throughout) toilets for disabled shop ⊗ (ex assist dogs) ▭

The Tall Ship at Glasgow Harbour

100 Stobcross Rd G3 8QQ

➲ *(from M8 junct 19 onto A814 follow signs for attraction)*

☎ 0141 222 2513

e-mail: info@thetallship.com

web: www.thetallship.com

Visit The Tall Ship at Glasgow Harbour and step back in time to the days of sail. Experience Glasgow's maritime history at first hand and explore the UK's only remaining Clydebuilt sailing ship, the Glenlee. Exhibitions on board and in the visitor centre on the quayside tell the story of the ship and the Glasgow Harbour area. If you have ever wondered what it would have been like to be a sailor on a tall ship, this is your chance to find out. Children can have fun by joining in the hunt for Jock, the ship's cat. An unmissable experience, The Tall Ship offers guided tours, changing exhibitions, children's activities, a nautical gift shop and café.

Times Open all year, daily Mar-Oct 10-5; Nov-Feb 10-4. **Fee** ✶ £4.95 (1 ch free with paying adult/concession, additional ch £2.50, concessions £3.75). **Facilities** ❷ 🍴 🎍 (indoor & outdoor) shop 🛒

The Tenement House

145 Buccleuch St, Garnethill G3 6QN

➲ *(N of Charing Cross)*

☎ 0844 493 2197

e-mail: information@nts.org.uk

web: www.nts.org.uk

This shows an unsung but once-typical side of Glasgow life: it is a first-floor flat, built in 1892, with a parlour, bedroom, kitchen and bathroom, furnished with the original recess beds, kitchen range, sink, and coal bunker, among other articles. The home of Agnes Toward from 1911 to 1965, the flat was bought by an actress who preserved it as a 'time capsule'. The contents vividly portray the life of one section of Glasgow society.

Times ✶ Open Mar-Oct, daily 1-5. **Facilities** ℗ (100yds) (restricted, recommend parking in town) ♿ (Partly accessible) (Braille guide, object handling collection) shop ❽ (ex assist dogs) 🐾

Trades Hall of Glasgow

85 Glassford St G1 1UH

➲ *(in city centre in Merchant City. Accessible from George Square & Argyle St)*

☎ 0141 552 2418

e-mail: info@tradeshallglasgow.co.uk

web: www.tradeshallglasgow.co.uk

The Trades Hall is one of Glasgow's most historic buildings and was home to the 14 incorporated crafts who regulated trade and played a vital role in shaping and making Glasgow the city it is today. Visitors can explore the impressive rooms of the building taking in the Grand Hall with its spectacular soaring windows, baroque chandeliers and striking dome, and the Saloon which features an original Adam fireplace and beautiful stained glass windows.

Times ✶ Open Mon-Fri, 10-4, subject to availability **Facilities** ℗ (NCP 100yds) (half price at NCP if visiting building) ♿ (electronic ramps for rise in levels of 3 & 4 stairs) toilets for disabled ❽ (ex assist dogs)

HIGHLAND

AVIEMORE   MAP 14 NH81

Strathspey Steam Railway

Aviemore Station, Dalfaber Rd PH22 1PY

➲ *(from A9 take B970 for Coylumbridge, on B9152, left after railway bridge, car park 0.25m on left. Other stations: Boat of Garten in village; Broomhill, off A95, 3.5m S of Grantown-on-Spey)*

☎ 01479 810725

e-mail: strathtrains@strathspeyrailway.co.uk

web: www.strathspeyrailway.co.uk

This steam railway covers the ten miles from Aviemore via Boat of Garten to Broomhill. The journey takes about 40 minutes, but allow around two hours for the round trip. Shorter trips are possible and timetables are available from the station and the tourist information centre. Telephone, visit website or see local press for details of events running throughout the year.

Times Phone for details. **Fee** Basic roundtrip £10.50 (ch £5.25) Family £26. Day Rover £14 (ch £7). **Facilities** ❷ 🍴 🍽️ licensed 🎍 (outdoor) ♿ (ramps) toilets for disabled shop 🛒

BALMACARA   MAP 14 NG82

Balmacara Estate & Lochalsh Woodland Garden

Lochalsh House IV40 8DN

➲ *(3m E of Kyle of Lochalsh, off A87)*

☎ 0844 493 2233

e-mail: information@nts.org.uk

web: www.nts.org.uk

The Balmacara Estate comprises some 5,600 acres and seven crofting villages, including Plockton, a conservation area. There are excellent views of Skye, Kintail and Applecross. The main attraction is the Lochalsh Woodland Garden, but the whole area is excellent for walking.

Times ✶ Estate open all year daily, Woodland Garden all year daily 9-sunset, Reception Kiosk 31 Mar-Sep daily 9-5, Balmacara Square Visitor Centre 31 Mar-Sep daily 9-5 (Fri 9-4). **Facilities** ❷ ♿ (Partly accessible) (Visual information, Audio information) 🐾

BETTYHILL   MAP 14 NC76

Strathnaver Museum   2 for 1

KW14 7SS

➲ *(By the A386 on outskirts of Bettyhill on the E of the village)*

☎ 01641 521418

e-mail: strathnavermus@ukonline.co.uk

The museum has displays on the Clearances, with a fine collection of Strathnaver Clearances furnishings, domestic and farm implements, and local books. There is also a Clan Mackay room. The museum's

CONTINUED

SCOTLAND

BETTYHILL CONTINUED

setting is a former church, a handsome stone building with a magnificent canopied pulpit dated 1774. The churchyard contains a carved stone known as the Farr Stone, which dates back to the 9th century and is a fine example of Pictish art.

Times Open Apr-Oct, Mon-Sat 10-1 & 2-5; Nov-Mar restricted opening. **Fee** £2 (ch 50p, under 5's free, concessions £1.50, student/groups £1). **Facilities** ♿ & (ground floor only accessible) (DVD, small wheelchair) shop ⊗ (ex assist dogs)

BOAT OF GARTEN   MAP 14 NH91

RSPB Loch Garten Osprey Centre

RSPB Reserve Abernethy Forest, Forest Lodge, Nethybridge PH25 3EF

➲ (signed from B970 & A9 at Aviemore, follow 'RSPB Ospreys' signs)

☎ 01479 821894

Home of the Loch Garten Osprey site, this reserve holds one of the most important remnants of Scots Pine forest in the Highlands. Within its 30,760 acres are forest bogs, moorland, mountain top, lochs and crofting land. In addition to the regular pair of nesting ospreys, there are breeding Scottish crossbills, capercaillies, black grouse and many others. The ospreys can be viewed through telescopes and there is a live TV link to the nest. Please telephone for details of special events running throughout the year.

Times Osprey Centre open daily, Apr-Aug 10-6. **Fee** ✳ £3 (ch 50p, concessions £2). **Facilities** ♿ & (low level viewing slots & optics) toilets for disabled shop ⊗ (ex assist dogs in centre) ▄

CARRBRIDGE   MAP 14 NH92

Landmark Forest Adventure Park

PH23 3AJ

➲ (off A9 between Aviemore & Inverness)

☎ 01479 841613 & 0800 731 3446

e-mail: landmarkcentre@btconnect.com

web: www.landmark-centre.co.uk

This innovative centre is designed to provide a fun and educational visit for all ages. Microworld takes a close-up look at the incredible microscopic world around us. There is a 70ft forest viewing tower and a treetop trail. There are also demonstrations of timber sawing on a steam-powered sawmill and log hauling by a Clydesdale horse throughout the day. Attractions include a 3-track Watercoaster, a maze and a large covered adventure play area, mini electric cars and remote-controlled truck arena. New features include; 'RopeworX', an aerial highwire obstacle course, and 'Skydive', a parachute jump simulator.

Times Open all year, daily, Apr-mid Jul 10-6; mid Jul-mid Aug 10-7; Sep-Oct 10-5.30; Nov-Mar 10-5. Closed 25 Dec and 1 Jan. **Fee** Apr-Oct £9.95 (ch & pen £7.80), Nov-Mar £3.50 (ch & pen £2.65) **Facilities** ♿ ⌷ ▯◎ licensed & (all areas accessible, some attractions not suitable) toilets for disabled shop ▄

CAWDOR   MAP 14 NH85

Cawdor Castle   `2 for 1`

IV12 5RD

➲ (on B9090, off A96)

☎ 01667 404401

e-mail: info@cawdorcastle.com

web: www.cawdorcastle.com

Home of the Thanes of Cawdor since the 14th century, this lovely castle has a drawbridge, an ancient tower built round a tree, and a freshwater well inside the house. Gardens Weekend takes place in June - guided tours of gardens with the head gardener.

Times Open May-11 Oct, daily 10-5.30 (last admission 5). **Fee** ✳ £7.90 (ch 5-15 £4.90, pen £6.90). Family ticket £24. Party 20+ £6.50 each. Gardens, grounds & nature trails only £4. **Facilities** ♿ ⌷ ▯◎ ᄆ (outdoor) & (ramps to restaurant, shops and garden, ground floor only of castle accessible) toilets for disabled shop ⊗ (ex assist dogs) ▄

CLAVA CAIRNS   MAP 14 NH74

Clava Cairns   `FREE`

➲ (6m E of Inverness, signed from B9091)

☎ 01667 460232

web: www.historic-scotland.gov.uk

A well-preserved Bronze Age cemetery complex of passage graves, ring cairns, kerb cairn and standing stones in a beautiful setting. In addition, the remains of a chapel of unknown date can be seen at this site.

Times ✳ Open at all reasonable times. **Facilities** ♿ ⊗ ᄆ

CROMARTY   MAP 14 NH76

Hugh Miller Museum & Birth Place Cottage

Church St IV11 8XA

➲ *(Via Kessock Bridge and A832 in Cromarty, 22m NE of Inverness.*

☎ 0844 493 2158

e-mail: information@nts.org.uk

web: www.nts.org.uk

The cottage houses an exhibition on the life and work of Hugh Miller, a stonemason born here in 1802 who became an eminent geologist and writer. It was built by his great-grandfather around 1698, and now has a charming cottage garden.

Times ✳ Open 31 Mar-Sep, daily 12.30-4.30. Oct Sun-Wed 12.30-4.30. **Facilities** ℗ (5mins) (disabled is directly outside) ও (Partly accessible) ⊗ (ex assist dogs) 🦮

CULLODEN MOOR   MAP 14 NH74

Culloden Battlefield

IV2 5EU

➲ *(B9006, 5m E of Inverness)*

☎ 0844 493 2159

e-mail: information@nts.org.uk

web: www.nts.org.uk

A cairn recalls this last battle fought on mainland Britain, on 16 April 1746, when the Duke of Cumberland's forces routed 'Bonnie' Prince Charles Edward Stuart's army. The battlefield has been restored to its state on the day of the battle, and in summer there are 'living history' enactments. This is a most atmospheric evocation of tragic events. Telephone for details of guided tours. A Visitors' Centre exploring the impact of the battle opened in 2007.

Times ✳ Visitor Centre, Restaurant & Shop: Feb-30 Mar daily 10-4. 31 Mar-Oct daily 9-6. Nov-Dec daily 10-4. (Closed 24-26 Dec). Site: All year daily. **Facilities** ℗ (charged) 🍽 ও (wheelchair, induction loop, raised map, Braille guidebook) toilets for disabled shop ⊗ (ex assist dogs) 🦮

DRUMNADROCHIT   MAP 14 NH52

Official Loch Ness Exhibition Centre, Loch Ness 2000

IV3 6TU

➲ *(on A82, 12m S Inverness)*

☎ 01456 450573 & 450218

web: www.lochness.com

This award-winning centre has a fascinating and popular multi-media presentation lasting 30 minutes. Seven themed areas cover the story of the Loch Ness Monster, from the pre-history of Scotland, through the cultural roots of the legend in Highland folklore, and into the 50-year controversy which surrounds it. The centre uses the latest technology in computer animation, lasers and multi-media projection systems.

Times Open all year; Nov-end Jan, 10-3.30, Xmas hols 10-5, Feb-end May & Oct 9.30-5, Jun & Sep, 9-6, Jul & Aug 9-6.30 **Fee** £6.50 (ch 6-16 £4.50, students £5.50, pen £5). Family ticket (2ad+2 or 3 ch) £18. **Facilities** ℗ ⊡ 🍽 licensed ⋒ (outdoor) ও (parking) toilets for disabled shop ⊗ (ex in grounds & assist dogs) ⚫

Urquhart Castle

IV63 6XJ

➲ *(on A82)*

☎ 01456 450551

web: www.historic-scotland.gov.uk

The castle was once Scotland's biggest and overlooks Loch Ness. It dates mainly from the 14th century, when it was built on the site of an earlier fort, and was destroyed before the 1715 Jacobite rebellion.

Times ✳ Open all year, Apr-Sep, daily 9.30-6.30; Oct-Mar, daily 9.30-4.30. Closed 25-26 Dec. **Facilities** ℗ shop ⊗ 🎖

DUNBEATH   MAP 15 ND12

Laidhay Croft Museum

KW6 6EH

➲ *(1m N of Dunbeath on A9)*

☎ 01593 731244

The museum gives visitors a glimpse of a long-vanished way of life. The main building is a thatched Caithness longhouse, with the dwelling quarters, byre and stable all under one roof. It dates back some 200 years, and is furnished as it might have been 100 years ago. A collection of early farm tools and machinery is also shown. Near the house is a thatched winnowing barn with its roof supported on three 'Highland couples', or crucks.

Times Open Jun-Sep, Mon-Sat 9.30-4.30. **Fee** £2 (ch 50p) **Facilities** ℗ ⊡ ও toilets for disabled

---

FORT GEORGE   MAP 14 NH75

Fort George

IV1 2TD

➲ *(11m NE of Inverness)*

☎ 01667 462777

web: www.historic-scotland.gov.uk

Built following the Battle of Culloden as a Highland fortress for the army of George II, this is one of the outstanding artillery fortifications in Europe and still an active army barracks.

Times ✳ Open all year, Apr-Sep daily 9.30-6.30; Oct-Mar daily 9.30-4.30. Closed 25-26 Dec. **Facilities** ℗ 🍽 ⋒ shop ⊗ 🎖

The Highlanders Regimental Museum Collection

IV2 7TD

➲ *(off A96 5m from Inverness)*

☎ 0131 310 8701

Fort George has been a military barracks since it was built in 1748-69, and was the Depot of the Seaforth Highlanders until 1961. The

CONTINUED

SCOTLAND

SCOTLAND

FORT GEORGE CONTINUED

museum of the Queen's Own Highlanders (Seaforth and Camerons) is sited in the former Lieutenant Governor's house, where uniforms, medals and pictures are displayed.

Times Open Apr-Sep daily 9.30-5.15; Oct-Mar Mon-Fri 10-4 (closed 24-25 Dec & BHs) **Fee** ✳ Free. (Admission charged by Historic Scotland for entry to Fort George). **Facilities** ❷ ᵭ (2nd floor accessible via stairs) (stair lift to 1st floor, wheelchair on 1st floor) toilets for disabled shop ❽ (ex assist dogs) ▬

FORT WILLIAM   **MAP 14 NN17**

Inverlochy Castle   `FREE`
PH33 6SN

➲ *(2m NE of Fort William, off A82)*

web: www.historic-scotland.gov.uk

A fine well-preserved 13th-century castle of the Comyn family; in the form of a square, with round towers at the corners. The largest tower was the donjon or keep. This is one of Scotland's earliest castles.

Times ✳ Open at all reasonable times. **Facilities** ❷ ❽ ▮

West Highland Museum
Cameron Square PH33 6AJ

➲ *(museum next door to tourist office)*

☎ 01397 702169

e-mail: info@westhighlandmuseum.org.uk
web: www.westhighlandmuseum.org.uk

The displays illustrate traditional Highland life and history, with numerous Jacobite relics. One of them is the 'secret portrait' of Bonnie Prince Charlie, which looks like meaningless daubs of paint but reveals a portrait when reflected in a metal cylinder.

Times ✳ Open all year Jun-Sep, Mon-Sat 10-5 (also Jul-Aug, Sun 2-5); Oct-May, Mon-Sat 10-4. **Facilities** Ⓟ (100yds) (charge all year) ᵭ (Partly accessible) toilets for disabled shop ❽ (ex assist dogs)

GAIRLOCH   **MAP 14 NG87**

Gairloch Heritage Museum   `2 for 1`
Achtercairn IV21 2BP

➲ *(on junct of A382 & B8021 near police station & public car park)*

☎ 01445 712287

e-mail: info@gairlochheritagemuseum.org.uk
web: www.gairlochheritagemuseum.org.uk

A converted farmstead now houses the award-winning museum, which shows the way of life in this West Highland parish from early times to the 20th century. There are hands-on activities for children and reconstructions of a croft house room, a school room, a shop, and a smugglers' cave. You can also view Gairloch through one of the largest lenses assembled by the Northern Lighthouse Board. Please visit website for details of regular events, such as craft demonstrations, free open evenings and special exhibitions.

Times Open Apr-Sep, Mon-Sat 10-5; Oct, Mon-Fri 10-1.30 (last admission 4.30). Winter months by arrangement. **Fee** ✳ £3 (ch 5-16yrs £1, under 5 free, concessions £2). Group rates available. **Facilities** ❷ ❶ ᵭ (Partly accessible) (Computer access to archive photographs) shop ❽ (ex assist dogs)

GLENCOE   **MAP 14 NN15**

Glencoe & Dalness
NTS Visitor Centre PH49 4LA

➲ *(on A82, 17m S of Fort William)*

☎ 0844 493 2222

e-mail: information@nts.org.uk
web: www.nts.org.uk

Glencoe has stunning scenery and some of the most challenging climbs and walks in the Highlands. Red deer, wildcats, eagles and ptarmigan are among the wildlife. It is also known as a place of treachery and infamy. The Macdonalds of Glencoe were hosts to a party of troops who, under government orders, fell upon the men, women and children in a bloody massacre in 1692. The Visitor Centre tells the story.

Times ✳ Visitor centre, shop, exhibition & café 2-6 Jan daily 10-4, 7 Jan-28 Feb Thu-Sun 10-4, Mar daily 10-4, Apr-Aug daily 9.30-5.30, Sep-Oct daily 10-5, Nov-16 Dec Thu-Sun 10-4, 26-31 Dec daily 10-4. Last entry to exhibition 30 mins before centre closes. Site all year daily **Facilities** ❷ ⬚ ⊟ ᵭ (Partly accessible) (induction loop in video programme room, object to handle) toilets for disabled shop ❽ (ex assist dogs) ☗

Glencoe & North Lorn Folk Museum
PH49 4HS

➲ *(turn off A82 at Glencoe x-roads then immediately right into Glencoe village)*

☎ 01855 811664

e-mail: info@glencoemuseum.com
web: www.glencoemuseum.com

Two heather-thatched cottages in the main street of Glencoe now house items connected with the Macdonalds and the Jacobite risings. A variety of local domestic and farming exhibits, dairying and slate-working equipment, costumes and embroidery are also shown. Activities for all ages inside the museum, plus special events, please see the website for details.

Times ✳ Open Apr-Oct, Mon-Sat 10-5.30. **Facilities** ❷ ᵭ (Disabled parking outside) shop

---

GLENFINNAN   **MAP 14 NM98**

Glenfinnan Monument   `FREE`
NTS Visitor Centre PH37 4LT

➲ *(on A830, 18.5m W of Fort William)*

☎ 0844 493 2221

e-mail: information@nts.org.uk
web: www.nts.org.uk

The monument commemorates the Highlanders who fought for Bonnie Prince Charlie in 1745. It stands in an awe-inspiring setting at the head of Loch Shiel. There is a visitor centre with information (commentary in four languages) on the Prince's campaign.

Times ✳ Visitor Centre, 31 Mar-30 Jun daily 10-5. Jul-Aug daily 9.30-5.30. Sep-Oct daily 10-5. Site: Daily all year. **Facilities** 🅿 ⯑ 🅿 ♿ (Partly accessible) (wheelchair available) shop 🍽

GOLSPIE   MAP 14 NH89

Dunrobin Castle

KW10 6SF

➲ *(1m NE on A9, from Golspie)*

☎ 01408 633177 & 633268

e-mail: info@dunrobincastle.net

web: www.dunrobincastle.co.uk

The ancient seat of the Earls and Dukes of Sutherland is a splendid, gleaming, turreted structure, thanks largely to 19th-century rebuilding, and has a beautiful setting overlooking the sea. Paintings, furniture and family heirlooms are on display, and the gardens are on a grand scale to match the house. There are also falconry displays in the gardens.

Times Open Apr-15 Oct, Mon-Sat 10.30-5.30, Sun 12-5.30. Closes 1 hr earlier Apr, May & Oct. (Last admission half hour before closing). **Fee** ✳ £7.50 (ch £5, pen £6.50). Family ticket (2ad+2ch) £20. **Facilities** 🅿 ⯑ 🅿 (outdoor) ♿ (garden access by prior arrangement) toilets for disabled shop ⊗ ➡

HELMSDALE   MAP 14 ND01

Timespan

Dunrobin St KW8 6JX

➲ *(off A9 in centre of village, by Telford Bridge)*

☎ 01431 821327

e-mail: enquiries@timespan.org.uk

web: www.timespan.org.uk

Located in a historic fishing village, this museum relates to the social and natural history of the area, and the art gallery has changing exhibitions of contemporary art and works by local artists. The garden has over 100 varieties of herbs and plants. There is a gift shop, and a café with beautiful views of the Telford Bridge.

Times Open Etr-end Oct, Mon-Sat 10-5, Sun 12-5. **Fee** ✳ £4 (ch £2, concessions £3). Family ticket £10. **Facilities** 🅿 ⯑ ♿ (lift) toilets for disabled shop ⊗ (ex assist dogs) ➡

KINCRAIG   MAP 14 NH80

Highland Wildlife Park

PH21 1NL

➲ *(on B9152, 7m S of Aviemore)*

☎ 01540 651270

e-mail: info@highlandwildlifepark.org

web: www.highlandwildlifepark.org

As you drive through the main reserve, you can see awe-inspiring European bison grazing alongside wild horses, red deer and highland cattle plus a wide variety of other species. Then in the walk-round forest, woodland and moorland habitats prepare for close encounters with animals such as wolves, capercaillie, arctic foxes, wildcats, pine

martens, otters and owls. Visit the snow monkeys in their beautiful lochside enclosure and the red pandas usually found climbing high up the trees.

Times Open all year, weather permitting. Apr-Oct, 10-5 (last entry 4); Nov-Mar 10-4. (Last entry 3). **Fee** £10.50 (ch £8, concessions £8.50). Family ticket (2ad+2ch) £34; (2ad+3ch) £38. Prices valid until March 2009. **Facilities** 🅿 ⯑ 🅿 (outdoor) shop ⊗ ➡

KINGUSSIE   MAP 14 NH70

Ruthven Barracks   [FREE]

➲ *(1m SE from Kingussie, signed from A9 and A86)*

☎ 01667 460232

web: www.historic-scotland.gov.uk

An infantry barracks erected in 1719 following the Jacobite rising of 1715, with two ranges of quarters and a stable block. Captured and burnt by Prince Charles Edward Stuart's army in 1746.

Times ✳ Open at any reasonable time. **Facilities** 🅿 ⊗ 🚩

KIRKHILL   MAP 14 NH54

Moniack Castle (Highland Winery)

IV5 7PQ

➲ *(7m from Inverness on A862, near Beauly, on S side of Beauly Firth)*

☎ 01463 831283

e-mail: jg@moniackcastle.co.uk

web: www.moniackcastle.co.uk

Commercial wine-making is not a typically Scottish industry, but nevertheless a wide range of country-style wines is produced, including elderflower and silver birch; mead and sloe gin are also made here. A selection of related products and tours of the production area are available at this unique attraction, situated in a 16th-century castle.

Times Open all year, Apr-Oct Mon-Sat 10-5. Nov-Mar, Mon-Fri 11-4. **Fee** ✳ £2 **Facilities** 🅿 🅿 (outdoor) ♿ (Partly accessible) shop ⊗ ➡

NEWTONMORE   MAP 14 NN79

Clan Macpherson House & Museum

Main St PH20 1DE

➲ *(off A9 at junct of Newtonmore and Kingussie, museum on left after entering village)*

☎ 01540 673332

e-mail: museum@clan-macpherson.org

web: www.clan-macpherson.org

Containing relics and memorials of the clan chiefs and other Macpherson families as well as those of Prince Charles Edward Stuart, this museum also displays the Prince's letters to the Clan Chief of 1745 and one to the Prince from his father, the Old Pretender, along with royal warrants and the green banner of the clan. Other interesting historic exhibits include James Macpherson's fiddle, swords, pictures, decorations and medals.

Times Open Apr-Oct, Mon-Sat 10-5, Sun 12-5. Other times by appointment. **Fee** Free. Donations welcome. **Facilities** 🅿 ♿ (ramp entrance from car park, subtitles on DVD) toilets for disabled shop ⊗ (ex assist dogs) ➡

NEWTONMORE CONTINUED

Highland Folk Museum `FREE`

Aultlarie Croft PH20 1AY

➲ *(on A86, follow signs off A9)*

☎ 01540 661307

e-mail: highland.folk@highland.gov.uk

web: www.highlandfolk.com

An early 18th-century farming township with turf houses has been reconstructed at this award-winning museum. A 1930s school houses old world maps, little wooden desks and a teacher rules! Other attractions include a working croft and tailor's workshop. Squirrels thrive in the pinewoods and there is an extensive play area at reception. A vintage bus runs throughout the site.

Times Open Apr-Aug, daily 10.30-5.30; Sep-Oct, daily 11-4.30. **Facilities** ♿ ⊡ ⊓ (outdoor) ♿ (vintage bus with full disabled access) toilets for disabled shop ⊗ (ex assist dogs) ⬛

POOLEWE　　　　　　　　**MAP 14 NG88**

Inverewe Garden

IV22 2LG

➲ *(6m NE of Gairloch, on A832 by Poolewe)*

☎ 0844 493 2225

e-mail: information@nts.org.uk

web: www.nts.org.uk

The influence of the North Atlantic Drift enables this remarkable garden to grow rare and sub-tropical plants. At its best in early June, but full of beauty from March to October, Inverewe has a backdrop of magnificent mountains and stands to the north of Loch Maree.

Times ✳ Open Garden: Jan-30 Mar daily 9.30-4. 31 Mar-Oct daily 9.30-9 or sunset if earlier. Visitor Centre & Shop: 31 Mar-Sep daily 9.30-5. Oct daily 9.30-4. **Facilities** ♿ ⊙⁴ ♿ (Partly accessible) (some paths difficult, Audio tour, mobiity scooter) toilets for disabled shop ⊗ (ex assist dogs) ⬤

ROSEMARKIE　　　　　　　**MAP 14 NH75**

Groam House Museum `FREE`

High St IV10 8UF

➲ *(off A9 at Tore onto A832)*

☎ 01381 620961　& 01463 811883

e-mail: curator@groamhouse.org.uk

web: www.groamhouse.org.uk

Opened in 1980, this community-based museum explores the history, culture and crafts of the mysterious Picts, who faded from history over a thousand years ago. Visitors can see the Rosemarkie symbol-bearing cross-slab and other Pictish sculptured stones; a replica Pictish harp, and a collection of photographs of Pictish stones all over the country. Thanks to a generous donation, the museum now holds the George Bain Collection of Celtic art for the Scottish Nation. Annual exhibitions take place, often with loans from other major museums. 2009 is the 20th anniversary of the museum.

Times Open Etr week, daily 2-4.30; closed Jan-Feb; May-Oct, Mon-Sat, 10-5, Sun 2-4.30; Apr, Sat-Sun 2-4.30. Nov-mid Dec, Sat-Sun 2-4 **Facilities** ♿ ♿ (wheelchair access to ground floor only) (Key held for disabled public toilets) shop ⊗ (ex assist dogs) ⬛

STRATHPEFFER　　　　　　**MAP 14 NH45**

Highland Museum of Childhood

The Old Station IV14 9DH

➲ *(5m W of Dingwall on A834)*

☎ 01997 421031

e-mail: info@highlandmuseumofchildhood.org.uk

web: www.highlandmuseumofchildhood.org.uk

Located in a renovated Victorian railway station of 1885, the museum tells the story of childhood in the Highlands amongst the crofters and townsfolk; a way of life recorded in oral testimony, displays and evocative photographs. An award-winning video, A Century of Highland Childhood is shown. There are also doll and toy collections.

Times Open Apr-Oct, daily 10-5, (Sun 2-5) also Jul & Aug evenings open to 7. Other times by arrangement. **Fee** £2.50 (ch £1.50, concessions £2). Family ticket (2ad+4ch) £6 **Facilities** ♿ ⊡ ⊓ (outdoor) ♿ (tape tour with induction loop, large print guide) shop ⊗ (ex assist dogs) ⬛

THURSO　　　　　　　　　**MAP 15 ND17**

Castle of Mey & Gardens of Mey `NEW`

KW14 8XH

➲ *(5m W of John O'Groats on A836)*

☎ 01847 851473

e-mail: castleofmey@totalise.co.uk

web: www.castleofmey.org.uk

Built in the 1560s, The Castle of Mey was bought by The Queen Mother in 1952. She restored the castle and created the beautiful gardens that can be seen today. For almost half a century The Queen Mother spent many happy summers at Mey. A tour of the castle and gardens affords visitors a rare opportunity to enjoy her summer home and gardens much as she left them after her last visit in October 2001.

Times Open May-Sep, 10.30-last entry 4. Closed 10 days late Jul-early Aug. **Fee** ✳ £7 (ch £3). Family ticket £20. Groups £7. **Facilities** ♿ ⊡ ♿ (1st floor possible, but not 2nd) toilets for disabled shop ⬛

TORRIDON　　　　　　　　**MAP 14 NG85**

Torridon Countryside Centre

The Mains IV22 2EZ

➲ *(N of A896, 9m SW of Kinlochewe).*

☎ 0844 493 2229

e-mail: information@nts.org.uk

web: www.nts.org.uk

Set amid some of Scotland's finest mountain scenery, the centre offers audio-visual presentations on the local wildlife. At the Mains nearby visitors may see deer.

Times ✳ Countryside Centre 31 Mar-Sep daily 10-5, Estate Deer Enclosure & Deer Museum (unstaffed) all year daily. **Facilities** ♿ ♿ (Partly accessible) (Ramp into centre, parking at centre) toilets for disabled ⬤

SCOTLAND

WICK

MAP 15 ND35

Castle of Old Wick

FREE

➲ *(1m S on Shore Rd)*

☎ 01667 460232

web: www.historic-scotland.gov.uk

The ruin of the best-preserved Norse castle in Scotland. Dating from the 12th-century this spectacular site is on a spine of rock projecting into the sea, between two deep, narrow gullies. Visitors must take great care and wear sensible shoes.

Times ✳ Open at all reasonable times. **Facilities** ⊗ ⋒

Wick Heritage Museum

18-27 Bank Row KW1 5EY

➲ *(close to the harbour)*

☎ 01955 605393

e-mail: museum@wickheritage.org

web: www.wickheritage.org

The heritage centre is near the harbour in a complex of eight houses, yards and outbuildings. The centre illustrates local history from Neolithic times to the herring fishing industry. In addition, there is a complete working 19th-century lighthouse, and the famous Johnston collection of photographs.

Times Open Apr-Oct, Mon-Sat 10-5, last admission 3.45. (Closed Sun). **Fee** £3 (ch 50p). **Facilities** ℗ ⋒ (outdoor) ♿ (Partly accessible) toilets for disabled

McLean Museum & Art Gallery

Times Open all year, Mon-Sat 10-5. Closed local & national PHs.
Facilities ℗ (200mtrs) ♿ (only ground floor accessible, ramped entrance with automatic doors) (induction loop) toilets for disabled shop ⊗ (ex assist dogs)

PORT GLASGOW

MAP 10 NS37

Newark Castle

PA14 5NH

➲ *(on A8)*

☎ 01475 741858

web: www.historic-scotland.gov.uk

The one-time house of the Maxwells, dating from the 15th and 17th centuries. The courtyard and hall are preserved. Fine turrets and the remains of painted ceilings can be seen, and the hall carries an inscription of 1597.

Times ✳ Open Apr-Sep, daily 9.30-6.30. **Facilities** ℗ shop ⋒

INVERCLYDE

GREENOCK

MAP 10 NS27

McLean Museum & Art Gallery

FREE

15 Kelly St PA16 8JX

➲ *(close to Greenock West Railway Station and Greenock Bus Station)*

☎ 01475 715624

e-mail: museum@inverclyde.gov.uk

web: www.inverclyde.gov.uk/

James Watt was born in Greenock, and various exhibits connected with him are shown. The museum also has an art collection, and displays on shipping, local and natural history, Egyptology and ethnography.

MIDLOTHIAN

CRICHTON

MAP 11 NT36

Crichton Castle

EH37 5QH

➲ *(2.5m SW of Pathhead, off A68)*

☎ 01875 320017

web: www.historic-scotland.gov.uk

The castle dates back to the 14th century, but most of what remains today was built over the following 300 years. A notable feature is the 16th-century wing built by the Earl of Bothwell in Italian style, with an arcade below.

Times ✳ Open Apr-Sep, daily 9.30-6.30. **Facilities** ℗ ⋒

SCOTLAND

SCOTLAND

Edinburgh Butterfly & Insect World
2 for 1

Dobbies Garden World, Lasswade EH18 1AZ

➲ *(0.5m S of Edinburgh city bypass at Gilmerton junct or Sherrifhall rdbt)*

☎ 0131 663 4932

e-mail: info@edinburgh-butterfly-world.co.uk
web: www.edinburgh-butterfly-world.co.uk

Rich coloured butterflies from all over the world can be seen flying among exotic rainforest plants, trees and flowers. The tropical pools are filled with giant waterlilies, colourful fish and are surrounded by lush vegetation. There are daily insect handling sessions and opportunities to see the leaf-cutting ants, scorpions, poison frogs, tarantulas and other remarkable creatures. There is also a unique honeybee hive that can be visited in season.

Times Open Summer daily 9.30-5.30; Winter daily 10-5. Closed 25-26 Dec & 1 Jan. **Fee** £5.95 (ch 3-15 £3.95, concessions £4.95). Family ticket from £18.50 (2ad+2ch). Party rates. **Facilities** ♿ ⬛ 🍴 ㅠ ♿ toilets for disabled shop garden centre ⊗ (ex assist dogs) ▬

Scottish Mining Museum
2 for 1

Lady Victoria Colliery EH22 4QN

➲ *(10m S of Edinburgh on A7, signed from bypass)*

☎ 0131 663 7519

e-mail: visitorservices@scottishminingmuseum.com
web: www.scottishminingmuseum.com

Scotland's National Mining Museum is based at one of Britain's finest Victorian colleries. Guided tours with miners, magic helmets, exhibitions, theatres, interactive displays and a visit to the coal face. Home to Scotland's largest steam engine.

Times Open all year, daily Mar-Oct, 10-5. Nov-Feb, daily, 10-4. **Fee** ✳ £5.95 (ch & concessions £3.95). Family ticket £17.95. Party 20+ (£4.95, ch £3.50) **Facilities** ♿ ⬛ 🍴 licensed ㅠ (outdoor) ♿ (tactile opportunities, audio tours, induction loop) toilets for disabled shop ⊗ (ex assist dogs) ▬

Edinburgh Crystal Visitor Centre
FREE

Eastfield EH26 8HB

➲ *(From Edinburgh City Bypass & A701/703 follow brown thistle signs)*

☎ 01968 675128

e-mail: visitorcentre@edinburgh-crystal.co.uk
web: www.edinburgh-crystal.com

Watch skilled craftsmen as they take molten crystal and turn it into intricately decorated glassware. Not only can you talk to the craftsmen themselves but there is also video footage, story boards, artefacts and audio listening posts to help you understand the 300-year-old history of glassmaking.

Times ✳ Open Mon-Sat 10-5, Sun 11-5. Closed 25-26 Dec & 1-2 Jan. **Facilities** ♿ ⬛ 🍴 ㅠ ♿ (ramp to first floor) toilets for disabled shop ⊗ (ex assist dogs) ▬

MORAY

The Glenlivet Distillery
FREE

Glenlivet AB37 9DB

➲ *(10m N of Tomintoul, off B9008)*

☎ 01340 821720

e-mail: betty.munro@chivas.com
web: www.theglenlivet.com

The visitor centre includes a guided tour of the whisky production facilities and a chance to see inside the vast bonded warehouses where the spirit matures. The multimedia exhibition and interactive presentations communicate the unique history, and traditions of Glenlivet Scotch Whisky. A complimentary dram is offered on return from the tour.

Times Open 6 Apr-30 Oct, Mon-Sat 9.30-4, Sun 12-4. **Facilities** ♿ ⬛ ♿ (access to visitor centre only, no disabled access on tour of distillery) (cafeteria, lift to exhibition) toilets for disabled shop ⊗ (ex assist dogs) ▬

Brodie Castle

IV36 2TE

➲ *(4.5m W of Forres, off A96 24m E of Inverness)*

☎ 0844 493 2156

e-mail: information@nts.org.uk
web: www.nts.org.uk

The Brodie family lived here for hundreds of years before passing the castle to the NTS in 1980. It contains many treasures, including furniture, porcelain and paintings. The extensive grounds include a woodland walk and an adventure playground. Wheelchairs for disabled visitors are available. Please telephone for details of recitals, concerts, open-air theatre etc.

Times ✳ Castle open 31 Mar-Apr daily 10.30-5. May-Jun Sun-Thu 10.30-5. Jul-Aug daily 10.30-5. Sep-Oct Sun-Thu 10.30-5. (Last tour starts at 4.30). Grounds open daily all year. **Facilities** ❷ 🖵 🗛 ⅙ (Partly accessible) (audio tape & information in Braille, wheelchair available) toilets for disabled shop ⊗ (ex assist dogs) ❦

CRAIGELLACHIE　　　　　MAP 15 NJ24

Speyside Cooperage Visitor Centre
Dufftown Rd AB38 9RS

➲ *(1m S of Craigellachie, on A941)*

☎ 01340 871108

e-mail: enquiries@speysidecooperage.co.uk

web: www.speysidecooperage.co.uk

A working cooperage with unique visitor centre, where skilled coopers and their apprentices practise this ancient craft. Each year they repair around 100,000 oak casks which will be used to mature many different whiskies. The 'Acorn to Cask' exhibition traces the history and development of the coopering industry.

Times Open all year, Mon-Fri 9.30-4. Closed Xmas & New Year. **Fee** ✳ £3.20 (ch £1.90 & concesssions £2.60). Family ticket £8.50. Party 15+. **Facilities** ❷ 🖵 🗛 (outdoor) ⅙ (picnic table, disabled viewing point) toilets for disabled shop ⊗ (ex assist dogs) ▭

DUFFTOWN　　　　　MAP 15 NJ34

Balvenie Castle
AB55 4DH

➲ *(on A941)*

☎ 01340 820121

web: www.historic-scotland.gov.uk

The ruined castle was the ancient stronghold of the Comyns, and became a stylish house in the 16th century.

Times ✳ Open Apr-Sep, daily 9.30-6.30. **Facilities** ❷ 🗛 🗮

Glenfiddich Distillery
AB55 4DH

➲ *(N of town, off A941)*

☎ 01340 820373

web: www.glenfiddich.com

Set close to Balvenie Castle, the distillery was founded in 1887 by William Grant and has stayed in the hands of the family ever since. Visitors can see the whisky-making process in its various stages, including bottling, and then sample the finished product.

Times ✳ Open all year Mon-Fri 9.30-4.30, also Etr-mid Oct, Sat 9.30-4.30, Sun 12-4.30. Closed Xmas & New Year **Facilities** ❷ 🖵 🗛 ⅙ (ramp access to production area & warehouse gallery) toilets for disabled shop ⊗ (ex assist dogs)

DUFFUS　　　　　MAP 15 NJ16

Duffus Castle ▐FREE▌
➲ *(5m NW of Elgin on B9012 to Burghead)*

☎ 01667 460232

web: www.historic-scotland.gov.uk

One of the finest examples of a motte and bailey castle in Scotland with a later, very fine, stone hall house and curtain wall. The original seat of the Moray family.

Times ✳ Open at all reasonable times. **Facilities** ❷ ⊗ 🗮

ELGIN　　　　　MAP 15 NJ26

Elgin Cathedral
North College St IV30 1EL

☎ 01343 547171

web: www.historic-scotland.gov.uk

Founded in 1224, the cathedral was known as the Lantern of the North and the Glory of the Kingdom because of its beauty. In 1390 it was burnt, along with most of the town. Although it was rebuilt, it fell into ruin after the Reformation. The ruins are quite substantial, however, and there is still a good deal to admire, including the fine west towers and the octagonal chapter house.

Times ✳ Open all year, Apr-Sep, daily 9.30-6.30; Oct-Mar, Mon-Wed & Sat-Sun 9.30-4.30. Closed 25-26 Dec & 1-2 Jan. **Facilities** Ⓟ shop 🗮

Elgin Museum
1 High St IV30 1EQ

➲ *(E end of High St, follow brown heritage signs)*

☎ 01343 543675

e-mail: curator@elginmuseum.org.uk

web: www.elginmuseum.org.uk

This award-winning museum is internationally famous for its fossil fish and fossil reptiles, and for its Pictish stones. The displays relate to the natural and human history of Moray.

Times Open Apr-Oct, Mon-Fri 10-5, Sat 11-4. **Fee** ✳ £3 (ch £1, concessions £1.50). Family £6. **Facilities** Ⓟ (50mtrs) (limited time) ⅙ (Partly accessible) (handrails, case displays at sitting level with large fonts) toilets for disabled shop ⊗ (ex assist dogs)

Pluscarden Abbey ▐FREE▌
IV30 8UA

➲ *(6m SW of Elgin on unclass road)*

☎ 01343 890257

web: www.pluscardenabbey.org

The original monastery was founded in 1230 by King Alexander II for monks of the Valliscaulian order from Burgundy, but it later became a Benedictine house. Monastic life was abandoned after the Reformation and the house passed through a succession of lay owners until it was bought by the third Marquess of Bute in 1898. His third son, Lord Colum Crichton Stuart gave the monastery to the Benedictines of Prinknash Abbey near Gloucester, and monastic life was recommenced in 1948. Today there are about two dozen monks who live here and

CONTINUED

SCOTLAND

ELGIN CONTINUED

lead a life of prayer, study and manual work. The services in the Abbey church are sung in Latin with Gregorian chant and are all open to the public.

Times Open all year, daily 4.45am-8.30pm **Facilities** ❷ ⛾ (induction loop, ramp, main entrance assistance required) toilets for disabled shop ❽ (ex assist dogs) ▬

FORRES
MAP 14 NJ05

Dallas Dhu Distillery
IV36 2RR

➲ *(1m S of Forres, off A940)*

☎ 01309 676548

web: www.historic-scotland.gov.uk

A perfectly preserved time capsule of the distiller's art. It was built in 1898 to supply malt whisky for Wright and Greig's 'Roderick Dhu' blend. Visitors are welcome to wander at will through this fine old Victorian distillery, or to take a guided tour, dram included.

Times ✳ Open all year, Apr-Sep, daily 9.30-6.30; Oct-Mar, Mon-Wed & Sat-Sun 9.30-4.30. Closed 25-26 Dec & 1-2 Jan. **Facilities** ❷ � shop ❽★

Falconer Museum
Tolbooth St IV36 1PH

➲ *(11m W of Elgin)*

☎ 01309 673701

e-mail: museums@moray.gov.uk

web: www.moray.gov.uk/museums

Founded by bequests made by two brothers, Alexander and Hugh Falconer. Hugh was a distinguished scientist, friend of Darwin, recipient of many honours and Vice-President of the Royal Society. On display are fossil mammals collected by him, and items relating to his involvement in the study of anthropology. Other displays are on local wildlife, geology, archaeology and history. Also you can see the Forres Quincentennial Time Capsule.

Times Open all year 24 Mar-Oct, Mon-Sat 10-5, (Jul-Aug Sun 1-4). Nov-Mar - please call to confirm times. Closed Xmas and New Year. **Fee** ✳ Donations welcome **Facilities** ❷ ⛾ (induction loop system) toilets for disabled shop ❽ (ex assist dogs)

Sueno's Stone
FREE

➲ *(E end of Forres, off A96)*

☎ 01667 460232

web: www.historic-scotland.gov.uk

The most remarkable sculptured monument in Britain, probably a cenotaph, standing over 20 feet high and dating back to the end of the first millennium AD. Covered by a protective glass enclosure.

Times ✳ Open at all reasonable times. **Facilities** ❷ ❽★

KEITH
MAP 15 NJ45

Strathisla Distillery
Seafield Av AB55 5BS

➲ *(A96 Aberdeen to Inverness road, attraction signed midway through town)*

☎ 01542 783044

e-mail: jeanett.grant@chivas.com

web: www.chivas.com

Tour the oldest distillery in the highlands, founded in 1786. A welcome dram of Chivas Regal 12-year-old is offered whilst guests view a DVD. A further dram of Chivas Regal 18-year-old or Strathisla 12-year-old single malt is offered on return from the distillery tour.

Times Open daily 6 Apr-30 Oct 9.30-4, Sun 12-4. **Fee** ✳ £5 per person (ch free, ch under 8 not admitted to production areas, but welcome in centre). Maybe subject to change. **Facilities** ❷ ⛾ (partial accessibility to Still House, Dram Room & gift shop) toilets for disabled shop ❽ (ex assist dogs) ▬

MARYPARK
MAP 15 NJ13

Glenfarclas Distillery
2 for 1
AB37 9BD

➲ *(4m S of Aberlour on A95 to Grantown-on-Spey)*

☎ 01807 500245 & 500257

e-mail: info@glenfarclas.co.uk

web: www.glenfarclas.co.uk

Established in 1836, Glenfarclas Distillery is proud of its independence. There is a guided tour illustrating their whisky's history and production, followed by a dram in the splendour of the Ships Room or a chance to browse in the gift shop.

Times Open Jan-Mar, Mon-Fri 10-4; Apr-Sep, Mon-Fri 10-5, Jul-Sep also open Sat 10-5; Oct-Dec, Mon-Fri 10-4. Closed Sun. (Last tour 1.5hr before closing) **Fee** ✳ £3.50. (Free admission to under 18's). **Facilities** ❷ ⛾ (only visitor centre is accessible) toilets for disabled shop ❽ (ex assist dogs in centre) ▬

ROTHES
MAP 15 NJ24

Glen Grant Distillery
AB38 7BS

➲ *(on A941 Elgin-Rothes road)*

☎ 01340 832118

e-mail: jennifer.robertson@glengrant.com

Founded in 1840 in a sheltered glen by the two Grant brothers. Discover the secrets of the distillery, including the delightful Victorian garden originally created by Major Grant, and now restored to its former glory, where you can enjoy a dram.

Times Open mid Jan-mid Dec, Mon-Sat 9.30-5, Sun 12-5. **Fee** ✳ £3.50 (under 18 free) **Facilities** ❷ ⛾⛃ (outdoor) ⛾ (access to ground floor only) (reception centre & still house, video) toilets for disabled shop ❽ (ex assist dogs) ▬

SPEY BAY   MAP 15 NJ36

The WDCS Wildlife Centre   FREE

IV32 7PJ

➲ *(off A96 onto B9014 at Fochabers, follow road approx 5m to village of Spey Bay. Turn left at Spey Bay Hotel and follow road for 500mtrs)*

☎ 01343 829109

e-mail: enquiries@mfwc.co.uk

web: www.mfwc.co.uk

The centre, owned and operated by the Whale and Dolphin Conservation Society, lies at the mouth of the River Spey and is housed in a former salmon fishing station, built in 1768. There is a free exhibition about the Moray Firth dolphins and the wildlife of Spey Bay. Visitors can browse through a well-stocked gift shop and enjoy refreshments in the cosy tea room.

Times ✱ Open Apr-Oct 10.30-5. Check for winter opening times **Facilities** ❷ ⬚ ⍤ (outdoor) shop ❽ (ex assist dogs) ▬

TOMINTOUL   MAP 15 NJ11

Tomintoul Museum

The Square AB37 9ET

➲ *(on A939, 13m E of Grantown)*

☎ 01309 673701

e-mail: museums@moray.gov.uk/museums

web: www.moray.gov.uk

Situated in one of the highest villages in Britain, the museum features a reconstructed crofter's kitchen and smiddy, with other displays on the local wildlife, the story of Tomintoul, and the local skiing industry.

Times Open 21 Mar-Oct, Mon-Sat, 9.30-5; Jul-Aug, Sun, 1-5. **Fee** Donations welcome. **Facilities** ❷ ⍤ (outdoor) ⚿ (induction loop, sound commentaries) shop ❽ (ex assist dogs)

NORTH AYRSHIRE

IRVINE   MAP 10 NS34

Scottish Maritime Museum   2 for 1

Harbourside KA12 8QE

➲ *(Follow AA signs from Irvine)*

☎ 01294 278283

e-mail: curator@scotmaritime.org.uk

web: www.scottishmaritimemuseum.org

The museum has displays that reflect all aspects of Scottish maritime history. Vessels can be seen afloat in the harbour and undercover. Experience life in a 1910 shipyard worker's tenement flat. Visit the Linthouse Engine Shop originally built in 1872, which is being developed and holds a substantial part of the museum's collection in open store.

Times Open Apr-Oct, 10-5 **Fee** £3.50 (ch & concessions £2.50). Family ticket £9.50. **Facilities** ❷ ⬚ ⚿ (audio tapes for blind) toilets for disabled shop ❽ (ex assist dogs)

LARGS   MAP 10 NS25

Kelburn Castle and Country Centre

Fairlie KA29 0BE

➲ *(2m S of Largs, on A78)*

☎ 01475 568685

e-mail: admin@kelburncountrycentre.com

web: www.kelburncountrycentre.com

Historic home of the Earls of Glasgow, Kelburn is famous for its romantic Glen, family gardens, unique trees and spectacular views over the Firth of Clyde. Glen walks, riding and trekking centre, adventure course, Kelburn Story Cartoon Exhibition and a family museum. The "Secret Forest" at the centre, Scotland's most unusual attraction, is a chance to explore the Giant's Castle, maze of the Green Man and secret grotto. Also included is a Falconry Centre, pottery craft studio and an indoor Sawmill Adventure Playground.

Times Open all year, Etr-end Oct, daily 10-6; Nov-Mar, 11-dusk. Grounds and Adventure Playbarn, wknds only **Fee** ✱ £7.50 (ch & concessions £5) Family ticket £25 **Facilities** ❷ ⬚ ⍢ ⍤ (outdoor) ⚿ (wheelchair access limited to main square area) (Ranger service to assist disabled) toilets for disabled shop ▬

Vikingar!

Greenock Rd KA30 8QL

➲ *(on A78, 0.5m into Largs, opposite RNLI lifeboat station)*

☎ 01475 689777

e-mail: cmcnaught@naleisure.co.uk

web: www.naleisure.co.uk

A multi-media experience that takes you from the first Viking raids in Scotland to their defeat at the Battle of Largs.

Times ✱ Open Apr-Sep, daily 10.30-5.30; Oct & Mar, daily 10.30-3.30; Nov & Feb, wknds only 10.30-3.30. Closed Dec & Jan. **Facilities** ❷ ⬚ ⚿ (Ramp to main door, Automatic doors) toilets for disabled shop ❽ (ex assist dogs) ▬

SALTCOATS   MAP 10 NS24

North Ayrshire Museum   FREE

Manse St, Kirkgate KA21 5AA

☎ 01294 464174

e-mail: namuseum@north-ayrshire.gov.uk

web: www.north-ayrshire.gov.uk/museums

This museum is housed in an 18th-century church, and features a rich variety of artefacts from the North Ayrshire area, including archaeological and social history material. There is a continuing programme of temporary exhibitions.

Times Open all year Tue-Sat, 10-1 & 2-5. **Facilities** Ⓟ (100mtrs) ⚿ toilets for disabled shop ❽ (ex assist dogs)

NORTH LANARKSHIRE

COATBRIDGE
MAP 11 NS76

Summerlee Heritage Park
FREE

Heritage Way, West Canal St ML5 1QD

➲ *(follow main routes towards town centre, adjacent to Coatbridge central station)*

☎ 01236 638460

e-mail: museums@northlan.gov.uk
web: www.nlcmuseums.bravehost.com

A 20-acre museum of social and industrial history centering on the remains of the Summerlee Ironworks which were put into blast in the 1830s. The exhibition hall features displays of social and industrial history including working machinery and recreated workshop interiors. Outside, Summerlee operates the only working tram in Scotland, a coal mine and reconstructed miners' rows with interiors dating from 1840.

Times Open summer 10-5, winter 10-4 **Facilities** ❷ 💵 🍴 (outdoor) ♿ (wheelchair available & staff assistance) toilets for disabled shop ⊗ (ex assist dogs)

MOTHERWELL
MAP 11 NS75

Motherwell Heritage Centre
FREE

High Rd ML1 3HU

➲ *(A723 for town centre. Left at top of hill, after pedestrian crossing and just before railway bridge)*

☎ 01698 251000

e-mail: museums@northlan.gov.uk
web: www.nlcmuseums.bravehost.com

The award-winning audio-visual experience, 'Technopolis', traces the history of the area from Roman times to the rise of 19th-century industry and the post-industrial era. There is also a fine viewing tower, an exhibition gallery and family history research facilities. A mixed programme of community events and touring exhibitions occur throughout the year.

Times Open all year Wed-Sat 10-5 (Thu 10-7), Sun 12-5. Also open BHs. Local studies library closed Sun **Facilities** ❷ ♿ (lifts, audio info & Braille buttons) toilets for disabled shop ⊗ (ex assist dogs)

PERTH & KINROSS

ABERFELDY
MAP 14 NN84

Dewar's World of Whisky
2 for 1

Aberfeldy Distillery PH15 2EB

➲ *(from A9 take A827 for Aberfeldy at Ballinluig)*

☎ 01887 822010

e-mail: worldofwhisky@dewars.com
web: www.dewarswow.com

This is an all-round whisky experience which challenges the skills and senses, and will educate you about the people and innovations of Dewar's. Try a dram of Aberfeldy single malt or Dewar's 12 before heading off for a guided tour of the working distillery.

Times Open Apr-Oct, Mon-Sat 10-6, Sun noon-4; Nov-Mar, Mon-Sat 10-4. Closed Xmas & New Year. **Fee** ✳ £6.50 (ch £4, concessions £4.50). **Facilities** ❷ 💵 🍴 (outdoor) ♿ (some parts of tour are inaccessible to wheelchair users) (lift) toilets for disabled shop ⊗ (ex assist dogs)

BLAIR ATHOLL
MAP 14 NN86

Blair Castle
2 for 1

PH18 5TL

➲ *(7m NW of Pitlochry, off A9 at Blair Atholl & follow signs to attraction)*

☎ 01796 481207

e-mail: office@blair-castle.co.uk
web: www.blair-castle.co.uk

Blair Castle is at the heart of the Atholl Estates set among glorious Highland scenery. The castle has been the ancient seat of the Dukes and Earls of Atholl for almost 740 years and is home to the Atholl Highlanders, Europe's only remaining private army. There are 30 rooms open to visitors, as well as historic gardens and grounds which include a deer park, pony trekking centre, farm tours and woodland. Highland Games in May, Horse Trials and Country Fair in August.

Times Open daily Etr-end Oct, 9.30-5.30 (last admission 4.30); Nov-Etr, Tue & Sat 9.30-2 (last admission 12.30). **Fee** ✳ £7.90 (ch £4.90, pen £6.90). Family ticket £20.50. Contact castle for 2009 prices. **Facilities** ❷ 💵 🍴 licensed 🍴 (outdoor) ♿ (access to ground floor only) (scooter, parking) shop ⊗ (ex assist dogs & on leads)

CRIEFF
MAP 11 NN82

Innerpeffray Library

PH7 3RF

➲ *(4.5m SE on B8062)*

☎ 01764 652819

e-mail: info@innerpeffraylibrary.co.uk
web: www.innerpeffraylibrary.co.uk

This is Scotland's oldest free lending library, founded in 1680. This Georgian Library (1762) with its associated school (1847), chapel (1508) and castle form an early complete group of educational and religious buildings. It houses the original 400 books in English, French, German, Latin and Italian presented by David Drummond, Lord Madertie, the Library's founder. It also has the books on law, history,

SCOTLAND

geography, maths and works by most of the Enlightenment authors. There are research facilities available and special events are planned.

Times Open Wed-Sat 10-12.45 & 2-4.45, Sun 2-4. (Closed Mon-Tue). Nov-Feb by arrangement. **Fee** ✶ £5 (ch with parents free) **Facilities** ℗ ⬚ 🛲 (outdoor) ♿ (Partly accessible) ⊗ (ex assist dogs)

The Famous Grouse Experience

The Hosh PH7 4HA

➲ (1.5m NW off A85)

☎ 01764 656565

e-mail: enquiries@thefamousgrouse.com

web: www.thefamousgrouse.com

A trip to Crieff is incomplete without a visit to The Famous Grouse Experience, set in Scotland's oldest, most visited and award-winning distillery. Opened in July 2002, this attraction is a fun and interesting day out which combines the traditional distillery visit with a unique exciting sensory experience. Spend a relaxing few hours absorbing the history of the brand. Test your senses and see if you have what it takes to become a 'Whisky Nose'. Have lunch, a snack or even a barbecue at the family restaurant. Visit the well-stocked shop or enjoy a peaceful woodland walk over The Brig O' Dram.

Times ✶ Open all year, daily 9-6 (last tour 4.30). Closed 25-26 Dec & 1 Jan **Facilities** ℗ ⬚ ⊙ 🛲 (outdoor) ♿ (lifts in all areas) toilets for disabled shop ⊗ (ex assist dogs) ⬛

DUNKELD   MAP 11 NO04

The Ell Shop & Little Houses   `FREE`

The Cross PH8 0AN

➲ (off A9, 15m N of Perth)

☎ 0844 4932192

e-mail: information@nts.org.uk

web: www.nts.org.uk

The National Trust owns two rows of 20 houses in Dunkeld, and has preserved their 17th/18th-century character. They are not open to the public, but there is a display and audio-visual show in the Information Centre.

Times ✶ Open Ell Shop mid 31 Mar-Sep, Mon-Sat, 10-5.30, Sun 12.30-5.30 (Sun during Jul-Aug 11-5.30). Nov-23 Dec, Mon-Sat 10-4.30, Sun 12.30-4.30. **Facilities** ℗ (300yds) shop ⊗ 🛇

KILLIECRANKIE   MAP 14 NN96

Killiecrankie Visitor Centre   `FREE`

NTS Visitor Centre PH16 5LG

➲ (3m N of Pitlochry on B8079)

☎ 0844 493 2194

e-mail: information@nts.org.uk

web: www.nts.org.uk

The visitor centre features an exhibition on the battle of 1689, when the Jacobite army routed the English, although the Jacobite leader, 'Bonnie Dundee', was mortally wounded in the attack. The wooded gorge is a notable beauty spot, admired by Queen Victoria, and there are some splendid walks.

Times ✶ Visitor Centre: Open 31 Mar-Oct, daily 10-5.30, Site: open all year daily. **Facilities** ℗ (charged) ⬚ 🛲 ♿ (Partly accessible) (visitor centre only, large print exhibition text.) toilets for disabled shop 🛇

KINROSS   MAP 11 NO10

Kinross House Gardens

KY13 8ET

➲ (M90 [Edinburgh to Perth] junct 6 to Kinross, signed in village)

☎ 01577 862900

e-mail: jm@kinrosshouse.com

web: www.kinrosshouse.com

Yew hedges, roses and herbaceous borders are the elegant attractions of these formal gardens. The 17th-century house was built by Sir William Bruce, but is not generally open to the public.

Times Gardens only open Apr-Sep, daily 10-7. **Fee** ✶ £3 (accompanied ch free, concessions £2.50). **Facilities** ℗ ♿ ⊗ (ex assist dogs)

Loch Leven Castle

Castle Island KY13 7AR

➲ (on an island in Loch Leven accessible by boat from Kinross)

☎ 01786 450000

web: www.historic-scotland.gov.uk

Mary, Queen of Scots was imprisoned here in this five-storey castle in 1567 - she escaped 11 months later and so gave the 14th-century castle its special place in history.

Times ✶ Open Apr-Sep, daily 9.30-6.30. **Facilities** ℗ 🛲 shop ⊗ 🎌

RSPB Nature Reserve Vane Farm

By Loch Leven KY13 9LX

➲ (2m E of M90 junct 5, on S shore of Loch Leven, entered off B9097 to Glenrothes)

☎ 01577 862355

e-mail: vane.farm@rspb.org.uk

web: www.rspb.org.uk

Well placed beside Loch Leven, with a nature trail and hides overlooking the Loch and a woodland trail with stunning panoramic views. Noted for its pink-footed geese. The area also attracts whooper swans, greylag geese and great spotted woodpeckers amongst others. Details of special events are available from the Visitors' Centre and the RSPB website.

Times Open all year daily, 10-5. Closed 25-26 Dec & 1-2 Jan. **Fee** £3 (ch 50p, concessions £2). Family £6. RSPB members free. **Facilities** ℗ ⬚ 🛲 (outdoor) ♿ (Visitor Centre accessible but not reserve without assistance) (wheelchair extensions, ramps, telescopes) toilets for disabled shop ⊗ (ex assist dogs) ⬛

SCOTLAND

SCOTLAND

MILNATHORT
MAP 11 NO10
Burleigh Castle
 FREE

KY13 7XZ

➲ *(0.5m E of Milnathort on A911)*

web: www.historic-scotland.gov.uk

The roofless but otherwise complete ruin of a tower house of about 1500, with a section of defensive barmkin wall and a remarkable corner tower with a square cap-house corbelled out. This castle was often visited by James IV.

Times ✳ Open summer only. Keys available locally, telephone 01786 45000. **Facilities** ⊗ ▮

MUTHILL
MAP 11 NN81
Drummond Gardens
PH7 4HZ

➲ *(2m S of Crieff on A822)*

☎ 01764 681433

e-mail: thegardens@drummondcastle.sol.co.uk

web: www.drummondcastlegardens.co.uk

The gardens of Drummond Castle were originally laid out in 1630 by John Drummond, 2nd Earl of Perth. In 1830, the parterre was changed to an Italian style. The multi-faceted sundial was designed by John Mylne, Master Mason to Charles I. These are Scotland's largest formal gardens and amongst the finest in Europe.

Times Open Gardens May-Oct, daily 1-6 (last admission 5). Also Etr for 4 days. **Fee** £4 (ch £1.50 & pen £3). **Facilities** ⊕ ⋈ (outdoor) �ਂ (viewing platform, wheelchair friendly route) toilets for disabled shop

PERTH
MAP 11 NO12
The Black Watch Regimental Museum
Balhousie Castle, Hay St PH1 5HR

➲ *(follow signs to Perth & attraction, approach via Dunkeld Rd)*

☎ 0131 310 8530

e-mail: rhq@theblackwatch.co.uk

web: www.theblackwatch.co.uk

The museum of Scotland's oldest highland regiment, which portrays the history of the Black Watch from 1725 to the present day. A memorial room remembers the soldiers of WWI with a lifelike figure in a trench, video footage and many artefacts from the period. Silver, uniforms, weapons and pictures are on display to give visitors an idea of what it was like to be in the regiment.

Times Open all year. May-Sep, Mon-Sat 10-4.30. Closed last Sat in Jun; Oct-Apr, Mon-Fri, 10-3.30. Closed 23 Dec-6 Jan. Other times & Parties 16+ by appointment. **Fee** Donations. **Facilities** ⊕ ⋈ (ground floor access only) (1 bay parking for disabled) toilets for disabled shop ⊗ (ex assist dogs) ▰

Branklyn Garden
116 Dundee Rd PH2 7BB

➲ *(on A85, Dundee Road, N of Perth)*

☎ 0844 493 2193

e-mail: information@nts.org.uk

web: www.nts.org.uk

The gardens cover two acres and are noted for their collections of rhododendrons, shrubs and alpines. Garden tours and botanical painting courses are held.

Times ✳ Open 31 Mar-Oct, daily 10-5. **Facilities** ⊕ (charged) ⋈ (Partly accessible) garden centre ⊗ (ex assist dogs) ☙

Caithness Glass Factory
& Visitor Centre
FREE

Inveralmond PH1 3TZ

➲ *(on Perth Western Bypass, A9, at Inveralmond Roundabout)*

☎ 01738 492320

e-mail: visitorcentre@caithnessglass.co.uk

web: www.caithnessglass.co.uk

All aspects of paperweight-making can be seen from the purpose-built viewing galleries. Visitors can now enter the glasshouse on a route which enables them to watch the glassmakers closely. There are talks in the glasshouse regularly throughout the day from Monday to Friday. There is also a factory shop, a best shop, children's play area and tourist information centre with internet access.

Times Open all year, Factory shop & restaurant Mon-Sat 9-5, Sun 10-5 (Jan-Feb 12-5). Glassmaking Mon-Sun 9-4.30. **Facilities** ⊕ ⊙ ⋈ (outdoor) ⋔ (wheelchair available) toilets for disabled shop ⊗ (ex assist dogs) ▰

Huntingtower Castle
PH1 3JL

➲ *(2m W)*

☎ 01738 627231

web: www.historic-scotland.gov.uk

Formerly known as Ruthven Castle and famous as the scene of the so-called 'Raid of Ruthven' in 1582, this structure was built in the 15th and 16th centuries and features a painted ceiling.

Times ✳ Open all year, Apr-Sep, daily 9.30-6.30; Oct-Mar, Mon-Wed & Sat-Sun 9.30-4.30. Closed 25-26 Dec & 1-2 Jan. **Facilities** ⊕ ⋈ shop ⊗ ▮

Perth Museum & Art Gallery
FREE

78 George St PH1 5LB

➲ *(in town centre, adjacent to Perth Concert Hall)*

☎ 01738 632488

e-mail: museum@pkc.gov.uk

web: www.pkc.gov.uk

Visit Perth Museum and Art Gallery for a fascinating look into Perthshire throughout the ages. Collections cover silver, glass, art, natural history, archaeology and human history.

Times Open all year, Mon-Sat 10-5, Sun 1-4.30, May-Sep. Closed Xmas-New Year. **Facilities** Ⓟ (800yds) (pay and display) ♿ (ramp, lifts, induction loops) toilets for disabled shop ⊗ (ex assist dogs)

PITLOCHRY MAP 14 NN95

Edradour Distillery

FREE

PH16 5JP

(2.5m E of Pitlochry on A924)

☎ 01796 472095

e-mail: info@signatoryvintage.com

web: www.edradour.co.uk

It was in 1825 that a group of local farmers founded Edradour, naming it after the bubbling burn that runs through it. It is Scotland's smallest distillery and is virtually unchanged since Victorian times. Have a dram of whisky while watching an audio-visual in the malt barn and then take a guided tour through the distillery itself.

Times Open Jan-Feb, Mon-Sat 10-4, Sun 12.4; Mar-Oct Mon-Sat 9.30-6, Sun 11.30-5; Nov-Dec, Mon-Sat 9.30-5, Sun 12-5. (Last tour 1hr before close, private tours arranged for a fee). **Facilities** Ⓟ ☕ ♿ (Partly accessible) toilets for disabled shop ⊗ (ex assist dogs)

Scottish Hydro Electric Visitor Centre, Dam & Fish Pass

FREE

PH16 5ND

(off A9, 24m N of Perth)

☎ 01796 473152

The visitor centre features an exhibition showing how electricity is brought from the power station to the customer, and there is access to the turbine viewing gallery. The salmon ladder viewing chamber allows you to see the fish as they travel upstream to their spawning ground.

Times Open Apr-Oct, Mon-Fri 10-5.30. Wknd opening Jul, Aug & BHs **Facilities** Ⓟ ♿ (access to shop only) (monitor viewing of salmon fish pass) toilets for disabled shop ⊗ (ex assist dogs)

QUEEN'S VIEW MAP 14 NN85

Queen's View Visitor Centre

FREE

PH16 5NR

(7m W of Pitlochry on B8019)

☎ 01350 727284

e-mail: peter.fullarton@forestry.gsi.gov.uk

web: www.forestry.gov.uk

Queen Victoria admired the view on a visit here in 1866; it is possibly one of the most famous views in Scotland. The area, in the heart of the Tay Forest Park, has a variety of woodlands that visitors can walk or cycle in.

Times ✳ Open Apr-Nov, daily 10-6. **Facilities** Ⓟ (charged) ☕ ⛩ (outdoor) shop 💳

SCONE MAP 11 NO12

Scone Palace

2 for 1

PH2 6BD

(2m NE of Perth on A93)

☎ 01738 552300

e-mail: visits@scone-palace.co.uk

web: www.scone-palace.co.uk

Visit Scone Palace, the crowning place of Scottish Kings and the home of the Earls of Mansfield. The Palace dates from 1803 but incorporates 16th century and earlier buildings, and is a unique treasury of furniture, fine art and other objets d'art. As well as beautiful gardens the grounds are home to the Murray Star Maze, the Pinetum, an adventure playground and livestock.

Times Open Apr-Oct, daily 9.30-5.30, Sat last admission 4. **Fee** ✳ Palace & Grounds £7.20 (ch £4.20, concessions £6.20). Family ticket £23. Grounds only £3.80 (ch £2.50, concessions £3.50). Group £6 (ch £4, concessions £5.30) **Facilities** Ⓟ ☕ 🍽 ⛩ (outdoor) ♿ (stairlift which gives access to all state rooms) toilets for disabled shop ⊗ (ex assist dogs & in grounds) 💳

WEEM MAP 14 NN84

Castle Menzies

PH15 2JD

(Follow signs from main roads)

☎ 01887 820982

e-mail: castlem@tiscali.co.uk

web: www.menzies.org

Restored seat of the Chiefs of Clan Menzies, and a fine example of a 16th-century Z-plan fortified tower house. Prince Charles Edward Stuart stayed here briefly on his way to Culloden in 1746. The whole of the 16th-century building can be explored, and there's a small clan museum.

Times Open Apr-mid Oct, Mon-Sat 10.30-5, Sun 2-5. **Facilities** Ⓟ ⛩ (outdoor) ♿ toilets for disabled shop ⊗ (ex assist dogs) 💳

RENFREWSHIRE

KILBARCHAN MAP 10 NS46

Weaver's Cottage

The Cross PA10 2JG

(off A737, 12m SW of Glasgow)

☎ 0844 493 2205

e-mail: information@nts.org.uk

web: www.nts.org.uk

The weaving craft is regularly demonstrated at this delightful 18th-century cottage museum, and there is a collection of weaving equipment and other domestic utensils.

Times ✳ Open 30 Mar-Sep Fri-Tues 1-5, Morning visits avail for pre-booked groups. **Facilities** Ⓟ (charged) ♿ (Partly accessible) (Scented plants, subtitled audio visual programme). ⊗ (ex assist dogs)

SCOTLAND

LANGBANK

MAP 10 NS37

Finlaystone Country Estate

2 for 1

PA14 6TJ

➲ *(off A8 W of Langbank, 10m W of Glasgow Airport, follow Thistle signs)*

☎ 01475 540505

e-mail: info@finlaystone.co.uk

web: www.finlaystone.co.uk

A beautiful country estate, historic formal gardens which are renowned for their natural beauty, with extensive woodland walks, picnic, BBQ and play areas. A tea room in the old walled garden, a gift shop and the 'Dolly Mixture', an international collection of dolls can be seen in The Visitor Centre.

Times Open all year. Woodland & Gardens daily, 10-5. **Fee** ✳ Garden & Woods £3.50 (ch & pen £2.50). 'The Dolly Mixture' Doll Museum free. **Facilities** ℗ ⬚ � (outdoor) ♿ (gardens and most walks accessible, lift to second floor and pathways for wheelchairs) toilets for disabled shop ▭

LOCHWINNOCH

MAP 10 NS35

RSPB Lochwinnoch Nature Reserve

2 for 1

Largs Rd PA12 4JF

➲ *(on A760, Largs road, opposite Lochwinnoch station, 16m SW of Glasgow)*

☎ 01505 842663

e-mail: lochwinnoch@rspb.org.uk

web: www.rspb.org.uk/reserves/lochwinnoch

The reserve, part of Clyde Muirshiel Regional Park and a Site of Special Scientific Interest, comprises two shallow lochs fringed by marsh which in turn is fringed by scrub and woodland. There are two trails with hides and a visitor centre with a viewing area. Please visit website for details of events running throughout the year.

Times Open all year, daily 10-5. Closed 1-2 Jan & 25-26 Dec. **Fee** Trails £2 (concessions £1, ch 50p). Family ticket £4. **Facilities** ℗ ㄷ (outdoor) ♿ (trails and hides all accessible, tower inaccessible) toilets for disabled shop ▭

PAISLEY

MAP 11 NS46

Coats Observatory

FREE

49 Oakshaw St West PA1 2DE

➲ *(M8 junct 27, follow signs to town centre until Gordon St (A761). Left onto Causeyside St, left onto Stone St then left onto High St)*

☎ 0141 889 2013

e-mail: ram.els@renfrewshire.gov.uk

web: www.renfrewshire.gov.uk

The Observatory, funded by Thomas Coats and designed by John Honeyman, was opened in 1883. It houses a 5 inch telescope under the dome at the top. Weather recording activities have been carried out here continuously since 1884. There is also earthquake-measuring equipment and the Renfrewshire Astronomical Society holds regular

meetings here. There are displays on the solar system, earthquakes and the telescope.

Times Open all year, Tue-Sat 10-5, Sun 2-5. Last entry 15 minutes before closing. **Facilities** ℗ (150yds) (meters/limited street parking) ❽ (ex assist dogs)

Paisley Museum

FREE

High St PA1 2BA

➲ *(M8 junct 27 (A741), rdbt 2nd exit (A761-town centre). At traffic lights take left lane towards Kilbride. Onto Gordon St, right onto Causeyside St, left onto Storie St, left onto High St)*

☎ 0141 889 3151

e-mail: ram.els@renfrewshire.gov.uk

web: www.renfrewshire.gov.uk

Pride of place here is given to a world-famous collection of Paisley shawls. Other collections illustrate local industrial and natural history, while the emphasis of the art gallery is on 19th-century Scottish artists and an important studio ceramics collection.

Times Open all year, Tue-Sat 10-5, Sun 2-5. BH 10-5. **Facilities** ℗ (330yds) ♿ (level access available through side entrance, lift gives access to main gallery, Shawl gallery is only available via rear entrance) toilets for disabled shop ❽ (ex assist dogs)

SCOTTISH BORDERS

COLDSTREAM

MAP 12 NT84

The Hirsel

Douglas & Angus Estates, Estate Office, The Hirsel TD12 4LP

➲ *(0.5m W on A697, on N outskirts of Coldstream)*

☎ 01573 224144

e-mail: rogerdodd@btconnect.com

web: www.hirselcountrypark.co.uk

The seat of the Home family, the grounds of which are open all year. The focal point is the Homestead Museum, craft centre and workshops. From there, nature trails lead around the lake, along the Leet Valley and into woodland noted for its rhododendrons and azaleas.

Times Garden & Grounds open all year, daylight hours. Museum 10-5. Craft Centre Mon-Fri, 10-5, wknds noon-5. **Fee** £2.50 per car **Facilities** ℗ (charged) ⬚ ⑪ ㄷ (outdoor) ♿ toilets for disabled shop ❽ (ex on lead)

DRYBURGH

MAP 12 NT53

Dryburgh Abbey

TD6 0RQ

➲ *(5m SE of Melrose on B6404)*

☎ 01835 822381

web: www.historic-scotland.gov.uk

The abbey was one of the Border monasteries founded by David I, and stands in a lovely setting on the River Tweed. The ruins are equally beautiful, and the church has the graves of Sir Walter Scott and Earl Haig.

Times ✳ Open all year, Apr-Sep daily 9.30-6.30; Oct-Mar daily 9.30-4.30. Closed 25-26 Dec & 1-2 Jan. **Facilities** ℗ 🚻 shop ⊗ ₪

DUNS
MAP 12 NT75

Manderston
TD11 3PP

➲ *(2m E of Duns on A6105)*

☎ 01361 883450 & 882636

e-mail: palmer@manderston.co.uk

web: www.manderston.co.uk

This grandest of grand houses gives a fascinating picture of Edwardian life above and below stairs. Completely remodelled for the millionaire racehorse owner Sir James Miller, the architect was told to spare no expense, and so the house boasts the world's only silver staircase. The staterooms are magnificent, and there are fine formal gardens, with a woodland garden and lakeside walks. Manderston has been the setting for a number of films.

Times Open 8 May-28 Sep, Thu & Sun (also late May & Aug English BH Mons). Gardens open, 11.30-dusk. House open, 1.30-4.15 **Fee** ✳ House & Gardens £8 (ch £4.50); Gardens only £4.50. **Facilities** ℗ 🚽 ♿ (Partly accessible) shop ⊗ (ex assist dogs on leads)

EYEMOUTH
MAP 12 NT96

Eyemouth Museum
Auld Kirk, Manse Rd TD14 5JE

➲ *(off A1 onto A1107, follow signs to town centre)*

☎ 018907 50678

The museum was opened in 1981 as a memorial to the 129 local fishermen lost in the Great Fishing Disaster of 1881. Its main feature is the 15ft Eyemouth tapestry, which was made for the centenary. There are also displays on local history.

Times ✳ Open Apr-Jun & Sep, Mon-Sat 10-5, Sun 10-1; Jul-Aug, Mon-Sat 10-5; Sun 10-2; Oct, Mon-Sat 10-4 (closed Sun) **Facilities** ℗ (250yds) (45min on street outside) shop ➿

GORDON
MAP 12 NT64

Mellerstain House
TD3 6LG

➲ *(signed on A6089 [Kelso-Gordon road], 1m W)*

☎ 01573 410225

e-mail: enquiries@mellerstain.com

web: www.mellerstain.com

One of Scotland's finest Georgian houses, begun by William Adam and completed by his son Robert in the 1770s. It has beautiful plasterwork, period furniture and pictures, terraced gardens and a lake. 2009 is Year of the Homecoming.

Times Open Etr, May-Jun & Sep, Sun, Wed, & BH; Jul & Aug Sun-Mon & Wed-Thu; Oct, Sun 12.30-5 (last admission 4.15) **Fee** House & Gardens £7.50. Gardens only £3.50 (ch free) **Facilities** ℗ 🚽 ♿ (main floor only accessible) toilets for disabled shop ⊗ (ex assist dogs) ➿

HERMITAGE
MAP 12 NY59

Hermitage Castle
TD9 0LU

➲ *(5.5m NE of Newcastleton, on B6399)*

☎ 01387 376222

web: www.historic-scotland.gov.uk

A vast, eerie ruin of the 14th and 15th centuries, associated with the de Soulis, the Douglases and Mary, Queen of Scots. Much restored in the 19th century.

Times ✳ Open Apr-Sep, daily 9.30-6.30. **Facilities** ℗ 🚻 ₪

SCOTLAND

INNERLEITHEN
MAP 11 NT33

Robert Smail's Printing Works

7/9 High St EH44 6HA.

➲ *(30m S of Edinburgh, A272, 6m from Peebles. Innerleithen Road)*

☎ 0844 493 2259

e-mail: information@nts.org.uk
web: www.nts.org.uk

These buildings contain a Victorian office, a paper store with reconstructed waterwheel, a composing room and a press room. The machinery is in full working order and visitors may view the printer at work and experience typesetting in the composing room.

Times ✳ Open 31 Mar-Oct , Thurs-Mon 12-5, Sun 1-5. **Facilities** ℗ (300yds) ♿ (Partly accessible) (Guidebook) shop ⊗ (ex assist dogs) ☒

JEDBURGH
MAP 12 NT62

Jedburgh Abbey

☎ 01835 863925
web: www.historic-scotland.gov.uk

Standing as the most complete of the Border monasteries (although it has been sacked and rebuilt many times) Jedburgh Abbey has been described as 'the most perfect and beautiful example of the Saxon and early Gothic in Scotland'. David I founded it as a priory in the 12th century and remains of some of the domestic buildings have been uncovered during excavations.

Times ✳ Open all year, Apr-Sep daily 9.30-6.30; Oct-Mar daily 9.30-4.30. Closed 25-26 Dec & 1-2 Jan. **Facilities** ❷ ♿ (limited access) toilets for disabled shop ⊗ ◪

Jedburgh Castle Jail & Museum `FREE`

Castlegate TD8 6QD

➲ *(off A68 towards town centre, follow signs to top of Castlegate)*

☎ 01835 864750
web: www.scotborders.gov.uk/museums

Relive the harsh realities of prison life in the 19th century with a visit to Jedburgh Castle Jail, built in the 1820s on the site of the Royal Burgh's medieval castle. Displays in the cell blocks recreate the lives of prisoners and staff, while the Jailer's House explores the history of the town. A children's activity guide is available, and there are plenty of hands-on activities for all the family.

Times Open late Mar-end Oct, Mon-Sat, 10-4.30, Sun 1-4 **Facilities** ❷ ⌂ (outdoor) ♿ (Partly accessible) (audio guide, touch screen, hearing loop, new guide book) toilets for disabled shop ⊗ (ex assist dogs)

KELSO
MAP 12 NT73

Floors Castle

Roxburghe Estates Office TD5 7SF

➲ *(from town centre follow Roxburghe St to main gates)*

☎ 01573 223333

e-mail: marketing@floorscastle.com
web: www.floorscastle.com

The home of the 10th Duke of Roxburghe, the Castle's lived-in atmosphere enhances the superb collection of French furniture, tapestries and paintings. The house was designed by William Adam in 1721 and enjoys a magnificent setting overlooking the River Tweed and the Cheviot Hills beyond. Regular events include massed pipe bands, open-air theatre, and garden festivals.

Times Open Etr, May-Oct daily 11-5 (last admission 4.30) **Fee** £7.50 (ch £3.50, concessions £6.50). Family ticket £19 **Facilities** ❷ ⌂ ◉ ⌂ (outdoor) ♿ (lift) toilets for disabled shop garden centre ⊗ (ex on leads & assist dogs)

Kelso Abbey `FREE`

☎ 0131 668 8800
web: www.historic-scotland.gov.uk

Founded by David I in 1128 and probably the greatest of the four famous Border abbeys, Kelso became extremely wealthy and acquired extensive lands. In 1545 it served as a fortress when the town was attacked by the Earl of Hertford, but now only fragments of the once-imposing abbey church give any clue to its long history.

Times ✳ Open at any reasonable time. **Facilities** ◪

LAUDER
MAP 12 NT54

Thirlestane Castle

TD2 6RU

➲ *(off A68, S of Lauder)*

☎ 01578 722430

e-mail: admin@thirlestanecastle.co.uk
web: www.thirlestanecastle.co.uk

This fairy-tale castle has been the home of the Maitland family, the Earls of Lauderdale, since the 12th century. Some of the most splendid plasterwork ceilings in Britain may be seen in the 17th-century state rooms. The family nurseries house a sizeable collection of antique toys and dolls. The informal riverside grounds, with their views of the grouse moors, include a woodland walk, picnic tables and adventure playground. Please visit website for details of events running throughout the year.

Times Open Jul-Aug Sun-Thu; 1-25 Sep Sun, Wed-Thu **Fee** ✳ £7.50 (ch £5.50, concessions £6.50) Family ticket (2ad+3ch) £20. Grounds only £3 (ch £1.50. Group rate £6.50 (ch £3.50) **Facilities** ❷ ⌂ ⌂ (outdoor) ♿ toilets for disabled ⊗ (ex assist dogs)

MELROSE   MAP 12 NT53

Abbotsford

TD6 9BQ

⮎ *(2m W off A6091, on B6360)*

☎ 01896 752043

e-mail: enquiries@scottsabbotsford.co.uk

web: www.scottsabbotsford.co.uk

Set on the River Tweed, Sir Walter Scott's romantic mansion remains much the same as it was in his day. Inside there are many mementoes and relics of his remarkable life and also his historical collections, armouries and library, with some 9,000 volumes. Scott built the mansion between 1811 and 1822, and lived here until his death ten years after its completion.

Times Open daily from 3rd Mon in Mar-Oct, Mon-Sat 9.30-5. Mar-May & Oct, Sun 2-5. Jun-Sep, Sun 9.30-5. **Fee** ✷ £6.20 (ch £3.10). Party £4.80 (ch £2.80) **Facilities ❷** 🍴 ⵗ (outdoor) ᕫ (ramps at entrance, show rooms, gift shop and tea rooms accessible) toilets for disabled shop ✪ (ex assist dogs) ◼

Harmony Garden

St Mary's Rd TD6 9LJ

⮎ *(opposite Melrose Abbey, off A6091 in Melrose)*

☎ 0844 493 2251

e-mail: information@nts.org.uk

web: www.nts.org.uk

Set around the early 19th-century Harmony Hall (not open to visitors), this attractive walled garden has magnificent views of Melrose Abbey and the Eildon Hills. The garden comprises lawns, herbaceous and mixed borders, vegetable and fruit areas, and a rich display of spring bulbs.

Times ✷ Open 31 Mar-Oct, Mon-Sat 10-5, Sun 1-5. **Facilities ❷** (charged) ᕫ ✪ ⵗ

Melrose Abbey & Abbey Museum

TD6 9LG

☎ 01896 822562

web: www.historic-scotland.gov.uk

The ruin of this Cistercian abbey is probably one of Scotland's finest, and has been given added glamour by its connection with Sir Walter Scott. The abbey was repeatedly wrecked during the Scottish wars of independence, but parts survive from the 14th century. The heart of Robert the Bruce is buried somewhere within the church.

Times ✷ Open all year, Apr-Sep daily 9.30-6.30; Oct-Mar daily 9.30-4.30. Closed 25-26 Dec & 1-2 Jan. **Facilities ❷** 🍴 shop ✪ ◼

Priorwood Garden & Dried Flower Shop

TD6 9PX

⮎ *(off A6091, in Melrose, adjacent to Abbey. On National Cycle Route 1)*

☎ 0844 493 2257

e-mail: information@nts.org.uk

web: www.nts.org.uk

This small garden specialises in flowers suitable for drying. It is formally designed with herbaceous and everlasting annual borders, and the attractive orchard has a display of 'apples through the ages'.

Times ✷ Garden 31 Mar-24 Dec (same opening times as shop).Shop open 5 Jan-Mar, Mon-Sat 12-4, Apr-24 Dec Mon-Sat 10-5, Sun 1-5. **Facilities ❷** 🍴 ᕫ (Partly accessible) (ramps, paths) shop ⵗ

PEEBLES   MAP 11 NT24

Kailzie Gardens   2 for 1

EH45 9HT

⮎ *(2.5m SE on B7062)*

☎ 01721 720007

e-mail: info@kailziegardens.com

web: www.kailziegardens.com

These extensive grounds, with their fine old trees, provide a burnside walk flanked by bulbs, rhododendrons and azaleas. A walled garden contains herbaceous, shrub rose borders, greenhouses and a formal rose garden. A garden for all seasons - don't miss the snowdrops. There is also a large stocked trout pond (rod hire available), and an 18-hole putting green, plus an open bait pond, ornamental duck pond and osprey viewing centre.

Times Open 25 Mar-Oct, daily 11-5.30. Grounds close 5.30. Garden open all year. **Fee** ✷ mid Mar-Jun £3.50, Jun-Oct £4.50, end Oct-mid Mar £2 honesty box (ch 5-12 80p) **Facilities ❷** ⵗ 🍴 (outdoor) ᕫ (Partly accessible) (ramps in garden) toilets for disabled shop

Neidpath Castle

EH45 8NW

⮎ *(0.5m W of Peebles on A72)*

☎ 01721 720333

e-mail: estateoffice@wemyssandmarch.co.uk

web: www.neidpathcastle.co.uk

Occupying a spectacular position on the Tweed, this 14th-century stronghold was adapted to 17th-century living; it contains a rock-hewn well, a pit prison and a small museum. There are fine walks and a picnic area.

Times ✷ Open Etr wknd, May-Sep Wed-Sat 10.30-5 Sun 12.30-5 (closed Mon & Tue except BHs) **Facilities ❷** 🍴 shop

SELKIRK   MAP 12 NT42

Bowhill House and Country Estate   2 for 1

TD7 5ET

➲ *(3m W of Selkirk off A708)*

☎ 01750 22204

e-mail: bht@buccleuch.com

web: www.bowhill.org

An outstanding collection of pictures, including works by Van Dyck, Canaletto, Reynolds, Gainsborough and Claude Lorraine are displayed here. Memorabilia and relics of people such as Queen Victoria and Sir Walter Scott, and a restored Victorian kitchen add further interest inside the house. Outside, the wooded grounds are perfect for walking. A small theatre provides a full programme of music and drama.

Times Park open May-Jun 10-5 wknd and BHs only. Jul gardens daily 10-5, house daily 1-4.30, house 28 Jun-Jul, 11-5. Aug park daily 10-5. **Fee** ✳ House & grounds £7 (ch under 3 & wheelchair users free, pen & groups £5). Grounds only £3. **Facilities** ❷ ⬚ ☜❶ licensed ☷ (outdoor) ♿ (guided tours for the blind by appointment) toilets for disabled shop ⊗ (ex assist & in park on leads) ➤

Halliwells House Museum   FREE

Halliwells Close, Market Place TD7 4BC

➲ *(off A7 in town centre)*

☎ 01750 20096

e-mail: museums@scotborders.gov.uk

A row of late 18th-century town cottages converted into a museum. Displays recreate the building's former use as an ironmonger's shop and home, and tell the story of the Royal Burgh of Selkirk. The Robson Gallery hosts a programme of contemporary art and craft exhibitions.

Times ✳ Open Apr-Sep, Mon-Sat 10-5, Sun 10-12; Jul-Aug, Mon-Sat 10-5.30, Sun 10-12; Oct, Mon-Sat 10-4. **Facilities** ❷ (charged) ♿ (lift to first floor, large print, interpretation) toilets for disabled shop ⊗ (ex assist dogs) ➤

Lochcarron of Scotland Visitor Centre

Waverley Mill, Rodgers Rd TD7 5DX

➲ *(On A7, follow signs to mill)*

☎ 01750 726000

e-mail: quality@lochcarron.com

web: www.quality@lochcarron.com

The museum brings the town's past to life and the focal point is a display on the woollen industry. Guided tours of the mill take about 40 minutes. (Please note that disabled toilets are built for members of staff who are disabled but are not in wheelchairs.)

Times ✳ Open all year, Mon-Sat 9-5, Sun (Jun-Sep) 12-5. Mill tours Mon-Thu at 10.30, 11.30, 1.30 & 2.30, Fri am only. **Facilities** ❷ ♿ toilets for disabled shop ➤

Sir Walter Scott's Courtroom   FREE

Market Place TD7 4BT

➲ *(on A7 in town centre)*

☎ 01750 20096

e-mail: museums@scotborders.gov.uk

Built in 1803-4 as a sheriff court and town hall this is where the famous novelist, Sir Walter Scott dispensed justice when he was Sheriff of Selkirkshire from 1804-1832. Displays tell of Scott's time as Sheriff, and of his place as a novelist as well as those of his contemporaries, writer, James Hogg and the explorer, Mungo Park.

Times ✳ Open Apr-Sep, Mon-Fri 10-4, Sat 10-2; May-Aug also Sun 10-2; Oct, Mon-Sat 1-4. **Facilities** ℗ (100mtrs) (30min on street, car park 50p for 2hrs) shop ⊗ (ex assist dogs) ➤

SMAILHOLM   MAP 12 NT63

Smailholm Tower

TD5 7RT

➲ *(6m W of Kelso on B6937)*

☎ 01573 460365

web: www.historic-scotland.gov.uk

An outstanding example of a classic Border tower-house, probably erected in the 15th century. It is 57 feet high and well preserved. The tower houses an exhibition of dolls and a display based on Sir Walter Scott's book *Minstrels of the Border*.

Times ✳ Open Apr-Sep, daily 9.30-6.30; Oct, Mon-Wed & Sat-Sun 9.30-4.30. Nov-Mar, wknds only. Closed 25-26 Dec & 1-2 Jan. **Facilities** ❷ shop ⊗ ◪

STOBO   MAP 11 NT13

Dawyck Botanic Garden

EH45 9JU

➲ *(8m SW of Peebles on B712)*

☎ 01721 760254

e-mail: dawyck@rbge.org.uk

web: www.rbge.org.uk

From the landscaped walks of this historic arboretum an impressive collection of mature specimen trees can be seen - some over 40 metres tall and including the unique Dawyck beech-stand. Notable features include the Swiss Bridge, a fine estate chapel and stonework/terracing produced by Italian craftsmen in the 1820s.

Times ✳ Open daily Feb-Nov. Feb & Nov 10-4. Mar-Oct 10-5. Apr-Sep 10-6 **Facilities** ❷ ⬚ ☷ (outdoor) shop garden centre ⊗ (ex assist dogs) ➤

TRAQUAIR

MAP 11 NT33

Traquair House

EH44 6PW

⮑ *(at Innerleithen take B709, house in 1m)*

☎ 01896 830323

e-mail: enquiries@traquair.co.uk

web: www.traquair.co.uk

Said to be Scotland's oldest inhabited house, dating back to the 12th century, 27 Scottish monarchs have stayed at Traquair House. William the Lion Heart held court here, and the house has associations with Mary, Queen of Scots and the Jacobite risings. The Bear Gates were closed in 1745, not to be reopened until the Stuarts should once again ascend the throne. There is a maze and woodland walks by the River Tweed, craft workshops and a children's adventure playground. Also an 18th-century working brewery with museum shop and tastings. Award-winning 1745 Cottage Restaurant open for lunches and teas.

Times Open Etr-Oct **Fee** ✳ Please telephone or visit website **Facilities** ❷ ⬚ ⦾| licensed ⌁ (outdoor) ⌂ (ground floor of house only accessible) toilets for disabled shop ▰

SOUTH AYRSHIRE

ALLOWAY

MAP 10 NS31

Burns National Heritage Park   `2 for 1`

Murdoch's Lone KA7 4PQ

⮑ *(2m S of Ayr)*

☎ 01292 443700

e-mail: info@burnsheritagepark.com

web: www.burnsheritagepark.com

The birthplace of Robert Burns, Scotland's National Poet, set in the gardens and countryside of Alloway. An introduction to the life of Robert Burns, with an audio-visual presentation - a multi-screen 3D experience describing the *Tale of Tam O'Shanter*. This attraction consists of the museum, Burn's Cottage, visitor centre, tranquil landscaped gardens and historical monuments. Please telephone for further details.

Times Open all year, Apr-Sep 10-5.30, Oct-Mar 10-5. Closed 25-26 Dec & 1-2 Jan **Fee** ✳ £5 (concessions £3) **Facilities** ❷ ⬚ ⦾| licensed ⌂ (access limited in some parts of property) (wheelchair available) toilets for disabled shop ⦻ (ex assist dogs) ▰

CULZEAN CASTLE

MAP 10 NS21

Culzean Castle & Country Park

KA19 8LE

⮑ *(4m W of Maybole, off A77, 12m S of Ayr)*

☎ 0844 493 2149

e-mail: information@nts.org.uk

web: www.nts.org.uk

This 18th-century castle stands on a cliff in spacious grounds and was designed by Robert Adam for the Earl of Cassillis. It is noted for its oval staircase, circular drawing room and plasterwork. The Eisenhower Room explores the American General's links with Culzean. The 563-acre country park has a wide range of attractions - shoreline, woodland walks, parkland, an adventure playground and gardens.

Times ✳ Castle & walled garden: 30 Mar-Oct daily 10.30-5 (last entry 4). Visitor centre: 30 Mar-Oct daily 9.30-5.30, Nov-29 Mar Thu-Sun 11-4. Other facilities 30 Mar-Oct daily 10.30-5.30. Country Park: open all year 9.30-sunset. **Facilities** ❷ ⬚ ⦾| ⌁ (outdoor) ⌂ (Partly accessible) (wheelchairs, lift in castle, Braille guides, Induct loop) toilets for disabled shop garden centre ⦻ (ex castle & assist dogs) ▰

KIRKOSWALD

MAP 10 NS20

Souter Johnnie's Cottage

Main Rd KA19 8HY

⮑ *(on A77, 4m SW of Maybole)*

☎ 0844 493 2147

e-mail: information@nts.org.uk

web: www.nts.org uk

'Souter' means cobbler and the village cobbler who lived in this 18th-century cottage was the inspiration for Burns' character Souter Johnnie, in his ballad *Tam O'Shanter*. The cottage is now a Burns museum and life-size stone figures of the poet's characters can be seen in the restored ale-house in the cottage garden.

Times ✳ Open 30 Mar-Sept, Fri-Tues 11.30-5. **Facilities** ℗ (75yds) ⌂ (Partly accessible) (only one small step into cottage) ⦻ (ex assist dogs) ▰

MAYBOLE

MAP 10 NS20

Crossraguel Abbey

KA19 5HQ

⮑ *(2m S)*

☎ 01655 883113

web: www.historic-scotland.gov.uk

The extensive remains of this 13th-century Cluniac monastery are impressive and architecturally important. The monastery was founded by Duncan, Earl of Carrick and the church, claustral buildings, abbot's house and an imposing castellated gatehouse can be seen.

Times ✳ Open Apr-Sep, daily 9.30-6.30. **Facilities** ❷ ⌁ ⦻ ▮

OLD DAILLY MAP 10 NX29
Bargany Gardens
KA26 9PH

➜ (4m NE on B734 from Girvan)

☎ 01465 871249

e-mail: bargany@btinternet.com

Woodland walks with a fine show of azaleas and rhododendrons. Plants on sale from the gardens.

Times Open Gardens, May 10-5. **Facilities** 🅿 ⌁ (outdoor) ♿ (Partly accessible) (rock garden not accessible)

TARBOLTON MAP 10 NS42
Bachelors' Club
Sandgate St KA5 5RB

➜ (In Tarbolton, off A77 S of Kilmarnock & off A76 at Mauchline. 7.5m NE of Ayr.)

☎ 0844 493 2146

e-mail: information@nts.org.uk

web: www.nts.org.uk

In this 17th-century thatched house, Robert Burns and his friends formed a debating club in 1780. Burns attended dancing lessons and was initiated into freemasonry here in 1781. The house is furnished in the style of the period.

Times ✳ Open 30 Mar-Sep, Fri-Tue 1-5. Morning visits available for pre-booked groups. **Facilities** Ⓟ (in village) ♿ (Partly accessible) ⊗ (ex assist dogs) ⛄

SOUTH LANARKSHIRE

BIGGAR MAP 11 NT03
Gladstone Court Museum
ML12 6DT

➜ (On A702 entrance by 113 High St)

☎ 01899 221050

e-mail: suzanne.bmt@googlemail.com

web: www.biggarmuseumtrust.co.uk

An old-fashioned village street is portrayed in this museum, which is set out in a century-old coach-house. On display are reconstructed shops, complete with old signs and advertisements - a bank, telephone exchange, photographer's booth and other interesting glimpses into the recent past.

Times Open May-Sep, Mon-Sat 11-4.30, Sun 2-4.30. **Fee** £2 (ch £1, pen £1.50). Family ticket £4. Party £1.25 each. **Facilities** 🅿 shop ⊗ (ex assist dogs)

Greenhill Covenanters House
Burn Braes ML12 6DT

➜ (On A702, 30m from Edinburgh, 40m from Glasgow)

☎ 01899 221050

e-mail: suzanne.bmt@googlemail.com

web: www.biggarmuseum.co.uk

This 17th-century farmhouse was brought, stone by stone, ten miles from Wiston and reconstructed at Biggar. It has relics of the turbulent 'Covenanting' period, when men and women defended the right to worship in Presbyterian style. Audio presentations.

Times Open mid May-Sep, wknds only 2-4.30. **Fee** ✳ £1 (ch 50p, pen 70p). Party 70p each. **Facilities** 🅿 ⌁ (outdoor) ⊗ (ex assist dogs)

Moat Park Heritage Centre
Kirkstyle ML12 6DT

➜ (On A702)

☎ 01899 221050

e-mail: suzanne.bmt@googlemail.com

web: www.biggarmuseumtrust.co.uk

The centre illustrates the history, archaeology and geology of the Upper Clyde and Tweed valleys with interesting displays.

Times Open May-Sep, Mon-Sat 11.30-4.30, Sun 2-4.30; Oct-Apr, open by appointment only. **Fee** £2 (ch £1, pen £1.50). Family ticket £4. Party £1.25 each. **Facilities** 🅿 ⌁ (outdoor) ♿ (upper floor with assistance on request) toilets for disabled shop ⊗ (ex assist dogs)

BLANTYRE MAP 11 NS65
David Livingstone Centre
165 Station Rd G72 9BT

➜ (M74 junct 5 onto A725, then A724, follow signs for Blantyre, right at lights. Centre is at foot of hill)

☎ 0844 493 2207

e-mail: information@nts.org.uk

web: www.nts.org.uk

Share the adventurous life of Scotland's greatest explorer, from his childhood in the Blantyre Mills to his explorations in the heart of Africa, dramatically illustrated in the historic tenement where he was born. Various events are planned throughout the season.

Times ✳ Open 30 Mar-24 Dec, Mon-Sat 10-5, Sun 12.30-5. **Facilities** 🅿 (charged) ⊡ ⌁ ♿ (Audio) toilets for disabled shop ⊗ (ex assist dogs) ⛄ ⊟

BOTHWELL MAP 11 NS75

Bothwell Castle

G71 8BL

(approach from Uddingston off B7071)

☎ 01698 816894

web: www.historic-scotland.gov.uk

Besieged, captured and 'knocked about' several times in the Scottish-English wars, the castle is a splendid ruin. Archibald the Grim built the curtain wall; later, in 1786, the Duke of Buccleuch carved graffiti - a coronet and initials - beside a basement well.

Times ✳ Open all year, Apr-Sep, daily 9.30-6.30; Oct-Mar, daily 9.30-4.30. Closed Thu & Fri in winter, 25-26 Dec & 1-2 Jan. **Facilities** Ⓟ ⛩ shop

EAST KILBRIDE MAP 11 NS65

National Museum of Rural Life Scotland

2 for 1

Wester Kittochside, Philipshill Rd, (off Stewartfield Way) G76 9HR

(From Glasgow take A749 to East Kilbride. From Edinburgh follow M8 to Glasgow, turn off junct 6 onto A725 to East Kilbride. Kittochside is signed before East Kilbride)

☎ 0131 225 7534

e-mail: info@nms.ac.uk

web: www.nms.ac.uk

Get a healthy dose of fresh air. Take in the sights, sounds and smells as you explore this 170-acre farm. Discover what life was like for country people in the past and how this has shaped Scotland's countryside today. Would you cope with life on a 1950s farm? Try milking 'Clover' by hand, hitch a ride on the farm explorer, meet Mairi the horse and the sheep, cows and hens. See the website for details of a wide range of special events and exhibitions. 2-for-1 Voucher not valid for special events.

Times Open daily 10-5. (Closed 25-26 Dec & 1Jan) **Fee** ✳ £5 (ch under 12 free, concessions £4) NMS and NTS members free. Charge for some events. **Facilities** Ⓟ ☕ ⛩ (outdoor) ♿ (wheelchair users have access to ground floor of farmhouse only, some steep paths) (disabled parking, induction loop, site transport, ramps) toilets for disabled shop ⊗ (ex assist dogs)

HAMILTON MAP 11 NS75

Chatelherault Country Park

FREE

Ferniegair ML3 7UE

(2.5km SE of Hamilton on A72 Hamilton-Larkhall/ Lanark Clyde Valley tourist route)

☎ 01698 426213

e-mail: phyllis.crosbie@southlanarkshire.gov.uk

web: www.southlanarkshire.gov.uk

Designed as a hunting lodge by William Adam in 1732, Chatelherault, built of unusual pink sandstone, has been described as a gem of Scottish architecture. Situated close to the motorway, there is a visitor's centre, shop and adventure playground. Also a herd of white Cadzow cattle.

Times ✳ Visitor Centre, open all year, Mon-Sat 10-5, Sun 12-5. House closed all day Fri & Sat. **Facilities** Ⓟ ☕ ⛩ (outdoor) ♿ (ramps, parking, large print guide) toilets for disabled shop garden centre ⊗ (ex in grounds & assist dogs)

Low Parks Museum

FREE

129 Muir St ML3 6BJ

(off M74 junct 6, by Asda Superstore)

☎ 01698 328232

e-mail: lowparksmuseum@southlanarkshire.gov.uk

web: www.southlanarkshire.gov.uk

The museum tells the story of both South Lanarkshire and The Cameronians (Scottish Rifles). The Cameronians were unique as they were the only Scottish rifle regiment, and the museum details their fascinating history from 1689 to 1968. Housed in the town's oldest building, dating from 1696, the museum also features a restored 18th-century assembly room and exhibitions on Hamilton Palace and The Covenanters.

Times Open all year, daily, Mon-Sat 10-5, Sun 12-5 **Facilities** Ⓟ ☕ shop ⊗ (ex assist dogs)

NEW LANARK MAP 11 NS84

New Lanark Visitor Centre

2 for 1

Mill 3, New Lanark Mills ML11 9DB

(1m S of Lanark. Signed from all major routes. Less than 1hr from Glasgow (M74/A72) and Edinburgh (A70).

☎ 01555 661345

e-mail: trust@newlanark.org

web: www.newlanark.org

Founded in 1785, New Lanark became well known in the early 19th century as a model community managed by enlightened industrialist and educational reformer Robert Owen. Surrounded by woodland and situated close to the Falls of Clyde, this unique world heritage site explores the philosophies of Robert Owen, using theatre, interactive displays, and the 'Millennium Experience', a magical ride through history. (Accommodation is available at the New Lanark Mill Hotel, and there's also a Youth Hostel.) Delicious meals and home-baking are available at the Mill Pantry, and the village is also home to the Scottish

CONTINUED

NEW LANARK CONTINUED

Wildlife Trust's Falls of Clyde Reserve. A wide variety of exciting, fun and educational events take place every year. There is a new roof garden and viewing platform which provides a birds eye view of this historic village and surrounding woodland.

Times Open all year daily. Jun-Aug 10.30-5; Sep-May 11-5. Closed 25 Dec & 1 Jan. **Fee** ✳ £6.95 (ch, concessions £5.95). Family ticket (2ad+2ch) £21.95. Family ticket (2ad+4ch) £27.95 **Facilities** ❷ ⬚ 🍽 licensed ⨅ (outdoor) ♿ (ramps, disabled parking, wheelchairs) toilets for disabled shop ⊗ (ex assist dogs) ⊟

STIRLING

BANNOCKBURN   MAP 11 NS89

Bannockburn Heritage Centre
Glasgow Rd FK7 0LJ

➲ (2m S of Stirling off M80/M9 junct 9, on A872)

☎ 0844 493 2139

e-mail: information@nts.org.uk
web: www.nts.org.uk

The Heritage Centre stands close to what is traditionally believed to have been Robert the Bruce's command post before the 1314 Battle of Bannockburn, a famous victory for the Scots and a turning point in Scottish history.

Times ✳ Heritage Centre, Shop & Cafe: Mar-Oct daily, 10-5.30. Site: All year daily. **Facilities** ❷ ⬚ ♿ (Partly accessible) (Induction loop, Visual info) toilets for disabled shop ⊗ ♨

BLAIR DRUMMOND   MAP 11 NS79

Blair Drummond Safari & Leisure Park
FK9 4UR

➲ (M9 junct 10, 4m on A84 towards Callander)

☎ 01786 841456 & 841396

e-mail: enquiries@blairdrummond.com
web: www.blairdrummond.com

Drive through the wild animal reserves where zebras, North American bison, antelope, lions, tigers, white rhino and camels can be seen at close range. Other attractions include the sea lion show, a ride on the boat safari through the waterfowl sanctuary and around Chimpanzee Island, an adventure playground, giant astraglide, and pedal boats. There are also African elephants, giraffes and ostriches.

Times ✳ Open 19 Mar-3 Oct, daily 10-5.30. (Last admission 4.30) **Facilities** ❷ ⬚ 🍽 ⨅ (outdoor) shop ⊗ (ex assist dogs) ⊟

DOUNE   MAP 11 NN70

Doune Castle
FK16 6EA

➲ (8m S of Callander on A84)

☎ 01786 841742

web: www.historic-scotland.gov.uk

The 14th-century stronghold with its two fine towers has been restored. It stands on the banks of the River Teith, and is associated with 'Bonnie' Prince Charlie and Sir Walter Scott.

Times ✳ Open all year, Apr-Sep, daily 9.30-6.30; Oct-Mar, Mon-Wed & Sat-Sun 9.30-4.30. Closed 25-26 Dec & 1-2 Jan. **Facilities** ❷ ⨅ shop ▯

KILLIN   MAP 11 NN53

Breadalbane Folklore Centre
Falls of Dochart FK21 8XE

➲ (A827 from Aberfeldy & Kenmore or A85 from Cairnlarich)

☎ 01567 820254

e-mail: info@breadalbanefolklorecentre.com
web: www.breadalbanefolklorecentre.com

Overlooking the beautiful Falls of Dochart, the centre gives a fascinating insight into the legends of Breadalbane - Scotland's 'high country'. Learn of the magical deeds of St Fillan and hear tales of mystical giants, ancient prophesies, traditional folklore and clan history. Housed in historic St Fillans Mill which features a restored waterwheel. Tourist Information and gift shop.

Times Open Apr-Jun, 10-5, daily. Jul-Aug, 10-5.30, daily. Sep-Oct, 10-5, daily. **Fee** ✳ £2.95 (ch £1.95 concessions £2.50). Family ticket £7.85. **Facilities** ℗ (30mtrs) ♿ shop ⊗ ⊟

PORT OF MENTEITH   MAP 11 NN50

Inchmahome Priory

FK8 3RA

➲ *(4m E of Aberfoyle, off A81)*

☎ 01877 385294

web: www.historic-scotland.gov.uk

Walter Comyn founded this Augustinian house in 1238, and it became famous as the retreat of the infant Mary, Queen of Scots in 1547. The ruins of the church and cloisters are situated on an island in the Lake of Monteith.

Times ✶ Open Apr-Sep, daily 9.30-6.30. **Facilities** ❷ ⊓ shop ▮

STIRLING   MAP 11 NS79

Mar's Wark   `FREE`

Broad St FK8 1EE

web: www.historic-scotland.gov.uk

A remarkable Renaissance mansion built by the Earl of Mar, Regent for James VI in 1570 and later used as the town workhouse. It was never completed and now the façade can be seen.

Times ✶ Open all reasonable times. **Facilities** ⊗ ▮

Museum of Argyll & Sutherland Highlanders

The Castle FK8 3PA

➲ *(museum in Stirling Castle)*

☎ 01786 475165

e-mail: museum@argylls.co.uk

web: www.argylls.co.uk

Situated in the King's Old Building in Stirling Castle, the museum tells the history of the Regiment from 1794 to the present day. Displays include uniforms, medals, silver, paintings, colours, pipe banners, and commentaries.

Times ✶ Open Etr-Sep, daily 9.30-5; Sep-Etr, daily 10-4.15. **Facilities** ℗ (Castle Esplanade) fee for parking on Esplanade ♿ (Partly accessible) shop ⊗

The National Wallace Monument

Hillfoots Rd, Causewayhead FK9 5LF

➲ *(Monument is signed from city centre & A91)*

☎ 01786 472140

e-mail: info@nationalwallacemonument.com

web: www.nationalwallacemonument.com

Meet Scotland's national hero, Sir William Wallace, and join his epic struggle for a free Scotland. Step into Westminster Hall and witness his trial. Climb the 220 foot tower and experience one of the finest views in Scotland. Each August there is an 'Encounter with Wallace', a programme of dramatic performances including traditional Scottish music. 2009 is the 140th anniversary of the opening of the monument.

Times Open all year Jan-Feb & Nov-Dec, daily 10.30-4; Mar-May & Oct, daily 10-5; Jun, daily 10-6; Jul-Aug, daily 9-6; Sep, daily 9.30-5.30. **Fee** ✶ £6.50 (ch £4, concessions £4.90). Family ticket £17. **Facilities** ❷ ⊒ ⊓ (outdoor) ♿ (limited access) shop ⊟

Stirling Castle

Upper Castle Hill FK8 1EJ

☎ 01786 450000

web: www.historic-scotland.gov.uk

Sitting on top of a 250ft rock, Stirling Castle has a strategic position on the Firth of Forth. As a result it has been the scene of many events in Scotland's history. James II was born at the castle in 1430. Mary, Queen of Scots spent some years there, and it was James IV's childhood home. Among its finest features are the splendid Renaissance palace built by James V, and the Chapel Royal, rebuilt by James VI.

Times ✶ Open all year, Apr-Sep, daily 9.30-6; Oct-Mar, daily 9.30-5. Closed 25-26. **Facilities** ❷ (charged) ⦿⌁ ⊓ shop ⊗ ▮

STIRLING CONTINUED

Stirling Old Town Jail

Saint John St FK8 1EA

➲ *(Located on St John's St main route to Stirling Castle)*

☎ 01786 450050

e-mail: info@oldtownjail.com

web: www.oldtownjail.com

Step inside an authentic Victorian jail at the heart of historic Stirling for a fascinating live prison tour. You'll meet the warden, the convict desperate to escape, and even the hangman. Look out from the rooftop viewpoint for a wonderful view, visit the exhibition area, and just for children, join the Beastie Hunt.

Times Open Apr-May 9.30-5.30; Jun-Sep 9-6; Oct 9.30-5; Nov-Mar 10-4 (last entry 1hr before closing) **Fee** ✳ £5-£5.95 (ch £3.20-£3.80, concessions £3.80-£4.50). Family ticket £13.25-£15.70. **Facilities** ❷ ♿ & toilets for disabled shop ⊗ ➡

Stirling Smith Art Gallery & Museum

Dumbarton Rd FK8 2RQ

➲ *(M9 junct 10, follow Stirling Castle signs)*

☎ 01786 471917

e-mail: museum@smithartgallery.demon.co.uk

web: www.smithartgallery.demon.co.uk

This award-winning museum and gallery presents a variety of exhibitions drawing on its own rich collections and works from elsewhere. Please telephone for details of events running throughout the year.

Times Open all year, Tue-Sat 10.30-5, Sun 2-5. Closed Mon, 25-26 Dec & 1-2 Jan. **Facilities** ❷ ♿ ⌐ (indoor & outdoor) & (wheelchair ramp available) (wheelchair lift, induction loop in theatre) toilets for disabled shop garden centre ➡

WEST DUNBARTONSHIRE

DUMBARTON — MAP 10 NS37

Dumbarton Castle

G82 1JJ

➲ *(the capital of the Celtic kingdom of Strathclyde)*

☎ 01389 732167

web: www.historic-scotland.gov.uk

The castle, set on the 240ft Dumbarton Rock above the River Clyde, dominates the town (the capital of the Celtic Kingdom of Strathclyde) and commands spectacular views. Most of what can be seen today dates from the 18th and 19th centuries, but there are a few earlier remains.

Times ✳ Open all year, Apr-Sep, daily 9.30-6.30. Oct-Mar, Mon-Wed & Sat-Sun 9.30-4.30. Closed 25-26 Dec & 1-2 Jan. **Facilities** ❷ ⌐ shop ⊗ ♬

WEST LOTHIAN

LINLITHGOW — MAP 11 NS97

Blackness Castle

EH49 7AL

➲ *(4m NE)*

☎ 01506 834807

web: www.historic-scotland.gov.uk

This was once one of the most important fortresses in Scotland. Used as a state prison during covenanting time and in the late 19th-century as a powder magazine, it was one of four castles left fortified by the Articles of Union. Most impressive are the massive 17th-century artillery emplacements.

Times ✳ Open all year, Apr-Sep, daily 9.30-6.30; Oct-Mar, daily 9.30-4.30. Closed Thu & Fri in winter, 25-26 Dec & 1-2 Jan. **Facilities** ❷ ⌐ shop ♬

House of The Binns

EH49 7NA

➲ *(4m E of Linlithgow, off A904)*

☎ 0844 493 2127

e-mail: information@nts.org.uk

web: www.nts.org.uk

An example of changing architectural tastes from 1612 onwards, this house reflects the transition from fortified stronghold to spacious mansion. The original three-storey building, with small windows and twin turrets, evolved into a fine crenellated house with beautiful moulded plaster ceilings - the ancestral home of the Dalyell family. There is a magnificent display of snowdrops and daffodils in spring.

Times ✳ Open House: Jun-Sep, Sat-Wed 2-5. Estate all year daily. **Facilities** ❷ (charged) ⌐ & (Partly accessible) (Braille sheets, Photo Album, Audio info) ⊗ (ex assist dogs) ♨

Linlithgow Palace

EH49 7AL

➲ (off M9)

☎ 01506 842896

web: www.historic-scotland.gov.uk

The magnificent ruin of a great Royal Palace, set in its own park or 'peel'. All the Stuart kings lived here, and work commissioned by James I, III, IV, and VI can be seen. The great hall and the chapel are particularly fine. James V was born here in 1512 and Mary, Queen of Scots in 1542.

Times ✳ Open all year, Apr-Sep, daily 9.30-6.30; Oct-Mar, daily 9.30-4.30. Closed 25-26 Dec & 1-2 Jan. **Facilities** ℗ ⊞ shop ⊗ ▮

LIVINGSTON   MAP 11 NT06

Almond Valley Heritage Trust

Millfield EH54 7AR

➲ (2m from M8 junct 3)

☎ 01506 414957

e-mail: info@almondvalley.co.uk

web: www.almondvalley.co.uk

A combination of fun and educational potential ideal for children, Almond Valley has a petting zoo of farm animals, an interactive museum on the shale oil industry, a narrow gauge railway, and tractor rides. Please telephone for details of events running throughout the year.

Times Open all year, daily 10-5. Closed Dec 25-26, Jan 1-2. **Fee** ✳ £5 (ch £3.50). Family (2ad+4ch) £17. **Facilities** ℗ ⊒ ⊞ (indoor & outdoor) ⅋ toilets for disabled shop ▭

SCOTTISH ISLANDS

ARRAN, ISLE OF

BRODICK   MAP 10 NS03

Brodick Castle, Garden & Country Park

KA27 8HY

➲ (Ferry from Ardrossan-Brodick or Lochranza-Kintyre - frequent in summer, limited in winter)

☎ 0844 493 2152

e-mail: information@nts.org.uk

web: www.nts.org.uk

The site has been fortified since Viking times, but the present castle dating from the 13th century was a stronghold of the Dukes of Hamilton. Splendid silver, fine porcelain and paintings acquired by generations of owners can be seen, including many sporting pictures and trophies. There is a magnificent woodland garden, started by the Duchess of Montrose in 1923, world famous for its rhododendrons and azaleas.

Times ✳ Castle 31 Mar-Apr daily 10.30-5, May-Jun Sun-Thu 10.30-5, Jul-Aug daily 10.30-5 Sep-Oct Sun-Thu 10.30-5 (last tour starts at 4.30). Grounds all year daily. **Facilities** ℗ ⏚ ⊞ ⅋ (Partly accessible) (Braille, wheelchairs, motorised buggy & stairlift) toilets for disabled shop ⊗ (ex assist dogs) ⅋

Isle of Arran Heritage Museum

Rosaburn KA27 8DP

➲ (right at Brodick Pier, approx 1m)

☎ 01770 302636

e-mail: tom.macleod@arranmuseum.co.uk

web: www.arranmuseum.co.uk

The setting is an 18th-century croft farm, including a cottage restored to its pre-1920 state and a 'smiddy' where a blacksmith worked until the late 1960s. There are also several demonstrations of horse-shoeing, sheep-shearing and weaving and spinning throughout the season - please ring for details. There is a large archaeology and geology section with archive, where help with research is available.

Times ✳ Open Apr-Oct, daily 10.30-4.30. **Facilities** ℗ ⊒ ⊞ (outdoor) shop ⊗ (ex assist dogs & in garden)

LOCHRANZA   MAP 10 NR95

Isle of Arran Distillery Visitor Centre   [2 for 1]

KA27 8HJ

➲ (from Brodick Ferry Terminal take coast road N for 14m. Distillery on left upon entering village)

☎ 01770 830264

e-mail: visitorcentre@arranwhisky.com

web: www.arranwhisky.com

Located amidst beautiful surroundings, the distillery was built to revive the dormant traditions of Arran single malt whisky production. After a guided tour of the distillery, visitors can now taste the highly-acclaimed 10 year old single malt and cask-matured whisky. From October 2008, 12 year old whisky will be available.

Times Open Jan-Feb, Mon, Wed, Fri-Sat 10-4; Mar-Oct, Mon-Sat 10-6, Sun 11-6; Nov-Dec Mon, Wed, Fri-Sat 10-4. **Fee** £4.50 (ch under 12 free, concessions £3.50). Party 15+ £3 **Facilities** ℗ ⑩ licensed ⊞ (outdoor) ⅋ (ground floor, shop, eating area, display area and toilets are accessible) (chair lift in visitor centre) toilets for disabled shop ⊗ (ex assist dogs) ▭

BUTE, ISLE OF

ROTHESAY   MAP 10 NS06

Bute Museum

7 Stuart St PA20 0EP

➲ (on road behind castle)

☎ 01700 505067

e-mail: Ivor@butemuseum.fsnet.co.uk

Local and natural history displays, including birds, mammals and seashore items; varied collections of recent bygones, information on WWII (especially midget submarines), a collection of early Christian crosses, and flints and pots from various Mesolithic and Neolithic burial cairns.

Times Open all year, Apr-Sep, Mon-Sat 10.30-4.30, Sun 2.30-4.30; Oct-Mar, Tue-Sat 2.30-4.30. Closed Sun & Mon. **Facilities** ℗ (3 mins walk) (50p per hour, free on street parking) ⅋ (touch table for blind, ramps) shop

SCOTLAND

433

ROTHESAY CONTINUED

Rothesay Castle

PA20 0DA

☎ 01700 502691

web: www.historic-scotland.gov.uk

The focal point of Rothesay is this 13th-century castle. It has lofty curtain walls defended by drum towers that enclose a circular courtyard.

Times ✳ Open all year, Apr-Sep, daily 9.30-6.30; Oct-Mar, Mon-Wed & Sat-Sun 9.30-4.30. Closed 25-26 Dec & 1-2 Jan. **Facilities** ℗ shop █

GREAT CUMBRAE ISLAND

MILLPORT   MAP 10 NS15

Museum of the Cumbraes   FREE

Garrison Grounds KA28 0DG

⟳ *(Ferry to Millport, from Largs Cal-Mac Terminal. Bus meets each ferry)*

☎ 01475 531191

e-mail: namuseum@north-ayrshire.gov.uk

web: www.north-ayrshire.gov.uk/museums

A small museum which displays the history and life of the Cumbraes. There is also a fine collection of local photographs.

Times Open Etr-Sep daily from 9 (Sat & Sun from 12). **Facilities** ❷ ⌷ Ꮭ shop ⊗ (ex assist dogs)

LEWIS, ISLE OF

ARNOL   MAP 13 NB34

Black House Museum

PA86 9DB

⟳ *(11m NW of Stornoway on A858)*

☎ 01851 710395

web: www.historic-scotland.gov.uk

A traditional Hebridean dwelling, built without mortar and roofed with thatch on a timber framework. It has a central peat fire in the kitchen, no chimney and a byre under the same roof.

Times ✳ Open all year, Apr-Sep, Mon-Sat 9.30-6.30; Oct-Mar, Mon-Sat 9.30-4.30. Closed 25-26 Dec & 1-2 Jan. **Facilities** ❷ shop ⊗ █

CALLANISH   MAP 13 NB23

Callanish Standing Stones

PA86 9DY

⟳ *(12m W of Stornoway off A859)*

☎ 01851 621422

web: www.historic-scotland.gov.uk

An avenue of 19 monoliths leads north from a circle of 13 stones with rows of more stones fanning out to south, east and west. Probably constructed between 3000 and 1500BC, this is a unique cruciform of megaliths.

Times ✳ Site accessible at all times. Visitor Centre open Apr-Sep, Mon-Sat 10-7; Oct-Mar, Mon-Sat 10-4. **Facilities** ❷ †◎⊣ shop █

CARLOWAY   MAP 13 NB24

Dun Carloway Broch   FREE

⟳ *(1.5m S of Carloway on A858)*

web: www.historic-scotland.gov.uk

Brochs are late-prehistoric circular stone towers, and their origins are mysterious. One of the best examples can be seen at Dun Carloway, where the tower still stands about 30ft high.

Times ✳ Open at all reasonable times. **Facilities** ❷ █

MULL, ISLE OF

CRAIGNURE   MAP 10 NM73

Mull & West Highland Narrow Gauge Railway

Craignure (old pier) Station PA65 6AY

⟳ *(0.25m from Craignure Ferry Terminal, just off road to Iona, by Police station)*

☎ 01680 812494 (in season) or 01680 812567

e-mail: mullrail@dee-emm.co.uk

web: www.mullrail.co.uk

The first passenger railway on a Scottish island, opened in 1983. Both steam and diesel trains operate on the ten-and-a-quarter inch gauge line, which runs from Craignure to Torosay Castle. The 1.25 mile line offers dramatic woodland and mountain views taking in Ben Nevis, Glencoe and the Isle of Lismore.

Times ✳ Open Etr-end Oct, 11-5 **Facilities** ❷ ⍨ (outdoor) ᏝᏝ (provision to carry person seated in wheelchair on trains) shop ▬

Torosay Castle & Gardens

PA65 6AY

⟳ *(1.5m S of Ferry Terminal at Craignure)*

☎ 01680 812421

e-mail: info@torosay.com

web: www.holidaymull.org/members/torosay

The Scottish baronial architecture of this Victorian castle is complemented by the magnificent setting, and inside the house there are displays of portraits and wildlife pictures, family scrapbooks and a study of the Antarctic. The gardens include a statue walk and water garden, an avenue of Australian gum trees, and an Oriental garden. Within the grounds there is a narrow gauge steam and diesel railway.

Times ✳ Open end Apr-Oct, daily 10.30-5. Gardens all year. **Facilities** ❷ ⌷⍨ (outdoor) shop ⊗ (ex assist dogs) ▬

SCOTLAND

ORKNEY

BIRSAY   MAP 16 HY22

Earl's Palace   FREE
KW15 1PD

➲ *(on A966)*

☎ 01856 721205 & 841815

web: www.historic-scotland.gov.uk

The gaunt remains of the residence of the 16th-century Earl of Orkney, constructed round a courtyard.

Times ✳ Open at all reasonable times. **Facilities** ⊗ 🖪

DOUNBY   MAP 16 HY22

The Brough of Birsay
➲ *(off A966)*

☎ 01856 841815

web: www.historic-scotland.gov.uk

This ruined Romanesque church stands next to the remains of a Norse village. The nave, chancel and semicircular apse can be seen, along with claustral buildings. Crossings must be made on foot at low-water - there is no boat.

Times ✳ Open mid Jun-Sep (tides permitting), daily 9.30-6.30. **Facilities** 🖪

Click Mill   FREE
➲ *(2.5m from Dounby on B905)*

☎ 01856 841815

web: www.historic-scotland.gov.uk

The last surviving horizontal water mill in Orkney, of a type well represented in Shetland and Lewis. The mill is in working condition and visitors should wear sensible footwear.

Times ✳ Open at all reasonable times. 🖪

Skara Brae
KW16 3LR

➲ *(19m W of Kirkwall on B9056)*

☎ 01856 841815

web: www.historic-scotland.gov.uk

Engulfed in drift sand, this remarkable group of well-preserved Stone Age dwellings is the most outstanding survivor of its kind in Britain. Stone furniture and a fireplace can be seen.

Times ✳ Open all year, Apr-Sep, daily 9.30-6.30; Oct-Mar, daily 9.30-4.30. Closed 25-26 Dec & 1-2 Jan. **Facilities** ❂ 🍽 🎋 shop ⊗ 🖪

FINSTOWN   MAP 16 HY31

Maes Howe Chambered Cairn
➲ *(9m W of Kirkwall, on A965)*

☎ 01856 761606

web: www.historic-scotland.gov.uk

The masonry of Britain's finest megalithic tomb is in a remarkably good state of preservation. Dating from neolithic times, it contains Viking carvings and runes.

Times ✳ Open all year, Apr-Sep daily 9.30-6.30; Oct-Mar, daily 9.30-4.30. Closed 25-26 Dec & 1-2 Jan. (Visits must be pre-booked). **Facilities** ❂ 🍽 shop ⊗ 🖪

Stones of Stenness Circle and Henge   FREE
➲ *(5m NE of Stromness on B9055)*

☎ 01856 841815

web: www.historic-scotland.gov.uk

Dating back to the second millennium BC, the remains of this stone circle are near the Ring of Brogar - a splendid circle of upright stones surrounded by a ditch.

Times ✳ Open at any reasonable time. **Facilities** ❂ 🖪

HARRAY   MAP 16 HY31

Corrigall Farm & Kirbuster Museum   FREE
KW17 2JR

➲ *(Off A986, main road through parish of Harray to parish of Birsay)*

☎ 01856 771411 & 771268

web: www.orkneyheritage.com

The museum consists of two Orkney farmhouses with outbuildings. Kirbuster (Birsay) has the last surviving example of a 'Firehoose' with its central hearth; Corrigall (Harray) represents an improved farmhouse and steading of the late 1800s.

Times Open Mar-Oct, Mon-Sat 10.30-1 & 2-5, Sun 2-7. **Facilities** ❂ 🎋 (outdoor) ♿ toilets for disabled shop ⊗ (ex assist dogs) ▭

KIRKWALL   MAP 16 HY41

Bishop's & Earl's Palaces
KW15 1PD

➲ *(In Kirkwall on A960)*

☎ 01856 875461

web: www.historic-scotland.gov.uk

The Bishop's Palace is a hall-house of the 12th century, later much altered, with a round tower built by Bishop Reid in 1541-48. A later addition was made by the notorious Patrick Stewart, Earl of Orkney, who built the adjacent Earl's Palace between 1600 and 1607 in a splendid Renaissance style.

Times ✳ Open Apr-Sep, daily 9.30-6.30. **Facilities** shop 🖪

SCOTLAND

KIRKWALL CONTINUED

Scapa Flow Visitor Centre & Museum FREE

Lyness, Hoy

➲ *(on A964 to Houton, ferry crossing takes 30 mins, visitors centre 2 mins from ferry terminal)*

☎ 01856 791300

e-mail: museum@orkney.gov.uk

web: www.orkneyheritage.com

Also known as the Lyness Interpretation Centre, this fascinating museum is home to a large collection of military equipment used in the defence of the Orkneys during the First and Second World Wars. There are also guns salvaged from the German ships scuppered in WWII. Visitors arrive at the island after a short boat trip from the Orkney mainland.

Times Open all year: Mon-Fri 9-4.30 (mid May-Oct also Sat, Sun 10.30-3.30)
Facilities ❷ ♲ ♿ toilets for disabled shop ⊗ (ex assist dogs) ▭

The Orkney Museum FREE

Broad St KW15 1DH

➲ *(town centre)*

☎ 01856 87355 ext 2523

e-mail: museum@orkney.gov.uk

web: www.orkneyheritage.com

One of the finest vernacular town houses in Scotland, this 16th-century building now contains a museum of Orkney history, including the islands' fascinating archaeology.

Times Open, Oct-Apr Mon-Sat, 10.30-12.30 & 1.30-5, May-Sep, 10.30-5 Mon-Sat. **Facilities** ℗ (50yds) ♿ (5 galleries at ground level, 8 galleries require use of stair lift) toilets for disabled shop ⊗ (ex assist dogs) ▭

STROMNESS   MAP 16 HY20

Orkney Maritime & Natural History Museum

52 Alfred St KW16 3DF

➲ *(0.5m from Stromess pier head)*

☎ 01856 850025

The museum focuses on Orkney's broad maritime connections, including fishing, whaling, the Hudson's Bay Company, the German Fleet in Scapa Flow, and the award-winning Pilot's House extension. The Natural History Gallery is fully restored, displaying a fine collection of curios and rare and interesting exhibits.

Times Open Apr-Sep, Mon-Sun 10-5; Oct-Mar, Mon-Sat 11-3.30. Closed Xmas, New Year & 3 wks Feb-Mar. **Fee** ✳ £3 (ch 50p, concessions £2). Family £6. (All tickets are valid for 1 week) **Facilities** ℗ (50yds) ♿ (stair lift and ramps) toilets for disabled shop ⊗ (ex assist dogs)

Pier Arts Centre FREE

KW16 3AA

☎ 01856 850209

e-mail: info@pierartscentre.com

web: www.pierartscentre.com

A permanent collection of modern art and sculpture including works by Barbara Hepworth and Ben Nicholson, given to Orkney by the late Margaret Gardiner. These works are housed in a landmark 18th-century building that has served as merchant's offices, a cooperage, stores and private lodgings. 2009 is the centre's 30th anniversary.

Times Open all year Mon-Sat 10.30-5, Jul-Sep open Sun 12-4 **Facilities** ℗ (100yds) ♿ toilets for disabled shop ⊗ (ex assist dogs) ▭

WESTRAY   MAP 16 HY44

Noltland Castle FREE

➲ *(1m W of Pierowall village)*

☎ 01856 841815

web: www.historic-scotland.gov.uk

A fine, ruined Z-plan tower, built between 1560 and 1573 but never completed. The tower is remarkable for its large number of gun loops and impressive staircase.

Times ✳ Open 11 Jun-Sep, daily 9.30-6.30. **Facilities** ⊗ ♞

SHETLAND

LERWICK   MAP 16 HU44

Clickimin FREE

ZE1 0QX

➲ *(1m SW of Lerwick on A970)*

☎ 01466 793191

web: www.historic-scotland.gov.uk

The remains of a prehistoric settlement that was fortified at the beginning of the Iron Age with a stone-built fort. The site was occupied for over 1000 years. The remains include a partially demolished broch (round tower) which still stands to a height of 17ft.

Times ✳ Open at all reasonable times. **Facilities** ♞

Fort Charlotte FREE

ZE1 0JN

➲ *(in centre of Lerwick)*

☎ 01466 793191

web: www.historic-scotland.gov.uk

A five-sided artillery fort with bastions projecting from each corner. The walls are high and massive. It was built in 1665 to protect the Sound of Bressay from the Dutch, but taken by them and burned in 1673. It was rebuilt in 1781.

Times ✳ Open at all reasonable times. Key available locally. **Facilities** ♞

Shetland Museum FREE

Hay's Dock ZE1 0WP

☎ 01595 695057

e-mail: info@shetlandmuseumandarchives.org.uk

web: www.shetlandmuseumandarchives.org.uk

After a grand re-opening in May 2007, the Museum and Archives sits in a unique dockside setting and is home to 3000 artefacts telling the story of Shetland.

Times Open all year Mon & Sat 10-5, Sun 12-7; Summer Tue-Thu 10-6, Fri 10-7; Winter Tue-Fri 10-5. Closed 25-26 Dec & 1-2 Jan. **Facilities** ❷ ♲ ♨ licensed ♿ (lift, wheelchair available) toilets for disabled shop ⊗ (ex assist dogs) ▭

MOUSA ISLAND — MAP 16 HU42

Mousa Broch `FREE`

➲ *(accessible by boat from Sandwick)*

☎ 01466 793191

web: www.historic-scotland.gov.uk

This broch is the best-preserved example of an Iron Age drystone tower in Scotland. The tower is nearly complete and rises to a height of 40ft. The outer and inner walls both contain staircases that may be climbed to the parapet. Boat not available all year. Contact 01950 431367 for more information.

Times ✳ Open at all reasonable times. **Facilities** ▮

SCALLOWAY — MAP 16 HU33

Scalloway Castle `FREE`

ZE1 0TP

➲ *(6m from Lerwick on A970)*

☎ 01466 793191

web: www.historic-scotland.gov.uk

The ruins of a castle designed on the medieval two-step plan. The castle was actually built in 1600 by Patrick Stewart, Earl of Orkney. When the Earl, who was renowned for his cruelty, was executed in 1615, the castle fell into disuse.

Times ✳ Open at all reasonable times. **Facilities** ℗▮

SUMBURGH — MAP 16 HU30

Jarlshof Prehistoric & Norse Settlement

➲ *(at Sumburgh Head, approx 22m S of Lerwick)*

☎ 01950 460112

web: www.historic-scotland.gov.uk

One of the most remarkable archaeological sites in Europe. There are remains of Bronze Age, Iron Age and Viking settlements as well as a medieval farm. There is also a 16th-century Laird's House, once the home of the Earls Robert and Patrick Stewart, and the basis of 'Jarlshof' in Sir Walter Scott's novel *The Pirate*.

Times ✳ Open Apr-Sep, daily 9.30-6.30. **Facilities** ℗ shop ▮

SKYE, ISLE OF

ARMADALE — MAP 13 NG60

Armadale Castle Gardens & Museum of the Isles

IV45 8RS

➲ *(16m S of Broadford on A851. Follow Clan Donald Centre or Armadale Castle Gardens & Museum of the Isles signs. Easily reached by Skye Bridge or the Mallaig A830 to Armdale Ferry)*

☎ 01471 844305 & 844227

e-mail: office@clandonald.com

web: www.clandonald.com

Armadale Castle and Gardens were built in 1815 as the home of Lord Macdonald. The warming effect of the Gulf Stream allows exotic trees and plants to flourish. Within the 40 acres of gardens is the Museum of the Isles, where visitors can discover the history of the Highlands.

Armadale Castle Gardens & Museum of the Isles

Times Open daily 9.30-5.30. Garden & Museum open Apr-Oct.
Facilities ℗ 🖙 🍴 🍺 (outdoor) ♿ (wheelchairs available) toilets for disabled shop garden centre ⊗ (ex on leads) ▬

DUNVEGAN — MAP 13 NG24

Dunvegan Castle and Gardens

IV55 8WF

➲ *(follow A87 over Skye Bridge. Turn onto A863 at Sligachan and continue to castle)*

☎ 01470 521206

e-mail: info@dunvegancastle.com

web: www.dunvegancastle.com

Dunvegan Castle is the oldest continuously inhabited castle in Scotland and has been the stronghold of the chiefs of MacLeod for nearly 800 years. Originally designed to keep people out, it was first opened to visitors in 1933. Romantic and historic, the castle is set amid stunning scenery and beautiful formal gardens. The castle and estate are steeped in history and clan legend, and you can take a boat trip onto Loch Dunvegan to see the seal colony, or stay in one of the charming estate cottages. Previous visitors to the castle have included Sir Walter Scott, Dr Johnson, Queen Elizabeth II and the Japanese Emperor Akihito.

Times Open Apr-15 Oct, daily 10-5.30 (last entry 5), 16 Oct-Mar, daily 11-4 (last entry 3.30). Closed 25-26 Dec & 1-3 Jan **Fee** Castle & Gardens: £7.50 (ch 5-15 yrs £4, pen & students £6). **Facilities** ℗ 🖙 🍴 licensed 🍺 (outdoor) ♿ (gardens, restaurant and shop fully accessible, parts of the castle are not accessible) (restaurant has ramps for wheelchair access) toilets for disabled shop ⊗ (ex assist dogs & in grounds) ▬

437

WALES

Skomer Island, Pembrokeshire Coast National Park

ANGLESEY, ISLE OF

BEAUMARIS — MAP 06 SH67

Beaumaris Castle

LL58 8AP

☎ 01248 810361

web: www.cadw.wales.gov.uk

Beaumaris was built by Edward I and took from 1295 to 1312 to complete. In later centuries it was plundered for its lead, timber and stone. Despite this it remains one of the most impressive and complete castles built by Edward I. It has a perfectly symmetrical, concentric plan, with a square inner bailey and curtain walls, round corner towers and D-shaped towers in between. There are also two great gatehouses, but these were never finished.

Times Open Apr-Oct, daily 9-5; Nov-Mar, Mon-Sat 9.30-4, Sun 11-4. **Fee** ✻ £3.70 (ch 5-15, concessions £3.30, disabled visitors and assisting companion free). Family ticket (2ad+all ch/grandch under 16) £10.70. Group rates available. Prices quoted apply until 31 Mar 2009. **Facilities** ℗ shop ⊗ ⊕ ◼

BRYNCELLI DDU — MAP 06 SH57

Bryn Celli Ddu Burial Chamber   FREE

➲ (3m W of Menai Bridge off A4080)

☎ 029 2050 0200

web: www.cadw.wales.gov.uk

Excavated in 1865, and then again in 1925-9, this is a prehistoric circular cairn covering a passage grave with a polygonal chamber.

Times Open at all times. **Facilities** ℗ ⊗ ⊕

BRYNSIENCYN — MAP 06 SH46

Anglesey Sea Zoo

LL61 6TQ

➲ (1st turning off Britannia Bridge onto Anglesey then follow Lobster signs along A4080 to zoo)

☎ 01248 430411

e-mail: info@angleseyseazoo.co.uk

web: www.angleseyseazoo.co.uk

Nestling by the Menai Straits, this all-weather undercover attraction contains a shipwreck bristling with conger eels, a lobster hatchery, a seahorse nursery, crashing waves and the enchanting fish forest.

Times ✻ Open Feb half term-late Oct half term. Telephone for times. **Facilities** ℗ ⊑ ⊚ ⊓ (outdoor) ♿ (2 wheelchairs available, Braille tour notes) toilets for disabled shop ⊗ (ex assist dogs) ◼

HOLYHEAD — MAP 06 SH28

RSPB Nature Reserve South Stack Cliffs   FREE

Plas Nico, South Stack LL65 1YH

➲ (A5 or A55 to Holyhead then follow brown heritage signs)

☎ 01407 764973

web: www.rspb.org.uk/reserves/southstack

South Stack Cliffs is an expanse of heathland with dramatic sea cliffs and a tremendous view. In summer breeding seabirds, including puffins, can be seen from the Information Centre at Ellins Tower where telescopes are provided and staff are on hand to help.

Times ✻ Open: Information Centre daily, Etr-Sep, 10-5.30. Reserve open daily at all times. **Facilities** ℗

LLANALLGO — MAP 06 SH58

Din Llugwy Ancient Village   FREE

➲ (0.75m NW off A5025)

web: www.cadw.wales.gov.uk

The remains of a 4th-century village can be seen here. There are two circular and seven rectangular buildings, still standing up to head height and encircled by a pentagonal stone wall some 4 to 5ft thick.

Times Open at all times. **Facilities** ⊗ ⊕

PLAS NEWYDD — MAP 06 SH56

Plas Newydd

LL61 6DQ

➲ (2m S of Llanfairpwll, on A4080)

☎ 01248 714795

e-mail: plasnewydd@nationaltrust.org.uk

web: www.nationaltrust.org.uk

Set amidst breathtakingly beautiful scenery and with spectacular views of Snowdonia, this elegant 18th-century house was built by James Wyatt and is an interesting mixture of Classical and Gothic. The comfortable interior, restyled in the 1930s, is famous for its association with Rex Whistler, whose largest painting is here. There is also an exhibition about his work. A military museum contains campaign relics of the 1st Marquess of Anglesey, who commanded the cavalry at the Battle of Waterloo. There is a fine spring garden and Australasian arboretum with an understorey of shrubs and wild flowers, as well as a summer terrace and, later, massed hydrangeas and autumn colour. A woodland walk gives access to a marine walk on the Menai Strait.

Times Open Apr-Oct, Sat-Wed. House 12-5, Garden 11-5.30. (Last admission 4.30) **Fee** ✻ House: £7 (ch £3.50). Family £17 (2ad+2ch). Parties 15+ £6. Garden: £5 (ch £2.50). **Facilities** ℗ ⊑ ⊓ (outdoor) ♿ (ground floor accessible for manual wheelchairs) (close parking, wheelchairs, garden shuttle, Braille guide) toilets for disabled shop ⊗ (ex assist dogs) ⋓ ◼

WALES

BRIDGEND

BRIDGEND MAP 03 SS97

Newcastle
FREE
☎ 01656 659515

web: www.cadw.wales.gov.uk

The small castle dates back to the 12th century. It is ruined, but a rectangular tower, a richly carved Norman gateway and massive curtain walls enclosing a polygonal courtyard can still be seen.

Times Open - accessible throughout the year. Key keeper arrangement. **Facilities** ⊕ ⊗ ⊕

COITY MAP 03 SS98

Coity Castle
FREE
CF35 6BG

➲ (2m NE of Bridgend, off A4061)

☎ 01656 652021

web: www.cadw.wales.gov.uk

A 12th to 16th-century stronghold, with a hall, chapel and the remains of a square keep.

Times Open all year, at all times. Key keeper arrangement. **Facilities** ⊕ ⊗ ⊕

CAERPHILLY

CAERPHILLY MAP 03 ST18

Caerphilly Castle
CF8 1JL

➲ (on A469)

☎ 029 2088 3143

web: www.cadw.wales.gov.uk

The concentrically planned castle was begun in 1268 by Gilbert de Clare and completed in 1326. It is the largest in Wales, and has extensive land and water defences. A unique feature is the ruined tower - the victim of subsidence - which manages to out-lean even Pisa. The south dam platform, once a tournament-field, now displays replica medieval siege-engines.

Times Open Apr-Oct, daily 9-5; Nov-Mar, Mon-Sat 9.30-4, Sun 11-4. **Fee** ✳ £3.70 (ch 5-15, concessions £3.30, disabled visitors and assisting companion free). Family ticket (2ad+all ch/grandch under 16) £10.70. Group rates available. Prices quoted apply until 31 Mar 2009. **Facilities** ⊕ shop ⊗ ⊕ ▬

Llancaiach Fawr Manor
2 for 1
Gelligaer Rd, Nelson CF46 6ER

➲ (M4 junct 32, A470 to Merthyr Tydfil. Towards Ystrad Mynach A472, follow brown heritage signs)

☎ 01443 412248

e-mail: llancaiachfawr@caerphilly.gov.uk
web: www.llancaiachfawr.co.uk

Step back in time to the Civil War period at this fascinating living history museum. The year is 1645 and visitors are invited into the Manor to meet the servants of 'Colonel' Edward Prichard - from the puritanical to the gossipy. Please telephone for details of events running throughout the year.

Times Open daily 10-5 (last admission 1hr before closing). Closed Mon, Nov-Feb and 24 Dec-1 Jan **Fee** ✳ £5.75 (ch £4.25) concessions £4.75. Family ticket £17 **Facilities** ⊕ ⊡ ⊙ licensed ⊼ (outdoor) ⊕ (2nd & 3rd floors not accessible as no lift) (DVD players) toilets for disabled shop ⊗ (ex assist dogs) ▬

CWMCARN MAP 03 ST29

Cwmcarn Forest & Campsite
Nantcarn Rd NP11 7FA

➲ (8m N of Newport on A467, follow brown tourist signs)

☎ 01495 272001

e-mail: cwmcarn-vc@caerphilly.gov.uk
web: www.cwmcarnforest.co.uk

A seven-mile scenic drive with spectacular views over the Bristol Channel and surrounding countryside. Facilities include barbecues, picnic and play areas, and forest and mountain walks. There is also a mountain bike trail and downhill trail on site. Special events are held throughout the year, please ring for details or visit the website.

Times Open Forest Drive: Mar & Oct 11-5; Apr-Aug 11-7 (11-9 wknds during Jul & Aug); Sep, 11-6; Nov-Feb 11-4 (wknds only). Visitor Centre open daily; Etr-Sep Mon-Thu 9-5, Fri-Sun 9-5; Oct-Etr, Mon-Thu & Sat-Sun 9-5, Fri 9-4.30. Please phone for Xmas & New Year opening times. **Fee** Cars & Motorcycles £3, Minibus £6, Coaches £20. Car season ticket £20. **Facilities** ⊕ ⊡ ⊼ (outdoor) ⊕ toilets for disabled shop ▬

CARDIFF

CARDIFF MAP 03 ST17

Cardiff Castle
Castle St CF10 3RB

➲ (from M4, A48 & A470 follow signs to city centre)

☎ 029 2087 8100

e-mail: cardiffcastle@cardiff.gov.uk
web: www.cardiffcastle.com

Cardiff Castle is situated in the heart of the city. Contained within its mighty walls is a history spanning nearly 2,000 years, dating from the coming of the Romans to the Norman Conquest and beyond. Discover spectacular interiors on your guided tour, and enjoy magnificent views of the city from the top of the 12th-century Norman keep. The new

CONTINUED

WALES

CARDIFF CONTINUED

Interpretation Centre includes a film presentation and a multimedia guide around the Castle grounds. Regular events throughout the year include a teddy bear's picnic, open air theatre, medieval and Roman re-enactments and much more.

Times Open all year, daily (ex 25-26 Dec & 1 Jan) including guided tours, Mar-Oct, 9.30-6 (last tour 5); Nov-Feb, 9.30-5.00 (last tour 4). Royal Regiment of Wales Museum closed Tue. **Fee** £8.95 (ch £6.35, concessions £7.50). Grounds only £3.75 (ch £2.25, concessions £3). There may be an additional charge for special events. **Facilities** ℗ (200 yds) ⚏ ᵬ (Castle apartments and Norman Keep not accessible to wheelchair users, cobblestone path at entrance.) (multi media guide, ramps, lift & tours visually impaired) toilets for disabled shop ⊗ (ex in grounds & assist dogs) ▬

Dyffryn Gardens

St Nicholas CF5 6SU

➲ *(A4232 towards Barry, rdbt take 1st exit, exit at junct with A48/A4050. At Culverhouse Cross rdbt take 4th exit A48 signed Cowbridge. Left at lights in St Nicholas village, Dyffryn on right after 1.5m)*

☎ 029 2059 3328

e-mail: dyffryn@valeofglamorgan.gov.uk

web: www.dyffryngardens.org.uk

Set in the heart of the Vale of Glamorgan, this exceptional example of Edwardian garden design is the result of a unique collaboration between landscape architect Thomas Mawson and plant collector Reginald Cory. The 55 acres of garden boast splendid lawns, an arboretum of rare and unusual trees, and a beautiful selection of intimate outdoor garden rooms.

Times Open Apr-Oct 10-6; Nov-Feb 11-4. **Facilities** ❷ ⚏ ⋔ (outdoor) ᵬ (wheelchairs for hire, parking) toilets for disabled shop ⊗ (ex on lead) ▬

Llandaff Cathedral

Llandaff CF5 2LA

➲ *(W on M4 junct 29 to A48(M), then onto A48 and follow brown signs. E on M4 junct 32 onto A470 towards Cardiff, leave A48 and follow brown signs)*

☎ 029 2056 4554

e-mail: office@llandaffcathedral.org.uk

web: www.llandaffcathedral.org.uk

A medieval cathedral begun in the 12th century on the site of an early Christian place of worship. The cathedral was severely damaged during the bombing raids on Cardiff during World War II. The interior is dominated by a modernistic post-war *Christ in Majesty* sculpture by Epstein. Please visit website for details of events running throughout the year.

Times Open all year, daily 8-7 (Sun 7-7 & Mon 8.30-7). **Fee** Donations expected. No group bookings on Sun or Holy Days. **Facilities** ℗ (100yds) (parking limited) ᵬ (Wheelchair access is provided at the East and West ends of the Cathedral) (wheelchair available) shop ⊗ (ex assist dogs)

Millennium Stadium Tours

Millennium Stadium, Westgate St, Gate 3 CF10 1JA

➲ *(A470 to city centre. Westgate St opposite Castle far end. Turn by Angel Hotel on corner of Westgate Street.)*

☎ 029 2082 2228

e-mail: mgibbons@wru.co.uk

web: millenniumstadium.com/tours

In the late 1990s this massive stadium was completed as part of an effort to revitalise Welsh fortunes. It replaced Cardiff Arms Park, and now hosts major music events, exhibitions, and international rugby and soccer matches. Its capacity of around 75,000 and its retractable roof make it unique in Europe. The home of Welsh Rugby and Welsh Football.

Times Open all year, Mon-Sat, 10-5; Sun 10-4 **Fee** £6.50 (ch up to 16 £4, ch under 5 free, concessions £4.50). Family (2ad+3ch) £18. **Facilities** ℗ (20mtrs) ᵬ (lifts, escalators, disabled parking) toilets for disabled shop ⊗ (ex assist dogs) ▬

National Museum Cardiff

Cathays Park CF10 3NP

➲ *(in Civic Centre. M4 junct 32, A470, 5 mins walk from city centre & 20 mins walk from bus & train station)*

☎ 029 2039 7951

e-mail: post@museumwales.ac.uk

web: www.museumwales.ac.uk

National Museum Cardiff is home to spectacular collections from Wales and all over the world. The Museum showcases displays of art, archaeology, geology and natural history all under one roof. The new archaeology gallery, 'Origins in search of early Wales', traces life in Wales from the earliest humans 230,000 years ago. Explore the past through themes such as conflict, power, wealth, family and the future. Discover stories behind some of Wales' most famous works of art in the new art galleries, which now include activity stations and touch screens to help bring the paintings to life. You can also enjoy changing displays drawn from the collection of Impressionist and Post-Impressionist paintings, including work by Monet, Renoir and Cézanne. Or how about a close encounter with The Big Bang, erupting volcanoes, dinosaurs and woolly mammoths on the journey through time and space?

Times Open all year, Tue-Sun 10-5. Closed Mon (ex BHs). Telephone for Xmas opening times. **Fee** Free admission but charge may be made for some events. **Facilities** ❷ (charged) ⚏ ⋔ licensed ᵬ (wheelchair available, Tel 029 2057 3509 for access guide) toilets for disabled shop ⊗ (ex assist dogs) ▬

Techniquest

Stuart St CF10 5BW

➲ *(A4232 to Cardiff Bay)*

☎ 029 2047 5475

e-mail: info@techniquest.org

web: www.techniquest.org

Located in the heart of the Cardiff Bay, there's always something new to explore at this exciting science discovery centre. Journey into space in the planetarium, enjoy an interactive Science Theatre Show or experience one of the 150 hands-on exhibits. Please visit website for details of events running throughout the year.

Times Open all year, Mon-Fri 9.30-4.30; Sat-Sun & BHs 10.30-5, school hols 9.30-5. Closed Xmas. **Fee** £6.90 (ch 5-16 & concessions £4.80). Family ticket £20 (2ad+3ch). Friend season ticket £47. Groups 10+ **Facilities** ℗ (50mtrs) (limited parking for disabled visitors) ⬜ ♿ (lift, hearing loop) toilets for disabled shop ⊗ (ex assist dogs) ▬

ST FAGANS   MAP 03 ST17

St Fagans: National History Museum

CF5 6XB

➲ *(4m W of Cardiff on A4232. From M4 exit at junct 33 and follow brown signs)*

☎ 029 2057 3500

web: www.museumwales.ac.uk

A stroll around the indoor galleries and 100 acres of beautiful grounds will give you a fascinating insight into how people in Wales have lived, worked and spent their leisure hours since Celtic times. You can see people practising the traditional means of earning a living, the animals they kept and at certain times of year, the ways in which they celebrated the seasons.

Times Open all year daily, 10-5. (Closed 24-26 Dec). **Fee** ✳ Free. Charge may apply to some events. **Facilities** ℗ (charged) ⬜ 🍴 licensed ㅈ (outdoor) ♿ (wheelchair access possible to most parts) (wheelchairs, motorised buggy-must pre-book) toilets for disabled shop ⊗ (ex in grounds if on lead) ▬

TONGWYNLAIS   MAP 03 ST18

Castell Coch

CF4 7YS

➲ *(A470 to Tongwynlais junct, then B4262 to castle on top of hill)*

☎ 029 2081 0101

web: www.cadw.wales.gov.uk

Castell Coch is Welsh for red castle, an appropriate name for this fairy-tale building with its red sandstone walls and conical towers. The castle was originally built in the 13th century but fell into ruins, and the present castle is a late-19th-century creation. Inside, the castle is decorated in fantasy style.

Times Open Apr-Oct, daily 9-5; Nov-Mar, Mon-Sat 9.30-4, Sun 11-4. The standard opening hours will apply ex between 5 Jan-8 Feb 2009 inclusive. During this period the monument will be closed for essential conservation works. **Fee** ✳ £3.70 (ch 5-15, concessions £3.30, disabled visitors and assisting companion free). Family ticket (2ad+all ch/grandch under 16) £10.70. Group rates available. Prices quoted apply until 31 Mar 2009. **Facilities** ℗ ㅈ shop ⊗ ⊕ ▬

CARMARTHENSHIRE

ABERGWILI   MAP 02 SN42

Carmarthenshire County Museum   FREE

SA31 2JG

➲ *(2m E of Carmarthen, just off A40, at Abergwili rdbt)*

☎ 01267 228696

e-mail: museums@carmarthenshire.gov.uk

web: www.carmarthenshire.gov.uk/

Housed in the old palace of the Bishop of St David's and set in seven acres of grounds, the museum offers a wide range of local subjects to explore, from geology and prehistory to butter making, Welsh furniture and folk art. Temporary exhibitions are held.

Times Open all year, Mon-Sat 10-4.30. Closed Xmas-New Year **Facilities** ℗ ⬜ ㅈ (outdoor) ♿ (lift) toilets for disabled shop ⊗ (ex assist dogs)

CARREG CENNEN CASTLE   MAP 03 SN61

Carreg Cennen Castle

SA19 6UA

➲ *(unclass road from A483 to Trapp village)*

☎ 01558 822291

web: www.cadw.wales.gov.uk

A steep path leads up to the castle, which is spectacularly sited on a limestone crag. It was first built as a stronghold of the native Welsh and then rebuilt in the late 13th century. Most remarkable among the impressive remains is a mysterious passage, cut into the side of the cliff and lit by loopholes. The farm at the site has a rare breeds centre.

Times Open all year, Apr-Oct, daily 9.30-6.30; Nov-Mar, daily, 9.30-4. **Fee** ✳ £3.70 (ch 5-15, concessions £3.30, disabled visitors & assisting companion free). Family ticket (2ad+all ch/grandch under 16) £10.70. Group rates available. Prices quoted apply until 31 Mar 2009. **Facilities** ℗ ⬜ shop ⊗ ⊕ ▬

DRE-FACH FELINDRE   MAP 02 SN33

National Woollen Museum

SA44 5UP

➲ *(16m W of Carmarthen off A484, 4m E of Newcastle Emlyn)*

☎ 01559 370929

e-mail: post@museumwales.ac.uk

web: www.museumwales.ac.uk

The museum is housed in the former Cambrian Mills and has a comprehensive display tracing the evolution of the industry from its
CONTINUED

WALES

DRE-FACH FELINDRE CONTINUED

beginnings to the present day. Demonstrations of the fleece to fabric process are given on 19th-century textile machinery.

Times Open Apr-Sep, daily 10-5; Oct-Mar, Tue-Sat 10-5. Phone for details of Xmas opening times. **Fee** Free admission but charge may be made for some events. **Facilities** ❷ ▭ ⊞ (outdoor) ♿ (wheelchair access to ground floor & ample seating) toilets for disabled shop ⊗ (ex assist dogs) ▬

DRYSLWYN
MAP 02 SN52

Dryslwyn Castle
FREE

➲ *(on B4279)*

☎ 029 2050 0200

web: www.cadw.wales.gov.uk

The ruined 13th-century castle was a stronghold of the native Welsh. It stands on a lofty mound, and was important in the struggles between English and Welsh. It is gradually being uncovered by excavation.

Times Open-entrance by arrangement with Dryslwyn Farm. **Facilities** ❷ ⊗ ⊕

KIDWELLY
MAP 02 SN40

Kidwelly Castle

SA17 5BQ

➲ *(via A484)*

☎ 01554 890104

web: www.cadw.wales.gov.uk

This is an outstanding example of late 13th-century castle design, with its 'walls within walls' defensive system. There were later additions made to the building, the chapel dating from about 1400. Of particular interest are two vast circular ovens.

Times Open Apr-Oct, daily 9-5; Nov-Mar, Mon-Sat 9.30-4, Sun 11-4. The monument will be closed for essential conservation/access works in Apr **Fee** ✳ £3.10 (ch 5-15, concessions £2.70, disabled visitors & assisting companion free). Family ticket (2ad+all ch/grandch under 16) £8.90. Group rates available. Prices quoted apply until 31 Mar 2009. **Facilities** ❷ shop ⊗ ⊕ ▬

Kidwelly Industrial Museum

Broadford SA17 4LW

➲ *(signed from Kidwelly bypass & town, stack visible from bypass)*

☎ 01554 891078

Two of the great industries of Wales are represented in this museum: tinplate and coal mining. The original buildings and machinery of the Kidwelly tinplate works, where tinplate was hand made, are now on display to the public. There is also an exhibition of coal mining with pit-head gear and a winding engine, while the more general history of the area is shown in a separate exhibition.

Times Open Etr, Jun-Sep, BH wknds, Mon-Fri 10-5, Sat-Sun 12-5. Last admission 4. Other times by arrangement for parties only. **Facilities** ❷ ▭ ⊞ (outdoor) ♿ (ramps on entrances) toilets for disabled shop

---

LAUGHARNE
MAP 02 SN31

Dylan Thomas' Boat House

Dylans Walk SA33 4SD

➲ *(14m SW of Carmarthen)*

☎ 01994 427420

e-mail: dylanthomas@carmarthenshire.gov.uk

web: www.dylanthomasboathouse.com

The home of Dylan Thomas and his family during the last four turbulent and creative years of his life. The house and its surrounding estuary, town and countryside feature considerably in the poet's work, including his famous *Under Milk Wood*. The house contains interpretive display, original furniture, bookshop and tearoom. Please telephone for details of events running throughout the year. 2009 is the 60th anniversary of Dylan Thomas and his family's move into the Boathouse.

Times Open all year, May-Oct & Etr wknd, daily 10-5.30 (last admission 5); Nov-Apr, daily 10.30-3.30 (last admission 3) **Fee** ✳ £3.50 (ch under 7 free, pen £2.75, concessions £2.50). Family and group rates available.
Facilities ℗ (200yds) ▭ (not accessible for wheelchairs) shop ⊗ (ex assist dogs & outside) ▬

Laugharne Castle

King St SA33 4SA

➲ *(on A4066)*

☎ 01994 427906

web: www.cadw.wales.gov.uk

Newly opened to the public, picturesque Laugharne Castle stands on a low ridge overlooking the wide Taff Estuary. A medieval fortress converted into an Elizabethan mansion, it suffered a civil war siege and later became the backdrop for elaborate Victorian gardens, now recreated. Laugharne Castle has also inspired two modern writers - Richard Hughes and Dylan Thomas.

Times Open Apr-Sep, daily 10-5. **Fee** ✳ £3.10 (ch 5-15, concessions £2.70, disabled visitors & assisting companion free). Family ticket (2ad+all ch/grandch under 16) £8.90. Group rates available. Prices quoted apply until 31 Mar 2009. **Facilities** ℗ (150mtrs) shop ⊗ ⊕ ▬

LLANARTHNE
MAP 02 SN52

The National Botanic Garden of Wales of Wales

SA32 8HG

➲ *(8m E of Carmarthen on A48, dedicated intersection - signed)*

☎ 01558 668768

e-mail: info@gardenofwales.org.uk

web: www.gardenofwales.org.uk

Set amongst 568 acres of Parkland in the beautiful Towy Valley in West Wales, just seven miles from Carmarthen. The Gardens centrepiece is the Great Glasshouse, an amazing tilted glass dome with a six-metre ravine. The Mediterranean landscape enables the visitor to experience the aftermath of an Australian bush fire, pause in an olive grove or wander through Fuchsia collections from Chile. The Tropical House features orchids, palms and other tropical plants.

A 220 metre herbaceous board walk forms the spine of the garden and leads to the children's play area and the 360-surround screen cinema to the Old Stables Courtyard. Here the visitor can view art exhibitions, wander in the gift shop or enjoy a meal in the restaurant. Land train tours will take the visitor around the necklace of lakes, which surround the central garden.

Times Open 24 Mar-26 Oct 10-6; 27 Oct-22 Mar 10-4.30 **Facilities** ❷ ⬚ ⑩ ㅈ (outdoor) ♿ (Braille interpretation wheelchairs/scooters shuttle svc) toilets for disabled shop garden centre ❽ (ex assist dogs) ☰

LLANDEILO
MAP 03 SN62

Dinefwr Park

SA19 6RT

➲ *(off A40 Carmarthenshire, on W outskirts of Llandeilo)*

☎ 01558 823902

e-mail: dinefwr@nationaltrust.org.uk

web: www.ukindex.co.uk/nationaltrust

At the heart of Welsh history for a thousand years, the Park as we know it today took shape in the years after 1775 when the medieval castle, house, gardens, woods and deer park were integrated into one vast and breathtaking landscape. Access to Church Woods and Dinefwr Castle is through the landscaped park.

Times ✳ Open Mar-Oct, daily Nov-20 Dec, Fri-Sun 11-4.30. (4pm winter) (Last admission 30 mins before closing) **Fee** ✳ £6.30 (ch £3.20) Family £15.80. **Facilities** ❷ (charged) ⬚ ♿ (Partly accessible) ❽ (ex outer park on lead) ⛵ ☰

LLANELLI
MAP 02 SN50

National Wetland Centre Wales

Penclacwydd, Llwynhendy SA14 9SH

➲ *(3m E of Llanelli, off A484)*

☎ 01554 741087

e-mail: info.llanelli@wwt.org.uk

web: www.wwt.org.uk

Stretching over 97 hectares on the Burry Inlet, the centre is Wales' premier site for water birds and waders and is home to countless wild species as diverse as dragonflies and Little Egrets. The beautifully landscaped grounds are home to over 650 of some of the world's most spectacular ducks, swans, geese and flamingos - many so tame they feed from the hand. There is also a discovery centre and outdoor activities for visitors including a Canoe Safari, Water Vole City, Pond Dipping Zone and Bike Trail.

Times Open daily 9.30-5 (ex 24-25 Dec). Grounds open until 6 in the summer. **Fee** ✳ Gift Aid donation: £6.95 (ch £3.85 age 4-16, ch under 4 and disability helpers free, concessions £5.20). Family (2ad+2ch) £19.45. WWT members free. **Facilities** ❷ ⬚ ⑩ licensed ㅈ (indoor & outdoor) ♿ (tower inaccessible) (wheelchair/mobility scooter, special viewing areas) toilets for disabled shop ❽ (ex assist dogs) ☰

LLANGATHEN
MAP 02 SN52

Aberglasney Gardens

SA32 8QH

➲ *(4m W of Llandeilo, follow signs from A40)*

☎ 01558 668998

e-mail: info@aberglasney.org

web: www.aberglasney.org

Aberglasney is a 10-acre garden, containing a variety of rare and unusual plants, providing interest throughout the seasons. At its heart is a unique and fully restored Elizabethan/Jacobean cloister and parapet walk, plus the award-winning garden created within the ruinous courtyard of the mansion. Please telephone for details of events running throughout the year. In July 2009 Aberglasney will be celebrating its 10th anniversary.

Times Open all year, Apr-Oct, daily 10-6 (last entry 5); Nov-Mar, daily 10.30-4. Closed 25 Dec **Fee** ✳ Gift Aid donation: £7 (ch £4, under 5 free, pen £7). Family (2ad+2ch) £18. Groups 10+ £6.50. **Facilities** ❷ ⬚ ⑩ ㅈ (outdoor) ♿ (access to garden restricted in some areas, steps, uneven ground & slopes) (garden route map, wheelchairs available, parking) toilets for disabled shop garden centre ❽ (ex assist dogs) ☰

LLANSTEFFAN
MAP 02 SN31

Llansteffan Castle

➲ *(off B4312)*

☎ 01267 241756

web: www.cadw.wales.gov.uk

The ruins of this 11th to 13th-century stronghold stand majestically on the west side of the Towy estuary.

Times Open - access throughout the year. **Facilities** ❽ ⟳

PUMSAINT MAP 03 SN64

Dolaucothi Gold Mines

SA19 8RR

➲ *(on A482, signed both directions)*

☎ 01558 650177

e-mail: dolaucothi@nationaltrust.org.uk

web: www.nationaltrust.org.uk

Here is an opportunity to spend a day exploring the gold mines and to wear a miner's helmet and lamp while touring the underground workings. The information centre and a walk along the Miners' Way disclose the secrets of 2,000 years of gold mining. This is the only place in Britain where the Romans mined gold.

Times Open end Mar-end Oct, daily 10-5. **Facilities** ❷ ⬛ ㅋ shop ⚄ ▰

CEREDIGION

ABERAERON MAP 02 SN46

Llanerchaeron `2 for 1`

Llanerchaeron, Ciliau Aeron SA48 8DG

➲ *(2.5m E of Aberaeron off A482)*

☎ 01545 570200

e-mail: llanerchaeron@nationaltrust.org.uk

web: www.nationaltrust.org.uk

Llanerchaeron, a few miles inland from Aberaeron on the Cardigan Bay coast, is centred round a Regency Villa designed by John Nash. The self sufficient country estate, villa, service courtyard, grounds, working organic farm and outbuildings remain virtually unaltered. The 18th-century estate features; the Walled Garden and farm complex, mature woodland and ornamental lake, vast parkland and farmland containing Llanwennog sheep and Welsh Black Cattle. Produce and plants from the walled gardens are sold in the visitor building. Please telephone for details of events running throughout the year.

Times ✴ Open late Mar-late Oct, Wed-Sun & BH Mons also open Tue during summer school holidays 11-5. (Last admission 1hr before closing). Park open all year dawn to dusk. **Fee** £6.70 (ch £3.40) Family (2ad+2ch) £16.80 **Facilities** ❷ ⬛ ㅋ (outdoor) ♿ (ramp access to villa, wheelchair, Braille guide) toilets for disabled shop ⊗ (except assist dogs) ⚄

ABERYSTWYTH MAP 06 SN58

The National Library of Wales

Penglais SY23 3BU

➲ *(Off Penglais Hill, A487 in N area of Aberystwyth)*

☎ 01970 632800

e-mail: holi@llgc.org.uk

web: www.llgc.org.uk

The largest library in Wales is just over one hundred years old. Its collections include books, manuscripts, archival documents, maps and photographs as well as paintings, film, video and sound recordings. The library is recognised as the leading research centre for Welsh and Celtic studies, and is popular with those studying family history.

Lectures, screenings and conferences throughout the year. There are constantly changing exhibitions in the galleries and exhibition halls.

Times Open on selected BHs. Please check details before travelling **Fee** ✴ Free. Admission to reading rooms available by readers ticket, two proofs of identity required, one including address. Free admission to all exhibitions **Facilities** ❷ ⬛ ⅼ⊙⅃ licensed ㅋ (outdoor) ♿ (lift) toilets for disabled shop ⊗ (ex assist dogs)

CENARTH MAP 02 SN24

The National Coracle Centre

Cenarth Falls SA38 9JL

➲ *(on A484 between Carmarthen and Cardigan, centre of Cenarth village, beside bridge and river)*

☎ 01239 710980

e-mail: martinfowler7@aol.com

web: www.coracle-centre.co.uk

Situated by the beautiful Cenarth Falls, this fascinating museum has a unique collection from all over the world, including Tibet, India, Iraq, Vietnam, and North America. Cenarth has long been a centre for coracle fishing, and coracle rides are often available in the village during the summer holiday. Look out for the salmon leap by the flour mill.

Times Open Etr-Oct, daily 10.30-5.30. All other times by appointment. **Facilities** ❷ ♿ (top floor of mill inaccessible for disabled) shop ▰

EGLWYSFACH MAP 06 SN69

RSPB Nature Reserve Ynys-hir

Visitor Centre, Cae'r Berllan SY20 8TA

➲ *(6m S of Machynlleth on A487 in Eglwysfach. Signed from main road)*

☎ 01654 700222

e-mail: ynyshir@rspb.org.uk

web: www.rspb.org.uk

The mixture of different habitats is home to an abundance of birds and wildlife. The saltmarshes in winter support the only regular wintering flock of Greenland white-fronted geese in England and Wales, in addition to peregrines, hen harriers and merlins. The sessile oak woodland is home to pied flycatchers, wood warblers, and redstarts in the summer, but woodpeckers, nuthatches, red kites, sparrowhawks and buzzards are here all year round. Otters, polecats, 30 butterfly and 15 dragonfly species are also present. Guided walks and children's activities. Please telephone for details of events running throughout the year.

Times Open daily, 9am-9pm (or sunset if earlier). Visitor Centre: Apr-Oct 9-5 daily; Nov-Mar 10-4 (Wed-Sun) **Fee** ✴ Non-members £2. RSPB members free. **Facilities** ❷ (charged) ㅋ (outdoor) (can take car to viewpoint) shop ⊗ (ex assist dogs) ▰

WALES

FELINWYNT
MAP 02 SN25

Felinwynt Rainforest Centre
2 for 1
SA43 1RT

➩ *(from A487 Blaenannerch Airfield turning, onto B4333. Signed 6m N of Cardigan)*

☎ 01239 810882 & 810250

e-mail: dandjdevereux@btinternet.com

web: www.butterflycentre.co.uk

A chance to wander amongst free-flying exotic butterflies accompanied by the recorded wildlife sounds of the Peruvian Amazon. A waterfall, ponds and streams contribute to a humid tropical atmosphere and provide a habitat for fish and native amphibians. See the exhibition of rainforests of Peru and around the world. Free paper and crayons to borrow for children.

Times Open daily, Apr-Oct, 10-5 (Oct 11-4) **Fee** ✳ £4 (ch 4-14 £2, concessions £3.75) **Facilities** ❷ ⬚ 🗐 (outdoor) ♿ toilets for disabled shop ❽ (ex assist dogs) ➡

STRATA FLORIDA
MAP 03 SN76

Strata Florida Abbey
SY25 6BT

➩ *(unclassified road from Pontrhydfendigaid, accessed from B4340)*

☎ 01974 831261

web: www.cadw.wales.gov.uk

Little remains of the Cistercian abbey founded in 1164, except the ruined church and cloister. Strata Florida was an important centre of learning in the Middle Ages, and it is believed that the 14th-century poet Dafydd ap Gwilym was buried here.

Times Open Apr-Sep, Wed-Sun 10-5. Monument will be opened and unstaffed with no admission charge on Mon and Tue (except BH Mon) between Apr-Sep. The monument will be open but unstaffed at all other times. During this period the opening hours will be between 10-4 daily. **Fee** ✳ £3.10 (ch 5-15, concessions £2.70, disabled visitors & assisting companion free). Family ticket (2ad+all ch/grandch under 16) £8.90. Group discounts available. Prices quoted apply until 31 Mar 2009. **Facilities** ❷ shop ❽ ⬧ ➡

CONWY

BETWS-Y-COED
MAP 06 SH75

Conwy Valley Railway Museum
Old Goods Yard LL24 0AL

➩ *(signed from A5 into Old Church Rd, adjacent to train station)*

☎ 01690 710568

e-mail: info@conwyrailwaymuseum.co.uk

web: www.conwyrailwaymuseum.co.uk

The two large museum buildings have displays on both the narrow and standard-gauge railways of North Wales, including railway stock and other memorabilia. There are working model railway layouts, a steam-hauled miniature railway in the grounds, which cover over four acres, and a 15inch-gauge tramway to the woods. The latest addition is the quarter-size steam 'Britannia' loco that is now on display. For children there are mini-dodgems, Postman Pat, a school bus and Toby Tram.

Times Open all year daily, 10-5.30. Closed Xmas **Fee** £1.50 (ch & concessions 80p). Family ticket £4. Steam train ride £1.50. Tram ride £1. **Facilities** ❷ ⬚ 🗐 (outdoor) ♿ (ramps & clearances for wheelchairs) toilets for disabled shop ➡

CERRIGYDRUDION
MAP 06 SH94

Llyn Brenig Visitor Centre
LL21 9TT

➩ *(on B4501 between Denbigh & Cerrigydrudion)*

☎ 01490 420463

e-mail: llyn.brenig@dwrcymru.com

web: www.dwrcymru.com

The 1800-acre estate has a unique archaeological trail and round-the-lake walk of ten miles. A hide is available and disabled anglers are catered for with a specially adapted fishing boat and an annual open day. The centre has an exhibition on archaeology, history and conservation, and an audio-visual programme.

Times Open mid Mar-Oct, daily 9-5. **Facilities** ❷ (charged) ⬚ 🗐 (outdoor) ♿ (boats for disabled & fishing open days) toilets for disabled shop

COLWYN BAY
MAP 06 SH87

Welsh Mountain Zoo
Old Highway LL28 5UY

➩ *(A55 junct 20 signed Rhos-on-Sea. Zoo signed)*

☎ 01492 532938

e-mail: info@welshmountainzoo.org

web: www.welshmountainzoo.org

Set high above Colwyn Bay with panoramic views and breath-taking scenery, this caring conservation zoo is set among beautiful gardens. Among the animals are many rare and endangered species, and there are daily shows which include Penguins Playtime, Chimp Encounter, Sealion Feeding and Birds of Prey.

Times Open all year, Mar-Oct, daily 9.30-6; Nov-Feb, daily 9.30-5. Closed 25 Dec. **Fee** ✳ £8.75 (ch & students £6.40, pen £7.60). Family ticket (2ad+2ch or 1ad+3ch) £27.45 **Facilities** ❷ ⬚ 🗐 (outdoor) ♿ (Partly accessible) toilets for disabled shop ❽ (ex car park area) ➡

WALES

CONWY

MAP 06 SH77

Aberconwy House

LL32 8AY

➲ *(Llanerchaeron is situated 2.5m E of Aberdeen off the A482 & signed off the A55 expressway)*

☎ 01492 592246

e-mail: aberconwyhouse@nationaltrust.org.uk

web: www.nationaltrust.org.uk

This house dates from the 14th century; it is the only medieval merchant's house in Conwy to have survived the centuries of turbulence, fire and pillage in this frontier town. Furnished rooms and an audio-visual presentation show daily life in the house at different periods in its history.

Times ✳ Open 31 Mar-4 Nov, Wed-Mon 11-5. (Last admission 30 mins before closing). **Facilities** ℗ (100yds & 0.5m) shop ⊗ (ex assist dogs) ⅍

Conwy Castle

LL32 8AY

➲ *(via A55 or B5106)*

☎ 01492 592358

web: www.cadw.wales.gov.uk

The castle is a magnificent fortress, built 1283-7 by Edward I. There is an exhibition on castle chapels on the ground floor of the Chapel Tower. The castle forms part of the same defensive system as the extensive town walls, which are among the most complete in Europe.

Times Open Apr-Oct, daily 9-5; Nov-Mar, Mon-Sat 9.30-4, Sun 11-4. **Fee** ✳ £4.70 (ch 5-15, concessions £4.20, disabled visitors & assisting companion free). Joint ticket for both monuments £7 (ch 5-15 & concessions £6, disabled visitors & assisting companion free). Group rates available. Prices quoted apply until 31 Mar 2009. **Facilities** ℗ shop ⊗ ⊕ ▬

Conwy Suspension Bridge

LL32 8LD

➲ *(adjacent to Conwy Castle)*

☎ 01492 573282

e-mail: kenneth.grover@nationaltrust.org.uk

Designed by Thomas Telford, one of the greatest engineers of the late 18th and early 19th century, this was the first bridge to span the river at Conwy. The bridge has been restored and the toll house furnished as it would have been a century ago.

Times ✳ Open daily 31 Mar-4 Nov, 10-5 **Facilities** ℗ 100 yds ⅋ (Partly accessible) ⅍

Plas Mawr

High St LL32 8DE

☎ 01492 580167

web: www.cadw.wales.gov.uk

Plas Mawr is an excellent example of an Elizabethan townhouse. Built by Robert Wynn between 1576 and 1585, the interior remains almost unaltered and displays decorated plaster ceilings and wooden screens.

Times Open Apr-Sep, Tue-Sun 9.30-5; Oct, Tue-Sun 9.30-4. The monument will be closed on Mon (except BHs) between Apr-Oct. **Fee** ✳ £5.10 (ch 5-15, concessions £4.70, disabled visitors & assisting companion free). Family (2ad+all ch/grandch under 16) £15. Joint ticket for both monuments £7 (ch 5-15, concessions £6, disabled visitors & assisting companion free). Family (2ad+all ch/grandch under 16) £22. **Facilities** shop ⊕ ▬

Smallest House
2 for 1

The Quay LL32 8BB

➲ *(leave A55 at Conwy sign, through town, at bottom of High St for the quay, turn left)*

☎ 01492 593484

The *Guinness Book of Records* lists this as the smallest house in Britain. Just 6ft wide by 10ft high, it is furnished in the style of a mid-Victorian Welsh cottage.

Times Open Apr-May & Oct 10-5; Jul-Sep 10-6. **Fee** £1 (ch under 16 50p, under 5 free). **Facilities** ℗ (100yds) ⅋ (access to ground floor only) shop

DOLWYDDELAN

MAP 06 SH75

Dolwyddelan Castle

LL25 0EJ

➲ *(on A470 Blaenau Ffestiniog to Betws-y-Coed)*

☎ 01690 750366

web: www.cadw.wales.gov.uk

The castle is reputed to be the birthplace of Llywelyn the Great. It was captured in 1283 by Edward I, who immediately began strengthening it for his own purposes. A restored keep of around 1200, and a 13th-century curtain wall can be seen. An exhibition on the castles of the Welsh Princes is located in the keep.

Times Open Apr-Sep, Mon-Sat 10-5 & Sun 11.30-4; Oct-Mar, Mon-Sat 10-4, Sun 11.30-4. On some occasions the site may be open but unstaffed with no admission charge. **Fee** ✳ £2.70 (ch 5-15, concessions £2.30, disabled visitors & assisting companion free). Family ticket (2ad+all ch/grandch under 16) £7.70. Group rates available. Prices quoted apply until 31 Mar 2009. **Facilities** ℗ ⊗ ⊕ ▬

LLANDUDNO

MAP 06 SH78

Great Orme Bronze Age Copper Mines

Pyliau Rd, Great Orme LL30 2XG

➲ *(Follow 'copper mine' signs from Llandudno Promenade)*

☎ 01492 870447

e-mail: gomines@greatorme.freeserve.co.uk

web: www.greatormemines.info

Browse in the visitor centre with a model of a Bronze Age village depicting life in Bronze Age times. Take a look at some original 4,000 year old Bronze Age artefacts and a selection of Bronze Age mining tools. After watching two short films take a helmet and make your way down to the mines. Walking through the tunnels and looking into some of the smaller tunnels gives you a feel for the conditions our prehistoric ancestors faced in their search for valuable copper ores. Excavation on the surface will continue for decades and one of the team is usually available to answer visitor's questions as they walk around the site and view the prehistoric landscape being uncovered.

Times Open mid Mar-end Oct, daily 10-5. **Fee** ✷ £6 (ch £4, under 5's free). Family ticket (2ad+2ch) £16, extra child £3. **Facilities** ❷ ⌂ ⏚ (outdoor) ♿ (no wheelchair access to underground mine) (paved walkways and ramps) toilets for disabled shop ➡

LLANDUDNO JUNCTION   MAP 06 SH77

RSPB Nature Reserve Conwy

LL31 9XZ

➲ (signed from junct 18 of A55)

☎ 01492 584091

e-mail: conwy@rspb.org.uk

web: www.rspb.org.uk

Explore the quiet nature trails, get close up experience with birds and other wildlife, or enjoy a leisurely cup of coffee or lunch while drinking in the magnificent views of Conwy Castle and Snowdonia. Lots of activities to keep children happy and lots to interest big kids too.

Times Open all year, daily, 9.30-5. **Fee** £2.50 (ch £1, concessions £1.50). Family £5 **Facilities** ❷ ⌂ ⏚ (outdoor) ♿ (free use of wheelchair) toilets for disabled shop ⊗ (ex assist dogs) ➡

LLANRWST   MAP 06 SH86

Gwydyr Uchaf Chapel   FREE

➲ (0.5m SW off B5106)

☎ 01492 640578

web: www.cadw.wales.gov.uk

Built in the 17th century by Sir John Wynn of Gwydir Castle, the chapel is noted for its painted ceiling and wonderfully varied woodwork.

Times Open any reasonable time. **Facilities** ❷ ⊗ 🚽 ⊕

PENMACHNO   MAP 06 SH75

Ty Mawr Wybrnant

LL25 0HJ

➲ (From A5 3m S of Betws-y-Coed take B4406 to Penmachno. House is 2.5m NW of Penmachno by forest road)

☎ 01690 760213

e-mail: tymawrwybrnant@nationaltrust.org.uk

web: www.nationaltrust.org.uk

Situated in the beautiful, secluded Wybrnant Valley, Ty Mawr was the birthplace of Bishop William Morgan (1545-1604), the first translator of the Bible into Welsh. The house has been restored to give an idea of its 16th-17th century appearance. The Wybrnant Nature Trail, a short walk, covers approximately one mile.

Times ✷ Open 5 Apr-28 Oct, Thu-Sun & BH Mon 12-5; Oct, Thu, Fri & Sun 12-4. (Last admission 30 mins before closing). **Facilities** ❷ ⊗ (ex in grounds) 🐾

TAL-Y-CAFN   MAP 06 SH77

Bodnant Garden

LL28 5RE

➲ (8m S of Llandudno & Colwyn Bay off A470. Signposted from the A55 exit at J19)

☎ 01492 650460

e-mail: ann.smith@nationaltrust.org.uk

web: www.bodnant-garden.co.uk

Set above the River Conwy with beautiful views over Snowdonia, this garden is a delight. Five Italian style terraces were constructed below the house - on the lowest terrace is a canal pool with an open-air yew hedge stage and a reconstructed Pin Mill. The garden is renowned for its collections of magnolias, camellias, rhododendrons and azaleas and the famous Laburnum Arch. The colourful displays in summer and autumn are a spectacular sight. Contact for details of events programme.

Times Open 28 Feb-1 Nov, daily 10-5 (last admission 4.30), 2-15 Nov, daily 10-4 (last admission 3.30). **Fee** With voluntary donation included: £7.50 (ch £3.75) Party of 15+ £6. NT & RHS members free. **Facilities** ❷ ⌂ ♿ (Garden is steep in places with many steps and is not easily accessible for wheelchairs) (ramps to gardens, wheelchairs & Braille guides) toilets for disabled shop garden centre ⊗ (ex assist dogs) 🐾 ➡

TREFRIW   MAP 06 SH76

Trefriw Woollen Mills   FREE

Main Rd LL27 0NQ

➲ (on B5106 in centre of Trefriw, 5m N of Betws-y-Coed)

☎ 01492 640462

e-mail: info@t-w-m.co.uk

web: www.t-w-m.co.uk

Established in 1859, the mill is situated beside the fast-flowing Afon Crafnant, which drives two hydro-electric turbines to power the looms. All the machinery of woollen manufacture can be seen here: blending, carding, spinning, dyeing, warping and weaving. In the Weaver's Garden, there are plants traditionally used in the textile industry, mainly for dyeing. Hand-spinning demonstrations are given. 2009 is the 150th anniversary of the mill.

Times Mill Museum open Etr-Sep, Mon-Fri 10-1 & 2-5 (ex BH's). Weaving demonstrations & turbine house: open all year (ex Xmas), Mon-Fri 10-1 & 2-5. Handspinning & weaver's garden Jun-Sep Tue-Thu. (Shop open all year ex 25-26 Dec & 1 Jan) **Facilities** ℗ (35yds) ⌂ ♿ (access limited to ground floor of Mill, stairs to top 2 floors) (ramp access to shop, cafe, weaving & turbine house) shop ⊗ (ex assist dogs) ➡

WALES

DENBIGHSHIRE

BODELWYDDAN
MAP 06 SJ07

Bodelwyddan Castle

LL18 5YA

➲ *(just off A55, near St Asaph, follow brown signs)*

☎ 01745 584060

e-mail: enquiries@bodelwyddan-castle.co.uk

web: www.bodelwyddan-castle.co.uk

Bodelwyddan Castle houses over 100 portraits from the National Portrait Gallery's 19th-century collection. The portraits hang in beautifully refurbished rooms and are complemented by sculpture and period furnishings. Interactive displays show how portraits were produced and used in the Victorian era. The Castle Gallery hosts a programme of temporary exhibitions and events. The castle is set within 200 acres of parkland, including formal gardens, an aviary, woodlands, a butterfly glade and an adventure playground. Lots of events, contact the castle for details. 21st Birthday - 13th July 2009.

Times Open Apr-Oct 10.30-5.30 (closed Fri), Aug open daily 10.30-5, Nov-Dec Thu 10-30-5, Sat-Sun 10.30-4. **Fee** ✶ £5 (ch 5-16 £2,ch under 4 free, concessions £4.50). Family ticket (4 people) £12. **Facilities** ❷ ⬛ ⑩ 🚻 ♿ (Partly accessible) (lift to first floor, Braille & audio guides) toilets for disabled shop ⊗ (ex assist dogs) ▬

CORWEN
MAP 06 SJ04

Ewe-Phoria Sheepdog Centre

Glanrafon, Llangwm LL21 0PE

➲ *(off A5 to Llangwm, follow signs)*

☎ 01490 460369

e-mail: info@adventure-mountain.co.uk

web: www.ewe-phoria.co.uk

Ewe-Phoria is an Agri-Theatre and Sheepdog Centre that details the life and work of the shepherd on a traditional Welsh farm. The Agri-Theatre has unusual living displays of sheep with accompanying lectures on their history and breed, while outside sheepdog handlers put their dogs through their paces. Try your hand at quad biking and off-road rally karting on Adventure Mountain.

Times Open Etr-end Oct, Wed-Fri & Sun. Closed Sat & Mon ex BHs
Facilities ❷ ⬛ ⑩ 🚻 ♿ toilets for disabled shop ⊗ (ex assist dogs) ▬

Rug Chapel

Rug LL21 9BT

☎ 01490 412025

web: www.cadw.wales.gov.uk

Rug Chapel was built in 1637 for Colonel William Salusbury, famous Civil War defender of Denbigh Castle. A rare, little altered example of a 17th-century private chapel, it reflects the Colonel's High Church religious views. Prettily set in a wooded landscape, the chapel's modest exterior gives little hint of the interior where local artists and carvers were given a free reign, with some spectacular results.

Times Open Apr-Sep, Wed-Sun 10-5. Access to Llangar is arranged Wed-Sun, 1-2.30 through Custodian at Rug Chapel, telephone 01490 412025 for details. Both monuments closed Mon & Tue (ex BH wknds) between Apr-Sep & are closed at all other times. **Fee** ✶ £3.70 (ch 5-15, concessions £3.30, disabled visitors & assisting companion free). Family ticket (2ad+all ch/grandch under 16) £10.70. Group rates available. Prices quoted apply until 31 Mar 2009. **Facilities** ❷ shop ⊗ ⬦ ▬

DENBIGH
MAP 06 SJ06

Denbigh Castle

➲ *(via A525, A543 & B5382)*

☎ 01745 813385

web: www.cadw.wales.gov.uk

The castle was begun by Henry de Lacy in 1282 and has an inspiring and impressive gatehouse, with a trio of towers and a superb archway, which is surmounted by a figure believed to be that of Edward I.

Times Open Apr-Oct, 10-5. (Monument open and unstaffed with no admission charge usually between 10-4 at all other times). **Fee** ✶ £3.10 (ch 5-15, concessions £2.70, disabled visitors & assisting companion free). Family ticket (2ad+all ch/grandch under 16) £8.90. Group rates available. Prices quoted apply until 31 Mar 2009. **Facilities** ❷ shop ⊗ ⬦ ▬

LLANGOLLEN
MAP 07 SJ24

Horse Drawn Boats Centre

The Wharf, Wharf Hill LL20 8TA

➲ *(A5 onto Llangollen High St, across river bridge to T-junct. Wharf opposite, up the hill)*

☎ 01978 860702 & 01691 690322

e-mail: bill@horsedrawnboats.co.uk

web: www.horsedrawnboats.co.uk

Take a horsedrawn boat trip along the beautiful Vale of Llangollen. Visit the canal museum, inside the motor museum, approx one mile along the towpath from the wharf, which illustrates the heyday of canals in Britain. The displays include working and static models, photographs, murals and slides. There is also a narrowboat trip that crosses Pontcysyllte Aqueduct, the largest navigable aqueduct in the world. Full bar on board, commentary throughout. Tea room serving light meals and breakfast.

Times Open Etr-end Oct, daily, 9.30-5; Tea room Nov-Mar, wknds 10-4.30.
Fee ✳ Horse Drawn Boat Trip from £5 (ch £2.50). Family £12.50 Aquaduct Trip £10 (ch £8). **Facilities** ℗ (400yds) ♿ (no access to motor boat) (alighting/pick-up point available) toilets for disabled shop ⊗ (ex assist dogs) ➡

Llangollen Railway

2 for 1

Abbey Rd LL20 8SN

➲ *(Llangollen Station - off A5 at Llangollen traffic lights onto A539, cross river bridge. Station on left at T-junct. Carrog Station - from A5 at Llidiart-y-Parc take B5437, station on right downhill after crossing railway bridge)*

☎ 01978 860979 & 860951(timetable)
e-mail: llangollen-railway@btinternet
web: www.llangollen-railway.co.uk

Heritage Railway featuring steam and classic diesel services along the picturesque Dee Valley. The journey consists of a 15-mile roundtrip between Llangollen and Carrog. A special coach for the disabled is available on all services. Please contact for more information.

Times Open: Services most wknds, daily services Apr-Oct, principally steam hauled. (Refer to timetable for diesel hauled services and off peak) **Fee** ✳ Return fare for full journey £9 (ch £4.50). Family £20 (2ad+2ch). Special fares apply for events. **Facilities** ℗ (400yds) (free parking at Carrog Station) ♿ (outdoor) ♿ (special coach for disabled on all trains) toilets for disabled shop ➡

Plas Newydd

Hill St LL20 8AW

➲ *(follow brown heritage signs from A5)*

☎ 01978 861314
e-mail: rose.mcmahon@denbighshire.gov.uk

The 'Ladies of Llangollen', Lady Eleanor Butler and Sarah Ponsonby, lived here from 1780 to 1831. The original stained-glass windows, carved panels, and domestic miscellany of two lives are exhibited along with prints, pictures and letters.

Times Open Etr-Oct, daily, 10-5. **Facilities** ℗ ♿ (outdoor) ♿ (Partly accessible) (virtual, signed & touch tours) toilets for disabled shop ⊗ (ex assist dogs or in grounds) ➡

Valle Crucis Abbey

LL29 8DD

➲ *(on B5103, off A5 W of Llangollen)*

☎ 01978 860326
web: www.cadw.wales.gov.uk

Set in a deep, narrow valley, the abbey was founded for the Cistercians in 1201 by Madog ap Gruffydd. Substantial remains of the church can be seen, and some beautifully carved grave slabs have been found. There is a small exhibition on the Cistercian monks and the abbey.

Times Open Apr-Sep, daily 10-5. Monument open and unstaffed with no admission charge at all other times between 10-4. **Fee** ✳ £2.70 (ch 5-15, concessions £2.30, disabled visitors & assisting companion free). Family ticket (2ad and all ch/grandch under 16) £7.70. Group rates available. Prices quoted apply until 31 Mar 2009. **Facilities** ℗ shop ⊗ ✛ ➡

RHUDDLAN   MAP 06 SJ07

Rhuddlan Castle

LL18 5AD

☎ 01745 590777
web: www.cadw.wales.gov.uk

The castle was begun by Edward I in 1277, on a simple 'diamond' plan with round towers linked by sections of nine feet thick curtain wall. The moat was linked to a deep-water canal, allowing Edward's ships to sail from the sea right up to the castle.

Times Open Apr-Sep, daily 10-5. **Fee** ✳ £3.10 (ch 5-15, concessions £2.70, disabled visitors & assisting companion free). Family ticket (2ad+all ch/grandch under 16) £8.90. Group discounts available. Prices quoted apply until 31 Mar 2009. **Facilities** ℗ shop ⊗ ✛ ➡

FLINTSHIRE

EWLOE   MAP 07 SJ36

Ewloe Castle

FREE

➲ *(1m NW of village on B5125)*

web: www.cadw.wales.gov.uk

Standing in Ewloe Wood are the remains of Ewloe Castle. It was a native Welsh castle, and Henry II was defeated nearby in 1157. Part of the Welsh Tower in the upper ward still stands to its original height, and there is a well in the lower ward. Remnants of walls and another tower can also be seen.

Times Open at all times. **Facilities** ⊗ ✛

FLINT   MAP 07 SJ27

Flint Castle

FREE

CH6 5PH

➲ *(NE side of Flint)*

☎ 01352 733078
web: www.cadw.wales.gov.uk

The castle was started by Edward I in 1277 and overlooks the River Dee. It is exceptional for its great tower, or Donjon, which is separated by a moat. Other buildings would have stood in the inner bailey, of which parts of the walls and corner towers remain.

Times Open at all times. **Facilities** ℗ ⊗ ✛

WALES

HOLYWELL — MAP 07 SJ17

Basingwerk Abbey — FREE

Greenfield Valley Heritage Pk, Greenfield CH8 7GH

➲ *(just S of A458)*

☎ 01352 714172

web: www.cadw.wales.gov.uk

The abbey was founded around 1131 by Ranulf de Gernon, Earl of Chester. The first stone church dates from the beginning of the 13th century. The last abbot surrendered the house to the crown in 1536. The Abbey is close to the Heritage Park Visitor Centre and access to the Museum and Farm Complex at Greenfield Valley.

Times Open all year, daily 9-6. **Facilities** ❷ ⏁⏁ ᗴ ᕼ (disabled facilities in Heritage Park) toilets for disabled shop ⊗ ⏁

GWYNEDD

BANGOR — MAP 06 SH57

Penrhyn Castle

LL57 4HN

➲ *(1m E of Bangor, off A5122 at Llandegai)*

☎ 01248 353084

e-mail: penrhyncastle@nationaltrust.org.uk

web: www.nationaltrust.org.uk

A massive 19th-century castle built on the profits of Jamaican sugar and Welsh slate, crammed with fascinating artefacts such as a one-ton slate bed made for Queen Victoria and a grand staircase that took ten years to build. Also houses a doll museum, two railway museums and one of the finest collections of Old Master paintings in Wales. Regular programme of events throughout the season.

Times Open 19 Mar-2 Nov, daily (ex Tue) Castle 12-5. Grounds and stableblock exhibitions 11-5 (Jul & Aug 10-5). (Last admission 4.30). Last audio tour 4. **Fee** ✳ All inclusive ticket: £9 (ch £4.50). Family ticket £22.50. Party 15+ £7.50 each. Grounds & stableblock only £5.60 (ch £2.80). **Facilities** ❷ ⏁⏁ᕼᗴ licensed ᕼ (outdoor) ᗴ (Partly accessible) (wheelchairs & golf buggies pre bookable) toilets for disabled shop ⨂

BEDDGELERT — MAP 06 SH54

Sygun Copper Mine — 2 for 1

LL55 4NE

➲ *(1m E of Beddgelert on A498)*

☎ 01766 890595 & 510101

e-mail: sygunmine@hotmail.com

web: www.syguncoppermine.co.uk

Spectacular audio-visual underground experience where visitors can explore the workings of this 19th-century coppermine and see the magnificent stalactite and stalagmite formations. Other activities include archery, panning for gold, metal detecting and coin making. Marvel at the fantastic coin collection from Julius Caesar to Queen Elizabeth II, and visit the Time-Line Museum with Bronze Age and Roman artefacts.

Sygun Copper Mine

Times Open Mar-end Oct 9.30-5. Feb half term, 10-4 **Fee** ✳ £7.99 (ch £5.99, pen £6.99). Family £26 **Facilities** ❷ ⏁⏁ᕼ (outdoor) ᗴ (gift shop, cafe & museum accessible for wheelchairs) shop ⊟

BLAENAU FFESTINIOG — MAP 06 SH74

Llechwedd Slate Caverns

LL41 3NB

➲ *(beside A470, 1m from Blaenau Ffestiniog)*

☎ 01766 830306

e-mail: quarrytours@aol.com

web: www.llechwedd-slate-caverns.co.uk

The Miners' Underground Tramway carries visitors into areas where early conditions have been recreated, while the Deep Mine is reached by an incline railway and has an unusual audio-visual presentation. Free surface attractions include several exhibitions and museums, slate mill and the Victorian village which has Victorian shops, bank, Miners Arms pub, lock-up and working smithy.

Times Open all year, daily from 10. (Last tour 5.15, Oct-Feb 4.15). Closed 25-26 Dec & 1 Jan **Fee** Single Tour £9.25 (ch £7, pen £7.75). Both tours £14.75 (ch £11.25, pen £12.50). Reductions for groups of 15+ **Facilities** ❷ ⏁⏁ᕼ (outdoor) ᗴ (access to underground mine tours via steps) toilets for disabled shop ⊗ (ex on surface) ⊟

CAERNARFON — MAP 06 SH46

Caernarfon Castle

LL55 2AY

☎ 01286 677617

web: www.cadw.wales.gov.uk

Edward I began building the castle and extensive town walls in 1283 after defeating the last independent ruler of Wales. Completed in 1328, it has unusual polygonal towers, notably the 10-sided Eagle Tower. There is a theory that these features were copied from the walls of Constantinople, to reflect a tradition that Constantine was born nearby. Edward I's son and heir was born and presented to the Welsh people here, setting a precedent that was followed in 1969, when Prince Charles was invested as Prince of Wales.

Times Open Apr-Oct, daily 9-5; Nov-Mar, Mon-Sat 9.30-4, Sun 11-4. **Fee** ✳ £5.10 (ch 5-15, pen & students £4.70, disabled visitors & assisting compainion free). Family ticket (2 ad & all ch/grandch under 16) £15. Group rates available. Prices quoted apply until 31 Mar 2009. **Facilities** Ⓟ shop ⊗ ⊕ ▬

Segontium Roman Museum ▐FREE▌

Beddgelert Rd LL55 2LN

➲ *(on A4085 to Beddgelert approx 1m from Caernarfon)*

☎ 01286 675625

e-mail: info@segontium.org.uk

web: www.segontium.org.uk

Segontium Roman Museum tells the story of the conquest and occupation of Wales by the Romans and displays the finds from the auxiliary fort of Segontium, one of the most famous in Britain. You can combine a visit to the museum with exploration of the site of the Roman Fort, which is in the care of Cadw: Welsh Historic Monuments. The exciting discoveries displayed at the museum vividly portray the daily life of the soldiers stationed in this most westerly outpost of the Roman Empire.

Times Open all year Tue-Sun 12.30-4. Closed Mon except BH **Facilities** Ⓟ shop ⊗ (ex assist dogs) ▬

Welsh Highland Railway

St. Helen's Rd LL55 2YD

➲ *(SW of Caernarfon Castle beside harbour. Follow brown signs)*

☎ 01286 677018 & 01766 516000

e-mail: enquiries@festrail.co.uk

web: www.festrail.co.uk

The Welsh Highland Railway is Snowdonia's newest narrow gauge railway. Running between Caernarfon and Rhyd Ddu, at the foot of Snowdon, passengers enjoy the spectacular scenery of Snowdonia from comfortable heated carriages, which provide an ideal form of transport into the Snowdonia National Park. The final extension of the line opens in 2009, providing a service stretching 40 miles, through Beddgelert and the Aberglaslyn Pass, to meet the Ffestiniog Railway at Porthmadog.

Times Open Etr-end Oct, limited service in Winter **Fee** ✳ £17.50 (1 ch under 16 free, concessions £15.75) - Caernarfon-Rhyd Ddu. **Facilities** Ⓟ (charged) ఈ (most main service trains accessible) (ramps, Braille & large print guides) toilets for disabled shop ⊗ (ex in 3rd class) ▬

CRICCIETH   MAP 06 SH43

Criccieth Castle

LL52 0DP

➲ *(off A497)*

☎ 01766 522227

web: www.cadw.wales.gov.uk

The castle dates from the 13th century and was taken and destroyed by Owain Glyndwr in 1404. Evidence of a fierce fire can still be seen. The gatehouse leading to the inner ward remains impressive, and parts of the walls are well preserved.

Times Open Apr-Oct, daily 10-5; Nov-Mar, Fri & Sat 9.30-4, Sun 11-4 (Monument open and unstaffed with no admission charge between 10-4 at all other times) **Fee** ✳ £3.10 (ch 5-15, concessions £2.70, disabled visitors & assisting companion free). Family ticket (2ad+all ch/grandch under 16) £8.90. Group rates available. Prices quoted apply until 31 Mar 2009. **Facilities** Ⓟ shop ⊗ ⊕ ▬

CYMER ABBEY   MAP 06 SH71

Cymer Abbey ▐FREE▌

➲ *(2m NW of Dolgellau on A494)*

☎ 01341 422854

web: www.cadw.wales.gov.uk

The abbey was built for the Cistercians in the 13th century. It was never very large, and does not seem to have been finished. The church is the best-preserved building, with ranges of windows and arcades still to be seen. The other buildings have been plundered for stone, but low outlines remain.

Times Open all year, early Apr-Oct, daily 9.30-6; Nov-Mar, daily 9.30-4. Closed 24-26 Dec & 1 Jan **Facilities** Ⓟ ⊗ ⊕ ▬

FAIRBOURNE   MAP 06 SH61

Fairbourne Railway

Beach Rd LL38 2EX

➲ *(on A493 follow signs for Fairbourne, main terminus is just past level crossing on left)*

☎ 01341 250362

web: www.fairbournerailway.com

One of the most unusual of Wales's 'little trains'; built in 1890 as a horse-drawn railway to carry building materials it was later converted to steam, and now covers two-and-a-half miles. Its route passes one of the loveliest beaches in Wales, with views of the beautiful Mawddach Estuary.

Times Open Feb half term (ex Fri). Apr-23 Sep (closed most Fri ex late Jul & all of Aug). Oct wknds & 20-28 Oct (ex Fri). **Fee** ✳ Return £7.20 (ch £4, pen £5.80). Family £18 (2ad+3ch) **Facilities** Ⓟ 30m ☐ ఈ (wheelchairs available upon request) toilets for disabled shop ▬

WALES

GROESLON MAP 06 SH45

Inigo Jones Slateworks `2 for 1`

LL54 7UE

⮑ *(on A487, 6m S of Caernarfon towards Porthmadog)*

☎ 01286 830242

e-mail: slate@inigojones.co.uk

web: www.inigojones.co.uk

Inigo Jones was established in 1861 primarily to make school writing slates. Today the company uses the same material to make architectural, monumental and craft products. A self-guided audio/video tour takes visitors round the slate workshops, and displays the various processes used in the extraction and working of Welsh slate. **Times** Open all year, daily 9-5. (Closed 25-26 Dec & 1 Jan.) **Fee** ✳ £4.50 (ch & concessions £4). **Facilities** ❷ ⌨️☂ shop ⊗ (ex assist dogs) ▬

HARLECH MAP 06 SH53

Harlech Castle

LL46 2YH

⮑ *(from A496)*

☎ 01766 780552

web: www.cadw.wales.gov.uk

Harlech Castle was built in 1283-89 by Edward I, with a sheer drop to the sea on one side. Owain Glyndwr starved the castle into submission in 1404 and made it his court and campaigning base. Later, the defence of the castle in the Wars of the Roses inspired the song *Men of Harlech*. Today the sea has slipped away, and the castle's great walls and round towers stand above the dunes. **Times** Open Apr-Oct, daily 9-5; Nov-Mar, Mon-Sat 9.30-4, Sun 11-4. **Fee** ✳ £3.70 (ch 5-15, concessions £3.30, disabled visitors & assisting companion free). Family ticket (2ad+all ch/grandch under 16) £10.70. Group rates available. Prices quoted apply until 31 Mar 2009. **Facilities** ❷ shop ⊗ ⊕ ▬

LLANBERIS MAP 06 SH56

Dolbadarn Castle `FREE`

LL55 4UD

⮑ (A4086)

web: www.cadw.wales.gov.uk

Built by Llywelyn the Great in the early 13th century, this Welsh castle overlooks Llyn Padarn in the Llanberis Pass. **Times** Open any reasonable time. **Facilities** ❷ ⊗ ⊕ ▬

Llanberis Lake Railway

Padarn Country Park LL55 4TY

⮑ *(off A4086 at Llanberis)*

☎ 01286 870549

e-mail: info@lake-railway.co.uk

web: www.lake-railway.co.uk

Starting near the foot of Snowdon, these vintage narrow-gauge steam trains, dating from 1899 to 1922, take you on a five mile return journey along the shore of Lake Padarn, following the route of the old slate railway. Passengers are treated to spectacular views of Snowdon and nearby mountains. The main station is adjacent to the Welsh Slate Museum in Padarn Country Park. There are Santa Train weekends in December, and an Easter Egg Hunt on Easter weekend, please telephone for details of these and other events. **Times** Open mid Mar-end Oct, Sun-Fri, 11-4 (Sat in Jun-Aug); Nov-mid Mar limited dates, send for free timetable or check the website. **Fee** £6.80 (ch £4.50). Family ticket (2ad+2ch) £19. Reduced rates for groups. **Facilities** ❷ (charged) ⌨️☂ (outdoor) ♿ (disabled carriage available) toilets for disabled shop ▬

Snowdon Mountain Railway

LL55 4TY

⮑ *(on A4086, Caernarfon to Capel Curig road. 7.5m from Caernarfon)*

☎ 0870 4580033

e-mail: info@snowdonrailway.co.uk

web: www.snowdonrailway.co.uk

The journey of just over four-and-a-half miles takes passengers more than 3,000ft up to the summit of Snowdon; breathtaking views include, on a clear day, the Isle of Man and the Wicklow Mountains in Ireland. The round trip to the summit and back takes two and a half hours including a half hour at the summit. **Times** Open daily mid Mar-Oct, (weather permitting). **Fee** ✳ Return £21 (ch £14). Early bird discount on 9am train, pre-booking only. 3/4 distance return £15 (ch £11). **Facilities** ❷ (charged) ⌨️☂ (outdoor) ♿ (some carriages suitable for wheelchairs - must notify) toilets for disabled shop ⊗ (ex assist dogs) ▬

Welsh Slate Museum

Gilfach Ddu, Padarn Country Park LL55 4TY

⮑ *(0.25m off A4086. Museum within Padarn Country Park)*

☎ 01286 870630

e-mail: slate@museumwales.ac.uk

web: www.museumwales.ac.uk

Set among the towering quarries at Llanberis, the Welsh Slate Museum is a living, working site located in the original workshops of Dinorwig Quarry, which once employed 15,000 men and boys. You can see the foundry, smithy, workshops and mess room which make up the old quarry, and view original machinery, much of which is still in working order. **Times** ✳ Open Etr-Oct, daily 10-5; Nov-Etr, Sun-Fri 10-4. **Facilities** ❷ (charged) ⌨️☂♿ (all parts accessible except patten loft) toilets for disabled shop ⊗ (ex assist dogs) ▬

LLANFIHANGEL-Y-PENNANT MAP 06 SH60

Castell-y-Bere `FREE`

⮑ *(off B4405)*

☎ 029 2050 0200

web: www.cadw.wales.gov.uk

The castle was begun around 1221 by Prince Llewelyn ap Iorwerth of Gwynedd to guard the southern flank of his principality. It is typically

Welsh in design with its D-shaped towers. Although a little off the beaten track, the castle lies in a spectacular setting, overshadowed by the Cader Idris range.

Times Open all reasonable times. **Facilities** ⊗ ⊕

LLANGYBI   MAP 06 SH44

St Cybi's Well   `FREE`

⮑ *(off B4354)*

☎ 01766 810047

web: www.cadw.wales.gov.uk

Cybi was a sixth-century Cornish saint, known as a healer of the sick, and St Cybi's Well (or Ffynnon Gybi) has been famous for its curative properties through the centuries. The corbelled beehive vaulting inside the roofless stone structure is Irish in style and unique in Wales.

Times Open at all times. **Facilities** ⊗ ⊕

LLANUWCHLLYN   MAP 06 SH83

Bala Lake Railway

The Station LL23 7DD

⮑ *(off A494 Bala to Dolgellau road)*

☎ 01678 540666

web: www.bala-lake-railway.co.uk

Steam locomotives which once worked in the slate quarries of North Wales now haul passenger coaches for four-and-a-half miles from Llanuwchllyn Station along the lake to Bala. The railway has one of the few remaining double-twist lever-locking framed GWR signal boxes, installed in 1896. Some of the coaches are open and some closed, so passengers can enjoy the beautiful views of the lake and mountains in all weathers.

Times Open Etr-last wknd in Sep, daily. (Closed certain Mon & Fri, telephone for details). **Fee** ✳ £7.50 return (pen £7). Family ticket (2ad+2ch) £18. **Facilities** ❷ ⧉ 🚻 (outdoor) ♿ (Partly accessible) (wheelchairs can be taken on train) shop

---

LLANYSTUMDWY   MAP 06 SH43

Lloyd George Museum

LL52 0SH

⮑ *(on A497 between Pwllheli & Criccieth)*

☎ 01766 522071

e-mail: amgueddfeydd-museums@gwynedd.gov.uk

web: www.gwynedd.gov.uk/museums

Explore the life and times of David Lloyd George in this museum. His boyhood home is recreated as it would have been when he lived there between 1864 and 1880, along with his Uncle Lloyd's shoemaking workshop.

Times ✳ Open Etr, daily 10.30-5; Apr-May, Mon-Fri 10.30-5 (open Sat in Jun); Jul-Sep daily 10.30-5; Oct, Mon-Fri 11-4. Open BHs; Other times by appointment, telephone 01286 679098 for details. **Facilities** ❷ 🚻 (outdoor) ♿ (induction loop in audio visual theatre, shop & cottage) toilets for disabled shop ⊗ (ex assist dogs) ▬

PENARTH FAWR   MAP 06 SH43

Penarth Fawr   `FREE`

⮑ *(3.5m NE of Pwllheli off A497)*

☎ 01766 810880

web: www.cadw.wales.gov.uk

The hall, buttery and screen are preserved in this house which was probably built in the 15th century.

Times Open at all times. **Facilities** ⊗ ⊕

PLAS-YN-RHIW   MAP 06 SH22

Plas-yn-Rhiw

LL53 8AB

⮑ *(12m from Pwllheli signed from B4413 to Aberdaron)*

☎ 01758 780219

e-mail: plasynrhiw@nationaltrust.org.uk

web: www.nationaltrust.org.uk

This is a small manor house, part medieval, with Tudor and Georgian additions. The ornamental gardens have flowering trees and shrubs including sub-tropical specimens, divided by box hedges and grass paths. There is a stream and waterfall, which descends from the snowdrop wood behind.

Times ✳ Open Apr-29 May, Thu-Mon, 12-5. 31 May-Sep, Wed-Mon, 12-5. 1-22 Oct, Sat-Sun, 12-4. 23-29 Oct, daily, 12-4. **Facilities** ❷ 🚻 ♿ (Braille guides/scented plants) toilets for disabled shop ⊗ (ex assist dogs) 🛒 ♨ ▬

PORTHMADOG   MAP 06 SH53

Ffestiniog Railway

Harbour Station LL49 9NF

⮑ *(SE end of town beside the harbour, on A487)*

☎ 01766 516000

e-mail: enquiries@festrail.co.uk

web: www.festrail.co.uk

A narrow gauge steam railway running for 13.5 miles through Snowdonia National Park, with breathtaking views and superb scenery.

CONTINUED

WALES

PORTHMADOG CONTINUED

Buffet service on all trains including licensed bar (in corridor carriages). Please telephone for details of special events. The company also runs the Welsh Highland Railway Caernarfon, which will link up with the Ffestiniog Railway, the final extension of which opens in 2009.

Times Open daily late Mar–late Oct. Limited Winter service mid wk trains Nov & early Dec. Santa specials in Dec. Open Feb half term. **Fee** ✳ Full distance return £17.50 (1 ch under 16 free, concessions £15.75). Other fares available. **Facilities** ❷ (charged) ⌨ ⁍◎⁌ licensed ⻗ (outdoor) ♿ (most train services accessible, phone in advance) (wheelchair ramps, Braille and large print guides) toilets for disabled shop ⊗ (ex 3rd class) ▬

PORTMEIRION   MAP 06 SH53

Portmeirion
LL48 6ER

➲ *(off A487 at Minffordd)*

☎ 01766 770000

e-mail: info@portmeirion-village.com

web: www.portmeirion-village.com

Welsh architect Sir Clough Williams Ellis built his fairy-tale, Italianate village on a rocky, tree-clad peninsula on the shores of Cardigan Bay. A bell-tower, castle and lighthouse mingle with a watch-tower, grottoes and cobbled squares among pastel-shaded picturesque cottages let as holiday accommodation. The 60-acre Gwyllt Gardens include miles of dense woodland paths and are famous for their fine displays of rhododendrons, azaleas, hydrangeas and sub-tropical flora. There is a mile of sandy beach and a playground for children. The village is probably best known as the major location for 1960s cult TV show, *The Prisoner*.

Times Open all year, daily 9.30–5.30 **Fee** £7.50 (ch £4, concessions £6). Family ticket (2ad+2ch) £19 **Facilities** ❷ ⌨ ⁍◎⁌ licensed ⻗ (outdoor) ♿ (steep slopes and many steps make access difficult to some areas) (w/chair available, disabled parking) toilets for disabled shop ⊗ (ex assist dogs) ▬

TYWYN   MAP 06 SH50

Talyllyn Railway
Wharf Station LL36 9EY

➲ *(A493 Machynlleth to Dolgellau for Tywyn station, B4405 for Abergynolwyn)*

☎ 01654 710472

e-mail: enquiries@talyllyn.co.uk

web: www.talyllyn.co.uk

The oldest 27in-gauge railway in the world, built in 1865 to run from Tywyn on Cardigan Bay to Abergynolwyn slate mine some seven miles inland. The railway climbs the steep sides of the Fathew Valley and with stops on the way at Dolgoch Falls and the Nant Gwernol forest. The return trip takes 2.5 hours. All scheduled passenger trains are steam hauled. There is a children's play area at Abergynolwyn. Special events take place throughout the year, please contact for details.

Times Open Sun mid Feb–Mar; Apr–early Nov & 26 Dec–1 Jan daily. Ring for timetable **Fee** £12 Day Rover (ch accompanied £2, under 5 free). Intermediate fare available **Facilities** ❷ (charged) ⌨ ⻗ (outdoor) ♿ (prior notice useful, wheelchair ramps into carriages) toilets for disabled shop ▬

Y FELINHELI   MAP 06 SH56

Greenwood Forest Park
LL56 4QN

➲ *(A55 junct 11, follow Llanberis signs onto A4244, signed from next rdbt. Located between Bangor and Caernarfon)*

☎ 01248 670076

e-mail: info@greenwoodforestpark.co.uk

web: www.greenwoodforestpark.co.uk

Family adventure and forest fun, whatever the weather. Ride the eco-friendly Green Dragon Rollercoaster, zoom down the 70 metre sledge slide, scramble through Tunnel Warren - tunnels, slides, ropes and towers for the under 7s, plus the giant Jumper - the Biggest Bouncing Pillow ever. Enjoy the Jungle Boat Adventure, drive mini-tractors, shoot traditional Longbows and build dens in the woods. Tackle the challenge of the Treetop Towers and find a crocodile in the Maze, Adventure Playgrounds, Puzzle Barn and Toddlers' Village plus the indoor interactive exhibition in the Great Hall. There'll be fabulous entertainment in the Forest Theatre and try the newest ride: Moon Karts.

Times Open daily mid Mar–late Oct 10–5.30 (Sep & Oct 10–5); Feb half-term **Fee** Seasonal £6.85–£9.80 (ch £5.75–£8.95, disabled & carers 50% discount) **Facilities** ❷ ⌨ ⁍◎⁌ ⻗ (indoor & outdoor) ♿ (grounds mostly accessible, some activities may not be accessible for visitors with disabilities) (parking) toilets for disabled shop ▬

MERTHYR TYDFIL

MERTHYR TYDFIL   MAP 03 SO00

Brecon Mountain Railway
Pant Station Dowlais CF48 2UP

➲ *(follow Mountain Railway signs from A470 or A465 N of Merthyr Tydfil)*

☎ 01685 722988

web: www.breconmountainrailway.co.uk

Opened in 1980, this narrow-gauge railway follows part of an old British Rail route which closed in 1964 when the iron industry in South Wales fell into decline. The present route starts at Pant Station and continues for 3.5 miles through the beautiful scenery of the Brecon Beacons National Park, as far as Taf Fechan reservoir. The train is pulled by a vintage steam locomotive and is one of the most popular railways in Wales.

Times Opening times on application to The Brecon Mountain Railway, Pant Station, Merthyr Tydfil. **Fee** ✳ Fares are under review, please ring for details. **Facilities** ❷ ⌨ ⁍◎⁌ licensed ⻗ (indoor & outdoor) ♿ (adapted carriage) toilets for disabled shop ▬

Cyfarthfa Castle Museum & Art Gallery   `FREE`

Cyfarthfa Park CF47 8RE

➲ *(off A470, N towards Brecon, follow brown heritage signs)*

☎ 01685 723112

e-mail: museum@merthyr.gov.uk

web: www.museums.merthyr.gov.uk

Set in wooded parkland beside a beautiful lake, this imposing Gothic mansion now houses a superb museum and art gallery. Providing a fascinating glimpse into 3,000 years of history, the museum displays wonderful collections of fine art, social history and objects from around the world in a Regency setting.

Times Open Apr-Sep, daily, 10-5.30 (last admission 5); Oct-Mar, Tue-Fri 10-4, Sat-Sun 12-4. Closed between Xmas & New Year **Facilities** ❷ ⌷ 🎋 (outdoor) ♿ (stair lift & wheelchair available) toilets for disabled shop ⊗ (ex assist dogs)

MONMOUTHSHIRE

CAERWENT   MAP 03 ST49

Caerwent Roman Town   `FREE`

➲ *(just off A48)*

☎ 029 2050 0200

web: www.cadw.wales.gov.uk

A complete circuit of the town wall of 'Venta Silurum', together with excavated areas of houses, shops and a temple.

Times Open - access throughout the year. There is a facilitator on site each Tue. For group bookings Tel: (01633) 430576. **Facilities** ⊗ ۞

CALDICOT   MAP 03 ST48

Caldicot Castle & Country Park

Church Rd NP26 4HU

➲ *(M4 junct 23A onto B4245. From M48 junct 2 follow A48 & B4245. Signed from B4245)*

☎ 01291 420241

e-mail: caldicotcastle@monmouthshire.gov.uk

web: www.caldicotcastle.co.uk

Caldicot Castle's well-preserved fortifications were founded by the Normans and fully developed by the late 14th century. Restored as a family home by a wealthy Victorian, the castle offers the chance to explore medieval walls and towers in a setting of tranquil gardens and wooded country parkland, plus the opportunity to play giant chess or draughts.

Times Open Apr-Oct, daily, 11-5. **Fee** ✳ £3.75 (ch, pen, student & disabled £2.50). Family (2ad+3ch) £12. Party 10+. **Facilities** ❷ ⌷ 🎋 (outdoor) ♿ (access to courtyard) (taped tour, level trails, induction loop, access guide) toilets for disabled shop ▬

CHEPSTOW   MAP 03 ST59

Chepstow Castle

NP6 5EZ

☎ 01291 624065

web: www.cadw.wales.gov.uk

Built by William FitzOsbern, Chepstow is the first recorded Norman stone castle. It stands in a strategic spot above the Wye. The castle was strengthened in the following centuries, but was not besieged (as far as is known) until the Civil War, when it was twice lost to the Parliamentarians. The remains of the domestic rooms and the massive gatehouse with its portcullis grooves and ancient gates are still impressive, as are the walls and towers.

Times Open Apr-Oct, daily 9-5; Nov-Mar, Mon-Sat 9.30-4, Sun 11-4. **Fee** ✳ £3.70 (ch 5-15, concessions £3.30, disabled visitors and assisting companion free). Family ticket (2ad+all ch/grandch under 16) £10.70. Group rates available. Prices quoted apply until 31 Mar 2009. **Facilities** ❷ shop ⊗ ۞ ▬

GROSMONT   MAP 03 SO42

Grosmont Castle   `FREE`

➲ *(on B4347)*

☎ 01981 240301

web: www.cadw.wales.gov.uk

Grosmont is one of the 'trilateral' castles of Hubert de Burgh (see also Skenfrith and White Castle). It stands on a mound with a dry moat, and the considerable remains of its 13th-century great hall can be seen. Three towers once guarded the curtain wall, and the western one is well preserved.

Times Open - access throughout the year. **Facilities** ⊗ ۞

LLANTHONY   MAP 03 SO22

Llanthony Priory   `FREE`

☎ 029 2050 0200

web: www.cadw.wales.gov.uk

William de Lacey discovered the remains of a hermitage dedicated to St David. By 1108 a church had been consecrated on the site and just over a decade later the priory was complete. After the priory was brought to a state of siege in an uprising, Hugh de Lacey provided the funds for a new church, and it is this that makes the picturesque ruin seen today. Visitors can still make out the west towers, north nave arcade and south transept.

Times Open - access throughout the year. **Facilities** ❷ ⊗ ۞

LLANTILIO CROSSENNY   MAP 03 SO31

Hen Gwrt   `FREE`

➲ *(off B4233)*

☎ 029 2050 0200

web: www.cadw.wales.gov.uk

The rectangular enclosure of the former medieval house, still surrounded by a moat.

Times Open - access throughout the year. **Facilities** ⊗ 🚳 ۞

WALES

457

MONMOUTH **MAP 03 SO51**

The Nelson Museum & Local History Centre `FREE`

New Market Hall, Priory St NP25 3XA

➲ *(in town centre)*

☎ 01600 710630

e-mail: nelsonmuseum@monmouthshire.gov.uk

One of the world's major collections of Admiral Nelson-related items, including original letters, glass, china, silver, medals, books, models, prints and Nelson's fighting sword. The local history displays deal with Monmouth's past as a fortress market town, and include a section on the co-founder of the Rolls Royce company, Charles Stewart Rolls, who was also a pioneer balloonist, aviator and, of course, motorist.

Times Open all year, Mar-Oct Mon-Sat & BH 11-1 & 2-5, Sun 2-5. Nov-Feb Mon-Sat 11-2 & 2-4, Sun 2-4 **Facilities** ℗ (200yds) (small daily charge) ♿ (mezzanine display area accessible only by stairs - 25% of whole museum display area) toilets for disabled shop ⊗ (ex assist dogs) ▬

RAGLAN **MAP 03 SO40**

Raglan Castle

NP5 2BT

➲ *(signed off A40)*

☎ 01291 690228

web: www.cadw.wales.gov.uk

This magnificent 15th-century castle is noted for its 'Yellow Tower of Gwent'. It was built by Sir William ap Thomas and destroyed during the Civil War, after a long siege. The ruins are still impressive however, and the castle's history is illustrated in an exhibition situated in the closet tower and two rooms of the gate passage.

Times Open Apr-Oct, daily 9-5; Nov-Mar, Mon-Sat 9.30-4, Sun 11-4. **Fee** ✱ £3.10 (ch 5-15, concessions £2.70, disabled visitors & assisting companion free). Family ticket (2ad+all ch/grandch under 16 £8.90). Group discounts available. Prices quoted apply until 31 Mar 2009. **Facilities** ℗ shop ⊗ ⊕ ▬

SKENFRITH **MAP 03 SO42**

Skenfrith Castle `FREE`

➲ *(on B4521)*

☎ 029 2050 0200

web: www.cadw.wales.gov.uk

This 13th-century castle has a round keep set inside an imposing towered curtain wall. Hubert de Burgh built it as one of three 'trilateral' castles to defend the Welsh Marches.

Times Open - access throughout the year. Key keeper arrangement. **Facilities** ℗ ⊗ ⊕ ▬

TINTERN PARVA **MAP 03 SO50**

Tintern Abbey

NP6 6SE

➲ *(via A466)*

☎ 01291 689251

web: www.cadw.wales.gov.uk

The ruins of this Cistercian monastery church are still surprisingly intact. The monastery was established in 1131 and became increasingly wealthy well into the 15th century. During the Dissolution, the monastery was closed and most of the buildings were completely destroyed. During the 18th century many poets and artists came to see the ruins and recorded their impressions.

Times Open Apr-Oct, daily 9-5; Nov-Mar, Mon-Sat 9.30-4, Sun 11-4. **Fee** ✱ £3.70 (ch 5-15, concessions £3.30, disabled visitors & assisting companion free). Family ticket (2ad+all ch/grandch under 16) £10.70. Group rates available. Prices quoted apply until 31 Mar 2009. **Facilities** ℗ shop ⊗ ⊕ ▬

WHITE CASTLE **MAP 03 SO31**

White Castle

NP7 8UD

➲ *(7m NE of Abergavenny, unclass road N of B4233)*

☎ 01600 780380

web: www.cadw.wales.gov.uk

The impressive 12th to 13th-century moated stronghold was built by Hubert de Burgh to defend the Welsh Marches. Substantial remains of walls, towers and a gatehouse can be seen. This is the finest of a trio of castles, the others being at Skenfrith and Grosmont.

Times Open Apr-Sep, Wed-Sun & BH Mon 10-5. Monument open and unstaffed on Mon & Tue between Apr-Sep. Monument open and unstaffed with no admission charge at all other times between 10-4. **Fee** ✱ £2.70 (ch 5-15, concessions £2.30, disabled visitors & assisting companion free). Family ticket (2ad+all ch/grandch under 16) £7.70. Group rates available. Prices quoted apply until 31 Mar 2009. **Facilities** ℗ ⊗ ⊕ ▬

WALES

NEATH PORT TALBOT

ABERDULAIS MAP 03 SS79

Aberdulais Falls

SA10 8EU

(from M4 junct 43, take A465 signed Vale of Neath. Onto A4109, Falls next to Dulais Rock Pub)

☎ 01639 636674

e-mail: aberdulaistic@nationaltrust.org.uk

web: www.nationaltrust.org.uk

The industrial heritage of this area goes back to 1584, when copper was first manufactured. Iron smelting and corn milling followed, with a tin plate works being built around 1830. As well as powering industries for over 400 years, this magnificent waterfall inspired artist J. M. W. Turner in 1795. Today, the site houses Europe's largest electricity-generating water wheel. An exciting exhibition shows how Aberdulais Falls played an important role in the industrialisation of South Wales.

Times Open Feb-22 Mar Sat & Sun 11-4, 23 Mar-25 Oct daily incl wknds, BH & Good Fri 10-5. 30 Oct-20 Dec Fri-Sun 11-4, 21-23 Dec 11-4 **Fee** ✳ £4 (ch £2) Family ticket £10. Parties 15+ £3 (ch £1.50) **Facilities** Ⓟ (outdoor) ♿ (lifts for disabled to view falls, ramp into tearoom) toilets for disabled shop

CRYNANT MAP 03 SN70

Cefn Coed Colliery Museum

FREE

SA10 8SN

(1m S of Crynant, on A4109)

☎ 01639 750556

e-mail: colliery@btconnect.com

The museum is on the site of a former working colliery, and tells the story of mining in the Dulais Valley. A steam-winding engine has been kept and is now operated by electricity, and there is also a simulated underground mining gallery, boilerhouse, compressor house, and exhibition area. Outdoor exhibits include a stationary colliery locomotive. Exhibitions relating to the coal mining industry are held on a regular basis.

Times Open Apr-Oct, daily 10.30-5; Nov-Mar, groups welcome by prior arrangement. **Facilities** Ⓟ (outdoor) ♿ (access to exhibition areas, but not to underground gallery) toilets for disabled shop

CYNONVILLE MAP 03 SS89

South Wales Miners' Museum

Afan Forest Park SA13 3HG

(M4 junct 40 onto A4107, 6m NE of Port Talbot)

☎ 01639 850564

e-mail: aandmboast@btinternet.com

web: www.southwalesminersmuseum.co.uk

The picturesquely placed museum gives a vivid picture of mining life, with coal faces, pit gear and miners' equipment. Guided tours of the museum on request. The country park has forest walks and picnic areas, as well as a visitor centre.

Times Open all year daily, Apr-Sep 10.30-5 (Sat & Sun 10.30-6); Oct-Feb 10.30-4 (Sat & Sun 10.30-5). Closed Xmas week. **Facilities** Ⓟ (charged) (outdoor) ♿ (mechanical & manual wheelchairs on request) toilets for disabled shop (ex assist dogs)

NEATH MAP 03 SS79

Gnoll Estate Country Park

SA11 3BS

(follow brown heritage signs from town centre)

☎ 01639 635808

e-mail: e.ford@npt.gov.uk

web: www.neath-porttalbot.gov.uk

The extensively landscaped Gnoll Estate offers tranquil woodland walks, picnic areas, stunning views, children's play areas, adventure playground, 9-hole golf course, and coarse fishing. Varied programme of events and school holiday activities.

Times Open all year. Vistor centre: daily from 10. Closed 24 Dec-2 Jan **Fee** ✳ Pitch & Putt closed for repairs until Etr 2009. Fishing permit £7 (ch £2). **Facilities** Ⓟ (outdoor) ♿ (wheelchair & scooter for hire, designated parking) toilets for disabled shop (ex assist dogs)

Neath Abbey

FREE

SA10 7DW

(1m W off A465)

☎ 01639 812387

web: www.cadw.wales.gov.uk

These ruins were originally a Cistercian abbey founded in 1130 by Richard de Grainville.

Times Open at all times. Key keeper arrangement. **Facilities** Ⓟ

WALES

WALES

NEWPORT

CAERLEON
MAP 03 ST39

Caerleon Roman Baths
NP6 1AE

➲ (on B4236)

☎ 01663 422518

web: www.cadw.wales.gov.uk

Caerleon was an important Roman military base, with accommodation for thousands of men. The foundations of barrack lines and parts of the ramparts can be seen, with remains of the cookhouse, latrines and baths. The amphitheatre nearby is one of the best examples in Britain.

Times Open Apr-Oct, daily 9.30-5; Nov-Mar, Mon-Sat, 9.30-5, Sun 11-4. **Fee** ✳ £3.10 (ch 5-15, concessions £2.70, disabled visitors & assisting companion free). Family ticket (2ad+all ch/grandch under 16) £8.90. Group rates available. Prices quoted apply until 31 Mar 2009. **Facilities** ❷ shop ⊗ ⊕ ▬

National Roman Legion Museum FREE
High St NP18 1AE

➲ (close to Newport, 20 min from M4, follow signs from Cardiff & Bristol)

☎ 01633 423134

e-mail: roman@museumwales.ac.uk

web: www.museumwales.ac.uk

The museum illustrates the history of Roman Caerleon and the daily life of its garrison. On display are arms, armour and equipment, with a collection of engraved gemstones, a labyrinth mosaic and finds from the legionary base at Usk. Please telephone for details of children's holiday activities.

Times Open all year: Mon-Sat 10-5, Sun 2-5. **Facilities** ℗ (100yds) ♿ toilets for disabled shop ⊗ (ex assist dogs) ▬

NEWPORT
MAP 03 ST38

Tredegar House & Park
NP10 8YW

➲ (2m W of Newport, signed from A48 & M4 junct 28)

☎ 01633 815880

e-mail: tredegar.house@newport.gov.uk

web: www.newport.gov.uk

Tredegar House is a magnificent 17th-century country house, which was the ancestral home of the Morgan family for 500 years. Parts of the house date back to medieval times, but most of it was built between 1664 and 1672. The house is set in 90 acres of landscaped park, and feature formal gardens, self-guided trails and craft workshops.

Times Open Etr-late Sep, Wed-Sun 11-4. **Facilities** ❷ (charged) ⌷ ⦿ ㋡ (outdoor) ♿ (wheelchairs for loan, 1st floor not accessible) toilets for disabled shop ⊗ (ex assist dogs & in park) ▬

PEMBROKESHIRE

AMROTH
MAP 02 SN10

Colby Woodland Garden
SA67 8PP

➲ (1.5m inland from Amroth beside Carmarthen Bay, follow brown signs from A477 Tenby-Carmarthen road, or off coast road at Amroth Castle Caravan Park)

☎ 01834 811885

e-mail: colby@nationaltrust.org.uk

web: www.nationaltrust.org.uk

From early spring to the end of June the garden is a blaze of colour, from the masses of daffodils to the rich hues of rhododendrons, azaleas and bluebells. Followed by hydrangeas in shaded walks through summer to glorious shades of autumn.

Times Open 15 Mar-2 Nov, daily 10-5. **Fee** ✳ £4.20 (ch £2.10). Family ticket £10.50. Group £3.60 (ch £1.80) NT members free. **Facilities** ❷ ⌷ ㋡ (outdoor) ♿ (grounds partly accessible. Map of accessible route available) (limited due to terrain) toilets for disabled shop ⊗ ❄ ▬

CAREW
MAP 02 SN00

Carew Castle & Tidal Mill
SA70 8SL

➲ (on A4075, just off A477 Pembroke to Kilgetty road)

☎ 01646 651782

e-mail: enquiries@carewcastle.com

web: www.carewcastle.com

This magnificent Norman castle has royal links with Henry Tudor and was the setting for the Great Tournament of 1507. Nearby is the Carew Cross (Cadw), an impressive 13ft Celtic cross dating from the 11th century. Carew Mill is one of only four restored tidal mills in Britain, with records dating back to 1558.

Times Open Castle Jan-Etr, Nov-Dec, daily 11-3 (closed Xmas). Castle & Mill Etr-Oct, daily 10-5. **Fee** ✳ £3.50 (concessions £2.50). Family ticket £9.50. **Facilities** ❷ ㋡ (outdoor) ♿ (ground floors, toilets and shop are acccessible) (audio tours, sign language, tours by arrangement) toilets for disabled shop ▬

CILGERRAN
MAP 02 SN14

Cilgerran Castle
SA43 2SF

➲ (off A484 & A478)

☎ 01239 615007

web: www.cadw.wales.gov.uk

Set above a gorge of the River Teifi - famed for its coracle fishermen - Cilgerran Castle dates from the 11th to 13th centuries. It decayed gradually after the Civil War, but its great round towers and high walls give a vivid impression of its former strength.

Times Open Apr-Sep, daily 9.30-6; Oct 9.30-5; Nov-Mar, daily 9.30-4. **Fee** ✳ £3.10 (ch 5-15, concessions £2.70, disabled visitors & assisting companion free). Family ticket (2ad+all ch/grandch under 16) £8.90 Group rates available. Prices quoted apply until 31 Mar 2009. **Facilities** shop ⊗ ⊕ ▬

CRYMYCH
MAP 02 SN13

Castell Henllys Iron Age Fort
Pant-Glas, Meline SA41 3UT

➲ *(off A487 between Cardigan and Newport)*

☎ 01239 891319

e-mail: celts@castellhenllys.com

web: www.castellhenllys.com

This Iron Age hill fort is set in the beautiful Pembrokeshire Coast National Park. Excavations began in 1981 and three roundhouses have been reconstructed, another roundhouse has been completed and is the largest on the site. Celtic roundhouses have been constructed in the original way using hazel wattle walls, oak rafters and thatched conical roofs. A forge, smithy and looms can be seen, with other attractions such as trails and a herb garden. Please telephone for details of special events.

Times ✳ Open Apr-early Nov, daily 10-5. Last entry 4.30 **Facilities** ❷ ⴲ (outdoor) ᬵ (ramp access to shop, hearing loop in shop) toilets for disabled shop ▬

FISHGUARD
MAP 02 SM93

OceanLab
The Parrog, Goodwick SA64 0DE

➲ *(A40 to Fishguard, turn at by-pass, follow signs for Stenaline ferry terminal, pass 2 garages, turn right at rdbt & follow signs to attraction)*

☎ 01348 874737

e-mail: fishguardharbour-tic@pembrokeshire.gov.uk

web: www.ocean-lab.co.uk

Overlooking the Pembrokeshire coastline, OceanLab is a multifunctional centre, which aims to provide a fun-filled experience for the family. There is also a hands-on ocean quest exhibition, a soft play area and a cybercafé. An exhibition is centred around 'Ollie the Octopus's Garden', with hands-on displays and activities.

Times Open Apr-Oct 9.30-5; Nov-Mar 10-4 **Fee** ✳ Telephone for details **Facilities** ❷ ⴲ ⴹ (outdoor) ᬵ (lift, flat even ground, low counter) toilets for disabled shop ⊗ (ex assist dogs) ▬

LAMPHEY
MAP 02 SN00

Lamphey Bishop's Palace
SA71 5NT

➲ *(off A4139)*

☎ 01646 672224

web: www.cadw.wales.gov.uk

This ruined 13th-century palace once belonged to the Bishops of St David's.

Times Open Apr-Mar, daily 10-5 The Visitor Centre will be closed at times during the Winter, but the side gate will be left open for access to the site between 10-4. **Fee** ✳ £3.10 (ch 5-15, concessions £2.70, disabled visitors & assisting companion free). Family ticket (2ad+all ch/grandch under 16) £8.90. Group discounts available. Price quoted apply until 31 Mar 2009. **Facilities** ❷ shop ⊗ ⊕ ▬

LLAWHADEN
MAP 02 SN01

Llawhaden Castle
FREE

➲ *(off A40, 3m NW of Narberth)*

☎ 01437 541201

web: www.cadw.wales.gov.uk

The castle was first built in the 12th century to protect the possessions of the Bishops of St David's. The 13th and 14th-century remains of the bishops' hall, kitchen, bakehouse and other buildings can be seen, all surrounded by a deep moat.

Times Open at all times. Key keeper arrangement. **Facilities** ⊗ ⊕

NARBERTH
MAP 02 SN11

Oakwood Park
Canaston Bridge SA67 8DE

➲ *(M4 W junct 49, take A48 to Carmarthen, signed)*

☎ 01834 861889

e-mail: info@oakwoodthemepark.co.uk

web: www.oakwoodthemepark.co.uk

Oakwood Theme Park offers over 30 rides and attractions. Thrill seekers can brave Speed, the UK's first roller-coaster with a beyond vertical drop, the award winning wooden roller coaster Megafobia, the 50 metre high sky coaster Vertigo and shot n' drop tower coaster The Bounce, or cool off on Hydro, the steepest and wettest ride in Europe. There are also plenty of family rides and lots of fun to be had for smaller kids with a designated children's area available with smaller rides.

Times Open 24 Mar-25 Sep daily, from 10 (closing times vary) **Fee** ✳ £14.95 (under 2's free, ch 3-9 £13.50, pen £10 & disabled £11.50). Family ticket (4) £53, (6) £77. Party 20+ tickets available £12.95 **Facilities** ❷ ⴹ ⏿⚲ ⴲ (outdoor) ᬵ (most areas of park are accessible apart from a few rides) (wheelchair hire, special access to some rides) toilets for disabled shop ⊗ (ex assist dogs) ▬

NEWPORT
MAP 02 SN03

Pentre Ifan Burial Chamber
FREE

➲ *(3m SE from B4329 or A487)*

☎ 029 2050 0200

web: www.cadw.wales.gov.uk

Found to be part of a vanished long barrow when excavated in 1936-37, the impressive remains of this chamber include the capstone, three uprights and a circular forecourt.

Times Open - access throughout the year. **Facilities** ⊗ ⊕

WALES

461

PEMBROKE   MAP 02 SM90

Pembroke Castle

SA71 4LA

➲ *(W end of main street)*

☎ 01646 681510 & 684585

e-mail: info@pembrokecastle.co.uk

web: www.pembrokecastle.co.uk

This magnificent castle commands stunning views over the Milford estuary. Discover its rich medieval history, and that of Henry VII, the first Tudor king, through a variety of exhibitions. There are lively guided tours and events each Sunday in July and August. Before leaving, pop into the Brass Rubbing Centre and make your own special souvenir. To complete the day, wander round the tranquil millpond and medieval town walls, which surround other architectural gems from Tudor and Georgian times. Special Events: 1st week in Sep 'Pembroke Festival'. Please telephone for details.

Times ✹ Open all year, daily, Apr-Sep 9.30-6; Mar & Oct 10-5; Nov-Feb, 10-4. Closed 24-26 Dec & 1 Jan. **Facilities** Ⓟ (100yds) ⊑ 🖪 (outdoor) ♿ (induction loop, handrails, portable ramp) toilets for disabled shop ▀

ST DAVID'S   MAP 02 SM72

St David's Bishop's Palace

SA62 6PE

➲ *(on A487)*

☎ 01437 720517

web: www.cadw.wales.gov.uk

These extensive and impressive ruins are all that remain of the principal residence of the Bishops of St David's. The palace shares a quiet valley with the cathedral, which was almost certainly built on the site of a monastery founded in the 6th century by St David. The Bishop's Palace houses an exhibition: 'Lords of the Palace'.

Times Open Apr-Oct, daily 9-5; Nov-Mar, Mon-Sat 9.30-4, Sun 11-4. **Fee** ✹ £3.10 (ch 5-15, concessions £2.70, disabled visitors & assisting companion free). Family ticket (2ad+all ch/grandch under16) £8.90. Group discounts available. Prices quoted apply until 31 Mar 2009. **Facilities** Ⓟ shop ⊗ ⊕ ▀

St David's Cathedral

The Close SA62 6PE

➲ *(from Haverfordwest A487 into St Davids, pass Cross Sq, left into car park)*

☎ 01437 720202

e-mail: info@stdavidscathedral.org.uk

web: www.stdavidscathedral.org.uk

Begun 1181 on the reputed site of St David's 6th-century monastic settlement, the present building was altered during the 12th to the 14th centuries and again in the 16th. The ceilings of oak, painted wood and stone vaulting are of considerable interest.

Times Open all year 8.30-5.30. **Facilities** Ⓟ (300yds) (no coach parking) ⊑ ♿ (hearing loop) toilets for disabled shop ⊗ (ex assist dogs) ▀

SCOLTON   MAP 02 SM92

Scolton Manor Museum & Country Park

Scolton Manor SA62 5QL

➲ *(5m N of Haverfordwest, on B4329)*

☎ 01437 731328 (Museum) & 731457 (Park)

Scolton Manor Museum is situated in Scolton Country Park. The early Victorian mansion, refurbished stables and the exhibition hall illustrate the history and natural history of Pembrokeshire. There are new displays in the house and stables, plus a 'Pembrokeshire Railways' exhibition. The 60-acre grounds, partly a nature reserve, have fine specimen trees and shrubs. Environmentally friendly Visitor Centre, alternative energy and woodland displays, guided walks and children's play areas. Classic Car show in June and Model Air show in July.

Times Open Museum Apr-Oct, Tue-Sun & BHs 10.30-1 & 1.30-5.30; Country Park all year, Etr-Sep 10-7, Oct-Etr 10-6. Closed 25-26 Dec **Fee** ✹ Museum: £2 (ch £1, concessions £1.50). Country Park car park £1 all day **Facilities** Ⓟ (charged) ⊑ 🖪 (outdoor) ♿ (ground floor only accessible only for wheelchairs) toilets for disabled shop ⊗ (ex assist dogs & in grounds)

WALES

TENBY   MAP 02 SN10

Tenby Museum & Art Gallery

Castle Hill SA70 7BP

➲ (near town centre above Harbour)

☎ 01834 842809

e-mail: info@tenbymuseum.org.uk

web: www.tenbymuseum.org.uk

The museum is situated on Castle Hill. It covers the local heritage from prehistory to the present in galleries devoted to archaeology, geology, maritime history, natural history, militaria and bygones. The art galleries concentrate on local associations with an important collection of works by Augustus John, Gwen John and others. There are child-friendly trails and art exhibitions that change monthly.

Times Open all year, 10-5. (Last admission 4.30). Winter Mon-Fri only. **Facilities** ℗ (10 mins walk) 🖵 ♿ (lifts, levelled floors, ramps, stair lift) toilets for disabled shop ⊗ (ex assist dogs)

Tudor Merchant's House

Quay Hill SA70 7BX

➲ (turn left off lower end of High St, past Lifeboat PH and Caldey Shop)

☎ 01834 842279

e-mail: alyson.bush@nationaltrust.org.uk

web: www.nationaltrust.org.uk

Recalling Tenby's history as a thriving and prosperous port, the Tudor Merchant's house is a fine example of gabled 15th-century architecture. There is a good Flemish chimney and on three walls the remains of seccos can be seen. A small herb garden has been created.

Times Open 30 Mar-1 Nov Sun-Fri 11-5 (last admission 4.30), open Sat BH wknds. **Fee** ✳ £2.50 (ch £1.20). Family £6.20. Group 15+ £2 (ch£1). NT members free **Facilities** ℗ (500yds) (no coaches nearby) ♿ (Partly accessible) (garden could be accessed, Braille guide, photo album) shop ⊗ (ex assist dogs) ⛟

POWYS

ABERCRAF   MAP 03 SN81

Dan-Yr-Ogof The National Showcaves Centre for Wales

SA9 1GJ

➲ (M4 junct 45, midway between Swansea & Brecon on A4067, follow brown tourist signs for Dan-Yr-Ogof)

☎ 01639 730284

e-mail: info@showcaves.co.uk

web: www.showcaves.co.uk

This award-winning attraction includes three separate caves, dinosaur park, Iron Age Farm, museum, shire horse centre and covered children's play area.

Times Open daily Apr-Oct, from 10.30 (last admission 3) **Fee** ✳ £11 (ch 3-16 £7). Group rates 20+ **Facilities** ❷ 🖵 🍴 (outdoor) shop ⊗ (ex assist dogs) ⛟

BERRIEW   MAP 07 SJ10

Glansevern Hall Gardens

Glansevern SY21 8AH

➲ (signed on A483 between Welshpool and Newtown)

☎ 01686 640644

e-mail: glansevern@yahoo.co.uk

web: www.glansevern.co.uk

Built in the Greek Revival style for Arthur Davies Owen, who chose a romantically positioned site on the banks of the River Severn. The current owners have developed the gardens, respecting the plantings and features of the past, and added a vast collection of new and interesting species. There are many fine and unusual trees, a lakeside walk, walled garden, water gardens and a rock garden with grotto.

Times Open May-Sep BH Mon & Thu-Sat 12-5. Parties other dates by arrangement. **Fee** ✳ £4 (ch under 15 free). **Facilities** ❷ 🖵 🍴 licensed 🍴 (outdoor) ♿ (most areas accessible) toilets for disabled shop garden centre

BRECON   MAP 03 SO02

Brecknock Museum & Art Gallery

Captain's Walk LD3 7DS

➲ (near town centre at junct of The Watton & Glamorgan St)

☎ 01874 624121

e-mail: brecknock.museum@powys.gov.uk

web: www.powys.gov.uk/breconmuseum

A wealth of local history is explored at the museum, which has archaeological and historical exhibits, with sections on folk life, decorative arts and natural history. Victorian Assize Court is interpreted with life-size figures, sound and light and there is one of the finest collections of Welsh Lovespoons. The museum also runs a lively programme of Welsh contemporary art exhibitions.

Times Open all year, Mon-Fri 10-5, Sat 10-1 & 2-5; Apr-Sep also open Sun 12-5. Closed Good Fri, 25-26 Dec & 1 Jan. **Fee** £1 (ch & residents free, concessions 50p) **Facilities** ❷ (charged) ♿ (limited parking, must be accompanied by able-bodied) toilets for disabled shop ⊗ (ex assist dogs)

Regimental Museum of The Royal Welsh

The Barracks, The Watton LD3 7EB

➲ (close to town centre, well signed)

☎ 01874 613310

e-mail: swb@rrw.org.uk

web: www.rrw.org.uk

The museum of the South Wales Borderers and Monmouthshire Regiment (now the Royal Welsh), which was raised in 1689 and has been awarded 23 Victoria Crosses. Amongst the collections is the Zulu War Room, devoted to the war and in particular to the events at Rorke's Drift, 1879, when 121 men fought 4,500 Zulus.

Times Open all year wkdys 10-5, Apr-Sep Sat & BHs 10-4. Call for special Sun opening times. **Fee** ✳ £3 (ch up to 16 free) **Facilities** ℗ (town centre 200yds) ♿ toilets for disabled shop ⊗ (ex assist dogs) ⛟

LLANFAIR CAEREINION — MAP 06 SJ10

Welshpool & Llanfair Light Railway

SY21 0SF

➲ *(beside A458, Shrewsbury-Dolgellau road)*

☎ 01938 810441
e-mail: info@wllr.org.uk
web: www.wllr.org.uk

The Llanfair Railway is one of the Great Little Trains of Wales. It offers a 16-mile round trip through glorious scenery by narrow-gauge steam train. The line is home to a collection of engines and coaches from all round the world. Please ring for details for special events.

Times Open Etr-late Oct wknds, (some extra days during Jun, Jul & Sep) daily during holiday periods, phone for timetable enquiries. **Fee** ✳ £11.20 return (one ch free per adult, extra ch £5.60, concessions £10.20). **Facilities** ❷ ⛱ ⊓ (outdoor) ⅋ (both termini have ramped access. No access from intermediate stations) (three coaches adapted for wheelchairs) toilets for disabled shop ➾

MACHYNLLETH — MAP 06 SH70

Bards' Quest

Corris Craft Centre, Corris SY20 9RF

➲ *(Situated at Corris Croft Centre on main A487 rd between Machynlleth & Dolgellau)*

☎ 01654 761584
e-mail: info@kingarthurslabyrinth.co.uk
web: www.kingarthurslabyrinth.com

Part of the Corris Craft Centre complex, Bard's Quest involves animated figures relating ancient myths and stories, in both English and Welsh. The Bard's maze is a self guided outdoor maze. It is easy to get around with level paths and seating.

Times Open daily 17 Mar-2 Nov, 10-5. **Fee** ✳ £4.10 (ch £2.35, concessions £3.60) **Facilities** ❷ ⛱ ⊓ (outdoor) ⅋ (Partly accessible) (designated parking nr entrance) toilets for disabled shop ❽ (ex assist dogs) ➾

Centre for Alternative Technology 2for1

SY20 9AZ

➲ *(3m N of Machynlleth, on A487)*

☎ 01654 705950
e-mail: info@cat.org.uk
web: www.cat.org.uk

The Centre for Alternative Technology promotes practical ideas and information on sustainable technologies. The exhibition includes displays of wind, water and solar power, organic gardens, low-energy buildings, and a unique water-powered railway which ascends a 200ft cliff from the car park. Free children's activities and guided tours during the summer holidays. Opening of WISE - The Wale's Institute for Sustainable Education Spring 2009.

Times Open all year (closed Dec 23-27 & 3-14 Jan), 10-5.30 or dusk in winter. **Fee** ✳ Summer £8.40 (ch over 5 £4.20, concessions £7.40); Winter, £6.40 (ch over 5 £4.20, concessions £5.40). **Facilities** ❷ ⛱ licensed ⊓ (indoor & outdoor) ⅋ (mobility scooter available) toilets for disabled shop ❽ (ex assist dogs) ➾

Corris Craft Centre FREE

Corris SY20 9RF

➲ *(on main A487 rd between Machynlleth & Dolgellau)*

☎ 01654 761584
e-mail: info@corriscraftcentre.co.uk
web: www.corriscraftcentre.co.uk

A large collection of workshops where visitors can see at first hand ancient and traditional crafts in progress. Among the crafts on display are furniture making, glassblowing, wood-turning, patchworking and quilting, leatherwork, jewellery, toy making, hand-made cards, pottery and candles. All the workshops have goods for sale, so this is the ideal place to purchase unusual gifts for friends and family.

Times Open daily Mar-Nov. From Nov-Mar, please call to check opening times. **Facilities** ❷ ⛱ ⊓ (outdoor) ⅋ (full access to craft units, café at the craft centre) (disabled parking spaces near entrance) toilets for disabled shop ❽ (ex assist dogs)

King Arthur's Labyrinth

King Arthur's Labyrinth, Corris SY20 9RF

➲ *(on A487 between Machynlleth and Dolgellau)*

☎ 01654 761584
e-mail: info@kingarthurslabyrinth.co.uk
web: www.kingarthurslabyrinth.com

A subterranean storybook, a boat ride through the great waterfall and into the Labyrinth of tunnels and caverns carved into the ancient rocks of Wales. Tales of King Arthur and other legends are re-told as you walk through this underground setting. Stories of dragons, giants, battles and more.

Times Open 17 Mar-2 Nov daily 10-5. **Fee** ✳ £6.50 (ch £4.65, concessions £5.85). **Facilities** ❷ ⛱ ⊓ (outdoor) ⅋ (full access to reception, shop & units of craft centre. Labyrinth tour includes 0.5m walk through caverns) toilets for disabled shop ❽ (ex assist dogs) ➾

MONTGOMERY — MAP 07 SO29

Montgomery Castle FREE

☎ 029 2050 0200
web: www.cadw.wales.gov.uk

Initially an earth and timber structure guarding an important ford in the River Severn, Montgomery was considered a 'suitable spot for the erection of an impregnable castle' in the 1220s. Building and modifications continued until 1251-53, but the final conquest of Wales by Edward I meant the castle lost much of its role.

Times Open all year, any reasonable time. **Facilities** ❽ ✛

PRESTEIGNE
MAP 03 SO36

The Judge's Lodging
`2 for 1`

Broad St LD8 2AD

➲ (in town centre, off B4362, signed from A44 & A49)

☎ 01544 260650

e-mail: info@judgeslodging.org.uk

web: www.judgeslodging.org.uk

A restored Victorian town house with integral courtroom, cells and service areas - step back into the 1860s, accompanied by an 'eavesdropping' audio tour of voices from the past. Explore the fascinating world of the Victorian judges, their servants and felonious guests at this award-winning, historic house. Various special events take place throughout the year, please telephone for details.

Times Open Mar-Oct daily 10-5; Nov-Dec, Wed-Sun 10-4. **Fee** ✳ £5.25 (ch £3.95, concessions £4.75). Family ticket £15. Party rates available.
Facilities Ⓟ (200mtrs) ♿ (Partly accessible) (lift, inaccessible items pack, audio/large print guides) shop ⊗ (ex assist dogs)

RHAYADER
MAP 06 SN96

Gilfach Nature Discovery Centre and Reserve

St Harmon LD6 5LF

➲ (From A470 turn right into reserve, before cattle grid turn right and follow road)

☎ 01597 823298

e-mail: info@radnorshirewildlifetrust.org.uk

web: www.radnorshirewildlifetrust.org.uk

Situated in the Cambrian Mountains, Gilfach is locally unique due to its wide variety of habitats; high moorland to enclosed meadow, oak woodland to rocky upland river. The reserve therefore supports a tremendous abundance of plants and animals within a relatively small area. This richness of wildlife has adapted to living in the various habitats created over the centuries through the practice of traditional farming. Visitors can take a number of planned walks including the Nature Trail, the Monks Trod Trail, and the Oakwood Path. The Nature Discovery Centre offers the opportunity to learn about the various habitats and wildlife featuring footage from cameras in nestboxes, games and quizzes. Please see the website or ring 01597 823298.

Times Open Reserve all year. Visitor Centre & Nature Discovery Centre open Etr-Sep during wknds, BHs & school hols. **Fee** ✳ Donations for parking
Facilities Ⓟ ⬚ ⼞ (outdoor) ♿ (wheelchair access path to viewpoint) toilets for disabled shop ⊗ (ex on lead)

TRETOWER
MAP 03 SO12

Tretower Court & Castle

NP8 2RF

➲ (3m NW of Crickhowell, off A479)

☎ 01874 730279

web: www.cadw.wales.gov.uk

The castle is a substantial ruin of an 11th-century motte and bailey, with a three-storey tower and 9ft-thick walls. Nearby is the Court, a 14th-century fortified manor house which has been altered and extended over the years. The two buildings show the shift from medieval castle to more domestic accommodation over the centuries.

Times Open Mar, Tue-Sun 9-4; Apr-Sep, Tue-Sun & BHs 10-5. The monument is closed at all other times. **Fee** ✳ £3.10 (ch 5-15, concessions £2.70, disabled visitors & assisting companion free). Family ticket (2ad+all ch/grandch under 16) £8.90. Group rates available. Prices quoted apply until 31 Mar 2009. **Facilities** Ⓟ shop ⊗ ⼞ ▬

WELSHPOOL
MAP 07 SJ20

Powis Castle & Garden

SY21 8RF

➲ (1m S of Welshpool, signed off A483)

☎ 01938 551920 & 551929

e-mail: powis.castle@nationaltrust.org.uk

web: www.nationaltrust.org.uk

Laid out in the Italian and French styles, the Garden retains its original lead statues, an Orangery and an aviary on the terraces. The medieval castle contains one of the finest collections of paintings and furniture in Wales and a beautiful collection of treasures from India. Please visit website for details of events running throughout the year.

Times Open 6 Apr-29 Oct, Thu-Mon (Wed-Mon during Jul-Aug). Castle and museum 1-5, gardens, 11-6. **Fee** ✳ Castle, Museum & Gardens £9.60, (ch under 17 £4.80) Family ticket £24. Group member £8.60. Garden only £6.60 (ch £3.30) Family £16, Group member £5.60. NT members & ch under 5 free. **Facilities** Ⓟ ⼞⌿ ⼞ (outdoor) ♿ (please phone for details) (photos of interior, braille guides, virtual tour)) toilets for disabled shop garden centre ⊗ (ex assist dogs) ⬚ ▬

WALES

RHONDDA CYNON TAFF

TREHAFOD
MAP 03 ST09

Rhondda Heritage Park
`2 for 1`

Lewis Merthyr Colliery, Coed Cae Rd CF37 2NP

➲ (between Pontypridd & Porth, off A470, follow brown heritage signs from M4 junct 32)

☎ 01443 682036

e-mail: reception@rhonddaheritagepark.com

web: www.rhonddaheritagepark.com

Based at the Lewis Merthyr Colliery, the Heritage Park is a fascinating 'living history' attraction. You can take the Cage Ride to 'Pit Bottom' and explore the underground workings of a 1950s pit, guided by men who were miners themselves. There are children's activities, an art gallery and a museum illustrating living conditions in the Rhondda Valley. Special events throughout the year, phone for details.

Times Open all year, daily 10-6. Closed Mon from Oct-Etr. (Last admission 4). Closed 25 Dec-early Jan. **Fee** £5.60 (ch £4.30, pen £4.95). Family(4) ticket from £16.50, (6) £21. **Facilities** Ⓟ ⼞⌿⼞ licensed ⼞ (indoor & outdoor) ♿ (Partly accessible) (wheelchair available, accessible parking, lifts) toilets for disabled shop ⊗ (ex assist dogs) ▬

SWANSEA

Weobley Castle

SA3 1HB

➲ *(from B4271 or B4295)*

☎ 01792 390012

web: www.cadw.wales.gov.uk

A 12th-to 14th-century fortified manor house with an exhibition on the history of Weobley and other historic sites on the Gower peninsula.

Times Open Apr-Oct, daily 9.30-6; Nov-Mar, daily 9.30-5. **Fee** ✷ £2.70 (ch 5-15, concessions £2.30, disabled visitors & assisting companion free). Family ticket (2ad+all ch/grandch under 16) £7.70. Group rates available. Prices quoted apply until 31 Mar 2009. **Facilities** ♿ shop ⊗ ⊕ ➦

Oxwich Castle

SA3 1NG

➲ *(A4118 from Swansea)*

☎ 01792 390359

web: www.cadw.wales.gov.uk

Situated on the Gower peninsula, this Tudor mansion is a striking testament in stone to the pride and ambitions of the Mansel dynasty of Welsh gentry. The E-shaped wing houses an exhibition on historical Gower and 'Chieftains and Princes of Wales'.

Times Open Apr-Sep, daily 10-5. **Fee** ✷ £2.70 (ch 5-15, concessions £2.30, disabled visitors & assisting companion free). Family ticket (2ad+all ch/grandch under 16) £7.70. Group rates available. Prices quoted apply until 31 Mar 2009. **Facilities** ♿ & (Radar key toilet) toilets for disabled ⊗ ⊕ ➦

Gower Heritage Centre

Y Felin Ddwr SA3 2EH

➲ *(follow signs for South Gower on A4118 W from Swansea. W side of Parkmill village)*

☎ 01792 371206

e-mail: info@gowerheritagecentre.co.uk

web: www.gowerheritagecentre.co.uk

Based around a 12th-century water-powered cornmill, the site also contains a number of craft workshops, two play areas, animals, a museum and a miller's cottage, all set in attractive countryside in an Area of Outstanding Natural Beauty.

Times ✷ Open daily, Mar-Oct 10-5.30; Nov-Feb 10-4.30. Closed 25 Dec. **Facilities** ♿ ⬚ ⑩ ⨉ & (ramp entrance access) toilets for disabled shop ➦

Glynn Vivain Art Gallery

Alexandra Rd SA1 5DZ

➲ *(M4 junct 42 along Fabian Way A483 up Wind St. Left at train station opposite Swansea Metropolitan University Art College)*

☎ 01792 516900

e-mail: glynn.vivian.gallery@swansea.gov.uk

web: www.glynnviviangallery.org

A broad spectrum of visual arts form the original bequest of Richard Glynn Vivian, including old masters and an international collection of porcelain and Swansea china. The 20th century is also well represented with modern painting and sculpture by British and foreign artists, with the emphasis on Welsh artists. On-going temporary exhibitions showcase the work of contemporary artists.

Times Open all year, Tue-Sun & BH Mon 10-5. Closed 25-26 Dec & 1 Jan. **Fee** Donations welcome. **Facilities** ℗ (200 yds) & (Partly accessible) (hearing loop, audio guides) toilets for disabled shop ⊗ (ex assist dogs) ➦

Plantasia   `2 for 1`

Parc Tawe SA1 2AL

➲ *(M4 junct 42, follow A483 into Swansea, follow car park signs for attraction)*

☎ 01792 474555

e-mail: swansea.plantasia@swansea.gov.uk

web: www.plantasia.org

Plantasia is a unique tropical haven of exotic plants and animals. Within the impressive glass pyramid is a luscious rainforest filled with over 500 tropical plants and a terraced waterfall flowing into a fish filled lagoon. There is also a mini-zoo where monkeys, reptiles, birds and insects can be seen.

Times Open daily 10-5, including BHs. Closed Mon in Dec & Jan and Xmas. **Fee** ✷ £3.70 (ch & concessions £2.70) Family ticket £12. **Facilities** ♿ ⬚ & toilets for disabled shop ⊗ (ex assist dogs) ➦

Swansea Museum   `FREE`

Victoria Rd, Maritime Quarter SA1 1SN

➲ *(M4 junct 42, on main road into city centre)*

☎ 01792 653763

e-mail: swansea.museum@swansea.gov.uk

web: www.swanseaheritage.co.uk

This is the oldest museum in Wales, showing the history of Swansea from the earliest times until today. The museum has a Tramshed and floating boats to explore (summer only). There is a continuous programme of temporary exhibitions and events all year around.

Times Open all year, Tue-Sun 10-5 (last admission 4.45). Closed Mon except BH Mon, 25-26 Dec & 1 Jan. **Facilities** ♿ ⨅ (outdoor) & (lower floor/gallery accessible) shop ⊗ (ex assist dogs) ➦

TORFAEN

BLAENAVON   MAP 03 SO20

Big Pit National Coal Museum   `FREE`
NP4 9XP

➲ *(M4 junct 25/26, follow signs on A4042 & A4043 to Pontypool & Blaenavon. Signed off A465)*

☎ 01495 790311

e-mail: post@museumwales.ac.uk
web: www.museumwales.ac.uk

The Real Underground Experience, Big Pit is the UK's leading mining museum. It is a real colliery and was the place of work for hundreds of men, woman and children for over 200 years. A daily struggle to extract the precious mineral that stoked furnaces and lit household fires across the world.

Times Open all year 9.30-5. Please call for underground guided tour availability **Facilities** ❶ ❑ ♿ (Partly accessible) (underground tours by prior arrangement) toilets for disabled shop ⊗ (ex assist dogs in some areas)

Blaenavon Ironworks   `FREE`
North St

☎ 01495 792615
web: www.cadw.wales.gov.uk

The Blaenavon Ironworks were a milestone in the history of the Industrial Revolution. Constructed in 1788-99, they were the first purpose-built, multi-furnace ironworks in Wales. By 1796, Blaenavon was the second largest ironworks in Wales, eventually closing down in 1904.

Times Open Apr-Oct, daily 10-5; Nov-Mar, Mon-Sat 9.30-5, Sun 11-4.
Facilities ❶ ⊗ ✿ ▬

CWMBRAN   MAP 03 ST29

Greenmeadow Community Farm   `2 for 1`
Greenforge Way NP44 5AJ

➲ *(M4 junct 26. Follow signs for Cwmbran then brown signs)*

☎ 01633 647662

e-mail: greenmeadowcommunityfarm@torfaen.gov.uk
web: www.greenmeadowcommunityfarm.org.uk

This is one of Wales' leading tourist attractions - a community farm that was created during the 1980s on land threatened by developers. There are milking demonstrations, tractor and trailer rides, a dragon, adventure play area, a farm trail, a nature trail and lots more. Please telephone for details of special events running throughout the year.

Times Open daily Summer 10-6, Winter 10-4. Closed 24 Dec-Jan. **Fee** £4.50 (ch £3.50). Family (2ad+3ch) £16. **Facilities** ❶ ❑ ☂ (outdoor) ♿ (some slopes and uneven paths, some rooms accessible by stairs only) (tractor & trailer rides for wheelchair users) toilets for disabled shop ▬

VALE OF GLAMORGAN

BARRY   MAP 03 ST16

Welsh Hawking Centre   `2 for 1`
Weycock Rd CF62 3AA

➲ *(on A4226)*

☎ 01446 734687
e-mail: norma@welsh-hawking.co.uk

There are over 200 birds of prey here, including eagles, hawks, owls, buzzards and falcons. They can be seen and photographed in the mews and some of the breeding aviaries. There are flying demonstrations at regular intervals during the day. A variety of tame, friendly animals, such as guinea pigs, horses and rabbits will delight younger visitors.

Times Open late Mar-late Sep, daily 10.30-5 (1hr before dusk in winter)
Fee ✳ £5 (ch & concessions £3). **Facilities** ❶ ❑ ☂ (outdoor) ♿ toilets for disabled shop ⊗ ▬

OGMORE   MAP 03 SS87

Ogmore Castle   `FREE`
➲ *(2.5m SW of Bridgend, on B4524)*

☎ 01656 653435
web: www.cadw.wales.gov.uk

Standing on the River Ogmore, the west wall of this castle is 40ft high. A hooded fireplace is preserved in the 12th-century, three-storey keep and a dry moat surrounds the inner ward.

Times Open - access throughout the year. Key keeper arrangement.
Facilities ❶ ⊗ ✿

PENARTH   MAP 03 ST17

Cosmeston Lakes Country Park & Medieval Village Village
Lavernock Rd CF64 5UY

➲ *(on B4267 between Barry and Penarth)*

☎ 029 2070 1678
e-mail: NColes@valeofglamorgan.gov.uk
web: www.valeofglamorgan.gov.uk

Deserted during the plagues and famines of the 14th century, the original village was rediscovered through archaeological excavations. The buildings have been faithfully reconstructed on the excavated remains, creating a living museum of medieval village life. Special events throughout the year include re-enactments and Living History.

Times ✳ Open all year, daily 11-5 in Summer, 11-4 in Winter. Closed 25 Dec. Country park open at all times. **Facilities** ❶ ❑ ⏍ ☂ ♿ (access ramps & wheelchair hire) toilets for disabled shop

467

ST HILARY   MAP 03 ST07

Old Beaupre Castle   `FREE`

➲ *(1m SW, off A48)*

☎ 01446 773034

web: www.cadw.wales.gov.uk

This ruined manor house was rebuilt during the 16th century. Its most notable features are an Italianate gatehouse and porch. The porch is an unusual three-storeyed structure.

Times Open - access throughout the year. Key keeper arrangement.
Facilities ℗ ⊗ ♿

WREXHAM

CHIRK   MAP 07 SJ23

Chirk Castle   `2 for 1`

LL14 5AF

➲ *(8m S of Wrexham, signed off A483)*

☎ 01691 777701

e-mail: chirkcastle@nationaltrust.org.uk

Chirk Castle is one of a chain of late 13th-century Marcher castles. Its high walls and drum towers have hardly changed, but the inside shows the varied tastes of 700 years of occupation. One of the least altered parts is Adam's Tower. Many of the medieval-looking decorations were created by Pugin in the 19th century. Varied furnishings include fine tapestries. In the garden there are beautiful views that take in seven counties.

Times Open Garden & Tower: 7-15 Feb Sat-Sun 11-4. 18-30 Mar Wed-Sun 11-4. Apr-28 Sep Wed-Sun & Tue in Jul-Aug 11-5. Oct-1 Nov Wed-Sun 11-4. **Fee** Castle & Garden £9.20 (ch £4.60). Family ticket £23. Garden only £6.50 (ch £3.25) Family ticket £16.25. **Facilities** ❷ ☑ 㞗 (outdoor) ♿ (access to east wing) (stairclimber, hearing loop, coach from car park) toilets for disabled shop ⊗ (ex assist dogs) ❦ ▬

WREXHAM   MAP 07 SJ35

Erddig

LL13 0YT

➲ *(off A525, 2m S of Wrexham & A483/A5152)*

☎ 01978 355314

e-mail: erddig@nationaltrust.org.uk

web: www.nationaltrust.org.uk

Built in 1680, the house was enlarged and improved by a wealthy London lawyer with a passion for gilt and silver furniture. Original furnishings remain, including a magnificent state bed in Chinese silk. The house is notable for the view it gives of both 'upstairs' and 'downstairs' life. The gardens, unusually, have been changed very little since the 18th century. The country park includes part of Wat's Dyke, a cup and saucer waterfall, examples of ridge and furrow field systems and a motte and bailey castle. Woodland walks and carriage rides available. Special events take place in spring, summer and autumn, please contact for details.

Times ✳ Open 25 Mar-28 Oct, Sat-Wed (open Good Fri), house 12-5, garden 11-6 (Jul-Aug gardens 10-6); Oct-1 Nov, Sat-Wed, house 12-4, garden 11-5.Open Thur in Jul & Aug. **Facilities** ❷ ☑ 㞗 (outdoor) ♿ (Partly accessible) (4 wheelchairs available, access to ground floor only) toilets for disabled shop garden centre ⊗ (ex assist dogs) ❦ ▬

Green Bridge of Wales along St Govans Headland in the Pembrokeshire Coast National Park

NORTHERN IRELAND

Glenarm, Ulster

BELFAST

BELFAST　　　　　　　　　　MAP 01 D5

Belfast Zoological Gardens

Antrim Rd BT36 7PN

➲ *(M2 junct 4 signed to Glengormley. Follow signs off rdbt to Zoo)*

☎ 028 9077 6277

e-mail: info@belfastzoo.co.uk

web: www.belfastzoo.co.uk

The 50-acre zoo has a dramatic setting on the face of Cave Hill, enjoying spectacular views. Attractions include the award-winning primate house (gorillas and chimpanzees), penguin enclosure, free-flight aviary, African enclosure, and underwater viewing of sealions and penguins. There are also red pandas, free-ranging lemurs and a group of very rare spectacled bears. Recent additions to the collection include Barbary lions, maned wolves, barn owls and a new Rainforest House.

Times Open all year, daily Apr-Sep 10-5; Oct-Mar 10-2.30. Closed 25 & 26 Dec. **Fee** ✳ Summer: £8.10 (ch £4.30), Winter: £6.70 (ch £3.40, ch under 4, pen and disabled free) **Facilities** ❷ ⛾ ⁋🍴 (outdoor) ♿ (free admission, reserved parking, scooters available) toilets for disabled shop ✪ (ex assist dogs) ➡

Botanic Gardens

3 College Park, Off Botanic Ave. BT7 1LP

➲ *(from City Hall, Bedford St then Dublin road for Botanic Avenue)*

☎ 028 9032 4902

e-mail: maxwellr@belfastcity.gov.uk

web: www.belfastcity.gov.uk

One highlight of the park is the beautiful glass-domed Victorian Palm House, built between 1839-52. This palm house pre-dates the one in Kew Gardens and is one of the earliest curved glass and iron structures in the world. Another feature is the Tropical Ravine - stand on a balcony to get a wonderful view through a steamy ravine full of exotic plants.

Times ✳ Open Palm House Tropical Ravine: Apr-Sep 10-12, 1-5; Oct-Mar 10-12, 1-4. Sat, Sun & BHs 1-5 (Summer), 1-4 (Winter). **Facilities** ℗ (street)

Giant's Ring　　　　　　　　FREE

➲ *(0.75m S of Shaws Bridge)*

☎ 028 9023 5000

web: www.ehsni.gov.uk

Circular, Bronze-age enclosure nearly 200 feet in diameter similar in style to Stonehenge, with a stone chambered grave in the centre and bordered by banks 20 feet wide and 12 feet high. Very little is known for certain about this site, except that it was used for ritual burial.

Times Open all times. **Facilities** ❷

Ulster Museum　　　　　　　FREE

Botanic Gardens BT9 5AB

➲ *(1m S of city centre on Stranmillis road)*

☎ 028 9038 3000

e-mail: uminfo@nmni.com

web: www.nmni.com

The Ulster Museum is the perfect place to explore the arts, ancient and modern history, and the nature of Ireland. Art displays change regularly but always include a rich variety of Irish and international paintings, drawings and sculpture, along with ceramics, glass and costume. The history galleries tell the story of the north of Ireland from the Ice Age to the present day. The natural environment is explored in the Habitas galleries.

Times Closed until 2009 for refurbishment. Please check website for futher details. **Facilities** ℗ (100yds on street) ⛾ ♿ (lifts, loop system) toilets for disabled shop ✪ (ex assist dogs) ➡

W5 at Odyssey

2 Queens Quay BT3 9QQ

☎ 028 9046 7700

web: www.w5online.co.uk

W5 investigates Who? What? Where? When? Why?… and that pretty much sums up the intent behind Ireland's first purpose built discovery centre. Visitors of any age will want to get their hands on interactive science and technology displays that include the laser harp, the fog knife, microscopes, robots and computers. W5 is part of a massive Millennium Landmark Project in the heart of Belfast.

Times ✳ Open all year Mon-Sat 10-6, Sun 12-6. Closed 25-26 Dec & 12 Jul. **Facilities** ❷ (charged) 🍴 ⁋ ♿ (hearing loop) toilets for disabled shop ✪ (ex assist dogs) ➡

CO ANTRIM

ANTRIM　　　　　　　　　　MAP 01 D5

Antrim Round Tower　　　　FREE

BT41 1BJ

➲ *(N of town)*

☎ 028 9023 5000

web: www.ehsni.gov.uk

Antrim round tower stands among lawns and trees but it was once surrounded by monastic buildings. Antrim was an important early monastery, probably a 6th-century foundation, closely linked with Bangor.

Times Open all year. **Facilities** ❷

BALLYCASTLE　　　MAP 01 D6

Bonamargy Friary　　FREE
➲ *(E of town, at golf course)*
☎ 028 9023 5000
web: www.ehsni.gov.uk
Founded by Rory MacQuillan around 1500 and later passed on to the MacDonnells, Earls of Antrim, there are still remains of the friary gatehouse, church and cloister for visitors to see.
Times Open all year. **Facilities** ❷ ♨

BALLYLUMFORD　　　MAP 01 D5

Ballylumford Dolmen　　FREE
➲ *(on B90 on NW tip of Island Magee)*
☎ 028 9023 5000
web: www.ehsni.gov.uk
Incorporated in the front garden of a house in Ballylumford Road are the remains of this huge 4-5,000-year-old single-chamber Neolithic tomb, also known as the Druid's Altar.
Times Open all year. **Facilities**

BALLYMENA　　　MAP 01 D5

Ecos Millennium Environmental Centre　　FREE
Ecos Centre, Kernohams Ln, Broughshane Rd BT43 7QA
➲ *(follow signs from M2 bypass at Ballymena)*
☎ 028 2566 4400
e-mail: www.ballymena.gov.uk/ecos
web: www.ballymena.gov.uk/ecos
Plenty of fun and adventure for all the family with duck feeding, toy tractors and sand pit. The centre hosts two interactive galleries, one on sustainability and one on biodiversity, and you can stroll through the willow tunnel and enjoy the play park.
Times Etr-Oct, Mon-Fri, 9-5. Jun-Aug, Sat & Sun, 12-5 (last admission 4). **Facilities** ❷ ♿ ☕ ⊼ (outdoor) ♿ toilets for disabled shop garden centre ⊗ (ex assist dogs)

Harryville Motte　　FREE
➲ *(N bank of River Braid)*
☎ 028 9023 5000
web: www.ehsni.gov.uk
On a ridge to the south of the town, this Norman fort, with its 40ft-high motte and rectangular bailey, is one of the finest examples of Norman earthworks left in Northern Ireland.
Times Open all year. **Facilities** ❷ ♨

BALLYMONEY　　　MAP 01 C6

Leslie Hill Open Farm　　2 for 1
Leslie Hill BT53 6QL
➲ *(1m NW of Ballymoney on Macfin Rd)*
☎ 028 2766 6803
web: www.lesliehillopenfarm.co.uk
An 18th-century estate with a Georgian house, magnificent period farm buildings, and fine grounds with paths, lakes and trees. Attractions include an extensive collection of rare breeds, poultry, horsedrawn machinery and carriages, exhibition rooms, a museum, working forge, deer park, walled garden and an adventure playground. 2009 is the farm's 20th anniversary.
Times Open Jul-Aug, Mon-Sat 11-6, Sun 2-6; Jun, Sat-Sun & BHs 2-6; Etr-May, Sun & BHs 2-6, open all Etr wk 11-6. **Fee** ✱ £4 (ch £3). Family ticket £10. **Facilities** ❷ ☕ ⊼ (indoor & outdoor) ♿ (ramps) toilets for disabled shop ⊗ (ex on lead)

BUSHMILLS　　　MAP 01 C6

Old Bushmills Distillery
BT57 8XH
➲ *(on Castlecatt Rd, in Bushmills Village)*
☎ 028 2073 1521
e-mail: sheelagh.croskery@diageo.com
web: www.bushmills.com
Old Bushmills was granted its licence in 1608 and is the oldest licenced whiskey distillery in the world. There's a guided tour, and afterwards you can take part in a comparative tasting session and become a whiskey expert.
Times ✱ Open Apr-Oct, Mon-Sat 9.30-5.30, Sun 12-5.30 (last tour 4); Nov-Mar, Mon-Fri 5 tours daily, 10.30, 11.30, 1.30, 2.30 & 3.30. Sat & Sun 3 tours, 1.30, 2.30, 3.30. Closed 12 July , Good Fri pm, Xmas & New Year **Facilities** ❷ ☕◉ ♿ (audio visual theatre, shops & restaurant) toilets for disabled shop ⊗ (ex assist dogs) ▬

CARRICK-A-REDE　　　MAP 01 D6

Carrick-a-rede Rope Bridge and Larrybane Visitors Centre
BT54 6LS
➲ *(E of Ballintoy on B15)*
☎ 028 2076 9839　& 2073 1582 (office)
e-mail: carrickarede@nationaltrust.org.uk
web: www.nationaltrust.org.uk
On the North Antrim Coastal Path is one of Northern Ireland's best-loved attractions: Carrick-a-Rede Rope Bridge and the disused limestone quarry of Larrybane. The island of Carrick is known as 'the rock in the road', as it is an obstacle on the path of migrating salmon, and fishermen have taken advantage of this to net the fish here for over 300 years.
Times Open Bridge daily (weather permitting), 28 Feb-24 May & Sep-1 Nov, 10-6; 25 May-Aug, 10-7. (Last admission 45 mins before closing). Coastal path open all year. **Fee** £4 (ch £2) Family £10 **Facilities** ❷ ☕ ⊼ (outdoor) ♿ (information centre, telescope at wheelchair height) toilets for disabled ⅍ ▬

IRELAND

CARRICKFERGUS MAP 01 D5

Carrickfergus Castle

BT38 7BG

➲ *(on N shore of Belfast Lough)*

☎ 028 9335 1273

web: www.ehsni.gov.uk

Imposingly placed on a rocky headland overlooking Belfast Lough, this is the best preserved and probably the most fought-over Norman castle in Ireland. Built by John de Courcy, Earl of Ulster, after 1180, it served a military purpose for more than eight centuries. Exhibits include a giant model of the castle, a short film, and a banqueting suite. The castle is often used as a venue for medieval banquets and fairs. There is a visitors' centre, shop and refreshment point.

Times ✳ Open all year, Apr-Sep, wkdays 10-6, Sun 2-6; Oct-Mar closes at 4.
Facilities ❷ ▱ shop ⊗

Town Walls FREE

☎ 028 9023 5000

web: www.ehsni.gov.uk

Lord Deputy Sir Arthur Chichester enclosed Carrickfergus with stone walls from 1611 onwards and more than half the circuit is still visible, often to its full height of 4 metres to the wall walk.

Times Visible at all times. **Facilities** ❷

CHURCHTOWN MAP 01 D5

Cranfield Church FREE

➲ *(3.75m SW of Randalstown)*

☎ 028 9023 5000

web: www.ehsni.gov.uk

This small medieval church is situated on the shores of Lough Neagh. Beside it is a famous holy well.

Times Open all year. **Facilities** ❷ ☴ ⬛

GIANT'S CAUSEWAY MAP 01 C6

Giant's Causeway Centre

44 Causeway Rd BT57 8SU

➲ *(2m N of Bushmills on B146)*

☎ 028 2073 1855

e-mail: causewaytic@hotmail.com

web: www.northantrim.com

This dramatic rock formation is undoubtedly one of the wonders of the natural world. The Centre provides an exhibition and audio-visual show, and Ulsterbus provides a minibus service to the stones and there are guided walks, and special facilities for the disabled.

Times ✳ Open all year, daily from 10 (closes 7 Jul & Aug). Closed 1 wk Xmas. **Facilities** ❷ (charged) ▱ ⬤◀ ☴ ⬛ (mini bus transport with wheelchair hoist, reserved parking) toilets for disabled shop ⊗ (ex assist dogs) ▬

LARNE MAP 01 D5

Olderfleet Castle FREE

☎ 028 9023 5000

web: www.ehsni.gov.uk

A 16th-century tower house, the last surviving of three which defended Larne.

Times Open at all times.

LISBURN MAP 01 D5

Duneight Motte and Bailey FREE

➲ *(2.3m S beside Ravernet River)*

☎ 028 9023 5000

web: www.ehsni.gov.uk

Impressive Anglo-Norman earthwork castle with high mound-embanked enclosure, making use of the defences of an earlier pre-Norman fort.

Times Open all year.

Irish Linen Centre & Lisburn Museum FREE

Market Square BT28 1AG

➲ *(Signed both in and outside town centre. Follow tourist signs from M1)*

☎ 028 9266 3377

e-mail: irishlinencentre@lisburn.gov.uk

web: www.lisburncity.gov.uk

The centre tells the story of the Irish linen industry past and present. The recreation of individual factory scenes brings the past to life and a series of imaginative hands-on activities describe the linen manufacturing processes. The Museum has a range of temporary exhibitions of local interest. 2009 is the 400th anniversary of Lisburn by exhibition.

Times Open all year, Mon-Sat, 9.30-5. **Facilities** ℗ (100 mtrs) (limited for disabled and coaches) ▱ ☴ (lift, induction loop, staff trained in sign language) toilets for disabled shop ⊗ (ex assist dogs) ▬

PORTBALLINTRAE MAP 01 C6

Dunluce Castle

➲ *(off A2)*

☎ 028 2073 1938

web: www.ehsni.gov.uk

Extensive and picturesque ruins of a 16th-century castle perched on a rocky crag high above the sea. Stronghold of the MacQuillans and MacDonnells, who significantly altered the original stonebuilt fortress. Randal MacDonnell built a house in the centre of the castle, of which parts of the Great Hall remain, as do the towers and early 17th-century gatehouse. The castle has new displays and there is an audio-visual show. The cave below the ruins provided a secret way into and out of the castle from the sea.

Times ✳ Open all year, Apr-Sep, wkdays 10-7, Sun 2-7; Oct-Mar, Tue-Sat 10-4, Sun 2-4. **Facilities** ❷ shop

IRELAND

TEMPLEPATRICK · MAP 01 D5

Pattersons Spade Mill

751 Antrim Rd BT39 0AP

➲ *(2m SE of Templepatrick on A6)*

☎ 028 9443 9713

e-mail: pattersons@nationaltrust.org.uk

web: www.nationaltrust.org.uk

See history literally forged in steel at the last working water-driven spade mill in daily use in the British Isles. Hear the hammers, smell the grit, feel the heat and witness the thrills of traditional spade making. Guided tours virtually capture life during the Industrial Revolution and dig up the history and culture of the humble spade.

Times Open wknds & BHs, 14 Mar-May & 5-27 Sep; daily, 10-19 Apr; Wed-Mon, Jun-Aug, 2-6. **Fee** £4.70 (ch £2.70). Family Ticket £12.10. **Facilities** 🅿 🍴 (outdoor) ♿ (ramps, wheelchair available) toilets for disabled 🍼

Templetown Mausoleum   `FREE`

BT39

➲ *(in Castle Upton graveyard on A6, Belfast-Antrim road)*

web: www.ntni.org.uk

Situated in the graveyard of Castle Upton, this family mausoleum is in the shape of a triumphal arch and was designed by Robert Adam.

Times ✳ Open daily during daylight hours. **Facilities** 🅿 🍴 🍼

CO ARMAGH

ARMAGH · MAP 01 C5

Armagh County Museum   `FREE`

The Mall East BT61 9BE

➲ *(in city centre)*

☎ 028 3752 3070

e-mail: acm.info@nmni.com

web: www.magni.org.uk

Housed in a 19th-century schoolhouse, this museum contains an art gallery and library, as well as a collection of local folkcrafts and natural history. Special events are planned thoughout the year.

Times Open all year, Mon-Fri 10-5, Sat 10-1 & 2-5. **Facilities** 🅿 (500yds) ♿ (entrance ramp and lift) toilets for disabled shop 🐾 (ex assist dogs) 🍴

Armagh Friary   `FREE`

➲ *(SE edge of town)*

☎ 028 9023 5000

web: www.ehsni.gov.uk

Situated just inside the gates of the former Archbishop's Palace are the remains of the longest friary church in Ireland (163ft). The friary was established in 1263 by Archbishop O'Scanail and destroyed by Shane O'Neill in the middle of the 16th century to prevent it being garrisoned by Elizabethan soldiers.

Times Open all year. **Facilities** 🅿

Armagh Planetarium

College Hill BT61 9DB

➲ *(on Armagh-Belfast road close to mall, city centre)*

☎ 028 3752 3689 & 4725

e-mail: info@armaghplanet.com

web: www.armaghplanet.com

The Planetarium is home to The Digital Theatre, a multi-media environment equipped with the latest projector technology and state-of-the-art sound system. Also featured are the space displays in the Galileo Hall, Copernicus Hall, Tycho, Cassini and Kepler rooms and surrounding the Planetarium is the Astropark, a 25-acre area where you can walk through the Solar System and the Universe. 2009 is the 40th anniversary of the moon landings.

Times Open all year, Sat 11.30-5. Sun 11.30-5, Mon during term time; May-Jun & Sep-Dec wkdys 1-5, July-Aug wkdys 11.30-5. **Fee** 🅿 £6 (ch, concessions £5). Family ticket (2ad+max 3 ch) £18. Exhibition area £2. **Facilities** 🅿 🍽 🍴 (outdoor) ♿ (loop system in theatre, lifts/ramps) toilets for disabled shop 🐾 (ex assist dogs) 🍴

Navan Centre & Fort

Killylea Rd BT60 4LD

➲ *(2.5m W on A28)*

☎ 028 3752 1801

e-mail: navan@armagh.gov.uk

web: www.visitarmagh.com

Navan was once known as Emain Macha, the ancient seat of kings and earliest capital of Ulster. Today it is an impressive archaeological site with its own museum and visitor centre located in a building that blends into the landscape. The Navan Centre uses audio-visuals and interactive devices to unravel history from myth. Travel into the 'Real World' of archaeology and the 'Other World' to hear the legends of the Ulster Cycle.

Times Open Apr, May & Sep, Sat 10-5, Sun 12-5, June, July & Aug Mon-Sat 10-5, Sun 12-5, Closed 12 July, BH (Other times by arrangement for tour groups and educational visits). **Fee** ✳ £5 (ch £3.25, concessions £4). Family ticket £15 **Facilities** 🅿 🍽 🍴 (outdoor) ♿ (loop for hearing aids, parking, full disabled facilities) toilets for disabled shop 🐾 (ex assist dogs) 🍴

Palace Stables Heritage Centre   `2 for 1`

The Palace Demesne BT60 4EL

➲ *(off Friary Rd beside council offices)*

☎ 028 3752 1801

e-mail: stables@armagh.gov.uk

web: www.visitarmagh.com

This picturesque Georgian building, set around a cobbled courtyard, has been lovingly restored and now houses a heritage centre. The building was home to the Archbishops of the Church of Ireland from 1770 up to the 1975. A daily Georgian interpretation is provided by authentic costumed characters. The centre also features a chapel, gardens, a Victorian conservatory, the ruins of a Franciscan Friary, and an ice house.

Times Open Apr-May, Sep & wknds Sat 10-5, Sun 2-5, Jun-Aug, Mon-Sat 10-5, Sun 2-5, (Other times by arrangement for groups & education). **Fee** ✳ £5 (ch £3.25, concessions £4). Family £15 **Facilities** 🅿 🍽 licensed 🍴 (outdoor) ♿ (ramps & lift in stables, full disabled facilities) toilets for disabled shop 🍴

IRELAND

ARMAGH CONTINUED

Saint Patrick's Trian Visitor Complex

2 for 1

40 English St BT61 7BA

➲ *(in city centre)*

☎ 028 3752 1801

e-mail: info@saintpatrickstrian.com

web: www.visitarmagh.com

An exciting visitor complex in the heart of the city. Incorporating three major exhibitions - The Armagh story: traces Armagh's historic Pagan monuments through to the coming of St Patrick and Celtic Christianity to the modern day city. Patrick's Testament: takes a closer look at Ireland's patron saint through the writings found in ancient manuscript the Book of Armagh. The Land of Lilliput: Jonathan Swift's most famous book, *Gulliver's Travels* is narrated by a 20-foot giant.

Times Open all year, Mon-Sat 10-5, Sun 2-5. Closed 12 Jul. **Fee** ✳ £5 (ch £3.25, concessions £4). Family ticket £15 **Facilities** ❷ (charged) ⑩✚ (specially designed for disabled) toilets for disabled shop ❽ (ex assist dogs) ➡

CAMLOUGH
MAP 01 D5

Killevy Churches

FREE

➲ *(3m S lower eastern slopes of Slieve Gullion)*

☎ 028 9023 5000

web: www.ehsni.gov.uk

The ruins of the two churches (10th and 13th-century) stand back to back, at the foot of Slieve Gullion sharing a common wall, but with no way through from one to the other. The churches stand on the site of an important nunnery founded by St Monenna in the 5th century. A huge granite slab in the graveyard supposedly marks the founder's grave. A holy well can be reached by climbing the path north of the graveyard. The nunnery was in use until the Dissolution in 1542.

Times Open all year. **Facilities**

JONESBOROUGH
MAP 01 D5

Kilnasaggart Inscribed Stone

FREE

➲ *(1.25m S)*

☎ 028 9023 5000

web: www.ehsni.gov.uk

A granite pillar stone dating back to 8th century, with numerous crosses and a long Irish inscription carved on it.

Times Open all year. **Facilities** ⓟ

MOY
MAP 01 C5

The Argory

Derrycaw Rd BT71 6NA

➲ *(3m NE)*

☎ 028 8778 4753

e-mail: argory@nationaltrust.org.uk

web: www.nationaltrust.org.uk

Built in the 1820s, this handsome Irish gentry house sits surveying its surrounding 320 acre wooded riverside estate. The former home of the McGeough family, a tour of this neo-classical masterpiece reveals it is unchanged since 1900 - the eclectic interior still evoking the family's Edwardian tastes and interests.

Times Open House: wknds & BHs, 14 Mar-Jun & 5-27 Sep; daily Good Fri-19 Apr, Jul & Aug 1-5.30. Grounds: daily Feb-Apr & Oct-Jun, 10-4; May-Sep 10-6. Last admission 1hr before closing. **Fee** £5.80 (ch £2.90). Family £14.50. Grounds £2.50 (ch £1). Family £6. **Facilities** ❷ (charged) ⌗ ⋔ (outdoor) ⅙ (Partly accessible) (parking facilities, wheelchair available, Braille) toilets for disabled shop ❽ (ex assist dogs) ⅗

NEWRY
MAP 01 D5

Moyry Castle

FREE

➲ *(7.5m S)*

☎ 028 9023 5000

web: www.ehsni.gov.uk

This tall, three-storey keep was built by Lord Mountjoy, Queen Elizabeth's deputy, in 1601, its purpose to secure the Gap of the North which was the main route into Ulster.

Times Open all year

OXFORD ISLAND
MAP 01 D5

Lough Neagh Discovery Centre

Oxford Island National Nature, Reserve BT66 6NJ

➲ *(signed from M1 junct 10)*

☎ 028 3832 2205

e-mail: oxford.island@craigavon.gov.uk

web: www.oxfordisland.com

In a spectacular setting on the water's edge, discover natural history, wildlife, family walks and much more.

Times Open Apr-Sep, Mon-Fri 9-5, Sat 10-5, Sun 10-6; Oct-Mar, Mon-Fri 9-5, Sat-Sun 10-5. **Fee** Free except for events **Facilities** ❷ ⌗ ⋔ (outdoor) ⅙ (bird watching hides) toilets for disabled shop ❽ (ex assist dogs) ➡

PORTADOWN　MAP 01 D5

Ardress House

64 Ardress Rd, Annaghmore BT62 1SQ

➲ *(on B28, 5m from Moy, 5m from Portadown, 3m from M1 junct 13)*

☎ 028 3885 1236 & 8778 4753

e-mail: ardress@nationaltrust.org.uk

web: www.nationaltrust.org.uk

A charming 17th-century farmhouse, elegantly remodelled in Georgian times by its visionary architect-owner George Ensor. The grounds are beautifully unspoilt and there is a traditional farmyard with livestock (popular with children) and a display of farm implements. Explore the apple orchards and scenic walks, and see the table where George V signed the Constitution of Northern Ireland in 1921.

Times Open wknds & BHs, 14 Mar-27 Sep, also Thu Jul & Aug 2-6, 21-22 Feb 12-4; daily, Good Fri-19 Apr 2-6. Last admission 1hr before closing. **Fee** £4.60 (ch £2.30). Family £11.50. Group £3.70. **Facilities** ℗ ⋒ (outdoor) & (Partly accessible) toilets for disabled shop ⊗ (ex assist dogs) ⚘

TYNAN　MAP 01 C5

Village Cross　FREE

☎ 028 9023 5000

web: www.ehsni.gov.uk

A carved High Cross, 11ft tall, which lay broken in two pieces for many years, but was skilfully mended in 1844.

Times Open all year **Facilities** ℗

CO DOWN

BALLYWALTER　MAP 01 D5

Grey Abbey　FREE

➲ *(on E edge of village)*

☎ 028 9054 6552

web: www.ehsni.gov.uk

Founded in 1193 by Affreca, daughter of the King of the Isle of Man, these extensive ruins of a Cistercian abbey, sitting in lovely sheltered parkland, are among the best preserved in Northern Ireland. The chancel, with its tall lancet windows, magnificent west doorway and an effigy tomb - believed to be Affreca's - in the north wall, are particularly interesting. The abbey was burned down in 1572, and then re-used as a parish church. There are many 17th and 18th-century memorials to be seen in the church ruins, which occupy a pleasant garden setting. The abbey now has a beautiful medieval herb garden, with over 50 varieties of plants, and a visitors' centre.

Times Open Apr-Sep; Tue-Sat 9-6, Sun 2-6; Oct-Mar, wknds 10-4. **Facilities** ℗

CASTLEWELLAN　MAP 01 D5

Drumena Cashel　FREE

➲ *(2.25m SW)*

☎ 028 9023 5000

web: www.ehsni.gov.uk

There are many stone ring forts in Northern Ireland, but few so well preserved as Drumena. Dating back to early Christian times, the fort is 30 metres in diameter and has an 11 metre accessible underground stone-built passage, probably used as a refuge and for storage.

Times Open all times **Facilities** ℗

COMBER　MAP 01 D5

WWT Castle Espie　2 for 1

Ballydrain Rd BT23 6EA

➲ *(12m SE of Belfast. A22 from Comber towards Killyleagh, 1st left into Ballydrain Rd)*

☎ 028 9187 4146

e-mail: info.castleespie@wwt.org.uk

web: www.wwt.org.uk

Home to the largest collection of wildfowl in Ireland. Comfortable hides enable you to watch the splendour of migratory waders and wildfowl. Beautiful landscaped gardens, a taxidermy collection and fine paintings by wildlife artists can be seen. Thousands of birds migrate to the reserve in winter and birdwatch mornings are held on the last Thursday of every month. The Centre's effluent is treated in a reed bed filtration system which can be seen on one walk.

Times Open all year (ex 23-25 Dec). Nov-Feb, Mon-Fri, 11-4. Sat & Sun 11-4.30. Mar-Jun, Mon-Fri 10.30-5. Sat & Sun 11-5.30. Jul-Aug, Mon-Fri, 10.30-5.30. Sat & Sun, 11-5.30. **Fee** ✳ £5.95 (ch £2.95, pen £4.50). Group 12+ £5 (ch £2.50, concessions £3.80) **Facilities** ℗ ⊡ ⋒ (outdoor) & (hides have wheelchair platforms, wheelchairs) toilets for disabled shop ⊗ (ex assist dogs) ▬

DOWNPATRICK　MAP 01 D5

Down County Museum　FREE

The Mall, County Down, Northern Ireland BT30 6AH

➲ *(on entry to town follow brown signs to museum)*

☎ 028 4461 5218

e-mail: museum@downdc.gov.uk

web: www.downcountymuseum.com

The museum is located in the restored buildings of the 18th-century county gaol. In addition to restored cells that tell the stories of some of the prisoners, there are exhibitions on the history of County Down. Plus temporary exhibits, events, tea-room and shop.

Times ✳ Open all year, Mon-Fri 10-5, wknds 1-5 **Facilities** ℗ (100yds) ⊡ ⋒ (outdoor) & (wheelchair available, handling boxes on application) toilets for disabled shop ⊗ (ex assist dogs) ▬

IRELAND

475

DOWNPATRICK CONTINUED

Inch Abbey

➲ *(0.75m NW off A7)*

☎ 028 9023 5000

web: www.ehsni.gov.uk

Beautiful riverside ruins of a Cistercian abbey founded by John de Courcy around 1180. Of particular note is the tall, pointed, triple east window.

Times Open all year Apr-Sep 10-7, Sun 2-7. Oct-Mar free access. **Fee** *Prices not confirmed for 2009* **Facilities** ᵽ

Loughinisland Churches   FREE

➲ *(4m W)*

☎ 028 9023 5000

web: www.ehsni.gov.uk

This remarkable group of three ancient churches stands on an island in the lough, accessible by a causeway. The middle church is the oldest, probably dating back to the 13th century, with a draw-bar hole to secure the door. The large North church was built in the 15th century, possibly to replace the middle church and continued in use until 1720. The smallest and most recent church is the South (MacCartan's) church.

Times Open all times **Facilities** ᵽ 🚲

Mound of Down   FREE

➲ *(on Quoile Marshes, from Mount Crescent)*

☎ 028 9023 5000

web: www.ehsni.gov.uk

A hill fort from the Early Christian period, conquered by Anglo-Norman troops in 1177, who then built an earthwork castle on top. This mound in the marshes, beside the River Quoile, was the first town before the present Downpatrick.

Times Open all times **Facilities** ᵽ

The St Patrick Centre   2 for 1

St Patrick Visitor Centre, Market St BT30 6LZ

➲ *(A7 from Belfast, follow brown heritage signs)*

☎ 028 4461 9000

e-mail: director@saintpatrickcentre.com

web: www.saintpatrickcentre.com

This 21st-century multimedia, interactive, audio-visual feast is dedicated to the fascinating story of Ireland's Patron Saint Patrick, who brought Christianity to Ireland in the 5th century. The Centre is located beside the saint's grave, in the heart of St. Patrick's country, forty minutes from Belfast and two hours from Dublin. Major events usually take place around the 17th of March, St Patrick's Day.

The St Patrick Centre

Times Open all year Oct-Mar, Mon-Sat, 10-5 & St Patricks Day 9.30-7; Apr-May & Sep, Mon-Sat 9.30-5.30, Sun 1-5.30 (morning opening on request), Jun-Aug Mon-Sat 9.30-6, Sun 10-6. (Last admission 1.5 hrs before closing). **Fee** ✳ £4.90 (ch £2.50, concessions £3.30). Family ticket (2ad+2ch) £11.70. Groups 25+, £3.25 (ch £2.20, concessions £2.65) **Facilities** ᵽ ⌂ ⅋ (lifts, wheelchairs, sensory gdn) toilets for disabled shop ⊗ (ex assist dogs)

Struell Wells   FREE

➲ *(1.5m E)*

☎ 028 9023 5000

web: www.ehsni.gov.uk

Pilgrims come to collect the healing waters from these holy drinking and eye wells which are fed by a swift underground stream. Nearby are the ruins of an 18th-century church, and, even more interesting, single-sex bath-houses. The men's bath-house is roofed, has an anteroom and a sunken bath, while the ladies' is smaller and roofless.

Times Open all times **Facilities** ᵽ 🚲

DROMARA   MAP 01 D5

Legananny Dolmen   FREE

➲ *(4m S)*

☎ 028 9023 5000

web: www.ehsni.gov.uk

Theatrically situated on the slopes of Slieve Croob, this tripod dolmen with its three tall uprights and huge capstone is the most graceful of Northern Ireland's Stone Age monuments. There are views to the Mourne Mountains.

Times Open at all times **Facilities** 🚲

HILLSBOROUGH   MAP 01 D5

Hillsborough Fort   FREE

☎ 028 9268 3285

web: www.ehsni.gov.uk

On a site that dates back to early Christian times, the existing fort was built in 1650 by Colonel Arthur Hill to command a view of the road

IRELAND

from Dublin to Carrickfergus. The building was ornamented in the 18th century. It is set in a forest park with a lake and pleasant walks.

Times Open all year; summer, Mon-Sat 10-7, Sun 2-7; winter, Mon-Sat 10-4, Sun 2-4 **Facilities** ♿ ㅈ

HOLYWOOD

Ulster Folk and Transport Museum

Cultra BT18 0EU

➲ *(12m outside Belfast on A2, past Holywood on main road to Bangor)*

☎ 028 9042 8428

e-mail: uftm.info@magni.org.uk

web: www.uftm.org.uk

This award-winning attraction illustrates the way of life and traditions of Northern Ireland. The galleries of the Transport Museum display collections of horse drawn carts, cars, steam locomotives and the history of ship and aircraft building. Please telephone for details of special events running throughout the year.

Times ✳ Open all year Mar-Jun, Mon-Fri 10-5, Sat 10-6, Sun 11-6; Jul-Sep, Mon-Sat 10-6, Sun 11-6; Oct-Feb, Mon-Fri 10-4, Sat 10-5, Sun 11-5. **Facilities** ♿ ⬚ ㅈ (outdoor) shop ▬

KILKEEL   MAP 01 D4

Greencastle

➲ *(4m SW)*

☎ 028 9023 5000

web: www.ehsni.gov.uk

Looking very much like an English Norman castle with its massive keep, gatehouse and curtain wall, this 13th-century royal fortress stands on the shores of Carlingford Lough, with fine views of the Mourne Mountains. Greencastle has an eventful military history, it was besieged and taken by Edward Bruce in 1316, attacked and spoiled by the Irish at least twice later in the 14th century, and maintained as a garrison for Elizabeth in the 1590s.

Times ✳ Open Jul-Aug, Tue-Sat 10-7, Sun 2-7. **Facilities** ♿

KILLINCHY   MAP 01 D5

Sketrick Castle   FREE

➲ *(3m E on W tip of Sketrick Islands)*

☎ 028 9023 5000

web: www.ehsni.gov.uk

A badly ruined tall tower house, probably 15th century. The ground floor rooms include a boat bay and prison. An underground passage leads from the north-east of the bawn to a freshwater spring.

Times Open at all times. **Facilities** ♿ ㅈ

NEWCASTLE   MAP 01 D5

Dundrum Castle   FREE

➲ *(4m N)*

☎ 028 9054 6518

web: www.ehsni.gov.uk

This medieval castle, one of the finest in Ireland, was built in 1777 by John De Courcy in a strategic position overlooking Dundrum Bay, a position which offers visitors fine views over the sea and to the Mourne Mountains. The castle was captured by King John in 1210 and was badly damaged by Cromwellian troops in 1652. Still an impressive ruin, it shows a massive round keep surrounded by a curtain wall, and a gatehouse which dates from the 13th century.

Times Open Apr-Sep, Tue-Sat 10-7, Sun 2-7; Oct-Mar, wknds, Sat 10-4, Sun 2-4. **Facilities** ♿ ㅈ

Maghera Church   FREE

➲ *(2m NNW)*

☎ 028 9023 5000

web: www.ehsni.gov.uk

The stump of a round tower, blown down in a storm in the early 18th century, survives from the early monastery, with a ruined 13th-century church nearby.

Times ✳ Open all year. **Facilities** ♿

NEWTOWNARDS   MAP 01 D5

Mount Stewart House & Gardens

Greyabbey BT22 2AD

➲ *(5m SE off A20)*

☎ 028 4278 8387

e-mail: mountstewart@nationaltrust.org.uk

web: www.nationaltrust.org.uk

On the east shore of Strangford Lough, is this fascinating house which has survived for three centuries, famous for its many illustrious owners and guests and well renowned for its magnificent gardens created by Edith Lady Londonderry, wife of the 7th Marquess. In the inspired gardens, which are now a nominated world heritage site, many rare and subtropical trees thrive. Located by the shore is the Temple of the Winds, built by James 'Athenian' Stuart in 1782 for the first Marquess.

Times Open Lakeside Gardens & Walks: Open all year daily, 10-sunset. Formal Gardens: wknds & BHs 21 Feb-29 Mar 10-4; daily Apr-Oct, 10-6, May-Sep 10-8. House: wknds & BHs, 7-29 Mar & May, 12-6; daily Good Fri, Jul-Sep 12-6 (May-Jun 1-6); Tue-Sun, 3 Oct-1 Nov, 12-6. Closed Tue May & Sep. Temple of the Winds: daily, Good Fri-Etr Tue, Sun & BHs, 4 Apr-1Nov, 2-5. Last admission 1 hr before closing. **Fee** House tour and gardens: £7.40 (ch £3.70). Family £18.40. Group £5.80. Gardens only: £5.60 (ch £2.80) Family £14. Group £4.40. **Facilities** ♿ ⬚⑩ㅈ (outdoor) ♿ (Partly accessible) (4 wheelchairs (2 electric) available) toilets for disabled shop ⅍ ▬

477

Scrabo Tower `FREE`

Scrabo Country Park, 203A Scrabo Rd BT23 4SJ

➲ *(1m W)*

☎ 028 9181 1491

web: www.ehsni.gov.uk

The 135 foot high Scrabo Tower, one of Northern Ireland's best-known landmarks, dominates the landscape of North Down and is also the centre of a country park around the slopes of Scrabo Hill. The Tower provides a fascinating series of interpretative displays about the surrounding countryside, and the viewing platform boasts spectacular views over Strangford Lough and County Down. The park provides walks through fine beech and hazel woodlands and the unique sandstone quarries display evidence of volcanic activity as well as being breeding sites for peregrine falcons.

Times Open late Mar-mid Sep, Sat-Thu 10.30-6. **Facilities** ♿ ⋒ shop ⊗

PORTAFERRY   MAP 01 D5

Exploris Aquarium

The Rope Walk, Castle St BT22 1NZ

➲ *(A20 or A2 or A25 to Strangford Ferry Service)*

☎ 028 4272 8062

e-mail: info@exploris.org.uk

web: www.exploris.org.uk

Exploris Aquarium is Northern Ireland's only public aquarium and now includes a seal sanctuary. Situated in Portaferry on the shores of Strangford Lough it houses some of Europe's finest displays. The Open Sea Tank holds 250 tonnes of sea water. The complex includes a park with duck pond, picnic area, children's playground, caravan site, woodland and bowling green.

Times Open all year, Mon-Fri 10-6, Sat 11-6, Sun 1-6. (Sep-Mar closing 1 hr earlier). **Fee** ✳ £7 (concessions £4). Family £22. **Facilities** ♿ ⊑ ⋒ (outdoor) ♿ (2 lifts within complex) toilets for disabled shop ⊗ (ex assist dogs) ▬

SAINTFIELD   MAP 01 D5

Rowallane Garden

BT24 7LH

➲ *(1m S of Saintfield on A7)*

☎ 028 9751 0131

e-mail: rowallane@nationaltrust.org.uk

web: www.nationaltrust.org.uk

Beautiful and exotic 52-acre gardens, started by the Rev John Moore in 1860, containing exquisite plants from all over the world. They are particularly noted for their rhododendrons and azaleas and for the wonderful floral displays in spring and summer.

Times Open daily, Jan-Apr & Nov-Dec, 10-4; May-Aug, 10-8; Sep-Oct, 10-6. Closed 25-26 Dec & 1 Jan. **Fee** £5 (ch £2.50). Family £12.50. Group £3.70. **Facilities** ♿ ⊑ ♿ (parking facilities, manual wheelchairs, scented plants) toilets for disabled ▮

STRANGFORD   MAP 01 D5

Castle Ward

BT30 7LS

➲ *(0.5m W of Strangford on A25)*

☎ 028 4488 1204

e-mail: castleward@nationaltrust.org.uk

web: www.nationaltrust.org.uk

Explore this exceptional 820-acre walled demesne dramatically set overlooking Strangford Lough and marvel at the quirky mid-Georgian mansion. An architectural curiosity, it is built inside and out in distinctly different styles of classical and gothic. Winding woodland, lakeside and parkland walks afford amazing unexpected vistas.

Times Open House: wknds & BHs, 21 Feb-Jun & 5 Sep-1 Nov, daily Good Fri-19 Apr & 4 Jul-Aug, 1-5. Grounds: daily Feb-Mar & Oct 10-4; Apr-Sep 10-8. Strangford Lough Wildlife Centre: wknds & BHs 21-22 Feb, 28 Feb-May & 5-27 Sep; daily Good Fri-19 Apr & Jun-Aug 12-5. **Fee** House tour: £2.80 (ch £1.90). Family £7.50. Grounds & centre £5 (ch £2.50). Family £12.50. **Facilities** ♿ (charged) ⊑ ⋒ ♿ (wheelchair available, may be driven to house, Braille) toilets for disabled shop ▮ ▬

Strangford Castle `FREE`

☎ 028 9023 5000

web: www.ehsni.gov.uk

A three-storey tower house built in the 16th century, overlooking the small double harbour of Strangford.

Times ✳ Open all reasonable times. **Facilities** ⊗

CO FERMANAGH

BELLEEK   MAP 01 B5

Belleek Pottery `2 for 1`

3 Main St BT93 3FY

➲ *(A46 from Enniskillen to Belleek. Pottery at entrance to village)*

☎ 028 6865 9300 & 6865 8501

e-mail: visitorcentre@belleek.ie

web: www.belleek.ie

Discover the secrets that make Belleek Pottery one of the most enduring success stories in Irish Craftsmanship. The award winning visitor centre offers guided tours along with a restaurant, audiovisual centre, showroom and museum.

Times Open all year, Jan-Feb, Mon-Fri 9-5.30; Mar-Oct, Mon-Fri 9-6, Sat 10-6, Sun 2-6 (Jul-Oct, Sun 12-6); Nov-Dec, Mon-Fri 9-5.30, Sat 10-5.30. Closed Xmas, New Year & 17 Mar **Fee** Guided tours £4 (ch under 12 free, concessions £2). **Facilities** ♿ ⏣ ⋒ (outdoor) ♿ (2 wheelchairs available) toilets for disabled shop ⊗ (ex assist dogs) ▬

CASTLE ARCHDALE BAY   MAP 01 C5

White Island Church

➲ *(in Castle Archdale Bay; ferry from marina)*
☎ 028 9023 5000
web: www.ehsni.gov.uk
Lined up on the far wall of a small, roofless 12th-century church are eight uncanny carved-stone figures. Part Christian and part pagan in appearance, their significance has been the subject of great debate. The church ruins sit on an early monastic site.

Times ✳ Open Jul-Aug, Tue-Sat 10-7, Sun 2-7. **Facilities** 🅿 ⊗ 🚌

DERRYGONNELLY   MAP 01 C5

Tully Castle   FREE

➲ *(3m N, on W shore of Lower Lough Erne)*
☎ 028 9054 6552
web: www.ehsni.gov.uk
Extensive ruins of a Scottish-style stronghouse with enclosing bawn overlooking Lough Erne. Built by Sir John Hume in the early 1600s, the castle was destroyed, and most of the occupants slaughtered, by the Maguires in the 1641 Rising. There is a replica of a 17th-century garden in the bawn.

Times Open Etr-Sep, 10-6. **Facilities** 🅿 ⊓ ⊗

ENNISKILLEN   MAP 01 C5

Castle Coole

BT74 6JY
➲ *(on A4, 1.5m from Enniskillen towards Belfast)*
☎ 028 6632 2690
e-mail: castlecoole@nationaltrust.org.uk
web: www.nationaltrust.org.uk
Savour the exquisite stately grandeur of this stunning 18th-century mansion, set in a historic wooded landscape park - ideal for family walks. As one of Ireland's finest neo-classical houses, the sumptuous Regency interior, boasting an especially fine state bedroom prepared for George IV, provides a rare treat for visitors to glimpse what life was like in the home of the Earls of Belmore.

Times Open House: wknds & BHs 14 Mar-May & 5-27 Sep; daily, Good Fri-19 Apr & Jun (closed Thu in Jun), 1-6; Jul-Aug, 12-6. Last tour 1 hr before closing. Grounds: daily, 14 Mar-Sep, 10-8 **Fee** House tour: £5 (ch £2). Family £12. Gardens & park £2.50 (ch £1). Family £6. **Facilities** 🅿 ⊓ & (may be driven to house, large print guide) toilets for disabled shop ⊗ (ex in park & assist dogs) 🐾 ▭

Enniskillen Castle

BT74 7HL
☎ 028 6632 2711
web: www.ehsni.gov.uk
Overlooking Lough Erne, this castle, a three-storey keep surrounded by massive stone-built barracks and with a turreted fairytale 17th-century water gate, now houses two museums and a heritage centre. In the castle keep is a small museum displaying Royal Enniskillen Fusiliers regimental exhibits, while the other rooms contain the Fermanagh County Museum's collection of local antiquities.

Times ✳ Open all year Mon 2-5, Tue-Fri 10-5 (closed 1-2, Oct-Apr), Sat 2-5 May-Aug, Sun 2-5 Jul-Aug, all day BHs. **Facilities** 🅿 ⊓ shop ⊗

Florence Court

BT92 1DB
➲ *(8m SW of Enniskillen via A4, then A32 to Swanlibar, well signed)*
☎ 028 6634 8249
e-mail: florencecourt@nationaltrust.org.uk
web: www.nationaltrust.org.uk
An 18th-century mansion overlooking wild and beautiful scenery towards the Mountains of Cuilcagh. The interior of the house, particularly noted for its flamboyant rococo plasterwork, was gutted by fire in 1955, but has been restored. There are pleasure grounds with an ice house, summer house, water powered sawmill and also a walled garden.

Times Open House: wknds & BHs, 21 Feb-10 May, 1-6; 19 Sep-1 Nov 1-5; daily, Good Fri-19 Apr, 16 May-Jun (except Tue) & 1-13 Sep, 1-6. Gardens & park: daily 21 Feb-9 Apr, 10-6; 10 Apr-1 Nov, 10-8; 2 Nov-20 Feb, 10-4 Last admission 1hr before closing **Fee** House tour: £5 (ch-£2). Family £12. Gardens & park £2.50 (ch £1). Family £6. **Facilities** 🅿 (charged) ⊒ ⊚ ⊓ (outdoor) & (wheelchair path) (electric wheelchair available, Braille) toilets for disabled shop 🐾 ▭

Marble Arch Caves European   2 for 1
Geopark

Marlbank Scenic Loop BT92 1EW
➲ *(off A4 Enniskillen to Sligo road. Left onto A32 and follow signs)*
☎ 028 6634 8855
e-mail: mac@fermanagh.gov.uk
web: www.marblearchcaves.net
One of Europe's finest cave systems, under Cuilcagh Mountain. Visitors are given a tour of a wonderland of stalagmites, stalactites and underground rivers and lakes, starting with a boat trip on the lower lake. The streams, which feed the caves, flow down into the mountain then emerge at Marble Arch, a 30ft detached limestone bridge. The geological, historical and economic benefits of Marble Arch Caves and Cuilcagh Mountain Park were recognised on an international scale when they were jointly awarded the title of European Geopark by UNESCO in 2001.

Times Open late Mar-Sep daily 10-4.30, Jul & Aug 10-5. **Fee** ✳ £8 (ch £5, pen & concessions £5.25). Family £18. Group rates available. **Facilities** 🅿 ⊒ ⊓ (outdoor) & (cave not accessible) (induction loop in AV theatre) toilets for disabled shop ⊗ (ex assist dogs) ▭

IRELAND

479

ENNISKILLEN CONTINUED

Monea Castle
FREE

➲ *(6m NW)*

☎ 028 9023 5000

web: www.ehsni.gov.uk

A fine example of a plantation castle still with much of its enclosing bawn wall intact, built around 1618. Of particular interest is the castle's stone corbelling - the Scottish method of giving additional support to turrets.

Times Open at any reasonable time. **Facilities** ℗

The Sheelin Irish Lace Museum
Ballanaleck BT92 2BA

➲ *(from Enniskillen take A4 onto A509. Thatched Sheelin Museum on left after 3m)*

☎ 028 6634 8052

e-mail: info@irishlacemuseum.com

web: www.irishlacemuseum.com

The Irish Lace Museum has the largest and most comprehensive display of antique lace anywhere in Ireland. There are around 700 exhibits, representing the five main types of Irish lace: Inishmacsaint Needlelace, Crochet, Limerick, Carrickmacross, and Youghal Needlelace. The history of the Irish lace-making industry is described, and antique items can be bought in the museum shop.

Times Open Apr-Oct 10-6 (closed 1-2 for lunch). **Fee** £3 (ch under 14 £1). Party 15+ £1.50 each **Facilities** ℗ ⅙ (toilets for disabled in teashop) toilets for disabled shop ⊗ (ex assist dogs) ⊟

LISNASKEA   MAP 01 C5

Castle Balfour
FREE

☎ 028 9023 5000

web: www.ehsni.gov.uk

Dating from 1618 and refortified in 1652, this is a T-plan house with vaulted rooms. Badly burnt in the early 1800s, this house has remained in ruins.

Times Open at all times. **Facilities** ℗

NEWTOWNBUTLER   MAP 01 C5

Crom
BT92 8AP

➲ *(3m from A34, well signed from Newtownbutler)*

☎ 028 6773 8118 & 8174

e-mail: crom@nationaltrust.org.uk

web: www.nationaltrust.org.uk

Featuring 2,000 acres of woodland, parkland and wetland, the Crom Estate is one of Northern Ireland's most important conservation areas. Nature trails are signposted through woodlands to the ruins of the old castle, and past the old boat house and picturesque summer house. Day tickets for pike fishing and boat hire are available from the Visitor Centre.

Times Open Grounds: 14 Mar-May & Sep-Nov, daily 10-6; Jun-Aug, 10-7. Visitor centre: 14-29 Mar, wknds & BHs 10-6; 4 Apr-13 Sep, daily 10-6; 14 Sep-11 Oct, wknds; 12 Oct-1 Nov 10-5. Last admission 1hr before closing. **Fee** £3 (ch £1). Family £7. Group £2.40 **Facilities** ℗ (charged) ⊡ ⊟ shop ⅙ ⊟

CO LONDONDERRY

COLERAINE   MAP 01 C6

Hezlett House
107 Sea Rd, Castlerock BT51 4TW

➲ *(5m W on Coleraine/Downhill coast road 1m from Castlerock)*

☎ 028 7084 8728

e-mail: hezletthouse@nationaltrust.org.uk

web: www.nationaltrust.org.uk

A low, thatched cottage built around 1690 with an interesting cruck truss roof, constructed by using pairs of curved timbers to form arches and infilling around this frame with clay, rubble and other locally available materials.

Times Open Fri-Tue, 4-19 Apr; wknds & BHs, 25 Apr-28 Jun, 5-27 Sep; Thu-Mon, Jul-Aug, 2-6. **Fee** £3.50 (ch £2.40). Family ticket £9.40. Group £2.50 each. **Facilities** ℗ ⊟ (outdoor) (parking) ⊗ (ex in gardens on lead) ⅙

Mount Sandel
FREE

➲ *(1.25m SSE)*

☎ 028 9023 0560

web: www.ehsni.gov.uk

This 200ft oval mound overlooking the River Bann is believed to have been fortified in the Iron Age. Nearby is the earliest known inhabited place in Ireland, where post holes and hearths of wooden dwellings, and flint implements dating back to 6650BC have been found. The fort was a stronghold of de Courcy in the late 12th century and was refortified for artillery in the 17th century.

Times Open at all times. **Facilities** ℗

DOWNHILL   MAP 01 C6

Mussenden Temple and Downhill Demesne
Mussenden Rd BT51 4RP

➲ *(1m W of Castlerock off A2, 6m from Coleraine)*

☎ 028 7084 8728

e-mail: downhillcastle@nationaltrust.org.uk

web: www.nationaltrust.org.uk

Spectacularly placed on a cliff edge overlooking the Atlantic, this perfect 18th-century rotunda was modelled on the Temple of Vesta at Tivoli. Visitors entering by the Bishop's Gate can enjoy a beautiful glen walk up to the headland where the temple stands.

Times Open Grounds, all year, dawn-dusk, daily & BHs, 24 Mar-4 Oct, 10-5
Fee £2.50 (ch £1.70). Family £6.70. Admission charged when facilities open.
Facilities ❷ �🄿 ⅋ toilets for disabled ♨

DUNGIVEN   MAP 01 C5

Banagher Church   FREE

➲ *(2m SW)*

☎ 028 9023 5000
web: www.ehsni.gov.uk

This church was founded by St Muiredach O'Heney in 1100 and altered in later centuries. Today impressive ruins remain. The nave is the oldest part and the square-headed lintelled west door is particularly impressive. Just outside, the perfect miniature stone house, complete with pitched roof and the sculpted figures of a saint at the doorway, is believed to be the tomb of St Muiredach. The saint was said to have endowed his large family with the power of bringing good luck. All they had to do was to sprinkle whoever or whatever needed luck with sand taken from the base of the saint's tomb.

Times Open at all times. **Facilities** ❷

Dungiven Priory   FREE

➲ *(SE of town overlooking River Roe)*

☎ 028 9023 5000
web: www.ehsni.gov.uk

Up until the 17th century Dungiven was the stronghold of the O'Cahan chiefs, and the Augustinian priory, of which extensive ruins remain, was founded by the O'Cahans around 1150. The church, which was altered many times in later centuries, contains one of Northern Ireland's finest medieval tombs. It is the tomb of Cooey na Gall O'Cahan who died in 1385. His sculpted effigy, dressed in Irish armour, lies under a stonework canopy. Below are six kilted warriors.

Times Open Church at all times, chancel only when caretaker available. Check with house at end of lane. **Facilities** ❷

LIMAVADY   MAP 01 C6

Rough Fort   FREE

➲ *(1m W off A2)*

☎ 028 7084 8728
e-mail: downhillcastle@nationaltrust.org.uk
web: www.ntni.org.uk

Early Christian rath picturesquely surrounded by pine and beech trees, making it a significant landscape feature. The Rough Fort is one of the best examples of an earthwork ring fort in Ireland.

Times ✳ Open at all times. **Facilities** 🐾 ♨

LONDONDERRY   MAP 01 C5

City Walls

☎ 028 9023 5000
web: www.ehsni.gov.uk

The finest and most complete city walls to be found in Ireland. The walls, 20-25ft high, are mounted with ancient cannon, and date back to the 17th century. The walled city is a conservation area with many fine

buildings. Visitors can walk round the city ramparts - a circuit of one mile.

Times ✳ Open all times. **Facilities** ❷ (charged)

Tower Museum

Union Hall Place BT48 6LU

➲ *(behind city wall, facing Guildhall)*

☎ 028 7137 2411
e-mail: museums@derrycity.gov.uk
web: www.derrycity.gov.uk/museums

Opened in 1992, the museum has won the Irish and British Museum of the Year Awards. It has two permanent exhibitions as well as hosting temporary and travelling exhibitions throughout the year. The multimedia 'Story of Derry' exhibition has reopened following extensive refurbishment. There is also an exhibition about the Spanish Armada which includes artefacts from a galleon shipwrecked in Kinnagoe Bay in 1588.

Times Open all year, Sep-Jun, Tue-Sat 10-5. Jul-Aug, Mon-Sat 10-5, Sun 10-1. Please check local press for opening details on BH. **Fee** ✳ £4 (concessions £2) **Facilities** ℗ (300yds) ⅋ toilets for disabled ❽ (ex assist dogs) ▭

MAGHERA   MAP 01 C5

Maghera Church   FREE

➲ *(E approach to the town)*

☎ 028 9023 5000
web: www.ehsni.gov.uk

Important 6th-century monastery founded by St Lurach, later a bishop's see and finally a parish church. This much-altered church has a magnificently decorated 12th-century west door. A cross-carved stone to the west of the church is supposed to be the grave of the founder.

Times Key from Leisure Centre. **Facilities** ❷

MONEYMORE   MAP 01 C5

Springhill House

BT45 7NQ

➲ *(1m from Moneymore on B18 to Coagh)*

☎ 028 8674 8210 & 7927
e-mail: springhill@nationaltrust.org.uk
web: www.nationaltrust.org.uk

Pretty 17th-century 'plantation' home with a significant costume collection. Today much of the family furniture, books and bric-a-brac have been retained. Outside, the laundry, stables, brewhouse, and old dovecote make interesting viewing. Inside is a family home with portraits, furniture and decorative arts that bring to life the many generations of the Lenox-Conynghams who lived here from 1680.

Times Open House: wknds & BHs, 14 Mar-28 Jun & 18-19 Apr, 5-7 Sep; daily Good Fri-14 Apr & Jul-Aug, 1-6. Grounds & costume collection: daily, Feb-Apr & Oct-Jan, 10-4; May-Sep, 10-6. **Fee** House, grounds and costume collection: £6.30 (ch £3.20). Family £10.30. Grounds & costume collection only: £3.20 (ch £1.60). Family £8. Group £5. Admission charged when house open. **Facilities** ❷ ▯ �🄿 (outdoor) ⅋ (Partly accessible) (lift, photograph album, wheelchair, scented plants) toilets for disabled shop ❽ (ex assist dogs) ♨

CO TYRONE

ARDBOE MAP 01 C5

Ardboe Cross FREE

(off B73)

☎ 028 9023 5000

web: www.ehsni.gov.uk

Situated at Ardboe Point, on the western shore of Lough Neagh, is the best example of a high cross to be found in Northern Ireland. Marking the site of an ancient monastery, the cross has 22 sculpted panels, many recognisably biblical, including Adam and Eve and the Last Judgment. It stands over 18ft high and dates back to the 10th century. It is still the rallying place of the annual Lammas, but praying at the cross and washing in the lake has been replaced by traditional music-making, singing and selling of local produce. The tradition of 'cross reading' or interpreting the pictures on the cross, is an honour passed from generation to generation among the men of the village.

Times Open at all times. **Facilities** Ⓟ

BALLYGAWLEY MAP 01 C5

U S Grant Ancestral Homestead & Visitor Centre

Dergenagh Rd BT70 1TW

(off A4, 2m on Dergenagh road, signed)

☎ 028 8555 7133

e-mail: killymaddy.reception@dungannon.gov.uk

web: www.dungannon.gov.uk

Ancestral homestead of Ulysses S Grant, 18th President of the United States of America. The homestead and farmyard have been restored to the style and appearance of a mid-19th-century Irish smallholding. There are many amenities including a children's play area, purpose built barbecue and picnic tables and butterfly garden.

Times Open Sep-Jun Mon-Fri 9-5; Jul-Aug Mon-Thu 9-6, Fri 9-7, Sat & Sun 9-5; Sep-Nov & Feb-Jun, Sat & Sun 10-4, Dec-Jan Sat &Sun 11-3 (extended opening hours on BHs). **Fee** Free admission. Charge made for AV show. **Facilities** Ⓟ (outdoor) ♿ (wide doorway to audio-visual area/entrances/exits) (ex assist dogs)

BEAGHMORE MAP 01 C5

Beaghmore Stone Circles and Alignments FREE

☎ 028 9023 5000

web: www.ehsni.gov.uk

Discovered in the 1930s, these impressive, ritualistic stones have been dated back to the early Bronze, and maybe even Neolithic Ages. There are three pairs of stone circles, one single circle, stone rows or alignments and cairns, which range in height from one to four feet. This is an area littered with historic monuments, many discovered by people cutting turf.

Times Open at all times. **Facilities** Ⓟ

BENBURB MAP 01 C5

Benburb Castle FREE

☎ 028 9023 5000

web: www.ehsni.gov.uk

The castle ruins - three towers and massive walls - are dramatically placed on a cliff-edge 120ft above the River Blackwater. The northwest tower is now restored and has dizzy cliff-edge views. The castle, built by Sir Richard Wingfield around 1615, is actually situated in the grounds of the Servite Priory. There are attractive walks down to the river.

Times Castle grounds open at all times. Special arrangements, made in advance, necessary for access to flanker tower. **Facilities** Ⓟ

CASTLECAULFIELD MAP 01 C5

Castle Caulfield FREE

☎ 028 9023 5000

web: www.ehsni.gov.uk

Sir Toby Caulfield, an Oxfordshire knight and ancestor of the Earls of Charlemont, built this manor house in 1619 on the site of an ancient fort. It was badly burnt in 1641, repaired and lived in by the Caulfield/Charlemont family until 1670. It boasts the rare distinction of having had Saint Oliver Plunkett and John Wesley preach in its grounds. Some fragments of the castle are re-used in the fine, large 17th-century parish church.

Times Open at all times. **Facilities** Ⓟ

COOKSTOWN MAP 01 C5

Tullaghoge Fort FREE

(2m S)

☎ 028 9023 5000

web: www.ehsni.gov.uk

This large hilltop earthwork, planted with trees, was once the headquarters of the O'Hagans, Chief Justices of the old kingdom of Tyrone. Between the 12th and 16th centuries the O'Neill Chiefs of Ulster were also crowned here - the King Elect was seated on a stone inauguration chair, new sandals were placed on his feet and he was then anointed and crowned. The last such ceremony was held here in the 1590s; in 1600 the stone throne was destroyed by order of Lord Mountjoy.

Times Open at all times. **Facilities** Ⓟ

Wellbrook Beetling Mill

20 Wellbrook Rd, Corkhill BT80 9RY

(4m W, 0.5m off A505)

☎ 028 8674 8210 & 8675 1735

e-mail: wellbrook@nationaltrust.org.uk

web: www.nationaltrust.org.uk

This 18th-century water-powered beetling mill was used for beetling and, until 1961, for finishing Irish linen. Beetling was the name given to the final process in linen making, when the material was beaten by 30 or so hammers (beetles) to achieve a smooth and slightly shiny finish.

Times Open wknds & BHs, 14 Mar-28 Jun, 18-19 Apr, 5-27 Sep; daily Good Fri-14 Apr & Jul-Aug (ex Fri) 2-6. **Fee** Mill tour: £4 (ch £2.30). Family £10.30. **Facilities** Ⓟ ♿ (Partly accessible) toilets for disabled shop

DUNGANNON
MAP 01 C5

Tyrone Crystal
2 for 1

Killybrackey BT71 6TT

➲ *(M1 junct 14/A45 to T-junct, left towards Dungannon. Attraction 2.5m on left, signed)*

☎ 028 8772 5335

e-mail: info@tyronecrystal.com

web: www.tyronecrystal.com

Crystal making in Tyrone dates its beginnings from the days of Benjamin Edwards in the 1770s. Tyrone Crystal is hand-cut, and visitors can see this craft in action on guided tours of the factory. The spacious visitor centre and facilities contribute to a fascinating insight of the history and heritage of this industry.

Times Open all year Visitor Centre Mon-Sat 9-5. Tour times Mon-Fri 11, 12, 2. **Fee** £5 for tour (ch under 12 £2.50, concessions & Groups 20+ £2.50). **Facilities** ❷ ⬚⬚◍ 🎋 (outdoor) ⛾ (disabled parking spaces) toilets for disabled shop ⊗ (ex assist dogs) ▄

NEWTOWNSTEWART
MAP 01 C5

Harry Avery's Castle
FREE

➲ *(0.75m SW)*

☎ 028 9023 5000

web: www.ehsni.gov.uk

The hilltop ruins of a Gaelic stone castle, built around the 14th century by one of the O'Neill chiefs, are the remains of the oldest surviving Irish-built castle in the north. Only the great twin towers of the gatehouse are left. A stairway enables the public to gain access to one of these.

Times Open at all times. **Facilities** ⊗ ⬚⬚

OMAGH
MAP 01 C5

Ulster American Folk Park

2 Mellon Rd, Castletown BT78 5QY

➲ *(5m NW Omagh on A5)*

☎ 028 8224 3292

e-mail: uafpinfo@nmni.com

web: www.nmni.com

An award winning outdoor museum of emigration which tells the story of millions of people who emigrated from these shores throughout the 18th and 19th centuries. The Old World and New World layout of the park illustrates the various aspects of emigrant life on both sides of the Atlantic. Traditional thatched buildings, American log houses and a full-scale replica emigrant ship plus the dockside gallery help to bring a bygone era back to life. Costumed demonstrators go about their everyday tasks including spinning, open hearth cookery, printing and textiles. The museum also includes an indoor Emigrants Exhibition and a centre for Migration Studies/library which is accessible to all visitors if they wish to find further information on the history of emigration and the place of their families in it.

Times Open all year Apr-Oct daily 10.30-6, Sun & BH 11-6.30; Nov-Mar Mon-Fri 10.30-5. (Last admission 1hr 30mins before closing). **Fee** ✳ Gift Aid admission £5.50 (under 5's free, ch 5-18 & concessions £3.50). Family ticket (2ad+2ch) £15.50, (1ad+3ch) £11. **Facilities** ❷ ⬚⬚◍ 🎋 (outdoor) ⛾ toilets for disabled shop ⊗ (ex assist dogs) ▄

STEWARTSTOWN
MAP 01 C5

Mountjoy Castle
FREE

Magheralamfield

➲ *(3m SE, off B161)*

☎ 028 9023 5000

web: www.ehsni.gov.uk

Ruins of an early 17th-century brick and stone fort, with four rectangular towers, overlooking Lough Neagh. The fort was built for Lord Deputy Mountjoy during his campaign against Hugh O'Neill, Earl of Tyrone. It was captured and re-captured by the Irish and English during the 17th century and was also used by the armies of James II and William III.

Times Open at all times. **Facilities** ❷

STRABANE
MAP 01 C5

Gray's Printing Press

49 Main St BT82 8AU

➲ *(in centre of Strabane)*

☎ 028 7188 0055 & 867 48210

e-mail: grays@nationaltrust.org.uk

web: www.nationaltrust.org.uk

Behind this 18th-century shopfront in the heart of Strabane, visitors can step back in time and hear the story of printing in what was once the leading printing town in Ulster. A treasure trove of history that tells the indelible story of ink, presses and emigration in the 18th-century printing house where John Dunlap, printer of the American Declaration of Independence, and James Wilson, grandfather of US President Woodrow Wilson, learnt their trade.

Times Please contact Property Manager 028 8674 8210. **Fee** ✳ £3.50 (ch £2.10). Family ticket £9.10. Group rate £2.80 each. Group rate outside normal hours £3.65 each. **Facilities** ⓟ (100yds) ⛾ (Partly accessible) toilets for disabled ⊗ (ex assist dogs) ▨

IRELAND

REPUBLIC OF IRELAND

Custom House, Dublin

CO CLARE

BALLYVAUGHAN
MAP 01 B3

Aillwee Cave
2 for 1

➲ (3m S of Ballyvaughan. Signed from Galway and Ennis)

☎ 065 707 7036
e-mail: barbara@aillweecave.ie
web: www.aillweecave.ie

An underground network of caves beneath the world famous Burren. Guided tours take you through large caverns, over bridged chasms and alongside thunderous waterfalls. There is a craftshop, a dairy where cheese is made, a speciality food shop and a tearoom. Santa uses the cave as a workshop around Christmas time, while Easter sees a massive egg hunt in the woods. The Burren Birds of Prey Centre, home to the largest display of birds of prey in Ireland. Visitors have the opportunity to view the birds in open fronted aviaries. Special Events: Santa's Workshop, appointments necessary.

Times Open all year, daily 10-5.30. End Nov & all Dec by appointment only. **Fee** €17 (ch€10, pen €15). Family ticket €39-€49 (all prices are joint tickets). **Facilities** ❶ ⬚ ⬚ 🍴 ⬚ (outdoor) ♿ (cave not accessible, but main cave building and birds of prey centre fully accessible) toilets for disabled shop ⊗ (ex assist dogs) ▬

BUNRATTY
MAP 01 B3

Bunratty Castle & Folk Park

➲ (Located 10km from Shannon Airport just off the main dual carriageway (N18) between Limerick and Ennis. Follow the tourist sign from the N18)

☎ 061 360788
e-mail: reservations@shannondev.ie
web: www.shannonheritage.com

Magnificent Bunratty Castle was built around 1425. The restored castle contains mainly 15th and 16th-century furnishings and tapestries. Within its grounds is Bunratty Folk Park where 19th-century Irish life is tellingly recreated. Rural farmhouses, a village street and Bunratty House with its formal Regency gardens are recreated and furnished, as they would have appeared at the time.

Times ✳ Open all year (ex Good Fri and 24-25 Dec). Low season 9.30-4.15. (Last admission 3.30). High season 9-5.30 (Last admission 4.15) Castle closes 4 all year round. Times subject to change. **Facilities** ❶ ⬚ 🍴 ⬚ (outdoor) shop garden centre ▬

KILLALOE
MAP 01 B3

Brian Boru Heritage Centre

➲ (N7 via Parkway Rdbt in Limerick city via Annacotty, Lisnagry and Birdhill. Turn left at Ballina R494)

☎ 061 360788
e-mail: reservations@shannondev.ie
web: www.shannonheritage.com

The 11th-century High King of Ireland, Brian Boru one of the most influential and colourful figures in Irish history. The heritage centre reveals the story of Brian Boru through a series of colourful exhibits, graphic illustrations and inter-active audio-visual presentation.

Times ✳ Open May-Sep, daily 10-6 **Facilities** ❶ shop ▬

LISCANNOR
MAP 01 B3

Cliffs of Moher Visitors Centre

➲ (6m NW of Lahinch)

☎ 065 708 6140
e-mail: marketing@cliffofmoher.ie
web: www.cliffsofmoher.ie

The Cliffs of Moher stand as a giant natural rampart against the aggressive might of the Atlantic Ocean. They rise in places to 700ft, and stretch for almost five miles. O'Brien's Tower was built in the early 19th century as a viewing point for tourists on the highest point. The famous site is the location for a new Visitor Experience, including a state-of-the-art interpretation element, Atlantic Edge, as well as extensive visitor facilities. Cliffs of Moher Rangers are now on site for visitor safety as well as cliff edge guiding and information.

Times Open all year. 9-5.30 Jan-Feb; 9-6 Mar-Apr & Oct; 8.30-9 May-Sep; 9.30-5 Nov-Dec **Facilities** ❶ (charged) ⬚ 🍴 ⬚ (outdoor) ♿ (induction loops at reception & audio visual theatre) toilets for disabled shop ⊗ (ex assist dogs in grounds) ▬

QUIN
MAP 01 B3

Craggaunowen The Living Past Experience

➲ (signed from N18 Limerick to Galway road, off R462 from Cratloe and R469 from Ennis)

☎ 061 360788
e-mail: reservations@shannondev.ie
web: www.shannonheritage.com

The project includes a reconstructed ring fort and replicas of furniture, tools and utensils. Also on display is the 'Brendan', a replica of the leather canoe used by St Brendan the Navigator in the 6th century. The boat was sailed across the Atlantic Ocean in 1976 and 1977. A major feature is the Bronze Age lake dwelling.

Times ✳ Open Apr-mid Oct, daily 10-6 (last admission 5). **Facilities** ❶ ⬚ ⬚ (outdoor) shop ▬

IRELAND

QUIN CONTINUED

Knappogue Castle & Walled Garden
➲ *(off N18 3m from Quin)*
☎ 061 360788
e-mail: reservations@shannondev.ie
web: www.shannonheritage.com

Built in 1467, Knappogue has a long and varied history. Occupied by Cromwell's troops in 1641 and completely restored in the mid-19th century, the castle fell into disrepair in the 1900s. In 1966 the careful restoration was completed and today the castle is famous for its medieval events. The attractive restored Victorian walled garden includes among many of its features a collection of plants from the Victorian era.

Times ✳ Open May-mid Sep daily 9.30-5.30 **Facilities** shop ▬

CO CORK

BLARNEY   **MAP 01 B2**

Blarney Castle & Rock Close   `2 for 1`
➲ *(5m from Cork on main road towards Limerick)*
☎ 021 4385252
e-mail: info@blarneycastle.ie
web: www.blarneycastle.ie

The site of the famous Blarney Stone, known the world over for the eloquence it is said to impart to those who kiss it. The stone is in the upper tower of the castle, and, held by your feet, you must lean backwards down the inside of the battlements in order to receive the 'gift of the gab'.

Times Open Blarney Castle & Rock Close. Mon-Fri, May & Sep 10-4, Jun-Aug 9-7. Oct-Apr 9-sundown or 6. Sun, Summer 9.30-5.30, Winter 9.30-sundown. Closed 24-25 Dec. **Fee** ✳ Blarney Castle & Rock Close €8 (ch 8-14 €2.50, concessions €6). Family ticket (2ad+2ch) €18 **Facilities** ❶ shop ⊗ (ex assist dogs & on leads)

CARRIGTWOHILL   **MAP 01 B2**
(CARRIGTOHILL)

Fota Arboretum & Gardens
Fota Estate
➲ *(14km from Cork on Cobh road)*
☎ 021 4812728
e-mail: info@heritageireland.ie
web: www.heritageireland.ie

Fota Arboretum contains an extensive collection of trees and shrubs extending over an area of approx 27 acres and includes features such as an ornamental pond and Italian walled gardens. The collection includes many tender plants that could not be grown at inland locations, with many examples of exotic plants from the Southern Hemisphere.

Times Arboretum: Open Apr-Oct, daily 9-6; Nov-Mar, daily 9-5. Walled Gardens: Apr-Oct, Mon-Thu 9-4.30, Fri 9-3.30, Sat & public hols 11-5, Sun 2-5. **Fee** Free admission. Parking fee €3. **Facilities** ❶ (charged) 戸

Fota Wildlife Park
Fota Estate
➲ *(16km E of Cork. From N25 (Cork to Waterford road) take Cobh road)*
☎ 021 4812678
e-mail: info@fotawildlife.ie
web: www.fotawildlife.ie

Established with the primary aim of conservation, Fota has more than 90 species of exotic wildlife in open, natural surroundings. Many of the animals wander freely around the park. Giraffes, zebras, ostriches, antelope, cheetahs and a wide array of waterfowl are among the species here.

Times Open 17 Mar-Oct, daily, 10-6 (Sun 11-6) (last admission 5); Nov-17 Mar 10-4.30 (Sun 11-4.30). (Last admission 3.30). **Fee** ✳ €13 (ch, concessions €8.50, ch under 3 free). Family day ticket €54. **Facilities** ❶ (charged) ⊑ 戸 (outdoor) ♿ (ramps where required) toilets for disabled shop ⊗ ▬

CLONAKILTY   **MAP 01 B2**

West Cork Model Village Railway
Inchydoney Rd
➲ *(From Cork N71 West Cork left at junct for Inchydoney Island, signed at road junct. Village on bay side of Clonakilty)*
☎ 023 33224
e-mail: modelvillage@eircom.net
web: www.modelvillage.ie

This miniature world depicts Irish towns as they were in the 1940s, with models of the West Cork Railway and various animated scenes. The tea room is set in authentic railway carriages that overlook picturesque Clonakilty Bay. Also take a guided tour of Clonakilty and the surrounding area on the road train.

Times ✳ Open daily Feb-Oct 11-5; Jul-Aug, 10-6. **Facilities** ❶ ⊑ 戸 shop ⊗ (ex assist dogs) ▬

COBH

MAP 01 B2

The Queentown Story

2 for 1

Cobh Railway Station

➲ *(off N25, follow signs for Cobh. Attraction at Deepwater Quay, adjacent to train station)*

☎ 021 4813591

e-mail: info@cobhheritage.com

web: www.cobhheritage.com

A dramatic exhibition of the origins, history and legends of Cobh. Between 1848 and 1950 over three million Irish people were deported from Cobh on convict ships. Visitors can explore the conditions onboard these vessels and learn about the harbour's connections with the *Lusitania* and the *Titanic*.

Times Open May-Nov, 10-6 (last admission 5). Nov-May, 10-5 (last admission 4) **Fee** €7.10 (ch €4, concessions €6). Family ticket €20 **Facilities** ❷ ⵑ〒◉ & (fully wheelchair accessible, wide access) toilets for disabled shop ⊗ (ex assist dogs) ▭

CORK

MAP 01 B2

Cork City Gaol

2 for 1

Convent Av, Sundays Well

➲ *(2km NW from Patrick St off Sundays Well Rd)*

☎ 021 4305022

e-mail: corkgaol@indigo.ie

web: www.corkcitygaol.com

A restored 19th-century prison building. Furnished cells, lifelike characters and sound effects combine to allow visitors to experience day-to-day life for prisoners and gaoler. There is an audio-visual presentation of the social history of Cork City. Individual sound tours are available in a number of languages. A permanent exhibition, the Radio Museum Experience, is located in the restored 1920s broadcasting studio, home to Cork's first radio station, 6CK. Unfortunately the 1st and 2nd floors are not accessible to wheelchair users.

Times Open all year Mar-Oct, daily 9.30-5; Nov-Feb, daily 10-4. Closed 23-28 Dec. **Fee** ✳ €7.50 (ch €4, concessions €6.50) Family ticket €20 **Facilities** ❷ ⵑ〒 (outdoor) & (3 cells on the first floor inaccessible) (customer care policy - individual attention) toilets for disabled shop ⊗ (ex assist dogs)

Cork Public Museum

FREE

Fitzgerald Park, Mardyke

➲ *(N of University College)*

☎ 021 4270679

e-mail: museum@corkcity.ie

Displays illustrating the history of the city are housed in this museum. The collections cover the economic, social and municipal history from the Mesolithic period onwards. There are fine collections of Cork silver and glass.

Times ✳ Open all year, Mon-Fri, 11-1 & 2.15-5; Sat 11-1 & 2.15-4; Sun (Apr-Oct only) 3-5. **Facilities** ❷ ⵑ & toilets for disabled ⊗ (ex assist dogs)

GLENGARRIFF

MAP 01 B2

Garinish Island

➲ *(1.5km boat trip from Glengarriff)*

☎ 027 63040

Ilnacullin is a small island of 37 acres known to horticulturists and lovers of trees and shrubs all around the world as an island garden of rare beauty. The gardens of Ilnacullin owe their existence to the creative partnership, some 80 years ago, of Annan Bryce, then owner of the island and Harold Peto, architect and garden designer.

Times Open Mar & Oct, Mon-Sat, 10-4, Sun 1-5; Apr, Mon-Sat, 10-6.30 Sun 1-6.30; May & Sep, Mon-Sat, 10-6.30, Sun 12-6.30; Jun, Mon-Sat, 10-6.30, Sun 11-6.30, Jul & Aug, Mon-Sat 9.30-6.30, Sun 11-6.30. Last landing 1 hour before closing. **Fee** €3.70 (ch & students €1.30, pen €2.60) Family ticket €8.70. Group rate €2.60 each. **Facilities** ⵑ & toilets for disabled

KINSALE

MAP 01 B2

Charles Fort

Summer Cove

➲ *(3km from Kinsale)*

☎ 021 4772263

e-mail: charlesfort@opw.ie

web: www.heritageireland.ie

Built as part of the fortifications of the Irish coast in the late 17th century, Charles Fort was named after King Charles II. After the Battle of the Boyne in 1690, Williamite forces attacked and successfully besieged Charles Fort and the nearby James Fort, both of which held out for King James. The Fort also played a role in the Napoleonic Wars and was made a National Monument in 1973.

Times Open mid Mar-Oct, daily 10-6; Nov-mid Mar, daily 10-5. Last admission 45 mins before closing. **Fee** €3.70 (ch & students €1.30, pen €2.60). Family ticket €8.70. Group rate €2.60 each. **Facilities** ℗ ⵑ 〒 & (lift) toilets for disabled ⊗ (ex assist dogs)

KINSALE CONTINUED

Desmond Castle

Cork St

➲ *(R600 from Cork city to Kinsale. From post office, 1st left then right, opposite Regional Museum then left and right again, castle on left)*

☎ 021 4774855

e-mail: desmondcastle@opw.ie
web: www.desmondcastle.ie

Built by the Earl of Desmond around the beginning of the 16th century, this tower was originally a custom house, but has also served as an ordnance office, prison, workhouse, stable and meeting place for the Local Defence Force during World War II. In 1938 it was declared a National Monument and restored. The Castle now houses the International Museum of Wine.

Times Open mid Apr-Oct, daily 10-6. Last admission 45 mins before closing. **Fee** €2.90, (ch & students €1.30, pen €2.10) Family €7.40 **Facilities** ℗ (200mtrs) (parking discs required in town) ⊗ (ex assist dogs)

MIDLETON   MAP 01 C2

Jameson Experience

The Old Distillery

➲ *(E end of main street on left. Well signed)*

☎ 021 4613594

e-mail: bookings@omd.ie
web: www.jamesonwhiskey.com

A tour of the Old Midleton Distillery commences with a 15-minute audio/visual presentation, followed by a 35-minute guided tour of the Old Distillery and then back to the Jameson Bar for a whiskey tasting - mineral water is available for children. The guided tour and audio-visual are available in seven languages.

Times Open Nov-Feb daily, tours 11.30, 1, 2.30 & 4. Mar-Oct daily 10-6 (last tour 5). Closed Good Fri, 24-26 & 31 Dec & 1 Jan. **Fee** ✳ €12.50 Family ticket €25 **Facilities** ℗ ⊑ ℉ licensed ঙ toilets for disabled shop ⊗ (ex certain areas/assist dogs) ▪

CO DONEGAL

BALLYSHANNON   MAP 01 B5

The Water Wheels   `FREE`

Abbey Assaroe

➲ *(cross Abbey River on Rossnowlagh Rd, next turning left & follow signs)*

☎ 071 9851580

Abbey Assaroe was founded by Cistercian Monks from Boyle Abbey in the late 12th century, who excelled in water engineering and canalised the river to turn water wheels for mechanical power. There are two restored 12th-century mills, one is used as coffee shop and restaurant; the other houses a small museum related to the history of the Cistercians. Interesting walks in the vicinity with views of the Erne Estuary and Atlantic Ocean.

Times Open May-Oct, daily 10.30-6.30 **Facilities** ℗ ⊑ ℉ ℉ (outdoor) ঙ toilets for disabled shop garden centre

---

DONEGAL   MAP 01 B5

Donegal Castle

➲ *(in town centre)*

☎ 074 9722405

e-mail: donegalcastle@opw.ie

This restored 15th-century castle and adjoining 17th-century ruined English manor house contain exhibitions of Irish historical events. Guided tours are available.

Times Open mid Mar-end Oct, daily 10-6; Nov-mid Mar Thu-Mon 9.30-4.30 Last admission 45 mins before closing. **Fee** €3.70 (ch & students €1.30, pen €2.60). Family ticket (2ad+3ch) €8.70 **Facilities** ℗ ⊗ (ex assist dogs)

LETTERKENNY   MAP 01 C5

Glebe House & Gallery

Churchill

➲ *(signed from Letterkenny on R251)*

☎ 074 9137071

web: www.glebegallery@opw.ie

This Regency house, set in beautiful woodland gardens along the shore of Lough Gartan, was given to the nation along with his art collection by artist Derek Hill. The interior of the house is decorated with original wallpapers and textiles by William Morris.

Times Open Etr daily 11-6.30 then Jun-Sep, Sat-Thu 11-6.30 (Closed Fri). Last tour 1 hour before closing. **Fee** €2.90 (ch & student €1.30, pen €2). Family ticket €7. Group rate €2.10 each. **Facilities** ℗ ⊑ ⊗ (ex assist dogs)

IRELAND

Glenveagh National Park & Castle

Churchill

➲ *(left off N56 from Letterkenny)*

☎ 074 9137090 & 9137262

e-mail: claire.bromley@environ.ie

web: www.glenreaghnationalpark.ie

Over 40,000 acres of mountains, glens, lakes and woods. A Scottish-style castle is surrounded by one of the finest gardens in Ireland, contrasting with the rugged surroundings.

Times Open all year daily 10-6 **Fee** ✳ Park: free, Castle €3 (ch & students €1.50, pen €2). Family ticket €7, group 20+ €2. Buses €1 & €2 **Facilities** ❷ ⛛🎞 (outdoor) ♿ (no lift access to first floor) (buses equipped to take wheelchair users) toilets for disabled ⊗ (dogs not permitted on buses)

LIFFORD   MAP 01 C5

Cavanacor Historic House & Art Gallery

Ballindrait

➲ *(1.5m from town off N14 Strabane/Letterkenny road)*

☎ 074 9141143

e-mail: art@cavanacorgallery.ie

web: www.cavanacorgallery.ie

Built in the early 1600s and commanding a view of the Clonleigh Valley and the River Deele, Cavanacor House is the ancestral home of James Knox Polk, 11th President of the USA (1845-1849). King James II dined under the sycamore tree in front of the house in 1689. There are over 10 acres of landscaped gardens and an old-fashioned walled garden. The Art Gallery will feature exhibitions of new work by national and international artists.

Times House open 1-23 Feb; May-15 Jun. Art gallery open all year. **Facilities** ❷ ♿ (Partly accessible) shop

The Old Courthouse

Visitor Centre, The Diamond

☎ 091 41733

e-mail: info@liffordoldcourthouse.com

web: www.liffordoldcourthouse.com

One of Ireland's oldest courthouse and jail provides an insight into legal history and some of the terrible conditions endured by prisoners in the 18th century. Witness re-enactments of famous trials held in this historic building.

Times ✳ Open all year, Mon-Fri, 10-5 & Sun 12.30-5 (last tour 4). Closed Sat & BHs. **Facilities** ⓟ 100mtrs ⛛🎞🎞 (outdoor) shop ⊗ (ex assist dogs) ▬

CO DUBLIN

BALBRIGGAN   MAP 01 D4

Ardgillan Castle

➲ *(R127 or M1 past Dublin Airport then follow signs)*

☎ 01 8492212

A large and elegant country manor house built in 1738, set in 194 acres of parkland, overlooking the sea and coast as far as the Mourne Mountains. There is a permanent exhibition of the 17th- century 'Down Survey' maps and various temporary exhibitions. Tours of the Gardens (June, July and August) begin at 3.30pm every Thursday. Guided tours of the house are conducted daily.

Times ✳ Open all year Apr-Sep, Tue-Sun & BHs 11-6 (daily Jul-Aug); Oct-Mar, Wed-Sun & BHs 11-4.30. Closed 23 Dec-1 Jan. **Facilities** ❷ ⛛🎞 (outdoor) ♿ toilets for disabled shop ⊗ (ex assist dogs)

DONABATE   MAP 01 D4

Newbridge House and Traditional Farm

Newbridge Demesne

➲ *(Take N1 and follow signs for Donabate.)*

☎ 01 8436534 & 8462184

e-mail: newbridgehouse@fingalcoco.ie

Newbridge House was designed by George Semple and built in 1737 for Charles Cobbe, Archbishop of Dublin. Set in 350 acres of parkland, the house contains many splendidly refurbished rooms featuring plasterwork, furniture and paintings. The house also features a fully restored courtyard surrounded by; a dairy, estate workers house, carpenters shop and blacksmiths forge. The grounds contain a 29 acre traditional farm with many rare breeds and children's playground.

Times ✳ Open Apr-Sep, Tue-Sat 10-5, Sun & PH 2-6; Oct-Mar, Sat-Sun & PH 2-5. Parties at other times by arrangement. **Facilities** ❷ ⛛🎞 (outdoor) shop ⊗ (ex assist dogs) ▬

DUBLIN   MAP 01 D4

The Casino

off Malahide Rd, Marino

➲ *(Turn left at pedestrian lights after Dublin Five Brigade Training HQ)*

☎ 01 8331618

e-mail: casinomarino@opw.ie

web: www.heritageireland.ie

Designed in 1757 by Sir William Chambers as a pleasure house for James Caulfield, 1st Earl of Charlemont, the Casino is possibly one of the finest 18th-century neo-Classical buildings in Europe. Its name means "small house", but the Casino surprisingly contains 16 finely-decorated rooms.

Times Open Feb, Mar & Nov, Sat, Sun & BH 12-4; Apr Sat & Sun 12-5; May & Oct daily 10-5; Jun-Sep, daily 10-6; Nov & Dec, Sat & Sun 12-4. Last admission 45 mins before closing. **Fee** €2.90 (ch & students €1.30, pen €2.10). Family ticket €7.40 **Facilities** ❷ ⊗ (ex assist dogs)

IRELAND

DUBLIN CONTINUED

Chester Beatty Library `FREE`

Dublin Castle

➲ *(2m from Dame St close to Christ Church Cathedral)*

☎ 01 4070750

e-mail: info@cbl.ie

web: www.cbl.ie

Situated in the heart of the city centre, the Chester Beatty Library is an art museum and library which houses the great collection of manuscripts, miniature paintings, prints, drawings, rare books and decorative arts assembled by Sir Alfred Chester Beatty (1875-1968). The exhibitions open a window on the artistic treasures of the great cultures and religions of the world. Egyptian papyrus texts, beautifully illustrated copies of the Qur'an and the Bible, and European medieval and renaissance manuscripts are among the highlights of the collection. Turkish and Persian miniatures and striking Buddhist paintings are also on display, as are Chinese dragon robes and Japanese woodblock prints.

Times Open all year, May-Sep, Mon-Fri 10-5; Oct-Apr, Tue-Fri 10-5, Sat 11-5, Sun 1-5. Closed 24-26 Dec, 1 Jan, BHs. **Facilities** ℗ (5mins walk) ⦿ licensed ♿ toilets for disabled shop ⓧ (ex assist dogs)

Christ Church Cathedral

Christchurch Place

➲ *(at top end of Dame St)*

☎ 01 6778099

e-mail: welcome@cccdub.ie

web: www.cccdub.ie

Founded in 1030, the present building dates from 1180 with a major restoration in the 1870s. The crypt is the second largest medieval crypt in Britain or Ireland. There are daily services and choral services on Sundays and during the week.

Times Open all year, daily Sep-May 9.45-5; Jun-Aug 9-6. Closed St Stephens Day & 27 Dec. **Fee** €6 (unwaged €4) **Facilities** ℗ (100yds) ⛩ (outdoor) ♿ (main cathedral accessible except area behind high altar) shop ⓧ (ex assist dogs) ▬

Drimnagh Castle

Long Mile Rd, Drimnagh D12

➲ *(Dame St, left at Christchurch Cathedral into Patrick St, right into Cork St, through Dolphins Barn up to Crumlin Rd, past Halfway House. 500yds on right)*

☎ 01 4502530 & 4508927

e-mail: drimnaghcastle@eircom.net

The last surviving medieval castle in Ireland with a flooded moat, Drimnagh dates back to the 13th century and was inhabited until 1954. The Castle consists of a restored Great Hall and medieval undercroft, a tall battlement tower and lookout posts, and other separate buildings including stables, an old coach house and a folly. One of the most attractive features of Drimnagh is the garden, a formal 17th-century layout with box hedges, yews and mop heads.

Times Open Apr-Oct Wed & Sun 12-5, Nov-Mar Sun 2-5. (Last tour 4). Other times by appointment. Large groups advisable to book **Fee** ✳ €4 (ch €2, concessions & students €3.50). Groups 20+ €3 each **Facilities** ℗ ♿ (limited access gravel courtyard and gardens) ⓧ (ex assist dogs)

Dublin Castle

Dame St

☎ 01 6777129

With two towers and a partial wall, this is the city's most outstanding legacy of the Middle Ages. Of interest are the Record Tower, state apartments, Church of the Most Holy Trinity and Heraldic Museum. The inauguration of the President of Ireland and related ceremonies are held in St. Patrick's Hall, an elegant state apartment.

Times ✳ Open all year, Mon-Fri 10-5, Sat-Sun & BH 2-5. Closed 24-26 Dec & Good Fri. **Facilities** ℗ ⦿

Dublin City Gallery The Hugh Lane `FREE`

Charlemont House, Parnell Square

➲ *(Off O'Connell St Parnell Monument. At the top of Parnell Square)*

☎ 01 2222550

e-mail: info.hughlane@dublincity.ie

web: www.hughlane.ie

Situated in Charlemont House, a fine Georgian building, the gallery's collection includes one of the most extensive collections of 20th-century Irish art. A superb range of international and Irish paintings, sculpture, works on paper and stained glass is also on show. Possibly the most fascinating aspect of the gallery is Francis Bacon's Studio, a complete reconstruction of the painter's studio, and a complete database of all the items in it. There are public lectures every Sunday and regular concerts (at noon on Sundays) throughout the year.

Times Open all year, Tue-Thu 10-6, Fri-Sat 10-5, Sun 11-5. Closed Mon, Good Fri & 24-25 Dec. **Facilities** ℗ (100mtrs) (meter parking) ⛩♿ (ramp & reserved parking) toilets for disabled shop ⓧ (ex assist dogs)

Dublinia & The Viking World `2 for 1`

St Michael's Hill, Christ Church

➲ *(in city centre)*

☎ 01 6794611

e-mail: info@dublinia.ie

web: www.dublinia.ie

The story of medieval Dublin. Housed in the former Synod Hall beside Christ Church Cathedral and developed by the Medieval Trust, Dublinia recreates the period from the arrival of Strongbow and the Anglo-Normans in 1170 to the closure of the monasteries by Henry VIII in 1540. Also included is the exhibition on the Viking World which tells the story of their way of life and turbulent voyages.

Times Open Apr-Sep 10-5; Oct-Mar 11-4. last admission 3.15 (winter) 4.15 (summer) **Fee** ✳ €6.25 (ch €3.95, concessions €5). Family ticket (2ad+3ch) €17 **Facilities** ℗ (100yds) ⛩♿ (2 floors accessible, but bridge and tower are not) toilets for disabled shop ⓧ (ex assist dogs) ▬

Dublin Writers Museum

18 Parnell Square

➲ *(on Parnell Sq, at North end of O'Connell St)*

☎ 01 8722077

e-mail: writers@dublintourism.ie
web: www.writersmuseum.com

The Dublin Writers Museum is housed in a restored 18th-century mansion and is a collection featuring personal items, portraits, books and letters relating to Dublin's most important literary figures, including Swift, Sheridan, Shaw, Wilde, Yeats, Joyce and Beckett. The mansion is a pleasure in itself, with sumptuous plasterwork and decorative stained windows. There is a special room dedicated to children's literature and a full programme of workshops, lectures and receptions.

Times ✱ Open all year, Mon-Sat 10-5, Sun & BH 11-5; Jun-Aug, Mon-Fri 10-6. **Facilities** ❷ (charged) 🖵 🍴 shop ⊗ (ex assist dogs) ◼

Dublin Zoo   [2 for 1]

Phoenix Park

➲ *(10mins bus ride from city centre)*

☎ 01 4748900

e-mail: info@dublinzoo.ie
web: www.dublinzoo.ie

Dublin Zoo first opened to the public in 1830, making it one of the oldest zoos in the world and has consistently been Ireland's favourite attraction. The Kaziranga Forest Trail is the latest development within Dublin Zoo. Visitors wander along winding paths to glimpse a breeding herd of Asian elephants. Dublin Zoo is a modern zoo with conservation, education and study as its mission. The majority of the animals here have been born and bred in zoos and are part of global breeding programmes to ensure their continued survival.

Times Open Mar-Oct, Mon-Sat 9.30-6, Sun 10.30-6; Nov-Feb, daily 10.30-dusk. **Fee** ✱ €14.50 (ch €10, concessions €12). Family tickets from €42 **Facilities** ❷ 🖵 🍴 🔥 (outdoor) 🔥 (Partly accessible) (wheelchairs available) toilets for disabled shop ⊗ ◼

Guinness Storehouse

St James's Gate Brewery

➲ *(from Dame St near Trinity College keep straight, follow road around passing Christchurch on right into Thomas St. Pass main brewery gates on left. At junct of James's St & Echlin St take left turn. At top of road turn left then 1st left on to Market St - pedestrian entrance on left)*

☎ 01 4084800 & 4714634

e-mail: guinness-storehouse@guinness.com
web: www.guinness-storehouse.com

The Guinness Storehouse is located in the heart of the Guinness brewery at St James's Gate. Housed in an old fermentation plant, this seven storey visitor experience tells the history of the making of this world famous beer. It is a dramatic story that begins 250 years ago and ends in Gravity Bar where visitors receive a complimentary pint of Guinness while relaxing and enjoying spectacular views over Dublin. The adventure begins the moment you walk through the door into the building's giant, pint-shaped heart of glass. You will discover what goes into making the "Black Stuff", the ingredients, the process, the passion. You'll learn about Arthur Guinness and find out how the drink that carries his name has been transported around the world. 2009 is the 250th anniversary of the company, and various celebratory events are planned.

Times Open daily 9.30-5 (last admission 5). Late summer opening Jul & Aug until 7. Closed Good Fri & 25-26 Dec. **Fee** €15 (ch 6-12 €5, pen & students over 18 €11, students under 18 €9). Family (2ad+2ch) €34.
Facilities ❷ 🖵 🍴 🔥 toilets for disabled shop ⊗ (ex assist dogs) ◼

Howth Castle Rhododendron Gardens   [FREE]

Howth

➲ *(9m NE of city centre, by coast road to Howth. Before Howth follow signs for Deer Park Hotel)*

☎ 01 8322624 & 8322256

e-mail: sales@deerpark.iol.ie

Overlooking the sea on the north side of Dublin Bay, the rhododendron walks command spectacular views of the Castle and Ireland's Eye. The flowers are at their best in May and June. Visitors should be aware that the gardens are in some disrepair and the paths somewhat rough and overgrown in parts.

Times Open all year, daily 8am-dusk. Closed 25 Dec. **Facilities** ❷ 🖵 🍴 licensed 🔥 (garden unsuitable) (ramped entrance) toilets for disabled ⊗ (ex assist dogs & in garden) ◼

Irish Museum of Modern Art   [FREE]

Royal Hospital, Military Rd, Kilmainham

➲ *(3.5km from city centre, just off N7 opposite Heuston Station)*

☎ 01 6129900

e-mail: info@imma.ie
web: www.imma.ie

Housed in the Royal Hospital Kilmainham, an impressive 17th-century building, the Irish Museum of Modern Art is Ireland's leading national institution for the collection and presentation of modern and contemporary art. It presents a wide variety of art and artists' ideas in a dynamic programme of exhibitions, which regularly includes bodies of work from the museum's own collection, its award-winning Education and Community Department and the Studio and National Programmes.

Times Open Jul-Sep, 27-30 Dec & BHs, Tue-Sun, 12-5.30. **Facilities** ❷ 🖵 shop ⊗ (ex assist dogs)

IRELAND

DUBLIN CONTINUED

James Joyce Centre

35 North Great George's St

➲ *(signed from N end of O'Connell Street and Parnell Square)*

☎ 01 8788547

e-mail: info@jamesjoyce.ie

web: www.jamesjoyce.ie

Situated in a beautifully restored 18th-century Georgian town house, the Centre is dedicated to the promotion of a greater interest in, and understanding of, the life and works of James Joyce. Visitors follow a self-guided tour through the house, that includes the door to No.7 Eccles Street, home of Leopold Bloom, the hero of *Ulysses*; furniture from Joyce's Paris flat, computer installations, video documentaries and a reconstruction of period rooms. Events are centred every year around 'Bloomsday', the 16th of June, which is when the events of *Ulysses* take place.

Times Open all year, Tue-Sat 10-5, Sun (Summer only) 12-5. Closed BHs **Fee** Admission €5 (concessions €4). Walking Tour €10 (concessions €8) group rates 10+ available €4.50 (concessions €3.50) **Facilities** Ⓟ (200mtrs) (pay & display) shop ⊗ (ex assist dogs) ═

Kilmainham Gaol

Inchicore Rd

➲ *(3.5km from city centre)*

☎ 01 4535984

web: www.kilmainhamgaol.opw.ie

One of the largest unoccupied gaols in Europe, covering some of the most heroic and tragic events in Ireland's emergence as a modern nation from the 1720s onwards. Attractions include a major exhibition detailing the political and penal history of the prison and its restoration.

Times Open Apr-Sep, daily 9.30-6 (last admission 5); Oct-Mar, Mon-Sat 9.30-5.30 (last admission 4), Sun 10-6 (last admission 5). Access by guided tour only. **Fee** €5.30 (ch & students €2.10, pen €3.70). Family ticket €11.50 **Facilities** Ⓟ (on street) ⊑ & (tours available by prior appointment) toilets for disabled ⊗

Marsh's Library

St Patrick's Close

➲ *(beside St Patrick Cathedral)*

☎ 01 4543511

e-mail: keeper@marshlibrary.ie

web: www.marshlibrary.ie

The first public library in Ireland, dating from 1701. Designed by William Robinson, the interior has been unchanged for 300 years. The collection is of approximately 25,000 volumes of 16th, 17th and early 18th-century books.

Times Open May-Sep Mon & Wed-Fri, 9.30-5, Sat 10.1. Oct-Apr, Mon & Wed-Fri, 10-1 & 2-5, Sat 10.30-1 **Fee** ✳ €2.50 (ch free, concessions €1.50). Maybe subject to change. **Facilities** Ⓟ (100mtrs) ⊗ (ex assist dogs) ▦

National Botanic Gardens

Glasnevin

➲ *(on Botanic Road, between N1 and N2)*

☎ 01 8374388 & 8570909

e-mail: botanicgardens@opw.ie

web: www.botanicgardens.ie

Ireland's premier Botanic Gardens, covers a total area of 19.5 hectares (48 acres), part of which is the natural flood plain of the River Tolka. The Gardens contain a large plant collection, which includes approximately 20,000 species and cultivated varieties. There are four ranges of glasshouses including the restored Curvilinear Range and the Great Palm House. Notable features include herbaceous borders, rose garden, rockery, alpine yard, arboretum, extensive shrub collections, wall plants and vegetable garden.

Times Open daily summer 9-6, winter 9-4.30 **Fee** Free admission. Parking €2. **Facilities** Ⓟ (charged) ⊑ ¶Ⓞ⊗ (ex assist dogs)

National Gallery of Ireland

Merrion Square

➲ *(N11, M50, follow signs to City Centre)*

☎ 01 6615133

e-mail: info@ngi.ie

web: www.nationalgallery.ie

The gallery, founded in 1854 by an Act of Parliament, houses the national collections of Irish art and European Old Masters including Rembrandt, Caravaggio, Poussin, and El Greco. There is also a special room dedicated to Jack B Yeats, and a National Portrait Collection.

Times Open all year, Mon-Sat 9.30-5.30 (Thu 9.30-8.30), Sun 12-5. Closed 24-26 Dec & Good Fri. **Facilities** Ⓟ (5 mins walk) (meter parking, around Merrion Sq) ⊑ ¶Ⓞ & (Braille/audio tours, lifts, ramps, disabled parking) toilets for disabled shop ⊗

National Library of Ireland

Kildare St

FREE

☎ 01 6030200

web: www.nli.ie

Founded in 1877 and based on collections from The Royal Dublin Society. The National Library holds an estimated five million items. There are collections of printed books, manuscripts, prints and drawings, photos, maps, newspapers, microfilms and ephemera. Included in the library's collection is the most significant exhibition on the life and works of the 20th century fine poet WB Yeats. The library's research facilities are open to all those with genuine research needs. In addition to research facilities, services include a regular programme of exhibitions open to the public and a Genealogy Service.

Times ✳ Open all year, Mon-Wed 9.30-7.45, Thu-Sat 9.30-4.45. Closed Sun, BHs, Good Fri & 23 Dec-2 Jan. **Facilities** shop ⊗ (ex assist dogs) ▦

National Photographic Archive

FREE

Meeting House Square, Temple Bar

➲ *(opposite The Gallery of Photography)*

☎ 01 6030200

e-mail: photoarchive@nli.ie

web: www.nli.ie

The National Photographic Archive, which is part of the National Library of Ireland, was opened in 1998 in an award-winning building in the Temple Bar area of Dublin. The archive holds an unrivalled collection of photographic images relating to Irish history, topography and cultural and social life. The collection is especially rich in late 19th and early 20th-century topographical views and studio portraits, but also includes photographs taken during the Rebellion of 1916 and the subsequent War of Independence and Civil War, as well as other historic events.

Times ✳ Open all year, Mon-Fri 10-5. (Closed BH's, Good Fri & 23 Dec-2 Jan). **Facilities** shop ⊗ (ex assist dogs) ▬

Natural History Museum

FREE

Merrion St

➲ *(in city centre)*

☎ 01 6777444

e-mail: education.nmi@indigo.ie

The Natural History Museum, which is part of The National Museum of Ireland, is a zoological museum containing diverse collections of world wildlife. The Irish Room, on the ground floor, is devoted largely to Irish mammals, sea creatures and insects. It includes the extinct giant Irish deer and the skeleton of a basking shark. The World Collection, has as its centre piece, the skeleton of a 60ft whale suspended from the roof. Other displays include the Giant Panda and a Pygmy Hippopotamus.

Times ✳ Open all year, Tue-Sat 10-5, Sun 2-5. Closed Mon, 25 Dec & Good Fri **Facilities** Ⓟ (parking meters wkdays) ⊗

Number Twenty Nine

2 for 1

29 Lower Fitzwilliam St

➲ *(on corner of Lower Fitzwilliam St & Mount Street Upper; adjacent to Merrion Square)*

☎ 01 7026165

e-mail: numbertwentynine@esb.ie

web: www.esb.ie/no29

Number Twenty-Nine is a lovingly restored middle class Dublin home from the late 18th and early 19th century, filled with a unique collection of original pieces, with excellent examples of Irish and international craftsmanship. Visitors are guided through the house from the basement kitchen to the attic nursery.

Times Open all year, Tue-Sat 10-5, Sun 12-5. Closed Mon & 2 wks prior to Xmas & Good Fri. **Fee** €6 (ch under 16 free, concessions €3). **Facilities** Ⓟ (on street/meter) ☕ ♿ (basement & ground floor accessible) toilets for disabled shop ⊗ (ex assist dogs) ▬

Phoenix Park Visitor Centre

FREE

Phoenix Park

➲ *(4km from Dublin)*

☎ 01 6770095

e-mail: phoenixparkvisitorcentre@opw.ie

Situated in Phoenix Park, the Visitor Centre provides an historical interpretation of the park from 3500BC, through a series of attractive displays. Part of the building is devoted to nature and there is a colourful film of Phoenix Park. The castle, probably dating from the early 17th century, has been restored to its former glory.

Times Open all year, Nov-mid Mar, Sat-Wed 10-6; mid Mar-end Oct, daily 10-6. **Facilities** Ⓟ ☕ ⊼ ⊗ (ex assist dogs)

DUN LAOGHAIRE — MAP 01 D4

The James Joyce Museum

Joyce Tower, Sandycove

➲ *(1m SE Dun Laoghaire by coast road to Sandycove Point or turn off main Dun Laoghaire-Dalkey road)*

☎ 01 2809265 & 8722077

e-mail: joycetower@dublintourism.ie

web: www.visitdublin.com/museums

Built by the British as a defence against a possible invasion by Napoleon, the tower has walls approximately 8ft thick and an original entrance door 13ft above the ground. The tower was once the temporary home of James Joyce, who depicted this setting in the opening scene of *Ulysses*. The structure is now a museum devoted to the author. Bloomsday, the day in 1904 on which all the action of *Ulysses* is set, is celebrated annually on 16th June. On this day, the museum is open from 8-6 for visits, readings from *Ulysses* and performances of various kinds, Edwardian costume is encouraged.

Times Open Apr-Sep, Mon-Sat 10-1 & 2-5, Sun & BHs 2-6; Oct-Mar by arrangement. **Fee** ✳ €7.25 (ch 3-11 €4.55, ch 12-17, pen & students €6.10). Family ticket €21. Parties 20+. **Facilities** Ⓟ (100yds) ♿ (access to ground floor only) shop ⊗ (ex assist dogs) ▬

MALAHIDE — MAP 01 D4

Malahide Castle

➲ *(from Dublin city centre follow signs for Malahide, then approaching village, main entrance to castle is signed to right off main road)*

☎ 01 8462184

e-mail: malahidecastle@dublintourism.ie

web: www.malahidecastle.com

One of Ireland's oldest castles, this romantic and beautiful structure, set in 250 acres of grounds, has changed very little in 800 years. Tours offer views of Irish period furniture and historical portrait collections. Additional paintings from the National Gallery depict figures from Irish life over the last few centuries.

Times ✳ Open Jan-Dec, Mon-Sat 10-5;. Apr-Sep, Sun & PHs, 10-6; Oct-Mar, Sun & PHs 11-5 **Facilities** Ⓟ ☕ 🍽 ⊼ (outdoor) shop ⊗ ▬

IRELAND

MALAHIDE CONTINUED

Talbot Botanic Gardens

Malahide Castle

➲ *(signed off M1/N1 Dublin-Belfast & Dublin-Malahide Rd)*

☎ 01 8462456

e-mail: gemma.ecarr@finga/coco.ie

web: www.finga/coco.ie

Malahide Castle has long been associated with ornamental gardening. Over seven hectares of shrubbery, and a Walled Garden of nearly two hectares are mainly the creation of Lord Milo Talbot de Malahide, whose family had lived at the estate for 800 years until his death in 1973. Lord Milo Talbot had travelled the world and brought home many exotic plants from Australia and Chile, among others. Visitors follow a path through the gardens, which gives them the best view of this impressive botanic garden.

Times Open May-Sep daily 2-5. Groups by appointment only. Guided tour of Walled Garden on Wed at 2. **Fee** €4.50 (ch under 12 & pen free). Guided tour €4.50. Groups €4 each. **Facilities** ❷ ▐◎▌ ☕ (outdoor) ♿ shop ❽ (ex assist dogs)

SKERRIES   MAP 01 D4

Skerries Mills   2 for 1

➲ *(signed off M1)*

☎ 01 8495208

e-mail: skerriesmills@indigo.ie

web: www.skerriesmills.org

A collection of restored mills, including a watermill, a five-sail, and a four-sail windmill, all in working order. The site dates from the 16th century and was originally part of a monastic establishment. It came into private ownership in 1538, and a bakery has been there since 1840. Nature lovers will enjoy the millpond, nearby wetlands and town park, of which the mills are the focal landmark.

Times Open all year Apr-Sep, daily 10-5.30; Oct-Mar, daily 10-4.30. (Closed Xmas). **Fee** Guided tours €6.50 (ch €3.50, pen & students €5). Family ticket €13 **Facilities** ❷ ▐◎▌ ♿ (Partly accessible) (stair lift, interactive tour) toilets for disabled shop ❽ ▬

CO GALWAY

GALWAY   MAP 01 B3

Galway Atlantaquaria

Salthill

➲ *(follow signs for Salthill. Next to Tourist Office at seafront rdbt)*

☎ 091 585100

e-mail: atlantaquaria@eircom.net

web: www.nationalaquarium.ie

Concentrating on the native Irish marine ecosystem, the Galway Atlantiquaria contains some 170 species of fish and sealife, and features both fresh and saltwater exhibits.

Times ✱ Open all year Apr-Jun & Sep daily 10-5; Jul & Aug daily 10-6; Oct-Mar Wed-Sun 10-5. Closed Mon & Tue. **Facilities** ❷ ▐◎▌ shop ❽ (ex assist dogs) ▬

Nora Barnacle House Museum

Bowling Green

➲ *(close to St Nicholas Collegiate Church, in city centre)*

☎ 091 564743

e-mail: norabarnaclehouse@eircom.net

web: www.norabarnacle.com

The smallest museum in Ireland, this tiny turn-of-century house was the home of Nora Barnacle, companion, wife and lifelong inspiration of James Joyce. Annie, Nora's mother, lived here until her death in 1940. Joyce himself visited the house twice, in 1909 and 1912. Letters, photographs and other exhibits of the lives of James Joyce and Nora Barnacle make a visit here a unique experience.

Times ✱ Open Jun-Aug, days may change during week, opening times posted on window. **Facilities** ❷ (100yds) (disc parking)

Royal Tara China Gift Centre   FREE

Tara Hall, Mervue

➲ *(N6 from Tourist Office. At rdbt take 2nd left & at lights turn right)*

☎ 091 705602

e-mail: mkilroy@royal-tara.com

web: www.royal-tara.com

Royal Tara China visitor centre, located minutes from Galway City Centre, operates from a 17th-century house situated on five acres.

Times Open all year, Mon-Sat 9-5, Sun 10-5 **Facilities** ❷ ♿ (all facilities accessible for disabled) toilets for disabled shop ❽ (ex assist dogs) ▬

GORT
MAP 01 B3

Coole Park & Gardens [FREE]

Coole Nature Reserve

⮑ *(3km N of Gort on N18 Limerick-Galway road, left turn signed)*

☎ 091 631804

e-mail: info@coolepark.ie

web: www.coolepark.ie

Once the home of Lady Gregory, dramatist and co-founder of the Abbey Theatre with W.B. Yeats and Edward Martyn, now a nature reserve, the Seven Woods celebrated by Yeats is part of a nature trail taking in woods and river to Coole lake. The restored courtyard has a visitor centre with exhibits and displays of Coole Park's history. Events around Biodiversity Day in May, and Heritage week at the end of August.

Times Park Open all year. Visitor Centre Open Apr-May & Sep, daily, 10-5; Jun-Aug, daily, 10-6. **Facilities** 🅿 ⌨️🍴🚻 (outdoor) ♿ (visitor centre is fully accessible. Nature trails are partly accessible. All main features are accessible) (hand rail, wide doors) toilets for disabled ⊗ (ex assist dogs & on lead)

Thoor Ballylee

⮑ *(1km off N18 & N66)*

☎ 091 631436 & 537733

This tower house is the former home of the poet William Butler Yeats and is where he completed most of his literary works. The tower, restored to appear exactly as it was when he lived there, houses an Interpretative Centre with audio-visual presentations and displays of his work.

Times Open 27 May-Sep, Mon-Sat 9.30-5 **Fee** ✳ €6 (concessions €5.50). Family ticket €12. Party. **Facilities** 🅿 🚻 ♿ (audio-visual presentation) toilets for disabled shop ⊗ (ex assist dogs) ▬

KINVARRA
MAP 01 B3

Dunguaire Castle

⮑ *(off N18 Ennis to Galway road, through Gort. Left at Ardrahan & continue to Kinvara)*

☎ 061 360768

e-mail: reservations@shannondev.ie

web: www.shannonheritage.com

The castle has stood for hundreds of years on the site of the 7th-century stronghold of Guaire, the King of Connaught. Today the restored castle gives an insight into the lifestyle of the people who lived there from 1520 to modern times.

Times ✳ Open May-Sep, daily 9.30-5 (last admission 4.30). Medieval banquet, Apr-Oct 5.30 & 8.45 (reservations necessary). **Facilities** 🅿 shop ⊗ (ex assist dogs) ▬

PORTUMNA
MAP 01 B3

Portumna Castle & Gardens

☎ 090 9741658

e-mail: portumnacastle@opw.ie

The great semi-fortified house at Portumna was built before 1618 by Richard Burke or de Burgo, 4th Earl of Clanricarde. This important Jacobean house, while influenced by Renaissance and English houses, remains distinctively Irish. It was the main seat of the de Burgo family for over 200 years, until it was gutted by fire in 1826. The ground floor of the house is now open to the public. To the north of the house is a formal, geometrically laid out garden, a feature often associated with large Jacobean mansions.

Times Open 13 Mar-end Oct, daily 10-6 (Last admission 45mins before closing). **Fee** €2.10 (ch, students & pen €1.10). Family ticket €5.80. Group rate €1.30 each. **Facilities** 🅿 ♿ ⊗ (ex assist dogs)

ROSSCAHILL
MAP 01 B4

Brigit's Garden [2 for 1]

Pollagh

⮑ *(signed from N59 between Moycullen & Oughterard)*

☎ 091 550905

e-mail: info@brigitsgarden.ie

web: www.brigitsgarden.ie

At the heart of Brigit's Garden are four unique gardens based on the old Celtic festivals and representing the cycle of life. Features include Irish sculpture and crafts designed to reflect the West of Ireland landscape. There are 11 acres of woodland and wildflower meadows to explore with a nature trail, a wind chamber, an original ring fort and the impressively large Brigit's Sundial. Special events on Bealtaine (May Day) and the Summer Solstice.

Times Open Feb-Oct, daily, 10-5.30 **Fee** ✳ €7.50 (ch €5, under 5 free, concessions €6.25). Family €22. **Facilities** 🅿 ⌨️🚻 (outdoor) ♿ (buildings and gardens fully accessible, only section of nature trail not accessible) toilets for disabled ▬

ROUNDSTONE
MAP 01 A4

Roundstone Music, Crafts & Fashion [FREE]

Craft Centre

⮑ *(N59 from Galway to Clifden. After approx 50m turn left at Roundstone sign, 7m to village. Attraction at top of village)*

☎ 095 35875

e-mail: bodhran@iol.ie

web: www.bodhran.com

The Roundstone Music Craft and Fashion shop is located within the walls of an old Franciscan Monastery. Here you can see the Bodhran being made, and regular talks and demonstrations are given. The first RiverDance stage drums were made here and are still on display in the Craftsman's Craftshop. There is an outdoor picnic area in a beautiful

CONTINUED

IRELAND

ROUNDSTONE CONTINUED

location alongside the bell tower by the water where the dolphins swim up to the wall in summer.

Times Open Apr-Oct 9.30-6, Jul-Sep 9-7, Winter 6 days 9.30-6.
Facilities ❷ ☐ ☴ (indoor & outdoor) ♿ toilets for disabled shop ⊗ (ex assist dogs)

CO KERRY

CASTLEISLAND   MAP 01 B2

Crag Cave

➲ *(1m N, signed off N21)*

☎ 066 7141244

e-mail: info@cragcave.com

web: www.cragcave.com

Crag Cave is one of the longest surveyed cave systems in Ireland, with a total length of 3.81km. It is a spectacular world, where pale forests of stalagmites and stalactites, thousands of years old, throw eerie shadows around vast echoing caverns complemented by dramatic sound and lighting effects. Now features new indoor and outdoor soft play areas, which are priced seperately. Tours of the caves last about 30 minutes.

Times Open daily all year, 10-6. (Dec-Mar telephone for times).
Facilities ❷ ☐ ⏻ ☴ (outdoor) ♿ (Partly accessible) (ramp to visitor centre) toilets for disabled shop ⊗ (ex assist dogs) ▬

KILLARNEY   MAP 01 B2

Muckross House, Gardens & Traditional Farms

Muckross

➲ *(4m on Kenmare road)*

☎ 066 31440 & 35571

e-mail: mucros@iol.ie

web: www.muckross-house.ie

The 19th-century mansion house of the formerly private Muckross Estate. It now houses a museum of Kerry folklife. In the basement craft centre, a weaver, blacksmith and potter demonstrate their trades. The grounds include Alpine and bog gardens, rhododendrons, azaleas and a rock garden.

Times Open all year Jul-Aug, daily 9-7; mid Mar-Jun & Sep-Oct, 9-6; Nov-16 Mar 9-5.30. **Fee** €5.75 (ch €2.35, students & pen €4.50) Family ticket €14.50. Group ticket €4.50. **Facilities** ❷ ⏻ ☴ shop ⊗ (ex assist dogs) ▬

Museum of Irish Transport

Scotts Hotel Gardens

➲ *(town centre, opposite railway station)*

☎ 064 34677

A unique collection of Irish veteran, vintage and classic cars, motorcycles, bicycles, carriages and fire engines. Exhibits include the

1907 Silver Stream, reputed to be the rarest car in the world, it was designed and built by an Irishman and he only made one.

Times ✳ Open Apr & Oct 11-4; May & Sep 11-5; Jun, Jul & Aug 10-6
Facilities ❷

TRALEE   MAP 01 A2

Kerry County Museum

Ashe Memorial Hall, Denny St

➲ *(in town centre, follow signs for museum & tourist information office)*

☎ 066 7127777

e-mail: info@kerrymuseum.com

web: www.kerrymuseum.com

The museum tells the story of Kerry (and Ireland) from the Stone Age to the present day. Archaeological treasures are displayed in the Museum Gallery, while a stroll through the Medieval Experience reveals the streets of Tralee as they were in 1450, with all the sights, sounds and smells of a bustling community. Discover what people wore, what they ate and where they lived, and find out why the Earls of Desmond, who founded the town, also destroyed it.

Times ✳ Open Jan-Mar, Tue-Fri 10-4.30; Apr-May, Tue-Sat 9.30-5.30; Jun-Aug, daily 9.30-5.30; Sep-Dec, Tue-Sat 9.30-5; BH wknds Sun & Mon 10-5. **Facilities** ❷ (charged) ☐ ♿ (special time car through Medieval Experience) toilets for disabled shop ⊗ (ex assist dogs) ▬

VALENCIA ISLAND   MAP 01 A2

The Skellig Experience

➲ *(Ring of Kerry road, signed after Cahersiveen then Valentia bridge, or ferry from Rena Rd Point)*

☎ 066 9476306

e-mail: info@skelligexperience.com

web: www.skelligexperience.com

The Skellig Rocks are renowned for their scenery, sea bird colonies, lighthouses, Early Christian monastic architecture and rich underwater life. The two islands - Skellig Michael and Small Skellig - stand like fairytale castles in the Atlantic Ocean, rising to 218 metres and their steep cliffs plunging 50 metres below the sea. The Heritage Centre, (on Valentia Island, reached from the mainland via a bridge), tells the story of the Skellig Islands in an exciting multimedia exhibition. Cruises around Valentia Habour are also available.

Times ✳ Open May-Jun 10-6; Jul-Aug 10-7; Sep 10-6. Mar, Apr & Oct-Nov 10-5 **Facilities** ❷ ☐ ♿ toilets for disabled shop ⊗ (ex assist dogs) ▬

IRELAND

CO KILDARE

CELBRIDGE
MAP 01 D4

Castletown
➲ *(13m from Dublin, follow signs to Celbridge from N4)*

☎ 01 628 8252

e-mail: castletown@opw.ie

web: www.heritageireland.ie

Ireland's largest and finest Palladian country house, begun c1722 for William Conolly, Speaker of the Irish House of Commons. The state rooms include the 'Pompeian' Long Gallery with its Venetian chandeliers, green silk drawing room and magnificent staircase hall with Lafranchini plasterwork. There is a fine collection of 18th-century Irish furniture and paintings.

Times Open St Patrick's Day-mid Nov Tue-Sun & BHs 10-6. Also open Xmas. **Fee** €4.50 (ch, students & pen €3.50). Family ticket €12.50. Pre-booked groups 20+ €3.50. **Facilities** ❷ ⌑ ⅙ (restricted access for disabled visitors) toilets for disabled ⊗ (ex assist dogs)

KILDARE
MAP 01 C3

Irish National Stud, Gardens & Horse Museum
2 for 1

Irish National Stud, Tully

➲ *(off M7, exit 13 then R415 towards Nurney & Kildare. Attraction well signed from rdbt)*

☎ 045 521617

e-mail: japanesegardens@eircom.net

web: www.irish-national-stud.ie

Situated in the grounds of the Irish National Stud, the gardens were established by Lord Wavertree between 1906 and 1910, and symbolise 'The Life of Man' in a Japanese-style landscape. You can also visit the Horse Museum which includes the skeleton of Arkle, an Irish racehorse that won a number of major races in the 1960s. The Commemorative Millennium Garden of St Fiachra has four acres of woodland and lakeside walks and features a Waterford Crystal garden and monastic cells of limestone.

Times Open 12 Feb-23 Dec, daily, 9.30-5. **Fee** €10.5. Family ticket (2ad+4ch) €27 **Facilities** ❷ ⍟ ⌐ ⅙ (outdoor) ⅙ (all parts of stud, garden & house accessible. Japanese gardens partly accessible) toilets for disabled shop ⊗ (ex on leads) ▄

CO KILKENNY

KILKENNY
MAP 01 C3

Kilkenny Castle
☎ 056 772 1450

Situated in a beautiful 50-acre park, the castle dates from 1172. The first stone castle was built 20 years later by William Marshall, Earl of Pembroke. It was the home of the very powerful Butler family, Earls and Dukes of Ormonde from 1391 to 1935. Due to major restoration works, the central block now includes a library, drawing room, and bedrooms decorated in 1830s splendour, as well as the beautiful Long Gallery.

Times Open all year, Apr-May, daily 10.30-5; Jun-Aug, daily 9.30-7; Sep, daily 10-6.30; Oct-Mar, daily 10.30-12.45 & 2-5. (Last tour 1hr before closing). Closed Xmas & Good Fri. **Fee** €5.30 (ch & students €2.10). Family ticket €11.50. Group rate €3.70 each. **Facilities** ℗ (local authority restrictions) ⌑ ⅙ shop ⊗ (ex assist dogs)

CO LIMERICK

FOYNES
MAP 01 B3

Foynes Flying Boat Museum
➲ *(on N69 in Foynes)*

☎ 069 65416

e-mail: info@flyingboatmuseum.com

web: www.flyingboatmuseum.com

The museum recalls the era of the flying boats during the 1930s and early 1940s when Foynes was an important airport for air traffic between the United States and Europe. There is a comprehensive range of exhibits, graphic illustrations and a 1940s style cinema featuring a 17-minute film - all original footage from the 30s and 40s. This is where Irish coffee was first invented by chef, Joe Sheridan, in 1942. Fly our B314 flight simulators and go on board the world's only full scale B314 flying boat model. July 2009 - special celebrations for the 70th anniversary of the first passenger flight across the North Atlantic. Also 20th anniversary of museum opening.

Times Open Mar-Sep daily 10-6, Oct-Dec daily 10-4 (last admission 1hr before closing). **Fee** €8.50 (ch €5). Family ticket €25. **Facilities** ❷ ⌑ ⅙ toilets for disabled shop ⊗ (ex assist dogs) ▄

HOLYCROSS
MAP 01 C3

Lough Gur Stone Age Centre
Bruff Rd

➲ *(17km S of Limerick, off R512 towards Kilmallock)*

☎ 061 360788

e-mail: reservations@shannondev.ie

web: www.shannonheritage.com

Lough Gur introduces visitors to the habitat of Neolithic Man on one of Ireland's most important archaeological sites. The visitor centre interprets the history of the area which dates back to 3000BC.

Times ✳ Open May-mid Sep, daily 10-6 (last admission 5.30) **Facilities** ❷ ⌐ (outdoor) shop ⊗ (ex assist dogs) ▄

IRELAND

LIMERICK
MAP 01 B3

The Hunt Museum
`2 for 1`

The Custom House, Rutland St

➲ *(a short walk from Arthur's Quay)*

☎ 061 312833

e-mail: info@huntmuseum.com

web: www.huntmuseum.com

On show at the Hunt Museum is one of Ireland's finest private collections of art and antiquities. Reflecting Ireland's Celtic past as well as masterworks by da Vinci and Renoir. Set in an 18th-century Custom House beside the River Shannon.

Times Open all year Mon-Sat 10-5, Sun 2-5, except Good Fri, 25 Dec & 1 Jan. **Fee** €7.75 (ch €4, concessions €6.25). Family ticket €17.50. **Facilities** Ⓟ (50mtrs) (parking discs for street parking) ♿🅇♿ toilets for disabled shop ⊗ (ex assist dogs) ▬

King John's Castle

Nicholas St

➲ *(on Kings Island in city)*

☎ 061 360788

e-mail: reservations@shannondev.ie

web: www.shannonheritage.com

The Castle was built between 1200 and 1210 and was repaired and extended many times in the following centuries. The interpretative centre at the Castle has been completely redesigned and now contains an imaginative historical exhibition. The courtyard and the Castle display some of the trades and traditions of the 16th century.

Times ✳ Open all year Mar, Apr, & Oct daily 9.30-5 (last admission 4); May-Sep 9.30-5.30 (last admission 4.30); Nov-Feb 10-4.30 (last admission 3.30). Closed Good Fri & 24-26 Dec. **Facilities** Ⓟ ⊓ (outdoor) ♿ (lifts and ramps) toilets for disabled shop ⊗ (ex assist dogs) ▬

CO LONGFORD

KEENAGH
MAP 01 C4

Corlea Trackway Visitor Centre
`FREE`

➲ *(off R397, 3km from village, 15km from Longford)*

☎ 043 22386

e-mail: ctrackwayvisitorcentre@opw.ie

The centre interprets an Iron Age bog road which was built in the year 148BC across the boglands close to the River Shannon. The oak road is the largest of its kind to have been uncovered in Europe and was excavated over the years by Professor Barry Raferty of University College Dublin. Inside the building, an 18-metre stretch of preserved road is on permanent display in a specially designed hall with humidifiers to prevent the ancient wood from cracking in the heat.

Times Open Apr-Sep, daily 10-6 **Facilities** Ⓟ ♿ ⊓ ⊗ (ex assist dogs)

CO MAYO

BALLYCASTLE
MAP 01 B5

Céide Fields

➲ *(5m W of Ballycastle on R314)*

☎ 096 43325

e-mail: ceidefields@opw.ie

web: www.heritageireland.ie

Beneath the wild boglands of North Mayo lies Céide Fields, the most extensive Stone-age monument in the world; field systems, dwelling areas and megalithic tombs of 5,000 years ago. In addition, the wild flora of the bog is of international importance and is bounded by some of the most spectacular rock formations and cliffs in Ireland.

Times Open mid Mar-May & Oct-Nov daily 10-5; Jun-Sep daily 10-6. Available for group bookings in winter months. Last tour 1 hr before closing time. **Fee** €3.70 (ch & students €1.30, pen €2.60). Family ticket €8.70. Group rate €2.60 each. **Facilities** Ⓟ ♿ ⊗ (ex assist dogs)

CO MONAGHAN

INNISKEEN
MAP 01 C4

Patrick Kavanagh Rural & Literary Resource Centre
`2 for 1`

Candlefort

➲ *(from Dublin take N2, exit at Carrickmacross, left along R178 to Essexford. Left at Kelly's pub for Inniskeen)*

☎ 042 937 8560

e-mail: infoatpkc@eircom.net

web: www.patrickkavanaghcountry.com

Birthplace of Patrick Kavanagh, one of Ireland's foremost 20th-century poets. The village grew around the ancient monastery of St Daig MacCairill, founded by 562, and its strong, 10th-century round tower still stands. The centre, housed in the former parish church, chronicles the ancient history of the region and its role in developing Kavanagh's work.

Times Open all year Tue-Fri 11-4.30. Jun-Sep Tue-Fri 11-4.30, Sat & Sun 2-5. **Fee** ✳ €5 (ch €2 - free when accompanied by an adult, concessions €3). **Facilities** Ⓟ ♿ ⊓ ♿ toilets for disabled shop ▬

IRELAND

MONAGHAN
MAP 01 C5

Monaghan County Museum
FREE

1-2 Hill St

➲ *(near town centre, opposite market house exhibition galleries)*

☎ 047 82928

e-mail: comuseum@monghancoco.ie

web: www.monaghan.ie

This is an award-winning museum of local archaeology, history, arts and crafts. Throughout the year various special exhibitions take place.

Times ✳ Open Sep-May, Tue-Fri 10-1 & 2-5 Sat 11-1 & 2-5. Jun-Aug, Mon-Fri 11-5, Thu 11-7, Sat 11-1 & 2-5. **Facilities** Ⓟ (near town centre) (restricted on-street parking) ⊗ (ex assist dogs)

CO OFFALY

BIRR
MAP 01 C3

Birr Castle Demesne

➲ *(N52 to Birr, turn right into Town Sq. At castle wall turn left, entrance is on right)*

☎ 057 9120 336

e-mail: mail@birrcastle.com

web: www.birrcastle.com

These award-winning gardens are the largest in the country, spanning over 120 acres of natural landscapes, with five miles of paths. The impressive plant collection boasts rare species from around the world, including over 40 champion trees of the British Isles. The Millennium Gardens, designed by the Sixth Countess of Rosse, include the world's tallest box hedges and beautiful pathways of hornbeam arches. The Demesne is also home to Ireland's Historic Science Centre which allows visitors to travel back to the time of the earlier Earls and Countesses of Rosse, when the Castle was a hub of scientific discovery and innovation. Many special events take place throughout the year, please see the website for details.

Times Open all year, Mar-Oct 9-6, Nov-Mar 10-4. **Facilities** Ⓟ ⫣ ⤢ (indoor & outdoor) ♿ toilets for disabled shop garden centre ▬

CO ROSCOMMON

BOYLE
MAP 01 B4

King House Interpretive Galleries & Museum
2 for 1

➲ *(in town centre)*

☎ 071 9663242

e-mail: kinghouse@roscommoncoco.ie

web: www.kinghouse.ie

King House is a magnificently restored Georgian mansion built around 1730 by Sir Henry King, whose family were one of the most powerful and wealthy in Ireland. After its first life as a home, King House became a military barracks to the famous Connaught Rangers from 1788-1922. In more recent years it has also been a barracks for the National Irish

Army. Today visitors can explore and delve into its history with interactive presentations on: Gaelic Ireland, the lives of the King family, the architecture and restoration of the building and its military history. The Boyle Arts Festival takes place in the last week of July.

Times Open Apr-Sep, daily 10-6 (last admission 5). Pre-booked groups welcome all year round, telephone for details. **Fee** €7 (ch €4, concessions €5). Family ticket €18. Party rates available **Facilities** Ⓟ ⏐◎⏐ ⤢ (outdoor) ♿ (lift to all areas, ramps, wide doors, parking) toilets for disabled shop ⊗ (ex assist dogs)

STROKESTOWN
MAP 01 C4

Strokestown Park House Garden & Famine Museum

Strokestown Park

➲ *(23km from Longford on N5)*

☎ 071 9633013

e-mail: info@strokestownpark.ie

web: www.strokestownpark.ie

A fine example of an early 18th-century gentleman farmer's country estate. Built in Palladian style the house reflects perfectly the confidence of the newly emergent ruling class. The pleasure garden has also been restored, and the Famine Museum, located in the stable yard, commemorates the Great Irish Famine of the 1840s.

Times Open 17 Mar-Oct, daily. **Fee** €14.50 (ch €7.50, concessions €13). Family ticket €30. Group 20+ €12 each **Facilities** Ⓟ ⏐◎⏐ ⤢ (no access to first floor of house) toilets for disabled shop garden centre ⊗ (ex assist dogs & in grounds) ▬

CO TIPPERARY

CASHEL
MAP 01 C3

Brú Ború Heritage Centre

➲ *(below Rock of Cashel in town)*

☎ 062 61122

e-mail: bruboru@comhaltas.com

web: www.comhaltas.com

At the foot of the Rock of Cashel, a 4th-century stone fort, this Heritage Centre is dedicated to the study and celebration of native Irish music, song, dance, story telling, theatre and Celtic studies. There's a Folk Theatre where performances are held daily in the summer, and in the evening, banquets evoke the Court of Brian Ború, 11th-century High King of Ireland with music, song and dance. Promoted by Comhaltas Ceoltóiri Éireann. There is also a Subterranean, "Sounds of History", experience.

Times Open Jan-May & Oct-Dec, Mon-Fri 9-5; Jun-Sep Tue-Sat 9-11, Sun-Mon 9-5. **Fee** ✳ Admission to centre free. Night show €20. Exhibition, 'Sounds of History' €5. Dinner Show/Option €50. **Facilities** Ⓟ (charged) ⫣⏐◎⏐ ♿ (wheelchair bay in theatre) toilets for disabled shop ⊗ (ex assist dogs) ▬

IRELAND

CO WATERFORD

LISMORE
MAP 01 C2

Lismore Castle Gardens & Art Gallery

➲ *(on N72 near town centre)*

☎ 058 54424

e-mail: lismoreestates@eircom.net

web: www.lismorecastle.com

Lismore Castle is the Irish home of the Duke of Devonshire. The beautifully situated walled and woodland gardens contain a fine collection of camellias, magnolias and other shrubs and a remarkable Yew Walk. Several pieces of contemporary sculpture have been installed in the garden. The West Wing has been converted into a contemporary art space and is planning to host art exhibitions from around the world.

Times Open 17 Mar-Sep, daily 11-4.45. **Fee** €7 (ch under 16: €3.50). Party 20+ €5. **Facilities** ❶ ➟ ⬤ (some of the grounds are accessible, stairs to upper gardens)

WATERFORD
MAP 01 C2

Waterford Crystal Visitor Centre

Kilbarry

➲ *(on N25, 1m from city centre)*

☎ 051 332500

e-mail: visitorreception@waterford.ie

web: www.waterfordvisitorcentre.com

There are factory tours to see mastercraftsmen mouth-blow and hand-cut this famous crystal. You can talk to the master engravers and see the crystal being sculpted. In the gallery there is the finest display of Waterford Crystal in the world.

Times Factory tours: Mar-Oct daily 8.30-4.15. Nov-Feb close Sat & Sun. **Facilities** ❶ ➟ ⬤ (special tours on request) toilets for disabled shop ⊗ (ex assist dogs) ➡

CO WEXFORD

FERRYCARRIG
MAP 01 D3

The Irish National Heritage Park ┃2 for 1┃

➲ *(3m from Wexford, on N11)*

☎ 053 912 0733

e-mail: info@inhp.com

web: www.inhp.com

Sixteen historical sites set in a magnificent 35-acre mature forest explaining Ireland's history from the Stone and Bronze Ages, through the Celtic period and concluding with the Vikings and Normans. Among the exhibits are a reconstructed Mesolithic camp, a Viking boatyard with two full-size ships and a Norman motte and bailey. Please visit website for details of events running throughout the year.

Times Open daily Oct-Mar, 9.30-5.30. Apr-Sep, 9.30-6.30. **Fee** €8 (concessions €6.50). Family (2 ad & upto 3 ch) €20. Group rates available on request. **Facilities** ❶ ➟ ⬤ licensed ➟ (outdoor) ⬤ toilets for disabled shop ⊗ (ex assist dogs) ➡

NEW ROSS
MAP 01 C3

Dunbrody Abbey Visitors Centre

Dunbrody Abbey, Campile

➲ *(10m from New Ross at base of Hook Peninsular)*

☎ 051 88603

e-mail: patrickbelfast@aol.com

web: www.dunbrodyabbey.com

The visitor centre is based around the Abbey itself and Dunbrody Castle. There is an intriguing yew hedge maze with 1,550 yew trees and a museum. In addition there is a golf pitch-and-putt course, a local craft centre and Dunbrody Abbey Cookery School.

Times Open May-Sep 10-6. **Fee** ✳ Abbey €2, Family ticket €5. Maze/Golf €5, (ch €2). Family €12. **Facilities** ❶ ➟ ⬤ (outdoor) ⬤ shop garden centre

John F Kennedy Arboretum

➲ *(12km S of New Ross, off R733)*

☎ 051 388171

e-mail: jfkarboretum@opn.ie

The Arboretum covers 623 acres across the hill of Slievecoiltia which overlooks the Kennedy ancestral home at Dunganstown. There are 4,500 types of trees and shrubs representing the temperate regions of the world, and laid out in botanical sequence. There's a lake and a visitor centre.

Times Open all year daily, May-Aug 10-8; Apr & Sep 10-6.30; Oct-Mar 10-5. (Last admission 45 mins before closing). Closed Good Fri & 25 Dec. **Fee** €2.90 (ch & student €1.30, pen €2.10). Family ticket €7.40 Heritage cards €21 (pen €16, ch & student €8) Family €55. **Facilities** ❶ ➟ ➟ shop

WEXFORD   MAP 01 D3

Johnstown Castle Gardens

Johnstown Castle Estate

➲ *(4m SW of town, signed off N25)*

☎ 053 9184671 & 9171247

e-mail: info@irishagrimuseum.ie

web: www.irishagrimuseum.ie

Johnstown Castle Garden consists of an exquisite Victorian castle set within 50 acres of onarmental grounds. The famous architect Daniel Robertson designed both Johnstown castle grounds and Powerscourt gardens. The grounds contain a wide variety of trees and shrubs representing the best aspects of a formal and wild garden. The grounds are greatly enhanced by two lakes with folly towers and are populated with a wide range of waterfowl. The Irish Agricultural Museum is located in the old farm and stable buildings of Johnstown Castle estate. Please note that Johnstown Castle itself is not open to the public.

Times Open all year, daily 9-5.30. Closed 25 Dec. **Fee** Car (inc passengers) €6. Pedestrians €2 (ch & students €0.50). Small coach €20, large coach €30. **Facilities** ♿ ⧠ ☂ (outdoor) & toilets for disabled garden centre

The Irish Agricultural Museum

Johnstown Castle Estate

➲ *(4m SW of town, signed off N25)*

☎ 053 9184671 & 9171247

e-mail: info@irishagrimuseum.ie

web: www.irishagrimuseum.ie

This museum is located in the old farm and stable buildings of the Johnstown castle Estate. There are a vast range of artefacts relating to a bygone era. Farming and rural life are the main themes explored, with exhibits covering rural transport, farming and the activities of the farmyard and farmhouse; and includes a large exhibition on the history of the potato and the Great Famine (1845-49). Large scale replicas of different workshops, including a blacksmith, cooper and basket worker, and include displays on the Ferguson tractor system and the history of the estate. Johnstown Castle Garden is a delightful 50 acres of ornamental grounds surrounding a Victorian castle. Famous architect Daniel Robertson designed both Johnstown Castle Gardens and Powerscourt Gardens. The grounds contain a wide variety of trees and shrubs, as well as two lakes and various follies.

Times Open all year: Museum Apr-Nov, Mon-Fri 9-5, Sat-Sun & BHs 11-5; Dec-Mar, Mon-Fri 9-5 (closed for lunch 12.30-1.30, wknds & BHs). Grounds open daily 9-5. **Fee** Museum €6 (ch & students €4, concessions €5). Family ticket €20. Grounds - car €6, coach €20-€30 **Facilities** ♿ ⧠ ☂ (outdoor) & (ground floor accessible) toilets for disabled shop ⊗ (ex on lead in grounds)

Wexford Wildfowl Reserve   `FREE`

North Slob

➲ *(8km NE from Wexford)*

☎ 053 23129

e-mail: info@heritageireland.ie

The reserve is of international importance for Greenland white-fronted geese, Brent geese, Bewick's swans and wigeon. The reserve is a superb place for birdwatching and there are hides and a tower hide available as well as a visitor centre.

Times Open all year daily, 9-5. Other hours by arrangement with the warden. Closed 25 Dec. Reserve may be closed temporarily for management operations - Notice on Gate. **Facilities** ♿ ☂ ⊗ (ex assist dogs)

CO WICKLOW

ENNISKERRY   MAP 01 D4

Powerscourt House & Gardens

Powerscourt Estate

➲ *(From Dublin city centre take N11 S, after 12m take exit left to Bray S, Enniskerry. Left at rdbt, over flyover, rejoin N11 N. Take 1st left for Enniskerry Village, entrance 600mtrs out of village)*

☎ 01 2046000

web: www.powerscourt.ie

In the foothills of the Wicklow Mountains, these gardens were begun by Richard Wingfield in the 1740s, and are a blend of formal plantings, sweeping terraces, statuary and ornamental lakes together with secret hollows, rambling walks and walled gardens. The gardens cover 19 hectares and contain more than two hundred varieties of tree and shrub. The house itself incorporates an audio visual exhibition which traces the history of the estate, and tells the story of the disastrous fire of 1974 which gutted the house. The grounds also contain Powerscourt Waterfall, Ireland's highest at 398ft.

Times Open Gardens & House daily 9.30-5.30 (Gardens close at dusk in winter), closed 25-26 Dec. Waterfall open daily, Mar-Apr & Sep-Oct 9.30-5.30; May-Aug 9.30-7; Nov-Feb 10.30-4 (closed 2 weeks before Xmas). Ballroom & Garden rooms open every Sun & Mon 9.30-1.30 (May-Sep) **Fee** House & Gardens €8 (ch under 16 €5 ch under 5 free, concession€7). Waterfall €5 (ch under 16 €3.50 ch under 2 free, concession €4.50). **Facilities** ♿ ⧠ � & (some areas in gardens are flat and suitable for wheelchair users) (lift to first floor, 2 wheelchairs available) toilets for disabled shop garden centre ⊗ (ex on leads, not in garden) ▬

IRELAND

KILQUADE   MAP 01 D3

National Garden Exhibitions Centre

Calumet Nurseries

➲ *(7m S of Bray - turn off N11 at Kilquade)*

☎ 01 281 9890

e-mail: ngec@eircom.net

web: www.gardenexhibition.ie

This Exhibition Centre has over 20 different gardens designed by some of Ireland's leading landscapers and designers. Ring for details and a calendar of events. The exhibitions are constantly changing and enjoy a high standard of maintenance. All plants are clearly labelled.

Times Open all year Mon-Sat 9-5.30; Sun 1-5.30. (Closed 24 Dec-1st Mon in Jan) **Fee** ✳ €4.50 (ch under 16 free, pen €3.50). **Facilities** ❷ ⬚ 🍽 ♿ (Partly accessible) shop garden centre ⊗ (ex assist dogs) ➡

RATHDRUM   MAP 01 D3

Avondale House & Forest Park   `2 for 1`

➲ *(S of Dublin on N11. At Rathnew on R752 to Glenealy and Rathdrum, L2149 to Avondale)*

☎ 0404 46111

e-mail: costelloe_j@coillte.ie

web: www.coillteoutdoors.ie

It was here in 1846 that one of the greatest political leaders of modern Irish history, Charles Stewart Parnell, was born. Parnell spent much of his time at Avondale until his death in October 1891. The house is set in a magnificent forest park with miles of forest trails, plus a children's play area, deer pen, orienteering courses and picnic areas.

Times Open: House 17 Mar-Oct, Tue-Sun, 11-4 (Mar-Apr & Sep-Oct); May-Aug, daily, 11-5 (last admission 1hr before closing). **Fee** €6 (pen €5.50). Family ticket (2ad+2ch) €18. **Facilities** ❷ (charged) ⬚ 🍽 licensed 🍴 (outdoor) ♿ (ground floor in house & one forest trail accessible) (special car park) ⊗ (ex on lead) ➡

Glendalough, County Wicklow

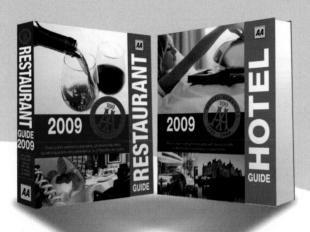

County Maps

The county map shown here will help you identify the counties within each country. You can look up each county in the guide using the county names at the top of each page. To find towns featured in the guide use the atlas and the index.

England
1 Bedfordshire
2 Berkshire
3 Bristol
4 Buckinghamshire
5 Cambridgeshire
6 Greater Manchester
7 Herefordshire
8 Hertfordshire
9 Leicestershire
10 Northamptonshire
11 Nottinghamshire
12 Rutland
13 Staffordshire
14 Warwickshire
15 West Midlands
16 Worcestershire

Scotland
17 City of Glasgow
18 Clackmannanshire
19 East Ayrshire
20 East Dunbartonshire
21 East Renfrewshire
22 Perth & Kinross
23 Renfrewshire
24 South Lanarkshire
25 West Dunbartonshire

Wales
26 Blaenau Gwent
27 Bridgend
28 Caerphilly
29 Denbighshire
30 Flintshire
31 Merthyr Tydfil
32 Monmouthshire
33 Neath Port Talbot
34 Newport
35 Rhondda Cynon Taff
36 Torfaen
37 Vale of Glamorgan
38 Wrexham

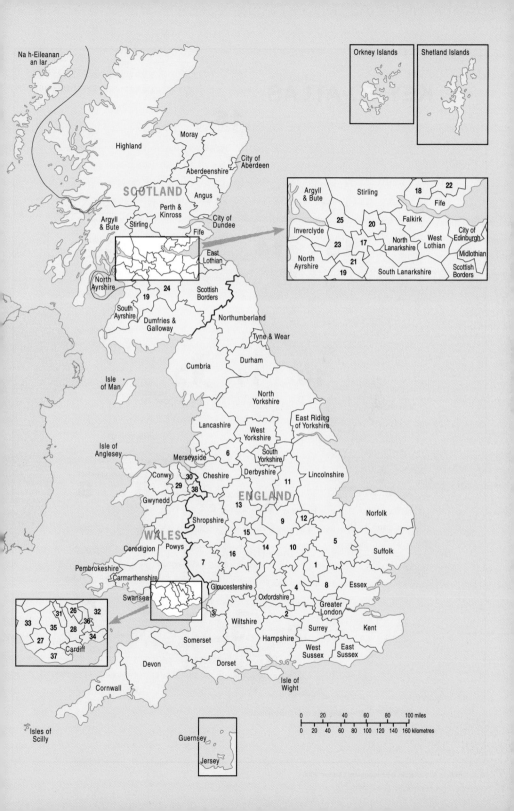

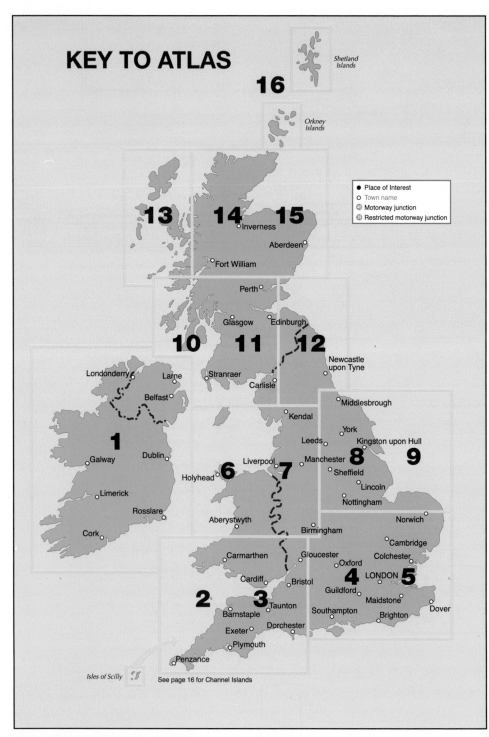

KEY TO ATLAS

16

Shetland Islands

Orkney Islands

- ● Place of Interest
- ○ Town name
- Motorway junction
- Restricted motorway junction

13   14   15

○Inverness

Aberdeen○

○Fort William

Perth○

Glasgow○   ○Edinburgh

10   11   12

Londonderry○   Larne○   Stranraer○   Carlisle○

Newcastle upon Tyne

Belfast○

Middlesbrough○

Kendal○

York○

Leeds○   Kingston upon Hull○

1   Galway○   Dublin○   Liverpool○   Manchester○   8   9

Holyhead○   6   7   ○Sheffield

Limerick○   Lincoln○

Rosslare○   Aberystwyth○   Nottingham○

Cork○   Birmingham○   Norwich○

Cambridge○

Carmarthen○   Gloucester○   Colchester○

Cardiff○   Oxford○   LONDON   5

2   3   Bristol○   4   Guildford○

Barnstaple○   Taunton○   Maidstone○   Dover○

Exeter○   Dorchester○   Southampton○   Brighton○

Plymouth○

Penzance○

Isles of Scilly   See page 16 for Channel Islands

© Automobile Association Developments Limited 2008

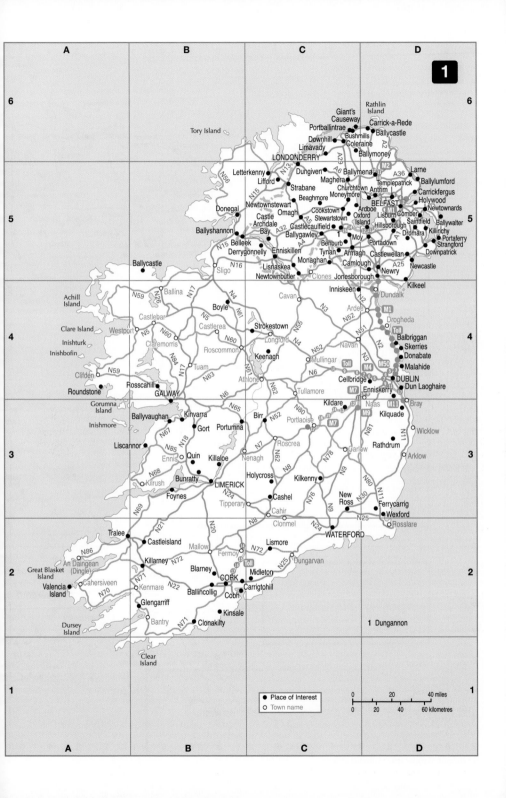

1

A   **B**   **C**   **D**

6

Rathlin
Island
Giant's
Causeway
Carrick-a-Rede
Portballintrae
Ballycastle
Downhill
Bushmills
Tory Island
Coleraine
Limavady
Ballymoney
A2
LONDONDERRY
A29
Ballymena
Larne
A36
Letterkenny
Dungiven
Templepatrick
Ballylumford
N13
Maghera
Antrim
Carrickfergus
Lifford
Churchtown
N56
Strabane
Moneymore
Holywood
N15
Beaghmore
BELFAST
Newtownards
Newtownstewart
Cookstown
Ardboe
Lisburn
Comber
Donegal
Omagh
Stewartstown
Oxford
Ballywalter
Castle
Castlecaulfield
Island
Hillsborough
Archdale
Ballygawley
Moy
Portaferry
Ballyshannon
Bay
A32
Benburb
Portadown
Dromara
Killinchy
N15
Belleek
A4
Tynan
Strangford
Derrygonnelly
Enniskillen
Armagh
Castlewellan
Downpatrick
Ballycastle
Lisnaskea
Monaghan
Camlough
A25
Newcastle
N16
Newtownbutler
Jonesborough
Newry
Sligo
Clones
Kilkeel
N59
Ballina
Cavan
Inniskeen
Dundalk
Achill
Island
N26
Boyle
Ardee
N2
Drogheda
Castlebar
N5
N61
N52
Toll
Balbriggan
Clare Island
Westport
N5
Castlerea
Strokestown
N55
N51
Skerries
Inishturk
N60
Longford
Navan
N2
Donabate
Inishbofin
Claremorris
Roscommon
N4
N52
M50
Malahide
Clifden
N84
N17
Keenagh
N6
N3
Toll
DUBLIN
N59
Tuam
N63
Mullingar
M4
Cellbridge
Dun Laoghaire
Roundstone
Rosscahill
Athlone
N62
Tullamore
Toll
Enniskerry
GALWAY
M7
Gorumna
N65
Kildare
Naas
M11
Bray
Island
Kinvarra
Birr
N52
N80
M9
Kilquade
Ballyvaughan
Portlaoise
Inishmore
N67
Gort
Portumna
M7
N81
Wicklow
N85
N18
Roscrea
Rathdrum
Liscannor
Ennis
Quin
N7
N62
Carlow
N11
Arklow
N68
Killaloe
Nenagh
N78
Kilrush
Bunratty
Holycross
N8
Kilkenny
N9
Foynes
LIMERICK
N24
Cashel
N76
New
N30
Ferrycarrig
N69
Tipperary
N80
Ross
N11
Cahir
N25
Wexford
Tralee
N21
Clonmel
N24
WATERFORD
Rosslare
N86
Castleisland
Lismore
Killarney
N72
Mallow
Fermoy
N72
Dungarvan
Great Blasket
An Daingean
N71
Blarney
Midleton
N25
Island
(Dingle)
Toll
Valencia
Cahersiveen
N22
CORK
Carrigtohill
Island
N70
Ballincollig
Cobh
Glengarriff
Kinsale
Dursey
Bantry
N71
Clonakilty
1 Dungannon
Island

Clear
Island

1

● Place of Interest   0   20   40 miles
○ Town name   0   20   40   60 kilometres

A   **B**   **C**   **D**

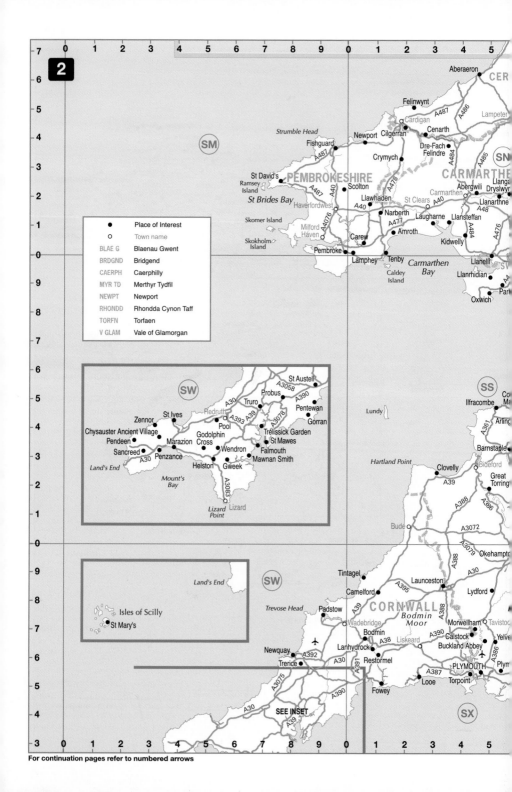

2

Place of Interest

○ Town name

BLAE G	Blaenau Gwent
BRDGND	Bridgend
CAERPH	Caerphilly
MYR TD	Merthyr Tydfil
NEWPT	Newport
RHONDD	Rhondda Cynon Taff
TORFN	Torfaen
V GLAM	Vale of Glamorgan

Aberaeron

CER

Felinwynt

Cardigan A487 A486 Lampeter

Strumble Head   Newport Cilgerran   Cenarth

Fishguard   Dre-Fach

A487   Crymych   Felindre A484   SN

St David's   PEMBROKESHIRE   CARMARTHE

Ramsey   Llanga

Island   A478   Abergwili Dryslwyr

St Brides Bay   A40   Scolton   Carmarthen A40

Haverfordwest   A40   Llawhaden   St Clears   Llanarthne

Skomer Island   Narberth   A48

Milford   A77   Laugharne Llansteffan

Haven   A476

Skokholm   Carew   Amroth   A484

Island   Pembroke   Kidwelly

Lamphey Tenby   Llanelli

Caldey   Carmarthen   SV

Island   Bay   Llanrhidian

Oxwich   Par

St Austell

SW   Probus A3058

A30   Truro   A390   Pentewan

Zennor   St Ives   Redruth   A39   Lundy   Ilfracombe   Co

Chysauster Ancient Village   Pool   A3078   Gorran   SS   Ma

Pendeen   Godolphin   Trelissick Garden   A361   Arling

Marazion   Cross   St Mawes

Sancreed   Wendron   Falmouth   Barnstaple

A30   Penzance   Mawnan Smith   Hartland Point   Clovelly   Bideford

Land's End   Helston   Gweek   A39   Great

Mount's   Torring

Bay   A3083

Lizard   Lizard

Point   Bude   A3072

Okehampto

A3079

Land's End   SW   Tintagel   Launceston   A30

Camelford   A395   Lydford

Isles of Scilly   Trevose Head Padstow   A39   CORNWALL   A388

St Mary's   Wadebridge   Bodmin   Morwellham Tavisto

Moor

Bodmin   Liskeard   A390   Calstock   Yelve

Newquay   A392   Lanhydrock   A38   Buckland Abbey   A386

Trerice   A30   Restormel   PLYMOUTH   Plym

A387   Looe   Torpoint

A3075   A390   Fowey

A30   SEE INSET   SX

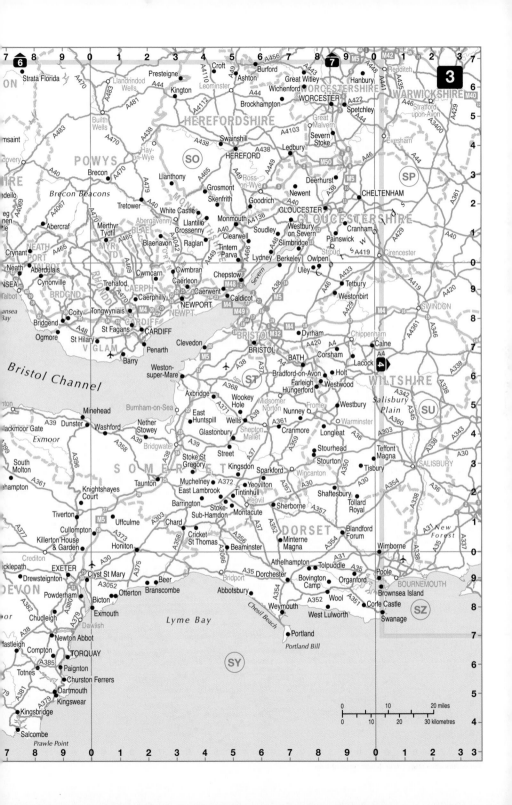

For continuation pages refer to numbered arrows

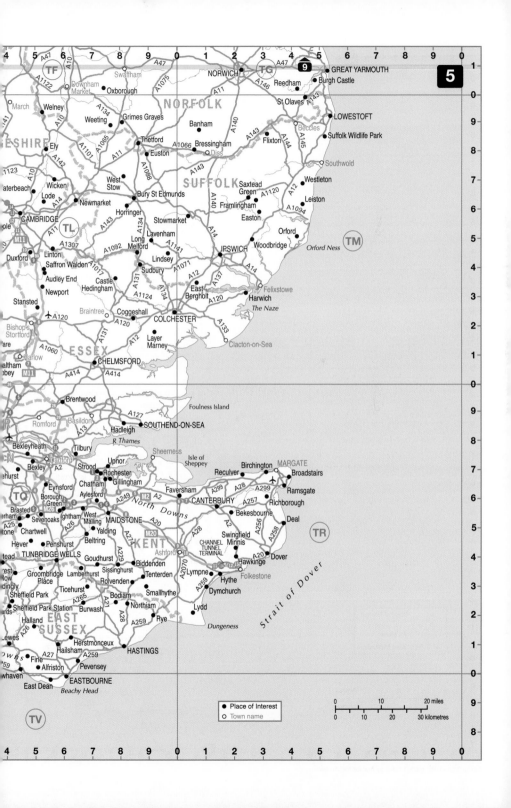

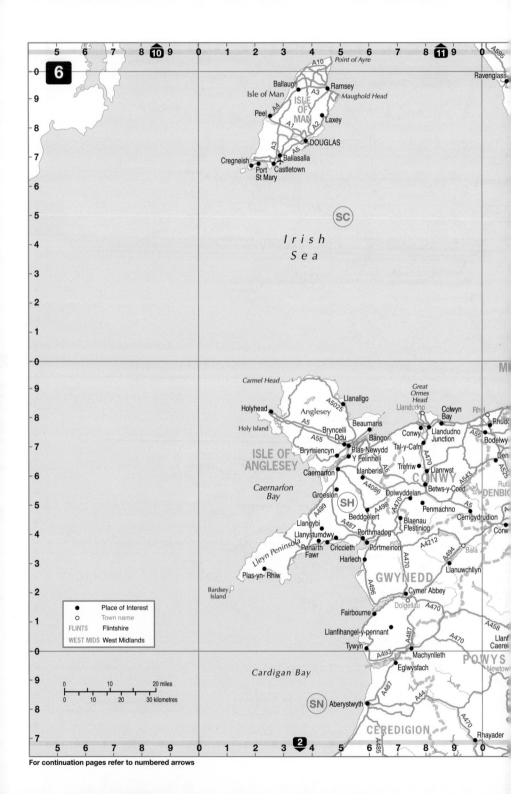

Point of Ayre
A595
Ravenglass

Ballaugh
Isle of Man
A10
Ramsey
Maughold Head
ISLE
OF
MAN
A3
A4
Peel
A1
A2
Laxey
A5
DOUGLAS
A3
Cregneish
Ballasalla
Port
St Mary
Castletown

SC

*I r i s h
S e a*

Carmel Head

Llanallgo
A5025
Holyhead
Anglesey
A5
Holy Island
Bryncelli
Ddu
Beaumaris
A55
Brynsiencyn
Plas Newydd
Y Felinheli
ISLE OF
ANGLESEY
Caernarfon
Bangor
Llanberis
A5

Great
Ormes
Head
Llandudno
Colwyn
Bay
Rhyl
Llandudno
Junction
A55
Conwy
Tal-y-Cafn
A470
Trefriw
Llanrwst
Betws-y-Coed
CONWY
A543
Ruth
DENBIG

Rhud
Bodelwy
Den
A5
A5

*Caernarfon
Bay*
Groeslon
SH
Beddgelert
A498
A470
Dolwyddelan
Penmachno
A5
Cerrigydrudion
Corw

A499
A487
Llangybi
Llanystumdwy
Penarth
Fawr
Criccieth
Porthmadog
Blaenau
Ffestiniog
A4212
A494
Bala

Lleyn Peninsula
Portmeirion
A470
Harlech
Llanuwchllyn
GWYNEDD

Plas-yn- Rhiw
Bardsey
Island
A496
Cymer Abbey
Dolgellau A470

Fairbourne
A458
Llanfihangel-y-pennant
A487
A470
Llanf
Caerei
Tywyn
A493
Machynlleth
POWYS
Newtow

Cardigan Bay
Eglwysfach

SN
Aberystwyth
A487
A44

CEREDIGION
A485
Rhayader

2

●	Place of Interest
○	Town name
FLINTS	Flintshire
WEST MIDS	West Midlands

0   10   20 miles
0   10   20   30 kilometres

For continuation pages refer to numbered arrows

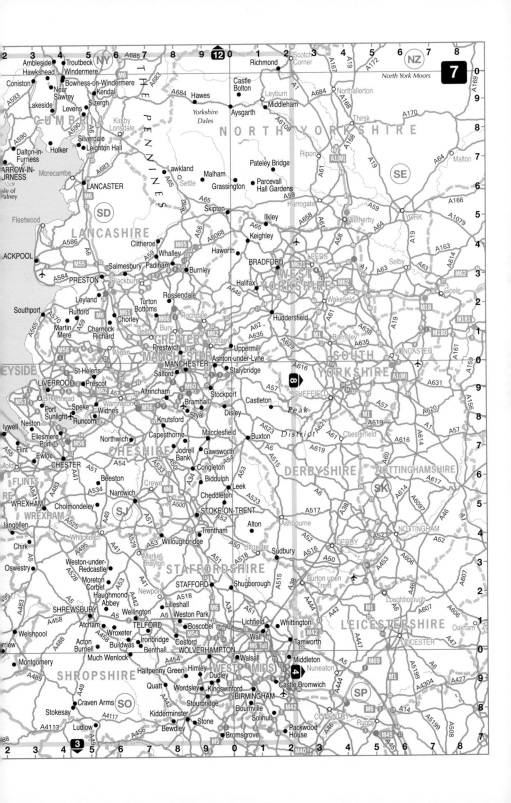

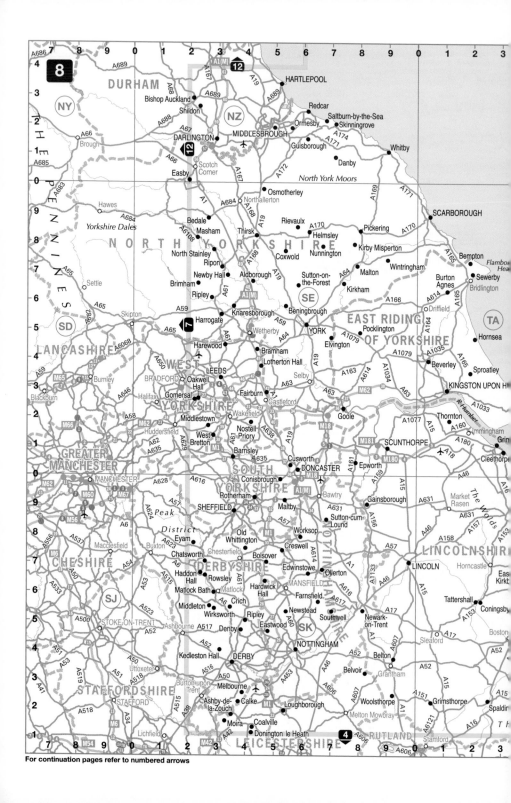

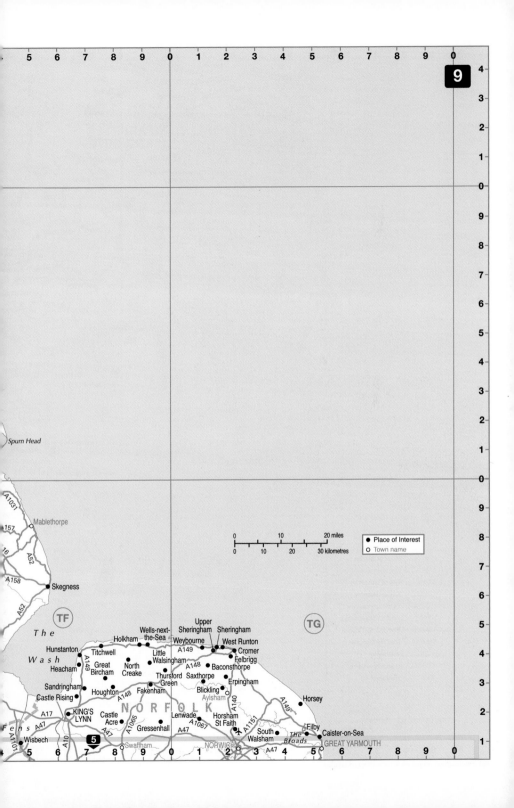

5 6 7 8 9 0 1 2 3 4 5 6 7 8 9 0

4
3
2
1
0
9
8
7
6
5
4
3
2
1
0
9
8
7
6
5
4
3
2
1

Spurn Head

A1031

Mablethorpe
157

16
A52

A158

Skegness

TF

The
Wash

NORFOLK

Holkham
Wells-next-the-Sea
Upper Sheringham
Sheringham
Weybourne
West Runton
Cromer
A149
Felbrigg
Hunstanton
Titchwell
Little Walsingham
Baconsthorpe
A148
Heacham
Great Bircham
North Creake
Thursford
Saxthorpe
A149
Green
Erpingham
Sandringham
Houghton
Fakenham
Blickling
Castle Rising
A148
Aylsham
KING'S LYNN
A17
Castle Acre
Lenwade
Horsham St Faith
Horsey
A1065
A149
A47
Gressenhall
A1067
South Walsham
A1151
Filby
Caister-on-Sea
Fens
A47
A10
Swaffham
A47
The Broads
GREAT YARMOUTH
A101
Wisbech
5
NORWICH

0 10 20 miles
0 10 20 30 kilometres

● Place of Interest
○ Town name

TG

5 6 7 8 9 0 1 2 3 4 5 6 7 8 9 0

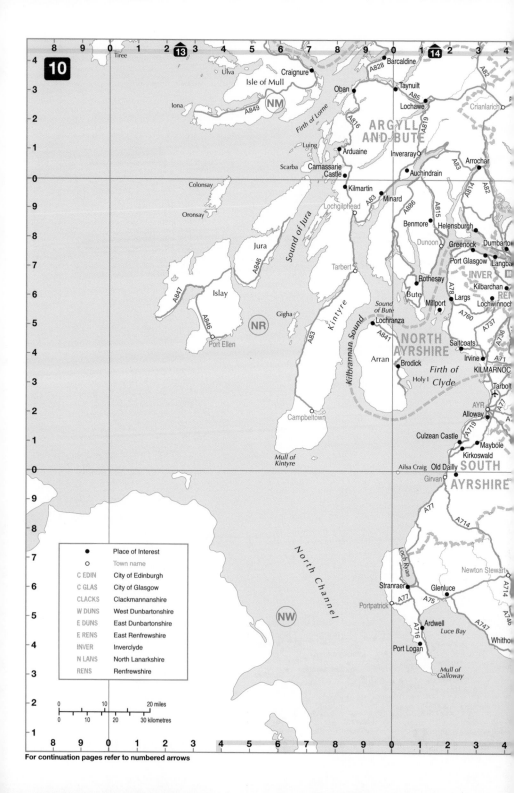

10

Tiree

13

14

Ulva
Isle of Mull
Iona
Craignure
Barcaldine
A828
Oban
Taynuilt
A85
Lochawe
A816
Crianlarich
ARGYLL
AND BUTE
NM
A849
Firth of Lorne
Luing
Arduaine
Inveraray
A83
Arrochar
A85
A819
Scarba
Carnassarie
Castle
Auchindrain
Colonsay
Kilmartin
A83
Minard
A886
A815
Oronsay
Lochgilphead
Benmore
Helensburgh
Jura
Dunoon
Greenock
Dumbarton
Port Glasgow
Langba
A846
Tarbert
Rothesay
INVER
A847
Islay
Kilbarchan
REN
Bute
Largs
Lochwinnoch
A846
Gigha
Millport
A760
A737
Sound
of Bute
NR
Lochranza
NORTH
AYRSHIRE
Saltcoats
Port Ellen
A841
Irvine
A71
Arran
Brodick
KILMARNOC
A83
Holy I
Firth of
Clyde
Tarbolt
AYR
Campbeltown
Alloway
A719
Culzean Castle
Maybole
Mull of
Kintyre
Kirkoswald
Ailsa Craig
Old Dailly
SOUTH
Girvan
AYRSHIRE
A77
A714
North Channel
Newton Stewart
Loch Ryan
A714
Stranraer
Glenluce
A716
Portpatrick
A77
A75
NW
Ardwell
Luce Bay
Whitho
Port Logan
Mull of
Galloway

Sound of Jura
Kintyre
Kilbrannan Sound

Place of Interest
Town name
C EDIN City of Edinburgh
C GLAS City of Glasgow
CLACKS Clackmannanshire
W DUNS West Dunbartonshire
E DUNS East Dunbartonshire
E RENS East Renfrewshire
INVER Inverclyde
N LANS North Lanarkshire
RENS Renfrewshire

0 10 20 miles
0 10 20 30 kilometres

For continuation pages refer to numbered arrows

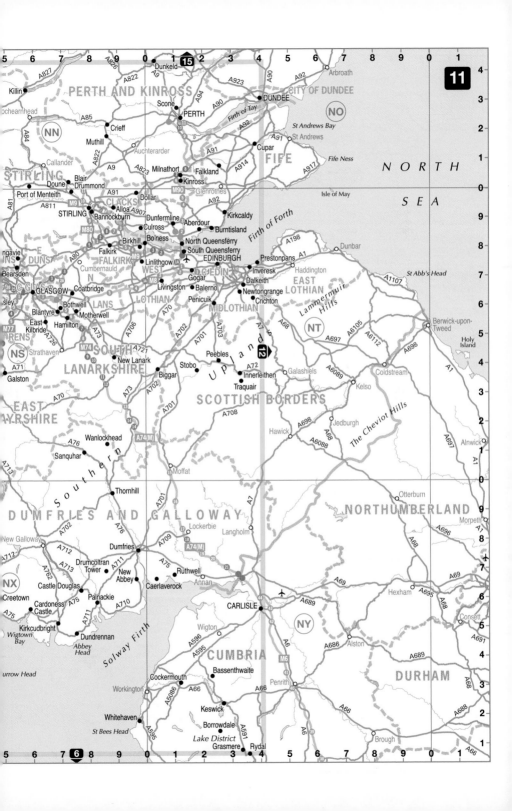

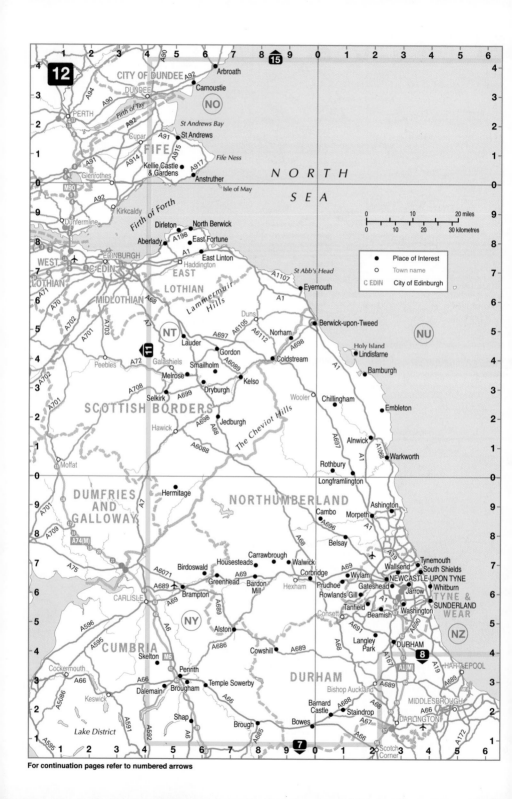

For continuation pages refer to numbered arrows

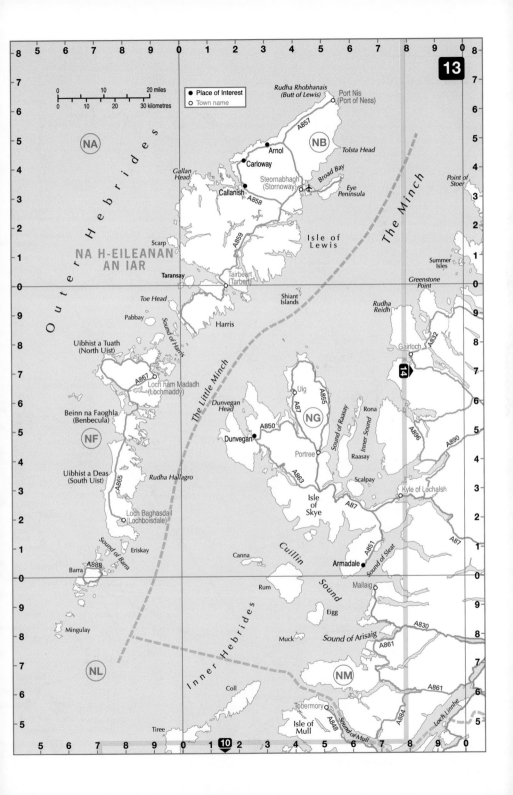

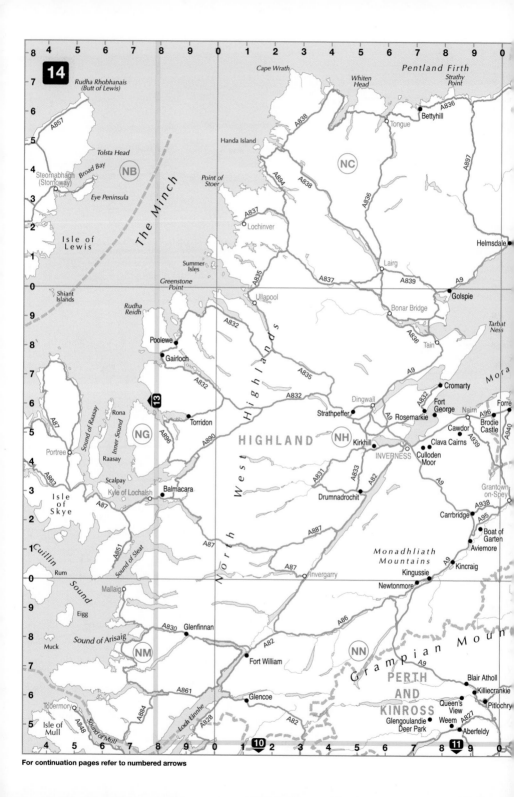

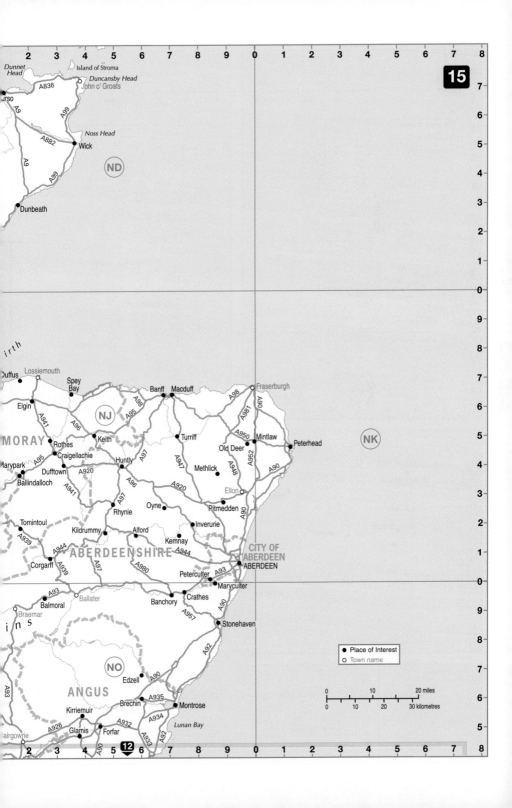

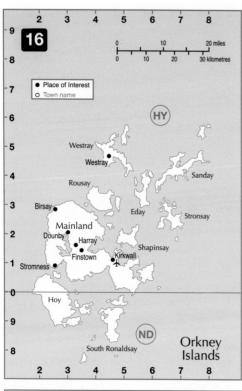

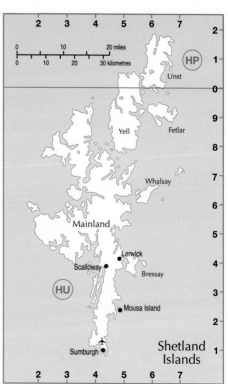

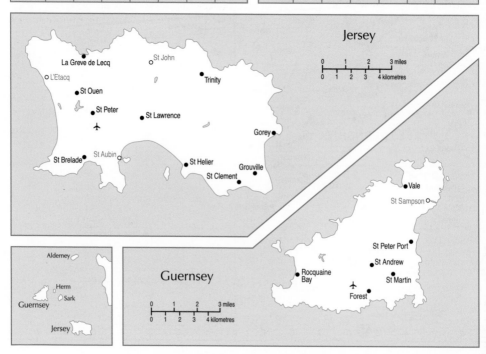

Index to Days Out

Index

Index

Index

Index

531

Index

Index

Index

Index

The Automobile Association would like to thank the following photographers, companies and picture libraries for their assistance in the preparation of this book.

Abbreviations for the picture credits are as follows: (t) top; (b) bottom; (l) left; (r) right; (AA) AA World Travel Library.

1 AA/M Jourdan; 2 AA/N Setchfield; 3t AA/M Jourdan; 3bl AA/J Wood; 3br Photodisc; 4 AA/M Jordan; 5t AA/M Jourdan; 5c AA/N Setchfield; 7 AA/M Birkitt; 10 AA/D Forss; 15 AA/S Day; 18 AA/M Birkitt; 23 AA/F Stephenson; 24 AA/M Moody; 31 AA/A J Hopkins; 38 AA/R Tennison; 48 AA/J Wood; 49 AA/T Mackie; 60 AA/T Mackie; 68 AA/N Hicks; 83 AA/A Burton; 92 AA/C Lees; 97 AA/M Birkitt; 102 AA/D Hall; 112 AA/S Day; 118 AA/A Burton; 133 AA/H Palmer; 136 AA/M Short; 137 AA/M Birkitt; 142 AA/M Busselle; 156 AA/J Beazley; 161 AA/P Baker; 166 AA/M Birkitt; 171 AA/J Tims; 200 AA/S Day; 206 AA/T Mackie; 218 AA/A Lawson; 221 AA/C Lees; 227 AA; 231 AA/P Baker; 232 AA/W Voysey; 240 AA/M Birkitt; 241 AA/P Grogan; 242 AA/M Hamblin; 247 AA/C Jones; 248 AA/C Jones; 258 AA/T Mackie; 264 AA/J Welsh; 265 AA/T Mackie; 271 AA/T Mackie; 272 AA/J Tims; 276 AA/J Miller; 277 AA/J Miller; 286 AA/J Miller; 293 AA/J Miller; 294 AA; 298 AA/V Greaves; 304 AA/J Welsh; 311 AA/A Burton; 316 AA/C Jones; 323 AA/D Hall; 324 AA/M Moody; 329 AA/C Jones; 330 AA/P Wilson; 334 AA/D Tarn; 349 AA/T Mackie; 350 AA; 353 AA/T Mackie; 360 AA/S Abrahams; 362 AA/P Trenchard; 366 AA; 369 AA/V Bates; 370/371 AA/M Hayward; 438/439 AA/C Warren; 468 AA/C Warren; 469 AA/D Forss; 484 AA/S Day; 502 AA/SlideFile;

Every effort has been made to trace the copyright holders, and we apologise in advance for any accidental errors. We would be happy to apply the corrections in the following edition of this publication.

Please send this form to:
Editor, The Days Out Guide,
Lifestyle Guides,
The Automobile Association,
Fanum House,
Basingstoke RG21 4EA

Readers' Report Form

e-mail: lifestyleguides@theAA.com

Please use this form to recommend any visitor attraction you have been to, whether it is in the guide or not currently listed. Feedback from readers helps us to keep our guide accurate and up to date. Please note, however, that if you have a complaint to make during a visit, we strongly recommend that you discuss the matter with the establishment management there and then so that they have a chance to put things right before your visit is spoilt. The AA does not undertake to arbitrate between you and the attraction's management, or to obtain compensation or engage in correspondence.

Date:

Your name (block capitals)

Your address (block capitals)

....

....

....

....

e-mail address:

Comments (Please include the name & address of the establishment) ....

....

....

....

....

....

....

....

....

(please attach a separate sheet if necessary)

Please tick here if you DO NOT wish to receive details of AA offers or products ☐

PTO

The Days Out Guide 2009

Have you bought this Guide before?   Yes   No

What other Days Out guides have you bought recently?

....

....

....

Why did you buy this Guide? (circle all that apply)

family holiday   short break   school holidays   special occasion

other ....

How often do you have a Day Out? (circle one choice)

more than once a month   once a month   once in 2-3 months

once in six months   once a year   less than once a year

Please answer these questions to help us make improvements to the guide:

Which of these factors are most important when choosing a Day Out?

price   location   previous experience

recommendation   type of attraction

other (please state) ....

Do you use the location atlas?   Yes   No

What elements of the guide do you find the most useful when choosing somewhere to visit?

description   photo   advertisement

Can you suggest any improvements to the guide?

....

....

....

....

Thank you for returning this form

2 for 1

Terms: This voucher is valid at any venue specified as accepting vouchers within the AA 'The Days Out Guide 2009'. This voucher admits one adult or child free when presented at the time of purchase of one fully priced adult ticket. Valid until 31 Oct 2009. Subject to availability at the venue when presented. Photocopies will not be accepted.

AA Lifestyle Guides

2 for 1

Terms: This voucher is valid at any venue specified as accepting vouchers within the AA 'The Days Out Guide 2009'. This voucher admits one adult or child free when presented at the time of purchase of one fully priced adult ticket. Valid until 31 Oct 2009. Subject to availability at the venue when presented. Photocopies will not be accepted.

AA Lifestyle Guides

2 for 1

Terms: This voucher is valid at any venue specified as accepting vouchers within the AA 'The Days Out Guide 2009'. This voucher admits one adult or child free when presented at the time of purchase of one fully priced adult ticket. Valid until 31 Oct 2009. Subject to availability at the venue when presented. Photocopies will not be accepted.

AA Lifestyle Guides

2 for 1

Terms: This voucher is valid at any venue specified as accepting vouchers within the AA 'The Days Out Guide 2009'. This voucher admits one adult or child free when presented at the time of purchase of one fully priced adult ticket. Valid until 31 Oct 2009. Subject to availability at the venue when presented. Photocopies will not be accepted.

AA Lifestyle Guides

2 for 1

Terms: This voucher is valid at any venue specified as accepting vouchers within the AA 'The Days Out Guide 2009'. This voucher admits one adult or child free when presented at the time of purchase of one fully priced adult ticket. Valid until 31 Oct 2009. Subject to availability at the venue when presented. Photocopies will not be accepted.

AA Lifestyle Guides

2 for 1

Terms: This voucher is valid at any venue specified as accepting vouchers within the AA 'The Days Out Guide 2009'. This voucher admits one adult or child free when presented at the time of purchase of one fully priced adult ticket. Valid until 31 Oct 2009. Subject to availability at the venue when presented. Photocopies will not be accepted.

AA Lifestyle Guides

2 for 1

Terms: This voucher is valid at any venue specified as accepting vouchers within the AA 'The Days Out Guide 2009'. This voucher admits one adult or child free when presented at the time of purchase of one fully priced adult ticket. Valid until 31 Oct 2009. Subject to availability at the venue when presented. Photocopies will not be accepted.

AA Lifestyle Guides

2 for 1

Terms: This voucher is valid at any venue specified as accepting vouchers within the AA 'The Days Out Guide 2009'. This voucher admits one adult or child free when presented at the time of purchase of one fully priced adult ticket. Valid until 31 Oct 2009. Subject to availability at the venue when presented. Photocopies will not be accepted.

AA Lifestyle Guides

2 for 1

Terms: This voucher is valid at any venue specified as accepting vouchers within the AA 'The Days Out Guide 2009'. This voucher admits one adult or child free when presented at the time of purchase of one fully priced adult ticket. Valid until 31 Oct 2009. Subject to availability at the venue when presented. Photocopies will not be accepted.

AA Lifestyle Guides

2 for 1

Terms: This voucher is valid at any venue specified as accepting vouchers within the AA 'The Days Out Guide 2009'. This voucher admits one adult or child free when presented at the time of purchase of one fully priced adult ticket. Valid until 31 Oct 2009. Subject to availability at the venue when presented. Photocopies will not be accepted.

AA Lifestyle Guides